CONTENTS

Introduction XIV

The Dictionary

CASSELL

Dictionary of Contemporary Quotations

Robert Andrews

CASSELL

Dedicated to Philip and Marina, in friendship and love

First published 1996
by Cassell
Wellington House
125 Strand
London WC2R 0BB

First published in paperback 1998

Distributed in the United States
by Sterling Publishing Co. Inc.
387 Park Avenue South, New York, NY 10016–8810

British Library Cataloguing in Publication Date
A catalogue record for this book is available from the British Library

ISBN 0–304–35032–X

Typeset by Gem Graphics, Trenance, Cornwall

Printed and bound in Finland

Front cover photographs show (clockwise from top left): Princess Diana, John F. Kennedy,
Mick Jagger, Salman Rushdie, Pope John Paul II, Margaret Thatcher, Marilyn Monroe,
Nelson Mandela and Stephen Hawking. Reproduced courtesy of Frank Spooner Pictures.

INTRODUCTION

All the 'contemporary quotations' in this book were first written or uttered after the end of the Second World War. This is more than a convenient starting-point, rather a recognition of a phase in history as significant in its way as the Renaissance or the Industrial Revolution. If the end of the First World War is sometimes cited as marking the birth of the 'Modern' mentality – the era of universal suffrage, imperial decline and intellectual revolt – then the Second World War might be said to signal the beginning of the 'post-modern' era. The age of James Joyce, Virginia Woolf and F. Scott Fitzgerald gave way to that of Samuel Beckett, Albert Camus and Allen Ginsberg, and just as *Winnie-the-Pooh* or the *Forsyte Saga* belong unquestionably to the interwar period, it is impossible to imagine such seminal works as *Catcher in the Rye, Junkie, Lolita* or *The Caretaker* being written pre-1945.

The 'post-modern' era unfolded in the wake of the atomic annihilation of entire cities and the attempted extermination of a whole people, and against the backdrop of an arms race that presented us with a vision of catastrophe as terrifying as any apocalyptic scenario found in the Bible. The Cold War, whose abrupt and dramatic end we are still coming to terms with, was played out to the accompaniment of rock 'n' roll, itself the delirious fanfare of a cult of youth which reached its revolutionary apotheosis in the sixties before being effortlessly re-absorbed into the mainstream – albeit a mainstream culture fundamentally altered. The triumph of materialism, the demise of ideology and the overwhelming impact of the information age now dominate our world-view, and though the mass media have focused attention on remote wars and natural calamities, bringing images of devastation, hunger and grief literally into our homes, the effect has been less to bestow us with any greater sense of control over our own destinies – let alone fostering a new spirit of altruism – but rather to transform us into a generation of impotent voyeurs. Perhaps the greatest challenge to our collective complacency is posed by the chilling awareness of how fragile we and our planet are, and how much irreversible damage we are capable of inflicting, even if what most excites us is the possibilities offered by the coming of the silicon chip and the introduction into our twentieth-century caves of terminals with an exponential range of potential uses, making the future teeming with possibility, yet impossible to predict.

These rapid changes have taken place against a ceaseless chatter of self-analysis, coruscating irony, and an obsessively probing, often wild, commentary, seeking above all to rationalize and understand. One might say that the most significant characteristic of the post-World War II age is this compulsion to communicate, a passion which simultaneously bombards us and motivates us, and of which this very book is both embodiment and beneficiary. Never before has there been such a plethora of words written, spoken and sung, for the most part trivial and ephemeral, but still somehow reassuring, since words are our one sustainable resource, endlessly recyclable and infinitely capable of surprising and inspiring us.

Out of this great torrent, certain phrases and passages have stuck with us, absorbed into common parlance and colouring our experience of these 50 years. In various ways, these quips and quotes have retained their original force, either by preserving a unique insight or because they stand as poignant emblems of some past significance. Steeping itself in this abundance of material, this collection endeavours to illustrate the period and its mores, to which end not just novels, essays and plays have been ransacked, but radio, TV, film, newspapers and gossip magazines, records and shows, even the Net, to present the most panoramic portrait of the age. The result is both a running commentary on the post-war era and a sort of picture gallery of the people who helped to shape it – presenting their opinions, revealing their prejudices and exposing their contradictions. The arrangement by subjects allows a multifaceted view of the major issues of the time – from AIDS to Vietnam, and from sex and violence in the cinema to soap operas on TV. Among the 1180 headings are the topics that have preoccupied post-war society – McCarthyism, the permissive society, the nuclear age, teenagers, abortion, computer technology, and the new world order – as well as contemporary slants on subjects which have absorbed all societies in all times: friendship, nature, sex, war, childhood, death, love, loyalty, virtue and vice.

The prime difficulty with this organization is that there are few quotes which can be tied exclusively to just one specific meaning. Verse, for example, is fiendishly difficult to pin down: how can you categorize the oft-quoted lines from the poem 'Not Waving but Drowning' or some of Bob Dylan's impressionistic sketches? As a rule, the choice has been made according to how illuminating or useful a passage is on a certain subject, though readers can use the key-word index to locate specific remembered quotes.

Inevitably an anthology of quotations entails an element of subjective choice, though I hope that the overall selection mirrors a general consensus on what are the most significant things said by the most relevant people. Where quotes are not familiar, they are chosen because they may contain a key phrase or idea which encapsulates the whole spirit of a book or philosophy or personality which itself is familiar to us.

If there is a bias it has more to do with the 'quotability' or otherwise of the person cited, and for this reason the choice veers towards those who have produced the crispest aperçus. Among these, such social commentators and essayists as Edmund White, Hannah Arendt and Susan Sontag are heavily represented; also, comics such as Woody Allen, Lenny Bruce and the Monty Python troupe; feminists such as Andrea Dworkin, Germaine Greer and Camille Paglia; influential doyens of the Left Bank such as Albert Camus, Michel Foucault, Jean Baudrillard and E.M. Cioran; polemicists such as Frantz Fanon, James Baldwin, Eldridge Cleaver, Malcolm X and Martin Luther King; maestros with a flair for piercing, caustic wit such as Andy Warhol, W.H. Auden and Philip Larkin, and demon provocateurs such as Valerie Solanas, P.J. O'Rourke and Amiri Baraku.

Songwriters such as Dylan, Lennon/McCartney and Hammerstein have been included on the same criteria as all other entries, represented here by lines which have a knack of bursting forth from us irresistibly, sometimes against our better judgement (think of: 'The hills are alive with the sound of music' or 'I get by with a little help from my friends...').

Film quotes have been ascribed to those most closely associated with them. This occasionally makes for inconsistencies, according to whether they are credited to film-makers, screenwriters or particular actors or actresses. Marlon Brando's 'contender' speech from *On the Waterfront* or Marilyn Monroe's famous lines from *Some Like It Hot*, Gloria Swanson's from *Sunset Boulevard* or Diane Keaton's 'La-di-da' are indelibly linked to the celluloid speaker, though screenwriter, director and actor are all identified.

In all cases, citations have been designed to include all the information essential for anyone interested in investigating further, without swamping the quote itself beneath a mass of data. Context and comment have been provided where these enhance the meaning and significance of the entries. With this in mind, I hope that this anthology proves as valuable and entertaining to read as it was to research. Although many of the 1825 names contained within have drifted in and out of fashion, none of them, I believe, deserves to be forgotten, and this book will have served its purpose well if it only helps to retrieve from oblivion some of the brilliant, beguiling and wayward characters who have helped mould the present age.

This book was a cooperative effort, and I owe a debt of gratitude to all those who shared the burden of research, and more important injected their enthusiasm into the project. Chief enthusiast was Kate Hughes, who applied her manifold talents at every phase of the work, from researching to word-processing to editing, not forgetting a magnificent job of indexing. Philip Krynsky threw himself into the task with characteristic generosity, in the process adding another thousand or so books to his sagging shelves. Derek Wall also came up with the goods, while satisfying his relish for scholarly investigations, delving into thickets of reading where no one else dared tread, especially in the fields of ecology, economics and modern history. Thanks are also due to Julian Dale, Kieran McGovern and Sara Jones for their scrupulous researchings, to Tim Munro for his computer know-how, and – for their past labours – thanks again to Will Ashon and Richard Davoll. At Cassell, Nigel Wilcockson was a steadfast presence on the end of the phone line, and never less than a perfect gent in the face of mangled schedules, while Sarah Chatwin was also a rallying force and an exemplary editor. Finally I would like to acknowledge the unflagging support of my family – Joyce and Gordon Murray, Jo Morgan, Quincy and Evelina, and Mango the Cat – who propped me up and kept me company through the long incubation of this book.

ROBERT ANDREWS

ABBREVIATIONS

Aph.	aphorism
b.	born
Bk.	book
c.	circa
Ch.	chapter
comp.	compiled
Cto.	canto
d.	died
ed.	edited
edn.	edition
No.	number
p.	page
Para.	paragraph
Pt.	part
publ.	published
rep.	reprinted
rev.	revised
Sct.	section
St.	stanza
tr.	translated
Vol.	volume

QUOTATIONS

ABORTION

1 Abortions will not let you forget.
You remember the children you got that you did not get.
Gwendolyn Brooks (b.1917), U.S. poet: 'The Mother', publ. in *Selected Poems* (1963)

2 The emphasis must be not on the right to abortion but on the right to privacy and reproductive control.
Ruth Bader Ginsberg (b.1933), U.S. educator and lawyer: quoted in *Ms.* (New York), April 1974

3 The compelled mother loves her child as the caged bird sings. The song does not justify the cage nor the love the enforcement.
Germaine Greer (b.1939), Australian feminist writer: 'Abortion', first publ. in *The Sunday Times* (London), 21 May 1972, rep. in *The Madwoman's Underclothes* (1986)

4 The cemetery of the victims of human cruelty in our century is extended to include yet another vast cemetery, that of the unborn.
Pope John Paul II [Karol Wojtyla] (b.1920), Polish ecclesiastic: quoted in *The Observer* (London), 9 June 1991

5 *It is not possible to speak of the right to choose when a clear moral evil is involved*, when what is at stake is the commandment *Do not kill!*
Pope John Paul II: *Crossing the Threshold of Hope* (1994), 'The Defense of Every Life'

6 The preservation of life seems to be rather a slogan than a genuine goal of the anti-abortion forces; what they want is control. Control over behavior: power over women. Women in the anti-choice movement want to share in male power over women, and do so by denying their own womanhood, their own rights and responsibilities.
Ursula K. Le Guin (b.1929), U.S. author: 'The Princess', address to National Abortion Rights Action League, Portland, Maine, Jan. 1982, rep. in *Dancing at the Edge of the World* (1989)

7 The greatest destroyer of peace is abortion because if a mother can kill her own child, what is left for me to kill you and you to kill me? There is nothing between.
Mother Teresa (1910–1997), Albanian-born Roman Catholic missionary: Nobel Peace Prize Lecture, 1979

ABROAD

1 Being abroad makes you conscious of the whole imitative side of human behavior. The ape in man.
Mary McCarthy (1912–1989), U.S. author and critic: *Birds of America* (1965), 'Epistle from Mother Carey's Chicken'

2 The British tourist is always happy abroad as long as the natives are waiters.
Robert Morley (1908–1992), British actor: quoted in *The Observer* (London), 20 April 1958

3 If any of you have got an A-level, it is because you have worked to get it. Go to any other country and when you have got an A-level you have bought it.
Michael Portillo (b.1953), British Conservative politican: speech to students of Southampton University, quoted in *The Guardian* (London), 31 Dec. 1994

4 The history of other cultures is non-existent until it erupts in confrontation with the United States; most of what counts about foreign societies is compressed into thirty-second items, 'sound-bites', and into the question of whether they are pro- or anti- America, freedom, capitalism, democracy.
Edward Said (b.1935), Lebanese-born U.S. social and literary critic: *Culture and Imperialism* (1993), Ch.4, Sct.2

See also Calvino on EMIGRATION & EXILE

ABSTINENCE

1 The best thing to do with the best things in life is to give them up.
Dorothy Day (1897–1980), U.S. religious leader: quoted in *Time* (New York), 29 Dec. 1975

2 An artist needs both knowledge and the power of observation only so that he can tell from what he is abstaining, and to be sure that his abstention will not appear artificial or false. For in the end it is important to confine yourself within a framework that will deepen your world, not impoverish it, help you to create it, excluding all pretentiousness and efforts to be original.
Andrey Tarkovsky (1932–1986), Russian film-maker: journal entry, 7 July 1980, publ. in *Time*

Within Time: The Diaries 1970–1986 (1989; tr.1994)

See also CELIBACY; DRINK: ABSTINENCE

ABSURDITY

1 Modern man must descend the spiral of his own absurdity to the lowest point; only then can he look beyond it. It is obviously impossible to get around it, jump over it, or simply avoid it.
Václav Havel (b.1936), Czech playwright and president: *Disturbing the Peace* (1986; tr.1990), Ch.2

2 We live in a time which has created the art of the absurd. It is our art. It contains happenings, Pop art, camp, a theater of the absurd. ... Do we have the art because the absurd is the patina of waste ... ? Or are we face to face with a desperate or most rational effort from the deepest resources of the unconscious of us all to rescue civilization from the pit and plague of its bedding?
Norman Mailer (b.1923), U.S. author: *Cannibals and Christians* (1966), 'Introducing Our Argument'

3 Great men of action ... never mind on occasion being ridiculous; in a sense it is part of their job, and at times they all are. A prophet or an achiever must never mind an occasional absurdity, it is an occupational risk.
Oswald Mosley (1896–1980), British fascist leader: *My Life* (1968), Ch.12

See also Havel on ALIENATION

ABUSE

1 Some guy hit my fender the other day, and I said unto him, 'Be fruitful, and multiply.' But not in those words.
Woody Allen (b.1935), U.S. film-maker: 'Private Life' live recording in Chicago, March 1964, on *Woody Allen* (album, 1964), publ. in *The Woody Allen Companion* by Stephen J. Spignesi (1993), Ch.7

2 People who treat other people as less than human must not be surprised when the bread they have cast on the waters comes floating back to them, poisoned.
James Baldwin (1924–1987), U.S. author: 'No Name in the Street' (1972), rep. in *The Price of the Ticket* (1985)

See also INSULTS

ACADEMIA

1 I realized early on that the academy and the literary world alike – and I don't think there really is a distinction between the two – are always dominated by fools, knaves, charlatans and bureaucrats. And that being the case, any human being, male or female, of whatever status, who has a voice of her or his own, is not going to be liked.
Harold Bloom (b.1930), U.S. literary critic and theorist: interview, 1985, publ. in *Criticism in Society* (ed. Imre Salusinski, 1987)

2 i would rather model harmonica holders than discuss aztec anthropology english literature. or the history of the united nations.
Bob Dylan (b.1941), U.S. singer and songwriter: sleevenotes to the album *Bringing it All Back Home* (1965)

3 If poetry is like an orgasm, an academic can be likened to someone who studies the passion-stains on the bedsheets.
Irving Layton (b.1912), Canadian poet: *The Whole Bloody Bird* (1969), 'Obs II'

4 A serious problem in America is the gap between academe and the mass media, which *is* our culture. Professors of humanities, with all their leftist fantasies, have little direct knowledge of American life and no impact whatever on public policy.
Camille Paglia (b.1947), U.S. author and critic: introduction to *Sex, Art, and American Culture* (1992)

5 In various academic departments – among them literature, philosophy, and history – theory is taught so as to make the student believe that he or she can become a Marxist, a feminist, an Afrocentrist, or a deconstructionist with about the same effort and commitment required in choosing items form a menu.
Edward Said (b.1935), Lebanese-born U.S. social and literary critic: *Culture and Imperialism* (1993), Ch.4, Sct.2

6 In universities and intellectual circles, academics can guarantee themselves popularity – or, which is just as satisfying, unpopularity – by being opinionated rather than by being learned.
A.N. Wilson (b.1950), British author: book review in *The Guardian* (London), 30 Sept. 1989

ACCEPTANCE

1 Always fall in with what you're asked to accept. Take what is given, and make it over your way. My aim in life has always been to hold my own with whatever's going. Not against: with.
Robert Frost (1874–1963), U.S. poet: in *Vogue* (New York), 14 March 1963

2 The art of acceptance is the art of making someone who has just done you a small favor wish that he might have done you a greater one.

Russell Lynes (1910–1991), U.S. editor and critic: in *Reader's Digest* (Pleasantville, NY), Dec. 1954

ACCIDENTS

1 A car crash harnesses elements of eroticism, aggression, desire, speed, drama, kinaesthetic factors, the stylizing of motion, consumer goods, status – all these in one event. I myself see the car crash as a tremendous sexual event really: a liberation of human and machine libido (if there is such a thing).
J.G. Ballard (b.1930), British author: interview in *Penthouse* (London), Sept. 1970, rep. in *Re/Search* (San Francisco), No.8/9, 1984

2 Depression moods lead, almost invariably, to accidents. But, when they occur, our mood changes again, since the accident shows we can draw the world in our wake, and that we still retain some degree of power even when our spirits are low. A series of accidents creates a positively light-hearted state, out of consideration for this strange power.
Jean Baudrillard (b.1929), French semiologist: *Cool Memories* (1987; tr.1990), Ch.4

3 We are all such accidents. We do not make up history and culture. We simply appear, not by our own choice. We make what we can of our condition with the means available. We must accept the mixture as we find it – the impurity of it, the tragedy of it, the hope of it.
Saul Bellow (b.1915), U.S. novelist: introduction to the Dell paperback edition of *Great Jewish Short Stories* (1963), in which Bellow discusses the plight of the Jewish writer in American society

4 Nothing is accidental in the universe – this is one of my Laws of Physics – except the entire universe itself, which is Pure Accident, pure divinity.
Joyce Carol Oates (b.1938), U.S. author: *Do What You Will* (1970), 'The Summing Up: Meredith Dawe'

5 Accidents, try to change them – it's impossible. The accidental reveals man.
Pablo Picasso (1881–1973), Spanish artist: in *Vogue* (New York), 1 Nov. 1956

6 I don't believe in accidents. There are only encounters in history. There are no accidents.
Elie Wiesel (b.1928), Rumanian-born U.S. writer: in the *International Herald Tribune* (Paris), 15 Sept. 1992

ACTING

1 Acting is the expression of a neurotic impulse. It's a bum's life…. The principal benefit acting has afforded me is the money to pay for my psychoanalysis.

Marlon Brando (b.1924), U.S. actor: quoted in *Marlon Brando: The Only Contender* by Gary Carey (1985), Ch.13

2 It is a simple fact that all of us use the techniques of acting to achieve whatever ends we seek. … Acting serves as the quintessential social lubricant and a device for protecting our interests and gaining advantage in every aspect of life.
Marlon Brando: introduction to *The Technique of Acting* by Stella Adler (1988)

3 You don't have to be smart to act – look at the outgoing president of the United States.
Cher (b.1946), U.S. singer and actress: remark Dec. 1988, quoted in *Brewer's Cinema* (1995)

4 You don't merely give over your creativity to making a film – you give over your life! In theatre, by contrast, you live these two rather strange lives simultaneously; you have no option but to confront the mould on last night's washing-up.
Daniel Day-Lewis (b.1957), British actor: interview in *City Limits* (London), 7 April 1988

5 I learnt to be in the light. The stage is like a cage of light. People are no longer afraid of you – they are the ones out there in the dark, watching.
Gérard Depardieu (b.1948), French actor: on how acting saved him from a life of crime, quoted in *Depardieu* by Marianne Gray (1991), Ch.3

6 Acting doesn't bring anything to a text. On the contrary, it detracts from it.
Marguerite Duras (1914–1996), French author and film-maker: in the *International Herald Tribune* (Paris), 28 March 1990

7 You spend all your life trying to do something they put people in asylums for.
Jane Fonda (b.1937), U.S. actress: quoted in *Halliwell's Filmgoer's Book of Quotes* (ed. Leslie Halliwell, 1973)

8 More than in any other performing arts the lack of respect for acting seems to spring from the fact that every layman considers himself a valid critic.
Uta Hagen (b.1919), U.S. actress: introduction to *Respect for Acting* (1973), Pt.1

9 What I do for a living is go to work and pretend I'm somebody else. … Acting is what I do and, unfortunately I can't do much of anything else. It's this or nothing. I can *pretend* to build automobiles.
Tom Hanks (b.1957), U.S. actor: quoted in *Tom Hanks* by Roy Trakin (1995), Ch.11

10 Acting is not about dressing up. Acting is about stripping bare. The whole essence of learning lines is to forget them so you can make

them sound like you thought of them that instant.

Glenda Jackson (b.1937), British actress and Labour politician: in *The Sunday Telegraph* (London), 26 July 1992

11 It's not a field, I think, for people who need to have success every day: if you can't live with a nightly sort of disaster, you should get out. I wouldn't describe myself as lacking in confidence, but I would just say that … the ghosts you chase you never catch.

John Malkovich (b.1953), U.S. actor: on acting in the theatre, in interview in the *Independent on Sunday* (London), 5 April 1992

12 My own desire is to do my best, the best I can from the moment the camera starts until it stops. … Lee says I have to start with myself, and I say, 'With *me*?' Well I'm not so important! Who does he think I am, Marilyn Monroe or something?

Marilyn Monroe (1926–1962), U.S. actress: quoted in *Marilyn Monroe: The Biography* by Donald Spoto (1993), Ch.15. Lee Strasberg was artistic director of the Actors Studio and proponent of The Method style of acting

13 Left eyebrow raised, right eyebrow raised.

Roger Moore (b.1928), British actor: of his acting range, quoted in *Star Billing* by David Brown (1985), 'Seven Comments on the Art of Acting'

14 Acting deals with very delicate emotions. It is not putting up a mask. Each time an actor acts he does not hide; he exposes himself.

Jeanne Moreau (b.1928), French actress: in the *New York Times*, 30 June 1976

15 Acting is a question of absorbing other people's personalities and adding some of your own experience.

Paul Newman (b.1925), U.S. actor: quoted in *Halliwell's Filmgoer's Companion* (ed. Leslie Halliwell, 1984)

16 An actor who knows his business ought to be able to make the London telephone directory sound enthralling.

Donald Sinden (b.1923), British actor: in *The Observer* (London), 12 Feb. 1989

17 I've spent my whole career playing myself.

John Wayne (1907–1979), U.S. actor: quoted in *The Film Greats* by Barry Norman (1985)

See also Bardot on THEATRE

ACTION

1 Action without a name, a 'who' attached to it, is meaningless.

Hannah Arendt (1906–1975), German-born U.S. political philosopher: *The Human Condition* (1958), 'Action' Ch.24

2 We understand things by means of what we do. That is to say, without doing something we tend to be blind to everything, but the moment we do do something that action opens our vision to the things in the past and the things in the future.

John Cage (1912–1992), U.S. composer: interview in *Biology and the History of the Future* by C. H. Waddington (1972), rep. in *Conversing with Cage* (ed. Richard Kostelanetz, 1988), 'Precursors'

3 I acted, and my action made me wise.

Thom Gunn (b.1929), British poet: 'Incident on a Journey', publ. in *Fighting Terms* (1954)

4 In our era, the road to holiness necessarily passes through the world of action.

Dag Hammarskjöld (1905–1961), Swedish statesman and secretary-general of U.N.: note written 1955, publ. in *Markings* (1963), 'Night is Drawing Nigh'

5 A human action becomes genuinely important when it springs from the soil of a clearsighted awareness of the temporality and the ephemerality of everything human. It is only this awareness that can breathe any greatness into an action.

Václav Havel (b.1936), Czech playwright and president: *Disturbing the Peace* (1986; tr.1990), Ch.3

6 Never confuse movement with action

Ernest Hemingway (1899–1961), U.S. author: quoted by Marlene Dietrich in *Papa Hemingway* by A. E. Hotchner (1966 edn.), Pt.1, Ch.1. 'In those five words,' Dietrich added, 'he gave me a whole philosophy'

7 Action is at bottom a swinging and flailing of the arms to regain one's balance and keep afloat.

Eric Hoffer (1902–1983), U.S. philosopher: *The Passionate State of Mind* (1955), Aph.25

8 Ideas in a void have never appealed to me; action must follow thought or political life is meaningless.

Oswald Mosley (1896–1980), British fascist leader: *My Life* (1968), Ch.17

9 Let's go to work.

Quentin Tarantino (b.1958), U.S. film-maker: Joe Cabot (Lawrence Tierney), in *Reservoir Dogs* (film; written and directed by Quentin Tarantino, 1992). The words featured on posters advertising the film

10 There should be less talk; a preaching point is not a meeting point. What do you do then? Take a broom and clean someone's house. That says enough.

Mother Teresa (1910–1997), Albanian-born Roman Catholic missionary: *A Gift for God* (1975), 'Carriers of Christ's Love'

ACTIVISM & PROTEST

1 What we've got is passion. All they've got is four quid an hour.
Anonymous anti-roads protester: on the hired security at the Newbury bypass protest, quoted in *The Guardian* (London), 6 April 1996

2 We shall overcome, we shall overcome,
We shall overcome some day.
Oh, deep in my heart I do believe
We shall overcome some day.
Anonymous: sung by supporters of the civil rights movement in the 1960s, originally a 19th-century song adapted as a Baptist hymn by C. Albert Tindley in 1901, and revived in the 1940s by black tobacco workers in Charleston, South Carolina

3 Let us be realistic and demand the impossible.
(Soyons réalistes, demandons l'impossible.)
Graffiti slogan in Paris 1968, publ. in *Paris '68* by Marc Rohan (1988), Ch.2

4 You do not become a 'dissident' just because you decide one day to take up this most unusual career. You are thown into it by your personal sense of responsibility, combined with a complex set of external circumstances. You are cast out of the existing structures and placed in a position of conflict with them. It begins as an attempt to do your work well, and ends with being branded an enemy of society.
Václav Havel (b.1936), Czech playwright and president: *Living in Truth* (1986), Pt.1, 'The Power of the Powerless', Sct.14

5 One-fifth of the people are against everything all the time.
Robert Kennedy (1925–1968), U.S. attorney-general and Democratic politician: speech, 6 May 1964, University of Pennsylvania, quoted in the *Philadelphia Inquirer*, 7 May 1964

6 I submit that an individual who breaks a law that conscience tells him is unjust, and willingly accepts the penalty by staying in jail in order to arouse the conscience of the community over its injustice, is in reality expressing the very highest respect for law.
Martin Luther King Jr. (1929–1968), U.S. clergyman and civil rights leader: 'Letter from Birmingham Jail', open letter addressed to clergymen, 16 April 1963, publ. in *Why We Can't Wait* (1963)

7 It wasn't just a protest camp. Life is a protest. We were trying to re-establish our roots as indigenous people. When it comes down to saving the land, we felt on a par with the Aborigines and Native Americans. We've all had our culture trashed.
Sam, Donga Tribe: remark in the summer of 1992, following the campaign against the extension of the M3 motorway at Twyford Down, quoted in *i-D* (London), July 1993

8 What I profess to do is help the oppressed and if I cause a load of discomfort in the white community and the black community, that in my opinion means I'm being effective, because I'm not trying to make them comfortable. The job of an activist is to make people tense and cause social change.
Al Sharpton (b.1954), U.S. civil rights campaigner: in the *Independent on Sunday* (London), 21 April 1991

9 Thank God for those who burn themselves alive in front of an impassive, wordless crowd, or who walk out into squares with placards and slogans condemning themselves to reprisals, and all those who say 'No' to the go-getters and the godless.
Andrey Tarkovsky (1932–1986), Russian film-maker: journal entry, 7 Sept. 1970, publ. in *Time Within Time: The Diaries 1970–1986* (1989; tr.1994)

10 I've always had the impression that real militants are like cleaning women, doing a thankless, daily but necessary job.
François Truffaut (1932–1984), French film director: letter, May-June 1973, to director Jean-Luc Godard, publ. in *Letters* (1988; tr.1989)

11 Notice the masochist tendency of leftist tactics. Leftists protest by lying down in front of vehicles, they intentionally provoke police or racists to abuse them, etc. These tactics may often be effective, but many leftists use them not as a means to an end but because they PREFER masochistic tactics. Self-hatred is a leftist trait.
Unabomber, U.S. radical: *Industrial Society and Its Future*, 'Feelings of Inferiority', Sct.20, publ. in the *Washington Post*, 19 Sept. 1995

12 All partisan movements add to the fullness of our understanding of society as a whole. They never detract; or, in any case, one must not allow them to do so. Experience adds to experience.
Alice Walker (b.1944), U.S. author and critic: 'Can I Be My Brother's Sister?', first publ. in *Ms.* (New York), Oct. 1975, rep. in *In Search of Our Mothers' Gardens* (1983), 'Brothers and Sisters'

See also ANIMAL LIB; BLACK CONSCIOUSNESS/ BLACK POWER; Adams on MARTYRDOM; Arendt on NONVIOLENCE; King on NONVIOLENCE; POLITICS; REVOLUTION

ACTORS

1 The actors today really need the whip hand. They're so lazy. They haven't got the sense of pride in their profession that the less socially

elevated musical comedy and music hall people or acrobats have. The theater has never been any good since the actors became gentlemen.

W.H. Auden (1907–1973), Anglo-American poet: *The Table Talk of W.H. Auden* (comp. Alan Ansen, ed. Nicholas Jenkins, 1990), 'November 16, 1946'

2 Directors like Satyajit Ray, Rossellini, Bresson, Buñuel, Forman, Scorsese, and Spike Lee have used non-professional actors precisely in order that the people we see on the screen may be scarcely more *explained* than reality itself. Professionals, except for the greatest, usually play not just the necessary role, but an explanation of the role.

John Berger (b.1926), British author and critic: 'Ev'ry Time We Say Goodbye', first publ. in *Expressen* (Stockholm), 3 Nov. 1990, rep. in *Keeping a Rendezvous* (1992)

3 To grasp the full significance of life is the actor's duty, to interpret it is his problem, and to express it his dedication.

Marlon Brando (b.1924), U.S. actor: said in 1960, quoted in *Marlon Brando* by David Shipman (1974, rev.1989), Ch.1

4 If it's a good script I'll do it. And if it's a bad script, and they pay me enough, I'll do it.

George Burns (1896–1996), U.S. comedian: in the *International Herald Tribune* (Paris), 9 Nov. 1988

5 The basic essential of a great actor is that he loves himself in acting.

Charlie Chaplin (1889–1977), British comic actor and film-maker: *My Autobiography* (1964), Ch.16

6 I was born at the age of twelve on a Metro-Goldwyn-Mayer lot.

Judy Garland (1922–1969), U.S. actress: quoted in *The Observer* (London), 18 Feb. 1951

7 An actor is a kind of guy who if you ain't talking about him ain't listening.

George Glass (1910–1984), U.S. film executive: quoted in *Brando* by Bob Thomas (1973), Ch.8. The quote is frequently attributed to Marlon Brando, who may have heard it from Glass; the actor Michael Wilding is also said to have uttered, 'You can pick out actors by the glazed look that comes into their eyes when the conversation wanders away from themselves'

8 Talk to them about things they don't know. Try to give them an inferiority complex. If the actress is beautiful, screw her. If she isn't, present her with a valuable painting she will not understand. If they insist on being boring, kick their asses or twist their noses. And that's about all there is to it.

John Huston (1906–1987), U.S. film-maker: advice to a young director on how to handle actors, quoted in *Things I Did ... and Things I Think I Did* by Jean Negulesco (1984)

9 We are born at the rise of the curtain and we die with its fall, and every night in the presence of our patrons we write our new creation, and every night it is blotted out forever; and of what use is it to say to audience or to critic, 'Ah, but you should have seen me last Tuesday?'

Micheál MacLiammóir (1899–1978), Irish actor: of acting in the theatre, from 'Hamlet in Elsinore', publ. in *The Bell*, Oct. 1952

10 In Europe an actor is an artist. In Hollywood, if he isn't working, he's a bum.

Antony Quinn (b.1915), Mexican-born U.S. actor: quoted in *Halliwell's Filmgoer's Companion* (ed. Leslie Halliwell, 1984)

11 Insecurity, commonly regarded as a weakness in normal people, is the basic tool of the actor's trade.

Miranda Richardson (b.1958), British actress: in *The Guardian* (London), 5 Dec. 1990

12 Miss Caswell is an actress, a graduate of the Copacabana school of dramatic arts.

George Sanders (1906-1972), British actor: Addison de Witt (George Sanders), introducing his protégée Miss Caswell (Marilyn Monroe) to Margo Channing (Bette Davis), in *All About Eve* (film; written and directed by Joseph L. Mankiewicz, 1950)

13 Actors ought to be larger than life. You come across quite enough ordinary, nondescript people in daily life and I don't see why you should be subjected to them on the stage too.

Donald Sinden (b.1923), British actor: in *The Observer* (London), 12 Feb. 1989

14 I just want to tell you all how happy I am to be back in the studio, making a picture again! You don't know much I've missed all of you. ... You see, this is my life. It always will be! There's nothing else. Just us, and the cameras, and those wonderful people out there in the dark. All right, Mr de Mille. I'm ready for my closeup.

Gloria Swanson (1897-1983), U.S. actress: Norma Desmond (Gloria Swanson), descending a staircase in the last lines of *Sunset Boulevard* (film; screenplay by Billy Wilder, Charles Brackett and D. M. Marsham Jr., directed by Billy Wilder, 1950)

15 I'm just an ordinary goddamn American and I talk for all the ordinary goddamn Americans, the butchers and bakers and plumbers. I know these people; I know what they think.

John Wayne (1907–1979), U.S. actor: quoted in *The Film Greats* by Barry Norman (1985), 'John Wayne'

See also BRIGITTE BARDOT; MARLON BRANDO; JAMES DEAN; Barthes on FACES; ELIZABETH TAYLOR

ADDICTIONS

1 Addictions do come in handy sometimes: at least you have to get out of bed for them.
Martin Amis (b.1949), British author: *Money* (1984), p.154 of Penguin edn. (1985)

2 All sin tends to be addictive, and the terminal point of addiction is what is called damnation.
W.H. Auden (1907–1973), Anglo-American poet: *A Certain World* (1970), 'Hell'

3 It is not heroin or cocaine that makes one an addict, it is the need to escape from a harsh reality. There are more television addicts, more baseball and football addicts, more movie addicts, and certainly more alcohol addicts in this country than there are narcotics addicts.
Shirley Chisholm (b.1924), U.S. congresswoman: testimony to House Select Committee on Crime, 17 Sept. 1969

4 Every form of addiction is bad, no matter whether the narcotic be alcohol or morphine or idealism.
Carl Jung (1875–1961), Swiss psychiatrist: *Memories, Dreams, Reflections* (1962), Ch.12, Sct.1

See also DRUGS: ADDICTION

ADMIRATION

1 I have always been an admirer, I regard the gift of admiration as indispensable if one is to amount to something; I don't know where I would be without it.
Thomas Mann (1875–1955), German author and critic: letter, 1950, quoted in *Thomas Mann and His Family* by Marcel Reich-Ranicki (1987; tr.1989), 'Thomas Mann – The Birth of Criticism'

2 At the risk of sounding more pompous than I am, I was always more loved than admired. I think musicians are admired, but I was always loved and I felt it. And I prefer that. Eric Clapton is admired, but who could love him? His own mother, perhaps.
Morrissey (b.1959), British rock musician: in *New Musical Express* (London), 1991, quoted in *NME Book of Quotes*, 4 Feb. 1995, 'Fame'

3 You always admire what you really don't understand.
Eleanor Roosevelt (1884–1962), U.S. columnist, lecturer and wife of F.D. Roosevelt: *Meet the Press*, NBC TV, 16 Sept. 1956

ADOLESCENCE

1 The big mistake that men make is that when they turn thirteen or fourteen and all of a sudden they've reached puberty, they believe that they like women. Actually, you're just horny. It doesn't mean you like women any more at twenty-one than you did at ten.
Jules Feiffer (b.1929), U.S. cartoonist: quoted in *Loose Talk* (ed. Linda Botts, 1980)

2 What we ought to see in the agonies of puberty is the result of the conditioning that maims the female personality in creating the feminine.
Germaine Greer (b.1939), Australian feminist writer: *The Female Eunuch* (1970), 'Puberty'

3 Perhaps a modern society can remain stable only by eliminating adolescence, by giving its young, from the age of ten, the skills, responsibilities, and rewards of grownups, and opportunites for action in all spheres of life. Adolescence should be a time of useful action, while book learning and scholarship should be a preoccupation of adults.
Eric Hoffer (1902–1983), U.S. philosopher: *Reflections on the Human Condition* (1973), Aph.58

4 I have no contempt for that time of life when our friendships are most passionate and our passions are incorrigible and none of our sentiments yet compromised by greed or cowardice or disappointment. The volatility and intensity of adolescence are qualities we should aspire to preserve.
Edmund White (b.1940), U.S. author: 'Paradise Found', first publ. in *Mother Jones*, June 1983, rep. in *The Burning Library* (1994)

See also TEENAGERS

ADULTERY

1 Life is a game in which the rules are constantly changing; nothing spoils a game more than those who take it seriously. Adultery? Phooey! You should never subjugate yourself to another nor seek the subjugation of someone else to yourself. If you follow that Crispian principle you will be able to say 'Phooey,' too, instead of reaching for your gun when you fancy yourself betrayed.
Quentin Crisp (b.1908), British author: *Manners from Heaven* (1984), Ch.7

2 The first breath of adultery is the freest; after it, constraints aping marriage develop.
John Updike (b.1932), U.S. author and critic: *Couples* (1968), Ch.5

ADULTHOOD

1 In my case, adulthood itself was not an advance, although it was a useful waymark.
Nicholson Baker (b.1957), U.S. author: *The Mezzanine* (1988), Ch.3

2 The distinction between children and adults, while probably useful for some purposes, is at bottom a specious one, I feel. There are only individual egos, crazy for love.
Don Barthelme (1931–1989), U.S. author: The narrator (Joseph), in 'Me and Miss Mandible', first publ. in *Come Back, Dr Caligari* (1964), rep. in *Sixty Stories* (1982)

3 Adults are just children who earn money.
Kenneth Branagh (b.1960), British actor and film-maker: quoted in *Sight and Sound* (London), Dec. 1992

4 We have not passed that subtle line between childhood and adulthood until we move from the passive voice to the active voice – that is, until we have stopped saying 'It got lost,' and say, 'I lost it.'
Sydney Harris (b.1917), U.S. journalist: *On the Contrary* (1962), Ch.7

5 Part of the reason for the ugliness of adults, in a child's eyes, is that the child is usually looking upwards, and few faces are at their best when seen from below.
George Orwell (1903–1950), British author: 'Such, Such were the Joys' (1947), rep. in *The Collected Essays, Journalism and Letters of George Orwell* (ed. Sonia Orwell and Ian Angus, 1968), Vol.IV

6 Adulthood is the ever-shrinking period between childhood and old age. It is the apparent aim of modern industrial societies to reduce this period to a minimum.
Thomas Szasz (b.1920), U.S. psychiatrist: *The Second Sin* (1973), 'Social Relations'

See also GROWING UP

ADVENTURE

1 There are two kinds of adventurers: those who go truly hoping to find adventure and those who go secretly hoping they won't.
William Least Heat-Moon [William Trogdon] (b.1939), U.S. author: opening words of *Blue Highways: A Journey into America* (1983), Pt.2, Ch.4

2 The test of an adventure is that when you're in the middle of it, you say to yourself, 'Oh, now I've got myself into an awful mess; I wish I were sitting quietly at home.' And the sign that something's wrong with you is when you sit quietly at home wishing you were out having lots of adventure.
Thornton Wilder (1897–1975), U.S. novelist and playwright: Barnaby, in *The Matchmaker* (1954), Act 4

ADVERSITY

1 It is possible to adapt to a given hard situation precisely because you have got to live it, and you have got to live with it every day. But adapting does not mean that you forget. You go to the mill every day – it is always unacceptable to you, it has always been unacceptable to you, and it remains so for life – but you adapt in the sense that you cannot continue to live in a state of conflict with yourself.
Steve Biko (1946–1977), South African anti-apartheid activist: *Steve Biko: Black Consciousness in South Africa* (ed. Millard Arnold, 1978), 'Day One: The Morning of May 3, 1976'

2 Life is truly known only to those who suffer, lose, endure adversity and stumble from defeat to defeat.
Ryszard Kapuściński (b.1932), Polish journalist: 'A Warsaw Diary', publ. in *Granta* (Cambridge), No.15, 1985

3 Christ, you know it ain't easy,
You know how hard it can be,
The way things are going
They're going to crucify me.
John Lennon (1940–1980), British rock musician: 'The Ballad of John and Yoko' (song, 1969), on the album *Shaved Fish* (1975). The song, which was banned for its perceived blasphemy, is also credited to Paul McCartney

4 It may be that the most interesting American struggle is the struggle to set oneself free from the limits one is born to, and then to learn something of the value of those limits.
Greil Marcus (b.1945), U.S. rock journalist: *Mystery Train* (1976), 'Robert Johnson, 1938'

See also HARD TIMES

ADVERTISING

1 An advertising agency is 85 per cent confusion and 15 per cent commission.
Fred Allen (1894–1957), U.S. radio comic: *Treadmill to Oblivion* (1954), Pt.2

2 If everything on television is, without exception, part of a low-calorie (or even no-calorie) diet, then what good is it complaining about the adverts? By their worthlessness, they at least help to make the programmes around them seem of a higher level.
Jean Baudrillard (b.1929), French semiologist: *America* (1986; tr.1988), 'Utopia Achieved'

3 We read advertisements ... to discover and enlarge our desires. We are always ready – even eager – to discover, from the announcement of

a new product, what we have all along wanted without really knowing it.
Daniel J. Boorstin (b.1914), U.S. historian: *The Image* (1961), Ch.5

4 It is pretty obvious that the debasement of the human mind caused by a constant flow of fraudulent advertising is no trivial thing. There is more than one way to conquer a country.
Raymond Chandler (1888–1959), U.S. author: letter, 15 Nov. 1951, to his New York literary agent Carl Brandt, publ. in *Raymond Chandler Speaking* (ed. Dorothy Gardiner and Kathrine S. Walker, 1962)

5 I first became fascinated with the Sears catalogue because all the people in its pages were perfect. Nearly everybody I knew had something missing, a finger cut off, a toe split, an ear half-chewed away, an eye clouded with blindness from a glancing fence staple.
Harry Crews (b.1935), U.S. author: *A Childhood* (1978), Ch.4

6 I find commercials fascinating. They are so exquisitely vulgar and so delightfully tasteless that they must be irresistible to everyone save the few who aren't enchanted by discussions of nasal passages and digestive tracts.
Alfred Hitchcock (1899–1980), British film-maker: Screen Producers Guild dinner, 7 March 1965, publ. in *Hitchcock on Hitchcock* (ed. Sidney Gottlieb, 1995), 'After-Dinner speech'. 'The television commercial' Hitchcock added, 'is the only instance where Man has invented a torture and then provided the victim with a means of escape'

7 Society drives people crazy with lust and calls it advertising.
John Lahr (b.1941), U.S. literary and drama critic: *The Guardian* (London), 2 Aug. 1989

8 Advertising is the greatest art form of the twentieth century.
Marshall McLuhan (1911–1980), Canadian communications theorist: in *Advertising Age* (Chicago), 3 Sept. 1976

9 Good wine needs no bush,
And perhaps products that people really want need no hard-sell or soft-sell TV push.
Why not?
Look at pot.
Ogden Nash (1902–1971), U.S. poet: 'Most Doctors Recommend or Yours For Fast Fast Fast Relief', publ. in *The Old Dog Barks Backwards* (1972)

10 The adverts do pay well. I turned one down for Ford dealers last year because I don't like people who drive Fords. I used to get round the Andrex thing by saying the sound of my voice made you want to wipe your bottom.
John Peel (b.1939), British disc jockey: in *New Musical Express* (London), 1994, quoted in *NME Book of Quotes* (1995), 'Fame'

11 Remove advertising, disable a person or firm from preconising its wares and their merits, and the whole of society and of the economy is transformed. The enemies of advertising are the enemies of freedom.
Enoch Powell (b.1912), British Conservative politician: in *The Listener* (London), 31 July 1969

12 People vary in their susceptibility to advertising and marketing techniques. Some people are so susceptible that, even if they make a great deal of money, they cannot satisfy their constant craving for the shiny new toys that the marketing industry dangles before their eyes. So they always feel hard-pressed financially even if their income is large, and their cravings are frustrated.
Unabomber, U.S. radical: *Industrial Society and Its Future*, 'How Some People Adjust', Sct.80, publ. in the *Washington Post*, 19 Sept. 1995

13 The series of triumphal arches in Rome is a prototype of the billboard. ... The triumphal arches in the Roman Forum were spatial markers channeling processional paths within a complex urban landscape. On Route 66 the billboards ... perform a similar formal-spatial function. Often the brightest, cleanest, and best-maintained elements in industrial sprawl, the billboards both cover and beautify that landscape.
Robert Venturi (b.1925), U.S. architect: *Learning from Las Vegas* by Robert Venturi, Denise Scott Brown and Stephen Izenour (1972; rev.1977), Pt.2, 'Silent-White Majority Architecture'

14 There is no more craven consumer than the advertising man.
Peter York (b.1950), British journalist: interview in *The Sunday Telegraph* (London), 31 Dec. 1995

See also McLuhan on ELOQUENCE; PUBLICITY; White on SPONSORSHIP

ADVICE

1 There is hardly a man on earth who will take advice unless he is certain that it is positively bad.
Edward Dahlberg (1900–1977), U.S. author and critic: *Alms for Oblivion* (1964), 'Moby-Dick: A Hamitic Dream'

2 Advice is what we ask for when we already know the answer but wish we didn't.
Erica Jong (b.1942), U.S. author: *How To Save Your Own Life* (1977), epigraph to 'A day in the life ...'

3 Advice almost never functions as a social lubricant; eight or nine times out of ten it makes people lose face, crushes their will, and creates a grudge.
Yukio Mishima (1925–1970), Japanese author:

Mishima on Hagakure (1977), '*Hagakure* and Its Author'

4 Some of these people need ten years of therapy – ten sentences of mine do not equal ten years of therapy.

Jeff Zaslow (b.1925), U.S. advice columnist: of his correspondents, in the *International Herald Tribune* (Paris), 24 Jan. 1990

AEROPLANES

1 A plane is a bad place for an all-out sleep, but a good place to begin rest and recovery from the trip to the faraway places you've been, a decompression chamber between Here and There. Though a plane is not the ideal place really to think, to reassess or reevaluate things, it is a great place to have the illusion of doing so, and often the illusion will suffice.

Shana Alexander (b.1925), U.S. writer and editor: 'Overcuddle and Megalull' (1967), rep. in *The Feminine Eye* (1970)

2 I don't mind flying. I always pass out before the plane leaves the ground.

Naomi Campbell (b.1970), British model: quoted in *Arthur Elgort's Models Manual* (1993)

3 I wish I could write well enough to write about aircraft. Faulkner did it very well in Pylon but you cannot do something someone else has done though you might have done it if they hadn't.

Ernest Hemingway (1899–1961), U.S. author: letter, 3 July 1956, publ. in *Selected Letters* (ed. Carlos Baker, 1981)

4 I feel about airplanes the way I feel about diets. It seems to me that they are wonderful things for other people to go on.

Jean Kerr (b.1923), U.S. author and playwright: *The Snake Has All the Lines* (1958), 'Mirror, Mirror on the Wall'

AESTHETICS

1 For aesthetics is the mother of ethics.... Were we to choose our leaders on the basis of their reading experience and not their political programs, there would be much less grief on earth. I believe – not empirically, alas, but only theoretically – that for someone who has read a lot of Dickens to shoot his like in the name of an idea is harder than for someone who has read no Dickens.

Joseph Brodsky (1940–1996), Russian-born U.S. poet and critic: speech, 1987 Nobel Prize acceptance

2 'Art' is an invention of aesthetics, which in turn is an invention of philosophers. ... What we call art is a game.

Octavio Paz (b.1914), Mexican poet and essayist: *Alternating Current* (1967), 'André Breton or the Quest of the Beginning'

3 'Form follows profit' is the aesthetic principle of our times.

Richard Rogers (b.1933), British architect: in *The Times* (London), 13 Feb. 1991

AFFECTION

1 It's not till sex has died out between a man and a woman that they can really love. And now I mean affection. Now I mean to be *fond of* (as one is fond of oneself) – to hope, to be disappointed, to live inside the other heart. When I look back on the pain of sex, the love like a wild fox so ready to bite, the antagonism that sits like a twin beside love, and contrast it with affection, so deeply unrepeatable, of two people who have lived a life together (and of whom one must die) it's the affection I find richer. It's that I would have again. Not all those doubtful rainbow colours.

Enid Bagnold (1889–1981), British novelist and playwright: *Autobiography* (1969), Ch.6

2 Affection is the mortal illness of lonely people.

Gary Indiana, U.S. author: *Horse Crazy* (1989), Ch.1

3 For me affection was more visible in terms of finance than in terms of words. People can talk and not mean what they say, but with money, you know it will not let you down.

Bienvenida Sokolow ['Lady Buck'] (b.1958), Spanish-born mistress of Sir Peter Harding: interview in *The Times* (London), 4 March 1995

4 One should never direct people towards happiness, because happiness too is an idol of the market-place. One should direct them towards mutual affection. A beast gnawing at its prey can be happy too, but only human beings can feel affection for each other, and this is the highest achievement they can aspire to.

Alexander Solzhenitsyn (b.1918), Russian novelist: Shulubin, in *Cancer Ward*, Pt 2, (1969), Ch.10

AFFIRMATIVE ACTION

1 Lots of white people think black people are stupid. They are stupid themselves for thinking so, but regulation will not make them smarter.

Stephen Carter (b.1954), U.S. lawyer and author: *Reflections of an Affirmative Action Baby* (1992), Ch.8

2 When they kept you out it was because you were black; when they let you in, it is because you are black. That's progress?
Marilyn French (b.1929), U.S. author and critic: Valerie, in *The Women's Room* (1977), Ch.4, Sct.19

3 It doesn't do good to open doors for someone who doesn't have the price to get in. If he has the price, he may not need the laws. There is no law saying the Negro has to live in Harlem or Watts.
Ronald Reagan (b.1911), U.S. Republican politician and president: in the *San Francisco Chronicle*, 9 Sept. 1967

AFRICA

1 While the rest of the world has been improving technology, Ghana has been improving the quality of man's humanity to man.
Maya Angelou (b.1928), U.S. author: 'Involvement in Black and White' interview in the *Oregonian* (Portland, Oreg.), 17 Feb. 1971, rep. in *Conversations with Maya Angelou* (ed. Jeffrey M. Elliot, 1989). Angelou lived and worked in Ghana and Egypt 1962–66

2 The ministers, the members of the cabinet, the ambassadors and local commissioners are chosen from the same ethnological group as the leader, sometimes directly from his own family. Such regimes of the family sort seem to go back to the old laws of inbreeding, and not anger but shame is felt when we are faced with such stupidity, such an imposture, such intellectual and spiritual poverty. These heads of the government are the true traitors in Africa, for they sell their country to the most terrifying of all its enemies: stupidity.
Frantz Fanon (1925–1961), Martiniquan psychiatrist, philosopher and political activist: *The Wretched of the Earth* (1961), Ch.3

3 Are you there, Africa with the bulging chest and oblong thigh? Sulking Africa, wrought of iron, in the fire, Africa of the millions of royal slaves, deported Africa, drifting continent, are you there? Slowly you vanish, you withdraw into the past, into the tales of castaways, colonial museums, the works of scholars.
Jean Genet (1910–1986), French playwright and novelist: Felicity, in *The Blacks* (1958; tr.1960)

4 Where do whites fit in the New Africa? *Nowhere*, I'm inclined to say ... and I do believe that it is true that even the gentlest and most westernised Africans would like the emotional idea of the continent entirely without the complication of the presence of the white man for a generation or two. But *nowhere*, as an answer for us whites, is in the same category as remarks like *What's the use of living?* in the face of the threat of atomic radiation. We are living; we are in Africa.
Nadine Gordimer (b.1923), South African author: 'Where Do Whites Fit In?', first publ. in *Twentieth Century*, April 1959, rep. in *The Essential Gesture* (ed. Stephen Clingman, 1988)

5 When old settlers say 'One has to understand the country,' what they mean is, 'You have to get used to our ideas about the native.' They are saying, in effect, 'Learn our ideas, or otherwise get out; we don't want you.'
Doris Lessing (b.1919), British novelist: *The Grass is Singing* (1950), Ch.1

6 In Africa, there is much confusion. ... Before, there was no radio, or other forms of communication.... Now, in Africa ... the government talks, people talk, the police talk, the people don't know anymore. They aren't free.
Youssou N'Dour (b.1959), Senegalese musician: interview in *Africa Beat* (London), summer 1987

7 Africa is a paradox which illustrates and highlights neo-colonialism. Her earth is rich, yet the products that come from above and below the soil continue to enrich, not Africans predominantly, but groups and individuals who operate to Africa's impoverishment.
Kwame Nkrumah (1900–1972), Ghanaian president: *Neo-Colonialism* (1965), Ch.1

8 The African is my brother – but he is my younger brother by several centuries.
Albert Schweitzer (1875–1965), French missionary, theologian and musician: quoted in *The Observer* (London), 23 Oct. 1955

See also Macmillan on DECOLONIZATION; Angelou on ROOTS; SOUTH AFRICA

AGE

1 The class distinctions proper to a democratic society are not those of rank or money, still less, as is apt to happen when these are abandoned, of race, but of age.
W.H. Auden (1907–1973), Anglo-American poet: *The Dyer's Hand* (1962), Pt.6, 'Postscript: Rome v. Monticello'

2 The age of a woman doesn't mean a thing. The best tunes are played on the oldest fiddles.
Sigmund Z. Engel (1869–?): aged 80, quoted in *Newsweek* (New York), 4 July 1949

3 People between twenty and forty are not sympathetic. The child has the capacity to do but it can't know. It only knows when it is no longer able to do – after forty. Between twenty and forty the will of the child to do gets stronger, more dangerous, but it has not begun to learn to know yet. Since his capacity to do is forced into channels of evil through environment and pressures, man is stong before he is

moral. The world's anguish is caused by people between twenty and forty.

William Faulkner (1897–1962), U.S. novelist: interview in *Writers at Work* (First Series, ed. Malcolm Cowley, 1958)

4 A man has every season while a woman only has the right to spring. That disgusts me.

Jane Fonda (b.1937), U.S. actress: in the *Daily Mail* (London), 13 Sept. 1989

5 Among the virtues and vices that make up the British character, we have one vice, at least, that Americans ought to view with sympathy. For they appear to be the only people who share it with us. I mean our worship of the antique. I do not refer to beauty or even historical association. I refer to age, to a quantity of years.

William Golding (1911–1993), British author: 'An Affection For Cathedrals', first publ. in *Holiday Magazine* (Indianapolis), Dec. 1965, rep. in *A Moving Target* (1982)

6 I have always felt that a woman has the right to treat the subject of her age with ambiguity until, perhaps, she passes into the realm of over ninety. Then it is better she be candid with herself and with the world.

Helena Rubinstein (1870–1965), Polish-born U.S. cosmetics manufacturer: *My Life for Beauty* (1966), Pt.1, Ch.1

7 When you are younger you get blamed for crimes you never committed and when you're older you begin to get credit for virtues you never possessed. It evens itself out.

I.F. Stone (1907–1989), U.S. author: in the *International Herald Tribune* (Paris), 16 March 1988

8 I'm 65 and I guess that puts me in with the geriatrics. But if there were fifteen months in every year, I'd only be 48. That's the trouble with us. We number everything. Take women, for example. I think they deserve to have more than twelve years between the ages of 28 and 40.

James Thurber (1894–1961), U.S. humorist and illustrator: in *Time* (New York), 15 Aug. 1960

See also ADOLESCENCE; CHILDHOOD; MIDDLE AGE; TEENAGERS; YOUTH

AGE: Aging

1 You can only perceive real beauty in a person as they get older.

Anouk Aimée (b.1932), French actress: in *The Guardian* (London), 24 Aug. 1988

2 A man does not get old because he nears death; a man gets old because he can no longer see the false from the good.

Charles Bukowski (1920–1994), U.S. author and poet: letter written early 1962, publ. in *Screams from the Balcony: Selected Letters* (1993)

3 I don't believe one grows older. I think that what happens early on in life is that at a certain age one stands still and stagnates.

T.S. Eliot (1888–1965), Anglo-American poet and critic: on his 70th birthday, quoted in the *New York Times*, 21 Sept. 1958

4 Self-parody is the first portent of age.

Larry McMurtry (b.1936), U.S. screenwriter, novelist and essayist: Danny Deck, in *Some Can Whistle*, (1989), Pt.1, Ch.14

5 The older you get the stronger the wind gets – and it's always in your face.

Jack Nicklaus (b.1940), U.S. golfer: on his 50th birthday, quoted in the *International Herald Tribune* (Paris), 28 Feb. 1990

6 Aging calls us outdoors, after the adult indoors of work and love-life and keeping stylish, into the lovely simplicities that we thought we had outgrown as children. We come again to love the plain world, its stone and wood, its air and water.

John Updike (b.1932), U.S. author and critic: *Self-Consciousness* (1989), Ch.6

See also Melly on MICK JAGGER

AGE: The 30s

1 But it's hard to be hip over thirty
When everyone else is nineteen,
When the last dance we learned was the Lindy,
And the last we heard, girls who looked like
  Barbra Streisand
Were trying to do something about it.

Judith Viorst (b.1935), U.S. poet and journalist: 'It's Hard to Be Hip Over Thirty', publ. in *It's Hard to Be Hip Over Thirty and Other Tragedies of Married Life* (1968)

AGE: The 40s

1 At twenty you have many desires which hide the truth, but beyond forty there are only real and fragile truths – your abilities and your failings.

Gérard Depardieu (b.1948), French actor: in the *Daily Mail* (London), 4 March 1991

2 At forty-five,
What next, what next?
I meet my father,
my age, still alive.

Robert Lowell (1917–1977), U.S. poet: 'Middle Age', Sct.2, publ. in *For The Union Dead* (1965)

3 At forty-seven the things which really matter and the things which are really fun are the

dreadful things that our parents really said mattered. Family and work and duty. Crap like that.

P.J. O'Rourke (b.1947), U.S. journalist: interview in *The Guardian* (London), 25 Nov. 1995

See also Lowell on THE 1950S

AGE: The 50s

1 I think when the full horror of being fifty hits you, you should stay home and have a good cry.

Alan Bleasdale (b.1946), British playwright and novelist: in *The Times* (London), 18 June 1992

2 I'm aiming by the time I'm fifty to stop being an adolescent.

Wendy Cope (b.1945), British poet: in *The Daily Telegraph* (London), 9 Dec. 1992

3 Women over fifty already form one of the largest groups in the population structure of the western world. As long as they like themselves, they will not be an oppressed minority. In order to like themselves they must reject trivialization by others of who and what they are. A grown woman should not have to masquerade as a girl in order to remain in the land of the living.

Germaine Greer (b.1939), Australian feminist writer: introduction to *The Change: Women, Ageing and the Menopause* (1991)

4 Nobody expects to trust his body overmuch after the age of fifty.

Edward Hoagland (b.1932), U.S. novelist and essayist: 'Heaven and Nature', first publ. in *Harper's Magazine* (New York), March 1988, rep. in *Heart's Desire* (1988)

5 When you get to fifty-two food becomes more important than sex.

Prue Leith (b.1940), British chef, caterer and writer on cookery: in *The Guardian* (London), 11 Nov. 1992

6 The real sadness of fifty is not that you change so much but that you change so little.

Max Lerner (1902–1992), U.S. author and columnist: 'Fifty', first publ. in the *New York Post*, 18 Dec. 1952, rep. in *The Unfinished Country* (1959), Pt.1

7 When you're 50 you start thinking about things you haven't thought about before. I used to think getting old was about vanity – but actually it's about losing people you love. Getting wrinkles is trivial.

Joyce Carol Oates (b.1938), U.S. author: interview in *The Guardian* (London), 18 Aug. 1989

8 'Except ye become as little children,' except you can wake on your fiftieth birthday with the same forward-looking excitement and interest in life that you enjoyed when you were five, 'ye cannot enter the kingdom of God.' One must not only die daily, but every day we must be born again.

Dorothy L. Sayers (1893–1957), British author: *Creed or Chaos? and Other Essays in Popular Mythology* (1947), 'Strong Meat'

AGE: The 60s

1 If I'd been out till quarter to three
Would you lock the door?
Will you still need me,
Will you still feed me,
When I'm sixty-four?

John Lennon (1940–1980) and **Paul McCartney** (b.1942), British rock musicians: 'When I'm Sixty-four' (song) on the album *Sgt. Pepper's Lonely Hearts Club Band* (The Beatles, 1967)

2 One starts to get young at the age of sixty and then it is too late.

Pablo Picasso (1881–1973), Spanish artist: in *The Sunday Times* (London), 20 Oct. 1963

3 With sixty staring me in the face, I have developed inflammation of the sentence structure and definite hardening of the paragraphs.

James Thurber (1894–1961), U.S. humorist and illustrator: written aged 59 in the *New York Post*, 30 June 1955

4 Now that I am sixty, I see why the idea of elder wisdom has passed from currency.

John Updike (b.1932), U.S. author and critic: in the *New Yorker*, Nov. 1992

AGE: The 70s

1 Being over seventy is like being engaged in a war. All our friends are going or gone and we survive amongst the dead and the dying as on a battlefield.

Muriel Spark (b.1918), British novelist: Miss Taylor, in *Memento Mori* (1959), Ch.4

AGE: Old Age

1 To me, old age is always fifteen years older than I am.

Bernard Baruch (1870–1965), U.S. financier: in *The Observer* (London), 21 Aug. 1955

2 It is old age, rather than death, that is to be contrasted with life. Old age is life's parody, whereas death transforms life into a destiny: in a way it preserves it by giving it the absolute dimension. ... Death does away with time.

Simone de Beauvoir (1908–1986), French novelist and essayist: conclusion to *The Coming of Age* (1970; tr.1972)

3 We lose our hair, our teeth! Our bloom, our ideals.
Samuel Beckett (1906–1989), Irish playwright and novelist: Hamm, in *Endgame* (1958), p.16 of Faber edn.

4 I hope I never get so old I get religious.
Ingmar Bergman (b.1918), Swedish stage and film writer-director: in the *International Herald Tribune* (Paris), 8 Sept. 1989

5 One of the reasons why old people make so many journeys into the past is to satisfy themselves that it is still there.
Ronald Blythe (b.1922), British author: introduction to *The View in Winter* (1979)

6 Age wins and one must learn to grow old.... I must learn to walk this long unlovely wintry way, looking for spectacles, shunning the cruel looking-glass, laughing at my clumsiness before others mistakenly condole, not expecting gallantry yet disappointed to receive none, apprehending every ache or shaft of pain, alive to blinding flashes of mortality, unarmed, totally vulnerable.
Diana Cooper (1892–1986), British actress, author and society figure: *Trumpets from the Steep* (1960), Ch.8

7 Old age is an insult. It's like being smacked.
Lawrence Durrell (1912–1990), British author: interview in *The Sunday Times* (London), 20 Nov. 1988

8 An ... important antidote to American democracy is American gerontocracy. The positions of eminence and authority in Congress are alloted in accordance with length of service, regardless of quality. Superficial observers have long criticized the United States for making a fetish of youth. This is unfair. Uniquely among modern organs of public and private administration, its national legislature rewards senility.
J.K. Galbraith (b.1908), U.S. economist: 'The United States', first publ. in *New York*, 15 Nov. 1971, rep. in *A View from the Stands* (1986)

9 The older woman's love is not love of herself, nor of herself mirrored in a lover's eyes, nor is it corrupted by need. It is a feeling of tenderness so still and deep and warm that it gilds every grassblade and blesses every fly. It includes the ones who have a claim on it, and a great deal else besides. I wouldn't have missed it for the world.
Germaine Greer (b.1939), Australian feminist writer: introduction to *The Change: Women, Ageing and the Menopause* (1991)

10 I don't generally feel anything until noon, then it's time for my nap.
Bob Hope (b.1903), U.S. comedian: in the *International Herald Tribune* (Paris), 3 Aug. 1990

11 Old age is not a disease – it is strength and survivorship, triumph over all kinds of vicissitudes and disappointments, trials and illnesses.
Maggie Kuhn (1905–1995), U.S. civil rights activist and author: quoted in *New Age*, Feb. 1979

12 Perhaps being old is having lighted rooms
Inside your head, and people in them, acting.
People you know, yet can't quite name.
Philip Larkin (1922–1986), British poet: 'The Old Fools', St.3, publ. in *High Windows* (1974)

13 Certainly the effort to remain unchanged, young, when the body gives so impressive a signal of change as the menopause, is gallant; but it is a stupid, self-sacrificial gallantry, better befitting a boy of twenty than a woman of forty-five or fifty. Let the athletes die young and laurel-crowned. Let the soldiers earn the Purple Hearts. Let women die old, white-crowned, with human hearts.
Ursula K. Le Guin (b.1929), U.S. author: 'The Space Crone', publ. in *The Co-Evolution Quarterly*, summer 1976, rep. in *Dancing at the Edge of the World* (1989)

14 The great secret that all old people share is that you really haven't changed in seventy or eighty years. Your body changes, but you don't change at all. And that, of course, causes great confusion.
Doris Lessing (b.1919), British novelist: in *The Sunday Times* (London), 10 May 1992

15 Age is not a particularly interesting subject. Anyone can get old. All you have to do is live long enough.
Groucho Marx (1895–1977), U.S. comic actor: *Groucho And Me* (1959), Ch.1

16 If you associate enough with older people who do enjoy their lives, who are not stored away in any golden ghettos, you will gain a sense of continuity and of the possibility for a full life.
Margaret Mead (1901–1978), U.S. anthropologist: quoted in *Family Circle* (New York), 26 July 1977

17 When you get to my age life seems little more than one long march to and from the lavatory.
John Mortimer (b.1923), British barrister and novelist: Haverford Downs, in *Summer's Lease* (1988), Pt.2, Ch.3

18 Here, with whitened hair, desires failing, strength ebbing out of him, with the sun gone down and with only the serenity and the calm warning of the evening star left to him, he drank to Life, to all it had been, to what it was, to what it would be. Hurrah!
Sean O'Casey (1884–1964), Irish playwright: final paragraph of *Sunset and Evening Star* (sixth and final volume of autobiography, 1954)

19 Old women snore violently. They are like bodies into which bizarre animals have crept at night; the animals are vicious, bawdy, noisy. How they snore! There is no shame to their snoring. Old women turn into old men.

Joyce Carol Oates (b.1938), U.S. author: 'What is the Connection Between Men and Women?', publ. in *Mademoiselle* (New York), Feb. 1970

20 Growing old's like being increasingly penalized for a crime you haven't committed.

Anthony Powell (b.1905), British novelist: Dick Umfraville, in *Temporary Kings* (1973), Ch.1

21 And now the end is near
And so I face the final curtain,
I'll state my case of which I'm certain.
I've lived a life that's full, I traveled each and
ev'ry highway,
And more, much more than this. I did it my
way.

Frank Sinatra (b.1915), U.S. singer and actor: 'My Way' (song, written by Claude François, Jacques Revaux and Paul Anka, 1969). The Canadian songwriter Paul Anka is generally credited with adapting this song – from a French original, *Comme D'Habitude* – for Sinatra, with whom it has become indelibly linked

22 You end up as you deserve. In old age you must put up with the face, the friends, the health, and the children you have earned.

Fay Weldon (b.1933), British novelist: narrator, Praxis Duveen, in *Praxis* (1978), Ch.21

See also LONGEVITY

AGENTS

1 The agent never receipts his bill, puts his hat on and bows himself out. He stays around forever, not only for as long as you can write anything that anyone will buy, but as long as anyone will buy any portion of any right to anything that you ever did write. He just takes ten per cent of your life.

Raymond Chandler (1888–1959), U.S. author: 'Ten Per Cent of your Life', publ. in the *Atlantic Monthly* (Boston, Mass.), Feb. 1952

2 If God had an agent, the world wouldn't be built yet. It'd only be about Thursday.

Jerry Reynolds, Sacramento Kings player personnel director: on how agents slow down the negotiating process, quoted in *Newsweek* (New York), 25 Nov. 1991

AGGRESSION

1 I love to see a young girl go out and grab the world by the lapels. Life's a bitch. You've got to go out and kick ass.

Maya Angelou (b.1928), U.S. author: interview in *Girl About Town*, 13 Oct. 1986, rep. in *Conversations with Maya Angelou* (ed. Jeffrey M. Elliot, 1989), 'Kicking Ass'

2 Does our ferocity not derive from the fact that our instincts are all too interested in other people? If we attended more to ourselves and became the centre, the object of our murderous inclinations, the sum of our intolerances would diminish.

E.M. Cioran (1911–1995), Rumanian-born French philosopher: title essay of *The Temptation to Exist* (1956)

3 When I pass a belt, I can't resist hitting below it.

Robert Maxwell (1923–1991), British tycoon: in the *International Herald Tribune* (Paris), 18 March 1991, quoted in *Maxwell: The Outsider* by Tom Bower (1988; rev.1991), Ch.16

4 He has a nasty instinct for the exposed groin, and always puts his knee in just to stir things up.

Austin Mitchell (b.1934), British Labour politician: of fellow MP and chat-show host Norman Tebbit, in the *Evening Standard* (London), 2 Feb. 1989

5 Aggression, the writer's main source of energy.

Ted Solotaroff (b.1928), U.S. editor: 'Writing in the Cold', publ. in *Granta* (Cambridge), No.15, 1985

AGNOSTICS

1 If only God would give me some clear sign! Like making a large deposit in my name at a Swiss bank.

Woody Allen (b.1935), U.S. film-maker: 'Selections from the Allen Notebooks', first publ. in the *New Yorker*, 5 Nov. 1973, rep. in *Without Feathers* (1976)

2 Lord I disbelieve – help thou my unbelief.

E.M. Forster (1879–1970), British novelist and essayist: *Two Cheers for Democracy* (1951), 'What I Believe'. A reference to Bible, New Testament, Mark 9:24, 'Lord, I believe, help thou mine unbelief'

3 Perhaps I am an agnostic, in the sense that I reject everything that humanity presents as new to the world, on the grounds that the methods used were inappropriate. The formula $E=mc^2$ cannot be right, because there can be no such thing as positive knowledge.

Andrey Tarkovsky (1932–1986), Russian film-maker: journal entry, 15 July 1981, publ. in *Time Within Time: The Diaries 1970–1986* (1989; tr.1994)

AGREEMENT

1 Thinking isn't agreeing or disagreeing. That's voting.

   Robert Frost (1874–1963), U.S. poet: interview in *Writers at Work* (Second Series, ed. George Plimpton, 1963)

2 There's nothing in this world more instinctively abhorrent to me than finding myself in agreement with my fellow-humans.

   Malcolm Muggeridge (1903–1990), British journalist and broadcaster: *Any Questions?* (radio broadcast, 29 April 1955), publ. in *Muggeridge Through the Microphone* (1967), 'Mini-Mania'

See also CONSENSUS

AID

1 Aid is ... like champagne: in success you deserve it, in failure you need it.

   Lord Bauer (b.1915), British economist: quoted in introduction to *Lords of Poverty* by Graham Hancock (1989)

2 It is not helpful to help a friend by putting coins in his pockets when he has got holes in his pockets.

   Douglas Hurd (b.1930), British Conservative politician: on aid to Russia, quoted in *The Observer* (London), 9 June 1991

3 To those people in the huts and villages of half the globe struggling to break the bonds of mass misery, we pledge our best efforts to help them help themselves, for whatever period is required, not because the Communists may be doing it, not because we seek their votes, but because it is right. If a free society cannot help the many who are poor, it cannot save the few who are rich.

   John F. Kennedy (1917–1963), U.S. Democratic politician and president: inaugural address, 20 Jan. 1961, Washington D.C., publ. in *Public Papers of the Presidents of the United States of America, John F. Kennedy, 1961*

4 Almsgiving tends to perpetuate poverty; aid does away with it once and for all. Almsgiving leaves a man just where he was before. Aid restores him to society as an individual worthy of all respect and not as a man with a grievance. Almsgiving is the generosity of the rich; social aid levels up social inequalities. Charity separates the rich from the poor; aid raises the needy and sets him on the same level with the rich.

   Eva Perón (1919–1952), Argentinian government official and politician: 'My Labour in the Field of Social Aid', speech to the American Congress of Industrial Medicine, 5 Dec. 1949

5 We are for aiding our allies by sharing some of our material blessings with those nations which share in our fundamental beliefs, but we are against doling out money government to government, creating bureaucracy, if not socialism, all over the world. We set out to help 19 countries. We are helping 107. We spent $146 billion. With that money, we bought a 2-million-dollar yacht for Haile Selassie. We bought dress suits for Greek undertakers, extra wives for Kenya government officials. We bought a thousand TV sets for a place where they have no electricity.

   Ronald Reagan (b.1911), U.S. Republican politician and president: TV address, 27 Oct. 1964, publ. in *Speaking My Mind* (1989), 'A Time for Choosing'

6 To keep a lamp burning we have to keep putting oil in it.

   Mother Teresa (1910–1997), Albanian-born Roman Catholic missionary: quoted in *Time* (New York), 29 Dec. 1975

AIDS

1 Both the Moral Majority, who are recycling medieval language to explain AIDS, and those ultra-leftists who attribute AIDS to some sort of conspiracy, have a clearly political analysis of the epidemic. But even if one attributes its cause to a microorganism rather than the wrath of God, or the workings of the CIA, it is clear that the way in which AIDS has been perceived, conceptualized, imagined, researched and financed makes this the most political of diseases.

   Dennis Altman (b.1943), Australian sociologist: *AIDS in the Mind of America* (1986), Ch.2

2 Everywhere I go I see increasing evidence of people swirling about in a human cesspit of their own making.

   James Anderton (b.1932), British senior police officer: on the AIDS epidemic, quoted in *City Limits* (London), 18 Dec. 1987

3 It could be said that the AIDS pandemic is a classic own-goal scored by the human race against itself.

   Anne, Princess Royal of Great Britain and Northern Ireland (b.1950): quoted in *The Daily Telegraph* (London), 27 Feb. 1988

4 We are aware for the first time in our history that the sexual act can bring about death. But we must not let AIDS become a banner that can be waved by right-wing elements to herald some new morality. AIDS is being used as a reason why nobody must experiment. But we have to be aware that everybody *must* feel comfortable in their sexuality.

   David Bowie (b.1947), British rock musician: interview in *Arena* (London), May/June 1993, rep.

in *Dispatches from the Front Line of Popular Culture* (Tony Parsons, 1994)

5 From the point of view of the pharmaceutical industry, the AIDS problem has already been solved. After all, we already have a drug which can be sold at the incredible price of $8,000 an annual dose, and which has the added virtue of not diminishing the market by actually curing anyone.
Barbara Ehrenreich (b.1941), U.S. author and columnist: 'Phallic Science' (1988), rep. in *The Worst Years of Our Lives* (1991)

6 We are all HIV-positive.
Diamanda Galás (b.1955), U.S. singer: tattooed on her knuckles. Discussing the tattoo in an interview in *Re/Search* (San Francisco), No.13, 1991, 'Angry Women', Galás stated 'if I wear the right clothes it will just say "HIV Positive". A lot of people already assume I've got AIDS because of my work, just as they assume I'm a lesbian'

7 AIDS was ... an illness in stages, a very long flight of steps that led assuredly to death, but whose every step represented a unique apprenticeship. It was a disease that gave death time to live and its victims time to die, time to discover time, and in the end to discover life.
Hervé Guibert (1955–1991), French author and AIDS victim: *To the Friend Who Did Not Save My Life* (1991), Ch.61

8 My thoughts are crowded with death
and it draws so oddly on the sexual
that I am confused
confused to be attracted
by, in effect, my own annihilation.
Thom Gunn (b.1929), British poet: 'In Time Of Plague', publ. in *The Man with Night Sweats* (1992)

9 The prejudice surrounding AIDS exacts a social death which precedes the actual physical one.
Tom Hanks (b.1957), U.S. actor: Andrew Beckett (Tom Hanks), in *Philadelphia* (film; screenplay by Ron Nyswaner, directed by Jonathan Demme, 1993). Hanks is reading a Supreme Court ruling from a previous case

10 Sometimes I have a terrible feeling that I am dying not from the virus, but from being untouchable.
Amanda Heggs, AIDS sufferer: quoted in *The Guardian* (London), 12 June 1989

11 We listen to the hum and throb of the hospital and watch the soundless river shatter light into thousands of white drops. It isn't fair. We used to say: How can we live like this? And now the question really is: How can we die like this?
Gary Indiana, U.S. author: *Horse Crazy* (1989), Ch.5

12 The slow-witted approach to the HIV epidemic was the result of a thousand years of Christian malpractice and the childlike approach of the church to sexuality. If any single man was responsible, it was Augustine of Hippo who murdered his way to sainthood spouting on about the sins located in his genitals.
Derek Jarman (1942–1994), British film-maker, artist and author: *At Your Own Risk: A Saint's Testament* (1992), '1980's'

13 I've spent fifteen years of my life fighting for our right to be free and make love whenever, wherever ... And you're telling me that all those years of what being gay stood for is wrong ... and I'm a murderer. We have been so oppressed! Don't you remember how it was? Can't you see how important it is for us to love openly, without hiding and without guilt?
Larry Kramer (b.1935), U.S. playwright and novelist: Mickey, in *The Normal Heart* (1985)

14 Then, strung out and spotty, you wriggle and sigh
and kiss all the fellows and make them all die.
Les Murray (b.1938), Australian poet: final couplet of 'Midnight Lake', publ. in *Dog Fox Field* (1991)

15 I have learned more about love, selflessness and human understanding in this great adventure in the world of Aids than I ever did in the cut-throat, competitive world in which I spent my life.
Anthony Perkins (1932–1992), U.S. actor: statement, publ. posthumously in the *Independent on Sunday* (London), 20 Sept. 1992

16 Any important disease whose causality is murky, and for which treatment is ineffectual, tends to be awash in significance.
Susan Sontag (b.1933), U.S. essayist: *Illness As Metaphor* (1978), Ch.8

17 Societies need to have one illness which becomes identified with evil, and attaches blame to its 'victims.'
Susan Sontag: *AIDS and Its Metaphors* (1989), Ch.1

18 The moral immune system of this country has been weakened and attacked, and the AIDS virus is the perfect metaphor for it. The malignant neglect of the last twelve years has led to breakdown of our country's immune system, environmentally, culturally, politically, spiritually and physically.
Barbra Streisand (b.1942), U.S. singer, actress and film-maker: 'The Way We Were', publ. in *The Guardian* (London), 26 Nov. 1992

19 The AIDS epidemic has rolled back a big rotting log and revealed all the squirming life underneath it, since it involves, all at once, the main themes of our existence: sex, death,

power, money, love, hate, disease and panic. No American phenomenon has been so compelling since the Vietnam War.
Edmund White (b.1940), U.S. author: *States of Desire: Travels in Gay America* (1980), 'Afterword – AIDS: An American Epidemic' (added to 1986 edn.)

MUHAMMAD ALI

1 Float like a butterfly, sting like a bee.
Muhammad Ali (b.1942), U.S. boxer: quoted in *The Story of Cassius Clay* by George Edward Sullivan (1964), Ch.8. Muhammad Ali's catchphrase was said to have originated with his aide Drew 'Bundini' Brown

2 That was always the difference between Muhammad Ali and the rest of us. He came, he saw, and if he didn't entirely conquer – he came as close as anybody we are likely to see in the lifetime of this doomed generation.
Hunter S. Thompson (b.1939), U.S. journalist: 'Last Tango in Vegas: Fear and Loathing in the Far Room', publ. in *Rolling Stone* (New York), 18 May 1978, rep. in *The Great Shark Hunt* (1979), Pt.4

ALIENATION

1 There is only one way left to escape the alienation of present day society: *to retreat ahead of it* .
Roland Barthes (1915–1980), French semiologist: *The Pleasure of the Text* (1975), 'Modern'

2 Although the masters make the rules
For the wise men and the fools
I got nothing, Ma, to live up to.
Bob Dylan (b.1941), U.S. singer and songwriter: 'It's Alright Ma (I'm Only Bleeding)' (song), on the album *Bringing it All Back Home* (1965)

3 Alienation is no longer a psychological aberration; it is defined by a historical moment.
Michel Foucault (1926–1984), French philosopher: *Mental Illness and Psychology* (1976)

4 By alienation is meant a mode of experience in which the person experiences himself as an alien. He has become, one might say, estranged from himself. He does not experience himself as the center of his world, as the creator of his own acts – but his acts and their consequences have become his masters, whom he obeys, or whom he may even worship. The alienated person is out of touch with himself as he is out of touch with any other person. He, like the others, are experienced as things are experienced; with the senses and with common sense, but at the same time without being related to oneself and to the world outside positively.

Erich Fromm (1900–1980), U.S. psychologist: *The Sane Society* (1955), Ch.5, 'Alienation'

5 The alienated human individual is bound to society as a whole by an invisible umbilical cord: the law of value. It acts upon all facets of his life, shaping his road and his destiny.
Ernesto 'Che' Guevara (1928–1967), Argentinian revolutionary leader: 'Socialism and Man in Cuba', open letter to the editor of the Uruguayan newspaper *La Marcha* , 1967, publ. in *Che Guevara on Revolution* (ed. Jay Mallin, 1969)

6 What else but a profound feeling of being excluded can enable a person better to see the absurdity of the world and his own existence or, to put it more soberly, the absurd dimensions of the world and his own existence?
Václav Havel (b.1936), Czech playwright and president: *Disturbing the Peace* (1986; tr. 1990), Ch.1

7 There is no religion in which everyday life is not considered a prison; there is no philosophy or ideology that does not think that we live in alienation.
Eugène Ionesco (1912–1994), Rumanian-born French playwright: *Present Past – Past Present* (1968), Ch.5

8 It seems to me as if that alienation which so long separated me from the world has become transferred into my own inner world, and has revealed to me an unexpected familiarity with myself.
Carl Jung (1875–1961), Swiss psychiatrist: closing words of *Memories, Dreams, Reflections* (1962), 'Retrospect'

9 Alienation as our present destiny is achieved only by outrageous violence perpetrated by human beings on human beings.
R.D. Laing (1927–1989), British psychiatrist: introduction to *The Politics of Experience* (1967)

10 Without alienation, there can be no politics.
Arthur Miller (b.1915), U.S. playwright: interview in *Marxism Today* (London), Jan. 1988

ALIENS

1 Have we been visited by aliens? ... I don't believe we have. I think that any such visit would be obvious and probably unpleasant. What would be the point of aliens revealing themselves only to a few cranks?
Stephen Hawking (b.1942), British theoretical physicist: in the *Radio Times* (London), 17 Feb. 1996, 'Hawking: the Big Questions'

2 You still don't know what you're dealing with, do you? ... Perfect organism. Its structural perfection is matched only by its hostility. I admire its purity, a survivor; unclouded

by conscience, remorse or delusions of morality.

Ian Holm (b.1932), British actor: Ash (Ian Holm) in *Alien* (film; screenplay by Dan O'Bannon, directed by Ridley Scott, 1979)

See also Didion on FICTION: SCIENCE FICTION

ALLIANCES

1 We cannot always assure the future of our friends; we have a better chance of assuring our future if we remember who our friends are.
Henry Kissinger (b.1923), U.S. Republican politician and secretary of state: on the changing U.S. policy towards the Shah of Iran, in *The White House Years* (1979), Ch.29, 'A Visit to the Shah of Iran'

2 An alliance is like a chain. It is not made stronger by adding weak links to it. A great power like the United States gains no advantage and it loses prestige by offering, indeed peddling, its alliances to all and sundry. An alliance should be hard diplomatic currency, valuable and hard to get, and not inflationary paper from the mimeograph machine in the State Department.
Walter Lippmann (1889–1974), U.S. journalist: in the *New York Herald Tribune*, 5 Aug. 1952

ALTRUISM

1 Much as we might wish to believe otherwise, universal love and the welfare of the species as a whole are concepts which simply do not make evolutionary sense.
Richard Dawkins (b.1941), British biologist and author: *The Selfish Gene* (1976), Ch.1

2 I don't mind giving them a reasonable amount, but a pint ... why that's very nearly an armful.
Tony Hancock (1924–1968), British comedian: *Hancock's Half-Hour*, BBC, 23 June 1961, (1956–1963 series written by Ray Galton and Alan Simpson), publ. in *Hancock's Half Hour* (1974), 'The Blood Donor'

3 The compulsion to do good is an innate American trait. Only North Americans seem to believe that they always should, may, and actually can choose somebody with whom to share their blessings. Ultimately this attitude leads to bombing people into the acceptance of gifts.
Ivan Illich (b.1926), Austrian-born U.S. theologian and author: *Celebration of Awareness* (1969), Preface to Ch.2

4 I think that more of our children would grow up happier and more stable if they were acquiring a conviction, all through childhood, that the most important thing that human beings can do is serve humanity in some function and to live by their ideals.
Dr Benjamin Spock (b.1903), U.S. paediatrician and author: *Baby and Child Care* (1946), 'The Parents' Part', Sct.11

AMBIGUITY

1 The human ability to entertain ambiguity is sadly limited and at any given moment most people have at least a hypothesis, if not an iron-clad theory, that explains the things that matter most to them.
Edmund White (b.1940), U.S. author: 'The Gay Philosopher' (essay written 1969), rep. in *The Burning Library* (1994)

AMBITION

1 Ambition is a Dead Sea fruit, and the greatest peril to the soul is that one is likely to get precisely what he is seeking.
Edward Dahlberg (1900–1977), U.S. author and critic: *Alms for Oblivion* (1964), 'No Love and No Thanks'

2 At the age of six I wanted to be a cook. At seven I wanted to be Napoleon. And my ambition has been growing steadily ever since.
Salvador Dali (1904–1989), Spanish painter: opening words of *The Secret Life of Salvador Dali* (1948), 'Prologue'

3 Man is the only creature that strives to surpass himself, and yearns for the impossible.
Eric Hoffer (1902–1983), U.S. philosopher: in the *New York Times*, 21 July 1969

4 Ambition if it feeds at all, does so on the ambition of others.
Susan Sontag (b.1933), U.S. essayist: *The Benefactor* (1963), Ch.1

THE AMERICAN DREAM

1 The American Dream has run out of gas. The car has stopped. It no longer supplies the world with its images, its dreams, its fantasies. No more. It's over. It supplies the world with its nightmares now: the Kennedy assassination, Watergate, Vietnam ...
J.G. Ballard (b.1930), British author: interview, first publ. in *Métaphors*, No.7, 1983, rep. in *Re/Search* (San Francisco), No.8/9, 1984

2 America has been a land of dreams. A land where the aspirations of people from countries cluttered with rich, cumbersome, aristocratic, ideological pasts can reach for what once seemed unattainable. Here they have tried to make dreams come true. ... Yet now ... we are threatened by a new and particularly American

menace. It is not the menace of class war, of ideology, of poverty, of disease, of illiteracy, or demagoguery, or of tyranny, though these now plague most of the world. It is the menace of unreality.

Daniel J. Boorstin (b.1914), U.S. historian: *The Image* (1961), Ch.6

3 I will keep America moving forward, always forward – for a better America, for an endless enduring dream and a thousand points of light.

George Bush (b.1924), U.S. Republican politician and president: acceptance speech, 18 August 1988, New Orleans, publ. in the *New York Times*, 19 Aug. 1988. The phrase 'a thousand points of light,' written for Bush by speechwriter Peggy Noonan, was used on various occasions during the 1988 presidential campaign. The words are not original, echoing similar phrases by Charles Dickens and Thomas Wolfe, among others. As president, Bush initiated a 'Points of Light' reform programme in June 1989

4 How can you get onto Route 66 when you live off the M1?

Jarvis Cocker (b.1963), British rock musician: interview in *The Observer* (London), quoted in *Pulp: The Tomorrow People* by Susan Wilson (1996), Ch.1

5 I am the living attestation of the American dream. I am the extolment of this great nation.

Don King (b.1931), U.S. boxing promoter: interview in the *Independent on Sunday* (London), 10 March 1996

6 Unfortunately, the balance of nature decrees that a super-abundance of dreams is paid for by a growing potential for nightmares.

Peter Ustinov (b.1921), British actor, writer and director: speaking of the U.S., in *The Independent* (London), 25 Feb. 1989

See also Le Guin on SUCCESS

AMERICANS *see under* THE UNITED STATES

ANGER

1 Rage cannot be hidden, it can only be dissembled. This dissembling deludes the thoughtless, and strengthens rage and adds, to rage, contempt.

James Baldwin (1924–1987), U.S. author: 'Stranger in the Village', first publ. in *Harper's Magazine* (New York), Oct. 1953, rep. in *Notes of a Native Son* (1955)

2 We are living in a very chaotic and confused world, and if we think that we're not in rage it's hypocritical. What we do is maybe suppress our rage and get sick from it; or you may take it out on your spouse or your family or the people

around you. And, actually, the rage is not against those people, it's against yourself; I think it's a rage that's there for a good reason, and that we should admit it and share it and use the energy of that anger to do something about it.

Yoko Ono (b.1933), Japanese-born U.S. artist: interview in *The Guardian* (London), 20 Jan. 1996

3 What I've learned about being angry with people is that it generally hurts you more than it hurts them.

Oprah Winfrey (b.1954), U.S. chat-show host: quoted in *Oprah!* by Robert Waldron (1987), Ch.2

THE ANGRY YOUNG MEN

1 I wish I knew why the hero is so dreadfully cross and what about? I should also like to know how, where and why he and his friend run a sweet-stall and if, considering the hero's unparalleled capacity for invective, they ever manage to sell any sweets? I expect my bewilderment is because I am very old indeed and cannot understand why the younger generation, instead of knocking at the door, should bash the fuck out of it.

Noël Coward (1899–1973), British playwright, actor and composer: on reading *Look Back in Anger*, in journal entry, 17 Feb. 1957, publ. in *The Noël Coward Diaries* (ed. Graham Payn and Sheridan Morley, 1982)

2 Damn you, England. You're rotting now, and quite soon you'll disappear. My hate will outrun you yet if only for a few seconds. I wish it could be eternal.

John Osborne (1929–1994), British playwright: letter to *Tribune*, 18 Aug. 1961

3 The theatre's press-agent, asked for a description of the iconoclastic young gate-crasher, said that he was first and foremost 'an angry young man'. Before long the phrase, in itself not particularly striking, had snowballed into a cult. It did so because it defined a phenomenon that was nationally recognizable. It gave a name to a generation of young intellectuals who disliked being called intellectuals, since they thought the word phony, affected, and 'wet'. There is nothing new in young men being angry: in fact, it would be news if they were anything else.

Kenneth Tynan (1927–1980), British critic: referring to George Fearon, press agent at the Royal Court Theatre which first staged *Look Back in Anger* in 1956, in 'The Angry Young Movement' (1958), rep. in *Tynan on Theatre* (1964)

4 I was never an angry young man, none of us was. On the contrary, we were all very happy young men and women. Who would not have been happy? Discovered, applauded, paid,

made internationally famous overnight? But I am an angry old man.

Arnold Wesker (b.1932), British playwright: quoted in the *Independent on Sunday* (London), 23 Oct. 1994

ANGST

1 Teenage angst has paid off well,
Now I'm bored and old.

Kurt Cobain (1967–1994), U.S. rock musician: 'Serve the Servants' (song), on the album *In Utero* (Nirvana, 1993)

2 I don't know if I'm free because I'm unhappy or unhappy because I'm free.

Jean-Luc Godard (b.1930), French film-maker and author: Patricia Franchini (Jean Seberg) in *À Bout de Souffle* (film; written and directed by Jean-Luc Goddard, 1959)

ANIMAL LIB

1 It takes up to 40 dumb animals to make a fur coat but only one to wear it.

Banner in David Bailey's celebrated video for the anti-fur trade group, Lynx, mid-1980s

2 If I could do anything about the way people behave towards each other, I would, but since I can't I'll stick to the animals.

Brigitte Bardot (b.1934), French actress: quoted in *Bardot* by Glenys Roberts (1984), Ch.15

3 Animals used to provide a lowlife way to kill and get away with it, as they do still, but, more intriguingly, for some people they are an aperture through which wounds drain. The scapegoat of olden times, driven off for the bystanders' sins, has become a tender thing, a running injury. There, running away … is me: hurt it and you are hurting me.

Edward Hoagland (b.1932), U.S. novelist and essayist: 'Lament the Red Wolf', first publ. in *Sports Illustrated* (New York), 14 Jan. 1974, rep. in *Heart's Desire* (1988)

4 Mankind's true moral test, its fundamental test (which lies deeply buried from view), consists of its attitude towards those who are at its mercy: animals. And in this respect mankind has suffered a fundamental debacle, a debacle so fundamental that all others stem from it.

Milan Kundera (b.1929), Czech-born French author and critic: *The Unbearable Lightness of Being* (1984), Pt.7, Ch.2

ANIMALS

1 A peasant becomes fond of his pig and is glad to salt away its pork. What is significant, and is so difficult for the urban stranger to understand, is that the two statements are connected by an *and* and not by a *but* .

John Berger (b.1926), British author and critic: *About Looking* (1980), 'Why Look at Animals?'

2 Bats have no bankers and they do not drink and cannot be arrested and pay no tax and, in general, bats have it made.

John Berryman (1914–1972), U.S. poet: *77 Dream Songs* (1964), No. 63

3 Animals are stylized characters in a kind of old saga – stylized because even the most acute of them have little leeway as they play out their parts.

Edward Hoagland (b.1932), U.S. novelist and essayist: 'Dogs and the Tug of Life', first publ. in *Harper's Magazine* (New York), Feb. 1975, rep. in *Heart's Desire* (1988)

4 Nothing to be done really about animals. Anything you do looks foolish. The answer isn't in us. It's almost as if we're put here on earth to show how silly they aren't.

Russell Hoban (b.1925), U.S. author: George Fairbairn, in *Turtle Diary* (1975), Ch.42

5 Animals often strike us as passionate machines.

Eric Hoffer (1902–1983), U.S. philosopher: *Reflections on the Human Condition* (1973), Aph.7

6 The surprise of animals … in and out, cats and dogs and a milk goat and chickens and guinea hens, all taken for granted, as if man was intended to live on terms of friendly intercourse with the rest of creation instead of huddling in isolation on the fourteenth floor of an apartment house in a city where animals occurred behind bars in the zoo.

Elizabeth Janeway (b.1913), U.S. author: *Accident on Route 37* (1964), 'Steven Benedict'

7 Camels are snobbish
and sheep, unintelligent;
water buffaloes, neurasthenic –
even murderous.
Reindeer seem over-serious.

Marianne Moore (1887–1972), U.S. poet: 'The Arctic Ox (Or Goat)', publ. in *O To Be a Dragon* (1959)

8 Four legs good, two legs bad.

George Orwell (1903–1950), British author: *Animal Farm* (1945), Ch.3. By the end of the story, the animals' revolutionary maxim has changed to 'Four legs good, two legs *better*' (Ch.10)

9 I've often said there's nothing better for the inside of a man than the outside of a horse.

Ronald Reagan (b.1911), U.S. Republican politician and president: remark, 13 Aug. 1987, North Platte, Nebraska. The *New York Times* had previously quoted this remark as early as 2 Oct. 1981

10 In reality, sheep are brave, enlightened
and sassy. They are walking clouds
and like clouds have forgotten
how to jump.
Jo Shapcott (b.1953), British poet: 'Lies', publ. in
Electroplating the Baby (1988)

11 The sense of smell in the animal is what
intuition is to the human spirit. It tells you of
the invisible, of what cannot be detected by
other means. It tells you the things that are not
there, yet are coming. You see into the blind
opaque past and round the corner of time.
Laurens van der Post (1906–1996), South African
writer and philosopher: *A Walk with a White
Bushman* (1986), p.18 of Chatto & Windus edn.

See also BIRDS; CATS; DOGS; Orwell on EQUALITY

ANTHROPOLOGY

1 Anthropology is the science which tells us that
people are the same the whole world over –
except when they are different.
Nancy Banks-Smith, British columnist: quoted in
The Guardian (London), 21 July 1988

2 Anthropologists are a connecting link between
poets and scientists; though their field-work
among primitive peoples has often made them
forget the language of science.
Robert Graves (1895–1985), British poet and
novelist: speech, 6 Dec. 1963, London School of
Economics, publ. in *Mammon and the Black
Goddess* (1965), 'Mammon'

3 No contact with savage Indian tribes has ever
daunted me more than the morning I spent
with an old lady swathed in woolies who compared herself to a rotten herring encased in a
block of ice.
Claude Lévi-Strauss (b.1908), French
anthropologist: *Tristes Tropiques* (1955), Ch.1

4 Anthropology has always struggled with an
intense, fascinated repulsion towards its
subject.... [The anthropologist] submits himself to the exotic to confirm his own inner
alienation as an urban intellectual.
Susan Sontag (b.1933), U.S. essayist: quoted in
'Structure and Infrastructure in Primitive Society'
by Neville Dyson-Hudson, publ. in *The
Structuralist Controversy* (ed. R. Macksey and E.
Donato, 1970)

ANTICIPATION

1 We know delay makes pleasure great.
In our eyes, on our tongues,
We savour the approaching delight
of things we know yet are fresh always.
Sweet things. Sweet things.
Thom Gunn (b.1929), British poet: 'Sweet Things',
publ. in *The Passages of Joy* (1982)

2 You know, sometimes, when they say you're
ahead of your time, it's just a polite way of
saying you have a real bad sense of timing.
George McGovern (b.1922), U.S. Democratic
politician: in *The Guardian* (London), 14 March
1990

ANTIPATHY

1 [They] exchanged the quick, brilliant smile of
women who dislike each other on sight.
Marshall Pugh (b.1925), British journalist and
author: *The Chancer* (1959), Ch.2

APATHY

1 I found it hard, it was hard to find,
Oh well, whatever, never mind.
Kurt Cobain (1967–1994), U.S. rock musician:
'Smells Like Teen Spirit' (song), on the album
Nevermind (Nirvana, 1991)

2 From the moment that a man no longer
responds in the slightest to the motives that
regulate the material world, that world appears
to be at complete repose.
Yukio Mishima (1925–1970), Japanese author:
Death in Midsummer and Other Stories (1966), 'The
Priest of Shiga Temple and His Love'

See also INDIFFERENCE

APHORISMS & EPIGRAMS

1 The test of a good classical moralization is that
it seems to have been written for oneself alone.
James Cameron (1911–1985), British journalist: of
the saying, *Video meliora proboque; deteriora sequor*,
in *Point of Departure* (1969), Ch.4

2 An aphorism
should be
like a burr:
sting,
stick,
and leave
a little soreness
afterwards.
Irving Layton (b.1912), Canadian poet: *The Whole
Bloody Bird* (1969), 'Aphs'

3 An epigram is only a wisecrack that's played at
Carnegie Hall.
Oscar Levant (1906–1972), U.S. pianist and
composer: in *Coronet Magazine*, Sept. 1968

4 It is the nature of aphoristic thinking to be
always in a state of concluding; a bid to have
the final word is inherent in all powerful
phrase-making.
Susan Sontag (b.1933), U.S. essayist: 'Writing
Itself: on Roland Barthes', introduction to *Barthes:
Selected Writings* (1982)

APPEARANCE

1 Everybody has that thing where they need to look one way but they come out looking another way and that's what people observe. You see someone on the street and essentially what you notice about them is the flaw. It's just extraordinary that we should have been given these peculiarities. ... Something is ironic in the world and it has to do with the fact that what you intend never comes out like you intend it.
Diane Arbus (1923–1971), U.S. photographer: from classes given in 1971, publ. in *Diane Arbus: An Aperture Monograph* (1972)

2 It's a stigma to have a pretty face and a good body. It's like you're not *allowed* to have everything – you can't be talented as well!
Naomi Campbell (b.1970), British model: on the resistance she encountered while trying to move into an acting career, quoted in *Naomi* by Lesley-Ann Jones (1993), Ch.10

3 Woman ... cannot be content with health and agility: she must make exorbitant efforts to appear something that never could exist without a diligent perversion of nature. Is it too much to ask that women be spared the daily struggle for superhuman beauty in order to offer it to the caresses of a subhumanly ugly mate?
Germaine Greer (b.1939), Australian feminist writer: *The Female Eunuch* (1970), 'Loathing and Disgust'

4 I do not think I had ever seen a nastier-looking man.... Under the black hat, when I had first seen them, the eyes had been those of an unsuccessful rapist.
Ernest Hemingway (1899–1961), U.S. author: of satirical author and painter (Percy) Wyndham Lewis, in *A Moveable Feast* (1964), Ch.12

5 I have observed many different kinds of people – swindlers, people who have killed or died for money, plagiarists – and they all look like normal people, so I am confused. In fact, more than 'normal', these people all have very nice faces and say very nice things, so I am all the more confused.
Akira Kurosawa (b.1910), Japanese filmmaker: *Something Like an Autobiography* (1982), 'Marriage'

6 The most common error made in matters of appearance is the belief that one should disdain the superficial and let the true beauty of one's soul shine through. If there are places on your body where this is a possibility, you are not attractive – you are leaking.
Fran Lebowitz (b.1951), U.S. journalist: *Metropolitan Life* (1978), 'Manners'

7 I am confident about my appearance now, but I always was. That's why I'm here. In this business you go up and down, but I never thought, 'Shit! Nose job!' Everyone has their insecurities ... but it's like 'fuck, that's the way I am' and if you get paranoid about changing, get neurotic about keeping up with the trends, you're gonna be fucked.
Kristen McMenamy (b.1965), U.S. model: interview in *i-D* (London), June 1993

8 I wish I was taller. I probably look taller 'cos I've got such a big mouth.
Madonna (b.1958), U.S. singer and actress: quoted in *Smash Hits* (London), 16 Feb. 1984, rep. in *The Faber Book of Pop* (ed. Hanif Kureishi and Jon Savage, 1995), Pt.8, '1984: Young, Bold and Aggressive'

9 A good man often appears *gauche* simply because he does not take advantage of the myriad mean little chances of making himself look stylish. Preferring truth to form, he is not constantly at work upon the façade of his appearance.
Iris Murdoch (b.1919), British novelist and philosopher: Bradley Pearson, in *The Black Prince* (1972), Pt.1

10 Think rich. Look poor.
Andy Warhol (c.1928–1987), U.S. Pop artist: *From A to B and Back Again* (1975), Ch.6

APPEASEMENT

1 An appeaser is one who feeds a crocodile, hoping it will eat him last.
Winston Churchill (1874–1965), British statesman and author: quoted in *Reader's Digest* (Pleasantville, NY), Dec. 1954

2 I trust that a graduate student some day will write a doctoral essay on the influence of the Munich analogy on the subsequent history of the twentieth century. Perhaps in the end he will conclude that the multitude of errors committed in the name of 'Munich' may exceed the original error of 1938.
Arthur M. Schlesinger Jr. (b.1917), U.S. historian: *The Bitter Heritage: Vietnam and American Democracy* (1967), 'The Inscrutability of History'

3 The world has been ruined by appeasement. Appeasement of whom? Of the Communists? Of the Neo-Nazis? No! Appeasement of the compulsive war-preparers. I can scarcely name a nation that has not lost most of its freedom and wealth in attempts to appease its own addicts to preparations for war.
Kurt Vonnegut (b.1922), U.S. novelist: *Fates Worse than Death* (1991), Ch.14

APPETITE

1 Appetite is essentially insatiable, and where it operates as a criterion of both action and enjoyment (that is, everywhere in the Western world since the sixteenth century) it will infallibly discover congenial agencies (mechanical and political) of expression.
Marshall McLuhan (1911–1980), Canadian communications theorist: in *Horizon* (London), Oct. 1947

APPLAUSE

1 Will the people in the cheaper seats clap your hands? All the rest of you, if you'll just rattle your jewelry.
John Lennon (1940–1980), British rock musician: said at Royal Variety Performance, London, 4 Nov. 1963, quoted in *John Winston Lennon* by R. Colman (1984), Pt.1, Ch.11

2 Applause that comes thundering with such force you might think the audience merely suffers the music as an excuse for its ovations.
Greil Marcus (b.1945), U.S. rock journalist: *Mystery Train* (1976), 'Elvis: Presliad'

3 Glorious bouquets and storms of applause ... are the trimmings which every artist naturally enjoys. But to *move* an audience in such a role, to hear in the applause that unmistakable note which breaks through good theatre manners and comes from the heart, is to feel that you have won through to life itself. Such pleasure does not vanish with the fall of the curtain, but becomes part of one's own life.
Alice Markova (b.1910), British ballerina: *Giselle and I* (1960), Ch.18

ARCHAEOLOGY

1 An archaeologist is the best husband any woman can have: the older she gets, the more interested he is in her.
Agatha Christie (1890–1976), British mystery writer: attributed remark referring to her own second husband Sir Max Mallowan, an archaeologist, quoted in news report, 9 March 1954 (later denied by her)

ARCHITECTS

1 'Where *do* architects and designers get their ideas?' The answer, of course, is mainly from other architects and designers, so is it mere casuistry to distinguish between tradition and plagiarism?
Stephen Bayley (b.1951), British design critic: *Commerce and Culture* (1989), Ch.3

2 All architects want to live beyond their deaths.
Philip Johnson (b.1906), U.S. architect: quoted in *The Observer* (London), 27 Dec. 1987

3 Le Corbusier was the sort of relentlessly rational intellectual that only France loves wholeheartedly, the logician who flies higher and higher in ever-decreasing circles until, with one last, utterly inevitable induction, he disappears up his own fundamental aperture and emerges in the fourth dimension as a needle-thin umber bird.
Tom Wolfe (b.1931), U.S. author and journalist: *From Bauhaus to Our House* (1981), Ch.1

4 The physician can bury his mistakes, but the architect can only advise his clients to plant vines.
Frank Lloyd Wright (1869–1959), U.S. architect: in the *New York Times Magazine*, 4 Oct. 1953

ARCHITECTURE

1 I want the Institute to teach its students *reverence* – reverence for the landscape and the soil; for the human spirit which is a reflection in some small measure of the Divine; and for the 'grammar' of architecture which, as in a language, enables an infinite variety of forms to be expressed within the context of harmonised sentences.
Charles, Prince of Wales (b.1948): memo, 9 June 1992, quoted in *The Prince of Wales: a Biography* by Jonathan Dimbleby (1994), Ch.23. Launched in 1991, The Prince of Wales Institute of Architecture was greeted, according to Dimbleby, with scepticism from the architectural establishment, but with approval from the media

2 We shape our buildings: thereafter they shape us.
Winston Churchill (1874–1965), British statesman and author: in *Time* (New York), 12 Sept. 1960

3 The job of buildings is to improve human relations: architecture must ease them, not make them worse.
Ralph Erskine (b.1914), British architect: in *The Times* (London), 16 Sept. 1992

4 Architecture is to make us know and remember who we are.
Geoffrey Jellicoe (b.1900), British architect: in the *International Herald Tribune* (Paris), 6 Nov. 1989

5 Architecture is the art of how to waste space.
Philip Johnson (b.1906), U.S. architect: in the *New York Times*, 27 Dec. 1964

6 All fine architectural values are human values, else not valuable.
Frank Lloyd Wright (1869–1959), U.S. architect: *The Living City* (1958), Pt.3 'Recapitulation'

See also Venturi on CHURCHES; Fenton on CITIES; Mies van der Rohe on MINIMALISM

ARCHITECTURE: Modern

1 In my experience, if you have to keep the lavatory door shut by extending your left leg, it's modern architecture.
Nancy Banks-Smith, British columnist: in *The Guardian* (London), 20 Feb. 1979

2 You have to give this much to the Luftwaffe: when it knocked down our buildings it did not replace them with anything more offensive than rubble. We did that.
Charles, Prince of Wales (b.1948): speech, 2 Dec. 1987, Mansion House, London

3 In short, the building becomes a theatrical demonstration of its functional ideal. In this romanticism, High-Tech architecture is, of course, no different in spirit – if totally different in form – from all the romantic architecture of the past.
Dan Cruickshank (b.1949), British architectural critic: *Commerce and Culture* (ed. Stephen Bailey, 1989), Ch.4 'Tradition'

4 Orthodox modern architecture is progressive, if not revolutionary, utopian, and puristic; it is dissatisfied with *existing* conditions. ... Architects have preferred to change the existing environment rather than enhance what is there. ... Modern architects work through anaogy, symbol, and image ... and they derive insights, analogies, and stimulation from unexpected images. There is a perversity in the learning process: We look back at history and tradition to go forward; we can also look downward to go upward.
Robert Venturi (b.1925), U.S. architect: *Learning from Las Vegas* by Robert Venturi, Denise Scott Brown and Stephen Izenour (1972; rev.1977), Pt.1, 'A Significance for AandP Parking Lots'

See also Charles, Prince of Wales on MUSEUMS & GALLERIES

ARGUMENT

1 When you argue with your inferiors,
you convince them of only one thing:
they are as clever as you.
Irving Layton (b.1912), Canadian poet: *The Whole Bloody Bird* (1969), 'Aphs'

2 No way dude.
Mike Myers (b.1964), Canadian comic actor and screenwriter: Wayne (Mike Myers) in *Wayne's World* (film; screenplay by Mike Myers, Bonnie Turner and Terry Turner, directed by Penelope Spheeris, 1992). This oft-repeated line was featured regularly on *Saturday Night Live*, on which Myers' character first appeared on U.S. TV from 1989

THE ARMS INDUSTRY

1 At the rate science proceeds, rockets and missiles will one day seem like buffalo – slow, endangered grazers in the black pasture of outer space.
Bernard Cooper (b.1936), U.S. physicist: in *Gettysburg Review* (Pennsylvania), summer 1989, rep. in *Harper's Magazine* (New York), Jan. 1990

2 In the councils of government, we must guard against the acquisition of unwarranted influence, whether sought or unsought, by the military-industrial complex. The potential for the disastrous rise of misplaced power exists and will persist. We must never let the weight of this combination endanger our liberties or democratic processes. We should take nothing for granted.
Dwight D. Eisenhower (1890–1969), U.S. general, Republican politician and president: farewell broadcast on radio and television, 17 Jan. 1961, publ. in *Public Papers of the Presidents of the United States, 1960–61*

3 The Prospero of poisons, the Faustus of the front,
bringing mental magic to modern armament.
Tony Harrison (b.1953), British poet: *Square Rounds* (1992), Pt.2. The speaker is intended to be the German chemist Fritz Haber, Nobel prizewinner and 'father' of chemical warfare

THE ARMS RACE

1 Weapons are like money; no one knows the meaning of *enough* .
Martin Amis (b.1949), British author: introduction to *Einstein's Monsters* (1987)

2 The ability to get to the verge without getting into the war is the necessary art. ... If you try to run away from it, if you are scared to go to the brink, you are lost.
John Foster Dulles (1888–1959), U.S. Republican politician: quoted in *Life* (New York), 16 Jan. 1956. The Democrat Adlai Stevenson characterized the Dulles-Eisenhower foreign policy as 'the power of positive brinking ...'

3 Every gun that is made, every warship launched, every rocket fired, signifies, in the final sense, a theft from those who hunger and are not fed, those who are cold and are not clothed. The world in arms is not spending money alone. It is spending the sweat of its labourers, the genius of its scientists, the hopes of its children.
Dwight D. Eisenhower (1890–1969), U.S. general, Republican politician and president: 'The Chance for Peace' speech to the American Society of Newspaper Editors, 16 April 1953, Washington D.C., publ. in *Public Papers of the Presidents of the United States, 1953*

4　We dare not tempt them with weakness. For only when our arms are sufficient beyond doubt can we be certain beyond doubt that they will never be employed.

John F. Kennedy (1917–1963), U.S. Democratic politician and president: inaugural address, 20 Jan. 1961, Washington D.C., quoted in *Kennedy* by Theodore C. Sorenson (1965), Pt.3, Ch.9

5　The emotional security and political stability in this country entitle us to be a nuclear power.

Ronald Mason (b.1930), British scientist and consultant on defence: said on his retirement, quoted in *The Observer* (London), 20 March 1983

6　So, in your discussions of the nuclear freeze proposals, I urge you to beware the temptation of pride – the temptation of blithely declaring yourselves above it all and label both sides equally at fault, to ignore the facts of history and the aggressive impulses of an evil empire, to simply call the arms race a giant misunderstanding and thereby remove yourself from the struggle between right and wrong and good and evil.

Ronald Reagan (b.1911), U.S. Republican politician and president: speech, 8 March 1983, Annual Convention of the National Association of Evangelicals, Orlando, Florida, publ. in *Speaking My Mind* (1989). Reagan added: 'Let us be aware that while they preach the supremacy of the state, declare its omnipotence over individual man, and predict its eventual domination of all peoples of the earth – they are the focus of evil in the modern world'

THE ARMY

1　Conscription may have been good for the country, but it damn near killed the army.

Richard Hull (1907–1989), British general: quoted in *Anatomy of Britain Today* by Anthony Sampson (1965), Ch.19

2　That was one nice thing about the Army ... someone else was paid to do the thinking.

William P. McGivern (1919–1982), U.S. author: *Odds Against Tomorrow* (1957), Ch.2

3　Do you know what a soldier is, young man? He's the chap who makes it possible for civilised folk to despise war.

Allan Massie (b.1938), British author: Colonel Fernie, in *A Question of Loyalties* (1989), Pt.2, Ch.1

4　We're Americans with a capital A. Do you know what that means? That means that our forefathers were kicked out of every decent country in the world. We are the wretched refuse. We're underdogs. We're mutts. ... We're all very, very different. But there is one thing we all have in common: we were all stupid enough to enlist in the army.

Bill Murray (b.1950), U.S. actor: John Winger (Bill Murray) in *Stripes* (film; screenplay by Len Blum, Dan Goldberg and Harold Ramis, directed and co-produced by Ivan Reirman, 1981)

5　The military mind is indeed a menace. Old-fashioned futurity that sees only men fighting and dying in smoke and fire; hears nothing more civilized than a cannonade; scents nothing but the stink of battle-wounds and blood.

Sean O'Casey (1884–1964), Irish playwright: *Sunset and Evening Star* (sixth volume of auto-biography, 1954), 'And Evening Star'

6　There are few men more superstitious than soldiers. They are, after all, the men who live closest to death.

Mary Stewart (b.1916), British novelist: *The Last Enchantment* (1979), Bk.2, Ch.3

7　The feeling about a soldier is, when all is said and done, he wasn't really going to do very much with his life anyway. The example usually is: 'he wasn't going to compose Beethoven's Fifth.'

Kurt Vonnegut (b.1922), U.S. novelist: interview in *City Limits* (London), 11 March 1983

See also GENERALS

ART

1　Art is an experience, not the formulation of a problem.

Lindsay Anderson (1923–1994), British film-maker: in *The Times* (London), 29 March 1989

2　Art is a fruit that grows in man, like a fruit on a plant, or a child in its mother's womb.

Jean Arp (1887–1948), French-German artist and poet: 'Art is a Fruit', publ. in *Cahiers d'Art* (Paris), Vol.XXII, 1947, rep. in *On My Way* (ed. Robert Motherwell, 1948)

3　The first mistake of Art is to assume that it's serious.

Lester Bangs (1948–1982), U.S. rock journalist: in *Who Put the Bomp*, winter/spring 1971, rep. in *Psychotic Reactions and Carburetor Dung* (1987), 'James Taylor Marked for Death'

4　Art can be a political reference, a sexual force, any force that you want, but it should be usable. What the hell do artists want? Museum pieces?

David Bowie (b.1947), British rock musician: interview in *Playboy* (Chicago), Sept. 1976, quoted in *David Bowie!* by Vivian Claire (1977), 'The Private Bowie'

5　Art is dangerous. It is one of the attractions: when it ceases to be dangerous you don't want it.

Anthony Burgess (1917–1993), British author and critic: interview in *The Face* (London), Dec. 1984

6　It is impossible to give a clear account of the world, but art can teach us to reproduce it – just as the world reproduces itself in the course of its eternal gyrations. The primordial sea indefatigably repeats the same words and casts up the same astonished beings on the same seashore.
Albert Camus (1913–1960), French-Algerian philosopher and author: *The Rebel* (1951; tr.1953), Pt.2, 'Absolute Affirmation'

7　Art for art's sake is a philosophy of the well-fed.
Cao Yu (b.1910), Chinese dramatist: in *The Observer* (London), 13 April 1980

8　Art is good when it springs from necessity. This kind of origin is the guarantee of its value; there is no other.
Neal Cassady (1926–1968), U.S. beat hero: letter 7–8 Jan. 1948, to Jack Kerouac, quoted in *Memory Babe* by Gerald Nicosia (1983), Ch.5, Sct.5

9　Without tradition, art is a flock of sheep without a shepherd. Without innovation, it is a corpse.
Winston Churchill (1874–1965), British statesman and author: address to Royal Academy of Arts, quoted in *Time* (New York), 11 May 1954

10　Art is aristocratic, not democratic, and probably the more people that like you, the worse you are.
Harry Crews (b.1935), U.S. author: interview in *Dazed and Confused* (London), No.11, April 1995

11　In art, one idea is as good as another. If one takes the idea of trembling, for instance, all of a sudden most art starts to tremble. Michelangelo starts to tremble. El Greco starts to tremble. All the Impressionists start to tremble.
Willem de Kooning (1904–1997), Dutch-born U.S. artist: 'A Desperate View', paper delivered to friends, 18 Feb. 1949, New York, first publ. in *William de Kooning* by Thomas B. Hess (1968)

12　Art is the most passionate orgy within man's grasp.
(*L'art est la plus passionate orgie à portée de l'homme.*)
Jean Dubuffet (1901–1985), French sculptor and painter: 'Notes for the Well-Read' (1946), rep. in *Jean Dubuffet: Towards an Alternative Reality* (ed. Marc Glimcher, 1987)

13　Art for art's sake? I should think so, and more so than ever at the present time. It is the one orderly product which our middling race has produced. It is the cry of a thousand sentinels, the echo from a thousand labyrinths, it is the lighthouse which cannot be hidden ... it is the best evidence we can have of our dignity.
E.M. Forster (1879–1970), British novelist and essayist: address to PEN Club Congress, quoted in *Monitor* (ed. Huw Weldon, 1962)

14　One thing that makes art different from life is that in art things have a shape ... it allows us to fix our emotions on events at the moment they occur, it permits a union of heart and mind and tongue and tear.
Marilyn French (b.1929), U.S. author and critic: *The Women's Room* (1977), Ch.3, Sct.1

15　Fortunately art is a community effort – a small but select community living in a spiritualized world endeavoring to interpret the wars and the solitudes of the flesh.
Allen Ginsberg (b.1926), U.S. poet: journal entry, 11 July 1954, publ. in *Journals: Early Fifties Early Sixties* (ed. Gordon Ball, 1977), 'Mexico and Return to U.S.'

16　Art attracts us only by what it reveals of our most secret self.
Jean-Luc Godard (b.1930), French film-maker and author: 'What is Cinema?' first publ. in *Les Amis du Cinéma* (Paris), 1 Oct. 1952, rep. in *Godard on Godard* (ed./tr. Tom Milne, 1968)

17　Art is so wonderfully irrational, exuberantly pointless, but necessary all the same. Pointless and yet necessary, that's hard for a puritan to understand.
Günter Grass (b.1927), German author: interview in *New Statesman and Society* (London), 22 June 1990

18　A work of art is above all an adventure of the mind.
Eugène Ionesco (1912–1994), Rumanian-born French playwright: 'An Address Delivered to a Gathering of French and German Writers', Feb. 1960, publ. in *Notes and Counter-Notes* (1962), Pt.2

19　Irresponsibility is part of the pleasure of all art, it is the part the schools cannot recognize.
Pauline Kael (b.1919), U.S. film critic: *Going Steady* (1968), 'Movies as Opera'

20　Art is the objectification of feeling.
Susanne K. Langer (1895–1985), U.S. philosopher: *Mind, An Essay on Human Feeling* (1967), Vol.I, Pt.2, Ch.4

21　Inwardly art is a means of expurgation, outwardly a means of battle, incumbent on men born and reared in sin and determined to rebel against it. Nothing else matters.
Naguib Mahfouz (b.1911), Egyptian novelist: *Wedding Song* (1981; tr.1984), 'Abas Karam Younis'

22　All art is a revolt against man's fate.
André Malraux (1901–1976), French man of letters and statesman: *The Voices of Silence* (1951), Pt.4, Ch.7

23 Art is the final cunning of the human soul which would rather do anything than face the gods.
Iris Murdoch (b.1919), British novelist and philosopher: Plato, in *Acastos: Two Platonic Dialogues* (1986), 'Art and Eros: A Dialogue about Art'. The dialogue was first performed on stage in Feb. 1980

24 I am for an art that is political-erotical-mystical, that does something other than sit on its ass in a museum.
I am for an art that grows up not knowing it is art at all, an art given the chance of having a starting point of zero.
I am for an art that employs itself with everyday crap and still comes out on top.
I am for an art that imitates the human, that is comic, if necessary, or violent, or whatever is necessary.
Claes Oldenburg (b.1929), Swedish-born U.S. artist: opening paragraph of 'I am for an Art', catalogue for exhibition in Martha Jackson Gallery, New York, June 1961, rep. in *Pop Art Redefined* by John Russell and Suzi Gablik (1969)

25 Wherever art appears, life disappears. (*Où apparaît l'art la vie disparaît.*)
Francis Picabia (1878–1953), French painter and poet: 'L'Humour Poetique', first publ. in *La Nef* (Paris), Dec. 1950/Jan. 1951, rep. in *Écrits*, Vol.II (ed. Olivier Revault d'Allones and Dominique Bouissou, 1978), '1950–1953'

26 Art is too serious to be taken seriously.
Ad Reinhardt (1913–1967), U.S. artist: notes quoted in *Ad Reinhardt* by Lucy R. Lippard (1981), Pt.1

27 Art, whose honesty must work through artifice, cannot avoid cheating truth.
Laura Riding (1901–1991), U.S. poet: preface to *Selected Poems: In Five Sets* (1975)

28 Every work of art exists under the shadow of the historian of its genre. Conservative and radical attitudes count for nothing as against the weight of data accumulated in support of interpretations that replace the work itself through the hearsay of the media. Who reads a novel, a poem, or a collection of critical essays except to collect evidence for or against its author?
Harold Rosenberg (1906–1978), U.S. art critic and author: 'The Cultural Situation Today', first publ. in *Partisan Review* (New Brunswick, N.J.), summer 1972, rep. as introduction to *Discovering the Present* (1973)

29 Not even the visionary or mystical experience ever lasts very long. It is for art to capture that experience, to offer it to, in the case of literature, its readers; to be, for a secular, materialist culture, some sort of replacement for what the love of god offers in the world of faith.

Salman Rushdie (b.1947), Indian-born British author: Herbert Read Memorial Lecture, read by Harold Pinter, publ. in *The Guardian* (London), 7 Feb. 1990

30 Art is seduction, not rape.
Susan Sontag (b.1933), U.S. essayist: *Against Interpretation* (1966), 'On Style'

31 Art should be Divine Inspiration. Art should be a yearning for the hereafter, the eternal, and the sublime. It should be the way to the truth, wisdom, immortality, and what we call love. Politics as an organizing principle for mediocre compromises needs the assistance of art, which always seeks justice and uses dreams to overcome death. Art is the reason for living, today as in the past.
Hans-Jurgen Syberberg (b.1935), German filmmaker: in *Semiotext(e)* (New York), 'The German Issue', Vol.IV, No.2, 1982

32 Art is parasitic on life, just as criticism is parasitic on art
Kenneth Tynan (1927–1980), British critic: 'Ionesco and the Phantom', first publ. in *The Observer* (London), 6 July 1958, rep. in *Notes and Counter-Notes* by Eugène Ionesco (1962)

33 Any authentic work of art must start an argument between the artist and his audience.
Rebecca West (1892–1983), British author: *The Court and the Castle* (1957), Pt.1, Ch.1

34 The moment you think you understand a great work of art, it's dead for you.
Robert Wilson (b.1941), U.S. theatre director and designer: in the *International Herald Tribune* (Paris), 22 May 1990

See also CARTOONS; André on CHANGE; André on CULTURE; Fischer on HUMANITY; Tynan on IDEOLOGY; Sontag on MORALITY; André on SYMBOLISM; Murdoch on VIRTUE

ART: and Commerce

1 Watteau is no less an artist for having painted a fascia board while Sainsbury's is no less effective a business for producing advertisements which entertain and educate instead of condescending and exploiting.
Stephen Bayley (b.1951), British design critic: *Commerce and Culture* (1989), Ch.1

2 Those who write for lucre or fame are grosser Iscariots than the cartel robbers, for they steal the genius of the people, which is its will to resist evil.
Edward Dahlberg (1900–1977), U.S. author and critic: *Alms for Oblivion* (1964), 'For Sale'

See also Warhol on BUSINESS

ART: Modern Art

1 Twentieth-century art may start with nothing but it flourishes by virtue of its belief in itself, in the possibility of control over what seems essentially uncontrollable, in the coherence of the inchoate, and in its ability to create its own values.
A. Alvarez (b.1929), British critic, poet and novelist: *The Savage God* (1971), Pt.4, 'Dada: Suicide as an Art'

2 A product of the untalented, sold by the unprincipled to the utterly bewildered.
Al Capp (1909–1979), U.S. cartoonist: of abstract art, quoted in the *National Observer* (Silver Spring, Maryland), 1 July 1963

3 This grandiose tragedy that we call modern art.
Salvador Dali (1904–1989), Spanish painter: *Dali by Dali* (1970), 'The Futuristic Dali'

4 The history of modern art is also the history of the progressive loss of art's audience. Art has increasingly become the concern of the artist and the bafflement of the public.
Henry Geldzahler (b.1935), Belgian-born U.S. curator and art critic: 'The Art Audience and the Critic', first publ. in *The Hudson Review* (New York), spring 1965, rep. in *The New Art: A Critical Anthology* (ed. Gregory Battcock, 1966, rev.1973)

5 The essential truth about art of the last thirty-five years, continually erased from consciousness by the ideology of international liberalism, is that fascism didn't die with the cessation of World War II but remains the repressed collective unconsciousness of the present.
Dan Graham (b.1942), U.S. artist: 'The End of Liberalism', publ. in *Rock My Religion* (ed. Brian Wallis, 1993). The article was first published in *ZG* (London), No.2, 1981, in a slightly different form

6 Whereas one tends to see what is in an Old Master before seeing it as a picture, one sees a Modernist painting as a picture first. This is, of course, the best way of seeing any kind of picture, Old Master or Modernist, but Modernism imposes it as the only and necessary way, and Modernism's success in doing so is a success of self-criticism.
Clement Greenberg (1909–1994), U.S. art critic: 'Modernist Painting', first publ. in *Forum Lectures* (1960), rep. in *Art in Theory* (ed. Charles Harrison and Paul Wood, 1992), Pt.6B

7 The public history of modern art is the story of conventional people not knowing what they are dealing with.
Robert Motherwell (1915–1991), U.S. artist: preface to *The Dada Painters and Poets: An Anthology* (ed. Robert Motherwell, 1951)

8 What distinguishes modern art from the art of other ages is criticism.
Octavio Paz (b.1914), Mexican poet and essayist: *Alternating Current* (1967), 'Invention, Underdevelopment, Modernity'

9 Modern art has been a series of individual explosions tearing at strata accumulated by centuries of communal inertia.
Harold Rosenberg (1906–1978), U.S. art critic and author: 'The Style of Today' (1940), rep. in *The Tradition of the New* (1960)

10 As far as I can see, the history of experimental art in the twentieth century is intimately bound up with the experience of intoxification.
Will Self (b.1961), British author: quoted in *The Face* (London), Nov. 1994

11 Much of modern art is devoted to lowering the threshold of what is terrible. By getting us used to what, formerly, we could not bear to see or hear, because it was too shocking, painful, or embarrassing, art changes morals.
Susan Sontag (b.1933), U.S. essayist: on *Photography* (1977), 'America, Seen Through Photographs, Darkly'

12 The notion that the public accepts or rejects anything in Modern Art … is merely a romantic fiction … the game is completed and the trophies distributed long before the public knows what has happened.
Tom Wolfe (b.1931), U.S. author and journalist: *The Painted Word* (1975), Ch.2

See also Dali on IMAGERY; Lacroix on PARODY

ART: and Nature

1 When I am finishing a picture I hold some God-made object up to it – a rock, a flower, the branch of a tree or my hand – as a kind of final test. If the painting stands up beside a thing man cannot make, the painting is authentic. If there's a clash between the two, it is bad art.
Marc Chagall (1889–1985), French artist: in the *Saturday Evening Post* (New York), 2 Dec. 1962

2 The attitude that nature is chaotic and that the artist puts order into it is a very absurd point of view, I think. All that we can hope for is to put some order into ourselves.
Willem de Kooning (1904–1997), Dutch-born U.S. artist: 'The Renaissance and Order', lecture, 1950, New York, publ. in *Collected Writings* (ed. George Scrivani, 1988)

3 Nature is inside art as its content, not outside as its model.
Northrop Frye (1912–1991), Canadian literary critic: *Fables of Identity* (1963), quoted in *Truth and Lies in Literature* by Stephen Vizinczey (1986), 'Rules of the Game'

ART: Painting

1 If you pick up some paint with your brush and make somebody's nose with it, this is rather ridiculous when you think of it, theoretically or philosophically. It's really absurd to make an image, like a human image, with paint, today.
Willem de Kooning (1904–1997), Dutch-born U.S. artist: 'Painting As Self Discovery', interview, BBC, 30 Dec. 1960, first publ. in *Location* (New York), spring 1963, as 'Content is a Glimpse ... ', quoted in *William de Kooning* by Diane Waldman (1988)

2 I don't very much enjoy looking at paintings in general. I know too much about them. I take them apart.
Georgia O'Keeffe (1887–1986), U.S. artist: quoted in the *San Francisco Examiner and Chronicle*, 16 March 1971

3 One does a whole painting for one peach and people think just the opposite – that that particular peach is but a detail.
Pablo Picasso (1881–1973), Spanish artist: in *Vogue* (New York), 1 Nov. 1956

4 The method of painting is the natural growth out of a need. I want to express my feelings rather than illustrate them. Technique is just a means of arriving at a statement. ... I *can* control the flow of paint: there is no accident, just as there is no beginning and no end.
Jackson Pollock (1912–1956), U.S. artist: 'Jackson Pollock', narrative to 1951 film made by Hans Nemuth and Paul Falkenberg, rep. in *Jackson Pollock* by Bryan Robertson (1960)

5 To me, a painter, if not the most useful, is the least harmful member of our society.
Man Ray (1890–1976), U.S. photographer: *Self Portrait* (1963), Ch.6

6 Pictures must be miraculous: the instant one is completed, the intimacy between the creation and the creator is ended. He is an outsider. The picture must be for him, as for anyone experiencing it later, a revelation, an unexpected and unprecedented resolution of an eternally familiar need.
Mark Rothko (1903–1970), U.S. artist: in *Possibilities* (New York), winter 1947/48, rep. in *Art in Theory* (ed. Charles Harrison and Paul Wood, 1992), Pt.5A

7 When I have to think about it, I know the picture is wrong. ... My instinct about painting says, 'If you don't think about it, it's right.' As soon as you have to decide and choose, it's wrong.
Andy Warhol (c.1928–1987), U.S. Pop artist: *From A to B and Back Again* (1975), Ch.10

8 Frankly, these days, without a theory to go with it, I can't *see* a painting.
Tom Wolfe (b.1931), U.S. author and journalist: *The Painted Word* (1975), Ch.1

ART: Political Art

1 Progressive art can assist people to learn not only about the objective forces at work in the society in which they live, but also about the intensely social character of their interior lives. Ultimately, it can propel people toward social emancipation.
Angela Davis (b.1944), U.S. political activist: 'Art on the Frontline', *Women, Culture and Politics* (1984)

2 Feminist art is not some tiny creek running off the great river of real art. It is not some crack in an otherwise flawless stone. It is, quite spectacularly I think, art which is not based on the subjugation of one half of the species. It is art which will take the great human themes – love, death, heroism, suffering, history itself – and render them fully human. It may also, though perhaps our imaginations are so mutilated now that we are incapable even of the ambition, introduce a new theme, one as great and as rich as those others – should we call it 'joy'?
Andrea Dworkin (b.1946), U.S. feminist critic: 'Feminism, Art, and My Mother Sylvia' speech, 16 April 1974, Smith College, Northampton, Massachusetts, rep. in *Our Blood* (1976), Ch.1

3 Good intentions and honest feelings, and a passionate belief in one's own ideals, may make excellent politics or influential social work (things which may be much more useful than the cinema) but they do not necessarily and indisputably make good films. And there is really nothing uglier or drearier – just because it is ineffectual and pointless – than a bad political film.
Federico Fellini (1920–1993), Italian film-maker: *Fellini on Fellini* (ed. Anna Keel and Christian Strich, 1974; tr.1977), 'Miscellany III', Sct.3

4 How contemptible it is to denounce any work of art on account of the artist's political beliefs, and how often has history held up the mirror of ridicule to the perpetrators of this philistine absurdity.
Oswald Mosley (1896–1980), British fascist leader: discussing the case of Ezra Pound, in *My Life* (1968), Ch.12

5 Only conservatives believe that subversion is still being carried on in the arts and that society is being shaken by it. ... Advanced art today is no longer a cause – it contains no moral imperative. There is no virtue in clinging to principles and standards, no vice in selling or in selling out.
Harold Rosenberg (1906–1978), U.S. art critic and author: 'The Cultural Situation Today', first publ.

in *Partisan Review* (New Brunswick, N.J.), summer 1972, rep. as introduction to *Discovering the Present* (1973)

ART: Pop Art

1 Pop artists deal with the lowly trivia of possessions and equipment that the present generation is lugging along with it on its safari into the future.
J.G. Ballard (b.1930), British author: interview in *Books and Bookmen* (London), April 1971, rep. in *Re/Search* (San Francisco), No.8/9, 1984

2 In England, pop art and fine art stand resolutely back to back.
Colin MacInnes (1914–1976), British author: 'Pop Songs and Teenagers', publ. in *Twentieth Century* (London), Feb. 1958, rep. in *England, Half English* (1961)

ART: Sculpture & Ceramics

1 The pot is the man: his virtues and his vices are shown therein – no disguise is possible.
Bernard Leach (1887–1979), British potter: *The Potter's Challenge* (1976), Ch.4

2 Sculpture is the best comment that a painter can make on painting.
Pablo Picasso (1881–1973), Spanish artist: remark, 2 Feb. 1964, quoted by artist Renato Guttuso in his journals, rep. in *Scritti di Picasso* by Mario de Micheli (1964)

ART: and Society

1 I never thought art could change things. To the degree that it's entertaining, it's got a use, but that's not the thing that changes people or countries or political systems, that's usually done through political action.
Woody Allen (b.1935), U.S. film-maker: interview in *Sight and Sound* (London), Feb. 1994

2 Every great work of art has two faces, one toward its own time and one toward the future, toward eternity.
Daniel Barenboim (b.1942), Argentinian-born Israeli pianist and conductor: in the *International Herald Tribune* (Paris), 20 Jan. 1989

3 In order for the artist to have a world to express he must first be situated in this world, oppressed or oppressing, resigned or rebellious, a man among men.
Simone de Beauvoir (1908–1986), French novelist and essayist: *The Ethics of Ambiguity* (1948), Ch.1

4 I can't tell you what art does and how it does it, but I know that often art has judged the judges, pleaded revenge to the innocent and shown to the future what the past suffered, so that it has

never been forgotten. ... Art, when it functions like this, becomes a meeting-place of the invisible, the irreducible, the enduring, guts, and honour.
John Berger (b.1926), British author and critic: *Miners* (exhibition catalogue 1989), rep. in *Keeping a Rendezvous* (1992)

5 To confer a socially *meritorious* nature to the production of art, making it an honored social function, is to seriously falsify its meaning, for the production of art is a strictly and strongly individual function, and consequently entirely antagonistic to any social function. It can only be an antisocial function, or at least an asocial one.
Jean Dubuffet (1901–1985), French sculptor and painter: 'Asphyxiating Culture' (1968), rep. in *Asphyxiating Culture and Other Writings* (1986; tr.1988)

6 In a decaying society, art, if it is truthful, must also reflect decay. And unless it wants to break faith with its social function, art must show the world as changeable. And help to change it.
Ernst Fischer (1899–1972), Austrian editor, poet and critic: *The Necessity of Art* (1959; tr.1963), Ch.2

7 The thing that's extraordinary is that no art remains shocking for more than ten or twelve years. There is no shocking art that doesn't reduce itself to triviality or beauty.
Henry Geldzahler (b.1935), Belgian-born U.S. curator and art critic: *Looking at Pictures* (1990), p.29 of Hanuman edn.

8 Art is on the side of the oppressed. Think before you shudder at the simplistic dictum and its heretical definition of the freedom of art. For if art is freedom of the spirit, how can it exist within the oppressors?
Nadine Gordimer (b.1923), South African author: 'The Essential Gesture', lecture 12 Oct. 1984, University of Michigan, first publ. in *The Tanner Lectures on Human Values* (ed. Sterling M. McMurrin, 1985), rep. in *The Essential Gesture* (ed. Stephen Clingman, 1988)

9 If we are to change our world view, images have to change. The artist now has a very important job to do. He's not a little peripheral figure entertaining rich people, he's really needed.
David Hockney (b.1937), British artist: *Hockney On Photography* (conversations with Paul Joyce, ed. Wendy Brown, 1988), 'New York: September 1986'

10 In free society art is not a weapon. ... Artists are not engineers of the soul.
John F. Kennedy (1917–1963), U.S. Democratic politician and president: speech, 26 Oct. 1963, Amherst College, Massachusetts, quoted in the *New York Times*, 27 Oct. 1963. The words 'Writers are the engineers of human souls' have been ascribed to Josef Stalin

11 Making social comment is an artificial place for an artist to start from. If an artist is touched by some social condition, what the artist creates will reflect that, but you can't force it.
Bella Lewitzky (b.1915), U.S. dancer: quoted in the *San Francisco Chronicle*, 4 March 1979

12 The final purpose of art is to intensify, even, if necessary, to exacerbate, the moral consciousness of people.
Norman Mailer (b.1923), U.S. author: 'Hip, Hell, and the Navigator', first publ. in *Western Review*, winter 1959, rep. in *Conversations with Norman Mailer* (ed. J. Michael Lennon, 1988)

13 I feel that America is essentially against the artist, that the enemy of America is the artist, because he stands for individuality and creativeness, and that's *un*-American somehow.
Henry Miller (1891–1980), U.S. author: interview in *Writers at Work* (Second Series, ed. George Plimpton, 1963)

14 There is the falsely mystical view of art that assumes a kind of supernatural inspiration, a possession by universal forces unrelated to questions of power and privilege or the artist's relation to bread and blood. In this view, the channel of art can only become clogged and misdirected by the artist's concern with merely temporary and local disturbances. The song is higher than the struggle.
Adrienne Rich (b.1929), U.S. poet: title essay of *Blood, Bread and Poetry* (1986)

15 The unfriendliness of society to his activity is difficult for the artist to accept. Yet this very hostility can act as a lever to true liberation.
Mark Rothko (1903–1970), Latvian-born U.S. painter: 'The Romantics Were Prompted', publ. in *Possibilities* (New York), winter 1947/48, rep. in *Theories of Modern Art* by Herschel B. Chipp (1968), Ch.9

16 A primary function of art and thought is to liberate the individual from the tyranny of his culture in the environmental sense and to permit him to stand beyond it in an autonomy of perception and judgment.
Lionel Trilling (1905–1975), U.S. critic: preface to *Beyond Culture* (1965)

17 All great art, and today all great artlessness, must appear extreme to the mass of men, as we know them today. It springs from the anguish of great souls. From the souls of men not formed, but deformed in factories whose inspiration is pelf.
Alexander Trocchi (1925–1983), Scottish novelist, poet and translator: *Cain's Book* (1960), p.145 of Quarto edn. (1973) ('pelf' = money, wealth, *OED*)

18 An artist must be a reactionary. He has to stand out against the tenor of the age and not go flopping along.
Evelyn Waugh (1903–1966), British novelist: interview in *Writers at Work* (Third Series, ed. George Plimpton, 1967)

ARTISTS

1 The primary distinction of the artist is that he must actively cultivate that state which most men, necessarily, must avoid: the state of being alone.
James Baldwin (1924–1987), U.S. author: 'The Creative Process' (1962), rep. in *The Price of the Ticket* (1985)

2 Any artist should be grateful for a naïve grace which puts him beyond the need to reason elaborately.
Saul Bellow (b.1915), U.S. novelist: foreword to *The Closing of the American Mind* by Allan Bloom (1987)

3 The artist is extremely lucky who is presented with the worst possible ordeal which will not actually kill him. At that point, he's in business.
John Berryman (1914–1972), U.S. poet: interview in *Writers at Work* (Fourth Series, ed. George Plimpton, 1976)

4 The emphasis placed on what people are saying, and whether they're profound or not, annoys me a little, 'cause I don't want to be profound. The aim of an artist is just to investigate. That's all I want to do: investigate and present the results.
David Bowie (b.1947), British rock musician: interview, 1972, rep. in *Bowie In His Own Words* (ed. Miles, 1980), 'Songwriting'

5 The more I produce the less I am certain. On the road along which the artist walks, night falls ever more densely. Finally he dies blind.
Albert Camus (1913–1960), French-Algerian philosopher and author: letter, quoted in *Camus: A Biography* by Herbert R. Lottman (1979), Ch.43

6 The creative artist seems to be almost the only kind of man that you could never meet on neutral ground. You can only meet him as an artist. He sees nothing objectively because his own ego is always in the foreground of every picture.
Raymond Chandler (1888–1959), U.S. author: letter to publisher Hamish Hamilton, 23 June 1950, publ. in *Raymond Chandler Speaking* (ed. Dorothy Gardiner and Kathrine S. Walker, 1962)

7 Artists are never allowed to let things alone. They're forever picking at the scabs. Writers, by their nature, spend their time thinking about, wondering about, delving into, trying to understand the very things that the rest of the world doesn't like to think about.

Harry Crews (b.1935), U.S. author: interview in
Dazed and Confused (London), April 1995

8 There is only one difference between a madman and me. I am not mad.

Salvador Dali (1904–1989), Spanish painter: entry,
May 1952, in *Diary of a Genius* (1966)

9 An artist is forced by others to paint out of his
own free will.

Willem de Kooning (1904–1997), Dutch-born
U.S. artist: 'A Desperate View', paper delivered
to friends, 18 Feb. 1949, New York, first publ.
in *William de Kooning* by Thomas B. Hess
(1968)

10 For us artists there waits the joyous compromise through art with all that wounded or
defeated us in daily life; in this way, not to
evade destiny, as the ordinary people try to do,
but to fulfil it in its true potential – the imagination.

Lawrence Durrell (1912–1990), British author:
Justine (1957), Pt.1

11 An artist is a creature driven by demons. He
don't know why they choose him and he's
usually too busy to wonder why. He is completely amoral in that he will rob, borrow, beg,
or steal from anybody and everybody to get the
work done.

William Faulkner (1897–1962), U.S. novelist:
interview in *Writers at Work* (First Series, ed.
Malcolm Cowley, 1958)

12 There really is no such thing as Art. There are
only artists.

E.H. Gombrich (b.1909), Austrian-born British art
critic and historian: opening words of introduction
to *The Story of Art* (1950)

13 No artist is ahead of his time. He *is* his time; it
is just that others are behind the times.

Martha Graham (1894–1991), U.S. dancer and
choreographer: quoted in *The Observer* (London),
8 July 1979

14 It is very important not to become hard. The
artist must always have one skin too few in
comparison to other people, so you feel the
slightest wind.

Shusha Guppy (b.1938), Persian singer and
author: interview in *The Guardian* (London),
6 April 1988

15 An artist's originality is balanced by a corres-
ponding conservatism, a superstitiousness,
about it; which might be boiled down to 'What
worked before will work again.'

Nancy Hale (b.1908), U.S. writer and editor: *Mary
Cassatt: A Biography of the Great American
Painter* (1975), Pt.2, Ch.6

16 I think the contemporary artist has a responsibility to humanity to continue celebrating
humanity and opposing the dehumanization of
our culture. This doesn't mean that technology shouldn't be utilized by the artist, only
that it should be at the service of humanity and
not vice-versa.

Keith Haring (1958–1990), U.S. artist: interview
in *Flash Art* (Milan), March 1984, quoted in
World Artists: 1980–1990 (ed. Claude Marks,
1991)

17 As an artist you have to reinvent yourself
everyday. Which I think is what you do anyway as a person, which is why people fall
out, split up, get together.... It's like turning
over.

Damien Hirst (b.1965), British artist: interview in
The Idler (London), July/Aug. 1995

18 We live in an age where the artist is forgotten.
He is a researcher. I see myself that way.

David Hockney (b.1937), British artist: quoted in
The Observer (London), 9 June 1991

19 I justified my drinking and drug use because I
was an artist, and artists must disorientate
their minds – you know, Arthur Rimbaud,
Baudelaire, Van Gogh, er ... John Barrymore,
W.C. Fields.

Denis Hopper (b.1935), U.S. actor and director:
interview in *The Face* (London), May 1993

20 There is nothing fiercer than a failed artist.
The energy remains, but, having no outlet, it
implodes in a great black fart of rage which
smokes up all the inner windows of the soul.
Horrible as successful artists often are, there is
nothing crueler or more vain than a failed
artist.

Erica Jong (b.1942), U.S. author: the narrator
(Isadora Wing), in *Fear of Flying* (1973), Ch.9

21 The first prerogative of an artist in any
medium is to make a fool of himself.

Pauline Kael (b.1919), U.S. film critic: *I Lost it at
the Movies* (1965), 'Is There a Cure for Film
Criticism?'

22 It seems likely that many of the young who
don't wait for others to call them artists, but
simply announce that they are, don't have the
patience to make art.

Pauline Kael: *Kiss Kiss Bang Bang* (1968), 'Movie
Brutalists'

23 The product of the artist has become less
important than the *fact* of the artist. We wish
to absorb this person. We wish to devour
someone who has experienced the tragic. In
our society this person is much more
important than anything he might create.

David Mamet (b.1947), U.S. playwright: *Writing
in Restaurants* (1986), 'Exuvial Magic: an Essay
Concerning Fashion'

24 You study, you learn, but you guard the
original naiveté. It has to be within you, as

desire for drink is within the drunkard or love is within the lover.
Henri Matisse (1869–1954), French artist: quoted in *Time* (New York), 26 June 1950

25 What is the *raison d'être*, what is the explanation of the seemingly insane drive of man to be painter and poet if it is not an act of defiance against man's fall and an assertion that he return to the Adam of the Garden of Eden? For the artists are the first men.
Barnett Newman (1905–1970), U.S. artist: 'The First Man Was an Artist', publ. in *Tiger's Eye* (New York), Oct. 1947, rep. in *Art in Theory* (ed. Charles Harrison and Paul Wood, 1992), Pt.5A

26 Everybody's an artist. Everybody's God. It's just that they're inhibited. I believe in people so much that if the whole of civilization is burned so we don't have any memory of it, even then people will start to build their own art. It is a necessity – a function. We don't need history.
Yoko Ono (b.1923), Japanese-born U.S. artist: interview by Abram Deswaan for Dutch TV, Oct. 1968, publ. in *Imagine* (ed. Andrew Solt and Sam Egan, 1988)

27 We artists are indestructible; even in a prison, or in a concentration camp, I would be almighty in my own world of art, even if I had to paint my pictures with my wet tongue on the dusty floor of my cell.
Pablo Picasso (1881–1973), Spanish artist: in *Der Monat* (Berlin), Dec. 1949, rep. in *Picasso on Art* by Dore Ashton (1972)

28 Human life itself may be almost pure chaos, but the work of the artist – the only thing he's good for – is to take these handfuls of confusion and disparate things, things that seem to be irreconcilable, and put them together in a frame to give them some kind of shape and meaning. Even if it's only his view of a meaning. That's what he's for – to give his view of life.
Katherine Anne Porter (1890–1980), U.S. short-story writer and novelist: interview in *Writers at Work* (Second Series, ed. George Plimpton, 1963)

29 The task of the artist at any time is uncompromisingly simple – to discover what has not yet been done, and to do it.
Craig Raine (b.1944), British poet and critic: in *The Guardian* (London), 19 Aug. 1988

30 To me the artist was that privileged being who could free himself from all social constraint – whose only objectives should be the pursuit of liberty and of pleasure. If the artist suffered and struggled, then he had not freed himself from the constraint.
Man Ray (1890–1976), U.S. photographer: *Self Portrait* (1963), Ch.4, 'Painters and Sculptors'

31 Today, each artist must undertake to invent himself, a lifelong act of creation that constitutes the essential content of the artist's work. The meaning of art in our time flows from this function of self-creation. Art is the laboratory for making new men.
Harold Rosenberg (1906–1978), U.S. art critic and author: *Discovering the Present* (1973), Pt.4, Ch.24

32 The artist is a being who strives (but not in secret or in hiding, nor moving in circles, nor in the spaciousness of some kind of ecological niche) to master ultimate truth.
The artist masters that truth every time he creates something perfect, something whole.
Andrey Tarkovsky (1932–1986), Russian film-maker: journal entry, 5 Dec. 1973, publ. in *Time Within Time: The Diaries 1970–1986* (1989; tr.1994)

33 A good artist should be isolated. If he isn't isolated, something is wrong.
Orson Welles (1915–1985), U.S. film-maker and actor: interview in *Hollywood Voices* (ed. Andrews Sarris, 1971)

34 One of the dangers of the American artist is that he finds himself almost exclusively thrown in with persons more or less in the arts. He lives among them, eats among them, quarrels with them, marries them.
Thornton Wilder (1897–1975), U.S. novelist and playwright: interview in *Writers at Work* (First Series, ed. Malcolm Cowley, 1958)

35 Most works of art are effectively treated as commodities and most artists, even when they justly claim quite other intentions, are effectively treated as a category of independent *craftsmen* or *skilled workers* producing a certain kind of marginal commodity.
Raymond Williams (1921–1988), British novelist and critic: *Keywords* (1976), 'Art'

See also Tarkovsky on ABSTINENCE; Wolfe on BOHEMIANS; Ustinov on MAGAZINES; Durrell on PATRIOTISM; PABLO PICASSO; Trilling on PLAGIARISM; Hamilton on POPULAR CULTURE; Bukowski on SIMPLICITY; Coppola on TALENT; ANDY WARHOL

THE ARTS

1 As for types like my own, obscurely motivated by the conviction that our existence was worthless if we didn't make a turning point of it, we were assigned to the humanities, to poetry, philosophy, painting – the nursery games of humankind, which had to be left behind when the age of science began. The humanities would be called upon to choose a wallpaper for the crypt, as the end drew near.

Saul Bellow (b.1915), U.S. novelist: *The Adventures of Augie Marsh* (1949), Ch.6

2 The arts are not just instantaneous pleasure – if you don't like it, the artist is wrong. I belong to the generation which says if you don't like it, you don't understand and you ought to find out.

John Drummond (b.1934), British writer and broadcaster: in *The Guardian* (London), 9 July 1992

3 That is one of the great advantages of the arts: they are a consolation for loneliness.

Lord Goodman (1913–1995), British lawyer and public figure: interview in *Singular Encounters* by Naim Attallah (1990), 'Lord Goodman'

4 Poetry = heightened talking. Novel = heightened story. Painting = a heightened seeing.

Philip Larkin (1922–85), British poet: letter, 23 May 1941, publ. in *Selected Letters of Philip Larkin 1940–1985* (ed. Anthony Thwaite, 1992)

5 As the unity of the modern world becomes increasingly a technological rather than a social affair, the techniques of the arts provide the most valuable means of insight into the real direction of our own collective purposes.

Marshall McLuhan (1911–1980), Canadian communications theorist: *The Mechanical Bride* (1951), 'Magic that Changes Mood'

6 Letting a hundred flowers blossom and a hundred schools of thought contend is the policy for promoting the progress of the arts and the sciences and a flourishing culture in our land.

Mao Zedong (1893–1976), Chinese leader: speech, 27 Feb. 1957, Peking, quoted in *Quotations from Chairman Mao Tse-Tung* (1966)

7 There is no true expertise in the humanities without knowing *all* of the humanities. Art is a vast, ancient interconnected web-work, a fabricated tradition. Overconcentration on any one point is a distortion.

Camille Paglia (b.1947), U.S. author and critic: in the *New York Times*, 5 May 1991

See also ARCHITECTURE; ART; THE AVANT-GARDE; CULTURE; DESIGN; MUSEUMS & GALLERIES; MUSIC; OPERA; SURREALISM; THEATRE; WOMEN: AND THE ARTS

ASIA

1 The delirium and horror of the East. The dusty catastrophe of Asia. Green only on the banner of the Prophet. Nothing grows here except mustaches.

Joseph Brodsky (1940–1996), Russian-born U.S. poet and critic: *Less Than One: Selected Essays* (1986), 'Flight from Byzantium', Sct.9

2 Be careful about Burma. Most people cannot remember whether it was Siam and has become Thailand, or whether it is now part of Malaysia and should be called Sri Lanka.

Alexander Cockburn (b.1941), Anglo-Irish journalist: 'How to be a Foreign Correspondent', first publ. in *More* (New York), May 1976, rep. in *Corruptions of Empire* (1988), Pt.1

3 This is Malaya. Everything takes a long, a very long time, in Malaya. Things get done, occasionally, but more often they don't, and the more in a hurry you are, the quicker you break down.

Han Suyin (b.1917), Chinese author: *And the Rain My Drink* (1956), Ch.2

4 Because the European does not know his own unconscious, he does not understand the East and projects into it everything he fears and despises in himself.

Carl Jung (1875–1961), Swiss psychiatrist: foreword to *Beelden uit het onbewuste* by R.J. Van Helsdingen (1957), rep. in *The Collected Works of Carl Jung*, Vol.XVIII (ed. William McGuire, 1977)

5 Now the long-feared Asiatic colossus takes its turn as world leader, and we – the white race – have become the yellow man's burden. Let us hope that he will treat us more kindly than we treated him.

Gore Vidal (b.1925), U.S. novelist and critic: *Armageddon? Essays 1983–1987* (1987), 'The Day the American Empire Ran Out of Gas'

See also CHINA; INDIA; JAPAN; VIETNAM

ASSASSINATION

1 The figure of the gunman in the window was inextricable from the victim and his history. This sustained Oswald in his cell. It gave him what he needed to live. The more time he spent in a cell, the stronger he would get. Everybody knew who he was now.

Don DeLillo (b.1926), U.S. author: of Lee Harvey Oswald, in *Libra* (1988), Pt.2, 'In Dallas'

2 One usually dies because one is alone, or because one has got into something over one's head. One often dies because one does not have the right alliances, because one is not given support. In Sicily the Mafia kills the servants of the State that the State has not been able to protect.

Giovanni Falcone (1939–1992), Italian judge: Closing words of *Men of Honor* (1992), Ch.6. Falcone, along with his wife and three bodyguards, was blown up outside Palermo, 23 May 1992

3 You never know what's hit you. A gunshot is the perfect way.

John F. Kennedy (1917–1963), U.S. Democratic politician and president: when asked how he would choose to die, quoted in *The Kennedys* by Peter Collier and David Horowitz (1984), Pt.3, Ch.3

4 In Pierre Elliot Trudeau, Canada has at last produced a political leader worthy of assassination.

Irving Layton (b.1912), Canadian poet: *The Whole Bloody Bird* (1969), 'Obs II'

5 The horror of Gandhi's murder lies not in the political motives behind it or in its consequences for Indian policy or for the future of non-violence; the horror lies simply in the fact that any man could look into the face of this extraordinary person and deliberately pull a trigger.

Mary McCarthy (1912–1989), U.S. author and critic: 'Gandhi' (1949), rep. in *On the Contrary* (1961), Pt.1

6 Honey, I forgot to duck.

Ronald Reagan (b.1911), U.S. Republican politician and president: remark, 30 March 1981 to Nancy Reagan, after John Hinckley III's assassination attempt. Reagan was echoing the celebrated excuse boxer Jack Dempsey made to his wife after losing a title fight in the 1920s

7 Before I was shot, I always thought that I was more half-there than all-there – I always suspected that I was watching TV instead of living life. … Right when I was being shot and ever since, I knew that I was watching television.

Andy Warhol (c.1928–1987), U.S. Pop artist: *From A to B and Back Again* (1975), Ch.6

See also DeLillo on THE KENNEDYS

ASTROLOGY

1 Faithful horoscope-watching, practiced daily, provides just the sort of small but warm and infinitely reassuring fillip that gets matters off to a spirited start.

Shana Alexander (b.1925), U.S. writer and editor: 'A Delicious Appeal to Unreason' (1966), rep. in *The Feminine Eye* (1970)

2 The stars which shone over Babylon and the stable in Bethlehem still shine as brightly over the Empire State Building and your front yard today. They perform their cycles with the same mathematical precision, and they will continue to affect each thing on earth, including man, as long as the earth exists.

Linda Goodman (b.1929), U.S. astrologer: afterword to *Linda Goodman's Sun Signs* (1968)

3 About astrology and palmistry: they are good because they make people vivid and full of possibilities. They are communism at its best. Everybody has a birthday and almost everybody has a palm.

Kurt Vonnegut (b.1922), U.S. novelist: *Wampeters, Foma and Granfallons* (1974), 'When I was Twenty-One'

See also Rado on THE NEW AGE; Vonnegut on SUPERSTITION

ASTRONOMY

1 Astronomy is not the apex of science or of invention. But it is a test of the cast of temperament and mind that underlies a culture.

Jacob Bronowski (1908–1974), British scientist and author: *The Ascent of Man* (1973), Ch.6

2 The pursuit of the good and evil are now linked in astronomy as in almost all science…. The fate of human civilization will depend on whether the rockets of the future carry the astronomer's telescope or a hydrogen bomb.

Bernard Lovell (b.1913), British astronomer: fourth Reith Lecture, publ. in *The Individual and the Universe*, p.72 of O.U.P. edn. (1959)

3 I try to forget what happiness was, and when that don't work, I study the stars.

Derek Walcott (b.1930), West Indian poet and playwright: '*The Schooner* Flight', Sct.11, publ. in *The Star-Apple Kingdom* (1980)

ATHEISM

1 I am a daylight atheist.

Brendan Behan (1923–1964), Irish playwright: quoted by Rae Jeffs, publicist and assistant to Behan, in *Sacred Monsters* by Daniel Farson (1988), 'Rousting in Dublin'

2 We find the most terrible form of atheism, not in the militant and passionate struggle against the idea of God himself, but in the practical atheism of everyday living, in indifference and torpor. We often encounter these forms of atheism among those who are formally Christians.

Nicolai A. Berdyaev (1874–1948), Russian Christian philosopher: *Truth and Revelation* (1953), rep. in *Christian Existentialism* (1965), Ch.5, 'Atheism'

3 To ignore the true God is in fact only half an evil; atheism is worth more than the piety bestowed on mythical gods.

Emmanuel Levinas (b.1905), French Jewish philosopher: 'A Religion for Adults' (1957), rep. in *Difficult Freedom* (1990), Pt.1

4 If you don't believe in God, all you have to believe in is decency. … Decency is very good.

Better decent than indecent. But I don't think it's enough.
Harold Macmillan (1894–1986), British Conservative politician and prime minister: said to William F. Buckley Jr. on *Firing Line*, recorded in New York, 20 Nov. 1980, quoted in *Macmillan* by Alistair Horne (1989), Vol.II, Ch.19

5 Here we are, we're alone in the universe, there's no God, it just seems that it all began by something as simple as sunlight striking on a piece of rock. And here we are. We've only got ourselves. Somehow, we've just got to make a go of it. *We've only ourselves.*
John Osborne (1929–1994), British playwright: Jean, in *The Entertainer* (1957), No.12

6 What you don't understand is that it is possible to be an atheist, it is possible not to know if God exists or why He should, and yet to believe that man does not live in a state of nature but in history, and that history as we know it now began with Christ, it was founded by Him on the Gospels.
Boris Pasternak (1890–1960), Russian poet, novelist and translator: Nikolay Nikolayevich, in *Doctor Zhivago* (1957; tr.1958), Ch.1, Sct.5

7 Among the repulsions of atheism for me has been its drastic uninterestingness as an intellectual position. Where was the ingenuity, the ambiguity, the humanity (in the Harvard sense) of saying that the universe just happened to happen and that when we're dead we're dead?
John Updike (b.1932), U.S. author and critic: *Self-Consciousness: Memoirs* (1989), Ch.4

See also Pasolini on COMMUNISM

ATHLETICS *see under* SPORT

ATTENTION

1 A state of dispersed attention seems to offer certain advantages. It may be compared to a sport like hang gliding. In distraction we are suspended, we hover, we reserve our opinions.
Saul Bellow (b.1915), U.S. novelist: *It All Adds Up* (1994), 'The Distracted Public'

2 Attention is the effort to counteract ... states of illusion. ... If I attend properly I will have no choices and this is the ultimate condition to be aimed at.
Iris Murdoch (b.1919), British novelist and philosopher: *The Sovereignty of Good* (1970), 'The Idea of Perfection'

CLEMENT ATTLEE

1 He seems determined to make a trumpet sound like a tin whistle.
Aneurin Bevan (1897–1960), British Labour politician: quoted in *Aneurin Bevan* by Michael Foot (1962), Vol.I, Ch.14. In playing second fiddle to Conservative Anthony Eden when the two were delegated to represent Britain at the U.N. conference in San Francisco, Attlee, according to Bevan, had 'consistently underplayed his position and opportunities. ... He brings to the fierce struggle of politics the tepid enthusiasm of a lazy summer afternoon at a cricket match'

2 He is a modest little man who has a good deal to be modest about.
Winston Churchill (1874–1965), British statesman and author: quoted in the *Chicago Sunday Tribune Magazine of Books*, 27 June 1954

AUDIENCES

1 I never let them cough. They wouldn't dare.
Ethel Barrymore (1879–1959), Anglo-American actress: the *New York Post*, 7 June 1956

2 Your audience gives you everything you need. They tell you. There is no director who can direct you like an audience.
Fanny Brice (1891–1951), U.S. entertainer: quoted in *The Fabulous Fanny* by Norman Katkov (1952), Ch.6

3 Theatergoing is a communal act, moviegoing a solitary one.
Robert Brustein (b.1927), U.S. stage director, author and critic: introduction to *Who Needs Theatre?* (1987)

4 Audiences can no longer be depended on to respond to conventional forms. Perhaps they want much more from entertainment than the civilized, but limited rational pleasures of genre pieces. ... Audiences ... don't care any longer about the conventions of the past, and are too restless and apathetic to pay attention to motivations and complications, cause and effect. They want less effort, more sensations, more knobs to turn.
Pauline Kael (b.1919), U.S. film critic: introduction to *I Lost it at the Movies* (1965)

5 I'm not here for your amusement. You're here for mine.
John Lydon [formerly Johnny Rotten] (b.1957), British rock musician: remark 1978, to audience in Memphis, Tennessee, quoted in *Sex Pistols File* (ed. Ray Stevenson, 1984)

6 My conception of the audience is of a public each member of which is carrying about with him what he thinks is an anxiety, or a hope, or a preoccupation which is his alone and isolates

him from mankind; and in this respect at least the function of a play is to reveal him to himself so that he may touch others by virtue of the revelation of his mutuality with them. If only for this reason I regard the theater as a serious business, one that makes or should make man more human, which is to say, less alone.

Arthur Miller (b.1915), U.S. playwright: introduction Sct.2 to *Collected Plays* (1958)

7   A concert audience has a face. It looks worked upon. Wild eyed. Stimulated from a distant source like a laboratory experiment. As though the stage event, the action being watched and heard, is only a mirror image of some unseen phenomenon.

Sam Shepard (b.1943), U.S. playwright and actor: *Rolling Thunder Logbook* (1977), 'Audience'

8   The audience is the most revered member of the theater. Without an audience there is no theater. Every technique learned by the actor, every curtain, every flat on the stage, every careful analysis by the director, every coordinated scene, is for the enjoyment of the audience. They are our guests, our evaluators, and the last spoke in the wheel which can then begin to roll. They make the performance meaningful.

Viola Spolin (b.1911), U.S. theatrical director and producer: *Improvisation for the Theater* (1963), Ch.1

9   An audience is never wrong. An individual member of it may be an imbecile, but a thousand imbeciles together in the dark – that is critical genius.

Billy Wilder (b.1906), U.S. film-maker: *Arena*, TV profile, BBC2, 24 Jan. 1992

See also Lennon on APPLAUSE; Tarantino on CINEMA; Scorsese on CINEMA: SEX & VIOLENCE; Dodd on COMEDIANS; Bangs on PERFORMANCE; Burchill on SPORT: BOXING

AUSTRALIA

1   One of the few moments of happiness a man knows in Australia is that moment of meeting the eyes of another man over the tops of two beer glasses.

Anonymous, scribbled on the flyleaf of a paperback copy of *Tristram Shandy* , bought in a second-hand bookstore in Alice Springs, Australia, quoted by Bruce Chatwin in *The Songlines* (1987), Ch.30, 'From the Notebooks'

2   We're built, as a nation, on the grounds of a concentration camp. It's like saying 'OK, here's Auschwitz. Here's where we'll start our country.'

Peter Carey (b.1943), Australian author: interview in *City Limits* (London), 7 April 1988

3   Where else in the world is a generous man defined as one who would give you his arsehole and shit through his ribs?

Germaine Greer (b.1939), Australian feminist writer: 'The New Maharajahs', first publ. in *The Sunday Times* (London), 16 Jan. 1972, rep. in *The Madwoman's Underclothes* (1986)

4   We have found that it *is* possible for Australians to have literary ideas about the place, that Australia is not outside the universe. In short Australia – which used to have one unifying rite, cricket – has now become pluralist. I cannot but predict it will be a disaster for Australian cricket.

Thomas Keneally (b.1935), Australian novelist: *Summer Days* (1981), 'The Cyclical Supremacy of Australia in World Cricket'

5   In a way Australia is like Catholicism. The company is sometimes questionable and the landscape is grotesque. But you always come back.

Thomas Keneally: *Woman's Day*, 4 July 1983

AUTHENTICITY

1   Some writers confuse authenticity, which they ought always to aim at, with originality, which they should never bother about.

W.H. Auden (1907–1973), Anglo-American poet: *The Dyer's Hand* (1962), Pt.1, 'Writing'

2   The things one shows need not be authentic. As a rule, they are better if they aren't. What must be authentic is the feeling one is trying to see and to express.

Federico Fellini (1920–1993), Italian film-maker: *Fellini on Fellini* (ed. Anna Keel and Christian Strich, 1974; tr.1977), 'Miscellany II', Sct.6

3   If you seek authenticity for authenticity's sake you are no longer authentic.

Jean-Paul Sartre (1905–1980), French philosopher and author: *Notebooks for an Ethics* (1983; tr.1992), Notebook 1

4   I'm not bothered by the provenance of things – to use a painter's analogy. I just think, 'Is it hot?'

Janet Street-Porter (b.1946), British broadcaster and programme-maker: interview in the *Independent on Sunday* (London), 20 Dec. 1992

AUTHORSHIP

1   Once the Author is removed, the claim to decipher a text becomes quite futile. To give a text an Author is to impose a limit on that text, to furnish it with a final signifier, to close the writing.

Roland Barthes (1915–1980), French semiologist: *Image-Music-Text* (1966; tr.1978), 'The Death of the Author'

2 What I find we're entering into now is not death of the author but diffusion of the author. Authorship gets spread through more and more people, you don't know who makes somehing now, where an idea comes from. I call this 'scenious' as opposed to genius. It's the intelligence of a whole situation, a whole network.

Brian Eno (b.1948), British musician: interview in *i-D* (London), Oct. 1993

3 I think somebody should be able to do all my paintings for me.

Andy Warhol (c.1928–1987), U.S. Pop artist: interview in 'What is Pop Art?' by G.R. Swenson, first publ. in *Art News* (New York), Nov. 1963, rep. in *Pop Art Redefined* by John Russell and Suzi Gablik (1969)

AUTOBIOGRAPHY

1 Every autobiography is concerned with two characters, a Don Quixote, the Ego, and a Sancho Panza, the Self.

W.H. Auden (1907–1973), Anglo-American poet: *The Dyer's Hand* (1962), Pt.3, 'Hic et Ille', Sct.B

2 Anyone who attempts to relate his life loses himself in the immediate. One can only speak of another.

Augusto Roa Bastos (b.1917), Paraguayan novelist: *I The Supreme* (1974; tr.1986), p.57 of Faber edn. (1988)

3 Autobiography begins with a sense of being alone. It is an orphan form.

John Berger (b.1926), British author and critic: 'Mother', first publ. in *Threepenny Review*, summer 1986, rep. in *Keeping a Rendezvous* (1992)

4 A man's memory is bound to be a distortion of his past in accordance with his present interests, and the most faithful autobiography is likely to mirror less what a man was than what he has become.

Fawn M. Brodie (1915–1981), U.S. biographer: *No Man Knows My History* (1945), Ch.19

5 Such reproductions may not interest the reader; but after all, this is my autobiography, not his; he is under no obligation to read further in it; he was under none to begin. ... A modest or inhibited autobiography is written without entertainment to the writer and read with distrust by the reader.

Neville Cardus (1889–1975), British journalist and critic: *Autobiography* (1947), Pt.1

6 An autobiography is an obituary in serial form with the last instalment missing.

Quentin Crisp (b.1908), British author: *The Naked Civil Servant* (1968), Ch.29

7 We can only write well about our sins because it is too difficult to recall a virtuous act or even whether it was the result of good or evil motives.

Edward Dahlberg (1900–1977), U.S. author and critic: *Alms for Oblivion* (1964), 'Moby-Dick: A Hamitic Dream'

8 Democratic societies are unfit for the publication of such thunderous revelations as I am in the habit of making.

Salvador Dali (1904–1989), Spanish painter: prologue to *Diary of a Genius* (1966)

9 *My Turn* is the distilled bathwater of Mrs Reagan's life, it is for the most part sweetish, with a tart edge of rebuke, but disappointingly free of dirt or particulate matter of any kind.

Barbara Ehrenreich (b.1941), U.S. author and columnist: 'The Bathtub Tapes', first publ. in *New Republic*, 1989, rep. in *The Worst Years of Our Lives* (1991)

10 Autobiography is now as common as adultery and hardly less reprehensible.

John Grigg (b.1924), British author and journalist: in *The Sunday Times* (London), 28 Feb. 1962

11 I am being frank about myself in this book. I tell of my first mistake on page 850.

Henry Kissinger (b.1923), U.S. Republican politician and secretary of state: of the second volume of his memoirs, *Years of Upheaval*, quoted in *The Observer* (London), 2 Jan. 1983

12 The trouble with writing a book about yourself is that you can't fool around. If you write about someone else, you can stretch the truth from here to Finland. If you write about yourself the slightest deviation makes you realize instantly that there may be honor among thieves, but *you* are just a dirty liar.

Groucho Marx (1895–1977), U.S. comic actor: opening sentence in *Groucho And Me* (1959), Ch.1

13 All those writers who write about their childhood! Gentle God, if I wrote about mine you wouldn't sit in the same room with me.

Dorothy Parker (1893–1967), U.S. humorous writer: interview in *Writers at Work* (First Series, ed. Malcolm Cowley, 1958)

14 I write fiction and I'm told it's autobiography, I write autobiography and I'm told it's fiction, so since I'm so dim and they're so smart, let *them* decide what it is or it isn't.

Philip Roth (b.1933), U.S. novelist: 'Philip', in *Deception* (1990), p.190 of Jonathan Cape edn.

15 If you really want to hear about it, the first thing you'll probably want to know is where I was born, and what my lousy childhood was like, and how my parents were occupied and all before they had me, and all that David Copperfield kind of crap, but I don't feel like going into it.

J.D. Salinger (b.1919), U.S. author: opening words of *Catcher in the Rye* (1951), Ch.1

16 Autobiographies ought to begin with Chapter Two.

Ellery Sedgwick (1872–1960), U.S. editor: *The Happy Profession* (autobiography, 1948), Ch.1

17 Don't give your opinions about Art and the Purpose of Life. They are of little interest and, anyway, you can't express them. Don't analyse yourself. Give the relevant facts and let your readers make their own judgments. Stick to your story. It is not the most important subject in history but it is one about which you are uniquely qualified to speak.

Evelyn Waugh (1903–1966), British novelist: advice to Stephen Spender in review of Spender's auto- biography, *World Within World* , publ. in *The Tablet* (London), 5 May 1951

18 There's no such thing as autobiography there's only art and lies.

Jeanette Winterson (b.1959), British author: *Art & Lies* (1994), 'Sappho', p.69 of Jonathan Cape edn. (1994)

THE AVANT-GARDE

1 An avant-garde man is like an enemy inside a city he is bent on destroying, against which he rebels; for like any system of government, an established form of expression is also a form of oppression. The avant-garde man is the oppo- nent of an existing system.

Eugène Ionesco (1912–1994), Rumanian-born French playwright: 'A Talk about the Avant-Garde' lecture, Helsinki, June 1959, rep. in *Notes and Counter Notes* (1962)

2 Avant-gardism is an addiction that can be appeased only by a revolution in permanence.

Harold Rosenberg (1906–1978), U.S. art critic and author: 'The Avant-Garde', first publ. in *Quality: Its Image* (ed. Louis Kronenberger, 1969), rep. in *Discovering the Present* (1973)

3 *Wake up*. The avant-garde is dead. It's been marketed.

Will Self (b.1961), British author: interview in *The Idler* (London), Nov./Dec. 1993

AWARDS

1 A new kind of award has been added – the deathbed award. It is not an award of any kind. Either the recipient has not acted at all, or was not nominated, or did not win the award the last few times around. It is intended to relieve the guilty conscience of the Academy members and save face in front of the public. The Academy has the horrible taste to have a star, choking with emotion, present this deathbed award so that there can be no doubt in any- body's mind why the award is so hurriedly given. Lucky is the actor who is too sick to watch the proceedings on television.

Marlene Dietrich (1904–1992), German-born U.S. film actress: *Marlene Dietrich's ABC* (1962), 'Academy Award'

2 I'm a prince of the Tuareg, a sheikh in the Order of the Two Niles, a chevalier in the Order of Leopold II, and a freeman of more fucking cities than I could ever hope to visit.

Bob Geldof (b.1954), Irish rock singer: in *New Musical Express* (London), 1994, quoted in *NME Book of Quotes*, 4 Feb. 1995, 'Fame'

3 Lots of people who complained about us receiving the MBE received theirs for heroism in the war – for killing people. We received ours for entertaining other people. I'd say we deserve ours more.

John Lennon (1940–1980), British rock musician: quoted in *Beatles Illustrated Lyrics* (1969), Vol.I

4 The Oscars demonstrate the will of the people to control and judge those they have elected to stand above them (much, perhaps, as in bygone days, an election celebrated the same).

David Mamet (b.1947), U.S. playwright: *Writing in Restaurants* (1986), 'Oscars'

5 Members rise from CMG (known sometimes in Whitehall as 'Call Me God') to KCMG ('Kindly Call Me God') to GCMG ('God Calls Me God').

Anthony Sampson (b.1926), British journalist and author: *Anatomy of Britain Today* (1965), Ch.18

6 To refuse awards … is another way of accept- ing them with more noise than is normal.

Peter Ustinov (b.1921), British actor, writer and director: of the refusal of Oscars by Marlon Brando and George C. Scott, quoted in *Marlon Brando* by David Shipman (1974; rev.1989), Ch.13

BABIES

1 From the moment of birth, when the stone-age baby confronts the twentieth-century mother, the baby is subjected to these forces of violence, called love, as its mother and father have been, and their parents and their parents before them. These forces are mainly con- cerned with destroying most of its poten- tialities. This enterprise is on the whole successful.

R.D. Laing (1927–1989), British psychiatrist: *The Politics of Experience* (1967), Ch.3

2 Babies are necessary to grown-ups. A new baby is like the beginning of all things – won- der, hope, a dream of possibilities. In a world that is cutting down its trees to build highways, losing its earth to concrete … babies are almost the only remaining link with nature, with the natural world of living things from which we spring.

Eda J. Le Shan (b.1922), U.S. educator and author: *The Conspiracy Against Childhood* (1967), Ch.2

3 Diaper backward spells repaid. Think about it.

Marshall McLuhan (1911–1980), Canadian communications theorist: remark, June 1969, made at American Booksellers Association luncheon, Washington D.C., quoted in the *Sun* (Vancouver), 7 June 1969

4 Every new baby is a blind desperate vote for survival: people who find themselves unable to register an effective political protest against extermination do so by a biological act.

Lewis Mumford (1895–1990), U.S. social philosopher: *The City in History* (1961), Ch.18

5 They resemble rubber, your ladyship, ha, ha, ha. Just a core of india-rubber, with an elastic centre. Oh yes, they are. Very, very much so. Resilience is no word for it – oh dear me, no. Every ounce, a bounce, ha, ha, ha! Every ounce, a bounce.

Mervyn Peake (1911–1968), British author and illustrator: Doctor Prunesquallor to the Countess of Groan, in *Titus Groan* (1946), 'Titus is Christened'

6 A baby is God's opinion that life should go on.

Carl Sandburg (1878–1967), U.S. poet: *Remembrance Rock* (1948), Ch.2

See also Auden on THE BODY: BODILY FUNCTIONS; Weldon on CHILDBIRTH

BACHELORS

1 Show me a man who lives alone and has a perpetually clean kitchen, and 8 times out of 9 I'll show you a man with detestable spiritual qualities.

Charles Bukowski (1920–1994), U.S. author and poet: *Tales of Ordinary Madness* (1967), 'Too Sensitive'

2 James Bond in his Sean Connery days ... was the first well-known bachelor on the American scene who was not a drifter or a degenerate and did not eat out of cans.

Barbara Ehrenreich (b.1941), U.S. author and columnist: 'Socialism in One Household', first publ. in *Mother Jones* (1987), *The Worst Years of Our Lives* (1991)

3 The most threatened group in human societies as in animal societies is the unmated male: the unmated male is more likely to wind up in prison or in an asylum or dead than his mated counterpart. He is less likely to be promoted at work and he is considered a poor credit risk.

Germaine Greer (b.1939), Australian feminist writer: *Sex and Destiny* (1984), Ch.2

BAN THE BOMB

1 Watching the Peace Movement grow in numbers and competence, I see it as talented citizenship. Citizenship is a tough occupation which obliges the citizen to make his own informed opinion and stand by it.

Martha Gellhorn (b.1908), U.S. journalist and author: conclusion to *The Face of War* (1959; rev.1967)

2 58% Don't Want Pershing.

Katharine Hamnett (b.1952), British fashion designer: T-shirt design, famously worn by Hamnett to meet Mrs Thatcher at a Downing Street reception in 1984, quoted in *Contemporary Fashion* (ed. Richard Martin, 1995)

3 Oh give me a land that is peaceful and grand
With concern for the whole human race,
So we can be proud that the dread mushroom cloud
In our future will not have a place.

Protest song on a march to the Atomic Weapons Research Establishment at Aldermaston, quoted in *Bertrand Russell* by Caroline Moorhead (1992), Ch.19

4 We used to think that Hitler was wicked when he wanted to kill all the Jews, but Kennedy and Macmillan and others both in the East and in the West pursue policies which will probably lead to killing not only all the Jews but all the rest of us too. They are much more wicked than Hitler and this idea of weapons of mass extermination is utterly and absolutely horrible and it is a thing which no man with one spark of humanity can tolerate and I will not pretend to obey a government which is organising the massacre of the whole of mankind.

Bertrand Russell (1872–1970), British philosopher and mathematician: extempore comment added to speech made by Russell, 15 April 1961, Birmingham, publ. in *The Autobiography of Bertrand Russell* (1967), Vol.III, Ch.3, 'Trafalgar Square'

BANALITY

1 The attitude I take is that everyday life is more interesting than forms of celebration, when we become aware of it. That *when* is when our intentions go down to zero. Then suddenly you notice that the world is magical.

John Cage (1912–1992), U.S. composer: interview in *Tulane Drama Review* Vol.II, No.2, 1965, rep. in *Conversing with Cage* (ed. Richard Kostelanetz, 1988), 'Esthetics'

2 A mental disease has swept the planet: banalization. ... Presented with the alternative of love or a garbage disposal unit, young people of

all countries have chosen the garbage disposal unit.

Ivan Chtcheglov (b.1934), French political theorist: 'Formulary for a New Urbanism', Oct. 1953, first publ. in *Internationale Situationiste* (Paris), No.1, June 1958, rep. in *Situationist International Anthology* (ed. Ken Knabb, 1981)

3 Banality is a symptom of non-communication. Men hide behind their clichés.

Eugène Ionesco (1912–1994), Rumanian-born French playwright: *Notes and Counter-Notes* (1962), Pt.4, 'Further Notes, 1960'

4 Both the sense of community and of security depend on the familiar. Freed of them, transcendental experience becomes possible.

Mark Rothko (1903–1970), Latvian-born U.S. painter: 'The Romantics Were Prompted', first publ. in *Possibilities* (New York), winter 1947/48, rep. in *Theories of Modern Art* by Herschel B. Chipp (1968), Ch.9

BRIGITTE BARDOT

1 I really am a cat transformed into a woman.

Brigitte Bardot (b.1934), French actress: quoted in *Bébé: The Films of Brigitte Bardot* by Tony Crawley (1975) 'The Bbeginning'

2 She represents the unavowed aspiration of the male human being, his potential infidelity – and infidelity of a very special kind, which would lead him to the opposite of his wife, to the 'woman of wax' whom he could model at will, make and unmake in any way he wished, even unto death.

Marguerite Duras (1914–1996), French author and film-maker: in 'Queen Bardot', first publ. in *France-Observateur* (Paris), 1958, rep. in *Outside: Selected Writings* (1984)

3 She was a wanton woman who had sacrificed her body to the god of success, perpetuating the myth of the film world in which depravity pays better than talent.

Roger Vadim (b.1927), French film-maker and former husband of Bardot: *Memoirs of the Devil* (1975), Ch.8. 'From the moment I liberated Brigitte,' Vadim was earlier quoted as saying, 'the moment I showed her how to be truly herself, our marriage was all downhill' (quoted in the *Sunday Express*, 2 July 1972)

BASEBALL *see under* SPORT

BATTLES

1 No battle is worth fighting except the last one.

Enoch Powell (b.1912), British Conservative politician: quoted in *The Observer* (London), 2 Jan. 1983

2 Dead battles, like dead generals, hold the military mind in their dead grip.

Barbara Tuchman (1912–1989), U.S. historian: *The Guns of August* (1962), Ch.2

See also Hussein on IRAQ & THE SECOND GULF WAR

THE BEAT GENERATION

1 Kerouac opened a million coffee bars and sold a million pairs of Levis to both sexes. Woodstock rises from his pages.

William Burroughs (1914–1997), U.S. author: *The Adding Machine* (1985), 'Remembering Jack Kerouac'

2 That isn't writing at all, it's typing.

Truman Capote (1924–1984), U.S. author: of the Beat novelists, quoted in report of television discussion in *New Republic* (Washington D.C.), 9 Feb. 1959

3 I saw the best minds of my generation
   destroyed by madness, starving hysterical naked,
dragging themselves through the negro streets
   at dawn looking for an angry fix,
angelheaded hipsters burning for the ancient
   heavenly connection to the starry dynamo in
   the machinery of night,
who poverty and tatters and hollow-eyed and
   high sat up smoking in the supernatural
   darkness of cold-water flats floating across
   the tops of cities contemplating jazz.

Allen Ginsberg (b.1926), U.S. poet: opening lines of 'Howl', publ. in *Howl and Other Poems* (1956)

4 But then they danced down the street like dingledodies, and I shambled after as I've been doing all my life after people who interest me, because the only people for me are the mad ones, the ones who are mad to live, mad to talk, mad to be saved, desirous of everything at the same time, the ones who never yawn or say a commonplace thing, but burn, burn, burn, like fabulous yellow roman candles exploding like spiders across the stars and in the middle you see the blue centerlight pop and everybody goes 'Awww!'

Jack Kerouac (1922–1969), U.S. author: *On The Road* (1957), Pt.1, Ch.1. In an interview in *Playboy* magazine in June 1959, Kerouac explained the origin of the label 'Beat Generation': 'John Clellon Holmes ... and I were sitting around trying to think up the meaning of the Lost Generation and the subsequent Existentialism and I said, "You know, this is really a beat generation" and he leapt up and said "That's it, that's right!"' The phrase also appeared in Holmes's novel *Go* (1952)

THE BEATLES

1 This place has become a haven for drop-outs. The trouble is, some of our best friends are drop-outs.
George Harrison (b.1943), British rock musician: of the Apple offices in Savile Row, London, quoted in *Shout! The True Story of the Beatles* by Philip Norman (1981), Pt.4, 'May 1969'

2 They sort of Europeanised us all. Before them, our society hadn't been the Great Society as much as it had been the Revlon Society.
Dustin Hoffman (b.1937), U.S. actor: in *The Observer* (London), 19 Feb. 1989

3 While the music is performed, the cameras linger savagely over the faces of the audience. What a bottomless chasm of vacuity they reveal! Those who flock round the Beatles, who scream themselves into hysteria, whose vacant faces flicker over the TV screen, are the least fortunate of their generation, the dull, the idle, the failures ...
Paul Johnson (b.1928), British journalist: 'The Menace of "Beatlism"', publ. in *New Statesman* (London), 28 Feb. 1964

4 The trumpets of the Beatles are not the trumpets of Jericho which will cause the walls of socialism to come tumbling down.
Wladyslaw Kozdra (b.1920), Polish Communist Party official: speech at eighth Plenary Session of the Central Committee of the Polish Communist Party, 16–17 May 1967, quoted in *Rock Around the Bloc* by Timothy Ryback (1990), Ch.6

5 I declare that the Beatles are mutants. Prototypes of evolutionary agents sent by God with a mysterious power to create a new species – a young race of laughing freemen. ... They are the wisest, holiest, most effective avatars the human race has ever produced.
Timothy Leary (1920–1996), U.S. psychologist: quoted in *Shout! The True Story of the Beatles* by Philip Norman (1981), Pt.4, 'August 1967'

6 One has to completely humiliate oneself to be what the Beatles were, and that's what I resent. I didn't know, I didn't foresee. It happened bit by bit, gradually, until this complete craziness is surrounding you, and you're doing exactly what you don't want to do with people you can't stand – the people you hated when you were ten.
John Lennon (1940–1980), British rock musician: interview in *Rolling Stone* (New York), 7 Jan. 1971

7 A poached egg on the Underground on the Bakerloo Line between Trafalgar Square and Charing Cross? Yes, Paul. A sock full of elephant shit on Otterspool Promenade? Give me 10 minutes, Ringo. Two Turkish dwarfs dancing the Charleston on a sideboard? Male or female, John? Pubic hair from Sonny Liston? It's early closing, George (gulp), but give me until noon tomorrow. The only gig I would do after this is the Queen. Their staff are terrified of them, and not without reason. They have fired more people than any comparable employer unit in the world. They make Lord Beaverbrook look like Jesus.
Derek Taylor (b. 1934), Beatles press officer: quoted in *Shout! The True Story of the Beatles* by Philip Norman (1981), Pt.4, 'May 1970'

See also Lennon on CHRISTIANITY; JOHN LENNON; Lennon on THE 1960S; Lennon on THE RAT RACE

BEAUTY

1 Beauty is one of the rare things that do not lead to doubt of God.
(*La beauté est une des rares choses qui ne font pas douter de Dieu.*)
Jean Anouilh (1910–1987), French playwright: Thomas à Becket, in *Becket* (1959; tr.1961), Act 1

2 Beauty is desired in order that it may be befouled; not for its own sake, but for the joy brought by the certainty of profaning it.
Georges Bataille (1897–1962), French novelist and critic: *Eroticism* (1962), Ch.13

3 The pursuit of beauty is much more dangerous nonsense than the pursuit of truth or goodness, because it affords a stronger temptation to the ego.
Northrop Frye (1912–1991), Canadian literary critic: *Anatomy of Criticism* (1957), 'Mythical Phase: Symbol as Archetype'

4 Beauty is a precious trace that eternity causes to appear to us and that it takes away from us. A manifestation of eternity, and a sign of death as well.
Eugène Ionesco (1912–1994), Rumanian-born French playwright: *Present Past – Past Present* (1968), Ch.5

5 I'm tired of all this nonsense about beauty being only skin-deep. That's deep enough. What do you want – an adorable pancreas?
Jean Kerr (b.1923), U.S. author and playwright: *The Snake Has All the Lines* (1958), 'Mirror, Mirror on the Wall'

6 At some point in life the world's beauty becomes enough. You don't need to photograph, paint or even remember it. It is enough.
Toni Morrison (b.1931), U.S. novelist and editor: *Tar Baby* (1981), p.244 of Chatto & Windus edn. (1981)

7 I have a horror of people who speak about the beautiful. What is the beautiful? One must speak of problems in painting!
Pablo Picasso (1881–1973), Spanish artist: in *Vogue* (New York), 1 Nov. 1956

8 The real sin against life is to abuse and destroy beauty, even one's own – even more, one's own, for that has been put in our care and we are responsible for its well-being.
Katherine Anne Porter (1890–1980), U.S. short-story writer and novelist: Herr Freytag, in *Ship of Fools* (1962), Pt.3

9 Beauty is the still birth of suffering, every woman knows that.
Emily Prager (b.1948), U.S. journalist and author: Lao Bing, in 'A Visit from the Footbinder', publ. in *Close Company: Stories of Mothers and Daughters* (ed. Christine Park and Caroline Heaton, 1987)

10 Beauty is always associated with the male fantasy of what the female body is.
Jenny Savile (b.1970), British artist: interview in the *Independent on Sunday* (London), 30 Jan. 1994

11 The beauty myth moves for men as a mirage; its power lies in its ever-receding nature. When the gap is closed, the lover embraces only his own disillusion.
Naomi Wolf (b.1962), U.S. author: *The Beauty Myth* (1990), 'Sex'

12 If beauty isn't genius it usually signals at least a high level of animal cunning.
Peter York (b.1950), British journalist: 'Discontinued Models', publ. in *London Collection Magazine*, April 1978, rep. in *Style Wars* (1980)

See also AESTHETICS; Aimée on AGE: AGING

BED

1 Don Juan needs no bed, being far too impatient to undress,
   nor do Tristan and Isolde, much too in love to care
for so mundane a matter, but unmythical mortals require one, and prefer to take their clothes off,
if only to sleep.
W.H. Auden (1907–1973), Anglo-American poet: 'Thanksgiving for a Habitat', Sct.11, 'The Cave of Nakedness', publ. in *About the House* (1965)

2 The bed is now as public as the dinner table and governed by the same rules of formal confrontation.
Angela Carter (1940–1992), British author: *The Sadeian Woman* (1979), 'Speculative Finale'

3 Talking in bed ought to be easiest,
Lying together there goes back so far,
An emblem of two people being honest.
Philip Larkin (1922–1985), British poet: 'Talking in Bed', written 1960, publ. in *The Whitsun Weddings* (1964)

4 You can do everything either from your bed or in your bed – eat, sleep, think, get exercise, smoke.... Everything is more glamorous when you do it in bed, anyway. Even peeling potatoes.
Andy Warhol (c.1928–1987), U.S. Pop artist: *From A to B and Back Again* (1975), Ch.10

BEGGARS

1 Begging defaces the city, degrades the spirit. It dehumanises you as well as them; it brutalises us all. You learn to walk past these people, you have to, and it makes it easier to turn away from the truly needy. These professional leeches, big strapping lads some of them, harden your heart, put callouses on your soul. They make every cry for help seem like junk mail.
Tony Parsons (b.1955), British journalist: 'Street Trash', publ. in *Arena* (London), Sept./Oct. 1991, rep. in *Dispatches from the Front Line of Popular Culture* (1994)

2 Give a beggar a dime and he'll bless you. Give him a dollar and he'll curse you for withholding the rest of your fortune. Poverty is a bag with a hole at the bottom.
Anzia Yezierska (c.1881–1970), Polish author: *Red Ribbon on a White Horse* (1950), Ch.9

BEHAVIOUR

1 When people are on their best behaviour they aren't always at their best.
Alan Bennett (b.1934), British playwright: 'Dinner at Noon', broadcast, in series *Byline*, BBC, April 1988, publ. in *Writing Home* (1994)

2 For his own behavior each one is responsible, but no behavior is final. It shapes human destiny – any behavior, all behavior – but it makes no last decision. Victory and defeat are both passing moments. There are no ends; there are only means.
Martha Gellhorn (b.1908), U.S. journalist and author: introduction (1959), to *The Face of War* (1967), Appendix

BEHAVIOURISM

1 Of course, Behaviourism 'works.' So does torture. Give me a no-nonsense, down-to-earth behaviourist, a few drugs, and simple electrical appliances, and in six months I will have him reciting the Athanasian Creed in public.

W.H. Auden (1907–1973), Anglo-American poet: *A Certain World* (1970), 'Behaviourism'

2   If we ever do end up acting just like rats or Pavlov's dogs, it will be largely because behaviorism has conditioned us to do so.
    Richard Dean Rosen (b.1949), U.S. journalist and critic: *Psychobabble: Fast Talk and Quick Cure in the Era of Feeling* (1977), 'Psychobabble'

BELIEF

1   I started out by believing God for a newer car than the one I was driving. I started out believing God for a nicer apartment than I had. Then I moved up.
    Jim Bakker (b.1940), U.S. evangelist: quoted in the *New Yorker*, 23 April 1990

2   We have all had the experience of finding that our reactions and perhaps even our deeds have denied beliefs we thought were ours.
    James Baldwin (1924–1987), U.S. author: 'The Crusade of Indignation', first publ. in *The Nation* (New York), 7 July 1956, rep. in *The Price of the Ticket* (1985)

3   As a first approximation, I define 'belief' not as the object of believing (a dogma, a program, etc.) but as the subject's investment in a proposition, the *act* of saying it and considering it as true.
    Michel de Certeau (1925–1986), French author and critic: *The Practice of Everyday Life* (1974), Ch.13

4   Well, I believe in the soul, the cock, the pussy, the small of a woman's back, the hangin' curved ball, high fiber, good Scotch, that the novels of Susan Sontag are self-indulgent overrated crap. I believe Lee Harvey Oswald acted alone, I believe there ought to be a constitutional amendment outlawing astroturf ... I believe in the sweet spot, soft-core pornography, opening your presents Christmas morning rather than Christmas Eve, and I believe in long slow deep soft wet kisses that last three days.
    Kevin Costner (b.1955), U.S. actor and film-maker: Crash Davis (Kevin Costner), in *Bull Durham* (film; written and directed by Ron Shelton, 1988)

5   Believing: it means believing in our own lies. And I can say that I am grateful that I got this lesson very early.
    Günter Grass (b.1927), German author: *Omnibus*, BBC1, 3 Nov. 1992

6   As I get older I seem to believe less and less and yet to believe what I do believe more and more.
    David Jenkins (b.1925), British ecclesiastic, Bishop of Durham: in *The Daily Telegraph* (London), 2 Nov. 1988

7   The word 'belief' is a difficult thing for me. I don't *believe*. I must have a reason for a certain hypothesis. Either I *know* a thing, and then I know it – I don't need to believe it.
    Carl Jung (1875–1961), Swiss psychiatrist: interview in 1959, publ. in *Face to Face* by Hugh Burnett (1964), p.51

8   Where there is no belief, there is no blasphemy.
    Salman Rushdie (b.1947), Indian-born British author: *The Satanic Verses* (1988), 'Return to Jahilia'

9   I confused things with their names: that is belief.
    Jean-Paul Sartre (1905–1980), French philosopher and author: *Les Mots* (1964), Pt.2, 'Écrire'

See also Russell on CREDULITY; Hampton on CREEDS; FAITH; MYTH; SUPERSTITION

BEREAVEMENT

1   Tears are sometimes an inappropriate response to death. When a life has been lived completely honestly, completely successfully, or just completely, the correct response to death's perfect punctuation mark is a smile.
    Julie Burchill (b.1960), British journalist and author: in *The Independent* (London), 5 Dec. 1989

2   It is extraordinary how the house and the simplest possessions of someone who has been left become so quickly sordid. ... Even the stain on the coffee cup seems not coffee but the physical manifestation of one's inner stain, the fatal blot that from the beginning had marked one for ultimate aloneness.
    Coleman Dowell (1925–1985), U.S. novelist, dramatist and lyricist: Entry in Mrs October's journals, in *Mrs October Was Here* (1973), Pt.3, 'Tasmania, Now'

3   Guilt is perhaps the most painful companion of death.
    Elisabeth Kübler-Ross (b.1926), Swiss-born U.S. psychiatrist: on *Death and Dying* (1969), Ch.9

4   If, as I can't help suspecting, the dead also feel the pains of separation (and this may be one of their purgatorial sufferings), then for both lovers, and for all pairs of lovers without exception, bereavement is a universal and integral part of our experience of love.
    C.S. Lewis (1898–1963), British author: *A Grief Observed* (1961), Pt.3. The book, published under the pseudonym N.W. Clerk, is an account of mourning for Lewis's dead wife

5   Bereavement is a darkness impenetrable to the imagination of the unbereaved.
    Iris Murdoch (b.1919), British novelist and philosopher: Montague Small, in *The Sacred and Profane Love Machine* (1974), p.30 of Chatto & Windus edn.

6 Widow. The word consumes itself …
Sylvia Plath (1932–1963), U.S. poet: 'Widow',
publ. in *Crossing the Water* (1971)

BERLIN *see under* GERMANY

BETRAYAL

1 It was the men I deceived the most that I loved
the most.
Marguerite Duras (1914–1996), French author and
film-maker: *Practicalities* (1987; tr.1990), 'The
Chimneys of *India Song*'

2 Anyone who hasn't experienced the ecstasy of
betrayal knows nothing about ecstasy at all.
Jean Genet (1910–1986), French playwright and
novelist: *Prisoner of Love* (1986; tr.1989), Pt.1

3 Under the spreading chestnut tree
I sold you and you sold me:
There lie they, and here lie we
Under the spreading chestnut tree.
George Orwell (1903–1950), British author:
popular song in *Nineteen Eighty-four* (1949), Pt.1,
Ch.7 and *passim*

See also Forster on CAUSES; Monroe on
HUSBANDS; Williams on SUSPICION

THE BIBLE

1 Never read the Bible as if it means something.
Or at any rate don't *try* and mean it. Nor
prayers. The liturgy is best treated and read as
if it's someone announcing the departure of
trains.
Alan Bennett (b.1934), British playwright: journal
entry, 30 June 1984, publ. in *Writing Home* (1994),
'Diaries 1980–1990'

2 Immorality, perversion, infidelity, canni-
balism, etc., are unassailable by church and
civic league if you dress them up in the togas
and talliths of the Good Book.
Ben Hecht (1893–1964), U.S. journalist, author and
screenwriter: on 'the fornication problem' in biblical
epics, in *A Child of the Century* (1954), Bk.5, 'Sex in
Hollywood'

3 We wonder, in fact, if the idea of prefiguration,
legitimate to the extent that it coincides with
that of prophecy, does not alter, when it is
raised into a system, the very essence of the
spirit which Judaism installed. If every pure
character in the Old Testament announces the
Messiah, if every unworthy person is his tor-
turer and every woman his Mother, does not
the Book of Books lose all life with this obsessive theme an endless repetition of the same
stereotyped gestures?
Emmanuel Levinas (b.1905), French Jewish
philosopher: 'Persons or Figures' (1950), rep. in
Difficult Freedom (1990), Pt.3

BICYCLES

1 Consider a man riding a bicycle. Whoever he
is, we can say three things about him. We know
he got on the bicycle and started to move. We
know that at some point he will stop and get
off. Most important of all, we know that if at
any point between the beginning and the end
of his journey he stops moving and does not get
off the bicycle he will fall off it. That is a
metaphor for the journey through life of any
living thing, and I think of any society of living
things.
William Golding (1911–1993), British author:
'Utopias and Antiutopias', address, 13 Feb. 1977, to
Les Anglicistes, Lille, France, rep. in *A Moving
Target* (1982)

2 The gross and net result of it is that people who
spent most of their natural lives riding iron
bicycles over the rocky roadsteads of this
parish get their personalities mixed up with the
personalities of their bicycle as a result of the
interchanging of the atoms of each of them and
you would be surprised at the number of
people in these parts who nearly are half people
and half bicycles.
Flann O'Brien (1911–1966), Irish author: Sergeant,
in *The Third Policeman* (1967), Ch.6

BIGOTRY

1 Those who believe in *their* truth – the only
ones whose imprint is retained by the memory
of men – leave the earth behind them strewn
with corpses. Religions number in their
ledgers more murders than the bloodiest
tyrannies account for, and those whom humanity has called divine far surpass the most
conscientious murderers in their thirst for
slaughter.
E.M. Cioran (1911–1995), Rumanian-born French
philosopher: *A Short History of Decay* (1949),
Ch.1, 'Itinerary of Hate'

2 When we believe ourselves in possession of the
only truth, we are likely to be indifferent to
common everyday truths.
Eric Hoffer (1902–1983), U.S. philosopher: *The
Passionate State of Mind* (1955), Aph.83

BIKERS

1 To me, this endless black-top is my sweet
eternity. I knew I was going to hell in a bread-
basket.

Kathryn Bigelow (b.1951), U.S. film-maker: Vance (Willem Dafoe), in *The Loveless* (film; written and directed by Kathryn Bigelow and Monty Montgomery, 1981)

2 These guys are nameless, faceless fry-cooks and grease monkeys all week, working at dreary jobs they hate. They've got to break out and *be* somebody, they've got to belong to something. They do violent things because they've been held down so long.

Marlon Brando (b.1924), U.S. actor: quoted in *The Fifties* by Peter Lewis (1978), 'Youthquake'. Brando glamorized the life of the biker in the 1954 film, *The Wild One* , though he later criticized the portrayal: 'Instead of finding out why young people bunch in groups that seek expression in violence, all we did was show the violence'

3 I had a motorbike before *he* did!

James Dean (1931–1955), U.S. actor: remark to photographer Roy Shatt on Marlon Brando, quoted in *James Dean in his Own Words* (ed. Mick St Michael, 1989), 'Acting'

4 Born to be wild.

Jerry Edmonton (b.1946), U.S. rock musician: 'Born to be Wild' (song, written by Jerry Edmonton), on the album *Steppenwolf* (Steppenwolf, 1968). The song became the archetypal biker slogan, featured in Dennis Hopper's film, *Easy Rider* (1969)

5 On motorcycles, up the road, they come:
Small, black, as flies hanging in heat, the Boys,
Until the distance throws them forth, their hum
Bulges to thunder held by calf and thigh.
In goggles, donned impersonality,
In gleaming jackets trophied with the dust,
They strap in doubt – by hiding it, robust –
And almost hear a meaning in their noise.

Thom Gunn (b.1929), British poet: 'On the Move', St.2, publ. in *The Sense of Movement* (1957)

6 I don't want a pickle,
Just want to ride on my motorsickle.

Arlo Guthrie (b.1947), U.S. singer and songwriter: 'The Motorcycle Song' (song, 1967), on the album *Alice's Restaurant* (1969)

7 I met him at the candy store,
He turned around and smiled at me,
You get the picture?
('Yes we see')
That's when I fell for the leader of the pack.

The Shangri-Las (1964–1977), U.S. vocal group: 'The Leader of the Pack' (song; written by George Morton, Jeff Barry and Ellie Greenwich, 1964)

8 Dirty, on her Harley,
(But her nails are clean.)
Super-powered, de-flowered,
Over-eighteen Irene.

Alexander 'Skip' Spence (b.1946), Canadian rock musician: 'Motorcycle Irene', on the album *Wow* (Moby Grape, 1968)

BIOGRAPHY

1 Biography is all about cutting people down to size. Getting an unruly quart into a pint pot.

Alan Bennett (b.1934), British playwright: quoted in *Beyond the Fringe … and Beyond* by Ronald Bergan (1989), Pt.4

2 In writing biography, fact and fiction shouldn't be mixed. And if they are, the fictional points should be printed in red ink, the facts printed in black ink.

Catherine Drinker Bowen (1897–1973), U.S. author: quoted in *Publisher's Weekly* (New York), 24 March 1958

3 Show me a character whose life arouses my curiosity, and my flesh begins crawling with suspense.

Fawn M. Brodie (1915–1981), U.S. biographer: quoted in the *Los Angeles Times Home Magazine*, 20 Feb. 1977

4 I am opposed to writing about the private lives of living authors and psychoanalyzing them while they are alive. Criticism is getting all mixed up with a combination of the Junior F.B.I.-men, discards from Freud and Jung and a sort of Columnist peep-hole and missing laundry list school. … Every young English professor sees gold in them dirty sheets now. Imagine what they can do with the soiled sheets of four legal beds by the same writer and you can see why their tongues are slavering.

Ernest Hemingway (1899–1961), U.S. author: letter, 21 Feb. 1952, publ. in *Selected Letters* (ed. Carlos Baker, 1981)

5 A biography is like a handshake down the years, that can become an arm-wrestle.

Richard Holmes (b.1945), British biographer: remark, 16 Oct. 1990, Waterstone's Debate, quoted in *The Sunday Times* (London), 21 Oct. 1990

6 A great biography should, like the close of a great drama, leave behind it a feeling of serenity. We collect into a small bunch the flowers, the few flowers, which brought sweetness into a life, and present it as an offering to an accomplished destiny. It is the dying refrain of a completed song, the final verse of a finished poem.

André Maurois (1885–1967), French author and critic: *The Art of Writing* (1960), 'The Writer's Craft', Sct.5

7 Biography is: a system in which the contradictions of a human life are unified.

José Ortega y Gasset (1883–1955), Spanish essayist and philosopher: 'In Search of Goethe from Within', first publ. in *Partisan Review* (New Brunswick), Dec. 1949, rep. in *The Dehumanization of Art and Other Essays* (1968)

8 The facts of a person's life will, like murder, come out.
Norman Sherry (b.1925), British educator and author: in the *International Herald Tribune* (Paris), 15 Sept. 1989

9 The immense majority of human biographies are a gray transit between domestic spasm and oblivion.
George Steiner (b.1929), French-born U.S. critic and novelist: *In Bluebeard's Castle* (1971), Ch.3

10 Just how difficult it is to write biography can be reckoned by anybody who sits down and considers just how many people know the real truth about his or her love affairs.
Rebecca West (1892–1983), British author: in *Vogue* (New York), 1 Nov. 1952, 'The Art of Skepticism'

See also AUTOBIOGRAPHY; PERSONALITY; Szasz on PSYCHOLOGY

BIRDS

1 People are interested in birds only inasmuch as they exhibit human behavior – greed and stupidity and anger – and by doing so free us from the unique sorrow of being human.
Douglas Coupland (b.1961), Canadian author: *Life After God* (1994), 'Things That Fly'

2 To a man, ornithologists are tall, slender, and bearded so that they can stand motionless for hours, imitating kindly trees, as they watch for birds.
Gore Vidal (b.1925), U.S. novelist and critic: *Armageddon? Essays 1983–1987* (1987), 'Mongolia!'

See also Cleese on THE DEAD; Ratushinskaya on PRISON

BIRTH

1 Birth was the death of him.
Samuel Beckett (1906–1989), Irish dramatist and novelist: 'A Piece of Monologue', publ. in *Three Occasional Pieces* (1982)

2 He not busy being born
Is busy dying.
Bob Dylan (b.1941), U.S. singer and songwriter: 'It's Alright Ma (I'm Only Bleeding)' (song), on the album *Bringing it All Back Home* (1965). In 'Communiqué 8' (1 May 1971), the anarchist Angry Brigade wrote: 'If you're not busy being born you're busy buying' (rep. in *The Angry Brigade 1967–84: Documents and Chronology*, 1985)

3 A man may be born, but in order to be born he must first die, and in order to die he must first awake.
George Gurdjieff (c.1877–1949), Greek-Armenian religious teacher and mystic: quoted in *In Search of the Miraculous* by P.D. Ouspensky (1949), Ch.11. Gurdjieff continued: 'If a man dies without having been awakened he cannot be born. If a man is born without having died he may become an "immortal thing". Thus the fact that he has not "died" prevents a man from being "born"; the fact of his not having awakened prevents him from "dying"; and should he be born without having died he is prevented from "being".'

4 Piece by piece I seem
to re-enter the world: I first began

a small, fixed dot, still see
that old myself, a dark-blue thumbtack

pushed into the scene,
a hard little head protruding

from the pointillist's buzz and bloom.
Adrienne Rich (b.1929), U.S. poet: opening lines of 'Necessities of Life', written 1962, publ. in *The Fact of a Doorframe* (1974)

5 Being born is like being kidnapped. And then sold into slavery.
Andy Warhol (c.1928–1987), U.S. Pop artist: *From A to B and Back Again* (1975), Ch.6

BIRTH CONTROL

1 I want to tell you a terrific story about oral contraception. I asked this girl to sleep with me and she said 'no.'
Woody Allen (b.1935), U.S. film-maker: quoted in *Woody Allen: Clown Prince of American Humor* by B. Adler and J. Feinman (1975), Ch.2

2 The blind conviction that we have to do something about other people's reproductive behaviour, and that we may have to do it whether they like it or not, derives from the assumption that the world belongs to us, who have so expertly depleted its resources, rather than to them, who have not.
Germaine Greer (b.1939), Australian feminist writer: *Sex and Destiny* (1984), Ch.14

3 If we can get that realistic feminine morality working for us, if we can trust ourselves and so let women think and feel that an unwanted child or an oversize family is wrong – not ethically wrong, not against the rules, but morally wrong, all wrong, wrong like a thalidomide birth, wrong like taking a wrong step that will break your neck – if we can get feminine and human morality out from under the yoke of a dead ethic, then maybe we'll begin to get somewhere on the road that leads to survival.
Ursula K. Le Guin (b.1929), U.S. author: 'Moral and Ethical Implications of Family Planning', speech to Planned Parenthood symposium, Portland, Maine, March 1978, rep. in *Dancing at the Edge of the World* (1989)

4 Contraceptives should be used on every conceivable occasion.

Spike Milligan (b.1918), British comedian and humorous writer: stage show, 30 April 1972, Camden Theatre, London, publ. in *The Last Goon Show of Them All* (1972)

5 No woman can call herself free who does not own and control her body. No woman can call herself free until she can choose consciously whether she will or will not be a mother.

Margaret Sanger (1883–1966), U.S. pioneer of birth control movement: in *Parade* (New York), 1 Dec. 1963

BIRTHDAYS

1 To divide one's life by years is of course to tumble into a trap set by our own arithmetic. The calendar consents to carry on its dull wall-existence by the arbitrary timetables we have drawn up in consultation with those permanent commuters, Earth and Sun. But we, unlike trees, need grow no annual rings.

Clifton Fadiman (b.1904), U.S. essayist: 'On Being Fifty', publ. in *Holiday* (Indianapolis), Feb. 1955

2 One of the sadder things, I think,
Is how our birthdays slowly sink:
Presents and parties disappear,
The cards grow fewer year by year,
Till, when one reaches sixty-five,
How many care we're still alive?

Philip Larkin (1922–1985), British poet: 'Dear CHARLES, My Muse, asleep or dead', written for the poet Charles Causley (1982), publ. in *Collected Poems* (1988)

BISEXUALITY

1 I see myself as a bisexual man who has never had a homosexual experience. That's the way I approach my songwriting. If you are asking am I insincere to pose as a sodomite when I've never had someone's cock up my arse, then no, I'm not. The sexuality you express is not limited to the things you've experienced. I mean, if you're a virgin, does that make you asexual?

Brett Anderson (b.1967), British rock musician: quoted by Tony Parsons in *Arena* (London), May/June 1993, rep. in *Dispatches from the Front Line of Popular Culture* (Tony Parsons, 1994). In an interview with Parsons in *Vox* (London), March 1994 (also published in this collection), Anderson refuted criticism from the gay community that he was 'hijacking gay imagery by posing as a sodomite', by denying that he was confining his comments to 'something as vulgar as sexuality'

2 It's true – I am a bisexual. But I can't deny that I've used that fact very well. I suppose it's the best thing that ever happened to me. Fun, too.

David Bowie (b.1947), British rock musician: interview, Feb. 1976, rep. in *Bowie In His Own Words* (ed. Miles, 1980), 'Love and Sex'

3 I am the kind of bisexual who sleeps only with men.

Todd Haynes (b.1961), U.S. film-maker: interview in *The Guardian* (London), 13 April 1996

BLACK CONSCIOUSNESS/BLACK POWER

1 The philosophy of Black Consciousness, therefore, expresses group pride and the determination by the Blacks to rise and attain the envisaged self. At the heart of this kind of thinking is the realization by the Blacks that the most potent weapon in the hands of the oppressor is the mind of the oppressed.

Steve Biko (1946–1977), South African anti-apartheid activist: writing in 1972, quoted in introduction to *Steve Biko: Black Consciousness in South Africa* (ed. Millard Arnold, 1978)

2 A great wind swept over the ghetto, carrying away shame, invisibility and four centuries of humiliation. But when the wind dropped people saw it had been only a little breeze, friendly, almost gentle.

Jean Genet (1910–1986), French playwright and novelist: of the rise and fall of the Black Panthers, in *Prisoner of Love* (1986; tr.1989), Pt.1

3 We have formed an organization known as the Organization of Afro-American Unity. ... To fight whoever gets in our way, to bring about the complete independence of people of African descent here in the Western hemisphere, and first here in the United States, and bring about the freedom of these people by any means necessary. That's our motto. We want freedom by any means necessary. We want justice by any means necessary. We want equality by any means necessary

Malcolm X (1925–1965), U.S. black leader: OAAU Founding Rally, 28 June 1964, Audubon Ballroom, New York, publ. in *Malcolm X By Any Means Necessary* (ed. George Breitman, 1970). The words 'by any means necessary' became a rallying-call among radical movements in the 1960s

4 Songs of liberation – who can lock them up? The spirit of freedom – who can jail it? A people's unity – what lash can beat it down? Civil rights – what doubletalk can satisfy our need?

Paul Robeson (1898–1976), U.S. singer and actor: 'A Lesson from Our South African Brothers and Sisters', publ. in *Freedom*, Sept. 1952

5 The black revolution has rocked middle America with militant agitation, angry denunciation, and violent insurrection. But the

object of the agitation is nevertheless cultural assimilation, if not always social integration. The excluded and exploited minorities do not by and large call for an end to technocratic capitalism, but for jobs, for 'black capitalism', and for greater access to the multiversities so that they too can rise in the meritocracy.

Theodore Roszak (b.1933), U.S. social critic: *Where the Wasteland Ends* (1972), Ch.2

6 What then did you expect when you unbound the gag that muted those black mouths? That they would chant your praises? Did you think that when those heads that our fathers had forcibly bowed down to the ground were raised again, you would find adoration in their eyes?

Jean-Paul Sartre (1905–1980), French philosopher and author: 'Orphée Noir', preface to *Anthologie de la Nouvelle Poésie Nègre et Malgache* (1948)

7 To be young, gifted and black
Is where it's at!

Nina Simone (b.1933), U.S. singer, songwriter and pianist: 'Young, Gifted and Black' (song; written by Weldon J. Irvine Jr., 1969), publ. in *The Poetry of Soul* (ed. A.X. Nicholas, 1971)

8 There are those who believe Black people possess the secret of joy and that it is this that will sustain them through any spiritual or moral or physical devastation.

Alice Walker (b.1944), U.S. author and critic: epigraph to *Possessing the Secret of Joy* (1992)

9 Black is the sorrow of a mourning band,
Black is a dream about a promised land.
Little baby, don't you cry,
You'll be free before you die.
Listen, child, to me.
Black is beautiful, don't you see?

Nancy Wilson (b.1937), U.S. soul singer: 'Black is Beautiful' (song; written by Charles Wood and John Cacavas, 1968), publ. in *The Poetry of Soul* (ed. A.X. Nicholas, 1971)

See also Baraka on LEGACIES; Lincoln on WHITES

BLACK CULTURE

---

1 There is a kind of strength that is almost frightening in black women. It's as if a steel rod runs right through the head down to the feet.

Maya Angelou (b.1928), U.S. author: 'A Conversation with Maya Angelou', interview broadcast 21 Nov. 1973, publ. in *Conversations with Maya Angelou* (ed. Jeffrey M. Elliot, 1989)

2 It is only in his music, which Americans are able to admire because a protective sentimentality limits their understanding of it, that the Negro in America has been able to tell his story.

James Baldwin (1924–1987), U.S. author: 'Many Thousands Gone' first publ. in *Partisan Review* (New Brunswick, N.J.), Nov-Dec 1951, rep. in *Notes of a Native Son* (1955), Pt.1

3 We're tired of beating our head against the wall
And working for someone else
We're people, we're like the birds and the bees
But we'd rather die on our feet than keep living
on our knees. ...
Say it loud! I'm black and I'm proud!

James Brown (b.1928), U.S. soul singer: 'Say it Loud! I'm Black and I'm Proud!' (song; written with Alfred Ellis, 1968), publ. in *The Poetry of Soul* (ed. A.X. Nicholas, 1971)

4 However painful it may be for me to accept this conclusion, I am obliged to state it: for the black man there is only one destiny. And it is white.

Frantz Fanon (1925–1961), Martiniquan psychiatrist, philosopher and political and activist: introduction to *Black Skins, White Masks* (1952; tr.1967)

5 I think one of the nicest things that we created as a generation was just the fact that we could say, Hey, I don't like white people.

Nikki Giovanni (b.1943), U.S. poet: conversation with James Baldwin , 4 Nov. 1971, London, publ. in *A Dialogue* (1973)

6 The burden of being black is that you have to be superior just to be equal. But the glory of it is that, once you achieve, you have achieved, indeed.

Jesse Jackson (b.1941), U.S. clergyman and civil rights leader: in *Christian Science Monitor* (Boston), 26 Sept. 1979

7 In America, the traditional routes to Black identity have hardly been normal. Suicide (disappearance by imitation, or willed extinction), violence (hysterical religiosity, crime, armed revolt), and exemplary moral courage; none of these is normal.

June Jordan (b.1936), U.S. poet and civil rights activist: 'Black Studies: Bringing Back the Person', publ. in *The Evergreen Review* (New York), Oct. 1969, rep. in *Moving Towards Home: Political Essays* (1989)

8 We do not need to minimize the poverty of the ghetto or the suffering inflicted by whites on blacks in order to see that the increasingly dangerous and unpredictable conditions of middle-class life have given rise to similar strategies for survival. Indeed the attraction of black culture for disaffected whites suggests that black culture now speaks to a general condition.

Christopher Lasch (1932–1994), U.S. historian: *The Culture of Narcissism* (1979), Ch.3, 'The Apotheosis of Individualism'

9 If we became students of Malcolm X, we would not have young black men out there

killing each other like they're killing each other now. Young black men would not be impregnating young black women at the rate going on now. We'd not have the drugs we have now, or the alcoholism.

Spike Lee (b.1956), U.S. film-maker: interview in *i-D* (London), Jan. 1993

See also Terrell on LABELS; Walker on RACE; Malcolm X on RACISM; THE UNITED STATES: AFRICAN AMERICANS; Angelou on WOMEN: THE MALE VIEW

TONY BLAIR

1 No rising hope on the political scene who offered his services to Labour when I happened to be its leader can be dismissed as an opportunist.

Michael Foot (b.1913), British Labour politician: quoted in the *Independent on Sunday* (London), 19 Feb. 1995

2 All the talk is Blair, Blair, Blair. SPD people say: 'BMW bought Rover, how can we buy Blair?' If Schmidt was the European left figure of the Seventies, and Felipe Gonzalez for the Eighties, it's Blair for the Nineties.

Denis MacShane (b.1948), British Labour politician: on returning from talks with SPD leaders in Germany, quoted in *The Independent* (London), 1 April 1996

BLAME

1 There's man all over for you, blaming on his boots the fault of his feet.

Samuel Beckett (1906–1989), Irish playwright and novelist: Vladimir, in *Waiting for Godot* (1952; tr.1954), Act 1

2 No one to blame! ... That was why most people led lives they hated, with people they hated. ... How wonderful to have someone to blame! How wonderful to live with one's nemesis! You may be miserable, but you feel forever in the right. You may be fragmented, but you feel absolved of all the blame for it. Take your life in your own hands, and what happens? A terrible thing: no one to blame.

Erica Jong (b.1942), U.S. author: *How To Save Your Own Life* (1977), 'Intuition, extuition ...'

BLUES *see under* MUSIC

THE BODY

1 Man consists of two parts, his mind and his body, only the body has more fun.

Woody Allen (b.1935), U.S. film-maker: Boris (Woody Allen), in *Love and Death* (film; written and directed by Woody Allen, 1975)

2 The basic Female body comes with the following accessories: garter belt, panti-girdle, crinoline, camisole, bustle, brassiere, stomacher, chemise, virgin zone, spike heels, nose ring, veil, kid gloves, fishnet stockings, fichu, bandeau, Merry Widow, weepers, chokers, barrettes, bangles, beads, lorgnette, feather boa, basic black, compact, Lycra stretch one-piece with modesty panel, designer peignoir, flannel nightie, lace teddy, bed, head.

Margaret Atwood (b.1939), Canadian novelist, poet and critic: 'The Female Body', publ. in *Michigan Quarterly Review* (1990), rep. in 'The Best American Essays, 1991' (ed. Joyce Carol Oates, 1991)

3 The human body is not a thing or substance, given, but a continuous creation. The human body is an energy system ... which is never a complete structure; never static; is in perpetual inner self-construction and self-destruction; we destroy in order to make it new.

Norman O. Brown (b.1913), U.S. philosopher: *Love's Body* (1967), Ch.8

4 Teeth. What God damn things they were. We had to eat. And eat and eat again. We are all disgusting, doomed to our dirty little tasks. Eating and farting and scratching and smiling and celebrating holidays.

Charles Bukowski (1920–1994), U.S. author: the narrator (Nicky Belane), in *Pulp* (1994), Ch.22

5 Which came first, the intestine or the tapeworm?

William Burroughs (1914–1997), U.S. author: interview on *The South Bank Show*, LWT, 12 April 1992

6 Why am I so determined to put the shoulder where it belongs? Women have very round shoulders that push forward slightly; this touches me and I say: 'One must not hide that!' Then someone tells you: 'The shoulder is on the back.' I've never seen women with shoulders on their backs.

Coco Chanel (1883–1971), French *couturière*: quoted in *Coco Chanel: Her Life, Her Secrets* by Marcel Haedrich (1971), Ch.21

7 A woman watches her body uneasily, as though it were an unreliable ally in the battle for love.

Leonard Cohen (b.1934), Canadian singer, poet and novelist: *The Favourite Game* (1963), Bk.3, Ch.8

8 Men renounce whatever they have in common with women so as to experience no commonality with women; and what is left, according to men, is one piece of flesh a few inches long, the penis. The penis is sensate; the penis

is the man; the man is human; the penis signifies humanity.

Andrea Dworkin (b.1946), U.S. feminist critic:
Pornography (1981), Ch.2

9 I travel light; as light,
   That is, as a man can travel who will
   Still carry his body around because
   Of its sentimental value.

   Christopher Fry (b.1907), British playwright:
   Thomas, in *The Lady's Not for Burning* (1949),
   Act 1

10 We are no longer entirely natural organisms –
    we've all of us got bits of metal and plastic in
    us, our body systems have been altered over
    the years.

    William Gibson (b.1948), U.S. author: interview in
    Rapid Eye 3 (ed. Simon Dwyer, 1995)

11 I have a head for business and a bod for sin. Is
    there anything wrong with that?

    Melanie Griffith (b.1957), U.S. actress: Tess
    McGill (Melanie Griffith), in *Working Girl* (film;
    screenplay by Kevin Wade, directed by Mike
    Nichols, 1988)

12 You know what frightens me about the human
    body? ... Well, it's like the most sophisticated
    mechanism in the entire universe, and yet it's
    so fucking quiet, isn't it? Know what I mean?
    ... It's like this wet, pink factory. What the
    fuck are they makin' in there? I mean, what's
    the product? You never see no delivery trucks
    comin' or goin', do you?

    Mike Leigh (b.1943), British film-maker: Johnny
    (David Thewlis) to Sophie, in *Naked* (film; written
    and directed by Mike Leigh, 1993)

13 Our own physical body possesses a wisdom
    which we who inhabit the body lack. We give it
    orders which make no sense.

    Henry Miller (1891–1980), U.S. author: *Big Sur
    and the Oranges of Hieronymous Bosch* (1957), Pt.3,
    'Paradise Lost' (Pt.3 also publ. separately as *A Devil
    in Paradise* , 1956)

14 Wondrous hole! Magical hole! Dazzlingly
    influential hole! Noble and effulgent hole!
    From this hole everything follows logically:
    first the baby, then the placenta, then, for years
    and years and years until death, a way of life. It
    is all logic, and she who lives by the hole will
    live also by its logic. It is, appropriately, logic
    with a hole in it.

    Cynthia Ozick (b.1928), U.S. novelist and short-
    story writer: 'The Hole/Birth Catalog', publ. in *The
    First Ms Reader* (ed. Francine Klagsbrun, 1972)

15 In order to live a fully human life we require
    not only *control* of our bodies (though control
    is a prerequisite); we must touch the unity and
    resonance of our physicality, our bond with the
    natural order, the corporeal grounds of our
    intelligence.

    Adrienne Rich (b.1929), U.S. poet: *Of Woman
    Born* (1976), Ch.1

16 The authority of any governing institution
    must stop at its citizen's skin.

    Gloria Steinem (b.1934), U.S. feminist writer and
    editor: 'Night Thoughts of a Media-Watcher', publ.
    in *Ms.* (New York), Nov. 1981

17 For male and female alike, the bodies of the
    other sex are messages signaling what we must
    do – they are glowing signifiers of our own
    necessities.

    John Updike (b.1932), U.S. author and critic: 'The
    Female Body', publ. in the *Michigan Quarterly
    Review* (1990), rep. in 'The Best American Essays,
    1991' (ed. Joyce Carol Oates, 1991)

See also BREASTS; FACES; HAIR; PHYSIQUE; TEETH

THE BODY: Bodily Functions

1 Where there is a stink of shit
   there is a smell of being.

   Antonin Artaud (1896–1948), French theatre
   producer, actor and theorist: *To Have Done with the
   Judgment of God* (1947), repr. in *Selected Writings*
   (ed. Susan Sontag, 1976), 'The Pursuit of Fecality'

2 Lifted off the potty,
   Infants from their mothers
   Hear their first impartial
   Words of wordly praise:
   Hence, to start the morning
   With a satisfactory
   Dump is a good omen
   All our adult days.

   W.H. Auden (1907–1973), Anglo-American poet:
   'Thanksgiving for a Habitat' Sct.6, 'The Geography
   of the House', publ. in *About the House* (1965)

3 What makes shit such a universal joke is that
   it's an unmistakable reminder of our duality, of
   our soiled nature and of our will to glory. It is
   the ultimate *lèse-majesté*.

   John Berger (b.1926), British author and critic:
   'Muck and Its Entanglements', first publ. in
   Harper's Magazine (New York), May 1989, rep. as
   'A Load of Shit' in *Keeping a Rendezvous* (1992)

4 Since man's highest mission on earth is to
   spiritualize everything, it is his excrement in
   particular that needs it most.

   Salvador Dali (1904–1989), Spanish painter: entry,
   2 Sept. 1952, in *Diary of a Genius* (1966)

5 The confidence and security of a people can be
   measured by their attitude toward laxatives. At
   the high noon of the British sun, soldiers in far-
   flung outposts of the Empire doctored themselves with 'a spoonful o' gunpowder in a
   cuppa 'ot tea.' Purveyors and users of harsh
   laxatives were not afraid of being thought
   mean and unfriendly just because their
   laxatives were. But in America, the need to be

nice is so consuming that nobody would dare take a laxative that makes you run up the stairs two at a time, pushing others aside and yelling 'Get out of the way!'

Florence King (b.1936), U.S. author: *Reflections in a Jaundiced Eye* (1989), 'Nice Guyism'

6 I honor shit for saying: we go on.

Maxine Kumin (b.1925), U.S. poet: 'The Excrement Poem', publ. in *Our Ground Time Here Will be Brief* (1973)

7 It amazes me that organs that piss
Can give human beings such perfect bliss.

Irving Layton (b.1912), Canadian poet: *The Whole Bloody Bird* (1969), 'Aphs'

8 Male urination really *is* a kind of accomplishment, an arc of transcendence. A woman merely waters the ground she stands on.

Camille Paglia (b.1947), U.S. author and critic: *Sexual Personae* (1990), Ch.1

See also DeLillo on WOMEN

BOHEMIANS

1 Our affluent society contains those of talent and insight who are driven to prefer poverty, to choose it, rather than to submit to the desolation of an empty abundance. It is a strange part of the other America that one finds in the intellectual slums.

Michael Harrington (1928–1989), U.S. social scientist and author: *The Other America* (1962), Ch.5, Sct.1

2 It is not my fault that certain so-called bohemian elements have found in my writings something to hang their peculiar beatnik theories on.

Jack Kerouac (1922–1969), U.S. author: in *The New York Journal-American*, 8 Dec. 1960

3 Bohemia has no banner. It survives by discretion.

Tennessee Williams (1911–1983), U.S. playwright: Marguerite Gautier, in *Camino Real* (1948), Block 7

4 The modern picture of The Artist began to form: The poor, but free spirit, plebeian but aspiring only to be classless, to cut himself forever free from the bonds of the greedy bourgeoisie, to be whatever the fat burghers feared most, to cross the line wherever they drew it, to look at the world in a way they couldn't *see* , to be high, live low, stay young forever – in short, to be the bohemian.

Tom Wolfe (b.1931), U.S. author and journalist: *The Painted Word* (1975), Ch.1

BOOKS

1 Some books are undeservedly forgotten; none are undeservedly remembered.

W.H. Auden (1907–1973), Anglo-American poet: *The Dyer's Hand* (1962), Pt.1, 'Reading'

2 Footnotes are the finer-suckered surfaces that allow tentacular paragraphs to hold fast to the wider reality of the library.

Nicholson Baker (b.1957), U.S. author: *The Mezzanine* (1988), footnote to Ch.14

3 There are worse crimes than burning books. One of them is not reading them.

Joseph Brodsky (1940–1996), Russian-born U.S. poet and critic: said at press conference, Washington D.C., on acceptance of U.S. poet laureateship, quoted in the *Independent on Sunday* (London), 19 May 1991

4 The lessons taught in great books are misleading. The commerce in life is rarely so simple and never so just.

Anita Brookner (b.1938), British novelist and art historian: *Novelists in Interview* (ed. John Haffenden, 1985)

5 The good of a book lies in its being read. A book is made up of signs that speak of other signs, which in their turn speak of things. Without an eye to read them, a book contains signs that produce no concepts; therefore it is dumb.

Umberto Eco (b.1932), Italian semiologist and novelist: Brother William, in *The Name of the Rose* (1980; tr.1983), 'Fifth Day: Vespers'

6 The only books that influence us are those for which we are ready, and which have gone a little farther down our particular path than we have yet got ourselves.

E.M. Forster (1879–1970), British novelist and essayist: *Two Cheers for Democracy* (1951), 'A Book that Influenced Me'

7 I don't think any good book is based on factual experience. Bad books are about things the writer already knew before he wrote them.

Carlos Fuentes (b.1928), Mexican novelist and short-story writer: in the *International Herald Tribune* (Paris), 5 Nov. 1991

8 Even bad books are books and therefore sacred.

Günter Grass (b.1927), German author: the narrator (Oskar Matzerath), in *The Tin Drum* (1959; tr.1961), Bk.1, 'Rasputin and the Alphabet'

9 For a good book has this quality, that it is not merely a petrification of its author, but that once it has been tossed behind, like

Deucalion's little stone, it acquires a separate and vivid life of its own.
Caroline Lejeune (1897–1973), British film critic: introduction to *Chestnuts in Her Lap, 1936–1946* (1947)

10 Until it is kindled by a spirit as flamingly alive as the one which gave it birth a book is dead to us. Words divested of their magic are but dead hieroglyphs.
Henry Miller (1891–1980), U.S. author: *The Books in My Life* (1951), Ch.7

11 A bibliophile of little means is likely to suffer often. Books don't slip from his hands but fly past him through the air, high as birds, high as prices.
Pablo Neruda (1904–1973), Chilean poet: *Memoirs* (1974; tr.1977), Ch.11

12 The books one reads in childhood, and perhaps most of all the bad and good bad books, create in one's mind a sort of false map of the world, a series of fabulous countries into which one can retreat at odd moments throughout the rest of life, and which in some cases can even survive a visit to the real countries which they are supposed to represent.
George Orwell (1903–1950), British author: 'Riding Down from Bangor' (1946), rep. in *The Collected Essays, Journalism and Letters of George Orwell* (ed. Sonia Orwell and Ian Angus, 1968), Vol.IV

13 A book is a version of the world. If you do not like it, ignore it; or offer your own version in return.
Salman Rushdie (b.1947), Indian-born British author: in the *Independent on Sunday* (London), 4 Feb. 1990

14 What I like best is a book that's at least funny once in a while. … What really knocks me out is a book that, when you're all done reading it, you wish the author that wrote it was a terrific friend of yours and you could call him up on the phone whenever you felt like it. That doesn't happen much, though.
J.D. Salinger (b.1919), U.S. author: the narrator (Holden Caulfield), in *The Catcher in the Rye* (1951), Ch.3

15 A book is like a man – clever and dull, brave and cowardly, beautiful and ugly. For every flowering thought there will be a page like a wet and mangy mongrel, and for every looping flight a tap on the wing and a reminder that wax cannot hold the feathers firm too near the sun.
John Steinbeck (1902–1968), U.S. author: *Writers at Work* (Fourth Series, ed. George Plimpton, 1977), 'On Publishing'

16 The age of the book is almost gone.
George Steiner (b.1929), French-born U.S. critic and novelist: in the *Daily Mail* (London), 27 June 1988

17 Old books that have ceased to be of service should no more be abandoned than should old friends who have ceased to give pleasure.
Peregrine Worsthorne (b.1923), British journalist: in the *Independent on Sunday* (London), 5 Aug. 1990

See also AUTOBIOGRAPHY; BIOGRAPHY; FICTION; LIBRARIES; PUBLISHING

BOOKS: Bestsellers

1 A best-seller is the golden touch of mediocre talent.
Cyril Connolly (1903–1974), British critic: quoted in *Journal and Memoir* by David Pryce-Jones (1983), Ch.11

2 The principle of procrastinated rape is said to be the ruling one in all the great bestsellers.
V.S. Pritchett (1900–1997), British author and critic: *The Living Novel* (1946), 'Clarissa'

BOOKS: Classics

1 Definition of a classic: a book everyone is assumed to have read and often thinks they have.
Alan Bennett (b.1934), British playwright: in the *Independent on Sunday* (London), 27 Jan. 1991

2 A classic is a book that has never finished saying what it has to say.
Italo Calvino (1923–1985), Italian author and critic: one of a series of definitions of 'a classic', in 'Why Read the Classics?' first publ. in *L'Espresso* (Rome), 28 June 1981, rep. in *The Literature Machine* (1987)

3 A truly great book should be read in youth, again in maturity and once more in old age, as a fine building should be seen by morning light, at noon and by moonlight.
Robertson Davies (1913–1995), Canadian novelist and journalist: 'Too Much, Too Fast', publ. in the *Peterborough Examiner* (Canada), 16 June 1962, rep. in *The Enthusiasms of Robertson Davies* (1990)

4 The light that radiates from the great novels time can never dim, for human existence is perpetually being forgotten by man and thus the novelists' discoveries, however old they may be, will never cease to astonish.
Milan Kundera (b.1929), Czech-born French author and critic: in *The Guardian* (London), 3 June 1988

5 There is but one way left to save a classic: to give up revering him and use him for our own salvation.
José Ortega y Gasset (1883–1955), Spanish essayist and philosopher: 'In Search of Goethe from Within',

first publ. in *The Partisan Review* (New Brunswick), Dec. 1949, rep. in *The Dehumanization of Art and Other Essays* (1968)

6   All … forms of consensus about 'great' books and 'perennial' problems, once stabilized, tend to deteriorate eventually into something philistine. The real life of the mind is always at the frontiers of 'what is already known'. Those great books don't only need custodians and transmitters. To stay alive, they also need adversaries. The most interesting ideas are heresies.
Susan Sontag (b.1933), U.S. essayist: interview, April 1975, publ. in *Salmagundi* (Saratoga Springs, N.Y.), fall 1975/winter 1976, rep. in *A Susan Sontag Reader* (1982)

BOREDOM

1   Is boredom anything less than the sense of one's faculties slowly dying?
John Berger (b.1926), British author and critic: *A Fortunate Man* (1967), p.133 of Writers and Readers Publishing Cooperative edn. (1976)

2   Life, friends, is boring. We must not say so.
After all, the sky flashes, the great sea yearns,
we ourselves flash and yearn,
and moreover my mother told me as a boy
(repeatedly) 'Ever to confess you're bored
means you have no
Inner Resources.' I conclude now I have no
inner resources, because I am heavy bored.
John Berryman (1914–1972), U.S. poet: *77 Dream Songs* (1964), No.14

3   Boredom is always counter-revolutionary. Always.
Guy Debord (1931–1994), French Situationist philosopher: 'The Bad Old Days Will End' (1963), rep. in *The Incomplete Works of the Situationist International* (ed. Christopher Gray, 1974)

4   Was I bored? No, I wasn't fuckin' bored. I'm never bored. That's the trouble with everybody – you're all so bored. You've 'ad nature explained to you and you're bored with it. You've 'ad the living body explained to you and you're bored with it. You've 'ad the universe explained to you and you're bored with it. So now you just want cheap thrills and like plenty of 'em, and it dun't matter 'ow tawdry or vacuous they are as long as it's new, as long as it's new, as long as it flushes and fuckin' bleeps in forty fuckin' different colours. Well, whatever else you can say about me, I'm not fuckin' bored!
Mike Leigh (b.1943), British film-maker: Johnny (David Thewlis) to Louise, in *Naked* (film; written and directed by Mike Leigh, 1993)

5   Boredom is just the reverse side of fascination: both depend on being outside rather than inside a situation, and one leads to the other.
Susan Sontag (b.1933), U.S. essayist: on *Photography* (1977), 'America, Seen Through Photographs, Darkly'

See also Mumford on TECHNOLOGY

BORES

1   What's wrong with being a boring kind of guy?
George Bush (b.1924), U.S. Republican politician and president: quoted in *The Daily Telegraph* (London), 28 April 1988

2   I don't know about bores. Maybe you shouldn't feel too sorry if you see some swell girl getting married to them. They don't hurt anybody most of them, and maybe they're all terrific whistlers or something. Who the hell knows? Not me.
J.D. Salinger (b.1919), U.S. author: the narrator (Holden Caulfield), in *The Catcher in the Rye* (1951), Ch.17

3   A healthy male adult bore consumes each year one and a half times his own weight in other people's patience.
John Updike (b.1932), U.S. author and critic: *Assorted Prose* (1965), 'Confessions of a Wild Bore'

BOSNIA

1   The political situation? A STUPID MESS. The 'kids' are trying to come to some agreement again. They're drawing maps, colouring with their crayons, but I think they're crossing out human beings, childhood and everything that's nice and normal. They are really just like kids.
Zlata Filipović (b.1980), Bosnian diarist: journal entry, 21 Aug. 1993, publ. in *Zlata's Diary* (1993)

2   I am not willing to risk the lives of German soldiers for countries whose names we cannot spell properly.
Volker Rühe (b.1942), German politician and defence minister: on intervening in the Bosnian conflict, in *The Independent* (London), 28 Aug. 1992

3   I have never been to Sarajevo, but I feel that I belong to it, in a way. … I … can claim to be, in some sense, an exile from Sarajevo, even though it is a city I do not know. There is a Sarajevo of the mind, an imagined Sarajevo whose ruination and torment exiles us all.
Salman Rushdie (b.1947), Indian-born British author: in *Index on Censorship* (London), May/June 1994

BOSTON *see under* THE UNITED
STATES

THE BOURGEOISIE

1 The petit-bourgeois is a man unable to
imagine the Other. If he comes face to face
with him, he blinds himself, ignores and denies
him, or else transforms him into himself.
Roland Barthes (1915–1980), French semiologist:
Mythologies (1957; tr.1972), 'Myth on the Right'

2 It is the corpse of the bourgeoisie that separates us. With us, it is that class that is the
carrier of the chromosome of banality.
Jean Baudrillard (b.1929), French semiologist:
America (1986; tr.1988), 'Astral America'

3 The discreet charms of the bourgeoisie have
been underrated for too long. They are the
most cultured class. The hardest working.
They believe in the welfare state but are
aware of its corrupting nature. Yes, there are
many things to despise about the middle class.
But, unlike the nobs and the riff-raff, they do
not know their place. They believe in self-
improvement.
Tony Parsons (b.1955), British journalist: 'The
Polenta Jungle', publ. in *Arena* (London), March/
April 1993, rep. in *Dispatches from the Front Line of
Popular Culture* (1994)

4 Our culture is ill-equipped to assert the bourgeois values which would be the salvation of
the under-class, because we have lost those
values ourselves.
Norman Podhoretz (b.1930), U.S. editor, critic
and essayist: in the *Daily Mail* (London), 10 Nov.
1989

5 If one defends the bourgeois, philistine virtues, one does not defend them merely from
the demonism or bohemianism of the artist but
from the present bourgeoisie itself.
Lionel Trilling (1905–1975), U.S. critic: notebook entry (c.1951), publ. in *Partisan Review 50th
Anniversary Edition* (ed. William Philips, 1985)

BOXING *see under* SPORT

BOYS

1 Timothy Winters comes to school
With eyes as wide as a football-pool,
Ears like bombs and teeth like splinters:
A blitz of a boy is Timothy Winters.
Charles Causley (b.1917), British poet: 'Timothy
Winters', *Union Street* (1957)

2 For a mother the *project* of raising a boy is the
most fulfilling project she can hope for. She
can watch him, as a child, play the games she
was not allowed to play; she can invest in him
her ideas, aspirations, ambitions, and values –
or whatever she has left of them; she can watch
her son, who came from her flesh and whose
life was sustained by her work and devotion,
embody her in the world. So while the project
of raising a boy is fraught with ambivalence
and leads inevitably to bitterness, it is the only
project that allows a woman *to be* – to be
through her son, to live through her son.
Andrea Dworkin (b.1946), U.S. feminist critic:
'The Sexual Politics of Fear and Courage', speech,
12 March 1975, Queens College, City University of
New York, publ. in *Our Blood* (1976), Ch.5

3 George – don't do that.
Joyce Grenfell (1910–1979), British actress and
writer: catch phrase in various sketches in the 1950s,
and the title of the collection, *George – Don't Do
That* (1977)

4 A fairly bright boy is far more intelligent and
far better company than the average adult.
J.B.S. Haldane (1892–1964), British scientist: in the
New York Times, 13 June 1948

5 Every genuine boy is a rebel and an anarch. If
he were allowed to develop according to his
own instincts, his own inclinations, society
would undergo such a radical transformation
as to make the adult revolutionary cower and
cringe.
Henry Miller (1891–1980), U.S. author: *The Books
in My Life* (1951), Ch.4

6 You silly twisted boy!
Peter Sellers (1925–1980), British comic: favourite
expression of Lance Brigadier Grytpype-Thynne
(Peter Sellers), in *The Goon Show* (BBC radio
comedy series, written by Spike Milligan), broadcast
1951–60, publ. in *The Goon Show Scripts*, ed. Spike
Milligan, 1972

THE BRAIN

1 It's my second favorite organ.
Woody Allen (b.1935), U.S. film-maker: Victor
Shakapopolis (Woody Allen), in *Sleeper* (film;
screenplay by Woody Allen and Marshall Brickman,
directed by Woody Allen, 1973)

2 I learned that the brain is an under-utilised
bio-computer, containing billions of un-
accessed neurons. I learned that normal
consciousness is one drop in an ocean of
intelligence. That consciousness and intelligence can be systematically expanded. That
the brain can be reprogrammed. The knowledge of how the brain works is the most pres-
sing scientific issue of our time.

Timothy Leary (1920–1996), U.S. psychologist: quoted in *The Guardian* (London), 2 Dec. 1995

3 I was taught that the human brain was the crowning glory of evolution so far, but I think it's a very poor scheme for survival.
Kurt Vonnegut (b.1922), U.S. novelist: quoted in *The Observer* (London), 27 Dec. 1987

MARLON BRANDO

1 If any man can harness atomic energy Mr Brando is the man for the job.
Jympson Harman, U.S. film critic: review of the film, *A Streetcar Named Desire* (1951), starring Brando as Kowalski, quoted in *Brando* by Robert Tanitch (1994), 'The 1950s'

2 Living with Marlon is like an afternoon at the races – short periods of orgiastic activity followed by long periods of boredom and anticipation. He's almost never home. ... He attracts women like faeces attract flies.
Anna Kashfi (b.1934), Indian-born U.S. actress: quoted in *People* (New York), 4 June 1990, rep. in *Marlon Brando: Larger Than Life* by Nellie Bly (1994), Ch.4. Brando and Kashfi's marriage lasted from 1957 to 1959

See also Brando on FACES

BREASTS

1 A full bosom is actually a millstone around a woman's neck: it endears her to the men who want to make their mammet of her, but she is never allowed to think that their popping eyes actually see her. Her breasts ... are not parts of a person but lures slung around her neck, to be kneaded and twisted like magic putty, or mumbled and mouthed like lolly ices.
Germaine Greer (b.1939), Australian feminist writer: *The Female Eunuch* (1970), 'Curves'

2 Thanks for the mammaries.
Mike Leigh (b.1943), British film-maker: remark made by Johnny (David Thewlis) to Sophie as he slips his hand inside her top, in *Naked* (film; written and directed by Mike Leigh, 1993)

3 Her protruding breasts were pressed flat between his body and hers. He had felt them, he had fondled them, he lifted them, he pressed them, he weighed them, he valued them, he counted them, he massaged them, he stood back from them, he pulled them, he sat on them and picking up a banjo he played them.
Spike Milligan (b.1918), British comedian and humorous writer: *Puckoon* (1963), Ch.10

BRITAIN

1 Great Britain has lost an Empire and has not yet found a role.
Dean Acheson (1893–1971), U.S. Democratic politician: speech, 5 Dec. 1962, West Point Academy, New York.

2 There is a marvelous turn and trick to British arrogance; its apparent unconsciousness makes it twice as effectual.
Catherine Drinker Bowen (1897–1973), U.S. author: *Adventures of a Biographer* (1946), Ch.14

3 There's nothing the British like better than a bloke who comes from nowhere, makes it, and then gets clobbered.
Melvyn Bragg (b.1939), British broadcaster and author: of actor Richard Burton, in *The Guardian* (London), 23 Sept. 1988

4 The British do not expect happiness. I had the impression, all the time that I lived there, that they do not want to be happy; they want to be right.
Quentin Crisp (b.1908), British author: 'Love Lies Bleeding', Channel 4, 6 Aug. 1991, publ. in *New Statesman and Society* (London), 9 Aug. 1991

5 Only in Britain could it be thought a defect to be 'too clever by half.' The probability is that too many people are too stupid by three-quarters.
John Major (b.1943), British Conservative politician and prime minister: quoted in *The Observer* (London), 7 July 1991

6 I find the word 'British' harder and harder to use as time passes.
Dennis Potter (1935–1994), British dramatist and screenwriter: interview with Melvyn Bragg, Channel 4, 5 April 1994

7 Of the general inadequacy of intellect in the conduct of life Britain is the most majestic exponent. She is instinctively disliked by such people as French, Persians, Hindus, who are clever by nature, and think that *intellect can rule*. The Italians strayed down this path and disliked us too. But they, and the Greeks, and the Arabs, have a natural perception of other and greater powers and this, I think, is an affinity that binds us. With the others, with the intellectual, it is not our stupidity, but the fact that we prove it possible to live by non-intellectual standards, which makes us disliked.
Freya Stark (1893–1993), British travel writer: *Perseus in the Wind* (1948), Ch.4

See also Tuchman on GOVERNMENT

BRITAIN: England

1 He was born an Englishman and remained one for years.
Brendan Behan (1923–1964), Irish playwright: Pat, referring to Monsewer, who later 'found out he was an Irishman', in *The Hostage* (1958), Act 1

2 I've always felt that English women had to be approached in a sisterly manner, rather than an erotic manner.
Anthony Burgess (1917–1993), British author and critic: in *The Times* (London), 27 July 1988

3 England has the most sordid literary scene I've ever seen. They all meet in the same pub. This guy's writing a foreword for this person. They all have to give radio programs, they *have* to do all this just in order to scrape by. They're all scratching each other's backs.
William Burroughs (1914–1997), U.S. author: taped conversation, 1980, New York City, in *With William Burroughs: A Report from the Bunker* by Victor Bockris (1981), 'Burroughs in London'

4 In the past, the English tried to impose a system wherever they went. They destroyed the nation's culture and one of the by-products of their systemisation was that they destroyed their own folk culture.
Martin Carthy (b.1941), English folk singer and musician: interview publ. in *The Guardian* (London), 29 Dec. 1988

5 No people in the world can make you feel so small as the English.
Robertson Davies (1913–1995), Canadian novelist and journalist: *The Enthusiasms of Robertson Davies* (1990), 'The Table Talk of Robertson Davies'

6 The English are probably the most tolerant, least religious people on earth.
David Goldberg (b.1939), Senior Rabbi, Liberal Jewish Synagogue, London: letter to *The Times* (London), 17 April 1980, on the furore that followed a controversial production of the documentary 'Death of a Princess', on BBC TV

7 English culture is basically homosexual in the sense that the men only really care about other men.
Germaine Greer (b.1939), Australian feminist writer: in the *Daily Mail* (London), 18 April 1988

8 We do not regard Englishmen as foreigners. We look on them only as rather mad Norwegians.
Halvard Lange (b.1918), Norwegian historian and politician: quoted in *The Observer* (London), 9 March 1957

9 Fifty years on from now, Britain will still be the country of long shadows on county grounds, warm beer, invincible green suburbs, dog lovers and – as George Orwell said – old maids bicycling to Holy Communion through the morning mist.
John Major (b.1943), British Conservative politician and prime minister: speech, 22 April 1993, to Conservative Group for Europe, Intercontinental Hotel, London, quoted in *The Daily Telegraph* (London), 23 April 1993. Orwell's essay, 'England Your England' (1941), described 'characteristic fragments of the English scene' which included 'the queues outside the Labour Exchange, the rattle of pin-tables in the Soho pubs, the old maids biking to Holy Communion through the mists of the autumn mornings.' Elsewhere in the essay, Orwell wrote, 'A family with the wrong members in control – that, perhaps, is as near as one can come to describing England in a phrase'

10 If an Englishman gets run down by a truck he apologizes to the truck.
Jackie Mason (b.1931), U.S. comic: in *The Independent* (London), 20 Sept. 1990

11 An Englishman, even if he is alone, forms an orderly queue of one.
George Mikes (1912–1987), Hungarian-born British humorist: *How To Be An Alien* (1946), Ch.1, Sct.14. Mikes elaborated further in *How To Be Decadent* (1977): 'In shops the English stand in queues; in government offices they sit in queues; in churches they kneel in queues; at sale times, they lie in queues all night'

12 English life, while very pleasant, is rather bland. I expected kindness and gentility and I found it, but there is such a thing as too much couth.
S.J. Perelman (1904–1979), U.S. humorist: quoted in *The Observer* (London), 24 Sept. 1971

13 Always in England if you had the type of brain that was capable of understanding T.S. Eliot's poetry or Kant's logic, you could be sure of finding large numbers of people who would hate you violently.
D.J. Taylor (b.1960), British author: in *The Guardian* (London), 14 Sept. 1989

14 You never find an Englishman among the under-dogs – except in England, of course.
Evelyn Waugh (1903–1966), British novelist: Sir Ambrose Abercrombie, in *The Loved One* (1948), p.13 of Penguin edn. (1951)

15 Ah don't hate the English. They're just wankers. We are colonised by wankers. We can't even pick a decent, healthy culture to be colonised by. No. We're ruled by effete arse-holes. What does that make us?
Irvine Welsh (b.1958), Scottish author: Renton, in *Trainspotting* (1994), 'Relapsing'

See also Osborne on ANGRY YOUNG MEN; MacInnes on ART: POP ART; THE ENGLISH LANGUAGE; Mason on FOOD; Mikes on FOOD; Albarn on MUSIC: COMPOSITION; Mikes on SEX; Orton on TASTE

BRITAIN: London

1 I firmly believe that London is the only civilized place in Britain. Go into the country-side and people are still living in 1953.
Brett Anderson (b.1967), British rock musician: interview in *i-D* (London), Oct. 1994

2 You don't go into Soho to see films, because Soho *is* a film.
Colin MacInnes (1914–1976), British author: *Absolute Beginners* (1959), 'in June'

3 London is a country coming down from its trip. We are sixty days from the end of this decade, and there's gonna be a lotta refugees. We are about to witness the world's biggest hangover, and there's fuck all Harold Wilson can do about it.
Bruce Robinson (b.1946), British film-maker: Danny (Ralph Brown), in *Withnail and I* (film; written and directed by Bruce Robinson, 1987)

See also Anderson on SUBURBS

BRITAIN: Scotland

1 Early morning on the coast of Scotland. Edinburgh: swans in the canals. The city encircling a false acropolis, mysterious and misty. The Athens of the North has nothing of the north. Chinese and Maltese in Princess [sic] Street. It's a port.
Albert Camus (1913–1960), French-Algerian philosopher and author: journal entry, May 1948, quoted in *Camus: A Biography* by Herbert R. Lottman (1979), Ch.33

2 Glasgow, the sort of industrial city where most people live nowadays but nobody imagines living.
Alasdair Gray (b.1934), Scottish novelist: *Lanark* (1981), Bk.3, Ch.11

3 In this country I don't think it is enough realized ... that Scotland has a case against England. On economic grounds it may not be a very strong case. ... The point is that many Scottish people, often quite moderate in outlook, are beginning to think about autonomy and to feel that they are pushed into an inferior position. They have a good deal of reason. In some areas, at any rate, Scotland is almost an occupied country. You have an English or anglicized upper class, and a Scottish working class which speaks with a markedly different accent, or even, part of the time, in a different language.
George Orwell (1903–1950), British author: in *Tribune* (London), 14 Feb. 1947, 'As I Please'

See also Welsh on BRITAIN: ENGLAND

BRITAIN: Wales

1 To live in Wales
is to love sheep
and to be afraid
of dragons.
Peter Finch (b.1947), Welsh poet: 'A Welsh Landscape', publ. in *End of the Vision* (1971)

2 The land of my fathers. My fathers can have it.
Dylan Thomas (1914–1953), Welsh poet: in *Adam* (London), Dec. 1953. 'Land of my Fathers' is the Welsh national anthem

3 An impotent people,
Sick with inbreeding,
Worrying the carcass of an old song.
R.S. Thomas (b.1913), Welsh poet and clergyman: 'Welsh Landscape', publ. in *An Acre of Land* (1952)

BROADWAY

1 I'm the end of the line; absurd and appalling as it may seem, serious New York theatre has died in my lifetime.
Arthur Miller (b.1915), U.S. playwright: in *The Times* (London), 11 Jan. 1989

2 The wide wonder of Broadway is disconsolate in the daytime; but gaudily glorious at night, with a milling crowd filling sidewalk and roadway, silent, going up, going down, between upstanding banks of brilliant lights, each building braided and embossed with glowing, many-coloured bulbs of man-rayed luminance. A glowing valley of the shadow of life. The strolling crowd went slowly by through the kinematically divine thoroughfare of New York.
Sean O'Casey (1884–1964), Irish playwright: *Rose And Crown* (fifth volume of autobiography, 1952), 'In New York Now'

3 We all know that the theater and every play that comes to Broadway have within themselves, like the human being, the seed of self-destruction and the certainty of death. The thing is to see how long the theater, the play, and the human being can last in spite of themselves.
James Thurber (1894–1961), U.S. humorist, illustrator: in the *New York Times*, 21 Feb. 1960. On the same subject, Thurber wrote: 'Surely no other American institution is so bound around and tightened up by rules, strictures, adages, and superstitions as the Broadway theater'

BROTHERHOOD

1 The ideal of brotherhood of man, the building of the Just City, is one that cannot be discarded without lifelong feelings of disappointment

and loss. But, if we are to live in the real world, discard it we must. Its very nobility makes the results of its breakdown doubly horrifying, and it breaks down, as it always will, not by some external agency but because it cannot work.

Kingsley Amis (1922–1995), British novelist and poet: in *The Sunday Telegraph* (London), 2 July 1967

2 We must love one another, yes, yes, that's all true enough, but nothing says we have to like each other. It may be the very recognition of all men as our brothers that accounts for the sibling rivalry, and even enmity, we have toward so many of them.

Peter de Vries (1910–1993), U.S. author: the narrator (Jim Tickler), opening sentences of *The Glory of the Hummingbird* (1974), Ch.1

3 The common erotic project of destroying women makes it possible for men to unite into a brotherhood; this project is the only firm and trustworthy groundwork for cooperation among males and all male bonding is based on it.

Andrea Dworkin (b.1946), U.S. feminist critic: 'The Root Cause', speech, 26 Sept. 1975, Massachusetts Institute of Technology, publ. in *Our Blood* (1976), Ch.9

4 The world has narrowed to a neighborhood before it has broadened to a brotherhood.

Lyndon B. Johnson (1908–1973), U.S. Democratic politician and president: speech, 17 Dec. 1963, New York City, publ. in *Public Papers of the Presidents of the United States, Lyndon B. Johnson, 1963–64*

5 I have a dream that one day on the red hills of Georgia the sons of former slaves and the sons of former slave owners will be able to sit down together at the table of brotherhood.

Martin Luther King Jr. (1929–1968), U.S. clergyman and civil rights leader: 'I Have a Dream', speech, 28 Aug. 1963, at civil rights march, Washington D.C., publ. in *A Testament of Hope: Essential Writings* (ed. James Melvin Washington, 1986), Ch.36

6 Nothing is more repugnant to me than brotherly feelings grounded in the common baseness people see in one another.

Milan Kundera (b.1929), Czech-born French author and critic: Ludvik, in *The Joke* (1967; tr.1982), Pt.3, Ch.9

7 The brotherhood of man is evoked by particular men according to their circumstances. But it seldom extends to all men. In the name of our freedom and our brotherhood we are prepared to blow up the other half of mankind and to be blown up in our turn.

R.D. Laing (1927–1989), British psychiatrist: *The Politics of Experience* (1967), Ch.4

8 I believe in the brotherhood of man, all men, but I don't believe in brotherhood with anybody who doesn't want brotherhood with me. I believe in treating people right, but I'm not going to waste my time trying to treat somebody right who doesn't know how to return the treatment.

Malcolm X (1925–1965), U.S. black leader: speech, 12 Dec. 1964, New York City, publ. in *Malcolm X: The Man and His Times* (ed. John Henrik Clarke, 1969), Pt.5, 'Communication and Reality'

9 The most dangerous word in any human tongue is the word for brother. It's inflammatory.

Tennessee Williams (1911–1983), U.S. playwright: Gutman, in *Camino Real* (1953), Block 2

BUDDHISM

1 The Buddha, the Godhead, resides quite as comfortably in the circuits of a digital computer or the gears of a cycle transmission as he does at the top of a mountain or in the petals of a flower.

Robert M. Pirsig (b.1928), U.S. author: *Zen and the Art of Motorcycle Maintenance* (1974), Pt.1, Ch.1

2 The idea that the whole of the external world is a treacherous fiction, that the self has no real existence, goes right against the Protestant, materialist American ethic. ... In every phase of post-colonial American history, Buddhism has offered a rhetoric of dissent.

Jonathan Raban (b.1942), British author and critic: 'New World', publ. in *Granta* (London), No.32, summer 1990

3 Zen ... does not confuse spirituality with thinking about God while one is peeling potatoes. Zen spirituality is just to peel the potatoes.

Alan Watts (1915–1973), British-born U.S. philosopher and author: *The Way of Zen* (1957), Pt.2, Ch.2

BUREAUCRACY

1 Poor fellow, he suffers from files.

Aneurin Bevan (1897–1960), British Labour politician: of administrator and trade unionist Sir Walter Citrine, quoted in Michael Foot's biography *Aneurin Bevan* Vol.I (1962), Ch.5. Citrine, Foot claimed, had a 'card-index mind'

2 It seems to me that there must be an ecological limit to the number of paper pushers the earth can sustain, and that human civilization will collapse when the number of, say, tax lawyers exceeds the world's total population of

farmers, weavers, fisherpersons, and pediatric nurses.

Barbara Ehrenreich (b.1941), U.S. author and columnist: 'Premature Pragmatism', first publ. in *Ms*, 1986, rep. in *The Worst Years of Our Lives* (1991)

3 The only thing that saves us from the bureaucracy is inefficiency. An efficient bureaucracy is the greatest threat to liberty.

Eugene J. McCarthy (b.1916), U.S. Democratic senator and author: in *Time* (New York), 12 Feb. 1979

4 Bureacracy, the rule of no one, has become the modern form of despotism.

Mary McCarthy (1912–1989), U.S. author and critic: 'The Vita Activa', first publ. in the *New Yorker*, 18 Oct. 1958, rep. in *On the Contrary* (1961)

5 Government proposes, bureaucracy disposes. And the bureaucracy must dispose of government proposals by dumping them on us.

P.J. O'Rourke (b.1947), U.S. journalist: *Parliament of Whores* (1991), 'The Bureaucracy'

6 If we did not have such a thing as an airplane today, we would probably create something the size of NASA to make one.

H. Ross Perot (b.1930), U.S. business executive and presidential candidate: in *Newsweek* (New York), 1 Dec. 1986

7 No government ever voluntarily reduces itself in size. Government programs, once launched, never disappear. Actually, a government bureau is the nearest thing to eternal life we'll ever see on this earth!

Ronald Reagan (b.1911), U.S. Republican politician and president: 'A Time for Choosing', television address, 27 Oct. 1964, publ. in *Speaking My Mind* (1989)

8 If you're going to sin, sin against God, not the bureaucracy, God will forgive you but the bureaucracy won't.

Hyman G. Rickover (1900–1986), U.S. admiral: quoted in the *New York Times*, 3 Nov. 1986

9 So many signatures for such a small heart.

Mother Teresa (1910–1997), Albanian-born Roman Catholic missionary: on form-filling in a Californian Hospital, quoted in the *Evening Standard* (London), 3 Jan. 1992

10 Modern man is strapped down by a network of rules and regulations, and his fate depends on the actions of a person remote from him whose decisions he cannot influence. This is not accidental or a result of the arbitrariness of arrogant bureaucrats. It is necessary and inevitable in any technologically advanced society. The system has to regulate human behavior closely in order to function.

Unabomber, U.S. radical: *Industrial Society and Its Future*, 'Restriction of Freedom is Unavoidable in Industrial Society', Sct.114, publ. in the *Washington Post*, 19 Sept. 1995

11 There is something about a bureaucrat that does not like a poem.

Gore Vidal (b.1925), U.S. novelist and critic: preface to *Sex, Death, and Money* (1968)

BURIAL

1 Just under the surface I shall be, all together at first, then separate and drift, through all the earth and perhaps in the end through a cliff into the sea, something of me. A ton of worms in an acre, that is a wonderful thought, a ton of worms, I believe it.

Samuel Beckett (1906–1989), Irish playwright and novelist: *From an Abandoned Work* (1958)

2 I could never bear to be buried with people to whom I had not been introduced.

Norman Parkinson (1913–1990), British fashion photographer: quoted in his obituary in *The Guardian* (London), 16 Feb. 1990

GEORGE BUSH

1 Let the others have the charisma. I've got the class.

George Bush (b.1924), U.S. Republican politician and president: said in California during presidential campaign, quoted in *The Guardian* (London), 3 Dec. 1988

2 Consider the vice president, George Bush, a man so bedeviled by bladder problems that he managed, for the last eight years, to be in the men's room whenever an important illegal decision was made.

Barbara Ehrenreich (b.1941), U.S. author and columnist: 'The Unbearable Being of Whiteness' (1988), rep. in *The Worst Years of Our Lives* (1991)

3 He's nice enough not to want to be associated with a nasty remark but not nice enough not to make it. Lacking the courage of one's nastiness does not make one nice.

Michael Kinsley (b.1951), U.S. journalist: in *Time* (New York), 16 July 1990

4 Poor George, he can't help it. He was born with a silver foot in his mouth.

Ann Richards (b.1933), U.S. Texas Democrat and state official: in *The Independent* (London), 20 July 1988

BUSINESS

1 There is no such thing as a free lunch.

Anonymous: popularized in the 1960s, the words have no known source, though have been dated to the 1840s, when they were used in saloons where snacks were offered to customers. The dictum was later ascribed to an Italian immigrant outside Grand Central Station, New York, in the epilogue of Alistair Cooke's *America* (1973) and it appears in Robert A. Heinlein's *The Moon is a Harsh Mistress* (1966), Ch.11 but has become most closely associated with economist Milton Friedman, who made it the title of a book in 1975

2   Executives are like joggers. If you stop a jogger, he goes on running on the spot. If you drag an executive away from his business, he goes on running on the spot, pawing the ground, talking business. He never stops hurtling onwards, making decisions and executing them.
Jean Baudrillard (b.1929), French semiologist: *Cool Memories* (1987; tr.1990), Ch.5

3   Such is the brutalization of commercial ethics in this country that no one can feel anything more delicate than the velvet touch of a soft buck.
Raymond Chandler (1888–1959), U.S. author: letter, 13 May 1949, to publisher Hamish Hamilton, publ. in *Raymond Chandler Speaking* (ed. Dorothy Gardiner and Katherine S. Walker, 1962)

4   Dream, diversify – and never miss an angle.
Walt Disney (1901–1966), U.S. animator and film-maker: quoted in introduction to *The Disney Studio Story* by Richard Holliss and Brian Sibley (1988)

5   When you are skinning your customers you should leave some skin on to grow again so that you can skin them again.
Nikita Khrushchev (1894–1971), Soviet premier: advice to British businessmen, quoted in *The Observer* (London), 28 May 1961

6   Captains go down with their ships, not businessmen.
Martin Landau (b.1933), U.S. actor: Abe Karatz (Martin Landau), in *Tucker – the Man and His Dream* (film; screenplay by Arnold Schulman, directed by Francis Ford Coppola, 1988)

7   If we decide to take this level of business creating ability nationwide, we'll all be plucking chickens for a living.
H. Ross Perot (b.1930), U.S. business executive and presidential candidate: of rival candidate Bill Clinton's initiatives in Arkansas, quoted in *Time* (New York), 16 Nov. 1992

8   In a hierarchy every employee tends to rise to his level of incompetence.
Laurence J. Peter (1919–1990), U.S.-Canadian author: *The Peter Principle* (1969), Ch.1. Compare with the *Paula Principle* : 'women stay below their level of competence, because they hold back from promotion' (formulated by Liz Filkin in *The Observer*, 19 Oct. 1986)

9   He's a businessman.... I'll make him an offer he can't refuse.
Mario Puzo (b.1920), U.S. novelist: Don Corleone, in *The Godfather* (1969), Bk.1, Ch.1. The line also

appears in Francis Ford Coppola's film version of the book, written in collaboration with Puzo (1972)

10   I am still looking for the modern equivalent of those Quakers who ran successful businesses, made money because they offered honest products and treated their people decently, worked hard, spent honestly, saved honestly, gave honest value for money, put back more than they took out and told no lies. This business creed, sadly, seems long forgotten.
Anita Roddick (b.1943), British businesswoman and founder of the Body Shop: *Body and Soul* (1991), Ch.1

11   Deals are my art form. Other people paint beautifully on canvas or write wonderful poetry. I like making deals, preferably big deals. That's how I get my kicks.
Donald Trump (b.1946), U.S. businessman: *Trump: The Art of the Deal* (written with Tony Schwartz, 1987), Ch.1

12   Being good in business is the most fascinating kind of art. ... Making money is art and working is art and good business is the best art.
Andy Warhol (c.1928–1987), U.S. Pop artist: *From A to B and Back Again* (1975), Ch.6

See also Roddick on ETHICS; Wilson on INDUSTRY; WOMEN: IN BUSINESS

CAMBRIDGE UNIVERSITY

1   I am ... willing to admit that some people might live there for years, or even a lifetime, so protected that they never sense the sweet stench of corruption that is all around them – the keen, thin scent of decay that pervades everything and accuses with a terrible accusation the superficial youthfulness, the abounding undergraduate noise, that fills those ancient buildings.
Thomas Merton (1915–1968), U.S. religious writer and poet: *The Seven Storey Mountain* (1948), Pt.1, Ch.3 of Merton's autobiography, describing his undergraduate days

2   Apparently, the most difficult feat for a Cambridge male is to accept a woman not merely as feeling, not merely as thinking, but as managing a complex, vital interweaving of both.
Sylvia Plath (1932–1963), U.S. poet: in *Isis* (Oxford students' magazine), 6 May 1956, written while Plath was a student at Cambridge

CAMP

1   The Camp attitude is essentially a mental set towards all sorts of objects which *fail from a serious* point of view. Instead of condemning these failures, it partially contemplates them

and partially enjoys them. ... Thus the epitome 'it's so bad that it's good.'

Charles Jencks (b.1939), U.S. architect and critic: *Modern Movements in Architecture* (1973), Ch.6

2   As the dandy is the nineteenth century's surrogate for the aristocrat in matters of culture, so Camp is the modern dandyism. Camp is the answer to the problem: how to be a dandy in the age of mass culture.

Susan Sontag (b.1933), U.S. essayist: 'Notes on "Camp"' (1964), Note 45, rep. in *Against Interpretation* (1966)

CANADA

1   The beginning of Canadian cultural nationalism was not 'Am I really that oppressed?' but 'Am I really that boring?'

Margaret Atwood (b.1939), Canadian novelist, poet and critic: 'Dancing on the Edge of the Precipice', interview with Joyce Carol Oates, publ. in the *Ontario Review*, fall/winter 1978, rep. in *Conversations* (ed. Earl G. Ingersoll, 1990)

2   Some say that no one ever leaves Montreal, for that city, like Canada itself, is designed to preserve the past, a past that happened somewhere else.

Leonard Cohen (b.1934), Canadian singer, poet and novelist: *The Favourite Game* (1963), Bk.2, Sct.19

3   Canada is not really a place where you are encouraged to have large spiritual adventures.

Robertson Davies (1913–1995), Canadian novelist and journalist: *The Enthusiasms of Robertson Davies* (1990), 'The Table Talk of Robertson Davies'

4   Long live Free Quebec!
    (*Vive le Québec Libre!*)

Charles de Gaulle (1890–1970), French general and president: speech, 24 July 1967, Montreal, publ. in *Speeches of General de Gaulle* (1970). The speech by de Gaulle aroused huge controversy, appearing to advocate the cause of Quebec separatists and inflaming an already volatile situation

5   Canadians look down on the United States and consider it Hell. They are right to do so. Canada is to the United States what, in Dante's scheme, Limbo is to Hell.

Irving Layton (b.1912), Canadian poet: *The Whole Bloody Bird* (1969), 'Obs II'

6   The past is still, for us, a place that is not safely settled.

Michael Ondaatje (b.1943), Canadian novelist: introduction to *The Faber Book of Contemporary Canadian Short Stories* (1990)

7   Canada is a country where nothing seems ever to happen. A country always dressed in its Sunday go-to-meeting clothes. A country you wouldn't ask to dance a second waltz. Clean. Christian. Dull. Quiescent. But growing. Yes, it must be admitted, the Dominion is growing.

Carol Shields (b.1935), U.S.-born Canadian author: *The Stone Diaries* (1993), Ch.3

See also Layton on ASSASSINATION

CANCER

1   We 'need' cancer because, by the very fact of its incurability, it makes all other diseases, however virulent, *not cancer*.

Gilbert Adair, British author and critic: *Myths and Memories* (1986), 'Under the Sign of Cancer'

2   My veins are filled, once a week with a Neapolitan carpet cleaner distilled from the Adriatic and I am as bald as an egg. However I still get around and am mean to cats.

John Cheever (1912–1982), U.S. author: of his cancer and its treatment, in letter, 10 May 1982, to Philip Roth, publ. in *The Letters of John Cheever* (1989)

3   I wish I had the voice of Homer
    To sing of rectal carcinoma.

J.B.S. Haldane (1892–1964), British scientist: 'Cancer's a Funny Thing', publ. in *New Statesman* (London), 21 Feb. 1964. Opening lines of a poem describing Haldane's colostomy. 'The main functions of my rhyme,' Haldane wrote, 'were to induce cancer patients to be operated on early and to be cheerful about it'

4   Cancer patients are lied to, not just because the disease is (or is thought to be) a death sentence, but because it is felt to be obscene – in the original meaning of that word: ill-omened, abominable, repugnant to the senses.

Susan Sontag (b.1933), U.S. essayist: *Illness As Metaphor* (1978), Ch.1

5   Every age seems to be accompanied by a sickness so peculiarly its own as to make one wonder if it is not merely a physical manifestation of the inner aberration of the time itself: and cancer certainly, within and without, is our very own.

Laurens van der Post (1906–1996), South African writer and philosopher: *A Walk with a White Bushman* (1986), p.285 of Chatto & Windus edn.

6   It was announced that the trouble was not 'malignant.' ... It was a typical triumph of modern science to find the only part of Randolph that was not malignant and remove it.

Evelyn Waugh (1903–1966), British novelist: journal entry, March 1964, publ. in *Diaries of Evelyn Waugh* (ed. Michael Davie, 1976), 'Irregular Notes 1960–65'. Waugh referred to Randolph Churchill (1911–1968), son of Winston Churchill and a forthright commentator on social affairs

CANDOUR

1 It is the weak and confused who worship the pseudosimplicities of brutal directness.
Marshall McLuhan (1911–1980), Canadian communications theorist: *The Mechanical Bride* (1951), 'The Tough as Narcissus'

2 Not to expose your true feelings to an adult seems to be instinctive from the age of seven or eight onwards.
George Orwell (1903–1950), British author: 'Such, Such were the Joys' (1947), rep. in *The Collected Essays, Journalism and Letters of George Orwell* (ed. Sonia Orwell and Ian Angus, 1968), Vol.IV

3 Let's face it. Let's talk sense to the American people. Let's tell them the truth, that there are no gains without pains, that we are now on the eve of great decisions, not easy decisions.
Adlai Stevenson (1900–1965), U.S. Democratic politician: acceptance speech, 26 July 1952, to the Democratic National Convention, Chicago, Illinois, publ. in *Speeches* (1953)

CAPITAL PUNISHMENT

1 Unlike other prisoners, death row inmates are not 'doing time.' Freedom does not shine at the end of the tunnel. Rather, the end of the tunnel brings extinction.
Mumia Abu-Jamal (b.1954), U.S. journalist and environmentalist: on being a death-row prisoner, in *Live From Death Row* (1995), Pt.1, 'Teetering on the brink between life and death'

2 What will be left of the power of example if it is proved that capital punishment has another power, and a very real one, which degrades men to the point of shame, madness, and murder?
Albert Camus (1913–1960), French-Algerian philosopher and author: *Resistance, Rebellion and Death* (1961), 'Reflections on the Guillotine'

3 Your Honor, I don't want to take up a lot of your time with my words. I believe I was given a fair trial and I think the sentence is proper and I am willing to accept it like a man. I don't wish to appeal. ... I desire to be executed on schedule, and I just wish to accept that with the grace and dignity of a man.
Gary Gilmore (1941–1977), U.S. convict: speech to the Supreme Court, 9 Nov. 1976, quoted in *The Executioner's Song* by Norman Mailer (1979), Bk.2, Pt.1, Ch.1, Sct.7. Gilmore's last words to the firing squad were, 'Let's do it!'

CAPITALISM

1 The most eloquent eulogy of capitalism was made by its greatest enemy. Marx is only anti-capitalist in so far as capitalism is out of date.
Albert Camus (1913–1960), French-Algerian philosopher and author: *The Rebel* (1951; tr.1953), Pt.3, 'State Terrorism and Rational Terror'

2 Predatory capitalism created a complex industrial system and an advanced technology; it permitted a considerable extension of democratic practice and fostered certain liberal values, but within limits that are now being pressed and must be overcome. It is not a fit system for the mid-twentieth century.
Noam Chomsky (b.1928), U.S. linguist and political analyst: 'Language and Freedom', lecture, Loyola University, Chicago, Jan. 1970, rep. in *For Reasons of State* (1973), first publ. 1970

3 History suggests that capitalism is a necessary condition for political freedom. Clearly it is not a sufficient condition.
Milton Friedman (b.1912), U.S. economist: *Capitalism and Freedom* (1962), Ch.1

4 In culture, capitalism has given all that it had to give and all that remains of it is the foretaste of a bad-smelling corpse; in art, its present decadence.
Ernesto 'Che' Guevara (1928–1967), Argentinian revolutionary leader: 'Socialism and Man in Cuba', *Che Guevara on Revolution* (ed. Jay Mallin, 1969), open letter to the editor of a Uruguayan newspaper, *La Marcha*, 1967

5 The unpleasant and unacceptable face of capitalism.
Edward Heath (b.1916), British Conservative politician and prime minister: speech, 15 May 1973, House of Commons, London, referring to the high payments made to company directors during a period of recession, publ. in Hansard Col.1243

6 Capitalism is at its liberating best in a noncapitalist environment. The crypto-businessman is the true revolutionary in a Communist country.
Eric Hoffer (1902–1983), U.S. philosopher: *Reflections on the Human Condition* (1973), Aph.73

7 Capitalism is an art form, an Apollonian fabrication to rival nature. It is hypocritical for feminists and intellectuals to enjoy the pleasures and conveniences of capitalism while sneering at it. ... Everyone born into capitalism has incurred a debt to it. Give Caesar his due.
Camille Paglia (b.1947), U.S. author and critic: *Sexual Personae* (1990), Ch.1

8 Let us look at the capitalist roots of the racial miseries of our own country, South Africa. The real question is not whether a system works, but for whom it works.
Joe Slovo (1926–1994), Lithuanian-born South African activist and politician: criticizing the notion that capitalism works and socialism has failed, quoted in obituary in *The Guardian* (London), 7 Jan. 1995

9 The ideology of capitalism makes us all into connoisseurs of liberty – of the indefinite expansion of possibility.

Susan Sontag (b.1933), U.S. essayist: *Aids and Its Metaphors* (1989), Ch.7

10 The first rule of venture capitalism should be Shoot the Inventor.

Richard Storey (b.1937), British newspaper publisher: quoted in Brian MacArthur's *Eddy Shah: Today and the Newspaper Revolution* (1988), Ch.21, referring to entrepreneur Eddie Shah. Sir Richard was one of Eddie Shah's backers

11 What breaks capitalism, all that will ever break capitalism, is capitalists. The faster they run the more strain on their heart.

Raymond Williams (1921–1988), British novelist and critic: Monkey Pitter, in Williams' last novel, *Loyalties* (1985), Pt.3, Ch.2

See also Stone on MCDONALD'S; Lerner on TRADE UNIONS

CAREERS

1 People don't choose their careers; they are engulfed by them.

John Dos Passos (1896–1970), U.S. novelist: in the *New York Times*, 25 Oct. 1959

2 Sometimes you wonder how you got on this mountain. But sometimes you wonder, 'How will I get off?'

Joan Manley (b.1932), U.S. publisher: quoted in the *Washington Post*, 8 April 1979

3 The life-fate of the modern individual depends not only upon the family into which he was born or which he enters by marriage, but increasingly upon the corporation in which he spends the most alert hours of his best years.

C. Wright Mills (1916–1962), U.S. sociologist: *The Power Elite* (1956), Ch.1

4 I have yet to hear a man ask for advice on how to combine marriage and a career.

Gloria Steinem (b.1934), U.S. feminist writer and editor: radio interview, 2 April 1984, LBC (London)

5 Never burn bridges. Today's junior prick, tomorrow's senior partner.

Sigourney Weaver (b.1949), U.S. actress: Katharine Parker (Sigourney Weaver), in *Working Girl* (film; screenplay by Kevin Wade, directed by Mike Nichols, 1988)

THE CARIBBEAN

1 You know people exaggerate that all is wild in Jamaica. I think that sometimes people fire a shot to try to make you nervous. They are not trying to hurt you.

Michael Manley (1924–1997), Jamaican politician and prime minister: in *The Daily Telegraph* (London), 8 Feb. 1989

2 I come from a place that likes grandeur; it likes large gestures; it is not inhibited by flourish; it is a rhetorical society; it is a society of physical performance; it is a society of style.

Derek Walcott (b.1930), West Indian poet and playwright: interview in *Writers at Work* (Eighth Series, ed. George Plimpton, 1988)

CARS

1 Freedom to Drive or Freedom to Breathe.

Anti-roads group: anti-roads protest banner from the Reclaim the Streets Action Network, Birmingham NEC, 15 May 1993, quoted in *i-D* (London), Nov. 1993

2 The car as we know it is on the way out. To a large extent, I deplore its passing, for as a basically old-fashioned machine, it enshrines a basically old-fashioned idea: freedom. In terms of pollution, noise and human life, the price of that freedom may be high, but perhaps the car, by the very muddle and confusion it causes, may be holding back the remorseless spread of the regimented, electronic society.

J.G. Ballard (b.1930), British author: 'The Car, The Future', first publ. in *Drive* (London), autumn 1971, rep. in *Re/Search* (San Francisco), No.8/9 1984

3 I think that cars today are almost the exact equivalent of the great Gothic cathedrals: I mean the supreme creation of an era, conceived with passion by unknown artists, and consumed in image if not in usage by a whole population which appropriates them as a purely magical object.

Roland Barthes (1915–1980), French semiologist: *Mythologies* (1957), 'The New Citroën'

4 Driving is a spectacular form of amnesia. Everything is to be discovered, everything to be obliterated.

Jean Baudrillard (b.1929), French semiologist: *America* (1986; tr.1988), 'Vanishing Point'

5 The reason American cars don't sell anymore is that they have forgotten how to design the American Dream. What does it matter if you buy a car today or six months from now, because cars are not beautiful. That's why the American auto industry is in trouble: no design, no desire.

Karl Lagerfeld (b.1938), German-born French fashion designer: quoted in *Vanity Fair* (New York), Feb. 1992

6 The Aquarium is gone. Everywhere, giant finned cars nose forward like fish;

a savage servility
slides by on grease.

Robert Lowell (1917–1977), U.S. poet: 'For The Union Dead', St.17, publ. in *For The Union Dead* (1964)

7 The car has become the carapace, the protective and aggressive shell, of urban and suburban man.

Marshall McLuhan (1911–1980), Canadian communications theorist: *Understanding Media* (1964), Ch.22

8 Automobiles are free of egotism, passion, prejudice and stupid ideas about where to have dinner. They are, literally, selfless. A world designed for automobiles instead of people would have wider streets, larger dining rooms, fewer stairs to climb and no smelly, dangerous subway stations.

P.J. O'Rourke (b.1947), U.S. journalist: *Give War A Chance* (1992), 'An Argument in Favor of Automobiles vs Pedestrians'

9 My auto is a hypochondriac. It lies to me, telling me its manifold, or whatever horseshit it can think up, is out of order. I kick it, I say: run you mother, drive, or whatever you call what you do. I can't believe so many parts and details have no sensation. Can't the bloody thing be proud for example of its steering wheel, its carburetor?

Claes Oldenburg (b.1929), Swedish-born U.S. artist: 'War and Sex, etc.', publ. in *Arts Magazine* (New York), summer 1967, rep. in *Icons and Images of the Sixties* by Nicholas and Elena Calas (1971), 'Pop Art: Claes Oldenburg's Contented Objects'

10 No other man-made device since the shields and lances of the ancient knights fulfils a man's ego like an automobile.

Lord Rootes (1894–1964), British automobile manufacturer: quoted on *Who Said That?*, BBC TV, 14 Jan. 1958

11 I don't even like *old* cars … I'd rather have a goddam horse. A horse is at least *human*, for God's sake.

J.D. Salinger (b.1919), U.S. author: the narrator (Holden Caulfield), in *The Catcher in the Rye* (1951), Ch.17

CARTOONS

1 I could draw *Bloom County* with my nose and pay my cleaning lady to write it, and I'd bet I wouldn't lose 10% of my papers over the next twenty years. Such is the nature of comic-strips. Once established, their half-life is usually more than nuclear waste.

Berke Breathed (b.1957), U.S. cartoonist and author: in *Time* (New York), 25 Dec. 1989

2 There is a relationship between cartooning and people like Miró and Picasso which may not be understood by the cartoonist, but it definitely is related even in the early Disney.

Roy Lichtenstein (1923–1997), U.S. Pop artist: 'Talking With Roy Lichtenstein', publ. in *Lichtenstein* by John Coplan (1972)

See also WALT DISNEY INC

CATHOLICISM

1 The thing with Catholicism, the same as all religions, is that it teaches what *should* be, which seems rather incorrect. This is 'what should be.' Now, if you're taught to live up to a 'what should be' that never existed – only an occult superstition, no proof of this 'should be' – then you can sit on a jury and indict easily, you can cast the first stone, you can burn Adolf Eichmann, like that!

Lenny Bruce (1925–1966), U.S. satirical comedian: *The Essential Lenny Bruce* (ed. John Cohen, 1967), 'Religions Inc.'

2 Anti-Catholicism is the anti-semitism of the intellectual.

Patrick Buchanan (b.1938), U.S. journalist, broadcaster and presidential candidate: in *The Observer* (London), 15 Dec. 1991. Peter Viereck, in *Shame and Glory of the Intellectuals* (1953) Ch.3, wrote: 'Catholic-baiting is the anti-Semitism of the liberals'

3 All human life is here, but the Holy Ghost seems to be somewhere else.

Anthony Burgess (1917–1993), British author and critic: of the Vatican, in book review in *The Observer* (London), 25 May 1986

4 Today's Catholic church seems to reward authoritarian personalities who are clearly ill, violent, sexually obsessed and unable to remember the past.

Matthew Fox (b.1940), U.S. clergyman and author: quoted in *The Independent* (London), 12 Nov. 1988

5 To care for the quarrels of the past, to identify oneself passionately with a cause that became, politically speaking, a losing cause with the birth of the modern world, is to experience a kind of straining against reality, a rebellious nonconformity that, again, is rare in America, where children are instructed in the virtues of the system they live under, as though history had achieved a happy ending in American civics.

Mary McCarthy (1912–1989), U.S. author and critic: *Memories of A Catholic Girlhood* (1957), 'To The Reader'

6 Catholicism is not a soothing religion. It's a painful religion. We're all gluttons for punishment.

Madonna (b.1959), U.S. singer and actress: interview in *Rolling Stone* (New York), 23 March 1989

7 You can't run the Church on Hail Marys.

Paul Marcinkus (b.1922), U.S. ecclesiastic and Vatican financier: quoted in *The Observer* (London), 25 May 1986

8 One cannot really be a Catholic & grown-up.

George Orwell (1903–1950), British author: 'Manuscript Notebook' (1949), publ. in *The Collected Essays, Journalism and Letters of George Orwell* (ed. Sonia Orwell and Ian Angus, 1968), Vol.IV

9 I vividly recall my own mind-murdering struggles with the Catholic catechism in childhood. Question and answer, question and answer ... a jackbooted parade of lifeless verbal formulas, every one of them to be recited letter perfect, every one of them to be literally believed under threat of corporal punishment. Dogma and doctrine were marched through my brain like storm troops flattening every natural barrier childish inquisitiveness might raise.

Theodore Roszak (b.1933), U.S. social critic: *Where the Wasteland Ends* (1972), Ch.11

10 I wouldn't take the Pope too seriously. He's a Pole first, a pope second, and maybe a Christian third.

Muriel Spark (b.1918), British novelist: in the *International Herald Tribune* (Paris), 29 May 1989

11 If you're going to do a thing, you should do it thoroughly. If you're going to be a Christian, you may as well be a Catholic.

Muriel Spark: in *The Independent* (London), 2 Aug. 1989

12 The Catholic Church has never really come to terms with women. What I object to is being treated either as Madonnas or Mary Magdalenes.

Shirley Williams (b.1930), British Liberal-Democrat politician: in *The Observer* (London), 22 March 1981

See also Greene on COMMUNISM

CATS

1 Your rat tail is all the fashion now. I prefer a bushy plume, carried straight up. You are Siamese and your ancestors lived in trees. Mine lived in palaces. It has been suggested to me that I am a bit of a snob. How true! I prefer to be.

Raymond Chandler (1888–1959), U.S. author: letter, Christmas 1948, from Chandler's cat, Taki, to Mike Gibbud, Esq., 'a Siamese Cat of imperfect blood line,' publ. in *Raymond Chandler Speaking* (ed. Dorothy Gardiner and Kathrine S. Walker, 1962)

2 One cat in a house is a sign of loneliness, two of barrenness, and three of sodomy.

Edward Dahlberg (1900–1977), U.S. author and critic: *Alms for Oblivion* (1964), 'Moby-Dick: A Hamitic Dream'

3 Authors like cats because they are such quiet, lovable, wise creatures, and cats like authors for the same reasons.

Robertson Davies (1913–1995), Canadian novelist and journalist: 'mehitabel', publ. in the *Toronto Daily Star*, 21 Nov. 1959, rep. in *The Enthusiasms of Robertson Davies* (1990)

4 Cats seem to go on the principle that it never does any harm to ask for what you want.

Joseph Wood Krutch (1893–1970), U.S. author and editor: *Twelve Seasons* (1949), 'February'

5 If a fish is the movement of water embodied, given shape, then cat is a diagram and pattern of subtle air.

Doris Lessing (b.1919), British novelist: *Particularly Cats* (1967), Ch.2

6 Cats are autocrats of naked self-interest. They are both amoral and immoral, consciously breaking rules. Their 'evil' look at such times is no human projection: the cat may be the only animal who savors the perverse or reflects upon it.

Camille Paglia (b.1947), U.S. author and critic: *Sexual Personae* (1990), Ch.2

See also Bardot on BRIGITTE BARDOT

CAUSES

1 No cause is left but the most ancient of all, the one, in fact, that from the beginning of our history has determined the very existence of politics, the cause of freedom versus tyranny.

Hannah Arendt (1906–1975), German-born U.S. political philosopher: introduction to *On Revolution* (1963)

2 The power of a movement lies in the fact that it can indeed change the habits of people. This change is not the result of force but of dedication, of moral persuasion.

Steve Biko (1946–1977), South African anti-apartheid activist: interview, July 1976, quoted in *Biko* by Donald Woods (1978), Ch.2

3 A good cause can become bad if we fight for it with means that are indiscriminatingly murderous. A bad cause can become good if enough people fight for it in a spirit of comradeship and self-sacrifice. In the end it is how you fight, as much as why you fight, that makes your cause good or bad.

Freeman Dyson (b.1923), British-born U.S. physicist and author: *Disturbing the Universe* (1979), Pt.1, Ch.4

4 I hate the idea of causes, and if I had to choose between betraying my country and betraying my friend, I hope I should have the guts to betray my country.

E.M. Forster (1879–1970), British novelist and essayist: *Two Cheers for Democracy* (1951), 'What I Believe'

5 Truth never damages a cause that is just.

Mohandas K. Gandhi (1869–1948), Indian political and spiritual leader: *Non-Violence in Peace and War* (1949), Vol.II, Ch.162

6 To gain that which is worth having, it may be necessary to lose everything else.

Bernadette McAliskey [formerly Bernadette Devlin] (b.1947), Northern Irish politician: preface to *The Price of my Soul* (1969)

7 The silent majority distrusts people who believe in causes.

Brian Moore (b.1921), Irish novelist: in *The Sunday Times* (London), 15 April 1990

8 It isn't until you begin to fight in your own cause that you (a) become really committed to winning, and (b) become a genuine ally of other people struggling for their freedom.

Robin Morgan (b.1941), U.S. feminist author and poet: introduction to *Sisterhood Is Powerful* (1970)

9 Perhaps misguided moral passion is better than confused indifference.

Iris Murdoch (b.1919), British novelist and philosopher: Jenkin Riderhood, in *The Book and the Brotherhood* (1987), Pt.2, 'Midwinter'

10 A man who has never lost himself in a cause bigger than himself has missed one of life's mountaintop experiences. Only in losing himself does he find himself. Only then does he discover all the latent strengths he never knew he had and which otherwise would have remained dormant.

Richard Nixon (1913–1992), U.S. Republican politician and president: introduction to *Six Crises* (1962)

11 There aren't any good, brave causes left. If the big bang does come, and we all get killed off, it won't be in aid of the old-fashioned grand design. It'll just be for the Brave New-nothing-very-much-thank-you. About as pointless and inglorious as stepping in front of a bus. No, there's nothing left for it, me boy, but to let yourself be butchered by the women.

John Osborne (1929–1994), British playwright: Jimmy Porter, in *Look Back in Anger* (1956), Act 3, Sc.1

See also Forster on LITERATURE: AND SOCIETY

CELIBACY

1 Some perks belong, though
  to all unwilling celibates: our rooms are seldom

battlefields, we enjoy the pleasure of reading in
  bed
(as we grow older, it's true, we may find it
  prudent
to get nodding drunk first), we retain the right
  to choose
our sacred image.

W.H. Auden (1907–1973), Anglo-American poet: 'The Cave of Nakedness', Sct.11 of 'Thanksgiving for a Habitat', in *About the House* (1965)

2 It's about time that we accepted total celibates are no more deranged, inefficient, unhappy or unhealthy than any other section of the population.

Germaine Greer (b.1939), Australian feminist writer: interview in *A Little Light Friction* by Val Hennessy (1989), 'Germaine Greer'

3 Celibacy is not just a matter of not having sex. It is a way of admiring a person for their humanity, maybe even for their beauty.

Timothy Radcliffe (b.1945), British theologian and Dominican Master General: in *The Guardian* (London), 3 Aug. 1992

4 I don't particularly have any great sexual urges or needs … But that's my good fortune, isn't it, really?

Cliff Richard (b.1940), British singer: quoted in the *Independent on Sunday* (London), 4 April 1993

See also VIRGINITY

CENSORSHIP

1 You can cage the singer but not the song.

Harry Belafonte (b.1927), U.S. singer and civil rights activist: on the arts in South Africa, in the *International Herald Tribune* (Paris), 3 Oct. 1988

2 Censors tend to do what only psychotics do: they confuse reality with illusion.

David Cronenberg (b.1943), Canadian film-maker: *Cronenberg on Cronenberg* (ed. Chris Rodley, 1992), Ch.5

3 Censorship is a way of admitting our own weakness and intellectual insufficiency.
  Censorship is always a political tool: certainly not an intellectual one. Criticism is an intellectual tool: it presupposes a knowledge of what one judges and opposes.
  Criticism does not destroy; it puts an object in its proper place among other objects.
  To censor is to destroy, or at least to oppose the process of reality.

Federico Fellini (1920–1993), Italian film-maker: *Fellini on Fellini* (ed. Anna Keel and Christian Strich, 1974; tr.1977), 'Notes on Censorship'

4 Censorship is never over for those who have experienced it. It is a brand on the imagination that affects the individual who has suffered it, forever.

Nadine Gordimer (b.1923), South African author: 'Censorship and its Aftermath', address at the International Writers' Day conference, London, June 1990, publ. in *Index on Censorship* (London), Aug. 1990

5 The crime of book purging is that it involves a rejection of the word. For the word is never absolute truth, but only man's frail and human effort to approach the truth. To reject the word is to reject the human search.
Max Lerner (1902–1992), U.S. author and columnist: of the McCarthy book burnings, in 'The Vigilantes and the Chain of Fear', first publ. in the *New York Post*, 24 June 1953, rep. in *The Unfinished Country* (1959), Pt.4

6 We live in oppressive times. We have, as a nation, become our own thought police; but instead of calling the process by which we limit our expression of dissent and wonder 'censorship,' we call it 'concern for commercial viability.'
David Mamet (b.1947), U.S. playwright: *Writing in Restaurants* (1986), 'Radio Drama'

7 Too often a great mistake is made in discussions about censorship: that of putting the debate in the terms proposed by the censors: that is of the moralistic-sexual. Instead it is quite otherwise: one must completely ignore their hypocritical pretext, and see what should be obvious to a child, that censorship is a political issue, with sex as a simple and shameless pretext.
Pier Paolo Pasolini (1922–1975), Italian filmmaker and essayist: 'Le belle bandiere' (column), in *Vie nuove*, 17 Dec. 1960, rep. in *Pasolini Requiem* by David Barth Schwartz (1992), Ch.16

8 When truth is no longer free, freedom is no longer real: the truths of the police are the truths of today.
(*Quand la vérité n'est pas libre la liberté n'est pas vrai: les vérités de la police sont les vérités d'aujourd'hui.*)
Jacques Prévert (1900–1977), French poet: 'Intermède', publ. in *Spectacle* (1951)

9 I am of course confident that I will fulfil my tasks as a writer in all circumstances – from my grave even more successfully and more irrefutably than in my lifetime. No one can bar the road to truth, and to advance its cause I am prepared to accept even death. But may it be that repeated lessons will finally teach us not to stop the writer's pen during his lifetime? At no time has this ennobled our history.
Alexander Solzhenitsyn (b.1918), Russian novelist: closing words to open letter to the Fourth Soviet Writers' Congress, 16 May 1967, publ. in *Problems of Communism*, July/Aug 1968, rep. in *Solzhenitsyn: A Documentary Record* (ed. Leopold Labedz, 1970)

10 Right now I think censorship is necessary; the things they're doing and saying in films right now just shouldn't be allowed. There's no dignity anymore and I think that's very important.
Mae West (1892–1980), U.S. actress: interview in *Take One* (Quebec), 22 Jan. 1974

See also Solzhenitsyn on FREEDOM OF EXPRESSION; Griffith-Jones on OBSCENITY

CEREMONY

1 Ceremony and ritual spring from our heart of hearts: those who govern us know it well, for they would sooner deny us bread than dare alter the observance of tradition.
F. Gonzalez-Crussi (b.1936), Mexican professor of pathology and author: *Notes of an Anatomist* (1985), 'On Embalming'

2 Every ceremony or rite has a value if it is performed without alteration. A ceremony is a book in which a great deal is written. Anyone who understands can read it. One rite often contains more than a hundred books.
George Gurdjieff (c.1877–1949), Greek-Armenian religious teacher and mystic: quoted in *In Search of the Miraculous* by P.D. Ouspensky (1949), Ch.15

3 We must learn which ceremonies may be breached occasionally at our convenience and which ones may never be if we are to live pleasantly with our fellow man.
Amy Vanderbilt (1908–1974), U.S. hostess and author: *New Complete Book of Etiquette* (1963), introduction to Pt.1

CERTAINTY

1 We are not certain, we are never certain. If we were we could reach some conclusions, and we could, at last, make others take us seriously.
Albert Camus (1913–1960), French-Algerian philosopher and author: the narrator (Jean-Baptiste Clamence), in *The Fall* (1956)

2 I'm frightened of all those people who show you the way, who know. Because really … nobody really knows, with a few exceptions. Unfortunately, the actions of these people usually end in tragedy – like the Second World War or Stalinism or something. I'm convinced that Stalin and Hitler knew exactly what they were to do. They knew very well. But that's how it is. That's fanaticism. That's knowing. That's the feeling of absolutely knowing. And the next minute, it's army boots. It always ends up like that.
Krzysztof Kieślowski (1941–1996), Polish filmmaker: *Kieślowski on Kieślowski* (1993), Ch.1

3 If you do know that *here is one hand*, we'll
grant you all the rest.
Ludwig Wittgenstein (1889–1951), Austrian-born
British philosopher: opening sentence of *On
Certainty* (ed. Anscombe and von Wright, 1969),
Sct.1. A response to a lecture by the philosopher
G.E. Moore, in which he refuted the premises of
scepticism

See also Weldon on THE NEW AGE

CHANGE

1 Change means movement. Movement means
friction. Only in the frictionless vacuum of a
nonexistent abstract world can movement or
change occur without that abrasive friction of
conflict.
Saul Alinsky (1909–1972), U.S. political activist:
Rules for Radicals (1971), 'The Purpose'

2 My works are in constant state of change.... As
people walk on them, as the steel rusts, as the
brick crumbles, as the materials weather, the
work becomes it's own record of everything
that's happened to it.
Carl André (b.1935), U.S. artist: symposium at
Wyndham College, Vermont, 30 April 1968, publ. in
Twentieth-Century Artists on Art (ed. Dore Ashton,
1985)

3 It is change, continuing change, inevitable
change, that is the dominant factor in society
today. No sensible decision can be made any
longer without taking into account not only the
world as it is, but the world as it will be. ...
This, in turn, means that our statesmen, our
businessmen, our everyman must take on a
science fictional way of thinking.
Isaac Asimov (1920–1992), Russian-born U.S.
author: 'My Own View', first publ. in *The
Encyclopedia of Science Fiction* (ed. Robert
Holdstock, 1978), rep. in *Asimov on Science Fiction*
(1981)

4 Most of us are about as eager to be changed as
we were to be born, and go through our
changes in a similar state of shock.
James Baldwin (1924–1987), U.S. author: 'Every
Good-Bye Ain't Gone', first publ. in *New York*, 19
Dec. 1977, rep. in *The Price of the Ticket* (1985)

5 If a man like Malcolm X could change and
repudiate racism, if I myself and other former
Muslims can change, if young whites can
change, then there is hope for America.
Eldridge Cleaver (b.1935), U.S. black leader and
writer: *Soul on Ice* (1968), 'The White Race and Its
Heroes'

6 It's been a long time coming
But I know a change is gonna come.
Sam Cooke (1931–1964), U.S. soul musician: 'A
Change is Gonna Come' (song, 1964), publ. in *The
Poetry of Soul* (ed. A.X. Nicholas, 1971)

7 Death to all modifiers.
Joseph Heller (b.1923), U.S. author: Yossarian, in
Catch-22 (1955), Ch.1

8 Only man is not content to leave things as they
are but must always be changing them, and
when he has done so, is seldom satisfied with
the result.
Elspeth Huxley (1907–1997), British author: *The
Mottled Lizard* (second volume of autobiography,
1962), Ch.4

9 The word *change*, so dear to our Europe, has
been given a new meaning: it no longer means *a
new stage of coherent development* (as it was
understood by Vico, Hegel or Marx), but a
shift from one side to another, from front to
back, from the back to the left, from the left to
the front (as understood by designers dreaming up the fashion for the next season).
Milan Kundera (b.1929), Czech-born French
author and critic: *Immortality* (1991), Pt.3
'Imagology'

10 Every moment of one's existence one is growing into more or retreating into less. One is
always living a little more or dying a little bit.
Norman Mailer (b.1923), U.S. author: 'Hip,
Hell, and the Navigator', first publ. in *The
Western Review*, winter 1959, rep. in *Conversations
with Norman Mailer* (ed. J. Michael Lennon,
1988)

11 Today the world changes so quickly that in
growing up we take leave not just of youth but
of the world we were young in. ... Fear and
resentment of what is new is really a lament for
the memories of our childhood.
Peter Medawar (1915–1987), British
immunologist: *Pluto's Republic* (1982), 'On "The
Effecting of All Things Possible"'

12 There are periods in history when change is
necessary, and other periods when it is better
to keep everything for the time as it is. The art
of life is to be in the rhythm of your age.
Oswald Mosley (1896–1980), British fascist leader:
My Life (1968), Ch.4

13 Wisdom lies neither in fixity nor in change, but
in the dialectic between the two.
Octavio Paz (b.1914), Mexican poet and essayist: in
The Times (London), 8 June 1989

See also Dylan on THE GENERATION GAP; Dylan
on THE 1960S

CHAOS

1 To find a form that accommodates the mess,
that is the task of the artist now.
Samuel Beckett (1906–1989), Irish playwright and
novelist: conversation with John Driver, 1961,
quoted in *Samuel Beckett, a Biography* by Deirdre
Bair (1978), Ch.21

2 Chaos is a name for any order that produces confusion in our minds.
George Santayana (1863–1952), U.S. philosopher, poet: *Dominations and Powers* (1951), Bk.1, Pt.1, Ch.1

3 Since we cannot hope for order let us withdraw with style from the chaos.
Tom Stoppard (b.1937), British playwright: Lord Malquist, in *Lord Malquist and Mr Moon* (1966), Pt.1, Ch.2

CHARACTER

1 Character contributes to beauty. It fortifies a woman as her youth fades. A mode of conduct, a standard of courage, discipline, fortitude and integrity can do a great deal to make a woman beautiful.
Jacqueline Bisset (b.1946), U.S. actress: quoted in the *Los Angeles Times*, 16 May 1974

2 Though intelligence is powerless to modify character, it is a dab hand at finding euphemisms for its weaknesses.
Quentin Crisp (b.1908), British author: *The Naked Civil Servant* (1968), Ch.29

3 I have only got down on to paper, really, three types of people: the person I think I am, the people who irritate me, and the people I'd like to be.
E.M. Forster (1879–1970), British novelist and essayist: address to PEN Club Congress, quoted in *Monitor* (ed. Huw Weldon, 1962)

4 Deep down, I'm pretty superficial.
Ava Gardner (1922–1990), U.S. actress: quoted in *Ava* by Roland Flamini (1983), Ch.8

5 To keep your character intact you cannot stoop to filthy acts. It makes it easier to stoop the next time.
Katharine Hepburn (b.1909), U.S. actress: quoted in the *Los Angeles Times*, 24 Nov. 1974

6 Look, we're all the same; a man is a fourteen-room house – in the bedroom he's asleep with his intelligent wife, in the living-room he's rolling around with some bareass girl, in the library he's paying his taxes, in the yard he's raising tomatoes, and in the cellar he's making a bomb to blow it all up.
Arthur Miller (b.1915), U.S. playwright: Lyman, in *The Ride down Mount Morgan* (1991), Act 2

7 You can tell a lot about a fellow's character by his way of eating jelly beans.
Ronald Reagan (b.1911), U.S. Republican politician and president: quoted in the *New York Times*, 15 Jan. 1981

8 The only thing that endures is character. Fame and wealth – all that is illusion. All that endures is character.

O.J. Simpson (b.1947), U.S. footballer and commentator: Nov. 1995, following his acquittal on murder charges, quoted in *The Guardian* (London), 30 Dec. 1995

CHARM

1 A man of such obvious and exemplary charm must be a liar.
Anita Brookner (b.1938), British novelist and art historian: Rachel, referring to Michael Sandberg, in *A Friend from England* (1987), Ch.3

2 You know what charm is: a way of getting the answer yes without having asked any clear question.
Albert Camus (1913–1960), French-Algerian philosopher and author: the narrator (Jean-Baptiste Clamence), in *The Fall* (1956), p.43 of Hamish Hamilton edn. (1957)

3 What is charm then? The free giving of a grace, the spending of something given by nature in her role of spendthrift … something extra, superfluous, unnecessary, essentially a power thrown away.
Doris Lessing (b.1919), British novelist: *Particularly Cats* (1967), Ch.9

4 If most men and women were forced to rely upon physical charm to attract lovers, their sexual lives would be not only meager but in a youth-worshiping country like America painfully brief.
Gore Vidal (b.1925), U.S. novelist and critic: 'Notes on Pornography', publ. in the *New York Review of Books*, 31 March 1966

CHAT SHOWS

1 The failures of the press have contributed immensely to the emergence of a talk-show nation, in which public discourse is reduced to ranting and raving and posturing. We now have a mainstream press whose news agenda is increasingly influenced by this netherworld.
Carl Bernstein (b.1944), U.S. journalist: in *The Guardian* (London), 3 June 1992

2 Here's Johnny!
Johnny Carson (b.1925), U.S. chat-show host and comedian: *Tonight Show Starring Johnny Carson* (U.S. TV variety show, 1962–92). Carson's opening was famously mimicked with manic glee by Jack Nicholson in *The Shining* (1980)

3 The talk shows are stuffed full of sufferers who have regained their health – congressmen who suffered through a serious spell of boozing and skirt-chasing, White House aides who were stricken cruelly with overweening ambition, movie stars and baseball players who came down with acute cases of wanting to trash hotel rooms while under the influence of recrea-

tional drugs. Most of them have found God, or at least a publisher.

Calvin Trillin (b.1935), U.S. journalist and author: 'Diseases of the Mighty', publ. in *The Nation* (New York), 19 Oct. 1985

See also Winfrey on SYMPATHY

CHEMISTRY

1 For me chemistry represented an indefinite cloud of future potentialities which enveloped my life to come in black volutes torn by fiery flashes, like those which had hidden Mount Sinai. Like Moses, from that cloud I expected my law, the principle of order in me, around me, and in the world. ... I would watch the buds swell in spring, the mica glint in the granite, my own hands, and I would say to myself: 'I will understand this, too, I will understand everything.'

Primo Levi (1919–1987), Italian chemist and author: *The Periodic Table* (1975; tr.1984), 'Hydrogen'

2 There's nothing colder than chemistry.

Anita Loos (1893–1981), U.S. novelist and screenwriter: *Kiss Hollywood Good-by* (1974), Ch.21

CHESS

1 The chess pieces are the block alphabet which shapes thoughts; and these thoughts, although making a visual design on the chess-board, express their beauty *abstractly* , like a poem. ... I have come to the personal conclusion that while all artists are not chess players, all chess players are artists.

Marcel Duchamp (1887–1968), French artist: address 30 Aug. 1952, New York State Chess Association, quoted in 'La Vie en Rrose' by Kynaston McShine, publ. in *Marcel Duchamp* (ed. Anne d'Harnoncourt and Kynaston McShine, 1989). Duchamp had given up painting in favour of chess 30 years before

2 Women, by their nature, are not exceptional chess players: they are not great fighters.

Gary Kasparov (b.1963), Russian chess player: in *The Times* (London), 9 Oct. 1990

3 Chess is ruthless: you've got to be prepared to kill people.

Nigel Short (b.1965), British chess player: in *The Observer* (London), 11 Aug. 1991

CHICAGO *see under* THE UNITED STATES

CHILD ABUSE

1 Child molestation is a touchy subject.... Read the papers! Half the country's doing it!

Woody Allen (b.1935), U.S. film-maker: Mickey Sachs (Woody Allen), in *Hannah and Her Sisters* (film; written and directed by Woody Allen, 1986)

2 Children's bodies aren't like automobiles with the assailant's fingerprints lingering on the wheel. The world of sexual abuse is quintessentially secret. It is the perfect crime.

Beatrix Campbell (b.1947), British journalist: *Unofficial Secrets* (1988), Ch.2

3 The germ of violence is laid bare in the child abuser by the sheer accident of his individual experience ... in a word, to a greater degree than we like to admit, we are all potential child abusers.

F. Gonzalez-Crussi (b.1936), Mexican professor of pathology and author: *Notes of an Anatomist* (1985), 'Reflections on Child Abuse'

4 I am not sure how many 'sins' I would recognize in the world. Some would surely be defused by changed circumstances. But I can imagine none that is more irredeemably sinful than the betrayal, the exploitation, of the young by those who should care for them.

Elizabeth Janeway (b.1913), U.S. author and critic: 'Incest: A Rational Look at the Oldest Taboo', publ. in *Ms.* (New York), Nov. 1981

5 The protection of a ten-year-old girl from her father's advances is a necessary condition of social order, but the protection of the father from temptation is a necessary condition of his continued social adjustment. The protections that are built up in the child against desire for the parent become the essential counterpart to the attitudes in the parent that protect the child.

Margaret Mead (1901–1978), U.S. anthropologist: *Male and Female* (1949), Ch.9

6 The farmer takes Jill down the well
& all the king's horses
& all the king's men
can't put that little girl together again
crooked man
crooked man
pumpkin eater
childhood stealer.

Sapphire (b.1950), U.S. author and poet: 'Mickey Mouse Was a Scorpio', publ. in *Re/Search* (San Francisco), No.13, 1991, 'Angry Women'. Sapphire recalled that it was the writing of this poem that first made her suspect she had been abused as a child

See also Janeway on SEXUAL DEVIATIONS

CHILDBIRTH

1 No phallic hero, no matter what he does to himself or to another to prove his courage, ever matches the solitary, existential courage of the woman who gives birth.
Andrea Dworkin (b.1946), U.S. feminist critic: 'The Sexual Politics of Fear and Courage', speech, first delivered 12 March 1975, Queens College, City University of New York, publ. in *Our Blood* (1976), Ch.5

2 Childbirth is more admirable than conquest, more amazing than self-defense, and as courageous as either one.
Gloria Steinem (b.1934), U.S. feminist writer and editor: 'In Praise Of Women's Bodies', publ. in *Ms.* (New York), April 1981, rep. in *Outrageous Acts and Everyday Rebellions* (1983)

3 Push, rend, slither, pop. Baby's here. Baby cries.
Fay Weldon (b.1933), British novelist: *Wicked Women* (1995), 'Pains'

CHILDHOOD

1 *Childhood lasts all through life.* It returns to animate broad sections of adult life. ... Poets will help us to find this living childhood within us, this permanent, durable immobile world.
Gaston Bachelard (1884–1962), French scientist, philosopher and literary theorist: *The Poetics of Reverie* (1960; tr.1969), 'Introduction', Sct.6

2 I generally assume that childhoods more or less ended with the First World War – halcyon childhoods certainly – and that most of them since have been the 'forgotten boredom' of Larkin's poem 'Coming'. Anyone born after 1940 got the Utility version, childhood according to the Authorized Economy Standard.
Alan Bennett (b.1934), British playwright: *Writing Home* (1994), 'Bad John'

3 Nothing fortuitous happens in a child's world. There are no accidents. Everything is connected with everything else and everything can be explained by everything else. ... For a young child everything that happens is a necessity.
John Berger (b.1926), British author and critic: *A Fortunate Man* (1967), p.122 of Writers and Readers Publishing Cooperative edn. (1976)

4 Being a child is horrible. It is slightly better than being a tree or a piece of heavy machinery but not half as good as being a domestic cat.
Julie Burchill (b.1960), British journalist and author: *Damaged Gods* (1986), 'Are You Sitting Comfortably?'

5 Seven to eleven is a huge chunk of life, full of dulling and forgetting. It is fabled that we slowly lose the gift of speech with animals, that birds no longer visit our windowsills to converse. As our eyes grow accustomed to sight they armour themselves against wonder.
Leonard Cohen (b.1934), Canadian singer, poet and novelist: *The Favourite Game* (1963), Bk.1, Ch.17

6 Childhood is a disease – a sickness that you grow out of.
William Golding (1911–1993), British author: quoted in *The Guardian* (London), 22 June 1990

7 For children, childhood is timeless. It's always the present. Everything is in the present tense. Of course they have memories. Of course, time shifts a little for them and Christmas comes round in the end. But they don't *feel* it. Today is what they feel, and when they say 'When I grow up ... ' there's always an edge of disbelief – how could they ever be other than what they are?
Ian McEwan (b.1948), British author: Charles Darke, in *The Child in Time* (1987), Ch.2

8 I think our childhood goes back thousands of years, farther back than the memory of any race.
Ben Okri (b.1959), Nigerian-born British author: quoted in *The Times* (London), 1 April 1995

9 I am convinced that, except in a few extraordinary cases, one form or another of an unhappy childhood is essential to the formation of exceptional gifts.
Thornton Wilder (1897–1975), U.S. novelist and playwright: interview in *Writers at Work* (First Series, ed. Malcolm Cowley, 1958)

CHILD-REARING

1 Anyone who has a child today should train him to be either a physicist or a ballet dancer. Then he'll escape.
W.H. Auden (1907–1973), Anglo-American poet: *The Table Talk of W.H. Auden* (comp. Alan Ansen, ed. Nicholas Jenkins, 1990), 'January 15, 1947'

2 For that's what a woman, a mother wants – to teach her children to take an interest in life. She knows it's safer for them to be interested in other people's happiness than to believe in their own.
Marguerite Duras (1914–1996), French author and film-maker: *Practicalities* (1987; tr.1990), 'House and Home'

3 No culture on earth outside of mid-century suburban America has ever deployed one woman per child without simultaneously assigning her such major productive activities as weaving, farming, gathering, temple maintenance, and tent-building. The reason is that

full-time, one-on-one child-raising is not good for women *or* children.

Barbara Ehrenreich (b.1941), U.S. author and columnist: 'Stop Ironing the Diapers' (1989), rep. in *The Worst Years of Our Lives* (1991)

4   Every luxury was lavished on you – atheism, breast-feeding, circumcision.

Joe Orton (1933–1967), British playwright: Hal, in *Loot* (1967), Act 1

CHILDREN

1   Children's talent to endure stems from their ignorance of alternatives.

Maya Angelou (b.1928), U.S. author: *I Know Why the Caged Bird Sings* (1969), Ch.17

2   The countenances of children, like those of animals, are masks, not faces, for they have not yet developed a significant profile of their own.

W.H. Auden (1907–1973), Anglo-American poet: *A Certain World* (1970), 'Face, The Human'

3   Even a minor event in the life of a child is an event of that child's world and thus a world event.

Gaston Bachelard (1884–1962), French scientist, philosopher and literary theorist: *Fragments of a Poetics of Fire* (1988; tr.1990), Ch.1, 'The Phoenix, a Linguistic Phenomenon'

4   Children have never been very good at listening to their elders, but they have never failed to imitate them.

James Baldwin (1924–1987), U.S. author: 'The Precarious Vogue of Ingmar Bergman', first publ. in *Esquire* (New York), April 1960, rep. in *Nobody Knows My Name* (1961)

5   A society in which adults are estranged from the world of children, and often from their own childhood, tends to hear children's speech only as a foreign language, or as a lie. ... Children have been treated ... as congenital fibbers, fakers and fantasisers.

Beatrix Campbell (b.1947), British journalist: *Unofficial Secrets* (1988), Ch.2

6   Adults find pleasure in deceiving a child. They consider it necessary, but they also enjoy it. The children very quickly figure it out and then practise deception themselves.

Elias Canetti (1905–1994), Austrian novelist and philosopher: *The Secret Heart Of The Clock: Notes, Aphorisms, Fragments 1973–1985* (1991), '1980'

7   It takes three to make a child.

e e cummings (1894–1962), U.S. poet: 'Jottings', first publ. in *Wake*, No.10, 1951, rep. in *A Miscellany* (ed. George J. Firmage, 1958)

8   Strange new problems are being reported in the growing generations of children whose mothers were always there, driving them around, helping them with their homework – an inability to endure pain or discipline or pursue any self-sustained goal of any sort, a devastating boredom with life.

Betty Friedan (b.1921), U.S. feminist writer: *The Feminine Mystique* (1963), Ch.1

9   She discovered with great delight that one does not love one's children just because they are one's children but because of the friendship formed while raising them.

Gabriel García Márquez (b.1928), Colombian author: of Fermina Daza, in *Love in the Time of Cholera* (1985; tr. 1988), p.207 of Penguin edn. (1988)

10 We in the West do not refrain from childbirth because we are concerned about the population explosion or because we feel we cannot afford children, but because we do not like children.

Germaine Greer (b.1939), Australian feminist writer: *Sex and Destiny* (1984), Ch.1

11 Our children will not survive our habits of thinking, our failures of the spirit, our wreck of the universe into which we bring new life as blithely as we do. Mostly, our children will resemble our own misery and spite and anger, because we give them no choice about it. In the name of motherhood and fatherhood and education and good manners, we threaten and suffocate and bind and ensnare and bribe and trick children into wholesale emulation of our ways.

June Jordan (b.1936), U.S. poet and civil rights activist: 'Old Stories: New Lives', keynote address to Child Welfare League of America, 1978, publ. in *Moving Towards Home: Political Essays* (1989)

12 Nothing you do for children is ever wasted. They seem not to notice us, hovering, averting our eyes, and they seldom offer thanks, but what we do for them is never wasted.

Garrison Keillor (b.1942), U.S. author: *Leaving Home* (1987), 'Easter'

13 All God's children are not beautiful. Most of God's children are, in fact, barely presentable.

Fran Lebowitz (b.1951), U.S. journalist: *Metropolitan Life* (1978), 'Manners'

14 For little boys are rancorous
    When robbed of any myth,
    And spiteful and cantankerous
    To all their kin and kith.
    But little girls can draw conclusions
    And profit from their lost illusions.

Phyllis McGinley (1905–1978), U.S. poet and author: last verse of 'What Every Woman Knows', publ. in *Times Three* (1960)

15 If help and salvation are to come, they can only come from the children, for the children are the makers of men.

Maria Montessori (1870–1952), Italian educationist: *The Absorbent Mind* (1949), Ch.1

16 One can love a child, perhaps, more deeply than one can love another adult, but it is rash to assume that the child feels any love in return.
George Orwell (1903–1950), British author: 'Such, Such were the Joys' (1947), rep. in *The Collected Essays, Journalism and Letters of George Orwell* (ed. Sonia Orwell and Ian Angus, 1968), Vol.IV. Orwell added: 'Looking back on my own childhood, after the infant years were over, I do not believe that I ever felt love for any mature person, except my mother.... Love, the spontaneous, unqualified emotion of love was something I could only feel for people who were young'

17 Children's liberation is the next item on our civil rights shopping list.
Letty Cottin Pogrebin (b.1939), U.S. journalist and author: 'Down with Sexist Upbringing', publ. in *The First Ms Reader* (ed. Francine Klagsbrun, 1972)

18 If you have a great passion it seems that the logical thing is to see the fruit of it, and the fruit are children.
Roman Polanski (b.1933), Polish film-maker: in the *Independent on Sunday* (London), 12 May 1991

19 I keep picturing all these little kids playing some game in this big field of rye and all. ... If they're running and they don't look where they're going I have to come out from somewhere and *catch* them. That's all I'd do all day. I'd just be the catcher in the rye and all. I know it's crazy, but that's the only thing I'd really like to be.
J.D. Salinger (b.1919), U.S. author: the narrator (Holden Caulfield), in *The Catcher in the Rye* (1951), Ch.22. The novel's title – and the image described above – derives from the Robert Burns poem, 'Comin' Through the Rye'

20 A child loves his play, not because it's easy, but because it's hard.
Benjamin Spock (b.1903), U.S. paediatrician and author: *Baby and Child Care* (1946), 'Managing Young Children'

21 When the human being loses interest in the child, he is in great peril. And we are in great peril because more and more children are being thrown into schools, into the hands of the professionals.
Laurens van der Post (1906–1996), South African writer and philosopher: *A Walk with a White Bushman* (1986), p.49 of Chatto & Windus edn.

22 Americans, indeed, often seem to be so overwhelmed by their children that they'll do anything for them except stay married to the co-producer.

Katharine Whitehorn (b.1926), British journalist: *Observations* (1970), 'Suffer How Many of the Little Children?'

23 Winning children (who appear so guileless) are children who have discovered how effective charm and modesty and a delicately calculated spontaneity are in winning what they want.
Thornton Wilder (1897–1975), U.S. novelist and playwright: interview in *Writers at Work* (First Series, ed. Malcolm Cowley, 1958)

See also Spock on ALTRUISM; McAliskey on ILLEGITIMACY; King on THE UNITED STATES

CHINA

1 Nothing and no one can destroy the Chinese people. They are relentless survivors. They are the oldest civilized people on earth. Their civilization passes through phases but its basic characteristics remain the same. They yield, they bend to the wind, but they never break.
Pearl S. Buck (1892–1973), U.S. author: *China, Past and Present* (1972), Ch.1

2 A black sun has appeared in the sky of my motherland.
Kaixi Wuer, Chinese student leader: on the massacre in Tiananmen Square, Beijing, quoted in *The Independent* (London), 29 June 1989

3 Even one billion Chinese do not a superpower make.
John Lukacs (b.1924), Hungarian-born U.S. historian: 'The Stirrings of History', publ. in *Harper's Magazine* (New York), Aug.1990

4 Apart from their other characteristics, the outstanding thing about China's 600 million people is that they are 'poor and blank.' This may seem a bad thing, but in reality it is a good thing. Poverty gives rise to the desire for change, the desire for action and the desire for revolution. On a blank sheet of paper free from any mark, the freshest and most beautiful pictures can be painted.
Mao Zedong (1893–1976), Chinese leader: 'Introducing a Co-operative' (15 April 1958), quoted in *Quotations from Chairman Mao Tse-Tung* (1967)

5 In a country where misery and want were the foundation of the social structure, famine was periodic, death from starvation common, disease pervasive, thievery normal, and graft and corruption taken for granted, the elimination of these conditions in Communist China is so striking that negative aspects of the new rule fade in relative importance.
Barbara Tuchman (1912–1989), U.S. historian: *Notes from China* (1972), Ch.1

CHIVALRY

1 When a man opens the car door for his wife, it's either a new car or a new wife.
Prince Philip, Duke of Edinburgh (b.1921): quoted in *Today* (London), 2 March 1988

2 There is a deep, natural obligation in men who are really men to be chivalrous to any woman in a way they need not be chivalrous to one another.
Laurens van der Post (1906–1996), South African writer and philosopher: *A Walk with a White Bushman* (1986), p.95 of Chatto & Windus edn.

CHRISTIANITY

1 The trouble with born-again Christians is that they are an even bigger pain the second time around.
Herb Caen (b.1916), U.S. columnist and author: in the *San Francisco Chronicle*, 20 July 1981

2 White people really deal more with God and black people with Jesus.
Nikki Giovanni (b.1943), U.S. poet: conversation with James Baldwin, 4 Nov. 1971, London, publ. in *A Dialogue* (1973)

3 Christianity will go. It will vanish and shrink. I needn't argue with that; I'm right and I will be proved right. We're more popular than Jesus now; I don't know which will go first – rock and roll or Christianity.
John Lennon (1940–1980), British rock musician: interview in the *Evening Standard* (London), 4 March 1966. The remark provoked a storm of reaction, especially in the U.S., causing Lennon to explain himself at a press conference in Chicago, 11 Aug. 1966: 'I'm not saying that we're better or greater, or comparing us with Jesus Christ as a person, or God as a thing, or whatever it is. I just said what I said, and it was wrong, or it was taken wrong. And now it's all this.' In his autobiography, *A Moveable Feast* (1964), Ch.18, Ernest Hemingway quoted Zelda Fitzgerald: 'Ernest, don't you think Al Jolson is greater than Jesus?'

4 The catholicity of Christianity integrates the small and touching household gods into the worship of saints, and local cults. Through sublimation, Christianity continues to give piety roots, nurturing itself on landscapes and memories culled from family, tribe and nation. That is why it conquered humanity.
Emmanuel Levinas (b.1905), French Jewish philosopher: 'Heidegger, Gagarin and Us' (1961), rep. in *Difficult Freedom* (1990), Pt.5

5 Nothing does more to activate Christian divisions than talk about Christian unity.
Conor Cruise O'Brien (b.1917), Irish historian, diplomat and critic: in *The Times* (London), 3 Oct. 1989

See also CATHOLICISM; THE CHURCH; EVANGELISM; King on FUNDAMENTALISM; JESUS CHRIST; PROTESTANTISM

CHRISTMAS

1 And is it true? And is it true,
This most tremendous tale of all,
Seen in a stained-glass window's hue,
A Baby in an ox's stall?
The Maker of the stars and sea
Become a Child on earth for me?
John Betjeman (1906–1984), British poet: 'Christmas', St.6, publ. in *A Few Late Chrysanthemums* (1954)

2 Is not Christmas the only occasion when one gets drunk *for the children's sake* ?
James Cameron (1911–1985), British journalist: quoted in the *Independent on Sunday* (London), 20 Dec. 1991

3 Midnight, and the clock strikes. It is Christmas Day, the werewolves' birthday, the door of the solstice still wide enough open to let them all slink through.
Angela Carter (1940–1992), British author: 'The Company of Wolves', publ. in *Bananas* (ed. Emma Tenant, 1977)

4 A lovely thing about Christmas is that it's compulsory, like a thunderstorm, and we all go through it together.
Garrison Keillor (b.1942), U.S. author: *Leaving Home* (1987), 'Exiles'

5 Please to put a nickel,
Please to put a dime.
How petitions trickle
In at Christmas time!
Phyllis McGinley (1905–1978), U.S. poet and author: 'Dear Madam: We Know You Will Want to Contribute ... ', publ. in *Times Three* (1960)

6 From a commercial point of view, if Christmas did not exist it would be necessary to invent it.
Katharine Whitehorn (b.1926), British journalist: *Roundabout* (1962), 'The Office Party'

THE CHURCH

1 I believe with all my heart that the Church of Jesus Christ should be a Church of blurred edges.
George Carey (b.1935), British ecclesiastic and Archbishop of Canterbury: in *The Independent* (London), 15 July 1992

2 A Church which has lost its memory is in a sad state of senility.
Henry Chadwick (b.1920), British educator and historian: in *The Daily Telegraph* (London), 10 Feb. 1988

3 Those who marry God can become domesticated too – it's just as hum-drum a marriage as all the others. The word 'Love' means a formal touch of the lips as in the ceremony of the Mass, and '*Ave Maria* ' like 'dearest' is a phrase to open a letter.
Graham Greene (1904–1991), British novelist: *A Burnt-Out Case* (1961), Pt.1, Ch.1, Sct.2

4 But a priest's life is not supposed to be well-rounded; it is supposed to be one-pointed – a compass, not a weathercock.
Aldous Huxley (1894–1963), British author: *The Devils of Loudun* (1952), Ch.1

5 The priesthood is a marriage. People often start by falling in love, and they go on for years without realizing that that love must change into some other love which is so unlike it that it can hardly be recognised as love at all.
Iris Murdoch (b.1919), British novelist and philosopher: Brendan Craddock, in *Henry and Cato* (1976), Pt.2, 'The Great Teacher'

6 Many are called but few are chosen. There are sayings of Christ which suggest that the Church he came to establish will always be a minority affair.
Edward Norman (b.1946), British ecclesiastic and educator: in *The Times* (London), 20 Feb. 1992

7 I think a bishop who doesn't give offence to anyone is probably not a good bishop.
James Thompson (b.1936), British cleric: in *The Daily Telegraph* (London), 30 May 1991

THE CHURCH: and Society

1 The question confronting the Church today is not any longer whether the man in the street can grasp a religious message, but how to employ the communications media so as to let him have the full impact of the Gospel message.
Pope John Paul II [Karol Wojtyla] (b.1920), Polish ecclesiastic: in the *International Herald Tribune* (Paris), 8 May 1989

2 Yes, I see the Church as the body of Christ. But, oh! How we have blemished and scarred that body through social neglect and through fear of being nonconformists.
Martin Luther King Jr. (1929–1968), U.S. clergyman and civil rights leader: 'Letter from Birmingham Jail', open letter addressed to clergymen, 16 April 1963, publ. in *Why We Can't Wait* (1963)

3 Standards of conduct appropriate to civil society or the workings of a democracy cannot be purely and simply applied to the Church.
Joseph Ratzinger (b.1927), German ecclesiastic and cardinal : in *The Independent* (London), 27 June 1990

4 I never liked the prospect of enquiring into what happened in a man's bedroom unless he was prepared to tell me.
Robert Runcie (b.1921), British ecclesiastic and Archbishop of Canterbury: in conversation with Anthony Howard, on *The Purple, the Blue and the Red*, BBC Radio 4, 16 May 1996, in reply to the question whether he had ever knowingly ordained practising homosexuals

5 The priesthood in many ways is the ultimate closet in Western civilization, where gay people particularly have hidden for the past two thousand years.
John Spong (b.1931), U.S. ecclesiastic: in *The Daily Telegraph* (London), 12 July 1990

See also Pius XII on TECHNOLOGY

THE CHURCH: and Women

1 A woman's asking for equality in the church would be comparable to a black person's demanding equality in the Ku Klux Klan.
Mary Daly (b.1928), U.S. educator, writer and theologian: new autobiographical preface to *The Church and the Second Sex* (1975)

2 I'm a priest, not a priestess. ... 'Priestess' implies mumbo jumbo and all sorts of pagan goings-on. Those who oppose us would love to call us priestesses. They can call us all the names in the world – it's better than being invisible.
Carter Heyward (b.1946), U.S. Episcopal priest: quoted in *Ms.* (New York), Dec. 1974

CHURCHES

1 It's a good job Mrs T[hatcher] isn't Archbishop of Canterbury, or we would just be left with the cathedrals and a few other 'viable places of worship'.
Alan Bennett (b.1934), British playwright: journal entry, 20 May 1985, publ. in *Writing Home* (1994), 'Diaries 1980–1990'

2 A serious house on serious earth it is,
In whose blent air all our compulsions meet,
Are recognised, and robed as destinies.
Philip Larkin (1922–1985), British poet: 'Church Going', publ. in *The Less Deceived* (1955)

3 In iconographic terms, the cathedral is a decorated shed.
Robert Venturi (b.1925), U.S. architect: *Learning from Las Vegas* by Robert Venturi, Denise Scott Brown and Stephen Izenour (1972; rev.1977), Pt.2, 'Historical and Other Precedents'

CHURCHGOING

1 He was of the faith chiefly in the sense that the church he currently did not attend was Catholic.
Kingsley Amis (1922–1995), British novelist and poet: referring to Roger Micheldene, in *One Fat Englishman* (1963), Ch.8

2 We praise Him, we bless Him, we adore Him, we glorify Him, and we wonder who is that baritone across the aisle and that pretty women on our right who smells of apple blossoms. Our bowels stir and our cod itches and we amend our prayers for the spiritual life with the hope that it will not be too spiritual.
John Cheever (1912–1982), U.S. author: journal entry, 1956, publ. in *John Cheever: The Journals* (ed. Robert Gottlieb, 1991), 'The Late Forties and the Fifties'

3 I don't go to church. Kneeling bags my nylons.
Jan Sterling (b.1923), U.S. actress: Lorraine (Jan Sterling), in *The Big Carnival* (film; screenplay by Billy Wilder, Lesser Samuel and Walter Newman, produced and directed by Billy Wilder, 1951). The film was originally released under the title *Ace in the Hole*

4 She say, Celie, tell the truth, have you ever found God in church? I never did. I just found a bunch of folks hoping for him to show. Any God I ever felt in church I brought in with me. And I think all the other folks did too. They come to church to *share* God, not find God.
Alice Walker (b.1944), U.S. author and critic: Shug, in *The Color Purple* (1982), p.165 of Women's Press edn. (1983)

WINSTON CHURCHILL

1 His ear is so sensitively attuned to the bugle note of history that he is often deaf to the more raucous clamour of contemporary life.
Aneurin Bevan (1897–1960), British Labour politician: quoted in *Aneurin Bevan*, Vol.I, by Michael Foot (1962), Ch.10. On another occasion, Bevan said of Churchill, 'He is a man suffering from petrified adolescence' (quoted in *Aneurin Bevan* by Vincent Brome (1953), Ch.11)

2 Thus, then, on the night of the tenth of May, at the outset of this mighty battle, I acquired the chief power in the State, which henceforth I wielded in ever-growing measure for five years and three months of world war, at the end of which time, all our enemies having surrendered unconditionally or being about to do so, I was immediately dismissed by the British electorate from all further conduct of their affairs.
Winston Churchill (1874–1965), British statesman and author: *The Second World War* (1948), Vol.I,

Bk.2, Ch.17, 'The Gathering Storm'. Churchill was re-elected prime minster in 1951

3 Old politicians, like old actors, revive in the limelight. The vacancy which afflicts them in private momentarily lifts when, once more, they feel the eyes of an audience upon them. Their old passion for holding the centre of the stage guides their uncertain footsteps to where the footlights shine, and summons up a wintry smile when the curtain rises.
Malcolm Muggeridge (1903–1990), British journalist and broadcaster: of Churchill's last years, in *Tread Softly For You Tread on My Jokes* (1966), 'Twilight of Greatness'

CINEMA

1 The cinema gives us a substitute world which fits our desires.
André Bazin (1918–1958), French film critic: quoted in *The New Wave* by James Monaco (1976), Ch.7. The quotation features in the closing credits of Jean-Luc Godard's film, *Le Mépris* (1963)

2 Film as dream, film as music. No art passes our conscience in the way film does, and goes directly to our feelings, deep down into the dark rooms of our souls.
Ingmar Bergman (b.1918), Swedish stage and film writer-director: quoted by John Berger in 'Ev'ry Time We Say Goodbye', publ. in *Sight and Sound* (London), June 1991

3 To moan more meaningfully than man has moaned before is the American cinema's aim.
Julie Burchill (b.1960), British journalist and author: *Girls on Film* (1986), Ch.14

4 The motion picture made in Hollywood, if it is to create art at all, must do so within such strangling limitations of subject and treatment that it is a blind wonder it ever achieves any distinction beyond the purely mechanical slickness of a glass and chromium bathroom.
Raymond Chandler (1880–1959), U.S. author: 'Oscar Night in Hollywood', publ. in *Atlantic Monthly* (Boston), March 1948

5 A film is a petrified fountain of thought.
Jean Cocteau (1889–1963), French author and film-maker: in *Esquire* (New York), Feb. 1961

6 If you can't *believe* a little in what you see on the screen, it's not worth wasting your time on cinema.
Serge Daney (1944–1992), French film critic: quoted in *Sight and Sound* (London), July 1992

7 Any movie that makes you a little uncomfortable is good news to me, because it means you're experiencing things that you are not familiar with.
Brian de Palma (b.1940), U.S. film-maker: interview in *Sight and Sound* (London), Dec. 1992

8 Film is more than the twentieth-century art. It's another part of the twentieth-century mind. It's the world seen from inside. We've come to a certain point in the history of film. If a thing can be filmed, the film is implied in the thing itself. This is where we are. The twentieth century is *on film*.... You have to ask yourself if there's anything about us more important than the fact that we're constantly on film, constantly watching ourselves.
Don DeLillo (b.1926), U.S. author: Frank Volterra, in *The Names* (1982), Ch.8

9 It struck me that the movies had spent more than half a century saying 'They lived happily ever after' and the following quarter-century warning that they'll be lucky to make it through the weekend. Possibly now we are entering a third era in which the movies will be sounding a note of cautious optimism: You know it just might work.
Nora Ephron (b.1941), U.S. author and journalist: on her screenplay for *When Harry Met Sally ...* (1989), quoted in the *Los Angeles Times*, 27 July 1989

10 Photography is truth. The cinema is truth twenty-four times per second.
Jean-Luc Godard (b.1930), French film-maker and author: *Le Petit Soldat* (film; written and directed by Jean-Luc Godard, 1960)

11 Films are created when there's no-one looking. They are the Invisible. What you can't see is the Incredible – and it's the task of the cinema to show you that.
Jean-Luc Godard: interview by Wim Wenders at the Cannes Film Festival, publ. in *The Logic of Images* (1988; tr.1991), 'Chambre 666'

12 Movies are one of the bad habits that corrupted our century. Of their many sins, I offer as the worst their effect on the intellectual side of the nation. It is chiefly from that viewpoint I write of them – as an eruption of trash that has lamed the American mind and retarded Americans from becoming a cultured people.
Ben Hecht (1893–1964), U.S. journalist, author and screenwriter: *A Child of the Century* (1954), Bk.5, 'What the Movies Are'. Hecht – who enjoyed a profitable career as a Hollywood screenwriter (*see* Hecht on CINEMA: THE SCREENWRITERS) – continued, 'They have slapped into the American mind more human misinformation in one evening than the Dark Ages could muster in a decade'

13 You write a book like that that you're fond of over the years, then you see that happen to it, it's like pissing in your father's beer.
Ernest Hemingway (1899–1961), U.S. author: after seeing David O. Selznick's remake of *A Farewell to Arms* (1957), quoted in *Papa Hemingway* by A.E. Hotchner (1966 edn.)

14 You should look straight at a film; that's the only way to see one. Film is not the art of scholars but of illiterates.
Werner Herzog (b.1942), German film-maker: in the *New York Times*, 11 Sept. 1977

15 Some films are slices of life. Mine are slices of cake.
Alfred Hitchcock (1899–1980), British film-maker: interview, Aug. 1962, publ. in *Hitchcock* by François Truffaut (1966; rev.1984), Ch.4. The quote appeared (more coherently) as 'For me, the cinema is not a slice of life, but a piece of cake,' quoted in *The Sunday Times* (London), 6 March 1977

16 All television ever did was shrink the demand for ordinary movies. The demand for extraordinary movies increased. If any one thing is wrong with the movie industry today, it is the unrelenting effort to astonish.
Clive James (b.1939), Australian writer and critic: in *The Observer* (London), 16 June 1979

17 The preserve of ambition and folly in pursuit of illusion, or ... delusion.
Derek Jarman (1942–1994), British film-maker, artist and author: of the film industry, in journal entry, 22 Feb. 1989, publ. in *Modern Nature: The Journals of Derek Jarman* (1991)

18 The movies are still where it happens, not for much longer perhaps, but the movies are still the art form that uses the material of our lives and the art form that we use.
Pauline Kael (b.1919), U.S. film critic: *I Lost it at the Movies* (1965), 'The Glamour of Delinquency'

19 The words 'Kiss Kiss Bang Bang,' which I saw on an Italian movie poster, are perhaps the briefest statement imaginable of the basic appeal of movies. This appeal is what attracts us, and ultimately what makes us despair when we begin to understand how seldom movies are more than this.
Pauline Kael: *Kiss Kiss Bang Bang* (1968), 'A Note on the Title'

20 Life in the movie business is like the beginning of a new love affair: it's full of surprises and you're constantly getting fucked.
David Mamet (b.1947), U.S. playwright: Charlie Fox, in *Speed The Plow* (1988), Sc.1

21 A film is difficult to explain because it is easy to understand.
Christian Metz (b.1941), French film theorist: quoted in *The New Wave* by James Monaco (1976), Ch.7

22 Cinema is the culmination of the obsessive, mechanistic male drive in western culture. The movie projector is an Apollonian straight-shooter, demonstrating the link between aggression and art. Every pictorial framing is a ritual limitation, a barred precinct.
Camille Paglia (b.1947), U.S. author and critic: *Sexual Personae* (1990), Ch.1

23 My belief is that no movie, nothing in life, leaves people neutral. You either leave them up or you leave them down.
David Puttnam (b.1941), British film-maker: in the *International Herald Tribune* (Paris), 23 Oct. 1989

24 Does art reflect life? In movies, yes. Because more than any other art form, films have been a mirror held up to society's porous face.
Marjorie Rosen (b.1942), U.S. film critic: preface to *Popcorn Venus* (1973)

25 Movies are about people who *do* things. The number one fantasy of the cinema is that we can do something – we are relatively impotent in our own lifes so we go to movies to watch people who are in control of their lives.
Paul Schrader (b.1946), U.S. film-maker: interview in *Schrader on Schrader* (ed. Kevin Jackson, 1990), Ch.5

26 In good films, there is always a directness that entirely frees us from the itch to interpret.
Susan Sontag (b.1933), U.S. essayist: 'Against Interpretation', Sct.7, first publ. in *The Evergreen Review* (New York), Dec. 1964, rep. in *Against Interpretation* (1966)

27 One of the joys of going to the movies was that it was trashy, and we should never lose that.
Oliver Stone (b.1946), U.S. film-maker: in the *International Herald Tribune* (Paris), 15 Feb. 1988

28 Film music should have the same relationship to the film drama that somebody's piano playing in my living room has to the book I am reading.
Igor Stravinsky (1882–1971), Russian-American composer: in *Music Digest*, Sept. 1946

29 Movies are an art form, and twenty per cent of that art form is supplied by what the audience brings to the movie.
Quentin Tarantino (b.1958), U.S. film-maker: quoted in *Quentin Tarantino: The Man and His Movies* by Jami Bernard (1995), Ch.10

30 People sometimes say that the way things happen in the movies is unreal, but actually it's the way things happen to you in life that's unreal. The movies make emotions look so strong and real, whereas when things really do happen to you, it's like watching television – you don't feel anything.
Andy Warhol (c.1928–1987), U.S. Pop artist: *From A to B and Back Again* (1975), Ch.6

31 Nobody should come to the movies unless he believes in heroes.
John Wayne (1907–1979), U.S. actor: quoted in *The Official John Wayne Reference Book* by Charles John Kieskalt (1985; rev.1993)

32 I rather think the cinema will die. Look at the energy being exerted to revive it – yesterday it was color, today three dimensions. I don't give it forty years more. Witness the decline of conversation. Only the Irish have remained incomparable conversationalists, maybe because technical progress has passed them by.
Orson Welles (1915–1985), U.S. film-maker and actor: *Les Nouvelles Littéraires* 1953, quoted in *Citizen Welles* by Frank Brady (1989), Ch.16

See also Brustein on AUDIENCES; Mamet on DISASTERS; Sontag on FICTION: SCIENCE FICTION; HOLLYWOOD; Goldman on STARDOM; Warhol on THE UNITED STATES

CINEMA: Horror & Suspense

1 I think of horror films as art, as films of confrontation. Films that make you confront aspects of your own life that are difficult to face. Just because you're making a horror film doesn't mean you can't make an artful film.
David Cronenberg (b.1943), Canadian film-maker: *Cronenberg on Cronenberg* (ed. Chris Rodley, 1992), Ch.4

2 One of the things that horror stories can do is show us the archetypes of the unconscious; we can see the dark side without having to confront it directly. Also, ghost stories appeal to our craving for immortality. If you can be afraid of a ghost, then you have to believe that a ghost may exist. And if a ghost exists then oblivion might not be the end.
Stanley Kubrick (b.1928), U.S. film-maker: *Newsweek* (New York), 26 May 1980, quoted in *Kubrick: Inside a Film Artist's Maze* by Thomas Allen Nelson (1982), Ch.8

3 We're gonna sell you this seat, but you're only going to use the edge of it.
Quentin Tarantino (b.1958), U.S. film-maker: quoted in advertising for *Reservoir Dogs* (film; written and directed by Quentin Tarantino, 1992)

CINEMA: The Movie-Makers

1 I'm not making films because I want to be in the movie business. I'm making them because I want to say something. And if I had nothing to say tomorrow, I wouldn't hire myself out as a director. I'd write plays or short stories, or retire or something.
Woody Allen (b.1935), U.S. film-maker: interview in *Moviegoer*, May 1985, rep. in *The Woody Allen Companion* by Stephen J. Spignesi (1993), Ch.3

2 Much of Hitchcock's limitations, I think, but also his greatness within them, are to be found in his heavy body. His way of always working in the studio, using a static camera, not moving about, he has erected it all into a system, using long scenes where he won't have to give himself the trouble of having to move about.

Ingmar Bergman (b.1918), Swedish stage and film writer-director: interview in *Bergman on Bergman* (1970), 'Solna, 25 June 1968'

3 My movie is born first in my head, dies on paper; is resuscitated by the living persons and real objects I use, which are killed on film but, placed in a certain order and projected onto a screen, come to life again like flowers in water.

Robert Bresson (b.1907), French film-maker: *Notes on the Cinematographer* (1975), '1950–1958: on Looks'

4 Some are able and humane men and some are low-grade individuals with the morals of a goat, the artistic integrity of a slot machine, and the manners of a floorwalker with delusions of grandeur.

Raymond Chandler (1880–1959), U.S. author: on producers, in 'Writers in Hollywood', publ. in *Atlantic Monthly* (Boston), Nov. 1945

5 The cinema is not a craft. It is an art. It does not mean team-work. One is always alone; on the set as before the blank page.

Jean-Luc Godard (b.1930), French film-maker and author: 'Bergmanorama', first publ. in *Cahiers du Cinéma* (Paris), July 1958, rep. in *Godard on Godard* (ed. Tom Milne, 1972)

6 When I hear the word culture, I take out my chequebook.

Jean-Luc Godard: Jeremy Prokosh (Jack Palance), a film producer, in *Le Mépris* (film; written by Jean-Luc Godard, adapted from Alberto Moravia's novel *A Ghost at Noon*, directed by Jean-Luc Godard, 1963)

7 All you need for a movie is a gun and a girl.

Jean-Luc Godard: journal entry, 16 May 1991, quoted in *Projections* (ed. John Boorman and Walter Donohue, 1992)

8 I discovered early in my movie work that a movie is never any better than the stupidest man connected with it. There are times when this distinction may be given to the writer or director. Most often it belongs to the producer.

Ben Hecht (1893–1964), U.S. journalist, author and screenwriter: *A Child of the Century* (1954), Bk.5, 'Illustrations by Doré (Gustave)'. 'The producer,' Hecht explained, 'is the shadow cast by the studio's owner. It falls across the entire studio product.' He said that he regarded the producer's chief task as 'the job of turning good writers into movie hacks. These sinister fellows were always my bosses'

9 Making a film means, first of all, to tell a story. That story can be an improbable one, but it should never be banal. It must be dramatic and human. What is drama, after all, but life with the dull bits cut out?

Alfred Hitchcock (1899–1980), British film-maker: interview, Aug. 1962, publ. in *Hitchcock* by François Truffaut (1966; rev.1984), Ch.4

10 Confront a man in his office with a nuclear alarm, and you have a documentary. If the news reaches him in his living room, you have a drama. If it catches him in the lavatory, the result is comedy.

Stanley Kubrick (b.1928), U.S. film-maker: discussing comic method in his film *Dr Strangelove* (1964), in Alexander Walker's *Stanley Kubrick Directs* (1972), quoted in *Kubrick: Inside a Film Artist's Maze* by Thomas Allen Nelson (1982), Ch.4

11 All my movies are about strange worlds that you can't go into unless you build them and film them. That's what's so important about film to me. I just like going into strange worlds.

David Lynch (b.1947), U.S. film-maker: interview in *Première* (New York), Sept. 1990, quoted in *David Lynch* by Michel Chion (1992), Ch.5

12 I guess I think that films have to be made totally by fascists – there's no room for democracy in making film.

Don Pennebaker (b.1930), U.S. film-maker: in *The Independent* (London), 29 July 1988

13 In this business we make movies, American movies. Leave the films to the French.

Sam Shepard (b.1943), U.S. playwright and actor: Saul, in *True West* (1980), Act 2, Sc.5

14 The most expensive habit in the world is celluloid, not heroin, and I need a fix every few years.

Steven Spielberg (b.1947), U.S. film-maker: interview in *Time* (New York), 16 April 1979

15 All film directors, whether famous or obscure, regard themselves as misunderstood or underrated. Because of that, they all lie. They're obliged to overstate their own importance.

François Truffaut (1932–1984), French film-maker: letter, 8 Jan. 1981, publ. in *Letters* (1988)

16 The biggest electric train set any boy ever had!

Orson Welles (1915–1985), U.S. film-maker and actor: of RKO studios, quoted in *The Fabulous Orson Welles* by Peter Noble (1956), Ch.7

17 The director is simply the audience. So the terrible burden of the director is to take the place of that yawning vacuum, to *be* the audience and to select from what happens during the day which movement shall be a disaster and which a gala night. His job is to preside over accidents.

Orson Welles: speech at Hollywood Foreign Press Association, broadcast at the memorial service for Welles in Los Angeles, 4 Nov. 1985, publ. in *Citizen Welles* by Frank Brady (1989), Ch.21

18 A lot of my films start off with roadmaps instead of scripts. Sometimes it feels like flying blind without instruments. You fly all night and in the morning you arrive somewhere.

That is: you have to try to make a landing somewhere so the film can end.

Wim Wenders (b.1945), German film-maker: *The Logic of Images* (1988; tr.1991), 'Like flying blind without instruments'

See also Kieślowski on PLAGIARISM; Tarantino on PLAGIARISM

CINEMA: The New Wave

1 The cinema is quite simply becoming a means of expression ... it is gradually becoming a language. By language, I mean a form in which and by which an artist can express his thoughts, however abstract they may be, or translate his obsessions exactly as he does in a contemporary essay or novel. That is why I would like to call this new age of cinema the age of *caméra-stylo* .

Alexander Astruc (b.1923), French film-maker and critic: 'The Birth of a New Avant-Garde: the Caméra-Stylo', publ. in *Écran Français*, 30 March 1948, quoted in preface to *The New Wave* by James Monaco (1976). The theories of Astruc were to become the programme of the New-Wave film-makers who followed ten years later

2 People complain that the Nouvelle Vague only shows people in bed; I'm going to show some who are in politics and don't have time to go to bed.

Jean-Luc Godard (b.1930), French film-maker and author: quoted by Nicholas Garnham, in introduction to *Le Petit Soldat* (film screenplay, tr. Nicholas Garnham, 1967)

CINEMA: The Screenwriters

1 I went out there for a thousand a week, and I worked Monday, and I got fired Wednesday. The guy that hired me was out of town Tuesday.

Nelson Algren (1909–1981), U.S. author: interview in *Writers at Work* (First Series, ed. Malcolm Cowley, 1958)

2 I don't think screenplay writing is the same as writing – I mean, I think it's blueprinting.

Robert Altman (b.1925), U.S. film-maker: quoted in the *Independent on Sunday* (London), 26 April 1992

3 The challenge of screenwriting is to say much in little and then take half of that little out and still preserve an effect of leisure and natural movement.

Raymond Chandler (1880–1959), U.S. author: 'Writers in Hollywood', publ. in *Atlantic Monthly* (Boston), Nov. 1945

4 That's one thing I like about Hollywood. The writer is there revealed in his ultimate corrup-

tion. He asks no praise, because his praise comes to him in the form of a salary check. In Hollywood the average writer is not young, not honest, not brave, and a bit overdressed. But he is darn good company, which book writers as a rule are not. He is better than what he writes. Most book writers are not as good.

Raymond Chandler: letter, 6 Dec. 1948, to the *San Francisco Chronicle* critic Lenore Glen Offord, publ. in *Raymond Chandler Speaking* (ed. Dorothy Gardiner and Kathrine S. Walker, 1962)

5 The wise screen writer is he who wears his second-best suit, artistically speaking, and doesn't take things too much to heart. He should have a touch of cynicism, but only a touch. The complete cynic is as useless to Hollywood as he is to himself. He should do the best he can without straining at it. He should be scrupulously honest about his work, but he should not expect scrupulous honesty in return. He won't get it. And when he has had enough, he should say goodbye with a smile, because for all he knows he may want to go back.

Raymond Chandler: letter, 10 Nov. 1950, to publisher Hamish Hamilton, publ. in *Raymond Chandler Speaking* (ed. Dorothy Gardiner and Kathrine S. Walker, 1962). Chandler was then working with Billy Wilder on the script of *Double Indemnity*

6 We don't need books to make films. It's the last thing we want – it turns cinema into the bastard art of illustration.

Peter Greenaway (b.1942), British film-maker: quoted in the *Independent on Sunday* (London), 10 July 1994

7 Hollywood held this double lure for me, tremendous sums of money for work that required no more effort than a game of pinochle.

Ben Hecht (1893–1964), U.S. journalist, author and screenwriter: *A Child of the Century* (1954), Bk.5, 'Enter, the Movies'. But a few pages further, Hecht maintained that, 'Half of the large sum paid me for writing a movie script was in payment for listening to the producer and obeying him. ... The movies pay as much for obedience as for creative work. An able writer is paid a larger sum than a man of small talent. But he is paid this added money not to use his superior talents'

8 Dialogue should simply be a sound among other sounds, just something that comes out of the mouths of people whose eyes tell the story in visual terms.

Alfred Hitchcock (1899–1980), British film-maker: quoted in *Hitchcock* by François Truffaut (1967), Ch.11

9 Sam Goldwyn said, 'How'm I gonna do decent pictures when all my good writers are in jail?' Then he added, the infallible Goldwyn, 'Don't

misunderstand me, they all ought to be hung'. Mr Goldwyn didn't know about 'hanged'. That's all there is to say.

Dorothy Parker (1893–1967), U.S. humorous writer: interview in *Writers at Work* (First Series, ed. Malcolm Cowley, 1958)

10 What's he know about what people wanna see on the screen! I drive on the freeway every day. I swallow the smog. I watch the news in color. I shop in the Safeway. I'm the one who's in touch! Not him!

Sam Shepard (b.1943), U.S. playwright and actor: Austin of his screenwriter brother, in *True West* (1980), Act 2, Sc.6

11 Dialogue is a necessary evil.

Fred Zinnemann (1907–1997), Austrian-born U.S. film-maker: interview in the *Independent on Sunday* (London), 31 May 1992

See also WRITING: SCRIPTS & SCREENPLAYS

CINEMA: Sex & Violence

1 Films don't cause violence, people do. Violence defines our existence. To shield oneself is more dangerous than trying to reflect it.

Kathryn Bigelow (b.1951), U.S. film-maker: interview in *The Guardian* (London), 23 Dec. 1995

2 Sexuality is such a part of life, but sexuality in movies – I have a hard time finding it.

Catherine Deneuve (b.1943), French actress: interview in *Première* (London), April 1993

3 Americans don't like sexual movies – they like sexy movies.

Jack Nicholson (b.1937), U.S. actor: in *Rolling Stone* (New York), March 1984

4 I saw *Taxi Driver* once in a theatre, on the opening night, I think, and everyone was yelling and screaming at the shoot-out. When I made it, I didn't intend to have the audience react with that feeling, 'Yes, do it! Let's go out and kill.' The idea was to create a violent catharsis, so that they'd find themselves saying, 'Yes, kill'; and then afterwards realize, 'My God, no' – like some strange Californian therapy session. That was the instinct I went with, but it's scary to hear what happens with the audience.

Martin Scorsese (b.1942), U.S. film-maker: *Scorsese on Scorsese* (1989), Ch.3

5 Rambo isn't violent. I see Rambo as a philanthropist.

Sylvester Stallone (b.1946), U.S. actor and film-maker: in *Today* (London), 27 May 1988

6 I get a kick out of violence in movies. The worst thing about movies is, no matter how far you can go, when it comes to violence you are wearing a pair of handcuffs that novelists … don't wear.

Quentin Tarantino (b.1958), U.S. film-maker: interview, May 1993, quoted in introduction to *Reservoir Dogs* (screenplay, 1995)

See also Reed on VIDEO CULTURE; Tarantino on VIOLENCE

CIRCUMCISION

1 There is no doubt that the practice is a means of suppressing and controlling the sexual behaviour of women. Female circumcision is a physiological chastity belt.

Sue Armstrong, South African journalist: in *New Scientist* (London), 2 Feb. 1991

2 Circumcision is startling, all right, particularly when performed by a garlicked old man upon the glory of a newborn body, but then maybe that's what the Jews had in mind and what makes the act seem quintessentially Jewish and the mark of their reality. Circumcision makes it clear as can be that you are here and not there, that you are out and not in – also that you're mine and not theirs. … Quite convincingly, circumcision gives the lie to the womb-dream of life in the beautiful state of innocent prehistory, the appealing idyll of living 'naturally,' unencumbered by man-made ritual. To be born is to lose all that. The heavy hand of human values falls upon you right at the start, marking your genitals as its own.

Philip Roth (b.1933), U.S. novelist: Nathan Zuckerman, writing to Maria, in *The Counterlife* (1986), Ch.5

3 They circumcised women, little girls, in Jesus's time. Did he know? Did the subject anger or embarrass him? Did the early church erase the record? Jesus himself was circumcised; perhaps he thought only the cutting done to him was done to women, and therefore, since he survived, it was all right.

Alice Walker (b.1944), U.S. author and critic: *Possessing the Secret of Joy* (1992), Pt.21, 'Tashi–Evelyn–Mrs Johnson'

THE CIRCUS

1 There's something of the madhouse in the circus. There's madness in it, and terrifying experiences.

… The threat of death, the feeling aroused by such shows, is connected with that felt in the ancient Circus Maximus in Rome.

There's blood on the sawdust.

Federico Fellini (1920–1993), Italian film-maker: *Fellini on Fellini* (ed. Anna Keel and Christian Strich, 1974; tr.1977), 'Why Clowns?'

2 Every country gets the circus it deserves.
Spain gets bullfights. Italy gets the Catholic
Church. America gets Hollywood.
Erica Jong (b.1942), U.S. author: *How To Save
Your Own Life* (1977), epigraph to 'Take the Red-
Eye ...'

3 The Hendersons will all be there
Late of Pablo Fanques Fair, what a scene.
Over men and horses hoops and garters
Lastly through a hogshead of real fire
In this way Mister K. will challenge the world.
John Lennon (1940–1980) and **Paul McCartney**
(b.1942), British rock musicians: 'Being for the
Benefit of Mr. Kite' (song), on the album *Sgt.
Pepper's Lonely Hearts Club Band* (The Beatles,
1967)

CITIES

1 The skyscraper establishes the block, the block
creates the street, the street offers itself to man.
Roland Barthes (1915–1980), French semiologist:
'Buffet Finishes off New York', first publ. in *Arts*
(Paris), 1959, rep. in *The Eiffel Tower and Other
Mythologies* (1979)

2 The cities of the world are concentric, isomor-
phic, synchronic. Only one exists and you are
always in the same one. It's the effect of their
permanent revolution, their intense circulation, their instantaneous magnetism.
Jean Baudrillard (b.1929), French semiologist:
Cool Memories (1987; tr.1990), Ch.3

3 Every city has a sex and an age which have
nothing to do with demography. Rome is feminine. So is Odessa. London is a teenager, an
urchin, and, in this, hasn't changed since the
time of Dickens. Paris, I believe, is a man in his
twenties in love with an older woman.
John Berger (b.1926), British author and critic:
'Imagine Paris' first publ. in *Harper's Magazine*
(New York), Jan. 1987 rep. in *Keeping a Rendezvous*
(1992)

4 The catalogue of forms is endless: until every
shape has found its city, new cities will continue to be born. When the forms exhaust their
variety and come apart, the end of cities
begins.
Italo Calvino (1923–1985), Italian author and critic:
Invisible Cities (1972; tr.1974), p.139 of Secker and
Warburg edn. (1974)

5 All that a city will ever allow you is an angle on
it – an oblique, indirect sample of what it contains, or what passes through it; a point of
view.
Peter Conrad (b.1948), Australian author and
critic: of New York, in the *Independent on Sunday*
(London), 11 March 1990

6 It is not what they built. It is what they
knocked down.

It is not the houses. It is the spaces between the
houses.
It is not the streets that exist. It is the streets
that no longer exist.
James Fenton (b.1949), British poet and critic:
'German Requiem' (1980), rep. in *The Memory of
War* (1982)

7 The Metropolis should have been aborted long
before it became New York, London or
Tokyo.
J.K. Galbraith (b.1908), U.S. economist: *The Age
of Uncertainty* (1977), Ch.9

8 There are eight million stories in the naked
city. This has been one of them.
Mark Hellinger (1903-1947), U.S. journalist,
scriptwriter and producer: voiceover, in *The Naked
City* (film; screenplay by Albert Maltz and Malvin
Wald, directed by Jules Dassin, 1948). This
afterword was spoken by Mark Hellinger – the film
was his last production – and was used at the end of
each episode of the TV series (1958–62)

9 There is a time of life somewhere between the
sullen fugues of adolescence and the retrench-
ments of middle age when human nature
becomes so absolutely absorbing one wants to
be in the city constantly, even at the height of
summer.
Edward Hoagland (b.1932), U.S. novelist and
essayist: 'City Walking' first publ. in the *New York
Times Book Review*, 1 June 1975, rep. in *Heart's
Desire* (1988)

10 A city is a place where there is no need to wait
for next week to get the answer to a question, to
taste the food of any country, to find new
voices to listen to and familiar ones to listen to
again.
Margaret Mead (1901–1978), U.S. anthropologist:
World Enough (1975), Ch.2

11 How soon country people forget. When they
fall in love with a city it is forever, and it is like
forever. As though there never was a time
when they didn't love it. The minute they
arrive at the train station or get off the ferry
and glimpse the wide streets and the wasteful
lamps lighting them, they know they are born
for it. There, in a city, they are not so much
new as themselves: their stronger, riskier
selves.
Toni Morrison (b.1931), U.S. novelist and editor:
Jazz (1991), Ch.2

12 The chief function of the city is to convert
power into form, energy into culture, dead
matter into the living symbols of art, biological
reproduction into social creativity.
Lewis Mumford (1895–1990), U.S. social
philosopher: *The City in History* (1961), Ch.18

13 There are dragons buried beneath our cities,
primordial energies greater than the power of

our bombs. Two thousand years of Judeo-Christian soul-shaping and three centuries of crusading scientific intellect have gone into their interment. ... But now they wake and stir.

Theodore Roszak (b.1933), U.S. social critic: introduction to *Where the Wasteland Ends* (1972)

14 My ideal city would be one long main street with no cross streets or side streets to jam up traffic. Just one long one-way street.

Andy Warhol (c.1928–1987), U.S. Pop artist: *From A to B and Back Again* (1975), Ch.10. On the same subject Warhol added, 'Buildings should be built to last for a short time. And if they are older than ten years, I say get rid of them'

15 To look at the cross-section of any plan of a big city is to look at something like the section of a fibrous tumor.

Frank Lloyd Wright (1869–1959), U.S. architect: *The Living City* (1958), Pt.2, 'Social and Economic Disease'

See also BRITAIN: LONDON; Camus on BRITAIN: SCOTLAND; Gray on BRITAIN: SCOTLAND; FRANCE: PARIS; GERMANY: BERLIN; ITALY: ROME; ITALY: VENICE; SUBURBS; THE UNITED STATES: BOSTON; THE UNITED STATES: CHICAGO; THE UNITED STATES: LOS ANGELES; THE UNITED STATES: NEW YORK; THE UNITED STATES: SAN FRANCISCO; THE UNITED STATES: WASHINGTON D.C.

CITIES: Ghettos

1 The needs of a society determine its ethics, and in the Black American ghettos the hero is that man who is offered only the crumbs from his country's table but by ingenuity and courage is able to take for himself a Lucullan feast.

Maya Angelou (b.1928), U.S. author: *I Know Why the Caged Bird Sings* (1969), Ch.29

2 All over Harlem, Negro boys and girls are growing into stunted maturity, trying desperately to find a place to stand; and the wonder is not that so many are ruined but that so many survive.

James Baldwin (1924–1987), U.S. author: 'The Harlem Ghetto', first publ. in *Commentary* (New York), Feb. 1948, rep. in *Notes of a Native Son* (1955), Pt.2

3 Ghetto space is wrong for America. It's wrong for people who are the same type to go and live together. There shouldn't be any huddling together in the same groups with the same food. In America it's got to mix 'n' mingle.

Andy Warhol (c.1928–1987), U.S. Pop artist: *From A to B and Back Again* (1975), Ch.10

CITIES: Slums

1 I've been in many of them and to some extent I would have to say this: If you've seen one city slum you've seen them all.

Spiro T. Agnew (1918–1996), U.S. Republican politician and vice president: speech, 18 Oct. 1968, Detroit, publ. in *Detroit Free Press*, 19 Oct. 1968

2 Life is lived in common, but not in community.

Michael Harrington (1928–1989), U.S. social scientist and author: of life in the slums, in *The Other America* (1962), Ch.7, Sct 4

CITIES: Urban Culture

1 The images I had were of people being driven mad by living in the city. Images of parents who were so hungry and unfulfilled that they ate their own children. Images of people, teenagers my own age, looking up from the asphalt and being blinded by the sun. These images stayed with me even after I left the city. Images so violent and malicious that they seemed to be my only point of reference for a long time afterwards. After I left.

Bret Easton Ellis (b.1964), U.S. author: Clay (narrator), in closing paragraph of *Less Than Zero* (1985)

2 One of the least pleasant aspects of life in America these days is the militarisation of city life. The infrastructure is there, there are controllable cameras everywhere, the helicopters are constantly overhead.

William Gibson (b.1948), U.S. science fiction author: interview in *i-D* (London), Oct. 1993

3 It's like a jungle sometimes,
It makes me wonder
How I keep from going under.

Grandmaster Flash (b.1958), U.S. rap singer: 'The Message' (song; written by Sylvia Robinson and Duke Bootee, 1982), on the album *Greatest Messages* (Grandmaster Flash and the Furious Five, 1984)

4 We New Yorkers see more death and violence than most soldiers do, grow a thick chitin on our backs, grimace like a rat and learn to do a disappearing act. Long ago we outgrew the need to be blowhards about our masculinity; we leave that to the Alaskans and Texans, who have more time for it.

Edward Hoagland (b.1932), U.S. novelist and essayist: 'City Rat', first publ. in *Audience* (Hollywood), March 1972, rep. in *Heart's Desire* (1988)

5 But look what we have built ... low-income projects that become worse centers of delinquency, vandalism and general social hopelessness than the slums they were supposed to

replace.... Cultural centers that are unable to support a good bookstore. Civic centers that are avoided by everyone but bums.... Promenades that go from no place to nowhere and have no promenaders. Expressways that eviscerate great cities. This is not the rebuilding of cities. This is the sacking of cities.
Jane Jacobs (b.1916), U.S. author: introduction to *The Death and Life of Great American Cities* (1961)

6 The city is not a concrete jungle, it is a human zoo.
Desmond Morris (b.1928), British zoologist: introduction to *The Human Zoo* (1969)

7 Today's city is the most vulnerable social structure ever conceived by man.
Martin Oppenheimer (b.1930), German-born U.S. sociologist: *Urban Guerrilla* (1969), Ch.7

8 Living in cities is an art, and we need the vocabulary of art, of style, to describe the peculiar relationship between man and material that exists in the continual creative play of urban living. The city as we imagine it, then, soft city of illusion, myth, aspiration, and nightmare, is as real, maybe more real, than the hard city one can locate on maps in statistics, in monographs on urban sociology and demography and architecture.
Jonathan Raban (b.1942), British author and critic: *Soft City* (1974), Ch.1

9 Hot town,
Summer in the city,
Back o' my neck gettin' dirty and gritty.
John Sebastian (b.1944), U.S. rock musician: 'Summer in the City' (song), on the album *Hums of The Lovin' Spoonful* (The Lovin' Spoonful, 1966)

10 Commuters give the city its tidal restlessness; natives give it solidity and continuity; but the settlers give it passion.
E.B. White (1899–1985), U.S. author and editor: 'Here is New York', publ. in *Holiday* (Indianapolis), April 1949

11 The screech and mechanical uproar of the big city turns the citified head, fills citified ears – as the song of birds, wind in the trees, animal cries, or as the voices and songs of his loved ones once filled his heart. He is sidewalk-happy.
Frank Lloyd Wright (1869–1959), U.S. architect: *The Living City* (1958), Pt.1, 'Earth'

CIVIL RIGHTS

1 Rights that do not flow from duty well performed are not worth having.
Mohandas K. Gandhi (1869–1948), Indian political and spiritual leader: *Non-Violence in Peace and War* (1949), Vol.II, Ch.269

2 Civil Rights: What black folks are given in the U.S. on the installment plan, as in civil-rights bills. Not to be confused with *human rights*, which are the dignity, stature, humanity, respect, and freedom belonging to all people by right of their birth.
Dick Gregory (b.1932), U.S. comedian and civil rights activist: *Dick Gregory's Political Primer* (1972). *See* Malcolm X on THE UNITED STATES: AFRICAN AMERICANS

3 A state that denies its citizens their basic rights becomes a danger to its neighbors as well: internal arbitrary rule will be reflected in arbitrary external relations. The suppression of public opinion, the abolition of public competition for power and its public exercise opens the way for the state power to arm itself in any way it sees fit. ... A state that does not hesitate to lie to its own people will not hesitate to lie to other states.
Václav Havel (b.1936), Czech playwright and president: *Living in Truth* (1986), Pt.1, 'An Anatomy of Reticence', Sct.9

4 There are those who say to you – we are rushing this issue of civil rights. I say we are 172 years late.
Hubert H. Humphrey (1911–1978), U.S. Democratic politician and vice president: address, 14 July 1948, to Democratic National Convention, Philadelphia, supporting his Civil Rights Amendment to the Party Platform; Humphrey was then Mayor of Minneapolis

5 Get up, stand up,
Stand up for your rights.
Get up, stand up,
Don't give up the fight.
Peter Tosh (1944–1987), Jamaican reggae musician: 'Get Up, Stand Up' (song; written with Bob Marley), on the album *Burnin'* (The Wailers, 1973)

See also HUMAN RIGHTS

CIVILIZATION

1 The skylines lit up at dead of night, the air-conditioning systems cooling empty hotels in the desert and artificial light in the middle of the day all have something both demented and admirable about them. The mindless luxury of a rich civilization, and yet of a civilization perhaps as scared to see the lights go out as was the hunter in his primitive night.
Jean Baudrillard (b.1929), French semiologist: *America* (1986; tr.1988), 'Astral America'

2 People sometimes tell me that they prefer barbarism to civilisation. I doubt if they have given it a long enough trial. Like the people of Alexandria, they are bored by civilisation; but then all the evidence suggests that the boredom of barbarism is infinitely greater.

Kenneth Clark (1903–1983), British art historian: *Civilisation* (1970), Ch.1

3 Civilization is a stream with banks. The stream is sometimes filled with blood from people killing, stealing, shouting and doing the things historians usually record, while on the banks, unnoticed, people build homes, make love, raise children, sing songs, write poetry and even whittle statues. The story of civilization is the story of what happened on the banks. Historians are pessimists because they ignore the banks for the river.
Will Durant (1885–1981), U.S. historian: in *Life* (New York), 18 Oct. 1963

4 Modern civilization, despite undisputed successes in many fields, has also made many mistakes and given rise to many abuses with regard to man, exploiting him in various ways. It is a civilization that constantly equips itself with power structures and structures of oppression, both political and cultural (especially through the media), in order to impose similar mistakes and abuses on all humanity.
Pope John Paul II [Karol Wojtyla] (b.1920), Polish ecclesiastic: *Crossing the Threshold of Hope* (1994), 'Was God at Work in the Fall of Communism'

5 The word 'civilization' to my mind is coupled with death. When I use the word, I see civilization as a crippling, thwarting thing, a stultifying thing. For me it was always so. I don't believe in the golden ages, you see.... Civilization is the arteriosclerosis of culture.
Henry Miller (1891–1980), U.S. author: interview in *Writers at Work* (Second Series, ed. George Plimpton, 1963)

6 Civilisation – a heap of rubble scavenged by scrawny English Lit vultures.
Malcolm Muggeridge (1903–1990), British journalist and broadcaster: quoted in *New Society* (London), 6 Oct. 1983

7 Civilization is a movement and not a condition, a voyage and not a harbour.
A.J. Toynbee (1889–1975), British historian: in *Reader's Digest* (Pleasantville, NY), Oct. 1958

CLASS

1 Class! Yes, it's still here. Terrific staying power, and against the historical odds. What *is* it with that old, *old* crap? The class system just doesn't know when to call it a day. Even a nuclear holocaust, I think, would fail to make that much of a dent in it.
Martin Amis (b.1949), British author: *London Fields* (1989), Ch.2

2 You'll never live like common people,
you'll never do what common people do,
you'll never fail like common people,
you'll never watch your life slide out of view
and dance and drink and screw
because there's nothing else to do.
Jarvis Cocker (b.1963), British rock musician: 'Common People' (song), on the album *Different Class* (Pulp, 1995)

3 When we say a woman is of a certain social class, we really mean her husband or father is.
Zoe Fairburns (b.1948), British author: quoted in *The Observer* (London), 9 Jan. 1983

4 The traveler to the United States will do well ... to prepare himself for the class-consciousness of the natives. This differs from the already familiar English version in being more extreme and based more firmly on the conviction that the class to which the speaker belongs is inherently superior to all others.
J.K. Galbraith (b.1908), U.S. economist: 'The United States', publ. in *New York*, 15 Nov. 1971, rep. in *A View from the Stands* (1986)

5 Classes struggle, some classes triumph, others are eliminated. Such is history; such is the history of civilization for thousands of years.
Mao Zedong (1893–1976), Chinese leader: said in Aug. 1949, quoted in *Mao and China: From Revolution to Revolution* by Stanley Karnow (1972)

6 The word of the moment is 'classless,' whether applied to Cockney Society photographers or sprigs of the aristocracy running little bistros round the corner. Mick Jagger, alternately slurring yob and lisping lordling, is classlessness apotheosised.
Philip Norman (b.1943), British author and journalist: *The Life and Good Times of the Rolling Stones* (1989), p.61

7 Throughout recorded time ... there have been three kinds of people in the world, the High, the Middle, and the Low. They have been subdivided in many ways, they have borne countless different names, and their relative numbers, as well as their attitude towards one another, have varied from age to age: but the essential structure of society has never altered. Even after enormous upheavals and seemingly irrevocable changes, the same pattern has always reasserted itself, just as a gyroscope will always return to equilibrium, however far it is pushed one way or the other. The aims of these three groups are entirely irreconcilable.
George Orwell (1903–1950), British author: first words of Goldstein's book in *Nineteen Eighty-four* (1949), Pt.2, Ch.9

8 NQOCD (not quite our class, darling) is an American joke. You might say 'He's a bit ordinaire ...'
Peter York (b.1950) and **Ann Barr**, British

journalists: *The Official Sloane Ranger's Handbook* (1982), 'The First Social Steps'

See also Chandler on SNOBBERY

CLICHÉS

1   The cliché organizes life; it expropriates people's identity; it becomes ruler, defence lawyer, judge, and the law.
    Václav Havel (b.1936), Czech playwright and president: *Disturbing the Peace* (1986; tr.1990), Ch.5

2   We make the oldest stories new when we succeed, and we are trapped by the old stories when we fail.
    Greil Marcus (b.1945), U.S. rock journalist: prologue to *Mystery Train* (1976)

3   If you want to use a cliché you must take full responsibility for it yourself and not try to job it off on anon., or on society.
    Lewis Thomas (1913–1993), U.S. physician and educator: *The Medusa and the Snail* (1979), 'Notes on Punctuation'

See also Gingrich on ELECTIONS

CLOWNS

1   Being a funny person does an awful lot of things to you. You feel that you mustn't get serious with people. They don't expect it from you, and they don't want to see it. You're not entitled to be serious, you're a clown, and they only want you to make them laugh.
    Fanny Brice (1891–1951), U.S. entertainer: quoted in *The Fabulous Fanny* by Norman Katkov (1952), Ch.9

2   I remain just one thing, and one thing only – and that is a clown. It places me on a far higher plane than any politician.
    Charlie Chaplin (1889–1977), British comic actor, film-maker: quoted in *The Observer* (London), 17 June 1960

3   The clown is the incarnation of a fantastic creature who expresses the irrational aspect of man; he stands for the instinct, for whatever is rebellious in each one of us and whatever stands up to the established order of things. He is a caricature of man's childish and animal aspects, the mocker and the mocked. The clown is a mirror in which man sees himself in a grotesque, deformed, ridiculous image. He is man's shadow. And so he will be forever.
    Federico Fellini (1920–1993), Italian film-maker: *Fellini on Fellini* (ed. Anna Keel and Christian Strich, 1974; tr.1977), 'Why Clowns?'

4   Much goodness exists in mankind; it is stupidity far more than wickedness which is the present trouble of the world. Falstaffs are

more common than Machiavellis, the clown is more frequent than the villain, in every continent.
Oswald Mosley (1896–1980), British fascist leader: *My Life* (1968), Ch.11

See also COMEDIANS

COCKTAILS

1   If you were to ask me if I'd ever had the bad luck to miss my daily cocktail, I'd have to say that I doubt it; where certain things are concerned, I plan ahead.
    Luis Buñuel (1900–1983), Spanish film-maker: *My Last Breath* (autobiography, 1983), Ch.6

2   A medium Vodka dry Martini – with a slice of lemon peel. Shaken and not stirred, please. I would prefer Russian or Polish vodka.
    Ian Fleming (1908–1964), British author: James Bond, ordering his favourite tipple, in *Dr. No* (1958), Ch.14

3   I misremember who first was cruel enough to nurture the cocktail party into life. But perhaps it would be not too much to say, in fact it would be not enough to say, that it was not worth the trouble.
    Dorothy Parker (1893–1967), U.S. humorous writer: in *Esquire* (New York), Nov. 1964

COFFEE

1   Coffee in England is just toasted milk.
    Christopher Fry (b.1907), British playwright: in the *New York Post*, 29 Nov. 1962

2   Damned fine cup of coffee!
    David Lynch (b.1946), U.S. film-maker: Agent Dale Cooper (Kyle MacLachlan), in *Twin Peaks* (TV series, written and created by David Lynch and Mark Frost, 1989–91). 'Damned fine cheese cake!' and 'Damned fine pie!' are other remarks associated with Agent Cooper

3   Caffeine has been the chemical adjunct of one of the most dramatic transformations of consciousness the human race has experienced. It has helped press the razor-sharp edge of wakefulness mercilessly against the mind; still today, only the pain of that blade will serve to convince most of us that we are alive and awake in the real world.
    Theodore Roszak (b.1933), U.S. social critic: *Where the Wasteland Ends* (1972), Ch.3

4   Not instant, darling. Grind some beans. That's not proper coffee … that's just beans that have been cremated. I want them entire with life force.
    Jennifer Saunders (b.1957), British comedienne: Edina (Jennifer Saunders), in *Absolutely Fabulous* (TV series, first shown 1993), 'Fashion'

THE COLD WAR

1 Let us not be deceived – we are today in the midst of a cold war.

Bernard Baruch (1870–1965), U.S. financier: speech, 16 April 1947, South Carolina Legislature, Columbia. A year later Baruch told the Senate War Investigating Committee, 'We are in the midst of a cold war which is getting warmer.' Baruch claimed the expression had been suggested to him by his speechwriter and former editor of *The New York World*, Herbert Bayard Swope

2 The Cold War began with the division of Europe. It can only end when Europe is whole.

George Bush (b.1924), U.S. Republican politician and president: quoted in *The Daily Telegraph* (London), 1 June 1989

3 A shadow has fallen upon the scenes so lately lighted by the Allied victory. … From Stettin in the Baltic to Trieste in the Adriatic, an iron curtain has descended across the Continent.

Winston Churchill (1874–1965), British statesman and author: speech, 5 March 1946, Fulton, Missouri, publ. in *Winston S. Churchill: His Complete Speeches, 1897–1963* , Vol.VI (ed. Robert Rhodes James, 1974). The first use of the phrase 'iron curtain' in this context is thought to have been by Joseph Goebbels in *Das Reich* (Nazi propaganda weekly), 23 Feb. 1945: 'Should the German people lay down their arms, the Soviets … would occupy all eastern and south-eastern Europe together with the greater part of the Reich. Over all this territory, which with the Soviet Union included, would be of enormous extent, an iron curtain (*ein eiserner Vorhang*), would at once descend.' Churchill had also used the phrase in early 1946 in a telegram to President Truman

4 If we cannot end now our differences, at least we can help make the world safe for diversity.

John F. Kennedy (1917–1963), U.S. Democratic politician and president: referring to Russo-American relations, in commencement address, 10 June 1963, American University, Washington D.C., publ. in *Public Papers of the Presidents of the United States: John F. Kennedy, 1963*

5 Whether you like it or not, history is on our side. We will bury you.

Nikita Khrushchev (1894–1971), Soviet premier: remark to Western diplomats, 18 Nov. 1956, Kremlin, Moscow, quoted in *The Times* (London), 19 Nov. 1956. Khrushchev later interpreted this remark to mean 'we will outlive you' (i.e. communism will triumph). On another occasion, 24 Aug. 1963, addressing a group of Westerners in Split, Yugoslavia, he referred to his controversial statement: 'Of course we will not bury you with a shovel. Your own working class will bury you'

6 It was *man* who ended the Cold War in case you didn't notice. It wasn't weaponry, or technology, or armies or campaigns. It was just *man*. Not even Western man either, as it happened, but our sworn enemy in the East, who went into the streets, faced the bullets and the batons and said: we've had enough. It was *their* emperor, not ours, who had the nerve to mount the rostrum and declare he had no clothes. And the ideologies trailed after these impossible events like condemned prisoners, as ideologies do when they've had their day.

John Le Carré (b.1931), British author: Smiley, in *The Secret Pilgrim* (1990), Ch.12

7 The Cold War isn't thawing; it is burning with a deadly heat. Communism isn't sleeping; it is, as always, plotting, scheming, working, fighting.

Richard Nixon (1913–1992), U.S. Republican politician and president: 'Cuba, Castro and John F. Kennedy', publ. in *Reader's Digest* (Pleasantville, N.Y.), Nov. 1964, rep. in the second volume of Stephen Ambrose's biography, *Nixon: The Triumph of a Politician* (1989), Ch.2

8 We're eyeball to eyeball, and I think the other fellow just blinked.

Dean Rusk (1909–1994), U.S. Democratic politician: remark, 24 Oct. 1962, referring to the Cuban missile crisis, in the *Saturday Evening Post* (New York), 8 Dec. 1962

9 We hear the Secretary of State boasting of his brinkmanship – the art of bringing us to the edge of the abyss.

Adlai Stevenson (1900–1965), U.S. Democratic politician: speech, 25 Feb. 1956, Hartford, Connecticut, quoted in the *New York Times*, 26 Feb. 1956, publ. in *The Papers of Adlai E. Stevenson*, Vol.V (1974). Stevenson was referring to John Foster Dulles (*see under* THE ARMS RACE)

See also Khrushchev on CUBA

COLONIALISM

1 Colonialism is not a thinking machine, nor a body endowed with reasoning faculties. It is violence in its natural state, and it will only yield when confronted with greater violence.

Frantz Fanon (1925–1961), Martiniquan psychiatrist, philosopher and political activist: *The Wretched of the Earth* (1961), Ch.1

2 Free up de lan, white man
free all African.

Mutabaruka (b.1952), Jamaican poet and singer: 'Free Up de Lan, White Man' (song), on the album *Check It* (1982)

3 A State in the grip of neo-colonialism is not master of its own destiny. It is this factor which makes neo-colonialism such a serious threat to world peace.

Kwame Nkrumah (1900–1972), Ghanaian president: introduction to *Consciencism* (1964)

4 In the colonies the truth stood naked, but the citizens of the mother country preferred it with clothes on: the natives had to love them, something in the way mothers are loved.
Jean-Paul Sartre (1905–1980), French philosopher and author: preface to *The Wretched of the Earth* by Frantz Fanon (1961)

5 There is no human failure greater than to launch a profoundly important endeavour and then leave it half done. This is what the West has done with its colonial system. It shook all the societies in the world loose from their old moorings. But it seems indifferent whether or not they reach safe harbour in the end.
Barbara Ward (1914–1981), British author and educator: *The Rich Nations and the Poor Nations* (1962), Ch.2

See also Nyerere on DANCE; DECOLONIZATION; Rushdie on THE ENGLISH LANGUAGE; Fanon on ENVY; IMPERIALISM

COLOUR

1 Why do two colours, put one next to the other, sing? Can one really explain this? No. Just as one can never learn how to paint.
Pablo Picasso (1881–1973), Spanish artist: *Arts de France* (Paris), No.6, 1946, quoted in Dore Ashton's *Picasso on Art* (1972)

2 I think it pisses God off if you walk by the color purple in a field somewhere and don't notice it.
Alice Walker (b.1944), U.S. author and critic: Shug, in *The Color Purple* (1982), p.167 of Women's Press edn. (1983)

See also Tarantino on NAMES

COMEDIANS

1 We are living in the machine age. For the first time in history the comedian has been compelled to supply himself with jokes and comedy material to compete with the machine. Whether he knows it or not, the comedian is on a treadmill to oblivion.
Fred Allen (1894–1957), U.S. comic: *Treadmill to Oblivion* (1954), Pt.4

2 I think being funny is not anyone's first choice.
Woody Allen (b.1935), U.S. film-maker: in *The Guardian* (London), 23 March 1992

3 Today's comedian has a cross to bear that he built himself. A comedian of the older generation did an 'act' and he told the audience, 'This is my act.' Today's comic is not doing an act. The audience assumes he's telling the truth. What is truth today may be a damn lie next week.
Lenny Bruce (1925–1966), U.S. satirical comedian:

The Essential Lenny Bruce (ed. John Cohen, 1967), 'Performing and the Art of Comedy'

4 Charlie Chaplin's genius was in comedy. He has no sense of humor, particularly about himself.
Lita Grey Chaplin (1908–1996), second wife of Charlie Chaplin: radio interview 1974, quoted in Richard Lamparski's *Whatever Became Of … ?* (Eighth Series, 1982)

5 If I get a hard audience they are not going to get away until they laugh. Those seven laughs a minute – I've got to have them.
Ken Dodd (b.1931), British comic: in *The Daily Telegraph* (London), 20 Sept. 1990

6 We mustn't complain too much of being comedians – it's an honourable profession. If only we could be good ones the world might gain at least a sense of style. We have failed – that's all. We are bad comedians, we aren't bad men.
Graham Greene (1904–1991), British novelist: the ambassador, in *The Comedians* (1966), Pt.1, Ch.5, Sct.2

7 There is not one female comic who was beautiful as a little girl.
Joan Rivers (b.1935), U.S. comedienne: quoted in the *Los Angeles Times*, 10 May 1974

8 The reason that there are so few women comics is that so few women can bear being laughed at.
Anna Russell (b.1911), Anglo-American comedienne and singer: in *The Sunday Times* (London), 25 Aug. 1957

See also CLOWNS

COMEDY

1 Comedy just pokes at problems, rarely confronts them squarely. Drama is like a plate of meat and potatoes, comedy is rather the dessert, a bit like meringue.
Woody Allen (b.1935), U.S. film-maker: quoted in *Woody Allen: New Yorker* by Graham McCann (1990), Ch.4

2 The only honest art form is laughter, comedy. You can't fake it … try to fake three laughs in an hour – ha ha ha ha ha – they'll take you away, man. You can't.
Lenny Bruce (1925–1966), U.S. satirical comedian: *The Essential Lenny Bruce* (ed. John Cohen, 1967), 'Performing and the Art of Comedy'

3 Comedy is tragedy that happens to *other* people.
Angela Carter (1940–1992), British author: *Wise Children* (1991), Ch.4

4 All I need to make a comedy is a park, a policeman and a pretty girl.

Charlie Chaplin (1889–1977), British comic actor and film-maker: *My Autobiography* (1964), Ch.10

5 Comedy, like sodomy, is an unnatural act.

Marty Feldman (1933–1982), British comedian: in *The Times* (London), 9 June 1969

6 Comedy is an escape, not from truth but from despair; a narrow escape into faith.

Christopher Fry (b.1907), British playwright: in *Time* (New York), 20 Nov. 1950

7 Comedy deflates the sense precisely so that the underlying lubricity and malice may bubble to the surface.

Paul Goodman (1911–1972), U.S. literary author and critic: 'Obsessed by Theatre', publ. in *The Nation* (New York), 29 Nov. 1958

8 Comedy comes from conflict, from hatred.

Warren Mitchell (b.1926), British actor: in *The Times* (London), 31 Dec. 1990

9 Farce is tragedy played at a thousand revolutions per minute.

John Mortimer (b.1923), British barrister and novelist: in *The Times* (London), 9 Sept. 1992

10 Laughter is a serious business and comedy a weapon more dangerous than tragedy. Which is why tyrants treat it with caution. The actual material of tragedy is equally viable as comedy – unless you happen to be writing in English, when the question of taste occurs.

Joe Orton (1933–1967), British playwright: in the *Radio Times* (London), 29 Aug. 1964, quoted in *Prick Up Your Ears: the Biography of Joe Orton* by John Lahr (1978), Ch.4

11 The only rules comedy can tolerate are those of taste, and the only limitations those of libel.

James Thurber (1894–1961), U.S. humorist and illustrator: *Lanterns and Lances* (1961), 'The Duchess and the Bugs'

12 The comic spirit is given to us in order that we may analyze, weigh, and clarify things in us which nettle us, or which we are outgrowing, or trying to reshape.

Thornton Wilder (1897–1975), U.S. novelist and playwright: interview in *Writers at Work* (First Series, ed. Malcolm Cowley, 1958)

See also JOKES

COMMITMENT

1 Commitment, I feel, prevents man from developing. ... Today I feel a profound hatred ... for all ideas that can be translated into formulas. I am committed to non-commitment.

Federico Fellini (1920–1993), Italian film-maker: *Fellini on Fellini* (ed. Anna Keel and Christian Strich, 1974; tr.1977), 'Miscellany III', Sct.4

2 The gap between the committed and the indifferent is a Sahara whose faint trails, followed by the mind's eye only, fade out in sand.

Nadine Gordimer (b.1923), South African author: 'Great Problems in the Street', first publ. in *I Will Still Be Moved* (ed. Marion Friedmann, 1963), rep. in *The Essential Gesture* (ed. Stephen Clingman, 1988)

3 The criminal and the soldier at least have the virtue of being against something or for something in a world where many people have learned to accept a kind of grey nothingness, to strike an unreal series of poses in order to be considered normal. ... It's difficult to say who is engaged in the greater conspiracy – the criminal, the soldier, or us.

Stanley Kubrick (b.1928), U.S. film-maker: in the *New York Times Magazine*, 12 Oct. 1958, rep. in *Kubrick: Inside a Film Artist's Maze* by Thomas Allen Nelson (1982), Ch.3

COMMITTEES

1 A committee is an animal with four back legs.

John Le Carré (b.1931), British author: Smiley, in *Tinker, Tailor, Soldier, Spy* (1974), Pt.3, Ch.34

2 A committee is organic rather than mechanical in its nature: it is not a structure but a plant. It takes root and grows, it flowers, wilts, and dies, scattering the seed from which other committees will bloom in their turn.

C. Northcote Parkinson (1909–1993), British historian and political scientist: *Parkinson's Law, or The Pursuit of Progress* (1958), 'Directors and Councils'

3 Muddle is the extra unknown personality in any committee.

Anthony Sampson (b.1926), British journalist and author: *Anatomy of Britain Today* (1965), Ch.15

4 When committees gather, each member is necessarily an actor, uncontrollably acting out the part of himself, reading the lines that identify him, asserting his identity. ... We are designed, coded, it seems, to place the highest priority on being individuals, and we must do this first, at whatever cost, even if it means disability for the group.

Lewis Thomas (1913–1993), U.S. physician and educator: *The Medusa and the Snail* (1979), 'On Committees'

5 Any committee that is the slightest use is composed of people who are too busy to want to sit on it for a second longer than they have to.

Katharine Whitehorn (b.1926), British journalist: *Observations* (1970), 'Are You Sitting Comfortably?'

COMMON SENSE

1 Common-sense is part of the home-made ideology of those who have been deprived of fundamental learning, of those who have been kept ignorant. This ideology is compounded from different sources: items that have survived from religion, items of empirical knowledge, items of protective scepticism, items culled for comfort from the superficial learning that *is* supplied. But the point is that common-sense can never teach itself, can never advance beyond its own limits, for as soon as the lack of fundamental learning has been made good, all items become questionable and the whole function of common-sense is destroyed. Common-sense can only exist as a category insofar as it can be distinguished from the spirit of enquiry, from philosophy.

John Berger (b.1926), British author and critic: *A Fortunate Man* (1967), p.102 of Writers and Readers Publishing Cooperative edn. (1976)

2 Common sense always speaks too late. Common sense is the guy who tells you you ought to have had your brakes relined last week before you smashed a front end this week. Common sense is the Monday morning quarterback who could have won the ball game if he had been on the team. But he never is. He's high up in the stands with a flask on his hip. Common sense is the little man in a grey suit who never makes a mistake in addition. But it's always somebody else's money he's adding up.

Raymond Chandler (1880–1959), U.S. author: Philip Marlowe, in *Playback* (1958), Ch.14

COMMUNICATION

1 If figures of speech based on sports and fornication were suddenly banned, American corporate communication would be reduced to pure mathematics.

Jay McInerney (b.1955), U.S. author: Harold Stone, in *Brightness Falls* (1992), Ch.24

2 What we've got here is a failure to communicate.

Strother Martin (1920-1980), U.S. actor: camp commandant (Strother Martin), in *Cool Hand Luke* (film; screenplay and original novel by Donn Pearce, directed by Stuart Rosenberg, 1967). The words appeared as a publicity slogan for the movie

3 We seem to live in a society that lacks communication. When you try to communicate, you're called a radical, a communist, dirty, a Republican, or something to let you know you're not speaking their language.

Richard Pryor (b.1940), U.S. actor: quoted in *Black and Blue* by Jeff Rovin (1983), Ch.10. Pryor is referring to the use of such words as 'nigger' and 'motherfucker' during his act

COMMUNISM

1 America's hysterical fear of Communism stems not from any real fear of brutality or oppression – but from the fear of not being able to wear the sloganized T-shirt of your choice, of not being an all-important (literally) individual.

Julie Burchill (b.1960), British journalist and author: *Damaged Gods* (1986), 'Damaged Gods'

2 The terrible thing is that one cannot be a Communist and not let oneself in for the shameful act of recantation. One cannot be a Communist and preserve an iota of one's personal integrity.

Milovan Djilas (1911–1995), Yugoslav political leader and writer: in *Encounter* (London), Dec. 1979. Djilas was a high-ranking member of the Yugoslav Communist Party and member of the government until his dismissal in 1956

3 I am a Communist, a convinced Communist! For some that may be a fantasy. But to me it is my main goal.

Mikhail Gorbachev (b.1931), Russian political leader: speech Dec. 1989, Second National Congress of People's Deputies, Moscow, quoted in the *New York Times*, 26 Dec. 1989. A week earlier, however, *Newsweek* had quoted Gorbachev as confiding to Prime Minister Margaret Thatcher, 'I don't even know if I'm a Communist any more.' Both pronouncements are discussed in Gail Sheehy's biography, *Gorbachev* (1991), Pt.6, 'Sakharov's Warning'

4 Communism, my friend, is more than Marxism, just as Catholicism ... is more than the Roman Curia. There is a *mystique* as well as a *politique*. ... Catholics and Communists have committed great crimes, but at least they have not stood aside, like an established society, and been indifferent. I would rather have blood on my hands than water like Pilate.

Graham Greene (1904–1991), British novelist: Dr Magiot, in *The Comedians* (1966), Pt.3, Ch.4, Sct.4

5 It would be simplistic to say that Divine Providence caused the fall of Communism. In a certain sense Communism as a system fell by itself. It fell as a consequence of its own mistakes and abuses, *It proved to be a medicine more dangerous than the disease itself*. It did not bring about true social reform, yet it did become a powerful threat and challenge to the entire world. But *it fell by itself, because of its own inherent weakness*.

Pope John Paul II [Karol Wojtyla] (b.1920), Polish ecclesiastic: *Crossing the Threshold of Hope* (1994), 'Was God at Work in the Fall of Communism?'

6 Many people feel empty, a world that seemed so strong just collapsed. Forty years have been wasted on stupid strife for the sake of an unsuccessful experiment. The values gathered together have vanished, the strategies for survival have become ridiculous. And so forty years of our lives have become a story, a bad anecdote. But it may be possible to remember these adventures with a kind of irony.

George Konrád (b.1933), Hungarian writer and politician: in the *Sunday Correspondent* (London), 15 April 1990

7 I can no longer sit back and allow Communist infiltration, Communist indoctrination, Communist subversion and the international Communist conspiracy to sap and impurify all of our precious bodily fluids.

Stanley Kubrick (b.1928), U.S. film-maker: General D. Ripper (Sterling Haydon), in *Dr Strangelove; or, How I Learned to Stop Worrying and Love the Bomb* (film; screenplay by Stanley Kubrick, Terry Southern and Peter George, based on Peter George's novel *Red Alert*, produced and directed by Stanley Kubrick, 1963)

8 The uninterrupted growth of the Communist Party, its conquest of the world, which was more rapid than the spread of Christianity or Islam, its catholic range, the faith, heroism and purity of its youth, its attachment, on the level of theory, to the great humanist ideals which it ultimately claimed for itself ... have accustomed us to hearing in this movement the very footsteps of Destiny.

Emmanuel Levinas (b.1905), French Jewish philosopher: 'Freedom of speech' (1957), rep. in *Difficult Freedom* (1990), Pt.5

9 Communists have always played an active role in the fight by colonial countries for their freedom, because the short-term objects of Communism would always correspond with the long-term objects of freedom movements.

Nelson Mandela (b.1918), South African political leader and president: statement to the court April/May 1964, in the Rivonia trial, South Africa, quoted in *Higher than Hope* by Fatima Meer (1988), Pt.4, Ch.24

10 Communism is not love. Communism is a hammer which we use to crush the enemy.

Mao Zedong (1893–1976), Chinese leader: quoted in *Time* (New York), 18 Dec. 1950

11 Dedicated communists are highly-trained political soldiers, equally prepared to sing in the choir of churches open to their infiltration, or to use machine-guns in the streets, which are conveniently carried beneath surplices.

Oswald Mosley (1896–1980), British fascist leader: *My Life* (1968), Ch.16

12 In the end we beat them with Levi 501 jeans. Seventy-two years of Communist indoctrination and propaganda was drowned out by a three-ounce Sony Walkman. A huge totalitarian system ... has been brought to its knees because nobody wants to wear Bulgarian shoes.... Now they're lunch, and we're number one on the planet.

P.J. O'Rourke (b.1947), U.S. journalist: 'The Death of Communism', publ. in *Rolling Stone* (New York), Nov. 1989, rep. in *Give War A Chance* (1992)

13 The atheism of a militant Communist is the essence of religion compared to the cynicism of a capitalist: in the first, one can always find those moments of idealism, of desperation, of psychological violence, of conscious will, of faith – which are elements, even degraded, of religion – in the second one finds only Mammon.

Pier Paolo Pasolini (1922–1975), Italian film-maker and essayist: 'Le belle bandiere' (column), in *Vie nuove*, 29 Oct. 1964, rep. in *Pasolini Requiem* by David Barth Schwartz (1992), Ch.18

14 We must conclude that it is not only a particular political ideology that has failed, but the idea that men and women could ever define themselves in terms that exclude their spiritual needs.

Salman Rushdie (b.1947), Indian-born British author: on the changes in Eastern Europe, in *The Independent* (London), 7 Feb. 1990

15 There are only two sorts of people in life you can trust – good Christians and good Communists.

Joe Slovo (1926–1994), South African leader of the Communist Party: in *The Independent* (London), 4 Nov. 1988

16 The crusade against Communism was even more imaginary than the spectre of Communism.

A.J.P. Taylor (1906–1990), British historian: *The Origins of the Second World War* (1961), Ch.2

17 Let's not talk about Communism. Communism was just an idea, just pie in the sky.

Boris Yeltsin (b.1931), Russian politician and president: remark during a visit to the U.S., quoted in *The Independent* (London), 13 Sept. 1989

18 Communists should be the first to be concerned about other people and country and the last to enjoy themselves.

Zhao Ziyang (b.1919), Chinese party official: in the *Financial Times* (London), 21 March 1988

19 I am a communist because I believe that the Communist idea is a state form of Christianity.

Alexander Zhuravlyov (b.1924), Byelorussian deputy: quoted in *The Observer* (London), 8 Sept. 1991

See also MARXISM; Koestler on RUSSIA; Solzhenitsyn on RUSSIA; SOCIALISM

COMMUNITIES

1 One of the weaknesses in the cooperative is that it has never been sufficiently leavened by the imagination. This is a quick-silver faculty, and likely to be a cause of worry to any collective settlement.
Edward Dahlberg (1900–1977), U.S. author and critic: *Alms for Oblivion* (1964), 'Our Vanishing Cooperative Colonies'

2 When a village ceases to be a community, it becomes oppressive in its narrow conformity. So one becomes an individual and migrates to the city. There, finding others likeminded, one re-establishes a village community. Nowadays only New Yorkers are yokels.
Paul Goodman (1911–1972), U.S. author, poet and critic: *Five Years* (1966), 'Winter and Spring 1956–1957', Sct.8

3 The village had institutionalized all human functions in forms of low intensity.... Participation was high and organization was low. This is the formula for stability.
Marshall McLuhan (1911–1980), Canadian communications theorist: *Understanding Media* (1964), Ch.10

4 Suddenly, it becomes a subversion of progress to assert the commonsensible principle that communities exist for the health and enjoyment of those who live in them, not for the convenience of those who drive through them, fly over them, or exploit their real estate for profit.
Theodore Roszak (b.1933), U.S. social critic: *Where the Wasteland Ends* (1972), Ch.7

5 One man's ceiling is another man's floor.
Paul Simon (b.1941), U.S. singer and songwriter: 'One Man's Ceiling is Another Man's Floor' (song), on the album *There Goes Rhymin' Simon* (1973)

6 Human beings *will* be happier – not when they cure cancer or get to Mars or eliminate racial prejudice or flush Lake Erie but when they find ways to inhabit primitive communities again. That's my utopia.
Kurt Vonnegut (b.1922), U.S. novelist: *Wampeters, Foma and Granfallons* (1974), 'Playboy Interview, 1973'

See also Carter on DISCIPLINE; Bloom on KNOWLEDGE; NEIGHBOURS; Debord on THE WORLD

COMPASSION

1 Compassion has no place in the natural order of the world which operates on the basis of necessity. Compassion opposes this order and is therefore best thought of as being in some way supernatural.
John Berger (b.1926), British author and critic: in *The Guardian* (London), 19 Dec. 1991

2 There is nothing heavier than compassion. Not even one's own pain weighs so heavy as the pain one feels with someone, for someone, a pain intensified by the imagination and prolonged by a hundred echoes.
Milan Kundera (b.1929), Czech-born French author and critic: *The Unbearable Lightness of Being* (1984), Pt.1, Ch.15

3 Minerva save us from the cloying syrup of coercive compassion!
Camille Paglia (b.1947), U.S. author and critic: 'The Big Udder', first publ. in the *Philadelphia Enquirer*, 12 May 1991, rep. in *Sex, Art, and American Culture* (1992)

4 No deep and strong feeling, such as we may come across here and there in the world, is unmixed with compassion. The more we love, the more the object of our love seems to us to be a victim.
Boris Pasternak (1890–1960), Russian poet, novelist and translator: *Doctor Zhivago* (1957; tr.1958), Ch.12, Sct.7

See also Miller on FAILURE; SYMPATHY

COMPETITION

1 It is better for a woman to compete impersonally in society, as men do, than to compete for dominance in her own home with her husband, compete with her neighbors for empty status, and so smother her son that he cannot compete at all.
Betty Friedan (b.1921), U.S. feminist writer: *The Feminine Mystique* (1963), Ch.18

2 Perfect competition is a theoretical concept like the Euclidean line, which has no width and no depth. Just as we've never seen that line there has never been truly free enterprise.
Milton Friedman (b.1912), U.S. economist: introduction to *There's No Such Thing as a Free Lunch* (1975)

3 Men often compete with one another until the day they die; comradeship consists of rubbing shoulders jocularly with a competitor.
Edward Hoagland (b.1932), U.S. novelist and essayist: 'Heaven and Nature', first publ. in *Harper's Magazine* (New York), March 1988, rep. in *Heart's Desire* (1988)

See also Durocher on SPORT

COMPLACENCY

1 In all life one should comfort the afflicted, but verily, also, one should afflict the comfortable, and especially when they are comfortably, contentedly, even happily wrong.
J.K. Galbraith (b.1908), U.S. economist: in *The Guardian* (London), 28 July 1989

2 He knew that he was precisely what he himself would have chosen to be had God consulted him on the subject of his birth; he fully appreciated and approved what had been bestowed, and realized that he couldn't have done the job better himself, in fact he would not have changed a single item.
Micheál MacLiammóir (1899–1978), Irish actor: on first meeting Orson Welles, in *All For Hecuba* (autobiography, 1947), Ch.4, 'Changes'

3 America is a hurricane, and the only people who do not hear the sound are those fortunate if incredibly stupid and smug White Protestants who live in the center, in the serene eye of the big wind.
Norman Mailer (b.1923), U.S. author: *Advertisements for Myself* (1959), Pt.5, 'Advertisement for "Games and Ends"'

COMPROMISE

1 If one cannot catch a bird of paradise, better take a wet hen.
Nikita Khrushchev (1894–1971), Soviet premier: quoted in *Time* (New York), 6 Jan. 1958

2 To be or not to be is not a question of compromise. Either you be or you don't be.
Golda Meir (1898–1978), Israeli politician and prime minister: on the question of Israel's future, quoted in the *New York Times*, 12 Dec. 1974

3 We will compromise on almost anything, but not on our values, or our asthetics, or our idealism, or our sense of curiosity.
Anita Roddick (b.1943), British businesswoman and founder of the Body Shop: *Body and Soul* (1991), Ch.11

See also Goodman on FREEDOM OF EXPRESSION; Bevan on INDECISION

COMPUTER TECHNOLOGY

1 Computer science only indicates the *retrospective* omnipotence of our technologies. In other words, an infinite capacity to process data (but only data – i.e. the *already given*) and in no sense a new vision. With that science, we are entering an era of exhaustivity, which is also an era of exhaustion.
Jean Baudrillard (b.1929), French semiologist: *Cool Memories* (1987; tr.1990), Ch.4

2 There is never finality in the display terminal's screen, but an irresponsible whimsicality, as words, sentences, and paragraphs are negated at the touch of a key. The significance of the past, as expressed in the manuscript by a deleted word or an inserted correction, is annulled in idle gusts of electronic massacre.
Alexander Cockburn (b.1941), Anglo-Irish journalist: on his preference for typewriters over word processors, in 'Pull the Plug', first publ. in *Mother Jones* (Boulder, Colorado), 11 Nov. 1986, rep. in *Corruptions of Empire* (1988), Pt.2

3 There is something about a monolithic tech culture like Microsoft that makes humans seriously rethink fundamental aspects of the relationship between their brains and their bodies – their souls and their ambitions; things and thoughts.
Douglas Coupland (b.1961), Canadian author: *Microserfs* (1995), 'Oop: Thursday-Later that week'

4 It is hardly surprising that children should enthusiastically start their education at an early age with the Absolute Knowledge of computer science; while they are unable to read, for reading demands making judgements at every line.... Conversation is almost dead, and soon so too will be those who knew how to speak.
Guy Debord (1931–1994), French Situationist philosopher: *Comments on the Society of the Spectacle* (1988; tr.1990), Ch.10

5 I think that the computer as some sort of discrete object that one owns and is very, very aware of ... will become a very quaint and antique concept.
William Gibson (b.1948), U.S. author: interview in *Rapid Eye 3* (ed. Simon Dwyer, 1995). Gibson predicted computers becoming 'small and transparent and finally invisible'

6 Media commentary on the virus scare has run not so much tongue-in-check as hand-in-glove with the rhetoric of AIDS hysteria ... the obsession with defence, security, and immunity; and the climate of suspicion generated around communitarian acts of sharing. The underlying moral imperative is this; you can't trust your best friend's software any more than you can trust his or her bodily fluids.
Andrew Ross (b.1956), British social theorist: *Strange Weather* (1991), Ch.2

7 This computer world offers a pretty sad, thin, painfully inadequate experience. I can't help feeling that access to this stuff isn't the big advantage they all think it is. I think the so-called data-rich may well turn out to be the losers: sad screen drones, plugging away with their mod cons and instant online access into

an empty space they think is exciting because it happens down a telephone line. ... In my world the privileged may well be the unplugged.

Janet Street-Porter (b.1946), British broadcaster and programme-maker: *Without Walls: J'Accuse – Technonerds* (Channel 4, 19 March 1996)

See also THE INTERNET

CONCENTRATION CAMPS

1 Despite the hundreds of attempts, police terror and the concentration camps have proved to be more or less impossible subjects for the artist; since what happened to them was beyond the imagination, it was therefore also beyond art and all those human values on which art is traditionally based.

A. Alvarez (b.1929), British critic, poet and novelist: *The Savage God* (1971), Pt.4, 'The Savage God'

2 The concentration camps, by making death itself anonymous (making it impossible to find out whether a prisoner is dead or alive), robbed death of its meaning as the end of a fulfilled life. In a sense they took away the individual's own death, proving that henceforth nothing belonged to him and he belonged to no one. His death merely set a seal on the fact that he had never existed.

Hannah Arendt (1906–1975), German-born U.S. political philosopher: *The Origins of Totalitarianism* (1951), Pt.3, Ch.12, Sct.3

3 If it is true that for a religious spirit the camps, like the torture of an innocent child by a brute, pose the supreme riddle, it is also true that for an agnostic spirit the same riddle springs up with the first act of compassion, heroism or love.

André Malraux (1901–1976), French man of letters and statesman: *Anti-Memoirs* (1967; tr.1968), 'The Human Condition', Sct.2

4 If you complain of people being shot down in the streets, of the absence of communication or social responsibility, of the rise of everyday violence which people have become accustomed to, and the dehumanization of feelings, then the ultimate development on an organized social level is the concentration camp. ... The concentration camp is the final expression of human separateness and its ultimate consequence. It is organized abandonment.

Arthur Miller (b.1915), U.S. playwright: in the *Paris Review* (Flushing, N.Y.), summer 1966. Miller regarded this concept as one of the prime themes of his 1964 play *After the Fall*, which featured a concentration camp in its staging

5 Here, lads, we live by the law of the *taiga*. But even here people manage to live. D'you know who are the ones the camps finish off? Those

who lick other men's left-overs, those who set store by the doctors, and those who peach on their mates.

Alexander Solzhenitsyn (b.1918), Russian novelist: Kuziomin, in *One Day in the Life of Ivan Denisovich* (1962; tr.1963), p.8 of Penguin edn.

6 I believe that all the survivors are mad. One time or another their madness will explode. You cannot absorb that much madness and not be influenced by it. That is why the children of survivors are so tragic. I see them in school. They don't know how to handle their parents. They see that their parents are traumatized: they scream and don't react normally.

Elie Wiesel (b.1928), Rumanian-born U.S. writer: interview in *Writers at Work* (Eighth Series, ed. George Plimpton, 1988)

CONFESSION

1 Literary confessors are contemptible, like beggars who exhibit their sores for money, but not so contemptible as the public that buys their books.

W.H. Auden (1907–1973), Anglo-American poet: *The Dyer's Hand* (1962), Pt.3, 'Hic et Ille', Sct.B

2 We have become a singularly confessing society. ... [The confession] plays a part in justice, medicine, education, family relationships, and love relations, in the most ordinary affairs of daily life, and in the most solemn rites: one confesses one's crimes, one's sins, one's thoughts and desires, one's illnesses and troubles; one goes about telling, with the greatest precision, whatever is most difficult to tell. ... One confesses – or is forced to confess.

Michel Foucault (1926–1984), French philosopher: *History of Sexuality* (1976; tr.1978), Vol.I

3 There are things to confess that enrich the world, and things that need not be said.

Joni Mitchell (b.1943), Canadian-born U.S. singer and songwriter: in *The Independent* (London), 13 May 1988

4 Confession, alas, is the new handshake.

Richard Dean Rosen (b.1949), U.S. journalist and critic: *Psychobabble: Fast Talk and Quick Cure in the Era of Feeling* (1977), 'Psychobabble'

See also Greer on STRANGERS

CONFORMITY

1 The American ideal, after all, is that everyone should be as much alike as possible.

James Baldwin (1924–1987), U.S. author: 'The Harlem Ghetto', first publ. in *Commentary* (New York), Feb. 1948, rep. in *Notes of a Native Son* (1955), Pt.2

2   If you give someone a white shirt and a tie and a ring of keys you'll find out what kind of a son of a bitch he is. Give them to him in the morning and you'll know before noon.
    Harry Crews (b.1935), U.S. author: interview in *Dazed and Confused* (London), April 1995

3   I find places where people are mixed up more compelling than places where everyone knows exactly what they are and what they should look like. ... You go to any city in the world, you walk into that one gay bar, and it's the same gay bar. It's a global village, it really is. And it's so uninteresting after a while.
    Todd Haynes (b.1961), U.S. film-maker: interview in *The Guardian* (London), 13 April 1996

4   Conformity is the jailer of freedom and the enemy of growth.
    John F. Kennedy (1917–1963), U.S. Democratic politician and president: address, 25 Sept. 1961, to the U.N. General Assembly, publ. in *Public Papers of the Presidents of the United States: John F. Kennedy, 1961*

5   What are we hoping to get out of it, what's it all in aid of – is it really just for the sake of a gloved hand waving at you from a golden coach?
    John Osborne (1929–1994), British playwright: Jean, in *The Entertainer* (1957), No.10

6   The concept of 'mental health' in our society is defined largely by the extent to which an individual behaves in accord with the needs of the system and does so without showing signs of stress.
    Unabomber, U.S. radical: *Industrial Society and Its Future*, 'Restriction of Freedom is Unavoidable in Industrial Society', Sct.119, publ. in the *Washington Post*, 19 Sept. 1995

See also Galbraith on INSTITUTIONS

CONSCIENCE

1   Freedom of conscience entails more dangers than authority and despotism.
    Michel Foucault (1926–1984), French philosopher: *Madness and Civilization* (1965), Ch.7

2   I cannot and will not cut my conscience to fit this year's fashions.
    Lillian Hellman (1905–1984), U.S. playwright: letter, 19 May 1952, to John S. Wood, Chairman of the House un-American Activities Committee, quoted in *The Nation* (New York), 31 May 1952. The letter explained Hellman's refusal to testify against colleagues accused of Communist affiliations

3   Conscience: self-esteem with a halo.
    Irving Layton (b.1912), Canadian poet: *The Whole Bloody Bird* (1969), 'Aphs'

4   There are some women ... in whom conscience is so strongly developed that it leaves little room for anything else. Love is scarcely felt before duty rushes to encase it, anger impossible because one must always be calm and see both sides, pity evaporates in expedients, even grief is felt as a sort of bruised sense of injury, a resentment that one should have grief forced upon one when one has always acted for the best.
    Sylvia Townsend Warner (1893–1978), British author: *Autumn River* (1966), 'Total Loss'

See also Solzhenitsyn on JUSTICE; Lee on THE MAJORITY

CONSCIOUSNESS

1   The real history of consciousness starts with one's first lie.
    Joseph Brodsky (1940–1996), Russian-born U.S. poet and critic: 'Less Than One', Sct.1 (1976), rep. in *Less Than One: Selected Essays* (1986)

2   Consciousness is much more than the thorn, it is the *dagger* in the flesh.
    E.M. Cioran (1911–1995), Rumanian-born French philosopher: *The Trouble with Being Born* (1973), Ch.3

3   The waking mind ... is the least serviceable in the arts.
    Henry Miller (1891–1980), U.S. author: interview in *Writers at Work* (Second Series, ed. George Plimpton, 1963)

CONSENSUS

1   Consensus Terrorism: The process that decides in-office attitudes and behavior.
    Douglas Coupland (b.1961), Canadian author: *Generation X* (1991), 'I Am Not a Target Market'

2   Consensus is what many people say in chorus but do not believe as individuals.
    Abba Eban (b.1915), Israeli politician: quoted in the *New Yorker*, 23 April 1990

3   Talk about the flag or drugs or crime (never about race or class or justice) and follow the yellow brick road to the wonderful land of 'consensus.' In place of honest argument among consenting adults the politicians substitute a lullaby for frightened children: the pretense that conflict doesn't really exist, that we have achieved the blessed state in which ... we no longer need politics.
    Lewis H. Lapham (b.1935), U.S. essayist and editor: 'Democracy in America?', publ. in *Harper's Magazine* (New York), Nov. 1990

4 A consensus politician is someone who does something that he doesn't believe is right because it keeps people quiet when he does it.
John Major (b.1943), British Conservative politician and prime minister: in the *Daily Mail* (London), 4 Jan. 1991

5 It is right always to try with the utmost patience to secure action by the gentle, English method of national agreement. More drastic action which bitterly divides the nation should only be undertaken if without it the nation may die.
Oswald Mosley (1896–1980), British fascist leader: *My Life* (1968), Ch.14

6 I am in favour of agreement but against consensus.
Margaret Thatcher (b.1925), British Conservative politician and prime minister: quoted in *One of Us* by Hugo Young (1989), Ch.18

See also Sontag on BOOKS: CLASSICS

THE CONSERVATIVE PARTY

1 Growing older, I have lost the need to be political, which means, in this country, the need to be left. I am driven into grudging toleration of the Conservative Party because it is the party of non-politics, of resistance to politics.
Kingsley Amis (1922–1995), British novelist and poet: in *The Sunday Telegraph* (London), 2 July 1967

2 No amount of cajolery, and no attempts at ethical or social seduction, can eradicate from my heart a deep burning hatred for the Tory Party. ... So far as I am concerned they are lower than vermin.
Aneurin Bevan (1897–1960), British Labour politician: speech, 4 July 1948, Manchester, quoted in *The Times* (London), 5 July 1948. Bevan was referring to the social policies of the Conservative Party, which 'condemned millions of first-class people to semi-starvation'. His invective, which formed part of a speech to inaugurate the National Health Service, provoked outrage in the press and embarrassment within his own party

3 The Conservative Party by long tradition and settled belief is the party of Empire. We are proud of its past. We see it as the surest hope in our own day. We proclaim our abiding faith in its destiny.
Conservative Party Manifesto: 'Britain Strong and Free', 1950: quoted by John Barnes in 'Ideology and Factions', publ. in *Conservative Century* (ed. Anthony Seldon and Stuart Ball, 1994), Pt.2

4 In order to succeed in our party the backbencher must be as wise as a dove and as

innocent as a serpent. He will, of course, have already recognised that what the party is presently suffering from is an addiction to an *idée en marche*, and he should promptly join the back of the column. Not to be a monetarist in today's party is to suffer from a severe handicap, it is the political equivalent of being young, black and unemployed.
Julian Critchley (b.1930), British Conservative politician: *Westminster Blues* (1985), Ch.12

5 Conservatives do not worship democracy. For them, majority rule is a device. ... And if it is leading to an end that is undesirable or inconsistent with itself, then there is a theoretical case for ending it.
Ian Gilmour (b.1926), British Conservative politician: *Inside Right* (1977), Pt.3, Ch.5

6 The cardinal point about Conservatism is that it binds the Conservatives together with one simple precept, which is respect for property. ... The respect that the Conservatives have for the initiative of the individual all turns on wealth, and there's no harm in that, but since it's a respect for a man who can amass wealth, it overrides any respect for intelligence, health or any other consideration.
Lord Goodman (1913–1995), British lawyer and public figure: interview in *Singular Encounters* by Naim Attallah (1990), 'Lord Goodman'

7 There is one thing you can be sure of with the Conservative Party, before anything else – they have a grand sense for where the votes are.
Enoch Powell (b.1912), British Conservative politician: in *The Listener* (London), 28 May 1981

See also JOHN MAJOR; MARGARET THATCHER

CONSERVATIVES

1 There are no black conservatives. Oh, there are neoconservatives with black skin, but they lack any claim to blackness other than the biological. They have forgotten their roots.
Stephen Carter (b.1954), U.S. lawyer and author: *Reflections of an Affirmative Action Baby* (1992), Ch.8

2 The world is burdened with young fogies. Old men with ossified minds are easily dealt with. But men who look young, act young and everlastingly harp on the fact that they are young, but who nevertheless think and act with a degree of caution that would be excessive in their grandfathers, are the curse of the world. Their very conservatism is secondhand, and they don't know what they are conserving.
Robertson Davies (1913–1995), Canadian novelist and journalist: *The Enthusiasms of Robertson Davies* (1990), 'The Table Talk of Robertson Davies'

3   We look like Republicans, and think like conservatives, but we drive a lot faster and keep vibrators and baby oil and a video camera behind the stack of sweaters on the bedroom closet shelf.
    P.J. O'Rourke (b.1947), U.S. journalist: introduction to *Republican Party Reptile* (1987)

4   The values to which the conservative appeals are inevitably caricatured by the individuals designated to put them into practice.
    Harold Rosenberg (1906–1978), U.S. art critic and author: 'The Cultural Situation Today', first publ. in the *Partisan Review* (New Brunswick, N.J.), summer 1972, rep. as introduction to *Discovering the Present* (1973)

5   The word 'conservative' is used by the BBC as a portmanteau word of abuse for anyone whose views differ from the insufferable, smug, sanctimonious, naive, guilt-ridden, wet, pink orthodoxy of that sunset home of the third-rate minds of that third-rate decade, the nineteen-sixties.
    Norman Tebbit (b.1931), British Conservative politician: quoted in *The Independent* (London), 24 Feb. 1990

6   The conservatives are fools: They whine about the decay of traditional values, yet they enthusiastically support technological progress and economic growth. Apparently it never occurs to them that you can't make rapid, drastic changes in the technology and the economy of a society without causing rapid changes in all other aspects of the society as well, and that such rapid changes inevitably break down traditional values.
    Unabomber, U.S. radical: *Industrial Society and Its Future*, 'Sources of Social Problems', Sct.50, publ. in the *Washington Post* 19 Sept. 1995

7   To be conservative requires no brains whatsoever. Cabbages, cows and conifers are conservatives, and are so stupid they don't even know it. All that is basically required is acceptance of what exists.
    Colin Welch (b.1924), British journalist: in *The Spectator* (London), 21 July 1967

See also Arendt on REVOLUTIONARIES

CONSPIRACIES

1   If we are on the outside, we assume a conspiracy is the perfect working of a scheme. Silent nameless men with unadorned hearts. A conspiracy is everything that ordinary life is not. It's the inside game, cold, sure, undistracted, forever closed off to us. We are the flawed ones, the innocents, trying to make some rough sense of the daily jostle. Conspirators have a logic and a daring beyond our reach. All conspiracies are the same taut story of men who find coherence in some criminal act.
    Don DeLillo (b.1926), U.S. author: *Libra* (1988), Pt.2, 'In Dallas'

2   The search for conspiracy only increases the elements of morbidity and paranoia and fantasy in this country. It romanticizes crimes that are terrible because of their lack of purpose. It obscures our necessary understanding, all of us, that in this life there is often tragedy without reason.
    Anthony Lewis (b.1927), U.S. journalist: in the *New York Times*, 25 Sept. 1975

3   Anyone who knows how difficult it is to keep a secret among three men – particularly if they are married – knows how absurd is the idea of a worldwide secret conspiracy consciously controlling all mankind by its financial power; in real, clear analysis these deep plots are seldom anything more sinister than the usual vast muddle.
    Oswald Mosley (1896–1980), British fascist leader: *My Life* (1968), Ch.18

CONSUMERISM

1   The technological landscape of the present day has enfranchised its own electorates – the inhabitants of marketing zones in the consumer goods society, television audiences and news magazine readerships ... vote with money at the cash counter rather than with the ballot paper at the polling booth.
    J.G. Ballard (b.1930), British author: 'The Consumer Consumer', first publ. in *Ink*, 5 June 1971, rep. in *Re/Search* (San Francisco), No.8/9, 1984

2   Large department stores, with their luxuriant abundance of canned goods, foods, and clothing, are like the primary landscape and the geometrical locus of affluence. Streets with overcrowded and glittering store windows ... the displays of delicacies, and all the scenes of alimentary and vestimentary festivity, stimulate a magical salivation. Accumulation is more than the sum of its products: the conspicuousness of surplus, the final and magical negation of scarcity ... mimic a new-found nature of prodigious fecundity.
    Jean Baudrillard (b.1929), French semiologist: 'Consumer Society', publ. in *La Société de Consommation* (1970), rep. in *Selected Writings* (ed. Mark Poster, 1988)

3   In our world it seems that as soon as a clear need appears, it is met falsely. It becomes a new occasion for exploitation. ... We are not sold real apples or real ice cream, we are sold

the idea of the apple, the memory of ice cream.

Saul Bellow (b.1915), U.S. novelist: 'A Matter of the Soul', first publ. in *Opera News*, 11 Jan. 1975, rep. in *It All Adds Up* (1994)

4 You really have to wonder why we even bother to get *up* in the morning. I mean, really: *Why work?* Simply to buy more *stuff?*

Douglas Coupland (b.1961), Canadian author: Dag, in *Generation X* (1991), 'Quit Your Job'

5 Living is more a question of what one spends than what one makes.

Marcel Duchamp (1887–1968), French artist: *Dialogues with Marcel Duchamp* (ed. Pierre Cabanne, 1967), Ch.4

6 ... Everything from toy guns that spark
To flesh-colored Christs that glow in the dark
It's easy to see without looking too far
That not much is really sacred.

Bob Dylan (b.1941), U.S. singer and songwriter: 'It's Alright Ma (I'm Only Bleeding),' (song), on the album *Bringing it all Back Home* (1965)

7 Modern man, if he dared to be articulate about his concept of heaven, would describe a vision which would look like the biggest department store in the world, showing new things and gadgets, and himself having plenty of money with which to buy them. He would wander around open-mouthed in this heaven of gadgets and commodities, provided only that there were ever more and newer things to buy, and perhaps that his neighbors were just a little less privileged than he.

Erich Fromm (1900–1980), U.S. psychologist: *The Sane Society* (1955), Ch.5, 'Alienation'

8 Consumer wants can have bizarre, frivolous, or even immoral origins, and an admirable case can still be made for a society that seeks to satisfy them. But the case cannot stand if it is the process of satisfying wants that creates the wants.

J.K. Galbraith (b.1908), U.S. economist: *The Affluent Society* (1958), Ch.11, Sct.2

9 The mystical nature of American consumption accounts for its joylessness. We spend a great deal of time in stores, but if we don't seem to take much pleasure in our buying, it's because we're engaged in the acts of sacrifice and self-definition. Abashed in the presence of expensive merchandise, we recognize ourselves ... as suppliants admitted to a shrine.

Lewis H. Lapham (b.1935), U.S. essayist and editor: *Money and Class in America* (1988), Ch.8

10 In our rich consumers' civilization we spin cocoons around ourselves and get possessed by our possessions.

Max Lerner (1902–1992), U.S. author and columnist: 'What Shall I Save?', first publ. in the *New York Post*, 10 Sept. 1952, rep. in *The Unfinished Country* (1959), Pt.1

11 Truly great brands are far more than just labels for products; they are symbols that encapsulate the desires of consumers; they are standards held aloft under which the masses congregate.

Tony O'Reilly (b.1936), Irish entrepreneur: speech to British Council of Shopping Centres, 1990, quoted by Fintan O'Toole in 'Brand Leader', publ. in *Granta* (London), No.53, spring 1996

12 The power of consumer goods ... has been engendered by the so-called liberal and progressive demands of freedom, and, by appropriating them, has emptied them of their meaning, and changed their nature.

Pier Paolo Pasolini (1922–1975), Italian film-maker and essayist: 'Sono Contro l'Aborto', publ. in *Il Corriere della Sera* (Milan), 19 Jan. 1975, rep. in *Scritti Corsari* (1975)

13 We're living in a shop. The world is one magnificent fucking shop, and if it hasn't got a price tag, it isn't worth having. There is no greater freedom than freedom of choice.

Bruce Robinson (b.1946), British film-maker: Dennis Bagley (Richard E. Grant), in *How to Get Ahead in Advertising* (film; written and directed by Bruce Robinson, 1989)

14 How do you ennoble the spirit when you are selling something as inconsequential as a cosmetic cream?

Anita Roddick (b.1943), British businesswoman and founder of the Body Shop: *Body and Soul* (1991), Ch.1

15 With the supermarket as our temple and the singing commercial as our litany, are we likely to fire the world with an irresistible vision of America's exalted purpose and inspiring way of life?

Adlai Stevenson (1900–1965), U.S. Democratic politician: in the *Wall Street Journal* (New York), 1 June 1960

16 It would be a bad strategy for the revolutionaries to condemn Americans for their habits of consumption. Instead, the average American should be portrayed as a victim of the advertising and marketing industry, which has suckered him into buying a lot of junk that he doesn't need and that is very poor compensation for his lost freedom. Either approach is consistent with the facts. It is merely a matter of attitude whether you blame the advertising industry for manipulating the public or blame the public for allowing itself to be manipulated. As a matter of strategy one should generally avoid blaming the public.

Unabomber, U.S. radical: *Industrial Society and Its Future*, 'Strategy', Sct.190, publ. in the *Washington Post*, 19 Sept. 1995

17 In the kingdom of consumption the citizen is king. A democratic monarchy: equality before consumption, fraternity in consumption, and freedom through consumption. The dictatorship of consumer goods has finally destroyed the barriers of blood, lineage and race.
Raoul Vaneigem (b.1934), Belgian Situationist philosopher: *The Revolution of Everyday Life* (1967; tr.1983), Ch.7 Sct.2. 'The ideology of consumption,' Vaneigem wrote, 'becomes the consumption of ideology.'

18 What's great about this country is that America started the tradition where the richest consumers buy essentially the same things as the poorest.
Andy Warhol (c.1928–1987), U.S. Pop artist: *From A to B and Back Again* (1975), Ch.6

See also York on ADVERTISING

CONTEMPLATION

1 I admire people who are suited to the contemplative life. ... They can sit inside themselves like honey in a jar and just be. It's wonderful to have someone like that around, you always feel you can count on them. You can go away and come back, you can change your mind and your hairdo and your politics, and when you get through doing all these upsetting things, you look around and there they are, just the way they were, just being.
Elizabeth Janeway (b.1913), U.S. author: *Accident on Route 37* (1964), 'Elizabeth Jowett'

2 The national distrust of the contemplative temperament arises less from an innate Philistinism than from a suspicion of anything that cannot be counted, stuffed, framed or mounted over the fireplace in the den.
Lewis H. Lapham (b.1935), U.S. essayist and editor: *Money and Class in America* (1988), Ch.8

CONTRADICTION

1 I happen to feel that the degree of a person's intelligence is directly reflected by the number of conflicting attitudes she can bring to bear on the same topic.
Lisa Alther (b.1944), U.S. novelist: Ginny Babcock, in *Kinflicks* (1976), Ch.7

2 What I claim is to live to the full the contradiction of my time, which may well make sarcasm the condition of truth.
Roland Barthes (1915–1980), French semiologist: preface to *Mythologies* (1957)

3 I believe that truth has only one face: that of a violent contradiction.
(*La vérité je crois n'a qu'un visage: celui d'un démenti violent.*)

Georges Bataille (1897–1962), French novelist and critic: preface to *The Deadman* (1967), rep. in *Violent Silence* (ed. Paul Buck, 1984)

4 I have forced myself to contradict myself in order to avoid conforming to my own taste.
Marcel Duchamp (1887–1968), French artist: quoted in 'Marcel Duchamp: Anti-Artist' by Harriet and Sidney Janis, first publ. in *View* (New York), 21 March 1945, rep. in *Dada Painters and Poets* by Robert Motherwell (1951)

5 I claim the right to contradict myself. I don't want to deprive myself of the right to talk nonsense, and I ask humbly to be allowed to be wrong sometimes.
Federico Fellini (1920–1993), Italian film-maker: *Fellini on Fellini* (ed. Anna Keel and Christian Strich, 1974; tr.1977), 'Miscellany I,' Sct.16

6 *Doublethink* means the power of holding two contradictory beliefs in one's mind simultaneously, and accepting both of them.
George Orwell (1903–1950), British author: extract from Goldstein's book, in *Nineteen Eighty-four* (1949), Pt.2, Ch.9

CONTROL

1 You can't control life. It doesn't wind up perfectly. Only ... only art you can control. Art and masturbation. Two areas in which I am an absolute expert.
Woody Allen (b.1935), U.S. film-maker: Sandy Bates (Woody Allen), in *Stardust Memories* (film; written and directed by Woody Allen, 1980)

2 When you sleep, you don't control your dream. I like to dive into a dream world that I've made, a world I chose and that I have complete contol over.
David Lynch (b.1947), U.S. film-maker: in *La Revue du Cinéma* (Paris), Feb. 1987, quoted in *David Lynch* by Michel Chion (1992), Ch.5

3 What the wretched of the earth need to improve their material lot is what the poor of our own country need. Nothing technological, but something through and through political. They need control over their own communities.
Theodore Roszak (b.1933), U.S. social critic: *Where the Wasteland Ends* (1972), Ch.12

4 If someone does something we disapprove of, we regard him as bad if we believe we can deter him from persisting in his conduct, but we regard him as mad if we believe we cannot. In either case, the crucial issue is our control of the other: the more we lose control over him, and the more he assumes control over himself, the more, in case of conflict, we are likely to consider him mad rather than just bad.
Thomas Szasz (b.1920), U.S. psychiatrist: *The Second Sin* (1973), 'Control and Self-control'

CONVERSATION

1   A sudden silence in the middle of a conversation suddenly brings us back to essentials: it reveals how dearly we must pay for the invention of speech.
E.M. Cioran (1911–1995), Rumanian-born French philosopher: *Anathemas and Admirations* (1986), 'On the Verge of Existence'

2   No collection of people who are all waiting for the same thing are capable of holding a natural conversation. Even if the thing they are waiting for is only a taxi.
Ben Elton (b.1959), British author and comic: *Stark* (1989), 'Airport Rescue'

3   The opposite of talking isn't listening. The opposite of talking is waiting.
Fran Lebowitz (b.1951), U.S. journalist: *Social Studies* (1981), 'People'

4   The techniques of opening conversation are universal. I knew long ago and rediscovered that the best way to attract attention, help, and conversation is to be lost. A man who seeing his mother starving to death on a path kicks her in the stomach to clear the way, will cheerfully devote several hours of his time giving wrong directions to a total stranger who claims to be lost.
John Steinbeck (1902–1968), U.S. author: *Travels With Charley: in Search of America* (1961), Pt.1

CONVERSION

1   Jesus tapped me on the shoulder and said, Bob, why are you resisting me? I said, I'm not resisting you! He said, You gonna follow me? I said, I've never thought about that before! He said, When you're not following me, you're resisting me.
Bob Dylan (b.1941), U.S. singer and songwriter: said on stage at Syracuse, New York, May 1980, quoted in *Q Magazine* (London), Jan.1990

2   I used to say: 'there is a God-shaped hole in me.' For a long time I stressed the absence, the hole. Now I find it is the shape which has become more important.
Salman Rushdie (b.1947), Indian-born British author: on his conversion to Islam after being branded an 'enemy of Islam' by the Iranian government, publ. in the *Independent on Sunday*, 30 Dec.1990

COOKERY

1   Life is too short to stuff a mushroom.
Shirley Conran (b.1932), British designer and journalist: epigraph to *Superwoman* (1975)

2   If cooking becomes an art form rather than a means of providing a reasonable diet, then something is clearly wrong.
Tom Jaine (b.1943), British editor of *The Good Food Guide*: in *The Daily Telegraph* (London), 19 Oct.1989

3   I did toy with the idea of doing a cook-book. ... The recipes were to be the routine ones: how to make dry toast, instant coffee, hearts of lettuce and brownies. But as an added attraction, at no extra charge, my idea was to put a fried egg on the cover. I think a lot of people who hate literature but love fried eggs would buy it if the price was right.
Groucho Marx (1895–1977), U.S. comic actor: *Groucho and Me* (1959), Ch.1

CORRUPTION

1   Life is a corrupting process from the time a child learns to play his mother off against his father in the politics of when to go to bed; he who fears corruption fears life.
Saul Alinsky (1909–1972), U.S. political activist: *Rules for Radicals* (1971), 'Of Means and Ends'

2   I wasn't strong enough to resist corruption, but I was strong enough to fight for a piece of it.
John Garfield (1913–1952), U.S. actor: Joe Morse (John Garfield), in *Force of Evil* (film; screenplay by Abraham Polonsky and Ira Wolfert, adapted from Ira Wolfert's novel, directed by Abraham Polonsky, 1948)

3   I have often noticed that a bribe ... has that effect – it changes a relation. The man who offers a bribe gives away a little of his own importance; the bribe once accepted, he becomes the inferior, like a man who has paid for a woman.
Graham Greene (1904–1991), British novelist: *The Comedians* (1966), Pt.1, Ch.4, Sct.3

4   The accomplice to the crime of corruption is frequently our own indifference.
Bess Myerson (b.1924), U.S. government official and columnist: quoted in 'Impeachment?' by Claire Safran, publ. in *Redbook* (New York), April 1974

5   I welcome this kind of examination because people have got to know whether or not their President is a crook. Well, I'm not a crook.
Richard Nixon (1913–1992), U.S. Republican politician and president: press conference, 17 Nov. 1973, publ. in the *New York Times*, 18 Nov. 1973

See also Berlusconi on ITALY

COSMETIC SURGERY

1 Look at the movie stars, they took the skin from their ass and stuck it on their face. The skin on the ass was the last to wrinkle. They all walked around in their later years with buttock faces.
Charles Bukowski (1920–1994), U.S. author and poet: the narrator (Nicky Belane), in *Pulp* (1994), Ch.4

2 The reason I come off being sexy and attractive – I still can't bring myself to say 'pretty' – is because I have had myself re-built. I had the hair under my arms taken care of. And I had an operation to firm up my breasts. And I spend about $1,000 a week to have my toenails, fingernails, eyebrows and hair put in top shape. I'm the female equivalent of a counterfeit $20 bill. Half of what you see is a pretty good reproduction, and the rest is a fraud.
Cher (b.1946), U.S. singer and actress: quoted in *Star Speak: Hollywood on Everything* (ed. Doug McClelland, 1987), 'Self-Improvement'

3 Women have face-lifts in a society in which women without them appear to vanish from sight.
Naomi Wolf (b.1962), U.S. author: *The Beauty Myth* (1990), 'Violence'

THE COSMOS

1 The Answer to the Great Question ... Of Life, the Universe and Everything ... Is ... Forty-two.
Douglas Adams (b.1952), British author: the computer Deep Thought, in *The Hitch Hiker's Guide to the Galaxy* (1979), Ch.27

2 If we find the answer to that, it would be the ultimate triumph of human reason – for then we would know the mind of God.
Stephen Hawking (b.1942), British theoretical physicist: closing words of *A Brief History of Time* (1988), Ch.11, referring to the question, 'why it is that we and the universe exist'

THE COUNTERCULTURE

1 Mis-shapes, mis-takes, mis-fits.
Raised on a diet of broken biscuits,
oh we don't look the same as you,
we don't do the things you do,
but we live round here too.
Jarvis Cocker (b.1963), British rock musician: 'Misshapes' (song), on the album *Different Class* (Pulp, 1995)

2 It is in our interests to let the police and their employers go on believing that the Underground is a conspiracy, because it increases their paranoia and their inability to deal with what is really happening. As long as they look for ringleaders and documents they will miss their mark, which is that proportion of every personality which belongs in the Underground.
Germaine Greer (b.1939), Australian feminist writer: 'The Million-Dollar Underground', first publ. in *Oz* (London), July 1969, rep. in *The Madwoman's Underclothes* (1986)

3 My advice to people today is as follows: If you take the game of life seriously, if you take your nervous system seriously, if you take your sense organs seriously, if you take the energy process seriously, you must turn on, tune in, and drop out.
Timothy Leary (1920–1996), U.S. psychologist: lecture, 1966, publ. in *The Politics of Ecstasy* (1968), Ch.21. Thirty years later, Leary suggested a variation of this slogan, 'Tune in, turn on, boot up,' quoted in an interview in *The Guardian* (London), 2 Dec. 1995

4 What concerns me here ... are the different conditions that exist today for recognising countercultural expression and activism. Twenty years later, the technology of hacking and viral guerilla warfare occupies a similar place in countercultural fantasy as the Molotov cocktail design once did.
Andrew Ross (b.1956), British social theorist: *Strange Weather* (1991), Ch.2

See also HIPPIES

COUNTRY LIFE

1 Cow dung and horse dung, as muck goes, are relatively agreeable. You can even become nostalgic about them. They smell of fermented grain, and on the far side of their smell there is hay and grass.
John Berger (b.1926), British author and critic: 'Muck and Its Entanglements', first publ. in *Harper's Magazine* (New York), May 1989, rep. in *Keeping a Rendezvous* (1992), as 'A Load of Shit'

2 The country is laid out in a haphazard, sloppy fashion, offensive to the tidy, organized mind.
Alan Brien (b.1925), British novelist and humorist: *Punch* (London), 22 March 1979

3 Country people do not behave as if they think life is short; they live on the principle that it is long, and savor variations of the kind best appreciated if most days are the same.
Edward Hoagland (b.1932), U.S. novelist and essayist: 'The Ridge-Slope Fox and the Knife Thrower', first publ. in *Harper's Magazine* (New York), Jan. 1977, rep. in *Heart's Desire* (1988)

4   To put it rather bluntly, I am not the type who wants to go back to the land; I am the type who wants to go back to the hotel.
Fran Lebowitz (b.1951), U.S. journalist: *Social Studies* (1981), 'Things'

5   I love the idea of being in the country, but then when I get there it comes back to me that:
I love to walk but I can't
I love to swim but I can't
I love to sit in the sun but I can't
I love to smell the flowers but I can't ...
The reason 'I can't' is simply because I'm *not the type*.
Andy Warhol (c.1928–1987), U.S. Pop artist: *From A to B and Back Again* (1975), Ch.10

COUNTRY MUSIC *see under* MUSIC

COUPLES

1   Constant togetherness is fine – but only for Siamese twins.
Victoria Billings (b.1945), U.S. journalist and author: *The Womansbook* (1974), 'A Love to Believe In'

2   The path of true love isn't smooth,
the ruffled feathers sex can soothe
ruffle again – for couples never
spend all their lives in bed together.
Gavin Ewart (1916–1995), British poet: '24th March 1986', publ. in *Late Pickings* (1987)

3   With my brains and your looks, we could go places.
John Garfield (1913-1952), U.S. actor: Frank Chambers (John Garfield), in *The Postman Always Rings Twice* (film; screenplay by Harry Ruskin and Niven Busch, adapted from James M. Cain's novel, directed by Tay Garnett, 1946)

4   Individually they were perhaps a little too attractive, but marriage neutered the appeal.
Jay McInerney (b.1955), U.S. author: *Brightness Falls* (1992), Ch.1

5   If we are a metaphor of the universe, the human couple is the metaphor par excellence, the point of intersection of all forces and the seed of all forms. The couple is time recaptured, the return to the time before time.
Octavio Paz (b.1914), Mexican poet and essayist: *Alternating Current* (1967), 'André Breton or the Quest of the Beginning'

COURAGE

1   Until the day of his death, no man can be sure of his courage.
(*Avant le jour de sa mort, personne ne sait exactement son courage.*)

Jean Anouilh (1910–1987), French playwright: Thomas à Becket, in *Becket* (1959; tr.1961), Act 1

2   Nothing gives a fearful man more courage than another's fear.
Umberto Eco (b.1932), Italian semiologist and novelist: *The Name of the Rose* (1980; tr.1983), 'Third Day: After Compline'

3   You take a number of small steps which you believe are right, thinking maybe tomorrow somebody will treat this as a dangerous provocation. And then you wait. If there is no reaction, you take another step: courage is only an accumulation of small steps.
George Konrád (b.1933), Hungarian writer and politician: on surviving as a writer in Communist Hungary, in the *Sunday Correspondent* (London), 15 April 1990

4   The idea was to prove at every foot of the way up that you were one of the elected and anointed ones who had *the right stuff* and could move higher and higher and even – ultimately, God willing, one day – that you might be able to join that special few at the very top, that elite who had the capacity to bring tears to men's eyes, the very Brotherhood of the Right Stuff itself.
Tom Wolfe (b.1931), U.S. author and journalist: on pilots and astronauts on the NASA training program, in the *Right Stuff* (1979), Ch.2

COWARDICE

1   When cowardice is made respectable, its followers are without number both from among the weak and the strong; it easily becomes a fashion.
Eric Hoffer (1902–1983), U.S. philosopher: *The Passionate State of Mind* (1955), Aph.203

2   I'm a hero wid coward's legs, I'm a hero from the waist up.
Spike Milligan (b.1918), British comedian and humorous writer: *Puckoon* (1963), Ch.2

CREATIVITY

1   No one has ever written, painted, sculpted, modeled, built, or invented except literally to get out of hell.
(*Nul n'a jamais écrit ou peint, sculpté, modelé, construit, inventé, que pour sortir en fait de l'enfer.*)
Antonin Artaud (1896–1948), French theatre producer, actor and theorist: *Van Gogh, the Man Suicided by Society* (1947), rep. in *Selected Writings* (ed. Susan Sontag, 1976), Pt.33

2   All works of art are commissioned in the sense that no artist can create one by a simple act of

will but must wait until what he believes to be a good idea for a work 'comes' to him.

W.H. Auden (1907–1973), Anglo-American poet: *The Dyer's Hand* (1962), Pt.1, 'Writing'

3 It's like driving a car at night. You never see further than your headlights, but you can make the whole trip that way.

E.L. Doctorow (b.1931), U.S. novelist: on his writing technique, in interview in *Writers at Work* (Eighth Series, ed. George Plimpton, 1988)

4 All in all, the creative act is not performed by the artist alone; the spectator brings the work in contact with the external world by deciphering and interpreting its inner qualifications and thus adds his contribution to the creative act. This becomes even more obvious when posterity gives its final verdict and sometimes rehabilitates forgotten artists.

Marcel Duchamp (1887–1968), French artist: 'The Creative Act', lecture, April 1957, Houston, Texas, publ. in *Art News* (New York), summer 1957, rep. in *Marcel Duchamp* by Robert Lebel (1959)

5 Our current obsession with creativity is the result of our continued striving for immortality in an era when most people no longer believe in an after-life.

Arianna Huffington [formerly Arianna Stassinopoulos] (b.1950), Greek author: *The Female Woman* (1973), 'The Working Woman'

6 Americans worship creativity the way they worship physical beauty – as a way of enjoying elitism without guilt: God did it.

Florence King (b.1936), U.S. author: *Reflections in a Jaundiced Eye* (1989), 'Democracy'

7 True creativity often starts where language ends.

Arthur Koestler (1905–1983), Hungarian-born British novelist and essayist: *The Act of Creation* (1964), Bk.1, Pt.2, Ch.7

8 I am beginning to think of the creative imagination as a fruit machine on which victories are rare and separated by much vain expense, and represent a rare alignment of mental and spiritual qualities that normally are quite at odds.

Philip Larkin (1912–1992), British poet: letter, 26 Feb. 1950, publ. in *Selected Letters of Philip Larkin 1940–1985* (ed. Anthony Thwaite, 1992)

9 Many of the creative spirits of our time do not realize that what seems to them to be the deepest expression of their being is often deadly poison injected into them by their most implacable enemies. Dying capitalism is filling the cup of human creation with a bitter brew.

Pablo Neruda (1904–1973), Chilean poet: *Let the Rail Splitter Awake and Other Poems* (1950), 'Our Duty Toward Life'

10 We try not to have ideas, preferring accidents. To create, you must empty yourself of every artistic thought.

Gilbert Proesch [of Gilbert and George] (b.1943), Italian-born British artist: in *The Independent* (London), 17 April 1989

11 Whoever undertakes to create soon finds himself engaged in creating himself. Self-transformation and the transformation of others have constituted the radical interest of our century, whether in painting, psychiatry, or political action.

Harold Rosenberg (1906–1978), U.S. art critic and author: preface to *The Tradition of the New* (1960)

12 The creative person, the person who moves from an irrational source of power, has to face the fact that this power antagonizes. Under all the superficial praise of the 'creative' is the desire to kill. It is the old war between the mystic and the nonmystic, a war to the death.

May Sarton (b.1912), U.S. poet and novelist: *Mrs Stevens Hears the Mermaids Singing* (1965), Pt.2

13 It is almost as if you were frantically constructing another world while the world that you live in dissolves beneath your feet, and that your survival depends on completing this construction at least one second before the old habitation collapses.

Tennessee Williams (1911–1983), U.S. playwright: author's foreword to *Camino Real* , written prior to the play's Broadway première and publ. in the *New York Times*, 15 March 1953

See also Chandler on REASON

CREDULITY

1 Our credulity is greatest concerning the things we know least about. And since we know least about ourselves, we are ready to believe all that is said about us. Hence the mysterious power of both flattery and calumny.

Eric Hoffer (1902–1983), U.S. philosopher: *The Passionate State of Mind* (1955), Aph. 128

2 One of the peculiar sins of the twentieth century which we've developed to a very high level is the sin of credulity. It has been said that when human beings stop believing in God they believe in nothing. The truth is much worse: they believe in anything.

Malcolm Muggeridge (1903–1990), British journalist and broadcaster: radio broadcast, *Woman's Hour*, 23 March 1966, publ. in *Muggeridge Through the Microphone* (1967), 'An Eighth Deadly Sin'

3 Man is a credulous animal, and must believe *something*; in the absence of good grounds for belief, he will be satisfied with bad ones.

Bertrand Russell (1872–1970), British philosopher and mathematician: *Unpopular Essays* (1950), 'An Outline of Intellectual Rubbish'

CREEDS

1   There lies at the back of every creed something terrible and hard for which the worshipper may one day be required to suffer.
E.M. Forster (1879–1970), British novelist and essayist: *Two Cheers for Democracy* (1951), 'What I Believe'

2   I always divide people into two groups. Those who live by what they know to be a lie, and those who live by what they believe, falsely, to be the truth.
Christopher Hampton (b.1946), British playwright: Don, in *The Philanthropist* (1970), Sc.6

3   If you have embraced a creed which appears to be free from the ordinary dirtiness of politics – a creed from which you yourself cannot expect to draw any material advantage – surely that proves that you are in the right?
George Orwell (1903–1950), British author: *Shooting an Elephant* (1950), 'Lear, Tolstoy and the Fool'

CRICKET *see under* SPORT

CRIME

1   Stripped of ethical rationalizations and philosophical pretensions, a crime is anything that a group in power chooses to prohibit.
Freda Adler (b.1934), U.S. educator and author: *Sisters in Crime* (1975), Ch.7

2   No punishment has ever possessed enough power of deterrence to prevent the commission of crimes. On the contrary, whatever the punishment, once a specific crime has appeared for the first time, its reappearance is more likely than its initial emergence could ever have been.
Hannah Arendt (1906–1975), German-born U.S. political philosopher: epilogue to *Eichmann in Jerusalem* (1963)

3   Crime is a fact of the human species, a fact of that species alone, but it is above all the secret aspect, impenetrable and hidden. Crime hides, and by far the most terrifying things are those which elude us.
Georges Bataille (1897–1962), French novelist and critic: *The Trial of Gilles de Rais* (1965, rev.1991), 'The Tragedy of Gilles de Rais: Sacred Monster'

4   The world of crime ... is a last refuge of the authentic, uncorrupted, spontaneous event.
Daniel J. Boorstin (b.1914), U.S. historian: *The Image* (1961), Ch.6

5   Crime seems to change character when it crosses a bridge or a tunnel. In the city, crime is taken as emblematic of class and race. In the suburbs though, it's intimate and psychological – resistant to generalization, a mystery of the individual soul.
Barbara Ehrenreich (b.1941), U.S. author and columnist: 'Marginal Men' (1989), rep. in *The Worst Years of Our Lives* (1991)

6   Crimes of which a people is ashamed constitute its real history. The same is true of man.
Jean Genet (1910–1986), French playwright and novelist: notes for *The Screens* (1961; tr.1973)

7   After all, crime is only a lefthanded form of human endeavor.
John Huston (1906-1987), U.S. film-maker: Emmerich (Louis Calhern), in *The Asphalt Jungle* (film; written and directed by John Huston, based on a novel by W.R. Burnett, 1950)

8   Crime is an equal-opportunity employer. It never discriminates. Anybody can enter the field. You don't need a college education. You don't need a G.E.D. You don't have to be any special color. You don't need white people to like you. You're self-employed. As a result, criminals are very independent people.
Ice-T (b.1958), U.S. rapper: *The Ice Opinion* (written with Heidi Sigmund, 1994), Ch.3

CRIMINALS

1   Repudiating the virtues of your world, criminals hopelessly agree to organize a forbidden universe. They agree to live in it. The air there is nauseating: they can breathe it.
Jean Genet (1910–1986), French playwright and novelist: *The Thief's Journal* (1949; tr.1965), p.5 of Penguin edn. (1967)

2   The truth of the matter is that muggers are very interesting people.
Michael Winner (b.1935), British film-maker: in the *Daily Express* (London), 11 May 1989

See also DELINQUENTS

CRISES

1   I think it's only in a crisis that Americans see other people. It has to be an American crisis, of course. If two countries fight that do not supply the Americans with some precious commodity, then the education of the public does not take place. But when the dictator falls, when the oil is threatened, then you turn on the television and they tell you where the country is, what the language is, how to pronounce the names of the leaders, what the religion is all about, and maybe you can cut out recipes in the newspaper of Persian dishes.
Don DeLillo (b.1926), U.S. author: Andreas Eliades, in *The Names* (1982), Ch.3

2   All history is nothing but a succession of 'crises' – of rupture, repudiation and

resistance.... When there is no 'crisis,' there is stagnation, petrification and death.

Eugène Ionesco (1912–1994), Rumanian-born French playwright: *Notes and Counter-Notes* (1962), Pt.4, 'Have I Written Anti-Theatre?'

3   There can't be a crisis next week. My schedule is already full.

Henry Kissinger (b.1923), U.S. Republican politician and secretary of state: in the *New York Times Magazine*, 1 June 1969

4   Crisis can indeed be an agony. But it is the exquisite agony which a man might not want to experience again – yet would not for the world have missed.

Richard Nixon (1913–1992), U.S. Republican politician and president: introduction to *Six Crises* (1962)

See also Moore on ROLE-PLAYING

CRITICISM

1   A negative judgement gives you more satisfaction than praise, provided it smacks of jealousy.

Jean Baudrillard (b.1929), French semiologist: *Cool Memories* (1987; tr.1990), Ch.5

2   It is very perplexing how an intrepid frontier people, who fought a wilderness, floods, tornadoes, and the Rockies, cower before criticism, which is regarded as a malignant tumor in the imagination.

Edward Dahlberg (1900–1977), U.S. author and critic: *Alms for Oblivion* (1964), 'No Love and No Thanks'

3   Critical remarks are only made by people who love you.

Federico Mayor (b.1934), Spanish biologist and politician, director-general of UNESCO: in *The Guardian* (London), 24 June 1988

See also Vorster on SOUTH AFRICA

CRITICISM: Professional

1   The avocation of assessing the failures of better men can be turned into a comfortable livelihood, providing you back it up with a Ph.D.

Nelson Algren (1909–1981), U.S. author: interview in *Writers at Work* (First Series, ed. Malcolm Cowley, 1958)

2   Criticism takes longer to change. The critics are a kind of dictatorship. ... They change much more slowly than the public itself.

Pedro Almodóvar (b.1951), Spanish film-maker: quoted in *Sight and Sound* (London), April 1992

3   Criticism should be a casual conversation.

W.H. Auden (1907–1973), Anglo-American poet: *The Table Talk of W.H. Auden* (comp. Alan Ansen, ed. Nicholas Jenkins, 1990), 'November 16, 1946'

4   Writing prejudicial, off-putting reviews is a precise exercise in applied black magic. The reviewer can draw free-floating disagreeable associations to a book by implying that the book is completely unimportant without saying exactly why, and carefully avoiding any clear images that could capture the reader's full attention.

William Burroughs (1914–1997), U.S. author: *The Western Lands* (1987), Ch.3

5   Good critical writing is measured by the perception and evaluation of the subject; bad critical writing by the necessity of maintaining the professional standing of the critic.

Raymond Chandler (1888–1959), U.S. author: letter, 7 May 1948, publ. in *Raymond Chandler Speaking* (ed. Dorothy Gardiner and Kathrine S. Walker, 1962)

6   Hardly a book of human worth, be it heaven's own secret, is honestly placed before the reader; it is either shunned, given a Periclean funeral oration in a hundred and fifty words, or interred in the potter's field of the newspapers' back pages.

Edward Dahlberg (1900–1977), U.S. author and critic: *Alms for Oblivion* (1964), 'For Sale'

7   The artist doesn't have time to listen to the critics. The ones who want to be writers read the reviews, the ones who want to write don't have the time to read reviews.

William Faulkner (1897–1962), U.S. novelist: interview in *Writers at Work* (First Series, ed. Malcolm Cowley, 1958)

8   Unless criticism refuses to take itself quite so seriously or at least to permit its readers not to, it will inevitably continue to reflect the finicky canons of the genteel tradition and the depressing pieties of the Culture Religion of Modernism.

Leslie Fiedler (b.1917), U.S. critic: 'Cross the Border – Close the Gap', first publ. in *Playboy* (Chicago), Dec. 1969, rep. in *Collected Essays* (1971), Vol.II

9   Without the meditative background that is criticism, works become isolated gestures, ahistorical accidents, soon forgotten.

Milan Kundera (b.1929), Czech-born French author and critic: 'On Criticism, Aesthetics, and Europe', publ. in *Review of Contemporary Fiction*, summer 1989, originally from Kundera's introduction to *La Littérature Contre Elle-Même* by François Ricard

10   When the reviews are bad I tell my staff that they can join me as I cry all the way to the bank.

Liberace (1919–1987), U.S. entertainer: *Liberace: An Autobiography* (1973), Ch.2. The words became a regular part of Liberace's stage act from the 1950s

11 Honest criticism means nothing: what one wants is unrestrained passion, fire for fire.
Henry Miller (1891–1980), U.S. author: *Sexus* (1949), Ch.2

12 A bad review is even less important than whether it is raining in Patagonia.
Iris Murdoch (b.1919), British novelist and philosopher: in *The Times* (London), 6 July 1989

13 The prolonged, indiscriminate reviewing of books is a quite exceptionally thankless, irritating and exhausting job. It not only involves praising trash ... but constantly *inventing* reactions towards books about which one has no spontaneous feelings whatever.
George Orwell (1903–1950), British author: 'Confessions of a Book Reviewer' (1946), rep. in *The Collected Essays, Journalism and Letters of George Orwell* (ed. Sonia Orwell and Ian Angus, 1968), Vol.IV

14 The greatest honor that can be paid to the work of art, on its pedestal of ritual display, is to *describe* it with sensory completeness. We need a science of description. ... Criticism is ceremonial revivification.
Camille Paglia (b.1947), U.S. author and critic: *Sex, Art, and American Culture* (1992), 'Sexual Personae: The Cancelled Preface'

15 The aim of all commentary on art now should be to make works of art – and, by analogy, our own experience – more, rather than less, real to us. The function of criticism should be to show *how it is what it is*, even *that it is what it is*, rather than to show *what it means*.
Susan Sontag (b.1933), U.S. essayist: 'Against Interpretation', Sct.9, first publ. in *The Evergreen Review* (New York), Dec. 1964, rep. in *Against Interpretation* (1966)

See also Fellini on CENSORSHIP; LITERARY CRITICISM

CRITICS

1 A critic is a bundle of biases held loosely together by a sense of taste.
Whitney Balliet (b.1926), U.S. author: *Dinosaurs in the Morning* (1962), 'introductory note'

2 Unlike other people, our reviewers are powerful because they believe in nothing.
Harold Clurman (1901–1980), U.S. stage director and critic: quoted in *Who Needs Theatre?* by Robert Brustein (1987), Pt.1, 'The Vitality of Harold Clurman'

3 The television critic, whatever his pretensions, does not labour in the same vineyard as those he criticizes; his grapes are all sour.
Frederic Raphael (b.1931), British author and critic: 'The Language of Television', publ. in *The State of the Language* (ed. Christopher Ricks, 1980)

4 Any critic is entitled to wrong judgments, of course. But certain lapses of judgment indicate the radical failure of an entire sensibility.
Susan Sontag (b.1933), U.S. essayist: *Against Interpretation* (1966), 'The Literary Criticism of George Lukács'

5 Give a critic an inch, he'll write a play.
John Steinbeck (1902–1968), U.S. author: *Writers at Work* (Fourth Series, ed. George Plimpton, 1977), 'On Critics'

6 A good drama critic is one who perceives what is happening in the theatre of his time. A great drama critic also perceives what is not happening.
Kenneth Tynan (1927–1980), British critic: foreword to *Tynan Right and Left* (1967)

7 It is healthier, in any case, to write for the adults one's children will become than for the children one's 'mature' critics often are.
Alice Walker (b.1944), U.S. author and critic: 'A Writer Because of, Not in Spite of, Her Children', first publ. in *Ms.* (New York), Jan. 1976, rep. in *In Search of Our Mothers' Gardens* (1983)

CROOKS

1 It takes a certain courage and a certain greatness to be truly base.
(*Il y a quelque courage aussi et quelque grandeur à être ignoble.*)
Jean Anouilh (1910–1987), French playwright: Le Générale, in *Ardèle* (1948), Act 1

2 Like art and politics, gangsterism is a very important avenue of assimilation into society.
E.L. Doctorow (b.1931), U.S. novelist: in the *International Herald Tribune* (Paris), 1 Oct. 1990

3 In the old days villains had moustaches and kicked the dog. Audiences are smarter today. They don't want their villain to be thrown at them with green limelight on his face. They want an ordinary human being with failings.
Alfred Hitchcock (1899–1980), British film-maker: quoted in *Halliwell's Filmgoer's Companion* (ed. Leslie Halliwell, 1984)

4 Like many businessmen of genius he learned that free competition was wasteful, monopoly efficient. And so he simply set about achieving that efficient monopoly.
Mario Puzo (b.1920), U.S. novelist: referring to Don Vito Corleone, in *The Godfather* (1969), Bk.3, Ch.14

5 Nowadays if you're a crook you're still considered up-there. You can write books, go on TV, give interviews – you're a big celebrity

and nobody even looks down on you because you're a crook. You're still really up-there. This is because more than anything people just want stars.

Andy Warhol (c.1928–1987), U.S. Pop artist: *From A to B and Back Again* (1975), Ch.5

6 In ways that we do not easily or willingly define, the gangster speaks for us, expressing that part of the American psyche which rejects the qualities and the demands of modern life, which rejects 'Americanism' itself.

Robert Warshow (1917–1955), U.S. author: 'The Gangster as Tragic Hero', first publ. in the *Partisan Review* (New Brunswick, N.J.), 1948, rep. in *The Immediate Experience* (1970)

CROSS-DRESSING

1 Like the veil, transvestism conceals and betrays; like the mirror, it presents reality in an illusion which masks reality while proffering it. ... It is an anti-nature which is mimicked and therefore warded off.

Michel Foucault (1926–1984), French philosopher: 'Un si cruel savoire', publ. in *Critique*, No.182, 1962, quoted in *The Lives of Michel Foucault* by David Macey (1993), Ch.6

2 I'm a lumberjack
And I'm OK,
I sleep all night
And I work all day.
I cut down trees, I skip and jump,
I like to press wild flowers.
I put on women's clothing
And hang around in bars.

Monty Python's Flying Circus: 'The Lumberjack Song' (song) in *Monty Python's Flying Circus* (TV series, 1969–74), episode 9, broadcast Dec. 1969. Monty Python episodes were written and performed by Graham Chapman (1941–1989), John Cleese (b.1939), Terry Gilliam (b.1940), Eric Idle (b.1943), Terry Jones (b.1942) and Michael Palin (b.1943)

3 The drag queen ... negotiates between sexual personae, day by day. ... Queens, unlike feminists, know that woman is dominatrix of the universe. They take on supernatural energy when ritualistically donning their opulent costume, the historical regalia of woman's power.

Camille Paglia (b.1947), U.S. author and critic: *Vamps and Tramps* (1994), 'No Law in the Arena', Sct.6

4 Among other things, drag queens are living testimony to the way women used to want to be, the way some people still want them to be, and the way some women still actually want to be. Drags are ambulatory archives of ideal moviestar womanhood. They perform a documentary service, usually consecrating their lives to keeping the glittering alternative

alive and available for (not-too-close) inspection.

Andy Warhol (c.1928–1987), U.S. Pop artist: *From A to B and Back Again* (1975), Ch.3

5 The scorn directed against drags is especially virulent; they have become the outcasts of gay life, the 'queers' of homosexuality. In fact, they are classic scapegoats. Our old fears about our sissiness, still with us though masked by the new macho fascism, are now located, isolated, quarantined through our persecution of the transvestite.

Edmund White (b.1940), U.S. author: *States of Desire: Travels in Gay America* (1980), Ch.2

CRUELTY

1 It is possible that the contemplation of cruelty will not make us humane but cruel; that the reiteration of the badness of our spiritual condition will make us consent to it.

Lionel Trilling (1905–1975), U.S. critic: on Plato's theory of art, in notebook entry, 1948, publ. in *The Partisan Review 50th Anniversary Edition* (ed. William Philips, 1985)

2 All cruel people describe themselves as paragons of frankness!

Tennessee Williams (1911–1983), U.S. playwright: Mrs Goforth, in *The Milk Train Doesn't Stop Here Anymore* (1963), Sc.1

CRYING

1 The tears of the world are a constant quality. For each one who begins to weep, somewhere else another stops. The same is true of the laugh.

Samuel Beckett (1906–1989), Irish playwright and novelist: Pozzo, in *Waiting for Godot* (1952; tr.1954), Act 1

2 Only to have a grief
equal to all these tears!

Adrienne Rich (b.1929), U.S. poet: 'Peeling Onions', publ. in *Snapshots of a Daughter-in-Law* (1963)

CUBA

1 I had to say something
To strike him very weird,
So I yelled out,
'I like Fidel Castro and his beard.'

Bob Dylan (b.1941), U.S. singer and songwriter: 'Motorpsycho Nightmare' (song), on the album *Another Side of Bob Dylan* (1964)

2 A small country existing under a relentless state of siege, persecuted by the strongest nation on earth, is not in the best shape for

flourishing freedom. If any American administration truly cared about Cuban political prisoners and Cuban civil liberties, it would let up on Cuba, leave Cuba alone, give Cuba a chance to breathe for a while and feel secure enough to afford more and more freedom.

Martha Gellhorn (b.1908), U.S. journalist and author: 'Cuba Revisited', first publ. in *Granta* (Cambridge), No.20, winter 1986, rep. in *The View from the Ground* (1990)

3 They talk about who won and who lost. Human reason won. Mankind won.

Nikita Khrushchev (1894–1971), Soviet premier: referring to the Cuban missile crisis, quoted in *The Observer* (London), 11 Nov. 1962

4 Castro couldn't even go to the bathroom unless the Soviet Union put the nickel in the toilet.

Richard Nixon (1913–1992), U.S. Republican politician and president: remark to interviewer, Sept. 1980, quoted in *Exile: The Unquiet Oblivion of Richard M. Nixon* by Robert Sam Anson (1984), Ch.17

5 Everything was blamed on Castro. Mudslides in California. The fact that you can't buy a decent tomato anymore. Was there an exceptionally high pollen count in Massapequa, Long Island, one day? It was Castro, exporting sneezes.

Calvin Trillin (b.1935), U.S. journalist and author: 'Castro Forgotten, Alas', syndicated column, 18 May 1986

CULTS

1 What is a cult? It just means not enough people to make a minority.

Robert Altman (b.1922), U.S. film-maker: quoted in *Halliwell's Filmgoer's Companion*, (ed. Leslie Halliwell, 1984)

2 The interminable unhappiness of the disciple may perhaps have to do with what he does not yet know or still conceals from himself: that the master, like real life, is, perhaps, always absent. We therefore have to break the glass, or rather the mirror, the reflection, the disciples' infinite speculation on the master. And begin to speak.

Jacques Derrida (b.1930), Algerian-born French literary theorist: *L'Écriture et la différence* (1967), 'Cogito et histoire de la folie'

3 One does not become a guru by accident.

James Fenton (b.1949), British poet and critic: referring to playwright Samuel Beckett, in *The Times* (London), 9 Aug. 1984

4 A cult is a religion with no political power.

Tom Wolfe (b.1931), U.S. author and journalist: *In Our Time* (1980), Ch.2, 'Jonestown'

CULTURE

1 Acceptance of the mass media entails a shift in our notion of what culture is. Instead of reserving the word for the highest artifacts and the noblest thoughts of history's top ten, it needs to be used more widely as a description of 'what a society does'.

Lawrence Alloway (b.1926), British artist and critic: 'The Long Front of Culture', publ. in *Cambridge Opinion* (Cambridge University), No.17, 1959, rep. in *Pop Art Redefined* by John Russell and Suzi Gablik (1969)

2 Art is what we do: culture is what is done to us.

Carl André (b.1935), U.S. sculptor: in *Interfunktionen* (Cologne), No.5, 1970, quoted in *Environments and Happenings* by Adrian Henri (1974), Ch.4

3 Here in the U.S., culture is not that delicious panacea which we Europeans consume in a sacramental mental space and which has its own special columns in the newspapers – and in people's minds. Culture is space, speed, cinema, technology. This culture is authentic, if anything can be said to be authentic.

Jean Baudrillard (b.1929), French semiologist: *America* (1986; tr.1988), 'Utopia Achieved'

4 Everything has to be tried out. Funnily enough, the same mind that takes in 'Dallas' or rap music is also accessible to Homer and Shakespeare.

Saul Bellow (b.1915), U.S. novelist: *It All Adds Up* (1994), 'Mozart: an Overture'

5 We are in the process of creating what deserves to be called the idiot culture. Not an idiot subculture, which every society has bubbling beneath the surface and which can provide harmless fun; but the culture itself. For the first time, the weird and the stupid and the coarse are becoming our cultural norm, even our cultural ideal.

Carl Bernstein (b.1944), U.S. journalist: in *The Guardian* (London), 3 June 1992

6 We are like ignorant shepherds living on a site where great civilizations once flourished. The shepherds play with the fragments that pop up to the surface, having no notion of the beautiful structures of which they were once a part.

Allan Bloom (1930–1992), U.S. educator and author: *The Closing of the American Mind* (1987), Pt.2, 'Our Ignorance'

7 Without culture, and the relative freedom it implies, society, even when perfect, is but a jungle. This is why any authentic creation is a gift to the future.

Albert Camus (1913–1960), French-Algerian philosopher and author: *The Myth of Sisyphus and Other Essays* (1955), 'The Artist and His Time'

8 A national culture is not a folklore, nor an abstract populism that believes it can discover the people's true nature. It is not made up of the inert dregs of gratuitous actions, that is to say actions which are less and less attached to the ever present reality of the people. A national culture is the whole body of efforts made by a people in the sphere of thought to describe, justify and praise the action through which that people has created itself and keeps itself in existence.

Frantz Fanon (1925–1961), Martiniquan psychiatrist, philosopher and political activist: *The Wretched of the Earth* (1961), Ch.4

9 It is of the essence of imaginative culture that it transcends the limits both of the naturally possible and of the morally acceptable.

Northrop Frye (1912–1991), Canadian literary critic: *Anatomy of Criticism* (1957), 'Anagogic Phase: Symbol as Monad'

10 A society person who is enthusiastic about modern painting or Truman Capote is already half a traitor to his class. It is middle-class people who, quite mistakenly, imagine that a lively pursuit of the latest in reading and painting will advance their status in the world.

Mary McCarthy (1912–1989), U.S. author and critic: 'Up the Ladder from *Charm* to *Vogue* ' (1950), rep. in *On the Contrary* (1961), Pt.2

11 All objects, all phases of culture are alive. They have voices. They speak of their history and interrelatedness. And they are all talking at once!

Camille Paglia (b.1947), U.S. author and critic: *Sex, Art, and American Culture* (1992), 'Sexual Personae: The Cancelled Preface'

12 Culture is a sort of theatre where various political and ideological causes engage one another. Far from being a placid realm of Apollonian gentility, culture can even be a battleground on which causes expose themselves to the light of day and contend with one another.

Edward Said (b.1935), Lebanese-born U.S. social and literary critic: introduction to *Culture and Imperialism* (1993)

13 We know that a man can read Goethe or Rilke in the evening, that he can play Bach and Schubert, and go to his day's work at Auschwitz in the morning.

George Steiner (b.1929), French-born U.S. critic and novelist: preface to *Language and Silence* (1967)

See also Mao Zedong on THE ARTS

CURIOSITY

1 All my life I've been harassed by questions: Why is something this way and not another?

How do you account for that? This rage to understand, to fill in the blanks, only makes life more banal. If we could only find the courage to leave our destiny to chance, to accept the fundamental mystery of our lives, then we might be closer to the sort of happiness that comes with innocence.

Luis Buñuel (1900–1983), Spanish film-maker: *My Last Breath* (autobiography, 1983), Ch.15

2 We never stop investigating. We are never satisfied that we know enough to get by. Every question we answer leads on to another question. This has become the greatest survival trick of our species.

Desmond Morris (b.1928), British zoologist: *The Naked Ape* (1967), Ch.5

3 I think, at a child's birth, if a mother could ask a fairy godmother to endow it with the most useful gift, that gift would be curiosity.

Eleanor Roosevelt (1884–1962), U.S. columnist, lecturer and wife of F.D. Roosevelt: quoted in *Today's Health* (Chicago), 2 Oct. 1966

CYNICISM

1 Cynicism is cheap – you can buy it at any Monoprix store – it's built into all poor-quality goods.

Graham Greene (1904–1991), British novelist: *The Comedians* (1966), Pt.1, Ch.1, Sct.3

2 A cynic is not merely one who reads bitter lessons from the past; he is one who is prematurely disappointed in the future.

Sydney Harris (b.1917), U.S. journalist: *On the Contrary* (1962), Ch.7

See also Oates on LUCK

DANCE

1 To shake your rump is to be environmentally aware.

David Byrne (b.1952), U.S. rock musician: sleevenotes to his compilation of Brazilian Samba music, *O Samba: Brazil Classics 2* (1989)

2 Dance then wherever you may be,
I am the Lord of the Dance, said he,
And I'll lead you all, wherever you may be
And I'll lead you all in the dance, said he.

Sydney Carter (b.1915), British songwriter: 'Lord of the Dance', publ. in *Nine Carols or Ballads* (1967)

3 The Twist was a guided missile, launched from the ghetto into the very heart of suburbia. The Twist succeeded, as politics, religion, and law could never do, in writing in the heart and soul what the Supreme Court could only write on the books.

Eldridge Cleaver (b.1935), U.S. black leader and writer: *Soul on Ice* (1968), 'Convalescence'

4 Stately as a galleon, I sail across the floor,
Doing the military two-step, as in the days of
   yore.
Joyce Grenfell (1910–1979), British actress and
writer: 'Stately as a Galleon' (song), publ. in *Stately
as a Galleon* (1977)

5 They seldom looked happy. They passed one
another without a word in the elevator, like
silent shades in hell, hell-bent on their next
look from a handsome stranger. Their next
rush from a popper. The next song that turned
their bones to jelly and left them all on the
dance floor with heads back, eyes nearly
closed, in the ecstasy of saints receiving the
stigmata.
Andrew Holleran (b.1943), U.S. journalist and
author: on club regulars, in *Dancer from the Dance*
(1978), Ch.2

6 When we were at school we were taught to sing
the songs of the Europeans. How many of us
were taught the songs of the Wanyamwezi or of
the Wahehe? Many of us have learnt to dance
the rumba, or the cha cha, to rock and roll and
to twist and even to dance the waltz and
foxtrot. But how many of us can dance, or have
even heard of the gombe sugu, the mangala,
nyang'umumi, kiduo, or lele mama?
Julius Nyerere (b.1922), Tanzanian president:
Tanzania National Assembly Official Reports
(1962), quoted in *African All-Stars* by Chris
Stapleton and Chris May (1987), Pt.1

7 Calling out around the world
Are you ready for a brand new beat?
Summer's here and the time is right
For dancing in the street.
Martha Reeves (b.1941), U.S. singer: 'Dancing in
the Street' (song; Martha and the Vandellas, 1964),
publ. in *The Poetry of Soul* (ed. A.X. Nicholas,
1971)

DANGER

1 For man, maximum excitement is the confrontation of death and the skillful defiance of
it by watching others fed to it as he survives
transfixed with rapture.
Ernest Becker (1924–1974), U.S. psychologist and
cultural anthropologist: *Escape from Evil* (1975),
Ch.8, 'The Logic of Scapegoating'

2 My point is not that everything is bad, but that
everything is dangerous, which is not exactly
the same as bad. If everything is dangerous,
then we always have something to do. So my
position leads not to apathy but to a hyper- and
pessimistic activism. I think that the ethico-
political choice we have to make every day is to
determine which is the main danger.
Michel Foucault (1926–1984), French philosopher:
quoted in *Michel Foucault: Beyond Structuralism
and Hermeneutics* by Hubert L. Dreyfus and Paul
Rabinow (1983)

3 When you go in search of honey you must
expect to be stung by bees.
Kenneth Kaunda (b.1924), Zambian politician and
president: quoted in *The Observer* (London), 2 Jan.
1983

DAYDREAMS

1 A daydream is a meal at which images are
eaten. Some of us are gourmets, some gour-
mands, and a good many take their images
precooked out of a can and swallow them down
whole, absent-mindedly and with little relish.
W.H. Auden (1907–1973), Anglo-American poet:
The Dyer's Hand (1962), Pt.3, 'Hic et Ille', Sct.C

2 Reverie is not a mind vacuum. It is rather the
gift of an hour which knows the plenitude of
the soul.
Gaston Bachelard (1884–1962), French scientist,
philosopher and literary theorist: *The Poetics of
Reverie* (1960; tr.1969), Ch.2, Sct.3

DAYS

1 What are days for?
Days are where we live.
Philip Larkin (1922–1986), British poet: 'Days',
St.1, (written 1953), publ. in *The Whitsun Weddings*
(1964)

2 There are more truths in twenty-four hours of
a man's life than in all the philosophies.
Raoul Vaneigem (b.1934), Belgian Situationist
philosopher: *The Revolution of Everyday Life*
(1967; tr.1983), Ch.1, Sct.1

THE DEAD

1 A man's death makes everything certain about
him. ... One does not know more facts about a
man because he is dead. But what one already
knows hardens and becomes definite. We
cannot hope for ambiguities to be clarified, we
cannot hope for further change, we cannot
hope for more. We are now the protagonists
and we have to make up our minds.
John Berger (b.1926), British author and critic: *A
Fortunate Man* (1967), p.160 of Writers and Readers
Publishing Cooperative edn. (1976)

2 This parrot is no more! It has ceased to be! It's
expired and gone to meet its maker! This is a
late parrot! It's a stiff! ... THIS IS AN EX-
PARROT!
John Cleese (b.1939), British comic actor: in 'Dead
Parrot Sketch', *Monty Python's Flying Circus* (TV
series, 1969–74), episode 8. Monty Python episodes
were written and performed by Graham Chapman
(1941–1989), John Cleese (b.1939), Terry Gilliam
(b.1940), Eric Idle (b.1943), Terry Jones (b.1942)
and Michael Palin (b.1943)

3 A considerable percentage of the people we meet on the street are people who are empty inside, that is, they are actually *already dead*. It is fortunate for us that we do not see and do not know it. If we knew what a number of people are actually dead and what a number of these dead people govern our lives, we should go mad with horror.

George Gurdjieff (c.1877–1949), Greek-Armenian religious teacher and mystic: quoted in *In Search of the Miraculous* by P.D. Ouspensky (1949), Ch.8

4 Their monument sticks like a fishbone
in the city's throat.

Robert Lowell (1917–1977), U.S. poet: 'For The Union Dead', St.8, publ. in *For The Union Dead* (1964)

5 Zed's dead, baby, Zed's dead.

Quentin Tarantino (b.1958), U.S. film-maker: Butch Coolidge (Bruce Willis), in *Pulp Fiction* (film; written and directed by Quentin Tarantino, 1994)

See also Yourcenar on MEMORY; Plath on SUICIDE

JAMES DEAN

1 Mr Dean appears to be wearing my last year's wardrobe and using my last year's talent ...

Marlon Brando (b.1924), U.S. actor: quoted in *James Dean in His Own Words* (ed. Mick St Michael, 1989), 'The Things They Said ... About Jimmy'. An intense hostility existed between the two actors

2 The main thing you felt about him is hurt. And the main thing the girls felt and the boys felt and the faggots felt about him was that you'd want to put your arm around him and protect him and look after him ... Don't cry kid, I'm on your side.

Elia Kazan (b.1909), U.S. film-maker: quoted in *The Fifties* by Peter Lewis (1978), 'Youthquake'

3 I knew by heart all the dialogue of James Dean's films; I could watch *Rebel Without a Cause* a hundred times over.

Elvis Presley (1935–1977), U.S. singer: quoted in *James Dean in His Own Words* (ed. Mick St Michael, 1989), 'The Things They Said ... About Jimmy'

DEATH

1 Don't tell me about the valley of the shadow of death. I live there. ...Welcome to Pennsylvania's death row.

Mumia Abu-Jamal (b.1954), U.S. journalist and environmentalist: on being a death-row prisoner, in preface to *Live from Death Row* (1995)

2 Personally I have no bone to pick with graveyards, I take the air there willingly, per-haps more willingly than elsewhere, when take the air I must.

Samuel Beckett (1906–1989), Irish playwright and novelist: *First Love* (1970; tr.1973)

3 No one's death comes to pass without making some impression, and those close to the deceased inherit part of the liberated soul and become richer in their humaneness.

Hermann Broch (1886–1951), Austrian novelist: *The Spell* (1976; tr.1987), Ch.2

4 Death is a displaced name for a linguistic predicament.

Paul de Man (1919–1983), Belgian-born U.S. literary critic: quoted in *Signs of the Times* by David Lehman (1991), Ch.4. Lehman called this 'the ultimate statement of the deconstructive credo'

5 When I die I want to decompose in a barrel of porter and have it served in all the pubs in Dublin.

J.P. Donleavy (b.1926), U.S. author: Sebastian Dangerfield, in *The Ginger Man* (1955), Ch.31

6 Life is a series of diminishments. Each cessation of an activity either from choice or some other variety of infirmity is a death, a putting to final rest. Each loss, of friend or precious enemy, can be equated with the closing off of a room containing blocks of nerves ... and soon after the closing off the nerves atrophy and that part of oneself, in essence, drops away. The self is lightened, is held on earth by a gram less of mass and will.

Coleman Dowell (1925–1985), U.S. novelist, dramatist and lyricist: entry in Mrs October's journals, in *Mrs October Was Here* (1973), Pt.3, 'Tasmania, Now'

7 Death is the last enemy: once we've got past that I think everything will be alright.

Alice Thomas Ellis (b.1932), British author: 'In the Psychiatrist's Chair', BBC Radio 4, 19 Aug. 1992

8 To die is poignantly bitter, but the idea of having to die without having lived is unbearable.

Erich Fromm (1900–1980), U.S. psychologist: *Man for Himself* (1947), Ch.4

9 This is the end, the redemption from Wilderness, way for the Wonderer, House sought for All, black handkerchief washed clean by weeping – page beyond Psalm – Last change of mine and Naomi – to God's perfect Darkness – Death, stay thy phantoms!

Allen Ginsberg (b.1926), U.S. poet: 'Kaddish', Sct.1, publ. in *Kaddish and Other Poems* (1960)

10 We are all of us resigned to death: it's life we aren't resigned to.

Graham Greene (1904–1991), British novelist: *The Heart of the Matter* (1948), Bk.3, Pt.2, Ch.2, Sct.1

11 Death's at the bottom of everything, Martins. Leave death to the professionals.

Graham Greene: Major Calloway (Trevor Howard), in *The Third Man* (film; screenplay by Graham Greene, directed by Carol Reed, 1950)

12 Your body must become familiar with its death – in all its possible forms and degrees – as a self-evident, imminent, and emotionally neutral step on the way towards the goal you have found worthy of your life.

Dag Hammarskjöld (1905–1961), Swedish statesman, secretary-general of U.N.: note, written 1957, publ. in *Markings* (1963), 'Night is Drawing Nigh'

13 The call of death is a call of love. Death can be sweet if we answer it in the affirmative, if we accept it as one of the great eternal forms of life and transformation.

Hermann Hesse (1877–1962), German novelist and poet: letter, 1950, publ. in *Hermann Hesse: A Pictorial Biography* (ed. Volker Michels, 1973), 'Montagnola'

14 We have the naive expectation that when we go, we won't be leaving any loose ends lying around: we will have made our peace with our children, left them happy and stable, and we will have achieved more or less everything that we wanted to with our lives. It's all nonsense, of course, and football fans contemplating their own mortality know that it is all nonsense. There will be hundreds of loose ends. Maybe we will die the night before our team appears at Wembley, or the day after a European Cup first-leg match, or in the middle of a promotion campaign or a relegation battle, and there is every prospect, according to many theories about the afterlife, that we will not be able to discover the eventual outcome. The whole *point* about death, metaphorically speaking, is that it is almost bound to occur before the major trophies have been awarded.

Nick Hornby (b.1957), British author: *Fever Pitch* (1992), '1968–1975: A Matter of Life and Death'

15 A belief in hell and the knowledge that every ambition is doomed to frustration at the hands of a skeleton have never prevented the majority of human beings from behaving as though death were no more than an unfounded rumour.

Aldous Huxley (1894–1963), British author: *Themes and Variations* (1950), 'Variations on a Baroque Tomb'

16 Since the death instinct exists in the heart of everything that lives, since we suffer from trying to repress it, since everything that lives longs for rest, let us unfasten the ties that bind us to life, let us cultivate our death wish, let us develop it, water it like a plant, let it grow unhindered. Suffering and fear are born from the repression of the death wish.

Eugène Ionesco (1912–1994), Rumanian-born French playwright: *Fragments of a Journal* (1967), p.56 of Grove Press edn. (1968)

17 It is hard to have patience with people who say 'There is no death' or 'Death doesn't matter.' There is death. And whatever is matters. And whatever happens has consequences, and it and they are irrevocable and irreversible. You might as well say that birth doesn't matter.

C.S. Lewis (1898–1963), British author: *A Grief Observed* (1961), Pt.1

18 Death is someone you see very clearly with eyes in the center of your heart: eyes that see not by reacting to light, but by reacting to a kind of a chill from within the marrow of your own life.

Thomas Merton (1915–1968), U.S. religious writer and poet: *The Seven Storey Mountain* (autobiography, 1948), Pt.1, Ch.3

19 If we value so highly the dignity of life, how can we not also value the dignity of death? No death may be called futile.

Yukio Mishima (1925–1970), Japanese author: *Mishima on Hagakure* (1977), 'How to Read Hagakure'

20 Our own death will be someone's
Milestone, whether we are teenaged
Riding pillion on grown-up machines,
Or old, hoping 'they'll find a cure'.

Anne Rouse (b.1954), U.S. poet: 'Night Song', publ. in *Sunset Grill* (1993)

21 For those who live neither with religious consolations about death nor with a sense of death (or of anything else) as natural, death is the obscene mystery, the ultimate affront, the thing that cannot be controlled. It can only be denied.

Susan Sontag (b.1933), U.S. essayist: *Illness As Metaphor* (1978), Ch.7

22 If I had my life over again I should form the habit of nightly composing myself to thoughts of death. I would practise, as it were, the remembrance of death. There is no other practice which so intensifies life. Death, when it approaches, ought not to take one by surprise. It should be part of the full expectancy of life. Without an ever-present sense of death life is insipid. You might as well live on the whites of eggs.

Muriel Spark (b.1918), British novelist: Henry Mortimer, in *Memento Mori* (1959), Ch.11

23 Death is an endless night so awful to contemplate that it can make us love life and value it with such passion that it may be the ultimate cause of all joy and all art.

Paul Theroux (b.1941), U.S. novelist and travel writer: 'D is for Death' – entry in *Hockney's Alphabet* (ed. Stephen Spender, 1991), a book published to raise money for AIDS victims

24 In the twentieth century, death terrifies men less than the absence of real life. All these dead, mechanized, specialized actions, stealing a little bit of life a thousand times a day until the mind and body are exhausted, until that death which is not the end of life but the final saturation with absence.

Raoul Vaneigem (b.1934), Belgian Situationist philosopher: *The Revolution of Everyday Life* (1967; tr.1983), Ch.4, Sct.2

25 In any man who dies there dies with him his first snow and kiss and fight ...
Not people die but worlds die in them.

Yevgeny Yevtushenko (b.1933), Russian poet: 'People', publ. in *Selected Poems* (1962)

See also BEREAVEMENT; FUNERALS; Dylan on IMMORTALITY; LIFE & DEATH; SUICIDE

DEATH: the Afterlife

1 I don't believe in an afterlife although I'm bringing a change of underwear.

Woody Allen (b.1935), U.S. film-maker: Boris Grushenko (Woody Allen), in *Love and Death* (film; written and directed by Woody Allen, 1975)

2 The chief problem about death, incidentally, is the fear that there may be no afterlife – a depressing thought, particularly for those who have bothered to shave. Also, there is the fear that there is an afterlife but no one will know where it's being held.

Woody Allen: *Without Feathers* (1976), 'The Early Essays'

3 If I were reincarnated, I'd want to come back a buzzard. Nothing hates him or envies him or wants him or needs him. He is never bothered or in danger, and he can eat anything.

William Faulkner (1897–1962), U.S. novelist: interview in *Writers at Work* (First Series, ed. Malcolm Cowley, 1958)

4 At the moment of death I hope to be surprised.

Ivan Illich (b.1926), Austrian-born U.S. theologian and author: reply to a question on his beliefs about the afterlife, quoted in *The Sunday Times* (London), 20 Nov. 1988

5 What time has been wasted during man's destiny in the struggle to decide what man's next world will be like! The keener the effort to find out, the less he knew about the present one he lived in.

Sean O'Casey (1884–1964), Irish playwright: *Sunset and Evening Star* (sixth volume of autobiography, 1954), 'Shaw's Corner'

6 I am by no means certain that after death there'll be nothing, a void, as clever people assure us, a dreamless sleep. Nobody has dreamless sleeps like that: as if a person could fall asleep (which he remembers) and then wake up again (he remembers that too) and remember nothing of what went on in between – something happened, only he cannot remember what.

Andrey Tarkovsky (1932–1986), Russian film-maker: journal entry, 5 Sept. 1970, publ. in *Time Within Time: The Diaries 1970–1986* (1989; tr.1994)

7 There will be sex after death; we just won't be able to feel it.

Lily Tomlin (b.1939), U.S. comedienne: quoted in *Hammer and Tongues* (ed. Michèle Brown and Ann O'Connor, 1986)

8 The yearning for an afterlife is the opposite of selfish: it is love and praise for the world that we are privileged, in this complex interval of light, to witness and experience.

John Updike (b.1932), U.S. author and critic: *Self-Consciousness: Memoirs* (1989), Ch.6

9 Eddie did not die. He is no longer on Channel 4, and our sets are tuned to Channel 4; he's on Channel 7, but he's still broadcasting. Physical incarnation is highly overrated; it is one corner of universal possibility.

Marianne Williamson (b.1953), U.S. benefactor: of dancer Edward Stierle, who died of AIDS, in *Vanity Fair* (New York), June 1991

DEATH: Dying

1 It's not that I'm afraid to die, I just don't want to be there when it happens.

Woody Allen (b.1935), U.S. film-maker: *Without Feathers* (1976), 'Death (A Play)'

2 There is a sense in which the dying *shake off* the concerns of the living, play them like a salmon plays the rod – seeming to get a little better so that relief replaces concern, then worsening again so that anxiety returns. It needs only a short dose of this before the living are quite glad to see them go.

Alan Bennett (b.1934), British playwright: journal entry, 26 May 1988, publ. in *Writing Home* (1994), 'Diaries 1980–1990'

3 To hell with reality! I want to die in music, not in reason or in prose.

Louis-Ferdinand Céline (1894–1961), French author: letter, 30 June 1947, publ. in *Critical Essays on Louis-Ferdinand Céline* (ed. William K. Buckley, 1989)

4 I'm trying to die correctly, but it's very difficult, you know.

Lawrence Durrell (1912–1990), British author: in *The Sunday Times* (London), 20 Nov. 1988

5 A person doesn't die when he should but when he can.

Gabriel García Márquez (b.1928), Colombian author: Colonel Aureliano Buendia, in *100 Years Of Solitude* (1967; tr.1970), p.199 of Picador edn. (1978)

6 I'm not afraid of death but I am afraid of dying. Pain can be alleviated by morphine but the pain of social ostracism cannot be taken away.

Derek Jarman (1942–1994), British film-maker, artist and author: on being HIV positive, in *At Your Own Risk: A Saint's Testament* (1992), '1980's'

7 Dying is something we human beings do continuously, not just at the end of our physical lives on this earth.

Elisabeth Kübler-Ross (b.1926), Swiss-born U.S. psychiatrist: *Death: The Final Stage of Growth* (1975), Ch.6

8 How you die is the most important thing you ever do. It's the exit, the final scene of the glorious epic of your life. It's the third act and, you know, everything builds up to the third act.

Timothy Leary (1920–1996), U.S. psychologist: interview in *The Guardian* (London), 2 Dec. 1995

9 Anyone who's never watched somebody die is suffering from a pretty bad case of virginity.

John Osborne (1929–1994), British playwright: Jimmy Porter, in *Look Back in Anger* (1956), Act 2, Sc.1

10 Dying
Is an art, like everything else.
I do it exceptionally well

I do it so it feels like hell.
I do it so it feels real.
I guess you could say I've a call.

Sylvia Plath (1932–1963), U.S. poet: 'Lady Lazarus', publ. in *Encounter* (London), Oct. 1963, rep. in *Ariel* (1965)

11 Things are both more trivial than they ever were, and more important than they ever were, and the difference between the trivial and the important doesn't seem to matter – but the *nowness* of everything is absolutely wondrous. And if people could see that – there's no way of telling you, you have to experience it – the glory of it, if you like, the comfort of it, the reassurance … Not that I'm interested in reassuring people you know – bugger that. The fact is, that if you see the present tense, boy do you see it, and boy can you celebrate it!

Dennis Potter (1935–1994), British dramatist and screenwriter: on the terminal stages of his illness, in interview with Melvyn Bragg, Channel 4, 5 April 1994

12 Just like those who are incurably ill, the aged know everything about their dying except exactly when.

Philip Roth (b.1933), U.S. novelist: opening letter to Zuckerman, in *The Facts* (1988), p.9 of Penguin edn. (1989)

13 Do not go gentle into that good night,
Old age should burn and rage at close of day;
Rage, rage, against the dying of the light.

Dylan Thomas (1914–1953), Welsh poet: 'Do Not Go Gentle into that Good Night' (1951), publ. in *Collected Poems* (1952)

14 Dying is the most embarrassing thing that can ever happen to you, because someone's got to take care of all your details.

Andy Warhol (c.1928–1987), U.S. Pop artist: quoted in *Warhol* by Victor Bokris (1989), 'Goodbye 1986–7'

DEBAUCHERY

1 True debauchery is liberating because it creates no obligations. In it you possess only yourself; hence it remains the favourite pastime of the great lovers of their own person.

Albert Camus (1913–1960), French-Algerian philosopher and author: the narrator (Jean-Baptiste Clamence), in *The Fall* (1956), p.77 of Hamish Hamilton edn. (1957)

2 My problem lies in reconciling my gross habits with my net income.

Errol Flynn (1909–1959), U.S. actor: quoted in *Great Lovers of the Movies* by Jane Mercer (1975), 'Errol Flynn'

DEBT

1 A man's indebtedness … is not virtue; his repayment is. Virtue begins when he dedicates himself actively to the job of gratitude.

Ruth Benedict (1887–1948), U.S. anthropologist: *The Chrysanthemum and the Sword* (1946), Ch.6

2 Bankruptcy is a sacred state, a condition beyond conditions, as theologians might say, and attempts to investigate it are necessarily obscene, like spiritualism. One knows only that he has passed into it and lives beyond us, in a condition not ours.

John Updike (b.1932), U.S. author and critic: *Hugging the Shore* (1983), 'The Bankrupt Man'

3 On 16 September 1985, when the Commerce Department announced that the United States had become a debtor nation, the American Empire died.

Gore Vidal (b.1925), U.S. novelist and critic: *Armageddon? Essays 1983–1987* (1987), 'The Day the American Empire Ran Out of Gas'

See also Pound on WAR

DECADENCE

1 A decadent civilization compromises with its disease, cherishes the virus infecting it, loses its self-respect.
E.M. Cioran (1911–1995), Rumanian-born French philosopher: *The Temptation to Exist* (1956), 'Rages and Resignations: Saint Paul'

2 I feel that decadence is indispensable to rebirth. I have already said that I love shipwrecks. So I am happy to be living at a time when everything is capsizing. It's a marvellous time, for the very reason that a whole series of ideologies, concepts and conventions is being wrecked.
Federico Fellini (1920–1993), Italian film-maker: *Fellini on Fellini* (ed. Anna Keel and Christian Strich, 1974; tr.1977), 'Miscellany III', Sct.16

3 The difference between our decadence and the Russians' is that while theirs is brutal, ours is apathetic.
James Thurber (1894–1961), U.S. humorist and illustrator: quoted in *The Observer* (London), 5 Feb. 1961

DECISIONS

1 Every decision is liberating, even if it leads to disaster. Otherwise, why do so many people walk upright and with open eyes into their misfortune?
Elias Canetti (1905–1994), Austrian novelist and philosopher: *The Secret Heart Of The Clock: Notes, Aphorisms, Fragments 1973–1985* (1991), '1980'

2 The myths have always condemned those who 'looked back'. Condemned them, whatever the paradise may have been which they were leaving. Hence this shadow over each departure from your decision.
Dag Hammarskjöld (1905–1961), Swedish statesman and secretary-general of U.N.: note written 1957, publ. in *Markings* (1963), 'Night is Drawing Nigh'

3 I've learned one thing in politics. You don't take a decision until you have to.
Margaret Thatcher (b.1925), British Conservative politician and prime minister: quoted by Alan Clark in journal entry, 19 Nov. 1986, publ. in *Diaries* (1994)

DECOLONIZATION

1 Decolonization, which sets out to change the order of the world, is, obviously, a programme of complete disorder.
Frantz Fanon (1925–1961), Martiniquan psychiatrist, philosopher and political activist: *The Wretched of the Earth* (1961), Ch.1

2 The wind of change is blowing through the continent. Whether we like it or not, this growth of national consciousness is a political fact.
Harold Macmillan (1894–1986), British Conservative politician and prime minister: speech to both houses of the South African Parliament, 3 Feb. 1960, Cape Town, publ. in *Pointing the Way* (1972)

3 It is far easier for the proverbial camel to pass through the needle's eye, hump and all, than for an erstwhile colonial administration to give sound and honest counsel of a *political* nature to its liberated territory.
Kwame Nkrumah (1900–1972), Ghanaian president: *Consciencism* (1964), Ch.4

See also COLONIALISM

DECONSTRUCTION

1 The fall into the abyss of deconstruction inspires us with as much pleasure as fear. We are intoxicated with the prospect of never hitting bottom.
Gayatri Chakravorty (b.1942), Indian-born U.S. educator, author and translator: translator's preface to *Of Grammatology* by Jacques Derrida (1967)

2 I would say that deconstruction is affirmation rather than questioning, in a sense which is not positive: I would distinguish between the positive, or positions, and affirmations. I think that deconstruction is affirmative rather than questioning: this affirmation goes *through* some radical questioning, but it is not questioning in the field of analysis.
Jacques Derrida (b.1930), Algerian-born French literary theorist: interview, 1985, publ. in *Criticism in Society* (ed. Imre Salusinski, 1987)

3 Deconstruction ... insists not that truth is illusory but that it is institutional.
Terry Eagleton (b.1943), British writer and critic: 'Frère Jacques: The Politics of Deconstruction' (1984), rep. in *Against The Grain* (1986), Ch.6

4 There is an air of last things, a brooding sense of impending annihilation, about so much deconstructive activity, in so many of its guises; it is not merely postmodernist but pre-apocalyptic.
David Lehman (b.1948), U.S. poet, editor and critic: *Signs of the Times* (1991), Ch.1, 'The End of the Word'

5 French rhetorical models are too narrow for the English tradition. Most pernicious of French imports is the notion that there is no person behind a text. Is there anything *more* affected, aggressive, and relentlessly concrete than a Parisian intellectual behind his/her

turgid text? The Parisian is a provincial when he pretends to speak for the universe.

Camille Paglia (b.1947), U.S. author and critic: *Sexual Personae* (1990), Ch.1

See also de Man on DEATH; Wolfe on STRUCTURALISM

DEFEAT

1 Man is not made for defeat. A man can be destroyed but not defeated.

Ernest Hemingway (1899–1961), U.S. author: *The Old Man and the Sea* (1952), quoted as the last words in A.E. Hotchner's biography, *Papa Hemingway* (1966 edn.)

2 It seems a rule of history that real men and real movements who finally change the course of events must first pass through the ordeal of recurrent defeat and long disaster; a natural test of greatness in any cause.

Oswald Mosley (1896–1980), British fascist leader: *My Life* (1968), Ch.16

3 Defeat doesn't finish a man – quit does. A man is not finished when he's defeated. He's finished when he quits.

Richard Nixon (1913–1992), U.S. Republican politician and president: note, written with reference to Edward Kennedy and the Chappaquiddick Bridge incident, July 1969, quoted in *Before the Fall* by William Safire (1975), Pt.3, Ch.4

4 All vanquished nations tend to see the hand of God in their misery and envisage their salvation only through redemption, with an implication of virtuous, spartan behaviour.

Guy de Rothschild (b.1909), French banker: on the German defeat of the French army in 1940, in *The Whims of Fortune* (1985), Ch.7

DEFENCE

1 There's no telling what might have happened to our defense budget if Saddam Hussein hadn't invaded Kuwait that August and set everyone gearing up for World War II½. Can we count on Saddam Hussein to come along every year and resolve our defense-policy debates? Given the history of the Middle East, it's possible.

P.J. O'Rourke (b.1947), U.S. journalist: *Parliament of Whores* (1991), 'Cry "Havoc!" and Let Slip the Hogs of Peace'

2 We're in greater danger today than we were the day after Pearl Harbor. Our military is absolutely incapable of defending this country.

Ronald Reagan (b.1911), U.S. Republican politician and president: in the *New York Times*, 12 April 1980, quoted in *Reagan's Reign of Error* (ed. Mark Green and Gail MacColl, 1987), 'Temptation of Pride'

DEFIANCE

1 Listen, if you guys want to do this your way, you have got to handcuff me and bind my feet together, so that I can't respond. If you allow me to respond, I'm certainly going to respond. And I'm afraid you may have to kill me in the process even if it's not your intention.

Steve Biko (1946–1977), South African anti-apartheid activist: to his gaolers, quoted in 'Biko on Death', publ. in *New Republic* (Washington D.C.), 7 Jan. 1978, rep. in *Steve Biko: Black Consciousness in South Africa* (ed. Millard Arnold, 1978), appendix. Biko thus forecast the manner of his death at the hands of the South African police at Port Elizabeth Jail, 12 Sept. 1977

2 She won't go quietly, that's the problem. I'll fight to the end.

Diana, Princess of Wales (1961–1997): interview on *Panorama*, BBC1, 20 Nov. 1995

DEFINITION

1 Men have defined the parameters of every subject. All feminist arguments, however radical in intent or consequence, are with or against assertions or premises implicit in the male system, which is made credible or authentic by the power of men to name.

Andrea Dworkin (b.1946), U.S. feminist critic: *Pornography* (1981), Ch.1

2 By speaking, by thinking, we undertake to clarify things, and that forces us to exacerbate them, dislocate them, schematize them. Every concept is in itself an exaggeration.

José Ortega y Gasset (1883–1955), Spanish essayist and philosopher: 'In Search of Goethe from Within', first publ. in *The Partisan Review* (New Brunswick, N.J.), Dec. 1949, rep. in *The Dehumanization of Art and Other Essays* (1968)

3 No one today is purely *one* thing. Labels like Indian, or woman, or Muslim, or American are no more than starting-points, which if followed into actual experience for one moment are quickly left behind.

Edward Said (b.1935), Lebanese-born U.S. social and literary critic: *Culture and Imperialism* (1993), Ch.4, Sct.3

4 In the animal kingdom, the rule is, eat or be eaten; in the human kingdom, define or be defined.

Thomas Szasz (b.1920), U.S. psychiatrist: *The Second Sin* (1973), 'Language'

5 Christa T said that she didn't like things to be fixed: that everything, once it's out there in existence – even this phrase which puts it out there – is so difficult to get moving again, so one should try in advance to keep alive while

it's still in the process of coming to be, in oneself. It must keep on *originating* , that's what matters. One should never, never let it become something finished.

But how can anyone do this?

Christa Wolf (b.1929), German novelist: *The Quest for Christa T* (1968; tr.1982), Ch.18

DELEGATION

1 Giving you something to do is like making love to an elephant. You might get a twitch if you are lucky, but it will still be 13 months before you actually produce something.

Robert Maxwell (1923–1991), British tycoon: quoted in *Maxwell* by Joe Haines (1988), Ch.1

2 Surround yourself with the best people you can find, delegate authority, and don't interfere.

Ronald Reagan (b.1911), U.S. Republican politician and president: in *Fortune* (New York), Sept. 1986, quoted in *Reagan's Reign of Error* (ed. Mark Green and Gail MacColl, 1987), 'Mission Impossible'

DELINQUENTS

1 Everything was exactly the way it was not meant to be. The police were bad because they were so good. Knifings were good because they had the potential to be so bad. The violence was good because it was so well organized. Crowd violence can be blamed not on the people causing it but on the ones stopping it.

Bill Buford (b.1954), U.S. editor and author: the views of a football 'thug', in *Among the Thugs* (1991), Pt.1, 'Manchester'

2 Violence among young people … is an aspect of their desire to create. They don't know how to use their energy creatively so they do the opposite and destroy.

Anthony Burgess (1917–1993), British author and critic: in *The Independent* (London), 31 Jan. 1990

3 Strange and predatory and truly dangerous, car thieves and muggers – they seem to jeopardize all our cherished concepts, even our self-esteem, our property rights, our powers of love, our laws and pleasures. The only relationship we seem to have with them is scorn or bewilderment, but they belong somewhere on the dark prairies of a country that is in the throes of self-discovery.

John Cheever (1912–1982), U.S. author: entry, 1955, in *John Cheever: The Journals* (ed. Robert Gottlieb, 1991), 'The Late Forties and the Fifties'

4 They're all animals anyway. All the criminals come out at night. Whores, skunk pussies, buggers, queens, fairies, dopers, junkies, sick, venal. Someday a *real* rain will come and wash all this scum off the streets.

Robert De Niro (b.1943), U.S. actor: voiceover by Travis Bickle (Robert De Niro), in *Taxi Driver* (film; screenplay by Paul Schrader, directed by Martin Scorsese, 1976)

5 Caprice, independence and rebellion, which are opposed to the social order, are essential to the good health of an ethnic group. We shall measure the good health of this group by the number of its delinquents. Nothing is more immobilizing than the spirit of *deference*.

Jean Dubuffet (1901–1985), French sculptor and painter: *Asphyxiating Culture* (1968), rep. in *Asphyxiating Culture and Other Writings* (1986; tr.1988)

6 If we were doing this in the Falklands they would love it. It's part of our heritage. The British have always been fighting wars.

Football fan: on hooliganism charge, quoted in *The Independent* (London), 23 Dec. 1988

7 We know that their adventures are childish. They themselves are fools. They are ready to kill or be killed over a card-game in which an opponent – or they themselves – was cheating. Yet, thanks to such fellows, tragedies are possible.

Jean Genet (1910–1986), French playwright and novelist: of petty criminals, in *The Thief's Journal* (1949; tr.1965), p.11 of Penguin edn. (1967)

See also Winner on CRIMINALS

DEMOCRACY

1 The function of a bourgeois democracy is to secure the consent of the masses to their own exploitation and oppression. … Political competition is permitted as long as the bourgeoisie's monopoly of legitimate violence is not challenged.

Tariq Ali (b.1943), Pakistani-born British activist and author: *1968 and After: Inside the Revolution* (1978), Ch.7

2 Democracy is the menopause of Western society, the Grand Climacteric of the body social. Fascism is its middle-aged lust.

Jean Baudrillard (b.1929), French semiologist: *Cool Memories* (1987; tr.1990), Ch.1

3 Democracy is largely a sham when the industrial system is controlled by any form of autocratic elite, whether of owners, managers, and technocrats, a 'vanguard' party, or a State bureaucracy.

Noam Chomsky (b.1928), U.S. linguist and political analyst: 'Notes on Anarchism', publ. in *New York Review of Books*, 21 May 1970

4 Sure the people are stupid: the human race is stupid. Sure Congress is an inefficient instrument of government. But the people are not stupid enough to abandon representative government for any other kind, including government by the guy who knows.

Bernard DeVoto (1897–1955), U.S. historian and critic: *The Easy Chair* (1955), 'Sometimes They Vote Right Too'

5 Democracy don't rule the world,
You'd better get that in your head;
This world is ruled by violence
But I guess that's better left unsaid.

Bob Dylan (b.1941), U.S. singer and songwriter: 'Union Sundown' (song), on the album *Infidels* (1983)

6 Two cheers for Democracy: one because it admits variety and two because it permits criticism.

E.M. Forster (1879–1970), British novelist and essayist: *Two Cheers for Democracy* (1951), 'What I Believe'. Forster thought two cheers 'quite enough'; three he reserved for 'Love the Beloved Republic' (from Swinburne's poem *Hertha*)

7 When people put their ballots in the boxes, they are, by that act, inoculated against the feeling that the government is not theirs. They then accept, in some measure, that its errors are their errors, its aberrations their aberrations, that any revolt will be against them. It's a remarkably shrewd and rather conservative arrangement when one thinks of it.

J.K. Galbraith (b.1908), U.S. economist: *The Age of Uncertainty* (1977), Ch.12

8 Democracy! Bah! When I hear that word I reach for my feather Boa!

Allen Ginsberg (b.1926), U.S. poet: 'Subliminal', written in journal, Oct. 1960, publ. in *Journals: Early Fifties Early Sixties* (ed. Gordon Ball, 1977), 'New York City'

9 I sometimes think that the critical difference between a democracy and a dictatorship is that in a dictatorship there are only two people out of every hundred who take a personal interest in politics; in a democracy there are three.

Denis Healey (b.1917), British Labour politician: *The Time of My Life* (1989), Pt.2, Ch.7

10 In the end you must either allow people liberty or you must shoot them. If a man claims a vote you must either give him a vote or be prepared to take his life.

William Rees-Mogg (b.1928), British journalist and public figure: quoted by Tony Parsons in 'The Tattooed Jungle' in *Arena* (London), Sept./Oct. 1989, rep. in *Dispatches from the Front Line of Popular Culture* (1994)

11 Democracy is supposed to give you the feeling of choice, like Painkiller X and Painkiller Y. But they're both just aspirin.

Gore Vidal (b.1925), U.S. novelist and critic: interview with author Martin Amis, in *The Observer* (London), 7 Feb. 1982

See also Stevenson on FREEDOM OF EXPRESSION; O'Rourke on GOVERNMENT

DENIAL

1 Negation is the mind's first freedom, yet a negative habit is fruitful only so long as we exert ourselves to overcome it, adapt it to our needs; once *acquired* it can imprison us.

E.M. Cioran (1911–1995), Rumanian-born French philosopher: title essay of *The Temptation to Exist* (1956)

2 In so far as one denies what is, one is possessed by what is not, the compulsions, the fantasies, the terrors that flock to fill the void.

Ursula K. Le Guin (b.1929), U.S. author: *The Lathe of Heaven* (1971), Ch.10

3 Over emphatic negatives always suggest that what is being denied may be what is really being asserted.

Jonathan Raban (b.1942), British author and critic: *Counterblasts* (1989)

DEPARTURES

1 It's interesting to leave a place, interesting even to think about it. Leaving reminds us of what we can part with and what we can't, then offers us something new to look forward to, to dream about.

Richard Ford (b.1944), U.S. author: 'An Urge for Going', publ. in *Harper's Magazine* (New York), Feb. 1992

2 Now is the time of departure. The last streamer that ties us to what is known, parts. We drift into a sea of storms.

Derek Jarman (1942–1994), British film-maker, artist and author: *Jubilee* (film; written and directed by Derek Jarman, 1977)

3 Beam me up, Scotty.

Gene Roddenberry (1921–1991), U.S. TV producer and writer: attributed to Capt. James T. Kirk (William Shatner), in *Star Trek* (TV series; creator and executive producer, Gene Roddenberry, 1966–69). These words were never actually spoken in the series: the nearest is 'Beam us up, Mr Scott,' said by Captain Kirk to his chief engineer

DEPRESSION

1 Lately, I've become accustomed to the way
The ground opens up and envelops me
Each time I go out to walk the dog.

Amiri Baraka [formerly Leroi Jones] (b.1934), U.S. poet and playwright: opening lines in *Preface to a Twenty Volume Suicide Note* (1961), title poem

2 The term clinical depression finds its way into too many conversations these days. One has a sense that a catastrophe has occurred in the psychic landscape.
Leonard Cohen (b.1934), Canadian singer, poet and novelist: in the *International Herald Tribune* (Paris), 4 Nov. 1988

3 Geez, if I could get through to you, kiddo, that depression is not sobbing and crying and *giving vent*, it is plain and simple *reduction of feeling*. Reduction, see? Of all feeling. People who keep stiff upper lips find that it's damn hard to smile.
Judith Guest (b.1936), U.S. author: the psychiatrist (Berger), to Conrad Jarrett, in *Ordinary People* (1976), Ch.27

4 The world leans on us. When we sag, the whole world seems to droop.
Eric Hoffer (1902–1983), U.S. philosopher: *The Passionate State of Mind* (1955), Aph.237

5 Depression is melancholy minus its charms – the animation, the fits.
Susan Sontag (b.1933), U.S. essayist: *Illness as Metaphor* (1978), Ch.7

See also DESPAIR

THE DESERT

1 The desert is a natural extension of the inner silence of the body. If humanity's language, technology, and buildings are an extension of its constructive faculties, the desert alone is an extension of its capacity for absence, the ideal schema of humanity's disappearance.
Jean Baudrillard (b.1929), French semiologist: *America* (1986; tr.1988), 'Astral America'

2 A desert is a place without expectation.
Nadine Gordimer (b.1923), South African author: 'Pula!', first publ. in *London Magazine*, Feb/March 1973, rep. in *The Essential Gesture* (ed. Stephen Clingman, 1988)

3 To say nothing is out here is incorrect; to say the desert is stingy with everything except space and light, stone and earth is closer to the truth.
William Least Heat-Moon [William Trogdon] (b.1939), U.S. author: *Blue Highways: A Journey into America* (1983), Pt.4, Ch.8

4 The Mojave is a big desert and a frightening one. It's as though nature tested a man for endurance and constancy to prove whether he was good enough to get to California.
John Steinbeck (1902–1968), U.S. author: *Travels with Charley: in Search of America* (1962), Pt.3

5 The man of the Kalahari is Esau and we are Jacob, and there is a great gulf between us. This sense of property, of possession that we have is utterly foreign to the Esaus of the world. We have, he is.
Laurens van der Post (1906–1996), South African writer, philosopher: *A Walk with a White Bushman* (1986), p.129 of Chatto & Windus edn.

DESIGN

1 Viewed holistically interior design is a travesty of the architectural process and a frightening condemnation of the credulity, helplessness and gullibility of the most formidable consumers – the rich.
Stephen Bayley (b.1951), British design critic: *Taste* (1991), Pt.2, 'Interiors: Vacuums of Taste'

2 Perhaps believing in good design is like believing in God, it ᴍakes you an optimist.
Terence Conran (b.1931), British businessman and designer: in *The Daily Telegraph* (London), 12 June 1989

3 Art has to move you and design does not, unless it's a good design for a bus.
David Hockney (b.1937), British artist: press conference, 25 Oct. 1988, at the Tate Gallery, London, quoted in *The Guardian* (London), 26 Oct. 1988

4 Design is not for philosophy – it's for life.
Issey Miyake (b.1939), Japanese fashion designer: in the *International Herald Tribune* (Paris), 23 March 1992

See also Bayley on FUNCTION

DESIRE

1 Man is a creation of desire, not a creation of need.
Gaston Bachelard (1884–1962), French scientist, philosopher and literary theorist: *The Psychoanalysis of Fire* (1938; tr.1964), Ch.2, 'Fire and Reverie'

2 Whenever we confront an unbridled desire we are surely in the presence of a tragedy-in-the-making.
Quentin Crisp (b.1908), British author: *Manners from Heaven* (1984), Ch.8

3 You can't always get what you want
But if you try sometimes
You just might find
You get what you need.
Mick Jagger (b.1943) and **Keith Richards** (b.1943), British rock musicians: 'You Can't Always Get What You Want' (song), on the album *Let It Bleed* (The Rolling Stones, 1970)

See also LUST

DESPAIR

1 Despair, in short, seeks its own environment as surely as water finds its own level.

A. Alvarez (b.1929), British critic, poet and novelist: *The Savage God* (1971), Pt.3, 'Theories'

2 Let judges secretly despair of justice: their verdicts will be more acute. Let generals secretly despair of triumph; killing will be defamed. Let priests secretly despair of faith: their compassion will be true.

Leonard Cohen (b.1934), Canadian singer, poet and novelist: *The Spice-Box of Earth* (1961), 'Lines from My Grandfather's Journal'

3 There is no logical explanation for despair. You can no more reason yourself into cheerfulness than you can reason yourself an extra six inches in height. You can only be better prepared.

Stephen Fry (b.1957), British comic actor and author: speech to launch the Samaritans' annual report, 17 May 1996, quoted in *The Guardian* (London), 18 May 1996

4 Despair is the price one pays for setting oneself an impossible aim. It is, one is told, the unforgivable sin, but it is a sin the corrupt or evil man never practises. He always has hope. He never reaches the freezing-point of knowing absolute failure. Only the man of goodwill carries always in his heart this capacity for damnation.

Graham Greene (1904–1991), British novelist: *The Heart of the Matter* (1948), Bk.1, Pt.1, Ch.2, Sct.4

5 A despairing humanity is not merely an unhappy humanity; it is an ugly humanity, ugly in its own eyes – dwarfed, diminished, stunted, and self-loathing. These are the buried sources of world war and despotic collectivism, of scapegoat hatred and exploitation. Ugly hates beautiful, hates gentle, hates loving, hates life. There is a politics of despair.

Theodore Roszak (b.1933), U.S. social critic: introduction to *Where the Wasteland Ends* (1972)

DESPERATION

1 Desperation is the raw material of drastic change. Only those who can leave behind everything they have ever believed in can hope to escape.

William Burroughs (1914–1997), U.S. author: *The Western Lands* (1987), Ch.5

2 What is most original in a man's nature is often that which is most desperate. Thus new systems are forced on the world by men who simply cannot bear the pain of living with what is.

Leonard Cohen (b.1934), Canadian singer, poet and novelist: the narrator in *Beautiful Losers* (1970), p.61 of Panther edn. (1972)

3 My interest in desperation lies only in that sometimes I find myself having become desperate. Very seldom do I start out that way. I can see of course that, in the abstract, thinking and all activity is rather desperate.

Willem de Kooning (1904–1997), Dutch-born U.S. artist: 'A Desperate View' paper delivered to friends, 18 Feb. 1949, New York, first publ. in *William de Kooning* by Thomas B. Hess (1968)

4 We all live in a house on fire, no fire department to call; no way out, just the upstairs window to look out of while the fire burns the house down with us trapped, locked in it.

Tennessee Williams (1911–1983), U.S. playwright: Chris, in *The Milk Train Doesn't Stop Here Anymore* (1963), Sc.6

DESTINY

1 What do I know of man's destiny? I could tell you more about radishes.

Samuel Beckett (1906–1989), Irish playwright and novelist: *Six Residua* (1978), 'Enough'

2 I happen to believe you make your own destiny. You have to do the best with what God gave you ... Life is a box of chocolates, Forrest. You never know what you're goin' to get.

Sally Field (b.1946), U.S. actress: Mrs Gump (Sally Field), in *Forrest Gump* (film; screen- play by Eric Roth, adapted from Winston Groom's novel, directed by Robert Zemeckis, 1994)

3 We are not permitted to choose the frame of our destiny. But what we put into it is ours.

Dag Hammarskjöld (1905–1961), Swedish statesman and secretary-general of U.N.: note, written 1950, publ. in *Markings* (1963), 'Night is Drawing Nigh'

4 A merciless fate threw me into this maelstrom. I wanted much, I began much, but the gale of the world carried away me and my work.

Draža Mihajlovic (1893–1946), Yugoslav soldier and Serbian guerrilla leader: final defence plea at his trial, 15 July 1946, Belgrade, before his execution by Tito's forces, against whom he had been engaged in civil war

5 The real test of a man is not how well he plays the role he has invented for himself, but how well he plays the role that destiny assigned to him.

Jan Patocka (1907–1977), Czech philosopher and activist: advice given to playwright Václav Havel, quoted by him in *Disturbing the Peace* (1986; tr. 1990), Ch.2

6 Destiny is something men select; women achieve it only by default or stupendous suffering.

Harriet Rosenstein (b.1932), U.S. author: quoted in *Ms.* (New York), July 1974

DETECTIVES

1 The detective must be either the official representative of the ethical or the exceptional individual who is in a state of grace.

W.H. Auden (1907–1973), Anglo-American poet: 'The Guilty Vicarage', first publ. in *Harper's Magazine* (New York), May 1948, rep. in *The Dyer's Hand* (1962), Pt.3

2 I needed a vacation. I needed 5 women. I needed to get the wax out of my ears. My car needed an oil change. I'd failed to file my damned income tax. ... I hadn't laughed in six years. I tended to worry when there was nothing to worry about. And when there was something to worry about, I got drunk.

Charles Bukowski (1920–1994), U.S. author and poet: the narrator (Nicky Belane), in *Pulp* (1994), Ch.45

3 A really good detective never gets married.

Raymond Chandler (1880–1959), U.S. author: 'Casual Notes on the Mystery Novel' (1949), first publ. in *Raymond Chandler Speaking* (ed. Dorothy Gardiner and Kathrine S. Walker, 1962)

4 At bottom, I mean profoundly at bottom, the FBI has nothing to do with Communism, it has nothing to do with catching criminals, it has nothing to do with the Mafia, the syndicate, it has nothing to do with trust-busting, it has nothing to do with interstate commerce, it has nothing to do with anything but serving as a church for the mediocre. A high church for the true mediocre.

Norman Mailer (b.1923), U.S. author: *The Presidential Papers* (1963), 'Sixth Presidential Paper – A Kennedy Miscellany: An Impolite Interview'. Mailer called the FBI 'the only absolute organization in America'

5 This is the city. Los Angeles, California. I work here. I carry a badge. My name's Friday. The story you are about to see is true; the names have been changed to protect the innocent.

Jack Webb (1920–1987), U.S actor and producer: Sgt. Joe Friday (Jack Webb), introducing *Dragnet* (radio and TV series created by Jack Webb and Richard L. Breen; written, produced, directed by and starring Jack Webb, 1949–1971). Originally produced for radio, then successfully on TV for another 18 years, the crime serial *Dragnet* started every episode with the above monologue. Friday's speech was also characterized by such expressions as, 'Just the facts, ma'am,' and 'that's my job'

See also Chandler on TELEVISION

THE DEVIL

1 Lucifer also has died with God, and from his ashes has arisen a spiteful demon who does not even understand the object of his venture.

Albert Camus (1913–1960), French-Algerian philosopher and author: *The Rebel* (1951; tr.1953), Pt.5, 'Moderation and Excess'

2 When the Devil quotes Scriptures, it's not, really, to deceive, but simply that the masses are so ignorant of theology that somebody has to teach them the elementary texts before he can seduce them.

Paul Goodman (1911–1972), U.S. author, poet and critic: *Five Years* (1966), 'Spring and Summer 1956', Sct.6

3 Those who consider the Devil to be a partisan of Evil and angels to be warriors for Good accept the demagogy of the angels. Things are clearly more complicated.

Milan Kundera (b.1929), Czech-born French author and critic: *The Book of Laughter and Forgetting* (1978; tr.1980), Pt.2, Ch.4

DIARIES

1 What the Journal posits is not the tragic question, the Madman's question: 'Who am I?', but the comic question, the Bewildered Man's question: 'Am I?' A comic – a comedian, that's what the Journal keeper is.

Roland Barthes (1915–1980), French semiologist: 'Deliberation', first publ. in *Tel Quel* (Paris), winter 1979, rep. in *Barthes: Selected Writings* (1982)

2 The Journal is not essentially a confession, a story about oneself. It is a Memorial. What does the writer have to remember? Himself, who he is when he is not writing, when he is living his daily life, when he alive and real, and not dying and without truth.

Maurice Blanchot (b.1907), French literary theorist and author: 'The Essential Solitude', first publ. in *The Space of Literature* (1955), rep. in *The Gaze of Orpheus, and Other Literary Essays* (ed. P. Adams Sitney, 1981)

3 After the writer's death, reading his journal is like receiving a long letter.

Jean Cocteau (1889–1963), French author and film-maker: journal entry, 7 June 1953, publ. in *Past Tense: Diaries* Vol.II (1988). Cocteau was writing of Kafka's journal, which he had 'read and re-read'

4 In Hollywood now when people die they don't say, 'Did he leave a will?' but 'Did he leave a diary?'

Liza Minelli (b.1946), U.S. actress: in *The Observer* (London), 13 Aug. 1989

5 I do not keep a diary. Never have. To write a diary every day is like returning to one's own vomit.
Enoch Powell (b.1912), British Conservative politician: in *The Sunday Times* (London), 6 Nov. 1977

6 Where I would like to discover facts, I find fancy. Where I would like to learn what I did, I learn only what I was thinking. They are loaded with opinion, moral thoughts, quick evaluations, youthful hopes and cares and sorrows. Occasionally, they manage to report something in exquisite honesty and accuracy. That is why I have refrained from burning them.
E.B. White (1899–1985), U.S. author and editor: of his own journals, in interview in *Writers at Work* (Eighth Series, ed. George Plimpton, 1988)

DINNER PARTIES

1 Conversation did not flow with the drink; it drowned in it.
Quentin Crisp (b.1908), British author: *The Naked Civil Servant* (1968), Ch.22

2 The best number for a dinner party is two – myself and a dam' good head waiter.
Nubar Gulbenkian (1896–1972), British oil tycoon and socialite: in *The Daily Telegraph* (London), 14 Jan. 1965

DIPLOMACY

1 If you are to stand up for your Government you must be able to stand up to your Government.
Lord Caccia (1905–1990), British ambassador: said while British ambassador at Washington D.C., quoted in *Anatomy of Britain* (1965), Ch.17

2 There are few ironclad rules of diplomacy but to one there is no exception. When an official reports that talks were useful, it can safely be concluded that nothing was accomplished.
J.K. Galbraith (b.1908), U.S. economist: 'The American Ambassador', publ. in *The Foreign Service Journal* (Washington D.C.), June 1969

3 My advice to any diplomat who wants to have a good press is to have two or three kids and a dog.
Carl Rowan (b.1925), U.S. diplomat: in the *New Yorker*, 7 Dec. 1963

4 A diplomat these days is nothing but a head-waiter who's allowed to sit down occasionally.
Peter Ustinov (b.1921), British actor, writer and director: the General, in *Romanoff and Juliet* (1956), Act 1. The part of the General was played by Ustinov himself in the first production of the play

DISABILITY

1 Now she's like everyone else.
(*Maintenant elle est comme les autres.*)
Charles de Gaulle (1890–1970), French general and president: remark at the funeral of his handicapped daughter, 1948, quoted in *De Gaulle* by Jean Lacouture (1965)

2 The very deaf, as I am, hear the most astounding things all round them, which have not, in fact, been said. This enlivens my replies until, through mishearing, a new level of communication is reached.
Henry Green (1905–1974), British novelist: interview in *Writers at Work* (Second Series, ed. George Plimpton, 1963)

DISAPPOINTMENT

1 It's precisely the disappointing stories, which have no proper ending and therefore no proper meaning, that sound true to life.
Max Frisch (1911–1991), Swiss author and architect: Stiller, in *I'm Not Stiller* (1954; tr.1958), 'First Notebook'

2 Disappointment is a sort of bankruptcy – the bankruptcy of a soul that expends too much in hope and expectation.
Eric Hoffer (1902–1983), U.S. philosopher: *The Passionate State of Mind* (1955), Aph.264

3 There can be no deep disappointment where there is not deep love.
Martin Luther King Jr. (1929–1968), U.S. clergyman and civil rights leader: 'Letter from Birmingham Jail', open letter to clergymen, 16 April 1963, publ. in *Why We Can't Wait* (1963)

DISARMAMENT

1 Bullets cannot be recalled. They cannot be uninvented. But they can be taken out of the gun.
Martin Amis (b.1949), British author: introduction to *Einstein's Monsters* (1987)

2 If you carry this resolution you will send Britain's Foreign Secretary naked into the conference chamber.
Aneurin Bevan (1897–1960), British Labour politician: speech, 2 Oct. 1957, Brighton, opposing a motion in favour of unilateral nuclear disarmament, quoted in the *Daily Herald* (London), 4 Oct. 1957

3 I would die for my country, but I could never let my country die for me.
Neil Kinnock (b.1942), British Labour politician: on nuclear disarmament, in speech to Labour Party Conference, 30 Sept. 1986, quoted in *The Guardian* (London), 1 Oct. 1986

DISASTERS

1 The earth is mankind's ultimate haven, our blessed *terra firma*. When it trembles and gives way beneath our feet, it's as though one of God's cheques has bounced.
Gilbert Adair, British author and critic: quoted in the *Sunday Correspondent* (London), 24 Dec. 1989

2 The bosses of our mass media, press, radio, film and television, succeed in their aim of taking our minds off disaster. Thus, the distraction they offer demands the antidote of maximum concentration on disaster.
Ernst Fischer (1899–1972), Austrian editor, poet and critic: *Art Against Ideology* (1966; tr. 1969), Ch.1

3 Perhaps catastrophe is the natural human environment, and even though we spend a good deal of energy trying to get away from it, we are programmed for survival amid catastrophe.
Germaine Greer (b.1939), Australian feminist writer: *Sex and Destiny* (1984), Ch.14

4 All safe as houses, fire
kennelled in a matchbox,
the water of drowned valleys
dammed behind taps.
Barring accidents, or malice –
nothing's disaster-proof.
David Malouf (b.1934), Australian novelist and poet: 'On Refusing an All-risk Insurance Policy', publ. in *Bicycle and Other Poems* (1970)

5 The popularity of disaster movies ... expresses a collective perception of a world threatened by irresistible and unforeseen forces which *nevertheless are thwarted at the last moment*. Their thinly veiled symbolic meaning might be translated thus: We are innocent of wrongdoing. We are attacked by unforeseeable forces come to harm us. We are, thus, innocent even of negligence. Though those forces are insuperable, *chance* will come to our aid and we shall emerge victorious.
David Mamet (b.1947), U.S. playwright: *Writing in Restaurants* (1986), 'Decadence'

DISC JOCKEYS

1 Do they merit vitriol, even a drop of it? Yes, because they corrupt the young, persuading them that the mature world, which produced Beethoven and Schweitzer, sets an even higher value on the transient anodynes of youth than does youth itself ... They are the Hollow Men. They are electronic lice.
Anthony Burgess (1917–1993), British author and critic: referring to disc jockeys, in *Punch* (London), 20 Sept. 1967

2 Radio news is bearable. This is due to the fact that while the news is being broadcast the disc jockey is not allowed to talk.
Fran Lebowitz (b.1951), U.S. journalist: *Metropolitan Life* (1978), 'No News is Bearable'

3 So, too, if, to our surprise, we should meet one of these morons whose remarks are so conspicuous a part of the folklore of the world of the radio – remarks made without using either the tongue or the brain, spouted much like the spoutings of small whales – we should recognize him as below the level of nature but not as below the level of the imagination.
Wallace Stevens (1879–1955), U.S. poet: 'Three Academic Pieces', No.1 (1947), rep. in *The Necessary Angel* (1951)

DISCIPLINE

1 What terrible discipline it takes to live harmoniously.
Angela Carter (1940–1992), British author: *Fireworks* (1974), 'A Souvenir of Japan'

2 Discipline is a political anatomy of detail.
Michel Foucault (1926–1984), French philosopher: *Discipline and Punish: The Birth of the Prison* (1975), 'Docile Bodies'

3 Reasonable orders are easy enough to obey; it is capricious, bureaucratic or plain idiotic demands that form the habit of discipline.
Barbara Tuchman (1912–1989), U.S. historian: *Stilwell and the American Experience in China: 1911–1945* (1970), Pt.1, Ch.1

DISEASE

1 Even diseases have lost their prestige, there aren't so many of them left. ... Think it over ... no more syphilis, no more clap, no more typhoid ... antibiotics have taken half the tragedy out of medicine.
Louis-Ferdinand Céline (1894–1961), French author: interview 1960, publ. in *Critical Essays on Louis-Ferdinand Céline* (ed. William F. Buckley, 1989)

2 Disease can never be conquered, can never be quelled by emotion's wailful screaming or faith's cymballic prayer. It can only be conquered by the energy of humanity and the cunning in the mind of man. In the patience of a Curie, in the enlightenment of a Faraday, a Rutherford, a Pasteur, a Nightingale, and all other apostles of light and cleanliness, rather than of a woebegone godliness, we shall find final deliverance from plague, pestilence, and famine.
Sean O'Casey (1884–1964), Irish playwright: *Inishfallen, Fare Thee Well* (fourth volume of autobiography, 1949), 'Inishfallen, Fare Thee Well'

3   With the modern diseases (once TB, now cancer) the romantic idea that the disease expresses the character is invariably extended to assert that the character causes the disease – because it has not expressed itself. Passion moves inward, striking and blighting the deepest cellular recesses.
    Susan Sontag (b.1933), U.S. essayist: *Illness As Metaphor* (1978), Ch.6

See also ILLNESS

WALT DISNEY, INC.

1   I must admit that the existence of Disneyland (which I *know* is real) proves that we are not living in Judaea in 50 AD. ... Saint Paul would never go near Disneyland. Only children, tourists, and visiting Soviet high officials ever go to Disneyland. Saints do not.
    Philip K. Dick (1928–1982), U.S. science fiction writer: *I Hope I Shall Arrive Soon* (1986), 'How to Build a Universe That Doesn't Fall Apart Two Days Later'

2   I love Mickey Mouse more than any woman I've ever known.
    Walt Disney (1901–1966), U.S. animator and filmmaker: quoted in *Halliwell's Filmgoer's Companion* (ed. John Walker, 1995)

3   To all who come to this happy place ... WELCOME. Disneyland is your land. Here age relives fond memories of the past ... and here you may savor the challenge and promise of the future. Disneyland is dedicated to the ideals, the dreams, and the hard facts that have created America ... with the hope that it will be a source of joy and inspiration to all the world.
    Disneyland Plaque, California, 1955: quoted in *Walt Disney: Hollywood's Dark Prince* by Mark Eliot (1994), 'Notes'

4   Disney World has acquired by now something of the air of a national shrine. American parents who don't take their children there sense obscurely that they have failed in some fundamental way, like Muslims who never made it to Mecca.
    Simon Hoggart (b.1946), British journalist: *America: A User's Guide* (1990), Ch.9

5   Take the serious side of Disney, the Confucian side of Disney. It's in having taken an ethos ... where you have the values of courage and tenderness asserted in a way that everybody can understand. You have got an absolute genius there. You have got a greater correlation of nature than you have had since the time of Alexander the Great.
    Ezra Pound (1885–1972), U.S. poet and critic: interview in *Writers at Work* (Second Series, ed. George Plimpton, 1963)

DISSATISFACTION

1   Man is the only creature who refuses to be what he is.
    Albert Camus (1913–1960), French-Algerian philosopher and author: introduction to *The Rebel* (1951; tr.1953)

2   The problem lay buried, unspoken for many years in the minds of American women. It was a strange stirring, a sense of dissatisfaction, a yearning that women suffered in the middle of the twentieth century in the United States. Each suburban housewife struggled with it alone. As she made the beds, shopped for groceries, matched slipcover material, ate peanut butter sandwiches with her children, chauffeured Cub Scouts and Brownies, lay beside her husband at night, she was afraid to ask even of herself the silent question: 'Is this all?'
    Betty Friedan (b.1921), U.S. feminist writer: opening paragraph of *The Feminine Mystique* (1963), Ch.1

3   No, no, we are not satisfied, and we will not be satisfied until justice rolls down like waters and righteousness like a mighty stream.
    Martin Luther King Jr., (1929–1968), U.S. clergyman and civil rights leader: 'I Have a Dream', speech, 28 Aug. 1963, at civil rights march, Washington D.C., publ. in *A Testament of Hope: Essential Writings* (ed. James Melvin Washington, 1986). King was quoting the Old Testament, Amos 5:24

4   Them belly full but we hungry
    A hungry mob is a angry mob.
    The Wailers, Jamaican reggae band: 'Them Belly Full' (song; written by Legon Cogil and Carlton Barrett), on the album *Natty Dread* (1974)

DISSENT

1   Has there ever been a society which has died of dissent? Several have died of conformity in our lifetime.
    Jacob Bronowski (1908–1974), British scientist and author: 'The Sense of Human Dignity', Sct.5, lecture given at the Massachusetts Institute of Technology, 19 March 1953, publ. in *Science and Human Values* (1961)

2   One does not arrest Voltaire.
    Charles de Gaulle (1890–1970), French general and president: referring to the Maoist and Communist activities of Jean-Paul Sartre during the 1960s, quoted in *Encounter* (London), June 1975

3   Wild intelligence abhors any narrow world; and the world of women must stay narrow, or the woman is an outlaw. No woman could be

Nietzsche or Rimbaud without ending up in a
whorehouse or lobotomized.

Andrea Dworkin (b.1946), U.S. feminist critic:
Right-Wing Women (1978), Ch.2

4 The dissident does not operate in the realm of
genuine power at all. He is not seeking power.
He has no desire for office and does not gather
votes. He does not attempt to charm the
public, he offers nothing and promises nothing. He can offer, if anything, only his own skin
– and he offers it solely because he has no other
way of affirming the truth he stands for. His
actions simply articulate his dignity as a
citizen, regardless of the cost.

Václav Havel (b.1936), Czech playwright and
president: *Living in Truth* (1986), Pt.1, 'An
Anatomy of Reticence,' Sct.10

5 Though dissenters seem to question everything in sight, they are actually bundles of
dusty answers and never conceived a new
question. What offends us most in the
literature of dissent is the lack of hesitation and
wonder.

Eric Hoffer (1902–1983), U.S. philosopher:
Reflections on the Human Condition (1973), Aph.49

6 The dissenter is every human being at those
moments of his life when he resigns momentarily from the herd and thinks for himself.

Archibald MacLeish (1892–1982), U.S. poet: 'In
Praise of Dissent', publ. in the *New York Times*,
16 Dec. 1956

7 The mark of our time is its revulsion against
imposed patterns.

Marshall McLuhan (1911–1980), Canadian
communications theorist: introduction to
Understanding Media (1964)

8 To shoot a man because one disagrees with his
interpretation of Darwin or Hegel is a sinister
tribute to the supremacy of ideas in human
affairs – but a tribute nevertheless.

George Steiner (b.1929), French-born U.S. critic
and novelist: *Language and Silence* (1967),
'Marxism and the Literary Critic'

9 Discussion in America means dissent.

James Thurber (1894–1961), U.S. humorist and
illustrator: *Lanterns and Lances* (1961), 'The
Duchess and the Bugs'

10 The original 'crime' of 'niggers' and lesbians is
that they prefer themselves.

Alice Walker (b.1944), U.S. author and critic:
'Breaking Chains and Encouraging Life', first publ.
in *Ms.* (New York), April 1980, rep. in *In Search of
our Mothers' Gardens* (1983)

See also Roszak on THE WEST

DISSIPATION

1 Sex and drugs and rock and roll.

Ian Dury (b.1942), British rock musician: 'Sex and
Drugs and Rock and Roll' (song), on the album *Sex
and Drugs and Rock and Roll* (Ian Dury and the
Blockheads, 1977)

2 Dissipation is a form of self-sacrifice. The
passage from this to other forms of self-sacrifice is not uncommon. Passionate sinning has
not infrequently been an apprenticeship to
sainthood.

Eric Hoffer (1902–1983), U.S. philosopher: *The
Passionate State of Mind* (1955), Aph.9

3 You think I've done bad things? I've always
tried to live a saintly life.

Shane MacGowan (b.1957), Anglo-Irish rock
musician: interview in *The Face* (London), Nov.
1994

4 They had both noticed that a life of dissipation
sometimes gave to a face the look of gaunt
suffering spirituality that a life of asceticism
was supposed to give and quite often did not.

Katherine Anne Porter (1890–1980), U.S. short-
story writer and novelist: of Herr Freytag and Mrs
Treadwell, in *Ship of Fools* (1962), Pt.3

5 All right, this is the plan. We'll get in there and
get wrecked. Then we'll eat a pork pie. Then
we'll go home and drop a couple of Surmontil
50s each. That means we'll miss out Monday,
but come up smiling Tuesday morning.

Bruce Robinson (b.1946), British film-maker:
Withnail (Richard E. Grant), in *Withnail and I*
(film; written and directed by Bruce Robinson,
1987)

DIVORCE

1 I know one husband and wife who, whatever
the official reasons given to the court for the
break up of their marriage, were really
divorced because the husband believed that
nobody ought to read while he was talking and
the wife that nobody ought to talk while she
was reading.

Vera Brittain (1893–1970), British author: quoted
in *Violets and Vinegar* by Jilly Cooper and Tom
Hartman (1980), 'The Battle Done'

2 People named John and Mary never divorce.
For better or for worser, in madness and in
saneness, they seem bound together for eternity by their rudimentary nomenclature. They
may loathe and despise one another, quarrel,
weep, and commit mayhem, but they are not
free to divorce. Tom, Dick, and Harry can go
to Reno on a whim, but nothing short of death
can separate John and Mary.

John Cheever (1912–1982), U.S. author: entry,
1966, in *John Cheever: The Journals* (ed. Robert

Gottlieb, 1991), 'The Sixties'. Cheever's wife was named Mary

3 Many divorces are not really the result of irreparable injury but involve, instead, a desire on the part of the man or woman to shatter the setup, start out from scratch alone, and make life work for them all over again. They want the risk of disaster, want to touch bottom, see where bottom is, and, coming up, to breathe the air with relief and relish again.
Edward Hoagland (b.1932), U.S. novelist and essayist: 'Other Lives', first publ. in *Harper's Magazine* (New York), July 1973, rep. in *Heart's Desire* (1988)

4 Being divorced is like being hit by a Mack truck. If you live through it, you start looking very carefully to the right and to the left.
Jean Kerr (b.1923), U.S. author and playwright: Mary, in *Mary, Mary* (1960), Act 1

5 Gimme the Plaza, the jet and $150 million, too.
New York Post: headline, 13 Feb. 1990, reporting on Ivana Trump's divorce settlement demands of husband Donald

6 A lot of people have asked me how short I am. Since my last divorce, I think I'm about $100,000 short.
Mickey Rooney (b.1920), U.S. actor and entertainer: in the *Chicago Sun-Times*, 22 June 1978

7 You can't stay married in a situation where you are afraid to go to sleep in case your wife might cut your throat.
Mike Tyson (b.1966), U.S. boxer: explaining his divorce, quoted in *The Daily Telegraph* (London), 1 Feb. 1989

See also MARRIAGE: FAILED

DOCTORS

1 A doctor, like anyone else who has to deal with human beings, each of them unique, cannot be a scientist; he is either, like the surgeon, a craftsman, or, like the physician and the psychologist, an artist. ... This means that in order to be a good doctor a man must also have a good character, that is to say, whatever weaknesses and foibles he may have, he must love his fellow human beings in the concrete and desire their good before his own.
W.H. Auden (1907–1973), Anglo-American poet: *A Certain World* (1970), 'Medicine'

2 When a man goes through six years' training to be a doctor he will never be the same. He knows too much.
Enid Bagnold (1889–1981), British novelist and playwright: *Autobiography* (1969), Ch.15

3 One of the fundamental reasons why so many doctors become cynical and disillusioned is precisely because, when the abstract idealism has worn thin, they are uncertain about the value of the actual lives of the patients they are treating. This is not because they are callous or personally inhuman: it is because they live in and accept a society which is incapable of knowing what a human life is worth.
John Berger (b.1926), British author and critic: *A Fortunate Man* (1967), p.165–6 of Writers and Readers Publishing Cooperative edn. (1976)

4 My doctor gave me six months to live but when I couldn't pay the bill, he gave me six months more.
Walter Matthau (b.1920), U.S. actor: said following a heart attack, quoted in *Star Billing* by David Brown (1985), p.31 of Weidenfeld & Nicolson edn.

5 I wasn't driven into medicine by a social conscience but by rampant curiosity.
Jonathan Miller (b.1936), British doctor, humorist and director: quoted in *The Observer* (London), 5 Feb. 1983

DOCTRINE

1 A faith is something you die for, a doctrine is something you kill for. There is all the difference in the world.
Tony Benn (b.1925), British Labour politician: television broadcast, BBC TV, 11 April 1989

2 A striking feature of moral and political argument in the modern world is the extent to which it is innovators, radicals, and revolutionaries who revive old doctrines, while their conservative and reactionary opponents are the inventors of new ones.
Alasdair MacIntyre (b.1929), British philosopher: *A Short History of Ethics* (1966), Ch.17

DOGS

1 If a dog doesn't put you first where are you both? In what relation? A dog needs God. It lives by your glances, your wishes. It even shares your humour. This happens about the fifth year. If it doesn't happen you are only keeping an animal.
Enid Bagnold (1889–1981), British novelist and playwright: *Autobiography* (1969), Ch.10

2 In order to really enjoy a dog, one doesn't merely try to train him to be semihuman. The point of it is to open oneself to the possibility of becoming partly a dog.
Edward Hoagland (b.1932), U.S. novelist and essayist: 'Dogs and the Tug of Life', first publ. in *Harper's Magazine* (New York), Feb. 1975, rep. in *Heart's Desire* (1988)

3 If you are a dog and your owner suggests that you wear a sweater ... suggest that he wear a tail.
Fran Lebowitz (b.1951), U.S. journalist: *Social Studies* (1981), 'Pointers for Pets'

4 A door is what a dog is perpetually on the wrong side of.
Ogden Nash (1902–1971), U.S. poet: 'A Dog's Best Friend is his Illiteracy', publ. in *The Private Dining Room* (1953)

DOUBT

1 Doubt, it seems to me, is the central condition of a human being in the twentieth century.
Salman Rushdie (b.1947), Indian-born British author: quoted in *The Observer* (London), 19 Feb. 1989

2 You may have your suspicions, your fears, you may even believe there is something, somewhere, terribly, drastically wrong, but because someone else is in charge, because there is a part of the system above you which you don't know, you don't question it, you even distrust your own doubts.
Graham Swift (b.1949), British author: *Shuttlecock* (1981), Ch.4

3 It would strike me as ridiculous to want to doubt the existence of Napoleon; but if someone doubted the existence of the earth 150 years ago, perhaps I should be more willing to listen, for now he is doubting our whole system of evidence.
Ludwig Wittgenstein (1889–1951), Austrian-born British philosopher: *On Certainty* (ed. Anscombe and von Wright, 1969), Sct.185

See also UNCERTAINTY

DREAMING

1 The armored cars of dreams, contrived to let us do
so many a dangerous thing.
Elizabeth Bishop (1911–1979), U.S. poet: 'Sleeping Standing Up', St.2, publ. in *Poems: North and South A Cold Spring* (1955)

2 There couldn't be a society of people who didn't dream. They'd be dead in two weeks.
William Burroughs (1914–1997), U.S. author: taped conversation, 1974, New York City, in *With William Burroughs: A Report from the Bunker* by Victor Bockris (1981), 'On Dreams'

3 I do not understand the capricious lewdness of the sleeping mind.
John Cheever (1912–1982), U.S. author: entry, 1955, in *John Cheever: The Journals* (ed. Robert Gottlieb, 1991), 'The Late Forties and the Fifties'

4 One of the characteristics of the dream is that nothing surprises us in it. With no regret, we agree to live in it with strangers, completely cut off from our habits and friends.
Jean Cocteau (1889–1963), French author and film-maker: *La Difficulté d'Etre* (1947), 'Du Rêve'

5 Oh, Jerry, don't let's ask for the moon – we have the stars.
Bette Davis (1908-88), U.S. actress: Charlotte Vale (Bette Davis), in *Now, Voyager* (film; screenplay by Casey Robinson, based on Olive Higgins Prouty's 1941 novel, directed by Irving Rapper, 1942)

6 A dream is a scripture, and many scriptures are nothing but dreams.
(*Un sogno è una scrittura, e molte scritture non sono altro che sogni.*)
Umberto Eco (b.1932), Italian semiologist and novelist: Brother William, in *The Name of the Rose* (1980; tr.1983), 'Sixth Day: After Terce'

7 Climb every mountain, ford every stream
Follow every rainbow, till you find your dream!
Oscar Hammerstein II (1895–1960), U.S. songwriter: 'Climb Every Mountain' (song), in *The Sound of Music* (stage musical, 1959; film, 1965)

8 We've removed the ceiling above our dreams. There are no more impossible dreams.
Jesse Jackson (b.1941), U.S. clergyman and civil rights leader: in *The Independent* (London), 9 June 1988

9 Dream is not a revelation. If a dream affords the dreamer some light on himself, it is not the person with closed eyes who makes the discovery but the person with open eyes lucid enough to fit thoughts together. Dream – a scintillating mirage surrounded by shadows – is essentially *poetry* .
Michel Leiris (1901–1990), French anthropologist and author: quoted in Roger Shattuck's introduction to *Nights as Day, Days as Nights* (1961)

10 You shoot me in a dream, you better wake up and apologize.
Quentin Tarantino (b.1958), U.S. film-maker: Mr White (Harvey Keitel), in *Reservoir Dogs* (film; written and directed by Quentin Tarantino, 1992)

11 Dreams come true; without that possibility, nature would not incite us to have them.
John Updike (b.1932), U.S. author and critic: *Self-Consciousness: Memoirs* (1989), Ch.3

See also THE AMERICAN DREAM; DAYDREAMS; Houston on IDEALISM

DRESS

1 The best-dressed woman is one whose clothes wouldn't look too strange in the country.
Hardy Amies (b.1909), British tailor and dressmaker to Queen Elizabeth II: in the *International Herald Tribune* (Paris), 20 June 1989

2 If you want to say something radical, you should dress conservative.
Steve Biko (1946–1977), South African antiapartheid activist: advice given to the young Barbara Follett, quoted by her in *The Observer* (London), 25 Feb.1996

3 Women's sexy underwear is a minor but significant growth industry of late-twentieth-century Britain in the twilight of capitalism.
Angela Carter (1940–1992), British author: 'The Bridled Sweeties' (1977), rep. in *Nothing Sacred* (1982)

4 Nothing goes out of fashion sooner than a long dress with a very low neck.
Coco Chanel (1883–1971), French *couturière*: quoted in *Coco Chanel: Her Life, Her Secrets* by Marcel Haedrich (1971), Ch.21

5 They look quite promising in the shop; and not entirely without hope when I get them back into my wardrobe. But then, when I put them on they tend to deteriorate with a very strange rapidity and one feels so sorry for them.
Joyce Grenfell (1910–1979), British actress and writer: on new clothes, in *Stately as a Galleon* (1978), 'English Lit.'

6 The origins of clothing are not practical. They are mystical and erotic. The primitive man in the wolf-pelt was not keeping dry; he was saying: 'Look what I killed. Aren't I the best?'
Katharine Hamnett (b.1948), British fashion designer: in the *Independent on Sunday* (London), 10 March 1991

7 Clothes make the poor invisible ... America has the best-dressed poverty the world has ever known.
Michael Harrington (1928–1989), U.S. social scientist, author: *The Other America* (1962), Ch.1, Sct.1

8 How did you get into that dress – with a spray gun?
Bob Hope (b.1903), U.S. actor: Hot Lips Barton (Bob Hope), to Lucia Maria de Andrade (Dorothy Lamour), in *Road To Rio* (film; screenplay by Edmund Beloin and Jack Rose, directed by Norman McLeod, 1947)

9 Conspicuous consumption in dress still survives in two locations: the private lives of the urban rich and the public lives of the urban poor.
Alison Lurie (b.1926), U.S. author: preface to *The Language of Clothes* (1981; rev.1992)

10 Where women are concerned, the rule is never to go out with anyone better dressed than you.
John Malkovich (b.1953), U.S. actor: interview in the *Independent on Sunday* (London), 5 April 1992

11 An accent mark, perhaps, instead of a whole western accent – a point of punctuation rather than a uniform twang. That is how it should be worn: as a quiet point of character reference, an apt phrase of sartorial allusion – macho, sotto voce.
Phil Patton (b.1953), U.S. author and journalist: of bolo ties, in *Esquire* (New York), Feb. 1990

12 I saw no reason why childhood shouldn't last for ever. I wanted everyone to retain the grace of a child and not to have to become stilted, confined, ugly beings. So I created clothes that worked and moved and allowed people to run, to jump, to leap, to retain their precious freedom.
Mary Quant (b.1934), British fashion designer: interview in *Harper's & Queen* (London), May 1973

13 Zippers are primal and modern at the very same time. On the one hand, your zipper is primitive and reptilian, on the other, mechanical and slick. A zipper is where the Industrial Revolution meets the Cobra Cult, don't you think? Ahh. Little alligators of ecstasy, that's what zippers are. Sexy, too. Now your button, a button is slim and persnickety. There's somethin' Victorian about a row o' buttons. But a zipper, why a zipper is the very snake at the gate of Eden, waitin' to escort a true believer into the Garden.
Tom Robbins (b.1936), U.S. author: Dr Dannyboy, in *Jitterbug Perfume* (1984), Pt.4

14 I have often said that I wish I had invented blue jeans: the most spectacular, the most practical, the most relaxed and nonchalant. They have expression, modesty, sex appeal, simplicity – all I hope for in my clothes.
Yves Saint Laurent (b.1936), French fashion designer: interview in *Ritz* (London), No.85, 1984

15 For women ... bras, panties, bathing suits, and other stereotypical gear are visual reminders of a commercial, idealized feminine image that our real and diverse female bodies can't possibly fit. Without these visual references, each individual woman's body demands to be accepted on its own terms. We stop being comparatives. We begin to be unique.
Gloria Steinem (b.1934), U.S. feminist writer and editor: 'In Praise of Women's Bodies', first publ. in *Ms.* (New York), April 1981, rep. in *Outrageous Acts and Everyday Rebellions* (1983)

16 There's nothing worse than going somewhere and wishing you had put on something more adventurous. ... When in doubt, overdress.

Vivienne Westwood (b.1941), British fashion designer: quoted in *Fashion and Perversity* by Fred Vermorel (1996), Pt.1

17 One of the less agreeable aspects of the communications age was the message T-shirt. Lacking in charisma? Get a message, get a T-shirt, get a brand. We became a nation of sandwich boards.

Peter York (b.1950), British journalist: interview in *The Sunday Telegraph* (London), 31 Dec. 1995

See also ELEGANCE; HATS; SHOES

DRINK

1 Other countries drink to get drunk, and this is accepted by everyone; in France, drunkenness is a consequence, never an intention. A drink is felt as the spinning out of a pleasure, not as the necessary cause of an effect which is sought: wine is not only a philtre, it is also the leisurely act of drinking.

Roland Barthes (1915–1980), French semiologist: *Mythologies* (1957; tr.1972), 'Wine and Milk'

2 The decline of the aperitif may well be one of the most depressing phenomena of our time.

Luis Buñuel (1900–1983), Spanish film-maker: *My Last Breath* (autobiography, 1983), Ch.6

3 Alcohol is like love. The first kiss is magic, the second is intimate, the third is routine. After that you take the girl's clothes off.

Raymond Chandler (1888–1959), U.S. author: Terry Lennox, in *The Long Goodbye* (1954), Ch.4

4 Alcohol doesn't console, it doesn't fill up anyone's psychological gaps, all it replaces is the lack of God. It doesn't comfort man. On the contrary, it encourages him in his folly, it transports him to the supreme regions where he is master of his own destiny.

Marguerite Duras (1914–1996), French author: *Practicalities* (1987; tr.1990), 'Alcohol'

5 Even though a number of people have tried, no one has yet found a way to drink for a living.

Jean Kerr (b.1923), U.S. author and playwright: Sydney, in *Poor Richard* (1963), Act 1

See also COCKTAILS; WINE

DRINK: Abstinence

1 I can maintain reasonably long periods of sobriety – one of the best things of being on the wagon is falling off and I do have that tendency.

Nick Cave (b.1957), Australian musician and author: interview in *Dazed and Confused* (London), Feb. 1996

2 The Wine, the Grape, the Visions that we saw –
And shared, it seemeth, with great Evelyn Waugh!
Ah, these the Liver faintly doth forbid.
Once Nightingales, but now the black Rook's Caw!

Gavin Ewart (1916–1995), British poet: 'Rubaiyat of the Prostate', publ. in *Late Pickings* (1987)

3 I'd hate to be a teetotaller. Imagine getting up in the morning and knowing that's as good as you're going to feel all day.

Dean Martin (1917–1995), U.S. actor and singer: quoted in *Halliwell's Filmgoer's Companion* (ed. Leslie Halliwelll, 1984)

DRINK: Alcoholism

1 An alcoholic has been lightly defined as a man who drinks more than his own doctor.

Alvan L. Barach (1895–1977), U.S. physician: quoted from *Journal of the American Medical Association* by John Illman in *The Guardian* (London), 29 Dec. 1989

2 One drink is too many for me and a thousand not enough.

Brendan Behan (1923–1964), Irish playwright: quoted by Rae Jeffs, publicist and assistant to Behan, in *Sacred Monsters* by Daniel Farson (1988), 'Rousting in Dublin'

3 When a woman drinks it's as if an animal were drinking, or a child. Alcoholism is scandalous in a woman, and a female alcoholic is rare, a serious matter. It's a slur on the divine in our nature.

Marguerite Duras (1914–1996), French author: *Practicalities* (1987; tr.1990), 'Alcohol'

DRINK: Drunks

1 When I played drunks I had to remain sober because I didn't know how to play them when I was drunk.

Richard Burton (1925–1984), British actor: quoted in *Halliwell's Filmgoer's Companion* (ed. Leslie Halliwell, 1984)

2 Alcohol is barren. The words a man speaks in the night of drunkenness fade like the darkness itself at the coming of day.

Marguerite Duras (1914–1996), French author: *Practicalities* (1987; tr.1990), 'Alcohol'

3 I often sit back and think 'I wish I'd done that' and find out later that I already have.

Richard Harris (b.1932), Irish actor: on his drinking, quoted in *The Sun* (London), 19 May 1988

4 The dark side of drunkenness is raised voices, casual violence, crazy laughter, unwise sex – it makes a man look like a fool. But it makes a woman look insane.

Tony Parsons (b.1955), British journalist: 'Gender Benders', publ. in *Arena* (London), Nov. 1993, rep. in *Dispatches from the Front Line of Popular Culture* (1994)

5 I do not live in the world of sobriety.

Oliver Reed (b.1938), British actor: quoted in *The Sunday Times* (London), 27 Dec. 1987

DRUGS

1 I don't respond well to mellow, you know what I mean, I-I have a tendency to ... if I get too mellow, I-I ripen and then rot.

Woody Allen (b.1935), U.S. film-maker: Alvy Singer (Woody Allen) passing on a marijuana party, in *Annie Hall* (film; written by Woody Allen and Marshall Brickman, directed by Woody Allen, 1977)

2 I give so much pleasure to so many people. Why can I not get some pleasure for myself? Why do I have to stop?

John Belushi (1949–1982), U.S. comedian, singer and actor: on his addiction, quoted in *Wired: The Short Life and Fast Times of John Belushi* by Bob Woodward (1984), Pt.1, Ch.7

3 The whole LSD, STP, marijuana, heroin, hashish, prescription cough medicine crowd suffers from the 'Watchtower' itch: you gotta be with us, man, or you're out, you're dead. This pitch is a continual and seeming MUST with those who use the stuff. It's no wonder they keep getting busted.

Charles Bukowski (1920–1994), U.S. author and poet: *Tales of Ordinary Madness* (1967), 'The Big Pot Game'

4 I experimented with marijuana a time or two. And I didn't like it, and I didn't inhale.

Bill Clinton (b.1946), U.S. Democratic politician and president: said during a television debate with Jerry Brown, a rival candidate for the Democratic Party nomination, quoted in the *Washington Post*, 30 March 1992. Under close questioning to ascertain whether the two men had ever broken state, federal or international laws, Clinton admitted his misdemeanour while a Rhodes Scholar at Oxford University

5 My heart is broke
but I have some glue.
Help me inhale
And mend it with you.

Kurt Cobain (1967–1994), U.S. rock musician: 'Dumb' (song), on the album *In Utero* (Nirvana, 1993)

6 Take me, I am the drug; take me, I am hallucinogenic.

Salvador Dali (1904–1989), Spanish painter: *Dali by Dali* (1970), 'The Hallucinogenic Dali'

7 Drug misuse is not a disease, it is a decision, like the decision to step out in front of a moving car. You would call that not a disease but an error of judgment.

Philip K. Dick (1928–1982), U.S. science fiction writer: *A Scanner Darkly* (1977), 'Author's Note'

8 There seems to be no stopping drug frenzy once it takes hold of a nation. What starts with an innocuous HUGS, NOT DRUGS bumper sticker soon leads to wild talk of shooting dealers and making urine tests a condition for employment – anywhere.

Barbara Ehrenreich (b.1941), U.S. author and columnist: 'Drug Frenzy' (1988), publ. in *The Worst Years of Our Lives* (1991)

9 Nobody stopped thinking about those psychedelic experiences. Once you've been to some of those places, you think, 'How can I get back there again but make it a little easier on myself?'

Jerry Garcia (1942–1995), U.S. rock musician: interview in *Rolling Stone* (New York), 30 Nov. 1989

10 No monster vibration, no snake universe hallucinations. Many tiny jeweled violet flowers along the path of a living brook that looked like Blake's illustration for a canal in grassy Eden: huge Pacific watery shore, Orlovsky dancing naked like Shiva long-haired before giant green waves, titanic cliffs that Wordsworth mentioned in his own Sublime, great yellow sun veiled with mist hanging over the planet's oceanic horizon. No harm.

Allen Ginsberg (b.1926), U.S. poet: description of an LSD experience in Big Sur, California, in letter, 2 June 1966, publ. in the *Paris Review*, summer 1966

11 Nobody saves America by sniffing cocaine
Jiggling yr knees blankeyed in the rain
When it snows in yr nose you catch cold in yr brain.

Allen Ginsberg: lines publ. in *Ginsberg: A Biography* by Barry Miles (1989), Ch.16

12 Only one thing is certain: if pot is legalized, it won't be for our benefit but for the authorities'. To have it legalized will also be to lose control of it.

Germaine Greer (b.1939), Australian feminist writer: 'Flip-top Legal Pot', first publ. in *Oz* (London), Oct. 1968, rep. in *The Madwoman's Underclothes* (1986)

13 Coming into Los Angeles, bringing in a couple of keys,

Don't touch my bags, if you please, Mister Customs Man.

Arlo Guthrie (b.1947), U.S. singer and songwriter: 'Coming into Los Angeles' (song), on the album *Running Down the Road* (1969)

14 If you think dope is for kicks and for thrills, you're out of your mind. There are more kicks to be had in a good case of paralytic polio or by living in an iron lung. If you think you need stuff to play music or sing, you're crazy. It can fix you so you can't play nothing or sing nothing.

Billie Holiday (1915–1959), U.S. blues singer: *Lady Sings the Blues* (written with William Dufty, 1956; rev.1975), Ch.23

15 If we could sniff or swallow something that would, for five or six hours each day, abolish our solitude as individuals, atone us with our fellows in a glowing exaltation of affection and make life in all its aspects seem not only worth living, but divinely beautiful and significant, and if this heavenly, world-transfiguring drug were of such a kind that we could wake up next morning with a clear head and an undamaged constitution – then, it seems to me, all our problems (and not merely the one small problem of discovering a novel pleasure) would be wholly solved and earth would become paradise.

Aldous Huxley (1894–1963), British author: *Music at Night and Other Essays* (1949), 'Wanted, a New Pleasure'. Huxley's earlier writings revealed a different attitude: 'I prefer being sober to even the rosiest and most agreeable intoxications,' he wrote in his introduction to *Texts and Pretexts* (1932). 'The peyotl-trances of Swinburne, for example, have always left me perfectly *compos mentis*; I do not catch the infection'

16 To punish drug takers is like a drunk striking the bleary face it sees in the mirror. Drugs will not be brought under control until society itself changes, enabling men to use them as primitive man did: welcoming the visions they provided not as fantasies, but as intimations of a different, and important, level of reality.

Brian Inglis (b.1916), British journalist and author: *The Forbidden Game: A Social History of Drugs* (1975), 'Postscript'

17 The basic thing nobody asks is why do people take drugs of any sort? ... Why do we have these accessories to normal living to live? I mean, is there something wrong with society that's making us so pressurized, that we cannot live without guarding ourselves against it?

John Lennon (1940–1980), British rock musician: interview on *The Dick Cavett Show*, 24 Sept. 1971, publ. in *Imagine* (ed. Andrew Solt and Sam Egan, 1988). Lennon added, 'If people take any notice of what we say, we say we've been through the drug scene, man, and there's nothing like being straight'

18 It's amazing how low you go to get high.

John Lennon: *Skywriting by Word of Mouth* (ed. Yoko Ono, 1986), 'The Art of Deception is in the Eye of the Beholder'

19 I'd love to turn you on.

John Lennon and **Paul McCartney** (b.1942), British rock musicians: 'A Day in the Life' (song), on the album *Sgt. Pepper's Lonely Hearts Club Band* (The Beatles, 1967)

20 Eight miles high,
And when you touch down
You'll find that
It's stranger than known.

Jim McGuin (b.1942), U.S. rock musician: 'Eight Miles High' (song), on the album *Fifth Dimension* (The Byrds, 1966)

21 One's condition on marijuana is always existential. One can feel the importance of each moment and how it is changing one. One feels one's being, one becomes aware of the enormous apparatus of nothingness – the hum of a hi-fi set, the emptiness of a pointless interruption, one becomes aware of the war between each of us, how the nothingness in each of us seeks to attack the being of others, how our being in turn is attacked by the nothingness in others.

Norman Mailer (b.1923), U.S. author: interview in *Writers at Work* (Third Series, ed. George Plimpton, 1967)

22 Is marijuana addictive? Yes, in the sense that most of the really pleasant things in life are worth endlessly repeating.

Richard Neville (b.1941), Australian journalist: *Playpower* (1971), 'Johnny Pot Wears Gold Sandals and a Black Derby Hat'

23 Marijuana is ... self-punishing. It makes you acutely sensitive, and in this world, what worse punishment could there be?

P.J. O'Rourke (b.1947), U.S. journalist: in *Rolling Stone* (New York), 30 Nov. 1989

24 My main experience is this: when you start taking drugs, it doesn't matter which kind. I was able to take them for a certain amount of time and hold it together somewhat. But there does come a time when, little by little, your whole body and mind will split apart and dissolve into a little puddle of piss. If I took anything now, in half an hour, believe me, this would not be a pretty sight. I can't. I *cannot*. I no longer have the capacity. I am a burnt French fry.

Iggy Pop (b.1947), U.S. rock musician: interview in *The Guardian* (London), 17 Feb. 1996

25 Let us not forget who we are. Drug abuse is a repudiation of everything America is.

Ronald Reagan (b.1911), U.S. Republican politician and president: joint television broadcast with Nancy Reagan, autumn 1986, announcing a national crusade against the use of drugs, quoted in *Money and Class in America* by Lewis H. Lapham (1988), Ch.5, Sct.1

26 I don't know just where I'm going
But I'm gonna try for the kingdom if I can
'Cause it makes me feel like I'm a man
When I put a spike into my vein
And I'll tell ya, things aren't quite the same.
Lou Reed (b.1944), U.S. rock musician: 'Heroin' (song), on the album *The Velvet Underground and Nico* (1967)

27 They shoulda called me Little Cocaine, I was sniffing so much of the stuff! My nose got big enough to back a diesel truck in, unload it, and drive it right out again.
Little Richard (b.1932), U.S. rock 'n' roll musician: quoted in *The Life and Times of Little Richard* by Charles White (1984), Pt.4

28 Speed, it's like a dozen transatlantic flights without ever getting off the plane. Time change. You lose. You gain. Makes no difference so long as you keep taking the pills.
Bruce Robinson (b.1946), British film-maker: Marwood (Paul McGann), in *Withnail and I* (film; written and directed by Bruce Robinson, 1987)

29 We have plenty of grass, and as we all know, dope will get you through times of no money better than money will get you through times of no dope.
Gilbert Shelton (b.1940), U.S. cartoonist: Freewheelin' Franklin, in *The Fabulous Furry Freak Brothers* (strip cartoon; created in 1968), 'The Freaks Pull a Heist' (1971), rep. in *Apex Treasury of Underground Comics* (ed. Don Donahue and Susan Goodrick, 1974). The line became a motto for the Freak Brothers and their following

30 One pill makes you larger
And one pill makes you small.
And the ones that mother gives you
Don't do anything at all.
Go ask Alice
When she's ten feet tall.
Grace Slick (b.1939), U.S. rock musician: 'White Rabbit' (song), on the album *Surrealistic Pillow* (Jefferson Airplane, 1967)

31 It's an ordinary day for Brian. Like, he died every day, you know.
Pete Townshend (b.1945), British rock musician: on Brian Jones's death by drowning in July 1969, quoted in *The Life and Good Times of the Rolling Stones* by Philip Norman (1989)

32 Take yir best orgasm, multiply the feeling by twenty, and you're still fuckin miles off the pace. Ma dry, cracking bones are soothed and liquefied by ma beautiful heroine's tender caresses. The earth moved, and it's still moving.

Irvine Welsh (b.1958), Scottish author: Renton, in *Trainspotting* (1994), 'Kicking'

33 In my day, we didn't have the cocaine, so we went out and knocked somebody over the head and *took* the money. But today, all this cocaine and crack, it doesn't give kids a chance.
Barry White (b.1944), U.S. singer: interview in *City Limits* (London), 7 April 1988

34 Here are some little tell-tale warning signs if you have a cocaine problem ... if you have this dream where you're doing cocaine in your sleep and you can't fall asleep, and you're doing cocaine in your sleep and you can't fall asleep, and you wake up, and you're still doing cocaine – Bingo!
Robin Williams (b.1951), U.S. actor and comedian: stand-up routine, recorded live at the Metropolitan Opera House, New York, 1986, on *A Night at the Met*, 'Cocaine'

35 A drug is neither moral nor immoral – it's a chemical compound. The compound itself is not a menace to society until a human being treats it as if consumption bestowed a temporary license to act like an asshole.
Frank Zappa (1940–1993), U.S. rock musician: *The Real Frank Zappa Book* (written with Peter Occhiogrosso, 1989), Ch.17

See also Self on ART: MODERN ART; Leary on THE COUNTERCULTURE; Garcia on PSYCHEDELIA; Reed on TOBACCO

DRUGS: Addiction

1 I'll die young but it's like kissing God.
Lenny Bruce (1925–1966), U.S. comic: on his drug addiction, quoted in *Playpower* by Richard Neville (1970), Ch.4

2 A junky runs on junk time. When his junk is cut off, the clock runs down and stops. All he can do is hang on and wait for non-junk time to start.
William Burroughs (1914–1997), U.S. author: *Junkie* (1953), Ch.10

3 Junk is just another nine to five gig in the end, only the hours are a bit more inclined towards shadows.
Jim Carroll (b.1950), U.S. author: *The Basketball Diaries* (1980), 'Summer 66'

4 In this country, don't forget, a habit is no damn private hell. There's no solitary confinement outside of jail. A habit is hell for those you love. And in this country it's the worst kind of hell for those who love you.
Billie Holiday (1915–1959), U.S. blues singer: *Lady Sings the Blues* (written with William Dufty, 1956; rev.1975), Ch.24

5 We are indeed drifting into the arena of the unwell, making an enemy of our own future.
Bruce Robinson (b.1946), British film-maker: Marwood (Paul McGann), in *Withnail and I* (film; written and directed by Bruce Robinson, 1987)

See also ADDICTION

DRUGS: The Dealers

1 God damn the pusher man.
Hoyt Axton (b.1938), U.S. rock musician: 'The Pusher' (song), on the album *Steppenwolf* (Steppenwolf, 1968)

2 I'm waiting for my man
Twenty-six dollars in my hand
Up to Lexington 125
Feeling sick and dirty more dead than alive
I'm waiting for my man.
Lou Reed (b.1944), U.S. rock musician: 'I'm Waiting for the Man' (song), on the album *The Velvet Underground and Nico* (1967)

3 Danny's here. Head-hunter to his friends. Head-hunter to everybody. He doesn't have any friends. The only people he converses with are his clients and occasionally the police. The purveyor of rare herbs and prescribed chemicals is back.
Bruce Robinson (b.1946), British film-maker: Marwood (Paul McGann), in *Withnail and I* (film; written and directed by Bruce Robinson, 1987)

DUTY

1 Duty largely consists of pretending that the trivial is critical.
John Fowles (b.1926), British novelist: *The Magus* (1965), Ch.18

2 A task becomes a duty from the moment you suspect it to be an essential part of that integrity which alone entitles a man to assume responsibility.
Dag Hammarskjöld (1905–1961), Swedish statesman and secretary-general of U.N.: note, written 1955, publ. in *Markings* (1963), 'Night is Drawing Nigh'

3 It is easier to do one's duty to others than to one's self. If you do your duty to others, you are considered reliable. If you do your duty to yourself, you are considered selfish.
Thomas Szasz (b.1920), U.S. psychiatrist: *The Second Sin* (1973), 'Personal Conduct'

BOB DYLAN

1 I'm glad I'm not me!
Bob Dylan (b.1941), U.S. singer and songwriter: reading newspaper report, 1965, in Donn Pennebaker's film, *Don't Look Back* (1967)

2 Dylan is to me the perfect symbol of the anti-artist in our society. He is against everything – the last resort of someone who doesn't really want to change the world. ... Dylan's songs accept the world as it is.
Ewan MacColl (1915–1989), British folk singer and songwriter: interview in *Melody Maker* (London), Sept. 1965, quoted in *No Direction Home* by Robert Shelton (biography, 1989), Ch.8

3 Dylan ... even in his most overt early songs, suggested a complicated universe where cause and effect, greed and exploitation, revolution and reaction are part of our fibre, not just nasty bogymen who can be exorcised with a guitar and a lyric. At most, he hoped to make us think, perhaps to act.
George Melly (b.1926), British jazz musician, critic and author: *Revolt into Style* (1970), 'British Pop Music: Rhythm and Blues'

4 If it is true that rock stars weather into institutions, then Dylan has started now to resemble the Church of England: the dwindling popularity of his product cannot diminish the intensity of the arguments among his congregation.
Robert Sandall, British journalist: in *The Sunday Times* (London), 19 May 1991

5 Bob freed your mind the way Elvis freed your body. He showed us that just because music was innately physical did not mean that it was anti-intellectual. He had the vision and the talent to make a pop record that contained the whole world.
Bruce Springsteen (b.1949), U.S. rock musician: speech, 20 Jan. 1988, Rock-and-Roll Hall of Fame induction dinner, New York City, publ. in *The Dylan Companion* (ed. Elizabeth Thomson and David Gutman, 1990), Pt.8

THE EARTH

1 The earth is the very quintessence of the human condition.
Hannah Arendt (1906–1975), German-born U.S. political philosopher: prologue to *The Human Condition* (1958)

2 After one look at this planet any visitor from outer space would say 'I WANT TO SEE THE MANAGER'.
William Burroughs (1914–1997), U.S. author: *The Adding Machine* (1985), 'Women: A Biological Mistake?'

3 Some of us still get all weepy when we think about the Gaia Hypothesis, the idea that earth is a big furry goddess-creature who resembles everybody's mom in that she knows what's best for us. But if you look at the historical record – Krakatoa, Mt. Vesuvius, Hurricane Charley, poison ivy, and so forth down the

ages – you have to ask yourself: Whose side is she on, anyway?

Barbara Ehrenreich (b.1941), U.S. author and columnist: 'The Great Syringe Tide', first publ. in *Mother Jones* (1988), rep. in *The Worst Years of Our Lives* (1991)

4   The earth only has so much bounty to offer and inventing ever larger and more notional prices for that bounty does not change its real value.

Ben Elton (b.1959), British author and comic: *Stark* (1989), 'Dinner in Los Angeles'

5   The question of whether it's God's green earth is not at center stage, except in the sense that if so, one is reminded with some regularity that He may be dying.

Edward Hoagland (b.1932), U.S. novelist and essayist: in *The Guardian* (London), 20 Jan. 1990

6   Our roots are in the dark; the earth is our country. Why did we look up for blessing – instead of around, and down? What hope we have lies there. Not in the sky full of orbiting spy-eyes and weaponry, but in the earth we have looked down upon. Not from above, but from below. Not in the light that blinds, but in the dark that nourishes, where human beings grow human souls.

Ursula K. Le Guin (b.1929), U.S. author: 'A Left-Handed Commencement Address', to Mills College Class of 1983, publ. in *Dancing at the Edge of the World* (1989)

7   To see the earth as we now see it, small and beautiful in that eternal silence where it floats, is to see ourselves as riders on the earth together, brothers on that bright loveliness in the unending night – brothers who *see* now they are truly brothers.

Archibald MacLeish (1892–1982), U.S. poet: on the first pictures of the earth from the moon, in 'Riders on Earth Together, Brothers in Eternal Cold', first publ. in the *New York Times*, 25 Dec. 1968, rep. in *Riders on Earth* (1978) as 'Bubble of Blue Air'

8   Is it possible that I am not alone in believing that in the dispute between Galileo and the Church, the Church was right and the centre of man's universe *is* the earth?

Stephen Vizinczey (b.1933), Hungarian novelist and critic: 'Rules of the Game' (review of Northrop Frye's *The Stubborn Structure*), publ. in *The Times* (London), 12 Nov. 1970, rep. in *Truth and Lies in Literature* (1986)

See also Vidal on POPULATION

ECCENTRICITY

1   The English like eccentrics. They just don't like them living next door.

Julian Clary (b.1959), British comedian and entertainer: in *The Daily Telegraph* (London), 2 Sept. 1992

2   Eccentricity is *not*, as dull people would have us believe, a form of madness. It is often a kind of innocent pride, and the man of genius and the aristocrat are frequently regarded as eccentrics because genius and aristocrat are entirely unafraid of and uninfluenced by the opinions and vagaries of the crowd.

Edith Sitwell (1887–1964), British poet and critic: *Taken Care Of* (1965), Ch.15

See also Maurois on ORIGINALITY

THE ECOLOGY MOVEMENT

1   Ecology is rather like sex – every new generation likes to think they were the first to discover it.

Michael Allaby (b.1933), British author and ecologist: in *The Times* (London), 6 Oct. 1989

2   Now that George Bush has declared himself an environmentalist and Time magazine has named this plundered Earth 'planet of the year', now that everyone expresses ecological concern, from the people living in contaminated communities to the businesses that contaminate them, it is time to regard environmentalism as a movement whose real promise remains unfulfilled. The insights of ecology have been debased to everyday clichés while the actual plunder and poisoning are accelerating.

George Bradford (b.1952), U.S. ecologist: preface to *How Deep is Deep Ecology?* (1989)

3   We cannot permit the extreme in the environmental movement to shut down the United States. We cannot shut down the lives of many Americans by going to the extreme on the environment.

George Bush (b.1924), U.S. Republican politician and president: speech on the Rio de Janeiro Earth Summit, 30 May 1992, at campaign rally, California

4   We, the generation that faces the next century, can add the ... solemn injunction 'If we don't do the impossible, we shall be faced with the unthinkable'.

Petra Kelly (1947–1992), German Green Party founder and spokeswoman: quoted in *Vanity Fair* (New York), Jan. 1993

5   How to be green? Many people have asked us this important question. It's really very simple and requires no expert knowledge or complex skills. Here's the answer. Consume less. Share more. Enjoy life.

Penny Kemp (b.1951) and **Derek Wall** (b.1965), British ecologists: dedication in *A Green Manifesto for the 1990s* (1990)

6 It entered the seventies as a vague critic of our society and exited as an institution, wrapped in the consumerism and political ambitions it once condemned. In their drive to win credibility with the government agencies and corporations ... the new professional environmentalists seemed to have wandered into the ambiguous world of George Orwell's Animal Farm, where it was increasingly difficult to tell the farmers from the pigs.
Christopher Manes (b.1957), U.S. ecologist: *Green Rage* (1990), Ch.3

7 The neo-hippie-dips, the sentimentality-crazed iguana anthropomorphizers, the Chicken Littles, the three-bong-hit William Blakes – thank God these people don't actually go outdoors much, or the environment would be even worse than it is already.
P.J. O'Rourke (b.1947), U.S. journalist: *Parliament of Whores* (1991), 'Dirt of The Earth: The Ecologists'

8 Green politics at its worst amounts to a sort of Zen fascism; less extreme, it denounces growth and seeks to stop the world so that we can all get off.
Chris Patten (b.1944), British Conservative politician: in *The Independent* (London), 19 April 1989. Patten was at the time secretary of state for the environment

9 The powerful appeal of ecology as a practical politics lies in its capacity to encourage people to make consistent links between the social and emotional shape of everyday actions and a quantitative world-picture of physical causes and effects. Above all, it is a politics of information and knowledge, exceptional among social and political movements in its overriding appeal to science for proof of the justice of ecological claims.
Andrew Ross (b.1956), British social theorist: *Strange Weather* (1991), Ch.6

See also Schumacher on ECONOMICS; THE ENVIRONMENT; Bookchin on HOLISM; POLLUTION

ECONOMICS

1 Economic growth may one day turn out to be a curse rather than a good, and under no conditions can it either lead into freedom or constitute a proof for its existence.
Hannah Arendt (1906–1975), German-born U.S. political philosopher: *On Revolution* (1963), Ch.6

2 It seems to be a law in American life that whatever enriches us anywhere except in the wallet inevitably becomes uneconomic.
Russell Baker (b.1925), U.S. journalist: in the *New York Times*, 24 March 1968

3 In the usual (though certainly not in every) public decision on economic policy, the choice is between courses that are almost equally good or equally bad. It is the narrowest decisions that are most ardently debated. If the world is lucky enough to enjoy peace, it may even one day make the discovery, to the horror of doctrinaire free-enterprisers and doctrinaire planners alike, that what is called capitalism and what is called socialism are both capable of working quite well.
J.K. Galbraith (b.1908), U.S. economist: 'The American Economy: Its Substance and Myth', first publ. in *Years of the Modern* (ed. J.W. Chase, 1949), rep. in *The Galbraith Reader* (1979)

4 From now the pound abroad is worth fourteen per cent or so less in terms of other currencies. It does not mean, of course, that the pound here in Britain, in your pocket or purse, or in your bank, has been devalued.
Harold Wilson (1916–1995), British Labour politician and prime minister: broadcast, 19 Nov. 1967, BBC TV, quoted in *The Times* (London), 20 Nov. 1967

THE ECONOMY

1 Unlimited economic growth has the marvelous quality of stilling discontent while maintaining privilege, a fact that has not gone unnoticed among liberal economists.
Noam Chomsky (b.1928), U.S. linguist and political analyst: introduction to *For Reasons of State* (1973)

2 Everyone is always in favour of general economy and particular expenditure.
Anthony Eden (1897–1977), British Conservative politician and prime minister: quoted in *The Observer* (London), 17 June 1958

3 We might come closer to balancing the Budget if all of us lived closer to the Commandments and the Golden Rule.
Ronald Reagan (b.1911), U.S. Republican politician and president: quoted in *The Observer* (London), 5 Feb. 1983

See also ECONOMICS

EDITING

1 The work was like peeling an onion. The outer skin came off with difficulty ... but in no time you'd be down to its innards, tears streaming

from your eyes as more and more beautiful reductions became possible.

Edward Blishen (1920–1996), British author: on his work adapting books for serial reading, from his autobiography, *Donkey Work* (1983), Pt.1, Ch.2

2   Would you convey my compliments to the purist who reads your proofs and tell him or her that I write in a sort of broken-down patois which is something like the way a Swiss waiter talks, and that when I split an infinitive, God damn it, I split it so it will stay split, and when I interrupt the velvety smoothness of my more or less literate syntax with a few sudden words of bar-room vernacular, that is done with the eyes wide open and the mind relaxed but attentive.

Raymond Chandler (1888–1959), U.S. author: letter, 18 Jan. 1948, to *Atlantic Monthly* editor Edward Weeks, publ. in *Raymond Chandler Speaking* (ed. Dorothy Gardiner and Kathrine S. Walker, 1962)

3   Editing is the same as quarreling with writers – same thing exactly.

Harold Ross (1892–1951), U.S. editor: in *Time* (New York), 6 March 1950

EDITORS

1   If they have a popular thought they have to go into a darkened room and lie down until it passes.

Kelvin MacKenzie (b.1946), British newspaper editor: on editors of the 'quality press', in *The Independent* (London), 19 Sept. 1989

2   It's the editors who interfere in the publisher's prerogative, not the other way round.

Robert Maxwell (1923–1991), British tycoon: comment, July 1985, regarding his relations with Mirror Group Newspapers, quoted in *Maxwell: The Outsider* by Tom Bower (1988, rev.1991), Ch.13

3   An editor is someone who separates the wheat from the chaff and then prints the chaff.

Adlai Stevenson (1900–1965), U.S. Democratic politician: quoted in *The Stevenson Wit* (1966). The aphorism has also been attributed to Elbert Hubbard

EDUCATION

1   Any parent wants the best for their children. I am not going to make a choice for my child on the basis of what is the politically correct thing to do.

Tony Blair (b.1953), British Labour politician: quoted in the *Independent on Sunday* (London), 1 Jan. 1995

2   Education [is not] a discipline at all. Half vocational, half an emptiness dressed up in garments borrowed from philosophy, psychology, literature.

Edward Blishen (1920–1996), British author: *Donkey Work* (autobiography, 1983), Pt.3, Ch.6

3   The liberally educated person is one who is able to resist the easy and preferred answers, not because he is obstinate but because he knows others worthy of consideration.

Allan Bloom (1930–1992), U.S. educator and author: preface to *The Closing of the American Mind* (1987)

4   A child's education should include at least a rudimentary grasp of religion, sex, and money. Without a basic knowledge of these three primary facts in a normal human being's life – subjects which stir the emotions, create events and opportunities, and if they do not wholly decide must greatly influence an individual's personality – no human being's education can have a safe foundation.

Phyllis Bottome (1884–1963), Anglo-American novelist: *Search for a Soul* (1947), Ch.9

5   Spoon feeding in the long run teaches us nothing but the shape of the spoon.

E.M. Forster (1879–1970), British novelist and essayist: quoted in *The Observer* (London), 7 Oct. 1951

6   The first president of the U.S. doesn't matter to me. I don't need that upstairs.

Tommy Lee (b.1962), U.S. rock musician: quoted in *FHM* (London), March 1996

7   The system – the American one, at least – is a vast and noble experiment. It has been polestar and exemplar for other nations. But from kindergarten until she graduates from college the girl is treated in it exactly like her brothers. She studies the same subjects, becomes proficient at the same sports. Oh, it is a magnificent lore she learns, education for the mind beyond anything Jane Austen or Saint Theresa or even Mrs Pankhurst ever dreamed. It is truly Utopian. But Utopia was never meant to exist on this disheveled planet.

Phyllis McGinley (1905–1978), U.S. poet and author: *The Province of the Heart* (1959), 'The Honor of Being a Woman'

8   The school system, custodian of print culture, has no place for the rugged individual. It is, indeed, the homogenizing hopper into which we toss our integral tots for processing.

Marshall McLuhan (1911–1980), Canadian communications theorist: *The Gutenberg Galaxy* (1962), 'Cervantes Confronted Typographic Man in the Figure of Don Quixote'

9   If education is always to be conceived along the same antiquated lines of a mere transmission of knowledge, there is little to be hoped from it in

the bettering of man's future. For what is the use of transmitting knowledge if the individual's total development lags behind?

Maria Montessori (1870–1952), Italian educationist: *The Absorbent Mind* (1949), Ch.1

10 Education costs money, but then so does ignorance.

Claus Moser (b.1922), German-born British academic and warden of Wadham College, Oxford: in *The Daily Telegraph* (London), 21 Aug. 1990

11 Education has become a prisoner of contemporaneity. It is the past, not the dizzy present, that is the best door to the future.

Camille Paglia (b.1947), U.S. author and critic: introduction to *Sex, Art, and American Culture* (1992)

12 The purpose of education is to keep a culture from being drowned in senseless repetitions, each of which claims to offer a new insight.

Harold Rosenberg (1906–1978), U.S. art critic and author: 'The Cultural Situation Today', first publ. in *Partisan Review* (New Brunswick, N.J.), summer 1972, rep. as introduction to *Discovering the Present* (1973)

13 To me education is a leading out of what is already there in the pupil's soul. To Miss Mackay it is a putting in of something that is not there, and that is not what I call education, I call it intrusion.

Muriel Spark (b.1918), British novelist: Miss Brodie, in *The Prime of Miss Jean Brodie* (1961), Ch.2

See also SCHOOL; Hughes on TELEVISION; UNIVERSITY

EFFORT

1 The human condition is such that pain and effort are not just symptoms which can be removed without changing life itself; they are the modes in which life itself, together with the necessity to which it is bound, makes itself felt. For mortals, the 'easy life of the gods' would be a lifeless life.

Hannah Arendt (1906–1975), German-born U.S. political philosopher: *The Human Condition* (1958), 'Labor', Ch.16

2 The secret of the truly successful, I believe, is that they learned very early in life how *not* to be busy. They saw through that adage, repeated to me so often in childhood, that anything worth doing is worth doing well. The truth is, many things are worth doing only in the most slovenly, halfhearted fashion possible, and many other things are not worth doing at all.

Barbara Ehrenreich (b.1941), U.S. author and columnist: 'The Cult Of Busyness' (1985), rep. in *The Worst Years of Our Lives* (1991)

3 God gives every bird his worm, but He does not throw it into the nest.

P.D. James (b.1920), British author: Jonah the tramp quoting a wayside pulpit, in *Devices and Desires* (1989), Ch.40

4 Effort is only effort when it begins to hurt.

José Ortega y Gasset (1883–1955), Spanish essayist and philosopher: 'In Search of Goethe from Within', first publ. in *Partisan Review* (New Brunswick, N.J.), Dec. 1949, rep. in *The Dehumanization of Art and Other Essays* (1968)

EGOTISM

1 The source of our actions resides in an unconscious propensity to regard ourselves as the centre, the cause, and the conclusion of time. Our reflexes and our pride transform into a planet the parcel of flesh and consciousness we are.

E.M. Cioran (1911–1995), Rumanian-born French philosopher: *A Short History of Decay* (1949), Ch.1, 'The Anti-Prophet'

2 There is nothing more natural than to consider everything as starting from oneself, chosen as the centre of the world; one finds oneself thus capable of condemning the world without even wanting to hear its deceitful chatter.

Guy Debord (1931–1994), French Situationist philosopher: *Panegyric* (first volume of autobiography, 1989), Pt.1

3 If being an egomaniac means I believe in what I do and in my art or my music, then in that respect you can call me that ... I believe in what I do, and I'll say it.

John Lennon (1940–1980), British rock musician: interview on *The Tomorrow Show* (NBC-TV, April 1975), publ. in *Imagine* (ed. Andrew Solt and Sam Egan, 1988)

See also Wolfe on THE 1970S

ALBERT EINSTEIN

1 Through the mythology of Einstein, the world blissfully regained the image of knowledge reduced to a formula.

Roland Barthes (1915–1980), French semiologist: *Mythologies* (1957; tr.1972), 'The Brain of Einstein'

2 The genius of Einstein leads to Hiroshima.

Pablo Picasso (1881–1973), Spanish artist: remark to Françoise Gilot in 1946, quoted in *Life with Picasso* by Françoise Gilot and Carlton Lake (1964), Pt.2

ELECTIONS

1 In every election in American history both parties have their clichés. The party that has the clichés that ring true wins.
Newt Gingrich (b.1943), U.S. Republican politician: in the *International Herald Tribune* (Paris), 1 Aug. 1988

2 It doesn't matter who you vote for, the government always gets in.
Graffiti in London, 1970s

3 I just received the following wire from my generous Daddy – 'Dear Jack, Don't buy a single vote more than is necessary. I'll be damned if I'm going to pay for a landslide'.
John F. Kennedy (1917–1963), U.S. Democratic politician and president: speech, 1958, Gridiron Dinner, Washington D.C., quoted in *The Wit of President Kennedy* by Bill Adler (1964), 'The Family'

4 Finishing second in the Olympics gets you silver. Finishing second in politics gets you oblivion.
Richard Nixon (1913–1992), U.S. Republican politician and president: on the defeat of Michael Dukakis by George Bush in the 1988 presidential election, quoted in *The Sunday Times* (London), 13 Nov. 1988

5 Maybe a nation that consumes as much booze and dope as we do and has our kind of divorce statistics should pipe down about 'character issues'. Either that or just go ahead and determine the presidency with three-legged races and pie-eating contests. It would make better TV.
P.J. O'Rourke (b.1947), U.S. journalist: *Parliament of Whores* (1991), 'Attack of the Midget Vote Suckers'

6 There is a sort of exotic preposterousness about a lot of elections, the way arguments are made even cruder.
Chris Patten (b.1944), British Conservative politician: quoted in *The Observer* (London), 30 June 1991. Patten managed the electoral campaign of 1992, which led to a fourth successive victory for the Conservative Party, though he himself lost his seat

7 Which one of the three candidates would you want your daughter to marry?
H. Ross Perot (b.1930), U.S. business executive and presidential candidate: in the *International Herald Tribune* (Paris), 29 Oct. 1992

8 Why should I? Someone is bound to do it for me.
Rickshaw driver, Bangladesh: when asked if he had voted in the Bangladesh election, quoted in *The Daily Telegraph* (London), 4 Feb. 1988

9 The advance planning and sense stimuli employed to capture a $10 million cigarette or soap market are nothing compared to the brainwashing and propaganda blitzes used to ensure control of the largest cash market in the world: the Executive Branch of the United States Government.
Phyllis Schlafly (b.1924), U.S. author and political activist: *A Choice Not an Echo* (1964), Ch.1

10 Indeed, you won the elections, but I won the count.
Anastasio Somoza (1925–1980), Nicaraguan dictator: said to an opponent accusing him of rigging the election, quoted in *The Guardian* (London), 17 June 1977

11 A funny thing happened to me on the way to the White House.
Adlai Stevenson (1900–1965), U.S. Democratic politician: speech, 13 Dec. 1952, Washington D.C., after his defeat in the presidential election, in which Eisenhower won a landslide victory, quoted in *Portrait: Adlai E. Stevenson* by Alden Whitman (1965), Ch.1

12 It Was The Sun Wot Won It.
The Sun: headline, 10 April 1992, following the unexpected Conservative victory in the general election, maintaining John Major in power and giving the Conservatives their fourth successive term in office

See also VOTING

ELEGANCE

1 Elegance does not consist in putting on a new dress.
Coco Chanel (1883–1971), French *couturière*: quoted in *Coco Chanel: Her Life, Her Secrets* by Marcel Haedrich (1971), Ch.21

2 For me, elegance is not to pass unnoticed but to get to the very soul of what one is.
Christian Lacroix (b.1951), French fashion designer: in the *International Herald Tribune* (Paris), 21 Jan. 1992

3 We must never confuse elegance with snobbery.
Yves Saint Laurent (b.1936), French fashion designer: interview in *Ritz* (London), No.85, 1984

4 It is elegance that is potent and subversive. Elegance in a world of vulgarity.
Vivienne Westwood (b.1941), British fashion designer: quoted in *Fashion and Perversity* by Fred Vermorel (1996), Pt.1

See also Westwood on MEN

ELOQUENCE

1 Verbal ability is a highly overrated thing in a guy, and it's our pathetic need for it that gets us into so much trouble.

Nora Ephron (b.1941), U.S. author and journalist: Becky (Rosie O'Donnell), in *Sleepless in Seattle* (film; screenplay by Jeff Ward, Nora Ephron and David S. Ward, directed by Nora Ephron, 1993)

2   Today it is not the classroom nor the classics which are the repositories of models of eloquence, but the ad agencies.
Marshall McLuhan (1911–1980), Canadian communications theorist: *The Mechanical Bride* (1951), 'Plain Talk'

EMBARRASSMENT

1   Well, la-de-da!
Diane Keaton (b.1946), U.S. actress: Annie (Diane Keaton), in *Annie Hall* (film; screenplay by Woody Allen and Marshall Brickman, directed by Woody Allen, 1977)

EMIGRATION & EXILE

1   Voyagers discover that the world can never be larger than the person that is in the world; but it is impossible to foresee this, it is impossible to be warned.
James Baldwin (1924–1987), U.S. author: on the futility of running from a situation, with particular reference to Baldwin's own 'exile' in Paris, in 'The New Lost Generation', publ. in *Esquire* (New York), July 1961, rep. in *The Price of the Ticket* (1985)

2   Emigration, forced or chosen, across national frontiers or from village to metropolis, is the quintessential experience of our time.
John Berger (b.1926), British author and critic: *And Our Faces, My Heart, Brief As Photos* (1984), Pt.2

3   It would be enough for me to have the system of a jury of twelve versus the system of one judge as a basis for preferring the U.S. to the Soviet Union. ... I would prefer the country you can leave to the country you cannot.
Joseph Brodsky (1940–1996), Russian-born U.S. poet and critic: *Writers at Work* (Eighth Series, ed. George Plimpton, 1988). Brodsky was 'asked' to leave the U.S.S.R. in 1972

4   The ideal place for me is the one in which it is most natural to live as a foreigner.
Italo Calvino (1923–1985), Italian author and critic: *Grand Bazaar* (Milan) Sept./Oct. 1980, rep. in *The Literature Machine* (1987)

5   Excluded by my birth and tastes from the social order, I was not aware of its diversity. ... Nothing in the world was irrelevant: the stars on a general's sleeve, the stock-market quotations, the olive harvest, the style of the judiciary, the wheat exchange, flower-beds. ... Nothing. This order, fearful and feared, whose details were all inter-related, had a meaning: my exile.

Jean Genet (1910–1986), French playwright and novelist: *The Thief's Journal* (1949; tr.1954), p.151 of Penguin edn. (1965)

6   Exile as a mode of genius no longer exists; in place of Joyce we have the fragments of work appearing in *Index on Censorship*.
Nadine Gordimer (b.1923), South African author: 'The Essential Gesture', lecture, 12 Oct. 1984, University of Michigan, first publ. in *The Tanner Lectures on Human Values* (ed. Sterling M. McMurrin, 1985), rep. in *The Essential Gesture* (ed. Stephen Clingman, 1988)

7   I believe a man should live in his own country and I think the deracination of human beings leads to frustration, in one way or another obstructing the light of the soul. I can live only in my own country. I cannot live without having my feet and my hands on it and my ear against it, without feeling the movement of its waters and its shadows, without feeling my roots reach down into its soil for maternal nourishment.
Pablo Neruda (1904–1973), Chilean poet: referring to his first period of exile in the course of World War II, in *Memoirs* (1974), Ch.8, 'Macchu Picchu'

8   Freedom-loving people around the world must say ... I am a refugee in a crowded boat foundering off the coast of Vietnam. I am Laotian, a Cambodian, a Cuban, and a Miskito Indian in Nicaragua. I, too, am a potential victim of totalitarianism.
Ronald Reagan (b.1911), U.S. Republican politician and president: speech, 27 May 1985, at Bergen-Belsen Concentration Camp, Germany, publ. in *Speaking My Mind* (1989)

9   Such is the miraculous nature of the future of exiles: what is first uttered in the impotence of an overheated apartment becomes the fate of nations.
Salman Rushdie (b.1947), Indian-born British author: of the Imam, exiled in London, in *The Satanic Verses* (1988), 'Ayesha'

EMOTION

1   The only questions worth asking today are whether humans are going to have any emotions tomorrow, and what the quality of life will be if the answer is no.
Lester Bangs (1948–1982), U.S. rock journalist: in *Gig*, Jan. 1978, rep. in *Psychotic Reactions & Carburetor Dung* (1987), 'Richard Hell'

2   You learn to put your emotional luggage where it will do some good, instead of using it to shit on other people, or blow up aeroplanes.
Margaret Drabble (b.1939), British novelist: quoted in *The Observer* (London), 6 Oct. 1991

3 You can't convey an emotion to the public unless you feel it yourself.
Alfred Hitchcock (1899–1980), British film-maker: interview, Aug. 1962, publ. in *Hitchcock* by François Truffaut (1966; rev.1984), Ch.4

4 Moral feeling is essential but emotion is disastrous in great affairs.
Oswald Mosley (1896–1980), British fascist leader: *My Life* (1968), Ch.8

THE END

1 The day the world ends, no one will be there, just as no one was there when it began. This is a scandal. Such a scandal for the human race that it is indeed capable collectively, out of spite, of hastening the end of the world by all means just so it can enjoy the show.
Jean Baudrillard (b.1929), French semiologist: *Cool Memories* (1987; tr.1990), Ch.5

2 I've a strong impression our world is about to go under. Our political systems are deeply compromised and have no further uses. Our social behaviour patterns – interior and exterior – have proved a fiasco. The tragic thing is, we neither can nor want to, nor have the strength to alter course. It's too late for revolutions, and deep down inside ourselves we no longer even believe in their positive effects. Just around the corner an insect world is waiting for us – and one day it's going to roll over our ultra-individualized existence. Otherwise I'm a respectable Social Democrat.
Ingmar Bergman (b.1918), Swedish stage and film writer-director: interview in *Bergman on Bergman* (1970), 'Solna, 25 June 1968'

3 You know how I know it's the end of the world? 'Cos everything's been done.
James Cameron (b.1954), Canadian director and screenwriter: *Strange Days* (film; screenplay by James Cameron, directed by Kathryn Bigelow, 1995)

4 The planet's survival has become so uncertain that any effort, any thought that presupposes an assured future amounts to a mad gamble.
Elias Canetti (1905–1994), Austrian novelist and philosopher: *The Secret Heart Of The Clock: Notes, Aphorisms, Fragments 1973–1985* (1991), '1979'

5 God seems to have left the receiver off the hook, and time is running out.
Arthur Koestler (1905–1983), Hungarian-born British novelist and essayist: *The Ghost in the Machine* (1967), Ch.18

6 The world began without man, and it will end without him.
Claude Lévi-Strauss (b.1908), French anthropologist: *Tristes Tropiques* (1955), Pt.9, Ch.40

7 We are close to dead. There are faces and bodies like gorged maggots on the dance floor, on the highway, in the city, in the stadium; they are a host of chemical machines who swallow the product of chemical factories, aspirin, preservatives, stimulant, relaxant, and breathe out their chemical wastes into a polluted air. The sense of a long last night over civilization is back again.
Norman Mailer (b.1923), U.S. author: *Cannibals and Christians* (1966), 'Introducing our Argument'

8 This is the end,
Beautiful friend.
This is the end,
My only friend, the end.
It hurts to set you free
But you'll never follow me.
Jim Morrison (1943–1971), U.S. rock musician: 'The End' (song), on the album *The Doors* (The Doors, 1967)

9 The Last Days were announced to St. John by a voice like the sound of many waters. But the voice that comes in our day summoning us to play out the dark myth of reckoning is our meager own, making casual conversation about the varieties of annihilation ... the thermonuclear Armageddon, the death of the seas, the vanishing atmosphere, the massacre of the innocents, the universal famine to come ...
Theodore Roszak (b.1933), U.S. social critic: preface to *Where the Wasteland Ends* (1972; rev. 1989)

10 We do not want our world to perish. But in our quest for knowledge, century by century, we have placed all our trust in a cold, impartial intellect which only brings us nearer to destruction. We have heeded no wisdom offering guidance. Only by learning to love one another can our world be saved. Only love can conquer all.
Dora Russell (1894–1986), British author and campaigner: final words of final volume of autobiography, *Challenge to the Cold War* (1985), Ch.14

11 Marches alone can't bring integratin'
When human respect is disintegratin'
This whole crazy world is just too frustratin'
And you tell me
Over and over and over again my friend
That you don't believe we're on the eve of destruction.
P.F. Sloan (b.1947), U.S. songwriter: 'Eve of Destruction' (song; recorded by Barry McGuire, 1965)

12 Cogito ergo boom.
Susan Sontag (b.1933), U.S. essayist: parenthetical comment on our sense that we stand 'in the ruins of thought, and on the verge of the ruins of history and of man himself', in *Styles of Radical Will* (1969), '"Thinking Against Oneself": Reflections on Cioran'

13 It isn't necessary to imagine the world ending in fire or ice – there are two other possibilities: one is paperwork, and the other is nostalgia.
Frank Zappa (1940–1993), U.S. rock musician: *The Real Frank Zappa Book* (written with Peter Occhiogrosso, 1989), Ch.9

See also NUCLEAR WAR; Walker on WHITES

ENDS & MEANS

1 Perfection of means and confusion of goals seem – in my opinion – to characterize our age.
Albert Einstein (1879–1955), German-born U.S. theoretical physicist: *Out of My Later Years* (1950), Ch.14

2 We have perhaps a natural fear of ends. We would rather be always on the way than arrive. Given the means, we hang on to them and often forget the ends.
Eric Hoffer (1902–1983), U.S. philosopher: *Reflections on the Human Condition* (1973), Aph.121

3 The means by which we live have outdistanced the ends for which we live. Our scientific power has outrun our spiritual power. We have guided missiles and misguided men.
Martin Luther King Jr. (1929–1968), U.S. clergyman and civil rights leader: *Strength to Love* (1963), Ch.7

4 It would be hopeless for revolutionaries to try to attack the system without using SOME modern technology. ... But they should use modern technology for only one purpose: to attack the technological system.
Unabomber, U.S. radical: *Industrial Society and Its Future*, 'Strategy', Sct.202, publ. in the *Washington Post*, 19 Sept. 1995

ENEMIES

1 Abatement in the hostility of one's enemies must never be thought to signify they have been won over. It only means that one has ceased to constitute a threat.
Quentin Crisp (b.1908), British author: *The Naked Civil Servant* (1968), Ch.24

2 I do not approve the extermination of the enemy; the policy of exterminating or, as it is barbarously said, liquidating enemies, is one of the most alarming developments of modern war and peace, from the point of view of those who desire the survival of culture. One needs the enemy.
T.S. Eliot (1888–1965), Anglo-American poet and critic: *Note Towards the Definition of Culture* (1948), Ch.3

3 Much has been written about her enemies. She picked them with care, and God knows they deserved her.

Jules Feiffer (b.1929), U.S. cartoonist and writer: of Lillian Hellman, in graveside eulogy quoted in appendix of *Lilly: Reminiscences of Lillian Hellman* by Peter Fiebleman (1988)

4 Our enemy is by tradition our savior, in preventing us from superficiality.
Joyce Carol Oates (b.1938), U.S. author: quoting an aphorism, in 'Master Race', publ in *Partisan Review 50th Anniversary Edition* (ed. William Phillips, 1985)

5 I hate admitting that my enemies have a point.
Salman Rushdie (b.1947), Indian-born British author: Hamza, in *The Satanic Verses* (1988), 'Mahound'

6 A very great man once said you should love your enemies, and that's not a bad piece of advice. We can love them, but, by God, that doesn't mean we're not going to fight them.
Norman Schwarzkopf (b.1934), U.S. general: in *The Daily Telegraph* (London), 1 Feb. 1991

7 I learned early in life that you get places by having the right enemies.
John Spong (b.1931), U.S. ecclesiastic: in *The Guardian* (London), 20 July 1988

ENGINEERING

1 A good scientist is a person with original ideas. A good engineer is a person who makes a design that works with as few original ideas as possible. There are no prima donnas in engineering.
Freeman Dyson (b.1923), British-born U.S. physicist and author: *Disturbing the Universe* (1979), Pt.1, Ch.10

2 One has to look out for engineers – they begin with sewing machines and end up with the atomic bomb
Marcel Pagnol (1895–1974), French playwright and film director: *Critique des Critiques* (1949), Ch.3

ENGLAND *see under* BRITAIN

THE ENGLISH LANGUAGE

1 All the people I have in my office, they can't speak English properly. All the letters sent from my office I have to correct myself. And that is because English is taught so bloody badly.
Charles, Prince of Wales (b.1948): off-the-cuff remark to business executives, 29 June 1989, quoted in *The Prince of Wales: a Biography* by Jonathan Dimbleby (1994), Ch.23

2 If English is spoken in heaven ... God undoubtedly employs Cranmer as his speechwriter. The angels of the lesser ministries probably use the language of the New English Bible and the Alternative Service Book for internal memos.

Charles, Prince of Wales: speech on judging a reading competition, quoted in *The Times* (London), 20 Dec. 1989

3   The problems of society will also be the problems of the predominant language of that society. It is the carrier of its perceptions, its attitudes, and its goals, for through it, the speakers absorb entrenched attitudes. The guilt of English then must be recognized and appreciated before its continued use can be advocated.

Njabulo Ndebele (b.1948), Lesotho educationist and writer: 'The English Language and Social Change', keynote paper delivered to the Jubilee Conference of the English Academy of Southern Africa, Johannesburg, 1986, quoted by Richard W. Bailey in 'English at its Twilight', in *The State of the Language* (ed. Christopher Ricks and Leonard Michaels, 1990)

4   My God! The English language is a *form of communication*! Conversation isn't just crossfire where you shoot and get shot at! Where you've got to duck for your life and aim to kill! Words aren't only bombs and bullets – no, they're little gifts, containing *meanings*!

Philip Roth (b.1933), U.S. novelist: *Portnoy's Complaint* (1967), 'The Most Prevalent Form of Degradation in Erotic Life'

5   I don't think it is always necessary to take up the anti-colonial – or is it post-colonial? – cudgels against English. What seems to me to be happening is that those people who were once colonized by the language are now rapidly remaking it, domesticating it, becoming more and more relaxed about the way they use it – assisted by the English language's enormous flexibility and size, they are carving out large territories for themselves within its frontiers.

Salman Rushdie (b.1947), Indian-born British author: '"Commonwealth Literature" Does Not Exist' (1983), rep. in *Imaginary Homelands* (1991)

6   The English language is nobody's special property. It is the property of the imagination: it is the property of the language itself.

Derek Walcott (b.1930), West Indian poet and playwright: interview in *Writers at Work* (Eighth Series, ed. George Plimpton, 1988)

ENTERTAINMENT

1   Meine Damen und Herren, Mesdames et Messieurs,
Ladies und Gentlemen – comment ça va?
Do you feel good? ... I am your host ...
Wilkommen! Bienvenue! Welcome!
Im Cabaret! Au Cabaret! To Cabaret!

Fred Ebb (b.1932), U.S. librettist: 'Wilkommen' (song), from *Cabaret* (stage musical, 1966; film, 1972). The words are spoken and sung by Joel Grey, as the master of ceremonies

2   I believe entertainment can aspire to be art, and can become art, but if you set out to make art you're an idiot.

Steve Martin (b.1945), U.S. comedian and comic actor: in *Today* (London), 17 May 1989

3   The essential is to excite the spectators. If that means playing *Hamlet* on a flying trapeze or in an aquarium, you do it.

Orson Welles (1915–1985), U.S. film-maker and actor: *Les Nouvelles Littéraires*, 1953, quoted in *Citizen Welles* by Frank Brady (1989), Ch.16

See also PERFORMANCE; SHOW BUSINESS

ENTROPY

1   Just as the constant increase of entropy is the basic law of the universe, so it is the basic law of life to be ever more highly structured and to struggle against entropy.

Václav Havel (b.1936), Czech playwright and president: *Living in Truth* (1986), Pt.1, 'Letter to Dr Gustáv Husák', 8 April 1975

2   Old age cannot be cured. An epoch or a civilization cannot be prevented from breathing its last. A natural process that happens to all flesh and all human manifestations cannot be arrested. You can only wring your hands and utter a beautiful swan song.

Renee Winegarten (b.1922), British author and critic: 'The Idea of Decadence', publ. in *Commentary* (New York) Sept. 1974

THE ENVIRONMENT

1   Conservation must come before recreation.

Charles, Prince of Wales (b.1948): in *The Times* (London), 5 July 1989

2   The poor tread lightest on the earth. The higher our income, the more resources we control and the more havoc we wreak.

Paul Harrison (b.1936), U.S. playwright and director: in *The Guardian* (London), 1 May 1992

3   Cities are expanding at an alarming rate. Intertidal zones are being polluted as mangrove gives way to marina. Over-consumption is leading to soil erosion and desertification, which in turn cause famine and exert pressure on formally fertile areas. We are pulling out the plugs of the system that keeps us alive. Every indicator is showing red: species diversity, water quality, weather patterns, the number of refugees.... We are unravelling nature like an old jumper.

Penny Kemp (b.1951) and **Derek Wall** (b.1965), British ecologists: *A Green Manifesto for the 1990s* (1990), Ch.4

4 Such is the scope of the environmental crisis that it makes us question our entire history on Earth, back to the origins of civilisation. People in the future may very well look back and wonder how the last generations could have gotten caught up in such minor distractions as two world wars, space flight, and the nuclear arms race.

Christopher Manes (b.1957), U.S. ecologist: *Green Rage* (1990), Ch.2

5 If the federal government had been around when the Creator was putting His hand to this state, Indiana wouldn't be here. It'd still be waiting for an environmental impact statement.

Ronald Reagan (b.1911), U.S. Republican politician and president: speech, 9 Feb. 1982, publ. in *Speaking My Mind* (1989), 'The Wit and Wisdom of Ronald Reagan'

6 They're cutting down jungles to breed hamburgers, turning the whole world into a car park. They'd sell off the sea to satisfy the needs of their great god greed. But it won't be satisfied, not till we're all squatting in one of its fucking hatch-backs on a motorway. There isn't going to be anywhere left to go except in slow revolutions towards the crest of the next slag-heap.

Bruce Robinson (b.1946), British film-maker: Dennis Bagley (Richard E. Grant), in *How to Get Ahead in Advertising* (film; written and directed by Bruce Robinson, 1989)

7 If I were a Brazilian without land or money or the means to feed my children, I would be burning the rain forest too.

Sting (b.1951), British rock musician: in the *International Herald Tribune* (Paris), 14 April 1989

8 It hurts the spirit, somehow, to read the word *environments*, when the plural means that there are so many alternatives there to be sorted through, as in a market, and voted on.

Lewis Thomas (1913–1993), U.S. physician and educator: *The Lives of a Cell* (1974), 'Natural Man'

9 We cannot cheat on DNA. We cannot get round photosynthesis. We cannot say I am not going to give a damn about phytoplankton. All these tiny mechanisms provide the preconditions of our planetary life. To say we do not care is to say in the most literal sense that 'we choose death'.

Barbara Ward (1914–1981), British author and educator: 'Only One Earth', publ. in *Who Speaks for Earth?* (ed. Maurice F. Strong, 1973)

10 Modern man's capacity for destruction is quixotic evidence of humanity's capacity for reconstruction. The powerful technological agents we have unleashed against the environment include many of the agents we require for its reconstruction.

George F. Will (b.1941), U.S. political columnist: *Statecraft as Soulcraft: What Government Does* (1984), Ch.7

See also THE ECOLOGY MOVEMENT; Leopold on THE LAND; POLLUTION

ENVY

1 The envied are like bureaucrats; the more impersonal they are, the greater the illusion (for themselves and for others) of their power.

John Berger (b.1926), British author and critic: *Ways of Seeing* (1972), Ch.7

2 The look that the native turns on the settler's town is a look of lust, a look of envy; it expresses his dream of possession – all manner of possession; to sit at the settler's table, to sleep in the settler's bed, with his wife if possible. The colonized man is an envious man.

Frantz Fanon (1925–1961), Martiniquan psychiatrist, philosopher and political activist: *The Wretched of the Earth* (1961), Ch.1

See also Layton on NEIGHBOURS

EPITAPHS

1 At last God caught his eye.

Harry Secombe (b.1921), Welsh comedian and singer: 'Epitaph for a head waiter', in *Punch* (London), 17 May 1962

2 Let it be said of me that I was born appalled, lived disaffected, and died in the height of fashion.

Tom Stoppard (b.1937), British playwright: Lord Malquist, in *Lord Malquist and Mr Moon* (1966), Pt.6, Ch.2

3 When I die, my epitaph should read: *She Paid the Bills*. That's the story of my private life.

Gloria Swanson (1897–1983), U.S. actress: quoted in the *Saturday Evening Post* (New York), 22 July 1950

EQUALITY

1 A commitment to sexual equality with males ... is a commitment to becoming the rich instead of the poor, the rapist instead of the raped, the murderer instead of the murdered.

Andrea Dworkin (b.1946), U.S. feminist critic: 'Renouncing Sexual "Equality"', speech, 12 Oct. 1974, National Organization for Women Conference on Sexuality, New York City, publ. in *Our Blood* (1976), Ch.2

2 All this talk about equality. The only thing people really have in common is that they are all going to die.

Bob Dylan (b.1941), U.S. singer and songwriter: remark 1966, quoted in *No Direction Home* by Robert Shelton (biography, 1986), Ch.1, '*Kaddish*'

3 When a bachelor of philosophy from the Antilles refuses to apply for certification as a teacher on the grounds of his colour I say that philosophy has never saved anyone. When someone else strives and strains to prove to me that black men are as intelligent as white men I say that intelligence has never saved anyone: and that is true, for, if philosophy and intelligence are invoked to proclaim the equality of men, they have also been employed to justify the extermination of men.

Frantz Fanon (1925–1961), Martiniquan psychiatrist, philosopher and political activist: introduction to *Black Skins, White Masks* (1952; tr.1967)

4 Just as modern mass production requires the standardization of commodities, so the social process requires standardization of man, and this standardization is called equality.

Erich Fromm (1900–1980), U.S. psychologist: *The Art of Loving* (1956), Ch.2

5 We understand the concept of equality, that we all want to be equal. But I think this is absolutely not true. I don't think anybody really wants to be equal. Everybody wants to be more equal.

Krzysztof Kieślowski (1941–1996), Polish film-maker: quoted in appreciation in *The Guardian* (London), 14 March 1996

6 If the worker and his boss enjoy the same television program and visit the same resort places, if the typist is as attractively made up as the daughter of her employer, if the Negro owns a Cadillac, if they all read the same newspaper, then this assimilation indicates not the disappearance of classes, but the extent to which the needs and satisfactions that serve the preservation of the Establishment are shared by the underlying population.

Herbert Marcuse (1898–1979), U.S. political philosopher: *One-Dimensional Man* (1964), Ch.1

7 All animals are equal but some animals are more equal than others.

George Orwell (1903–1950), British author: *Animal Farm* (1945), Ch.10. The animals' Commandment at the end of the story, originally formulated as 'All animals are equal'

8 No advance in wealth, no softening of manners, no reform or revolution has ever brought human equality a millimetre nearer.

George Orwell: extract from Goldstein's book in *Nineteen Eighty-four* (1949), Pt.2, Ch.9

9 The trauma of the Sixties persuaded me that my generation's egalitarianism was a senti-mental error. ... I now see the hierarchical as both beautiful and necessary. Efficiency liberates; egalitarianism tangles, delays, blocks, deadens.

Camille Paglia (b.1947), U.S. author and critic: *Sex, Art, and American Culture* (1992), 'Sexual Personae: The Cancelled Preface'

10 Prosperity or egalitarianism – you have to choose. I favour freedom – you never achieve real equality anyway: you simply sacrifice prosperity for an illusion.

Mario Vargas Llosa (b.1936), Peruvian novelist: in the *Independent on Sunday* (London), 5 May 1991

See also Malcolm X on BROTHERHOOD; Picabia on INEQUALITY; Trilling on LIBERALS

EROTICISM

1 Eroticism is assenting to life even in death.

Georges Bataille (1897–1962), French novelist and critic: introduction to *Eroticism* (1957)

2 Erotica is simply high-class pornography; better produced, better conceived, better executed, better packaged, designed for a better class of consumer.

Andrea Dworkin (b.1946), U.S. feminist critic: preface to *Pornography* (1981)

3 Eroticism is like a dance: one always leads the other.

Milan Kundera (b.1929), Czech-born French author and critic: *Immortality* (1991), Pt.3, 'The Cat'

4 In this loveless everyday life eroticism is a substitute for love.

Henri Lefebvre (b.1901), French philosopher: *Everyday Life in the Modern World* (1962), Ch.4

5 Pornography is about dominance. Erotica is about mutuality.

Gloria Steinem (b.1934), U.S. feminist writer and editor: 'Erotica vs. Pornography', adapted from articles in *Ms.* (New York), Aug. 1977 and Nov. 1978, rep. in *Outrageous Acts and Everyday Rebellions* (1983)

6 Eroticism has its own moral justification because it says that pleasure is enough for me; it is a statement of the individual's sovereignty.

Mario Vargas Llosa (b.1936), Peruvian novelist: in the *International Herald Tribune* (Paris), 23 Oct. 1990

ERROR

1 There is no original truth, only original error.

Gaston Bachelard (1884–1962), French scientist, philosopher and literary theorist: *Fragments of a Poetics of Fire* (1988; tr.1990), 'A Retrospective Glance at the Lifework of a Master of Books'

2 People like watching people who make mistakes, but they prefer watching a man who survives his mistakes. ... The so-called rebel figures are not popular because they're rebels, but because they've made mistakes and got over them.
David Bowie (b.1947), British rock musician: interview, March 1976, rep. in *Bowie in His Own Words* (ed. Miles, 1980), 'Rock 'n' Roll'

3 Mistakes are almost always of a sacred nature. Never try to correct them. On the contrary: rationalise them, understand them thoroughly. After that, it will be possible for you to sublimate them.
Salvador Dali (1904–1989), Spanish painter: journal entry, 30 June 1952, in *Diary of a Genius* (1966)

4 Mistakes are a fact of life
It is the response to error that counts.
Nikki Giovanni (b.1943), U.S. poet: 'Of Liberation', St.16, publ. in *Black Feeling/Black Talk/Black Judgement* (1970)

5 Mistakes are, after all, the foundations of truth, and if a man does not know what a thing *is*, it is at least an increase in knowledge if he knows what it is *not*.
Carl Jung (1875–1961), Swiss psychiatrist: 'Aion' (1951), rep. in *Collected Works* (ed. William McGuire), Vol.IX (1959), Pt.2, Para.429

6 So long as a person who has made mistakes ... honestly and sincerely wishes to be cured and to mend his ways, we should welcome him and cure his sickness so that he can become a good comrade. We can never succeed if we just let ourselves go and lash at him.
Mao Zedong (1893–1976), Chinese leader: speech in Peking, 1965, publ. in *Selected Works*, Vol.III, p.50

7 If the individual, or heretic, gets hold of some essential truth, or sees some error in the system being practised, he commits so many marginal errors himself that he is worn out before he can establish his point.
Ezra Pound (1885–1972), U.S. poet and critic: interview in *Writers at Work* (Second Series, ed. George Plimpton, 1963). Pound was obliquely referring to his own experience, and his incarceration in an American mental institution for ten years following his arrest for treason in 1945

8 We are built to make mistakes, coded for error.
Lewis Thomas (1913–1993), U.S. physician and educator: *The Medusa and the Snail* (1979), 'To Err is Human'

See also FAUX-PAS; Auden on THEATRE

ESCAPISM

1 Man seeks to escape himself in myth, and does so by any means at his disposal. Drugs, alcohol, or lies. Unable to withdraw into himself, he disguises himself. Lies and inaccuracy give him a few moments of comfort.
Jean Cocteau (1889–1963), French author and film-maker: *Diary of an Unknown* (1953; tr.1988), 'On Invisibility'

2 Man staggers through life yapped at by his reason, pulled and shoved by his appetites, whispered to by fears, beckoned by hopes. Small wonder that what he craves most is self-forgetting.
Eric Hoffer (1902–1983), U.S. philosopher: *The Passionate State of Mind* (1955), Aph.219

3 Choose us. Choose life. Choose mortgage payments; choose washing machines; choose cars; choose sitting oan a couch watching mind-numbing and spirit-crushing game shows, stuffing fuckin junk food intae yir mooth. Choose rotting away, pishing and shiteing yersel in a home, a total fuckin embarrassment tae the selfish, fucked-up brats ye've produced. Choose life.
Well, ah choose no tae choose life.
Irvine Welsh (b.1958), Scottish author: Renton, in *Trainspotting* (1994), 'Blowing It: Searching for the Inner Man'

See also Plath on THE MIND

ESPIONAGE

1 What do you think spies are: priests, saints and martyrs? They're a squalid procession of vain fools, traitors too, yes; pansies, sadists and drunkards, people who play cowboys and Indians to brighten their rotten lives.
John Le Carré (b.1931), British author: Leamas, in *The Spy Who Came in From the Cold* (1963), Ch.25

2 It's easy to forget what intelligence consists of: luck and speculation. Here and there a windfall, here and there a scoop.
John Le Carré: Leclerc, in *The Looking-Glass War* (1965), Pt.2, Ch.9

3 There are some who become spies for money, or out of vanity and megalomania, or out of ambition, or out of a desire for thrills. But the malady of our time is of those who become spies out of idealism.
Max Lerner (1902–1992), U.S. author and columnist: of the atomic secrets spy Julius Rosenberg, in 'The Tragedy of the Rosenbergs', first publ. in the *New York Post* 9 April 1952, rep. in *The Unfinished Country* (1959), Pt.4

4 I cannot think that espionage can be recommended as a technique for building an impressive civilisation. It's a lout's game.
Rebecca West (1892–1983), British author: introduction (1982) to *The Meaning of Treason* (1949)

5 He smiled rather too much. He smiled at breakfast, you know.
Charles Wheeler (b.1923), British journalist and broadcaster: remembering the spy George Blake on *Inside Story*, BBC 1, quoted in *The Independent* (London), 20 Sept. 1990

THE ESTABLISHMENT

1 If you attack the establishment long enough and hard enough, they will make you a member of it.
Art Buchwald (b.1925), U.S. humorist: in the *International Herald Tribune* (Paris), 24 May 1989

2 Our establishment has presided over economic decline and bequeathed a culture of mediocrity. Why join a bunch of losers?
Andrew Neil (b.1949), British journalist and editor: in *The Evening Standard* (London), 26 May 1993

3 There is nothing more agreeable in life than to make peace with the Establishment – and nothing more corrupting.
A.J.P. Taylor (1906–1990), British historian: in the *New Statesman* (London), 29 Aug. 1953

See also Marcuse on EQUALITY; Lapham on THE 1990s

ETHICS

1 Ethics is an optics of the Divine. Henceforth, no relations with God is direct or immediate. The Divine can be manifested only through my neighbour. For a Jew, Incarnation is neither possible nor necessary.
Emmanuel Levinas (b.1905), French Jewish philosopher: 'Jewish Thought Today' (1961), rep. in *Difficult Freedom* (1990), Pt.4

2 It is immoral to trade on fear. It is immoral constantly to make women feel dissatisfied with their bodies. It is immoral to deceive a customer by making miracle claims for a product. It is immoral to use a photograph of a glowing sixteen-year-old to sell a cream aimed at preventing wrinkles in a forty-year-old.
Anita Roddick (b.1943), British businesswoman and founder of the Body Shop: *Body and Soul* (1991), Ch.1

ETIQUETTE

1 Nothing more rapidly inclines a person to go into a monastery than reading a book on etiquette. There are so many trivial ways in which it is possible to commit some social sin.
Quentin Crisp (b.1908), British author: *Manners from Heaven* (1984), Ch.1

2 A commercial society whose members are essentially ascetic and indifferent in social ritual has to be provided with blueprints and specifications for evoking the right tone for every occasion.
Marshall McLuhan (1911–1980), Canadian communications theorist: *The Mechanical Bride* (1951), 'Emily Post'

EUROPE

1 Europe has lived on its contradictions, flourished on its differences, and, constantly transcending itself thereby, has created a civilization on which the whole world depends even when rejecting it. This is why I do not believe in a Europe unified under the weight of an ideology or of a technocracy that overlooked these differences.
Albert Camus (1913–1960), French-Algerian philosopher and author: interview in *Demain* (Paris), 24 Oct. 1957, rep. in *Resistance, Rebellion and Death* (1961), 'The Wager of Our Generation'

2 The European game has finally ended; we must find something different. WE today can do everything, so long as we do not imitate Europe, so long as we are not obsessed by the desire to catch up with Europe.
Frantz Fanon (1925–1961), Martiniquan psychiatrist, philosopher and political activist: *The Wretched of the Earth* (1961), Ch.6

3 If you live in Europe ... things change ... but continuity never seems to break. You don't have to throw the past away.
Nadine Gordimer (b.1923), South African author: Madame Bagnelli, in *Burger's Daughter* (1979), Pt.2

4 War and culture, those are the two poles of Europe, her heaven and hell, her glory and shame, and they cannot be separated from one another. When one comes to an end, the other will end also and one cannot end without the other. The fact that no war has broken out in Europe for fifty years is connected in some mysterious way with the fact that for fifty years no new Picasso has appeared either.
Milan Kundera (b.1929), Czech-born French author and critic: Paul, in *Immortality* (1991), Pt.3, 'The Brilliant Ally of his own Gravediggers'

5 When an American heiress wants to buy a man, she at once crosses the Atlantic. The only really materialistic people I have ever met have been Europeans.
Mary McCarthy (1912–1989), U.S. author and critic: 'America the Beautiful', first publ. in *Commentary* (New York), Sept. 1947, rep. in *On the Contrary* (1961)

6 Never say, for example, as European politicians continually do, that Britain will lead Europe; say rather that Britain will play a vital

part within Europe; in these large affairs he does most who boasts least.

Oswald Mosley (1896–1980), British fascist leader: *My Life* (1968), Ch.2

7 You can see it's the end; Europe is springing leaks everywhere. What then has happened? It simply is that in the past we made history and now it is being made of us. The ratio of forces has been inverted.

Jean-Paul Sartre (1905–1980), French philosopher and author: preface to *The Wretched of the Earth* by Frantz Fanon (1961)

8 Almost overwhelmingly, European culture, at the close of this millennium, is that of the museum. Who among us believes that we shall witness a new Dante, a Shakespeare of the 21st Century, a Mozart to come?

George Steiner (b.1929), French-born U.S. critic and novelist: 'Modernity, Mythology and Magic', lecture 1994, at the Salzburg Festival, rep. in *The Guardian* (London), 6 Aug. 1994

See also BRITAIN; FRANCE; GERMANY; HOLLAND; IRELAND; ITALY; POLAND; SWITZERLAND

EUROPE: and America

1 Europe has what we do not have yet, a sense of the mysterious and inexorable limits of life, a sense, in a word, of tragedy. And we have what they sorely need: a sense of life's possibilities.

James Baldwin (1924–1987), U.S. author: *Nobody Knows My Name* (1961), 'The Discovery of What it Means to be an American'

2 No one is stirred to the bowels by Europe of the ancient parapets. A huge force has lost its power over the imagination. This force began to weaken in the fifties, and by the sixties it was entirely gone.

Saul Bellow (b.1915), U.S. novelist: 'My Paris', first publ. in the *New York Times Magazine*, 13 March 1983, rep. in *It All Adds Up* (1994)

3 I've come to think of Europe as a hardcover book, America as the paperback version.

Don DeLillo (b.1926), U.S. author: Owen Brademas, in *The Names* (1982), Ch.1

4 The immense popularity of American movies abroad demonstrates that Europe is the unfinished negative of which America is the proof.

Mary McCarthy (1912–1989), U.S. author and critic: 'America the Beautiful', first publ. in *Commentary* (New York) Sept. 1947, rep. in *On the Contrary* (1961)

See also Wenders on THE SUBCONSCIOUS

EUROPE: Eastern Europe

1 There is no Soviet domination of Eastern Europe and there never will be under a Ford administration. ... The United States does not concede that those countries are under the domination of the Soviet Union.

Gerald Ford (b.1913), U.S. Republican politician and president: TV debate, 6 Oct. 1976, with presidential candidate Jimmy Carter, publ. in *Great Debates* by S. Kraus (1979). When asked to clarify this statement, Ford admitted he may not have been as precise as he might have been

2 We are finding out that what looked like a neglected house a year ago is in fact a ruin.

Václav Havel (b.1936), Czech playwright and president: on the state of Czechoslovakia and other ex-Soviet Bloc countries, in *The Daily Telegraph* (London), 3 Jan. 1991

3 The era of long parades past an official podium filled with cold faces is gone. Celebrating is now a right, not a duty.

Lothar de Maizière (b.1940), German lawyer and politician: speech, on May Day, while East German prime minister, quoted in *The Independent* (London), 5 May 1990

4 I indispensably contributed to saving eastern Europe.

Robert Maxwell (1923–1991), British tycoon: referring to his business investments and relations with Gorbachev, in *The Guardian* (London), 5 March 1990, quoted in *Maxwell: The Outsider* by Tom Bower (1988, rev.1991), Ch.16

5 Reality has become so absorbing that the streets, the television, and the journals have confiscated the public interest and people are no longer thirsty for culture on a higher level.

Andre Plesu (b.1948), Rumanian culture minister: in the *International Herald Tribune* (Paris), 14 Nov. 1990

See also Kennedy on GERMANY: BERLIN

THE EUROPEAN UNION

1 Their Europeanism is nothing but imperialism with an inferiority complex.

Denis Healey (b.1917), British Labour politician: of the Conservative Party, quoted in *The Observer* (London) 7 Oct. 1962

2 The movement of science since 1939 compels a commensurate development in political thinking.... The union of Europe is now necessary to the survival of every nation in this continent. The new science presents at once the best opportunity and the worst danger of all history. It has destroyed for ever the island immunity of Britain and compelled the organisation of life in wider areas. It has accelerated

evolution, and imposed union with our kindred of Europe if we are to survive.

Oswald Mosley (1896–1980), British fascist leader: *My Life* (1968), Ch.23. In an earlier section of the book, Mosley wrote, 'In the European future the fierce passions which divided and destroyed us can be overcome, and the sublime spirit of duty, sacrifice and high endeavour then imprisoned within them and distorted to the service of war will be released in a union of all high things to make Europe and save mankind' (Ch.3)

3 Decisions of great consequence will simply unfold as matters of inexorable economic necessity – as interpreted by the Brussels-based bureaucracy of the EEC. The near non-existence of popular control over the Common Market's Council of Ministers and its economic planners promises to make the EEC the most effective suave technocracy in the world. For how else to compete with the dynamism of the American corporate establishment?

Theodore Roszak (b.1933), U.S. social critic: *Where the Wasteland Ends* (1972), Ch.2

4 The Europe which might have sprung into being during Churchill's visit to Strasbourg in 1945 has, at best, been transformed into a self-important bureaucracy. Tribalism, religious detestations, chauvinism of every tint, characterise relations between members of what is, in fact, a Byzantine system of commercial and technocratic arrangements. Nostalgias for both a fascist and a communist past sicken the enfeebled democracies of both East and West. The very word Maastricht has become an obscure mockery of the stately dreams of *communitas*.

George Steiner (b.1929), French-born U.S. critic and novelist: 'Modernity, Mythology and Magic', lecture at the 1994 Salzburg Festival, publ. in *The Guardian* (London), 6 Aug. 1994

5 We have not successfully rolled back the frontiers of the State in Britain only to see them reimposed at a European level, with a European super-State exercising a new dominance from Brussels.

Margaret Thatcher (b.1925), British Conservative politician and prime minister: 'The Bruges Speech', 20 Sept. 1988, publ. in *The Penguin Book of Twentieth-Century Speeches* (ed. Brian MacArthur, 1992)

EUTHANASIA

1 Euthanasia is a long, smooth-sounding word, and it conceals its danger as long, smooth words do, but the danger is there, nevertheless.

Pearl S. Buck (1892–1973), U.S. author: *The Child Who Never Grew* (1950), Ch.2

2 What does terrorise me is to be an invalid strapped to a couch with ten different tubes coming into me, immobile, consciousness

barely functioning at all, barely able to speak, having my diapers changed. It is better to die than become a victim of the whole dying industry – religion, morticians, politicians.

Timothy Leary (1920–1996), U.S. psychologist: on being diagnosed as suffering from cancer in Jan. 1995, in interview in *The Guardian* (London), 2 Dec. 1995

EVANGELISM

1 Why should I apologize because God throws in crystal chandeliers, mahogany floors, and the best construction in the world?

Jim Bakker (b.1940), U.S. evangelist: of his luxury religious centre, Heritage U.S.A., quoted in the *New Yorker*, 23 April 1990

2 In soliciting donations from his flock, a preacher may promise eternal life in a celestial city whose streets are paved with gold, and that's none of the law's business. But if he promises an annual free stay in a luxury hotel on Earth, he'd better have the rooms available.

Charlotte Observer (North Carolina), 6 Oct. 1989: commenting on the prosecution of local televangelist Jim Bakker on charges of fraud and conspiracy.

3 There is no arguing with the pretenders to a divine knowledge and to a divine mission. They are possessed with the sin of pride, they have yielded to the perennial temptation.

Walter Lippmann (1889–1974), U.S. journalist: *The Public Philosophy* (1955), Ch.7, Sct.5

4 Religion was inevitably going to contract into a small nucleus of enthusiasts, and all they've achieved is to change the enthusiasts; the new enthusiasts happen to be the ones who like clapping their hands and looking soppy. They repel me.

Auberon Waugh (b.1939), British journalist and novelist: on new trends within the Catholic church, in interview in *Singular Encounters* by Naim Attallah (1990), 'Auberon Waugh'

5 God is definitely out of the closet.

Marianne Williamson (b.1953), U.S. benefactor: quoted in *Vanity Fair* (New York), June 1991

EVENTS

1 A pseudo-event ... comes about because someone has planned it, planted, or incited it. Typically, it is not a train wreck or an earthquake, but an interview.

Daniel J. Boorstin (b.1914), U.S. historian: *The Image* (1961), Ch.1

2 The enemy of the conventional wisdom is not ideas but the march of events.

J.K. Galbraith (b.1908), U.S. economist: quoted in introduction to *The Affluent Society* (1958, rev. 1977)

3 Like a kick in the butt, the force of events wakes slumberous talents.
Edward Hoagland (b.1932), U.S. novelist and essayist: in *The Guardian* (London), 11 Aug. 1990

4 One of the extraordinary things about human events is that the unthinkable becomes thinkable.
Salman Rushdie (b.1947), Indian-born British author: interview in *The Guardian* (London), 8 Nov. 1990

EVIL

1 Evil is being involved in the glamour and charm aspect of material existence – glamour in its old Gaelic sense, meaning enchantment with the look of things, rather than the soul of things.
Kenneth Anger (b.1929), U.S. film-maker and author: quoted in the *Sunday Correspondent* (London), 14 Jan. 1990

2 The fearsome, word-and-thought-defying *banality of evil*.
Hannah Arendt (1906–1975), German-born U.S. political philosopher: *Eichmann in Jerusalem* (1963), Ch.15

3 There are evils ... that have the ability to survive identification and go on for ever ... money, for instance, or war.
Saul Bellow (b.1915), U.S. novelist: Albert Corde, in *The Dean's December* (1982), Ch.13

4 Nothing in the nature around us is evil. This needs to be repeated since one of the human ways of *talking oneself into* inhuman acts is to cite the supposed cruelty of nature.
John Berger (b.1926), British author and critic: 'Muck and Its Entanglements' first publ. in *Harper's Magazine* (New York), May 1989, rep. in *Keeping a Rendezvous* (1992), as 'A Load of Shit'

5 The surest defense against Evil is extreme individualism, originality of thinking, whimsicality, even – if you will – eccentricity. That is, something that can't be feigned, faked, imitated; something even a seasoned imposter couldn't be happy with.
Joseph Brodsky (1940–1996), Russian-born U.S. poet and critic: 'A Commencement Address', Williams College, 1984, publ. in *Less Than One: Selected Essays* (1986)

6 The face of 'evil' is always the face of total need.
William Burroughs (1914–1997), U.S. author: 'Deposition: Testimony Concerning a Sickness', publ. in *The Evergreen Review* (New York), Jan./Feb. 1960, rep. as introduction to *The Naked Lunch* (1962 edn.)

7 Must I do all the evil I can before I learn to shun it? Is it not enough to know the evil to shun it? If not, we should be sincere enough to admit that we love evil too well to give it up.
Mohandas K. Gandhi (1869–1948), Indian political and spiritual leader: *Non-Violence in Peace and War* (1949), Vol.II, Ch.74

8 Some people show evil as a great racehorse shows breeding. They have the dignity of a hard chancre.
Ernest Hemingway (1899–1961), U.S. author: *A Moveable Feast* (1964), Ch.12

9 Evil is not a mystical principle that can be effaced by a ritual, it is an offence perpetrated on man by man. No one, not even God, can substitute himself for the victim.
Emmanuel Levinas (b.1905), French Jewish philosopher: 'A Religion for Adults' (1957), rep. in *Difficult Freedom* (1990), Pt.1

10 But what is the greatest evil? If you are going to epitomize evil, what is it? Is it the bomb? The greatest evil that one has to fight constantly, every minute of the day until one dies, is the worse part of oneself.
Patrick McGoohan (b.1928), Anglo-American actor: quoted in *The Prisoner and Danger Man* by Dave Rogers (1989), 'I Am Not a Number, I Am a Free Man'

11 Evil is something you recognise immediately you see it: it works through charm.
Brian Masters (b.1939), British author: in *The Daily Telegraph* (London), 31 May 1991

12 There is, of course, always a small minority among all peoples who like being brutal if they get the chance; the number may vary in different countries and on divers occasions, but it is always there. They are not the real problem, because society can always deal with this sadistic criminal element if it has the will. The real question is presented by those who do vile things for ideal reasons.
Oswald Mosley (1896–1980), British fascist leader: *My Life* (1968), Ch.8

13 I couldn't claim that I have never felt the urge to explore evil, but when you descend into hell you have to be very careful.
Kathleen Raine (b.1908), British poet: in *The Times* (London), 18 April 1992

EVOLUTION

1 Natural selection, the blind, unconscious, automatic process which Darwin discovered, and which we now know is the explanation for the existence and apparently purposeful form of all life, has no purpose in mind. It has no mind and no mind's eye. It does not plan for the future. It has no vision, no foresight, no sight at all. If it can be said to play the role of

the watchmaker in nature, it is the *blind* watchmaker.

Richard Dawkins (b.1941), British biologist: *The Blind Watchmaker* (1986), Ch.1

2 Natural selection, as it has operated in human history, favors not only the clever but the murderous.

Barbara Ehrenreich (b.1941), U.S. author and columnist: *The Worst Years of Our Lives* (1991), 'Iranscam: Oliver North and the Warrior Caste'

3 God ... created a number of possibilities in case some of his prototypes failed – that is the meaning of evolution.

Graham Greene (1904–1991), British novelist: Mr Visconti, in *Travels With My Aunt* (1969), Pt.2, Ch.7

4 If you think about it, 3,000 years ago we were writing with a piece of rock on shell. In my opinion, human beings, the species, have not yet even been born. We are still embryonic.

Timothy Leary (1920–1996), U.S. psychologist: interview in *The Guardian* (London), 2 Dec. 1995

5 Historians will have to face the fact that natural selection determined the evolution of cultures in the same manner as it did that of species.

Konrad Lorenz (1903–1989), Austrian ethologist: *On Aggression* (1963; tr.1966), 'Ecce Homo!', Ch.13

6 It is disturbing to discover in oneself these curious revelations of the validity of the Darwinian theory. If it is true that we have sprung from the ape, there are occasions when my own spring appears not to have been very far.

Cornelia Otis Skinner (1901–1979), U.S. author and actress: *The Ape in Me* (1959), 'The Ape in Me'

7 We are the products of editing, rather than of authorship.

George Wald (1906–1997), U.S. biochemist: 'The Origin of Optical Activity', publ. in *Annals of the New York Academy of Sciences* (1957), Vol.LXIX

EXCELLENCE

1 The sad truth is that excellence makes people nervous.

Shana Alexander (b.1925), U.S. writer and editor: 'Neglected Kids – the Bright Ones' (1966), rep. in *The Feminine Eye* (1970)

2 Always strive to excel, but only on weekends.

Richard Rorty (b.1931), U.S. philosopher: quoted in the *New York Times Magazine*, 12 Feb. 1990

See also GREATNESS

EXCESS

1 We have almost succeeded in leveling all human activities to the common denominator of securing the necessities of life and providing for their abundance.

Hannah Arendt (1906–1975), German-born U.S. political philosopher: *The Human Condition* (1958), Pt.3, Ch.17

2 Let's not quibble! I'm the foe of moderation, the champion of excess. If I may lift a line from a die-hard whose identity is lost in the shuffle, 'I'd rather be strongly wrong than weakly right'.

Tallulah Bankhead (1903–1968), U.S. actress: *Tallulah* (1952), Ch.4

3 Americans are overreaching; overreaching is the most admirable and most American of the many American excesses.

George F. Will (b.1941), U.S. political columnist: *Statecraft as Soulcraft: What Government Does* (1984), Ch.4

EXISTENCE

1 There is no means of *proving* it is preferable to be than not to be.

E.M. Cioran (1911–1995), Rumanian-born French philosopher: *The New Gods* (*Le Mauvais Démiurge*, 1969; tr. 1974), 'Strangled Thoughts', Sct.1

2 Being is a fiction invented by those who suffer from becoming.

Coleman Dowell (1925–1985), U.S. novelist, playwright and lyricist: entry in Mrs October's journals, in *Mrs October Was Here* (1973), Pt.3, 'Tasmania, Now'

3 Man is the only animal for whom his own existence is a problem which he has to solve.

Erich Fromm (1900–1980), U.S. psychologist: *Man For Himself* (1947), Ch.3

4 As far as we can discern, the sole purpose of human existence is to kindle a light in the darkness of mere being.

Carl Jung (1875–1961), Swiss psychiatrist: *Memories, Dreams, Reflections* (1962), Ch.11

5 Her drama was a drama not of heaviness but of lightness. What fell to her lot was not the burden but the unbearable lightness of being.

Milan Kundera (b.1929), Czech-born French author and critic: of Sabina, in *The Unbearable Lightness of Being* (1984), Pt.3, Ch.10

6 There's nothing that makes you so aware of the improvisation of human existence as a song unfinished. Or an old address book.

Carson McCullers (1917–1967), U.S. author: Ferris, in 'The Sojourner', publ. in *The Ballad of the Sad Café* (1951)

7 The cradle rocks above an abyss, and common sense tells us that our existence is but a brief

crack of light between two eternities of darkness.

Vladimir Nabokov (1899–1977), Russian-born U.S. novelist and poet: opening words of auto-biography, *Speak, Memory* (1955; rev.1966), Ch.1, Sct.1

8 One is still what one is going to cease to be and already what one is going to become. One lives one's death, one dies one's life.

Jean-Paul Sartre (1905–1980), French philosopher and author: *Saint Genet: Actor and Martyr* (1952; tr.1963), Bk.2, 'The Melodious Child Dead in Me ...'

9 Existence is no more than the precarious attainment of relevance in an intensely mobile flux of past, present, and future.

Susan Sontag (b.1933), U.S. essayist: *Styles of Radical Will* (1969), 'Thinking Against Oneself: Reflections on Cioran'

10 Existence itself does not feel horrible; it feels like an ecstasy, rather, which we have only to be still to experience.

John Updike (b.1932), U.S. author and critic: *Self-Consciousness: Memoirs* (1989), Ch.6

See also Cioran on HABIT

EXISTENTIALISM

1 Existentialism is about being a saint without God; being your own hero, without all the sanction and support of religion or society.

Anita Brookner (b.1938), British novelist and art historian: interview in *Writers at Work* (Eighth Series, ed. George Plimpton, 1988)

2 Then we are assured by Sartre that owing to the final disappearance of God our liberty is *absolute!* At this the entire audience waves its hat or claps its hands. But this natural enthusiasm is turned abruptly into something much less buoyant when it is learnt that this liberty weighs us down immediately with tremendous *responsibilities*. We now have to take all God's worries on our shoulders – now that we are become 'men like gods'. It is at this point that the Anxiety and Despondency begin, ending in utter despair.

Wyndham Lewis (1882–1957), British author and painter: *The Writer and the Absolute* (1952), 'Twentieth Century Nihilism'

3 To be an existentialist, one must be able to feel oneself – one must know one's desires, one's rages, one's anguish, one must be aware of the character of one's frustration and know what would satisfy it. The overcivilized man can be an existentialist only if it is chic, and deserts it quickly for the next chic.

Norman Mailer (b.1923), U.S. author: 'The White Negro', Sct.2, first publ. in *Dissent*, summer 1957, rep. in *Advertisements for Myself* (1959)

EXPERIENCE

1 The notion of a universality of human experience is a confidence trick and the notion of a universality of female experience is a clever confidence trick.

Angela Carter (1940–1992), British author: *The Sadeian Woman* (1979), 'Polemical Preface'

2 Experience is a dim lamp, which only lights the one who bears it.

Louis-Ferdinand Céline (1894–1961), French author: interview in *Writers at Work* (Third Series, ed. George Plimpton, 1967)

3 I try to avoid experience if I can. Most experience is bad.

E.L. Doctorow (b.1931), U.S. novelist: interview in *Writers at Work* (Eighth Series, ed. George Plimpton, 1988)

4 You learn from a conglomeration of the incredible past – whatever experience gotten in any way whatsoever.

Bob Dylan (b.1941), U.S. singer and songwriter: *Tarantula* (1970), 'Subterranean Homesick Blues and the Blond Waltz'

5 We learn through experience and experiencing, and no one teaches anyone anything. This is as true for the infant moving from kicking to crawling to walking as it is for the scientist with his equations. If the environment permits it, anyone can learn whatever he chooses to learn; and if the individual permits it, the environment will teach him everything it has to teach.

Viola Spolin (b.1911), U.S. theatrical director and producer: *Improvisation for the Theater* (1963), Ch.1

EXPERTS

1 Too bad that all the people who know how to run the country are busy driving taxicabs and cutting hair.

George Burns (1896–1996), U.S. comedian: in *Life* (New York), Dec. 1979

2 It is, after all, the responsibility of the expert to operate the familiar and that of the leader to transcend it.

Henry Kissinger (b.1923), U.S. Republican politician and secretary of state: *Years of Upheaval* (1982), Ch.10, 'The Foreign Service'

3 This world is run by people who know how to do things. They know how things work. They are *equipped*. Up there, there's a layer of people who run everything. But we – we're just peasants. We don't understand what's going on, and we can't do anything.

Doris Lessing (b.1919), British novelist: Dorothy, in *The Good Terrorist* (1985), p.330 of Jonathan Cape edn.

4 A specialist is someone who does everything else worse.

Ruggiero Ricci (b.1918), U.S. violinist: in *The Daily Telegraph* (London), 25 May 1990

5 Experts are never in real danger. Everyone needs them. The chambermaid always survives the palace revolution. Someone has to make the beds.

Fay Weldon (b.1933), British novelist: Defoe Desmond, in 'End of the Line', publ. in *Wicked Women* (1995)

EXTREMISM

1 I'm not one for delicate social niceties. If I take a jump into the pool, I generally swallow all the water.

David Bowie (b.1947), British rock musician: interview, Oct. 1977, rep. in *Bowie In His Own Words* (ed. Miles, 1980), 'Politics'

2 This woman did not fly to extremes; she lived there.

Quentin Crisp (b.1908), British author: *The Naked Civil Servant* (1968), Ch.3

3 I would remind you that extremism in the defense of liberty is no vice! And let me remind you also that moderation in the pursuit of justice is no virtue!

Barry Goldwater (b.1909), U.S. Republican politician: speech, 16 July 1964, accepting presidential nomination, Republican National Convention, San Francisco, quoted in the *New York Times*, 17 July 1964. Goldwater later attributed these words to Cicero. On 31 Oct. 1964, Lyndon B. Johnson, as Democratic contender for the presidency, replied in a speech in New York: 'Extremism in the pursuit of the Presidency is an unpardonable vice. Moderation in the affairs of the nation is the highest virtue.' Johnson won a sweeping victory against Goldwater in the presidential election three days later

4 Polarization is addictive. It is the crack of politics – a short intense rush that the system craves again and again, until it begins to collapse.

Robert Hughes (b.1938), Australian author and critic: *Culture of Complaint* (1993), Ch.1

5 What is objectionable, what is dangerous, about extremists is not that they are extreme, but that they are intolerant. The evil is not what they say about their cause, but what they say about their opponents.

Robert Kennedy (1925–1968), U.S. attorney general and Democratic politician: *The Pursuit of Justice* (1964), Pt.3, 'Extremism, Left and Right'

6 The question is not whether we will be extremist but what kind of extremist will we be.

Martin Luther King Jr. (1929–1968), U.S. clergyman and civil rights leader: 'Letter from Birmingham Jail', open letter to clergymen, 16 April 1963, publ. in *Why We Can't Wait* (1964)

FACES

1 My face looks like a wedding-cake left out in the rain.

W.H. Auden (1907–1973), Anglo-American poet: quoted in *W.H. Auden* by Humphrey Carpenter (1981), Pt.2, Ch.6

2 I think your whole life shows in your face and you should be proud of that.

Lauren Bacall (b.1924), U.S. actress: in *The Daily Telegraph* (London), 2 March 1988

3 The face of Garbo is an Idea, that of Hepburn an Event.

Roland Barthes (1915–1980), French semiologist: *Mythologies* (1957; tr.1972), 'The Face of Garbo'

4 I have the eyes of a dead pig.

Marlon Brando (b.1924), U.S. actor: quoted in *Screen International* (London), 18 Jan 1991

5 It has been said that a pretty face is a passport. But it's not, it's a visa, and it runs out fast.

Julie Burchill (b.1960), British journalist and author: 'Kiss and Sell', first publ. in *The Mail on Sunday* (London) 1988, rep. in *Sex and Sensibility* (1992)

6 A blank helpless sort of face, rather like a rose just before you drench it with DDT.

John Carey (b.1934), British author and critic: of photographs of society figure Lady Diana Cooper, in *The Sunday Times* (London) 20 Sept. 1981, rep. in *Original Copy* (1987), Pt.2, 'Keeping Up With the Coopers'

7 It has to be displayed, this face, on a more or less horizontal plane. Imagine a man wearing a mask, and imagine that the elastic which holds the mask on has just broken, so that the man (rather than let the mask slip off) has to tilt his head back and balance the mask on his real face. This is the kind of tyranny which Lawson's face exerts over the rest of his body as he cruises along the corridors. ... He doesn't look down his nose at you, he looks along his nose.

James Fenton (b.1949), British poet and critic: of former chancellor Nigel Lawson, in the *New Statesman* (London), 23 July 1976

8 I said I liked it, I didn't say I wanted to kiss it.

Gloria Grahame (1924–1981), U.S. actor: Laurel Gray (Gloria Grahame) to Humphrey Bogart, in *In a Lonely Place* (film; screenplay by Andrew Salt and Edmund North, adapted from Dorothy B. Hughes's novel, directed by Nicholas Ray, 1950)

9 Our masks, always in peril of smearing or cracking,

In need of continuous check in the mirror or silverware,
Keep us in thrall to ourselves, concerned with our surfaces.
Carolyn Kizer (b.1925), U.S. poet, educator: 'Pro Femina', publ. in *Knock upon Silence* (1963)

10 The serial number of a human specimen is the face, that accidental and unrepeatable combination of features. It reflects neither character nor soul, nor what we call the self. The face is only the serial number of a specimen.
Milan Kundera (b.1929), Czech-born French author and critic: *Immortality* (1991), Pt.1, Ch.3

11 That the public can grow accustomed to any face is proved by the increasing prevalence of Keith's ruined physiognomy on TV documentaries and chat shows, as familiar and homely a horror as Grandpa in *The Munsters*.
Philip Norman (b.1943), British author and journalist: of Keith Richards, in introduction to *The Life and Good Times of the Rolling Stones* (1989). Richards, Norman wrote, 'is as endearing a personality as ever lurked within the aspect of Count Dracula on a bad morning. Who, looking into that grave-hollowed face, would ever suspect quick wit, authentic humour or the boozy, affectionate voice of some old-time theatrical actor-manager?'

12 At 50, everyone has the face he deserves.
George Orwell (1903–1950), British author: last entry in Orwell's notebook, 17 April 1949, publ. in *The Collected Essays, Journalism and Letters of George Orwell* (ed. Sonia Orwell and Ian Angus, 1968), Vol.IV. Albert Camus, in *The Fall* (1956), expressed much the same notion: 'After a certain age every man is responsible for his face'

13 What is a face, really? Its own photo? Its make-up? Or is it a face as painted by such or such painter? That which is in front? Inside? Behind? And the rest? Doesn't everyone look at himself in his own particular way? Deformations simply do not exist.
Pablo Picasso (1881–1973), Spanish artist: *Arts de France* (Paris) No.6, 1946, quoted in *Picasso on Art* (ed. Dore Ashton, 1972)

FACTS

1 Facts all come with points of view
Facts don't do what I want them to.
David Byrne (b.1952), U.S. rock musician: 'Crosseyed and Painless' (song, written with Brian Eno), on the album *Remain in Light* (Talking Heads, 1980)

2 Anyone who knows a strange fact shares in its singularity.
Jean Genet (1910–1986), French playwright and novelist: *Prisoner of Love* (1986: tr.1989), Pt.1

3 I'm not afraid of facts, I welcome facts *but a congeries of facts is not equivalent to an idea.*

This is the essential fallacy of the so-called 'scientific' mind. People who mistake facts for ideas are incomplete thinkers; they are gossips.
Cynthia Ozick (b.1928), U.S. novelist and short-story writer: 'We are the Crazy Lady and Other Feisty Feminist Fables', publ. in *The First Ms. Reader* (ed. Francine Klagsbrun, 1972)

4 Obviously the facts are never just coming at you but are incorporated by an imagination that is formed by your previous experience. Memories of the past are not memories of facts but memories of your imaginings of the facts.
Philip Roth (b.1933), U.S. novelist: opening letter to Zuckerman, in *The Facts* (1988), p.8 of Penguin edn. (1989)

5 Facts are generally overesteemed. For most practical purposes, a thing is what men think it is. When they judged the earth flat, it was flat. As long as men thought slavery tolerable, tolerable it was. We live down here among shadows, shadows among shadows.
John Updike (b.1932), U.S. author and critic: the statesman Buchanan, in *Buchanan Dying* (1974), Act 1

6 It is the spirit of the age to believe that any fact, no matter how suspect, is superior to any imaginative exercise, no matter how true.
Gore Vidal (b.1925), U.S. novelist and critic: 'French Letters: Theories of the New Novel', in *Encounter* (London), Dec. 1967

FAILURE

1 There are few things more dreadful than dealing with a man who knows he is going under, in his own eyes, and in the eyes of others. Nothing can help that man. What is left of that man flees from what is left of human attention.
James Baldwin (1924–1987), U.S. author: introduction to *The Price of the Ticket* (1985)

2 Ever tried. Ever failed. No matter. Try again. Fail again. Fail better.
Samuel Beckett (1906–1989), Irish playwright and novelist: *Worstward Ho* (1984)

3 What do I get – a couple of bucks and a one-way ticket to Palookaville. It was you, Charley. You was my brother. You should've looked out for me. Instead of making me take them dives for the short-end money. ... You don't understand! I could've been a contender. I could've had class and been somebody. Real class. Instead of a bum, which is what I am. It was you, Charley.
Marlon Brando (b.1924), U.S. actor: Terry Mallon (Marlon Brando), in *On The Waterfront* (film; screenplay by Budd Schulberg, directed by Elia Kazan, 1954). The lines are spoken to Mallon's brother (Rod Steiger), whom he blamed for his failed boxing career

4 She knows there's no success like failure
And that failure's no success at all.
Bob Dylan (b.1941), U.S. singer and songwriter:
'Love Minus Zero/No Limit' (song), on the album
Bringing it All Back Home (1965)

5 Failure brings a feeling of solitude, and that is
anything but cheerful. All the same, if something I have done is not liked, I care very little.
What saddens me is unlimited admiration
from someone who praises me for the wrong
reasons.
Federico Fellini (1920–1993), Italian film-maker:
Fellini on Fellini (ed. Anna Keel and Christian
Strich, 1974; tr.1977), 'Miscellany I', Sct.26

6 He was a self-made man who owed his lack of
success to nobody.
Joseph Heller (b.1923), U.S. novelist: referring to
Colonel Cargill, in *Catch-22* (1961), Ch.3

7 No failure in America, whether of love or
money, is ever simple; it is always a kind of betrayal, of a mass of shadowy, shared hopes.
Greil Marcus (b.1945), U.S. rock journalist:
Mystery Train (1976), 'Robert Johnson'

8 I don't say he's a great man. Willy Loman
never made a lot of money. His name was never
in the paper. He's not the finest character that
ever lived. But he's a human being, and a
terrible thing is happening to him. So attention
must be paid.
Arthur Miller (b.1915), U.S. playwright: Linda,
referring to her husband Willy Loman, in *Death of a
Salesman* (1949), Act 1

9 It is only possible to succeed at second-rate
pursuits – like becoming a millionaire or a
prime minister, winning a war, seducing beautiful women, flying through the stratosphere
or landing on the moon. First-rate pursuits –
involving, as they must, trying to understand
what life is about and trying to convey that
understanding – inevitably result in a sense of
failure. A Napoleon, a Churchill, a Roosevelt
can feel themselves to be successful, but never
a Socrates, a Pascal, a Blake. Understanding is
for ever unattainable. Therein lies the inevit-
ablility of failure in embarking upon its quest,
which is none the less the only one worthy of
serious attention.
Malcolm Muggeridge (1903–1990), British
journalist and broadcaster: *Woman's Hour* (radio
broadcast), 5 Aug. 1965, publ. in *Muggeridge
Through the Microphone* (1967), 'Failure'

10 Why are plots in which people win by far the
most common, in literature, theatre and film?
Of course, that sort of development corresponds with how people live through the hero's
experience, but they would still live it through
if the hero were to be a total loser. Stories of
failure could well be a fruitful new departure in
art.

Andrey Tarkovsky (1932–1986), Russian film-
maker: journal entry, 14 Aug 1981, publ. in *Time
Within Time: The Diaries 1970–1986* (1989;
tr.1994)

FAITH

1 May it not be that, just as we have to have faith
in Him, God has to have faith in us and,
considering the history of the human race so
far, may it not be that 'faith' is even more difficult for Him than it is for us?
W.H. Auden (1907–1973), Anglo-American poet: *A
Certain World* (1970), 'God'

2 You don't decide to build a church because you
have money in the bank. You build because
God says this is what I should do. Faith is the
supplier of things hoped for and the evidence
of things not seen.
Jim Bakker (b.1940), U.S. evangelist: quoted in the
New Yorker, 23 April 1990

3 Faith, to my mind, is a stiffening process, a sort
of mental starch, which ought to be applied as
sparingly as possible.
E.M. Forster (1879–1970), British novelist and
essayist: *Two Cheers for Democracy* (1951), 'What I
Believe'

4 If you have abandoned one faith, do not abandon all faith. There is always an alternative to
the faith we lose. Or is it the same faith under
another mask?
Graham Greene (1904–1991), British novelist:
Dr Magiot, in *The Comedians* (1966), Pt.2, Ch.4,
Sct.4

5 Absolute faith corrupts as absolutely as abso-
lute power.
Eric Hoffer (1902–1983), U.S. philosopher:
Reflections on the Human Condition (1973), Aph.13

6 The faith that moves mountains and conceives
of a world without slaves immediately trans-
ports itself to utopia, separating the reign of
God from the reign of Caesar. This reassures
Caesar.
Emmanuel Levinas (b.1905), French Jewish
philosopher: 'Place and Utopia' (1950), rep. in
Difficult Freedom (1990), Pt.3

7 My faith is the grand drama of my life. I'm a
believer, so I sing words of God to those who
have no faith. I give bird songs to those who
dwell in cities and have never heard them,
make rhythms for those who know only military marches or jazz, and paint colours for
those who see none.
Oliver Messiaen (1908–1992), French composer
and organist: in *The Independent* (London), 9 Dec.
1988

8 In an age of declining faith, sir, surely it's
enough for the young to hold spiritual convic-

tions. It's an act of pedantry to ask that they should be the right ones.

Joe Orton (1933–1967), British playwright: notes for dialogue in *What the Butler Saw*, quoted in *Prick Up Your Ears: the Biography of Joe Orton* by John Lahr (1978), Ch.6

9 My faith
is a great weight
hung on a small wire,
as doth the spider
hang her baby on a thin web.

Anne Sexton (1928–1974), U.S. poet: 'Small Wire', publ. in *The Awful Rowing Toward God* (1975)

See also BELIEF

THE FALKLANDS CONFLICT

1 The Falklands thing was a fight between two bald men over a comb.

Jorge Luis Borges (1899–1986), Argentinian author: in *Time* (New York), 14 Feb. 1983

2 GOTCHA!

The Sun: headline, 4 May 1982, on the sinking of the Agentinian cruiser *General Belgrano*

See also Thatcher on VICTORY

FAME

1 Those who have known the famous are publicly debriefed of their memories, knowing as their own dusk falls that they will only be remembered for remembering someone else.

Alan Bennett (b.1934), British playwright: Peggy, in *Prick up Your Ears: The Screenplay* (1987)

2 The celebrity is a person who is known for his well-knownness.

Daniel J. Boorstin (b.1914), U.S. historian: *The Image* (1961), Ch.2

3 Fame! In the best of cases, a misunderstanding.

Albert Camus (1913–1960), French-Algerian philosopher and author: journal entry, Sept. 1945, quoted in *Camus: A Biography* by Herbert R. Lottman (1979), Ch.28

4 A legend is an old man with a cane known for what he used to do. I'm still doing it.

Miles Davis (1926–1991), U.S. jazz musician: in the *International Herald Tribune* (Paris), 17 July 1991

5 It is a mark of many famous people that they cannot part with their brightest hour.

Lillian Hellman (1905–1984), U.S. playwright: *Pentimento* (1973), 'Theatre'

6 In the world of the celebrity, the hierarchy of publicity has replaced the hierarchy of descent and even of great wealth.

C. Wright Mills (1916–1962), U.S. sociologist: quoted in *Talking to Myself* by Studs Terkel (1977), Bk.4, Ch.1

7 Fame will go by and, so long, I've had you, fame. If it goes by, I've always known it was fickle. So at least it's something I experienced, but that's not where I live.

Marilyn Monroe (1926–1962), U.S. actress: conclusion of taped conversation, publ. the day that Monroe died in *Life* (New York), 3 Aug. 1962

8 I always thought being famous was the only thing worth doing in human life, and anything else was just perfunctory. I thought anonymity was easy: it was easy to be a simple, nodding individual who got on the bus. I wasn't terribly impressed by obscurity.

Morrissey (b.1959), British rock musician: interview in *Melody Maker* (London), 12 March 1988, rep. in *Classic Rock Interviews* (ed. Allan Jones, 1994), 'Viva Hate'

9 To become a celebrity is to become a brand name. There is Ivory Soap, Rice Krispies, and Philip Roth. Ivory is the soap that floats; Rice Krispies the breakfast cereal that goes snap-crackle-pop; Philip Roth the Jew who masturbates with a piece of liver.

Philip Roth (b.1933), U.S. novelist: *Reading Myself and Others* (1975, rev.1985), 'Interview with Le Nouvel Observateur' (May 1981)

10 Celebrity is good for kick-starting ideas, but often celebrity is a lead weight around your neck. It's like you pointing at the moon, but people are looking at your finger.

Sting (b.1951), British rock musician: on his campaign to protect the rain forest, in interview in *Mojo* (London), Feb. 95

11 Celebrity is a mask that eats into the face. As soon as one is aware of being 'somebody,' to be watched and listened to with extra interest, input ceases, and the performer goes blind and deaf in his overanimation. One can either see or be seen.

John Updike (b.1932), U.S. author and critic: *Self-Consciousness: Memoirs* (1989), Ch.6

12 In the future everybody will be world famous for fifteen minutes.

Andy Warhol (c.1928–1987), U.S. Pop artist: *Andy Warhol* (exhibition catalogue, 1968). In *Andy Warhol's Exposures* (1954), 'Studio 54', the artist wrote, 'I'm bored with that line. I never use it any more. My new line is, "In fifteen minutes everybody will be famous"'

See also Presley on ELVIS PRESLEY; STARDOM

FAME: Ups & Downs

1 When you're on the way up there are plenty of people climbing over each other to buy you

drinks, but when things start going wrong, more often than not, you drink alone.

Ian Botham (b.1955), British cricketer: *Botham: My Autobiography* (1994), Ch.7

2 You have all these secretaries. Limos pick you up at the airport and people bring you diet caffeine-free Cokes all the time and tell you you're fabulous, the show you're working on is great – until it comes out. And then you're yesterday's Danish.

Tom Hanks (b.1957), U.S. actor: quoted in *Tom Hanks* by Roy Trakin (1995), Ch.11

3 It is better to be a has-been than a never-was.

Cecil Parkinson (b.1932), British Conservative politician: in *The Guardian* (London), 29 June 1990

4 I hate that word. It's *return* – a return to the millions of people who've never forgiven me for deserting the screen.

Gloria Swanson (1897–1983), U.S. actress: Norma Desmond (Gloria Swanson), on her 'comeback', in *Sunset Boulevard* (film; screenplay by Billy Wilder, Charles Brackett and D.M. Marsham Jr., directed by Billy Wilder, 1950)

FAMILIES

1 There's a kind of blackmail that only the family can exercise over you and it is more powerful than anything the whole of society can do to you. In all societies there have been families and I think the family is the most repressive invention that exists.

Pedro Almodóvar (b.1951), Spanish film-maker: quoted in *Sight and Sound* (London), April 1992

2 You hear a lot of dialogue on the death of the American family. Families aren't dying. They're merging into big conglomerates.

Erma Bombeck (1927–1996), U.S. journalist: 'Empty Fridge, Empty Nest', publ. in the *San Francisco Examiner*, 1 Oct. 1978

3 If Mr Vincent Price were to be co-starred with Miss Bette Davis in a story by Mr Edgar Allan Poe directed by Mr Roger Corman, it could not fully express the pent-up violence and depravity of a single day in the life of the average family.

Quentin Crisp (b.1908), British author: *Manners from Heaven* (1984), Ch.2

4 Families suck! I wish they would all disappear.

Macaulay Culkin (b.1980), U.S. actor: Kevin (Macaulay Culkin), in *Home Alone* (film; screenplay by John Hughes, directed by Chris Columbus, 1990)

5 Families should spend more time talking to each other, rather than glued in front of the television.

Diana, Princess of Wales (1961–1997): remark, at Great Ormond Street Hospital, quoted in the *Independent on Sunday* (London), 16 May 1993

6 The only perfect love to be found on earth is not sexual love, which is riddled with hostility and insecurity, but the wordless commitment of families, which takes as its model mother-love. This is not to say that fathers have no place, for father-love, with its driving for self-improvement and discipline, is also essential to survival, but that uncorrected father-love, father-love as it were practised by both parents, is a way to annihilation.

Germaine Greer (b.1939), Australian feminist writer: introduction to *The Madwoman's Underclothes* (1986)

7 The striking point about our model family is not simply the compete-compete, consume-consume style of life it urges us to follow.... The striking point, in the face of all the propaganda, is how few Americans actually live this way.

Louise Kapp Howe (b.1934), U.S. author and editor: introduction to *The Future of The Family* (1972)

8 As the family goes, so goes the nation and so goes the whole world in which we live.

Pope John Paul II [Karol Wojtyla] (b.1920), Polish ecclesiastic: quoted in *The Observer* (London), 7 Dec. 1986

9 The most socially subversive institution of our time is the one-parent family.

Paul Johnson (b.1928), British journalist: quoted in the *Sunday Correspondent* (London), 24 Dec. 1989

10 The proliferation of support groups suggests to me that too many Americans are growing up in homes that do not contain a grandmother. A home without a grandmother is like an egg without salt and Helpists know it. They have jumped into the void left by the disappearance of morbid old ladies from the bosom of the American family.

Florence King (b.1936), U.S. author: *Reflections in a Jaundiced Eye* (1989), 'Does Your Child Taste Salty?'

11 As to the family, I have never understood how that fits in with the other ideals – or, indeed, why it should be an ideal at all. A group of closely related persons living under one roof; it is a convenience, often a necessity, sometimes a pleasure, sometimes the reverse; but who first exalted it as admirable, an almost religious ideal?

Rose Macaulay (1881–1958), British novelist and essayist: *The World My Wilderness* (1950), Ch.20

12 Sisters are always drying their hair.
    Locked into rooms, alone,
They pose at the mirror, shoulders bare,
Trying this way and that their hair,
Or fly importunate down the stair
    To answer the telephone.

Phyllis McGinley (1905–1978), U.S. poet and author: 'Girl's-Eye View of Relatives: Triolet Against Sisters', publ. in *Times Three* (1960)

13 Families are nothing other than the idolatry of duty.
Ann Oakley (b.1944), British sociologist and author: *Taking It Like a Woman* (1984), 'The War Between Love and the Family II'

14 To me, a good family is the basis of democracy and is democratic to the core. That's why the feminists had to destroy it.
Erin Pizzey (b.1939), British novelist and activist: quoted in *The Observer* (London), 11 Feb. 1996. Pizzey opened the first shelter for battered women in 1971

15 In our family, as far as we are concerned, we were born and what happened before that is myth.
V.S. Pritchett (1900–1997), British author: opening words of *A Cab at the Door* (first volume of autobiography, 1968)

16 One of the oddest features of western Christianized culture is its ready acceptance of the myth of the stable family and the happy marriage. We have been taught to accept the myth not as an heroic ideal, something good, brave, and nearly impossible to fulfil, but as the very fibre of normal life. Given most families and most marriages, the belief seems admirable but foolhardly.
Jonathan Raban (b.1942), British author and critic: *For Love and Money* (1987), Pt.3

17 Family indivisibility, the first commandment.
Philip Roth (b.1933), U.S. novelist: prologue to *The Facts* (1988)

18 Big sisters are the crab grass in the lawn of life.
Charles Schulz (b.1922), U.S. cartoonist: Linus, in *Peanuts* (strip cartoon, 1952)

19 A family's photograph album is generally about the extended family – and, often, is all that remains of it.
Susan Sontag (b.1933), U.S. essayist: *On Photography* (1977), 'In Plato's Cave'

20 The family is the basic cell of government: it is where we are trained to believe that we are human beings or that we are chattel, it is where we are trained to see the sex and race divisions and become callous to injustice even if it is done to ourselves, to accept as biological a full system of authoritarian government.
Gloria Steinem (b.1934), U.S. feminist writer and editor: speech, July 1981, National Women's Political Causus Conference, Albuquerque, New Mexico, quoted in *The Quotable Woman* (ed. Elaine Partnow, 1982)

See also CHILD-REARING; FATHERS; MOTHERS; PARENTS

FAMINE

1 When the Somalians were merely another hungry third world people, we sent them guns. Now that they are falling down dead from starvation, we send them troops. Some may see in this a tidy metaphor for the entire relationship between north and south. But it would make a whole lot more sense nutritionally – as well as providing infinitely more vivid viewing – if the Somalians could be persuaded to eat the troops.
Barbara Ehrenreich (b.1941), U.S. author and columnist: in *The Guardian* (London), 9 Jan. 1993

2 They were like the grotesque creatures of some distorted imagination. I stood and watched their slow, apathetic movements and fended off the awful truth that these were human beings. ... Their eyes ... were glazed, blank, and vacuous. They looked but did not see. They were the eyes of people who had given up.
Bob Geldof (b.1954), Irish rock singer: on his first visit to see the victims of the famine in Ethiopia, Jan 1985, in *Is That It?* (written with Paul Vallely, 1986), Ch.14

3 Famine sighs like a scythe
across the field of statistics and the desert
is a moving mouth. In the hold of this earth
10,000,000 shoreless souls are drifting.
Somalia: 765,000, their skeletons will go under
    the tidal sand.
Derek Walcott (b.1930), West Indian poet and playwright: 'The Fortunate Traveller' Pt.1, publ. in *The Fortunate Traveller* (1981)

FANATICS

1 A fanatic is one who can't change his mind and won't change the subject.
Winston Churchill (1874–1965), British statesman and author: quoted in the *New York Times*, 5 July 1954

2 The fanatic is incorruptible: if he kills for an idea, he can just as well get himself killed for one; in either case, tyrant or martyr, he is a monster.
E.M. Cioran (1911–1995), Rumanian-born French philosopher: *A Short History of Decay* (1949), Ch.1, 'Genealogy of Fanaticism'

3 Fervour is the weapon of choice of the impotent.
Frantz Fanon (1925–1961), Martiniquan psychiatrist, philosopher and political activist: introduction to *Black Skins, White Masks* (1952; tr.1967)

4 Throughout human history, the apostles of purity, those who have claimed to possess a

total explanation, have wrought havoc among mere mixed-up human beings.

Salman Rushdie (b.1947), Indian-born British author: 'In Good Faith', publ. in the *Independent on Sunday* (London), 4 Feb. 1990

See also OBSESSION

FANS

1 I'm your number-one fan.
Kathy Bates (b.1948), U.S. actress: Annie Wilkes (Kathy Bates), in *Misery* (film; screenplay by William Goldman, based on Stephen King's 1987 short story *Misery*, directed and co-produced by Rob Reiner, 1990)

2 The natural state of the football fan is bitter disappointment, no matter what the score.
Nick Hornby (b.1957), British author: *Fever Pitch* (1992), '1968–1975: Home Début'

3 Let's face it, they're not that bright.
Madonna (b.1959), U.S. singer and actress: of the fans camped outside her New York apartment, quoted in 'Madonna', by Martin Amis, first publ. in *The Observer* (London), 1992, rep. in *Visiting Mrs Nabokov* (1993)

4 We look forward to Saturdays all week long. It's the most meaningful thing in our lives. It's a religion, really. That's how important it is to us. Saturday is our day of worship.
Manchester United fan: quoted in *Among the Thugs* by Bill Buford (1991), Pt.1, 'Manchester'

5 Fans are more dangerous than a man with a weapon because they're after something invisible. Some imagined 'something'. At least with a gun you know what you're facing.
Sam Shepard (b.1943), U.S. playwright and actor: *Rolling Thunder Logbook* (1977), 'Fans'

6 To be an intelligent fan is to participate in something. It is an activity, a form of appreciating that is good for the individual's soul, and hence for society.
George F. Will (b.1941), U.S. political columnist: introduction to *Men at Work: The Craft of Baseball* (1990)

See also Football fan on DELINQUENTS

FANTASY

1 Fantasies are more than substitutes for unpleasant reality; they are also dress rehearsals, plans. All acts performed in the world begin in the imagination.
Barbara Grizzuti Harrison (b.1941), U.S. author and publicist: 'Talking Dirty', publ. in *Ms.* (New York), Oct. 1973

2 But fantasy *kills* imagination, pornography is death to art.

Iris Murdoch (b.1919), British novelist and philosopher: Alfred Ludens, in *The Message to the Planet* (1989), Pt.1

3 We live under continual threat of two equally fearful, but seemingly opposed, destinies: unremitting banality and inconceivable terror. It is fantasy, served out in large rations by the popular arts, which allows most people to cope with these twin specters.
Susan Sontag (b.1933), U.S. essayist: *Against Interpretation* (1966), 'The Imagination of Disaster'

See also DAYDREAMS; SEXUAL FANTASY

FAREWELLS

1 So long, and thanks for all the fish.
Douglas Adams (b.1952), British author: The dolphins' farewell message to humanity, in *So Long, and Thanks For all the Fish* (4th book in the *Hitch Hiker's Guide to the Galaxy* series, 1984), Ch.31

2 Hasta la vista, baby.
Arnold Schwarzenegger (b.1947), U.S. actor: the Terminator (Arnold Schwarzenegger), in *Terminator 2: Judgment Day* (film; written, directed and produced by James Cameron, 1991)

3 Faithless is he that says farewell when the road darkens.
J.R.R. Tolkien (1892–1973), British novelist and scholar: the dwarf Gimli, in *The Fellowship of the Ring* (Pt.1 of *The Lord of the Rings* trilogy) (1954), Bk.2, Ch.3

FARMING

1 There is, of course, a gold mine or a buried treasure on every mortgaged homestead. Whether the farmer ever digs for it or not, it is there, haunting his daydreams when the burden of debt is most unbearable.
Fawn M. Brodie (1915–1981), U.S. biographer: *No Man Knows My History* (1945), Ch.2

2 There are only three things that can kill a farmer: lightning, rolling over in a tractor, and old age.
Bill Bryson (b.1951), U.S. author and journalist: *The Lost Continent: Travels in Small Town America* (1989), Ch.4

FASCISM

1 A particularly nasty nationalism has gained ground in England. ... This is the old fascism of Oswald Mosley presented today in a new garb by the National Front. If any organisation has made a thorough and unscrupulous use of the decline of the British Empire it has been the fascist leaders of the National Front.

Tariq Ali (b.1943), Pakistani-born British activist and author: *1968 and After: Inside the Revolution* (1978), Ch.6

2 Fascism is not in itself a new order of society. It is the future refusing to be born.

Aneurin Bevan (1897–1960), British Labour politician: quoted in *Aneurin Bevan* by Michael Foot (1962), Vol.I, Ch.10

3 Yes, I believe very strongly in fascism. The only way we can speed up the sort of liberalism that's hanging foul in the air at the moment is to speed up the progress of a right-wing, totally dictatorial tyranny and get it over as fast as possible. People have always responded with greater efficiency under a regimental leadership. A liberal wastes time saying, 'Well, now, what ideas have you got?' Show them what to do, for God's sake. If you don't, nothing will get done. I can't stand people just hanging about.

David Bowie (b.1947), British rock musician: interview, Feb. 1976, rep. in *Bowie In His Own Words* (ed. Miles, 1980), 'Politics'. Bowie had earlier voiced similar opinions in an interview in Aug. 1975, though he later repudiated his remarks, which he called 'glib, theatrical observations', and called himself 'apolitical'

4 I have often thought that if a rational Fascist dictatorship were to exist, then it would choose the American system.

Noam Chomsky (b.1928), U.S. linguist and political analyst: *Language and Responsibility* (with Mitsou Ronat, 1979), Pt.1, Ch.1

5 The strategic adversary is fascism ... the fascism in us all, in our heads and in our everyday behaviour, the fascism that causes us to love power, to desire the very thing that dominates and exploits us.

Michel Foucault (1926–1984), French philosopher: preface to *Anti-Oedipus* by Gilles Deleuze and Félix Guattari (1972)

6 When the bystanders see an elephant coming down the street, it is idle to tell them it is a pleasant Sunday afternoon outing organised by the Young Men's Christian Association. We were a distinctive movement of intense national patriotism, but in the age of fascism it was clearly jejune and possibly dishonest to deny that we were fascist.

Oswald Mosley (1896–1980), British fascist leader: *My Life* (1968), Ch.16. In the same chapter, Mosley wrote: 'Fascism does not exist at present, not because it has been answered, but because it belongs to the epoch before the Second World War. Since that period science has presented us with a new set of facts, the errors of fascism have provided their lessons, and nationalism has been extended to a European patriotism'

7 Fascism is not defined by the number of its victims, but by the way it kills them.

Jean-Paul Sartre (1905–1980), French philosopher and author on the execution of Julius and Ethel Rosenberg, in *Libération* (Paris), 22 June 1953

FASHION

1 I would like to be remembered as the person who created a modern elegance.

Giorgio Armani (b.1935), Italian fashion designer: interview in *The Guardian* (London), 4 Feb. 1995

2 I never cared for fashion much, amusing little seams and witty little pleats: it was the girls I liked.

David Bailey (b.1938), British photographer: in *The Independent* (London), 5 Nov. 1990

3 Fashions are born and they die too quickly for anyone to learn to love them.

Bettina Ballard (1903–1961), U.S. editor: *In My Fashion* (1960), Ch.1

4 Fashion is primitive in its insistence on exhibitionism, which withers in isolation. The catwalk fashion show with its incandescent hype is its apotheosis. A ritualized gathering of connoisseurs and the spoilt at a spotlit parade of snazzy pulchritude, it is an industrialized version of the pagan festivals of renewal. At the end of each seasonal display, a priesthood is enjoined to carry news of the omens to the masses.

Stephen Bayley (b.1951), British design critic: *Taste* (1991), Pt.2, 'Fashion: Being and Dressing'

5 Fashion – turn to the left;
fashion – turn to the right.

David Bowie (b.1947), British rock musician: 'Fashion' (song), on the album *Scary Monsters and Super Creeps* (1980)

6 Fashion is made to become unfashionable.

Coco Chanel (1883–1971), French *couturière*: in *Life* (New York), 19 Aug. 1957

7 Fashion is architecture: it is a matter of proportions.

Coco Chanel: quoted in *Coco Chanel: Her Life, Her Secrets* by Marcel Haedrich (1971), Ch.21

8 Fashion is like the ashes left behind by the uniquely shaped flames of the fire, the trace alone revealing that a fire actually took place.

Paul de Man (1919–1983), Belgian-born U.S. literary critic: 'Literary History and Literary Modernity', lecture, Sept. 1969, rep. in *Blindness and Insight* (1971, rev.1983)

9 Only the minute and the future are interesting in fashion – it exists to be destroyed. If everybody did everything with respect, you'd go nowhere.

Karl Lagerfeld (b.1938), German-born French fashion designer: quoted in *Vanity Fair* (New York), Feb. 1992

10 Fashion designers must give a social reflection of the things which are going on. Fashion is a kind of communication. It's a language without words. Fashion is about attitude, not hemlines.
Helmut Lang (b.1956), Austrian fashion designer: interview in *i-D* (London), Dec. 1993

11 People ask how can a Jewish kid from the Bronx do preppy clothes? Does it have to do with class and money? It has to do with dreams.
Ralph Lauren (b.1939), U.S. fashion designer: in the *International Herald Tribune* (Paris), 7 April 1992

12 The fashion industry has taught me insanity.
Kristen McMenamy (b.1965), U.S. model: interview in *i-D* (London), June 1993

13 The pursuit of Fashion is the attempt of the middle class to co-opt tragedy. In adopting the clothing, speech, and personal habits of those in straitened, dangerous, or pitiful circumstances, the middle class seeks to have what it feels to be the exigent and nonequivocal experiences had by those it emulates.
David Mamet (b.1947), U.S. playwright: *Writing in Restaurants* (1986), 'Exuvial Magic: an Essay Concerning Fashion'

14 It pains me physically to see a woman victimized, rendered pathetic, by fashion.
Yves Saint Laurent (b.1936), French fashion designer: interview in *Ritz* (London), No.85, 1984. In the same article, Saint Laurent described fashion as a 'kind of vitamin for style'

15 Fashion is born by small facts, trends, or even politics, never by trying to make little pleats and furbelows, by trinkets, by clothes easy to copy, or by the shortening or lengthening of a skirt.
Elsa Schiaparelli (1890–1973), Italian fashion designer: *Shocking Life* (1954), Ch.9

16 Fashion is really about being naked.
Vivienne Westwood (b.1941), British fashion designer: quoted in *Fashion and Perversity* by Fred Vermorel (1996), Pt.1

17 The great attraction of fashion is that it diverted attention from the insoluble problems of beauty and provided an easy way – which money could buy ... to a simply stated, easily reproduced ideal of beauty, however temporary that ideal.
Theodore Zeldin (b.1923), U.S. author: quoted in *Beauty in History* by Arthur Marwick (1988), Pt.1, Ch.2

See also HAUTE COUTURE; MODELS

FATHERS

1 A father is always making his baby into a little woman. And when she is a woman he turns her back again.
Enid Bagnold (1889–1981), British novelist and playwright: *Autobiography* (1969), Ch.4

2 As my bones grew, they did hurt
They hurt really bad.
I tried hard to have a father
But instead I had a dad.
Kurt Cobain (1967–1994), U.S. rock musician: 'Serve the Servants' (song), on the album *In Utero* (Nirvana, 1991)

3 If the new American father feels bewildered and even defeated, let him take comfort from the fact that whatever he does in any fathering situation has a fifty percent chance of being right.
Bill Cosby (b.1937), U.S. comedian and actor: *Fatherhood* (1986), Ch.5

4 Like many other women, I could not understand why every man who changed a diaper has felt impelled, in recent years, to write a book about it.
Barbara Ehrenreich (b.1941), U.S. author and columnist: 'Wimps', first publ. in the *New York Times*, 1985, rep. in *The Worst Years of Our Lives* (1991)

5 A man knows when he is growing old because he begins to look like his father.
Gabriel García Márquez (b.1928), Colombian author: *Love in the Time of Cholera* (1985; tr.1988), p.170 of Penguin edn. (1989)

6 To be a successful father ... there's one absolute rule: when you have a kid, don't look at it for the first two years.
Ernest Hemingway (1899–1961), U.S. author: quoted in *Papa Hemingway* by A.E. Hotchner (1966), Pt.2, Ch.5

7 There must be many fathers around the country who have experienced the cruellest, most crushing rejection of all: their children have ended up supporting the wrong team.
Nick Hornby (b.1957), British author: *Fever Pitch* (1992), '1976–1986: My Brother'

8 The thing to remember about fathers is,
they're men.
A girl has to keep it in mind:
They are dragon-seekers, bent on improbable
rescues.
Scratch any father, you find
Someone chock-full of qualms and romantic
terrors,
Believing change is a threat –

Like your first shoes with heels on, like your first bicycle
It took such months to get.
Phyllis McGinley (1905–1978), U.S. poet and author: 'Girl's-Eye View of Relatives: First Lesson', publ. in *Times Three* (1960)

9 I stopped loving my father a long time ago. What remained was the slavery to a pattern.
Anaïs Nin (1903–1977), Franco-American novelist and diarist: *Under a Glass Bell* (1948), 'Birth'

10 It doesn't matter who my father was; it matters who I remember he was.
Anne Sexton (1928–1974), U.S. poet: journal entry, 1 Jan. 1972, in 'A Small Journal', publ. in *The Poet's Story* (ed. Howard Moss, 1974)

11 It no longer bothers me that I may be constantly searching for father figures; by this time, I have found several and dearly enjoyed knowing them all.
Alice Walker (b.1944), U.S. author and critic: 'In Search of Zora Neale Hurston', publ. in *Ms.* (New York) March 1975, rep. in *In Search of Our Mothers' Gardens* (1983), 'Looking for Zora'

See also Pasolini on PARENTS

FAULTS

1 Both men and women are fallible. The difference is, women know it.
Eleanor Bron (b.1934), British actress and author: in *The Times* (London), 28 July 1992

2 We all carry within us our places of exile, our crimes, and our ravages. But our task is not to unleash them on the world; it is to fight them in ourselves and in others.
Albert Camus (1913–1960), French-Algerian philosopher and author: *The Rebel* (1951; tr.1953), Pt.5, 'Moderation and Excess'

3 The organizations of men, like men themselves, seem subject to deafness, nearsightedness, lameness, and involuntary cruelty. We seem tragically unable to help one another, to understand one another.
John Cheever (1912–1982), U.S. author: journal entry, 1963, in *John Cheever: The Journals* (ed. Robert Gottlieb, 1991), 'The Sixties'

4 It is always well to accept your own shortcomings with candor but to regard those of your friends with polite incredulity.
Russell Lynes (1910–1991), U.S. editor and critic: 'The Art of Accepting', publ. in *Vogue* (New York), 1 Sept. 1952

5 If I have any justification for having lived it's simply, I'm nothing but faults, failures and so on, but I have tried to make a good pair of shoes. There's some value in that.

Arthur Miller (b.1915), U.S. playwright: interview in *Marxism Today* (London), Jan. 1988

6 The essence of a man is found in his faults.
(*La verité d'un homme ce sont ses erreurs*.)
Francis Picabia (1878–1953), French painter and poet: '591' (Paris), 21 Jan. 1952, rep. in *Écrits* Vol.II (ed. Olivier Revault d'Allones and Dominique Bouissou, 1978), '1950–1953'

FAUX-PAS

1 A gaffe is when a politician tells the truth.
Michael Kinsley (b.1951), U.S. journalist: in *The Guardian* (London), 14 Jan. 1992

2 Dentopedalogy is the science of opening your mouth and putting your foot in it. I've been practising it for years.
Prince Philip, Duke of Edinburgh (b.1921): address to General Dental Council, quoted in *Time* (New York), 21 Nov. 1960

FAVOURS

1 Go ahead. Make my day.
Clint Eastwood (b.1930), U.S. actor and film-maker: Harry Callahan (Clint Eastwood), in *Sudden Impact* (film; screenplay by Joseph Stinson; produced and directed by Clint Eastwood, 1983)

2 The pleasure we derive from doing favors is partly in the feeling it gives us that we are not altogether worthless. It is a pleasant surprise to ourselves.
Eric Hoffer (1902–1983), U.S. philosopher: *The Passionate State of Mind* (1955), Aph.113

FEAR

1 By the time we are women, fear is as familiar to us as air. It is our element. We live in it, we inhale it, we exhale it, and most of the time we do not even notice it. Instead of 'I am afraid,' we say, 'I don't want to,' or 'I don't know how,' or 'I can't.'
Andrea Dworkin (b.1946), U.S. feminist critic: 'The Sexual Politics of Fear and Courage', speech, 12 March 1975, Queens College, City University of New York, publ. in *Our Blood* (1976), Ch.5

2 The truth is that there is no terror untempered by some great moral idea.
Jean-Luc Godard (b.1930), French film-maker and author: 'Strangers on a Train', first publ. in *Cahiers du Cinéma* (Paris), 10 March 1952, rep. in *Godard on Godard* (ed./tr. Tom Milne, 1968)

3 There is no terror in a bang, only in the anticipation of it.
Alfred Hitchcock (1899–1980), British film-maker: quoted in *Halliwell's Filmgoer's Companion* (ed. Leslie Halliwell, 1984)

4 *In order to set contemporary man free from fear of himself, of the world, of others, of earthly powers, of oppressive systems, in order to set him free from every manifestation of a servile fear before that 'prevailing force' which believers call God, it is necessary to pray fervently that he will bear and cultivate in his heart that true fear of God, which is the beginning of wisdom.*
Pope John Paul II [Karol Wojtyla] (b.1920), Polish ecclesiastic: *Crossing the Threshold of Hope* (1994), 'Crossing the Threshold of Hope'

5 People react to fear, not love – they don't teach that in Sunday School, but it's true.
Richard Nixon (1913–1992), U.S. Republican politician and president: quoted in prologue to *Before the Fall* by William Safire (1975)

6 Fear is the main source of superstition, and one of the main sources of cruelty. To conquer fear is the beginning of wisdom, in the pursuit of truth as in the endeavour after a worthy manner of life.
Bertrand Russell (1872–1970), British philosopher and mathematician: *Unpopular Essays* (1950), 'An Outline of Intellectual Rubbish'

FEASTS & FESTIVITIES

1 The only way to spend New Year's Eve is either quietly with friends or in a brothel. Otherwise when the evening ends and people pair off, someone is bound to be left in tears.
W.H. Auden (1907–1973), Anglo-American poet: *The Table Talk of W.H. Auden* (comp. Alan Ansen, ed. Nicholas Jenkins, 1990), '31 December, 1947'

2 Christmas and Easter can be subjects for poetry, but Good Friday, like Auschwitz, cannot. The reality is so horrible, it is not surprising that people should have found it a stumbling block to faith.
W.H. Auden: *A Certain World* (1970), 'Friday, Good'

3 There is nothing funny about Halloween. This sarcastic festival reflects, rather, an infernal demand for revenge by children on the adult world.
Jean Baudrillard (b.1929), French semiologist: *America* (1986; tr.1988) 'Astral America'

See also CHRISTMAS

FEMININITY

1 Femininity appears to be one of those pivotal qualities that is so important no one can define it.
Caroline Bird (b.1915), U.S. author and social commentator: *Born Female* (1968), Ch.11

2 The feminine mystique has succeeded in burying millions of American women alive.
Betty Friedan (b.1921), U.S. feminist writer: *The Feminine Mystique* (1963), Ch.13

3 Older women can afford to agree that femininity is a charade, a matter of coloured hair, écru lace and whalebones, the kind of slap and tat that transvestites are in love with, and no more.
Germaine Greer (b.1939), Australian feminist writer: *The Change: Women, Ageing and the Menopause* (1991), Ch.2

4 Prim, pink-breasted, feminine, she nurses Chocolate Fancies in rose-papered rooms.
Sylvia Plath (1932–1963), U.S. poet: 'Female Author', publ. in *Collected Poems* (ed. Ted Hughes, 1981), 'Juvenilia'

FEMINISM

1 The sadness of the women's movement is that they don't allow the necessity of love. See, I don't personally trust any revolution where love is not allowed.
Maya Angelou (b.1928), U.S. author: 'Listening to Maya Angelou', first publ. in *California Living*, 14 May 1975, rep. in *Conversations with Maya Angelou* (ed. Jeffrey M. Elliot, 1989)

2 Feminism is an entire world view or gestalt, not just a laundry list of 'women's issues.'
Charlotte Bunch (b.1944), U.S. editor and author: 'Understanding Feminist Theory', publ. in *New Directions for Women* (New York), Sept./Oct. 1981

3 The freedom that women were supposed to have found in the Sixties largely boiled down to easy contraception and abortion; things to make life easier for men, in fact.
Julie Burchill (b.1960), British journalist and author: *Damaged Gods* (1986), 'Born Again Cows'

4 A good part – and definitely the most fun part – of being a feminist is about frightening men.
Julie Burchill: in *Time Out* (London), 16 Nov. 1989

5 Just because we're sisters under the skin doesn't mean we've got much in common.
Angela Carter (1940–1992), British author: in *The Guardian* (London), 25 Oct. 1990

6 One of the reasons for the failure of feminism to dislodge deeply held perceptions of male and female behaviour was its insistence that women were victims, and men powerful patriarchs, which made a travesty of ordinary people's experience of the mutual interdependence of men and women.
Rosalind Coward (b.1953), British author: *Our Treacherous Hearts* (1992), Ch.9

7 The embattled gates to equal rights indeed opened up for modern women, but I sometimes think to myself: 'That is not what I meant by freedom – it is only "social progress"'.
Helene Deutsch (1884–1982), U.S. psychiatrist: *Confrontations With Myself* (1973), Ch.1

8 Women have been taught that, for us, the earth is flat, and that if we venture out, we will fall off the edge. Some of us have ventured out nevertheless, and so far we have not fallen off. It is my faith, my feminist faith, that we will not.
Andrea Dworkin (b.1946), U.S. feminist critic: 'Redefining Nonviolence', speech, 5 April 1975, Boston College, publ. in *Our Blood* (1976), Ch.6, Sct.2

9 Feminism is hated because women are hated. Anti-feminism is a direct expression of misogyny; it is the political defense of women hating.
Andrea Dworkin: *Right-Wing Women* (1978), Ch.6

10 'I hate discussions of feminism that end up with who does the dishes,' she said. So do I. But at the end, there are always the damned dishes.
Marilyn French (b.1929), U.S. author and critic: Isolde, in *The Women's Room* (1977), Ch.1, Sct.21

11 Surely women's liberation is a most unpromising panacea. But the movement is working politically, because our sexuality is so confused, our masculinity so uncertain, and our families so beleaguered that no one knows what they are for or how they are sustained.
George Gilder (b.1939), U.S. editor, speechwriter and author: introduction to *Sexual Suicide* (1973)

12 Women's liberation, if it abolishes the patriarchal family, will abolish a necessary substructure of the authoritarian state, and once that withers away Marx will have come true willy-nilly, so let's get on with it.
Germaine Greer (b.1939), Australian feminist writer: *The Female Eunuch* (1970), 'Revolution'

13 Movements born in hatred very quickly take on the characteristics of the thing they oppose.
J.S. Habgood (b.1927), British ecclesiastic and archbishop of York: of ultra-feminists, quoted in *The Observer* (London), 4 May 1986

14 Liberation is an evershifting horizon, a total ideology that can never fulfill its promises. ... It has the therapeutic quality of providing emotionally charged rituals of solidarity in hatred – it is the amphetamine of its believers.
Arianna Huffington [formerly Stassinopoulos] (b.1950), Greek author: *The Female Woman* (1973), 'The Liberated Woman? ... and Her Liberators'

15 *Contemporary feminism* finds its roots in the absence of true respect for woman. Revealed truth teaches us something different. Respect for woman, amazement at the mystery of womanhood, and finally the nuptial love of God Himself and of Christ, as expressed in the Redemption, are all elements that have never been completely absent in the faith and life of the Church. This can be seen in a rich tradition of customs and practices that, regrettably, is nowadays being eroded. In our civilization woman has become, before all else, an object of pleasure.
Pope John Paul II [Karol Wojtyla] (b.1920), Polish ecclesiastic: *Crossing the Threshold of Hope* (1994), 'Women'

16 I am a feminist, and what that means to me is much the same as the meaning of the fact that I am Black: it means that I must undertake to love myself and to respect myself as though my very life depends upon self-love and self-respect.
June Jordan (b.1936), U.S. poet and civil rights activist: 'Where is the Love?', address, 1978, Black Writers' Conference, Howard University, publ. in *Moving Towards Home: Political Essays* (1989)

17 I became a feminist as an alternative to becoming a masochist.
Sally Kempton (b.1943), U.S. author: 'Cutting Loose', publ. in *Esquire* (New York), July 1970

18 Women's liberation is the liberation of the feminine in the man and the masculine in the woman.
Corita Kent (b.1918), U.S. artist: quoted in the *Los Angeles Times*, 11 July 1974

19 The people I'm furious with are the Women's Liberationists. They keep getting up on soapboxes and proclaiming women are brighter than men. That's true, but it should be kept quiet or it ruins the whole racket.
Anita Loos (1893–1981), U.S. novelist and screenwriter: quoted in *The Observer* (London), 30 Dec. 1973

20 Oh, I believe in everything they do – but I was too impatient. I couldn't wait.
Madonna (b.1958), U.S. singer and actress: of feminists, quoted in *Sex and Sensibility* by Julie Burchill (1992), 'Madonna'

21 We need a new kind of feminism, one that stresses personal responsibility and is open to art and sex in all their dark, unconsoling mysteries. The feminist of the *fin de siècle* will be bawdy, streetwise, and on-the-spot confrontational, in the prankish Sixties way.
Camille Paglia (b.1947), U.S. author and critic: introduction to *Sex, Art, and American Culture* (1992)

22 There must be a world revolution which puts an end to all materialistic conditions hindering woman from performing her natural role in life

and driving her to carry out man's duties in order to be equal in rights.

Muhammar Qaddafi (b.1938), Libyan leader: *The Green Book* (1976–79), Pt.3, 'Woman'

23 The modern woman is the curse of the universe. A disaster, that's what. She thinks that before her arrival on the scene no woman ever did anything worthwhile before, no woman was ever liberated until her time, no woman really ever amounted to anything.

Adela Rogers St. Johns (1894–1988), U.S. journalist: quoted in the *Los Angeles Herald-Examiner*, 13 Oct. 1974

See also Paglia on MADONNA; Paglia on WOMEN

FEMINISM: and Men

1 The fundamental impulse of the movement is neither masturbatory nor concretely lesbian – although it of course offers warm houseroom to both these possibilities; it is an impulse to maidenhood – to that condition in which a woman might pretend to a false fear or loathing of the penis in order to escape from any responsibility for the pleasure and well-being of the man who possesses it.

Midge Decter (b.1927), U.S. author, editor and social critic: *The New Chastity and Other Arguments Against Women's Liberation* (1972), Ch.2

2 Men who want to support women in our struggle for freedom and justice should understand that it is not terrifically important to us that they learn to cry; it is important to us that they stop the crimes of violence against us.

Andrea Dworkin (b.1946), U.S. feminist critic: 'The Rape Atrocity and the Boy Next Door', speech, 1 March 1975, at State University of New York, Stony Brook, publ. in *Our Blood* (1976), Ch.4

3 There has come into existence, chiefly in America, a breed of men who claim to be feminists. They imagine that they have understood 'what women want' and that they are capable of giving it to them. They help with the dishes at home and make their own coffee in the office, basking the while in the refulgent consciousness of virtue. ... Such men are apt to think of the true male feminists as utterly chauvinistic.

Germaine Greer (b.1939), Australian feminist writer: 'Eternal War: Strindberg's View of Sex', first publ. in *The Spectator* (London), 3 June 1978, rep. in *The Madwoman's Underclothes* (1986)

4 Women's Liberation is just a lot of foolishness. It's the men who are discriminated against. They can't bear children. And no one's likely to do anything about that.

Golda Meir (1898–1978), Israeli politician and prime minister: quoted in *Newsweek* (New York), 23 Oct. 1972

5 If I were a woman, I would never trust men who say they are feminists. Either they are acting out of guilt, trying to establish credentials, or they think they might be able to pick up more girls. If I were a woman, I would say, go away and have your first period. Then come back and tell me you are a feminist.

David Thomas (b.1959), British editor: in *The Guardian/Elle Supplement* (London), 9 Jan. 1992

FERTILITY

1 I don't know what it is about fecundity that so appals. I suppose it is the teeming evidence that birth and growth, which we value, are ubiquitous and blind, that life itself is so astonishingly cheap, that nature is as careless as it is bountiful, and that with extravagance goes a crushing waste that will one day include our own cheap lives.

Annie Dillard (b.1945), U.S. author and poet: *Pilgrim at Tinker Creek* (1974), Ch.10

2 The management of fertility is one of the most important functions of adulthood.

Germaine Greer (b.1939), Australian feminist writer: *Sex and Destiny* (1984), Ch.2

3 Virginity is now a mere preamble or waiting room to be got out of as soon as possible; it is without significance. Old age is similarly a waiting room, where you go after life's over and wait for cancer or a stroke. The years before and after the menstrual years are vestigial: the only meaningful condition left to women is that of fruitfulness.

Ursula K. Le Guin (b.1929), U.S. author: 'The Space Crone', publ. in *The Co-Evolution Quarterly*, summer 1976, rep. in *Dancing at the Edge of the World* (1989)

FESTIVALS

1 Is this the way they say the future's meant to feel?
Or just 20,000 people standing in a field.
And I don't quite understand just what this feeling is.
But that's okay 'cos we're all sorted out for E's and wizz.

Jarvis Cocker (b.1963), British rock musician: 'Sorted for E's and Wizz' (song), on the album *Different Class* (Pulp, 1995)

2 I realize that to many ageing flower children it is heresy to say it, but the Woodstock festival was a catastrophe mitigated only by the camaraderie often seen at floods or train crashes.

Kieran Crowley, U.S. journalist: quoted in *The Daily Telegraph* (London), 18 Aug. 1989

FICTION

1 We live in a world ruled by fictions of every kind – mass merchandising, advertising, politics conducted as a branch of advertising, the instant translation of science and technology into popular imagery, the increasing blurring and intermingling of identities within the realm of consumer goods, the preempting of any free or original imaginative response to experience by the television screen. We live inside an enormous novel. For the writer in particular it is less and less necessary for him to invent the fictional content of his novel. The fiction is already there. The writer's task is to invent the reality.

J.G. Ballard (b.1930), British novelist: introduction (1974) to the French edition of *Crash* (1973)

2 Writing novels preserves you in a state of innocence – a lot passes you by – simply because your attention is otherwise diverted.

Anita Brookner (b.1938), British novelist and art historian: *Novelists in Interview* (ed. John Haffenden, 1985)

3 If you write fiction you are, in a sense, corrupted. There's a tremendous corruptibility for the fiction writer because you're dealing mainly with sex and violence. These remain the basic themes, they're the basic themes of Shakespeare whether you like it or not.

Anthony Burgess (1917–1993), British author and critic: interview in *The Face* (London), Dec. 1984

4 If I were a writer, how I would enjoy being told the novel is dead. How liberating to work in the margins, outside a central perception. You are the ghoul of literature. Lovely.

Don DeLillo (b.1926), U.S. author: Owen Brademas, in *The Names* (1982), Ch.4

5 Writing a novel is not merely going on a shopping expedition across the border to an unreal land: it is hours and years spent in the factories, the streets, the cathedrals of the imagination.

Janet Frame (b.1924), New Zealand novelist and poet: *The Envoy from Mirror City* (first volume of autobiography, 1985), Ch.20

6 By its very nature, the novel indicates that we are becoming. There is no final solution. There is no last word.

Carlos Fuentes (b.1928), Mexican novelist and short-story writer: in *The Guardian* (London), 24 Feb.1989

7 Novelists do not write as birds sing, by the push of nature. It is part of the job that there should be much routine and some daily stuff on the level of carpentry.

William Golding (1911–1993), British author: 'Rough Magic', lecture, 16 Feb. 1977, Canterbury, rep. in *A Moving Target* (1982)

8 You know that fiction, prose rather, is possibly the roughest trade of all in writing. You do not have the reference, the old important reference. You have the sheet of blank paper, the pencil, and the obligation to invent truer than things can be true. You have to take what is not palpable and make it completely palpable and also have it seem normal and so that it can become a part of experience of the person who reads it.

Ernest Hemingway (1899–1961), U.S. author: letter, 24 Sept. 1954, to the critic Bernard Berenson, publ. in *Selected Letters* (ed. Carlos Baker, 1981)

9 It's with bad sentiments that one makes good novels.

Aldous Huxley (1894–1963), British author: letter, 10 July 1962, quoted in *Aldous Huxley: the Critical Heritage* (ed. Donald Watt, 1975). Huxley believed this to be the explanation for why his novel *Island* – published that year and greatly criticized – was 'so inadequate'

10 A novel that does not uncover a hitherto unknown segment of existence is immoral. Knowledge is the novel's only morality.

Milan Kundera (b.1929), Czech-born French author and critic: in the *New York Review of Books*, 19 July 1984

11 For a novelist, a given historic situation is an *anthropologic laboratory* in which he explores his basic question: *What is human existence?*

Milan Kundera: postscript to 1986 edn. of *Life Is Elsewhere* (1973)

12 The really great novel ... tends to be the exact negative of its author's life.

André Maurois (1885–1967), French author and critic: *The Art of Writing* (1960), 'The Writer's Craft', Sct.4

13 A novelist is, like all mortals, more fully at home on the surface of the present than in the ooze of the past.

Vladimir Nabokov (1899–1977), Russian-born U.S. novelist and poet: *Strong Opinions* (1973), Ch.20

14 For a Jewish Puritan of the middle class, the novel is serious, the novel is work, the novel is conscientious application – why, the novel is practically the retail business all over again.

Howard Nemerov (1920–1991), U.S. poet, novelist and critic: *Journal of the Fictive Life* (1965), 'Reflexions of the Novelist Felix Ledger', Sct.C

15 The first sentence of every novel should be: 'Trust me, this will take time but there is order

here, very faint, very human.' Meander if you want to get to town.

Michael Ondaatje (b.1943), Canadian novelist: *In the Skin of a Lion* (1987), Bk.2, 'Palace of Purification'

16 The acceptance that all that is solid has melted into the air, that reality and morality are not givens but imperfect human constructs, is the point from which fiction begins.

Salman Rushdie (b.1947), Indian-born British author: 'Is Nothing Sacred?', Herbert Read Memorial Lecture (read by Harold Pinter), 6 Feb. 1990, publ. in *The Guardian* (London), 7 Feb. 1990

17 Writing fiction has become a priestly business in countries that have lost their faith.

Gore Vidal (b.1925), U.S. novelist and critic: in *The Independent* (London), 16 Aug. 1989

See also Greene on JOURNALISM; Doctorow on NARRATIVE

FICTION: Science Fiction

1 Science fiction writers foresee the inevitable, and although problems and catastrophes may be inevitable, solutions are not.

Isaac Asimov (1920–1992), Russian-born U.S. author: 'How Easy to See the Future', first publ. in *Natural History* (New York), April 1975, rep. in *Asimov on Science Fiction* (1981)

2 Individual science fiction stories may seem as trivial as ever to the blinder critics and philosophers of today – but the core of science fiction, its essence ... has become crucial to our salvation if we are to be saved at all.

Isaac Asimov: 'My Own View', first publ. in *The Encyclopedia of Science Fiction* (ed. Robert Holdstock, 1978), rep. in *Asimov on Science Fiction* (1981)

3 Everything is becoming science fiction. From the margins of an almost invisible literature has sprung the intact reality of the 20th century.

J.G. Ballard (b.1930), British author: 'Fictions of Every Kind', first publ. in *Books and Bookmen* (London) Feb. 1971, rep. in *Re/Search* (San Francisco) No.8/9, 1984. Ballard continued: 'Even the worst science fiction is better ... than the best conventional fiction. The future is a better key to the present than the past'

4 Science fiction writers, I am sorry to say, really do not know anything. We can't talk about science, because our knowledge of it is limited and unofficial, and usually our fiction is dreadful.

Philip K. Dick (1928–1982), U.S. science fiction writer: *I Hope I Shall Arrive Soon* (1986), 'How to Build a Universe That Doesn't Fall Apart Two Days Later'

5 The fancy that extraterrestrial life is by definition of a higher order than our own is one that soothes all children, and many writers.

Joan Didion (b.1934), U.S. essayist: *The White Album* (1979), 'Doris Lessing'

6 A predilection for genre fiction is symptomatic of a kind of arrested development.

Thomas M. Disch (b.1940), U.S. author and ex-science fiction writer: quoted in *The Face* (London), March 1986

7 In sci-fi convention, life-forms that hadn't developed space travel were mere prehistory – horse-shoe crabs of the cosmic scene – and something of the humiliation of being stuck on a provincial planet in a galactic backwater has stayed with me ever since.

Barbara Ehrenreich (b.1941), U.S. author and columnist: 'Blocking the Gates to Heaven' (1986), rep. in *The Worst Years of Our Lives* (1991)

8 I love *E.T.* 'cos it reminds me of me. Someone from another world coming down and you becoming friends with them and this person is, like, 800 years old and he's filling you with all kinds of wisdom and he can teach you how to fly. That whole fantasy thing which I think is great. I mean, who don't wanna fly?

Michael Jackson (b.1958), U.S. singer and dancer: interview in *Smash Hits* (London), 20 Jan. 1983. Jackson collaborated with *E.T.* director Steven Spielberg on the 'E.T. Storybook' album

9 What the hell is nostalgia doing in a science-fiction film? With the whole universe and all the future to play in, Lucas took his marvelous toys and crawled under the fringed cloth on the parlor table, back into a nice safe hideyhole, along with Flash Gordon and the Cowardly Lion and Huck Skywalker and the Flying Aces and the Hitler Jugend. If there's a message there, I don't think I want to hear it.

Ursula K. Le Guin (b.1929), U.S. author: of the film *Star Wars*, in 'Close Encounters, Star Wars, and the Tertium Quid', first publ. in *Future*, Aug. 1978, rep. in *Dancing at the Edge of the World* (1989)

10 If science fiction is the mythology of modern technology, then its myth is tragic.

Ursula K. Le Guin: 'The Carrier Bag Theory of Fiction', written 1986, first publ. in *Women of Vision* (ed. Denise M. Du Pont, 1988), rep. in *Dancing at the Edge of the World* (1989)

11 Space or science fiction has become a dialect for our time.

Doris Lessing (b.1919), British novelist: in *The Guardian* (London), 7 Nov. 1988

12 May the Force be with you!

George Lucas (b.1944), U.S. film-maker: Ben 'Obi-wan' Kenobi (Alec Guinness), in *Star Wars* (film; written and directed by George Lucas, 1977)

13 The question grows more troubling with each passing year: how much of what yesterday's science fiction regarded as unspeakably dreadful has become today's award-winning research?
Theodore Roszak (b.1933), U.S. social critic: *Where the Wasteland Ends* (1972), Ch.7

14 Science fiction films are not about science. They are about disaster, which is one of the oldest subjects of art.
Susan Sontag (b.1933), U.S. essayist: *Against Interpretation* (1966), 'The Imagination of Disaster'

15 If poets are the unacknowledged legislators of the world, science-fiction writers are its court jesters. We are Wise Fools who can leap, caper, utter prophecies, and scratch ourselves in public. We can play with Big Ideas because the garish motley of our pulp origins makes us seem harmless.
Bruce Sterling (b.1954), U.S. science fiction author: preface to William Gibson's *Burning Chrome* (1986)

16 I have been a soreheaded occupant of a file drawer labeled 'Science Fiction' ... and I would like out, particularly since so many serious critics regularly mistake the drawer for a urinal.
Kurt Vonnegut (b.1922), U.S. novelist: *Wampeters, Foma and Granfallons* (1974), 'Science Fiction'

FICTION: Thrillers

1 It is just possible that the tensions in a novel of murder are the simplest and yet most complete pattern of the tensions on which we live in this generation.
Raymond Chandler (1888–1959), U.S. author: letter, 17 Oct. 1948, to critic James Sandoe, publ. in *Raymond Chandler Speaking* (ed. Dorothy Gardiner and Kathrine S. Walker, 1962)

2 Let us never accept the point of view that mysteries are written by hacks. The poorest of us shed our blood over every chapter. The best of us start from scratch with every new book.
Raymond Chandler: letter, Oct. 1955, publ. in *Raymond Chandler Speaking* (ed. Dorothy Gardiner and Kathrine S. Walker, 1962)

3 We ignore thriller writers at our peril. Their genre is the political condition. They massage our dreams and magnify our nightmares. If it is true that we always need enemies, then we will always need writers of fiction to encode our fears and fantasies.
Daniel Easterman (b.1949), Irish author: in *Million Magazine* (London), Sept./Oct. 1991

4 The mystery form is like gymnastic equipment: you can grasp hold of it and show off what you can do.
Mickey Friedman (b.1944), U.S. author: in the *International Herald Tribune* (Paris), 31 Jan. 1990

5 The main question raised by the thriller is not what kind of world we live in, or what reality is like, but what it has done to us.
Ralph Harper (b.1915), U.S. cleric and author: *The World of the Thriller* (1969), Pt.3, 'The Emotions'

6 What the detective story is about is not murder but the restoration of order.
P.D. James (b.1920), British author: interview in *The Face* (London), Dec. 1986

7 For decades to come the spy world will continue to be the collective couch where the subconscious of each nation is confessed.
John Le Carré (b.1931), British author: quoted in *The Observer* (London), 19 Nov. 1989

8 The detective novel is the art-for-art's-sake of our yawning Philistinism, the classic example of a specialized form of art removed from contact with the life it pretends to build on.
V.S. Pritchett (1900–1997), British author and critic: 'The Roots of Detection', first publ. in the *New Statesman* (London) 16 June 1951, rep. in *Books in General* (1953)

FIN DE SIÈCLE

1 As the end of the century approaches, all our culture is like the culture of flies at the beginning of winter. Having lost their agility, dreamy and demented, they turn slowly about the window in the first icy mists of morning. They give themselves a last wash and brush-up, their ocellated eyes roll, and they fall down the curtains.
Jean Baudrillard (b.1929), French semiologist: *Cool Memories* (1987; tr.1990), Ch.5

2 I confidently predict the collapse of capitalism and the beginning of history. Something will go wrong in the machinery that converts money into money, the banking system will collapse totally, and we will be left having to barter to stay alive. Those who can dig in their garden will have a better chance than the rest. I'll be all right; I've got a few veg.
Margaret Drabble (b.1939), British novelist: predictions for the year, in *The Guardian* (London), 2 Jan. 1993

3 The turn of the century raises expectations. The end of a millennium promises apocalypse and revelation. But at the close of the twentieth century the golden age seems behind us, not ahead. The end game of the 1990s promises neither nirvana nor armageddon, but entropy.
Robert Hewison (b.1943), British cultural historian: *Future Tense* (1990), Ch.1

FINANCE

1 What we now call 'finance' is, I hold, an intellectual perversion of what began as warm human love.
Robert Graves (1895–1985), British poet and novelist: speech, 6 Dec. 1963, London School of Economics, publ. in *Mammon and the Black Goddess* (1965), 'Mammon'

2 Women's battle for financial equality has barely been joined, much less won. Society still traditionally assigns to woman the role of money-handler rather than money-maker, and our assigned specialty is far more likely to be home economics than financial economics.
Paula Nelson (b.1945), U.S. business executive: *The Joy of Money* (1975), Ch.1

3 The Law of Triviality ... briefly stated, it means that the time spent on any item of the agenda will be in inverse proportion to the sum involved.
C. Northcote Parkinson (1909–1993), British historian and political scientist: *Parkinson's Law, or The Pursuit of Progress* (1958), 'High Finance'

4 When it comes to finances, remember that there are no withholding taxes on the wages of sin.
Mae West (1892–1980), U.S. actress: *On Sex, Health and ESP* (1975), 'Last Word'

FLOWERS

1 A perfect beauty of a sunflower! a perfect
    excellent lovely sunflower
existence! a sweet natural eye to the new hip
    moon, woke up alive and
excited grasping in the sunset shadow sunrise
    golden monthly breeze.
Allen Ginsberg (b.1926), U.S. poet: 'Sunflower Sutra', publ. in *Howl and Other Poems* (1956)

2 I hate flowers – I paint them because they're cheaper than models and they don't move.
Georgia O'Keeffe (1887–1986), U.S. artist: quoted in the *New York Herald Tribune*, 18 April 1954, rep. in *Portrait of an Artist* by Laurie Lisle (1986). O'Keeffe – famously a painter of flowers – was responding to the remark, 'How perfect to meet you with flowers in your hands!'

3 Where have all the flowers gone?
Pete Seeger (b.1919), U.S. folk singer and songwriter: 'Where Have All the Flowers Gone?' (song, 1961)

FOLK MUSIC *see under* MUSIC

FOOD

1 Brains evolved after bowels, therefore,

Great assets as fine raiment and good looks
    can be on festive occasions,
they are not essential like artful cooks
    and stalwart digestions.
W.H. Auden (1907–1973), Anglo-American poet: 'Thanksgiving for a Habitat', No.10: 'Tonight at Seven-Thirty', publ. in *About the House* (1965)

2 Sadder than destitution, sadder than a beggar is the man who eats alone in public. Nothing more contradicts the laws of man or beast, for animals always do each other the honour of sharing or disputing each other's food.
Jean Baudrillard (b.1929), French semiologist: *America* (1986; tr.1988), 'New York'

3 We consider the mystery of the truffle. Why is it so highly prized? ... It is digestive, it is sexual, it is a mortality odor.
Saul Bellow (b.1915), U.S. novelist: *It All Adds Up* (1994), 'Winter in Tuscany'

4 Clearly, some time ago makers and consumers of American junk food passed jointly through some kind of sensibility barrier in the endless quest for new taste sensations. Now they are a little like those desperate junkies who have tried every known drug and are finally reduced to mainlining toilet bowl cleanser in an effort to get still higher.
Bill Bryson (b.1951), U.S. author and journalist: *The Lost Continent: Travels in Small Town America* (1989), Ch.3

5 The right diet directs sexual energy into the parts that matter.
Barbara Cartland (b.1901), British novelist: quoted in *The Observer* (London), 11 Jan. 1981

6 Gluttony is an emotional escape, a sign something is eating us.
Peter De Vries (1910–1993), U.S. author: Crystal, in *Comfort Me With Apples* (1956), Ch.15

7 Upscale people are fixated with food simply because they are now able to eat so much of it without getting fat, and the reason they don't get fat is that they maintain a profligate level of calorie expenditure. The very same people whose evenings begin with melted goats cheese ... get up at dawn to run, break for a mid-morning aerobics class, and watch the evening news while racing on a stationary bicycle.
Barbara Ehrenreich (b.1941), U.S. author and columnist: 'Food Worship' (1985), rep. in *The Worst Years of Our Lives* (1991)

8 A cheese may disappoint. It may be dull, it may be naive, it may be oversophisticated. Yet it remains cheese, milk's leap toward immortality.
Clifton Fadiman (b.1904), U.S. essayist: *Any Number Can Play* (1957), p.105

9 Sharing food with another human being is an intimate act that should not be indulged in lightly.

M.F.K. Fisher (b.1908), U.S. culinary writer: *An Alphabet for Gourmets* (1949), 'A is for dining Alone'

10 There is such a thing as food and such a thing as poison. But the damage done by those who pass off poison as food is far less than that done by those who generation after generation convince people that food is poison.

Paul Goodman (1911–1972), U.S. author, poet and critic: *Five Years* (1966), 'Ireland, Spring 1958', Sct.2

11 The act of putting into your mouth what the earth has grown is perhaps your most direct interaction with the earth.

Frances Moore Lappë (b.1944), U.S. ecologist and author: *Diet For A Small Planet* (1971), Pt.1

12 If you're going to America, bring your own food.

Fran Lebowitz (b.1951), U.S. journalist: *Social Studies* (1981), 'Fran Lebowitz's Travel Hints'

13 This is the only country in the world where the food is more dangerous than sex.

Jackie Mason (b.1931), U.S. comic: of England, in *The Daily Telegraph* (London), 17 Feb. 1989

14 On the Continent people have good food; in England people have good table manners.

George Mikes (1912–1987), Hungarian-born British humorist: *How To Be An Alien* (1946), Ch.1, Sct.1. Commenting in 1977 on this oft-quoted remark, Mikes wrote, 'Since then, food in England has improved, table manners have deteriorated. In those days food was hardly ever discussed, it was taboo, like sex' (*How To Be Decadent*)

15 Lunch is for wimps.

Oliver Stone (b.1946), U.S. film-maker: Gordon Gekko (Michael Douglas), in *Wall Street* (film; written by Oliver Stone and Stanley Weiser, directed by Oliver Stone, 1987)

16 All recipes are built on the belief that somewhere at the beginning of the chain there is a cook who does not use them. This is the great nostalgia of our cuisine, ever invoking an absent mother-cook who once laid her hands on the body of the world for us and worked it into food. The promise of every cookbook is that it offers a way back onto her lap.

John Thorne (b.1943), U.S. writer on cookery: 'Cuisine Mécanique', publ. in *The Journal of Gastronomy* (San Francisco), spring 1990

FOOLS

1 In days gone by, we were afraid of dying in dishonour or a state of sin. Nowadays, we are afraid of dying fools. Now the fact is that there is no Extreme Unction to absolve us of foolish-ness. We endure it here on earth as subjective eternity.

Jean Baudrillard (b.1929), French semiologist: *Cool Memories* (1987; tr.1990), Ch.4

2 The wise man who is not heeded is counted a fool, and the fool who proclaims the general folly first and loudest passes for a prophet and Führer, and sometimes it is luckily the other way round as well, or else mankind would long since have perished of stupidity.

Carl Jung (1875–1961), Swiss psychiatrist: *Mysterium Coniunctionis* (1955–6), rep. in *Collected Works* (ed. William McGuire), Vol.XIV (1963), para.783

3 The great God endows His children variously. To some he gives intellect – and they move the earth. To some he allots heart – and the beating pulse of humanity is theirs. But to some He gives only a soul, without intelligence – and these, who never grow up, but remain always His children, are God's fools, kindly, elemental, simple, as if from His palette the Artist of all had taken one color instead of many.

Mary Roberts Rinehart (1876–1958), U.S. author: *Love Stories* (1920), 'God's Fool'

4 Looking foolish does the spirit good. The need not to look foolish is one of youth's many burdens; as we get older we are exempted from more and more, and float upward in our heed-lessness, singing *Gratia Dei sum quod sum*.

John Updike (b.1932), U.S. author and critic: *Self-Consciousness: Memoirs* (1989), Ch.6. *Gratia Dei sum quod sum* ('Thanks be to God that I am what I am') – one of the epigraphs of Updike's volume of memoirs – is inscribed on the tomb of Bishop West in Ely Cathedral.

FOOTBALL *see under* SPORT

GERALD FORD

1 I am a Ford, not a Lincoln.

Gerald Ford (b.1913), U.S. Republican politician and president: address, on taking vice-presidential oath, 6 Dec. 1973, quoted in *A Ford, Not a Lincoln* by Richard Reeves (1975), Ch.2. Ford explained, 'My addresses will never be as eloquent as Lincoln's. But I will do my best to equal his brevity and plain speaking.' Eight months later, Ford was sworn in as president. He told Congress, 'The truth is I am the people's man' (12 Aug. 1974)

2 Jerry Ford is so dumb he can't fart and chew gum at the same time.

Lyndon B. Johnson (1908–1973), U.S. Democratic politician and president: quoted in *A Ford, Not a Lincoln* by Richard Reeves (1975), Ch.1. Reeves alleges that Johnson's remark was 'cleaned up' by 'the late President's aides and history'

FOREIGN POLICY

1 Domestic policy can only defeat us; foreign policy can kill us.
   John F. Kennedy (1917–1963), U.S. Democratic politician and president: quoted in *The Imperial Presidency* by Arthur M. Schlesinger Jr. (1973), Ch. 11, Sct. 7

2 Most foreign policies that history has marked highly, in whatever country, have been originated by leaders who were opposed by experts.
   Henry Kissinger (b. 1923), U.S. Republican politician and secretary of state: *Years of Upheaval* (1982), Ch. 10, 'The Foreign Service'

3 In foreign policy you have to wait twenty-five years to see how it comes out.
   James Reston (b. 1909), U.S. journalist: in the *International Herald Tribune* (Paris), 18 Nov. 1991

4 We are apt to say that a foreign policy is successful only when the country, or at any rate the governing class, is united behind it. In reality, every line of policy is repudiated by a section, often by an influential section, of the country concerned. A foreign minister who waited until everyone agreed with him would have no foreign policy at all.
   A.J.P. Taylor (1906–1990), British historian: *The Trouble Makers* (1957), Ch. 1

See also THE UNITED STATES: FOREIGN POLICY

FOREIGNERS

1 The less sophisticated of my forbears avoided foreigners at all costs, for the very good reason that, in their circles, speaking in tongues was commonly a prelude to snake handling. The more tolerant among us regarded foreign languages as a kind of speech impediment that could be overcome by willpower.
   Barbara Ehrenreich (b. 1941), U.S. author and columnist: 'Language Barrier' (1989), rep. in *The Worst Years of Our Lives* (1991)

2 Xenophobia looks like becoming the mass ideology of the 20th-century *fin-de-siècle*. What holds humanity together today is the denial of what the human race has in common.
   Eric Hobsbawm (b. 1917), British historian: lecture to the American Anthropological Association, rep. in the *New Statesman* (London), 24 April 1992

FORGIVENESS

1 In contrast to revenge, which is the natural, automatic reaction to transgression and which, because of the irreversibility of the action process can be expected and even calculated, the act of forgiving can never be predicted; it is the only reaction that acts in an unexpected way and thus retains, though being a reaction, something of the original character of action.
   Hannah Arendt (1906–1975), German-born U.S. political philosopher: *The Human Condition* (1958), 'Action', Ch. 33

2 Once a woman has forgiven her man, she must not reheat his sins for breakfast.
   Marlene Dietrich (1904–1992), German-born U.S. actress: *Marlene Dietrich's ABC* (1962), 'Forgiveness'

3 'To forgive oneself' – ? No, that doesn't work: we have to *be forgiven*. But we can only believe this is possible if we ourselves can forgive.
   Dag Hammarskjöld (1905–1961), Swedish statesman and secretary-general of U.N.: note written 3 Sept. 1959, publ. in *Markings* (1963), 'Night is Drawing Nigh'

4 The stupid neither forgive nor forget; the naïve forgive and forget; the wise forgive but do not forget.
   Thomas Szasz (b. 1920), U.S. psychiatrist: *The Second Sin* (1973), 'Personal Conduct'

FRANCE

1 Everything ends this way in France. Weddings, christenings, duels, burials, swindlings, affairs of state – everything is a pretext for a good dinner.
   Jean Anouilh (1910–1987), French playwright: Monsieur Orlas, in *Cécile* (1951)

2 The sickly cultural pathos which the whole of France indulges in, that fetishism of the cultural heritage.
   Jean Baudrillard (b. 1929), French semiologist: *America* (1986; tr. 1988), 'Utopia Achieved'

3 God would be perfectly happy in France because he would not be troubled by prayers, observances, blessings, and demands for the interpretation of difficult dietary questions. Surrounded by unbelievers, He too, could relax toward evening, just as thousands of Parisians do at their favorite cafés.
   Saul Bellow (b. 1915), U.S. novelist: 'My Paris', first publ. in the *New York Times Magazine*, 13 March 1983, rep. in *It All Adds Up* (1994)

4 A bad liver is to a Frenchman what a nervous breakdown is to an American. Everyone has had one and everyone wants to talk about it.
   Art Buchwald (b. 1925), U.S. humorist: in the *New York Herald Tribune*, 16 Jan. 1958

5 The French are very smug, which may come of their having had an empire *and* a revolution; like measles, people believe these things only happen once. It is fitting that *bourgeois* is a

French word, because a lot of French people fit the description.

Julie Burchill (b.1960), British journalist and author: *Girls on Film* (1986), Ch.11

6 France is the only place where you can make love in the afternoon without people hammering on your door.

Barbara Cartland (b.1901), British novelist: quoted in *The Guardian* (London), 24 Dec. 1984

7 Old France, weighed down with history, prostrated by wars and revolutions, endlessly vacillating from greatness to decline, but revived, century after century, by the genius of renewal!

(*Vieille France, accablée d'Histoire, meurtrie de guerres et des révolutions, allant et venant sans relâche de la grandeur au déclin, mais redressée, de siècle en siècle, par le génie du renouveau!*)

Charles de Gaulle (1890–1970), French general and president: *War Memoirs*, Vol.III (1959), Ch.7

8 How can anyone govern a nation that has two hundred and forty-six different kinds of cheese?

Charles de Gaulle: quoted in *Newsweek* (New York), 1 Oct. 1962

9 Conservatism, colonialism, racism, and religious intolerance are part of the make-up of the French bourgeois, who is just as bigoted, brainlessly selfish, and frightened as his counterparts in the other countries. ... France is now entirely dominated, owned, manipulated, exploited, milked, policed, by *les bourgeois* for *les bourgeois*.

Maurice Girodias (1919–1990), French publisher: introduction to *The Olympia Reader* (ed. Maurice Girodias, 1965)

10 *Liberté! Fraternité! Sexualité!*

Graffiti in Paris Métro, 1980s

11 You gave the world the guillotine
But still we don't know why the heck
You have to drop it on our neck.
We're glad of what we did to you,
At Agincourt and Waterloo.
And now the Franco-Prussian War
Is something we are strongly for.
So damn your food and damn your wines,
Your twisted loaves and twisting vines,
Your *table d'hôte*, your *à la carte*,
Your land, your history, your art.
From now on you can keep the lot.
Take every single thing you've got,
Your land, your wealth, your men, your dames,
Your dream of independent power,
And dear old Konrad Adenauer,
And stick them up your Eiffel Tower.

Anthony Jay (b.1930), British writer and journalist: on France's rejection of Britain's entry into the Common Market, in *Time* (New York), 8 Feb. 1963

12 It's true that the French have a certain obsession with sex, but it's a particularly adult obsession. France is the thriftiest of all nations; to a Frenchman sex provides the most economical way to have fun. The French are a logical race.

Anita Loos (1893–1981), U.S. novelist and screenwriter: *Kiss Hollywood Good-by* (1974), Ch.21

13 One becomes aware in France, after having lived in America, that sex pervades the air. It's there all around you, like a fluid.

Henry Miller (1891–1980), U.S. author: interview in *Writers at Work* (Second Series, ed. George Plimpton, 1963)

14 The French are a logical people, which is one reason the English dislike them so intensely. The other is that they own France, a country which we have always judged to be much too good for them.

Robert Morley (1908–1992), British actor: *A Musing Morley* (1974), 'France and the French'

15 The French, whether hypocritical or irrational, it doesn't matter, have no trouble in getting round their own contradiction: they simply cherish their own possessions while condemning everyone else's. ... The French cling to their pathological distinction between their little nest egg and anonymous riches labelled 'finance'.

Guy de Rothschild (b.1909), French banker: *The Whims of Fortune* (1985), Ch.1

16 The French bourgeois doesn't dislike shit, provided it is served up to him at the right time.

Jean-Paul Sartre (1905–1980), French philosopher and author: *Saint Genet: Actor and Martyr* (1952; tr.1963), Bk.2, 'To Succeed in Being All, Strive to be Nothing in Anything'

17 [France is] a country where the money falls apart but you can't tear the toilet paper.

Billy Wilder (b.1906), U.S. film-maker: quoted in *Billy Wilder in Hollywood* by Maurice Zolotow (1977), Ch.18

See also Barthes on DRINK

FRANCE: Paris

1 The American arrives in Paris with a few French phrases he has culled from a conversational guide or picked up from a friend who owns a beret.

Fred Allen (1894–1957), U.S. radio comic: quoted in introduction to *Paris After Dark* by Art Buchwald (1954)

2　The heart of Paris is like nothing so much as the unending interior of a house. Buildings become furniture, courtyards become carpets and arrases, the streets are like galleries, the boulevards conservatories. It is a house, one or two centuries old, rich, bourgeois, distinguished. The only way of going out, or shutting the door behind you, is to leave the centre.

John Berger (b.1926), British author and critic: 'Imagine Paris', first publ. in *Harper's Magazine* (New York), Jan. 1987, rep. in *Keeping a Rendezvous* (1992)

3　Nowhere is one more alone than in Paris ... and yet surrounded by crowds. Nowhere is one more likely to incur greater ridicule. And no visit is more essential.

Marguerite Duras (1914–1996), French author and film-maker: 'Tourists in Paris', first publ. in *France-Observateur* (Paris) 1957, rep. in *Outside: Selected Writings* (1984)

4　If you are lucky enough to have lived in Paris as a young man, then wherever you go for the rest of your life it stays with you, for Paris is a moveable feast.

Ernest Hemingway (1899–1961), U.S. author: quoted in *Papa Hemingway* by A.E. Hotchner (1966), Pt.1, Ch.3. The words 'a moveable feast' were used – on Hotchner's recommendation – as the title for Hemingway's posthumously published Paris memoirs. This paragraph appears as the book's epigraph

See also Paglia on DECONSTRUCTION

FREAKS

1　There's a quality of legend about freaks. Like a person in a fairy tale who stops you and demands that you answer a riddle. Most people go through life dreading they'll have a traumatic experience. Freaks were born with their trauma. They've already passed their test in life. They're aristocrats.

Diane Arbus (1923–1971), U.S. photographer: from classes given in 1971, publ. in *Diane Arbus: An Aperture Monograph* (1972), p.3 of Phaidon edn.

2　The freakish is no longer a private zone, difficult of access. People who are bizarre, in sexual disgrace, emotionally violent are seen daily on the newsstands, on TV, in the subways. Hobbesian man roams the streets, quite visible, with glitter in his hair.

Susan Sontag (b.1933), U.S. essayist: *On Photography* (1977), 'America, Seen Through Photographs, Darkly'

FREE ENTERPRISE

1　That's free enterprise, friends: freedom to gamble, freedom to lose. And the great thing – the truly democratic thing about it – is that you don't even have to be a player to lose.

Barbara Ehrenreich (b.1941), U.S. author and columnist: 'How You Can Save Wall St' (1988), rep. in *The Worst Years of Our Lives* (1991)

2　If a chemist feels it is immoral to make napalm, he can solve his problem by getting a job where he doesn't have to. He will pay a price. but the ultimate effect will be that if many, many people feel that way, the cost of hiring people to make napalm will be high, napalm will be expensive, and less of it will be used. This is another way in which the free market does provide a much more sensitive and subtle voting mechanism than does the political system.

Milton Friedman (b.1912), U.S. economist: *There's No Such Thing as a Free Lunch* (1975), Ch.11

3　The market came with the dawn of civilization and it is not an invention of capitalism.... If it leads to improving the well-being of the people there is no contradiction with socialism.

Mikhail Gorbachev (b.1931), Russian political leader: quoted in *The Guardian* (London), 21 June 1990

FREE WILL

1　The will is never free – it is always attached to an object, a purpose. It is simply the engine in the car – it can't steer.

Joyce Cary (1888–1957), British author: interview in *Writers at Work* (First Series, ed. Malcolm Cowley, 1958)

2　One of the annoying things about believing in free will and individual responsibility is the difficulty of finding somebody to blame your problems on. And when you do find somebody, it's remarkable how often his picture turns up on your driver's license.

P.J. O'Rourke (b.1947), U.S. journalist: in *Rolling Stone* (New York), 30 Nov. 1989

3　How strangely people live. They seem to be in command of the situation – and they do not understand that they have been given the chance of living and actually using the opportunity to be free. Everything in this life is terrible, apart from the freedom of will that we possess. Once we are united with God we shall no longer be able to exercise it, it will have been taken away from us.

Andrey Tarkovsky (1932–1986), Russian film-maker: journal entry, 22 June 1980, publ. in *Time Within Time: The Diaries 1970–1986* (1989; tr.1994)

4 We human beings do have some genuine freedom of choice and therefore some effective control over our own destinies. I am not a determinist. But I also believe that the decisive choice is seldom the latest choice in the series. More often than not, it will turn out to be some choice made relatively far back in the past.

A.J. Toynbee (1889–1975), British historian: 'Some Great "If's" Of History', publ. in the *New York Times*, 5 March 1961

FREEDOM

1 The caged bird sings
with a fearful trill
of things unknown
but longed for still ...
... the caged bird
sings of freedom.

Maya Angelou (b.1928), U.S. author: 'Caged Bird', publ. in *Shaker, Why Don't You Sing?* (1983)

2 It is always the same: once you are liberated, you are forced to ask who you are.

Jean Baudrillard (b.1929), French semiologist: *America* (1986; tr.1988), 'Astral America'

3 Freedom is the by-product of economic surplus.

Aneurin Bevan (1897–1960), British Labour politician: quoted in *Aneurin Bevan*, Vol.I by Michael Foot (1962), Ch.3

4 Freedom is poetry, taking liberties with words, breaking the rules of normal speech, violating common sense. Freedom is violence.

Norman O. Brown (b.1913), U.S. philosopher: *Love's Body* (1966), Ch.15

5 Without freedom, no art; art lives only on the restraints it imposes on itself, and dies of all others. But without freedom, no socialism either, except the socialism of the gallows.

Albert Camus (1913–1960), French-Algerian philosopher and author: 'Socialism of the Gallows', interview first publ. in *Demain* (Paris), 21 Feb. 1957, rep. in *Resistance, Rebellion, and Death* (1961)

6 It doesn't say much for human nature to see what happened with the American experiment in freedom. It's been taken advantage of so much that now there is nothing left.

Robert Crumb (b.1943), U.S. cartoonist: interview in *The Apex Treasury of Underground Comics* (ed. Susan Goodrick and Don Donahue, 1974)

7 The guarantee of freedom is freedom.

Michel Foucault (1926–1984), French philosopher: interview 1982, publ. in *The Foucault Reader* (ed.

Paul Rabinow, 1984), 'Space, Knowledge, and Power'

8 Give us this day our television, and an automobile, but deliver us from freedom.

Jean-Luc Godard (b.1930), French film-maker and author: Madeleine (Chantal Goya), in *Masculin-Féminin* (film; written by Jean-Luc Godard, based on two short stories by Guy de Maupassant, directed by Jean-Luc Godard, 1966)

9 Only very slowly and late have men come to realize that unless freedom is universal it is only extended privilege.

Christopher Hill (b.1912), British historian: *The Century of Revolution* (1961), Ch.20

10 The free way of life proposes ends, but it does not prescribe means.

Robert Kennedy (1925–1968), U.S. Democratic politician and attorney general: *The Pursuit of Justice* (1964), Pt.5, 'Berlin East and West'

11 Our mouths are full of such words as freedom, but what does it really mean? Does it not perhaps mean being totally alone, living in a total vacuum?

Krzysztof Kieślowski (1941–1996), Polish film-maker: quoted in appreciation in *The Guardian* (London), 14 March 1996

12 Freedom is never voluntarily given by the oppressor; it must be demanded by the oppressed.

Martin Luther King Jr. (1929–1968), U.S. clergyman and civil rights leader: 'Letter from Birmingham Jail', open letter to clergymen, 16 April 1963, publ. in *Why We Can't Wait* (1963)

13 Freedom's just another word for nothing left to lose.

Kris Kristofferson (b.1936), U.S. singer and song-writer: 'Me and Bobby McGhee' (song, written with Fred Foster, 1969) on the album of the same name (1972)

14 Emancipate yourselves from mental slavery. None but ourselves can free our minds.

Bob Marley (1945–1981), Jamaican reggae musician: 'Redemption Song' (song), on the album *Uprising* (Bob Marley and the Wailers, 1980)

15 There's something contagious about demanding freedom.

Robin Morgan (b.1941), U.S. feminist author and poet: introduction to *Sisterhood Is Powerful* (1970)

16 It is possible either to kill freedom by force or to smother it by the power of money with the connivance of the State. There is not much freedom left to the individual with a new opinion, when the Press, radio and television are denied to him.

Oswald Mosley (1896–1980), British fascist leader: *My Life* (1968), Ch.16

17 I mean, it's real hard to be free when you're bought and sold in the market-place.

Jack Nicholson (b.1937), U.S. actor: George Hanson, in *Easy Rider* (film; written by Dennis Hopper, Peter Fonda and Terry Southern, directed by Dennis Hopper, 1969)

18 Freedom is the freedom to say that two plus two make four. If that is granted, all else follows.

George Orwell (1903–1950), British author: Winston Smith writing in his diary, in *Nineteen Eighty-four* (1949), Pt.2, Ch.7

19 Freedom prospers when religion is vibrant and the rule of law under God is acknowledged.

Ronald Reagan (b.1911), U.S. Republican politician and president: speech, 8 March 1983, Annual Convention of the National Association of Evangelicals, Orlando, Florida, publ. in *Speaking My Mind* (1989)

20 Freedom is not an ideal, it is not even a protection, if it means nothing more than freedom to stagnate, to live without dreams, to have no greater aim than a second car and another television set.

Adlai Stevenson (1900–1965), U.S. Democratic politician: 'Putting First Things First', publ. in *Foreign Affairs* (New York), Jan. 1960

See also Crisp on NAGGING; Arendt on NECESSITY; Malcolm X on PEACE

FREEDOM OF EXPRESSION

1 If we don't believe in freedom of expression for people we despise, we don't believe in it at all.

Noam Chomsky (b.1928), U.S. linguist and political analyst: interview with John Pilger on *The Late Show*, BBC2, 25 Nov. 1992, excerpted in *The Guardian* (London), 23 Nov. 1992

2 We who officially value freedom of speech above life itself seem to have nothing to talk about but the weather.

Barbara Ehrenreich (b.1941), U.S. author and columnist: 'The Moral Bypass' (1985), rep. in *The Worst Years of Our Lives* (1991)

3 We are willing enough to praise freedom when she is safely tucked away in the past and cannot be a nuisance. In the present, amidst dangers whose outcome we cannot foresee, we get nervous about her, and admit censorship.

E.M. Forster (1879–1970), British novelist and essayist: *Two Cheers for Democracy* (1951), 'The Tercentenary of the Areopagitica'

4 Here we have the beautiful British compromise: a man can say anything, he mustn't do anything; a man can listen to anything, but he musn't be roused to do anything. By freedom of speech is meant freedom to talk *about*; speech is not saying-as-an-action.

Paul Goodman (1911–1972), U.S. author, poet and critic: 'Censorship and Pornography on the Stage' (1959), Pt.2, lecture publ. in *Creator Spirit Come* (1977)

5 The primacy of the word, basis of the human psyche, that has in our age been used for mind-bending persuasion and brain-washing pulp, disgraced by Goebbels and debased by advertising copy, remains a force for freedom that flies out between all bars.

Nadine Gordimer (b.1923), South African author: 'The Unkillable Word', address, 17 April 1980, first publ. as 'Censorship and the Word' in *The Bloody Horse*, Sept./Oct. 1980, rep. in *The Essential Gesture* (ed. Stephen Clingman, 1988)

6 Free speech is the whole thing, the whole ball game. Free speech is life itself.

Salman Rushdie (b.1947), Indian-born British author: interview in *The Guardian* (London), 8 Nov. 1990

7 Woe to that nation whose literature is cut short by the intrusion of force. This is not merely interference with freedom of the press but the sealing up of a nation's heart, the excision of its memory.

Alexander Solzhenitsyn (b.1918), Russian novelist: in *Time* (New York), 25 Feb. 1974

8 The sound of tireless voices is the price we pay for the right to hear the music of our own opinions. But there is also, it seems to me, a moment at which democracy must prove its capacity to act. Every man has a right to be heard; but no man has the right to strangle democracy with a single set of vocal chords.

Adlai Stevenson (1900–1965), U.S. Democratic politician: speech, 28 Aug. 1952, New York City, publ. in *The Papers of Adlai E. Stevenson*, Vol.IV (1974)

9 I'm a free-speech absolutist. I defend the most extreme speech from the Left or from the Right. My father was a Holocaust survivor, I am a Jew: I know from logic and from observation and from experience that the more powerless you are as a group, gender or ideology, the more you should defend your freedom of speech.

Nadine Strossen, U.S. civil rights lawyer and author: on calls to censor negative images of women, in interview in *The Observer* (London), 28 Jan. 1996

10 When a man says that he is Jesus or Napoleon, or that the Martians are after him, or claims something else that seems outrageous to common sense, he is labeled psychotic and locked up in a madhouse. Freedom of speech is only for normal people.

Thomas Szasz (b.1920), U.S. psychiatrist: *The Second Sin* (1973), 'Schizophrenia'

FRIENDS

1 Between friends differences in taste or opinion are irritating in direct proportion to their triviality.
W.H. Auden (1907–1973), Anglo-American poet: *The Dyer's Hand* (1962), Pt.3, 'Hic et Ille', Sct.D

2 Friends, both the imaginary ones you build for yourself out of phrases taken from a living writer, or real ones from college, and relatives, despite all the waste of ceremony and fakery and the fact that out of an hour of conversation you may have only five minutes in which the old entente reappears, are the only real means for foreign ideas to enter your brain.
Nicholson Baker (b.1957), U.S. author: *U And I: A True Story* (1991), Ch.4

3 My friends are all either married, boring, and depressed; single, bored, and depressed; or moved out of town to avoid boredom and depression.
Douglas Coupland (b.1961), Canadian author: the narrator (Andy), in *Generation X* (1991), 'MTV Not Bullets'

4 It pays to know who your friends are but it also pays to know you aint got any friends.
Bob Dylan (b.1941), U.S. singer and songwriter: *Tarantula* (1970), 'Prelude to the Flatpick'

5 In a bad marriage, friends are the invisible glue. If we have enough friends, we may go on for years, intending to leave, talking about leaving – instead of actually getting up and leaving.
Erica Jong (b.1942), U.S. author: *How To Save Your Own Life* (1977), 'A day in the life ...'

6 I get by with a little help from my friends.
John Lennon (1940–1980) and **Paul McCartney** (b.1942), British rock musicians: 'With a Little Help from my Friends' (song), on the album *Sgt. Pepper's Lonely Hearts Club Band* (The Beatles, 1967)

7 I do not believe that friends are necessarily the people you like best, they are merely the people who got there first.
Peter Ustinov (b.1921), British actor, writer and director: *Dear Me* (1977), Ch.5

8 Whenever a friend succeeds, a little something in me dies.
Gore Vidal (b.1925), U.S. novelist and critic: quoted in *The Sunday Times* (London), 16 Sept. 1973

9 You should have contact with your closest friends through the most intimate and exclusive of all media – the telephone.
Andy Warhol (c.1928–1987), U.S. Pop artist: *From A to B and Back Again* (1975), Ch.10

10 We shelter children for a time; we live side by side with men; and that is all. We owe them nothing, and are owed nothing. I think we owe our friends more, especially our female friends.
Fay Weldon (b.1933), British novelist: the narrator (Praxis Duveen), in *Praxis* (1978), Ch.19

See also Bukowski on PRISON

FRIENDSHIP

1 Friendship is one of the most tangible things in a world which offers fewer and fewer supports.
Kenneth Branagh (b.1960), British actor and director: in *The Daily Telegraph* (London), 4 Nov. 1992

2 Accountability in friendship is the equivalent of love without strategy.
Anita Brookner (b.1938), British novelist and art historian: interview in *Women Writers Talk* (ed. Olga Kenyon, 1989)

3 Friendship is a pretty full-time occupation if you really are friendly with somebody. You can't have too many friends because then you're just not really friends.
Truman Capote (1924–1984), U.S. author: *Conversations With Truman Capote* (ed. Lawrence Grobel, 1985), Ch.3, 'Love, Sex, and Fear'

4 No man can be friends with a woman he finds attractive. He always wants to have sex with her. Sex is always out there. Friendship is ultimately doomed and that is the end of the story.
Nora Ephron (b.1941), U.S. author and journalist: Harry Burns (Billy Crystal), in *When Harry Met Sally ...* (film; screenplay by Nora Ephron, directed and co-produced by Rob Reiner, 1989)

5 It is easy enough to be friendly to one's friends. But to befriend the one who regards himself as your enemy is the quintessence of true religion. The other is mere business.
Mohandas K. Gandhi (1869–1948), Indian political and spiritual leader: *Non-Violence in Peace and War* (1948), Vol.II, Ch.248

FRIGIDITY

1 Men always fall for frigid women because they put on the best show.
Fanny Brice (1891–1951), U.S. entertainer: quoted in Ben Hecht's autobiography, *A Child of the Century* (1954), Bk.5, 'Don Juan in Hollywood'. Hecht added, 'Don Juan is apt to prefer the hullaballoo of spurious passion to the simpler noises of honest sex'

2 Show me a frigid woman and, nine times out of ten, I'll show you a little man.
Julie Burchill (b.1960), British journalist and author: 'Where's the Beef?', first publ. in *Arena* (London), 1988, rep. in *Sex and Sensibility* (1992)

3 Frigidity is desire imagined by a woman who doesn't desire the man offering himself to her. It's the desire of a woman for a man who hasn't yet come to her, whom she doesn't yet know. She's faithful to this stranger even before she belongs to him. Frigidity is the non-desire for whatever is not him.
Marguerite Duras (1914–1996), French author and film-maker: *Practicalities* (1987; tr.1990), 'Men'

4 Frigidity is largely nonsense. It is this generation's catchword, one only vaguely understood and constantly misused. Frigid women are few. There is a host of diffident and slow-ripening ones.
Phyllis McGinley (1905–1978), U.S. poet and author: *The Province of the Heart* (1959), 'The Honor of Being a Woman'

FUN

1 Most people get a fair amount of fun out of their lives, but on balance life is suffering, and only the very young or the very foolish imagine otherwise.
George Orwell (1903–1950), British author: *Shooting an Elephant* (1950), 'Lear, Tolstoy and the Fool'

2 No fun, my babe. No Fun.
No fun to hang around feeling the same old way.
No fun to hang around, freaked out for another day.
No fun to be all alone, walking by myself.
No fun to be alone in love with nobody else.
Iggy Pop (b.1947), U.S. rock musician: 'No Fun' (song), on the album *The Stooges* (The Stooges, 1969)

3 Every time I hear that word, I cringe. Fun! I think it's disgusting; it's just running around. It's not my idea of pleasure.
Vivienne Westwood (b.1941), British fashion designer: in the *Independent on Sunday* (London), 18 Feb. 1990

FUNCTION

1 In product design, functional excellence is now the baseline and to be successful consumer goods have to offer something more culturally seductive than mere efficiency.
Stephen Bayley (b.1951), British design critic: *Commerce and Culture* (1989), Ch.1

2 Virtue is simply happiness, and happiness is a by-product of function. You are happy when you are functioning.
William Burroughs (1914–1997), U.S. author: *Painting and Guns* (1992), 'The Creative Observer'

3 Form and function are a unity, two sides of one coin. In order to enhance function, appropriate form must exist or be created.
Ida P. Rolf (1896–1979), U.S. biochemist and physical therapist: preface to *Rolfing: The Integration of Human Structures* (1977)

FUNDAMENTALISM

1 Any hope that America would finally grow up vanished with the rise of fundamentalist Christianity. Fundamentalism, with its born-again regression, its pink-and-gold concept of heaven, its literal-mindedness, its rambunctious good cheer ... its anti-intellectualism ... its puerile hymns ... and its faith-healing ... are made to order for King Kid America.
Florence King (b.1936), U.S. author: *Reflections in a Jaundiced Eye* (1989), 'Good King Herod'

2 For all the jeremiads that fundamentalism, Islamic and Christian, lances at Western 'materialism', it is fundamentalism that is hard, factualistic and philistine, impervious to the multi-layered nuances of meaning that reside in texts, in fictions, in music and iconographies, in the cells of art and culture where modernity – that universal modernity created by a vibrant, still dynamic 'West' – stores its spiritual wealth. ... Fundamentalism is the most materialistic of contemporary ideologies, a throwback to the mechanistic values of the Victorians. It thrives among the deracinated, who compensate for physical displacement by seeking impious certainties in language.
Malise Ruthven (b.1942), British author: *A Satanic Affair* (1990), Ch.6

3 Truly this has been the age of Ayatollahs, in which a phalanx of guardians (Khomeni, the Pope, Margaret Thatcher) simplify and protect one or another creed, essence, primordial faith. One fundamentalism invidiously attacks the others in the name of sanity, freedom, and goodness.
Edward Said (b.1935), Lebanese-born U.S. social and literary critic: *Culture and Imperialism* (1993), Ch.4, Sct.3

FUND-RAISING

1 There are times when you feel you simply can't go on. The last five miles of every stage are awful. Terrible. That is the point where you are like a human cabbage: you can see the destination but it just won't come any closer. It

is then that I pinch myself and remind myself just what I am doing, why I am on this road.

Ian Botham (b.1955), British cricketer: on sponsored walks, in *Botham: My Autobiography* (1994), Ch.15

2 A cheque or credit card, a Gucci bag strap, anything of value will do. Give as you live.

Jesse Jackson (b.1941), U.S. clergyman and civil rights leader: fund-raising in Aspen, Colorado, quoted in *The Daily Telegraph* (London), 6 April 1988

3 Let us more and more insist on raising funds of love, of kindness, of understanding, of peace. Money will come if we seek first the Kingdom of God – the rest will be given.

Mother Teresa (1910–1997), Albanian-born Roman Catholic missionary: *A Gift for God* (1975), 'Carriers of Christ's Love'

FUNERALS

1 The only reason I might go to the funeral is to make absolutely sure that he's dead.

'An eminent editor': of press baron Lord Beaverbrook, quoted in *Anatomy of Britain Today* by Anthony Sampson (1965), Ch.9

2 Memorial services are the cocktail parties of the geriatric set.

Harold Macmillan (1894–1986), British Conservative politician and prime minister: quoted in *Macmillan* by Alistair Horne, Vol.II (1989), Ch.20

FUTILITY

1 If man merely sat back and thought about his impending termination, and his terrifying insignificance and aloneness in the cosmos, he would surely go mad, or succumb to a numbing sense of futility. Why, he might ask himself, should he bother to write a great symphony, or strive to make a living, or even to love another, when he is no more than a momentary microbe on a dust mote whirling through the unimaginable immensity of space?

Stanley Kubrick (b.1928), U.S. film-maker: interview in *Playboy* (Chicago), Sept. 1968, rep. in *Kubrick: Inside a Film Artist's Maze* by Thomas Allen Nelson (1982), Ch.1

2 He's a real nowhere man
Sitting in his nowhere land
Making all his nowhere plans for nobody.

John Lennon (1940–1980) and **Paul McCartney** (b.1942), British rock musicians: 'Nowhere Man' (song), on the album *Rubber Soul* (The Beatles, 1966)

3 If only I could get down to Sidcup! I've been waiting for the weather to break. He's got my papers, this man I left them with, it's got it all down there, I could prove everything.

Harold Pinter (b.1930), British playwright: Davies, in *The Caretaker* (1960), Act 1

GAMBLING

1 He was ... a degenerate gambler. That is, a man who gambled simply to gamble and must lose. As a hero who goes to war must die. Show me a gambler and I'll show you a loser, show me a hero and I'll show you a corpse.

Mario Puzo (b.1920), U.S. novelist: of Jordan Hawley, in *Fools Die* (1978), Ch.2

2 Someone once asked me why women don't gamble as much as men do, and I gave the common-sensical reply that we don't have as much money. That was a true but incomplete answer. In fact, women's total instinct for gambling is satisfied by marriage.

Gloria Steinem (b.1934), U.S. feminist writer and editor: 'Night Thoughts of a Media Watcher', publ. in *Ms.* (New York), Nov. 1981, rep. in *Outrageous Acts and Everyday Rebellions* (1983)

See also THE LOTTERY

GAMES

1 No human being is innocent, but there is a class of innocent human actions called Games.

W.H. Auden (1907–1973), Anglo-American poet: *The Dyer's Hand* (1962), Pt.7, 'Dingly Dell and The Fleet'

2 Intelligence and war are games, perhaps the only meaningful games left. If any player becomes too proficient, the game is threatened with termination.

William Burroughs (1914–1997), U.S. author: *The Adding Machine* (1985), 'The Hundred Year Plan'

3 I've been around a lot of heavy, degenerate gamblers, so I can see what it does to people. It's a lifestyle. People killing each other over games. There's more passion at a Wembley soccer match than in St Patrick's Cathedral.

Abel Ferrara (b.1952), U.S. film-maker: interview in *Sight and Sound* (London), Feb. 1993

See also CHESS; GOLF; SPORT

GARDENS

1 I just come and talk to the plants, really – very important to talk to them, they respond I find.

Charles, Prince of Wales (b.1948): television interview, 21 Sept. 1986, quoted in *The Daily Telegraph* (London), 22 Dec. 1986. Charles's half-joking remark helped to establish his reputation as a new-age eccentric. Responding humorously to this, he was later quoted as saying, 'Only the other day I was inquiring of an entire bed of old-fashioned roses, forced to listen to my ramblings on the meaning of the universe as I sat cross-legged in the lotus position in front of them' (*The Daily Telegraph*, 15 Nov. 1988)

2   Paradise haunts gardens, and some gardens are paradises. Mine is one of them. Others are like bad children – spoilt by their parents, over-watered and covered with noxious chemicals.

Derek Jarman (1942–1994), British film-maker, artist and author: of Jarman's garden at Prospect Cottage near Dungeness, in *Derek Jarman's Garden* (text by Derek Jarman, photographs by Howard Sooley, 1995)

3   The true gardener ... brushes over the ground with slow and gentle hand, to liberate a space for breath round some favourite; but he is not thinking about destruction except incidentally. It is only the amateur like myself who becomes obsessed and rejoices with a sadistic pleasure in weeds that are big and bad enough to pull, and at last, almost forgetting the flowers altogether, turns into a Reformer.

Freya Stark (1893–1993), British travel writer: *Perseus in the Wind* (1948), Ch.17

GENDER

1   It would be futile to attempt to fit women into a masculine pattern of attitudes, skills and abilities and disastrous to force them to suppress their specifically female characteristics and abilities by keeping up the pretense that there are no differences between the sexes.

Arianna Huffington [formerly Arianna Stassinopoulos] (b.1950), Greek author: *The Female Woman* (1973), 'The Natural Woman'

2   The mind is not sex-typed.

Margaret Mead (1901–1978), U.S. anthropologist: *Blackberry Winter* (1972), Ch.5

3   In the theory of gender I began from zero. There is no masculine power or privilege I did not covet. But slowly, step by step, decade by decade, I was forced to acknowledge that even a woman of abnormal will cannot escape her hormonal identity.

Camille Paglia (b.1947), U.S. author and critic: *Sex, Art, and American Culture* (1992), 'Sexual Personae: The Cancelled Preface'

4   To be sure he's a 'Man,' the male must see to it that the female be clearly a 'Woman,' the opposite of a 'Man,' that is, the female must act like a faggot.

Valerie Solanas (1936–1988), U.S. actress and writer: *The SCUM Manifesto* (1968). The acronym *SCUM* stood for 'Society for Cutting Up Men'

5   Except for their genitals, I don't know what immutable differences exist between men and women. Perhaps there are some other un-changeable differences; probably there are a number of irrelevant differences. But it is clear that until social expectations for men and women are equal, until we provide equal respect for both sexes, answers to this question will simply reflect our prejudices.

Naomi Weisstein (b.1939), U.S. psychologist and author: 'Woman as Nigger', publ. in *Psychology Today* (New York), Oct. 1969

6   Well, nobody's perfect.

Billy Wilder (b.1906), U.S. film-maker: Osgood E. Fielding III (Joe E. Brown), in *Some Like It Hot* (film; screenplay by Billy Wilder and I.A.L. Diamond, produced and directed by Billy Wilder, 1959). Osgood utters these final words of the film on discovering that his bride-to-be (Jack Lemmon) is a man

See also MEN; MEN & WOMEN; WOMEN

GENERALIZATIONS

1   We are more prone to generalize the bad than the good. We assume that the bad is more potent and contagious.

Eric Hoffer (1902–1983), U.S. philosopher: *Reflections on the Human Condition* (1973), Aph.162

2   Obvious enough that generalities work to protect the mind from the great outdoors; is it possible that this was in fact their first purpose?

Howard Nemerov (1920–1991), U.S. poet, novelist and critic: *Journal of the Fictive Life* (1965), 'Reflexions of the Novelist Felix Ledger', Sct.C

GENERALS

1   I am convinced that the best service a retired general can perform is to turn in his tongue along with his suit, and to mothball his opinions.

Omar Nelson Bradley (1893–1981), U.S. general: Armed Forces Day address, quoted in the *New York Times*, 17 May 1959

2   In defeat unbeatable: in victory unbearable.

Winston Churchill (1874–1965), British statesman and author: referring to Viscount Montgomery, quoted in *Ambrosia and Small Beer* by Edward Marsh (1964), Ch.5

3   Like the old soldier of the ballad, I now close my military career and just fade away, an old soldier who tried to do his duty as God gave him the light to see that duty. Goodbye.

Douglas MacArthur (1880–1964), U.S. general: speech to Congress, 19 April 1951, on his dismissal as commander of U.N. forces in Korea, for dissenting with the Truman administration's conduct of the war. Truman called the speech 'nothing but a bunch of damn bullshit,' in Merle Miller's *Plain Speaking: Conversations with Harry S Truman* (1973), Ch.25. The 'ballad' referred to by

MacArthur was a popular barrack-room ditty, which originated as a British army song during World War I

4 The nearest the modern general or admiral comes to a small-arms encounter of any sort is at a duck hunt in the company of corporation executives at the retreat of Continental Motors, Inc.
C. Wright Mills (1916–1962), U.S. sociologist: *The Power Elite* (1956), Ch.8

5 Perfect soldier, perfect gentleman ... never gave offence to anyone not even the enemy.
A.J.P. Taylor (1906–1990), British historian: of Field Marshal Alexander, in letter, 16 March 1973, publ. in *Letters to Eva* (ed. Eva Haraszti Talyor, 1991)

THE GENERATION GAP

1 What really distinguishes this generation in all countries from earlier generations ... is its determination to act, its joy in action, the assurance of being able to change things by one's own efforts.
Hannah Arendt (1906–1975), German-born U.S. political philosopher: *Crises of the Republic* (1972), 'Thoughts on Politics and Revolution'

2 Can sixty make sense to sixteen-Plus?
What has my camp in common with theirs,
With buttons and beards and Be-Ins?
Much, I hope. In *Acts* it is written
Taste was no problem at Pentecost.
W.H. Auden (1907–1973), Anglo-American poet: 'Prologue at Sixty', publ. in *City Without Walls* (1969)

3 Oh You Pretty Things
Don't you know you're driving your
Mamas and papas insane?
Let me make it plain
You gotta make way for Homo Superior
David Bowie (b.1947), British rock musician: 'Oh! You Pretty Things' (song), on the album *Hunky Dory* (1971)

4 The white youth of today have begun to react to the fact that the 'American Way of Life' is a fossil of history. What do they care if their old baldheaded and crew-cut elders don't dig their caveman mops? They couldn't care less about the old, stiffassed honkies who don't like their new dances: Frug, Monkey, Jerk, Swim, Watusi. All they know is that it feels good to swing to way-out body-rhythms instead of dragassing across the dance floor like zombies to the dead beat of mind-smothered Mickey Mouse music.
Eldridge Cleaver (b.1935), U.S. black leader and writer: *Soul on Ice* (1968), 'The White Race and Its Heroes'

5 Come mothers and fathers
Throughout the land
And don't criticize
What you can't understand
Your sons and your daughters
Are beyond your command
Your old road is rapidly agin'.
Bob Dylan (b.1941), U.S. singer and songwriter: 'The Times They Are A-Changin'' (song), on the album *The Times They Are A-Changin'* (1964)

6 There is no such thing as a 'generation gap' any more; how can you rebel against the generation of Coltrane or Brando or MacInnes? What we have is a heritage that you can draw succour and inspiration from; and there's those who do and those who don't. That's the only gap.
Robert Elms (b.1959), British journalist: *The Face* (London), 29 Sept. 1982, rep. in *The Faber Book of Pop* (ed. Hanif Kureishi and Jon Savage, 1995), Pt.8, '1982: Hard Times'

7 Well let's face it, what right have you to a life, unless you devote it to dispelling the confines that our parents worked so hard to achieve ... although don't forget that we're all parents now.
Dennis Hopper (b.1935), U.S. actor and director: interview in *Blitz* (London), May 1983

8 Today, age is needy and, as its powers decline, so does its income; but full-blooded youth has wealth as well as vigour. In this decade, we witness the second Children's Crusade, armed with strength and beauty, against all 'squares', all adult nay-sayers.
Colin MacInnes (1914–1976), British author: 'Pop Songs and Teenagers', publ. in *Twentieth Century* (London), Feb. 1958, rep. in *England, Half English* (1961)

9 Our parents are waging a genocidal war against their own kids. The economy has no use or need for youth. Everything is already built. *Our existence is a crime.*
Jerry Rubin (1938–1994), U.S. essayist and radical leader: *Do It!* (1970), 'Yippie!', Extract 14

10 People try to put us down
(Talkin' 'bout my generation)
Just because we get around... .
Things they do look awful c-c-cold... .
Hope I die before I get old.
Pete Townshend (b.1945), British rock musician: 'My Generation' (song), on the album *My Generation* (The Who, 1965)

See also Bowie on THE MEDIA

GENERATIONS

1 If the flower children believed they owed nothing to the Republic except an encore of

'Blowin' in the Wind', their middle-aged avatars believe they owe nothing to the Republic except a demonstration of their golf swings.

Lewis H. Lapham (b.1935), U.S. essayist and editor: in *Harper's Magazine* (New York), March 1996

2 Youth doesn't reason, it acts. The old man reasons and would like to make the others act in his place.

(*La jeunesse ne raisonne pas, elle agit. Le vieillard raisonne et voudrait faire agir les autres à sa place.*)

Francis Picabia (1878–1953), French painter and poet: *591* (Paris), 21 Jan. 1952, rep. in *Écrits* Vol. II (ed. Olivier Revault d'Allones and Dominique Bouissou, 1978), '1925–1932'

3 Infantilism is possibly the hallmark of our generation.

John Wells (b.1936), British writer, actor and director: quoted in *Beyond the Fringe ... and Beyond* by Ronald Bergan (1989), Pt.4

GENIUS

1 Almost everybody is born a genius and buried an idiot.

Charles Bukowski (1920–1994), U.S. author and poet: *Notes of a Dirty Old Man* (1969), p.165 of City Lights edn. (1973)

2 What Romantic terminology called genius or talent or inspiration is nothing other than finding the right road empirically, following one's nose, taking short cuts.

Italo Calvino (1923–1985), Italian author and critic: 'Cybernetics and Ghosts', lecture, Turin, Nov. 1969, publ. in *The Literature Machine* (1987)

3 Few people can see genius in someone who has offended them.

Robertson Davies (1913–1995), Canadian novelist and journalist: 'Dylan Thomas and Hector Berlioz', publ. in *Saturday Night* (Canada), 9 June 1956, rep. in *The Enthusiasms of Robertson Davies* (1990)

4 Everybody denies I am a genius – but nobody ever called me one!

Orson Welles (1915–1985), U.S. film-maker and actor: quoted in *Halliwell's Filmgoer's Companion* (ed. Leslie Halliwell, 1984)

See also Picasso on ALBERT EINSTEIN

GENOCIDE

1 Genocide begins, however improbably, in the conviction that classes of biological distinction indisputably sanction social and political discrimination.

Andrea Dworkin (b.1946), U.S. feminist critic: 'Biological Superiority: The World's Most

Dangerous and Deadly Idea' (1978), rep. in *Letters from a War-Zone* (1987), Sct.3

2 People are inexterminable – like flies and bedbugs. There will always be some that survive in cracks and crevices – that's us.

Robert Frost (1874–1963), U.S. poet: quoted in *The Observer* (London), 29 March 1959

3 I know for sure that there is only one step from insecticide to genocide.

Werner Herzog (b.1942), German film-maker: in the *New York Times*, 11 Sept. 1977

4 Genocide requires three kinds of people: killers, strategists and ideologues. Rwanda's shadow armies and political parties and radio broadcasts provided all three.

Lindsey Hilsum, British journalist: 'Where is Kigali?', publ. in *Granta* (London), No.51, autumn 95

GENTLEMEN

1 Gentleman. A man who buys two of the same morning paper from the doorman of his favorite nightclub when he leaves with his girl.

Marlene Dietrich (1904–1992), German-born U.S. actress: *Marlene Dietrich's ABC* (1962), 'Gentleman'

2 Being a gentleman is the number one priority, the chief question integral to our national life.

Edward Fox (b.1934), British actor: in *The Daily Telegraph* (London), 14 Feb. 1992

GERMANY

1 Don't mention the war.

John Cleese (b.1939), British comic actor and author: Basil Fawlty, on the pending arrival of German guests, in *Fawlty Towers*, 24 Oct. 1975, 'The Germans' (TV series, co-written with Connie Booth), publ. in *The Complete Fawlty Towers* (1988)

2 The tears I have cried over Germany have dried. I have washed my face.

Marlene Dietrich (1904–1992), German-born U.S. film actress: *Marlene Dietrich's ABC* (1962), 'Germany'

3 It's like the Beatles coming together again – let's hope they don't go on a world tour.

Matt Frei, British journalist: on German reunification, in *The Listener* (London), 21 June 1990

4 They came, they saw, they did a little shopping.

Graffiti: on the Berlin wall, following the influx of thousands of East Berliners into West Berlin after the lifting of travel restrictions, reported in *Newsweek* (New York), 4 Dec. 1989

5 How much atonement is enough? The bombing must be allowed as at least part-payment:

those of our young people who are concerned about the moral problem posed by the Allied air offensive should at least consider the moral problem that would have been posed if the German civilian population had not suffered at all.
Clive James (b.1939), Australian writer and critic: 'Postcard from Munich', first publ. in *The Observer* (London), 13 Feb. 1983, rep. in *Flying Visits* (1984)

6 Everybody should know that Germany will not go it alone: there will be no restless Reich.
Helmut Kohl (b.1930), German politician and chancellor: in the *International Herald Tribune* (Paris), 3 Oct. 1990

7 I love Germany so dearly that I hope there will always be two of them.
François Mauriac (1885–1970), French author: quoted in *Newsweek* (New York), 20 Nov. 1989

8 The Teutons have been singing the swan song ever since they entered the ranks of history. They have always confounded truth with death.
Henry Miller (1891–1980), U.S. author: discussing Nietzsche and Spengler, in *Plexus* (1963), Ch.17

9 No nation is generically more evil than any other, not even the German nation of half a century ago. History and example, religion and patriotism can make monsters of us all: and if you and I had been born into the Germany of the Thirties, we might have been among Hitler's willing executioners ourselves.
Jan Morris (b.1926), British journalist and travel writer: review of the book, *Hitler's Willing Executioners* by Daniel Jonah Goldhagen, in *The Independent* (London), 30 March 1996

10 When they fall, the Germans rest like Atlas on the earth, and when the giant rises much depends on what voice is whispering in his ear.
Oswald Mosley (1896–1980), British fascist leader: *My Life* (1968), Ch.13

See also THE NAZIS

GERMANY: Berlin

---

1 Berlin is not only Berlin, but is also the symbol of the division of the world, and something even more: a 'point in the universe', the place in which the question of a unity which is both necessary and impossible confronts every individual who resides there, and who, in residing there, experiences not only a place of residence but also the absence of a place of residence.
Maurice Blanchot (b.1907), French literary theorist and author: 'The Word Berlin', publ. in *Semiotext(e)* (New York), 'The German Issue', Vol.IV, No.2, 1982

2 Berlin, an etching by Churchill, after an idea by Hitler.
Bertolt Brecht (1898–1956), German playwright and author: journal entry, 27 Oct. 1948, publ. in *Arbeitsjournal* (1973), Vol.II

3 All free men, wherever they may live, are citizens of Berlin, and therefore, as a free man, I take pride in the words, *Ich bin ein Berliner*.
John F. Kennedy (1917–1963), U.S. Democratic politician and president: speech, 26 June 1963, West Berlin, quoted in *Kennedy* by Theodore C. Sorenson (1965), Pt.5, Ch.21. Kennedy's words recalled Cicero, *Civis Romanus sum* ('I am a Roman citizen'), from *In Verrem*, speech 5

GHETTOS *see under* CITIES

GIRLS

---

1 Thank heaven for little girls!
For little girls get bigger every day.
Alan Jay Lerner (1918–1986), U.S. songwriter: 'Thank Heaven for Little Girls' (song), in the film *Gigi* (1958). The song was sung and recorded by Maurice Chevalier, whose signature tune it became

2 The knowingness of little girls
Is hidden underneath their curls.
Phyllis McGinley (1905–1978), U.S. poet and author: 'What Every Woman Knows', publ. in *Times Three* (1960)

3 I only have two rules for my newly born daughter: she will dress well and never have sex.
John Malkovich (b.1953), U.S. actor: interview in the *Independent on Sunday* (London), 5 April 1992

4 You know something – you're a pretty nice guy, for a girl.
Robert Mitchum (1917–1997), U.S. actor: Frank Jessup (Robert Mitchum), in *Angel Face* (film; screenplay by Frank Nugent and Oscar Millard, directed and produced by Otto Preminger, 1953)

5 Between the age limits of nine and fourteen there occur maidens who, to certain bewitched travelers, twice or many times older than they, reveal their true nature which is not human, but nymphic (that is, demoniac); and these chosen creatures I propose to designate as 'nymphets.'
Vladimir Nabokov (1899–1977), Russian-born U.S. novelist and poet: Humbert Humbert (narrator), in *Lolita* (1955), Pt.1, Ch.5. This passage was cut in the 1962 film directed by Stanley Kubrick

6 Diamonds are a girl's best friend.
Leo Robin (1900–1984), U.S. songwriter: 'Diamonds Are a Girl's Best Friend' (song), from

Gentleman Prefer Blondes (stage show, 1949; film, 1953)

7   There are no good girls gone wrong, just bad girls found out.
Mae West (1892–1980), U.S. actress: *On Sex, Health and ESP* (1975), 'Last Word'

See also Greer on ADOLESCENCE

GIVING

1   Real giving had its joy in imagining the joy of the receiver. It means choosing, expending time, going out of one's way, thinking of the other as a subject: the opposite of distraction.
Theodor W. Adorno (1903–1969), German philosopher, sociologist and music critic: *Minima Moralia* (1951; tr.1978), Ch.21

2   It is rare indeed that people give. Most people guard and keep; they suppose that it is they themselves and what they identify with themselves that they are guarding and keeping, whereas what they are actually guarding and keeping is their system of reality and what they assume themselves to be.
James Baldwin (1924–1987), U.S. author: 'Letter from a Region in My Mind', first publ. in the *New Yorker*, 17 Nov. 1962, rep. in *The Fire Next Time* (1963)

3   People who think they're generous to a fault usually think that's their only fault.
Sydney Harris (b.1917), U.S. journalist: *On the Contrary* (1962), Ch.7

4   There is sublime thieving in all giving. Someone gives us all he has and we are his.
Eric Hoffer (1902–1983), U.S. philosopher: *The Passionate State of Mind* (1955), Aph.236

5   We ourselves feel that what we are doing is just a drop in the ocean. But if that drop was not in the ocean, I think the ocean would be less because of that missing drop. I do not agree with the big way of doing things.
Mother Teresa (1910–1997), Albanian-born Roman Catholic missionary: *A Gift for God* (1975), 'Carriers of Christ's Love'

GLAMOUR

1   Glamour cannot exist without personal social envy being a common and widespread emotion.
John Berger (b.1926), British author and critic: *Ways of Seeing* (1972), Ch.7

2   In England, glamour's in the gutter, it's everywhere, anywhere you want to find it.
Boy George (b.1961), British singer: interview in *Smash Hits* (London), 23 Dec. 1982

GOD

1   The important thing, I think, is not to be bitter. If it turns out that there is a God, I don't think that he's evil. But the worst thing you can say about him is that he's basically an under-achiever. After all, you know, there are worse things in life than death.
Woody Allen (b.1935), U.S. film-maker: Boris Grushenko (Woody Allen), in *Love and Death* (film; written and directed by Woody Allen, 1975)

2   I find it interesting that the meanest life, the poorest existence, is attributed to God's will, but as human beings become more affluent, as their living standard and style begin to ascend the material scale, God descends the scale of responsibility at a commensurate speed.
Maya Angelou (b.1928), U.S. author: *I Know Why the Caged Bird Sings* (first volume of autobiography, 1969), Ch.18

3   With God, what is terrible is that one never knows whether it's not just a trick of the devil. (*Avec Dieu, ce qu'il y a de terrible, c'est qu'on ne sait jamais si ce n'est pas un coup du diable.*)
Jean Anouilh (1910–1987), French playwright: the Archbishop, in *The Lark* (1953; tr.1955)

4   What reverence is rightly paid
    To a divinity so odd
    He lets the Adam whom he made
        Perform the Acts of God?
W.H. Auden (1907–1973), Anglo-American poet: 'Friday's Child', publ. in *Homage to Clio* (1960)

5   To place oneself in the position of God is painful: being God is equivalent to being tortured. For being God means that one is in harmony with all that is, including the worst. The existence of the worst evils is unimaginable unless God willed them.
Georges Bataille (1897–1962), French novelist and critic: 'Bataille, Feydeau and God', interview by Marguerite Duras in *France-Observateur* (Paris), 1957, rep. in *Outside: Selected Writings* by Marguerite Duras (1984)

6   The bastard! He doesn't exist!
Samuel Beckett (1906–1989), Irish playwright and novelist: Hamm, in *Endgame* (1957; tr.1958). Hamm's exclamation after attempting to pray. Clov replies, 'Not yet'

7   How can one better magnify the Almighty than by sniggering with him at his little jokes, particularly the poorer ones.
Samuel Beckett: Winnie, in *Happy Days* (1961), Act 1

8   If someone were to prove to me – right this minute – that God, in all his luminousness,

exists, it wouldn't change a single aspect of my behaviour.

Luis Buñuel (1900–1983), Spanish film-maker: *My Last Breath* (autobiography, 1983), Ch.15

9 Whether or not God is dead: it is impossible to keep silent about him who was there for so long.

Elias Canetti (1905–1994), Austrian novelist and philosopher: *The Secret Heart Of The Clock: Notes, Aphorisms, Fragments 1973–1985* (1991), '1973'

10 Mother goddesses are just as silly a notion as father gods. If a revival of the myths of these cults gives woman emotional satisfaction, it does so at the price of obscuring the real conditions of life. This is why they were invented in the first place.

Angela Carter (1940–1992), British author: *The Sadeian Woman* (1979), 'Polemical Preface'

11 All the gods are dead except the god of war.

Eldridge Cleaver (b.1935), U.S. black leader and writer: *Soul on Ice* (1968), Pt.1 'Four Vignettes: "The Christ" and His Teachings'

12 If God is male, then male is God. The divine patriarch castrates women as long as he is allowed to live on in the human imagination.

Mary Daly (b.1928), U.S. educator, writer and theologian: *Beyond God the Father* (1973), Ch.1

13 Forgive, O Lord, my little jokes on Thee
And I'll forgive Thy great big one on me.

Robert Frost (1874–1963), U.S. poet: 'Cluster of Faith', publ. in *In the Clearing* (1962)

14 I admit that the generation which produced Stalin, Auschwitz and Hiroshima will take some beating; but the radical and universal consciousness of the death of God is still ahead of us; perhaps we shall have to colonize the stars before it is finally borne in upon us that God is not out there.

R.J. Hollingdale (b.1930), British author, critic and translator: *Thomas Mann: A Critical Study* (1971), Ch.8

15 No statement about God is simply, literally true. God is far more than can be measured, described, defined in ordinary language, or pinned down to any particular happening.

David Jenkins (b.1925), British theologian and bishop of Durham: in *The Guardian* (London), 24 Dec.1984

16 God is indeed dead.
He died of self-horror
when He saw the creature He had made
in His own image.

Irving Layton (b.1912), Canadian poet: *The Whole Bloody Bird* (1969), 'Aphs'

17 What if God just put us 'ere for his own entertainment? That's all we are. Just somethin' for 'im to 'ave a bit of a laugh at.

Mike Leigh (b.1943), British film-maker: Johnny (David Thewlis) to Louise, in *Naked* (film; written and directed by Mike Leigh, 1993)

18 God is a concept by which we measure our pain.

John Lennon (1940–1980), British rock musician: 'God' (song), on the album *John Lennon/Plastic Ono Band* (1970)

19 God the Director effaces God the Creator. He commands actors rather than freedoms. Is the image that, in its marvellous precociousness, Judaism conceived in the midst of peoples who were extremely happy in their enthusiasm, not alienated when the shadow of a destiny falls on our intentions?

Emmanuel Levinas (b.1905), French Jewish philosopher: 'Persons or Figures' (1950), rep. in *Difficult Freedom* (1990), Pt.3

20 Can a mortal ask questions which God finds unanswerable? Quite easily, I should think. All nonsense questions are unanswerable.

C.S. Lewis (1898–1963), British author: *A Grief Observed* (1961), Pt.4

21 God is really only another artist. He invented the giraffe, the elephant, and the cat. He has no real style. He just keeps on trying other things.

Pablo Picasso (1881–1973), Spanish artist: quoted in *Life with Picasso* by Françoise Gilot and Carlton Lake (1964), Pt.1

22 God's a rumour.... I see God in us or with us, if I see God at all, as shreds and particles and rumours, some knowledge that we have, some feeling why we sing and dance and act, why we paint, why we love, why we make art. ... All the things that separate us from the purely animal in us are palpably there ... and I have no means of knowing whether that thereness in some sense doesn't cling to what I call 'me'.

Dennis Potter (1935–1994), British dramatist and screenwriter: interview with Melvyn Bragg, Channel 4, 5 April 1994

23 If God has at last died in our culture, he has not been buried. For the casually religious, he lingers on like a fond old relative who has been so expertly embalmed that we may prop him up in the far corner of the living room and pretend the old fellow is still with us. We have even taken pains to bend his fallen mouth into a benign and permissive smile ... and that is a comfort. It makes him so much *easier* to live with. No more of the old hellfire and brimstone; no more of the terrible mystery and paradox that require the crucifixion of the intellect; no more dark nights of the soul.

Theodore Roszak (b.1933), U.S. social critic: *Where the Wasteland Ends* (1972), Ch.6

24 So long as one believes in God one has the right *to do* the Good in order *to be* moral.

Jean-Paul Sartre (1905–1980), French philosopher and author: *Notebooks for an Ethics* (1983; tr.1992), Notebook 1

25 If we really think about it, God exists for any single individual who puts his trust in Him, not for the whole of humanity, with its laws, its organizations, and its violence. Humanity is the demon which God does not succeed in destroying.

Salvatore Satta (1902–1975), Italian jurist and novelist: *The Day of Judgment* (1979), Ch.15

26 God owns heaven
but He craves the earth.

Anne Sexton (1928–1974), U.S. poet: 'The Earth', St.2, publ. in *The Awful Rowing Toward God* (1975)

27 It is an insult to God to believe in God. For on the one hand it is to suppose that he has perpetrated acts of incalculable cruelty. On the other hand, it is to suppose that he has perversely given his human creatures an instrument – their intellect – which must inevitably lead them, if they are dispassionate and honest, to deny his existence. It is tempting to conclude that if he exists, it is the atheists and agnostics that he loves best, among those with any pretensions to education. For they are the ones who have taken him most seriously.

Galen Strawson (b.1952), British philosopher and literary critic: in *The Independent* (London), 24 June 1990

28 If you talk to God, you are praying; if God talks to you, you have schizophrenia.

Thomas Szasz (b.1920), U.S. psychiatrist: *The Second Sin* (1973), 'Schizophrenia'

29 'God' is a word, however problematical, we do not have to look up in the dictionary. We seem to have its acquaintance from birth.

John Updike (b.1932), U.S. author and critic: *Self-Consciousness: Memoirs* (1989), Ch.6

30 I rarely speak about God. To God, yes. I protest against Him. I shout at Him. But to open a discourse about the qualities of God, about the problems that God imposes, theodicy, no. And yet He is there, in silence, in filigree.

Elie Wiesel (b.1928), Rumanian-born U.S. writer: interview in *Writers at Work* (Eighth Series, ed. George Plimpton, 1988)

See also Allen on AGNOSTICS; Hawking on THE COSMOS; Auden on FAITH; Bellow on FRANCE; Prévert on PRAYER

GOLF

1 If there is any larceny in a man, golf will bring it out.

Paul Gallico (1897–1976), U.S. novelist: in the *New York Times*, 6 March 1977

2 If you watch a game, it's fun. If you play it, it's recreation. If you work at it, it's golf.

Bob Hope (b.1903), U.S. comedian: quoted in *Reader's Digest* (Pleasantville, N.Y.), Oct. 1958

3 If you think it's hard to meet new people, try picking up the wrong golf ball.

Jack Lemmon (b.1925), U.S. actor: in *Sports Illustrated* (New York), 9 Dec. 1985

GOODNESS

1 As if one could know the good a person is capable of, when one doesn't know the bad he might do.

Elias Canetti (1905–1994), Austrian novelist and philosopher: *The Secret Heart Of The Clock: Notes, Aphorisms, Fragments 1973–1985* (1991), '1975'

2 True human goodness, in all its purity and freedom, can come to the fore only when its recipient has no power.

Milan Kundera (b.1929), Czech-born French author and critic: *The Unbearable Lightness of Being* (1984), Pt.7, Ch.2

3 The Crucifixion and other historical precedents notwithstanding, many of us still believe that outstanding goodness is a kind of armor, that virtue, seen plain and bare, gives pause to criminality. But perhaps it is the other way around.

Mary McCarthy (1912–1989), U.S. author and critic: 'Gandhi' (1949), rep. in *On the Contrary* (1961), Pt.1

4 Being good is just a matter of temperament in the end.

Iris Murdoch (b.1919), British novelist and philosopher: Kate Gray, in *The Nice and the Good* (1968), Ch.14

5 The final measure of damnation: to hate the good precisely because we know it is good and know that its beauty calls our whole being into question.

Theodore Roszak (b.1933), U.S. social critic: introduction to *Where the Wasteland Ends* (1972)

6 We are not born bad: everybody has something good inside them. Some hide it, some neglect it, but it is there.

Mother Teresa (1910–1997), Albanian-born Roman Catholic missionary: *A Simple Path* (ed. Lucinda Vardey, 1995), 'Faith'

See also KINDNESS

GOSSIP

1 Gossip is the new pornography.
Woody Allen (b.1935), U.S. film-maker: Yale (Michael Murphy), in *Manhattan* (film; screenplay by Woody Allen and Marshall Brickman, directed by Woody Allen, 1979)

2 While gossip among women is universally ridiculed as low and trivial, gossip among men, especially if it is about women, is called theory, or idea, or fact.
Andrea Dworkin (b.1946), U.S. feminist critic: *Right-Wing Women* (1978), Ch.1

3 Gossip is the opiate of the oppressed.
Erica Jong (b.1942), U.S. author: the narrator (Isadora Wing), in *Fear of Flying* (1973), Ch.6

4 Anyone who has obeyed nature by transmitting a piece of gossip experiences the explosive relief that accompanies the satisfying of a primary need.
Primo Levi (1919–1987), Italian chemist and author: 'About Gossip', first publ. in *La Stampa* (Turin), 24 June 1986, rep. in *The Mirror Maker* (1989)

5 Gossip isn't scandal and it's not merely malicious. It's chatter about the human race by lovers of the same. Gossip is the tool of the poet, the shop-talk of the scientist, and the consolation of the housewife, wit, tycoon and intellectual. It begins in the nursery and ends when speech is past.
Phyllis McGinley (1905–1978), U.S. poet and author: 'A New Year and No Resolutions', publ. in *Woman's Home Companion*, Jan. 1957

6 Ah, well, the truth is always one thing, but in a way it's the other thing, the gossip, that counts. It shows where people's hearts lie.
Paul Scott (1920–1978), British author: Count Bronowsky, in *The Day of the Scorpion* (1968), Bk.1, Pt.3, Ch.3

7 Gossip is news running ahead of itself in a red satin dress.
Liz Smith (b.1923), U.S. journalist and author: in *American Way*, syndicated column, 3 Sept. 1985. 'Most good gossip columnists,' Smith went on to write in 1991, 'have a touch of Savonarola in them'

GOVERNMENT

1 But their determination to banish fools foundered
ultimately in the installation of absolute idiots.
Basil Bunting (1900–1985), British poet: on the decline of government under the Turkish Seljuk dynasty, in 'The Spoils', first publ. in *Poetry* (Chicago), 1951, rep. in *Collected Poems* (1968)

2 I say to myself that I mustn't let myself be cut off in there, and yet the moment I enter my bag is taken out of my hand, I'm pushed in, shepherded, nursed and above all cut off, alone. Whitehall envelops me.
Richard Crossman (1907–1974), British Labour politician: journal entry, 22 Oct. 1964, after his first week in the Cabinet, publ. in *Diaries* Vol. II (1976)

3 Truth is the glue that holds government together.
Gerald Ford (b.1913), U.S. Republican politician and president: speech, 9 Aug. 1974, on succeeding Richard Nixon as president, publ. in *Public Papers of the Presidents* (1974). Ford had used the words on various previous occasions

4 To govern is to choose. To appear to be unable to choose is to appear to be unable to govern.
Nigel Lawson (b.1932), British Conservative politician: in the *Daily Mail* (London), 26 March 1991

5 Generosity is a part of my character, and I therefore hasten to assure this Government that I will never make an allegation of dishonesty against it wherever a simple explanation of stupidity will suffice.
Leslie Lever (1905–1977), British solicitor and Labour politician: speech in House of Commons, quoted in *The Fine Art of Political Wit* by Leon Harris (1964), Ch.12

6 In government offices which are sensitive to the vehemence and passion of mass sentiment public men have no sure tenure. They are in effect perpetual office seekers, always on trial for their political lives, always required to court their restless constituents.
Walter Lippmann (1889–1974), U.S. journalist: *The Public Philosophy* (1955), Ch.2, Sct.4

7 If you join government, calmly make your contribution and move on. Don't go along to get along; do your best and when you have to – and you will – leave, and be something else.
Peggy Noonan (b.1950), U.S. author and presidential speechwriter: *What I Saw at the Revolution* (1990), 'Another Epilogue'

8 Every government is a parliament of whores. The trouble is, in a democracy the whores are us.
P.J. O'Rourke (b.1947), U.S. journalist: *Parliament of Whores* (1991), 'At Home in the Parliament of Whores'

9 Government does not solve problems; it subsidizes them.
Ronald Reagan (b.1911), U.S. Republican politician and president: speech, 11 Dec. 1972, publ. in *Speaking My Mind* (1989), 'The Wit and Wisdom of Ronald Reagan'

10 No more distressing moment can ever face a British government than that which requires it to come to a hard, fast and specific decision.

Barbara Tuchman (1912–1989), U.S. historian: *The Guns of August* (1962), Ch.9

11 I love my government not least for the extent to which it leaves me alone.

John Updike (b.1932), U.S. author and critic: testimony, 30 Jan. 1978, given before the Subcommittee on Select Education of the House of Representatives Committee on Education and Labor, Boston, publ. in Appendix to Updike's *Hugging the Shore* (1983)

See also Friedman on RESPONSIBILITY; Baudrillard on SCANDAL; Mosley on TRICKERY

GRAFFITI

1 In New York – whose subway trains in particular have been 'tattooed' with a brio and an energy to put our own rude practitioners to shame – not an inch of free space is spared *except that of advertisements.* ... Even the most chronically dispossessed appear prepared to endorse the legitimacy of the 'haves'.

Gilbert Adair, British author and critic: *Myths and Memories* (1986), 'Cleaning and Cleansing'

2 In the dime stores and bus stations,
People talk of situations,
Read books, repeat quotations,
Draw conclusions on the wall.

Bob Dylan (b.1941), U.S. singer and songwriter: 'Love Minus Zero/No Limit' (song), on the album *Bringing it All Back Home* (1965)

GRATITUDE

1 Gratitude is the most exquisite form of courtesy.

Jacques Maritain (1882–1973), French philosopher: *Reflections on America* (1948), Ch.17

2 Gratitude – the meanest and most snivelling attribute in the world.

Dorothy Parker (1893–1967), U.S. humorous writer: interview in *Writers at Work* (First Series, ed. Malcolm Cowley, 1958)

GREATNESS

1 Everybody comes along at the right time.... Leonardo was lucky because he came along at the right time. Oscar Wilde was lucky because he came at the right time – if he hadn't gone to court and been martyred he wouldn't be such a cult hero now. Or Jesus Christ – if he came back now he would really be up the shit because there's no capital punishment.

David Bailey (b.1938), British photographer: interview in *The Face* (London), Dec. 1984

2 We shall never resolve the enigma of the relation between the negative foundations of greatness and that greatness itself.

Jean Baudrillard (b.1929), French semiologist: *America* (1986; tr.1988), 'Utopia Achieved'

3 It is not men who are great. It is man who is great. It is not wonderful to be exceptional. It is wonderful to be a man.

Jean Dubuffet (1901–1985), French sculptor and painter: 'Notes for the Well-Lettered', first publ. in *Prospectus* (1946) rep. in *Art in Theory* (ed. Charles Harrison and Paul Wood, 1992), Pt.5B

4 I distrust Great Men. They produce a desert of uniformity around them and often a pool of blood too, and I always feel a little man's pleasure when they come a cropper.

E.M. Forster (1879–1970), British novelist and essayist: *Two Cheers for Democracy* (1951), 'What I Believe'

5 A great man's greatest good luck is to die at the right time.

Eric Hoffer (1902–1983), U.S. philosopher: *The Passionate State of Mind* (1955), Aph.276

6 I dare to be great. The man without imagination stands unhurt and hath no wings. This is my credo, this is my forte.

Don King (b.1931), U.S. boxing promoter: interview in the *Independent on Sunday* (London), 10 March 1996

7 In my opinion, most of the great men of the past were only there for the beer – the wealth, prestige and grandeur that went with the power.

A.J.P. Taylor (1906–1990), British historian: quoted in introduction to *Voices 1870–1914* by Peter Vansittart (1984)

See also McGovern on ANTICIPATION

GREED

1 Greed is all right, by the way... I think greed is healthy. You can be greedy and still feel good about yourself.

Ivan F. Boesky (b.1937), U.S. arbitrageur: commencement address, 18 May 1986, School of Business Administration, University of California, Berkeley. Boesky was later convicted of conspiring to file false documents with the federal government, involving insider trading violations. His words were echoed in Oliver Stone's film, *Wall Street* (1987), spoken by Gordon Gekko (Michael Douglas): 'Greed is good. Greed is right. Greed clarifies, cuts through, and captures. Greed has marked the upward surge of mankind'

2   There is enough in the world for everyone's need, but not enough for everyone's greed.
Frank Buchman (1878–1961), U.S. evangelist: *Remaking the World* (1947)

3   What kind of society isn't structured on greed?
Milton Friedman (b.1912), U.S. economist: introduction to *There's No Such Thing as a Free Lunch* (1975)

4   The point is that you can't be too greedy.
Donald Trump (b.1946), U.S. businessman: *Trump: The Art of the Deal* (written with Tony Schwartz, 1987), Ch.2

See also De Vries on FOOD

GRIEF

1   In deep sadness there is no place for sentimentality.
William Burroughs (1914–1997), U.S. author: *Queer* (1985), Ch.8

2   Pain hardens, and great pain hardens greatly, whatever the comforters say, and suffering does not ennoble, though it may occasionally lend a certain rigid dignity of manner to the suffering frame.
A.S. Byatt (b.1936), British author: quoted in *The Daily Telegraph* (London), 21 July 1986

3   No one ever told me that grief felt so like fear.
C.S. Lewis (1898–1963), British author: opening words of *A Grief Observed* (1961), a book of mourning for Lewis's dead wife

4   The human heart dares not stay away too long from that which hurt it most. There is a return journey to anguish that few of us are released from making.
Lillian Smith (1897–1966), U.S. author: *Killers of the Dream* (1949; rev.1961), Pt.1, Ch.1

5   Your generation does too much sharing. To share grief is to double grief, not halve it; each spouse likes to believe in the other's strength; wants the other to stay grown-up for the moments when he, she, becomes the weeping child again.
Fay Weldon (b.1933), British novelist: Christobel, in *A Good Sound Marriage* (1991), publ. in *Wicked Women* (1995)

See also BEREAVEMENT; SORROW; UNHAPPINESS

GROWING UP

1   It's worth the pain to be born and to grow up. But must one live after that? All life then finds itself justified.
Albert Camus (1913–1960), French-Algerian philosopher and author: journal entry, 27 May 1950, quoted in *Camus: A Biography* by Herbert R. Lottman (1979), Ch.36

2   I used to believe, although I don't now, that growing and growing up are analogous, that both are inevitable and uncontrollable processes. Now it seems to me that growing up is governed by the will, that one can *choose* to become an adult, but only at given moments. These moments come along fairly infrequently – during crises in relationships, for example, or when one has been given the chance to start afresh somewhere – and one can ignore them or seize them.
Nick Hornby (b.1957), British author: *Fever Pitch* (1992), '1976–1986: A Fourth Division Town'

3   The child thinks of growing old as an almost obscene calamity, which for some mysterious reason will never happen to itself. All who have passed the age of thirty are joyless grotesques, endlessly fussing about things of no importance and staying alive without, so far as the child can see, having anything to live for. Only child life is real life.
George Orwell (1903–1950), British author: 'Such, Such were the Joys' (1947), rep. in *The Collected Essays, Journalism and Letters of George Orwell* (ed. Sonia Orwell and Ian Angus, 1968), Vol.IV

4   Our message: Don't grow up. Growing up means *giving up your dreams*.
Jerry Rubin (1938–1994), U.S. essayist, radical leader: *Do It!* (1970), 'Yippie!', Extract 13

See also ADULTHOOD; MATURITY

GUERRILLA WARFARE

1   The conventional army loses if it does not win. The guerrilla wins if he does not lose.
Henry Kissinger (b.1923), U.S. Republican politician and secretary of state: commenting on the war in Vietnam, in *Foreign Affairs* (New York), Jan. 1969

2   It is necessary to turn political crisis into armed crisis by performing violent actions that will force those in power to transform the military situation into a political situation. That will alienate the masses, who, from then on, will revolt against the army and the police and blame them for this state of things.
Carlos Marighella (d.1969), Brazilian guerrilla leader: *Minimanual of the Urban Guerrilla* (1969)

GUILT

1   It is quite gratifying to feel guilty if you haven't done anything wrong: how noble! Whereas it is

rather hard and certainly depressing to admit guilt and to repent.
Hannah Arendt (1906–1975), German-born U.S. political philosopher: *Eichmann in Jerusalem* (1963), Ch.15

2   Guilt always hurries towards its complement, punishment; only there does its satisfaction lie.
Lawrence Durrell (1912–1990), British author: *Justine* (1957), Pt.3

3   The extent of one man's guilt may be defined by how much of it is experienced by the party he injured.
Ryszard Kapuściński (b.1932), Polish journalist: 'A Warsaw Diary', publ. in *Granta* (Cambridge), No.15, 1985

4   True guilt is guilt at the obligation one owes to oneself to be oneself. False guilt is guilt felt at not being what other people feel one ought to be or assume that one is.
R.D. Laing (1927–1989), British psychiatrist: *The Self and Others* (1961), Ch.10

5   How extraordinary it is that one feels most guilt about the sins one is unable to commit.
V.S. Pritchett (1900–1997), British author and critic: *Midnight Oil* (second volume of memoirs, 1971), Ch.10

See also Kübler-Ross on BEREAVEMENT

GUNS

1   My, my. Such a lot of guns around town and so few brains.
Humphrey Bogart (1899–1957), U.S. actor: Philip Marlowe (Humphrey Bogart), in *The Big Sleep* (film; screenplay by William Faulkner, Leigh Brackett and Jules Furthman, adapted from Raymond Chandler's novel, directed by Howard Hawks, 1946)

2   After a shooting spree, they always want to take the guns away from the people who *didn't* do it. I sure as hell wouldn't want to live in a society where the only people allowed guns are the police and the military.
William Burroughs (1914–1997), U.S. author: 'The War Universe', taped conversation first publ. in *Grand Street* (New York), No.37, rep. in *Painting and Guns* (1992) in a slightly different form

3   When I hold you in my arms
And I feel my finger on your trigger
I know no one can do me no harm
Because happiness is a warm gun.
John Lennon (1940–1980) and **Paul McCartney** (b.1942), British rock musicians: 'Happiness is a Warm Gun' (song) on *The BEATLES (White Album)*, (The Beatles, 1968)

4   It's the thing that shows there is no aristocracy,

that there is no class division, and it's an absolutely vital right to retain.
P.J. O'Rourke (b.1947), U.S. journalist: on gun rights, in interview in *The Guardian* (London), 25 Nov. 1995

5   But you see Sheriff, that's the way it is. When you've got a gun, you are a sort of god. If you had the gun, I'd be the chump and you'd be the god. The gun gives you the power of life and death. ... Without the gun, I'm nothing.
Frank Sinatra (b.1915), U.S. singer and actor: Johnny Baron (Frank Sinatra), in *Suddenly* (film; screenplay by Richard Sale, directed by Lewis Allen, 1954)

See also Tarantino on KILLING

HABIT

1   To *exist* is a habit I do not despair of acquiring.
E.M. Cioran (1911–1995), Rumanian-born French philosopher: title essay of *The Temptation to Exist* (1956)

2   *Good* Habits: they are never good, because they are habits.
Jean-Paul Sartre (1905–1980), French philosopher and author: *Notebooks for an Ethics* (1983; tr.1992), Notebook 1

HAIR

1   What does it say about racial purity that the best blondes have all been brunettes (Harlow, Monroe, Bardot)? I think it says that we are not as white as we think. I think it says that Pure is a Bore.
Julie Burchill (b.1960), British journalist and author: *Girls on Film* (1986), Ch.6

2   People get real comfortable with their features. Nobody gets comfortable with their hair. Hair trauma. It's the universal thing.
Jamie Lee Curtis (b.1958), U.S. actress: in *U.S.*, (New York), 21 Feb. 1991

3   Blondes are the best victims. They're like virgin snow which shows up the bloody footprints.
Alfred Hitchcock (1899–1980), British film-maker: in *The Sunday Times* (London), 1 Sept. 1973

4   Robert Redford ... has turned almost alarmingly blond – he's gone past platinum, he must be into plutonium; his hair is coordinated with his teeth.
Pauline Kael (b.1919), U.S. film critic: *Reeling* (1976), Pt.2, 'The Sting'

5   Being blond is definitely a different state of mind. I can't really put my finger on it, but the artifice of being blond has some incredible sort of sexual connotation.

Madonna (b.1959), U.S. singer and actress: interview in *Rolling Stone* (New York) 23 March 1989

6 I don't advise a haircut, man. All hairdressers are in the employment of the government. Hairs are your aerials. They pick up signals from the cosmos, and transmit them directly into the brain. This is the reason bald-headed men are uptight.
Bruce Robinson (b.1946), British film-maker: Danny (Ralph Brown), in *Withnail and I* (film; written and directed by Bruce Robinson, 1987)

See also Hammerstein II on INFATUATION; Walker on JESUS CHRIST

HAPPINESS

1 Happiness is always a by-product. It is probably a matter of temperament, and for anything I know it may be glandular. But it is not something that can be demanded from life, and if you are not happy you had better stop worrying about it and see what treasures you can pluck from your own brand of unhappiness.
Robertson Davies (1913–1995), Canadian novelist and journalist: 'The Table Talk of Robertson Davies', first publ. in *Maclean's* (Toronto), Sept. 1972, rep. in *The Enthusiasms of Robertson Davies* (1990)

2 Point me out the happy man and I will point you out either egotism, selfishness, evil – or else an absolute ignorance.
Graham Greene (1904–1991), British novelist: *The Heart of the Matter* (1948), Bk.2, Pt.1, Ch.1, Sct.3

3 There is something ridiculous and even quite indecent in an individual *claiming* to be happy. Still more a people or a nation making such a claim. ... This lamentable phrase 'the pursuit of happiness' is responsible for a good part of the ills and miseries of the modern world.
Malcolm Muggeridge (1903–1990), British journalist and broadcaster: *Woman's Hour* (radio broadcast), 5 Oct. 1965, publ. in *Muggeridge Through the Microphone* (1967), 'Happiness'

4 Happiness is a matter of one's most ordinary everyday mode of consciousness being busy and lively and unconcerned with self. To be damned is for one's ordinary everyday mode of consciousness to be unremitting agonising preoccupation with self.
Iris Murdoch (b.1919), British novelist and philosopher: Willy Kost, in *The Nice and the Good* (1968), Ch.22

5 Even if happiness forgets you a little bit, never completely forget about it.
(*Même si le bonheur t'oublie un peu, ne l'oublie jamais tout à fait.*)
Jacques Prévert (1900–1977), French poet: 'Intermède', publ. in *Spectacle* (1951)

6 Happiness is an imaginary condition, formerly often attributed by the living to the dead, now usually attributed by adults to children, and by children to adults.
Thomas Szasz (b.1920), U.S. psychiatrist: *The Second Sin* (1973), 'Emotions'

HARD TIMES

1 Hardship makes the world obscure.
Don DeLillo (b.1926), U.S. author: James Axton, in *The Names* (1982), Ch.12

2 Life isn't meant to be easy. It's hard to take being on the top – or on the bottom. I guess I'm something of a fatalist. You have to have a sense of history, I think, to survive some of these things.... Life is one crisis after another.
Richard Nixon (1913–1992), U.S. Republican politician and president: on the Watergate scandal, to interviewer, Sept. 1980, quoted in *Exile: The Unquiet Oblivion of Richard M. Nixon* by Robert Sam Anson (1984), Ch.17

3 Born down in a dead man's town
The first kick I took was when I hit the ground
You end up like a dog that's been beat too
    much
Till you spend half your life just covering up.
Bruce Springsteen (b.1949), U.S. rock musician: 'Born in the U.S.A.' (song), on the album *Born in the U.S.A.* (Bruce Springsteen and the E Street Band, 1984)

4 When you are down and out something always turns up – and it is usually the noses of your friends.
Orson Welles (1915–1985), U.S. film-maker and actor: in the *New York Times*, 1 April 1962

HATE

1 While love ceaselessly strives toward that which lies at the hiddenmost centre, hatred only perceives the topmost surface and perceives it so exclusively that the devil of hatred, despite all his terror-inspiring cruelty, never is entirely free of ridicule and of a somewhat dilettantish aspect. One who hates is a man holding a magnifying-glass, and when he hates someone, he knows precisely that person's surface, from the soles of his feet all the way up to each hair on the hated head. Were one merely to seek information, one should inquire of the man who hates, but if one wishes to know what truly is, one better ask the one who loves.
Hermann Broch (1886–1951), Austrian novelist: *The Spell* (1976; tr.1987), Ch.9

2   When Love becomes a command, Hatred be-
    comes a pleasure.
    Charles Bukowski (1920–1994), U.S. author and
    poet: *Notes of a Dirty Old Man* (1969), p.165 of City
    Lights edn. (1973)

3   You are done for – a living dead man – not
    when you stop loving but stop hating. Hatred
    preserves: in it, in its chemistry, resides the
    'mystery' of life. Not for nothing is hatred still
    the best tonic ever discovered, for which any
    organism, however feeble, has a tolerance.
    E.M. Cioran (1911–1995), Rumanian-born French
    philosopher: *The New Gods* (*Le Mauvais Démiurge*
    1969; tr. 1974), 'Strangled Thoughts', Sct.1

4   The price of hating other human beings is
    loving oneself less.
    Eldridge Cleaver (b.1935), U.S. black leader and
    writer: closing words of 'On Becoming', written
    from Folsom Prison, California, 25 June 1965, publ.
    in *Soul on Ice* (1968)

5   I never hated a man enough to give him
    diamonds back.
    Zsa Zsa Gabor (b.1919), Hungarian-born U.S.
    actress: quoted in *The Observer* (London), 28 Aug.
    1957

6   What we need is hatred. From it our ideas are
    born.
    Jean Genet (1910–1986), French playwright and
    novelist: epigraph to *The Blacks* (1959; tr.1960)

7   Hate traps us by binding us too tightly to our
    adversary.
    Milan Kundera (b.1929), Czech-born French
    author and critic: *Immortality* (1991), Pt.1, Ch.5

8   I don't believe that people are capable of real
    hate. We are too lonely for that. We vanish too
    quickly for that. Do you ever hate a cloud?
    How could anyone hate people who are on
    their deathbeds? That's where we all are since
    the day of birth.
    Yoko Ono (b.1933), Japanese-born U.S. artist:
    sleevenotes on *Feeling the Space* (album, 1973)

9   To make oneself hated is more difficult than to
    make oneself loved.
    Pablo Picasso (1881–1973), Spanish artist: in *Vogue*
    (New York), 1 Nov. 1956

HATS

1   The hat is not for the street: it will never be
    democratized. But there are certain houses
    that one cannot enter without a hat. And one
    must always wear a hat when lunching with
    people whom one does not know well. One
    appears to one's best advantage.
    Coco Chanel (1883–1971), French *couturière*:
    quoted in *Coco Chanel: Her Life, Her Secrets* by
    Marcel Haedrich (1971), Ch.21

2   Well, you look so pretty in it
    Honey, can I jump on it sometime?
    Yes, I just wanna see
    If it's really that expensive kind
    You know it balances on your head
    Just like a mattress balances
    On a bottle of wine
    Your brand new leopard-skin pill-box hat.
    Bob Dylan (b.1941), U.S. singer and songwriter:
    'Leopard-Skin Pill-Box Hat' (song), on the album
    Blonde on Blonde (1968)

3   Hats divide generally into three classes:
    offensive hats, defensive hats, and shrapnel.
    Katharine Whitehorn (b.1926), British journalist:
    Shouts and Murmurs (1963), 'Hats'

HAUTE COUTURE

1   Haute Couture should be fun, foolish and
    almost unwearable.
    Christian Lacroix (b.1951), French fashion
    designer: quoted in *The Observer* (London), 27 Dec.
    1987

2   A designer who is not also a couturier, who
    hasn't learned the most refined mysteries of
    physically creating his models, is like a
    sculptor who gives his drawings to another
    man, an artisan, to accomplish. For him the
    truncated process of creating will always be an
    interrupted act of love, and his style will bear
    the shame of it, the impoverishment.
    Yves Saint Laurent (b.1936), French fashion
    designer: interview in *Ritz* (London), No.85, 1984

See also FASHION; MODELS

HEALTH

1   'Healing,'
    Papa would tell me,
    'is not a science,
    but the intuitive art
    of wooing Nature.'
    W.H. Auden (1907–1973), Anglo-American poet:
    'The Art of Healing' (1969), rep. in *Collected Poems*
    (1976)

2   Bad health is a sign of the moral failing that
    only recently was attributed to repressed
    sexuality ... the perpetual, paranoid main-
    tenance of a cleansed, purified body, immune
    to all sorts of external pollution, tends to feed
    into a social philosophy saturated with the
    historical barbarism of the politics of quaran-
    tine, natural selection, and social apartheid.
    Andrew Ross (b.1956), British social theorist:
    Strange Weather (1991), Ch.1

3   We are all ill: but even a universal sickness im-
    plies an idea of health.

Lionel Trilling (1905–1975), U.S. critic: *The Liberal Imagination* (1950), 'Art and Neurosis'

4   Health is a state of complete physical, mental and social well-being, and not merely the absence of disease or infirmity.
World Health Organisation: Constitution, 1948

See also DISEASE; DOCTORS; ILLNESS; MEDICINE

HELL

1   A valid hell is one from which there is a possibility of redemption, even if this is never achieved, the dungeons of an architecture of grace whose spires point to some kind of heaven. The institutional hells of the present century are reached with one-way tickets, marked Nagasaki and Buchenwald, worlds of terminal horror even more final than the grave.
J.G. Ballard (b.1930), British author: 'Visions of Hell', review of *The Human Age* by Wyndham Lewis, first publ. in *New Worlds* (London), March 1966, rep. in *Re/Search* (San Francisco), No.8/9, 1984

2   Hell is oneself,
Hell is alone, the other figures in it
Merely projections. There is nothing to escape from
And nothing to escape to. One is always alone.
T.S. Eliot (1888–1965), Anglo-American poet, critic: Edward, in *The Cocktail Party* (1950), Act 1, Sc.3

3   To be in a world which is a hell, to be *of* that world and neither to believe in or guess at anything *but* that world, is not merely hell but the only possible damnation: the act of a man damning himself.
William Golding (1911–1993), British author: 'Belief and Creativity', lecture, 11 April 1980, Hamburg, rep. in *A Moving Target* (1982)

4   Hell is not horror; hell is being degraded to the point of death, whether death comes or passes by: the appalling abjection of the victim, the mysterious abjection of the executioner. Satan is the Degrader.
André Malraux (1901–1976), French man of letters and statesman: referring to the concentration camps in Nazi Germany, in *Anti-Memoirs* (1967; tr.1968), 'The Human Condition', Sct.2

5   It is an open question whether any behavior based on fear of eternal punishment can be regarded as ethical or should be regarded as merely cowardly.
Margaret Mead (1901–1978), U.S. anthropologist: quoted in *Redbook* (New York), Feb. 1971

HERITAGE

1   The use of the word 'heritage' as a term of obligation, binding people not only to respect relics of the past but also to understand them in one prescribed way as 'national symbols', is not spontaneous. It is a form of manipulation, devised by politicians and quangocrats to make the tatty, dishevelled building-site of the present look more imposing.
Neal Ascherson (b.1932), British journalist: in the *Independent on Sunday* (London), 19 Feb. 1995

2   Had Jerusalem been builded here and the site of the Crucifixion discovered, it would be promptly built over and christened the Golgotha Centre.
Alan Bennett (b.1934), British playwright: journal entry, 14 May 1989, publ. in *Writing Home* (1994), 'Diaries 1980–1990'

3   If the only new thing we have to offer is an improved version of the past, then today can only be inferior to yesterday. Hypnotised by images of the past, we risk losing all capacity for creative change.
Robert Hewison (b.1943), British cultural historian: introduction to *The Heritage Industry* (1987)

4   Our culture has become something that is completely and utterly in love with its parent. It's become a notion of boredom that is bought and sold, where nothing will happen except that people will become more and more terrified of tomorrow, because the new continues to look old, and the old will always look cute.
Malcolm McLaren (b.1946), British rock impresario: discussion, 24 Sept. 1988, New York City, publ. in *Discourses: Conversations in Postmodern Art and Culture* (ed. Russell Ferguson *et al.*, 1990), 'Punk and History'

See also Baudrillard on FRANCE; ROOTS

HEROES

1   They wouldn't be heroes if they were infallible, in fact they wouldn't be heroes if they weren't miserable wretched dogs, the pariahs of the earth, besides which the only reason to build up an idol is to tear it down again.
Lester Bangs (1948–1982), U.S. rock journalist: in *Creem* (London), March 1975, rep. in *Psychotic Reactions & Carburetor Dung* (1987), 'Let Us Now Praise Famous Death Dwarves'

2   What is a society without a heroic dimension?
Jean Baudrillard (b.1929), French semiologist: *America* (1986; tr.1988), 'Utopia Achieved'

3   In our world of big names, curiously, our true heroes tend to be anonymous. In this life of

illusion and quasi-illusion, the person of solid virtues who can be admired for something more substantial than his well-knownness often proves to be the unsung hero: the teacher, the nurse, the mother, the honest cop, the hard worker at lonely, underpaid, unglamorous, unpublicized jobs.

Daniel J. Boorstin (b.1914), U.S. historian: *The Image* (1961), Ch.2

4 I – I will be king
and you – you will be queen,
though nothing will drive them away
We can be heroes
Just for one day.

David Bowie (b.1947), British rock musician: 'Heroes' (song), on the album *Heroes* (1977)

5 The 'paper tiger' hero, James Bond, offering the whites a triumphant image of themselves, is saying what many whites want desperately to hear reaffirmed: *I am still the White Man, lord of the land, licensed to kill, and the world is still an empire at my feet.*

Eldridge Cleaver (b.1935), U.S. black leader and writer: *Soul on Ice* (1968), 'The White Race and Its Heroes'

6 I think of a hero as someone who understands the degree of responsibility that comes with his freedom.

Bob Dylan (b.1941), U.S. singer and songwriter: interview 1985, publ. in sleevenotes to the album *Biograph* (1985)

7 Bardot, Byron, Hitler, Hemingway, Monroe, Sade: we do not require our heroes to be subtle, just to be big. Then we can depend on someone to make them subtle.

D.J. Enright (b.1920), British poet and critic: 'The Marquis and the Madame' (1953), rep. in *Conspirators and Poets* (1966)

8 The fame of heroes owes little to the extent of their conquests and all to the success of the tributes paid to them.

Jean Genet (1910–1986), French playwright and novelist: *Prisoner of Love* (1986: tr.1989), Pt.1

9 The world doesn't make any heroes anymore.

Graham Greene (1904–1991), British novelist: Major Calloway (Trevor Howard), in *The Third Man* (film; screenplay by Graham Greene, directed by Carol Reed, 1950)

10 It was involuntary. They sank my boat.

John F. Kennedy (1917–1963), U.S. Democratic politician and president: on being asked by a small boy how he became a war hero, quoted in *A Thousand Days* by Arthur M. Schlesinger Jr. (1965), Ch.4

11 Ultimately a hero is a man who would argue with the gods, and so awakens devils to contest his vision. The more a man can achieve, the

more he may be certain that the devil will inhabit a part of his creation.

Norman Mailer (b.1923), U.S. author: preface to *The Presidential Papers* (1963)

12 The ordinary man is involved in action, the hero acts. An immense difference.

Henry Miller (1891–1980), U.S. author: *The Books in My Life* (1951), Ch.10

13 Most people aren't appreciated enough, and the bravest things we do in our lives are usually known only to ourselves. No one throws ticker tape on the man who chose to be faithful to his wife, on the lawyer who didn't take the drug money, or the daughter who held her tongue again and again. All this anonymous heroism.

Peggy Noonan (b.1950), U.S. author and presidential speechwriter: *What I Saw at the Revolution* (1990), Ch.13

14 No bastard ever won a war by dying for his country. He won it by making the other poor dumb bastard die for his country.

George C. Scott (b.1926), U.S. actor: General George S. Patton Jr. (George C. Scott), in *Patton* (film; screenplay by Francis Ford Coppola and Edmund H. North, directed by Franklin J. Schaffner, 1970). In the film's opening speech, Patton addresses the audience as if they were his troops

15 The opportunities for heroism are limited in this kind of world: the most people can do is sometimes not to be as weak as they've been at other times.

Angus Wilson (1913–1991), British author: interview in *Writers at Work* (First Series, ed. Malcolm Cowley, 1958)

16 It's true that heroes are inspiring, but mustn't they also do some rescuing if they are to be worthy of their name? Would Wonder Woman matter if she only sent commiserating telegrams to the distressed?

Jeanette Winterson (b.1959), British author: in *The Independent* (London), 6 Jan. 1990

See also Moore on MEDIOCRITY

HETEROSEXUALITY

1 Such figures as Boy George do not disturb me nearly so much as do those relentlessly hetero (sexual?) keepers of the keys and seals, those who know what the world needs in the way of order and who are ready and willing to supply that order.

James Baldwin (1924–1987), U.S. author: 'Freaks and the American Ideal of Manhood', first publ. in *Playboy* (Chicago), Jan. 1985, rep. in *The Price of the Ticket* (1985), 'Here Be Dragons'

2 In heterosexual love there's no solution. Man and woman are irreconcilable, and it's the

doomed attempt to do the impossible, repeated in each new affair, that lends heterosexual love its grandeur.

Marguerite Duras (1914–1996), French author and film-maker: *Practicalities* (1987; tr.1990), 'Men'

3 Constant conditioning in my youth and social pressure in every department of my life all failed to convert me to heterosexuality.

Ian McKellen (b.1939), British actor: in *The Times* (London), 5 Dec. 1991

4 Competence in heterosexuality, or at least the appearance or pretense of such competence, is as much a public affair as a private one. Thus, going steady is a high school diploma in heterosexuality; engagement a BA; marriage an MA; and children a PhD.

Thomas Szasz (b.1920), U.S. psychiatrist: *The Second Sin* (1973), 'Sex'

See also Mailer on HOMOSEXUALITY; Wandor on LESBIANISM; Jarman on MEN

HIPPIES

1 I was always a sort of throwback to the Beat period in my early thinking. And when the hippies came along with all their funny tie-dyes and things, it all seemed naïve and wrong. It didn't have a backbone. ... I wanted to hit everybody that came along wearing love beads.

David Bowie (b.1947), British rock musician: interview Feb. 1976, rep. in *Bowie In His Own Words* (ed. Miles, 1980), 'Politics'

2 Keep on truckin'...truckin' on down the line ...
  hey, hey, hey
I said keep on truckin' ... truckin' my blues
  away.

Robert Crumb (b.1943), U.S. cartoonist: cartoon (1967), publ. in *R. Crumb's Head Comix* (1968; rev.1988)

3 The appropriation of radical thinking by lazy, self-obsessed hippies is a public relations disaster that could cost the earth.

Ben Elton (b.1959), British author and comic: *Stark* (1989), 'Court, Hippies and Love at First Sight'

4 Old hippies don't die, they just lie low until the laughter stops and their time comes round again.

Joseph Gallivan (b.1964), British journalist: in *The Independent* (London), 30 Aug. 1990

5 The hippie is the scion of surplus value. The dropout can only claim sanctity in a society which offers something to be dropped out of – career, ambition, conspicuous consumption. The effects of hippie sanctimony can only be felt in the context of others who plunder his lifestyle for what they find good or profitable, a process known as rip-off by the hippie, who will not see how savagely he has pillaged intricate and demanding civilizations for his own parodic lifestyle.

Germaine Greer (b.1939), Australian feminist writer: 'Hippies in Asia', first publ. in *The Sunday Times* (London), 27 Aug. 1972, rep. in *The Madwoman's Underclothes* (1986)

6 When we heard about the hippies, the barely more than boys and girls who decided to try something different ... we laughed at them. Smug in our certain awareness that ... communal life must be more difficult even than nuclear family life, which we know, to our very nerve endings, is disastrous, we condemned them, our children, for seeking a different future. We hated them for their flowers, for their love, and for their unmistakable rejection of every hideous, mistaken compromise that we had made throughout our hollow, money-bitten, frightened, adult lives.

June Jordan (b.1936), U.S. poet and civil rights activist: 'Old Stories: New Lives', keynote address, 1978, Child Welfare League of America, publ. in *Moving Towards Home: Political Essays* (1989)

7 It has to be acknowledged that in capitalist society, with its herds of hippies, originality has become a sort of fringe benefit, a *mere* convention, accepted obsolescence, the Beatnik model being turned in for the Hippie model, as though strangely obedient to capitalist laws of marketing.

Mary McCarthy (1912–1989), U.S. author and critic: *Hanoi* (1968), 'Language'

8 We are stardust,
We are golden,
And we got to get ourselves
Back to the garden.

Joni Mitchell (b.1943), Canadian-born U.S. singer and songwriter: 'Woodstock' (song, 1969)

9 The hippy movement seemed like a worldwide movement, in concept, but still the establishment was bigger. The only criticism I have of that movement was that, although we were talking about freedom, women still got a very raw deal. It was a very chauvinistic movement.

Yoko Ono (b.1933), Japanese-born U.S. artist: interview in *The Guardian* (London), 20 Jan. 1996

10 His hair has the long jesuschrist look. He is wearing the costume clothes. But most of all, he now has a very tolerant and therefore withering attitude toward all those who are still struggling in the old activist political ways ... while he, with the help of psychedelic chemicals, is exploring the infinite regions of human consciousness.

Tom Wolfe (b.1931), U.S. author and journalist: *The Electric Kool-Aid Acid Test* (1968), Ch.26

See also PSYCHEDELIA

HISTORIANS

1 The historian's job is to aggrandize, promoting accident to inevitability and innocuous circumstance to portent.
Peter Conrad (b.1948), Australian author and critic: *The Art of the City* (1984), Ch.1

2 I am not a professional historian; nobody is perfect.
Michel Foucault (1926–1984), French philosopher: comment at the University of Vermont, 27 Oct. 1982, quoted in 'Foucault and the History of Madness' by Gary Gutting, publ. in *The Cambridge Companion to Foucault* (1994)

3 Historians are left forever chasing shadows, painfully aware of their inability ever to reconstruct a dead world in its completeness however thorough or revealing their documentation. ... We are doomed to be forever hailing someone who has just gone around the corner and out of earshot.
Simon Schama (b.1945), British historian: *Dead Certainties* (1991), 'Afterword'

See also Hobsbawm on NATIONALISM

HISTORY

1 History is a relay of revolutions.
Saul Alinsky (1909–1972), U.S. political activist: *Rules for Radicals* (1971), 'Of Means and Ends'

2 History is, strictly speaking, the study of questions; the study of answers belongs to anthropology and sociology.
W.H. Auden (1907–1973), Anglo-American poet: *The Dyer's Hand* (1962), Pt.3, 'Hic et Ille', Sct.B

3 English history is all about men liking their fathers, and American history is all about men hating their fathers and trying to burn down everything they ever did.
Malcolm Bradbury (b.1932), British author: *Stepping Westward* (1965), Bk.2, Ch.5

4 History, as an entirety, could only exist in the eyes of an observer outside it and outside the world. History, only exists, in the final analysis, for God.
Albert Camus (1913–1960), French-Algerian philosopher and author: *The Rebel* (1951; tr.1953), Pt.5, 'Historic Murder'

5 History is a needle
for putting men asleep
anointed with the poison
Of all they want to keep.
Leonard Cohen (b.1934), Canadian singer, poet and novelist: 'On Hearing A Name Long Unspoken', St.3, publ. in *Flowers For Hitler* (1964)

6 The bases for historical knowledge are not empirical facts but written texts, even if these texts masquerade in the guise of wars or revolutions.
Paul de Man (1919–1983), Belgian-born U.S. literary critic: 'Literary History and Literary Modernity', lecture, Sept. 1969, publ. in *Blindness and Insight* (1971, rev. 1983)

7 History is the present. That's why every generation writes it anew. But what most people think of as history is its end product, myth.
E.L. Doctorow (b.1931), U.S. novelist: interview in *Writers at Work* (Eighth Series, ed. George Plimpton, 1988)

8 We as women know that there are no disembodied processes; that all history originates in human flesh; that all oppression is inflicted by the body of one against the body of another; that all social change is built on the bone and muscle, and out of the flesh and blood, of human creators.
Andrea Dworkin (b.1946), U.S. feminist critic: 'Our Blood: The Slavery of Women in Amerika', speech, 23 Aug. 1975, to the National Organization for Women, Washington D.C., publ. in *Our Blood* (1976), Ch.8

9 History has no 'meaning,' though this is not to say that it is absurd or incoherent. On the contrary, it is intelligible and should be susceptible to analysis down to the smallest detail – but this in accordance with the intelligibility of struggles, of strategies and tactics.
Michel Foucault (1926–1984), French philosopher: interview publ. in *Power/Knowledge* (1980), 'Truth and Power'

10 Written by the victors, and meditating on the victories, our Western history and our philosophy of history announce the realization of a humanist ideal while ignoring the vanquished, the victims and the persecuted, as if they were of no significance. They denounce the violence through which this history was none the less achieved without being concerned by this contradiction. This is humanism for the arrogant!
Emmanuel Levinas (b.1905), French Jewish philosopher: 'Jacob Gordin' (1972–3), rep. in *Difficult Freedom* (1990), Pt.4

11 History is the myth, the true myth, of man's fall made manifest in time.
Henry Miller (1891–1980), U.S. author: *Plexus* (1949), Ch.12

12 I have always felt a clear choice existed between two states of mind, the writing of history and the making of history. He who is interested in the latter should only be detained by the former just long enough to absorb its lessons.

Oswald Mosley (1896–1980), British fascist leader: *My Life* (1968), Ch.3

13 I believe that history has shape, order, and meaning; that exceptional men, as much as economic forces, produce change; and that passé abstractions like beauty, nobility, and greatness have a shifting but continuing validity.

Camille Paglia (b.1947), U.S. author and critic: *Sex, Art, and American Culture* (1992), 'Sexual Personae: The Cancelled Preface'

14 What is history? Its beginning is that of the centuries of systematic work devoted to the solution of the enigma of death, so that death itself may eventually be overcome. That is why people write symphonies, and why they discover mathematical infinity and electromagnetic waves.

Boris Pasternak (1890–1960), Russian poet, novelist and translator: Nikolay Nikolayevich, in *Doctor Zhivago* (1957; tr.1958), Ch.1, Sct.5

15 Science and Technology revolutionize our lives, but memory, tradition and myth frame our response. Expelled from individual consciousness by the rush of change, history finds its revenge by stamping the collective unconscious with habits, values, expectations, dreams. The dialectic between past and future will continue to form our lives.

Arthur M. Schlesinger Jr. (b.1917), U.S. historian: 'The Challenge of Change', publ. in the *New York Times Magazine*, 27 July 1986

16 There is nothing new in the world except the history you do not know.

Harry S Truman (1884–1972), U.S. Democratic politician and president: quoted in *Mr President* by William Hillman (1952), Pt.2, Ch.1

17 A country losing touch with its own history is like an old man losing his glasses, a distressing sight, at once vulnerable, unsure, and easily disoriented.

George Walden (b.1939), British Conservative politician: in *The Times* (London), 20 Dec. 1986

See also HERITAGE; Castro on POSTERITY; Guare on TIME: PAST

ADOLF HITLER

1 Adolf Hitler was one of the first rock stars. Look at some of his films and see how he moved. I think he was quite as good as Jagger. It's astounding. And, boy, when he hit that stage, he worked an audience. Good God! He was no politician, he was a media artist himself. He used politics and theatrics and created this thing that governed and controlled the show for those twelve years. The world will never see his like. He staged a country.

David Bowie (b.1947), British rock musician: interview, Feb. 1976, rep. in *Bowie In His Own Words* (ed. Miles, 1980), 'Politics'

2 It is true that this man was nothing but an elemental force in motion, directed and rendered more effective by extreme cunning and by a relentless tactical clairvoyance.... Hitler was history in its purest form.

Albert Camus (1913–1960), French-Algerian philosopher and author: *The Rebel* (1951; tr.1953), Pt.3, 'State Terrorism and Irrational Terror'

3 If Hitler invaded hell I would make at least a favourable reference to the devil in the House of Commons.

Winston Churchill (1874–1965), British statesman and author: *The Second World War: The Grand Alliance* (1950), Ch.20

4 He was simple, and treated me throughout the occasion with a gentle, almost feminine charm. Naturally, it was much easier for me to deal with him than some politicians, because in the international issues under discussion we had nothing to quarrel about. The men with whom we quarrel in life are those who want the same thing as we do, with consequent clash of interest; Hitler and I pursued different paths.

Oswald Mosley (1896–1980), British fascist leader: *My Life* (1968), Ch.19

See also Jakobovits on PASSIVITY

HOLIDAYS

1 Holidays arc in no sense an alternative to the congestion and bustle of cities and work. Quite the contrary. People look to escape into an intensification of the conditions of ordinary life, into a deliberate aggravation of those conditions: further from nature, nearer to artifice, to abstraction, to total pollution, to well above average levels of stress, pressure, concentration and monotony – this is the ideal of popular entertainment. No one is interested in overcoming alienation; the point is to plunge into it to the point of ecstasy. That is what holidays are for.

Jean Baudrillard (b.1929), French semiologist: *Cool Memories* (1987; tr.1990), Ch.2

2 Total physical and mental inertia are highly agreeable, much more so than we allow ourselves to imagine. A beach not only permits such inertia but enforces it, thus neatly eliminating all problems of guilt. It is now the only place in our overly active world that does.

J.K. Galbraith (b.1908), U.S. economist: foreword to 'The Beach Book', by Gloria Steinem (1963), rep. in *A View from the Stands* (1986)

3　We're all going on a summer holiday,
　　No more worries for a week or two.
　　Cliff Richard (b.1940), British singer: 'Summer
　　Holiday' (song, written by Bruce Welch and Brian
　　Bennett; performed by Cliff Richard and the
　　Shadows, 1963). The song featured in the film
　　Summer Holiday, directed by Peter Yates, 1963

4　We've gone on holiday by mistake.
　　Bruce Robinson (b.1946), British film-maker:
　　Withnail (Richard E. Grant), in *Withnail and I*
　　(film; written and directed by Bruce Robinson,
　　1987)

HOLISM

1　It's very hard to get your heart and head to-
　　gether in life. In my case, they're not even
　　friendly.
　　Woody Allen (b.1935), U.S. film-maker: Gabe Roth
　　(Woody Allen), in *Husbands and Wives* (film;
　　written and directed by Woody Allen, 1992)

2　Humanity has passed through a long history of
　　one-sidedness and of a social condition that has
　　always contained the potential of destruction,
　　despite its creative achievements in tech-
　　nology. The great project of our time must be
　　to open the other eye: to see all-sidedly and
　　wholly, to heal and transcend the cleavage
　　between humanity and nature that came with
　　early wisdom.
　　Murray Bookchin (b.1941), U.S. ecologist: *The
　　Ecology of Freedom* (1982), Ch.1

3　The appearance of the epithet 'Western' is like
　　the mark of Satan for the holistic health com-
　　munity, which systematically conceives of us
　　as victims rather than beneficiaries of specifi-
　　cally Western technology.
　　Andrew Ross (b.1956), British social theorist:
　　Strange Weather (1991), Ch.1

4　What is most threatening and destructive in
　　human society today is the human being who is
　　split in his own nucleus: it is the fission in the
　　modern soul which makes nuclear fission so
　　dangerous – he is a split atom. He has got to
　　heal himself, make himself whole.
　　Laurens van der Post (1906–1996), South African
　　writer and philosopher: *A Walk with a White
　　Bushman* (1986), p.50 of Chatto & Windus edn.

HOLLAND

1　Holland is a dream, Monsieur, a dream of gold
　　and smoke – smokier by day, more gilded by
　　night. And night and day that dream is peopled
　　with Lohengrins like these, dreamily riding
　　their black bicycles with high handle-bars,
　　funereal swans constantly drifting throughout
　　the whole country, around the seas, along the
　　canals.
　　Albert Camus (1913–1960), French-Algerian
　　philosopher and author: the narrator (Jean-Baptiste
　　Clamence), in *The Fall* (1956), p.12 of Hamish
　　Hamilton edn. (1957)

2　Apart from cheese and tulips, the main pro-
　　duct of the country is advocaat, a drink made
　　from lawyers.
　　Alan Coren (b.1938), British editor and humorist:
　　The Sanity Inspector (1974), 'All You Need to Know
　　about Europe'

HOLLYWOOD

1　Hollywood is a place where people from Iowa
　　mistake each other for stars.
　　Fred Allen (1894–1957), U.S. radio comic: quoted
　　in *No People Like Show People* by Maurice Zolotow
　　(1951), Ch.8

2　In Beverly Hills ... they don't throw their gar-
　　bage away. They make it into television shows.
　　Woody Allen (b.1935), U.S. film-maker: Alvy
　　Singer (Woody Allen), in *Annie Hall* (film;
　　screenplay by Woody Allen and Marshall Brickman,
　　directed by Woody Allen, 1977)

3　The sumptuous age of stars and images is
　　reduced to a few artificial tornado effects,
　　pathetic fake buildings, and childish tricks
　　which the crowd pretends to be taken in by to
　　avoid feeling too disappointed. Ghost towns,
　　ghost people. The whole place has the same air
　　of obsolescence about it as Sunset or Holly-
　　wood Boulevard.
　　Jean Baudrillard (b.1929), French semiologist:
　　America (1986; tr.1988), 'Astral America'

4　If New York is the Big Apple, tonight Holly-
　　wood is the Big Nipple.
　　Bernardo Bertolucci (b.1940), Italian film-maker:
　　said at Oscar presentation ceremony, at which *The
　　Last Emperor* scored nine awards, quoted in *The
　　Guardian* (London), 13 April 1988

5　To survive there, you need the ambition of a
　　Latin-American revolutionary, the ego of a
　　grand opera tenor, and the physical stamina of
　　a cow pony.
　　Billie Burke (1885–1970), U.S. actress: quoted in
　　Halliwell's Filmgoer's Companion (ed. Leslie
　　Halliwell, 1984)

6　Its idea of 'production value' is spending a
　　million dollars dressing up a story that any
　　good writer would throw away. Its vision of the
　　rewarding movie is a vehicle for some glamor-
　　puss with two expressions and eighteen
　　changes of costume, or for some male idol of
　　the muddled millions with a permanent hang-
　　over, six worn-out acting tricks, the build of a
　　lifeguard, and the mentality of a chicken-
　　strangler.
　　Raymond Chandler (1880–1959), U.S. author:

'Writers in Hollywood', publ. in *Atlantic Monthly* (Boston), Nov. 1945

7 If my books had been any worse, I should not have been invited to Hollywood, and ... if they had been any better, I should not have come.
Raymond Chandler: letter, publ. in *Atlantic Monthly* (Boston), 12 Dec. 1945, publ. in *Raymond Chandler Speaking* (ed. Dorothy Gardiner and Kathrine S. Walker, 1962)

8 There is in Hollywood, as in all cultures in which gambling is the central activity, a lowered sexual energy, an inability to devote more than token attention to the preoccupations of the society outside. The action is everything, more consuming than sex, more immediate than politics; more important always than the acquisition of money, which is never, for the gambler, the true point of the exercise.
Joan Didion (b.1934), U.S. essayist: *The White Album* (1979), 'In Hollywood'

9 There's a big trend in Hollywood of taking very good European films and turning them into very bad American films. It's really a perverse activity. I'd rather go on the dole.
Roddy Doyle (b.1958), Irish author: quoted in the *Independent on Sunday* (London), 1 May 1994

10 Studio executives are intelligent, brutally overworked men and women who share one thing in common with baseball managers: They wake up every morning of the world with the knowledge that sooner or later they're going to get fired.
William Goldman (b.1931), U.S. screenwriter and novelist: *Adventures in the Screen Trade* (1983), Ch.1

11 Much more frequent in Hollywood than the emergence of Cinderella is her sudden vanishing. At our party, even in those glowing days, the clock was always striking twelve for someone at the height of greatness; and there was never a prince to fetch her back to the happy scene.
Ben Hecht (1893–1964), U.S. journalist, author and screenwriter: *A Child of the Century* (1954), Bk.5, 'My Poverty Row'

12 The average Hollywood film star's ambition is to be admired by an American, courted by an Italian, married to an Englishman and have a French boyfriend.
Katharine Hepburn (b.1909), U.S. actress: in the *New York Journal-American*, 22 Feb. 1954

13 Hollywood has always been a cage ... a cage to catch our dreams.
John Huston (1906–1987), U.S. film-maker: quoted in *The Sunday Times* (London), 27 Dec. 1987

14 Where is Hollywood located? Chiefly between the ears. In that part of the American brain lately vacated by God.

Erica Jong (b.1942), U.S. author: *How To Save Your Own Life* (1977), epigraph to 'Hello to Hollywood...'

15 Just like those other black holes from outer space, Hollywood is postmodern to this extent: it has no center, only a spreading dead zone of exhaustion, inertia, and brilliant decay.
Arthur Kroker (b.1945), **Marilouise Kroker** and **David Cook** (b.1946), Canadian sociologists: *Panic Encyclopedia* (1989), 'Panic Hollywood'

16 Strip away the phoney tinsel of Hollywood and you find the real tinsel underneath.
Oscar Levant (1906–1972), U.S. pianist and composer: *Inquisition in Eden* (1965)

17 You can fool all the people all the time if the advertising is right and the budget is big enough.
Joseph E. Levine (1905–1987), U.S. film producer and executive: quoted in *Halliwell's Filmgoer's Companion* (ed. Leslie Halliwell, 1984)

18 If we have to tell Hollywood good-by, it may be with one of those tender, old-fashioned, seven-second kisses exchanged between two people of the *opposite* sex, with all their clothes on.
Anita Loos (1893–1981), U.S. novelist and screenwriter: last lines of *Kiss Hollywood Good-by* (1974), Ch.21

19 We Americans have always considered Hollywood, at best, a sinkhole of depraved venality. And, of course, it is. It is not a Protective Monastery of Aesthetic Truth. It is a place where everything is incredibly expensive.
David Mamet (b.1947), U.S. playwright: *Writing in Restaurants* (1986), 'A Playwright in Hollywood'

20 Hollywood's a place where they'll pay you a thousand dollars for a kiss, and fifty cents for your soul. I know, because I turned down the first offer often enough and held out for the fifty cents.
Marilyn Monroe (1926–1962), U.S. actress: quoted in *Marilyn Monroe In Her Own Words* (1990), 'Acting'

21 The twentieth century is not the Age of Anxiety but the Age of Hollywood. The pagan cult of personality has reawakened and dominates all art, all thought. It is morally empty but ritually profound. We worship it by the power of the western eye. Movie screen and television screen are its sacred precincts.
Camille Paglia (b.1947), U.S. author and critic: *Sexual Personae* (1990), Ch.1

22 Hollywood money isn't money. It's congealed snow, melts in your hand, and there you are.
Dorothy Parker (1893–1967), U.S. humorous writer: interview in *Writers at Work* (First Series, ed. Malcolm Cowley, 1958). 'I can't talk about

Hollywood,' Parker declared. 'It was a horror to me when I was there and it's a horror to look back on. I can't imagine how I did it. When I got away from it I couldn't even refer to the place by name. "Out there," I called it'

23 Hollywood is a place that attracts people with massive holes in their souls.
Julia Phillips (b.1945), U.S. film producer: in *The Times* (London), 3 April 1991

24 Hollywood's like Egypt, full of crumbled pyramids. It'll never come back. It'll just keep on crumbling until finally the wind blows the last studio prop across the sands.
David O. Selznick (1902–1965), U.S. film producer: said in 1951 to journalist and author Ben Hecht, quoted in Hecht's autobiography, *A Child of the Century* (1954), Bk.5, 'Enter, the Movies'

25 You don't resign from these jobs, you escape from them.
Dawn Steel (b.1946), U.S. film producer and executive: quitting as president of Columbia Pictures, quoted in the *International Herald Tribune* (Paris), 10 Jan. 1990

26 If you have a vagina *and* an attitude in this town, then that's a lethal combination.
Sharon Stone (b.1958), U.S. actress: in *Empire* (London), June 1992

See also Quinn on ACTORS; Chandler on CINEMA; Jong on THE CIRCUS; Hecht on PROMISCUITY

THE HOLOCAUST

1 It is painful to recall a past intensity, to estimate your distance from the Belsen heap, to make your peace with numbers. Just to get up each morning is to make a kind of peace.
Leonard Cohen (b.1934), Canadian singer, poet and novelist: *The Spice-Box of Earth* (1965), 'Lines From My Grandfather's Journal'

2 I have not made a study of it, but believe that it is a minor point in the history of the war.
Jean-Marie Le Pen (b.1928), French nationalist politician: of the Holocaust, quoted in *The Sunday Times* (London) 27 Dec. 1987

3 Without centuries of Christian antisemitism, Hitler's passionate hatred would never have been so fervently echoed.
Robert Runcie (b.1921), British ecclesiastic and archbishop of Canterbury: in *The Daily Telegraph* (London), 10 Nov. 1988

4 Today, almost forty years later, I grow dizzy when I recall that the number of manufactured tanks seems to have been more important to me than the vanished victims of racism.
Albert Speer (1905–1981), German architect and Nazi official: *The Slave State* (1981), Ch.21

5 How do you describe the sorting out on arriving at Auschwitz, the separation of children who see a father or mother going away, never to be seen again? How do you express the dumb grief of a little girl and the endless lines of women, children and rabbis being driven across the Polish or Ukrainian landscapes to their deaths? No, I can't do it. And because I'm a writer and teacher, I don't understand how Europe's most cultured nation could have done that. For these men who killed with submachine-guns in the Ukraine were university graduates. Afterwards they would go home and read a poem by Heine. So what happened?
Elie Wiesel (b.1928), Rumanian-born U.S. writer: testifying at the trial of Klaus Barbie in Lyons, 2 June 1987, quoted in *Le Monde* (Paris), 4 June 1987. Wiesel was himself a survivor of the concentration camps. In an interview he spoke of the continuing impact of the Holocaust on his life: 'There isn't a day, there simply isn't a day without my thinking of death or of looking into death, darkness, or seeing that fire or trying to understand what happened. There isn't a day' (*Writers at Work*, Eighth Series, ed. George Plimpton, 1988)

THE HOMELESS

1 How does it feel
To be without a home
Like a complete unknown
Like a rolling stone?
Bob Dylan (b.1941), U.S. singer and songwriter: 'Like a Rolling Stone' (song), on the album *Highway 61 Revisited* (1965)

2 You scour the Bowery, ransack the Bronx, Through funeral parlors and honky-tonks. From river to river you comb the town For a place to lay your family down.
Ogden Nash (1902–1971), U.S. poet: 'Nature Abhors a Vacancy', publ. in *Versus* (1949)

3 What we have found in this country, and maybe we're more aware of it now, is one problem that we've had, even in the best of times, and that is the people who are sleeping on the grates, the homeless, you might say, by choice.
Ronald Reagan (b.1911), U.S. Republican politician and president: statement, 31 Jan. 1984, quoted in *Reagan's Reign of Error* (ed. Mark Green and Gail MacColl, 1987), 'A Deficit of Economics'

4 I am my brother's keeper, and he's sleeping pretty rough these days.
Derek Worlock (1920–1996), British Roman Catholic cleric and archbishop: in *The Observer* (London), 16 Dec. 1990

See also TRAMPS

HOMOSEXUALITY

1   Human beings are distinguished by a capacity
    for experience as well as by their behavior, and
    homosexuality is as much a matter of emotion
    as of genital manipulation. ... As we each
    examine our own sense of identity we realize
    how much more complex is the question of
    homosexuality than a mere Kinsey-like com-
    putation of orgasms.
    Dennis Altman (b.1943), Australian sociologist:
    Homosexual Oppression and Liberation (1971), Ch.1

2   Sexual fidelity is more important in a homo-
    sexual relationship than in any other. In other
    relationships there are a variety of ties. But
    here, fidelity is the only bond.
    W.H. Auden (1907–1973), Anglo-American poet:
    The Table Talk of W.H. Auden (comp. Alan Ansen,
    ed. Nicholas Jenkins, 1990), 'October 20, 1947'

3   The condition that is now called gay was then
    called queer. The operative word was *faggot*
    and, later, pussy, but those epithets really had
    nothing to do with the question of sexual
    preference: You were being told simply that
    you had no balls.
    James Baldwin (1924–1987), U.S. author: 'Freaks
    and the American Ideal of Manhood', first publ. in
    Playboy (Chicago), Jan. 1985, rep. in *The Price of the
    Ticket* (1985), 'Here Be Dragons'

4   He said 'Next time can I bring my friend?'
    And I thought 'Does he mean friend?'
    And I thought 'Yes he *does* mean friend.'
    Which was quite bold in those days.
    It was the Dark Ages. Men and men.
    And they could still put you in prison for it.
    And did, dear.
    Alan Bennett (b.1934), British playwright: Peggy,
    in *Prick up Your Ears: The Screenplay* (1987), p.4 of
    Faber & Faber edn.

5   The world dictates that heteros make love
    while gays have sex.
    Boy George (b.1961), British singer: in *New
    Musical Express* (London), 1984, quoted in *NME
    Book of Quotes* (1995), 'Sex'

6   Feminine homosexual men, *queens* if you
    must, exist in inverse ratio amongst a country's
    homosexual population to their existence in
    that country's minds and nightmares.
    Julie Burchill (b.1960), British journalist and
    author: *Girls on Film* (1986), Ch.7

7   I think that what we call love is a fraud per-
    petrated by the female sex, and that the point
    of sexual relations between men is nothing that
    we could call love, but rather what we might
    call *recognition*.
    William Burroughs (1914–1997), U.S. author:
    quoted in 'This is Not a Mammal', by Edmund

White, first publ. in *Soho News*, 18 Feb. 1981, rep. in
The Burning Library (1994)

8   At my back I hear the word – 'homosexual' –
    and it seems to split my world in two. ... It is
    ignorance, our ignorance of one another, that
    creates this terrifying erotic chaos. Infor-
    mation, a crumb of information, seems to light
    the world.
    John Cheever (1912–1982), U.S. author: journal
    entry 1966, in *John Cheever: The Journals* (ed.
    Robert Gottlieb, 1991), 'The Sixties'

9   I, for one, do not think homosexuality is the
    latest advance over heterosexuality in the scale
    of human evolution. Homosexuality is a
    sickness, just as are baby-rape or wanting to
    become head of General Motors.
    Eldridge Cleaver (b.1935), U.S. black leader and
    writer: *Soul on Ice* (1968), 'Notes on a Native Son'

10 The ... problem that confronts homosexuals is
    that they set out to win the love of a 'real' man.
    If they succeed, they fail. A man who 'goes
    with' other men is not what they would call a
    real man. The conundrum is incapable of reso-
    lution, but that does not make homosexuals
    give it up.
    Quentin Crisp (b.1908), British author: *The Naked
    Civil Servant* (1968), Ch.9

11 I became one of the stately homos of England.
    Quentin Crisp: *The Naked Civil Servant* (1968),
    Ch.24. Crisp was echoing the opening lines of Felicia
    Hemans's 1849 poem 'The Homes of England': 'The
    stately homes of England,/ How beautiful they
    stand!'

12 In homosexual love the passion is homo-
    sexuality itself. What a homosexual loves, as if
    it were his lover, his country, his art, his land,
    is homosexuality.
    Marguerite Duras (1914–1996), French author and
    film-maker: *Practicalities* (1987; tr.1990), 'Men'

13 We think that we live in a heterosexual society
    because most men are fixated on women as
    sexual objects; but, in fact, we live in a homo-
    sexual society because all credible transactions
    of power, authority, and authenticity take
    place among men; all transactions based on
    equity and individuality take place among
    men. Men are real; therefore, all real relation-
    ship is between men; all real communication is
    between men; all real reciprocity is between
    men; all real mutuality is between men.
    Andrea Dworkin (b.1946), U.S. feminist critic:
    'The Root Cause', speech, 26 Sept. 1975,
    Massachusetts Institute of Technology, publ. in *Our
    Blood* (1976), Ch.9

14 One of the concessions we make to others is
    presenting homosexuality purely in the form
    of immediate pleasure, of two young men
    meeting in the street, seducing one another

with their eyes, putting their hands on each other's bums and having it off in a few minutes. We have there a neat and tidy image of homosexuality, which takes away all its potential to disturb for two reasons: it corresponds to a reassuring canon of beauty, and it destroys the disturbing element in affection, tenderness, fidelity, comradeship, companionship, for which a fairly controlled society cannot make room, for fear that alliances will be formed, that unexpected lines of force will appear. I think it's that that makes homosexuality 'unsettling': the homosexual way of life, rather than the sexual act itself ... when individuals begin to love one another, it does become problematical.

Michel Foucault (1926–1984), French philosopher: from 'De l'Amitié comme mode de la vie', publ. in *Gai Pied*, 25 April 1981, quoted in *The Lives of Michel Foucault* by David Macey (1993), Ch.14

15 Is it possible to create a homosexual mode of life? This notion of mode of life seems important to me. ... It seems to me that a way of life can yield a culture and an ethics. To be 'gay', I think, is not to identify with the psychological traits and the visible marks of the homosexual, but to try to define and develop a way of life.

Michel Foucault: 'Subjectivité et vérité, 1980–81', publ. in *Resumé des Cours, 1970–1982* (1989), quoted in 'Ethics as ascetics' by Arnold I. Davison in *The Cambridge Companion to Foucault* (1994)

16 Understand that sexuality is as wide as the sea. Understand that your morality is not law. Understand that we are you. Understand that if we decide to have sex whether safe, safer, or unsafe, it is our decision and you have no rights in our lovemaking.

Derek Jarman (1942–1994), British film-maker, artist and author: *At Your Own Risk: A Saint's Testament* (1992), '1940's'

17 The modern queer was invented by Tennessee Williams. Brando in blue jeans, sneakers, white T-shirt and leather jacket. When you saw that, you knew they were available.

Derek Jarman: *At Your Own Risk: A Saint's Testament* (1992), '1960's'

18 For men who want to flee Family Man America and never come back, there is a guaranteed solution: homosexuality is the new French Foreign Legion.

Florence King (b.1936), U.S. author: *Reflections in a Jaundiced Eye* (1989), 'From Captain Marvel to Captain Valium'

19 The only way we'll have real pride is when we demand recognition of a culture that isn't just sexual. It's all there – all through history we've been there; but we have to claim it, and identify who was in it, and articulate what's in our minds and hearts and all our creative contri-

butions to this earth. And until we do that, and until we organize ourselves block by neighborhood by city by state into a united visible community that fights back, we're doomed.

Larry Kramer (b.1935), U.S. playwright and novelist: Ned, in *The Normal Heart* (1985)

20 There is probably no sensitive heterosexual alive who is not preoccupied with his latent homosexuality.

Norman Mailer (b.1923), U.S. author: *Advertisements for Myself* (1959), 'The Homosexual Villain'

21 I think a lot of gay people who are not dealing with their homosexuality get into right-wing politics.

Armistead Maupin (b.1944), U.S. journalist and author: in *The Guardian* (London), 22 April 1988

22 I have heard some say ... that such practices are allowed in France and in other NATO countries. We are not French, and we are not other nationals. We are British, thank God!

Viscount Montgomery (1887–1976), British soldier: speech to House of Lords, 26 May 1965, debating Homosexuality Bill, publ. in *Hansard*, col.648

23 Gay men are guardians of the masculine impulse. To have anonymous sex in a dark alleyway is to pay homage to the dream of male freedom. The unknown stranger is a wandering pagan god. The altar, as in prehistory, is anywhere you kneel.

Camille Paglia (b.1947), U.S. author and critic: 'Homosexuality at the Fin de Siècle', first publ. in *Esquire* (New York), Oct. 1991, rep. in *Sex, Art, and American Culture* (1992)

24 I have suffered the sufferable, but I have never accepted my sin, I have never come to terms with my nature and am not even used to it. ...

My homosexuality was something more, outside, had nothing to do with me. But I always saw it as something next to me, like an enemy, never feeling it inside me.

Pier Paolo Pasolini (1922–1975), Italian film-maker and essayist: letter, 10 Feb. 1950, publ. in *Pasolini Requiem* by David Barth Schwartz (1992), Ch.12

25 A person's sexuality is so much more than one word 'gay'. No one refers to anyone as just 'hetero' because that doesn't say anything. Sexual identity is broader than a label.

Gus Van Sant (b.1953), U.S. film-maker: quoted in *Sight and Sound* (London), Aug. 1992

26 From the perspective of the present, we can now look back at the beginning of gay liberation and observe that it flowered exactly at the moment when gays became identified, by themselves and by the market, as a distinct group of affluent and avid consumers.

Edmund White (b.1940), U.S. author: 'Paradise Found', first publ. in *Mother Jones*, June 1983, rep. in *The Burning Library* (1994)

See also Jarman on LABELS; White on LUST; Jarman on MEN; Sontag on MINORITIES; White on PROMISCUITY

HOMOSEXUALITY: Homophobia

1 Homophobia may be offensive but the other side of the coin is just as noisome, whatever they may tell you in Euroboy or Zipper.
John Osborne (1929–1994), British playwright: in *The Spectator* (London), 17 Dec. 1994

2 I don't want to be in bed with anybody who's stronger than me or that has more hair on their chest than I do. Now you can call me old-fashioned, you can call me conservative ... just call me a man.
Denzel Washington (b.1954), U.S. actor: Joe Miller (Denzel Washington), in *Philadelphia* (film; screenplay by Ron Nyswaner, directed by Jonathan Demme, 1993)

HOPE

1 Hope is definitely not the same thing as optimism. It is not the conviction that something will turn out well, but the certainty that something makes sense, regardless of how it turns out.
Václav Havel (b.1936), Czech playwright and president: *Disturbing the Peace* (1986; tr.1990), Ch.5

2 Hope is the feeling you have that the feeling you have isn't permanent.
Jean Kerr (b.1923), U.S. author and playwright: Felicia, in *Finishing Touches* (1973), Act 3

3 Hope? I have none and furthermore I condemn it with everything in my power. Hope is the flag, the special marker of hypocrisy ... I don't believe in it. I believe only in my own vitality
Pier Paolo Pasolini (1922–1975), Italian filmmaker and essayist: quoted in *Pasolini Requiem* by David Barth Schwartz (1992), Ch.19

HORROR

1 I don't believe in evil, I believe only in horror. In nature there is no evil, only an abundance of horror: the plagues and the blights and the ants and the maggots.
Isak Dinesen (1885–1962), Danish author: said to author and poet Frederic Prokosch, quoted in *Voices: A Memoir* by Prokosch (1983), 'Phantoms'

2 What is it that our horror literature and science fiction haul in whenever they seek to make our skin crawl? Anything alive, mindless, and gooey ... anything sloppy, slobbering, liquescent, smelly, slimy, gurgling, putrescent, mushy, grubby ... things amoeboid or fungoid that stick and cling, that creep and seep and grow ... things that have the feel of spit or shit, snot or piss, sweat or pus or blood. ... In a word, anything *organic*, and as messy as birth, sex, death, and decay.
Theodore Roszak (b.1933), U.S. social critic: *Where the Wasteland Ends* (1972), Ch.3

See also CINEMA: HORROR & SUSPENSE

HOSTAGES

1 People are capable of doing an awful lot when they have no choice and I had no choice. Courage is when you have choices.
Terry Anderson (b.1947), U.S. journalist and hostage: in the *International Herald Tribune* (Paris), 6 May 1992

2 Neither dead nor alive, the hostage is suspended by an incalculable outcome. It is not his destiny that awaits for him, nor his own death, but anonymous chance, which can only seem to him something absolutely arbitrary. ... He is in a state of radical emergency, of virtual extermination.
Jean Baudrillard (b.1929), French semiologist: *Fatal Strategies* (1983; tr.1990), 'Figures of the Transpolitical'

3 Hostage is a crucifying aloneness. It is a silent, screaming slide into the bowels of ultimate despair. Hostage is a man hanging by his fingernails over the edge of chaos, feeling his fingers slowly straightening. Hostage is the humiliating stripping away of every sense and fibre of body and mind and spirit that make us what we are. Hostage is a mutant creation filled with fear, self-loathing, guilt and death-wishing. But he is a man, a rare, unique and beautiful creation of which these things are no part.
Brian Keenan (b.1950), Irish teacher and hostage in Lebanon: on his 4½-year ordeal as a hostage, quoted in *The Independent* (London), 31 Aug. 1990

4 Freeing hostages is like putting up a stage set, which you do with the captors, agreeing on each piece as you slowly put it together; then you leave an exit through which both the captor and the captive can walk with sincerity and dignity.
Terry Waite (b.1939), British religious adviser: television broadcast (ABC TV), 3 Nov. 1986, on his trips to Lebanon as special envoy of the archbishop of Canterbury to negotiate the release of hostages held by terrorists. On 20 Jan. 1987 Waite was himself kidnapped and not freed until November 1991

HOTELS

1   It's the business of hotels to be one step behind the times – hotels, like colonies, keeping up a way of life that is already outmoded.
Alan Bennett (b.1934), British playwright: 'Dinner at Noon', broadcast April 1988 in BBC series *Byline*, publ. in *Writing Home* (1994)

2   Of course great hotels have always been social ideas, flawless mirrors to the particular societies they service.
Joan Didion (b.1934), U.S. essayist: *The White Album* (1979), 'In the Islands'

3   Doorman – a genius who can open the door of your car with one hand, help you in with the other, and still have one left for the tip.
Dorothy Kilgallen (1913–1965), U.S. columnist and television personality: quoted in *Violets and Vinegar* (ed. Jilly Cooper and Tom Hartman, 1980), 'Come Away, Poverty's Catching'

4   The hotel was once where things coalesced, where you could meet both townspeople and travelers. Not so in a motel. No matter how you build it, the motel remains the haunt of the quick and dirty, where the only locals are Chamber of Commerce boys every fourth Thursday. Who ever heard the returning traveler exclaim over one of the great motels of the world he stayed in? Motels can be big, but never grand.
William Least Heat-Moon [William Trogdon] (b.1939), U.S. author: *Blue Highways: A Journey into America* (1983), Pt.5, Ch.2

5   I've always thought a hotel ought to offer optional small animals. ... I mean a cat to sleep on your bed at night, or a dog of some kind to act pleased when you come in. You ever notice how a hotel room feels so lifeless?
Anne Tyler (b.1941), U.S. author: Macon Leary, in *The Accidental Tourist* (1985), Ch.9

HOUSE & HOME

1   If I were asked to name the chief benefit of the house, I should say: the house shelters daydreaming, the house protects the dreamer, the house allows one to dream in peace.
Gaston Bachelard (1884–1962), French scientist, philosopher and literary theorist: *The Poetics of Space* (1958; tr.1964), Ch.1, 'The House'

2   People's backyards are much more interesting than their front gardens, and houses that back on to railways are public benefactors.
John Betjeman (1906–1984), British poet: quoted in *The Observer* (London), 20 March 1983

3   When someone tells you they've just bought a house, they might as well tell you they no longer have a personality. You can immediately assume so many things: that they're locked into jobs they hate; that they're broke; that they spend every night watching videos; that they're fifteen pounds overweight; that they no longer listen to new ideas. It's profoundly depressing.
Douglas Coupland (b.1961), Canadian author: the narrator, Andy, in *Generation X* (1991), 'MTV Not Bullets'

4   When I can no longer bear to think of the victims of broken homes, I begin to think of the victims of intact ones.
Peter De Vries (1910–1993), U.S. author: Augie, in *The Tunnel of Love* (1954), Ch.8

5   The house a woman creates is a Utopia. She can't help it – can't help trying to interest her nearest and dearest not in happiness itself but in the search for it.
Marguerite Duras (1914–1996), French author and film-maker: *Practicalities* (1987; tr.1990), 'House and Home'

6   Construed ... as turf, home just seems a provisional claim, a designation you make upon a place, not one it makes on you. A certain set of buildings, a glimpsed, smudged window-view across a schoolyard, a musty aroma sniffed behind a garage when you were a child, all of which come crowding in upon your latter-day senses – those are pungent things and vivid, even consoling. But to me they are also inert and nostalgic and unlikely to connect you to the real, to that essence art can sometimes achieve, which is permanence.
Richard Ford (b.1944), U.S. author: 'An Urge for Going', publ. in *Harper's Magazine* (New York), Feb. 1992

7   Any interior is a set of anachronisms, a museum with the lingering residues of decorative styles that an inhabited space collects. Banal or beautiful, exquisite or sordid, each says a lot about its owner and something about humanity in general.
Richard Hamilton (b.1922), British Pop artist: interview in *Vanguard* (Vancouver), Sept. 1978, rep. in *Collected Words 1953–1982* (1982), 'Interiors'

8   Own Your Own Cave and Be Secure.
William Denby Hanna (b.1910) and **Joseph Roland Barbera** (b.1911), U.S. animators: slogan at the quarry where Fred Flintstone worked as operator of a dinosaur-powered crane, in *The Flintstones* (TV cartoon, from 1960, produced by Hanna and Barbera)

9   The house is so ideally suited to my living habits that it's a world unto itself, and in most respects, far better than the world outside.
Hugh Hefner (b.1926), U.S. publisher: referring to the Playboy Mansion, quoted in *Hefner* by Frank Brady (1974), Ch.1

10 One never reaches home, but wherever friendly paths intersect the whole world looks like home for a time.

Hermann Hesse (1877–1962), German novelist and poet: Frau Eva, in *Demian* (1960), Ch.5

11 Home is so sad. It stays as it was left,
Shaped to the comfort of the last to go
As if to win them back.

Philip Larkin (1922–1985), British poet: 'Home is so Sad', written 1958, publ. in *The Whitsun Weddings* (1964)

12 Nothing succeeds like address.

Fran Lebowitz (b.1951), U.S. journalist: *Metropolitan Life* (1978), 'The Nail Bank: Not Just Another Clip Joint'

13 I live in my house as I live inside my skin: I know more beautiful, more ample, more sturdy and more picturesque skins: but it would seem to me unnatural to exchange them for mine.

Primo Levi (1919–1987), Italian chemist and author: *Other People's Trades* (1985; tr.1989), 'My House'

14 Little boxes on the hillside
Little boxes all the same.

There's a green one, and a pink one,
And a blue one, and a yellow one
And they're all made out of ticky tacky,
and they all look just the same.

Malvina Reynolds (1900–1978), U.S. songwriter: 'Little Boxes' (song, 1962)

15 Home is where you come to when you have nothing better to do.

Margaret Thatcher (b.1925), British Conservative politician and prime minister: interview in *Vanity Fair* (New York), June 1991

HOUSEWIVES

1 I hate the word housewife; I don't like the word home-maker either. I want to be called – domestic goddess.

Roseanne Barr (b.1952), U.S. stand-up comedienne and actress: *Roseanne* (U.S. sitcom, from 1988), quoted in *Funny Business* by David Housham and John Frank-Keyes (1992)

2 The suburban housewife – she was the dream image of the young American women and the envy, it was said, of women all over the world. The American housewife – freed by science and labor-saving appliances from the drudgery, the dangers of childbirth, and the illnesses of her grandmother ... had found true feminine fulfilment

Betty Friedan (b.1921), U.S. feminist writer: *The Feminine Mystique* (1963), Ch.1

3 Now, as always, the most automated appliance in a household is the mother.

Beverly Jones (b.1927), U.S. feminist writer: 'The Dynamics of Marriage and Motherhood', publ. in *The Florida Paper on Women's Liberation* (1970)

4 Perhaps all artists were, in a sense, housewives: tenders of the earth household.

Erica Jong (b.1942), U.S. author: 'The Artist as Housewife: the Housewife as Artist', publ. in *The First Ms. Reader* (ed. Francine Klagsbrun, 1972)

5 Each home has been reduced to the bare essentials – to barer essentials than most primitive people would consider possible. Only one woman's hands to feed the baby, answer the telephone, turn off the gas under the pot that is boiling over, soothe the older child who has broken a toy, and open both doors at once. She is a nutritionist, a child psychologist, an engineer, a production manager, an expert buyer, all in one. Her husband sees her as free to plan her own time, and envies her; she sees him as having regular hours and envies him.

Margaret Mead (1901–1978), U.S. anthropologist: *Male and Female* (1949), Ch.16

6 For a woman to get a rewarding sense of total creation by way of the multiple monotonous chores that are her daily lot would be as irrational as for an assembly line worker to rejoice that he had created an automobile because he tightened a bolt.

Edith Mendel Stern (1901–1975), U.S. author and critic: 'Women are Household Slaves', publ. in *American Mercury* (California), Jan. 1949

HOUSEWORK

1 I make no secret of the fact that I would rather lie on a sofa than sweep beneath it. But you have to be efficient if you're going to be lazy.

Shirley Conran (b.1932), British designer and journalist: *Superwoman* (1975), 'The Reason Why'

2 Cleaning your house while your kids are still growing is like shoveling the walk before it stops snowing.

Phyllis Diller (b.1917), U.S. author and actress: quoted in *Violets and Vinegar* by Jilly Cooper and Tom Hartman (1980), 'I Liked You Better Smaller'

3 The labor of keeping house is labor in its most naked state, for labor is toil that never finishes, toil that has to be begun again the moment it is completed, toil that is destroyed and consumed by the life process.

Mary McCarthy (1912–1989), U.S. author and critic: 'The Vita Activa', first publ. in the *New Yorker*, 18 Oct. 1958, rep. in *On the Contrary* (1961)

4 I hate housework! You make the beds, you do the dishes – and six months later you have to start all over again.

Joan Rivers (b.1935), U.S. comedienne: quoted in *Woman Talk* (ed. Michèle Brown and Ann O'Connor, 1984), 'Work'

5   We are not actually incapable of cleaning our homes: but we are liable to reorganize instead of scrub; we do our cleaning in a series of periodic assaults. A mother-in-law has only to appear over the horizon and we act like the murderer in a Ray Bradbury story who kept on wiping the finger prints off the fruit at the bottom of the bowl. We work in a frenzy; but ... the frenzy usually subsides before we have got everything back into the cupboards again.
     Katharine Whitehorn (b.1926), British journalist: *Roundabout* (1962), 'Nought for Homework'

See also Thomas on THE SUN

HUMAN NATURE

1   We all want to be happy, and we're all going to die.... You might say those are the only two unchallengeably true facts that apply to every human being on this planet.
     William Boyd (b.1952), British novelist: Loomis Gage, in *Stars and Bars* (1984), Pt.2, Ch.6

2   We are all murderers and prostitutes – no matter to what culture, society, class, nation one belongs, no matter how normal, moral, or mature, one takes oneself to be.
     R.D. Laing (1927–1989), British psychiatrist: introduction to *The Politics of Experience* (1967)

3   It is fascinating to realize that what distinguishes man so sharply from other creatures are those attitudes he develops soon after the age of 5: his inhibition and sublimation of sexuality, his interest in symbols, abstractions, systems and rules, his capacity for being inspired by heroes, God and spiritual ideals.
     Benjamin Spock (b.1903), U.S. paediatrician and author: *Baby and Child Care* (1946), 'The Parents' Part', Sct.13

HUMAN RIGHTS

1   Perhaps we can shrug off and shed some of the dangerous myths laid on our minds like a second skin – such as the 'right' to a fair and impartial jury of our peers; the 'right' to represent oneself; the 'right' to a fair trial, even. They're *not* rights – they're privileges of the powerful and rich. For the powerless and the poor, they are chimera that vanish once one reaches out to claim them as something real or substantial.
     Mumia Abu-Jamal (b.1954), U.S. journalist and environmentalist: preface to *Live from Death Row* (1995)

2   A right is not what someone gives you; it's what no one can take from you.
     Ramsey Clark (b.1927), U.S. attorney general: in the *New York Times*, 2 Oct. 1977

3   *The Gospel is the fullest confirmation of all of human rights.* Without it we can easily find ourselves far from the truth about man.
     Pope John Paul II [Karol Wojtyla] (b.1920), Polish ecclesiastic: *Crossing the Threshold of Hope* (1994), 'Human Rights'

HUMANISM

1   A humanist has four leading characteristics – curiosity, a free mind, belief in good taste, and belief in the human race.
     E.M. Forster (1879–1970), British novelist and essayist: *Two Cheers for Democracy* (1951), 'Gide and George'

2   As soon as man began considering himself the source of the highest meaning in the world and the measure of everything, the world began to lose its human dimension, and man began to lose control of it.
     Václav Havel (b.1936), Czech playwright and president: *Disturbing the Peace* (1986; tr.1990), Ch.1

3   Humanism, it seems, is almost impossible in America where material progress is part of the national romance whereas in Europe such progress is relished because it feels nice.
     Paul West (b.1930), British author and critic: *The Wine of Absurdity* (1966), 'George Santayana'

HUMANITY

1   There is no doubt: the study of man is just beginning, at the same time that his end is in sight.
     Elias Canetti (1905–1994), Austrian novelist and philosopher: *The Secret Heart of the Clock: Notes, Aphorisms, Fragments 1973–1985* (1991), '1980'

2   The only thing that separates us from the animals is our ability to accessorize.
     Olympia Dukakis (b.1931), U.S. actress: Clairee Belcher (Olympia Dukakis), in *Steel Magnolias* (film; screenplay by Robert Harling based on his own play, directed by Herbert Ross, 1989)

3   Man, became man through work, who stepped out of the animal kingdom as transformer of the natural into the artificial, who became therefore the magician, man the creator of social reality, will always stay the great magician, will always be Prometheus bringing fire from heaven to earth, will always be Orpheus enthralling nature with his music. Not until humanity itself dies will art die.
     Ernst Fischer (1899–1972), Austrian editor, poet and critic: *The Necessity of Art* (1959; tr.1963), Ch.5

4   More and more I see the human predicament as a dialogue between lovers.
     Jean-Luc Godard (b.1930), French film-maker and author: Natasha von Braun (Anna Karina), in

Alphaville (film; written and directed by Jean-Luc Godard, 1965)

5 What constitutes a real, live human being is more of a mystery than ever these days, and men – each one of whom is a valuable, unique experiment on the part of nature – are shot down wholesale.
Hermann Hesse (1877–1962), German novelist and poet: the narrator (Sinclair), in prologue to *Demian* (1960)

6 Humankind can generally be divided into hunters and people who cope with the consequences.
Miroslav Holub (b.1923), Czech biologist and poet: 'Shedding Life', essay first publ. in *Science 86*, rep. in *The Dimension of the Present Moment and Other Essays* (1990)

7 Somebody has said that man is the missing link between primitive apes and civilized human beings. You might say that the idea is inherent in *2001*. We are semi-civilized, capable of cooperation and affection, but needing some sort of transfiguration into a higher form of life. Since the means to obliterate life on Earth exists, it will take more than just careful planning and reasonable cooperation to avoid some eventual catastrophe. The problem exists, and the problem is essentially a moral and spiritual one.
Stanley Kubrick (b.1928), U.S. film-maker: discussing his film *2001: A Space Odyssey* (1968), in *Stanley Kubrick: A Film Odyssey* by Gene D. Phillips (1975), quoted in *Kubrick: Inside a Film Artist's Maze* by Thomas Allen Nelson (1982), Ch.5

8 The man who is forever disturbed about the condition of humanity either has no problems of his own or has refused to face them.
Henry Miller (1891–1980), U.S. author: *Sexus* (1949), Ch.9

9 We are, to put it mildly, in a mess, and there is a strong chance that we shall have exterminated ourselves by the end of the century. Our only consolation will have to be that, as a species, we have had an exciting term of office.
Desmond Morris (b.1928), British zoologist: *The Naked Ape* (1967), Ch.5

10 Human affairs are not serious, but they have to be taken seriously.
Iris Murdoch (b.1919), British novelist and philosopher: Brendan Craddock, in *Henry and Cato* (1976), Pt.2, 'The Great Teacher'

11 The whole race is a poet that writes down
The eccentric propositions of its fate.
Wallace Stevens 1879–1955, U.S. poet: last lines of poem, 'Men Made Out of Words', publ. in *Transport to Summer* (1947)

12 We're all of us guinea pigs in the laboratory of God. Humanity is just a work in progress.
Tennessee Williams (1911–1983), U.S. playwright: the Gipsy, in *Camino Real* (1953), Block 12

See also Bastos on IMITATION; John Paul II on RESPONSIBILITY; Updike on SOLITUDE; Charles, Prince of Wales on THE SOUL; Calvino on THE WORLD

HUMILIATION

1 You will find that you survive humiliation. And that's an experience of incalculable value.
T.S. Eliot (1888–1965), Anglo-American poet, critic: Unidentified Guest (later identified as Sir Henry Harcourt-Reilly), in *The Cocktail Party* (1950), Act 1, Sc.1

2 Avoiding humiliation is the core of tragedy and comedy.
John Guare (b.1938), U.S. playwright: in *The Independent* (London), 17 Oct. 1988

3 If every day a man takes orders in silence from an incompetent superior, if every day he solemnly performs ritual acts which he privately finds ridiculous, if he unhesitatingly gives answers to questionnaires which are contrary to his real opinions and is prepared to deny his own self in public, if he sees no difficulty in feigning sympathy or even affection where, in fact, he feels only indifference or aversion, it still does not mean that he has entirely lost the use of one of the basic human senses, namely, the sense of *humiliation*.
Václav Havel (b.1936), Czech playwright and president: *Living in Truth* (1986), Pt.1, 'Letter to Dr Gustáv Husák', 8 April 1975

HUMILITY

1 At home I am a nice guy: but I don't want the world to know. Humble people, I've found, don't get very far.
Muhammad Ali (b.1942), U.S. boxer: in the *Sunday Express* (London), 13 Jan. 1963

2 I've never had a humble opinion in my life. If you're going to have one, why bother to be humble about it?
Joan Baez (b.1941), U.S. singer: in the *International Herald Tribune* (Paris), 2 Dec. 1992

3 To make us feel small in the right way is a function of art; men can only make us feel small in the wrong way.
E.M. Forster (1879–1970), British novelist and essayist: *Two Cheers for Democracy* (1951), 'A Book that Influenced Me'

4 A man who has humility will have acquired in the last reaches of his beliefs the saving doubt of his own certainty.
Walter Lippmann (1889–1974), U.S. journalist: *The Public Philosophy* (1955), Ch.10, Sct.4

HUMOUR

1 Among those whom I like or admire, I can find no common denominator, but among those whom I love, I can: all of them make me laugh.
W.H. Auden (1907–1973), Anglo-American poet: *The Dyer's Hand* (1962), Pt.7, 'Notes on the Comic'

2 Humorists can never start to take themselves seriously. It's literary suicide.
Erma Bombeck (1927–1996), U.S. journalist: quoted in the *Detroit Free Press*, 10 Aug. 1978

3 All my humor is based upon destruction and despair. If the whole world were tranquil, without disease and violence, I'd be standing on the breadline right in back of J. Edgar Hoover.
Lenny Bruce (1925–1966), U.S. satirical comedian: *The Essential Lenny Bruce* (ed. John Cohen, 1967), 'Performing and the Art of Comedy'. The passage also appears as the book's epigraph

4 Humour is by far the most significant activity of the human brain.
Edward De Bono (b.1933), British writer on thinking processes: in the *Daily Mail* (London), 29 Jan. 1990

5 The comic is the perception of the opposite; humour is the feeling of it.
Umberto Eco (b.1932), Italian semiologist and novelist: 'The Comic and the Rule' (1980), rep. in *Travels in Hyperreality* (1986)

6 Humour, just like the dramatic, the tragic, the visionary, is the collocation of reality in a particular climate. Humour is a type of view, of rapport, of feeling one has about things, and is, above all, a natural characteristic which one has or doesn't have.
Federico Fellini (1920–1993), Italian film-maker: *Fellini on Fellini* (ed. Anna Keel and Christian Strich, 1974; tr.1977), 'Miscellany III', Sct.11

7 His hilarity was like a scream from a crevasse.
Graham Greene (1904–1991), British novelist: of Major Scobie, in *The Heart of the Matter* (1948), Bk.3, Pt.1, Ch.1, Sct.1

8 I do think that a sense of humor gets you much farther in the movies than it does in real life. There was a long period of time where I swear to God being funny just didn't get you laid no matter how funny you were.
Tom Hanks (b.1957), U.S. actor: quoted in *Tom Hanks* by Roy Trakin (1995), Ch.15

9 Humor, a good sense of it, is to Americans what manhood is to Spaniards and we will go to great lengths to prove it. Experiments with laboratory rats have shown that, if one psychologist in the room laughs at something a rat does, all of the other psychologists in the room will laugh equally. Nobody wants to be left holding the joke.
Garrison Keillor (b.1942), U.S. author: introduction to *We Are Still Married* (1989)

10 Good taste and humour are a contradiction in terms, like a chaste whore.
Malcolm Muggeridge (1903–1990), British journalist and broadcaster: defending his editorship of *Punch*, in *Time* (New York), 14 Sept. 1953

11 Wit is a weapon. Jokes are a masculine way of inflicting superiority. But humour is the pursuit of a gentle grin, usually in solitude.
Frank Muir (b.1920), British humorist: in the *Daily Mail* (London), 26 April 1990

12 Humor is emotional chaos remembered in tranquility.
James Thurber (1894–1961), U.S. humorist and illustrator: in the *New York Post*, 29 Feb. 1960. An earlier version of Thurber's quip was attributed to him by Max Eastman in *Enjoyment of Laughter* (1936): 'Humor is a kind of emotional chaos told about calmly and quietly in retrospect. There is always a laugh in the utterly familiar.' The words derive from Wordsworth

13 When humour can be made to alternate with melancholy, one has a success, but when the *same* things are funny and melancholic at the same time, it's just wonderful.
François Truffaut (1932–1984), French film-maker: letter, 15 Jan. 1980, publ. in *Letters* (1988; tr.1989)

14 I used to think that everything was just being funny but now I don't know. I mean, how can you tell?
Andy Warhol (c.1928–1987), U.S. Pop artist: quoted in *Vogue* (New York), 1 March 1970

15 Humour is not a mood but a way of looking at the world. So if it is correct to say that humour was stamped out in Nazi Germany, that does not mean that people were not in good spirits, or anything of that sort, but something much deeper and more important.
Ludwig Wittgenstein (1889–1951), Austrian-born British philosopher: journal entry, 1948, publ. in *Culture and Value* (ed. G.H. von Wright with Heikki Nyman, 1980)

See also Parker on WIT; Thurber on WIT

HUNGER

1 Where people go hungry, to say that man does not live by bread alone is too easily misunderstood as an argument in favor of starvation.

Theodore Roszak (b.1933), U.S. social critic: introduction to *Where the Wasteland Ends* (1972)

2 A hungry man is not a free man.

Adlai Stevenson (1900–1965), U.S. Democratic politician: 'Farm Policy', speech, 6 Sept. 1952, Kasson (Minnesota), publ. in *The Speeches of Adlai Stevenson* (1952)

3 If sometimes our poor people have had to die of starvation, it is not that God didn't care for them, but because you and I didn't give, were not an instrument of love in the hands of God, to give them that bread, to give them that clothing; because we did not recognize him, when once more Christ came in distressing disguise, in the hungry man, in the lonely man, in the homeless child, and seeking for shelter.

Mother Teresa (1910–1997), Albanian-born Roman Catholic missionary: *A Gift for God* (1975), 'Suffering'

See also FAMINE

HUSBANDS

1 No man worth his salt, no man of spirit and spine, no man for whom I could have any respect, could rejoice in the identification of Tallulah's husband. It's tough enough to be bogged down in a legend. It would be even tougher to marry one.

Tallulah Bankhead (1903–1968), U.S. actress: *Tallulah* (1952), Ch.14

2 You may marry the man of your dreams, ladies, but 14 years later you're married to a couch that burps.

Roseanne Barr (b.1952), U.S. stand-up comedienne and actress: *Roseanne* (U.S. sitcom, from 1988), quoted in *Funny Business* by David Housham and John Frank-Keyes (1992)

3 I've never yet met a man who could look after me. I don't need a husband. What I need is a wife.

Joan Collins (b.1933), British actress: quoted in *The Sunday Times* (London), 27 Dec. 1987

4 *Do* let him read the papers. But not while you accusingly tiptoe around the room, or perch much like a silent bird of prey on the edge of your most uncomfortable chair. (He will read them anyway, and he *should* read them, so let him choose his own good time.) Don't make a big exit. Just go. But kiss him quickly, before you go, otherwise he might think you are angry; *he is used to suspecting he is doing something wrong.*

Marlene Dietrich (1904–1992), German-born U.S. actress: *Marlene Dietrich's ABC* (1962), 'Married Love'

5 Personally, I can't see why it would be any less romantic to find a husband in a nice four-color catalogue than in the average downtown bar at happy hour.

Barbara Ehrenreich (b.1941), U.S. author and columnist: 'Tales of the Man Shortage', first publ. in *Mother Jones*, 1986, rep. in *The Worst Years of Our Lives* (1991)

6 Husbands are like fires. They go out when unattended.

Zsa Zsa Gabor (b.1919), Hungarian-born U.S. actress: in *Newsweek* (New York), 28 March 1960

7 An early-rising man ... a good spouse but a bad husband.

Gabriel García Márquez (b.1928), Colombian author: the widow Monteil, in *In Evil Hour* (1968; tr.1979), p.154 of Jonathan Cape edn. (1980)

8 I've had the boyhood thing of being Elvis. Now I want to be with my best friend, and my best friend's my wife. Who could ask for anything more?

John Lennon (1940–1980), British rock musician: interview for KFRC RKO Radio (San Francisco), 8 Dec. 1980, the day of Lennon's murder, publ. in *Imagine* (ed. Andrew Solt and Sam Egan, 1988)

9 Husbands should be like kleenex: soft, strong, and disposable.

Jonathan Lynn (b.1943), British film-maker: Mrs White (Madeline Kahn), in *Clue* (film; written and directed by Jonathan Lynn, 1986)

10 Husbands are chiefly good as lovers when they are betraying their wives.

Marilyn Monroe (1926–1962), U.S. actress: quoted in *Marilyn Monroe In Her Own Words* (1990), 'Weddings and Divorces'

11 I think every woman's entitled to a middle husband she can forget.

Adela Rogers St. Johns (1894–1988), U.S. journalist: quoted in the *Los Angeles Times*, 13 Oct. 1974

HYPOCRISY

1 What makes it so plausible to assume that hypocrisy is the vice of vices is that integrity can indeed exist under the cover of all other vices except this one. Only crime and the criminal, it is true, confront us with the perplexity of radical evil; but only the hypocrite is really rotten to the core.

Hannah Arendt (1906–1975), German-born U.S. political philosopher: *On Revolution* (1963), Ch.2

2 Man is the only animal that learns by being hypocritical. He pretends to be polite and then, eventually, he *becomes* polite.

Jean Kerr (b.1923), U.S. author and playwright: Jeff, in *Finishing Touches* (1973), Act 1

3 My right hand hasn't seen my left hand in thirty years.
Burt Lancaster (1913–1994), U.S. actor: J.J. Hunsecker (Burt Lancaster), in *Sweet Smell of Success* (film; screenplay by Clifford Odets and Ernest Lehman, adapted from Ernest Lehman's short story, directed by Alexander Mackendrick, 1957)

4 The only thing worse than a liar is a liar that's also a hypocrite!
Tennessee Williams (1911–1983), U.S. playwright: Rosa, in *The Rose Tattoo* (1951), Act 3

See also Rice-Davies on PROSTITUTION

IDEALISM

1 The idealist walks on tiptoe, the materialist on his heels.
(*L'idéaliste a la marche des orteils; et le matérialiste a la marche des talons.*)
Malcolm de Chazal (1902–1981), French writer: *Sens Plastique*, Vol.II (1946), p.3

2 When your dreams tire, they go underground and out of kindness that's where they stay.
Libby Houston (b.1941), British poet: 'Gold', publ. in *Necessity* (1988)

3 Our salvation is in striving to achieve what we know we'll never achieve.
Ryszard Kapuściński (b.1932), Polish journalist: 'A Warsaw Diary', publ. in *Granta* (Cambridge), No.15, 1985

4 The enemy of idealism is zealotry.
Neil Kinnock (b.1942), British Labour politician: quoted in *The Observer* (London), 27 Dec. 1987

5 Idealist: a cynic in the making.
Irving Layton (b.1912), Canadian poet: *The Whole Bloody Bird* (1969), 'Aphs'

6 No one is crueller than an idealist. ... Who's responsible for all the carnage in this world? Idealists.
Naguib Mahfouz (b.1911), Egyptian novelist: al-Hilaly, in *Wedding Song* (1981; tr.1984), 'Tariq Ramadan the Actor'

7 Most idealistic people are skint. I have discovered that people with money have no imagination, and people with imagination have no money.
George Weiss (b.1940), British eccentric: in *The Guardian* (London), 3 Nov. 1984

IDEAS

1 Ideas are refined and multiplied in the commerce of minds. In their splendour, images effect a very simple communion of souls.
Gaston Bachelard (1884–1962), French scientist, philosopher and literary theorist: *The Poetics of Reverie* (1960; tr.1969), 'Introduction', Sct.4

2 I can't understand why people are frightened of new ideas. I'm frightened of the old ones.
John Cage (1912–1992), U.S. composer: interview in *down beat*, 20 Oct. 1977, rep. in *Conversing with Cage* (ed. Richard Kostelanetz, 1988), 'Esthetics'

3 It doesn't matter how new an idea *is*: what matters is how new it *becomes*.
Elias Canetti (1905–1994), Austrian novelist and philosopher: *The Secret Heart Of The Clock: Notes, Aphorisms, Fragments 1973–1985* (1991), '1981'

4 Ideas are powerful things, requiring not a studious contemplation but an action, even if it is only an inner action. Their acquisition obligates each man in some way to change his life, even if it is only his inner life. They demand to be stood for. They dictate where a man must concentrate his vision. They determine his moral and intellectual priorities. They provide him with allies and make him enemies. In short, ideas impose an interest in their ultimate fate which goes far beyond the realm of the merely reasonable.
Midge Decter (b.1927), U.S. author, editor and social critic: *The Liberated Woman and Other Americans* (1971), Pt.2, Ch.2

5 It's very good for an idea to be commonplace. The important thing is that a new idea should develop out of what is already there so that it soon becomes an old acquaintance. Old acquaintances aren't by any means always welcome, but at least one can't be mistaken as to who or what they are.
Penelope Fitzgerald (b.1916), British author: Fred Fairly lecturing to his students at Cambridge, in *The Gate of Angels* (1990), Ch.20

6 Ideas do not rule the world. But it is because the world has ideas ... that it is not passively ruled by those who are its leaders or those who would like to teach it, once and for all, what it must think.
Michel Foucault (1926–1984), French philosopher: 'Les Reportages d'Idées', publ. in *Il Corriere della Sera* (Milan), 12 Nov. 1978, rep. in *Michel Foucault* by Didier Eribon (1989; tr.1991)

7 I think the idea is more important than the object. The object can look after itself. It will probably last long after I'm dead. ... You can always get another shark.
Damien Hirst (b.1965), British artist: interview by Will Self in *Modern Painters* (London), summer 1994, rep. in *Junk Mail* by Will Self (1995). Hirst was referring to one of his installations of a shark preserved in formaldehyde. Ironically, the day after this interview, one of his new exhibits at the Serpentine Gallery, also a preserved animal, was vandalized

8   One does not *adopt* an idea, one slips into it.
    Jean-Paul Sartre (1905–1980), French philosopher
    and author: *Notebooks for an Ethics* (1983; tr.1992),
    Notebook 1

9   My ideas are a curse.
    They spring from a radical discontent
    With the awful order of things.
    Anne Sexton (1928–1974), U.S. poet: 'February
    3rd', publ. in *Scorpio, Bad Spider, Die: the
    Horoscope Poems* (1978)

10 A person fulfils his duty to society in the name
    of an idea, always doing violence to someone or
    something.
    Andrey Tarkovsky (1932–1986), Russian film-
    maker: journal entry, 22 Jan. 1981, publ. in *Time
    Within Time: The Diaries 1970–1986* (1989;
    tr.1994)

11 Say it! No ideas but in things.
    William Carlos Williams (1883–1963), U.S. poet:
    Paterson (1946, rev. 1963), Bk.1, 'The Delineaments
    of the Giants,' Sct.1. Williams's poetic dictum – to
    present the subject concretely, without literary
    artifice – was influential on the Beat writers, notably
    Allen Ginsberg

See also Genet on HATE

IDENTITY

1   An identity would seem to be arrived at by the
    way in which the person faces and uses his
    experience.
    James Baldwin (1924–1987), U.S. author: 'No
    Name in the Street' (1972), rep. in *The Price Of The
    Ticket* (1985)

2   Man may be defined as the animal that can say
    'I,' that can be aware of himself as a separate
    entity.
    Erich Fromm (1900–1980), U.S. psychologist: *The
    Sane Society* (1955), Ch.3, 'Sense of Identity'

3   Human beings have an inalienable right to
    invent themselves; when that right is pre-
    empted it is called brain-washing.
    Germaine Greer (b.1939), Australian feminist
    writer: in *The Times* (London), 1 Feb. 1986

4   I'd like to be a better me, a cleverer me, a more
    organized me. And wouldn't mind being a me
    of 28 knowing what I knew at 40. But the
    thought of being somebody else is incon-
    ceivable. Not because I'm particularly pleased
    with myself – I just can't imagine *being* some-
    body else. Perhaps you only want to be
    somebody else when you are very much in
    love. You want to become the other person.
    Peter Hall (b.1930), British theatre, opera and film
    director: on being asked, 'Who would you like to be if
    you weren't Peter Hall?', in journal entry, 2 July
    1973, publ. in *Diaries* (1983)

5   I guess I've always been suspicious about what
    identity means – how we desperately need it,
    but also what it demands of us. ... Whether it's
    saying 'I love you' in the mirror, or saying, 'yes
    I killed Jesus Christ and I will live my life in
    repentance', it's all part of the same impulse.
    We all do it.
    Todd Haynes (b.1961), U.S. film-maker: interview
    in *The Guardian* (London), 13 April 1996

IDEOLOGY

1   Ideology has very little to do with 'con-
    sciousness' .... It is profoundly *unconscious*.
    Louis Althusser (1918–1990), Algerian-born
    French Marxist philosopher: *For Marx* (1965),
    Ch.7, Sct.4

2   Whoever today speaks of human existence in
    terms of power, efficiency, and 'historical
    tasks' ... is an actual or potential assassin.
    Albert Camus (1913–1960), French-Algerian
    philosopher and author: address, 1946, Columbia
    University, New York City, quoted in *The Wine of
    Absurdity* by Paul West (1966), 'Albert Camus'

3   What persuades men and women to mistake
    each other from time to time for gods or ver-
    min is ideology. One can understand well
    enough how human beings may struggle and
    murder for good material reasons – reasons
    connected, for instance, with their physical
    survival. It is much harder to grasp how they
    may come to do so in the name of something as
    apparently abstract as ideas. Yet ideas are what
    men and women live by, and will occasionally
    die for.
    Terry Eagleton (b.1943), British critic: intro-
    duction to *Ideology* (1991)

4   Our blight is ideologies – they are the long-
    expected Antichrist!
    Carl Jung (1875–1961), Swiss psychiatrist: *The
    Tibetan Book of the Great Liberation* (1954), rep. in
    Collected Works (ed. William McGuire), Vol.XI
    (1958), para.778

5   Ideologies ... have no heart of their own.
    They're the whores and angels of our striving
    selves.
    John Le Carré (b.1931), British author: Smiley, in
    The Secret Pilgrim (1990), Ch.12

6   If you take away ideology, you are left with a
    case by case ethics which in practice ends up as
    me first, me only, and in rampant greed.
    Richard Nelson (b.1950), U.S. playwright: in *The
    Independent* (London), 12 July 1989

7   We must have an ideology. The other side have
    got an ideology they can test their policies
    against. We must have one as well.
    Margaret Thatcher (b.1925), British Conservative
    politician and prime minister: speech to the

Conservative Philosophy Group in 1975, shortly after being elected leader of the Conservative Party, quoted in *One of Us* by Hugo Young (1989), Ch.18

8 Art and ideology often interact on each other; but the plain fact is that both spring from a common source. Both draw on human experience to explain mankind to itself; both attempt, in very different ways, to assemble coherence from seemingly unrelated phenomena; both stand guard for us against chaos.
   Kenneth Tynan (1927–1980), British critic: 'Ionesco and the Phantom', first publ. in *The Observer* (London), 6 July 1958, rep. in *Notes and Counter-Notes* by Eugène Ionesco (1962)

See also Jiang Qing on INTERNATIONAL RELATIONS; Chomsky on THE MEDIA

IGNORANCE

1 The ground for taking ignorance to be restrictive of freedom is that it causes people to make choices which they would not have made if they had seen what the realization of their choices involved.
   A.J. Ayer (1910–1989), British philosopher: *The Meaning of Life and Other Essays* (1990), 'The Concept of Freedom'

2 Only Socrates knew, after a lifetime of unceasing labor, that he was ignorant. Now every high-school student knows that. How did it become so easy?
   Allan Bloom (1930–1992), U.S. educator and author: introduction to *The Closing of the American Mind* (1987)

3 There can be no more ancient and traditional American value than ignorance. English-only speakers brought it with them to this country three centuries ago, and they quickly imposed it on the Africans – who were not allowed to learn to read and write – and on the Native Americans, who were simply not allowed.
   Barbara Ehrenreich (b.1941), U.S. author and columnist: 'Language Barrier' (1989), rep. in *The Worst Years of Our Lives* (1991)

4 It's always like that. One never understands anything, then suddenly, one evening, you end up dying of it.
   Jean-Luc Godard (b.1930), French film-maker and author: Lemmy Caution (Eddie Constantine), in *Alphaville* (film; written and directed by Jean-Luc Godard, 1965)

5 Nothing in all the world is more dangerous than sincere ignorance and conscientious stupidity.
   Martin Luther King Jr. (1929–1968), U.S. clergyman and civil rights leader: *Strength to Love* (1963), Ch.4, Sct.3

6 There is natural ignorance and there is artificial ignorance. I should say at the present moment the artificial ignorance is about eighty-five per cent.
   Ezra Pound (1885–1972), U.S. poet and critic: interview in *Writers at Work* (Second Series, ed. George Plimpton, 1963)

7 The truth is that our race survived ignorance; it is our scientific genius that will do us in.
   Stephen Vizinczey (b.1933), Hungarian novelist and critic: 'Leonardo's Regret' (review of Richie Calder's *The Age of the Eye*), publ. in *The Times* (London), 21 Sept. 1970, rep. in *Truth and Lies in Literature* (1986)

See also STUPIDITY

ILLEGITIMACY

1 There are no illegitimate children, only illegitimate parents – if the term is to be used at all.
   Bernadette McAliskey [formerly Bernadette Devlin] (b.1947), Northern Irish politician: quoted in the *Irish Times* (Dublin), 31 July 1971. The words are not original – the lawyer Léon Yankwich said the same during a hearing at the State District Court, Southern District of California, in June 1928, and he was quoting the journalist O.O. McIntyre

2 Oh these illegitimate babies!
   Oh girls, girls,
   Silly little valuable things,
   You should have said, No, I am valuable,
   And again, It is because I am valuable
   I say, No.
   Stevie Smith (1902–1971), British poet and novelist: 'Valuable' (1962), rep. in *The Collected Poems of Stevie Smith* (1975)

ILLNESS

1 The sick man is taken away by the institution that takes charge not of the individual, but of his illness, an isolated object transformed or eliminated by technicians devoted to the defence of health the way others are attached to the defence of law and order or tidiness.
   Michel de Certeau (1925–1986), French author and critic: *The Practice of Everyday Life* (1974), Ch.14, 'An Unthinkable Practice'

2 You aren't ill: it is just that you are made of second-rate materials.
   Natalia Ginzburg (1916–1991), Italian novelist: Alberto to his wife Miranda, in *Family Sayings* (1963; tr.1967, rev.1984), p.98 of Carcanet edn. (1984)

3 As a cure for the cold, take your toddy to bed, put one bowler hat at the foot, and drink until you see two.

Robert Lockhart (1886–1970), British author, diplomat and journalist: quoted in *The Independent* (London), 25 Nov. 1989

4 Illness is the night-side of life, a more onerous citizenship. Everyone who is born holds dual citizenship, in the kingdom of the well and in the kingdom of the sick. Although we all prefer to use only the good passport, sooner or later each of us is obliged, at least for a spell, to identify ourselves as citizens of that other place.
Susan Sontag (b.1933), U.S. essayist: opening words of preface to *Illness As Metaphor* (1978)

5 Dearest Lord, may I see you today and every day in the person of your sick, and, whilst nursing them, minister unto you. Though you hide yourself behind the unattractive disguise of the irritable, the exacting, the unreasonable, may I still recognize you, and say: 'Jesus, my patient, how sweet it is to serve you.'
Mother Teresa (1910–1997), Albanian-born Roman Catholic missionary: *A Gift for God* (1975), 'Love to Pray'

6 We are such docile creatures, normally, that it takes a virus to jolt us out of life's routine. A couple of days in a fever bed are, in a sense, health-giving; the change in body temperature, the change in pulse rate, and the change of scene have a restorative effect on the system equal to the hell they raise.
E.B. White (1899–1985), U.S. author and editor: 'The Cold', publ. in the *New Yorker*, 10 Nov. 1951, rep. in *Writings from the New Yorker 1927–1976* (ed. Rebecca M. Dale, 1991)

7 Sickness disgusts us with death, and we wish to get well, which is a way of wishing to live. But weakness and suffering, with manifold bodily woes, soon discourage the invalid from trying to regain ground: he tires of those respites which are but snares, of that faltering strength, those ardours cut short, and that perpetual lying in wait for the next attack.
Marguerite Yourcenar (1903–1987), French novelist: *Memoirs of Hadrian* (1954), 'Patientia'

See also DISEASE; Auden on HEALTH; Trilling on HEALTH

ILLUSION

1 I search myself for illusions like a monkey looking for fleas.
Philip Larkin (1922–85), British poet: letter, 13 July 1949, publ. in *Selected Letters of Philip Larkin 1940–1985* (ed. Anthony Thwaite, 1992)

2 No illusion is more crucial than the illusion that great success and huge money buy you immunity from the common ills of mankind, such as cars that won't start.

Larry McMurtry (b.1936), U.S. screenwriter, novelist and essayist: Danny Deck, in *Some Can Whistle* (1989), Pt.1, Ch.11

3 This world cannot ever hope to really exist and so it exists entirely through illusion, but illusion is employed as subversively, as convincingly as possible. This critical moment is my act of seeing.
Claes Oldenburg (b.1929), Swedish-born U.S. artist: *Store Days* (1966), rep. in *Twentieth-Century Artists on Art* (ed. Dore Ashton, 1985)

4 'Oh what an artistic animal is our little Man',
Sneered the wind, 'It is wonderful how he can
Invent fairy stories about everything, pit pat,
Will he ever face fact and not feel flat?'
Stevie Smith (1902–1971), British poet and novelist: 'Will Man Ever Face Fact and not Feel Flat?', publ. in *Not Waving But Drowning* (1957)

5 Artists use frauds to make human beings seem more wonderful than they really are. Dancers show us human beings who move much more gracefully than human beings really move. Films and books and plays show us people talking much more entertainingly than people really talk, make paltry human enterprises seem important. Singers and musicians show us human beings making sounds far more lovely than human beings really make. Architects give us temples in which something marvelous is obviously going on. Actually, practically nothing is going on.
Kurt Vonnegut (b.1922), U.S. novelist: *Wampeters, Foma and Granfalloons* (1974), 'When I Was Twenty-One'

IMAGERY

1 We are all hungry and thirsty for concrete images. Abstract art will have been good for one thing: to restore its exact virginity to figurative art.
Salvador Dali (1904–1989), Spanish painter: journal entry, 2 Aug. 1953, in *Diary of a Genius* (1966)

2 In societies where modern conditions of production prevail, all of life presents itself as an immense accumulation of *spectacles*. Everything that was directly lived has moved away into a representation.
Guy Debord (1931–1994), French Situationist philosopher: *The Society of the Spectacle* (1967; tr. 1977), Ch.1, Sct.1

3 Metaphors are much more tenacious than facts.
Paul de Man (1919–1983), Belgian-born U.S. literary critic: *Allegories of Reading* (1979), Pt.1, Ch.1, 'Semiology and Rhetoric'

4 For such an advanced civilization as ours to be without images that are adequate to it is as serious a defect as being without memory.
Werner Herzog (b.1942), German film-maker: in the *New York Times*, 11 Sept. 1977

5 The visual is sorely undervalued in modern scholarship. ... Drunk with self-love, criticism has hugely overestimated the centrality of language to western culture. It has failed to see the electrifying sign language of images.
Camille Paglia (b.1947), U.S. author and critic: *Sexual Personae* (1990), Ch.1

6 Industrial societies turn their citizens into image-junkies; it is the most irresistible form of mental pollution. Poignant longings for beauty, for an end to probing below the surface, for a redemption and celebration of the body of the world. Ultimately, having an experience becomes identical with taking a photograph of it.
Susan Sontag (b.1933), U.S. essayist: *On Photography* (1977), 'In Plato's Cave'

7 Isn't life a series of images that change as they repeat themselves?
Andy Warhol (c.1928–1987), U.S. Pop artist: quoted in *Warhol* by Victor Bokris (1989), 'Too Much Work 1980–84'

8 What I fear most is an overdose of images. I fear losing the ability to discriminate between the good and the ugly.
Wim Wenders (b.1945), German film-maker: interview in the *Independent on Sunday* (London), 19 April 1992

See also McLuhan on POLITICS

IMAGINATION

1 Man is an imagining being.
Gaston Bachelard (1884–1962), French scientist, philosopher and literary theorist: *The Poetics of Reverie* (1960; tr.1969), Ch.2, Sct.10

2 The human imagination ... has great difficulty in living strictly within the confines of a materialist practice or philosophy. It dreams, like a dog in its basket, of hares in the open.
John Berger (b.1926), British author and critic: 'The Soul and the Operator', first publ. in *Expressen* (Stockholm), 19 March 1990, rep. in *Keeping a Rendezvous* (1992)

3 Fortunately, somewhere between chance and mystery lies imagination, the only thing that protects our freedom, despite the fact that people keep trying to reduce it or kill it off altogether.
Luis Buñuel (1900–1983), Spanish film-maker: *My Last Breath* (autobiography, 1983), Ch.15

4 Imagination has seized power.
(*L'imagination prend le pouvoir*.)
Graffiti: publ. in *Paris, '68* by Marc Rohan (1988), Ch.2, Paris, 1968

5 My imagination makes me human and makes me a fool; it gives me all the world and exiles me from it.
Ursula K. Le Guin (b.1929), U.S. author: 'Winged: the Creatures on my Mind', publ. in *Harper's Magazine* (New York), Aug. 1990

6 Imagination is the voice of daring. If there is anything Godlike about God it is that. He dared to imagine everything.
Henry Miller (1891–1980), U.S. author: *Sexus* (1949), Ch.14

7 The genius of Man in our time has gone into jet-propulsion, atom-splitting, penicillin-curing, etc. There is none over for works of imagination; of spiritual insight or mystical enlightenment. I asked for bread and was given a tranquilliser. It is important to recognise that in our time man has not written one word, thought one thought, put two notes or two bricks together, splashed colour on to canvas or concrete into space, in a manner which will be of any conceivable *imaginative* interest to posterity.
Malcolm Muggeridge (1903–1990), British journalist and broadcaster: *Tread Softly for You Tread on My Jokes* (1966), 'I Like Dwight'

8 Imagination, the supreme delight of the immortal and the immature, should be limited. In order to enjoy life, we should not enjoy it too much.
Vladimir Nabokov (1899–1977), Russian-born U.S. novelist and poet: *Speak, Memory* (1955; rev.1966), Ch.1, Sct.1

9 There is a fifth dimension beyond those known to man. It is a dimension vast as space and timeless as infinity. It is the middle ground between light and shadow, between the pit of his fears and the summit of his knowledge. This is the dimension of imagination. It is an area called the Twilight Zone.
Rod Serling (1924–1975), U.S. writer and producer for television: preamble to *The Twilight Zone* (TV series, written, created and narrated by Rod Serling, 1959–64)

10 To regard the imagination as metaphysics is to think of it as part of life, and to think of it as part of life is to realize the extent of artifice. We live in the mind.
Wallace Stevens (1879–1955), U.S. poet: 'Imagination as Value', lecture (1949), rep. in *The Necessary Angel* (1951)

See also FANTASY

IMITATION

1 Man is an idiot. He doesn't know how to do anything without copying, without imitating, without plagiarizing, without aping. It might even have been that man invented generation by coitus after seeing the grasshopper copulate.
Augusto Roa Bastos (b.1917), Paraguayan novelist: *I The Supreme* (1974; tr.1986), p.133 of Faber edn. (1988)

2 Those who do not want to imitate anything, produce nothing.
Salvador Dali (1904–1989), Spanish painter: *Dali by Dali* (1970), 'The Futuristic Dali'

3 Imitation, if it is not forgery, is a fine thing. It stems from a generous impulse, and a realistic sense of what can and cannot be done.
James Fenton (b.1949), British poet and critic: 'Ars Poetica', No.47, in the *Independent on Sunday* (London), 16 Dec. 1990

4 When people are free to do as they please, they usually imitate each other.
Eric Hoffer (1902–1983), U.S. philosopher: *The Passionate State of Mind* (1955), Aph.33. Hoffer adds, 'A society which gives unlimited freedom to the individual, more often than not attains a disconcerting sameness. On the other hand, where communal discipline is strict but not ruthless ... originality is likely to thrive'

See also PLAGIARISM

IMMIGRATION

1 The making of an American begins at the point where he himself rejects all other ties, any other history, and himself adopts the vesture of his adopted land.
James Baldwin (1924–1987), U.S. author: 'Many Thousands Gone', first publ. in *Partisan Review* (New Brunswick, N.J.), Nov./Dec. 1951, rep. in *Notes of a Native Son* (1955), Pt.1

2 The proposition that Muslims are welcome in Britain if, and only if, they stop behaving like Muslims is a doctrine which is incompatible with the principles that guide a free society.
Roy Hattersley (b.1932), British Labour politician: in *The Independent* (London), 21 July 1989

3 It is like watching a nation busily engaged in heaping up its own funeral pyre. ... As I look ahead, I am filled with foreboding. Like the Roman, I seem to see 'the River Tiber foaming with much blood'.
Enoch Powell (b.1912), British Conservative politician: speech, 20 April 1968, to West Midlands Conservatives, Birmingham, quoted in *The Observer* (London), 21 April 1968. The day after making this notorious warning about the consequences of large-scale immigration into Britain from Commonwealth countries, Powell was dropped from the Shadow Cabinet. According to *Brewer's Quotations* (Nigel Rees, 1994), Powell afterwards commented that he should have quoted the remark in Latin to emphasize that he was not predicting a bloodbath, only evoking the Sybil's prophecy in Virgil's *Aeneid* Bk.6, l.86: 'Et Thybrim multo spumantem sanguine cerno.' The phrase 'rivers of blood' was also used by, among others, Thomas Jefferson and Winston Churchill

4 The feeling they exuded towards the world was: 'We don't really care what you think. What you say doesn't touch us because you're not really part of our world.' ... We were born here. We haven't got another world that we carry around in our heads. We have to compete. We had to take on a lot of the battles that they couldn't or wouldn't engage in. We had to redefine the image they'd given of Indians as these ethereal, exotic people, clannish, never quite involved.
Meera Syal (b.1963), British actress and writer: contrasting the attitudes of her parents and their generation with the experience of their children, in interview in *The Guardian* (London), 6 April 1996

IMMORTALITY

1 I don't want to achieve immortality through my work ... I want to achieve it through not dying.
Woody Allen (b.1935), U.S. film-maker: quoted in *Woody Allen and His Comedy* by Eric Lax (1975), Ch.12

2 For them that think death's honesty
Won't fall upon them naturally
Life sometimes
Must get lonely.
Bob Dylan (b.1941), U.S. singer and songwriter: 'It's Alright Ma (I'm Only Bleeding)' (song), on the album *Bringing it All Back Home* (1965)

3 You may want to live forever but do you want your parents to live forever? Do you want Ronald Reagan to live forever?
William Gibson (b.1948), U.S. science fiction author: interview in *Rapid Eye 3* (ed. Simon Dwyer, 1995)

4 He had decided to live for ever or die in the attempt.
Joseph Heller (b.1923), U.S. novelist: referring to Yossarian, in *Catch-22* (1961), Ch.3

5 Immortality
Is not mere repetition:
It is a blue flash,
A kingfisher vision
It is a new-feathered
And procreant love,

Seen where the halcyon
   Nests on the waves.
Anne Ridler (b.1912), British poet: 'The Halcyons',
publ. in *New and Selected Poems* (1988)

6   Man, as long as he lives, is immortal. One minute before his death he shall be immortal. But
one minute later, God wins.
Elie Wiesel (b.1928), Rumanian-born U.S. writer:
paraphrasing Jewish tradition, in interview in
Writers at Work (Eighth Series, ed. George
Plimpton, 1988)

See also Tarkovsky on MORTALITY

IMPERIALISM

1   The good old imperialism was a bloody sight
wiser and healthier than all this woolly-
headed, muddled, 'all men are equal' humani-
tarianism which has lost us so much pride and
dignity and prestige in the modern world. The
British Empire was a great and wonderful
social, economic and even spiritual experiment, and all the parlour pinks and eager, ill-
informed intellectuals cannot convince me to
the contrary.
Noël Coward (1899–1973), British playwright,
actor and composer: journal entry, 3 Feb. 1957, publ.
in *The Noël Coward Diaries* (ed. Graham Payn and
Sheridan Morley, 1982)

2   Exploitation and oppression is not a matter of
race. It is the system, the apparatus of worldwide brigandage called imperialism, which
made the Powers behave the way they did. I
have no illusions on this score, nor do I believe
that any Asian nation or African nation, in the
same state of dominance, and with the same
system of colonial profit-amassing and plunder, would have behaved otherwise.
Han Suyin (b.1917), Chinese author: *The Crippled
Tree* (1965), Pt.1, Ch.9

3   Never was it the case that the imperial encounter pitted an active Western intruder
against a supine or inert non-Western native;
there was *always* some form of active resistance and, in the overwhelming majority of
cases, the resistance finally won out.
Edward Said (b.1935), Lebanese-born U.S. social
and literary critic: introduction to *Culture and
Imperialism* (1993)

See also COLONIALISM

IMPOTENCE

1   I am tortured by impotence – that utterly negative feeling, a void; zero between the loins.
Alan Clark (b.1928), British Conservative
politician: journal entry, 17 July 1989, publ. in
Diaries (1993)

2   All it means, if you wilt that way with a lady, is
that you haven't yet really met her. You're not
trying to make love to a woman, you're trying
not to miss an opportunity.
Clive James (b.1939), Australian writer and critic:
Falling Towards England (1985), Ch.8

3   What a let-down! I was ready for a tour round
his Eiffel Tower, but all I got was a limp excuse
and not-tonight-Josephine. Next time it had
better be the real French stick, François, not a
soggy brioche.
Ruth Morgan (1920–1978), U.S. novelist: Roberta,
in *Jeu d'Esprit* (1968), Ch.9

See also Abish on THE UNITED STATES

IMPROVISATION

1   Improvisation is too good to leave to chance.
Paul Simon (b.1941), U.S. singer and songwriter: in
the *International Herald Tribune* (Paris), 12 Oct.
1990

2   Through spontaneity we are re-formed into
ourselves. It creates an explosion that for the
moment frees us from handed-down frames of
reference, memory choked with old facts and
information and undigested theories and
techniques of other people's findings. Spontaneity is the moment of personal freedom
when we are faced with reality, and see it,
explore it and act accordingly. In this reality
the bits and pieces of ourselves function as an
organic whole. It is the time of discovery, of
experiencing, of creative expression.
Viola Spolin (b.1911), U.S. theatrical director and
producer: *Improvisation for the Theater* (1963),
Ch.1

INDECISION

1   He has conferred on the practice of vacillation
the aura of statesmanship.
Kenneth Baker (b.1934), British Conservative
politician: of SDP leader Dr David Owen, in *The
Daily Telegraph* (London), 11 Oct. 1989

2   We know what happens to people who stay in
the middle of the road. They get run over.
Aneurin Bevan (1897–1960), British Labour
politician: quoted in *The Observer* (London), 6 Dec.
1953

INDEPENDENCE

1   It's easy to be independent when you've got
money. But to be independent when you
haven't got a thing – that's the Lord's test.
Mahalia Jackson (1911–1972), U.S. gospel singer:
Movin' On Up (written with Evan McLoud Wylie,
1966), Ch.1

2 Our treatment of both older people and children reflects the value we place on independence and autonomy. We do our best to make our children independent from birth. We leave them all alone in rooms with the lights out and tell them, 'Go to sleep by yourselves.' And the old people we respect most are the ones who will fight for their independence, who would sooner starve to death than ask for help.

Margaret Mead (1901–1978), U.S. anthropologist: quoted in *Family Circle* (New York), 26 July 1977

3 We prefer self-government with danger to servitude in tranquillity.

Kwame Nkrumah (1900–1972), Ghanaian president: motto of the *Accra Evening News*, founded 1948, quoted in *Axioms of Kwame Nkrumah* (1967), p.50

See also Smith on JESUS CHRIST

INDIA

1 There are moments in India, and no doubt always have been, when every function of human domestic behaviour appears to be performed with a futility, a hopeless and infuriating lack of the meanest dexterity that drives one almost to mania. At such times it seems past understanding how this ancient and numerous people ever contrived to get their race propagated at all, let alone produce undying work of beauty and scientific permanence. At other times there is the corrective – some unexpected demonstration of extraordinary skill and resource, some extravagant dinner prepared in a tin-can oven; a delicate bauble suddenly moulded from coloured mud.

James Cameron (1911–1985), British journalist: *Point of Departure* (1969), Ch.12

2 There exists no politician in India daring enough to attempt to explain to the masses that cows can be eaten.

Indira Gandhi (1917–1984), Indian politician and prime minister: quoted by Oriana Fallaci in 'Indira's Coup', publ. in the *New York Review of Books*, 18 Sept. 1975

3 Remote from ourselves in dream and in time, India belongs to the Ancient Orient of our soul. ... What is Zeus, compared with Shiva? The only god of antiquity whose language is worthy of India is the god without temples – Fate.

André Malraux (1901–1976), French man of letters and statesman: *Anti-Memoirs* (1967; tr.1968), 'The Temptation of the West', Sct.1

See also van der Post on WILLIAM SHAKESPEARE

INDIFFERENCE

1 Make sense who may. I switch off.

Samuel Beckett (1906–1989), Irish playwright and novelist: Bam, in *What Where* (1984)

2 It means nothing to me. I have no opinion about it, and I don't care.

Pablo Picasso (1881–1973), Spanish artist: reaction to the first moon-landing, publ. in the *New York Times*, 21 July 1969

3 We're pretty ... pretty vacant
And we don't care.

Sex Pistols (1976–1979), British punk band: 'Pretty Vacant' song, on the album *Never Mind the Bollocks* (1977)

4 Men are accomplices to that which leaves them indifferent.

George Steiner (b.1929), French-born U.S. critic and novelist: *Language and Silence* (1967), 'A Kind of Survivor'

5 The opposite of love is not hate, it's indifference. The opposite of art is not ugliness, it's indifference. The opposite of faith is not heresy, it's indifference. And the opposite of life is not death, it's indifference.

Elie Wiesel (b.1928), Rumanian-born U.S. writer: *U.S. News and World Report* (New York), 27 Oct. 1986

See also APATHY

INDIVIDUALITY

1 The greatest enemy of individual freedom is the individual himself.

Saul Alinsky (1909–1972), U.S. political activist: prologue to *Rules for Radicals* (1971)

2 Today the individual has become the highest form and the greatest bane of artistic creation. The smallest wound or pain of the ego is examined under the microscope as if it were of eternal importance. The artist considers his isolation, his subjectivity, his individualism almost holy. Thus we finally gather in one large pen, where we stand and bleat about our loneliness without listening to each other and without realizing that we are smothering each other to death.

Ingmar Bergman (b.1918), Swedish stage and film writer-director: spoken introduction to *The Seventh Seal* (film; written and directed by Ingmar Bergman, 1956)

3 It is the individual man
In his individual freedom who can mature
With his warm spirit the unripe world.

Christopher Fry (b.1907), British playwright: Moses in *The Firstborn* (1946), Act 1, Sc.1

4 In each individual the spirit is made flesh, in each one the whole of creation suffers, in each one a Saviour is crucified.

Hermann Hesse (1877–1962), German novelist and poet: the narrator (Sinclair), in prologue to *Demian* (1960)

5 Resistance to the organized mass can be effected only by the man who is as well organized in his individuality as the mass itself.

Carl Jung (1875–1961), Swiss psychiatrist: *The Undiscovered Self* (1957), Ch.4

6 Comrades! We must abolish the cult of the individual decisively, once and for all.

Nikita Khrushchev (1894–1971), Soviet premier: speech, 25 Feb. 1956, to the secret session of the 20th Congress of the Communist Party, quoted in *The Manchester Guardian*, 11 June 1956. Khrushchev used the occasion to identify Stalin as the chief exponent of the cult of the individual (also translated 'cult of the personality') by 'the glorification of his own person'. He expanded: 'Everyone can err, but Stalin considered that he never erred, that he was always right. He never acknowledged to anyone that he made any mistake, large or small, despite the fact that he made not a few mistakes in the matter of theory and in his practical activity' (quoted in *Stalin*, Pt.2, Ch.6, ed. T.H. Rigby, 1966)

7 Except in a few well-publicized instances (enough to lend credence to the iconography painted on the walls of the media), the rigorous practice of rugged individualism usually leads to poverty, ostracism and disgrace. The rugged individualist is too often mistaken for the misfit, the maverick, the spoilsport, the sore thumb.

Lewis H. Lapham (b.1935), U.S. essayist and editor: *Money and Class in America* (1988), Ch.9

8 I am not a number – I am a free man!

Patrick McGoohan (b.1928), Anglo-American actor: Number Six (Patrick McGoohan), in preamble to each episode of *The Prisoner* (TV series created by Patrick McGoohan, George Markstein and David Tomblin, 1967–1968). Elsewhere in the series, Number Six (who is never named), states, 'I will not be pushed, stamped, filed, indexed, briefed, debriefed or numbered. My life is my own'

9 Those who talk about individuality the most are the ones who most object to deviation, and in a few years it may be the other way around. Some day everybody will just think what they want to think, and then everybody will probably be thinking alike; that seems to be what is happening.

Andy Warhol (c.1928–1987), U.S. Pop artist: in *Art News* (New York), Nov. 1963

See also Winterson on SELF ; Advertisement on SPORT: ATHLETICS

INDUSTRY

1 It is an axiom, enforced by all the experience of the ages, that they who rule industrially will rule politically.

Aneurin Bevan (1897–1960), British Labour politician: quoted in *Aneurin Bevan* Vol.I, by Michael Foot (1962), Ch.2

2 We have created an industrial order geared to automatism, where feeble-mindedness, native or acquired, is necessary for docile productivity in the factory; and where a pervasive neurosis is the final gift of the meaningless life that issues forth at the other end.

Lewis Mumford (1895–1990), U.S. social philosopher: *The Conduct of Life* (1951), 'The Fulfillment of Man'

3 Properly, urban-industrialism must be regarded as an experiment. And if the scientific spirit has taught us anything of value, it is that honest experiments may well fail.

Theodore Roszak (b.1933), U.S. social critic: introduction to *Where the Wasteland Ends* (1972)

4 The Industrial Revolution and its consequences have been a disaster for the human race. They have greatly increased the life-expectancy of those of us who live in 'advanced' countries, but they have destabilized society, have made life unfulfilling, have subjected human beings to indignities, have led to widespread psychological suffering (in the Third World to physical suffering as well) and have inflicted severe damage on the natural world. The continued development of technology will worsen the situation.

Unabomber, U.S. radical: *Industrial Society and Its Future*, 'Introduction, 1', publ. in the *Washington Post*, 19 Sept. 1995

5 In an industrial society which confuses work and productivity, the necessity of producing has always been an enemy of the desire to create.

Raoul Vaneigem (b.1934), Belgian Situationist philosopher: *The Revolution of Everyday Life* (1967; tr.1983), Ch.5

6 For years I thought what was good for our country was good for General Motors and vice versa. The difference did not exist. Our company is too big. It goes with the welfare of the country.

Charles E. Wilson (1890–1961), U.S. industrialist and secretary of defense: statement to a U.S. Senate committee, Jan. 1953, quoted in the *New York Times*, 24 Feb. 1953. Wilson was head of General Motors Corporation 1941–53; his words (usually quoted 'What's good for the country is good for General Motors, and *vice versa*') were pounced upon by the Democrats on the Committee, who were in a majority, to question his true loyalties

INEQUALITY

1 The only inequalities that matter begin in the mind. It is not income levels but differences in mental equipment that keep people apart, breed feelings of inferiority.
Jacquetta Hawkes (1910–1996), British archaeologist and writer: in the *New Statesman* (London), Jan. 1957

2 There is always inequity in life. Some men are killed in a war and some men are wounded and some men never leave the country. ... Life is unfair.
John F. Kennedy (1917–1963), U.S. Democratic politician and president: press conference, 21 March 1962, quoted in *A Thousand Days* by Arthur M. Schlesinger Jr. (1965)

3 Inequality is the only bearable thing, the monotony of equality can only lead us to boredom.
(*L'inégalité est la seul chose supportable, la monotonie de l'égalité ne peut nous mener à l'ennui.*)
Francis Picabia (1878–1953), French painter and poet: 'L'Humour Poétique', first publ. in *La Nef* (Paris), Dec. 1950/Jan. 1951, rep. in *Yes No: Poems and Sayings* (ed. Rémy Hall, 1990), 'Sayings'

4 We have so many people who can't see a fat man standing beside a thin one without coming to the conclusion that the fat man got that way by taking advantage of the thin one!
Ronald Reagan (b.1911), U.S. Republican politician and president: 'A Time for Choosing', television address, 27 Oct. 1964, publ. in *Speaking My Mind* (1989)

INERTIA

1 Estragon: Charming spot. Inspiring prospects. Let's go.
Vladimir: We can't.
Estragon: Why not?
Vladimir: We're waiting for Godot.
Samuel Beckett (1906–1989), Irish playwright and novelist: *Waiting for Godot* (1952; tr.1954), Act 1

2 Nothing happens, nobody comes, nobody goes, it's awful.
Samuel Beckett: Estragon, in *Waiting for Godot* (1952; tr.1954), Act 1

See also Galbraith on HOLIDAYS

INFATUATION

1 I was born when you kissed me. I died when you left me. I lived a few weeks while you loved me.
Gloria Grahame (1924–1981), U.S. actress: Laurel Gray (Gloria Grahame), quoting the unfinished

script of screenwriter Dixon Steele (Humphrey Bogart) at the end of *In a Lonely Place* (film; screenplay by Andrew Solt, adapted from Dorothy B. Hughes's novel, directed by Nicholas Ray, 1950)

2 I'm gonna wash that man right out of my hair.
Oscar Hammerstein II (1895–1960), U.S. songwriter: 'I'm Gonna Wash That Man Right Out of my Hair' (song), performed in *South Pacific* (stage musical, 1949; film, 1958)

3 Lolita, light of my life, fire of my loins. My sin, my soul. Lo-lee-ta: the tip of the tongue taking a trip of three steps down the palate to tap, at three, on the teeth. Lo. Lee. Ta.
Vladimir Nabokov (1899–1977), Russian-born U.S. novelist and poet: Humbert Humbert (narrator), in opening paragraph of *Lolita* (1955)

4 Men who care passionately for women attach themselves at least as much to the temple and to the accessories of the cult as to their goddess herself.
Marguerite Yourcenar (1903–1987), French novelist: *Memoirs of Hadrian* (1954), 'Varius Multiplex Multi Formis'

INFLATION

1 People are out of work. Interest rates go up. Money gets tight. It's unpleasant. Only later do the good effects of an end to rising prices show up. The problem is getting through the painful cure without wanting another drink. The greatest difficulty in curtailing inflation is that, after a while, people begin to think they'd rather have the sickness than the cure.
Milton Friedman (b.1912), U.S. economist: introduction to *There's No Such Thing as a Free Lunch* (1975)

2 Inflation is as violent as a mugger, as frightening as an armed robber and as deadly as a hit man.
Ronald Reagan (b.1911), U.S. Republican politician and president: speech to Republican party fund-raising dinner, quoted in the *Los Angeles Times*, 20 Oct. 1978

INFORMATION

1 Information can tell us everything. It has all the answers. But they are answers to questions we have not asked, and which doubtless don't even arise.
Jean Baudrillard (b.1929), French semiologist: *Cool Memories* (1987; tr.1990), Ch.5

2 Information networks straddle the world. Nothing remains concealed. But the sheer volume of information dissolves the information. We are unable to take it all in.
Günter Grass (b.1927), German author: interview in the *New Statesman and Society* (London), 22 June 1990

3 Knowledge in the form of an informational commodity indispensable to productive power is already, and will continue to be, a major – perhaps *the* major – stake in the worldwide competition for power. It is conceivable that the nation-states will one day fight for control of information, just as they battled in the past for control over territory, and afterwards for control over access to and exploitation of raw materials and cheap labor.
Jean François Lyotard (b.1924), French philosopher: introduction to *The Postmodern Condition: A Report on Knowledge* (1979)

4 The more the data banks record about each one of us, the less we exist.
Marshall McLuhan (1911–1980), Canadian communications theorist: interview in *Playboy* (Chicago), March 1969

5 I was brought up to believe that the only thing worth doing was to add to the sum of accurate information in the world.
Margaret Mead (1901–1978), U.S. anthropologist: in the *New York Times*, 9 Aug. 1964

6 Information is the oxygen of the modern age. It seeps through the walls topped by barbed wire, it wafts across the electrified borders.
Ronald Reagan (b.1911), U.S. Republican politician and president: quoted in *The Guardian* (London), 14 June 1989

See also KNOWLEDGE

INHIBITION

1 Men would rather take their trousers off in public when they're drunk than open the shield of their hearts when they are sober.
Stephen Fry (b.1957), British comic actor and author: speech to launch the Samaritans' annual report, 17 May 1996, quoted in *The Guardian* (London), 18 May 1996

2 Yet if a woman never lets herself go, how will she ever know how far she might have got? If she never takes off her high-heeled shoes, how will she ever know how far she could walk or how fast she could run?
Germaine Greer (b.1939), Australian feminist writer: *The Change: Women, Ageing and the Menopause* (1991), Ch.2

3 My defences were so great. The cocky rock and roll hero who knows all the answers was actually a terrified guy who didn't know how to cry. Simple.
John Lennon (1940–1980), British rock musician: interview in *Playboy* (Chicago), Sept. 1980

See also SHYNESS

INJURY

1 To live is to hurt others, and through others, to hurt oneself. Cruel earth! How can we manage not to touch anything? To find what ultimate exile?
Albert Camus (1913–1960), French-Algerian philosopher and author: journal entry, 1 Aug. 1949, publ. in *American Journals* (1978; tr. 1988)

2 Children show scars like medals. Lovers use them as secrets to reveal. A scar is what happens when the word is made flesh.
Leonard Cohen (b.1934), Canadian singer, poet and novelist: *The Favourite Game* (1963), Bk.1, Ch.1

INJUSTICE

1 Children will still die unjustly even in a perfect society. Even by his greatest effort, man can only propose to diminish, arithmetically, the sufferings of the world.
Albert Camus (1913–1960), French-Algerian philosopher and author: *The Rebel* (1951; tr.1953), Pt.5, 'Beyond Nihilism'

2 Progress is the injustice each generation commits with regard to its predecessors.
E.M. Cioran (1911–1995), Rumanian-born French philosopher: *The Trouble with Being Born* (1973), Ch.8

INNOCENCE

1 I believe we are still so innocent. The species is still so innocent that a person who is apt to be murdered believes that the murderer, just before he puts the final wrench on his throat, will have enough compassion to give him one sweet cup of water.
Maya Angelou (b.1928), U.S. author: 'Work in Progress', interview, first publ. June 1973, rep. in *Conversations with Maya Angelou* (ed. Jeffrey M. Elliot, 1989)

2 People who shut their eyes to reality simply invite their own destruction, and anyone who insists on remaining in a state of innocence long after that innocence is dead turns himself into a monster.
James Baldwin (1924–1987), U.S. author: 'Stranger in the Village', first publ. in *Harper's Magazine* (New York), Oct. 1953, rep. in *Notes of a Native Son* (1955), Pt.2

3 There is no aphrodisiac like innocence.
Jean Baudrillard (b.1929), French semiologist: *Cool Memories* (1987; tr.1990), Ch.5

4 Only the old are innocent. That is what the Victorians understood, and the Christians.

Original sin is a property of the young. The old grow beyond corruption very quickly.

Malcolm Bradbury (b.1932), British author: Dr Jochum, in *Stepping Westward* (1965), Bk.1, Ch.1

5 Innocence always calls mutely for protection when we would be so much wiser to guard ourselves against it: innocence is like a dumb leper who has lost his bell, wandering the world, meaning no harm.

Graham Greene (1904–1991), British novelist: *The Quiet American* (1955), Pt.1, Ch.3, Sct.3. Later in the book, the narrator describes Pyle – the idealistic 'quiet American' of the title – in similar terms: 'What's the good? He'll always be innocent, you can't blame the innocent, they are always guiltless. All you can do is control them or eliminate them. Innocence is a kind of insanity' (Pt.3, Ch.2, Sct.1)

6 All things truly wicked start from an innocence.

Ernest Hemingway (1899–1961), U.S. author: *A Moveable Feast* (1964), Ch.17

7 An innocent man is a sin before God. Inhuman and therefore untrustworthy. No man should live without absorbing the sins of his kind, the foul air of his innocence, even if it did wilt rows of angel trumpets and cause them to fall from their vines.

Toni Morrison (b.1931), U.S. novelist and editor: *Tar Baby* (1981), p.245 of Chatto & Windus edn. (1981)

8 The essential self is innocent, and when it tastes its own innocence knows that it lives for ever.

John Updike (b.1932), U.S. author and critic: *Self-Consciousness: Memoirs* (1989), Ch.1

INNOCENCE: Loss of

1 In my desperation there is no more purity, no more innocence. ... Now I am a desert completely explored; there is no way to save me. I am all consciousness.

Pier Paolo Pasolini (1922–1975), Italian filmmaker and essayist: journal entry, 21 Nov. 1946, in the second of Pasolini's 'Red Notebooks', publ. in *Pasolini Requiem* by David Barth Schwartz (1992), Ch.9

2 The idea of a fall from childhood grace, pinned on one particular moment – a moment over which we had no control, much lamented – gives our lives a compelling narrative structure. It's easy to see why the seventeen-year-old likes it. It's easy to see why the rape-crisis feminists like it. It's a natural human impulse put to political purpose. But in generating and perpetuating these kinds of myths we should keep in mind that myths surrounding female innocence have been used to keep women inside and behind veils. They have been used to keep them out of work and in labor.

Katie Roiphe (b.1969), U.S. feminist writer: *The Morning After* (1993), 'The Rape-Crisis, or "Is Dating Dangerous?"'

3 The ingenuous open heart preserves one's ability to say 'I' to a stranger, until a moment comes when this strange 'I' returns and enters into 'me' again. Then at one blow the heart is captive, one is pre-possessed; that much can be foretold.

Christa Wolf (b.1929), German novelist: *The Quest for Christa T* (1968: tr.1982), Ch.1

INNOVATION

1 Innovation! One cannot be forever innovating. I want to create classics.

Coco Chanel (1883–1971), French *couturière*: quoted in *Coco Chanel: Her Life, Her Secrets* by Marcel Haedrich (1971), Ch.21

2 Anyone who has invented a better mousetrap, or the contemporary equivalent, can expect to be harassed by strangers demanding that you read their unpublished manuscripts or undergo the humiliation of public speaking, usually on remote Midwestern campuses.

Barbara Ehrenreich (b.1941), U.S. author and columnist: 'The Cult of Busyness', first publ. in the *New York Times*, 1985, rep. in *The Worst Years of Our Lives* (1991)

INNUENDO

1 You might say that, my dear: I couldn't possibly comment.

Andrew Davies (b.1936), British screenwriter: Francis Urquhart (Iain Richardson) to Mattie Storin (Susannah Harker), in *House of Cards* (TV series, 1992, based on the original novel by Michael Dobbs)

2 Nudge, nudge, wink, wink, say no more, know what I mean...

Monty Python's Flying Circus: Eric Idle, posing as a pestering, inquisitive bore, in *Monty Python's Flying Circus* (TV series, 1969–74), first series, broadcast 19 Nov. 1969. Monty Python episodes were written and performed by Graham Chapman (1941–1989), John Cleese (b.1939), Terry Gilliam (b.1940), Eric Idle (b.1943), Terry Jones (b.1942) and Michael Palin (b.1943)

INSECTS

1 Now what sort of man or woman or monster would stroke a centipede I have ever seen? 'And here is my good big centipede!' If such a

man exists, I say kill him without more ado. He is a traitor to the human race.
William Burroughs (1914–1997), U.S. author: *The Western Lands* (1987), Ch.4

2   Long after the bomb falls and you and your good deeds are gone, cockroaches will still be here, prowling the streets like armored cars.
Tama Janowitz (b.1957), U.S. author: *Slaves of New York* (1986), 'Modern Saint 271'

3   After the planet becomes theirs, many millions of years will have to pass before a beetle particularly loved by God, at the end of its calculations will find written on a sheet of paper in letters of fire that energy is equal to the mass multiplied by the square of the velocity of light. The new kings of the world will live tranquilly for a long time, confining themselves to devouring each other and being parasites among each other on a cottage industry scale.
Primo Levi (1919–1987), Italian chemist and author: *Other People's Trades* (1985; tr.1989), 'Beetles'

4   I saw the spiders marching through the air,
Swimming from tree to tree that mildewed day
    In latter August when the hay
    Came creaking to the barn.
Robert Lowell (1917–1977), U.S. poet: 'Mr Edwards and the Spider', St.1 (1946), publ. in *Poems 1938–1949* (1950)

See also Herzog on GENOCIDE

INSECURITY

1   I have three phobias which, could I mute them, would make my life as slick as a sonnet, but as dull as ditch water: I hate to go to bed, I hate to get up, and I hate to be alone.
Tallulah Bankhead (1903–1968), U.S. actress: *Tallulah* (1952), Ch.1

2   Don't touch me! Don't question me! Don't speak to me! Stay with me!
Samuel Beckett (1906–1989), Irish playwright and novelist: Estragon, in *Waiting for Godot* (1952; tr.1954), Act 2

3   Wouldn't this be a great world if insecurity and desperation made us more attractive?
James L. Brooks (b.1940), U.S. film-maker: Aaron Altman (Albert Brooks), in *Broadcast News* (film; written, directed and co-produced by James L. Brooks, 1987)

4   Probably the only place where a man can feel really secure is in a maximum security prison, except for the imminent threat of release.
Germaine Greer (b.1939), Australian feminist writer: *The Female Eunuch* (1970), 'Security'

5   The man who looks for security, even in the mind, is like a man who would chop off his limbs in order to have artificial ones which will give him no pain or trouble.
Henry Miller (1891–1980), U.S. author: *Sexus* (1949), Ch.14

6   Our lives depend on whether safety standards at a nuclear power plant are properly maintained; on how much pesticide is allowed to get into our food or how much pollution into our air; on how skillful (or incompetent) our doctor is; whether we lose or get a job may depend on decisions made by government economists or corporation executives; and so forth. Most individuals are not in a position to secure themselves against these threats to more [than] a very limited extent. The individual's search for security is therefore frustrated, which leads to a sense of powerlessness.
Unabomber, U.S. radical: *Industrial Society and Its Future*, 'Disruption of the Power Process in Modern Society', Sct.67, publ. in the *Washington Post*, 19 Sept. 1995

INSIGNIFICANCE

1   You'll come to learn a great deal if you study the Insignificant in depth.
Odysseus Elytis (b.1911), Greek poet and essayist: *To Axion Asti – It Is Worthy* (1959), quoted as Epigraph to *Discontent and Liberal Opinion* by Roman Baczynski (1987)

2   A small man can be just as exhausted as a great man.
Arthur Miller (b.1915), U.S. playwright: Linda, referring to her husband Willy Loman, in *Death of a Salesman* (1949), Act 1

3   Nothing is the history of the world viewed from a suitable distance. Revolution is a trivial shift in the emphasis of suffering; the capacity for self-indulgence changes hands. But the world does not alter its shape or its course. The seasons are inexorable, the elements constant. Against such vast immutability the human struggles take place on the same scale as the insect movement in the grass, and carnage in the streets is no more than the spider-sucked husk of a fly on a dusty window-sill.
Tom Stoppard (b.1937), British playwright: Lord Malquist, in *Lord Malquist and Mr Moon* (1966), Pt.1, Ch.1

INSPIRATION

1   *When you do not know what you are doing* and what you are doing is the best – that is inspiration.
Robert Bresson (b.1907), French film-maker: *Notes on the Cinematographer* (1975), '1950–1958: The Real'

2 The moment of truth, the sudden emergence of a new insight, is an act of intuition. Such intuitions give the appearance of miraculous flashes, or short-circuits of reasoning. In fact they may be likened to an immersed chain, of which only the beginning and the end are visible above the surface of consciousness. The diver vanishes at one end of the chain and comes up at the other end, guided by invisible links.
Arthur Koestler (1905–1983), Hungarian-born British novelist and essayist: *The Act of Creation* (1964), Pt.2, Ch.8

3 Deprivation is for me what daffodils were for Wordsworth.
Philip Larkin (1922–1985), British poet: interview in *The Observer* (London) 1979, rep. in *Required Writing* (1983)

4 I didn't have to think up so much as a comma or a semicolon; it was all given, straight from the celestial recording room. Weary, I would beg for a break, an intermission, time enough, let's say, to go to the toilet or take a breath of fresh air on the balcony. Nothing doing!
Henry Miller (1891–1980), U.S. author: on the composition of *Tropic of Capricorn*, in *Big Sur and the Oranges of Hieronymous Bosch* (1957), Pt.2, 'A Fortune in Francs'. Miller added, 'How could I possibly imagine then that some few years later a judicial triumvirate, eager to prove me a sinner, would accuse me of having written such passages "for gain"?'

5 Everyone has left me
except my muse,
that good nurse.
She stays in my hand,
a mild white mouse.
Anne Sexton (1928–1974), U.S. poet: 'Flee on Your Donkey', St.3, publ. in *Live or Die* (1966). The title quotes from Rimbaud's work *Fêtes de la Faim* (1872)

6 Why does my Muse only speak when she is unhappy?
She does not, I only listen when I am unhappy.
Stevie Smith (1902–1971), British poet and novelist: 'My Muse' (1962), publ. in *Selected Poems* (1964)

INSTINCT

1 When people are forced to deny their natural urges they get weird, twisted and mean.
Robert Crumb (b.1943), U.S. cartoonist: interview in *The Apex Treasury of Underground Comics* (ed. Susan Goodrick and Don Donahue, 1974)

2 If men as individuals surrender to the call of their elementary instincts, avoiding pain and seeking satisfaction only for their own selves, the result for them all taken together must be a state of insecurity, of fear, and of promiscuous misery.
Albert Einstein (1879–1955), German-born U.S. theoretical physicist: *Out of My Later Years* (1950), Ch.7

3 Even when we feel we are most overwhelmed by our instinctual urgings, what we are usually doing is reworking the scripts which tell us about our 'needs' and 'desires', about what is 'right' and 'wrong'.
Jeffrey Weeks (b.1945), British sexologist: introduction to *Against Nature* (1991)

INSTITUTIONS

1 In any great organization it is far, far safer to be wrong with the majority than to be right alone.
J.K. Galbraith (b.1908), U.S. economist: in *The Guardian* (London), 28 July 1989

2 Power is not of a man. Wealth does not center in the person of the wealthy. Celebrity is not inherent in any personality. To be celebrated, to be wealthy, to have power requires access to major institutions.
C. Wright Mills (1916–1962), U.S. sociologist: *The Power Elite* (1956), Ch.1

INSULTS

1 No one can be as calculatedly rude as the British, which amazes Americans, who do not understand studied insult and can only offer abuse as a substitute.
Paul Gallico (1897–1976), U.S. novelist: in the *New York Times*, 14 Jan. 1962

2 Daily life is governed by an economic system in which the production and consumption of insults tends to balance out.
Raoul Vaneigem (b.1934), Belgian Situationist philosopher: *The Revolution of Everyday Life* (1967; tr.1983), Ch.2, Sct.1

See also ABUSE

INSURANCE

1 The Act of God designation on all insurance policies: which means, roughly, that you cannot be insured for the accidents that are most likely to happen to you. If your ox kicks a hole in your neighbour's Maserati, however, indemnity is instantaneous.
Alan Coren (b.1938), British editor and humorist: *The Lady from Stalingrad Mansions* (1977), 'A Short History of Insurance'

2 For almost seventy years the life insurance industry has been a smug sacred cow feeding the public a steady line of sacred bull.

Ralph Nader (b.1934), U.S. consumer rights activist: testimony to U.S. Senate subcommittee, quoted in the *New York Times*, 19 May 1974

See also Malouf on DISASTERS

INTELLECTUALS

1 A spirit of national masochism prevails, encouraged by an effete corps of impudent snobs who characterize themselves as intellectuals.

Spiro T. Agnew (1918–1996), U.S. Republican politician and vice president: speech, 19 Oct. 1969, New Orleans, publ. in *Collected Speeches of Spiro Agnew* (1971)

2 I've never been an intellectual but I have this look.

Woody Allen (b.1935), U.S. film-maker: in the *International Herald Tribune* (Paris), 18 March 1992

3 I've been called many things, but never an intellectual.

Tallulah Bankhead (1903–1968), U.S. actress: *Tallulah* (1952), Ch.15

4 The intellectual tradition is one of servility to power, and if I didn't betray it I'd be ashamed of myself.

Noam Chomsky (b.1928), U.S. linguist and political analyst: responding to an accusation of betrayal by Arthur Schlesinger Jr., in television interview on *The Late Show* (BBC2), 25 Nov. 1992, excerpted in *The Guardian* (London), 23 Nov. 1992

5 Intellectual sodomy, which comes from the refusal to be simple about plain matters, is as gross and abundant today as sexual perversion and they are nowise different from one another.

Edward Dahlberg (1900–1977), U.S. author and critic: *Alms for Oblivion* (1964), 'Moby-Dick: A Hamitic Dream'

6 We should take care not to make the intellect our god; it has, of course, powerful muscles, but no personality.

Albert Einstein (1879–1955), German-born U.S. scientist: *Out of My Later Life* (1950), Ch.51

7 The native intellectual has thrown himself greedily upon Western culture. Like adopted children who only stop investigating the new family framework at the moment when a minimum nucleus of security crystallizes in their psyche, the native intellectual will try to make European culture his own. He will not be content to get to know Rabelais and Diderot, Shakespeare and Edgar Allen Poe; he will bind them to his intelligence as closely as possible.

Frantz Fanon (1925–1961), Martiniquan psychiatrist, philosopher and political activist: *The Wretched of the Earth* (1961), Ch.4

8 The work of an intellectual is not to mould the political will of others; it is, through the analyses that he does in his own field, to re-examine evidence and assumptions, to shake up habitual ways of working and thinking, to dissipate conventional familiarities, to re-evaluate rules and institutions and ... to participate in the formation of a political will (where he has his role as citizen to play).

Michel Foucault (1926–1984), French philosopher: 'The Concern for Truth', interview first publ. in *Le Magazine Littéraire* (Paris), May 1984, rep. in *Foucault Live* (ed. Sylvère Lotringer, 1989)

9 There's always something suspect about an intellectual on the winning side.

Václav Havel (b.1936), Czech playwright and president: *Disturbing the Peace* (1986; tr.1990), Ch.5

10 Intellectuals can tell themselves anything, sell themselves any bill of goods, which is why they were so often patsies for the ruling classes in nineteenth-century France and England, or twentieth-century Russia and America.

Lillian Hellman (1905–1984), U.S. playwright: journal entry, 30 April 1967, publ. in Hellman's memoir, *An Unfinished Woman* (1969), Ch.13

11 *I think, therefore I am* is the statement of an intellectual who underrates toothaches.

Milan Kundera (b.1929), Czech-born French author and critic: *Immortality* (1991), Pt.4, Ch.11

12 We suffer from a hubris of the mind. We have abolished superstition of the heart only to install a superstition of the intellect in its place.

Laurens van der Post (1906–1996), South African writer, philosopher: *The Heart of the Hunter* (1961), p.129 of Penguin edn. (1971)

See also Carter on THE UNITED STATES: AFRICAN AMERICANS

INTELLIGENCE

1 Undernourished, intelligence becomes like the bloated belly of a starving child: swollen, filled with nothing the body can use.

Andrea Dworkin (b.1946), U.S. feminist critic: *Right-Wing Women* (1978), Ch.2

2 Reason is man's faculty for *grasping* the world by thought, in contradiction to intelligence, which is man's ability to *manipulate* the world with the help of thought. Reason is man's instrument for arriving at the truth, intelligence is man's instrument for manipulating the world more successfully; the former is

essentially human, the latter belongs to the animal part of man.

Erich Fromm (1900–1980), U.S. psychologist: *The Sane Society* (1955), Ch.3, 'The Need for a Frame of Orientation and Devotion – Reason vs. Irrationality'

3   Man is an intelligence, not served by, but in servitude to his organs.

Aldous Huxley (1894–1963), British author: *Themes and Variations* (1950), 'Variations on a Philosopher'

4   Intelligence ... is really a kind of taste: taste in ideas.

Susan Sontag (b.1933), U.S. essayist: 'Notes on "Camp"' (1964), rep. in *Against Interpretation* (1966)

See also Fowles on RACE

INTERNATIONAL RELATIONS

1   There cannot be peaceful coexistence in the ideological realm. Peaceful coexistence corrupts.

Jiang Qing (1914–1991), Chinese party official, wife of Mao Tse-tung: said in April 1967, quoted in *Mao and China: From Revolution to Revolution* by Stanley Karnow (1972), Ch.15

2   If you live among wolves you have to act like a wolf.

Nikita Khrushchev (1894–1971), Soviet premier: quoted in *The Observer* (London), 26 Sept. 1971

THE INTERNET

1   It's what I always wanted – to be in touch with a community of ideas like this. ... There's something thrilling about the internet. ... It almost doesn't matter what anyone says. It's more the thrill of knowing you're in touch with people laterally, rather than through a filter of some kind.

Brian Eno (b.1948), British rock musician: interview in *i-D* (London), Oct. 1993

2   Cyberspace is where a long distance phone call takes place. Cyberspace is where the bank keeps your money. Where your medical records are stored. All of this stuff is out there somewhere. There is really no point in thinking about its geographical location. Information is extra-geographical.

William Gibson (b.1948), U.S. science fiction author: interview in *Rapid Eye 3* (ed. Simon Dwyer, 1995)

3   Enthusiasm for a medium that keeps you away from human beings strikes me as worrying. That you would rather live in an unreal time and space, with unreal people who don't even give their names – you can say what you like, you can be whoever you like – means that

people aren't anyone, they become more and more unreal.

Ian Hislop (b.1960), British journalist: *Without Walls: J'Accuse – Technonerds* (Channel 4), 19 March 1996

4   The new electronic interdependence recreates the world in the image of a global village.

Marshall McLuhan (1911–1980), Canadian communications theorist: chapter gloss in *The Gutenberg Galaxy* (1962), p.31 of University of Toronto Press edn.

5   We've now invented the ultimate tool for keeping the sads busy: the internet. But behind all the techno-babble about cyberspace and hyper-text and virtual worlds, behind all the promises of total immersion in a parallel universe, there's a boring reality: a bunch of screeching modems, lost jobs, and boring computer-nerds getting all excited over a glorified telephone exchange. I'm sick of the spurious claims devotees make for the internet, and I'm particularly sick of the internerds.

Janet Street-Porter (b.1946), British broadcaster and programme-maker: *Without Walls: J'Accuse – Technonerds* (Channel 4), 19 March 1996

6   Anyone wishing to communicate with Americans should do so by e-mail, which has been specially invented for the purpose, involving neither physical proximity nor speech.

Auberon Waugh (b.1939), British journalist and novelist: on the 'perils' of visiting New York, in 'Way of the World', column in *The Daily Telegraph* (London), 1 Nov. 1995

INTERPRETATION

1   Have you never despaired of understanding an ancient text? Have you not been scared by the many interpretations lying between the text and yourself? Have you never been discouraged by the ambiguity in every word, however straight and precise, as it immediately fades into adulteration and interpretation?

Emmanuel Levinas (b.1905), French Jewish philosopher: *Difficult Freedom* (1990), Pt.2, 'Messianic Texts'

2   Interpretation is the revenge of the intellect upon art. Even more. It is the revenge of the intellect upon the world. To interpret is to impoverish, to deplete the world – in order to set up a shadow world of 'meanings'.

Susan Sontag (b.1933), U.S. essayist: 'Against Interpretation', Sct.4, first publ. in *The Evergreen Review* (New York), Dec. 1964, rep. in *Against Interpretation* (1966)

INTERVENTION

1 Most of the trouble in this world has been caused by folks who can't mind their own business, because they have no business of their own to mind, any more than a smallpox virus has.
William Burroughs (1914–1997), U.S. author: *The Adding Machine* (1985), 'My Own Business'

2 All of Western tradition, from the late bloom of the British Empire right through the early doom of Vietnam, dictates that *you do something spectacular and irreversible* whenever you find yourself in or whenever you impose yourself upon a wholly unfamiliar situation belonging to somebody else. Frequently it's your soul or your honor or your manhood, or democracy itself, at stake.
June Jordan (b.1936), U.S. poet and civil rights activist: 'Beyond Apocalypse Now', speech, 1980, Lewis and Clark University, Oregon, publ. in *Moving Towards Home: Political Essays* (1989)

INTERVIEWS

1 The literary interview won't tell you what a writer is *like*. Far more compellingly, to some, it will tell you what a writer is *like to interview*.
Martin Amis (b.1949), British author: in *The Observer* (London), 30 Aug. 1987, rep. in *Visiting Mrs Nabokov* (1993), 'John Updike'

2 The best interviews – like the best biographies – should sing the strangeness and variety of the human race.
Lynn Barber (b.1944), British journalist: in the *Independent on Sunday*, (London) 24 Feb. 1991

3 The media no longer ask those who know something ... to share that knowledge with the public. Instead they ask those who know nothing to represent the ignorance of the public and, in so doing, to legitimate it.
Serge Daney (1944–1992), French film critic: quoted in *Sight and Sound* (London), July 1992

4 Listening to someone talk isn't at all like listening to their words played over on a machine. What you hear when you have a face before you is never what you hear when you have before you a winding tape.
Oriana Fallaci (b.1930), Italian author: foreword to *The Egotists* (1963)

5 I'd like to keep a note of the replies I've already given and then say to the journalists – who always ask the same questions, anyway – 'Look at reply No.2005'.
Federico Fellini (1920–1993), Italian film-maker: *Fellini on Fellini* (ed. Anna Keel and Christian Strich, 1974; tr.1977), 'Miscellany I', Sct.3

6 If, sir, I possessed ... the power of conveying unlimited sexual attraction through the potency of my voice, I would not be reduced to accepting a miserable pittance from the BBC for interviewing a faded female in a damp basement.
Gilbert Harding (1907–1960), British broadcaster: on being asked to sound more sexy when interviewing Mae West, recalled by Wynford Vaughan Thomas in *Gilbert Harding By His Friends* (ed. Stephen Grenfell, 1961)

7 I'm notorious for giving a bad interview. I'm an actor and I can't help but feel I'm boring when I'm on as myself.
Rock Hudson (1925–1985), U.S. actor: quoted in *TV Times* (London), 19 Oct. 1972

8 Never try to look into both eyes at the same time. ... Switch your gaze from one eye to the other. That signals warmth and sincerity.
Dorothy Sarnoff (b.1917), U.S. publicist: in *The Times* (London), 27 April 1988

9 It rots a writer's brain, it cretinises you. You say the same thing again and again, and when you do that happily you're well on the way to being a cretin. Or a politician.
John Updike (b.1932), U.S. author and critic: interviewed by novelist Martin Amis in *The Observer* (London), 30 Aug. 1987, rep. in *Visiting Mrs Nabokov* by Martin Amis (1993), 'John Updike'

10 Almost every journalist never wants to know what you really think – they just want the answers that fit the questions that fit the story they want to write, and their idea usually is that you shouldn't let your own personality butt in on the article they're writing about you or else they'll really hate you for sure for giving them more work, because the more answers you give, the more answers they have to twist to fit their story. So it's better just to smile.
Andy Warhol (c.1928–1987), U.S. Pop artist: *From A to B and Back Again* (1975), Ch.11

See also Boorstin on EVENTS

INTIMACY

1 What people don't realize is that intimacy has its conventions as well as ordinary social intercourse. There are three cardinal rules – don't take somebody else's boyfriend unless you've been specifically invited to do so, don't take a drink without being asked, and keep a scrupulous accounting in financial matters.
W.H. Auden (1907–1973), Anglo-American poet: *The Table Talk of W.H. Auden* (comp. Alan Ansen, ed. Nicholas Jenkins, 1990), '31 December, 1947'

2 Women's propensity to share confidences is universal. We confirm our reality by sharing.
Barbara Grizzuti Harrison (b.1941), U.S. author and publicist: 'Secrets Women Tell Each Other', publ. in *McCall's* (New York), Aug. 1975

3 The many faces of intimacy: the Victorians could experience it through correspondence, but not through cohabitation; contemporary men and women can experience it through fornication, but not through friendship.
Thomas Szasz (b.1920), U.S. psychiatrist: *The Second Sin* (1973), 'Social Relations'

See also Heilbrun on MARRIAGE

INTROSPECTION

1 What is interesting about self-analysis is that it leads nowhere – it is an art form in itself.
Anita Brookner (b.1938), British novelist and art historian: interview in *Writers at Work* (Eighth Series, ed. George Plimpton, 1988)

2 Self-revelation is a cruel process. The real picture, the real 'you' never emerges. Looking for it is as bewildering as trying to know how you really look. Ten different mirrors show you ten different faces.
Shashi Deshpande (b.1938), Indian author: *That Long Silence* (1988), Ch.1

See also SELF-ABSORPTION

INVESTMENT

1 Money itself isn't lost or made, it's simply transferred from one perception to another. This painting here. I bought it 10 years ago for 60 thousand dollars. I could sell it today for 600. The illusion has become real and the more real it becomes, the more desperately they want it.
Oliver Stone (b.1946), U.S. film-maker: Gordon Gekko (Michael Douglas), in *Wall Street* (film; written by Oliver Stone and Stanley Weiser, directed by Oliver Stone, 1987)

2 Sometimes your best investments are the ones you don't make.
Donald Trump (b.1946), U.S. businessman: *Trump: The Art of the Deal* (written with Tony Schwartz, 1987), Ch.1

See also THE STOCK MARKET

IRAQ & THE SECOND GULF WAR

1 According to U.S. strategy, if you never *see* the other, his destruction will be more acceptable ... so that when Iraqi soldiers surrendered, sooner than expected, it was as if they emerged from a dream, a flash-back, a lost epoch – an epoch when the enemy still had a body and was still 'like us'.
Serge Daney (1944–1992), French film critic: quoted in *Sight and Sound* (London), July 1992

2 The Gulf War was like teenage sex. We got in too soon and out too soon.
Tom Harkin (b.1939), U.S. Democratic politician and senator: quoted in the *Independent on Sunday* (London), 29 Sept. 1991

3 The great, the jewel and the mother of battles has begun.
Saddam Hussein (b.1937), Iraqi president: speech, 6 Jan. 1991, at the start of the Gulf War, quoted in *The Independent* (London), 19 Jan. 1991

4 If Kuwait grew carrots we wouldn't give a damn.
Lawrence Korb (b.1939), U.S. Republican politician and former assistant defense secretary: on the motives for 'Operation Desert Storm', in the *International Herald Tribune*, 21 Aug. 1990

5 Experts are saying that President Bush's goal now is to politically humiliate Saddam Hussein. Why don't we just make him the next Democratic presidential nominee?
Jay Leno (b.1950), U.S. comedian and actor: in the *International Herald Tribune* (Paris), 18 March 1991

6 We spend all day broadcasting on the radio and TV telling people back home what's happening here. And we learn what's happening here by spending all day monitoring the radio and TV broadcasts from back home.
P.J. O'Rourke (b.1947), U.S. journalist: 'Gulf Diary', 31 Jan. 1991, first publ. in *Rolling Stone* (New York), rep. in *Give War A Chance* (1992)

7 Our leaders had the audacity to say the Gulf War made America feel good again. How morally corrupt are we that we need a war to feel good about ourselves?
Tim Robbins (b.1958), U.S. film-maker: in the *Independent on Sunday* (London), 10 Sept. 1992

8 Here, in a war waged explicitly over neo-colonial control of nonrenewable resources, the state and the media jointly offered a spectacular advertisement for another forty years of the permanent war economy, sustained by the uninterrupted flow of cheap fossil fuels.'
Andrew Ross (b.1956), British social theorist: introduction to *Strange Weather* (1991)

9 For at least a decade movies about American commandos pitted a hulking Rambo or technically whizz-like Delta Force against Arab/Muslim terrorist-desperadoes; in 1991 it was as if an almost metaphysical intention to rout Iraq had sprung into being, not because Iraq's offence, though great, was cataclysmic, but

because a small non-white country had disturbed or rankled a suddenly energized supernation imbued with a fervor that could only be satisfied with compliance or subservience from 'sheikhs', dictators and camel-jockeys.

Edward Said (b.1935), Lebanese-born U.S. social and literary critic: *Culture and Imperialism* (1993), Ch.4, Sct.1

IRELAND

1 Pat: He was an Anglo-Irishman.
Meg: In the blessed name of God, what's that?
Pat: A Protestant with a horse.

Brendan Behan (1923–1964), Irish playwright: of Monsewer, in *The Hostage* (1958), Act 1

2 I'm sick and tired of Irish Americans coming up to me, who haven't been back to their country in years, and talking about the glory of the revolution. Where's the glory in taking a man out in front of his wife and kids and shooting him? In leaving people out with their medals all brushed up laying under the rubble, dying for the glory of the revolution? Fuck the revolution.

Bono (b.1960), Irish rock musician: in *New Musical Express* (London), 1988, quoted in *NME Book of Quotes* (1995), 'Politics'

3 To marry the Irish is to look for poverty.

J.P. Donleavy (b.1926), U.S. author: *The Ginger Man* (1955), Ch.2

4 The Irish are the blacks of Europe; Dubliners are the blacks of Ireland, and on our side, we're the blacks of Dublin. So say it: I'm black and I'm proud.

Roddy Doyle (b.1950), Irish author: Jimmy Rabbitte (Robert Arkins), in *The Commitments* (film; screenplay by Ian LaFrenais, Dick Clement and Roddy Doyle, based on Roddy Doyle's novel, directed by Alan Parker, 1991)

5 Irish Americans are about as Irish as black Americans are African.

Bob Geldof (b.1954), Irish rock singer: quoted in *The Observer* (London), 22 June 1986

6 Ireland is where strange tales begin and happy endings are possible.

Charles Haughey (b.1925), Irish Fianna Fáil politician and prime minister: in *The Daily Telegraph* (London), 14 July 1988

7 The Irish are often nervous about having the appropriate face for the occasion. They have to be happy at weddings, which is a strain, so they get depressed; they have to be sad at funerals, which is easy, so they get happy.

Peggy Noonan (b.1950), U.S. author and presidential speechwriter: *What I Saw at the Revolution* (1990), Ch.13

8 Irishness is not primarily a question of birth or blood or language; it is the condition of being involved in the Irish situation, and usually of being mauled by it.

Conor Cruise O'Brien (b.1917), Irish historian, diplomat and critic: 'Irishness', publ. in the *New Statesman* (London) Jan. 1959

9 Here we have bishops, priests, and deacons, a Censorship Board, vigilant librarians, confraternities and sodalities, Duce Maria, Legions of Mary, Knights of this Christian order and Knights of that one, all surrounding the sinner's free will in an embattled circle.

Sean O'Casey (1884–1964), Irish playwright: letter, to the *Irish Times* (Dublin), 8 June 1957

10 It is often said that in Ireland there is an excess of genius unsustained by talent; but there is talent in the tongues.

V.S. Pritchett (1900–1997), British author and critic: *Midnight Oil* (second volume of memoirs, 1971), Ch.6

See also Behan on BRITAIN: ENGLAND

IRELAND: Northern Ireland

1 I'll wear no convict's uniform
Nor merely serve my time
That England might
brand Ireland's fight
800 years of crime.

Francie Brolly: 'The Politics of Irish Freedom' (1986), publ. in *Gerry Adams: Selected Writings* (1994)

2 The Troubles are a pigmentation in our lives here, a constant irritation that detracts from real life. But life has to do with something else as well, and it's the other things which are the more permanent and real.

Brian Friel (b.1929), Irish playwright and author: in *Vanity Fair* (New York), Oct. 1991

3 The tragedy of Northern Ireland is that it is now a society in which the dead console the living.

Jack Holland (b.1947), Irish poet and journalist: in the *New York Times Magazine*, 15 July 1979

4 Belfast is a big city. At one time it was quite small, even worse, there has been an occasion when there was no Belfast City at all. Thank heaven, those days are gone and there is now a plentiful supply of Belfast.

Spike Milligan (b.1918), British comedian and humorous writer: *Puckoon* (1963), Ch.5

5 For generations, a wide range of shooting in Northern Ireland has provided all sections of the population with a pastime which ... has occupied a great deal of leisure time. Unlike many other countries, the outstanding charac-

teristic of the sport has been that it was not confined to any one class.

Northern Irish Tourist Board: quoted in the *New Statesman* (London), 29 Aug. 1969

6 How could Southern Ireland keep a bridal North in the manner to which she is accustomed?

Terence O'Neill (1914–1990), Northern Irish politician and prime minister: quoted in the *Irish Times* (Dublin), 16 Jan. 1971

7 People who live in this heck's half acre have been worked-over by social scientists until there's hardly one of them who's not a footnote on somebody's master's thesis. And they're so thoroughly journalized that urchins in the street ask, 'Will you be needing a sound bite?' and criticize your choice of shutter speeds.

P.J. O'Rourke (b.1947), U.S. journalist: *Holidays in Hell* (1988), 'The Piece of Ireland that Passeth all Understanding'

See also Anonymous Belfast resident on TERRORISM

IRRITANTS

1 There's always somebody about to ruin your day, if not your life.

Charles Bukowski (1920–1994), U.S. author and poet: the narrator (Nicky Belane), in *Pulp* (1994), Ch.28

2 The only thing that could spoil a day was people.... People were always the limiters of happiness except for the very few that were as good as spring itself.

Ernest Hemingway (1899–1961), U.S. author: *A Moveable Feast* (1964), Ch.6

3 There aren't many irritations to match the condescension which a woman metes out to a man who she believes has loved her vainly for the past umpteen years.

Edward Hoagland (b.1932), U.S. novelist and essayist: *Heart's Desire* (1988), 'The Lapping, Itchy Edge of Love'

4 The two things in life you can do without are neighbours and piles.

Spike Milligan (b.1918), British comedian and humorous writer: quoting his father, in the *Radio Times* (London), 13 April 1996, 'My Kind of Day'

ISLAM

1 Sooner or later we must absorb Islam if our own culture is not to die of anemia.

Basil Bunting (1900–1985), British poet: foreword to *Arabic and Persian Poems* by Omar Pound (1970)

2 The exact objectives of Islam Inc. are obscure. Needless to say everyone involved has a different angle, and they all intend to cross each other up somewhere along the line.

William Burroughs (1914–1997), U.S. author: *The Naked Lunch* (1959), 'Islam Inc. and the Parties of Interzone'

3 Islam is the youngest of the major religions and it has the arrogance of youth.

James Cameron (1911–1985), British journalist: quoted by Moni Cameron (James Cameron's wife) in letter publ. in *The Guardian* (London), 15 March 1989

4 There is nothing in our book, the Koran, that teaches us to suffer peacefully. Our religion teaches us to be intelligent. Be peaceful, be courteous, obey the law, respect everyone; but if someone puts his hand on you, send him to the cemetery. That's a good religion.

Malcolm X (1925–1965), U.S. black leader: 'Message to the Grass Roots', speech, Nov. 1963, Detroit, publ. in *Malcolm X Speaks* (1965), Ch.1

5 Our religion doesn't give women any human dignity. Women are considered slaves. ... I write against the religion because if women want to live like human beings, they will have to live outside the religion and Islamic law.

Taslima Nasreen (b.1958), Bangladeshi author: in *The Times* (London), 22 June 1994

6 If Woody Allen were a Muslim, he'd be dead by now.

Salman Rushdie (b.1947), Indian-born British author: of the death threats by Muslim extremists following the publication of Rushdie's novel, *The Satanic Verses* (1988), quoted in *The Independent* (London), 18 Feb. 1989

7 As for those who think the Arab world promises freedom, the briefest study of its routine traditional treatment of blacks (slavery) and women (purdah) will provide relief from all illusion. If Malcolm X had been a black woman his last message to the world would have been entirely different. The brotherhood of Moslem men – all colors – may exist there, but part of the glue that holds them together is the thorough suppression of women.

Alice Walker (b.1944), U.S. author, critic: *In Search of Our Mothers' Gardens* (1983), 'To the Editors of *Ms*. Magazine'

See also Hattersley on IMMIGRATION

ISOLATION

1 We allow our ignorance to prevail upon us and make us think we can survive alone, alone in

patches, alone in groups, alone in races, even alone in genders.

Maya Angelou (b.1928), U.S. author: address, March 1990, Centenary College of Louisiana, publ. in the *New York Times*, 11 March 1990

2 We're all of us sentenced to solitary confinement inside our own skins, for life!

Tennessee Williams (1911–1983), U.S. playwright: Val Xavier, in *Orpheus Descending* (1957), Act 2, Sc.1

ISRAEL

1 My generation, dear Ron, swore on the Altar of God that whoever proclaims the intent of destroying the Jewish state or the Jewish people, or both, seals his fate.

Menachem Begin (1913–1992), Israeli politician and prime minister: letter to Ronald Reagan, quoted in *The Observer* (London), 2 Jan. 1983

2 Listen, my friend, I've just come back from Mississippi and over there when you talk about the West Bank they think you mean Arkansas.

Patrick Buchanan (b.1938), U.S. journalist, broadcaster and presidential candidate: in *The Spectator* (London), 13 March 1992

3 Israel, and you who call yourself Israel, the Church that calls itself Israel, and the revolt that calls itself Israel, and every nation chosen to be a nation – none of these lands is yours, all of you are thieves of holiness, all of you at war with Mercy.

Leonard Cohen (b.1934), Canadian singer, poet and novelist: *Book of Mercy* (1984), Sct.27

4 We are a generation of settlers, and without the steel helmet and the cannon we cannot plant a tree and build a home. Let us not shrink back when we see the hatred fomenting and filling the lives of hundreds and thousands of Arabs, who sit all around us. Let us not avert our gaze, so that our hands shall not slip. This is the fate of our generation, the choice of our life – to be prepared and armed, strong and tough – or otherwise the sword shall slip from our fist and our life will be snuffed out.

Moshe Dayan (1915–1981), Israeli soldier and politician: quoted in *Israel Without Zionism: A Plea for Peace in the Middle East* by Yuri Avneri (1968), p.134 of Collier Macmillan edn.

5 Israel has not become worse than the surrounding world, whatever the anti-Semites say, but it has ceased to be better. The worst thing is that this was precisely one of its ambitions.

Emmanuel Levinas (b.1905), French Jewish philosopher: 'Ethics and Spirit' (1952), rep. in *Difficult Freedom* (1990), Pt.1

6 We have always said that in our war with the Arabs we had a secret weapon – no alternative.

Golda Meir (1898–1978), Israeli politician and prime minister: in *Life* (New York), 3 Oct. 1969

7 The greatest security for Israel is to create new Egypts.

Ronald Reagan (b.1911), U.S. Republican politician and president: quoted in *The Observer* (London), 27 Feb. 1983

8 Our image has undergone change from David fighting Goliath to being Goliath.

Yitzhak Shamir (b.1915), Israeli politician and prime minister: quoted in *The Daily Telegraph* (London), 25 Jan. 1989

9 There is Israel, for us at least. What no other generation had, we have. We have Israel in spite of all the dangers, the threats and the wars, we have Israel. We can go to Jerusalem. Generations and generations could not and we can.

Elie Wiesel (b.1928), Rumanian-born U.S. writer: interview in *Writers at Work* (Eighth Series, ed. George Plimpton, 1988)

ITALY

1 If all corporations were run like Fininvest, there would be no problems of public morality in Italy.

Silvio Berlusconi (b.1936), Italian businessman and politician: said in Aug. 1994, shortly before investigations into corrupt practices within Berlusconi's Fininvest consortium, quoted in *The Guardian* (London), 31 Dec. 1994

2 It is unjust that Italy should claim musical pre-eminence, even forcing Italian on music as its international language, when Italy's genius is so visual. No nation can build towns as beautiful nor claim a better right to regard nature as a shapeless substance to be redeemed by urbifaction. The Italians are not Wordsworthian. Man fulfils himself in the town. There is too much wild nature in music, and it has to be tamed into simple four-square patterns, as in Verdi and Bellini. The tenor does not proclaim Byronically to the woods and hills: he is a kind of sexy politician for the town *piazza*. The Italians would listen to Aaron, but not to Moses.

Anthony Burgess (1917–1993), British author and critic: *You've Had Your Time* (1990), Pt.4

3 Better than all the museums, this strolling folk
Who sun themselves in the apricot light of
    antiquity
And take its prestige for granted. Cameo faces,
Contessa or contadina; bronze boys skylarking
As if they had just wriggled free from a
    sculptor's hand –
How easily art and nature overlap here!

Cecil Day Lewis (1904–1972), British poet and author: *An Italian Visit* (1953), Pt.3, 'A Letter from Rome'

4 Italy is a poor country full of rich people.

Richard Gardner (b.1927), U.S. diplomat and former ambassador in Rome: quoted in *The Observer* (London), 16 Aug. 1981

5 Whatever else an Italian may lack, he has an Ego. Sometimes two. It is nice to think that even the poorest Italian may possess two Egos while even the richest Englishman, as a rule, has none.

George Mikes (1912–1987), Hungarian-born British humorist: *Italy for Beginners* (1956), 'Tourists and Natives: Two Redeeming Sins'

ITALY: Rome

1 Hurry! We burn
For Rome so near us, for the Phoenix moment
When we have thrown off this traveller's
    trance,
And mother-naked and ageless-ancient
Wake in her warm nest of renaissance.

Cecil Day Lewis (1904–1972), British poet and author: *An Italian Visit* (1953), Pt.2, 'Flight to Italy'

2 eternal it is not,
with its nine-digit numbers
and children's games, graffiti
chipped from the ruins of a third declension,
The New Jerusalem –
Rome-Babylon.

David Malouf (b.1934), Australian novelist and poet: 'Eternal City', publ. in *Neighbours in a Thicket* (1974)

3 In every act or undertaking there is an undercurrent of irony: nothing must be done seriously, and therefore each one of their passions (fishing, killing lizards) slides on an ironic base, and makes them hostile, ambiguous. This is part of the street-smart philosophy of the quarter, where it is necessary not to be different. They are ever competing with each other in boredom, the possibility of being able to do without others, the immediate capacity for catching others red-handed in credulity, faith, commitment – in naivety.

Pier Paolo Pasolini (1922–1975), Italian film-maker and essayist: describing the boys of Testaccio (a quarter of Rome), in 'Studies in the Life of Testaccio', first publ. in *Ali degli occhi azzurri* (1951), rep. in *Pasolini Requiem* by David Barth Schwartz (1992), Ch.12

ITALY: the South

1 The southerner ... wants above all to be obeyed, admired, respected, feared and envied. He wants wealth too, of course, but as an instrument to influence people, and, for that,
the appearance of wealth is as useful as wealth itself. ... Generally speaking, southerners tend to make money in order to rule, northerners to rule in order to make money.

Luigi Barzini (1908-1984), Italian author: *The Italians* (1964), Ch.10

2 Don't forget that even our most obscene vices nearly always bear the seal of sullen greatness.

Gesualdo Bufalino (1920–1996), Sicilian author: of the Sicilians, in *The Guardian* (London), 21 May 1992

3 A Neapolitan will tell you that he has never paid to watch a football match with as much pride as if he were telling you, for instance, that his ancestors fought in the Crusades. If, on the other hand, anyone in Naples finds himself having to pay for a ticket, it means he's a failure, he knows nobody and counts for nothing.

Luciano De Crescenzo (b.1928), Italian author: Antonio Caramanna, in *Thus Spake Bellavista* (1977; tr.1988), Ch.6

ITALY: Venice

1 Venice is like eating an entire box of chocolate liqueurs at one go.

Truman Capote (1924–1984), U.S. author: quoted in *The Observer* (London), 26 Nov. 1961

2 The things of *this* world reveal their essential absurdity when they are put in the Venetian context. In the unreal realm of the canals, as in a Swiftian Lilliput, the real world, with its contrivances, appears as a vast folly.

Mary McCarthy (1912–1989), U.S. author and critic: *Venice Observed* (1956), Ch.1

3 A new Venice is being born, protected, restored, no longer sufficient to itself, but adopted by the world at large as a universal heritage. While I acknowledge the excitement of this new fulfilment, I cannot altogether share it. For one thing I believe the idea of Venice to be unreconcilable with the modern world. For another, selfishly perhaps, foolishly even, I miss the tristesse. The sad magic has gone for me. Incomparable though Venice remains, I miss the pathos of her decline. I wish her well, admire her always, hope on the whole they keep her standing: but I am out of love with her.

Jan Morris (b.1926), British journalist and travel writer: foreword (1982) to *Venice* (1960)

MICK JAGGER

1 This well-put-together, vitamin-packed unit of a human being does not really dance any more: it's simply that his head, his shoulders,

his pelvis, both his arms, both his legs, both his huge feet and both his buttocks are wriggling, at great speed, independently, all the time. ... No question: Mick is, without doubt, one of our least sedentary millionaires.

Martin Amis (b.1949), British author: in the *New Statesman*, 1976, rep. in *Visiting Mrs Nabokov* (1993), 'The Rolling Stones at Earls Court'

2   A slinky mod Frankenstein monster – lurching, jerking, writhing, convulsing – like a marionette being zapped every few seconds by a jolt of electricity. Through these contortions he flawlessly telegraphed the whole Stones' posture – swaggering, sullen, arrogant, androgynous. You got it entirely from Mick's dancing.

Marianne Faithfull (b.1946), British singer: on seeing Jagger perform for the first time, the prelude to her relationship with him, in *Faithfull* (1994), 'Colston Hall'

3   Surely nothing could be that funny.

George Melly (b.1926), British jazz musician, critic and author: on being told by Mick Jagger that his wrinkles were laughter lines, quoted in the *Independent on Sunday* (London), 1 Jan. 1995

4   You don't have to, you know, prance around and run five miles round a stadium in a poofy football suit to prove anything. There's no point pretending to be Peter Pan.

Keith Richards (b.1943), British rock musician: in *New Musical Express* (London), 1988, quoted in *NME Book of Quotes* (1995), 'Rivals'

JAPAN

1   The Japanese are full of surprises, because the women are so refined and elegant and the men fundamentally so crude and rough.

Harold Acton (1904–1994), British author: interview in *Singular Encounters* by Naim Attallah (1990), 'Sir Harold Acton'

2   The Japanese are, to the highest degree, both aggressive and unaggressive, both militaristic and aesthetic, both insolent and polite, rigid and adaptable, submissive and resentful of being pushed around, loyal and treacherous, brave and timid, conservative and hospitable to new ways.

Ruth Benedict (1887–1948), U.S. anthropologist: *The Chrysanthemum and the Sword* (1946), Ch.1

3   For the building of a new Japan
Let's put our mind and strength together,
Doing our best to promote production,
Sending our goods to the peoples of the world,
Endlessly and continuously,
Like water gushing from a fountain.
Grow, industry, grow, grow, grow,
Harmony and sincerity. Matsushita Electrical.

Matsushita Electrical Company: company anthem, sung on official occasions, quoted in *Iemoto, The Heart of Japan* by F.L.K. Hsu (1975)

4   The Japanese have perfected good manners and made them indistinguishable from rudeness.

Paul Theroux (b.1941), U.S. novelist and travel writer: *The Great Railway Bazaar* (1975), Ch.28

JAZZ *see under* MUSIC

JEALOUSY

1   Jealousy is all the fun you *think* they had....

Erica Jong (b.1942), U.S. author: *How To Save Your Own Life* (1977), epigraph to 'Bennett tells all in Woodstock...'

2   To jealousy, nothing is more frightful than laughter.
(*Rien n'est plus affreux que le rire pour la jalousie.*)

Françoise Sagan (b.1935), French novelist and playwright: Lucile, in *La Chamade* (1965), Ch.9

JESUS CHRIST

1   A lot of people say to me, 'Why did you kill Christ?' 'I dunno ... it was one of those parties, got out of hand, you know.' We killed him because he didn't want to become a doctor, that's why we killed him.

Lenny Bruce (1925–1966), U.S. satirical comedian: *The Essential Lenny Bruce* (ed. John Cohen, 1967), 'The Jews'

2   A man who was completely innocent, offered himself as a sacrifice for the good of others, including his enemies, and became the ransom of the world. It was a perfect act.

Mohandas K. Gandhi (1869–1948), Indian political and spiritual leader: of Jesus, in *Non-Violence in Peace and War* (1949), Vol.II, Ch.166

3   Jesus was the first socialist, the first to seek a better life for mankind.

Mikhail Gorbachev (b.1931), Russian political leader: in *The Daily Telegraph* (London), 16 June 1992

4   I wouldn't put it past God to arrange a virgin birth if He wanted, but I very much doubt if He would.

David Jenkins (b.1925), British ecclesiastic and bishop of Durham: in the *Church Times* (London), 4 May 1984

5   Jesus was all right, but his disciples were thick and ordinary. It's them twisting it that ruins it for me.

John Lennon (1940–1980), British rock musician: interview in the *Evening Standard* (London), 4 March 1966

6 Jesus was a brilliant Jewish stand-up comedian, a phenomenal improvisor. His parables are great one-liners.
Camille Paglia (b.1947), U.S. author and critic: in *Harper's Magazine* (New York), March 1991

7 Jesus died for somebody's sins but not mine.
Patti Smith (b.1946), U.S. rock musician and poet: 'Gloria' (song), on the album *Horses* (1975)

8 There is but one love of Jesus, as there is but one person in the poor – Jesus. We take vows of chastity to love Christ with undivided love; to be able to love him with undivided love we take a vow of poverty which frees us from all material possessions, and with that freedom we can love him with undivided love, and from this vow of undivided love we surrender ourselves totally to him in the person who takes his place.
Mother Teresa (1910–1997), Albanian-born Roman Catholic missionary: *A Gift for God* (1975), 'Carriers of Christ's Love'

9 Somewhere in the bible it say Jesus' hair was like lamb's wool, I say. Well, say Shug, if he came to any of these churches we talking bout he'd have to have it conked before anybody paid him any attention. The last thing niggers want to think about they God is that his hair kinky.
Alice Walker (b.1944), U.S. author, critic: *The Color Purple* (1982), p.166 of Women's Press edn. (1983)

See also Ustinov on PROPHETS; Serrano on SYMBOLISM

JOKES

1 My life has been one great big joke,
A dance that's walked
A song that's spoke,
I laugh so hard I almost choke
When I think about myself.
Maya Angelou (b.1928), U.S. author: 'When I Think About Myself', publ. in *Just Give Me a Cool Drink of Water 'fore I Diiie* (1971)

2 They say the seeds of what we will do are in all of us, but it always seemed to me that in those who make jokes in life the seeds are covered with better soil and with a higher grade of manure.
Ernest Hemingway (1899–1961), U.S. author: *A Moveable Feast* (1964), Ch.11

3 The funniest line in English is 'Get it?' When you say that, *everyone* chortles.
Garrison Keillor (b.1942), U.S. author: introduction to *We Are Still Married* (1989)

4 Jokes are grievances.
Marshall McLuhan (1911–1980), Canadian communications theorist: remark, June 1969, made at American Booksellers Association luncheon, Washington D.C., quoted in the *Sun* (Vancouver), 7 June 1969

5 Jokes have little to do with spontaneous humour. The teller has the same relationship to them that he or she might have to Hertz Rent-a-Car. A joke is a hired object, with many previous users, and very often its ashtrays are filled with other people's cigarettes, and its gears are worn and slipping, because other people have driven this joke very badly before you got behind the wheel.
Jonathan Miller (b.1936), British doctor, humorist and director: 'Among Chickens', publ. in *Granta* (Cambridge), No.23, spring 1988

See also Frost on GOD

JOURNALISM

1 The lowest form of popular culture – lack of information, misinformation, disinformation, and a contempt for the truth or the reality of most people's lives – has overrun real journalism. Today, ordinary Americans are being stuffed with garbage.
Carl Bernstein (b.1944), U.S. journalist: in *The Guardian* (London), 3 June 1992

2 My experience with journalists authorises me to record that a very large number of them are ignorant, lazy, opinionated, intellectually dishonest and inadequately supervised.
Conrad Black (b.1944), Canadian newspaper proprietor: testimony to a Canadian Senate Committee, quoted in *The Observer* (London), 28 Jan. 1996

3 We need not be theologians to see that we have shifted responsibility for making the world interesting from God to the newspaperman.
Daniel J. Boorstin (b.1914), U.S. historian: *The Image* (1961), Ch.1

4 Rage is the only quality which has kept me, or anybody I have ever studied, writing columns for newspapers.
Jimmy Breslin (b.1929), U.S. journalist and author: in *The Times* (London), 9 May 1990

5 Journalism could be described as turning one's enemies into money.
Craig Brown (b.1957), British journalist: in *The Daily Telegraph* (London), 28 Sept. 1990

6 Objectivity in some circumstances is both meaningless and impossible. I still do not see how a reporter attempting to define a situation involving some sort of ethical conflict can do it with sufficient demonstrable neutrality to

fulfil some arbitrary concept of 'objectivity'. It never occurred to me, in such a situation, to be other than subjective, and as obviously so as I could manage to be. I may not always have been satisfactorily balanced; I always tended to argue that objectivity was of less importance than the truth, and that the reporter whose technique was informed by no opinion lacked a very serious dimension.

James Cameron (1911–1985), British journalist: *Point of Departure* (1967), Ch.4

7 Evidently there are plenty of people in journalism who have neither got what they liked nor quite grown to like what they get. They write pieces they do not much enjoy writing, for papers they totally despise, and the sad process ends by ruining their style and disintegrating their personality, two developments which in a writer cannot be separate, since his personality and style must progress or deteriorate together, like a married couple in a country where death is the only permissible divorce.

Claud Cockburn (1904–1981), British author and journalist: *I, Claud* (1967), 'Mr Capone, Philosopher'

8 I see journalists as the manual workers, the labourers of the word. Journalism can only be literature when it is passionate.

Marguerite Duras (1914–1996), French author and film-maker: *Practicalities* (1987; tr.1990), 'Walesa's Wife'

9 In journalism it is simpler to sound off than it is to find out. It is more elegant to pontificate than it is to sweat.

Harold Evans (b.1928), British journalist and publisher: said at memorial service for journalist David Blundy, 24 Jan. 1990, quoted in *The Guardian* (London), 25 Jan. 1990

10 Serious, careful, honest, journalism is essential, not because it is a guiding light but because it is a form of honourable behavior, involving the reporter and the reader.

Martha Gellhorn (b.1908), U.S. journalist and author: introduction (1959) to *The Face of War*, pub. in appendix to 1967 edn.

11 A petty reason perhaps why novelists more and more try to keep a distance from journalists is that novelists are trying to write the truth and journalists are trying to write fiction.

Graham Greene (1904–1991), British novelist: letter, 18 Jan. 1981, to critic Stephen Pile, in *The Sunday Times*, rep. in *Yours, Etc: Letters to the Press, 1945–1989* (1989)

12 If you can't get a job as a pianist in a brothel you become a royal reporter.

Max Hastings (b.1945), British journalist and editor: in the *Daily Express* (London), 9 June 1992

13 Our job is like a baker's work – his rolls are tasty as long as they're fresh; after two days they're stale; after a week, they're covered with mould and fit only to be thrown out.

Ryszard Kapuściński (b.1932), Polish journalist: *The Soccer War* (1990), 'The Plan of the Never-Written Book', Sct.33

14 What a squalid and irresponsible little profession it is.... Nothing prepares you for how bad Fleet Street really is until it craps on you from a great height.

Ken Livingstone (b.1945), British Labour politician: quoted in *City Limits* (London), 1 May 1986

15 Opinionated writing is always the most difficult ... simply because it involves retaining in the cold morning-after crystal of the printed word the burning flow of molten feeling.

Gavin Lyall (b.1932), British journalist and novelist: introduction to *Roundabout* by Katharine Whitehorn (1962)

16 Every journalist who is not too stupid or too full of himself to notice what is going on knows that what he does is morally indefensible. He is a kind of confidence man, preying on people's vanity, ignorance, or loneliness, gaining their trust and betraying them without remorse.

Janet Malcolm (b.1934), U.S. author: *The Journalist and the Murderer* (1990), Pt.1. This paragraph opens the book, which is a study of the case of journalist Joe McGinniss, who won the trust of an alleged murderer, then wrote a best-seller, *Fatal Vision* (1984), proclaiming his guilt

17 I am a journalist and, under the modern journalist's code of Olympian objectivity (and total purity of motive), I am absolved of responsibility. We journalists don't have to step on roaches. All we have to do is turn on the kitchen light and watch the critters scurry.

P.J. O'Rourke (b.1947), U.S. journalist: *Parliament of Whores* (1991), 'Why God is a Republican and Santa Claus is a Democrat'

18 Don't think for a moment that the middle-class journalist cares at all for the truth; to be in some way honest; to be personal. He completely depersonalizes himself, to allow himself to speak to a hypothetical public, one which he naturally considers right-thinking but idiotic, normal but ferocious, uncensored but vile.

Pier Paolo Pasolini (1922–1975), Italian film-maker and essayist: 'Le belle bandiere' (column) in *Vie nuove*, 15 Oct. 1960, rep. in *Pasolini Requiem* by David Barth Schwartz (1992), Ch.16

19 Journalists belong in the gutter because that is where the ruling classes throw their guilty secrets.

Gerald Priestland (1927–1991), British broadcaster: Radio London, 19 May 1988

20 In America journalism is apt to be regarded as an extension of history: in Britain, as an extension of conversation.
Anthony Sampson (b.1926), British journalist and author: *Anatomy of Britain Today* (1965), Ch.9

21 I still believe that if your aim is to change the world, journalism is a more immediate short-term weapon.
Tom Stoppard (b.1937), British playwright: in *The Guardian* (London), 18 March 1988

22 *Gonzo* journalism ... is a style of 'reporting' based on William Faulkner's idea that the best fiction is far more *true* than any kind of journalism – and the best journalists have always known this. ... True *gonzo* reporting needs the talents of a master journalist, the eye of an artist/photographer and the heavy balls of an actor. Because the writer *must* be a participant in the scene, while he's writing it – or at least taping it, or even sketching it. Or all three. Probably the closest analogy to the ideal would be a film director/producer who writes his own scripts, does his own camera work and somehow manages to film himself in action, as the protagonist or at least a main character.
Hunter S. Thompson (b.1939), U.S. journalist: *The Great Shark Hunt* (1979), 'Jacket Copy for Fear and Loathing in Las Vegas'

23 Most rock journalism is people who can't write, interviewing people who can't talk, for people who can't read.
Frank Zappa (1940–1993), U.S. rock musician: in the *Chicago Tribune*, 18 Jan. 1978

See also Warhol on INTERVIEWS; Graham on NEWS; Reston on NEWS; THE PRESS; Malcolm on QUOTATION; WAR CORRESPONDENTS

JOY

1 If we bring a little joy into your humdrum lives, it makes us feel our work ain't been in vain for nothin'.
Jean Hagen (1924–1977), U.S. actress: Lina Lamont (Jean Hagen), in *Singin' in the Rain* (film musical; screenplay by Betty Comden and Adolph Green, directed by Gene Kelly and Stanley Donen, 1952)

2 Yabba dabba do!
William Denby Hanna (b.1910) and **Joseph Roland Barbera** (b.1911), U.S. animators: Fred Flintstone, in *The Flintstones* (TV cartoon, from 1960, produced by Hanna and Barbera). Fred Flintstone (voiced by Alan Reed) and Barney Rubble were modelled on Jackie Gleason and and Art Carney in the TV sitcom *The Honeymooners*

3 Joy is prayer – Joy is strength – Joy is love – Joy is a net of love by which you can catch souls. God loves a cheerful giver. She gives most who gives with joy. The best way to show our gratitude to God and the people is to accept everything with joy. A joyful heart is the inevitable result of a heart burning with love. Never let anything so fill you with sorrow as to make you forget the joy of the Christ risen.
Mother Teresa (1910–1997), Albanian-born Roman Catholic missionary: *A Gift for God* (1975), 'Joy'

4 Zip a dee doo dah,
Zip a dee ay,
My, oh my, what a wonderful day.
Allie Wrubel (1905–1973), U.S. composer and musician: 'Zip A Dee Doo Dah' (song), in *Song of The South* (film musical, 1946)

JUDAISM

1 In a certain sense I lump the Jewish religion in with all other religions as an organised religion and consequently baneful. I think all organised religions are not to the good of the human race.
Woody Allen (b.1935), U.S. film-maker: interview in *Sight and Sound* (London), Feb. 1994

2 You can never betray the people who are dead, so you go on being a public Jew; the dead can't answer slurs, but I'm here. I would love to think that Jesus wants me for a sunbeam, but he doesn't.
Anita Brookner (b.1938), British novelist and art historian: *Novelists in Interview* (ed. John Haffenden, 1985)

3 Now a Jew, in the dictionary, is one who is descended from the ancient tribes of Judea, or one who is regarded as descended from that tribe. That's what it says in the dictionary; but you and I know what a Jew is – *One Who Killed Our Lord*. ... And although there should be a statute of limitations for that crime, it seems that those who neither have the actions nor the gait of Christians, pagan or not, will bust us out, unrelenting dues, for another deuce.
Lenny Bruce (1925–1966), U.S. satirical comedian: *The Essential Lenny Bruce* (ed. John Cohen, 1967), 'The Jews'

4 Being a Jew, one learns to believe in the reality of cruelty and one learns to recognize indifference to human suffering as a fact.
Andrea Dworkin (b.1946), U.S. feminist critic: 'A Feminist Looks at Saudi-Arabia' (1978), rep. in *Letters from a War-Zone* (1987)

5 The Jews always complained, kvetching about false gods, and erected the
biggest false God, Jehovah, in middle of western civilization.
Allen Ginsberg (b.1926), U.S. poet: 'World Karma', publ. in *White Shroud* (1986)

6 Judaism also appeals to a humanity devoid of myths – not because the marvellous is repug-

nant to its narrow soul but because myth, albeit sublime, introduces into the soul that troubled element, that impure element of magic and sorcery and that drunkenness of the Sacred and of war that prolong the animal within the civilised.

Emmanuel Levinas (b.1905), French Jewish philosopher: 'Being a Westerner' (1951), rep. in *Difficult Freedom* (1990), Pt.1

7 Judaism, like an objective institution, like a Synagogue, teaches only the truths that concern the Good of the community and the public order. It teaches and prophesies justice. It is not an insurance company.

Emmanuel Levinas: *Difficult Freedom* (1990), Pt.2, 'Messianic Texts'

8 Pessimism is a luxury that a Jew can never allow himself.

Golda Meir (1898–1978), Israeli politician and prime minister: quoted in *The Observer* (London), 29 Dec. 1974

9 A Jewish man with parents alive is a fifteen-year-old boy, and will remain a fifteen-year-old boy until *they die!*

Philip Roth (b.1933), U.S. novelist: *Portnoy's Complaint* (1967), 'Cunt Crazy'

10 England's made a Jew of me in only eight weeks, which, on reflection, might be the least painful method. A Jew without Jews, without Judaism, without Zionism, without Jewishness, without a temple or an army or even a pistol, a Jew clearly without a home, just the object itself, like a glass or an apple.

Philip Roth: Nathan Zuckerman, describing his new-found sense of difference after living in England, in *The Counterlife* (1986), Ch.5

11 We Jews walk closer to our children than other men ... because to have children is possibly to condemn them.

George Steiner (b.1929), French-born U.S. critic and novelist: interview in *The Guardian* (London), 6 Jan. 1996

12 I marvel at the resilience of the Jewish people. Their best characteristic is their desire to remember. No other people has such an obsession with memory.

Elie Wiesel (b.1928), Rumanian-born U.S. writer: in the *Daily Mail* (London), 15 July 1988

13 In my blood there is no Jewish blood.
In their callous rage, all antisemites must hate me now as a Jew.
For that reason I am a true Russian.

Yevgeny Yevtushenko (b.1933), Russian poet: 'Babi Yar' (1961; tr. George Reavey, 1966). Last lines of the poem which described the massacre of 96,000 Jews in the Ukraine by the Nazis. The poem caused controversy by implying that the Soviet régime was antisemitic

See also THE HOLOCAUST; ISRAEL; Bruce on JESUS CHRIST; Sontag on MINORITIES

JUDGES

1 Judges don't age. Time decorates them.

Enid Bagnold (1889–1981), British novelist and playwright: Judge, in *The Chalk Garden* (1953), Act 2

2 The judges of normality are present everywhere. We are in the society of the teacher-judge, the doctor-judge, the educator-judge, the 'social worker'-judge.

Michel Foucault (1926–1984), French philosopher: *Discipline and Punish: The Birth of the Prison* (1975), Pt.4, Ch.3

3 I have a lifetime appointment and I intend to serve it. I expect to die at 110, shot by a jealous husband.

Thurgood Marshall (1908–1993), U.S. judge: in the *International Herald Tribune* (Paris), 15 Jan. 1990. Marshall was the first black judge on the U.S. Supreme Court

4 A judge is not supposed to know anything about the facts of life until they have been presented in evidence and explained to him at least three times.

Lord Parker (1900–1972), British judge: quoted in *The Observer* (London), 12 March 1961

JUSTICE

1 I don't know what the face of justice is – sometimes it's masculine, sometimes it's feminine – that is where ambiguity resides: in questions of morality.

Pedro Almodóvar (b.1951), Spanish film-maker: quoted in *Sight and Sound* (London), April 1992

2 If one really wishes to know how justice is administered in a country, one does not question the policemen, the lawyers, the judges, or the protected members of the middle class. One goes to the unprotected – those, precisely, who need the law's protection most! – and listens to their testimony.

James Baldwin (1924–1987), U.S. author: 'No Name in the Street' (1972), rep. in *The Price Of The Ticket* (1985)

3 Absolute justice is achieved by the suppression of all contradiction: therefore it destroys freedom.

Albert Camus (1913–1960), French-Algerian philosopher and author: *The Rebel* (1951; tr.1953), Pt.5, 'Historic Murder'

4 Justice ... limps along, but it gets there all the same.

Gabriel García Márquez (b.1928), Colombian author: Guardiola to Judge Arcadio, in *In Evil*

Hour (1968; tr.1979), p.155 of Jonathan Cape edn. (1980)

5 Humanity is born in man to the extent that he manages to reduce a mortal offence to the level of a civil lawsuit, to the extent that punishing becomes a question of putting right what can be put right and re-educating the wicked. Justice without passion is not the only thing man must possess. He must also have justice without killing.

Emmanuel Levinas (b.1905), French Jewish philosopher: *Difficult Freedom* (1990), Pt.3, 'An Eye for an Eye'

6 Ordinary people may not understand the meaning of democracy but they've a passionate regard for fair play.

Robert Maxwell (1923–1991), British tycoon: quoted in *Maxwell* by Joe Haines (1988), Ch.1

7 Justice *is* conscience, not a personal conscience but the conscience of the whole of humanity. Those who clearly recognize the voice of their own conscience usually recognize also the voice of justice.

Alexander Solzhenitsyn (b.1918), Russian novelist: letter, Oct. 1967, from Solzhenitsyn to three students, publ. in *Solzhenitsyn: A Documentary Record* (ed. Leopold Labedz, 1970), 'The Struggle Intensifies'

See also McIlvanney on LAW

THE KENNEDYS

1 One would never have guessed that the world had such a capacity for genuine grief. The most we can do is exploit our memories of his excellence.

John Cheever (1912–1982), U.S. author: journal entry 1963, referring to the assassination of John F. Kennedy, in *John Cheever: The Journals* (ed. Robert Gottlieb, 1991), 'The Sixties'

2 There's never a dearth of reasons to shoot at the President.

Don DeLillo (b.1926), U.S. author: Larry Parmenter, in *Libra* (1988), Pt.1, '26 April'

3 I shouted out, 'Who killed the Kennedy's?' When after all, it was you and me.

Mick Jagger (b.1943), and **Keith Richards** (b.1943), British rock musicians: 'Sympathy for the Devil' (song), on the album *Beggars Banquet* (The Rolling Stones, 1969)

4 It all began so beautifully. After a drizzle in the morning, the sun came out bright and clear. We were driving into Dallas. In the lead car were President and Mrs Kennedy....

Lady Bird Johnson (b.1912), U.S. First Lady: first entry, 22 Nov. 1963, in *A White House Diary* (1970)

5 I do not think it altogether inappropriate to introduce myself to this audience. I am the man who accompanied Jacqueline Kennedy to Paris, and I have enjoyed it.

John F. Kennedy (1917–1963), U.S. Democratic politician and president: speech, 2 June 1961, SHAPE Headquarters, Paris, publ. in *Public Papers of the Presidents of the United States: John F. Kennedy, 1961*. Kennedy was referring to the huge media interest in the Kennedys' visit to Paris – focused particularly on Jackie Kennedy

6 Don't let it be forgot
That once there was a spot
For one brief shining moment that was known
As Camelot.

Alan Jay Lerner (1918–1986), U.S. composer and lyricist: 'Camelot' (song), in *Camelot* (stage musical, 1960; film, 1967). In an interview shortly after John F. Kennedy's assassination, Jackie Kennedy named the song as one of which her husband was particularly fond. Official biographer William Manchester called his book *One Brief Shining Moment* (1983)

7 What a terrible thing has happened to us all! To you there, to us here, to all everywhere. Peace who was becoming bright-eyed, now sits in the shadow of death; her handsome champion has been killed as he walked by her very side. Her gallant boy is dead. What a cruel, foul, and most unnatural murder! We mourn here with you, poor, sad American people.

Sean O'Casey (1884–1964), Irish playwright: referring to President Kennedy's assassination, in letter to Mrs Rose Russell (leader of New York City Teachers' Union), publ. in the *New York Times*, 27 Nov. 1963

8 We have no one to blame for the Kennedys but ourselves. We took the Kennedys to heart of our own accord. And it is my opinion that we did it not because we respected them or thought what they proposed was good, but because they were pretty. We, the electorate, were smitten by this handsome, vivacious family. ... We wanted to hug their golden tousled heads to our dumpy breasts.

P.J. O'Rourke (b.1947), U.S. journalist: *Give War A Chance* (1992), 'Mordred Had a Point – Camelot Revisited'. 'Two were shot,' O'Rourke wrote of the Kennedys, 'but under the most romantic circumstances and not, as might have been hoped, after due process of law'

9 She's got to reconcile herself to being Mrs Aristotle Onassis, because the only place she'll find sympathy from now on is in the dictionary between shit and syphilis.

Aristotle Onassis (1906–1975), Greek shipping magnate: of Jacqueline Kennedy, whom he married in 1968, quoted in *The Observer* (London), 23 Oct. 1988

10 When we think of him, he is without a hat, standing in the wind and weather. He was impatient of topcoats and hats, preferring to be exposed, and he was young enough and tough

enough to enjoy the cold and the wind of those times. ... It can be said of him, as of few men in a like position, that he did not fear the weather, and did not trim his sails, but instead challenged the wind itself, to improve its direction and to cause it to blow more softly and more kindly over the world and its people.

E.B. White (1899–1985), U.S. author and editor: 'John F. Kennedy', publ. in the *New Yorker*, 30 Nov. 1963, rep. in *Writings from the New Yorker 1927–1976* (ed. Rebecca M. Dale, 1991)

KILLING

1   The new rite of passage into the adult world – at least in some sections of the gun-crazy United States – is no longer losing your virginity, but taking a life.
    A. Alvarez (b.1929), British critic, poet and novelist: *Night: An Exploration Of Night Life, Night Language, Sleep and Dreams* (1995), 'The Dark at the Top of the Stairs', Sct.2

2   If anything in this life is certain, if history has taught us anything, it's that everyone can be killed.
    Francis Ford Coppola (b.1939), U.S. film-maker: Michael Corleone (Al Pacino), in *The Godfather Part II* (film; screenplay by Francis Ford Coppola and Mario Puzo, directed by Francis Ford Coppola, 1974)

3   The force of a death should be enormous but how can you know what kind of man you've killed or who was the braver and stronger if you have to peer through layers of glass that deliver the image but obscure the meaning of the act? War has a conscience or it's ordinary murder.
    Don DeLillo (b.1926), U.S. author: Frank Vásquez, in *Libra* (1988), Pt.2, '6 September'

4   For some men the power to destroy life becomes the equivalent to the female power to create life.
    Myriam Miedzian, U.S. author: *Boys Will Be Boys* (1991), Ch.4

5   Everybody thought I'd gone crazy. ... I wasn't crazy. But when I was holding the shotgun, it all became clear. I realized for the first time my one true calling in life. I'm a natural born killer.
    Quentin Tarantino (b.1958), U.S. film-maker: Mickey Knox (Woody Harrelson), in *Natural Born Killers* (film; screenplay by Quentin Tarantino, directed by Oliver Stone, 1995). In a dispute with Stone, Tarantino later disowned the film

6   The urge to kill, like the urge to beget,
    Is blind and sinister. Its craving is set
    Today on the flesh of a hare: tomorrow it can
    Howl the same way for the flesh of a man.

Andrei Voznesensky (b.1933), Russian poet: 'Hunting a Hare', St.5 (1964; tr. W.H. Auden), publ. in *Antiworlds and the Fifth Ace* (ed. Patricia Blake and Max Hayward, 1966)

See also ASSASSINATION; Herzog on GENOCIDE; Camus on KNOWLEDGE; MURDER

KINDNESS

1   Human kindness is like a defective tap, the first gush may be impressive but the stream soon dries up.
    P.D. James (b.1920), British author: Jonah the tramp, in *Devices and Desires* (1989), Ch.40

2   It is a terrible thing, this kindness that human beings do not lose. Terrible because when we are finally naked in the dark and cold, it is all we have. We who are so rich, so full of strength, wind up with that small change. We have nothing else to give.
    Ursula K. Le Guin (b.1929), U.S. author: *The Left Hand of Darkness* (1969), Ch.13

3   Kindness is a virtue neither modern nor urban. One almost unlearns it in a city. Towns have their own beatitude; they are not unfriendly; they offer a vast and solacing anonymity or an equally vast and solacing gregariousness. But one needs a neighbor on whom to practice compassion.
    Phyllis McGinley (1905–1978), U.S. poet and author: *The Province of the Heart* (1959), 'A Garland of Kindness'

4   Kindness glides about my house.
    Dame Kindness, she is so nice!
    The blue and red jewels of her rings smoke
    In the windows, the mirrors
    Are filling with smiles.
    Sylvia Plath (1932–1963), U.S. poet: 'Kindness' (written 1963), publ. in *Collected Poems* (ed. Ted Hughes, 1981)

See also Williams on STRANGERS; Bush on THE UNITED STATES

MARTIN LUTHER KING

1   The secret lies, I think, in his intimate knowledge of the people he is addressing be they black or white, and in the forthrightness with which he speaks of those things which hurt and baffle them. ... He allows them their self-respect – indeed, he insists on it.
    James Baldwin (1924–1987), U.S. author: of Martin Luther King's power as a public speaker and leader, in 'The Dangerous Road Before Martin Luther King', first publ. in *Harper's Magazine* (New York), Feb. 1961, rep. in *The Price Of The Ticket* (1985)

2 Free at last, Free at last
Thank God Almighty
I'm free at last

Epitaph: on King's tomb, in South View Cemetery, Atlanta, Georgia, the words of the spiritual with which he often closed his speeches

3 You know I have grown very, very tired of talking, and listening to talk. King and his kind have betrayed our bosom interests with their demagogic delirium. The poor fool knows nothing of the antagonist's true nature and has not the perception to read and learn by history and past events.

George Jackson (1942–1971), U.S. black activist: letter to his mother, March 1967, from Soledad Prison, publ. in *Soledad Brother* (1970)

4 When that devil's bullet lodged itself inside the body of Martin Luther King, he had already begun an astonishing mobilization of poor, Black, white, latino Americans who had nothing to lose. They would challenge our government to eliminate exploitative, merciless, and war-mongering policies, nationwide, or else 'tie up the country' through 'means of civil disobedience.' Dr King intended to organize those legions into 'coercive direct actions' that would make of Babylon a dysfunctional behemoth begging for relief. Is it any wonder he was killed?

June Jordan (b.1936), U.S. poet and civil rights activist: 'The Mountain and the Man Who Was Not God', lecture, 20 Jan. 1987, Stanford University, California, publ. in *Moving Towards Home: Political Essays* (1989)

KITSCH

1 Kitsch ... is one of the major categories of the modern object. Knick-knacks, rustic odds-and-ends, souvenirs, lampshades, and African masks: the kitsch-object is collectively this whole plethora of 'trashy,' sham or faked objects, this whole museum of junk which proliferates everywhere.... Kitsch is the equivalent to the 'cliché' in discourse.

Jean Baudrillard (b.1929), French semiologist: 'Mass Media Culture', first publ. in *The Society of Consumption* (1970), rep. in *Revenge of the Crystal: Selected Writings 1968–83* (ed. Paul Foss and Julian Pefanis, 1990)

2 No matter how much we scorn it, kitsch is an integral part of the human condition.

Milan Kundera (b.1929), Czech-born French author and critic: *The Unbearable Lightness of Being* (1984), Pt.6, Ch.12

3 Kitsch is the daily art of our time, as the vase or the hymn was for earlier generations. For the sensibility it has that arbitrariness and importance which works take on when they are no longer noticeable elements of the environment. In America kitsch is Nature. The Rocky Mountains have resembled fake art for a century.

Harold Rosenberg (1906–1978), U.S. art critic and author: *The Tradition of the New* (1960), Ch.18

KNOWLEDGE

1 Knowledge divorced from life equals sickness.

Saul Bellow (b.1915), U.S. novelist: *More Die of Heartbreak* (1987), Ch.1

2 The real community of man ... is the community of those who seek the truth, of the potential knowers.

Allan Bloom (1930–1992), U.S. educator and author: *The Closing of the American Mind* (1987), Pt.3, 'The Student and the University'

3 Those who claim to know everything and to settle everything end up killing everything. The day comes when they have no other rule but murder, no other science than the poor scholastic arguments which occasionally serve to justify murder.

Albert Camus (1913–1960), French-Algerian philosopher and author: 'Où est la mystification?', publ. in *Caliban*, June/July 1948, quoted in *Camus: A Biography* by Herbert R. Lottman (1979), Ch.31. The article was a response to D'Astier's accusation of Camus's complicity with bourgeois society

4 There's a theory, one I find persuasive, that the quest for knowledge is, at bottom, the search for the answer to the question: 'Where was I before I was born.' In the beginning was ... what? Perhaps, in the beginning, there was a curious room, a room like this one, crammed with wonders; and now the room and all it contains are forbidden you, although it was made just for you, had been prepared for you since time began, and you will spend all your life trying to remember it.

Angela Carter (1940–1992), British author: 'The Curious Room', uncollected short story read at Basel University conference, excerpted in *New Writing* (ed. Malcolm Bradbury and Judy Cooke, 1992)

5 To know all is not to forgive all. It is to despise everybody.

Quentin Crisp (b.1908), British author: *The Naked Civil Servant* (1968), Ch.11

6 You have to believe in God before you can say there are things that man was not meant to know. I don't think there's anything man wasn't meant to know. There are just some stupid things that people shouldn't do.

David Cronenberg (b.1943), Canadian film-maker: *Cronenberg on Cronenberg* (ed. Chris Rodley, 1992), Ch.1

7   Knowledge is a polite word for dead but not buried imagination.

e e cummings (1894–1962), U.S. poet: 'Jottings', publ. in *Wake*, No.10, 1951, rep. in *A Miscellany* (ed. George J. Firmage, 1958)

8   A man can only attain knowledge with the help of those who possess it. This must be understood from the very beginning. *One must learn from him who knows.*

George Gurdjieff (c.1877–1949), Greek-Armenian religious teacher and mystic: quoted in *In Search of the Miraculous* by P.D. Ouspensky (1949), Ch.2

9   All knowledge is ambiguous.

J.S. Habgood (b.1927), British ecclesiastic and archbishop of York: in *The Observer* (London), 14 April 1991

10 Knowledge is what we get when an observer, preferably a scientifically trained observer, provides us with a copy of reality that we can all recognize.

Christopher Lasch (1932–1994), U.S. historian: 'Journalism, Publicity, and the Lost Art of Political Argument', first publ. in *Gannett Center Journal* (New York), spring 1990, rep. in *Harper's Magazine* (New York), Sept. 1990 as 'The Lost Art of Political Argument'

11 Knowledge is and will be produced in order to be sold, it is and will be consumed in order to be valorized in a new production: in both cases, the goal is exchange. Knowledge ceases to be an end in itself, it loses its 'use-value'.

Jean François Lyotard (b.1924), French philosopher: introduction to *The Postmodern Condition: A Report on Knowledge* (1979)

12 Knowledge is ancient error reflecting on its youth.
(*La connaissance est une vieille erreur qui pense à sa jeunesse.*)

Francis Picabia (1878–1953), French painter and poet: *491* (Paris), 4 March 1949, rep. in *Yes No: Poems and Sayings* (1990), 'Sayings'

13 What our competitive and careerist knowledge industry has produced already hopelessly exceeds our ability to make graceful use of it. The abundance does not cohere. Like the physicist's particle zoo, it increases as the focus tightens; but no enduring patterns emerge.

Theodore Roszak (b.1933), U.S. social critic: *Where the Wasteland Ends* (1972), Ch.5

14 Knowledge is the most democratic source of power.

Alvin Toffler (b.1928), U.S. author: *Powershift: Knowledge, Wealth, and Violence at the Edge of the 21st Century* (1990), Pt.1, Ch.2, 'The Democratic Difference'

15 Knowledge is in the end based on acknowledgement.

Ludwig Wittgenstein (1889–1951), Austrian-born British philosopher: *On Certainty* (ed. G.H. Anscombe and von Wright, 1969), Sct.378

See also INFORMATION

LABELS

1   These names: gay, queer, homosexual are limiting. I would love to finish with them. We're going to have to decide which terms to use and where we use them. ... For me to use the word 'queer' is a liberation; it was a word that frightened me, but no longer.

Derek Jarman (1942–1994), British film-maker, artist and author: *At Your Own Risk: A Saint's Testament* (1992), '1950's'

2   I came to live in a country I love; some people label me a defector. I have loved men and women in my life; I've been labeled 'the bisexual defector' in print. Want to know another secret? I'm even ambidextrous. I don't like labels. Just call me Martina.

Martina Navratilova (b.1956), Czech-born U.S. tennis player: *Martina Navratilova – Being Myself* (1985), Ch.1

3   Please stop using the word 'Negro.' ... We are the only human beings in the world with fifty-seven variety of complexions who are classed together as a single racial unit. Therefore, we are really truly colored people, and that is the only name in the English language which accurately describes us.

Mary Church Terrell (1863–1954), U.S. educator and suffragist: letter to the editor, in the *Washington Post*, 14 May 1949

See also Said on DEFINITION

THE LABOUR PARTY

1   I did not enter the Labour Party forty-seven years ago to have our manifesto written by Dr Mori, Dr Gallup and Mr Harris.

Tony Benn (b.1925), British Labour politician: in *The Guardian* (London), 13 June 1988

2   I know that the right kind of leader for the Labour Party is a kind of desiccated calculating machine.

Aneurin Bevan (1897–1960), British Labour politician: speech to Tribune Group, 29 Sept. 1954, Labour Party Conference, quoted in *Aneurin Bevan* by Michael Foot (1973), Vol.II, Ch.11. The remark was taken as referring to Hugh Gaitskell, though Bevan later denied this

3   We have never yet had a Labour Government that knew what taking power really means; they always act like second-class citizens.

Dora Russell (1894–1986), British author and campaigner: quoted in *The Observer* (London), 30 Jan. 1983

4   If the church to which you went decided to stop worshipping God and started worshipping the devil, you would have second thoughts. The leadership of New Labour has abandoned their socialist faith and embraced capitalism which is tantamount to embracing the devil!
Arthur Scargill (b.1938), British trade union leader: interview in *The Guardian* (London), 4 May 1996

5   No new ideas have come out of the Labour Party since the manifesto of 1848. There is nothing that is of the modern age – not their structure, their concept of life or their concept of society. Their concept of society is a partial society ruled by social workers.
Laurens van der Post (1906–1996), South African writer and philosopher: *A Walk with a White Bushman* (1986), p.99 of Chatto & Windus edn.

6   This Party is a moral crusade or it is nothing.
Harold Wilson (1916–1995), British Labour politician and prime minister: speech to Labour Party Conference, 1 Oct. 1962, quoted in *The Times* (London), 2 Oct. 1962. The words were recalled by party leader Tony Blair on Wilson's death

See also CLEMENT ATTLEE; TONY BLAIR; Kaufman on POLICY

LADIES

1   Girls who put out are tramps. Girls who don't are ladies. This is, however, a rather archaic usage of the word. Should one of you boys happen upon a girl who doesn't put out, do not jump to the conclusion that you have found a lady. What you have probably found is a lesbian.
Fran Lebowitz (b.1951), U.S. journalist: *Metropolitan Life* (1978), 'The Word *Lady*: Most Often Used to Describe Someone You Wouldn't Want to Talk to for Even Five Minutes'

2   A lady is nothing very specific. One man's lady is another man's woman; sometimes, one man's lady is another man's wife. Definitions overlap but they almost never coincide.
Russell Lynes (1910–1991), U.S. editor and critic: 'Is There a Lady in the House?', publ. in *Look* (New York), 22 July 1958

THE LAND

1   To every people the land is given on condition. Perceived or not, there is a Covenant, beyond the constitution, beyond sovereign guarantee, beyond the nation's sweetest dreams of itself.
Leonard Cohen (b.1934), Canadian singer, poet and novelist: *Book of Mercy* (1984), Sct.27

2   This land is your land, this land is my land,
From California to the New York Island.
From the redwood forest to the Gulf Stream
    waters
This land was made for you and me.
Woody Guthrie (1912–1967), U.S. singer and songwriter: 'This Land Is Your Land' (song, 1956). 'This land is your land and this land is my land – sure,' Bob Dylan wrote in *Tarantula* (1970), 'but the world is run by those that never listen to music anyway'

3   We abuse land because we regard it as a commodity belonging to us. When we see land as a community to which we belong, we may begin to use it with love and respect.
Aldo Leopold (1886–1948), U.S. forester: foreword to *A Sand Country Almanac* (1949)

4   Grab this land! Take it, hold it, my brothers, make it, my brothers, shake it, squeeze it, turn it, twist it, beat it, kick it, kiss it, whip it, stomp it, dig it, plow it, seed it, reap it, rent it, buy it, sell it, own it, build it, multiply it, and pass it on – can you hear me? Pass it on!
Toni Morrison (b.1931), U.S. novelist and editor: *Song of Solomon* (1977), Ch.10

5   All the land has been discovered. Some parts of hidden South America maybe still lie out of sight, but this land here has been discovered. Every inch. Now the move is inner space. New religions. est. Gurus. Meditation. Outer space is too expensive and only lies within the reach of the government or corporate industry.
Sam Shepard (b.1943), U.S. playwright and actor: *Rolling Thunder Logbook* (1977), 'Explore'

LANGUAGE

1   All true language
is incomprehensible,
Like the chatter
of a beggar's teeth.
(*Tout vrai langage
est incompréhensible,
Comme la claque
du claque-dents.*)
Antonin Artaud (1896–1948), French theatre producer, actor and theorist: 'Ci-Gît' (1947), rep. in *Selected Writings* (ed. Susan Sontag, 1976), Pt.36, '*Indian Culture* and *Here Lies*'

2   A special kind of beauty exists which is born in language, of language, and for language.
Gaston Bachelard (1884–1962), French scientist, philosopher and literary theorist: *Fragments of a Poetics of Fire* (1988; tr.1990), 'A Retrospective Glance at the Lifework of a Master of Books'

3   Language is a skin: I rub my language against the other. It is as if I had words instead of

fingers, or fingers at the tip of my words. My language trembles with desire.

Roland Barthes (1915–1980), French semiologist: *A Lovers Discourse: Fragments* (1977), 'Talking'

4 One can say of language that it is potentially the only human home, the only dwelling place that cannot be hostile to man.

John Berger (b.1926), British author and critic: *And Our Faces, My Heart, Brief As Photos* (1984), Pt.2

5 Everything can change, but not the language that we carry inside us, like a world more exclusive and final than one's mother's womb.

Italo Calvino (1923–1985), Italian author and critic: in *Grand Bazaar* (Milan), Sept./Oct. 1980, rep. in *The Literature Machine* (1987)

6 There is no such thing as an ugly language. Today I hear every language as if it were the only one, and when I hear of one that is dying, it overwhelms me as though it were the death of the earth.

Elias Canetti (1905–1994), Austrian novelist and philosopher: *The Secret Heart Of The Clock: Notes, Aphorisms, Fragments 1973–1985* (1991), '1976'

7 Language is a process of free creation; its laws and principles are fixed, but the manner in which the principles of generation are used is free and infinitely varied. Even the interpretation and use of words involves a process of free creation.

Noam Chomsky (b.1928), U.S. linguist and political analyst: 'Language and Freedom', lecture, Jan. 1970, Loyola University, Chicago, first publ.1970, rep. in *For Reasons of State* (1973)

8 One does not inhabit a country; one inhabits a language. That is our country, our fatherland – and no other.

E.M. Cioran (1911–1995), Rumanian-born French philosopher: *Anathemas and Admirations* (1986), 'On the Verge of Existence'

9 Curiously enough, it seems to be only in describing a mode of language which does not mean what it says that one can actually say what one means.

Paul de Man (1919–1983), Belgian-born U.S. literary critic: 'The Rhetoric of Temporality', Sct.2, first published in *Interpretation* (ed. Charles Singelton, 1969), rep. in *Blindness and Insight* (1971; rev.1983)

10 Male supremacy is fused into the language, so that every sentence both heralds and affirms it.

Andrea Dworkin (b.1946), U.S. feminist critic: *Pornography* (1981), Ch.1

11 I ascribe a basic importance to the phenomenon of language. ... To speak means to be in a position to use a certain syntax, to grasp the morphology of this or that language, but it means above all to assume a culture, to support the weight of a civilization.

Frantz Fanon (1925–1961), Martiniquan psychiatrist, philosopher and political activist: *Black Skins, White Masks* (1952; tr.1967), 'The Negro and Language'

12 A language near extinction best preserves the deepest grammer of our nothingness.

Tony Harrison (b.1953), British poet: 'Art and Extinction', No.6, publ. in *Continuous: School of Eloquence* (1981)

13 Man acts as though *he* were the shaper and master of language, while in fact *language* remains the master of man.

Martin Heidegger (1889–1976), German philosopher: 'Building Dwelling Thinking', lecture, 5 Aug. 1951, publ. in *Poetry, Language, Thought* (1971)

14 After all, when you come right down to it, how many people speak the same language even when they speak the same language?

Russell Hoban (b.1932), U.S. author: Boaz-Jachin, in *The Lion of Boaz-Jachin and Jachin-Boaz* (1973), Ch.27

15 Language is political. That's why you and me, my Brother and Sister, that's why we sposed to choke our natural self into the weird, lying, barbarous, unreal, white speech and writing habits that the schools lay down like holy law. Because, in other words, the powerful don't play; they mean to keep that power, and those who are the powerless (you and me) better shape up – mimic/ape/suck – in the very image of the powerful, or the powerful will destroy you – you and our children.

June Jordan (b.1936), U.S. poet and civil rights activist: 'White English/Black English: The Politics of Translation' (1972), rep. in *Moving Towards Home: Political Essays* (1989)

16 Public speaking is done in the public tongue, the national or tribal language; and the language of our tribe is the men's language. Of course women learn it. We're not dumb. If you can tell Margaret Thatcher from Ronald Reagan, or Indira Gandhi from General Somoza, by anything they say, tell me how. This is a man's world, so it talks a man's language.

Ursula K. Le Guin (b.1929), U.S. author: 'A Left-Handed Commencement Address' to Mills College Class of 1983, publ. in *Dancing at the Edge of the World* (1989),

17 Language is a form of human reason, which has its internal logic of which man knows nothing.

Claude Lévi-Strauss (b.1908), French anthropologist: *The Savage Mind* (1962), Ch.9

18 Syntax and vocabulary are overwhelming constraints – the rules that run us. Language is using *us* to talk – we think we're using the

language, but language is doing the thinking, we're its slavish agents.

Harry Mathews (b.1930), U.S. novelist: in *City Limits* (London), 26 May 1988

19 There is ... in every child a painstaking teacher, so skilful that he obtains identical results in all children in all parts of the world. The only language men ever speak perfectly is the one they learn in babyhood, when no one can teach them anything!

Maria Montessori (1870–1952), Italian educationist: *The Absorbent Mind* (1949), Ch.1

20 The human in language is literature, not communication. Man's first cry was a song. Man's first address to a neighbor was a cry of power and solemn weakness, not a request for a drink of water.

Barnett Newman (1905–1970), U.S. artist: 'The First Man Was an Artist', publ. in *Tiger's Eye* (New York), Oct. 1947, rep. in *Art in Theory* (ed. Charles Harrison and Paul Wood, 1992), Pt.5A

21 The great enemy of clear language is insincerity. When there is a gap between one's real and one's declared aims, one turns as it were instinctively to long words and exhausted idioms, like a cuttlefish squirting out ink.

George Orwell (1903–1950), British author: 'Politics and the English Language' (1946), rep. in *Shooting an Elephant* (1950)

22 Don't you see that the whole aim of Newspeak is to narrow the range of thought? In the end we shall make thoughtcrime literally impossible, because there will be no words in which to express it.

George Orwell: Symes, in *Nineteen Eighty-four* (1949), Pt.1, Ch.5

23 Man, even man debased by the neocapitalism and pseudosocialism of our time, is a marvelous being because he sometimes *speaks*. Language is the mark, the sign, not of his fall but of his original innocence. Through the Word we may regain the lost kingdom and recover powers we possessed in the far-distant past.

Octavio Paz (b.1914), Mexican poet and essayist: *Alternating Current* (1967), 'André Breton or the Quest of the Beginning'

24 We might hypothetically possess ourselves of every technological resource on the North American continent, but as long as our language is inadequate, our vision remains formless, our thinking and feeling are still running in the old cycles, our process may be 'revolutionary' but not transformative.

Adrienne Rich (b.1929), U.S. poet: 'Power and Danger: Works of a Common Woman', introduction to *The Work of a Common Woman: The Collected Poetry of Judy Grahn, 1964–1977* (1977), rep. in *On Lies, Secrets, and Silence* (1980)

25 When a language creates – as it does – a community within the present, it does so only by courtesy of a community between the present and the past.

Christopher Ricks (b.1933), British critic: preface to *The State of the Language* (ed. Christopher Ricks, 1980)

26 If you want to tell the untold stories, if you want to give voice to the voiceless, you've got to find a language. Which goes for film as well as prose, for documentary as well as autobiography. Use the wrong language, and you're dumb and blind.

Salman Rushdie (b.1947), Indian-born British author: '*Songs* Don't Know the Score', book review in *The Guardian* (London), 12 Jan. 1987

27 Language can only deal meaningfully with a special, restricted segment of reality. The rest, and it is presumably the much larger part, is silence.

George Steiner (b.1929), French-born U.S. critic and novelist: *Language and Silence* (1967), 'The Retreat from the Word'

28 As societies grow decadent, the language grows decadent, too. Words are used to disguise, not to illuminate, action: you liberate a city by destroying it. Words are to confuse, so that at election time people will solemnly vote against their own interests.

Gore Vidal (b.1925), U.S. novelist and critic: *Armageddon? Essays 1983–1987* (1987), 'The Day the American Empire Ran Out of Gas'

29 We are all one-syllable people now, two at the most. So we mumble and stumble into our futures. But it is still our task and our reward to scavenge through the universe, picking up the detritus of lost concepts, dusting them down, making them shine. Latin was the best polishing cloth of all, but we threw it away.

Fay Weldon (b.1933), British novelist: Elaine Desmond, in 'The End of the Line', publ. in *Wicked Women* (1995)

30 The living language is like a cowpath: it is the creation of the cows themselves, who, having created it, follow it or depart from it according to their whims or their needs. From daily use, the path undergoes change. A cow is under no obligation to stay in the narrow path she helped make, following the contour of the land, but she often profits by staying with it and she would be handicapped if she didn't know where it was or where it led to.

E.B. White (1899–1985), U.S. author and editor: 'The Living Language', publ. in the *New Yorker*, 23 Feb. 1957, rep. in *Writings from the New Yorker 1927–1976* (ed. Rebecca M. Dale, 1991)

See also CLICHÉS; McInerney on COMMUNICATION; THE ENGLISH LANGUAGE; Neruda on STYLE; WORDS

LANGUAGE: Grammar, Spelling & Punctuation

1 Colorless green ideas sleep furiously.
Noam Chomsky (b.1928), U.S. linguist and
political analyst: example of the independence of
syntax from meaning, in *Syntactic Structures* (1957),
Ch.2. Chomsky gave the following example of a
sentence lacking both meaning and syntactic form:
'Furiously sleep ideas green colorless'

2 You can be a little ungrammatical if you come
from the right part of the country.
Robert Frost (1874–1963), U.S. poet: in *Atlantic
Monthly* (Boston), Jan. 1962

3 What the devil to do with the sentence 'Who
the devil does he think he's fooling?' You can't
write 'Whom the devil –'
Paul Goodman (1911–1972), U.S. author, poet and
critic: *Five Years* (1966), 'September to December
1958', Sct.2

4 Could we gain access to they mystery of religions without philology? Vocabulary, con-
junctions, syntax only encumber the tortuous
paths of profane civilizations. A whole youth
must be spent in explaining three lines of the
Odyssey.
Emmanuel Levinas (b.1905), French Jewish
philosopher: 'Persons or Figures' (1950), rep. in
Difficult Freedom (1990), Pt.3

5 Nothing is more astounding in our resources
of syntax than the evolution of optatives, of
subjunctives, of counter-factual propositions.
What complex worlds of reasoned imagining
underwrite sentences beginning with 'if': *if
Napoleon had won at Waterloo, if we discover
a remedy for Aids, if there had been no
Mozart*. Such sentences say 'no' to reality,
they allow us to inhabit manifold orders of possibility, to dream argumentatively.
George Steiner (b.1929), French-born U.S. critic
and novelist: 'Modernity, Mythology and Magic',
lecture at the Salzburg Festival, 1994, rep. in *The
Guardian* (London), 6 Aug. 1994

6 Sometimes you get a glimpse of a semicolon
coming, a few lines farther on, and it is like
climbing a steep path through woods and seeing a wooden bench just at a bend in the road
ahead, a place where you can expect to sit for a
moment, catching your breath.
Lewis Thomas (1913–1993), U.S. physician and
educator: *The Medusa and the Snail* (1979), 'Notes
on Punctuation'

7 As far as I'm concerned, 'whom' is a word that
was invented to make everyone sound like a
butler.
Calvin Trillin (b.1935), U.S. journalist and author:
'Whom Says So?', publ. in *The Nation* (New York),
8 June 1985

8 Ultimately it's all a matter of style. What it
comes down to is this: Do you spell Jennifer
with a *J* or *G*? That's a class division. As a
populist, I'm all for *G*.
Gore Vidal (b.1925), U.S. novelist and critic:
interview in *Time* (New York), 28 Sept. 1992

See also Chandler on EDITING; Thurber on
MAGAZINES

LANGUAGE: Jargon

1 Jargon is the verbal sleight of hand that makes
the old hat seem newly fashionable; it gives an
air of novelty and specious profundity to ideas
that, if stated directly, would seem superficial,
stale, frivolous, or false. The line between
serious and spurious scholarship is an easy one
to blur, with jargon on your side.
David Lehman (b.1948), U.S. poet, editor and
critic: *Signs of the Times* (1991), Ch.3, 'Archie
Debunking'

2 Psychobabble is ... a set of repetitive verbal
formalities that kills off the very spontaneity,
candor, and understanding it pretends to
promote. It's an idiom that reduces psychological insight to a collection of standardized
observations, that provides a frozen lexicon to
deal with an infinite variety of problems.
Richard Dean Rosen (b.1949), U.S. journalist and
critic: on 'psychobabble', the term first coined by
Rosen to describe speech patterns in the Bay Area of
San Francisco, in *Psychobabble: Fast Talk and
Quick Cure in the Era of Feeling* (1977),
'Psychobabble'

3 Where people arguing politics used to talk of
justice, freedom and moral rights and wrongs,
the new expertise talks of 'parameters', 'trade-
offs', 'interfaces', 'inputs', 'optimizations',
'cost-benefits', and 'cross matrix impact
analyses'. Nothing is straightforwardly accessible to the layman.
Theodore Roszak (b.1933), U.S. social critic:
Where the Wasteland Ends (1972), Ch.2

LANGUAGE: Slang

1 I've found that there are only two kinds that
are any good: slang that has established itself in
the language, and slang that you make up
yourself. Everything else is apt to be passé
before it gets into print.
Raymond Chandler (1880–1959), U.S. author:
letter, 18 March 1949, publ. in *Raymond Chandler
Speaking* (ed. Dorothy Gardiner and Kathrine S.
Walker, 1962)

2 The language of the younger generation ... has
the brutality of the city and an assertion of
threatening power at hand, not to come. It is
military, theatrical, and at its most coherent

probably a lasting repudiation of empty courtesy and bureaucratic euphemism.

Elizabeth Hardwick (b.1916), U.S. critic and author: 'The Apotheosis of Martin Luther King' (1968), rep. in *Bartleby in Manhattan and Other Essays* (1983)

3 Slang is a language that rolls up its sleeves, spits on its hands and goes to work.

Carl Sandburg (1878–1967), U.S. poet: in the *New York Times*, 13 Feb. 1959

LATIN AMERICA

1 Everything is in order now; the U.S. has taken over Panama in its usual style, with a friendly native government. 'Democracy', which has the sound of silver bells in Central Europe, is a mean joke in Central America.

Martha Gellhorn (b.1908), U.S. journalist and author: 'The Invasion of Panama', publ. in *Granta* (London), No.32, summer 1990

2 Not only does the world scarcely know who the Latin American man is, the world has barely *cared*.

Georgie Anne Geyer (b.1935), U.S. author and columnist: introduction to *The New Latins* (1970)

3 Latin America can no longer tolerate being a haven for United States liberals who cannot make their point at home, an outlet for apostles too 'apostolic' to find their vocation as competent professionals within their own community. The hardware salesman threatens to dump second-rate imitations of parishes, schools and catechisms – out-moded even in the United States – all around the continent. The traveling escapist threatens further to confuse a foreign world with his superficial protests, which are not viable even at home.

Ivan Illich (b.1926), Austrian-born U.S. theologian and author: *Celebration of Awareness* (1969), Ch.5

4 Night, snow, and sand make up the form
of my thin country,
all silence lies in its long line,
all foam flows from its marine beard,
all coal covers it with mysterious kisses.
Gold burns in its fingers like an ember
and silver illuminates like a green moon
its thickened shadow of a sullen planet.

Pablo Neruda (1904–1973), Chilean poet: 'Descubridores de Chile' ('Discoverers of Chile'), publ. in *Canto General* (1950)

5 Latin America is very fond of the word 'hope.' We like to be called the 'continent of hope.' Candidates for deputy, senator, president, call themselves 'candidates of hope.' This hope is really something like a promise of heaven, an IOU whose payment is always being put off. It is put off until the next legislative campaign, until next year, until the next century.

Pablo Neruda: *Memoirs* (1974: tr.1977), Ch.11

6 Well, I learned a lot. ... You'd be surprised. They're all individual countries.

Ronald Reagan (b.1911), U.S. Republican politician and president: following a tour of South America, quoted in the *Washington Post*, 6 Dec. 1982

7 Mexico is a nineteenth-century country arranged for gaslight. Once brought into the harsh light of the twentieth-century media, Mexico can only seem false. In its male, in its public, its city aspect, Mexico is an arch-transvestite, a tragic buffoon. Dogs bark and babies cry when Mother Mexico walks abroad in the light of day. The policeman, the Marxist mayor – Mother Mexico doesn't even bother to shave her mustachios. Swords and rifles and spurs and bags of money chink and clatter beneath her skirts. A chain of martyred priests dangles from her waist, for she is an austere, pious lady. Ay, how much – clutching her jangling bosoms; spilling cigars – how much she has suffered.

Richard Rodriguez (b.1944), U.S. author and journalist: *Frontiers* (1990), 'Night and Day'

8 Surely these societies, where the think tank overlooks the concentration camp, are the most grotesque hybrids of the urban-industrial world.

Theodore Roszak (b.1933), U.S. social critic: on Brazil and other South American dictatorships of the 1970s supported by the U.S., in *Where the Wasteland Ends* (1972), Ch.2

9 Since it is impossible to know what's really happening, we Peruvians lie, invent, dream and take refuge in illusion. Because of these strange circumstances, Peruvian life, a life in which so few actually do read, has become literary.

Mario Vargas Llosa (b.1936), Peruvian novelist: the narrator, in *The Real Life of Alejandro Mayta* (1984; tr.1986), Ch.9

See also CUBA; Sting on THE ENVIRONMENT; Illich on MISSIONARIES; NICARAGUA

LAUGHTER

1 There comes a time when suddenly you realize that laughter is something you remember and that *you* were the one laughing.

Marlene Dietrich (1904–1992), German-born U.S. actress: *Marlene Dietrich's ABC* (1962), 'Laughter'

2 In laughter we stretch the mouth from ear to ear,
or at least in that direction,

we bare our teeth and in that way reveal
long-past stages in evolution
when laughter still was an expression of
triumph over a slain neighbour.

Miroslav Holub (b.1923), Czech biologist and poet:
'Brief Reflection on Laughter', publ. in *On the
Contrary and Other Poems* (1984)

3   The sound of laughter is like the vaulted dome
of a temple of happiness.

Milan Kundera (b.1929), Czech-born French
author and critic: *The Book of Laughter and
Forgetting* (1978; tr.1980), Pt.3, Ch.2

4   There is a kind of laughter that sickens the
soul. Laughter when it is out of control: when
it screams and stamps its feet, and sets the bells
jangling in the next town. Laughter in all its
ignorance and cruelty. Laughter with the seed
of Satan in it. It tramples upon shrines; the
belly-roarer. It roars, it yells, it is delirious:
and yet it is as cold as ice. It has no humour. It
is naked noise and naked malice.

Mervyn Peake (1911–1968), British author and
illustrator: *Sometime, Never* (1956), 'Boy in
Darkness'

5   We are a nation that has always gone in for the
loud laugh, the wow, the yak, the belly laugh,
and the dozen other labels for the roll-'em-in-
the-aisles gagerissimo. This is the kind of
laugh that delights actors, directors, and producers, but dismays writers of comedy because
it is the laugh that often dies in the lobby. The
appreciative smile, the chuckle, the soundless
mirth, so important to the success of comedy,
cannot be understood unless one sits among
the audience and feels the warmth created by
the quality of laughter that the audience takes
home with it.

James Thurber (1894–1961), U.S. humorist and
illustrator: in the *New York Times*, 21 Feb. 1960

See also Greene on HUMOUR; Melly on MICK
JAGGER; Eco on TRUTH

LAW

1   No civilization ... would ever have been possible without a framework of stability, to
provide the wherein for the flux of change.
Foremost among the stabilizing factors, more
enduring than customs, manners and traditions, are the legal systems that regulate our
life in the world and our daily affairs with each
other.

Hannah Arendt (1906–1975), German-born U.S.
political philosopher: *Crises of the Republic* (1972),
'Civil Disobedience'

2   The law isn't justice. It's a very imperfect
mechanism. If you press exactly the right

buttons and are also lucky, justice may show
up in the answer. A mechanism is all the law
was ever intended to be.

Raymond Chandler (1880–1959), U.S. author:
Sewell Endicott, in *The Long Goodbye* (1953),
Ch.8

3   The law is simply expediency wearing a long
white dress.

Quentin Crisp (b.1908), British author: *Manners
from Heaven* (1984), Ch.8

4   An unjust law is itself a species of violence.
Arrest for its breach is more so.

Mohandas K. Gandhi (1869–1948), Indian political
and spiritual leader: *Non-Violence in Peace and War*
(1949), Vol.II, Ch.150

5   In a democracy – even if it is a so-called
democracy like our white-élitist one – the
greatest veneration one can show the rule of
law is to keep a watch on it, and to reserve the
right to judge unjust laws and the subversion
of the function of the law by the power of the
state. That vigilance is the most important
proof of respect for the law.

Nadine Gordimer (b.1923), South African author:
'Speak Out: The Necessity for Protest', lecture, 11
Aug. 1971, University of Natal, South Africa, publ.
in *The Essential Gesture* (ed. Stephen Clingman,
1988)

6   The law is only one of several imperfect and
more or less external ways of defending what is
better in life against what is worse. By itself,
the law can never create anything better. ...
Establishing respect for the law does not automatically ensure a better life for that, after all,
is a job for people and not for laws and institutions.

Václav Havel (b.1936), Czech playwright and
president: *Living in Truth* (1986), Pt.1, 'The Power
of the Powerless', Sct.17

7   Every time I hear the word 'law' I visualise
gangs of militiamen or Pinkertons busting
strikes, pigs wearing sheets and caps that fit
over their pointed heads. I see a white oak and a
barefoot black hanging, or snake-eyes peeping
down the lenses of telescopic rifles, or conspiracy trials.

George Jackson (1942–1971), U.S. black activist:
Blood in my Eye (1972), 'Classes at War'

8   It may be true that the law cannot make a man
love me, but it can keep him from lynching me,
and I think that's pretty important.

Martin Luther King Jr. (1929–1968), U.S.
clergyman and civil rights leader: quoted in *The
Wall Street Journal* (New York), 13 Nov. 1962

9   Law and order exist for the purpose of
establishing justice, and ... when they fail to do
this purpose they become dangerously struc-

tured dams that block the flow of social progress.
Martin Luther King Jr.: 'Letter from Birmingham Jail', open letter to clergymen, 16 April 1963, rep. in *Why We Can't Wait* (1963)

10 Who thinks the law has anything to do with justice? It's what we have because we can't have justice.
William McIlvanney (b.1936), British novelist: Laidlaw, in *Laidlaw* (1977), Ch.35

11 The business of the law is to make sense of the confusion of what we call human life – to reduce it to order but at the same time to give it possibility, scope, even dignity.
Archibald MacLeish (1892–1982), U.S. poet: 'Apologia', publ. in the *Harvard Law Review*, June 1972, rep. in *Riders on Earth* (1978), as 'Art and Law'

See also King on ACTIVISM & PROTEST

LAWYERS

1 Some men are heterosexual, and some men are homosexual, and some men don't think about sex at all. They become lawyers.
Woody Allen (b.1935), U.S. film-maker: Boris Grushenko (Woody Allen), in *Love and Death* (film; written and directed by Woody Allen, 1975)

2 The kind of lawyer you hope the other fellow has.
Raymond Chandler (1880–1959), U.S. author: *The Long Goodbye* (1954), Ch.17

3 Of course he's upset, he's a lawyer. He's paid to be upset.
Jack Lemmon (b.1925), U.S. actor: Stanley Ford (Jack Lemmon), in *How to Murder Your Wife* (film; written and produced by George Axelrod, directed by Richard Quine, 1965)

4 Lawyers are like rhinoceroses: thick-skinned, short-sighted, and always ready to charge.
David Mellor (b.1949), British Conservative politician: on *Question Time*, BBC1, 3 Dec. 1992

5 A lawyer with his briefcase can steal more than a hundred men with guns.
Mario Puzo (b.1920), U.S. novelist: a favourite saying of Don Corleone, in *The Godfather* (1969), Bk.1, Ch.1

6 Going to trial with a lawyer who considers your whole life-style a Crime in Progress is not a happy prospect.
Hunter S. Thompson (b.1939), U.S. journalist: 'A Letter to *The Champion*: a publication of the National Assoc. of Criminal Defense Lawyers', July 1990, publ. in *Songs of the Doomed* (1991)

LEADERS

1 The art of leadership is saying no, not saying yes. It is very easy to say yes.
Tony Blair (b.1953), British Labour politician: quoted in the *Independent on Sunday* (London), 1 Jan. 1995

2 All of the great leaders have had one characteristic in common: it was the willingness to confront unequivocally the major anxiety of their people in their time. This, and not much else, is the essence of leadership.
J.K. Galbraith (b.1908), U.S. economist: on his experience of the Nuremburg Trials of Nazi war criminals, in *The Age of Uncertainty* (1977), Ch.12

3 Blessed are the people whose leaders can look destiny in the eye without flinching but also without attempting to play God.
Henry Kissinger (b.1923), U.S. Republican politician and secretary of state: *Years of Upheaval* (1982), Ch.25, 'The End of the Road'

4 Most of the ladies and gentlemen who mourn the passing of the nation's leaders wouldn't know a leader if they saw one. If they had the bad luck to come across a leader, they would find out that he might demand something from them, and this impertinence would put an abrupt and indignant end to their wish for his return.
Lewis H. Lapham (b.1935), U.S. essayist and editor: *Money and Class in America* (1988), Ch.10. 'Leadership,' Lapham wrote, 'consists not in degrees of technique but in traits of character; it requires moral rather than athletic or intellectual effort, and it imposes on both leader and follower alike the burdens of self-restraint'

5 There is no such thing as a perfect leader either in the past or present, in China or elsewhere. If there is one, he is only pretending, like a pig inserting scallions into its nose in an effort to look like an elephant.
Liu Shao-Ch'i (1898–?), Chinese leader: spoken 13 July 1947, quoted in *Mao and China: From Revolution to Revolution* by Stanley Karnow (1972), Ch.4

6 Follow me if I advance! Kill me if I retreat! Revenge me if I die!
Ngo Dinh Diem (d.1963), Vietnamese politician: on becoming president of Vietnam, 1954, reported in *Time* (New York), 8 Nov. 1963. The same exhortation had been used by Mussolini to his officers after an attempt on his life, quoted in Christopher Hibbert's *Benito Mussolini* (1962), Pt.1, Ch.5

7 I don't think that a leader can control to any great extent his destiny. Very seldom can he step in and change the situation if the

forces of history are running in another direction.

Richard Nixon (1913–1992), U.S. Republican politician and president: quoted in *Richard Nixon: A Political and Personal Portrait* by Earl Mazo (1959), Ch.18

8   The secret of a leader lies in the tests he has faced over the whole course of his life and the *habit of action* he develops in meeting those tests.

Gail Sheehy (b.1937), U.S. journalist and author: *Gorbachev* (1991), 'Looking for Mikhail Gorbachev'

9   I am a leader by default, only because nature does not allow a vacuum.

Desmond Tutu (b.1931), South African churchman and archbishop: in the *Christian Science Monitor* (Boston), 20 Dec. 1984

10   It is very comforting to believe that leaders who do terrible things are, in fact, mad. That way, all we have to do is make sure we don't put psychotics in high places and we've got the problem solved.

Tom Wolfe (b.1931), U.S. author and journalist: *In Our Time* (1980), Ch.2, 'Jonestown'

LEBANON

1   We are going to pull out the plug. We have reached the point where shells do not hurt us any more.

Michel Aoun (b.1935), Lebanese army officer: in *The Independent* (London), 19 April 1989

2   A process of genocide is being carried out before the eyes of the world.

Pope John Paul II [Karol Wojtyla] (b.1920), Polish ecclesiastic: of the situation in Beirut, quoted in *The Independent* (London), 16 Aug. 1989

3   Here, even the law of the jungle has broken down.

Walid Jumblatt (b.1949), leader of the Druze: quoted in *The Sunday Times* (London), 29 Dec. 1985

4   The beaches, though shell-pocked and occasionally mined, are not crowded. Ruins of historical interest abound; in fact, block most streets. Hotel rooms are plentiful.

P.J. O'Rourke (b.1947), U.S. journalist: of Beirut in 1984, in *Holidays in Hell* (1988), 'A Ramble through Lebanon'

LEGACIES

1   When I die, the consciousness I carry I will to black people. May they pick me apart and take the useful parts, the sweet meat of my feelings. And leave the bitter bullshit rotten white parts alone.

Amiri Baraka [formerly Leroi Jones] (b.1934), U.S. poet and playwright: 'leroy', publ. in *Black Magic* (1969)

2   We are earthworms of the earth, and all that has gone through us is what will be our trace.

Seamus Heaney (b.1939), Irish poet: 'Station Island', Pt.2, publ. in *Station Island* (1984)

3   Our mothers and grandmothers have, more often than not anonymously, handed on the creative spark, the seed of the flower they themselves never hoped to see: or like a sealed letter they could not plainly read. ... Guided by my heritage of a love of beauty and a respect for strength – in search of my mother's garden, I found my own.

Alice Walker (b.1944), U.S. author and critic: 'In Search of Our Mothers' Gardens', first publ. in *Ms.* (New York), May 1974, rep. in *In Search of Our Mothers' Gardens* (1983)

LEISURE

1   It is already possible to imagine a society in which the majority of the population, that is to say, its labourers, will have almost as much leisure as in earlier times was enjoyed by the aristocracy. When one recalls how aristocracies in the past actually behaved, the prospect is not cheerful.

W.H. Auden (1907–1973), Anglo-American poet: *A Certain World* (1970), 'Work, Labor, and Play'

2   We're not built for free time as a species. We think we are, but we aren't.

Douglas Coupland (b.1961), Canadian author: Margaret, in *Generation X* (1991), 'Quit Your Job'

3   I do not see plays because I can nap at home for free, and I don't see movies because they're trash and they've got nothing but naked people in 'em, and I don't read books because if they're any good they're going to make them into mini-series.

Shirley Maclaine (b.1934), U.S. actress: Ouiser Boudreaux (Shirley MacLaine), in *Steel Magnolias* (film; screenplay by Robert Harling, adapted from his play, directed by Herbert Ross, 1989)

JOHN LENNON

1   John was a very political animal. The thing that politics did and that fame as an entertainer *didn't* do was provide you with an engine for propagating your theories and beliefs. The one thing John would have liked more than anything else was his own political machine. Even though he would profess that politics is bullshit, he just wouldn't call it 'politics'. He'd call it 'peace'.

John Brower (b.1946), Canadian rock impresario: quoted in *The Lives of John Lennon* by Albert

Goldman (1988), 'A Vote for Peace is a Vote for Lennon'

2 I'm not gonna change the way I look or the way I feel to conform to anything. I've always been a freak. So I've been a freak all my life and I have to live with that, you know. I'm one of those people.
John Lennon (1940–1980), British rock musician: interview in *Playboy* (Chicago), Sept. 1980

3 My role in society, or any artist or poet's role, is to try and express what we all feel. Not to tell people how to feel. Not as a preacher, not as a leader, but as a reflection of us all.
John Lennon: interview in New York, for KFRC RKO Radio (San Francisco), 8 Dec. 1980, the day of his death, publ. in *Imagine* (ed. Andrew Solt and Sam Egan, 1988)

4 His motives are admirable, but his means are childish. The years of worship have given him a sense of omnipotence, and it just won't do to arrive on the steps of a cathedral to fast on behalf of the starving Biafrans in a custombuilt white Rolls. A film of his penis is an exhibitionist rather than a revolutionary act. He seems unable to disassociate indignation from self-advertisement. He and Yoko Ono trivialize. They sit down in front of the wall which blocks the advance of pop culture and by turning their backs on it pretend it's not there.
George Melly (b.1926), British jazz musician, critic and author: *Revolt into Style* (1970), 'For My Next Trick'

5 John used to say he'd had two great partnerships – one with Paul McCartney, the other with Yoko Ono. 'And I discovered both of them,' he used to say. 'That isn't bad going, is it?'
Yoko Ono (b.1933), Japanese-born U.S. artist: quoted in *Shout! The True Story of the Beatles* by Philip Norman (1981; rev.1982), 'Postscript, 1982'

See also THE BEATLES

LESBIANISM

1 Then the question began to live under my blankets: How did lesbianism begin? What were the symptoms? The public library gave information on the finished lesbian – and that woefully sketchy – but on the growth of a lesbian, there was nothing. I did discover that the difference between hermaphrodites and lesbians was that hermaphrodites were 'born that way'. It was impossible to determine whether lesbians budded gradually, or burst into being with a suddenness that dismayed them as much as it repelled society.
Maya Angelou (b.1928), U.S. author: *I Know Why the Caged Bird Sings* (first volume of autobiography, 1969), Ch.35

2 Between women love is contemplative; caresses are intended less to gain possession of the other than gradually to re-create the self through her; separateness is abolished, there is no struggle, no victory, no defeat; in exact reciprocity each is at once subject and object, sovereign and slave; duality become mutuality.
Simone de Beauvoir (1908–1986), French novelist and essayist: *The Second Sex* (1949; tr.1953), Bk.2, Pt.4, Ch.4

3 I love, cherish, and respect women in my mind, in my heart, and in my soul. This love of women is the soil in which my life is rooted. It is the soil of our common life together. My life grows out of this soil. In any other soil, I would die. In whatever ways I am strong, I am strong because of the power and passion of this nurturant love.
Andrea Dworkin (b.1946), U.S. feminist critic: 'Lesbian Pride', speech, 28 June 1975, Central Park, New York City, publ. in *Our Blood* (1976), Ch.7

4 I do
And then again
She does
And then sometimes
Neither of us
Wears any trousers at all.
Maria Jastrzębska (1953), Polish-born British poet: 'Which of Us Wears the Trousers', publ. in *Naming the Waves – Contemporary Lesbian Poetry* (ed. Christine McEwen, 1988)

5 'Lesbianism' would appear to be so little a threat at the moment that it is hardly ever mentioned. ... Whatever its potentiality in sexual politics, female homosexuality is currently so dead an issue that while male homosexuality gains a grudging tolerance, in women the event is observed in scorn or in silence.
Kate Millett (b.1934), U.S. feminist author: note in *Sexual Politics* (1970), Pt.3, Ch.8

6 Gay men may seek sex without emotion; lesbians often end up in emotion without sex.
Camille Paglia (b.1947), U.S. author and critic: 'Homosexuality at the Fin de Siècle', first publ. in *Esquire* (New York), Oct. 1991, rep. in *Sex, Art, and American Culture* (1992)

7 It is ... crucial that we understand lesbian/ feminism in the deepest, most radical sense: as that love for ourselves and other women, that commitment to the freedom of all of us, which transcends the category of 'sexual preference' and the issue of civil rights, to become a politics of *asking women's questions*, demanding a world in which the integrity of all women

– not a chosen few – shall be honored and validated in every respect of culture.

Adrienne Rich (b.1929), U.S. poet: foreword to *On Lies, Secrets, and Silence* (1980)

8 I have decided to give up heterosexuality. I have decided that, while the project of altering the balance of power within heterosexual relationships is still a valid one, it is no longer one I can espouse – so to speak. There is no revolutionary hope for the heterosexual, and I have therefore decided to love myself and become a lesbian.

Michelene Wandor (b.1940), British poet, playwright and critic: in conversation with her mother, in 'Meet My Mother', publ. in *Close Company: Stories of Mothers and Daughters* (ed. Christine Park and Caroline Heaton, 1987)

LETTERS

1 How frail and ephemeral ... is the material substance of letters, which makes their very survival so hazardous. Print has a permanence of its own, though it may not be much worth preserving, but a letter! Conveyed by uncertain transportation, over which the sender has no control; committed to a single individual who may be careless or inappreciative; left to the mercy of future generations, of families maybe anxious to suppress the past, of the accidents of removals and house-cleanings, or of mere ignorance. How often it has been by the veriest chance that they have survived at all.

Elizabeth Drew (1887–1965), Anglo-American author and critic: *The Literature of Gossip* (1964), 'The Literature of Gossip'

2 A woman's best love letters are always written to the man she is betraying.

Lawrence Durrell (1912–1990), British author: Justine, in *Clea* (1960), Pt.1, Ch.4

3 Letters are above all useful as a means of expressing the ideal self; and no other method of communication is quite so good for this purpose. ... In letters we can reform without practice, beg without humiliation, snip and shape embarrassing experiences to the measure of our own desires. ...

Elizabeth Hardwick (b.1916), U.S. author and critic: 'Anderson, Millay and Crane in Their Letters' (1953), rep. in *A View of My Own* (1962)

4 It does me good to write a letter which is not a response to a demand, a gratuitous leter, so to speak, which has accumulated in me like the waters of a reservoir.

Henry Miller (1891–1980), U.S. author: *The Books in My Life* (1951), Ch.12

5 His vocation was orderliness, which is the basis of creation. Accordingly, when a letter came, he would turn it over in his hands for a long time, gazing at it meditatively; then he would put it away in a file without opening it, because everything had its own time.

Salvatore Satta (1902–1975), Italian jurist and novelist: of Ludovico, in *The Day of Judgment* (1979), Ch.20

6 His courtesy was somewhat extravagant. He would write and thank people who wrote to thank him for wedding presents and when he encountered anyone as punctilious as himself the correspondence ended only with death.

Evelyn Waugh (1903–1966), British novelist: in *Life* (New York), 8 April 1946

LIBERALS

1 Ultraliberalism today translates into a whimpering isolationism in foreign policy, a mulish obstructionism in domestic policy, and a pusillanimous pussyfooting on the critical issue of law and order.

Spiro T. Agnew (1918–1996), U.S. Republican politician and vice president: speech, 10 Sept. 1970, Springfield, Illinois, publ. in *Collected Speeches of Spiro Agnew* (1971)

2 There are two kinds of liberalism. A liberalism which is always, subterraneously authoritative and paternalistic, on the side of one's good conscience. And then there is a liberalism which is more ethical than political; one would have to find another name for this. Something like a profound suspension of judgement.

Roland Barthes (1915–1980), French semiologist: interview by Bernard-Henri Lévy in *Art and Text* (1977), No.8, rep. in *Discourses: Conversations in Postmodern Art and Culture* (ed. Russell Ferguson et al., 1990)

3 There's some form of ghost-force liberalism permeating the air in America, but it's got to go, because it's got no foundation at all, apart from a set of laws that were established way back in the bloody Fifties and early Sixties and have no bearing at all in the Seventies.

David Bowie (b.1947), British rock musician: interview, Aug. 1975, rep. in *Bowie In His Own Words* (ed. Miles, 1980), 'Politics'

4 The liberals can understand everything but people who don't understand them.

Lenny Bruce (1925–1966), U.S. satirical comedian: *The Essential Lenny Bruce* (ed. John Cohen, 1967), 'Politics'

5 As with most liberal sexual ideas, what makes the world a better place for men invariably makes it a duller and more dangerous place for women.

Julie Burchill (b.1960), British journalist and author: 'Where's the Beef?', first publ. in *Arena* (London), 1988, rep. in *Sex and Sensibility* (1992)

6 The label of liberalism is hardly a sentence to public ignominy: otherwise Bruce Springsteen would still be rehabilitating used Cadillacs in Asbury Park and Jane Fonda, for all we know, would be just another overweight housewife.
Barbara Ehrenreich (b.1941), U.S. author and columnist: 'The Liberals' Disappearing Act', first publ. in *Mother Jones*, 1986, rep. in *The Worst Years of Our Lives* (1991)

7 I have almost reached the regrettable conclusion that the Negro's great stumbling block in his stride toward freedom is not the White Citizen's Counciler or the Ku Klux Klanner, but the white moderate.
Martin Luther King Jr. (1929–1968), U.S. clergyman and civil rights leader: 'Letter from Birmingham Jail', open letter addressed to clergymen, 16 April 1963, publ. in *Why We Can't Wait* (1964)

8 The liberals have not softened their view of actuality to make themselves live closer to the dream, but instead sharpen their perceptions and fight to make the dream actuality or give up the battle in despair.
Margaret Mead (1901–1978), U.S. anthropologist: *Male and Female* (1949), Ch.12

9 The principle feature of American liberalism is sanctimoniousness. By loudly denouncing all bad things – war and hunger and date rape – liberals testify to their own terrific goodness. More important, they promote themselves to membership in a self-selecting elite of those who care deeply about such things. ... It's a kind of natural aristocracy, and the wonderful thing about this aristocracy is that you don't have to be brave, smart, strong or even lucky to join it, you just have to be liberal.
P.J. O'Rourke (b.1947), U.S. journalist: introduction to *Give War A Chance* (1992)

10 Liberal – a power worshipper without power.
George Orwell (1903–1950), British author: 'Politics and the English Language' (1946), rep. in *Shooting an Elephant* (1950)

11 The essence of the Liberal outlook lies not in *what* opinions are held, but in *how* they are held: instead of being held dogmatically, they are held tentatively, and with a consciousness that new evidence may at any moment lead to their abandonment.
Bertrand Russell (1872–1970), British philosopher and mathematician: *Unpopular Essays* (1950), 'Philosophy and Politics'

12 We who are liberal and progressive know that the poor are our equals in every sense except that of being equal to us.
Lionel Trilling (1905–1975), U.S. critic: *The Liberal Imagination* (1950), 'The Princess Casamassima'

13 The liberal holds that he is true to the republic when he is true to himself. (It may not be as cozy an attitude as it sounds.) He greets with enthusiasm the fact of the journey, as a dog greets a man's invitation to take a walk. And he acts in the dog's way too, swinging wide, racing ahead, doubling back, covering many miles of territory that the man never traverses, all in the spirit of inquiry and the zest for truth. He leaves a crazy trail, but he ranges far beyond the genteel old party he walks with and he is usually in a better position to discover a skunk.
E.B. White (1899–1985), U.S. author and editor: 'Liberalism', publ. in the *New Yorker*, 17 Jan. 1948, rep. in *Writings from the New Yorker 1927–1976* (ed. Rebecca M. Dale, 1991)

14 A liberal is a conservative who has been arrested.
Tom Wolfe (b.1931), U.S. author and journalist: *The Bonfire of the Vanities* (1987), Ch.24

15 Why is it that right-wing bastards always stand shoulder to shoulder in solidarity, while liberals fall out among themselves?
Yevgeny Yevtushenko (b.1933), Russian poet: quoted in *The Observer* (London), 15 Dec. 1991

See also Major on UNDERSTANDING

LIBERTY

1 Liberty, as it is conceived by current opinion, has nothing inherent about it; it is a sort of gift or trust bestowed on the individual by the state pending *good behavior*.
Mary McCarthy (1912–1989), U.S. author and critic: 'The Contagion of Ideas', speech, 1952, publ. in *On the Contrary* (1961)

2 We are as great as our belief in human liberty – no greater. And our belief in human liberty is only ours when it is larger than ourselves.
Archibald MacLeish (1892–1982), U.S. poet: 'Now Let Us Address the Main Question: Bicentennial of What?', publ. in the *New York Times*, 3 July 1976, rep. in *Riders on Earth* (1978), as 'The Ghost of Thomas Jefferson'

3 A free spirit takes liberties even with liberty itself.
(*Un esprit libre prend des libertés même à l'égard de la liberté.*)
Francis Picabia (1878–1953), French painter and poet: *591* (Paris), 21 Jan. 1952, rep. in *Écrits*, Vol.II (ed. Olivier Revault d' Allones and Dominique Bouissou, 1978), '1950–1953'

LIBRARIES

1 I've always found them close relations of the walking dead.
Alan Bennett (b.1934), British playwright: of librarians, in *Writing Home* (1994), 'Instead of a Present'

2 Libraries are reservoirs of strength, grace and wit, reminders of order, calm and continuity, lakes of mental energy, neither warm nor cold, light nor dark. The pleasure they give is steady, unorgastic, reliable, deep and long-lasting. In any library in the world, I am at home, unselfconscious, still and absorbed.
Germaine Greer (b.1939), Australian feminist writer: *Daddy, We Hardly Knew You* (1989), 'Still in Melbourne, January 1987'

3 What is more important in a library than anything else – than everything else – is the fact that it exists.
Archibald MacLeish (1892–1982), U.S. poet: 'The Premise of Meaning', publ. in *American Scholar* (Washington D.C.), 5 June 1972, rep. in *Riders on Earth* (1978), as 'The Premise at the Center'

4 I was enraged that there were so many rubbishy novels and rubbishy books. It reminded me of the Bible: 'Of the making of books, there is no end', because there isn't. Libraries might as well not exist; they've got endless shelves of rubbish and hardly any space for good books.
Joe Orton (1933–1967), British playwright: explaining his defacement of library books, in the *Evening News* (London), 9 June 1967, quoted in *Prick Up Your Ears: the Biography of Joe Orton* by John Lahr (1978), Ch.3. Orton and his lover, Kenneth Halliwell, were convicted of stealing and defacing library books, resulting in a six-month jail sentence in 1962

5 To a historian libraries are food, shelter, and even muse. They are of two kinds: the library of published material, books, pamphlets, periodicals, and the archive of unpublished papers and documents.
Barbara Tuchman (1912–1989), U.S. historian: *Practising History* (1981), 'The Houses of Research'

LIES

1 Of course I lie to people. But I lie altruistically – for our mutual good. The lie is the basic building block of good manners. That may seem mildly shocking to a moralist – but then what isn't?
Quentin Crisp (b.1908), British author: *Manners from Heaven* (1984), Ch.4

2 He entered the territory of lies without a passport for return.
Graham Greene (1904–1991), British novelist: of Major Scobie, in *The Heart of the Matter* (1948), Bk.2, Pt.3, Ch.2, Sct.1

3 Good lies need a leavening of truth to make them palatable.
William McIlvanney (b.1936), British novelist: *The Papers of Tony Veitch* (1983), Ch.17

4 Each day a few more lies eat into the seed with which we are born, little institutional lies from the print of newspapers, the shock waves of television, and the sentimental cheats of the movie screen.
Norman Mailer (b.1923), U.S. author: *Advertisements for Myself* (1959), 'First Advertisement for Myself'

5 Grow your tree of falsehood from a small grain of truth.
Do not follow those who lie in contempt of reality.
Let your lie be even more logical than the truth itself,
So the weary travellers may find repose.
Czeslaw Milosz (b.1911), Lithuanian-born Polish poet: 'Child of Europe', Sct.4, publ. in *Selected Poems* (1973)

6 Lying is like alcoholism. You are always recovering.
Steven Soderbergh (b.1963), U.S. film-maker: Graham Dalton (James Spader), in *Sex, Lies and Videotape* (film; written and directed by Steven Soderbergh, 1989)

7 I would dodge, not lie, in the national interest.
Larry Speakes (b.1939), U.S. executive and former White House official: in the *New York Times*, 10 Oct. 1986

8 Mendacity is a system that we live in. Liquor is one way out an' death's the other.
Tennessee Williams (1911–1983), U.S. playwright: Brick, in *Cat on a Hot Tin Roof* (1955), Act 2

9 Someone who knows too much finds it hard not to lie.
Ludwig Wittgenstein (1889–1951), Austrian-born British philosopher: journal entry, 1947, publ. in *Culture and Value* (ed. G. H. von Wright with Heikki Nyman, 1980)

See also Williams on HYPOCRISY; Fellini on STORY-TELLING

LIFE

1 Life is divided up into the horrible and the miserable.
Woody Allen (b.1935), U.S. film-maker: Alvy Singer (Allen), in *Annie Hall* (film; screenplay by Woody Allen and Marshall Brickman, directed by Woody Allen, 1977)

2 Why is life worth living? That's a very good question. Ummm ... Well there are certain things, I guess, that make it worthwhile. Uh, like what? Okay. Um, for me ... oh, I would say ... what, Groucho Marx, to name one thing, and ... Willie Mays, and ... the second movement of the Jupiter Symphony, and ... Louis Armstrong's recording of 'Potatohead Blues' ... Swedish movies, naturally ... *Sentimental Education* by Flaubert ... and Marlon Brando, Frank Sinatra ... those incredible apples and pears by Cézanne.

Woody Allen: Isaac Davis (Woody Allen), recording some ideas on to a tape for a short story, in *Manhattan* (film; screenplay by Woody Allen and Marshall Brickman, directed by Woody Allen, 1979)

3 Life doesn't imitate art, it imitates bad television.

Woody Allen: Rain (Juliette Lewis), in *Husbands and Wives* (film; written and directed by Woody Allen, 1992)

4 Life loves the liver of it.

Maya Angelou (b.1928), U.S. author: 'The Black Scholar Interviews Maya Angelou' (Jan./Feb. 1977), rep. in *Conversations with Maya Angelou* (ed. Jeffrey M. Elliot, 1989)

5 One should not confuse the craving for life with endorsement of it.

Elias Canetti (1905–1994), Bulgarian-born novelist and philosopher: *The Secret Heart Of The Clock: Notes, Aphorisms, Fragments 1973–1985* (1991), '1981'

6 Life is filigree work. ... What is written clearly is not worth much, it's the transparency that counts.

Louis-Ferdinand Céline (1894–1961), French author: *Féerie pour une Autre Fois* (1952), quoted in *Céline* by Patrick McCarthy (1975), Ch.8

7 Life is a tragedy when seen in close-up, but a comedy in long-shot.

Charlie Chaplin (1889–1977), British comic actor and film-maker: quoted in obituary, in *The Guardian* (London), 28 Dec. 1977

8 When you're young, you always feel that life hasn't yet begun – that 'life' is always scheduled to begin next week, next month, next year, after the holidays – whenever. But then suddenly you're old and the scheduled life didn't arrive. You find yourself asking 'well then, exactly what was it I was having – that interlude – the scrambly madness – all that time I had before?'

Douglas Coupland (b.1961), Canadian author: *Life After God* (1994), 'Gettysburg'

9 Life was a funny thing that happened to me on the way to the grave.

Quentin Crisp (b.1908), British author: *The Naked Civil Servant* (1968), Ch.18

10 Life is – or has – meaning and meaninglessness. I cherish the anxious hope that meaning will preponderate and win the battle.

Carl Jung (1875–1961), Swiss psychiatrist: *Memories, Dreams, Reflections* (1962), 'Retrospect'

11 All of life is a foreign country.

Jack Kerouac (1922–1969), U.S. author: letter, 24 June 1949, publ. in *The Beat Vision: A Primary Sourcebook* (ed. Arthur and Kit Knight, 1987)

12 Most people, I'm convinced, don't think about life at all. They grab what they think they want and the subsequent consequences keep them busy in an endless chain till they're carried out feet first.

Philip Larkin (1922–85), British poet: letter, 30 Oct. 1949, publ. in *Selected Letters of Philip Larkin 1940–1985* (ed. Anthony Thwaite, 1992)

13 Life is what happens to you while you're busy making other plans.

John Lennon (1940–1980), British rock musician: 'Beautiful Boy' (song) on the album *Starting Over* (John Lennon, 1980). The line has also been attributed to Betty Talmadge (divorced wife of Senator Herman Talmadge) and to Thomas La Mance

14 Life is not a matter of place, things or comfort; rather, it concerns the basic human rights of family, country, justice and human dignity.

Imelda Marcos (b.1929), Filipino First Lady and society figure: quoted in *Newsweek* (New York), 12 June 1989

15 Life is constantly providing us with new funds, new resources, even when we are reduced to immobility. In life's ledger there is no such thing as frozen assets.

Henry Miller (1891–1980), U.S. author: *Quiet Days in Clichy* (1956), p.33 of Allison and Busby edn., 1991

16 Life – how curious is that habit that makes us think it is not here, but elsewhere.

V.S. Pritchett (1900–1997), British author and critic: *Midnight Oil* (second volume of memoirs, 1971), Ch.6. 'Life is elsewhere' is a loose translation of Rimbaud's line *La vraie vie est absente*, from his poem 'Délires'. The words were adopted by Milan Kundera as the title of his novel (written 1969, publ.1973), in which he cites the conclusion of André Breton's Surrealist Manifesto and mentions the line's use as a slogan by Paris students in May 1968

17 Life is like Sanskrit read to a pony.

Lou Reed (b.1944), U.S. rock musician: 'What's Good' (song) on the album *Magic and Loss* (1992)

18 The slightest living thing answers a deeper need than all the works of man because it is *transitory*. It has an evanescence of life, or growth, or change: it passes, as we do, from one stage to another, from darkness to darkness,

into a distance where we, too, vanish out of sight. A work of art is static; and its value and its weakness lie in being so: but the tuft of grass and the clouds above it belong to our own travelling brotherhood.
Freya Stark (1893–1993), British travel writer: *Perseus in the Wind* (1948), Ch.14

19 Life is a means of extracting fiction.
Robert Stone (b.1937), U.S. novelist: interview in *Writers at Work* (Eighth Series, ed. George Plimpton, 1988)

20 Life is like a B-movie. You don't want to leave in the middle of it but you don't want to see it again.
Ted Turner (b.1938), U.S. broadcasting and sports executive: in the *International Herald Tribune* (Paris), 2 March 1990

21 Along a parabola life like a rocket flies,
Mainly in darkness, now and then on a
rainbow.
Andrei Voznesensky (b.1933), Russian poet: opening lines of 'Parabolic Ballad', St.1 (1960; tr. W.H. Auden)

See also Conran on COOKERY; Warhol on IMAGERY; Williams on MEMORY

LIFE: and Death

1 The aims of life are the best defence against death.
Primo Levi (1919–1987), Italian author: *The Drowned and the Saved* (1988), Ch.6

2 Death does determine life. ... Once life is finished it acquires a sense; up to that point it has not got a sense; its sense is suspended and therefore ambiguous.
Pier Paolo Pasolini (1922–1975), Italian film-maker and essayist: *Pasolini On Pasolini: Interviews With Oswald Stack* (1969), Ch.3

LIFE: Purpose of Life

1 To find the point where hypothesis and fact meet; the delicate equilibrium between dream and reality; the place where fantasy and earthly things are metamorphosed into a work of art; the hour when faith in the future becomes knowledge of the past; to lay down one's power for others in need; to shake off the old ordeal and get ready for the new; to question, knowing that never can the full answer be found; to accept uncertainties quietly, even our incomplete knowledge of God; this is what man's journey is about, I think.
Lillian Smith (1897–1966), U.S. author: *The Journey* (1954), Ch.15

2 There is one thing that matters – to set a chime of words tinkling in the minds of a few fastidious people.
Logan Pearsall Smith (1865–1946), U.S.-born British essayist, aphorist: in answer to the question, two weeks before his death, whether he had discovered any meaning in life, quoted by Cyril Connolly in obituary, the *New Statesman* (London), 9 March 1946

3 Of course life has no point. If it had man would not be free, he'd become a slave to that point and his life would be governed by completely new criteria: the criteria of slavery.
Andrey Tarkovsky (1932–1986), Russian film-maker: journal entry, 5 Sept. 1970, publ. in *Time Within Time: The Diaries 1970–1986* (1989; tr.1994)

LITERARY CRITICISM

1 Criticism is a misconception: we must read not to understand others but to understand ourselves.
E.M. Cioran (1911–1995), Rumanian-born French philosopher: *Anathemas and Admirations* (1986), 'On the Verge of Existence'

2 The critical method which denies literary modernity would appear – and even, in certain respects, would be – the most modern of critical movements.
Paul de Man (1919–1983), Belgian-born U.S. literary critic: 'Literary History and Literary Modernity', lecture, Sept. 1969, rep. in *Blindness and Insight* (1971; rev.1983)

3 The 'text' is merely one of the contexts of a piece of literature, its lexical or verbal one, no more or less important than the sociological, psychological, historical, anthropological or generic.
Leslie Fiedler (b.1917), U.S. critic: preface to the first edition of *Love and Death in the American Novel* (1960)

4 Much literary criticism comes from people for whom extreme specialization is a cover for either grave cerebral inadequacy or terminal laziness, the latter being a much cherished aspect of academic freedom.
J.K. Galbraith (b.1908), U.S. economist: 'H.L. Mencken', publ. in the *Washington Post*, 14 Sept. 1980, rep. in *A View from the Stands* (1986)

5 You know lots of criticism is written by characters who are very academic and think it is a sign you are worthless if you make jokes or kid or even clown. I wouldn't kid Our Lord if he was on the cross. But I would attempt a joke with him if I ran into him chasing the money changers out of the temple.
Ernest Hemingway (1899–1961), U.S. author: letter, 21 June 1952, publ. in *Selected Letters* (ed. Carlos Baker, 1981)

6　The literary critic, or the critic of any other specific form of artistic expression, may detach himself from the world for as long as the work of art he is contemplating appears to do the same.
Clive James (b.1939), Australian writer and critic: introduction to *Glued to the Box* (1983)

7　I have, then, given my hostages. What I think and judge I have stated as responsibly and clearly as I can. Jane Austen, George Eliot, Henry James, Conrad, and D.H. Lawrence: the great tradition of the English novel is *there*.
F.R. Leavis (1895–1978), British literary critic: introduction to *The Great Tradition* (1948), Ch.1

8　Writing criticism is to writing fiction and poetry as hugging the shore is to sailing in the open sea.
John Updike (b.1932), U.S. author and critic: foreword to *Hugging the Shore* (1984)

See also CRITICISM: PROFESSIONAL; DECONSTRUCTION

LITERATURE

1　Literature is *without proofs*. By which it must be understood that it cannot prove, not only *what* it says, but even that it is worth the trouble of saying it.
Roland Barthes (1915–1980), French semiologist: 'Deliberation', first publ. in *Tel Quel* (Paris), winter 1979, rep. in *Barthes: Selected Writings* (1982)

2　Literature is not exhaustible, for the sufficient and simple reason that a single book is not. A book is not an isolated entity: it is a narration, an axis of innumerable narrations. One literature differs from another, either before or after it, not so much because of the text as for the manner in which it is read.
Jorge Luis Borges (1899–1986), Argentinian author: *For Bernard Shaw* (1952), rep. in *Other Inquisitions* (1960; tr.1964),

3　The struggle of literature is in fact a struggle to escape from the confines of language; it stretches out from the utmost limits of what can be said; what stirs literature is the call and attraction of what is not in the dictionary.
Italo Calvino (1923–1985), Italian author and critic: 'Cybernetics and Ghosts', lecture, Nov. 1969, Turin, publ. in *The Literature Machine* (1987)

4　When a book, any sort of book, reaches a certain intensity of artistic performance it becomes literature. That intensity may be a matter of style, situation, character, emotional tone, or idea, or half a dozen other things. It may also be a perfection of control over the movement of a story similar to the control a great pitcher has over the ball.

Raymond Chandler (1880–1959), U.S. author: letter, 29 Jan. 1946, to crime writer Erle Stanley Gardner, refuting Gardner's denigration of his own books, publ. in *Raymond Chandler Speaking* (ed. Dorothy Gardiner and Kathrine S. Walker, 1962)

5　Literature ... is condemned (or privileged) to be forever the most rigorous and, consequently, the most reliable of terms in which man names and transforms himself.
Paul de Man (1919–1983), Belgian-born U.S. literary critic: *Allegories of Reading* (1979), Pt.1, Ch.1, 'Semiology and Rhetoric'

6　To provoke dreams of terror in the slumber of prosperity has become the moral duty of literature.
Ernst Fischer (1899–1972), Austrian editor, poet and critic: *Art Against Ideology* (1966; tr.1969), Ch.1

7　In our day the conventional element in literature is elaborately disguised by a law of copyright pretending that every work of art is an invention distinctive enough to be patented.
Northrop Frye (1912–1991), Canadian literary critic: *Anatomy of Criticism* (1957), 'Mythical Phase: Symbol as Archetype'

8　The world must be all fucked up when men travel first class and literature goes as freight.
Gabriel García Márquez (b.1928), Colombian author: the Catalan bookstore owner in Macondo, in *100 Years Of Solitude* (1967; tr.1970), p.323 of Picador edn. (1978)

9　[The] attempt to devote oneself to literature alone is a most deceptive thing, and ... often, paradoxically, it is literature that suffers for it.
Václav Havel (b.1936), Czech playwright and president: *Disturbing the Peace* (1986; tr.1990), Ch.3

10　How simple the writing of literature would be if it were only necessary to write in another way what has been well written. It is because we have had such great writers in the past that a writer is driven far out past where he can go, out to where no one can help him.
Ernest Hemingway (1899–1961), U.S. author: address accepting the Nobel Prize for literature, 10 Dec. 1954, publ. in *Hemingway: the Writer as Artist* by Carlos Baker (edn. 1963), Ch.13

11　Great literature cannot grow from a neglected or impoverished soil. Only if we actually tend or care will it transpire that every hundred years or so we might get a *Middlemarch*.
P.D. James (b.1920), British author: in *The Daily Telegraph* (London), 14 April 1988

12　In the electronic age, books, words and reading are not likely to remain sufficiently authoritative and central to knowledge to justify literature.
Alvin Kernan (b.1923), U.S. educator: in the *International Herald Tribune* (Paris), 12 Dec. 1990

13 The present era grabs everything that was ever written in order to transform it into films, TV programmes; or cartoons. What is essential in a novel is precisely what can only be expressed in a novel, and so every adaptation contains nothing but the non-essential. If a person is still crazy enough to write novels nowadays and wants to protect them, he has to write them in such a way that they cannot be adapted, in other words, in such a way that they cannot be retold.

Milan Kundera (b.1929), Czech-born French author and critic: the narrator, in *Immortality* (1991), Pt.5, Ch.9

14 Literature is analysis after the event.

Doris Lessing (b.1919), British novelist: quoted in *Children of Albion: Poetry of the Underground in Britain* (ed. Michael Horovitz, 1969), 'Afterwords', Sct.2

15 Literature is mostly about having sex and not much about having children. Life is the other way round.

David Lodge (b.1935), British novelist and critic: Adam Appleby, in *The British Museum is Falling Down* (1965), Ch.4

16 What makes literature interesting is that it does not survive its translation. The characters in a novel are made out of the sentences. That's what their substance is.

Jonathan Miller (b.1936), British doctor, humorist and director: in *The Sunday Times* (London), 12 Feb. 1989

17 Literary art takes its materials from life, but although life is thus the mother of literature, it is also her bitter enemy; although life is inherent in the author himself, it is also the eternal antithesis of art.

Yukio Mishima (1925–1970), Japanese author: *Mishima on Hagakure* (1977), '*Hagakure* and I'

18 The existence of good bad literature – the fact that one can be amused or excited or even moved by a book that one's intellect simply refuses to take seriously – is a reminder that art is not the same thing as cerebration.

George Orwell (1903–1950), British author: *Shooting an Elephant* (1950), 'Good Bad Books'

19 The truth is that literature, particularly fiction, is not the pure medium we sometimes assume it to be. Response to it is affected by things other than its own intrinsic quality; by a curiosity or lack of it about the people it deals with, their outlook, their way of life.

Vance Palmer (1885–1959), Australian author and poet: 'Fragment of Autobiography' (1958), rep. in *Intimate Portraits* (ed. H.P. Heseltine, 1969)

20 Literature is the expression of a feeling of deprivation, a recourse against a sense of something missing. But the contrary is also true: language is what makes us human. It is a recourse against the meaningless noise and silence of nature and history.

Octavio Paz (b.1914), Mexican poet and essayist: *Alternating Current* (1967), 'The Exception to the Rule'

21 The party of God and the party of Literature have more in common than either will admit; their texts may conflict, but their bigotries coincide. Both insist on being the sole custodians of the true word and its only interpreters.

Frederic Raphael (b.1931), British author and critic: in *The Sunday Times* (London), 12 Feb. 1989

22 The liveliness of literature lies in its exceptionality, in being the individual, idiosyncratic vision of one human being, in which, to our delight and great surprise, we may find our own vision reflected.

Salman Rushdie (b.1947), Indian-born British author: 'In Good Faith', publ. in the *Independent on Sunday* (London), 4 Feb. 1990

23 Of course the illusion of art is to make one believe that great literature is very close to life, but exactly the opposite is true. Life is amorphous, literature is formal.

Françoise Sagan (b.1935), French novelist and playwright: interview in *Writers at Work* (First Series, ed. Malcolm Cowley, 1958)

24 The function of literature, through all its mutations, has been to make us aware of the particularity of selves, and the high authority of the self in its quarrel with its society and its culture. Literature is in that sense subversive.

Lionel Trilling (1905–1975), U.S. critic: *Beyond Culture* (1965), 'Freud: Within and Beyond Culture', Sct.2

25 Literature is the orchestration of platitudes.

Thornton Wilder (1897–1975), U.S. author: in *Time* (New York), 12 Jan. 1953

26 Professors of literature, who for the most part are genteel but mediocre men, can make but a poor defense of their profession, and the professors of science, who are frequently men of great intelligence but of limited interests and education, feel a politely disguised contempt for it; and thus the study of one of the most pervasive and powerful influences on human life is traduced and neglected.

Yvor Winters (1900–1968), U.S. literary critic: foreword to *In Defense of Reason* (1960)

See also WILLIAM SHAKESPEARE

LITERATURE: Modern Literature

1 The hacker and the rocker are this decade's pop-culture idols, and cyberpunk is very much a pop phenomenon: spontaneous, energetic,

close to its roots. Cyberpunk comes from the realm where the computer hacker and the rocker overlap, a cultural Petri dish where writhing gene lines splice.

Bruce Sterling (b.1954), U.S. science fiction author: preface to *Mirrorshades* (ed. Bruce Sterling, 1986)

2 Any historian of the literature of the modern age will take virtually for granted the adversary intention, the actually subversive intention, that characterizes modern writing – he will perceive its clear purpose of detaching the reader from the habits of thought and feeling that the larger culture imposes, of giving him a ground and a vantage point from which to judge and condemn, and perhaps revise, the culture that produces him.

Lionel Trilling (1905–1975), U.S. critic: preface to *Beyond Culture* (1965)

3 People are a wee bit fed up with the lack of substance in middle class postmodern writing. You know, that somehow the Oxbridge writer goes into this kind of supermarket and just picks whatever style or voices that they like. ... You can't do subcultures as an Oxford twat hanging around the fucking streets, sitting in pubs and listening in on people.

Irvine Welsh (b.1958), Scottish author: interview in *Dazed and Confused* (London), Feb. 1996

See also de Man on LITERARY CRITICISM

LITERATURE: and Society

1 The writer in western civilization has become not a voice of his tribe, but of his individuality. This is a very narrow-minded situation.

Aharon Appelfeld (b.1932), Israeli novelist: in the *International Herald Tribune* (Paris), 10 Aug. 1989

2 If the most significant characteristic of man is the complex of biological needs he shares with all members of his species, then the best lives for the writer to observe are those in which the role of natural necessity is clearest, namely, the lives of the very poor.

W.H. Auden (1907–1973), Anglo-American poet: *The Dyer's Hand* (1962), Pt.8, 'Cav And Pag'

3 As a poet there is only one political duty, and that is to defend one's language against corruption. When it is corrupted, people lose faith in what they hear and this leads to violence.

W.H. Auden: quoted in *The Observer* (London), 31 Oct. 1971

4 If a poet has any obligation toward society, it is to write well. Being in the minority, he has no other choice. Failing this duty, he sinks into oblivion. Society, on the other hand, has no obligation toward the poet. A majority by

definition, society thinks of itself as having other options than reading verses, no matter how well written. Its failure to do so results in its sinking to that level of locution at which society falls easy prey to a demagogue or a tyrant. This is society's own equivalent of oblivion.

Joseph Brodsky (1940–1996), Russian-born U.S. poet and critic: 'To Please a Shadow', Sct.2 (1983), rep. in *Less Than One: Selected Essays* (1986)

5 English literature is a kind of training in social ethics. ... English trains you to handle a body of information in a way that is conducive to action.

Marilyn Butler (b.1937), British educator and author: in *The Guardian* (London), 3 March 1989

6 When politicians and politically minded people pay too much attention to literature, it is a bad sign – a bad sign mostly for literature.... But it is also a bad sign when they don't want to hear the word mentioned.

Italo Calvino (1923–1985), Italian author and critic: 'Right and Wrong Political Uses of Literature', lecture, Feb. 1976, delivered at Amherst College, Massachusetts, publ. in *The Literature Machine* (1987)

7 The writer isn't made in a vacuum. Writers are witnesses. The reason we need writers is because we need witnesses to this terrifying century.

E.L. Doctorow (b.1931), U.S. novelist: interview in *Writers at Work* (Eighth Series, ed. George Plimpton, 1988)

8 Chaucer was a class traitor
Shakespeare hated the mob
Donne sold out a bit later
Sidney was a nob.

Terry Eagleton (b.1943), British critic: 'The Ballad of English Literature' (to be sung to the tune of 'Land of Hope and Glory'), publ. in *Against The Grain* (1986), Ch.14

9 Creative writers are always greater than the causes that they represent.

E.M. Forster (1879–1970), British novelist and essayist: *Two Cheers for Democracy* (1951), 'Gide and George'

10 A great number of the disappointments and mishaps of the troubled world are the direct result of literature and the allied arts. It is our belief that no human being who devotes his life and energy to the manufacture of fantasies can be anything but fundamentally inadequate.

Christopher Hampton (b.1946), British playwright: Celia, in *The Philanthropist* (1970), Sc.5

11 I really do inhabit a system in which words are capable of shaking the entire structure of government, where words can prove mightier than ten military divisions.

Václav Havel (b.1936), Czech playwright and president: speech, Oct 1989, Germany, accepting a peace prize, quoted in *The Independent* (London), 9 Dec. 1989

12 All you can be sure about in a political-minded writer is that if his work should last you will have to skip the politics when you read it. Many of the so-called politically enlisted writers change their politics frequently. ... Perhaps it can be respected as a form of the pursuit of happiness.

Ernest Hemingway (1899–1961), U.S. author: interview in *Writers at Work* (Second Series, ed. George Plimpton, 1963),

13 It is not the first duty of the novelist to provide blueprints for insurrection, or uplifting tales of successful resistance for the benefit of the opposition. The naming of what is there is what is important.

Ian McEwan (b.1948), British author: preface to *A Move Abroad* (1989)

14 I've never read a political poem that's accomplished anything. Poetry makes things happen, but rarely what the poet wants.

Howard Nemerov (1920–1991), U.S. poet, novelist and critic: in the *International Herald Tribune* (Paris), 14 Oct 1988

15 It seems that the fiction writer has a revolting attachment to the poor, for even when he writes about the rich, he is more concerned with what they lack than with what they have.

Flannery O'Connor (1925–1964), U.S. author: 'The Teaching of Literature', publ. in *Mystery and Manners* (ed. Sally and Robert Fitzgerald, 1972)

16 Writers and politicians are natural rivals. Both groups try to make the world in their own images; they fight for the same territory.

Salman Rushdie (b.1947), Indian-born British author: quoted in *The Observer* (London), 19 Feb. 1989

17 Literature is the one place in any society where, within the secrecy of our own heads, we can hear *voices talking about everything in every possible way*. The reason for ensuring that that privileged arena is preserved is not that writers want the absolute freedom to say and do whatever they please. It is that we, all of us, readers and writers and citizens and generals and godmen, need that little, unimportant-looking room. We do not need to call it sacred, but we do need to remember that it is necessary.

Salman Rushdie: 'Is Nothing Sacred?', Herbert Read Memorial Lecture, 6 Feb. 1990, ICA, London,

publ. in *The Guardian* (London), 7 Feb. 1990. In the wake of the fatwa made twelve months earlier by the Ayatollah Khomeini, Rushdie's lecture was read by Harold Pinter

18 Just as the office worker dreams of murdering his hated boss and so is saved from really murdering him, so it is with the author; with his great dreams he helps his readers to survive, to avoid their worst intentions. And society, without realizing it ... respects and even exalts him, albeit with a kind of jealousy, fear and even repulsion, since few people want to discover the horrors that lurk in the depths of their souls. This is the highest mission of great literature, and there is no other.

Ernesto Sábato (b.1911), Argentinian novelist and essayist: interview in *The Independent* (London), 20 June 1992

19 Reading and writing texts are never neutral activities: there are interests, powers, pleasures entailed no matter how aesthetic or entertaining the work. Media, political economy, mass institutions – in fine, the tracings of secular power and the influence of the state – are part of what we call literature.

Edward Said (b.1935), Lebanese-born U.S. social and literary critic: *Culture and Imperialism* (1993), Ch.4, Sct.2

20 Writing is the continuation of politics by other means.

Philippe Sollers (b.1936), French author and critic: *Tel Quel: Théorie d'Ensemble* (1968), 'Écriture et Révolution'

21 Literature that is not the breath of contemporary society, that dares not transmit the pains and fears of that society, that does not warn in time against threatening moral and social dangers – such literature does not deserve the name of literature; it is only a façade. Such literature loses the confidence of its own people, and its published works are used as wastepaper instead of being read.

Alexander Solzhenitsyn (b.1918), Russian novelist: open letter to the Fourth Soviet Writers' Congress, 16 May 1967, rep. in *Solzhenitsyn: A Documentary Record* (ed. Leopold Labedz, 1970), 'The Struggle Intensifies'

22 For a country to have a great writer ... is like having another government. That's why no régime has ever loved great writers, only minor ones.

Alexander Solzhenitsyn: Innokenty, in *The First Circle* (1968), Ch.57

23 Already the writers are complaining that there is too much freedom. They need some pressure. The worse your daily life, the better your art. If you have to be careful because of oppression and censorship, this pressure produces diamonds.

Tatyana Tolstaya (b.1951), Russian author: on Russian writers, in *The Independent* (London), 31 May 1990

24 There is an incompatibility between literary creation and political activity.

Mario Vargas Llosa (b.1936), Peruvian novelist: in the *International Herald Tribune* (Paris), 1 April 1988

See also Solzhenitsyn on FREEDOM OF EXPRESSION

LITIGATION

1 If your lawyers tell you that you have a very good case, you should settle immediately.

Richard Ingrams (b.1937), British journalist and editor: on losing a libel action taken out by Robert Maxwell against *Private Eye*, Nov. 1985, quoted in *Maxwell: The Outsider* by Tom Bower (1988; rev.1991), Ch.14. The suit concerned allegations in July 1985 that Maxwell had paid for Labour party leader Neil Kinnock's travel expenses in the hope of a peerage. Ingrams blamed his losing the case on the jury, who 'while good and true [are] immensely thick'

2 The most important things in their lives ... was to have a lawsuit going. It was not a question of winning or losing it, and indeed it was vital to do neither, for otherwise the suit would be over and done with. A lawsuit was part of the personality, if not the only visible sign of it, to such an extent that there was often no real animosity between the litigants, because they both needed each other.

Salvatore Satta (1902–1975), Italian jurist and novelist: of the people of Nuoro, in *The Day of Judgment* (1979), Ch.20. The novel recounts the lives of the inhabitants of an inland mountain town in Sardinia around the turn of the century

LIVE FAST, DIE YOUNG

1 In your 20s, you feel like you're indestructible, that nothing can kill you and you laugh at death. You go on and stay up for days and do as many things as you can and then, in your 30s, you think, well, maybe I'll be around here a little longer, so I'm going to maybe take better care of myself.

John Belushi (1949–1982), U.S. comedian, singer and actor: interview in *Rolling Stone* (New York), 21 Jan 1982. Belushi died of a drugs overdose two months later

2 Live fast, die young and have a good-looking corpse.

John Derek (b.1926), U.S. actor: Nick Romano (John Derek), in *Knock On Any Door* (film; screenplay by Daniel Taradash and John Monks Jr.,

based on Willard Motley's novel, directed by Nicholas Ray, 1949)

3 Life careers gravewards at a breakneck rate, so drink and love, and leave the rest to fate.

Tony Harrison (b.1953), British poet: *Palladas: Poems* (1975), No.11. The poems are versions of Greek originals by the 4th-century Alexandrian poet, Palladas

4 Let me die a youngman's death
Not a free from sin tiptoe in
Candle wax & waning death
Not a curtains drawn by angels borne
'What a nice way to go' death

Roger McGough (b.1937), British poet: 'Let Me Die a Youngman's Death', publ. in *Penguin Modern Poets: The Mersey Sound* (1968)

5 Now he's gone and joined that stupid club.

Wendy O'Connor, Kurt Cobain's mother: on her son's suicide, referring to the number of other deaths by young rock stars, quoted by Tony Parsons in *The Daily Telegraph* (London), 14 April 1994, rep. in *Dispatches from the Front Line of Popular Culture* (Tony Parsons, 1994)

6 Name me, if you can, a better feeling than the one you get when you've half a bottle of Chivas in the bag with a gram of coke up your nose and a teenage lovely pulling off her tube top in the next seat over while you're doing a hundred miles an hour in a suburban side street.

P.J. O'Rourke (b.1947), U.S. journalist: *Republican Party Reptile* (1987), 'How to Drive Fast On Drugs While Getting Your Wing Wang Squeezed and Not Spill Your Drink'

LONDON *see under* BRITAIN

LONELINESS

1 A lonely man is a lonesome thing, a stone, a bone, a stick, a receptacle for Gilbey's gin, a stooped figure sitting at the edge of a hotel bed, heaving copious sighs like the autumn wind.

John Cheever (1912–1982), U.S. author: journal entry 1966, in *John Cheever: The Journals* (ed. Robert Gottlieb, 1991), 'The Sixties'

2 Our trouble, as modern men, is loneliness, and this begins in the very depths of our being. No public celebration or political symphony can hope to be rid of it.

Federico Fellini (1920–1993), Italian film-maker: *Fellini on Fellini* (ed. Anna Keel and Christian Strich, 1974; tr.1977), 'Letter to a Marxist Critic'

3 Loneliness is never more cruel than when it is felt in close propinquity with someone who has ceased to communicate.

Germaine Greer (b.1939), Australian feminist writer: *The Female Eunuch* (1970), 'Security'

4 What makes loneliness an anguish
   Is not that I have no one to share my burden,
   But this:
   I have only my own burden to bear.
   Dag Hammarskjöld (1905–1961), Swedish
   statesman and secretary-general of U.N.: note
   written 1952, publ. in *Markings* (1963), 'Night is
   Drawing Nigh'

5 When Christ said: 'I was hungry and you fed
   me', he didn't mean only the hunger for bread
   and for food; he also meant the hunger to be
   loved. Jesus himself experienced this loneliness. He came amongst his own and his own
   received him not, and it hurt him then and it
   has kept on hurting him. The same hunger, the
   same loneliness, the same having no one to be
   accepted by and to be loved and wanted by.
   Every human being in that case resembles
   Christ in his loneliness; and that is the hardest
   part, that's real hunger.
   Mother Teresa (1910–1997), Albanian-born
   Roman Catholic missionary: *A Gift for God* (1975),
   'Imitation of Christ'

6 The gift of loneliness is sometimes a radical
   vision of society or one's people that has not
   previously been taken into account.
   Alice Walker (b.1944), U.S. author and critic:
   interview first publ. in *Interviews with Black
   Writers* (ed. John O'Brien, 1973), rep. in *In
   Search of our Mothers' Gardens* (1983), 'From
   an Interview'

7 When so many are lonely as seem to be lonely,
   it would be inexcusably selfish to be lonely
   alone.
   Tennessee Williams (1911–1983), U.S. playwright:
   Don Quixote, in *Camino Real* (1953), 'Prologue'

LONGEVITY

1 In the name of Hippocrates, doctors have
   invented the most exquisite form of torture
   ever known to man: survival.
   Luis Buñuel (1900–1983), Spanish film-maker: *My
   Last Breath* (autobiography, 1983), Ch.21

2 My mother, not content with being motion-
   less, deaf and speechless, is now going blind.
   That's what you get for not dying, you see.
   Philip Larkin (1922–1985), British poet: letter to
   Kingsley Amis, 24 Oct. 1941, publ. in *Selected
   Letters of Philip Larkin 1940–1985* (ed. Anthony
   Thwaite, 1992)

3 Ours is an age in which everything is based on
   the premise that it is best to live as long as
   possible. The average life span has become the
   longest in history, and a monotonous plan for
   humanity unrolls before us.
   Yukio Mishima (1925–1970), Japanese author:
   Mishima on Hagakure (1977), '*Hagakure* is Alive
   Today'

4 Since people are going to be living longer and
   getting older, they'll just have to learn how to
   be babies longer.
   Andy Warhol (c.1928–1987), U.S. Pop artist: *From
   A to B and Back Again* (1975), Ch.7

See also AGE: OLD AGE; EUTHANASIA

LOQUACITY

1 We never say so much as when we do not quite
   know what we want to say. We need few words
   when we have something to say, but all the
   words in all the dictionaries will not suffice
   when we have nothing to say and want desperately to say it.
   Eric Hoffer (1902–1983), U.S. philosopher:
   Reflections on the Human Condition (1973), Aph.173

2 It's apparent that we can't proceed any further
   without a name for this institutionalized garru-
   lousness, this psychological patter, this need to
   catalogue the ego's condition. Let's call it
   psychobabble, this spirit which now tyrannizes conversation in the seventies.
   Richard Dean Rosen (b.1949), U.S. journalist and
   critic: *Psychobabble: Fast Talk and Quick Cure in
   the Era of Feeling* (1977), 'Psychobabble'. Rosen
   added: 'Psychobabble is difficult to avoid and there
   is often an embarrassment involved in not using it,
   somewhat akin to the mild humiliation experienced
   by American tourists in Paris who cannot speak the
   native tongue. Psychobabble is now spoken by
   magazine editors, management consultants, sandal
   makers, tool and die workers, chiefs of state, Ph.D.s
   in clinical psychology, and just about everyone else'

LOS ANGELES *see under* THE UNITED STATES

THE LOTTERY

1 I object to the National Lottery because it encourages gambling and because it takes money
   from those who are least able to afford it, but
   who are desperate to escape their situation... I
   am not impressed by the argument that it
   raises money for good causes. If we think
   things are worth supporting then we should
   be prepared to pay for them out of the tax
   coffers. Gambling profits are a sleazy way of
   doing it.
   Stephen Hawking (b.1942), British theoretical
   physicist: in the *Radio Times* (London), 17 Feb.
   1996, 'Hawking: the Big Questions'

2 The lottery's a regressive tax foisted on the
   classes that can least afford it by the fascist
   state.
   Jay McInerney (b.1955), U.S. author: man in
   queue, in *Brightness Falls* (1992), Ch.8

LOVE

1 The Impossible Generalized Man today is the critic who believes in loving those unworthy of love as well as those worthy – yet believes this only insofar as no personal risk is entailed. Meaning he loves no one, worthy or no. This is what makes him impossible.

Nelson Algren (1909–1981), U.S. author: *Notes from a Sea Diary: Hemingway All the Way* (1966), 'Prefatory'

2 To love is to suffer. To avoid suffering one must not love. But then one suffers from not loving. Therefore to love is to suffer, not to love is to suffer. To suffer is to suffer. To be happy is to love. To be happy then is to suffer. But suffering makes one unhappy. Therefore, to be unhappy one must love, or love to suffer, or suffer from too much happiness. I hope you're getting this down.

Woody Allen (b.1935), U.S. film-maker: Sonja (Diane Keaton) giving advice to Natasha, in *Love and Death* (film; written and directed by Woody Allen, 1975)

3 We men have got love well weighed up; our stuff
    Can get by without it.
Women don't seem to think that's good enough;
    They will write about it.

Kingsley Amis (1922–1995), British novelist and poet: 'A Bookshop Idyll', publ. in *A Case of Samples* (1956)

4 There is love of course. And then there's life, its enemy.
(*Il y a l'amour bien sûr. Et puis il y a la vie, son ennemie.*)

Jean Anouilh (1910–1987), French playwright: Le Général, in *Ardèle* (1947), Act 1

5 Love, by its very nature, is unworldly, and it is for this reason rather than its rarity that it is not only apolitical but antipolitical, perhaps the most powerful of all antipolitical human forces.

Hannah Arendt (1906–1975), German-born U.S. political philosopher: *The Human Condition* (1958), Pt.5, Ch.33

6 We are not commanded (or forbidden) to love our mates, our children, our friends, our country because such affections come naturally to us and are good in themselves, although we may corrupt them. We are commanded to love our neighbour because our 'natural' attitude toward the 'other' is one of either indifference or hostility.

W.H. Auden (1907–1973), Anglo-American poet: *A Certain World* (1970), 'Neighbor, Love of One's'

7 To try to write love is to confront the *muck* of language: that region of hysteria where language is both *too much* and *too little*, excessive … and impoverished.

Roland Barthes (1915–1980), French semiologist: *A Lover's Discourse* (1977; tr.1979), 'Inexpressible Love'

8 When we understand that man is the only animal who must *create* meaning, who must open a wedge into neutral nature, we already understand the essence of love. Love is the problem of an animal who must *find* life, *create* a dialogue with nature in order to experience his own being.

Ernest Becker (1924–1974), U.S. psychologist and cultural anthropologist: *The Structure of Evil* (1968), Pt.2, Ch.9, 'A Brief Ontology of Love'

9 Real love is a pilgrimage. It happens when there is no strategy, but it is very rare because most people are strategists.

Anita Brookner (b.1938), British novelist and art historian: interview in *Women Writers Talk* (ed. Olga Kenyon, 1989)

10 What is insane about love is that one wishes to precipitate and to *lose* the days of waiting. Thus one desires to approach the end. So by one of its characteristics love coincides with death.

Albert Camus (1913–1960), French-Algerian philosopher and author: journal entry, April 1950, quoted in *Camus: A Biography* by Herbert R. Lottman (1979), Ch.36

11 Love is the extra effort we make in our dealings with those whom we do not like and once you understand that, you understand all. This idea that love overtakes you is nonsense. This is but a polite manifestation of sex. To love another you have to undertake some fragment of their destiny.

Quentin Crisp (b.1908), British author: 'Love Lies Bleeding', broadcast on Channel 4, 6 Aug. 1991, publ. in the *New Statesman and Society* (London), 9 Aug. 1991

12 If we seek the pleasures of love, passion should be occasional, and common sense continual.

Robertson Davies (1913–1995), Canadian novelist and journalist: 'The Pleasures of Love', first publ. in *Saturday Night* (Canada), 23 Dec. 1961, rep. in *The Enthusiasms of Robertson Davies* (1990)

13 Love is not enough. It must be the foundation, the cornerstone – but not the complete structure. It is much too pliable, too yielding.

Bette Davis (1908–1989), U.S. actress: *The Lonely Life* (autobiography, 1962), Ch.19

14 To love one child and to love all children, whether living or dead – somewhere these two loves come together. To love a no-good but humble punk and to love an honest man who

believes himself to be an honest man – somewhere these, too, come together.

Marguerite Duras (1914–1996), French author and film-maker: 'The Path Of Joyful Despair', interview first publ. in *Le Monde* (Paris), 1977, rep. in *Outside: Selected Writings* (1984)

15 It's unthinkable not to love – you'd have a severe nervous breakdown. Or you'd have to be Philip Larkin.

Lawrence Durrell (1912–1990), British author: interview in *The Observer* (London), 11 Nov. 1990

16 Romantic love, in pornography as in life, is the mythic celebration of female negation. For a woman, love is defined as her willingness to submit to her own annihilation. ... The proof of love is that she is willing to be destroyed by the one whom she loves, for his sake. For the woman, love is always self-sacrifice, the sacrifice of identity, will, and bodily integrity, in order to fulfill and redeem the masculinity of her lover.

Andrea Dworkin (b.1946), U.S. feminist critic: 'The Root Cause', speech, 26 Sept. 1975, Massachusetts Institute of Technology, publ. in *Our Blood* (1976), Ch.9

17 If only the strength of the love that people feel when it is reciprocated could be as intense and obsessive as the love we feel when it is not; then marriages would be truly made in heaven.

Ben Elton (b.1959), British author and comic: *Stark* (1989), 'Private Investigations'

18 Well, love is insanity. The ancient Greeks knew that. It is the taking over of a rational and lucid mind by delusion and self-destruction. You lose yourself, you have no power over yourself, you can't even think straight.

Marilyn French (b.1929), U.S. author and critic: Valerie, in *The Women's Room* (1977), Ch.4, Sct.10

19 Love is often nothing but a favorable exchange between two people who get the most of what they can expect, considering their value on the personality market.

Erich Fromm (1900–1980), U.S. psychologist: *The Sane Society* (1955), Ch.5, 'Alienation'

20 *Je t'aime moi non plus.*

Serge Gainsbourg (1928–1991), French singer, songwriter and director: 'Je t'Aime Moi Non Plus' (song, 1969)

21 Love, love, love – all the wretched cant of it, masking egotism, lust, masochism, fantasy under a mythology of sentimental postures, a welter of self-induced miseries and joys, blinding and masking the essential personalities in the frozen gestures of courtship, in the kissing and the dating and the desire, the compliments and the quarrels which vivify its barrenness.

Germaine Greer (b.1939), Australian feminist writer: *The Female Eunuch* (1970), 'Obsession'

22 The ones we choose to love become our anchor when the hawser of the blood-tie's hacked, or frays.

Tony Harrison (b.1953), British poet: *v* (1985)

23 One would always want to think of oneself as being on the side of love, ready to recognize it and wish it well – but, when confronted with it in others, one so often resented it, questioned its true nature, secretly dismissed the particular instance as folly or promiscuity. Was it merely jealousy, or a reluctance to admit so noble and enviable a sentiment in anyone but oneself?

Shirley Hazzard (b.1931), Australian-American author: *The Evening of the Holiday* (1965), Ch.9

24 Only the really plain people know about love – the very fascinating ones try so hard to create an impression that they very soon exhaust their talents.

Katharine Hepburn (b.1909), U.S. actress: in *Look* (New York), 18 Feb. 1958

25 Love cannot be irresponsible. Its beauty is the fruit of responsibility. When love is truly responsible, it is also truly free.

Pope John Paul II [Karol Wojtyla] (b.1920), Polish ecclesiastic: *Crossing the Threshold of Hope* (1994), 'The Defense of Every Life'

26 Do you want me to tell you something really subversive? Love *is* everything it's cracked up to be. That's why people are so cynical about it. ... It really *is* worth fighting for, being brave for, risking everything for. And the trouble is, if you don't risk anything, you risk even *more*.

Erica Jong (b.1942), U.S. author: Hans, in *How To Save Your Own Life* (1977), 'Intuition, extuition...'

27 We love in another's soul
whatever of ourselves
we can deposit in it;
the greater the deposit,
the greater the love.

Irving Layton (b.1912), Canadian poet: *The Whole Bloody Bird* (1969), 'Aphs'

28 We've got this gift of love, but love is like a precious plant. You can't just accept it and leave it in the cupboard or just think it's going to get on by itself. You've got to keep watering it. You've got to really look after it and nurture it.

John Lennon (1940–1980), British rock musician: *Man of the Decade* television broadcast, ATV, 30 Dec. 1969, publ. in *Imagine* (ed. Andrew Solt and Sam Egan, 1988)

29 All you need is love.

John Lennon and **Paul McCartney** (b.1942), British rock musicians: 'All You Need is Love' (song) on the album *Yellow Submarine* (The Beatles, 1968)

30 And in the end, the love you take
Is equal to the love you make.
John Lennon and **Paul McCartney**: 'The End'
(song) on the album *Abbey Road* (The Beatles, 1970)

31 There's no love at all. ... You can't love anything. Love is what you feel for a dog or a pussy cat. It doesn't apply to humans, and if it does it just shows how low you are.
John Lydon [formerly Johnny Rotten] (b.1957), British rock musician: interview, 19 Nov. 1976, publ. in *1988: The New Wave Punk Rock Explosion* by Caroline Coon (1977), 'The Sex Pistols'

32 Great passions, my dear, don't exist: they're liars' fantasies. What do exist are little loves that may last for a short or a longer while.
Anna Magnani (1918–1973), Egyptian-born Italian actress: quoted in *The Egotists* by Oriana Fallaci (1963), 'Anna Magnani'

33 Love is losing its scope; lovers are losing the courage to surmount obstacles, the revolutionary passion to change social morality; love is losing its abstract meaning. In concrete terms, the lover loses the joy of having won his love and the sorrow of having failed to win her: he loses the wide spectrum of human emotion, the power to idealize the object of his affection. Love is relative, and if the other person's stature is lessened one's own stature is equally lessened.
Yukio Mishima (1925–1970), Japanese author: *Mishima on Hagakure* (1977), '*Hagakure* and Its Author'

34 Maybe love is like luck. You have to go all the way to find it.
Robert Mitchum (1917–1997), U.S. actor: Jeff Bailey (Robert Mitchum), in *Out Of The Past* (film; screenplay by Geoffrey Homes, directed by Jacques Tourneur, 1947)

35 No love is entirely without worth, even when the frivolous calls to the frivolous and the base to the base.
Iris Murdoch (b.1919), British novelist and philosopher: *The Nice and the Good* (1968), Ch.39

36 If love ... means that one person absorbs the other, then no real relationship exists any more. Love evaporates; there is nothing left to love. The integrity of self is gone.
Ann Oakley (b.1944), British sociologist and author: *Taking It Like a Woman* (1984), 'Love: Irresolution'

37 All we have to do is just admire each other and love each other 24 hours a day until we vanish... The rest is just foreplay to get to that.
Yoko Ono (b.1933), Japanese-born U.S. artist: sleevenotes on the album *Feeling the Space* (1973)

38 If all of us just loved and cared for one person each. That is all it takes. Love breeds love. Maybe then we will be able to prevent each other from going insane. Maybe then we will be able to prevent each other from becoming violent, as violence is in our hearts and not in our weapons. Guilt is not in the one who pulls the trigger, but in each of us who allows it.
Yoko Ono: letter to the world's press, following the murder of John Lennon in 1980

39 To an ordinary human being, love means nothing if it does not mean loving some people more than others.
George Orwell (1903–1950), British author: *Shooting an Elephant* (1950), 'Reflections on Gandhi'

40 It's no good trying to fool yourself about love. You can't fall into it like a soft job, without dirtying up your hands. It takes muscle and guts. And if you can't bear the thought of messing up your nice, clean soul, you'd better give up the whole idea of life, and become a saint. Because you'll never make it as a human being. It's either this world or the next.
John Osborne (1929–1994), British playwright: Jimmy Porter, in *Look Back in Anger* (1956), Act 3, Sc.2

41 One does not kill oneself for love of *a* woman, but because love – any love – reveals us in our nakedness, our misery, our vulnerability, our nothingness.
Cesare Pavese (1908–1950), Italian poet, novelist and translator: journal entry, 25 March 1950, publ. in *This Business of Living* (1952; tr.1961)

42 Birds do it, bees do it,
Even educated fleas do it.
Let's do it, let's fall in love.
Cole Porter (1893–1964), U.S. composer and lyricist: 'Let's Do It' (song, 1954). The song was first featured in a 1928 musical, *Paris*, without this verse

43 Love is the direct opposite of hate. By *definition* it's something you can't feel for more than a few minutes at a time, so what's all this bullshit about loving somebody for the rest of your life?
Judith Rossner (b.1935), U.S. author: *Nine Months in the Life of an Old Maid* (1969), Pt.2

44 It is the privilege of those who fear love to murder those who do not fear it!
May Sarton (b.1912), U.S. poet and novelist: Hilary Stevens, in *Mrs Stevens Hears the Mermaids Singing* (1965), Pt.2

45 Love means never having to say you're sorry.
Erich Segal (b.1937), U.S. author: Jenny Cavilleri (Ali MacGraw), in *Love Story* (film; screenplay by Erich Segal, directed by Arthur Hiller, 1970). The words (which appear in Ch.13 of Segal's novelization

of the film as 'Love means not ever having to say you're sorry') were used to promote the film, subsequently spawning endless variations on the theme

46 We often speak of love when we really should be speaking of the drive to dominate or to master, so as to confirm ourselves as active agents, in control of our own destinies and worthy of respect from others.
Thomas Szasz (b.1920), U.S. psychiatrist: *The Second Sin* (1973), 'Love'

47 I try to give to the poor people for love what the rich could get for money. No, I wouldn't touch a leper for a thousand pounds; yet I willingly cure him for the love of God.
Mother Teresa (1910–1997), Albanian-born Roman Catholic missionary: *A Gift for God* (1975), 'Riches'

48 If love is the answer, could you rephrase the question?
Lily Tomlin (b.1939), U.S. comedienne: quoted in *Funny Business* by David Housham and John Frank-Keyes (1992)

49 An affair wants to spill, to share its glory with the world. No act is so private it does not seek applause.
John Updike (b.1932), U.S. author and critic: *Couples* (1968), Ch.2

50 Love is an act of endless forgiveness, a tender look which becomes a habit.
Peter Ustinov (b.1921), British actor, writer and director: in the *Christian Science Monitor* (Boston), 9 Dec. 1958

51 I've only been in love with a beer bottle and a mirror.
Sid Vicious (1957–1979), British punk rocker: in *Sounds* (London), 9 Oct. 1976

52 If somebody says, 'I love you,' to me, I feel as though I had a pistol pointed at my head. What can anybody reply under such conditions but that which the pistol-holder requires? 'I love you, *too*.'
Kurt Vonnegut (b.1922), U.S. novelist: address at dedication of Wheaton College Library, 1973, publ. in *Wampeters, Foma and Granfalloons* (1974)

53 Fantasy love is much better than reality love. Never doing it is very exciting. The most exciting attractions are between two opposites that never meet.
Andy Warhol (c.1928–1987), U.S. Pop artist: *From A to B and Back Again* (1975), Ch.3

54 A man in love is like a clipped coupon – it's time to cash in.
Mae West (1892–1980), U.S. actress: *On Sex, Health and ESP* (1975), 'That Four-Letter Word!'

55 Oh, Jacques, we're used to each other, we're a pair of captive hawks caught in the same cage, and so we've grown used to each other. That's

what passes for love at this dim, shadowy end of the Camino Real....
Tennessee Williams (1911–1983), U.S. playwright: Marguerite Gautier to Jacques Casanova, in *Camino Real* (1953), Block 15

56 However it is debased or misinterpreted, love is a redemptive feature. To focus on one individual so that their desires become superior to yours is a very cleansing experience.
Jeanette Winterson (b.1959), British author: in *The Times* (London), 26 Aug. 1992

57 Why is it that the most unoriginal thing we can say to one another is still the thing we long to hear? 'I love you' is always a quotation. You did not say it first and neither did I, yet when you say it and when I say it we speak like savages who have found three words and worship them.
Jeanette Winterson: *Written on the Body* (1992), p.9 of Jonathan Cape edn.

58 A man falls in love through his eyes, a woman through her ears.
Woodrow Wyatt (b.1918), British journalist: *To the Point* (1981), 'The Ears Have It'. Wyatt's reasoning, apropos of women, was that 'what is said to them and what they believe about a man's status is usually more important than the superficiality of good looks'

See also Duras on BETRAYAL; Bukowski on HATE; MARRIAGE: AND LOVE; Parsons on THE MIDDLE CLASS; Pavese on SUICIDE

LOVE: Ended

1 A bizarre sensation pervades a relationship of pretense. No truth seems true. A simple morning's greeting and response appear loaded with innuendo and fraught with implications. ... Each nicety becomes more sterile and each withdrawal more permanent.
Maya Angelou (b.1928), U.S. author: *Singin' and Swingin' and Gettin' Merry Like Christmas* (third volume of autobiography, 1976), Ch.5

2 I leave before being left. I decide.
Brigitte Bardot (b.1933), French actress: quoted in *Newsweek* (New York), 5 March 1973

3 It's afterwards you realize that the feeling of happiness you had with a man didn't necessarily prove that you loved him.
Marguerite Duras (1914–1996), French author and film-maker: *Practicalities* (1987; tr.1990), 'The Chimneys of *India Song*'

4 Two separate, distinct personalities, not separate at all, but inextricably bound, soul and body and mind, to each other, how did we get so far apart so fast?
Judith Guest (b.1936), U.S. author: *Ordinary People* (1976), Ch.19

5 Falling out of love is chiefly a matter of *forgetting* how charming someone is.
Iris Murdoch (b.1919), British novelist and philosopher: Anderson Palmer, in *A Severed Head* (1961), Ch.24

6 In every question and every remark tossed back and forth between lovers who have not played out the last fugue, there is one question and it is this: 'Is there someone new?'
Edna O'Brien (b.1936), Irish author: *Lantern Slides* (1990), 'Long Distance'

7 We who were loved will never unlive that crippling fever.
Adrienne Rich (b.1929), U.S. poet: 'After a Sentence in "Malte Laurids Brigge"', publ. in *Snapshots of a Daughter-in-Law* (1963)

See also MARRIAGE: FAILED

LOVE: and Sex

1 I think men get more and more in love with the person they're [fucking] and women get more and more attracted to the person they love.
Steven Soderbergh (b.1963), U.S. film-maker: Graham Dalton (James Spader), in *sex, lies and videotape* (film; written and directed by Steven Soderbergh, 1989). The rapt Anne (Andy MacDowell) replies, 'That's beautiful...'

2 Love and sex can go together and sex and un-love can go together and love and unsex can go together. But personal love and personal sex is bad.
Andy Warhol (c.1928–1987), U.S. Pop artist: *From A to B and Back Again* (1975), Ch.3

LOVERS

1 A man can go from being a lover to being a stranger in three moves flat ... but a woman under the guise of friendship will engage in acts of duplicity which come to light very much later. There are different species of self-justification.
Anita Brookner (b.1938), British novelist and art historian: *Novelists in Interview* (ed. John Haffenden, 1985)

2 Every man needs two women, a quiet home-maker, and a thrilling nymph.
Iris Murdoch (b.1919), British novelist and philosopher: Gildas Hearne, in *The Message to the Planet* (1989), Pt.1

3 An orange on the table
Your dress on the rug
And you in my bed
Sweet present of the present
Cool of night

Warmth of my life.
(*Une orange sur la table
Ta robe sur le tapis
Et toi dans mon lit
Doux présent du présent
Fraîcheur de la nuit.*)
Jacques Prévert (1900–1977), French poet: 'Alicante', publ. in *Paroles* (1946; tr. Lawrence Ferlinghetti, 1958)

4 I'm a bit of a P.T. Barnum. I make stars out of everyone.
Donald Trump (b.1946), U.S. businessman: on the women in his life, quoted in *The Observer* (London), 7 July 1991

LOYALTY

1 Total loyalty is possible only when fidelity is emptied of all concrete content, from which changes of mind might naturally arise.
Hannah Arendt (1906–1975), German-born U.S. political philosopher: *The Origins of Totalitarianism* (1951), Ch.10, Sct.1

2 We are all the President's men.
Henry Kissinger (b.1923), U.S. Republican politician and secretary of state: spoken in 1970, after the invasion of Cambodia, quoted in *The Sunday Times* (London), 4 May 1975

LUCK

1 Chance is a part of reality: we are continually shaped by the forces of coincidence, the unexpected occurs with almost numbing regularity in our lives.
Paul Auster (b.1947), U.S. author: interview with Larry McCaffery and Sinda Gregory in 1989/90, publ. in *The Red Notebook* (1995)

2 All good fortune is a gift of the gods, and ... you don't win the favour of the ancient gods by being good, but by being *bold*.
Anita Brookner (b.1938), British novelist and art historian: interview in *Writers at Work* (Eighth Series, ed. George Plimpton, 1988)

3 What we call luck is the inner man externalized. We make things happen to us.
Robertson Davies (1913–1995), Canadian novelist and journalist: Simon Darcourt, in *What's Bred in the Bone* (1985), Pt.1, 'Who Asked the Question?'

4 Chance is the one thing you can't buy.... You have to pay for it and you have to pay for it with your life, spending a lot of time, you pay for it with time, not the wasting of time but the spending of time.
Robert Doisneau (1912–1994), French photographer: interview in *The Guardian* (London), 4 April 1992

5 I know what you're thinking. Did he fire six shots or only five? Well, to tell you the truth, in all this excitement I've kinda lost track myself. But being this is a .44 Magnum, the most powerful handgun in the world, and would blow your head clean off – you've got to ask yourself one question: Do I feel lucky? Well, do ya, punk?

Clint Eastwood (b.1930), U.S. actor and film-maker: Harry Callahan (Clint Eastwood), holding his gun to the head of a bank-robber after a foiled raid, in *Dirty Harry* (film; screenplay by Harry and Rita Fink and Dean Riesner, directed by Don Siegel, 1971)

6 I always get the fuzzy end of the lollipop.

Marilyn Monroe (1926–1962), U.S. actress: Sugar Kane (Marilyn Monroe), in *Some Like It Hot* (film; screenplay by Billy Wilder and I.A.L. Diamond, produced and directed by Billy Wilder, 1959)

7 The worst cynicism: a belief in luck.

Joyce Carol Oates (b.1938), U.S. author: *Do What You Will* (1970), Pt.2, Ch.15

LUST

1 Guys would sleep with a bicycle if it had the right colour lip-gloss on. They have no shame. They're like bull elks in a field. It's a scent to them, a smell.

Tori Amos (b.1963), U.S. rock singer: in *New Musical Express* (London), 1994, quoted in *NME Book of Quotes* (1995), 'Sex'

2 I've looked on a lot of women with lust. I've committed adultery in my heart many times. This is something God recognizes I will do – and I have done it – and God forgives me for it.

Jimmy Carter (b.1924), U.S. Democratic politician and president: interview in *Playboy* (Chicago), Nov. 1976, during the presidential campaign against Gerald Ford

3 What most men desire is a virgin who is a whore.

Edward Dahlberg (1900–1977), U.S. author and critic: *Reasons of the Heart* (1965), 'On Lust'

4 If you live in rock and roll, as I do, you see the reality of sex, of male lust and women being aroused by male lust. It attracts women. It doesn't repel them.

Camille Paglia (b.1947), U.S. author and critic: interview in *Playboy* (Chicago), Oct. 1991, rep. in *Sex, Art, and American Culture* (1992), 'The Rape Debate'

5 All men want quick, uncomplicated sexual adventure (as well as sustained romantic passion); in a world of all men, that desire is granted.

Edmund White (b.1940), U.S. author: 'Sexual Culture', first publ. in *Vanity Fair*, 1983, rep. in *The Burning Library* (1994)

6 It is no longer enough to be lusty. One must be a sexual gourmet.

George F. Will (b.1941), U.S. political columnist: 'The Ploy of Sex' (1974), rep. in *The Pursuit of Happiness, and Other Sobering Thoughts* (1978)

McCARTHYISM

1 It was an infringement of liberty but it was only a tiny inconvenience compared with having no job. I weighed it by priority.

Joseph Heller (b.1923), U.S. author: on his signing the 'loyalty oath' at Penn State University, quoted in *The Fifties* by Peter Lewis (1978), Ch.3

2 There is a hate layer of opinion and emotion in America. There will be other McCarthys to come who will be hailed as its heroes.

Max Lerner (1902–1992), U.S. author and columnist: 'McCarthyism: The Smell of Decay', first publ. in the *New York Post*, 5 April 1950, rep. in *The Unfinished Country* (1959), Pt.4. In this article the word 'McCarthyism' was first coined, as Lerner affirmed in a later column, 3 Feb. 1954: 'For my own part I doubt seriously whether the word will outlast the political power of the man from whom it derives'

3 McCarthyism is Americanism with its sleeves rolled.

Joseph McCarthy (1908–1957), U.S. Republican politician: speech, 1952, Wisconsin, quoted in *Senator Joe McCarthy* by Richard Rovere (1973), Ch.1

4 No one can terrorize a whole nation, unless we are all his accomplices.

Edward R. Murrow (1908–1965), U.S. newscaster: 'See It Now', CBS-TV, 7 March 1954

5 The nation that complacently and fearfully allows its artists and writers to become suspected rather than respected is no longer regarded as a nation possessed with humor in depth.

James Thurber (1894–1961), U.S. humorist and illustrator: in response to the question whether humour was in decline in the United States, in the *New York Times Magazine*, 7 Dec. 1958

McDONALD'S

1 I believe that everything went downhill from the moment McDonald's was given licence to invade England. ... To me, it was like the outbreak of war and I couldn't understand why English troops weren't retaliating.

Morrissey (b.1959), British rock musician: quoted in *The Guardian* (London), 26 Feb. 1994

2 McDonald's is good for the world, that's my opinion.... The Pax Americana to me, is the dollar sign. It works. It may not be attractive. It's not pretty to see American businessmen running all around the world in plaid trousers,

drinking whiskey. But what they're doing makes sense.

Oliver Stone (b.1946), U.S. film-maker: interview in *Playboy* (Chicago), Feb. 1980, quoted in *The Cinema of Oliver Stone* (1995), Ch.5

3   The most beautiful thing in Tokyo is
        McDonald's.
     The most beautiful thing in Stockholm is
        McDonald's.
     The most beautiful thing in Florence is
        McDonald's.
     Peking and Moscow don't have anything
        beautiful yet.

Andy Warhol (c.1928–1987), U.S. Pop artist: *From A to B and Back Again* (1975), Ch.4

MACHINES

1   The machine has had a pernicious effect upon virtue, pity, and love, and young men used to machines which induce inertia, and fear, are near impotents.

Edward Dahlberg (1900–1977), U.S. author and critic: *Alms for Oblivion* (1964), 'No Love and No Thanks'

2   As machines become more and more efficient and perfect, so it will become clear that *imperfection is the greatness of man*.

Ernst Fischer (1899–1972), Austrian editor, poet and critic: *The Necessity of Art* (1959; tr.1963), Ch.5

3   I declare that World War III is now being waged by short-haired robots whose deliberate aim is to destroy the complex web of free wild life by the imposition of mechanical order.

Timothy Leary (1920–1996), U.S. psychologist: *Manifesto* (1970), publ. in *Counterculture and Revolution* (ed. David Horowitz, Michael P. Lerner and Craig Pykes, 1972). Leary's *Manifesto* was written after escaping prison and fleeing to Algeria

4   Never let anything mechanical know you are in a hurry.

Andrew Ross (b.1956), British social theorist: on photocopiers, in introduction to *Strange Weather* (1991)

MADNESS

1   And what is an authentic madman? It is a man who preferred to become mad, in the socially accepted sense of the word, rather than forfeit a certain superior idea of human honour. So society has strangled in its asylums all those it wanted to get rid of or protect itself from, because they refused to become its accomplices in certain great nastinesses. For a madman is also a man whom society did not want to hear and whom it wanted to prevent from uttering certain intolerable truths.

Antonin Artaud (1896–1948), French theatre producer, actor and theorist: *Van Gogh, the Man Suicided by Society* (1947), rep. in *Selected Writings*, Pt.33 (ed. Susan Sontag, 1976)

2   In a completely sane world, *madness* is the only freedom!

J.G. Ballard (b.1930), British author: interview, 30 Oct. 1982, in *Re/Search* (San Francisco), No.8/9, 1984

3   We all are born mad. Some remain so.

Samuel Beckett (1906–1989), Irish playwright and novelist: Estragon, in *Waiting for Godot* (1952; tr.1954), Act 2

4   The world has always gone through periods of madness so as to advance a bit on the road to reason.

Hermann Broch (1886–1951), Austrian novelist: the doctor, in *The Spell* (1976; tr.1987), Ch.11

5   Men are mad most of their lives; few live sane, fewer die so. … The acts of people are baffling unless we realize that their wits are disordered. Man is driven to justice by his lunacy.

Edward Dahlberg (1900–1977), U.S. author and critic: *The Carnal Myth* (1968), Ch.2

6   In this century the writer has carried on a conversation with madness. We might almost say of the twentieth-century writer that he aspires to madness. Some have made it, of course, and they hold special places in our regard. To a writer, madness is a final distillation of self, a final editing down. It's the drowning out of false voices.

Don DeLillo (b.1926), U.S. author: Owen Brademas, in *The Names* (1982), Ch.5

7   Madness cannot be found in a wild state. Madness exists only within a society, it does not exist outside the forms of sensibility which isolate it and the forms of repulsion which exclude it or capture it.

Michel Foucault (1926–1984), French philosopher: interview in *Le Monde* (Paris), 22 July 1961, quoted in *The Lives of Michel Foucault* by David Macey (1993), Ch.5

8   There is a supreme lucidity, which is the precisely calculated awareness which is called madness.

Martha Graham (1894–1991), U.S. dancer and choreographer: *The Notebooks of Martha Graham* (1973), 'The Trysting Tent'

9   Madness need not be all breakdown. It may also be break-through. It is potential liberation and renewal as well as enslavement and existential death.

R.D. Laing (1927–1989), British psychiatrist: *The Politics of Experience* (1967), Ch.6

10   Our society is run by insane people for insane objectives. … I think we're being run by

maniacs for maniacal ends ... and I think I'm liable to be put away as insane for expressing that. That's what's insane about it.

John Lennon (1940–1980), British rock musician: interview, BBC, 22 June 1968, publ. in *Imagine* (ed. Andrew Solt and Sam Egan, 1988)

11 What can you do against the lunatic who is more intelligent than yourself, who gives your arguments a fair hearing and then simply persists in his lunacy?

George Orwell (1903–1950), British author: Winston Smith of O'Brien, in *Nineteen Eighty-four* (1949), Pt.3, Ch.3

12 The usefulness of madmen is famous: they demonstrate society's logic flagrantly carried out down to its last scrimshaw scrap.

Cynthia Ozick (b.1928), U.S. novelist and short-story writer: 'The Hole/Birth Catalog', publ. in *The First Ms. Reader* (ed. Francine Klagsbrun, 1972)

13 We all go a little mad sometimes.

Anthony Perkins (1932–1992), U.S. actor: Norman Bates (Anthony Perkins), in *Psycho* (film; screenplay by Joseph Stefano, based on Robert Bloch's novel *Psycho*, 1959, produced and directed by Alfred Hitchcock, 1960)

14 You're only given a little spark of madness. You mustn't lose it.

Robin Williams (b.1952), U.S. actor and comedian: quoted in *Funny Business* by David Housham and John Frank-Keyes (1992)

MADONNA

1 Madonna's protean quality, her ability to re-design herself ... represents an emphasis of will over talent. Not greatly gifted, not deeply beautiful, Madonna tells America that fame comes from *wanting* it badly enough. And everyone is terribly good at badly wanting things.

Martin Amis (b.1949), British author: in *The Observer* (London) 1992, rep. in *Visiting Mrs Nabokov* (1993), 'Madonna'

2 Madonna's ambition is to rule the world, but now it seems unlikely that she will ever receive even an Oscar nomination. But she's still a good thing. And most importantly, she still looks like a whore and thinks like a pimp. Which everyone knows is the very best sort of modern girl.

Julie Burchill (b.1960), British journalist and author: *Sex and Sensibility* (1992), 'Madonna'

3 They used to say that I was a slut, a pig, an easy lay, a sex bomb, Minnie Mouse or even Marlene Dietrich's daughter, but I'd rather say that I'm just a hyperactive adult.

Madonna (b.1958), U.S. singer and actress: quoted in *Madonna In Her Own Words* (ed. Mick St. Michael, 1990), 'Me'

4 Madonna is the true feminist. She exposes the puritanism and suffocating ideology of American feminism, which is stuck in an adolescent whining mode. Madonna has taught young women to be fully female and sexual while still exercising control over their lives.

Camille Paglia (b.1947), U.S. author and critic: 'Madonna 1: Animality and Artifice', first publ. in the *New York Times*, 14 Dec. 1991, rep. in *Sex, Art, and American Culture* (1992)

See also Madonna on NAMES

MAGAZINES

1 Having a high-profile magazine that loses lots of money, being a vanity publisher if you like, is rather like having a trophy wife. It's nice to have her on your arm, but you can't do anything with her because you are too old and clapped out – and it's as expensive as running an Ivana Trump, I can tell you. Rich men do it because it gets them invited to the right dinner parties and to meet politicians, that sort of thing. It also means that when they are asked what they do they can say, 'I own the Spectator' rather than, 'I export pipe linings'.

Alan Coren (b.1938), British editor and humorist: quoted in *The Observer* (London), 11 Feb. 1996

2 You have a great danger with a magazine. It's true with any company but it's very clear with a magazine: just keep your friends around you and grow old together and just watch the magazine go right into the toilet.

Hugh Hefner (b.1926), U.S. publisher: quoted in *Hefner* by Frank Brady (1974), Ch.11

3 That's where *Time* magazine lives ... way out there on the puzzled, masturbating edge, peering through the keyhole and selling what they see to the big wide world of chamber of commerce voyeurs who support the public prints.

Hunter S. Thompson (b.1939), U.S. journalist: 'The Ultimate Free Lancer', publ. in *Distant Drummer*, Nov. 1967, rep. in *The Great Shark Hunt* (1979)

4 I consider that that 'that' that worries us so much should be forgotten. Rats desert a sinking ship. Thats infest a sinking magazine.

James Thurber (1894–1961), U.S. humorist and illustrator: memo to the *New Yorker* in 1959, first publ. in the *New York Times Book Review*, 4 Dec. 1988

5 If Botticelli were alive today he'd be working for *Vogue*.

Peter Ustinov (b.1921), British actor, writer and director: quoted in *The Observer* (London), 21 Oct 1968

See also Hefner on PORNOGRAPHY

MAGIC

1 Black magic operates most effectively in pre-conscious, marginal areas. Casual curses are the most effective.
William Burroughs (1914–1997), U.S. author: *The Western Lands* (1987), Ch.3

2 Why not walk in the aura of magic that gives to the small things of life their uniqueness and importance? Why not befriend a toad today?
Germaine Greer (b.1939), Australian feminist writer: *The Change: Women, Ageing and the Menopause* (1991), Ch.16

3 I put a spell on you, 'cos your mine
You'd better stop the things you do
Ha! Haa! Haa! – What's up! – I ain't lyin'!
Yeaaaaahhhh! I can't stand it, oh no,
Your runnin' around,
I can't stand no – I can't stand you putting me down.
Screamin' Jay Hawkins (b.1929), U.S. rock singer: 'I Put a Spell on You' (song, co-written with Herb Slotkin, 1956)

JOHN MAJOR

1 It makes me laugh now when I hear him called a grey man. That's just a cover. It's a mask.
Jean Kierans, former girlfriend of John Major: quoted in the *Independent on Sunday* (London), 19 Feb. 1995

2 John Major is the Antichrist. There's something in Nostradamus about him: 'A pearled isle will be destroyed by a man from the circus who has turned to politics.' It's a bit like *The Omen*, innit?
Mark E. Smith (b.1960), British rock musician: in *New Musical Express* (London), 1994, quoted in *NME Book of Quotes* (1995), 'Politics'

THE MAJORITY

1 There is something wonderful in seeing a wrong-headed majority assailed by truth.
J.K. Galbraith (b.1908), U.S. economist: in *The Guardian* (London), 28 July 1989

2 The one thing that doesn't abide by majority rule is a person's conscience.
Harper Lee (b.1926), U.S. author: Atticus Finch, in *To Kill a Mockingbird* (1960), Pt.1, Ch.11

3 Majority rule is a precious, sacred thing worth dying for. But – like other precious, sacred things, such as the home and the family – it's not only worth dying for; it can make you wish you were dead. Imagine if all of life were deter-mined by majority rule. Every meal would be a pizza. Every pair of pants, even those in a Brooks Brothers suit, would be stonewashed denim. Celebrity diet and exercise books would be the only thing on the shelves at the library. And – since women are a majority of the population – we'd all be married to Mel Gibson.
P.J. O'Rourke (b.1947), U.S. journalist: *Parliament of Whores* (1991), 'The Mystery of Government'

MAKE-UP

1 Lipstick is power.
Barbara Follett (b.1942), British Labour politician: Follett's most quoted soundbite, which she later repudiated, quoted in *The Observer* (London), 25 Feb. 1996

2 Isn't that the problem? That women have been swindled for centuries into substituting adornment for love, fashion (as it were) for passion? ... All the cosmetics names seemed obscenely obvious to me in their promises of sexual bliss. They were all firming or uplifting or invigorating. They made you *tingle*. Or *glow*. Or feel *young*. They were prepared with hormones or placentas or royal jelly. All the juice and joy missing in the lives of these women were to be supplied by the contents of jars and bottles. No wonder they would spend twenty dollars for an ounce of face makeup or thirty for a half-ounce of hormone cream. What price bliss? What price sexual ecstasy?
Erica Jong (b.1942), U.S. author: *How To Save Your Own Life* (1977), 'A day in the life...'

3 Waits at the window,
Wearing the face that she keeps in a jar by the door.
Who is it for?
John Lennon (1940–1980) and **Paul McCartney** (b.1942), British rock musicians: 'Eleanor Rigby' (song) on the album *Revolver* (The Beatles, 1966)

MALICE

1 It is remarkable by how much a pinch of malice enhances the penetrating power of an idea or an opinion. Our ears, it seems, are wonderfully attuned to sneers and evil reports about our fellow men.
Eric Hoffer (1902–1983), U.S. philosopher: *The Passionate State of Mind* (1955), Aph.167

2 Malice is only another name for mediocrity.
Patrick Kavanagh (1905–1967), Irish poet and author: *Collected Pruse* (1967), 'Signposts'

MANAGEMENT

1 I couldn't motivate a bee to sting you if it didn't have the equipment. I couldn't motivate a snake to bite you if it didn't have the teeth. You can only bring out of people what they are capable of giving. Two of the great myths circulating now are that Heinz's beans are the best and that I can get more out of men than they have inside them.
Brian Clough (b.1935), British footballer and manager: quoted by Hugh McIlvanney, in *The Observer* (London), 15 Nov. 1975, rep. in *McIlvanney on Football* (1994), 'The Big Man and Other Giants'

2 You don't need a Harvard MBA to know that the bedroom and the boardroom are just two sides of the same ballgame.
Stephen Fry (b.1957), British comic actor and author: Stephen, in *A Bit of Fry and Laurie* (1990), 'Troubleshooters'

3 When you overpay small people you frighten them. They know that their merits or activites entitle them to no such sums as they are receiving. As a result their boss soars out of economic into magic significance. He becomes a source of blessings rather than wages. Criticism is sacrilege, doubt is heresy.
Ben Hecht (1893–1964), U.S. journalist, author and screenwriter: *A Child of the Century* (1954), Bk.5, 'The Captive Muse'

4 I am the proprietor. I am the boss. And I want that to be understood very clearly. There can only be one boss and that is me.
Robert Maxwell (1923–1991), British tycoon: speech, 13 July 1984, to union leaders of the newly purchased Mirror Group Newspapers, quoted in *Maxwell: The Outsider* by Tom Bower (1988; rev.1991), Ch.13

5 A man may be a tough, concentrated, successful money-maker and never contribute to his country anything more than a horrible example. A manager may be tough and practical, squeezing out, while the going is good, the last ounce of profit and dividend, and may leave behind him an exhausted industry and a legacy of industrial hatred. A tough manager may never look outside his own factory walls or be conscious of his partnership in a wider world. I often wonder what strange cud such men sit chewing when their working days are over, and the accumulating riches of the mind have eluded them.
Robert Menzies (1894–1978), Australian Liberal politician and prime minister: First William Queale Memorial Lecture, 1954, quoted in *Wit and Wisdom of Robert Menzies* (ed. Colin Bingham, 1982)

MANNERS

1 I don't mind if you don't like my manners. I don't like them myself. They're pretty bad. I grieve over them on longer winter evenings.
Humphrey Bogart (1899–1957), U.S. actor: Philip Marlowe (Humphrey Bogart), in *The Big Sleep* (film; screenplay by William Faulkner, Leigh Brackett and Jules Furthman, adapted from Raymond Chandler's novel, directed by Howard Hawks, 1946)

2 The English are polite by telling lies. The Americans are polite by telling the truth.
Malcolm Bradbury (b.1932), British author: Dr Bernard Froelich, in *Stepping Westward* (1965), Bk.2, Ch.5

3 Manners are love in a cool climate.
Quentin Crisp (b.1908), British author: *Manners from Heaven* (1984), Ch.2

4 The purpose of polite behavior is never virtuous. Deceit, surrender, and concealment: these are not virtues. The goal of the mannerly is comfort, per se.
June Jordan (b.1936), U.S. poet and civil rights activist: 'Civil Wars' (1981), rep. in *Moving Towards Home: Political Essays* (1989)

5 Manners are of such great consequence to the novelist that any kind will do. Bad manners are better than no manners at all, and because we are losing our customary manners, we are probably overly conscious of them; this seems to be a condition that produces writers.
Flannery O'Connor (1925–1964), U.S. author: 'The Fiction Writer and His Country', publ. in *The Living Novel: A Symposium* (ed. Granville Hicks, 1957), rep. in *Mystery and Manners* (ed. Sally and Robert Fitzgerald, 1972)

6 Good manners have much to do with the emotions. To make them ring true, one must feel them, not merely exhibit them.
Amy Vanderbilt (1908–1974), U.S. hostess and author: *New Complete Book of Etiquette* (1963), introduction to Pt.2

7 Manners are especially the need of the plain. The pretty can get away with anything.
Evelyn Waugh (1903–1966), British novelist: quoted in *The Observer* (London), 15 April 1962

MARRIAGE

1 When two people marry they become in the eyes of the law one person, and that one person is the husband!
Shana Alexander (b.1925), U.S. writer and editor: introduction to *State-by-State Guide to Women's Legal Rights* (1975)

2 In marriage there are no manners to keep up, and beneath the wildest accusations no real criticism. Each is familiar with that ancient child in the other who may erupt again. ... We are not ridiculous to ourselves. We are ageless. That is the luxury of the wedding ring.

Enid Bagnold (1889–1981), British novelist and playwright: *Autobiography* (1969), Ch.6

3 The curse which lies upon marriage is that too often the individuals are joined in their weakness rather than in their strength – each asking from the other instead of finding pleasure in giving. It is even more deceptive to dream of gaining through the child a plenitude, a warmth, a value, which one is unable to create for oneself; the child brings joy only to the woman who is capable of disinterestedly desiring the happiness of another, to one who without being wrapped up in self seeks to transcend her own existence.

Simone de Beauvoir (1908–1986), French novelist and essayist: *The Second Sex* (1949; tr.1953), Bk.2, Pt.5, Ch.2

4 In Europe we tend to see marital love as an eternity which encompasses hate and also indifference: when we promise to love we really mean that we promise to honour a contract. Americans, seeming to take marriage with not enough seriousness, are really taking love and sex with too much.

Anthony Burgess (1917–1993), British author and critic: *You've Had Your Time* (1990), Ch.2

5 A man will teach his wife what is needed to arouse his desires. And there is no reason for a woman to know any more than what her husband is prepared to teach her. If she gets married knowing far too much about what she wants and doesn't want then she will be ready to find fault with her husband.

Barbara Cartland (b.1901), British novelist: interview in *Speaking Frankly* by Wendy Leigh (1978)

6 Marriages will survive despite enormous strains. A lover will ask, 'Is he happy? Can he still love her?' They don't realise that's not the point, it's all the normal things they do together – going to the supermarket, choosing wallpaper, doing things with the children.

Carol Clewlow (b.1947), British novelist: interview in *The Observer* (London), 19 Feb. 1989

7 You can't bring logic into this. We're talking about marriage. Marriage is like the Middle East. There's no solution.

Pauline Collins (b.1940), British actress: Shirley (Pauline Collins), in *Shirley Valentine* (film; screenplay by Willy Russell, based on his 1986 play, directed by Lewis Gilbert, 1989)

8 So basically you're saying marriage is just a way of getting out of an embarrassing pause in conversation.

Richard Curtis (b.1956), British screenwriter: Charles (Hugh Grant) to Gareth, in *Four Weddings and a Funeral* (film; screenplay by Richard Curtis, directed by Mike Newell, 1994)

9 There were three of us in this marriage.

Diana, Princess of Wales (1961–1997): on the alleged adultery of Prince Charles, in interview on *Panorama*, BBC1, 20 Nov. 1995

10 Marriage as an institution developed from rape as a practice. Rape, originally defined as abduction, became marriage by capture. Marriage meant the taking was to extend in time, to be not only use of but possession of, or ownership.

Andrea Dworkin (b.1946), U.S. feminist critic: *Pornography* (1981), Ch.1

11 Marriage is socialism among two people.

Barbara Ehrenreich (b.1941), U.S. author and columnist: 'Socialism in One Household', first publ. in *Mother Jones*, 1987, rep. in *The Worst Years of Our Lives* (1991)

12 Married life requires shared mystery even when all the facts are known.

Richard Ford (b.1944), U.S. author: *The Sportswriter* (1986), p.137 of Flamingo edn. (1987)

13 Marriage accustomed one to the good things, so one came to take them for granted, but magnified the bad things, so they came to feel as painful as a grain in one's eye. An open window, a forgotten quart of milk, a TV set left blaring, socks on the bathroom floor could become occasions for incredible rage.

Marilyn French (b.1929), U.S. author and critic: Mira, in *The Women's Room* (1977), Ch.5, Sct.12

14 The problem with marriage is that it ends every night after making love, and it must be rebuilt every morning before breakfast.

Gabriel García Márquez (b.1928), Colombian author: Dr Urbino, in *Love in the Time of Cholera* (1985; tr.1988), p.209 of Penguin edn. (1989)

15 Every time a woman makes herself laugh at her husband's often-told jokes she betrays him. The man who looks at his woman and says 'What would I do without you?' is already destroyed.

Germaine Greer (b.1939), Australian feminist writer: *The Female Eunuch* (1970), 'Egotism'

16 The married are those who have taken the terrible risk of intimacy and, having taken it, know life without intimacy to be impossible.

Carolyn Heilbrun (b.1926), U.S. author and educator: 'Marriage is the Message', publ. in *Ms.* (New York), Aug. 1974

17 Marriage is an act of will that signifies and involves a mutual gift, which unites the spouses and binds them to their eventual souls, with whom they make up a sole family – a domestic church.

Pope John Paul II [Karol Wojtyla] (b.1920), Polish ecclesiastic: quoted in *The Observer* (London), 31 Jan. 1982

18 Marrying a man is like buying something you've been admiring for a long time in a shop window. You may love it when you get it home, but it doesn't always go with everything else in the house.

Jean Kerr (b.1923), U.S. author and playwright: *The Snake Has All the Lines* (1958), 'The Ten Worst Things About a Man'

19 The American woman's concept of marriage is a clearly etched picture of something un-inflated on the floor. A sleeping-bag without air, a beanbag without beans, a padded bra without pads. To work on it, you start pumping – what the magazines call 'breathing life into your marriage'. Do enough of this and the marriage becomes a kind of Banquo's ghost, a quasi-living entity.

Florence King (b.1936), U.S. author: *Reflections in a Jaundiced Eye* (1989), 'From Captain Marvel to Captain Valium'

20 All married couples should learn the art of battle as they should learn the art of making love. Good battle is objective and honest – never vicious or cruel. Good battle is healthy and constructive, and brings to a marriage the principle of equal partnership.

Ann Landers (b.1918), U.S. columnist: *Ann Landers Says Truth Is Stranger...* (1968), Ch.11

21 Marriage, well. I think of it as a marvellous thing for other people, like going to the stake.

Philip Larkin (1922–1985), British poet: letter, 12 March 1965, publ. in *Selected Letters of Philip Larkin 1940–1985* (ed. Anthony Thwaite 1992)

22 Progress of a marriage:
'There was a time when you couldn't
make me happy.
Now the time has come when you can't
make me unhappy.'

Irving Layton (b.1912), Canadian poet: *The Whole Bloody Bird* (1969), 'Aphs'

23 Rituals are important. Nowadays it's hip not be married. I'm not interested in being hip.

John Lennon (1940–1980), British rock musician: in *Playboy* (Chicago), Sept. 1980

24 Two by two in the ark of
the ache of it.

Denise Levertov (b.1923), U.S. poet: 'The Ache of Marriage', publ. in *O Taste and See* (1964)

25 There is, hidden or flaunted, a sword between the sexes till an entire marriage reconciles them.

C.S. Lewis (1898–1963), British author: *A Grief Observed* (1961), Pt.3

26 Say what you will, making marriage work is a woman's business. The institution was invented to do her homage; it was contrived for her protection. Unless she accepts it as such – as a beautiful, bountiful, but quite unequal association – the going will be hard indeed.

Phyllis McGinley (1905–1978), U.S. poet and author: *The Province of the Heart* (1959), 'The Honor of Being a Woman'

27 When it comes to marriage there's just this one basic variety. You're supposed to live together monogamously. You see what I'm saying? One size fits all? No way. Why can't we have different brands of marriage?

Jay McInerney (b.1955), U.S. author: Washington, in *Brightness Falls* (1992), Ch.1

28 The institution of marriage in all societies is a pattern within which the strains put by civilization on males and females alike must be resolved, a pattern within which men must learn, in return for a variety of elaborate rewards, new forms in which sexual spontaneity is still possible, and women must learn to discipline their receptivity to a thousand other considerations.

Margaret Mead (1901–1978), U.S. anthropologist: *Male and Female* (1949), Ch.10

29 In almost every marriage there is a selfish and an unselfish partner. A pattern is set up and soon becomes inflexible, of one person always making the demands and one person always giving way.

Iris Murdoch (b.1919), British novelist and philosopher: Martin Lynch-Gibbon, in *A Severed Head* (1961), Ch.2

30 Garth, marriage is punishment for shoplifting, in some countries.

Mike Myers (b.1964), Canadian comic and screenwriter: Wayne Campbell (Mike Myers), in *Wayne's World* (film; screenplay by Mike Myers and Bonnie and Terry Turner, directed by Penelope Spheeris, 1992)

31 Chains do not hold a marriage together. It is threads, hundreds of tiny threads which sew people together through the years. That is what makes a marriage last – more than passion or even sex!

Simone Signoret (b.1921), French actress: in the *Daily Mail* (London), 4 July 1978

32 The concerts you enjoy together
Neighbors you annoy together
Children you destroy together
That make marriage a joy.

Stephen Sondheim (b.1930), U.S. songwriter:
'The Little Things You Do Together' (song) in
Company (stage musical, 1970)

33 A happy marriage perhaps represents the ideal
of human relationship – a setting in which each
partner, while acknowledging the need of the
other, feels free to be what he or she by nature
is: a relationship in which instinct as well as
intellect can find expression; in which giving
and taking are equal; in which each accepts the
other, and I confronts Thou.

Anthony Storr (b.1920), British psychiatrist: *The
Integrity of the Personality* (1960), Ch.9

34 Marriage is nothing like being in prison!
Women are let out every day to go to the shops
and stuff, and quite a lot go to work.

Sue Townsend (b.1946), British author: Adrian
Mole's journal entry for 2 March, in *The Secret
Diary of Adrian Mole Aged 13¾* (1982)

35 Every marriage tends to consist of an aristocrat
and a peasant. Of a teacher and a learner.

John Updike (b.1932), U.S. author and critic:
Couples (1968), Ch.1

36 In this brave new cannibalistic world of ours,
all proper men are married, all proper women
too. It's our prudence, our reality, our safe
familiarity while we nibble and guzzle the
private parts of comparative strangers. Oh
strange new wondrous delicacies!

Fay Weldon (b.1933), British novelist: *Wicked
Women* (1995), 'Baked Alaska'

See also McInerney on COUPLES; Jong on
FRIENDS; WEDDINGS

MARRIAGE: Failed

1 There is a rhythm to the ending of a marriage
just like the rhythm of a courtship – only
backward. You try to start again but get into
blaming over and over. Finally you are both
worn out, exhausted, hopeless. Then lawyers
are called in to pick clean the corpses. The
death has occurred much earlier.

Erica Jong (b.1942), U.S. author: *How To Save
Your Own Life* (1977), 'There is a rhythm to the
ending...'

2 That a marriage ends is less than ideal; but all
things end under heaven, and if temporality is
held to be invalidating, then nothing real succeeds.

John Updike (b.1932), U.S. author and critic:
foreword to *Too Far To Go* (1979)

3 We treat the failure of marriage as though it
were the failure of individuals to achieve it – a
decline in grit or maturity or commitment or
stamina rather than the unraveling of a poorly
tied knot. Bourgeois marriage was meant to
concentrate friendship, romance, and sex into
an institution at once familial and economic.
Only the most intense surveillance could keep
such a bulky, ill-assorted load from bursting at
the seams.

Edmund White (b.1940), U.S. author: 'Sexual
Culture', first publ. in *Vanity Fair*, 1983, rep. in *The
Burning Library* (1994)

See also DIVORCE

MARRIAGE: and Love

1 Like everything which is not the involuntary
result of fleeting emotion but the creation of
time and will, any marriage, happy or unhappy, is infinitely more interesting than any
romance, however passionate.

W.H. Auden (1907–1973), Anglo-American poet: *A
Certain World* (1970), 'Marriage'

2 Love and marriage, love and marriage
Go together like a horse and carriage
Dad was told by mother
You can't have one without the other.

Sammy Cahn (1913–1993), U.S. songwriter: 'Love
and Marriage' (song, 1955). The song is best known
for Frank Sinatra's version

3 A man in love is incomplete until he has
married – then he's finished.

Zsa Zsa Gabor (b.1919), Hungarian-born U.S.
actress: quoted in *Newsweek* (New York), 28 March
1960

MARTYRDOM

1 Hunger strike is unlike any other form of
struggle. An IRA volunteer does not go out to
get killed; if he or she gets killed it is because he
or she makes a mistake or some circumstance
arises. But a hunger striker embarks on a
process which, from day one, is designed to
end in his or her death.

Gerry Adams (b.1948), Irish politician and leader of
Sinn Féin: 'Political Status', publ. in *Selected
Writings* (1994)

2 You are either alive and proud or you are dead,
and when you are dead, you can't care anyway.
And your method of death can itself be a
politicizing thing. So you die in the riots. For a
hell of a lot of them, in fact, there's really
nothing to lose – almost literally, given the
kind of situations they come from. So if you
can overcome the personal fear of death, which

is a highly irrational thing, you know, then you're on the way.

Steve Biko (1946–1977), South African anti-apartheid activist: 'Biko on Death', publ. in the *New Republic* (Washington D.C.), 7 Jan. 1978, rep. in *Steve Biko: Black Consciousness in South Africa* (ed. Millard Arnold, 1978), appendix

3 Martyrs, *cher ami*, must choose between being forgotten, mocked or made use of. As for being understood – never!

Albert Camus (1913–1960), French-Algerian philosopher and author: the narrator (Jean-Baptiste Clamence), in *The Fall* (1956), p.57 of Hamish Hamilton edn. (1957)

4 No human beings more dangerous than those who have suffered for a belief: the great persecutors are recruited from the martyrs not quite beheaded. Far from diminishing the appetite for power, suffering exasperates it.

E.M. Cioran (1911–1995), Rumanian-born French philosopher: *A Short History of Decay* (1949), Ch.1, 'Genealogy of Fanaticism'

5 If a man hasn't discovered something that he will die for, he isn't fit to live.

Martin Luther King Jr. (1929–1968), U.S. clergyman and civil rights leader: speech, 23 June 1963, Detroit, quoted in *The Days of Martin Luther King* by James Bishop (1971), Ch.4

See also Tarkovsky on ACTIVISM & PROTEST

MARXISM

1 Our tradition of political thought had its definite beginning in the teachings of Plato and Aristotle. I believe it came to a no less definite end in the theories of Karl Marx.

Hannah Arendt (1906–1975), German-born U.S. political philosopher: *Between Past and Future* (1961), Ch.1

2 The Marxist analysis has got nothing to do with what happened in Stalin's Russia: it's like blaming Jesus Christ for the Inquisition in Spain.

Tony Benn (b.1925), British Labour politician: quoted in *The Observer* (London), 27 April 1980

3 Marxism is not scientific: at the best, it has scientific prejudices.

Albert Camus (1913–1960), French-Algerian philosopher and author: *The Rebel* (1951; tr.1953), Pt.3, 'State Terrorism and Rational Terror'

4 One good reason for the popularity of 'reductionism' among the philosophical outposts of the Western Establishment is that it can be, and is, used as a device for trying to take the wind, so to speak, out of the sails of Marxism. ... In essence reductionism is a kind of anti-Marxist caricature of Marxist deter-

minism. It is what anti-Marxists pretend that Marxist determinism is.

Claud Cockburn (1904–1981), British author and journalist: *Cockburn Sums Up* (1981), 'Days of Hope'

5 Ask anyone committed to Marxist analysis how many angels on the head of a pin, and you will be asked in return to never mind the angels, tell me who controls the production of pins.

Joan Didion (b.1934), U.S. essayist: *The White Album* (1979), 'The Women's Movement'

6 Marxism exists in nineteenth-century thought as a fish exists in water; that is, it ceases to breathe anywhere else.

Michel Foucault (1926–1984), French philosopher: *The Order of Things: An Archaeology of the Human* (in French, *Les Mots et les Choses*, 1966; tr.1971), quoted in *The Lives of Michel Foucault* by David Macey (1993), Ch.7

7 It has been the acknowledged right of every Marxist scholar to read into Marx the particular meaning that he himself prefers and to treat all others with indignation.

J.K. Galbraith (b.1908), U.S. economist: *The Age of Uncertainty* (1977), Ch.3

8 Workers of the world forgive me.

Graffiti: on the bust of Karl Marx in Bucharest, reported in the *The Times* (London), 4 May 1990

9 When asked whether or not we are Marxists, our position is the same as that of a physicist or a biologist who is asked if he is a 'Newtonian', or if he is a 'Pasteurian'.

Ernesto 'Che' Guevara (1928–1967), Argentinian revolutionary leader: 'We Are Not Practical Revolutionaries', publ. in *Verde Olivo* (Havana), 8 Oct. 1960, rep. in *Venceremos!: The Speeches and Writings of Ernesto Che Guevara* (ed. John Gerassi, 1968)

10 There's something about Marxism that brings out warts – the only kind of growth this economic system encourages.

P.J. O'Rourke (b.1947), U.S. journalist: 'The Death of Communism', first publ. in *Rolling Stone* (New York), Nov. 1989, rep. in *Give War A Chance* (1992)

11 The Marxist vision of man without God must eventually be seen as an empty and a false faith – the second oldest in the world – first proclaimed in the Garden of Eden with whispered words of temptation: 'Ye shall be as gods.'

Ronald Reagan (b.1911), U.S. Republican politician and president: speech, 20 March 1981, to Conservative Political Action Conference, Washington D.C., publ. in *Speaking My Mind* (1990)

MASCULINITY

1   The masculine imagination lives in a state of perpetual revolt against the limitations of human life. In theological terms, one might say that all men, left to themselves, become gnostics. They may swagger like peacocks, but in their heart of hearts they all think sex an indignity and wish they could beget themselves on themselves. Hence the aggressive hostility toward women so manifest in most club-car stories.

W.H. Auden (1907–1973), Anglo-American poet: foreword to Phyllis McGinley's *Times Three: Selected Verse from Three Decades* (1960)

2   The American ideal of masculinity ... has created cowboys and Indians, good guys and bad guys, punks and studs, tough guys and softies, butch and faggot, black and white. It is an ideal so paralytically infantile that it is virtually forbidden – as an unpatriotic act – that the American boy evolves into the complexity of manhood.

James Baldwin (1924–1987), U.S. author: *The Price of the Ticket* (1985), 'Here Be Dragons'

3   Every modern male has, lying at the bottom of his psyche, a large, primitive being covered with hair down to his feet. Making contact with this Wild Man is the step the Eighties male or the Nineties male has yet to take. That bucketing-out process has yet to begin in our contemporary culture.

Robert Bly (b.1926), U.S. poet and author: *Iron John* (1990), Ch.1, 'Finding Iron John'

4   In this society, the norm of masculinity is phallic aggression. Male sexuality is, by definition, intensely and rigidly phallic. A man's identity is located in his conception of himself as the possessor of a phallus; a man's worth is located in his *pride* in phallic identity. The main characteristic of phallic identity is that *worth* is entirely contingent on the possession of a phallus. Since men have no other criteria for worth, no other notion of identity, those who do not have phalluses are not recognized as fully human.

Andrea Dworkin (b.1946), U.S. feminist critic: 'The Rape Atrocity and the Boy Next Door', speech, 1 March 1975, State University of New York, Stony Brook, publ. in *Our Blood* (1976), Ch.4

5   Unlike femininity, relaxed masculinity is at bottom empty, a limp nullity. While the female body is full of internal potentiality, the male is internally barren.... Manhood at the most basic level can be validated and expressed only in action.

George Gilder (b.1939), U.S. editor, speechwriter and author: *Sexual Suicide* (1973), Pt.1, Ch.1

6   The tragedy of machismo is that a man is never quite man enough.

Germaine Greer (b.1939), Australian feminist writer: 'My Mailer Problem', first publ. in *Esquire* (New York), Sept. 1971, rep. in *The Madwoman's Underclothes* (1986)

7   Masculinity is not something given to you, but something you gain. And you gain it by winning small battles with honor.

Norman Mailer (b.1923), U.S. author: 'Petty Notes on Some Sex in America', first publ. in *Playboy*, 1961–2, rep. in *Cannibals and Christians* (1966)

8   In the United States adherence to the values of the masculine mystique makes intimate, self-revealing, deep friendships between men unusual.

Myriam Miedzian, U.S. author: introduction to *Boys Will Be Boys* (1991)

9   A woman simply is, but a man must become. Masculinity is risky and elusive. It is achieved by a revolt from woman, and it is confirmed only by other men. ... Manhood coerced into sensitivity is no manhood at all.

Camille Paglia (b.1947), U.S. author and critic: 'Alice in Muscle Land', book review in the *Boston Globe*, 27 Jan. 1991, rep. in *Sex, Art, and American Culture* (1992)

THE MASSES

1   What will happen once the authentic mass man takes over, we do not know yet, although it may be a fair guess that he will have more in common with the meticulous, calculated correctness of Himmler than with the hysterical fanaticism of Hitler, will more resemble the stubborn dullness of Molotov than the sensual vindictive cruelty of Stalin.

Hannah Arendt (1906–1975), German-born U.S. political philosopher: of the masses in a totalitarian society, in *The Origins of Totalitarianism* (1951), Ch.10, Sct.2

2   The only freedom supposed to be left to the masses is that of grazing on the ration of simulacra the system distributes to each individual.

Michel de Certeau (1925–1986), French author and critic: *The Practice of Everyday Life* (1974), Ch.12

3   None of us knows all the potentialities that slumber in the spirit of the population, or all the ways in which that population can surprise us when there is the right interplay of events.

Václav Havel (b.1936), Czech playwright and president: *Disturbing the Peace* (1986; tr.1990), Ch.3

4 There is a grandeur in the uniformity of the mass. When a fashion, a dance, a song, a slogan or a joke sweeps like wildfire from one end of the continent to the other, and a hundred million people roar with laughter, sway their bodies in unison, hum one song or break forth in anger and denunciation, there is the over-powering feeling that in this country we have come nearer the brotherhood of man than ever before.

Eric Hoffer (1902–1983), U.S. philosopher: *The Passionate State of Mind* (1955), Aph.169

5 I have witnessed the tremendous energy of the masses. On this foundation it is possible to accomplish any task whatsoever.

Mao Zedong (1893–1976), Chinese leader: said in Sept. 1958, quoted in *Mao and China: From Revolution to Revolution* by Stanley Karnow (1972), Ch.5

6 I can't help feeling wary when I hear anything said about the masses. First you take their faces from 'em, calling them the masses, and then you accuse 'em of not having any faces.

J.B. Priestley (1894–1984), British author: *Saturn Over the Water* (1961), Ch.2

7 Men tied fast to the absolute, bled of their differences, drained of their dreams by authoritarian leeches until nothing but pulp is left, become a massive, sick Thing whose sheer weight is used ruthlessly by ambitious men. Here is the real enemy of the people: our own selves dehumanized into 'the masses'. And where is the David who can slay this giant?

Lillian Smith (1897–1966), U.S. author: prologue to *The Journey* (1954)

MASTURBATION

1 Hey, don't knock masturbation! It's sex with someone I love.

Woody Allen (b.1935), U.S. film-maker: Alvy Singer (Allen), in *Annie Hall* (film; screenplay by Woody Allen and Marshall Brickman, directed by Woody Allen, 1977)

2 I tell women, 'Go and masturbate! Get loads of kinky books and masturbate every day! *They* do it from the age of nine!'

Björk (b.1967), Icelandic singer: in *New Musical Express* (London) 1993, quoted in *NME Book of Quotes* (1995), 'Sex'

3 Masturbation is not only an expression of self-regard: it is also the natural emotional outlet of those who ... have already accepted as inevitable the wide gulf between their real futures and the expectations of their fantasies.

Quentin Crisp (b.1908), British author: *The Naked Civil Servant* (1968), Ch.2

4 Removed from its more restrictive sense, masturbation has become an expression for everything that has proved, for lack of human contact, to be void of meaning. We have communication problems, suffer from egocentrism and narcissism, are frustrated by information glut and loss of environment; we stagnate despite the rising GNP.

Günter Grass (b.1927), German author: *From the Diary of a Snail* (1972), 'On Stasis in Progress'

5 Women are denied masturbation even more severely than men and that's another method of control – they're not taught to please themselves. ... Most women – it takes them a while to warm up to the 'situation', but once they get into it, I'm sure they're going to get just as hooked as – well, everyone I know is!

Lydia Lunch (b.1959), U.S. rock singer: interview in *Angry Women* issue of *Re/Search* (San Francisco), No.13, 1991

6 Masturbation: the primary sexual activity of mankind. In the nineteenth century, it was a disease; in the twentieth, it's a cure.

Thomas Szasz (b.1920), U.S. psychiatrist: *The Second Sin* (1973), 'Sex'

MATERIALISM

1 Young people everywhere have been allowed to choose between love and a garbage disposal unit. Everywhere they have chosen the garbage disposal unit.

Guy Debord (1931–1994), French Situationist philosopher: *The Incomplete Works of the Situationist International* (ed. Christopher Gray, 1974), 'Formula for a New City'

2 The strongest argument for the un-materialistic character of American life is the fact that we tolerate conditions that are, from a negative point of view, intolerable. What the foreigner finds most objectionable in American life is its lack of basic comfort. No nation with any sense of material well-being would endure the food we eat, the cramped apartments we live in, the noise, the traffic, the crowded subways and buses. American life, in large cities, is a perpetual assault on the senses and the nerves; it is out of asceticism, out of unworldliness, precisely, that we bear it.

Mary McCarthy (1912–1989), U.S. author and critic: 'America the Beautiful', first publ. in *Commentary* (New York) Sept. 1947, rep. in *On the Contrary* (1961)

3 The people recognize themselves in their commodities; they find their soul in their automobile, hi-fi set, split-level home, kitchen equipment.

Herbert Marcuse (1898–1979), U.S. political philosopher: *One-Dimensional Man* (1964), Ch.1

4 When we try in good faith to believe in materialism, in the exclusive reality of the physical, we are asking our selves to step aside; we are disavowing the very realm where we exist and where all things precious are kept – the realm of emotion and conscience, of memory and intention and sensation.

John Updike (b.1932), U.S. author and critic: *Self-Consciousness: Memoirs* (1989), Ch.6

5 The organization controlling the material equipment of our everyday life is such that what in itself would enable us to construct it richly plunges us instead into a poverty of abundance, making alienation all the more intolerable as each convenience promises liberation and turns out to be only one more burden. We are condemned to slavery to the means of liberation.

Raoul Vaneigem (b.1934), Belgian Situationist philosopher: 'Basic Banalities II', first publ. in *Internationale Situationiste* (Paris), Jan. 1963, rep. in *Situationist International Anthology* (ed. Ken Knabb, 1981)

See also McCarthy on EUROPE; Ruthven on FUNDAMENTALISM; POSSESSIONS; Muggeridge on SEX

MATHEMATICS

1 How happy the lot of the mathematician! He is judged solely by his peers, and the standard is so high that no colleague or rival can ever win a reputation he does not deserve. No cashier writes a letter to the press complaining about the incomprehensibility of Modern Mathematics and comparing it unfavourably with the good old days when mathematicians were content to paper irregularly shaped rooms and fill bathtubs without closing the waste pipe.

W.H. Auden (1907–1973), Anglo-American poet: *The Dyer's Hand* (1962), Pt.1, 'Writing'

2 As far as the laws of mathematics refer to reality, they are not certain, and as far as they are certain, they do not refer to reality.

Albert Einstein (1879–1955), German-born U.S. theoretical physicist: quoted in *The Tao of Physics* by Fritjof Capra (1975), Ch.2

3 Nobody before the Pythagoreans had thought that mathematical relations held the secret of the universe. Twenty-five centuries later, Europe is still blessed and cursed with their heritage. To non-European civilizations, the idea that numbers are the key to both wisdom and power, seems never to have occurred.

Arthur Koestler (1905–1983), Hungarian-born British novelist and essayist: *The Sleepwalkers* (1959), Pt.1, Ch.2, Sct.4

4 Stand firm in your refusal to remain conscious during algebra. In real life, I assure you, there is no such thing as algebra.

Fran Lebowitz (b.1951), U.S. journalist: *Social Studies* (1981), 'Tips for Teens'

5 Only mathematical thought manages to free itself from the camouflaged egoism of scholastic knowledge and its mystical and rationalist relics.

Emmanuel Levinas (b.1905), French Jewish philosopher: 'Being a Westerner' (1951), rep. in *Difficult Freedom* (1990), Pt.1

6 You've got many refinements. I don't think you need to worry about your failure at long division. I mean, after all, you got through short division, and short division is all that a lady ought to be called on to cope with...

Tennessee Williams (1911–1983), U.S. playwright: Silva (Karl Malden) speaking to Baby Doll, in *Baby Doll* (film; screenplay by Tennessee Williams, directed by Elia Kazan, 1956)

See also Bronowski on NUMBERS

MATURITY

1 Ah, but I was so much older then,
   I'm younger than that now.

Bob Dylan (b.1941), U.S. singer and songwriter: 'My Back Pages' (song) on the album *Another Side of Bob Dylan* (1964)

2 Maturity: among other things, the unclouded happiness of the child at play, who takes it for granted that he is at one with his play-mates.

Dag Hammarskjöld (1905–1961), Swedish statesman and secretary-general of U.N.: note, written 1953, publ. in *Markings* (1963), 'Night is Drawing Nigh'

3 True maturity is only reached when a man realizes he has become a father figure to his girlfriends' boyfriends – and he accepts it.

Larry McMurtry (b.1936), U.S. screenwriter, novelist and essayist: Danny Deck, in *Some Can Whistle* (1989), Pt.1, Ch.12

See also Kael on TEENAGERS

MEANING

1 Everywhere one seeks to produce meaning, to make the world signify, to render it visible. We are not, however, in danger of lacking meaning; quite the contrary, we are gorged with meaning and it is killing us.

Jean Baudrillard (b.1929), French semiologist: *The Ecstasy of Communication* (1987), 'Seduction, or the Superficial Abyss'

2 Just as all thought, and primarily that of non-signification, signifies something, so there is no art that has no signification.
Albert Camus (1913–1960), French-Algerian philosopher and author: *The Rebel* (1951; tr.1953), Pt.4

3 The fact that life has no meaning is a reason to live – moreover, the only one.
E.M. Cioran (1911–1995), Rumanian-born French philosopher: *Anathemas and Admirations* (1986), 'Fractures'

4 The deeper the experience of an absence of meaning – in other words, of absurdity – the more energetically meaning is sought.
Václav Havel (b.1936), Czech playwright and president: *Disturbing the Peace* (1986; tr.1990), Ch.5

5 Social criticism begins with grammar and the re-establishing of meanings.
Octavio Paz (b.1914), Mexican poet and essayist: *The Other Mexico: Critique of the Pyramid* (1972), 'Development and Other Mirages'

See also de Man on LANGUAGE; Chomsky on LANGUAGE: GRAMMAR, SPELLING & PUNCTUATION

MEAT

1 I've always been very moved by pictures about slaughterhouses and meat, and to me they belong very much to the whole thing of the Crucifixion.
Francis Bacon (1910–1992), British artist: interview, recorded Oct. 1962 (broadcast BBC, 23 March 1963), publ. in *The Brutality of Fact: Interviews with Francis Bacon* by David Sylvester (1975)

2 To eat steak rare ... represents both a nature and a morality.
Roland Barthes (1915–1980), French semiologist: *Mythologies* (1957; tr.1972), 'Steak and Chips'

3 Don't get a job in an abattoir. Don't be a butcher. The idea that people have to do these jobs for a livelihood is ridiculous. They can get other jobs. Shoplift, man. Better to be a prostitute than cut an animal's head off for a living.
Chrissie Hynde (b.1952), U.S. rock musician: in *New Musical Express* (London), 1989, quoted in *NME Book of Quotes* (1995), 'Politics'

4 The fact is that our beef is as safe as the Rock of Gibraltar, even though we still have things to learn about BSE itself.
Colin Maclean (b.1938), British director of the Meat and Livestock Commission: quoted in *The Guardian* (London), 31 Dec. 1994

5 Our meat comes to us from factory farms where immobilized, fast-fatted cattle and pigs are fed by the time clock and scientifically

tranquilized to hold down the often violent anxiety that comes of lifelong close confinement. These beasts we eat are all but a fabricated counterfeit; we do not even grant them the dignity of setting foot in the open air once in a lifetime. For after all, what difference does their dignity make to us? Meat is meat, isn't it?
Theodore Roszak (b.1933), U.S. social critic: *Where the Wasteland Ends* (1972), Ch.1

THE MEDIA

1 The futility of everything that comes to us from the media is the inescapable consequence of the absolute inability of that particular stage to remain silent. Music, commercial breaks, news flashes, adverts, news broadcasts, movies, presenters – there is no alternative but to fill the screen; otherwise there would be an irremediable void. ... That's why the slightest technical hitch, the slightest slip on the part of the presenter becomes so exciting, for it reveals the depth of the emptiness squinting out at us through this little window.
Jean Baudrillard (b.1929), French semiologist: *Cool Memories* (1987; tr.1990), Ch.4

2 The media network has its idols, but its principal idol is its own style which generates an aura of winning and leaves the rest in darkness. It recognises neither pity nor pitilessness.
John Berger (b.1926), British author and critic: 'The Third Week of August, 1991', first publ. in *The Guardian* (London), 4 Sept. 1991, rep. in *Keeping a Rendezvous* (1992)

3 I think that we have created a new kind of person in a way. We have created a child who will be so exposed to the media that he will be lost to his parents by the time he is twelve.
David Bowie (b.1947), British pop singer: quoted in *Melody Maker* (London), 22 Jan. 1972, rep. in *The Faber Book of Pop* (ed. Hanif Kureishi and Jon Savage, 1995), Pt.6, '1972: Oh You Pretty Thing'

4 Society cannot share a common communication system so long as it is split into warring factions.
Bertolt Brecht (1898–1956), German playwright and poet: 'A Short Organum for the Theatre' (1949), para.55, rep. in *Brecht on Theatre* (ed. and tr. John Willett, 1964)

5 Cinema, radio, television, magazines are a school of inattention: people look without seeing, listen in without hearing.
Robert Bresson (b.1907), French film-maker: *Notes on the Cinematographer* (1975), '1950–1958: Exercises'

6 The media transforms the great silence of things into its opposite. Formerly constituting a secret, the real now talks constantly. News

reports, information, statistics, and surveys are everywhere.

Michel de Certeau (1925–1986), French author and critic: *The Practice of Everyday Life* (1974), Ch.13, 'The Establishment of the Real'

7 The United States is unusual among the industrial democracies in the rigidity of the system of ideological control – 'indoctrination', we might say – exercised through the mass media.
Noam Chomsky (b.1928), U.S. linguist and political analyst: *Language and Responsibility* (1979), 'Politics'

8 The medium is the message. This is merely to say that the personal and social consequences of any medium – that is, of any extension of ourselves – result from the new scale that is introduced into our affairs by each extension of ourselves, or by any new technology.
Marshall McLuhan (1911–1980), Canadian communications theorist: *Understanding Media* (1964), Ch.1

9 Commercial jazz, soap opera, pulp fiction, comic strips, the movies set the images, mannerisms, standards, and aims of the urban masses. In one way or another, everyone is equal before these cultural machines; like technology itself, the mass media are nearly universal in their incidence and appeal. They are a kind of common denominator, a kind of scheme for pre-scheduled, mass emotions.
C. Wright Mills (1916–1962), U.S. sociologist: *White Collar* (1951), Ch.15, Sct.3

10 If I use the media, even with tricks, to publicize a black youth being shot in the back in Teaneck, New Jersey ... then I should be praised for it, and it's more of a comment on them than me that it would take tricks to make them cover the loss of life.
Al Sharpton (b.1954), U.S. civil rights campaigner: in the *Independent on Sunday* (London), 21 April 1991

11 The media overestimates its own importance. I was on the cover of everything for three years but I still only had half a bottle of milk in the fridge.
Mark E. Smith (b.1960), British rock musician: in *New Musical Express* (London), 1990, quoted in *NME Book of Quotes* (1995), 'Fame'

12 The corporate grip on opinion in the United States is one of the wonders of the Western World. No First World country has ever managed to eliminate so entirely from its media all objectivity – much less dissent.
Gore Vidal (b.1925), U.S. novelist and critic: *A View from the Diner's Club* (1991), 'Cue the Green God, Ted'

See also Alloway on CULTURE; McLuhan on THE INTERNET; JOURNALISM; MAGAZINES; NEWSPAPERS; THE PRESS; RADIO; TELEVISION

MEDICINE

1 Just a spoonful of sugar helps the medicine go down.
Julie Andrews (b.1934), British actress and singer: 'A Spoonful of Sugar' (song, written by Richard and Robert Sherman) in *Mary Poppins* (film, 1964)

2 I sing the love homeopathic:
it cures you before very long.
You just take a speck
of that pain-in-the-neck
and let it dissolve on your tongue.
Connie Bensley (b.1929), British poet: 'A Cure for Love', publ. in *Choosing to be a Swan* (1994)

3 The whole imposing edifice of modern medicine is like the celebrated tower of Pisa – slightly off balance.
Charles, Prince of Wales (b.1948): quoted in *The Observer* (London), 2 Jan. 1983

4 Injections ... are the best thing ever invented for feeding doctors.
Gabriel García Márquez (b.1928), Colombian author: Doctor Giraldo, in *In Evil Hour* (1968; tr.1979), p.139 of Jonathan Cape edn. (1980)

5 We have to ask ourselves whether medicine is to remain a humanitarian and respected profession or a new but depersonalized science in the service of prolonging life rather than diminishing human suffering.
Elisabeth Kübler-Ross (b.1926), Swiss-born U.S. psychiatrist: *On Death and Dying* (1969), Ch.2

MEDIOCRITY

1 Some men are born mediocre, some men achieve mediocrity, and some men have mediocrity thrust upon them. With Major Major it had been all three.
Joseph Heller (b.1923), U.S. novelist: *Catch-22* (1961), Ch.9

2 The real antichrist is he who turns the wine of an original idea into the water of mediocrity.
Eric Hoffer (1902–1983), U.S. philosopher: *Reflections on the Human Condition* (1973), Aph.109

3 The world's made up of individuals who don't want to be heroes.
Brian Moore (b.1921), Irish novelist: in *The Sunday Times* (London), 15 April 1990

See also Anderson on PERFORMANCE

MEETINGS

1 Meetings are a great trap. Soon you find yourself trying to get agreement and then the people who disagree come to think they have a right to be persuaded.... However, they are indispensable when you don't want to do anything.
J.K. Galbraith (b.1908), U.S. economist: written while serving as U.S. ambassador to India 1961–63, publ. in *Ambassador's Journal* (1969), Ch.5

2 Whoever invented the meeting must have had Hollywood in mind. I think they should consider giving Oscars for meetings: Best Meeting of the Year, Best Supporting Meeting, Best Meeting Based on Material from Another Meeting.
William Goldman (b.1931), U.S. screenwriter and novelist: *Adventures in the Screen Trade* (1983), Ch.2

3 I love meetings with suits. I *live* for meetings with suits. I love them because I know they had a really boring week and I walk in there with my orange velvet leggings and drop popcorn in my cleavage and then fish it out and eat it. I like that. I know I'm entertaining them and I know that they know. Obviously, the best meetings are with suits that are intelligent, because then things are operating on a whole other level.
Madonna (b.1959), U.S. singer and actress: in *Vanity Fair* (New York), April 1991

MEMORY

1 The charm, one might say the genius of memory, is that it is choosy, chancy, and temperamental: it rejects the edifying cathedral and indelibly photographs the small boy outside, chewing a hunk of melon in the dust.
Elizabeth Bowen (1899–1973), Anglo-Irish novelist: in *Vogue* (New York), 15 Sept. 1955

2 You have to begin to lose your memory, if only in bits and pieces, to realize that memory is what makes our lives. Life without memory is no life at all, just as an intelligence without the possibility of expression is not really an intelligence. Our memory is our coherence, our reason, our feeling, even our action. Without it, we are nothing.
Luis Buñuel (1900–1983), Spanish film-maker: *My Last Breath* (autobiography, 1983), Ch.1

3 You've had most of your important memories by the time you're thirty. After that, memory becomes water overflowing into an already full cup.
Douglas Coupland (b.1961), Canadian author: *Life After God* (1994), 'My Hotel Year'

4 All stimulation generates a memory – and these memories have to *go* somewhere. Our bodies are essentially diskettes.
Douglas Coupland: Karla, in *Microserfs* (1995), 'Oop: Thursday – Later that week'

5 The difference between false memories and true ones is the same as for jewels: it is always the false ones that look the most real, the most brilliant.
Salvador Dali (1904–1989), Spanish painter: *The Secret Life of Salvador Dali* (1948), Ch.4

6 People may correctly remember the events of twenty years ago (a remarkable feat), but who remembers his fears, his disgusts, his tone of voice? It is like trying to bring back the weather of that time.
Martha Gellhorn (b.1908), U.S. journalist and author: *The Face of War* (1959, rev.1986), introduction to 'The War in Finland'

7 The light of memory, or rather the light that memory lends to things, is the palest light of all. ... I am not quite sure whether I am dreaming or remembering, whether I have lived my life or dreamed it. Just as dreams do, memory makes me profoundly aware of the unreality, the evanescence of the world, a fleeting image in the moving water.
Eugène Ionesco (1912–1994), Rumanian-born French playwright: *Present Past – Past Present* (1968), Ch.5

8 The struggle of man against power is the struggle of memory against forgetting.
Milan Kundera (b.1929), Czech-born French author and critic: Mirek, in *The Book of Laughter and Forgetting* (1978; tr.1980), Pt.1, Ch.2

9 Human memory is a marvellous but fallacious instrument. ... The memories which lie within us are not carved in stone; not only do they tend to become erased as the years go by, but often they change, or even increase by incorporating extraneous features.
Primo Levi (1919–1987), Italian chemist and author: *The Drowned and the Saved* (1988), Ch.1

10 The selective memory isn't selective enough.
Blake Morrison (b.1950), British poet and critic: in the *Independent on Sunday* (London), 16 June 1991

11 Memory is a parade of dead men.
Oswald Mosley (1896–1980), British fascist leader: *My Life* (1968), Ch.3

12 What we remember is what we become. What we have forgotten is more kindly and disturbs only our dreams. We become resemblances of our past.
John Osborne (1929–1994), British playwright: *Almost a Gentleman* (1991), Ch.26

13 My memory is so very untrustworthy. It's as fickle as a fox. Ask me to name the third lateral

bloodvessel that runs east to west when I lie on my face at sundown, or the percentage of chalk to be found in the knuckles of an average spinster in her fifty-seventh year, ha, ha, ha! – or even ask me, my dear boy, to give details of the pulse rate of frogs two minutes before they die of scabies – these things are no tax upon my memory, ha, ha, ha! but ask me to remember exactly what you said your problems were, a minute ago, and you will find that my memory has forsaken me utterly.

Mervyn Peake (1911–1968), British author and illustrator: Doctor Prunesquallor to Steerpike, in *Titus Groan* (1946), 'At the Prunesquallors'

14 It's a pleasure to share one's memories. Everything remembered is dear, endearing, touching, precious. At least the past is safe – though we didn't know it at the time. We know it now. Because it's in the past; because we have survived.

Susan Sontag (b.1933), U.S. essayist: 'Debriefing', first publ. in the *American Review* (New York), Sept. 1973, rep. in *I, Etcetera* (1978)

15 That is my major preoccupation – memory, the kingdom of memory. I want to protect and enrich that kingdom, glorify that kingdom and serve it.

Elie Wiesel (b.1928), Rumanian-born U.S. writer: interview in *Writers at Work* (Eighth Series, ed. George Plimpton, 1988)

16 Life is all memory except for the one present moment that goes by you so quick you hardly catch it going.

Tennessee Williams (1911–1983), U.S. playwright: Mrs Goforth, in *The Milk Train Doesn't Stop Here Anymore* (1963), Sc.3

17 The effectiveness of our memory banks is determined not by the total number of facts we take in, but the number we wish to reject.

Jon Wynne-Tyson (b.1924), British author: *Food for a Future* (1975), Ch.2

18 The memory of most men is an abandoned cemetery where lie, unsung and unhonoured, the dead whom they have ceased to cherish. Any lasting grief is reproof to their forgetfulness.

Marguerite Yourcenar (1903–1987), French novelist: *Memoirs of Hadrian* (1954), 'Saeculum Aureum'

See also Havel on STORY-TELLING

MEN

1 Poor little men, poor little cocks! As soon as they're old enough, they swell their plumage to be conquerors... If they only knew that it's enough to be just a little bit wounded and sad in order to obtain everything without fighting for it.

Jean Anouilh (1910–1987), French playwright: Araminthe, in *Cécile* (1951)

2 Men are not to be told anything they might find too painful; the secret depths of human nature, the sordid physicalities, might overwhelm or damage them. For instance, men often faint at the sight of their own blood, to which they are not accustomed. For this reason you should never stand behind one in the line at the Red Cross donor clinic.

Margaret Atwood (b.1939), Canadian novelist, poet and critic: describing her mother's beliefs, in 'Significant Moments in the Life of my Mother', publ. in *Close Company: Stories of Mothers and Daughters* (ed. Christine Park and Caroline Heaton, 1987)

3 Left to itself the masculine imagination has very little appreciation for the here and now; it prefers to dwell on what is absent, on what has been or may be. If men are more punctual than women, it is because they know that, without the external discipline of clock time, they would never get anything done.

W.H. Auden (1907–1973), Anglo-American poet: foreword to *Times Three: Selected Verse from Three Decades* by Phyllis McGinley (1960)

4 Men's private self-worlds are rather like our geographical world's seasons, storm, and sun, deserts, oases, mountains and abysses, the endless-seeming plateaus, darkness and light, and always the sowing and the reaping.

Faith Baldwin (1893–1978), U.S. author: *Harvest of Hope* (1962), 'April'

5 The question arises as to whether it is possible *not* to live in the world of men and still to live in the world.

Louise Bernikow (b.1940), U.S. journalist: introduction to *The World Split Open* (1974)

6 Bloody men are like bloody buses –
You wait for about a year
And as soon as one approaches your stop
Two or three others appear.

Wendy Cope (b.1945), British poet: 'Bloody Men', publ. in *Serious Concerns* (1992)

7 Men are not in any sense irreplaceable, except in one's private life.

Edith Cresson (b.1934), French politician and prime minister: quoted in the *International Herald Tribune* (Paris), 20 May 1991

8 All real men are gentle; without tenderness, a man is uninteresting.

Marlene Dietrich (1904–1992), German-born U.S. actress: referring to Ernest Hemingway (described as 'gentle'), quoted in *Papa Hemingway* by A.E. Hotchner (1966 edn.), Pt.1, Ch.1

9 Before they're plumbers or writers or taxi drivers or unemployed or journalists, before everything else, men are men. Whether heterosexual or homosexual. The only difference is that some of them remind you of it as soon as you meet them, and others wait for a little while.
Marguerite Duras (1914–1996), French author and film-maker: *Practicalities* (1987; tr.1990), 'Men'

10 Only when manhood is dead – and it will perish when ravaged femininity no longer sustains it – only then will we know what it is to be free.
Andrea Dworkin (b.1946), U.S. feminist critic: 'The Root Cause', speech, 26 Sept. 1975, Massachusetts Institute of Technology, publ. in *Our Blood* (1976), Ch.9

11 Considering the absence of legal coercion, the surprising thing is that men have for so long, and, on the whole, so reliably, adhered to what we might call the 'breadwinner ethic'.
Barbara Ehrenreich (b.1941), U.S. author and columnist: *The Hearts of Men* (1983), Ch.1

12 Providing for one's family as a good husband and father is a water-tight excuse for making money hand over fist. Greed may be a sin, exploitation of other people might, on the face of it, look rather nasty, but who can blame a man for 'doing the best' for his children?
Eva Figes (b.1932), Anglo-German author: 'A View of My Own', publ. in *Nova* (London), Jan. 1973

13 The world men inhabit ... is rather bleak. It is a world full of doubt and confusion, where vulnerability must be hidden, not shared; where competition, not co-operation, is the order of the day; where men sacrifice the possibility of knowing their own children and sharing in their upbringing, for the sake of a job they may have chosen by chance, which may not suit them and which in many cases dominates their lives to the exclusion of much else.
Anna Ford (b.1943), British radio and television journalist: concluding chapter of *Men* (1985)

14 I find that my years of research have confirmed something even the most uninstructed woman takes as given: Inside every adult male is a denied little boy. He loved his father, but was taught to show that love only through mindless imitation of his father's mindless imitation of *his* father's Victorian authoritarianism. He loved his mother, but feared her power.
Nancy Friday (b.1937), U.S. author: *Men in Love* (1980), Ch.22

15 All societies on the verge of death are masculine. A society can survive with only one man; no society will survive a shortage of women.
Germaine Greer (b.1939), Australian feminist writer: *Sex and Destiny* (1984), Ch.3

16 Not only is it harder to be a man, it is also harder to become one.
Arianna Huffington [formerly Arianna Stassinopoulos] (b.1950), Greek author: *The Female Woman* (1973), 'The Male Man'

17 All men are homosexual, some turn straight. It must be very odd to be a straight man because your sexuality is hopelessly defensive. It's like an ideal of racial purity.
Derek Jarman (1942–1994), British film-maker, artist and author: *At Your Own Risk: A Saint's Testament* (1992), '1940's'

18 Next to the striking of fire and the discovery of the wheel, the greatest triumph of what we call civilization was the domestication of the human male.
Max Lerner (1902–1992), U.S. author and columnist: 'The Revolt of the American Father', first publ. in the *New York Post*, 16 June 1958, rep. in *The Unfinished Country* (1959), Pt.2

19 Effeminate men intrigue me more than anything in the world. I see them as my alter egos. I feel very drawn to them. I think like a guy, but I'm feminine. So I relate to feminine men.
Madonna (b.1959), U.S. singer and actress: in *Vanity Fair* (New York), April 1991

20 Because there is very little honor left in American life, there is a certain built-in tendency to destroy masculinity in American men.
Norman Mailer (b.1923), U.S. author: 'Petty Notes on Some Sex in America' (1962–3), rep. in *Cannibals and Christians* (1966)

21 As long as male behavior is taken to be the norm, there can be no serious questioning of male traits and behavior. A norm is by definition a standard for judging; it is not itself subject to judgment.
Myriam Miedzian, U.S. author: *Boys Will Be Boys* (1991), Ch.1

22 Don't accept rides from strange men,
and remember that all men are as strange as hell.
Robin Morgan (b.1941), U.S. feminist author and poet: 'Letter to a Sister Underground', in introduction to *Sisterhood is Powerful* (1970)

23 I love the male body, it's better designed than the male mind.
Andrea Newman (b.1938), British author: in *Today* (London), 30 Sept. 1988

24 Men are the enemies of women. Promising sublime intimacy, unequalled passion, amazing security and grace, they nevertheless exploit and injure in a myriad subtle ways. Without men the world would be a better place: softer, kinder, more loving; calmer, quieter, more humane.
Ann Oakley (b.1944), British sociologist and author: *Taking It Like a Woman* (1984), 'A French Letter'

25 Men know they are sexual exiles. They wander the earth seeking satisfaction, craving and despising, never content. There is nothing in that anguished motion for women to envy.
Camille Paglia (b.1947), U.S. author and critic: *Sexual Personae* (1990), Ch.1

26 Most men act so tough and strong on the outside because on the inside, we are scared, weak, and fragile. Men, not women, are the weaker sex.
Jerry Rubin (1938–1994), U.S. essayist and radical leader: in the *Chicago Tribune*, 16 March 1978

27 Show me a guy who has feelings, and I'll show you a sucker.
Frank Sinatra (b.1915), U.S. singer and actor: Johnny Baron (Frank Sinatra), in *Suddenly* (film; screenplay by Richard Sale, directed by Lewis Allen, 1954)

28 To call a man an animal is to flatter him; he's a machine, a walking dildo.
Valerie Solanas (1936–1988), U.S. actress and writer: *The SCUM Manifesto* (1968). The acronym *SCUM* stood for 'Society for Cutting Up Men'

29 There is hardly an American male of my generation who has not at one time or another tried to master the victory cry of the great ape as it issued from the androgynous chest of Johnny Weissmuller, to the accompaniment of thousands of arms and legs snapping during attempts to swing from tree to tree in the backyards of the Republic.
Gore Vidal (b.1925), U.S. novelist and critic: 'The Waking Dream: Tarzan Revisited', publ. in *Esquire* (New York), Dec. 1963

30 I think we're a kind of desperation. We're sort of a maddening luxury. The basic and essential human is the woman, and all that we're doing is trying to brighten up the place. That's why all the birds who belong to our sex have prettier feathers – because males have got to try and justify their existence.
Orson Welles (1915–1985), U.S. film-maker and actor: interview with David Frost in *The Americans* by David Frost (1970), 'Can a Martian Survive by Pretending to be a Leading American Actor?'

31 It is not possible for a man to be elegant without a touch of femininity.
Vivienne Westwood (b.1941), British fashion designer: in *The Independent* (London), 12 July 1990

32 Hooray Henries are aged between 18 and 30; main interest, getting drunk together; ambition, if ambitious: to get drunk enough to do some crazy thing which will go down in the Hooray annals as a Historic Act of Hilarity.
Peter York (b.1950), and **Ann Barr**, British journalists: *The Official Sloane Ranger's Handbook* (1982), 'Hooray Henry'

See also Dworkin on THE BODY; White on LUST; MASCULINITY; Billings on MONEY; Dworkin on NIGHT; WIMPS; Mead on WOMEN; WOMEN: AND MEN

MEN: the Female View

1 The trouble with some women is that they get all excited about nothing – and then marry him.
Cher (b.1946), U.S. singer and actress: quoted in *Hammer and Tongues* (ed. Michèle Brown and Ann O'Connor, 1986)

2 You have to be very fond of men. Very, very fond. You have to be very fond of them to love them. Otherwise they're simply unbearable.
Marguerite Duras (1914–1996), French author and film-maker: *Practicalities* (1987; tr.1990), 'Men'

3 Whatever they may be in public life, whatever their relations with men, in their relations with women, all men are rapists and that's all they are. They rape us with their eyes, their laws, their codes.
Marilyn French (b.1929), U.S. author: Valerie, in *The Women's Room* (1977), Ch.5, Sct.19

4 I have always been principally interested in men for sex. I've always thought any sane woman would be a lover of women because loving men is such a mess. I have always wished I'd fall in love with a woman. Damn.
Germaine Greer (b.1939), Australian feminist writer: in the *New York Times Book Review*, 11 Oct. 1992

5 They're either married or gay. And if they're not gay, they've just broken up with the most wonderful woman in the world or they've just broken up with a bitch who looks just like me. They're in transition from a monogamous relationship and they need more space or they're tired of space but they just can't commit or they want to commit but they're afraid to get close. They want to get close, you don't want to get near them.
Lawrence Kasdan (b.1949), U.S. film-maker: Meg (Mary Kay Place) to Sarah, in *The Big Chill* (film; screenplay by Lawrence Kasdan and Barabara Benedek, directed by Lawrence Kasdan, 1983)

6 For a young man's a beauty, so firm and so fresh,
No widening of girth and no sagging of flesh.
No '*Where are my slippers?*' or '*Please, not tonight*'.
His chin is not twinning, his eyes are still bright.
Susan Kelly, British poet: 'Blind Cupid', publ. in *The Virago Book of Wicked Verse* (ed. Jill Dawson, 1992)

7 Sometimes I have a notion that what might improve the situation is to have women take over the occupations of government and trade and to give men their freedom. Let them do what they are best at. While we scrawl inter-office memos and direct national or extra-national affairs, men could spend *all* their time inventing wheels, peering at stars, composing poems, carving statues, exploring continents – discovering, reforming, or crying out in a sacramental wilderness. Efficiency would probably increase, and no one would have to worry so much about the Gaza Strip or an election.

Phyllis McGinley (1905–1978), U.S. poet and author: *The Province of the Heart* (1959), 'Some of My Best Friends...'

8 He may have hair upon his chest
But, sister, so has Lassie.

Cole Porter (1891–1964), U.S. composer and lyricist: 'I Hate Men' (song), in *Kiss Me Kate* (stage musical, 1948)

9 Just as humans have a prior right to existence over dogs by virtue of being more highly evolved and having a superior consciousness, so women have a prior right to existence over men. The elimination of any male is, therefore, a righteous and good act, an act highly bene-ficial to women as well as an act of mercy.

Valerie Solanas (1936–1988), U.S. actress and writer: *The SCUM Manifesto* (1968)

See also Turner on STUPIDITY

MEN: the New Man

1 It is the marketplace that calls most clearly for men to be softer, more narcissistic and recep-tive, and the new man is the result.

Barbara Ehrenreich (b.1941), U.S. author and columnist: 'At Last, a New Man', first publ. in the *New York Times*, 1984, rep. in *The Worst Years of Our Lives* (1991)

2 My husband cooked my son an egg this morning.
He thinks he has bonded with him for life.
I'll have mine scrambled.

Ronnie Hughes (b.1957), British poet: 'The Hard-Boiled Husband', publ. in *Narrow Thoughts from Home* (1995)

3 During the feminist seventies men were caught between a rock and a hard-on; in the fathering eighties they are caught between good hugs and bad hugs.

Florence King (b.1936), U.S. author: *Reflections in a Jaundiced Eye* (1989), 'From Captain Marvel to Captain Valium'

MEN & WOMEN

1 Men act and women appear. Men look at women. Women watch themselves being looked at.

John Berger (b.1926), British author and critic: *Ways of Seeing* (1972), Ch.3

2 The woman is the home. That's where she used to be, and that's where she still is. You might ask me, What if a man tries to be part of the home – will the woman let him? I answer yes. Because then he becomes one of the children.

Marguerite Duras (1914–1996), French author and film-maker: *Practicalities* (1987; tr.1990), 'House and Home'

3 Given the cultural barriers to intersex con-versation, the amazing thing is that we would even expect women and men to have anything to say to each other for more than ten minutes at a stretch. The barriers are ancient – perhaps rooted, as some paleontologist may soon discover, in the contrast between the occa-sional guttural utterances exchanged in male hunting bands and the extended discussions characteristic of female food-gathering groups.

Barbara Ehrenreich (b.1941), U.S. author and columnist: 'Tales of the Man Shortage', first publ. in *Mother Jones*, 1986, rep. in *The Worst Years of Our Lives* (1991)

4 Men should be saying 'I want to become a woman.' The world would be a far better place if more men wanted to become women, than women wanted to become men.

Albert Halsey (b.1923), British author and educator: in *The Independent* (London), 14 Oct. 1992

5 Men greet each other with a sock on the arm, women with a hug, and the hug wears better in the long run.

Edward Hoagland (b.1932), U.S. novelist and essayist: 'Heaven and Nature', first publ. in *Harper's Magazine* (New York), March 1988, rep. in *Heart's Desire* (1988)

6 Sometimes I think that the biggest difference between men and women is that more men need to seek out some terrible lurking thing in existence and hurl themselves upon it.... Women know where it lives but they can let it alone.

Russell Hoban (b.1932), U.S. author: Neaera, in *Turtle Diary* (1975), Ch.18

7 Men and women, women and men. It will never work.

Erica Jong (b.1942), U.S. author: the narrator (Isadora Wing), in *Fear of Flying* (1973), Ch.16

8   I do not know who first invented the myth of sexual equality. But it is a myth willfully fostered and nourished by certain semi-scientists and other fiction writers. And it has done more, I suspect, to unsettle marital happiness than any other false doctrine of this myth-ridden age.
     Phyllis McGinley (1905–1978), U.S. poet and author: *The Province of the Heart* (1959), 'The Honor of Being a Woman'

9   The suffering of either sex – of the male who is unable, because of the way in which he was reared, to take the strong initiating or patriarchal role that is still demanded of him, or of the female who has been given too much freedom of movement as a child to stay placidly within the house as an adult – this suffering, this discrepancy, this sense of failure in an enjoined role, is the point of leverage for social change.
     Margaret Mead (1901–1978), U.S. anthropologist: *Male and Female* (1949), Ch.15

10   Because of our social circumstances, male and female are really two cultures and their life experiences are utterly different.
     Kate Millett (b.1934), U.S. feminist author: *Sexual Politics* (1970), Ch.2, Sct.2

11   Men are gentle, honest and straightforward. Women are convoluted, deceptive and dangerous.
     Erin Pizzey (b.1939), British novelist and activist: in the *Daily Mail* (London), 24 Aug. 1988

12   In our civilization, men are afraid that they will not be men enough and women are afraid that they may be considered only women.
     Theodor Reik (1888–1969), U.S. psychologist: in *Esquire* (New York), Nov. 1958

13   How we dwelt in two worlds
     the daughters and the mothers
     in the kingdom of the sons.
     Adrienne Rich (b.1929), U.S. poet: 'Sibling Mysteries', publ. in *The Dream of a Common Language* (1978),

14   There is very little difference between men and women in space.
     Helen Sharman (b.1963), British scientist and astronaut: in the *Independent on Sunday* (London), 9 June 1991. Sharman was Britain's first astronaut in space

15   What is most beautiful in virile men is something feminine; what is most beautiful in feminine women is something masculine.
     Susan Sontag (b.1933), U.S. essayist: 'Notes on "Camp"', Note 9, first publ. in *Partisan Review* (New Brunswick, N.J.), 1964, rep. in *Against Interpretation* (1966)

16   The anger that appears to be building up between the sexes becomes more virulent with every day that passes. And far from women

taking the blame ... the fact is that men are invariably portrayed as the bad guys. Being a good man is like being a good Nazi.
David Thomas (b.1959), British editor: *Fifth Column*, BBC2, Oct. 1991, quoted in the *Independent on Sunday* (London), 22 March 1992

See also Amis on LOVE

THE MENOPAUSE

1   The climacteric marks the end of apologizing. The chrysalis of conditioning has once for all to break and the female woman finally to emerge.
     Germaine Greer (b.1939), Australian feminist writer: *The Change: Women, Ageing and the Menopause* (1991), Ch.17

2   The menopause is probably the least glamorous topic imaginable; and this is interesting, because it is one of the very few topics to which cling some shreds and remnants of taboo. A serious mention of menopause is usually met with uneasy silence; a sneering reference to it is usually met with relieved sniggers. Both the silence and the sniggering are pretty sure indications of taboo.
     Ursula K. Le Guin (b.1929), U.S. author: 'The Space Crone', publ. in *The Co-Evolution Quarterly*, Summer 1976, rep. in *Dancing at the Edge of the World* (1989)

See also Le Guin on AGE: OLD AGE

MENSTRUATION

1   If you think you are emancipated, you might consider the idea of tasting your menstrual blood – if it makes you sick, you've a long way to go, baby.
     Germaine Greer (b.1939), Australian feminist writer: *The Female Eunuch* (1970), 'The Wicked Womb'

2   Each month
     the blood sheets down
     like good red rain.
     Erica Jong (b.1942), U.S. author: 'Gardener', publ. in *Half Lives* (1973)

3   It is not menstrual blood per se which disturbs the imagination – unstanchable as that red flood may be – but rather the albumen in the blood, the uterine shreds, placental jellyfish of the female sea. This is the chthonian matrix from which we rose. We have an evolutionary revulsion from slime, our site of biologic origins. Every month, it is woman's fate to face the abyss of time and being, the abyss which is herself.
     Camille Paglia (b.1947), U.S. author and critic: *Sexual Personae* (1990), Ch.1

4 In man, the shedding of blood is always associated with injury, disease, or death. Only the female half of humanity was seen to have the magical ability to bleed profusely and still rise phoenix-like each month from the gore.

Estelle R. Ramey (b.1917), U.S. scientist and educator: 'Men's Monthly Cycles (They Have Them Too, You Know)', publ. in *The First Ms. Reader* (ed. Francine Klagsbrun, 1972)

5 When people say women can't be trusted because they cycle every month, my response is that men cycle every day, so they should only be allowed to negotiate peace treaties in the evening.

June Reinisch (b.1943), U.S. psychologist: in *The Times* (London), 20 Jan. 1992

6 If men could menstruate ... clearly, menstruation would become an enviable, boastworthy, masculine event: Men would brag about how long and how much.... Sanitary supplies would be federally funded and free. Of course, some men would still pay for the prestige of such commercial brands as Paul Newman Tampons, Muhammed Ali's Rope-a-Dope Pads, John Wayne Maxi Pads, and Joe Namath Jock Shields – 'For Those Light Bachelor Days'.

Gloria Steinem (b.1934), U.S. feminist writer and editor: 'If Men Could Menstruate', first publ. in *Ms.* (New York), Oct. 1978, rep. in *Outrageous Acts and Everyday Rebellions* (1983)

7 Stupid word, that. Period. In America it means 'full stop', like in punctuation. That's stupid as well. A period isn't a full stop. It's a new beginning. I don't mean all that creativity, life-giving force, earth-mother stuff, I mean it's a new beginning to the month, relief that you're not pregnant, when you don't have to have a child.

Michelene Wandor (b.1940), British poet, playwright and critic: *Guests in the Body* (1986), 'Mother's Pride'

MENTAL ILLNESS

---

1 Nothing defines the quality of life in a community more clearly than people who regard themselves, or whom the consensus chooses to regard, as mentally unwell.

Renata Adler (b.1938), U.S. author and film critic: 'The Thursday Group' (1967), rep. in *Toward a Radical Middle* (1971)

2 It is thus that the few rare lucid well-disposed people who have had to struggle on the earth find themselves at certain hours of the day or night in the depth of certain authentic and waking nightmare states, surrounded by the formidable suction, the formidable tentacular oppression of a kind of civic magic which will soon be seen appearing openly in social behaviour.

Antonin Artaud (1896–1948), French theatre producer, actor and theorist: *Van Gogh, the Man Suicided by Society* (1947), rep. in *Selected Writings* (ed. Susan Sontag, 1976), Pt.33

3 Schizophrenia cannot be understood without understanding despair.

R.D. Laing (1927–1989), British psychiatrist: *The Divided Self* (1959), Ch.2

4 The experience and behaviour that gets labelled schizophrenic is a special strategy that a person invents in order to live in an unlivable situation.

R.D. Laing: *The Politics of Experience* (1967), Ch.5

5 There is no such 'condition' as 'schizophrenia', but the label is a social fact and the social fact a *political event*.

R.D. Laing: *The Politics of Experience* (1967), Ch.5

6 Schizophrenia may be a necessary consequence of literacy.

Marshall Mcluhan (1911–1980), Canadian communications theorist: *The Gutenberg Galaxy* (1962), 'Typographic Man Can Express But is Helpless to Read the Configuration of Print Technology'

7 In the past, men created witches; now they create mental patients.

Thomas Szasz (b.1920), U.S. psychiatrist: introduction to *The Manufacture of Madness* (1971). This sentence summarizes the book's theme. *See* Szasz on PSYCHIATRY

8 No further evidence is needed to show that 'mental illness' is not the name of a biological condition whose nature awaits to be elucidated, but is the name of a concept whose purpose is to obscure the obvious.

Thomas Szasz: *The Second Sin* (1973), 'Mental Illness'

9 You must always be puzzled by mental illness. The thing I would dread most, if I became mentally ill, would be your adopting a common sense attitude; that you could take it for granted that I was deluded.

Ludwig Wittgenstein (1889–1951), Austrian-born British philosopher: conversations, 1947–48, publ. in *Personal Recollections* (ed. Rush Rhees, 1981), Ch.6

See also Szasz on GOD; MADNESS; NEUROSIS; PSYCHIATRIC INSTITUTIONS; PSYCHIATRY

THE MESSIAH

---

1 One has failed to say anything about the Messiah if one represents him as a person who comes to put a miraculous end to the violence in the world, the injustice and contradictions which destroy humanity but have their source

in the nature of humanity, and simply in Nature.

Emmanuel Levinas (b.1905), French Jewish philosopher: *Difficult Freedom* (1990), Pt.2, 'Messianic Texts'

2   I think the Messianic concept, which is the Jewish offering to mankind, is a great victory. What does it mean? It means that history has a sense, a meaning, a direction; it goes somewhere, and necessarily in a good direction – the Messiah.

Elie Wiesel (b.1928), Rumanian-born U.S. writer: interview in *Writers at Work* (Eighth Series, ed. George Plimpton, 1988)

See also Levinas on PROPHECY

METAPHYSICS

1   I was thrown out of NYU my freshman year ... for cheating on my metaphysics final. You know, I looked within the soul of the boy sitting next to me.

Woody Allen (b.1935), U.S. film-maker: Alvy Singer (Allen), doing stand-up comedy in front of a college audience, in *Annie Hall* (film; screenplay by Woody Allen with Marshall Brickman, directed by Woody Allen, 1977)

2   Two half philosophers will probably never a whole metaphysician make.

Gaston Bachelard (1884–1962), French scientist, philosopher and literary theorist: *Fragments of a Poetics of Fire* (1988; tr.1990), 'A Retrospective Glance at the Lifework of a Master of Books'

3   That's metaphysics, my dear fellow. It's forbidden me by my doctor, my stomach won't take it.

Boris Pasternak (1890–1960), Russian poet, novelist and translator: Ivan Ivanovich, in *Doctor Zhivago* (1957; tr.1958), Ch.1, Sct.5

MIDDLE AGE

1   She was a handsome woman of forty-five and would remain so for many years.

Anita Brookner (b.1938), British novelist and art historian: *Hotel du Lac* (1984), Ch.4

2   The years between fifty and seventy are the hardest. You are always being asked to do things, and yet you are not decrepit enough to turn them down.

T.S. Eliot (1888–1965), Anglo-American poet and critic: in *Time* (New York), 23 Oct. 1950

3   The misery of the middle-aged woman is a grey and hopeless thing, born of having nothing to live for, of disappointment and resentment at having been gypped by consumer society, and surviving merely to be the butt of its unthinking scorn.

Germaine Greer (b.1939), Australian feminist writer: introduction to *The Change: Women, Ageing and the Menopause* (1991)

4   At last now you can be
What the old cannot recall
And the young long for in dreams,
Yet still include them all.

Elizabeth Jennings (b.1926), British poet: 'Accepted', publ. in *Growing Pains* (1975)

5   Men of my age live in a state of continual desperation.

Trevor McDonald (b.1939), British journalist and broadcaster: in *Today* (London), 8 Dec. 1989

6   In mid-life the man wants to see how irresistible he still is to younger women. How they turn their hearts to stone and more or less commit a murder of their marriage I just don't know, but they do.

Patricia Neal (b.1926), U.S. actress: in *The Daily Telegraph* (London), 22 June 1988

7   Irascibility, muse of middle age.

Derek Walcott (b.1930), West Indian poet and playwright: 'The Estranging Sea', Ch.18, Sct.3, publ. in *Another Life* (1973)

8   In middle life, the human back is spoiling for a technical knockout and will use the flimsiest excuse, even a sneeze, to fall apart.

E.B. White (1899–1985), U.S. author and editor: 'Radiography', publ. in the *New Yorker*, 24 Feb. 1951, rep. in *Writings from the New Yorker 1927–1976* (ed. Rebecca M. Dale, 1991)

See also AGE; Lowell on THE 1950S

THE MIDDLE CLASS

1   What I call middle-class society is any society that becomes rigidified in predetermined forms, forbidding all evolution, all gains, all progress, all discovery. I call middle-class a closed society in which life has no taste, in which the air is tainted, in which ideas and men are corrupt. And I think that a man who takes a stand against this death is in a sense a revolutionary.

Frantz Fanon (1925–1961), Martiniquan psychiatrist, philosopher and political activist: *Black Skins, White Masks* (1952; tr.1967), Ch.8

2   In the affluent society, a man who has a full plate whisked away from in front of him can be quicker to react than the down-and-out of the pre-war period who was accustomed to protracted conditions of unemployment and poverty. It is the ruined middle class which makes revolutions, and in pre-war terms nearly everyone is middle class now.

Oswald Mosley (1896–1980), British fascist leader: *My Life* (1968), Ch.15

3 Being middle class means always having to say you're sorry.

Tony Parsons (b.1955), British journalist: 'The Polenta Jungle', publ. in *Arena* (London), March/April 1993, rep. in *Dispatches from the Front Line of Popular Culture* (1994)

See also THE WORKING CLASS

THE MIDDLE EAST

1 We have proved we are not modern. We have proved we are not religious in the real sense of the word. We have proved that we cannot afford democracy.

Muhammad Heikal (b.1923), Egyptian journalist: on the Arab world after the Gulf War, in *The Independent* (London), 11 March 1992

2 America is the world's policeman, all right – a big, dumb, mick flatfoot in the middle of the one thing cops dread most, a 'domestic disturbance'.

P.J. O'Rourke (b.1947), U.S. journalist: 'Jordan', first publ. in *Rolling Stone* (New York), Aug. 1990, rep. in *Give War a Chance* (1992)

3 It is crystal clear to me that if Arabs put down a draft resolution blaming Israel for the recent earthquake in Iran it would probably have a majority, the U.S. would veto it and Britain and France would abstain.

Amos Oz (b.1939), Israeli novelist: in *The Times* (London), 24 Oct. 1990

4 We know that this mad dog of the Middle East has a goal of a world revolution, Muslim fundamentalist revolution, which is targeted on many of his own Arab compatriots and where we figure in that I don't know.

Ronald Reagan (b.1911), U.S. Republican politician and president: of Libyan leader Colonel Qaddafi, at press conference, 9 April 1986, quoted in the *New York Times*, 10 April 1986. Six days later, Reagan launched a bombing raid on Tripoli, killing about a hundred civilians

5 The tormenting dilemma of the Middle East is this: either we have one people too many, or one state too few.

Afif Safieh, London representative of P.L.O.: quoted by Neal Ascherson in the *Independent on Sunday* (London), 3 March 1991

6 I often think that one reason for our powerlessness is that we feel self-hatred. Otherwise it is impossible to explain how over 200 million people with human and natural resources of a high order can continuously hurt themselves, continuously prevent themselves from accumulating the kind of power that brings self-respect and seriousness of purpose. I have no other explanation for our situation, which cannot be extenuated or explained away by appeals to the ravages of imperialism, or to corrupt regimes, or any of the other litanies of self-exculpation. The problem is Arab powerlessness.

Edward Said (b.1935), Lebanese-born U.S. social and literary critic: 'A Powerless People', publ. in *The Guardian* (London), 25 April 1996

See also IRAQ & THE SECOND GULF WAR; ISRAEL; LEBANON; PALESTINE; SUEZ

THE MIND

1 Nothing worth knowing can be understood with the mind.

Woody Allen (b.1935), U.S. film-maker: Isaac Davis (Allen), in *Manhattan* (film; screenplay by Woody Allen and Marshall Brickman, directed by Woody Allen, 1979)

2 The mind is the result of the torments the flesh undergoes or inflicts upon itself.

E.M. Cioran (1911–1995), Rumanian-born French philosopher: title essay of *The Temptation to Exist* (1956)

3 The human head is bigger than the globe. It conceives itself as containing more. It can think and rethink itself and ourselves from any desired point outside the gravitational pull of the earth. It starts by writing one thing and later reads itself as something else. The human head is monstrous.

Günter Grass (b.1927), German author: 'Racing with the Utopias', first publ. in *Die Zeit*, 16 June 1978, rep. in *On Writing and Politics 1967–1983* (1984; tr.1985)

4 Is there no way out of the mind?

Sylvia Plath (1932–1963), U.S. poet: 'Apprehensions', publ. in *Crossing the Water* (1971)

See also Mead on GENDER

MINERS

1 From the days when the miners' leaders thought they owned the Government to the day when every miner owns part of his own mine – that's the British revolution.

Cecil Parkinson (b.1932), British Conservative politician: in the *Daily Mail* (London), 13 Oct 1988

2 Down there for eight hours, you're away from God's fresh air and sunshine and there's nothing that can compensate for that. There's nothing as dark as the darkness down a pit, the blackness that closes in on you if your lamp goes out. You'd think you would see some kind of shapes but you can see nothing, nothing but the inside of your head. I think everybody should go down the pit at least once to know what darkness is.

Jock Stein (1922–1985), Scottish footballer and manager: quoted in appreciation by Hugh McIlvanney, in *The Observer* (London), 15 Sept. 1985, rep. in *McIlvanney on Football* (1994). Stein spent 11 years as a miner before turning to full-time professional football aged 27

MINIMALISM

1 Less is more.

Ludwig Mies van der Rohe (1886–1969), German-born U.S. architect: in the *New York Herald Tribune*, 28 June 1959

2 Less is a bore.

Robert Venturi (b.1925), U.S. architect: quoted in *Icons* (ed. James Park, 1991)

3 Less is only more where more is no good.

Frank Lloyd Wright (1869–1959), U.S. architect: preface to *The Future of Architecture* (1953)

MINORITIES

1 We cannot discuss the state of our minorities until we first have some sense of what we are, who we are, what our goals are, and what we take life to be. The question is not what we can do now for the hypothetical Mexican, the hypothetical Negro. The question is what we really want out of life, for ourselves, what we think is real.

James Baldwin (1924–1987), U.S. author: address, 1960, Kalamazoo College, publ. in *Nobody Knows My Name* (1961)

2 Niggerization is the result of oppression – and it doesn't just apply to the black people. Old people, poor people, and students can also get niggerized.

Florynce R. Kennedy (b.1916), U.S. lawyer and civil rights activist: quoted by Gloria Steinem in 'The Verbal Karate of Florynce R. Kennedy, Esq.', publ. in *Ms.* (New York), March 1973

3 What characterizes a member of a minority group is that he is forced to see himself as both exceptional and insignificant, marvelous and awful, good and evil.

Norman Mailer (b.1923), U.S. author: *Cannibals and Christians* (1966), 'A Speech at Berkeley on Vietnam Day'

4 Unfortunately, I am involved in a freedom ride protesting the loss of the minority rights belonging to the few remaining earthbound stars. All we demanded was our right to twinkle.

Marilyn Monroe (1926–1962), U.S. actress: telegram, 13 June 1962, to Mr and Mrs Robert Kennedy, turning down a party invitation, shown on *Marilyn: Something's Got to Give*, Channel 4, 2 Aug. 1992

5 Jews and homosexuals are the outstanding creative minorities in contemporary urban culture. Creative, that is in the truest sense: they are creators of sensibilities. The two pioneering forces of modern sensibility are Jewish moral seriousness and homosexual aestheticism and irony.

Susan Sontag (b.1933), U.S. essayist: 'Notes on "Camp"', Note 51 (1964), rep. in *Against Interpretation* (1966)

6 History is made by active, determined minorities, not by the majority, which seldom has a clear and consistent idea of what it really wants. Until the time comes for the final push toward revolution, the task of revolutionaries will be less to win the shallow support of the majority than to build a small core of deeply committed people.

Unabomber, U.S. radical: *Industrial Society and Its Future*, 'Strategy', Sct.189, publ. in the *Washington Post*, 19 Sept. 1995

MIRACLES

1 God is a character, a real and consistent being, or He is nothing. If God did a miracle He would deny His own nature and the universe would simply blow up, vanish, become nothing.

Joyce Cary (1888–1957), British author: interview in *Writers at Work* (First Series, ed. Malcolm Cowley, 1958)

2 A miracle entails a degree of irrationality – not only because it shocks reason, but because it makes no appeal to it.

Emmanuel Levinas (b.1905), French Jewish philosopher: Pt.1 'Ethics and Spirit' (1952), rep. in *Difficult Freedom* (1990)

MISANTHROPY

1 It is a sign of creeping inner death when we can no longer praise the living.

Eric Hoffer (1902–1983), U.S. philosopher: *Reflections on the Human Condition* (1973), Aph.147

2 Since I no longer expect
anything from mankind except
madness,
meanness, and mendacity;
egotism,
cowardice,
and
self-delusion,
I have stopped
being a
misanthrope.

Irving Layton (b.1912), Canadian poet: *The Whole Bloody Bird* (1969), 'Aphs'

3 It is true that we are weak and sick and ugly and quarrelsome but if that is all we ever were, we would millenniums ago have disappeared from the face of the earth.
John Steinbeck (1902–1968), U.S. author: *Writers at Work* (Fourth Series, ed. George Plimpton, 1977), 'On Intent'

MISERY

1 People talk about the courage of condemned men walking to the place of execution: sometimes it needs as much courage to walk with any kind of bearing towards another person's habitual misery.
Graham Greene (1904–1991), British novelist: *The Heart of the Matter* (1948), Bk.1, Pt.1, Ch.2, Sct.3

2 Friends *love* misery, in fact. Sometimes, especially if we are too lucky or too successful or too pretty, our misery is the only thing that endears us to our friends.
Erica Jong (b.1942), U.S. author: *How To Save Your Own Life* (1977), 'A day in the life ...'

3 Man hands on misery to man.
It deepens like a coastal shelf.
Get out as early as you can,
And don't have any kids yourself.
Philip Larkin (1922–1986), British poet: 'This Be The Verse', St.3, publ. in *High Windows* (1974)

4 Part of every misery is, so to speak, the misery's shadow or reflection: the fact that you don't merely suffer but have to keep on thinking about the fact that you suffer. I not only live each endless day in grief, but live each day thinking about living each day in grief.
C.S. Lewis (1898–1963), British author: *A Grief Observed* (1961), Pt.1

5 Maybe men are only separated from each other by the degree of their misery.
(*Peut-être les hommes ne sont séparés les uns des autres que par les dégrés de leur misère.*)
Francis Picabia (1878–1953), French painter and poet: *591* (Paris), 21 Jan. 1952, rep. in *Écrits*, Vol.II (ed. Olivier Revault d'Allones and Dominique Bouissou, 1978), '1950–1953'

MISSIONARIES

1 They're not going to catch us. We're on a mission from God.
Dan Aykroyd (b.1950), Canadian actor and comic: Elwood (Aykroyd), in *The Blues Brothers* (film; screenplay by John Landis and Dan Aykroyd, directed by John Landis, 1980)

2 Read the Bible. Work hard and honestly. And don't complain.
Billy Graham (b.1918), U.S. evangelist: message to the Chinese, reported in the *International Herald Tribune* (Paris), 18 April 1988

3 Exporting Church employees to Latin America masks a universal and unconscious fear of a new Church. North and South American authorities, differently motivated but equally fearful, become accomplices in maintaining a clerical and irrelevant Church. Sacralizing employees and property, this Church becomes progressively more blind to the possibilities of sacralizing person and community.
Ivan Illich (b.1926), Austrian-born U.S. theologian and author: *Celebration of Awareness* (1969), Ch.5

4 As each Sister is to become a Co-Worker of Christ in the slums, each ought to understand what God and the Missionaries of Charity expect from her. Let Christ radiate and live his life in her and through her in the slums. Let the poor, seeing her, be drawn to Christ and invite him to enter their homes and their lives. Let the sick and suffering find in her a real angel of comfort and consolation. Let the little ones of the streets cling to her because she reminds them of him, the friend of the little ones.
Mother Teresa (1910–1997), Albanian-born Roman Catholic missionary: *A Gift for God* (1975), 'Carriers of Christ's Love'

MOCKERY

1 No great movement designed to change the world can bear to be laughed at or belittled. Mockery is a rust that corrodes all it touches.
Milan Kundera (b.1929), Czech-born French author and critic: Kostka, in *The Joke* (1967; tr.1982), Pt.6, Ch.18

2 When a person can no longer laugh at himself, it is time for others to laugh at him.
Thomas Szasz (b.1920), U.S. psychiatrist: *The Second Sin* (1973), 'Social Relations'

3 Laughing at someone else is an excellent way of learning how to laugh at oneself; and questioning what seem to be the absurd beliefs of another group is a good way of recognizing the potential absurdity of many of one's own cherished beliefs.
Gore Vidal (b.1925), U.S. novelist and critic: 'Satire in the 1950's', first publ. in *The Nation* (New York), 26 April 1958, rep. in *Homage to Daniel Shays: Collected Essays 1952–1972* (1974)

MODELS

1 I think that if most guys in America could somehow get their fave-rave poster girl in bed and have total license to do whatever they wanted with this legendary body for one

afternoon, at least 75 percent of the guys in the country would elect to beat her up.

Lester Bangs (1948–1982), U.S. rock journalist: quoted in *Sound Effects: Youth, Leisure and the Politics of Rock* by Simon Frith (1979), Ch.10

2 Model. Two mobile eyes in a mobile head, itself on a mobile body.

Robert Bresson (b.1907), French film-maker: *Notes on the Cinematographer* (1975), '1950–1958: on Automatism'

3 We don't wake up for less than $10,000 a day.

Linda Evangelista (b.1965), Italian-Canadian model: quoted in *Vogue* (New York), fall 1991, repr. in *Model* by Michael Gross (1995), '$10,000 a Day'

4 Models are the physical mirror of femininity. They *should* come in all sizes, shapes, and ages, and now they do. If my two careers mean anything, it's that.

Lauren Hutton (b.1943), U.S. actress and model: quoted in *Model* by Michael Gross (1995), Pt.2

5 She ... lies back on the bed like Manet's Olympia, ripe and haughty, a bored odalisque. She is a woman whose image is expensively employed to arouse desire in conjunction with certain consumer goods.

Jay McInerney (b.1955), U.S. author: 'Philomena', publ. in the *New Yorker*, 25 Dec. 1995

6 I foresee the future and I know, I just know, that in two months I'll be out. I mean, what the fuck is a supermodel? I'm a super human being and a super woman, and everyone can be and everyone should be. I wanna live the rest of my life, I don't wanna have to jump off a bridge in two years. But I'll be out and someone else will be in and that's the nature of this business and it's horrible.

Kristen McMenamy (b.1965), U.S. model: interview in *i-D* (London), June 1993

7 Four straight limbs in search of a woman's body.

Newsweek (New York), April 1967, of Twiggy, featured on the cover of that month's issue. In *Model* by Michael Gross (1995), Twiggy is quoted as saying, 'I used to be a thing. I'm a person now'

8 A good model can advance fashion by ten years.

Yves Saint Laurent (b.1936), French fashion designer: interview in *Ritz* (London), No.85, 1984

9 The catwalk is theatre. It's about provocation and outrage.

Vivienne Westwood (b.1941), British fashion designer: quoted in *Fashion and Perversity* by Fred Vermorel (1996), Pt.1

See also McMenamy on FASHION; HAUTE COUTURE

MODERN ART *see under* ART

MODERN LIFE

1 I sometimes think of what future historians will say of us. A single sentence will suffice for modern man: he fornicated and read the papers.

Albert Camus (1913–1960), French-Algerian philosopher and author: the narrator (Jean-Baptiste Clamence), in *The Fall* (1956), p.7 of Hamish Hamilton edn. (1957)

2 I don't even know how to use a parking meter, let alone a phone box.

Diana, Princess of Wales (1961–1997): to the *Daily Mail*'s Royal correspondent, Richard Kay, on allegations that she had pestered art dealer Oliver Hoare with telephone calls, quoted in *The Guardian* (London), 31 Dec. 1994

3 It takes a kind of shabby arrogance to survive in our time, and a fairly romantic nature to want to.

Edgar Z. Friedenberg (b.1921), U.S. sociologist: *The Vanishing Adolescent* (1959), 'The Vanishing Adolescent'

4 By all but the pathologically romantic, it is now recognized that this is not the age of the small man.

J.K. Galbraith (b.1908), U.S. economist: *The New Industrial State* (1967), Ch.3

5 If work and leisure are soon to be subordinated to this one utopian principle – absolute busyness – then utopia and melancholy will come to coincide: an age without conflict will dawn, perpetually busy – and without consciousness.

Günter Grass (b.1927), German author: *From the Diary of a Snail* (1972), 'On Stasis in Progress'

6 Even in a time of elephantine vanity and greed, one never has to look far to see the campfires of gentle people.

Garrison Keillor (b.1942), U.S. author: *We Are Still Married* (1989), 'The Meaning of Life'

7 The trouble with our age is that it is all signpost and no destination.

Louis Kronenberger (1904–1980), U.S. critic, editor and author: *Company Manners* (1954), 'The Spirit of the Age'

8 It is a tribute to the peculiar horror of contemporary life that it makes the worst features of earlier times – the stupefaction of the masses, the obsessed and driven lives of the bourgeoisie – seem attractive by comparison.

Christopher Lasch (1932–1994), U.S. historian: *The Culture of Narcissism* (1979), Ch.4, 'No Exit'

9 The sickness of our times for me has been just this damn thing that everything has been get-

ting smaller and smaller and less and less important, that the romantic spirit has dried up, that there is no shame today.... We're all getting so mean and small and petty and ridiculous, and we all live under the threat of extermination.

Norman Mailer (b.1923), U.S. author: 'Hip, Hell, and the Navigator', first publ. in the *Western Review*, winter 1959, rep. in *Conversations with Norman Mailer* (ed. J. Michael Lennon, 1988)

10 The new man is born too old to tolerate the new world. The present conditions of life have not yet erased the traces of the past. We run too fast, but we still do not move enough. ... He looks but he does not contemplate, he sees but he does not think. He runs away from time, which is made of thought, and yet all he can feel is his own time, the present.

Eugenio Montale (1896–1981), Italian poet: *Poet In Our Time* (1972), p.17 of Marion Boyars edn. (1976)

11 Unable to create a meaningful life for itself, the personality takes its own revenge: from the lower depths comes a regressive form of spontaneity: raw animality forms a counterpoise to the meaningless stimuli and the vicarious life to which the ordinary man is conditioned. Getting spiritual nourishment from this chaos of events, sensations, and devious interpretations is the equivalent of trying to pick through a garbage pile for food.

Lewis Mumford (1895–1990), U.S. social philosopher: of the condition of man in the modern city, in *The Conduct Of Life* (1951), Ch.1

12 You don't have to be old in America to say of a world you lived in, That world is gone.

Peggy Noonan (b.1950), U.S. author and presidential speechwriter: *What I Saw at the Revolution* (1990), Ch.1

13 The atom bombs are piling up in the factories, the police are prowling through the cities, the lies are streaming from the loudspeakers, but the earth is still going round the sun.

George Orwell (1903–1950), British author: *Shooting an Elephant* (1950), 'Thoughts on the Common Toad'

14 Today we all speak, if not the same tongue, the same universal language. There is no one centre, and time has lost its former coherence: East and West, yesterday and tomorrow exist as a confused jumble in each one of us. Different times and different spaces are combined in a here and now that is everywhere at once.

Octavio Paz (b.1914), Mexican poet and essayist: *Alternating Current* (1967), 'Invention, Underdevelopment, Modernity'

15 Anyone who lives in this time is concerned with grottiness.

Peter Reading (b.1946), British poet: in the *International Herald Tribune* (Paris), 10 March 1988

16 Never before so much power, knowledge, daring, opulence, dynamism. Never so many great adventures in the making. And that is the worst of it – that even the genocidal end we prepare for our species shines with a Promethean grandeur. Who can escape being torn between the yes and the no?

Theodore Roszak (b.1933), U.S. social critic: introduction to *Where the Wasteland Ends* (1972)

17 We're living in a funny world, kid, a peculiar civilization. The police are playing crooks in it, and the crooks are doing police duty. The politicians are preachers, and the preachers are politicians. The tax collectors collect for themselves. The Bad People want us to have more dough, and the Good People are fighting to keep it from us.

Jim Thompson (1906–1977), U.S. author: Lou Ford, in *The Killer Inside Me* (1952), Ch.12

18 Among the abnormal conditions present in modern industrial society are excessive density of population, isolation of man from nature, excessive rapidity of social change and the break-down of natural small-scale communities such as the extended family, the village or the tribe.

Unabomber, U.S. radical: *Industrial Society and Its Future*, 'Sources of Social Problems', Sct.47, publ. in the *Washington Post*, 19 Sept. 1995

MODERNISM

1 Modernism may be seen as an attempt to reconstruct the world in the absence of God.

Bryan Appleyard (b.1951), British author: *The Culture Club: Crisis in the Arts* (1984), Ch.6

2 A 'modern' man has nothing to add to modernism, if only because he had nothing to oppose it with. The well-adapted drop off the dead limb of time like lice.

Elias Canetti (1905–1994), Austrian novelist and philosopher: *The Secret Heart Of The Clock: Notes, Aphorisms, Fragments 1973–1985* (1991), '1980'

3 By Modernism I mean the positive rejection of the past and the blind belief in the process of change, in novelty for its own sake, in the idea that progress through time equates with cultural progress; in the cult of individuality, originality and self-expression.

Dan Cruickshank (b.1949), British architectural critic: *Commerce and Culture* (1989), Ch.4

4 I don't think we can ignore the Modern Movement. But I wouldn't have minded at all if it hadn't happened. I think the world would be a much nicer place.

Quinlan Terry (b.1937), British architect: in the *International Herald Tribune* (Paris), 25 April 1988

See also Greenberg on ART: MODERN ART; Adair on POSTMODERNISM; Hewison on POST-MODERNISM; Lyotard on POSTMODERNISM

MODERNITY

1 You are born modern, you do not become so.
Jean Baudrillard (b.1929), French semiologist: *America* (1986; tr.1988), 'Astral America'

2 Now 'modern' is a curious term: it can be used to degrade as well as (or more often than) to elevate. It can mean decadent, degenerate, nihilistic, abysmal, at one end – or it can signify a capacity to overcome contemporary disorder, or to adumbrate a stage in the formation of a new superiority, or to begin to distill a new essence.
Saul Bellow (b.1915), U.S. novelist: *It All Adds Up* (1994), 'Mozart: an Overture'

3 Don't bother about being modern. Unfortunately it is the one thing that, whatever you do, you cannot avoid.
Salvador Dali (1904–1989), Spanish painter: journal entry, 15 July 1952, in *Diary of a Genius* (1966)

4 Modernity exists in the form of a desire to wipe out whatever came earlier, in the hope of reaching at least a point that could be called a true present, a point of origin that marks a new departure.
Paul de Man (1919–1983), Belgian-born U.S. literary critic': 'Literary History and Literary Modernity', lecture, Sept. 1969, rep. in *Blindness and Insight* (1971; rev.1983)

5 Modernity is distinct from fashion, which does no more than call into question the course of time; modernity is the attitude that makes it possible to grasp the 'heroic' aspect of the present moment. Modernity is not a phenomenon of sensitivity to the fleeting present; it is the will to 'heroize' the present.
Michel Foucault (1926–1984), French philosopher: 'What Is Enlightenment?', Pt.2, based on unpublished manuscript, publ. in *The Foucault Reader* (ed. Paul Rabinow, 1984)

MONEY

1 Money is better than poverty, if only for financial reasons.
Woody Allen (b.1935), U.S. film-maker: *Without Feathers* (1976), 'The Early Essays'

2 Making lots of money – it's not that hard, you know. It's overestimated. Making lots of money is a breeze. You watch.
Martin Amis (b.1949), British author: *Money* (1984), p.19 of Penguin edn. (1985)

3 Money doesn't mind if we say it's evil, it goes from strength to strength. It's a fiction, an addiction, and a tacit conspiracy.
Martin Amis: *Novelists in Interview* (ed. John Haffenden, 1985)

4 Whether he admits it or not, a man has been brought up to look at money as a sign of his virility, a symbol of his power, a bigger phallic symbol than a Porsche.
Victoria Billings (b.1945), U.S. journalist and author: *The Womansbook* (1974), 'Getting It Together'

5 The money complex is the demonic, and the demonic is God's ape; the money complex is therefore the heir to and substitute for the religious complex, an attempt to find God in things.
Norman O. Brown (b.1913), U.S. philosopher: of the Protestant view of money, in *Life Against Death* (1959), Ch.15, 'Sacred and Secular'

6 We all need money, but there are degrees of desperation.
Anthony Burgess (1917–1993), British author and critic: interview in *The Face* (London), Dec. 1984

7 However toplofty and idealistic a man may be, he can always rationalize his right to earn money.
Raymond Chandler (1880–1959), U.S. author: letter, 15 Nov. 1951, to his New York literary agent Carl Brandt, publ. in *Raymond Chandler Speaking* (ed. Dorothy Gardiner and Kathrine S. Walker, 1962)

8 Comparatively few people know what a million dollars actually is. To the majority it is a gaseous concept, swelling or decreasing as the occasion suggests. In the minds of politicians, perhaps more than anywhere, the notion of a million dollars has this accordion-like ability to expand or contract; if they are disposing of it, the million is a pleasing sum, reflecting warmly upon themselves; if somebody else wants it, it becomes a figure of inordinate size, not to be compassed by the rational mind.
Robertson Davies (1913–1995), Canadian novelist and journalist: *What's Bred in the Bone* (1985), Pt.6

9 Money speaks, but it speaks with a male voice.
Andrea Dworkin (b.1946), U.S. feminist critic: *Pornography* (1981), Ch.1

10 Money doesn't talk, it swears.
Bob Dylan (b.1941), U.S. singer and songwriter: 'It's Alright Ma (I'm Only Bleeding)' (song) on the album *Bringing it All Back Home* (1965)

11 Money makes the world go round
the world go round
the world go round,
Money makes the world go round
That clinking clanking sound!
Money! Money! Money!

Money! Money! Money!
It makes the world go round.

Fred Ebb (b.1932), U.S. librettist: 'Money' (song) in *Cabaret* (stage musical, 1966; film, 1972). The words are sung by Sally Bowles (Liza Minelli) and the master of ceremonies (Joel Grey)

12 Money is a singular thing. It ranks with love as man's greatest source of joy. And with death as his greatest source of anxiety. Over all history it has oppressed nearly all people in one of two ways: either it has been abundant and very unreliable, or reliable and very scarce.

J.K. Galbraith (b.1908), U.S. economist: *The Age of Uncertainty* (1977), Ch.6

13 Money is like fire, an element as little troubled by moralizing as earth, air and water. Men can employ it as a tool or they can dance around it as if it were the incarnation of a god. Money votes socialist or monarchist, finds a profit in pornography or translations from the Bible, commissions Rembrandt and underwrites the technology of Auschwitz. It acquires its meaning from the uses to which it is put.

Lewis H. Lapham (b.1935), U.S. essayist and editor: *Money and Class in America* (1988), Ch.8

14 Quarterly, is it, money reproaches me:
    'Why do you let me lie here wastefully?
I am all you never had of goods and sex.
    You could get them still by writing a few cheques.'

Philip Larkin (1922–1985), British poet: 'Money', publ. in *High Windows* (1974)

15 Money is a poor man's credit card.

Marshall McLuhan (1911–1980), Canadian communications theorist: quoted in *Maclean's* (Toronto), June 1971

16 I get so tired listening to one million dollars here, one million dollars there, it's so petty.

Imelda Marcos (b.1929), Filipino First Lady and society figure: complaining of the numerous witnesses called to testify to her financial profligacy during her trial on charges of embezzlement in New York, quoted in *The Times* (London), 22 June 1990

17 Money couldn't buy friends, but you got a better class of enemy.

Spike Milligan (b.1918), British comedian and humorous writer: Mrs Doonan, in *Puckoon* (1963), Ch.6

18 Americans want action for their money. They are fascinated by its self-reproducing qualities if it's put to work. ... Gold-hoarding goes against the American grain; it fits in better with European pessimism than with America's traditional optimism.

Paula Nelson (b.1945), U.S. business executive: *The Joy of Money* (1975), Ch.15

19 I told you he had a cash register mind. Rings every time he opens his mouth.

Dennis O'Keefe (1908–1968), U.S. actor: Joe Sullivan (O'Keefe), in *Raw Deal* (film; screenplay by Leopold Atlas and John C. Higgins, directed by Anthony Mann, 1948)

20 Having money is rather like being a blond. It is more fun but not vital.

Mary Quant (b.1936), British fashion designer: quoted in *The Observer* (London), 2 Nov. 1986

21 A phantasmagorical god, it is implored and dreaded. It is the scapegoat for our misfortunes. Created for our convenience, we make it bear out emotions; it was a means, it has become an end.

Guy de Rothschild (b.1909), French banker: *The Whims of Fortune* (1985), Ch.1

22 Money isn't lost or made. It's simply transformed from one perception to another.

Oliver Stone (b.1946), U.S. film-maker: Gordon Gekko (Michael Douglas), in *Wall Street* (film; screenplay by Stanley Weiser and Oliver Stone, directed by Oliver Stone, 1987)

23 No one would remember the Good Samaritan if he'd only had good intentions – he had money as well.

Margaret Thatcher (b.1925), British Conservative politician and prime minister: television interview, 6 Jan. 1986, quoted in *The Times* (London), 12 Jan. 1986

24 You can be young without money but you can't be old without it.

Tennessee Williams (1911–1983), U.S. playwright: Margaret, in *Cat on a Hot Tin Roof* (1955), Act 1

See also Sokolow on AFFECTION; FINANCE; Stone on INVESTMENT; TAXES

MONOGAMY

1 I'm old-fashioned. I don't believe in extra-marital relationships. I think people should mate for life, like pigeons or Catholics.

Woody Allen (b.1935), U.S. film-maker: Isaac Davis (Allen), in *Manhattan* (film; screenplay by Woody Allen and Marshall Brickman, directed by Woody Allen, 1979)

2 The highest level of sexual excitement is in a monogamous relationship.

Warren Beatty (b.1937), U.S. actor: quoted in *The Observer* (London), 27 Oct. 1991

See also McInerney on MARRIAGE

MARILYN MONROE

1 In death Marilyn has become strangely sexless – she is a MARILYN, a species apart. In life she was a man's woman because men wanted her; now she is a man's woman because a lot of men want to be her.

Julie Burchill (b.1960), British journalist and author: *Girls on Film* (1986), Ch.11

2 The essence of the physicality of the most famous blonde in the world is a wholesome eroticism blurred a little round the edges by the fact she is not quite sure what eroticism is. This gives her her tentative luminosity and what makes her, somehow, always more like her own image in the mirror than she is like herself.
Angela Carter (1940–1992), British author: *The Sadeian Woman* (1979), 'Desecration of the Temple'

3 Monroe, the consummate sexual doll, is empowered to act but afraid to act, perhaps because no amount of acting, however inspired, can convince the actor herself that her ideal female life is not a dreadful form of dying.
Andrea Dworkin (b.1946), U.S. feminist critic: *Right-Wing Women* (1978), Ch.1

4 And it seems to me you lived your life
Like a candle in the wind.
Elton John (b.1947), British rock musician: 'Candle in the Wind' (song; lyrics by Bernie Taupin), on the album *Goodbye Yellow Brick Road* (1973)

5 So we think of Marilyn who was every man's love affair with America. Marilyn Monroe who was blonde and beautiful and had a sweet little rinky-dink of a voice and all the cleanliness of all the clean American backyards.
Norman Mailer (b.1923), U.S. author: *Marilyn* (1973), Ch.1

6 All my energy and attention were devoted to trying to help her solve her problems. Unfortunately I didn't have much success.
Arthur Miller (b.1915), U.S. playwright: in the *International Herald Tribune* (Paris), 5 Aug. 1992

7 My work is the only ground I've ever had to stand on. I seem to have a whole superstructure with no foundation – but I'm working on the foundation.
Marilyn Monroe (1926–1962), U.S. actor: quoted in *Marilyn Monroe In Her Own Words* (1990), 'Acting'

8 I remember her on the screen, huge as a colossus doll, mincing and whispering and simply hoping her way into total vulnerability.
Gloria Steinem (b.1934), U.S. feminist writer and editor: 'Marilyn Monroe: The Woman who Died Too Soon', publ. in *Ms.* (New York), Aug. 1972, rep. in *Outrageous Acts and Everyday Rebellions* (1983)

9 Ah, Marilyn, Hollywood's Joan of Arc, our Ultimate Sacrificial Lamb. Well, let me tell you, she was mean, terribly mean. The meanest woman I have ever known in this town. I am appalled by this Marilyn Monroe cult. Perhaps it's getting to be an act of courage to say the truth about her. Well, let me be

courageous. I have never met anyone as utterly mean as Marilyn Monroe. Nor as utterly fabulous on the screen, and that includes Garbo.
Billy Wilder (b.1906), U.S. film-maker: interview in the *Los Angeles Times*, 1968, quoted in *Billy Wilder in Hollywood* by Maurice Zolotow (1977), Ch.19

See also Sanders on ACTORS

THE MOON

1 The Eagle has landed.
Neil Armstrong (b.1930), U.S. astronaut: radio message, spoken as the lunar module 'Eagle' touched down, announcing the first landing on the moon, 20 July 1969, quoted in the *Washington Post*, 21 July 1969

2 That's one small step for a man, one giant leap for mankind.
Neil Armstrong: on first stepping on to the moon's surface, 10.56pm (EDT), 20 July 1969, quoted in the *New York Times*, 21 July 1969. Armstrong's message was garbled, and was originally transmitted as 'one small step for man, one giant leap for mankind'

3 It's natural the Boys should whoop it up for
so huge a phallic triumph, and adventure
   it would not have occurred to women
   to think worthwhile, made possible only
because we like huddling in gangs and
   knowing
the exact time.
W.H. Auden (1907–1973), Anglo-American poet: 'Moon Landing', publ. in *Epistles to a Godson* (1972)

4 So there he is at last. Man on the moon. The poor magnificent bungler! He can't even get to the office without undergoing the agonies of the damned, but give him a little metal, a few chemicals, some wire and twenty or thirty billion dollars and, vroom! there he is, up on a rock a quarter of a million miles up in the sky.
Russell Baker (b.1925), U.S. journalist: in the *New York Times*, 21 July 1969

5 The moon is nothing
But a circumambulating aphrodisiac
Divinely subsidized to provoke the world
Into a rising birth-rate.
Christopher Fry (b.1907), British playwright: Thomas Mendip, in *The Lady's Not for Burning* (1949), Act 3

6 The hardness and the brightness and the plain
Far-reaching singleness of that wide stare
Is a reminder of the strength and pain
Of being young; that it can't come again,
But is for others undiminished somewhere.
Philip Larkin (1922–1985), British poet: 'Sad Steps', written 1968, publ. in *High Windows* (1974)

7 Treading the soil of the moon, palpating its pebbles, tasting the panic and splendor of the event, feeling in the pit of one's stomach the separation from terra ... these form the most romantic sensation an explorer has ever known ... this is the only thing I can say about the matter. The utilitarian results do not interest me.

Vladimir Nabokov (1899–1977), Russian-born U.S. novelist and poet: referring to the first moon-landing, in the *New York Times*, 21 July 1969

8 This is the greatest week in the history of the world since the Creation, because as a result of what happened in this week, the world is bigger, infinitely.

Richard Nixon (1913–1992), U.S. Republican politician and president: remark, 24 July 1969, on *U.S.S. Hornet*, welcoming back the crew of Apollo 11, four days after the first moon-landing, quoted in *Nixon: The Triumph of a Politician* by Stephen Ambrose (1989), Vol. II, Ch. 13. A few days later, Ambrose narrates, the evangelist Billy Graham mentioned three greater days: Christ's birth, Christ's death, and Christ's resurrection. Nixon's scribbled response was: 'tell Billy RN referred to a *week* not *a day*'

9 HERE MEN FROM THE PLANET
 EARTH
 FIRST SET FOOT UPON THE MOON
 JULY, 1969 AD
 WE CAME IN PEACE FOR ALL
 MANKIND

Plaque: left on the moon's surface by the crew of Apollo 11

10 Nothing is more symptomatic of the enervation, of the decompression of the Western imagination, than our incapacity to respond to the landings on the Moon. Not a single great poem, picture, metaphor has come of this breathtaking act, of Prometheus's rescue of Icarus or of Phaeton in flight towards the stars.

George Steiner (b.1929), French-born U.S. critic and novelist: 'Modernity, Mythology and Magic', lecture at the 1994 Salzburg Festival, publ. in *The Guardian* (London), 6 Aug. 1994

See also Picasso on INDIFFERENCE

MORALITY

1 The only immorality ... is not to do what one has to do when one has to do it.
 (*La seule chose qui soit immorale ... c'est de ne pas faire ce qu'il faut, quand il le faut.*)
 Jean Anouilh (1910–1987), French playwright: Thomas à Becket, in *Becket* (1959; tr.1961), Act 2

2 While moral rules may be propounded by authority the fact that these were so propounded would not validate them.

A.J. Ayer (1910–1989), British philosopher: title essay in *The Meaning of Life and Other Essays* (1990)

3 The essence of morality is a questioning about morality; and the decisive move of human life is to use ceaselessly all light to look for the origin of the opposition between good and evil.

Georges Bataille (1897–1962), French novelist and critic: 'Du Rapport entre le Divin et le Mal', first publ. in *Critique* (Paris), March 1947, quoted in 'The Dualist Materialism of Georges Bataille' by Denis Hollier in *On Bataille* (ed. Allan Stoekl, 1990)

4 Professionally, morals aren't too much of a problem. Over the years one has learned certain things by experience. They mount up. And gradually they crystallize into a pattern of behaviour which afterwards – to use a superior expression – one calls one's professional ethics.

Ingmar Bergman (b.1918), Swedish stage and film writer-director: interview in *Bergman on Bergman* (1970), 'Rasunda, 3 July 1968'

5 Morality's *not* practical. Morality's a gesture. A complicated gesture learned from books.

Robert Bolt (1924–1995), British playwright: Sir Thomas More, in *A Man for All Seasons* (1960), Act 2

6 It is far easier for a woman to lead a blameless life than it is for a man; all she has to do is to avoid sexual intercourse like the plague.

Angela Carter (1940–1992), British author: introduction to *Wayward Girls and Wicked Women* (ed. Angela Carter, 1986)

7 When we start deceiving ourselves into thinking not that we want something or need something, not that it is a pragmatic necessity for us to have it, but that it is a *moral imperative* that we have it, then is when we join the fashionable madmen, and then is when the thin whine of hysteria is heard in the land, and then is when we are in bad trouble.

Joan Didion (b.1934), U.S. essayist: *Slouching Towards Bethlehem* (1968), 'On Morality'

8 Morality comes with the sad wisdom of age, when the sense of curiosity has withered.

Graham Greene (1904–1991), British novelist: *A Sort of Life* (1971), Ch.7, Sct.1

9 We may pretend that we're basically moral people who make mistakes, but the whole of history proves otherwise.

Terry Hands (b.1941), British theatre and opera director: in *The Times* (London), 11 Aug. 1992

10 Morality and expediency coincide more than the cynics allow.

Roy Hattersley (b.1932), British Labour politician: in *The Guardian* (London), 30 Sept. 1988

11 Even a purely moral act that has no hope of any immediate and visible political effect can

gradually and indirectly, over time, gain in political significance.

Václav Havel (b.1936), Czech playwright and president: from letter written to Czech leader Alexander Dubcek, Aug. 1969, quoted by Havel in *Disturbing the Peace* (1986; tr.1990), Ch.3

12 Moral choices do not depend on personal preference and private decision but on right reason and, I would add, divine order.

Basil Hume (b.1923), British churchman and archbishop of Westminster: in *The Times* (London), 16 March 1990

13 There are few things more disturbing than to find, in somebody we detest, a moral quality which seems to us demonstrably superior to anything we ourselves possess. It augurs not merely an unfairness on the part of creation, but a lack of artistic judgement. ... Sainthood is acceptable only in saints.

Pamela Hansford Johnson (1912–1981), British author and critic: *Night and Silence, Who is Here? – An American Comedy* (1962), Ch.23

14 Morals are a matter of taste.

Mike Leigh (b.1943), British film-maker: interview in *Naked and Other Screenplays* (1995)

15 Moral action must not be confused with the tedium of sermons. It involves the reasoning and the humour of the talmudists, the overwhelming certainties of the prophets, and virile confidence of the psalms. It even involves the possibility of those feelings that have lost their innocence.

Emmanuel Levinas (b.1905), French Jewish philosopher: 'Place and Utopia' (1950), rep. in *Difficult Freedom* (1990), Pt.3

16 It is a purely relative matter where one draws the plimsoll-line of condemnation, and ... if you find the whole of humanity falls below it you have simply made a mistake and drawn it too high. And are probably below it yourself.

Frances Partridge (b.1900), British translator and author: journal entry, 3 Sept. 1959, publ. in *Julia* (1983), Ch.17

17 Morality has to transcend itself toward an end that is not itself. Give someone who is thirsty something to drink not in order to give him something or in order to be good but in order to overcome his thirst.

Jean-Paul Sartre (1905–1980), French philosopher and author: *Notebooks for an Ethics* (1983; tr.1992), Notebook 1

18 Unfortunately, moral beauty in art – like physical beauty in a person – is extremely perishable. It is nowhere so durable as artistic or intellectual beauty. Moral beauty has a tendency to decay very rapidly into sententiousness or untimeliness.

Susan Sontag (b.1933), U.S. essayist: 'Camus' Notebooks' (1963), rep. in *Against Interpretation* (1966)

19 Moral power is probably best when it is not used. The less you use it the more you have.

Andrew Young (b.1932), U.S. Democratic politician and diplomat: in *The Observer* (London), 8 Sept. 1979

MORTALITY

---

1 In the decade of Vietnam, in the century of Hiroshima and Buchenwald, we are as perpetually aware of mortality as any generation ever was. It is small wonder that so many people are taking the dandy's way of asking unanswerable questions. The pursuit of magnificence starts as play and ends as nihilism or metaphysics or a new examination of the nature of goals.

Angela Carter (1940–1992), British author: in *New Society* (London), 1967, rep. in *The Faber Book of Pop* (ed. Hanif Kureishi and Jon Savage, 1995), Pt.5, '1967: Notes for a Theory of Sixties Style'

2 It has been drummed into man that's he's mortal, but faced with something that really threatens to take away his right to Immortality he will resist as if he were about to be killed.

Andrey Tarkovsky (1932–1986), Russian film-maker: journal entry, 7 Sept. 1970, publ. in *Time Within Time: The Diaries 1970–1986* (1989; tr.1994)

3 Maybe I'm gonna die. You've got even bigger problems – you're gonna live.

James Warren (b.1936), U.S. actor: Johnny Rico (Warren) to his brother, in *The Brothers Rico* (film; screenplay by Lewis Meltzer and Ben Perry, adapted from Georges Simenon's novelette, directed by Phil Karlson, 1957)

MOTHERS

---

1 The best thing that could happen to motherhood already has. Fewer women are going into it.

Victoria Billings (b.1945), U.S. journalist and author: *The Womansbook* (1974), 'Meeting Your Personal Needs'

2 The kind of power mothers have is enormous. Take the skyline of Istambul – enormous breasts, pathetic little willies, a final revenge on Islam. I was so scared I had to crouch in the bottom of the boat when I saw it.

Angela Carter (1940–1992), British author: interview in *New Writing* (ed. Malcolm Bradbury and Judy Cooke, 1992)

3 I believe that always, or almost always, in all childhoods and in all the lives that follow them, the mother represents madness. Our mothers always remain the strangest, craziest people we've ever met.

Marguerite Duras (1914–1996), French author and film-maker: *Practicalities* (1987; tr.1990), 'House and Home'

4 The fact that we are all trained to be mothers from infancy on means that we are all trained to devote our lives to men, whether they are our sons or not; that we are all trained to force other women to exemplify the lack of qualities which characterizes the cultural construct of femininity.

Andrea Dworkin (b.1946), U.S. feminist critic: 'The Sexual Politics of Fear and Courage', speech, 12 March 1975, City University of New York, publ. in *Our Blood* (1976), Ch.5

5 Take motherhood: nobody ever thought of putting it on a moral pedestal until some brash feminists pointed out, about a century ago, that the pay is lousy and the career ladder nonexistent.

Barbara Ehrenreich (b.1941), U.S. author and columnist: 'Premature Pragmatism', first publ. in *Ms.* (New York), 1986, rep. in *The Worst Years of Our Lives* (1991)

6 All that remains to the mother in modern consumer society is the role of scapegoat; psychoanalysis uses huge amounts of money and time to persuade analysands to foist their problems on to the absent mother, who has no opportunity to utter a word in her own defence. Hostility to the mother in our societies is an index of mental health.

Germaine Greer (b.1939), Australian feminist writer: *The Change: Women, Ageing and the Menopause* (1991), Ch.3

7 I love you, mama, but I must be frank. Why did Papa die alone and hungry? Why did you think me insane for wanting a new bicycle instead of the old one I stole piece by piece and put together? Why did you allow us to worship at a white altar? Why even now, following tragedy after tragedy, crisis after crisis, do you still send Jon to that school where he is taught to feel inferior, and why do you continue to send me Easter cards? This is the height of the disrespect you show me. You never wanted me to be a man nor Jon either. You don't want us to resist and defeat our enemies. What is wrong with you, Mama?

George Jackson (1942–1971), U.S. black activist: letter, 26 March 1967, to his mother from Soledad Prison, publ. in *Soledad Brother* (1970)

8 A Mother's hardest to forgive.
Life is the fruit she longs to hand you,
Ripe on a plate. And while you live,
Relentlessly she understands you.

Phyllis McGinley (1905–1978), U.S. poet and author: 'The Adversary', publ. in *A Certain Age* (1960)

9 My very photogenic mother died in a freak accident (picnic, lightning) when I was three, and, save for a pocket of warmth in the darkest past, nothing of her subsists within the hollows and dells of memory.

Vladimir Nabokov (1899–1977), Russian-born U.S. novelist and poet: the narrator (Humbert Humbert), in *Lolita* (1955), Pt.1, Ch.1

10 Clearly, society has a tremendous stake in insisting on a woman's natural fitness for the career of mother: the alternatives are all too expensive.

Ann Oakley (b.1944), British sociologist and author: *Woman's Work: The Housewife, Past and Present* (1974), Ch.8

11 Every man must define his identity against his mother. If he does not, he just falls back into her and is swallowed up.

Camille Paglia (b.1947), U.S. author and critic: 'Homosexuality at the Fin de Siècle', first publ. in *Esquire* (New York), Oct. 1991, rep. in *Sex, Art, and American Culture* (1992)

12 A boy's best friend is his mother.

Anthony Perkins (1932–1992), U.S. actor: Norman Bates (Perkins), in *Psycho* (film; screenplay by Joseph Stefano, based on Robert Bloch's novel *Psycho*, 1959, directed by Alfred Hitchcock, 1960)

13 As her sons have seen her: the mother in patriarchy: controlling, erotic, castrating, heart-suffering, guilt-ridden, and guilt-provoking; a marble brow, a huge breast, an avid cave; between her legs snakes, swampgrass, or teeth; on her lap a helpless infant or a martyred son. She exists for one purpose: to bear and nourish the son.

Adrienne Rich (b.1929), U.S. poet: *Of Woman Born* (1976), Ch.8

14 Only in America ... do these peasants, our mothers, get their hair dyed platinum at the age of sixty, and walk up and down Collins Avenue in Florida in pedalpushers and mink stoles – and with opinions on every subject under the sun. It isn't their fault they were given a gift like speech – look, if cows could talk, they would say things just as idiotic.

Philip Roth (b.1933), U.S. novelist: *Portnoy's Complaint* (1967), 'Cunt Crazy'

15 How simple a thing it seems to me that to know ourselves as we are, we must know our mothers' names.

Alice Walker (b.1944), U.S. author and critic: 'A Letter to the Editor of *Ms.*', publ. in *Ms.* (New

York), Aug. 1974, rep. in *In Search of Our Mothers' Gardens* (1983)

16 Young women especially have something invested in being *nice people*, and it's only when you have children that you realise you're not a nice person at all, but generally a selfish bully.
Fay Weldon (b.1933), British novelist: in the *Independent on Sunday* (London), 5 May 1991

17 Motherhood is the strangest thing, it can be like being one's own Trojan horse.
Rebecca West (1892–1983), British author: letter, 20 Aug. 1959, quoted in *Rebecca West: A Life* by Victoria Glendinning (1987), Pt.5, Ch.8

See also Fenton on SONG

MOTTOS & MAXIMS

1 Never play cards with a man called Doc. Never eat at a place called Mom's. Never sleep with a woman whose troubles are worse than your own.
Nelson Algren (1909–1981), U.S. author: quoted in *Newsweek* (New York), 2 July 1956

2 Never let the other fellow set the agenda.
James Baker (b.1930), U.S. Republican politician and secretary of state: in *The Daily Telegraph* (London), 15 Nov. 1988

3 Until a friend or relative has applied a particular proverb to your own life, or until you've watched him apply the proverb to his own life, it has no power to sway you.
Nicholson Baker (b.1957), U.S. author: *U And I: A True Story* (1991), Ch.4

4 If you have to be in a soap opera try not to get the worst role.
Boy George (b.1961), British singer: interview in *The Face* (London), Dec. 1984

5 There are things you just can't do in life. You can't beat the phone company, you can't make a waiter see you until he's ready to see you, and you can't go home again.
Bill Bryson (b.1951), U.S. author and journalist: *The Lost Continent: Travels in Small Town America* (1989), Ch.2

6 Moral of the Work. In war: resolution. In defeat: defiance. In victory: magnanimity. In peace: goodwill.
Winston Churchill (1874–1965), British statesman and author: epigraph in each volume of *The Second World War* (1948–54). Churchill first used the words with reference to World War I

7 Don't follow leaders
And watch the parkin' meters.
Bob Dylan (b.1941), U.S. singer and songwriter: 'Subterranean Homesick Blues' (song) on the album *Bringing it All Back Home* (1965)

8 Early to bed, early to rise, work like hell and organize.
Albert Gore (b.1948), U.S. Democratic politician and vice president: campaigning slogan as presidential contender, quoted in *The Daily Telegraph* (London), 2 Feb. 1988

9 Life is not a dress rehearsal.
Rose Tremain (b.1943), British author: personal motto, as told to *The Sunday Correspondent* (London), 24 Dec. 1989

10 Never be the only one, except, possibly, in your own home.
Alice Walker (b.1944), U.S. author and critic: 'Breaking Chains and Encouraging Life', first publ. in *Ms.* (New York), April 1980, rep. in *In Search of our Mothers' Gardens* (1983)

MULTICULTURALISM

1 The establishment of democracy on the American continent was scarcely as radical a break with the past as was the necessity, which Americans faced, of broadening this concept to include black men.
James Baldwin (1924–1987), U.S. author: 'Stranger In The Village', first publ. in *Harper's Magazine* (New York), Oct. 1953, rep. in *Notes of a Native Son* (1955)

2 We Americans have the chance to become someday a nation in which all radical stocks and classes can exist in their own selfhoods, but meet on a basis of respect and equality and live together, socially, economically, and politically. We can become a dynamic equilibrium, a harmony of many different elements, in which the whole will be greater than all its parts and greater than any society the world has seen before. It can still happen.
Shirley Chisholm (b.1924), U.S. congresswoman: *The Good Fight* (1973), Ch.14

3 Once the visitor was told rather repetitively that this city was the melting pot; never before in history had so many people of such varied languages, customs, colors and culinary habits lived so amicably together. Although New York remains peaceful by most standards, this self-congratulation is now less often heard, since it was discovered some years ago that racial harmony depended unduly on the willingness of the blacks (and latterly the Puerto Ricans) to do for the other races the meanest jobs at the lowest wages and then to return to live by themselves in the worst slums.
J.K. Galbraith (b.1908), U.S. economist: of New York City, in 'The United States', publ. in *New York*, 15 Nov. 1971, rep. in *A View from the Stands* (1986)

4 I hear that melting-pot stuff a lot, and all I can say is that we haven't melted.

Jesse Jackson (b.1941), U.S. clergyman and civil rights leader: in *Playboy* (Chicago), Nov. 1969

5 It's just like when you've got some coffee that's too black, which means it's too strong. What do you do? You integrate it with cream, you make it weak. But if you pour too much cream in it, you won't even know you ever had coffee. It used to be hot, it becomes cool. It used to be strong, it becomes weak. It used to wake you up, now it puts you to sleep.
Malcolm X (1925–1965), U.S. black leader: 'Message to the Grass Roots', speech, Nov. 1963, Detroit, publ. in *Malcolm X Speaks* (1965), Ch.1

6 All cultures are involved in one another; none is single and pure, all are hybrid, heterogeneous, extraordinarily differentiated, and unmonolithic. This, I believe, is as true of the contemporary United States as it is of the modern Arab world, where in each instance respectively so much has been made of the angers of 'un-Americanism' and the threats to 'Arabism'.
Edward Said (b.1935), Lebanese-born U.S. social and literary critic: introduction to *Culture and Imperialism* (1993)

See also PLURALISM

MURDER

1 It's frightening how easy it is to commit murder in America. Just a drink too much. I can see myself doing it. In England, one feels all the social restraints holding one back. But here, anything can happen.
W.H. Auden (1907–1973), Anglo-American poet: *The Table Talk of W.H. Auden* (comp. Alan Ansen, ed. Nicholas Jenkins, 1990), 'November 16, 1946'

2 Murder is unique in that it abolishes the party it injures, so that society has to take the place of the victim and on his behalf demand atonement or grant forgiveness; it is the one crime in which society has a direct interest.
W.H. Auden: 'The Guilty Vicarage', first publ. in *Harper's Magazine* (New York), May 1948, rep. in *The Dyer's Hand* (1962), Pt.3

3 All that seems desirable to me at this time is that in the middle of a universe of murder, we decide to think about murder, and to choose.
Albert Camus (1913–1960), French-Algerian philosopher and author: 'Neither Victims nor Executioners', publ. in *Combat*, Nov. 1947, rep. in *Actuelles*, 1950, quoted in *Camus: A Biography* by Herbert R. Lottman (1979), Ch.30

4 After all, every murderer when he kills runs the risk of the most dreadful of deaths, whereas those who kill him risk nothing except promotion.
Albert Camus: *Resistance, Rebellion and Death* (1961), 'Reflections on the Guillotine'

5 Murders are exciting and lift people into a heart-beating awe as religion is supposed to do, after seeing one in the street young couples will go back to bed and make love, people will cross themselves and thank God for the gift of their stuporous lives, old folks will talk to each other over cups of hot water with lemon because murders are enlivened sermons to be analyzed and considered and relished, they speak to the timid of the dangers of rebellion, murders are perceived as momentary descents of God and so provide joy and hope and righteous satisfaction to parishioners, who will talk about them for years afterward to anyone who will listen.
E.L. Doctorow (b.1931), U.S. novelist: *Billy Bathgate* (1989), Ch.19

6 I wasn't thinking, I wasn't planning, I was just doing. I'm just saying murder vents rage. Rage is not reason. The murders were without reason.
Gary Gilmore (1941–1977), U.S. murderer: quoted in *The Guardian* (London), 30 Sep 1995

7 Every murder turns on a bright hot light, and a lot of people ... have to walk out of the shadows.
Mark Hellinger (1903–1947), U.S. journalist, scriptwriter and producer: narrator, in *The Naked City* (film; screenplay by Albert Maltz and Malvin Wald, directed by Jules Dassin, 1948). Hellinger's last production was narrated by himself

8 Under the rules of a society that cannot distinguish between profit and profiteering, between money defined as necessity and money defined as luxury, murder is occasionally obligatory and always permissible.
Lewis H. Lapham (b.1935), U.S. essayist and editor: *Money and Class in America* (1988), Ch.4

9 You can always count on a murderer for a fancy prose style.
Vladimir Nabokov (1899–1977), Russian-born U.S. novelist and poet: *Lolita* (1955), Pt.1, Ch.1

10 Killing you and what you represent is a statement. I'm not exactly sure what it's saying...
Quentin Tarantino (b.1958), U.S. film-maker: Mickey Knox (Woody Harrelson) to a TV show host, in *Natural Born Killers* (film; screenplay by Quentin Tarantino, directed by Oliver Stone, 1995). During their interview earlier from prison, Mickey explains, 'It's just murder. All creatures and species do it. I know a lot of people who deserve to die. That's where I come in, fate's messenger.' In a dispute with Stone, Tarantino later disowned the film

11 Murder does not rank as a scandal, in the way that financial impropriety or (to a lesser extent) sexual misbehaviour might. Murder is more of a misfortune, part of the American way of life. It is considered in bad taste to bring up the subject in conversation.

Auberon Waugh (b.1939), British journalist and novelist: on doubts surrounding the alleged suicide note of Vincent Foster, White House official and friend of Hillary Clinton, in 'Way of the World' column in *The Daily Telegraph* (London), 28 Oct. 1995

See also Hitchcock on TELEVISION

MUSEUMS & GALLERIES

1 It looks as if we may be presented with a kind of vast municipal fire station. ... What is proposed is like a monstrous carbuncle on the face of a much loved and elegant friend.

Charles, Prince of Wales (b.1948): referring to the proposed extension to London's National Gallery, in speech, 30 May 1984, to Royal Institute of British Architects, quoted in *The Times* (London), 31 May 1984. In the furore which followed Charles's attack, the design was rejected in favour of a more classical structure. Charles's words may have been inspired by a passage recently written by Princess Diana's stepmother, Raine Spencer, in *The Spencers on Spas* (1983): 'Alas, for our towns and cities. Monstrous carbuncles of concrete have erupted in gentle Georgian squares'

2 The Louvre is a morgue; you go there to identify your friends.

Jean Cocteau (1889–1963), French author and filmmaker: quoted in 'A Native Son of Paris', by Roger Shattuck, in the anthology *Jean Cocteau and the French Scene* (1984)

3 Individually, museums are fine institutions, dedicated to the high values of preservation, education and truth; collectively, their growth in numbers points to the imaginative death of this country.

Robert Hewison (b.1943), British cultural historian: introduction to *The Heritage Industry* (1987),

4 I never can pass by the Metropolitan Museum of Art in New York without thinking of it not as a gallery of living portraits but as a cemetery of tax-deductible wealth.

Lewis H. Lapham (b.1935), U.S. essayist and editor: *Money and Class in America* (1988), Ch.9

5 Nothing seems more like a whorehouse to me than a museum. In it you find the same equivocal aspect, the same frozen quality.

Michel Leiris (1901–1990), French anthropologist and author: *Manhood* (1946; tr.1963), Ch.2, 'Brothels and Museums'

6 Attitudes to museums have changed. If it had Marilyn Monroe's knickers or Laurence Olivier's jockstrap they would flock to it.

Jonathan Miller (b.1936), British doctor, humorist and director: on the low attendances at his recently opened Theatre Museum, in *The Daily Telegraph* (London), 7 June 1989

MUSIC

1 Today, music heralds ... the establishment of a society of repetition in which nothing will happen anymore.

Jacques Attali (b.1943), Algerian-born French economist and writer: *Noise: The Political Economy of Music* (1977), Ch.1

2 A verbal art like poetry is reflective; it stops to think. Music is immediate, it goes on to become.

W.H. Auden (1907–1973), Anglo-American poet: *The Dyer's Hand* (1962), Pt.8, 'Notes on Music and Opera'

3 People basically only want very little from music, and I want a lot from it. It's capable of amazing journeys and meanings. And if you understand that, the problem with the kind of music I write is no problem at all.

Harrison Birtwistle (b.1934), British composer: interview in the *Independent on Sunday* (London), 7 April 1996. In the same interview, Birtwistle explained: 'I look at a piece of music as if it were a three-dimensional object ... at no point do you see the whole object'

4 It is better to make a piece of music than to perform one, better to perform one than to listen to one, better to listen to one than to misuse it as a means of distraction, entertainment, or acquisition of 'culture'.

John Cage (1912–1992), U.S. composer: 'Forerunners of Modern Music: At Random', first publ. in *Tiger's Eye* (New York), March 1949, rep. in *Silence* (1961)

5 If the music doesn't say it, how can the words say it for the music?

John Coltrane (1926–1967), U.S. jazz musician: quoted in *Jazz is* by Nat Hentoff (1976), Ch.5

6 Nothing separates the generations more than music. By the time a child is eight or nine, he has developed a passion for his own music that is even stronger than his passions for procrastination and weird clothes.

Bill Cosby (b.1937), U.S. comedian and actor: *Fatherhood* (1986), Ch.10

7 Music was invented to confirm human loneliness.

Lawrence Durrell (1912–1990), British author: Clea, in *Clea* (1960), Ch.1, Sct.4

8 Perhaps all music, even the newest, is not so much something discovered as something that re-emerges from where it lay buried in the memory, inaudible as a melody cut in a disc of flesh. A composer lets me hear a song that has always been shut up silent within me.

Jean Genet (1910–1986), French playwright and novelist: *Prisoner of Love* (1986; tr.1989), Pt.1

9   The hills are alive with the sound of music.

Oscar Hammerstein II (1895–1960), U.S. songwriter: 'The Sound of Music' (song) in *The Sound of Music* (stage musical, 1959; film, 1965)

10   I am fond of music I think because it is so amoral. Everything else is moral and I am after something that isn't. I have always found moralizing intolerable.

Hermann Hesse (1877–1962), German novelist and poet: Sinclair, in *Demian* (1960), Ch.5

11   Since music is a language with some meaning at least for the immense majority of mankind, although only a tiny minority of people are capable of formulating a meaning in it, and since it is the only language with the contra-dictory attributes of being at once intelligible and untranslatable, the musical creator is a being comparable to the gods, and music itself the supreme mystery of the science of man, a mystery that all the various disciplines come up against and which holds the key to their progress.

Claude Lévi-Strauss (b.1908), French anthropologist: *The Raw and the Cooked* (1964), 'Overture'

12   A woman's two cents worth is worth two cents in the music business.

Loretta Lynn (b.1930), U.S. singer: quoted in the *Los Angeles Times*, 26 May 1974

13   Music is spiritual. The music business is not.

Van Morrison (b.1945), Irish rock musician: in *The Times* (London), 6 July 1990

14   There once was a brainy baboon
Who always breathed down a bassoon,
    For he said, 'It appears
    That in billions of years
I shall certainly hit on a tune.'

Ezra Pound (1885–1972), U.S. poet and critic: letter to Huntingdon Cairns of the National Gallery of Art in Washington D.C., 21 July 1949, quoted in *A Serious Character* by Humphrey Carpenter (biography, 1988), Pt.2, Ch.16. Pound took up the bassoon for a few months in 1921

15   If anyone has conducted a Beethoven perfor-mance, and then doesn't have to go to an osteopath, then there's something wrong.

Simon Rattle (b.1955), British conductor: in *The Guardian* (London), 31 May 1990

16   Music is not a cheap spectacle – not the enter-tainment of the brothel. It is like prayer.

Vikram Seth (b.1952), Indian author: Ustad Majeed Khan, in *A Suitable Boy* (1993), Ch.6, Sct.2

17   The most perfect expression of human be-haviour is a string quartet.

Jeffrey Tate (b.1943), British conductor: in the *New Yorker*, 30 April 1990

18   Oh, I'm a martyr to music.

Dylan Thomas (1914–1953), Welsh poet: Mrs Organ Morgan, in *Under Milk Wood* (1954),

19   Music is the effort we make to explain to ourselves how our brains work. We listen to Bach transfixed because this is listening to a human mind.

Lewis Thomas (1913–1993), U.S. physician and educator: *The Medusa and the Snail* (1979), 'On Thinking About Thinking'

20   There's a basic rule which runs through all kinds of music, kind of an unwritten rule. I don't know what it is. But I've got it.

Ron Wood (b.1947), British rock musician: in *The Independent* (London), 10 Sept. 1992

21   Music, in performance, is a type of sculpture. The air in the performance is sculpted into something.

Frank Zappa (1940–1993), U.S. rock musician: *The Real Frank Zappa Book* (written with Peter Occhiogrosso, 1989), Ch.8

See also Cage on NOISE; OPERA; Anderson on PERFORMANCE; PUNK; SONG; Zappa on TIME

MUSIC: Blues

1   Blues is easy to play, but hard to feel.

Jimi Hendrix (1942–1970), U.S. rock musician: quoted in *Crosstown Traffic* by Charles Shaar Murray (1989), Ch.6

2   It's never hard to sing the blues. Everyone in the world has the blues ... poor people have the blues because they're poor and hungry. Rich people can't sleep at night because they're try-ing to hold on to their money and everything they have.

John Lee Hooker (b.1917), U.S. blues musician: in the *Detroit Free Press*, 8 Sept. 1991

3   Blues are the songs of despair, but gospel songs are the songs of hope.

Mahalia Jackson (1911–1972), U.S. gospel singer: *Movin' On Up* (written with Evan McLoud Wylie, 1966), Ch.6

4   When you get your ass kicked that hard, it makes you go to the innermost depths of what you are all about as a human being. Now, maybe most people have not been kicked that hard, but it's still in everybody, and this music rings a bell that you can hear throughout the fucking world.

Quincy Jones (b.1933), U.S. musician, arranger and producer: quoted in *Rolling Stone* (New York), 1 July 1976

5 The blues was like that problem child that you may have had in the family. You was a little bit ashamed to let anybody see him, but you loved him. You just didn't know how other people would take it.

B.B. King (b.1925), U.S. blues guitarist: interview in *The Sunday Times* (London), 4 Nov. 1984

6 For a long time even the black people looked down on the blues. It wasn't middle-class. Then Elvis Presley came along, twisting and singing and everything ... and we were making *all kinds* of money. I ain't got no problem with that.

Reverend Arnold 'Gatemouth' Moore (b.1914), U.S. blues musician: quoted in *Mojo* (London), March 1996

MUSIC: Composition

---

1 Whenever I don't know what to write about, I just close my eyes and think of Essex.

Damon Albarn (b.1967), British rock musician: interview in *Blah Blah Blah* (London), April 1996

2 All I try to do in my writing is assemble points that interest me and puzzle through it, and that becomes a song and other people who listen to that song must take what they can from it and see if information that they've assembled fits in with anything I've assembled and what do we do now?

David Bowie (b.1947), British rock musician: interview, Jan. 1973, rep. in *Bowie In His Own Words* (ed. Miles, 1980), 'Songwriting'

3 I think perhaps my own best piece, at least the one I like the most, is the silent piece. It has three movements and in all of these movements there are no sounds. I wanted my work to be free of my own likes and dislikes, because I think music should be free of the feelings of the composer.

John Cage (1912–1992), U.S. composer: of his composition, *4'33"* (1952), in interview in *Soho Weekly News* (New York), 12 Sept. 1974, rep. in *Conversing with Cage* (ed. Richard Kostelanetz, 1988), 'His Own Music (to 1970)'

4 In writing songs I've learned as much from Cézanne as I have from Woody Guthrie.

Bob Dylan (b.1941), U.S. singer and songwriter: quoted in *Dylan: Behind the Shades* by Clinton Heylin (1991), Ch.25

5 Composing a piece of music is very feminine. It is sensitive, emotional, contemplative. By comparison, doing housework is positively masculine.

Barbara Kolb (b.1939), U.S. composer: quoted in *Time* (New York), 10 Nov. 1975

6 The diatonic scale is what you use if you want to write a national anthem, or a love song, or a lullaby. The chromatic scale is what you use to give the effect of drinking a quinine martini and having an enema at the same time.

Philip Larkin (1922–1985), British poet: interview in the *Paris Review*, 1982, rep. in *Required Writing* (1983)

7 Songwriting is about getting the demon out of me. It's like being possessed. You try to go to sleep, but the song won't let you. So you have to get up and make it into something, and then you're allowed to sleep. It's always in the middle of the bloody night, or when you're half-awake or tired, when your critical faculties are switched off. So letting go is what the whole game is. Every time you try to put your finger on it, it slips away. You turn on the lights and the cockroaches run away. You can never grasp them.

John Lennon (1940–1980), British rock musician: in *Playboy* (Chicago), Sept. 1980

8 The collection of antiques which is a symphony orchestra belongs more properly to the past. A modern composer is forced to translate into the language of these old instruments what his imagination proposes to him in a form which has nothing in common with them.

Witold Lutoslawski (1913–1994), Polish composer: *Conversations with Witold Lutoslawski* (ed. Tadeusz Kaczyński, 1972; tr.1984), Ch.13

9 A composer is a guy who goes around forcing his will on unsuspecting air molecules, often with the assistance of unsuspecting musicians.

Frank Zappa (1940–1993), U.S. rock musician: *The Real Frank Zappa Book* (written with Peter Occhiogrosso, 1989), Ch.8

See also Cage on MYSTERY

MUSIC: Country

---

1 I'm a country songwriter and we write cry-in-your-beer songs. That's what we do. Something that you can slow dance to.

Willie Nelson (b.1933), U.S. singer and songwriter: interview in *The Independent* (London), 11 May 1996

2 You've got to have smelled a lot of mule manure before you can sing like a hillbilly.

Hank Williams (1923–1953), U.S. country musician: quoted in *All You Need is Love* by Tony Palmer (1976), 'Making Moonshine'

MUSIC: Folk

---

1 Nowadays, you go to see a folk singer – what's the folk singer doin'? He's singin' all his own songs. *That* ain't no folk singer. Folk singers

sing those old folk songs, ballads. ... There's no *dedication* to folk music now, no *appreciation* of the art form.

Bob Dylan (b.1941), U.S. singer and songwriter: interview in *Rolling Stone* (New York), June 1984

2 My idea of heaven is a place where the Tyne meets the Delta, where folk music meets the blues.

Mark Knopfler (b.1949), British rock musician: interview in *Mojo* (London), April 1996

3 I had thought that folk music was something old, back in the library, and pop music was new – it was something you could hear on the radio. All of a sudden I realized that was a phony distinction. Millions of people were making music which grew out of the old traditions, mostly making up new words to fit old tunes. New words to fit new circumstances. This is what I call the folk process.

Pete Seeger (b.1919), U.S. folk singer: quoted in *All You Need is Love* by Tony Palmer (1976), 'Go Down Moses!'

MUSIC: Jazz

1 The further jazz moves away from the stark blue continuum and the collective realities of Afro-American and American life, the more it moves into academic concert-hall lifelessness, which can be replicated by any middle class showing off its music lessons.

Amiri Baraka [formerly Leroi Jones] (b.1934), U.S. poet and playwright: *Daggers and Javelins* (1984), 'Jazz: Speech At Black Film Festival'

2 I've come close to matching the feeling of that night in 1944 in music, when I first heard Diz and Bird, but I've never got there ... I'm always looking for it, listening and feeling for it, though, trying to always feel it in and through the music I play everyday.

Miles Davis (1926–1991), U.S. jazz musician: of Dizzy Gillespie and Charlie Parker, in Prologue to *Miles: The Autobiography* (1989)

3 Playing 'bop' is like playing Scrabble with all the vowels missing.

Duke Ellington (1899–1974), U.S. jazz musician: in *Look* (New York), 10 Aug. 1954

4 Jazz is the big brother of the blues. If a guy's playing blues like we play, he's in high school. When he starts playing jazz it's like going on to college, to a school of higher learning.

B.B. King (b.1925), U.S. blues guitarist: interview in *The Sunday Times* (London), 4 Nov. 1984

5 The great thing about the jazz world, and all the kids that enter into it, is that no one, not a soul, cares what your class is, or what your race is, or what your income, or if you're a boy, or girl, or bent, or versatile, or what you are – so long as you dig the scene and can behave your-self, and have left all that crap behind you, too, when you come in the jazz club door.

Colin MacInnes (1914–1976), British author: *Absolute Beginners* (1959), 'in June'

6 For jazz is orgasm, it is the music of orgasm, good orgasm and bad, and so it spoke across a nation, it had the communication of art even where it was watered, perverted, corrupted, and almost killed, it spoke in no matter what laundered popular way of instantaneous existential states to which some whites could respond, it was indeed a communication by art because it said, 'I feel this, and now you do too'.

Norman Mailer (b.1923), U.S. author: 'The White Negro', Sct.2, first publ. in *Dissent*, summer 1957, rep. in *Advertisements for Myself* (1959)

7 Jazz is music that really deals with what it means to be an American. The irony is when they wrote the Declaration of Independence and the United States Constitution, they didn't even think of a Black man. Yet Louis Armstrong, the grandson of a slave, is the one more than anybody else [who] could translate into music that feeling of what it is to be an American.

Wynton Marsalis (b.1961), U.S. jazz musician: 'We Must Preserve Our Jazz Heritage', publ. in *Ebony* (Chicago), Feb. 1986

8 There's more bad music in jazz than any other form. Maybe that's because the audience doesn't really know what's happening.

Pat Metheny (b.1954), U.S. jazz guitarist: in the *International Herald Tribune* (Paris), 7 July 1992

9 Music is your own experience, your own thoughts, your wisdom. If you don't live it, it won't come out of your horn. They teach you there's a boundary line to music. But, man, there's no boundary line to art.

Charlie Parker (1920–1955), U.S. jazz musician: quoted in *Children of Albion: Poetry of the Underground in Britain* (ed. Michael Horovitz, 1969), 'Afterwords', Sct.3

10 Jazz music is an intensified feeling of nonchalance.
(*La musique de jazz, c'est une insouciance accelerée.*)

Françoise Sagan (b.1935), French novelist and playwright: Dominique, in *A Certain Smile* (1956), Pt.1, Ch.7

11 Something was still there, that something that distinguishes an artist from a performer: the revealing of self. Here I be. Not for long, but here I be. In sensing her mortality, we sensed our own.

Studs Terkel (b.1912), U.S. author and broadcaster: on seeing Billie Holiday perform in Chicago, 1956, in *Talking to Myself* (1977), Bk.4, Ch.4

MUSIC: Muzak

1   The thing that makes Muzak tolerable is its very narrow dynamic range. ... You can hear many other things at the same time as you hear Muzak. And if you pay attention carefully enough, I think you can put up with Muzak – if you pay attention, I mean, to the things that are not Muzak.
John Cage (1912–1992), U.S. composer: interview, 1985, rep. in *Conversing with Cage* (ed. Richard Kostelanetz, 1988), 'Esthetics'

2   I hate it, hate it. It seems to me there is silence, and there is conversation, and there is a place you choose to go to, to listen to music. I hate the presumption.
Simon Gray (b.1936), British playwright: interview in the *Independent on Sunday* (London), 19 Feb. 1995

3   People whose sensibility is destroyed by music in trains, airports, lifts, cannot concentrate on a Beethoven quartet.
Witold Lutoslawski (1913–1994), Polish composer: in the *Independent on Sunday* (London), 13 Jan. 1991

4   The manner in which Americans 'consume' music has a lot to do with leaving it on their coffee tables, or using it as wallpaper for their lifestyles, like the score of a movie – it's consumed that way without any regard for how and why it's made.
Frank Zappa (1940–1993), U.S. rock musician: interview quoted in *The Real Frank Zappa Book* (written with Peter Occhiogrosso, 1989), Ch.11

MUSIC: Rap

1   Don't mock the rap-artist: envy him. A rap-artist is definitely the thing to be. As well as the affection, reverence and erotic perks traditionally due to the musician, he is also accorded the status of poet, philosopher, dissident and redeemer. Nobody ever had it so good.
Martin Amis (b.1949), British author: in the *Evening Standard* (London), 1989, rep. in *Visiting Mrs Nabokov* (1993), 'Carnival'

2   You better think it out
We should be able to say anything
Our lungs were meant to shout.
Say what you feel, yell out what's real
Even though it may not bring mass appeal
Your opinion is yours, mine is mine
If you don't like what I'm sayin' fine.
Ice-T (b.1958), U.S. rapper: 'Freedom of Speech' (song; written by Ice-T and Afrika Islam, 1990)

3   Rap is poetry to music – like beatniks without beards and bongos.
Dave Lee Roth (b.1955), U.S. rock musician: quoted in *Rolling Stone* (New York), Dec. 1990

MUSIC: Reggae

1   It's just a fun, joke kinda word that means the ragged rhythm and the body feelin'. If it's got a greater meanin', it doesn't matter.
Hux Brown, Jamaican musician: quoted in *Catch a Fire* by Timothy White (1991), Ch.1

2   Brothers and sisters rocking,
a dread beat pulsing fire, burning.
Linton Kwesi Johnson (b.1952), Anglo-Jamaican poet and singer: 'Dread Beat an Blood' (poem, 1975; set to music and released on the album *Dread, Beat and Blood*, 1978)

3   The real reggae must come from Jamaica, because other people could not play it all the while, anyway – it would go against the whole life. Reggae has t'be inside you. ... Reggae music is simple, all the while. ... Cannot be taught, that's a fact.
Bob Marley (1945–1981), Jamaican reggae musician: interview in *Melody Maker* (London), 12 June 1976, rep. in *Melody Maker: Classic Rock Interviews* (ed. Allan Jones, 1994)

MUSIC: Rock & Pop

1   Pop is all about doing something that connects really easily, and that's why I've never had any time for classical music. ... It just bores me because it's too easy. Anyone can be that complicated. Three notes is far cleverer than three hundred if they're arranged in the right way, and that's what pop music is all about.
Brett Anderson (b.1967), British rock musician: interview in *i-D* (London), Oct. 1994

2   A lot of pop music is about stealing pocket money from children.
Ian Anderson (b.1947), British rock musician: in *Rolling Stone* (New York), 30 Nov. 1989

3   The essential misapprehension about popular music is that it is anything other than a totally capitalistic enterprise. In fact, it has absolutely nothing to do with anything except making money and getting rich. Some popular musicians start out with revolutionary rhetoric, but all they want is cars and girls and champagne. It's nonsense to think that popular music is anything but conspicuous consumption and the good life.
Lester Bangs (1948–1982), U.S. rock journalist: quoted in *All You Need is Love* by Tony Palmer (1976), 'Imagine...'

4 James Brown and Frank Sinatra are two different quantities in the universe. They represent two different experiences of the world.

Amiri Baraka [formerly Leroi Jones] (b.1934), U.S. poet and playwright: interview with David Frost in *The Americans* by David Frost (1970), 'Is Democracy a White Man's Word?'

5 Rock 'n' roll has been really bringing me down lately. It's in great danger of becoming an immobile, sterile fascist that constantly spews its propaganda on every arm of the media. It rules and dictates a level of thought and clarity of intelligence that you'll never rise above. ... It lets in lower elements and shadows that I don't think are necessary. Rock has always been the devil's music. You can't convince me that it isn't.

David Bowie (b.1947), British rock musician: interview, Feb. 1976, rep. in *Bowie In His Own Words* (ed. Miles, 1980), 'Rock 'n' Roll'

6 As I define it, rock and roll is dead. The attitude isn't dead, but the music is no longer vital. It doesn't have the same meaning. The attitude, though, is still very much alive – and it still informs other kinds of music.

David Byrne (b.1952), U.S. rock musician: quoted in *Rolling Stone* (New York), Dec. 1990

7 Rock music should be gross: that's the fun of it. It gets up and drops its trousers.

Bruce Dickinson (b.1958), British rock guitarist: in *The Guardian* (London), 10 Jan. 1991

8 One-two-three o'clock, four o'clock rock! Five-six-seven o'clock, eight o'clock rock! Nine-ten-eleven o'clock, twelve o'clock rock! We're gonna rock around the clock tonight!

Max Freedman (1893–1962), U.S. songwriter: 'Rock Around the Clock' (song). The song was a minor hit in 1952 for Sunny Dae, but, recorded by Bill Haley and the Comets two years later, and adopted as the title music to the film, *Blackboard Jungle* (1955), became the biggest hit of the rock and roll era, selling more than 25 million copies

9 What people have got to understand is that we are lads. We have burgled houses and nicked car stereos, and we like girls and we swear and we go to the football and take the piss.

Noel Gallagher (b.1967), British rock musician: interview in *Melody Maker* (London), March 1996, quoted in *The Guardian* (London), 6 April 1996. The confession prompted an investigation by Greater Manchester police, and a defence by the mother of Noel and Liam Gallagher, of the group Oasis, who declared, 'As far as I know they were never involved in any crime. They were just normal boys. ... Really, they are very thoughtful and kind and all they think about are their family and friends'

10 What we do is as American as lynch mobs. America has always been a complex place.

Jerry Garcia (1942–1995), U.S. rock musician: in *Rolling Stone* (New York), 30 Nov. 1989

11 There is no clandestine value to rock 'n' roll music. No excitement. It's totally unrevolutionary. It's totally accepted and part of everything. It's totally pushed.

Debbie Harry (b.1945), U.S. singer: in *New Musical Express* (London), 1987, quoted in *NME Book of Quotes* (1995), 'Music'

12 I know it's only rock 'n' roll but I like it.

Mick Jagger (b.1943) and **Keith Richards** (b.1943), British rock musicians: 'It's only Rock 'n' Roll' (song) on the album *It's only Rock 'n' Roll* (The Rolling Stones, 1974)

13 That ain't working, that's the way you do it
Get your money for nothing and your chicks
for free.

Mark Knopfler (b.1949), British rock musician: 'Money For Nothing' (song) on the album *Brothers in Arms* (Dire Straits, 1985)

14 There are two kinds of artists left: those who endorse Pepsi and those who simply won't.

Annie Lennox (b.1954), British singer: in *The Guardian* (London), 30 Nov. 1990

15 For those even more ignorant than I was, I should say that the team is guitar-led, though unfortunately not by Segovia. I expected a great deal of raucous noise, and got it, but listening carefully, I realised that this stuff is not just shouting, and is even up to making a musical point. Yet I knew that it would fail the crucial test; I do not believe that I would or could continue to listen to such music, and the reason is surely obvious: it is ultimately without roots.

Bernard Levin (b.1928), British author and critic: of the rock group 'Nirvana', the day after their lead singer, Kurt Cobain, shot himself, in *The Times* (London), 8 April 1994. Of Cobain, Levin wrote, 'Why should not ten million youths find their idol in a foul-mouthed, brutish, violent singer-guitarist, drugged to the eyebrows and hating himself and his way of life?'

16 No one in this band is a musician. We all hate the term. We're something close to factory workers. Machinists. Skilled operators.

John Lydon [formerly Johnny Rotten] (b.1957), British rock musician: quoted in *Rock 'n' Roll Babylon* by Gary Herman (1982), Ch.4

17 Rock and roll doesn't necessarily mean a band. It doesn't mean a singer, and it doesn't mean a lyric, really. ... It's that question of trying to be immortal.

Malcolm McLaren (b.1946), British rock impresario: 'Punk and History', transcript of discussion 24 Sept. 1988, New York City, publ. in *Discourses: Conversations in Postmodern Art and Culture* (ed. Russell Ferguson *et al.*, 1990)

18 Rock 'n' roll is a combination of good ideas dried up by fads, terrible junk, hideous failings in taste and judgment, gullibility and manipulation, moments of unbelievable clarity and invention, pleasure, fun, vulgarity, excess, novelty and utter enervation.
Greil Marcus (b.1945), U.S. rock journalist: *Mystery Train* (1976), 'Randy Newman'

19 Jazz enthusiasts despised rock 'n' roll as musically illiterate, although it produced one or two fine artists like Presley and Little Richard. It was a thinned-down derivative of Negro urban Blues reduced to their most boring element – the rhythm. Why this, which had been around for ever, should suddenly have sparked off a whole generation is a mystery. I think it had to do with military service. There was no point in getting on with your life after leaving school and while waiting to be called up. So they earned high wages in dead-end jobs and wanted something to spend them on. In this gap rock 'n' roll flourished.
George Melly (b.1926), British jazz musician, critic and author: quoted in *The Fifties* by Peter Lewis (1978), 'Youthquake'

20 I can't carry on rocking the way I have done in the past. It is all too much. It's no way for a grown man to behave.
Freddy Mercury (1946–1991), Anglo-Iranian rock musician: quoted in *Q/Omnibus Rock 'n' Roll Reader* (ed. Danny Kelly, 1994)

21 In classical music, people were doing very complex things, for the sake of being complex. I learned that rock, with two simple chords, can bring an incredible communication of the spirit.
Yoko Ono (b.1933), Japanese-born U.S. artist: interview in *The Wire* (London), April 1996

22 Awop-bop-a-loo-mop alop-bam-boom!
Little Richard (b.1932), U.S. rock musician: 'Tutti-Frutti' (song; written by Little Richard – as Richard Penniman – J. Lubin and Dorothy La Bostrie, 1955)

23 Music for the neck downwards.
Keith Richards (b.1943), British rock guitarist: quoted in *Sound Effects: Youth, Leisure and the Politics of Rock* by Simon Frith (1979), Ch.7

24 The most brutal, ugly, desperate, vicious form of expression it has been my misfortune to hear.
Frank Sinatra (b.1915), U.S. singer and actor: quoted in *Sound Effects: Youth, Leisure and the Politics of Rock* by Simon Frith (1979), Ch.5

25 There's no bullshit going down with rock and roll. It's an honest form and one of the most open. It encompasses poetry, jazz and just about anything you can imagine ... it is the highest form. It goes beyond color, gender – anything.
Patti Smith (b.1946), U.S. poet and rock musician: in *Cash Box*, 24 Jan. 1976

26 The new sound-sphere is global. It ripples at great speed across languages, ideologies, frontiers and races. ... The economics of this musical esperanto are staggering. Rock and pop breed concentric worlds of fashion, setting and life-style. Popular music has brought with it sociologies of private and public manner, of group solidarity. The politics of Eden come loud.
George Steiner (b.1929), French-born U.S. critic and novelist: *In Bluebeard's Castle* (1971), Ch.4

27 Music has ceased to belong to the young. ... The rock rebel is defunct. He's meaningless.
Sting (b.1951), British rock musician: interview in *Smash Hits* (London), 19 Aug. 1982

28 Every gimmick-hungry yob digging gold from rock 'n' roll
Grabs the mike to tell us he'll die before he's sold
But I believe in this – and it's been tested by research –
That he who fucks nuns will later join the church.
Joe Strummer (b.1952) and **Mick Jones** (b.1956), British rock musicians: 'Death or Glory' (song) on the album *London Calling* (The Clash, 1979)

29 It is amorphous, but basically it always has the same job, which is to get you through the day. And that seems to me to be a profoundly important job; it is like fresh bread.
Pete Townshend (b.1945), British rock musician: in reply to the question 'What is pop music anyway?' in interview in *The Observer* (London), 25 Feb. 1996

30 Pop music is collective music; it is as archaic as tribal music without the innocence of tribal music, and as impregnated with warning and somnambulism as Wagner at his worst.
Laurens van der Post (1906–1996), South African writer and philosopher: *A Walk with a White Bushman* (1986), p.221 of Chatto & Windus edn.

31 There are beautiful sounds in rock. Very lazy, dreamlike noises. You can forget about the lyrics in most songs. Just dig the noise, and you've got our sound. ... We're musical primitives.
Andy Warhol (c.1928–1987), U.S. Pop artist: on the Velvet Underground, quoted in the *New York Magazine*, 1967, rep. in *The Faber Book of Pop* (ed. Hanif Kureishi and Jon Savage, 1995), Pt.5, '1966: A Quiet Evening at the Balloon Farm'

32 I was working at York Sainsbury's, and people were walking past saying, 'What a wanker'. Now, because I'm in a group, people are going

to be saying that in national magazines. It's the next step.

Rick Witter, British rock musician: in *New Musical Express* (London), 1994, quoted in *NME Book of Quotes* (1995), 'Fame'

33 No change in musical style will survive unless it is accompanied by a change in clothing style. Rock is to dress up to.

Frank Zappa (1940–1993), U.S. rock musician: *The Real Frank Zappa Book* (written with Peter Occhiogrosso, 1989), Ch.9

See also THE BEATLES; BOB DYLAN; MICK JAGGER; Zappa on JOURNALISM; JOHN LENNON; MADONNA; Townshend on PERFORMANCE; ELVIS PRESLEY; Marcus on RADIO; Bowie on SELF-EXPRESSION

MYSTERY

1 I'm on the side of keeping things mysterious, and I have never enjoyed understanding things. If I understand something, I have no further use for it. So I try to make a music which I don't understand and which will be difficult for other people to understand, too.

John Cage (1912–1992), U.S. composer: interview in *Sonus*, Vol.III, 1983, rep. in *Conversing with Cage* (ed. Richard Kostelanetz, 1988), 'Esthetics'

2 Give me a mystery – just a plain and simple one – a mystery which is diffidence and silence, a slim little, barefoot mystery: give me a mystery – just one!

Yevgeny Yevtushenko (b.1933), Russian poet: 'Mysteries', St.10 (1960; tr.1965)

MYSTICISM

1 The most beautiful emotion we can experience is the mystical. It is the power of all true art and science. He to whom this emotion is a stranger, who can no longer wonder and stand rapt in awe, is as good as dead. To know that what is impenetrable to us really exists, manifesting itself as the highest wisdom and the most radiant beauty, which our dull faculties can comprehend only in their most primitive forms – this knowledge, this feeling, is at the centre of true religiousness. In this sense, and in this sense only, I belong to the rank of devoutly religious men.

Albert Einstein (1879–1955), German-born U.S. theoretical physicist: quoted in *Einstein: His Life and Times* by Philipp Frank (1947), Ch.12, Sct.5

2 We follow the mystics. They know where they are going. They, too, go astray, but when they go astray they do so in a way that is mystical, dark, and mysterious.

Ryszard Kapuściński (b.1932), Polish journalist: 'A Warsaw Diary', publ. in *Granta* (Cambridge), No.15, 1985

3 Mysticism and exaggeration go together. A mystic must not fear ridicule if he is to push all the way to the limits of humility or the limits of delight.

Milan Kundera (b.1929), Czech-born French author and critic: *The Book of Laughter and Forgetting* (1978; tr.1980), Pt.3, Ch.2

4 If we know the mystical only in its most extravagant forms, it is because we are like children raised wholly in the metropolis. We are more likely to have seen tigers in the zoo than barnyard cows, more apt to have seen hothouse orchids than ordinary wild flowers.

Theodore Roszak (b.1933), U.S. social critic: *Where the Wasteland Ends* (1972), Ch.3

5 What does mysticism really mean? It means the way to attain knowledge. It's close to philosophy, except in philosophy you go horizontally while in mysticism you go vertically.

Elie Wiesel (b.1928), Rumanian-born U.S. writer: interview in *Writers at Work* (Eighth Series, ed. George Plimpton, 1988)

MYTH

1 Myth is neither a lie nor a confession: it is an inflexion.

Roland Barthes (1915–1980), French semiologist: *Mythologies* (1957; tr.1972), 'Myth Today: Reading and Deciphering Myth'

2 Myth is the hidden part of every story, the buried part, the region that is still unexplored because there are as yet no words to enable us to get there. ... Myth is nourished by silence as well as by words.

Italo Calvino (1923–1985), Italian author and critic: 'Cybernetics and Ghosts', lecture, Nov. 1969, Turin, publ. in *The Literature Machine* (1987)

3 There are times when reality beomes too complex for Oral Communication. But Legend gives it a form by which it pervades the whole world.

Jean-Luc Godard (b.1930), French film-maker and author: the computer, Alpha 60, in opening voice-over of *Alphaville* (film; written and directed by Jean-Luc Godard, 1965)

4 The act of mythmaking has been transferred from the subject-matter of the work to the artist himself as the content of his art.

Richard Hamilton (b.1922), British Pop artist: 'For the Finest Art Try – POP', first publ. in *Gazette*, No.1, 1961, rep. in *Collected Words 1953–1982* (1982)

5 There is nothing truer than myth: history, in its attempt to 'realize' myth, distorts it, stops

halfway; when history claims to have 'succeeded,' this is nothing but humbug and mystification. Everything we dream is 'realizable'. Reality does not have to be: it is simply what it is.

Eugène Ionesco (1912–1994), Rumanian-born French playwright: 'Experience of the Theatre', publ. in *Nouvelle N.R.F.*(Paris) No.62, 1958, rep. in *Notes and Counter Notes* (1962)

6 I therefore claim to show, not how men think in myths, but how myths operate in men's minds without their being aware of the fact.

Claude Lévi-Strauss (b.1908), French anthropologist: *The Raw and the Cooked* (1964), 'Overture', Sct.1

7 It is a sure sign that a culture has reached a dead end when it is no longer intrigued by its myths.

Greil Marcus (b.1945), U.S. rock journalist: *Mystery Train* (1976), 'Elvis: Presliad'

8 The primary function of myth is to validate an existing social order. Myth enshrines conservative social values, raising tradition on a pedestal. It expresses and confirms, rather than explains or questions, the sources of cultural attitudes and values. ... Because myth anchors the present in the past it is a sociological charter for a future society which is an exact replica of the present one.

Ann Oakley (b.1944), British sociologist and author: *Woman's Work: The Housewife, Past and Present* (1974), Ch.7

9 Myths make history. The mythic symbol taps unconscious reservoirs of energy in all of us, winning our assent and motivating action by its imaginative power. Perhaps nothing has more to do with determining what we will decide to regard as truth than the force of an empowered symbol superbly projected upon the cultural stage.

Theodore Roszak (b.1933), U.S. social critic: *Where the Wasteland Ends* (1972), Ch.6

10 Sometimes legends make reality, and become more useful than the facts.

Salman Rushdie (b.1947), Indian-born British author: *Midnight's Children* (1981), Bk.1, 'Hit-the-spittoon'

11 A myth is, of course, not a fairy story. It is the presentation of facts belonging to one category in the idioms appropriate to one another. To explode a myth is accordingly not to deny the facts but to re-allocate them.

Gilbert Ryle (1900–1976), British philosopher: introduction to *The Concept of Mind* (1949)

12 Myths and legends die hard in America. We love them for the extra dimension they provide, the illusion of near-infinite possibility to erase the narrow confines of most men's

reality. Weird heroes and mould-breaking champions exist as living proof to those who need it that the tyranny of 'the rat race' is not yet final.

Hunter S. Thompson (b.1939), U.S. journalist: 'Those Daring Young Men in their Flying Machines... Ain't What They Used to Be!', publ. in *Pageant*, Sept. 1969, rep. in *The Great Shark Hunt* (1979), Pt.3

NAGGING

1 It is not the simple statement of facts that ushers in freedom; it is the constant repetition of them that has this liberating effect. Tolerance is the result not of enlightenment, but of boredom.

Quentin Crisp (b.1908), British author: *The Naked Civil Servant* (1968), Ch.28

2 Naggers always know what they are doing. They weigh up the risks, then they go on and on and on until they get what they want or until they get punched.

Jools Holland (b.1958), British rock musician and television presenter: quoted in the *Independent on Sunday* (London), 4 Oct. 1992

3 Nagging is the repetition of unpalatable truths.

Edith Summerskill (1901–1980), British Labour politician: speech, 14 July 1960, to Married Women's Association, House of Commons, quoted in *The Times* (London), 15 July 1960

NAMES

1 Proper names are poetry in the raw. Like all poetry they are untranslatable.

W.H. Auden (1907–1973), Anglo-American poet: *A Certain World* (1970), 'Names, Proper'

2 To name oneself is the first act of both the poet and the revolutionary. When we take away the right to an individual name, we symbolically take away the right to be an individual. Immigration officials did this to refugees; husbands routinely do it to wives.

Erica Jong (b.1942), U.S. author: *How To Save Your Own Life* (1977), epigraph to 'My posthumous life...'

3 In its purest sense, nicknaming is an elitist ritual practiced by those who cherish hierarchy. For preppies it's a smoke signal that allows Bunny to tell Pooky that they belong to the same tribe, while among the good ole boys it serves the cause of masculine dominance by identifying Bear and Wrecker as Alpha males.

Florence King (b.1936), U.S. author: *Reflections in a Jaundiced Eye* (1989), 'Democracy'

4 We don't know when our name came into being or how some distant ancestor acquired it.

We don't understand our name at all, we don't know its history and yet we bear it with exalted fidelity, we merge with it, we like it, we are ridiculously proud of it as if we had thought it up ourselves in a moment of brilliant inspiration.

Milan Kundera (b.1929), Czech-born French author and critic: Agnes, in *Immortality* (1991), Pt.1, Ch.7

5   The name of a man is a numbing blow from which he never recovers.

Marshall McLuhan (1911–1980), Canadian communications theorist: *Understanding Media* (1964), Ch.2

6   I sometimes think I was born to live up to my name. How could I be anything else but what I am having been named Madonna? I would either have ended up a nun or this.

Madonna (b.1959), U.S. singer and actress: in *Vanity Fair* (New York), April 1991. Madonna Ciccione was named after her mother

7   No one can claim the name of Pedro, nobody is Rosa or Maria, all of us are dust or sand, all of us are rain under rain. They have spoken to me of Venezuelas, of Chiles and Paraguays; I have no idea what they are saying. I know only the skin of the earth and I know it has no name.

Pablo Neruda (1904–1973), Chilean poet: 'Demasiados nombres' ('Too Many Names'), publ. in *Estravagario* (1958)

8   Names, once they are in common use, quickly become mere sounds, their etymology being buried, like so many of the earth's marvels, beneath the dust of habit.

Salman Rushdie (b.1947), Indian-born British author: *The Satanic Verses* (1988), 'Ayesha'

9   Why am I Mr Pink? ... Why can't we pick our own color? ... Mr Pink sounds like Mr Pussy. Tell you what, let me be Mr Purple. That sounds good to me.

Quentin Tarantino (b.1958), U.S. film-maker: Mr Pink (Steve Buscemi), arguing over the choice of alias in the run up to the heist, in *Reservoir Dogs* (film; written and directed by Quentin Tarantino, 1992). Tarantino's character adds: 'Mr Brown, that's a little too close to Mr Shit'

See also Sartre on BELIEF; Cheever on DIVORCE; Berger on NATIONALISM

NARRATIVE

1   We construct a narrative for ourselves, and that's the thread that we follow from one day to the next. People who disintegrate as personalities are the ones who lose that thread.

Paul Auster (b.1947), U.S. author: in *The Sunday Times* (London), 16 April 1989

2   The narrative impulse is always with us; we couldn't imagine ourselves through a day without it.

Robert Coover (b.1932), U.S. author: in *Time Out* (London), 7 May 1986

3   There is no longer any such thing as fiction or nonfiction; there's only narrative.

E.L. Doctorow (b.1931), U.S. novelist: in the *New York Times Book Review*, 27 Jan. 1988

4   We inherit plots.... There are only two or three in the world, five or six at most. We ride them like treadmills.

Janette Turner Hospital (b.1942), Australian author: in *The Independent* (London), 7 April 1990

See also STORY-TELLING

NATIONALISM

1   All nationalisms are at heart deeply concerned with names: with the most immaterial and original human invention. Those who dismiss names as a detail have never been displaced; but the peoples on the peripheries are always being displaced. That is why they insist upon their continuity – their links with their dead and the unborn.

John Berger (b.1926), British author and critic: 'The Soul and the Operator', first publ. in *Expressen* (Stockholm), 19 March 1990, rep. in *Keeping a Rendezvous* (1992)

2   Nationalism, that magnificent song that made the people rise against their oppressors, stops short, falters and dies away on the day that independence is proclaimed.

Frantz Fanon (1925–1961), Martiniquan psychiatrist, philosopher and political activist: *The Wretched of the Earth* (1961), Ch.3

3   While it is often the enemy of democracy, nationalism has also been democracy's handmaiden, from the time of the French Revolution.

Francis Fukuyama (b.1952), U.S. historian: in *The Independent* (London), 3 March 1992

4   Historians are to nationalism what poppy-growers in Pakistan are to heroin-addicts: we supply the essential raw material for the market.

Eric Hobsbawm (b.1917), British historian: lecture to the American Anthropological Association, publ. in the *New Statesman* (London), 24 April 1992

5   All the isms are wasms – except one, the most powerful ism of this century, indeed, of the entire democratic age, which is nationalism.

John Lukacs (b.1924), Hungarian-born U.S. historian: 'The Stirrings of History', publ. in *Harper's Magazine* (New York), Aug. 1990

6 An exaggerated nationalism must be counted both the strength and the weakness of fascism. It was strong because nationalism is always a quick starter in popular favour, but it was weak because narrow nationalism has the same short legs as lies, and is soon overtaken by facts.
Oswald Mosley (1896–1980), British fascist leader: *My Life* (1968), Ch.16

7 Nations whose nationalism is destroyed are subject to ruin.
Muhammar Qaddafi (b.1938), Libyan leader: *The Green Book* (1976–9), Pt.3, 'The Social Basis of the Third Universal Theory'

NATIONS

1 The great nations have always acted like gangsters, and the small nations like prostitutes.
Stanley Kubrick (b.1928), U.S. film-maker: in *The Guardian* (London), 5 June 1963

2 Without a country, I am not a man.
Nawaf al-Nasir al-Sabah, grand-nephew of the Emir of Kuwait: quoted in *The Guardian* (London), 9 Aug. 1990

3 The lesson of the century has been that the people feel far more comfortable and more stable with a nation state. It is the nation state which is the unit of loyalty. Ours is the United Kingdom.
Margaret Thatcher (b.1925), British Conservative politician and prime minister: in *The Sunday Telegraph* (London), 13 Dec. 1992

4 You can't be a Real Country unless you have A BEER and an airline – it helps if you have some kind of a football team, or some nuclear weapons, but at the very least you need a BEER.
Frank Zappa (1940–1993), U.S. rock musician: *The Real Frank Zappa Book* (written with Peter Occhiogrosso, 1989), Ch.12

NATURE

1 To me nature is ... spiders and bugs, and big fish eating little fish, and plants eating plants, and animals eating... It's like an enormous restaurant, that's the way I see it.
Woody Allen (b.1935), U.S. film-maker: Boris Grushenko (Allen), in *Love and Death* (film; written and directed by Woody Allen, 1975)

2 Nature has no mercy at all. Nature says, 'I'm going to snow. If you have on a bikini and no snowshoes, that's tough. I am going to snow anyway.'
Maya Angelou (b.1928), U.S. author: 'Maya Angelou: an Interview' (Oct. 1974), rep. in *Conversations with Maya Angelou* (ed. Jeffrey M. Elliot, 1989)

3 Nature is not cruel, only pitilessly indifferent. This is one of the hardest lessons for humans to learn. We cannot admit that things might be neither good nor evil, neither cruel nor kind, but simply callous – indifferent to all suffering, lacking all purpose.
Richard Dawkins (b.1941), British biologist: *River Out of Eden* (1995), Ch.4

4 I am against nature. I don't dig nature at all. I think nature is very unnatural. I think the truly natural things are dreams, which nature can't touch with decay.
Bob Dylan (b.1941), U.S. singer and songwriter: remark, 1966, quoted in *No Direction Home* by Robert Shelton (biography, 1986), Ch.1, '*Kaddish*'

5 A man who lives with nature is used to violence and is companionable with death. There is more violence in an English hedgerow than in the meanest streets of a great city.
P.D. James (b.1920), British author: Jonah the tramp, in *Devices and Desires* (1989), Ch.40

6 There are no accidents, only nature throwing her weight around. Even the bomb merely releases energy that nature has put there. Nuclear war would be just a spark in the grandeur of space. Nor can radiation 'alter' nature: she will absorb it all. After the bomb, nature will pick up the cards we have spilled, shuffle them, and begin her game again.
Camille Paglia (b.1947), U.S. author and critic: *Sexual Personae* (1990), Ch.1

7 In the modern period of Western culture, Nature has been personified as, respectively God's (medieval) deputy or minister, an absolute (Renaissance) monarch, an (Enlightenment) constitutional lawyer, a (Darwinian) selective breeder, and a (laissez-faire) free marketeer, among others. It could easily be argued that none of those roles guaranteed the general population anything but a passive, dominated fate, subject to the brutal 'natural' scarcity and necessity as created or interpreted by ruling interests.
Andrew Ross (b.1956), British social theorist: *Strange Weather* (1991), Ch.6

8 The embrace of nature may often have been rough, even murderous, as when nature assumed the formidable aspect of Mother Kali; but it was nonetheless an embrace.
Theodore Roszak (b.1933), U.S. social critic: *Where the Wasteland Ends* (1972), Ch.1

9 Nature in America has always been suspect, on the defensive, cannibalized by progress. In America, every specimen becomes a relic.
Susan Sontag (b.1933), U.S. essayist: *On Photography* (1977), 'Melancholy Objects'

10 The positive ideal that we propose is Nature. That is, WILD nature; those aspects of the functioning of the Earth and its living things that are independent of human management and free of human interference and control. And with wild nature we include human nature.

Unabomber, U.S. radical: *Industrial Society and Its Future*, 'Strategy', Sct.183, publ. in the *Washington Post*, 19 Sept. 1995

11 Our task is not to rediscover nature but to remake it.

Raoul Vaneigem (b.1934), Belgian situationist philosopher: *The Revolution of Everyday Life* (1967; tr.1983), Ch.9, Sct.2

See also ART: AND NATURE; THE ECOLOGY MOVEMENT; THE ENVIRONMENT; Berger on EVIL; Walker on WHITES

THE NAZIS

1 The trouble with Eichmann was precisely that so many were like him, and that the many were neither perverted nor sadistic, that they were, and still are, terribly and terrifyingly normal. From the viewpoint of our legal institutions and of our moral standards of judgment, this normality was much more terrifying than all the atrocities put together.

Hannah Arendt (1906–1975), German-born U.S. political philosopher: epilogue to *Eichmann in Jerusalem* (1963)

2 A régime which invented a biological foreign policy was obviously acting against its own best interests. But at least it obeyed its own particular logic.

Albert Camus (1913–1960), French-Algerian philosopher and author: *The Rebel* (1951; tr.1953), Pt.3, 'State Terrorism and Irrational Terror'

3 Hermann Goering, Joachim von Ribbentrop, Albert Speer, Walther Frank, Julius Streicher and Robert Ley did pass under my inspection and interrogation in 1945 but they only proved that National Socialism was a gangster interlude at a rather low order of mental capacity and with a surprisingly high incidence of alcoholism.

J.K. Galbraith (b.1908), U.S. economist: *The Age of Uncertainty* (1977), Ch.12

4 Hitler has paled the memory of the Jewish blood spilled before 1933–45. People have ended up believing that anti-Semitism was born with National Socialism and that the fall of the Third Reich essentially rid humanity of it, leaving it to lead an anachronistic existence among certain underdeveloped peoples and a few sick spirits who have no grasp of the way things really work.

Emmanuel Levinas (b.1905), French Jewish philosopher: 'Poetry and the Impossible' (1969), rep. in *Difficult Freedom* (1990), Pt.3

5 There is always of course a disadvantage in bearing a resemblance to foreign parties, however superficial, particularly if in essence you are a movement of ardent patriotism.

Oswald Mosley (1896–1980), British fascist leader: *My Life* (1968), Ch.16

6 Left-wing movements have tended to be unisex, and asexual in their imagery. Right-wing movements, however puritanical and repressive the realities they usher in, have an erotic surface. Certainly Nazism is 'sexier' than communism.

Susan Sontag (b.1933), U.S. essayist: 'Fascinating Fascism' (1974), rep. in *Under the Sign of Saturn* (1980). This fact, Sontag parenthetically added, 'is not to the Nazis' credit, but rather shows something of the nature and limits of the sexual imagination.' *See* Sontag on SADISM

See also Morris on GERMANY; ADOLF HITLER

NECESSITY

1 Man cannot be free if he does not know that he is subject to necessity, because his freedom is always won in his never wholly successful attempts to liberate himself from necessity.

Hannah Arendt (1906–1975), German-born U.S. political philosopher: *The Human Condition* (1958), Pt.3, Ch.16

2 We come into the world laden with the weight of an infinite necessity.

Albert Camus (1913–1960), French-Algerian philosopher and author: *Resistance, Rebellion and Death* (1961), 'Reflections on the Guillotine'

3 Arguably the only goods people need these days are food and nappies.

Terence Conran (b.1931), British businessman and designer: in *The Observer* (London), 21 Feb. 1988

4 Necessity has the face of a dog.

Gabriel García Márquez (b.1928), Colombian author: Mina, in *In Evil Hour* (1968; tr.1979), p.148 of Jonathan Cape edn. (1980)

5 The bare necessities, the simple bare
    necessities
Forget about your worries and your strife.

Terry Gilkyson, U.S. songwriter: 'Bare Necessities' (song) in *The Jungle Book* (film, 1967)

6 The necessary has never been man's top priority. The passionate pursuit of the non-essential and the extravagant is one of the chief traits of human uniqueness. Unlike other forms of life, man's greatest exertions are made in the pursuit not of necessities but of superfluities.

Eric Hoffer (1902–1983), U.S. philosopher: in the *New York Times*, 21 July 1969

NEGOTIATION

1 Better to jaw-jaw than to war-war.
Winston Churchill (1874–1965), British statesman and author: remark, 26 June 1954, at the White House, quoted in the *New York Times*, 27 June 1954. The words were reported with slight variations in different newspapers, and also within the same edition of the *New York Times*

2 Let us never negotiate out of fear, but let us never fear to negotiate.
John F. Kennedy (1917–1963), U.S. Democratic politician and president: inaugural address, 20 Jan. 1961, quoted in *Kennedy* by Theodore C. Sorenson (1965), Pt.3, Ch.9

3 Only free men can negotiate. Prisoners cannot enter into contracts.
Nelson Mandela (b.1918), South African political leader and president: statement from prison, 10 Feb. 1985, refusing the terms set for his release by South African president P.W. Botha, quoted in *Higher than Hope* by Fatima Meer (1988), Pt.4, Ch.30. The statement was read by Zindzi Mandela, Nelson's daughter, at a U.D.F. rally at the Jabulani Stadium, Soweto

NEIGHBOURS

1 Keeping up with the Joneses was a full-time job with my mother and father. It was not until many years later when I lived alone that I realized how much cheaper it was to drag the Joneses down to my level.
Quentin Crisp (b.1908), British author: *The Naked Civil Servant* (1968), Ch.1

2 Christ didn't say 'Love humanity as thyself', but 'Love thy neighbour as thyself', and do you know why? Because your neighbour, by definition, is the person nearby, the man sitting next to you in the underground who smells, perhaps, the man next to you in the queue who maybe tries to barge ahead of you, in short, your neighbour is the person who threatens your own liberty.
Luciano De Crescenzo (b.1928), Italian author: the Professor, in *Thus Spake Bellavista* (1977; tr.1988), Ch.7

3 My neighbour
doesn't want to be loved
as much as
he wants to be envied.
Irving Layton (b.1912), Canadian poet: *The Whole Bloody Bird* (1969), 'Aphs'

See also FRIENDS

NEUROSIS

1 If you get hung up on everybody else's hang-ups, then the whole world's going to be nothing more than one huge gallows.
Richard Brautigan (1935–1984), U.S. novelist and poet: *The Abortion: An Historical Romance 1966* (1970), p.63 of Pocket Books edn.

2 I love her too, but our neuroses just don't match.
Arthur Miller (b.1915), U.S. playwright: Lyman, discussing his wife with his lawyer, in *The Ride Down Mount Morgan* (1991), Act 1

3 If neurotic is wanting two mutually exclusive things at one and the same time, then I'm neurotic as hell. I'll be flying back and forth between one mutually exclusive thing and another for the rest of my days.
Sylvia Plath (1932–1963), U.S. poet: the narrator (Esther Greenwood), in *The Bell Jar* (1963), Ch.8

4 Doubt is to certainty as neurosis is to psychosis. The neurotic is in doubt and has fears about persons and things; the psychotic has convictions and makes claims about them. In short, the neurotic has problems, the psychotic has solutions.
Thomas Szasz (b.1920), U.S. psychiatrist: *The Second Sin* (1973), 'Mental Illness'

5 Every neurosis is a primitive form of legal proceeding in which the accused carries on the prosecution, imposes judgment and executes the sentence: *all to the end that someone else should not perform the same process.*
Lionel Trilling (1905–1975), U.S. critic: notebook entry, 1946, publ. in *Partisan Review 50th Anniversary Edition* (ed. William Philips, 1985)

See also Trilling on HEALTH

THE NEW AGE

1 This is the dawning of the age of Aquarius.
James Rado (b.1939), U.S. songwriter: 'Aquarius' (song; lyrics by James Rado and Jerome Ragni) in *Hair* (stage musical, 1967)

2 The New Age? It's just the old age stuck in a microwave oven for fifteen seconds.
James Randi (b.1928), Canadian-born U.S. magician, psychic investigator and author: in *The Observer* (London), 14 April 1991

3 Therapists, New Agers and Born Again Christians seldom blink. A blink marks the mind's registration of a new idea. Converts have no intention of receiving new ideas. They know already all they want to know.

Fay Weldon (b.1933), British novelist: Elaine Desmond, in 'End of the Line', publ. in *Wicked Women* (1995)

NEW ENGLAND *see under* THE UNITED STATES

THE NEW MAN *see under* MEN

THE NEW WORLD

1 What passes for identity in America is a series of myths about one's heroic ancestors. It's astounding to me, for example, that so many people really seem to believe that the country was founded by a band of heroes who wanted to be free. That happens not to be true. What happened was that some people left Europe because they couldn't stay there any longer and had to go someplace else to make it. They were hungry, they were poor, they were convicts.
James Baldwin (1924–1987), U.S. author: 'A Talk To Teachers', 16 Oct. 1963, publ. in *The Price of the Ticket* (1985)

2 If you are prepared to accept the consequences of your dreams ... then you must still regard America today with the same naive enthusiasm as the generations that discovered the New World.
Jean Baudrillard (b.1929), French semiologist: *America* (1986; tr.1988), 'Utopia Achieved'

3 I asked the captain what his name was
And how come he didn't drive a truck
He said his name was Columbus
I just said, 'Good luck'.
Bob Dylan (b.1941), U.S. singer and songwriter: 'Bob Dylan's 115th Dream' (song) on the album *Bringing it All Back Home* (1965)

4 Being human signifies, for each one of us, belonging to a class, a society, a country, a continent and a civilization; and for us European earth-dwellers, the adventure played out in the heart of the New World signifies in the first place that it was not our world and that we bear responsibility for the crime of its destruction.
Claude Lévi-Strauss (b.1908), French anthropologist: *Tristes Tropiques* (1955), Ch.38

5 Europe and the U.K. are yesterday's world. Tomorrow is in the United States.
Tiny Rowland (b.1917), British businessman: quoted in *The Observer* (London), 16 Jan. 1983

6 The open frontier, the hardships of homesteading from scratch, the wealth of natural resources, the whole vast challenge of a continent waiting to be exploited, combined

to produce a prevailing materialism and an American drive bent as much, if not more, on money, property, and power than was true of the Old World from which we had fled.
Barbara Tuchman (1912–1989), U.S. historian: 'On Our Birthday – America as Idea', publ. in *Newsweek* (New York), 12 July 1976

7 Adam had an idea.
He and the snake would share
the loss of Eden for a profit.
So both made the New World. And it looked good.
Derek Walcott (b.1930), West Indian poet and playwright: 'New World', publ. in *Sea Grapes* (1976)

THE NEW WORLD ORDER

1 If the Soviet Union can give up the Brezhnev Doctrine for the Sinatra Doctrine, the United States can give up the James Monroe Doctrine for the Marilyn Monroe Doctrine: Let's all go to bed wearing the perfume we like best.
Carlos Fuentes (b.1928), Mexican novelist and short-story writer: quoted in *The Times* (London), 23 Feb. 1990

2 What we may be witnessing is not just the end of the Cold War but the end of history as such: that is, the end point of man's ideological evolution and the universalisation of Western liberal democracy.
Francis Fukuyama (b.1952), U.S. historian: in *The Independent* (London), 20 Sept. 1989

3 My life's work has been accomplished. I did all that I could.
Mikhail Gorbachev (b.1931), Russian political leader: on being ousted as Soviet president, quoted in *The Observer* (London), 15 Dec. 1991

4 People have passed through a very dark tunnel at the end of which there was a light of freedom. Unexpectedly they passed through the prison gates and found themselves in a square. They are now free and they don't know where to go.
Václav Havel (b.1936), Czech playwright and president: address to Institute of Contemporary Arts, London, quoted in *The Independent* (London), 22 March 1990

5 Ideology, politics and journalism, which luxuriate in failure, are impotent in the face of hope and joy.
P.J. O'Rourke (b.1947), U.S. journalist: 'The Death of Communism', first publ. in *Rolling Stone* (New York), Nov. 1989, rep. in *Give War A Chance* (1992)

6 The old invented histories and traditions and efforts to rule are giving way to newer, more elastic and relaxed theories of what is so

discrepant and intense in the contemporary moment. In the west, post-modernism has seized upon the ahistorical weightlessness, consumerism, and spectacle of the new order.

Edward Said (b.1935), Lebanese-born U.S. social and literary critic: *Culture and Imperialism* (1993), Ch.4, Sct.3

NEW YORK *see under* THE UNITED STATES

NEWS

1 The greatest felony in the news business today is to be behind, or to miss a big story. So speed and quantity substitute for thoroughness and quality, for accuracy and context. The pressure to compete, the fear somebody else will make the splash first, creates a frenzied environment in which a blizzard of information is presented and serious questions may not be raised.

Carl Bernstein (b.1944), U.S. journalist: in *The Guardian* (London), 3 June 1992

2 You don't need a weather man
To know which way the wind blows.

Bob Dylan (b.1941), U.S. singer and songwriter: 'Subterranean Homesick Blues' (song), on the album *Bringing it All Back Home* (1965)

3 News is the first rough draft of history.

Philip L. Graham (1915–1963), U.S. newspaper publisher: attributed. The aphorism has also been ascribed to the *Washington Post* editor Ben C. Bradlee, but Bradlee himself, in an interview in *Vanity Fair* (New York), Sept. 1991, credited it to Phil Graham, formerly his boss at the *Post*

4 Listening to a news broadcast is like smoking a cigarette and crushing the butt in the ashtray.

Milan Kundera (b.1929), Czech-born French author and critic: Paul, in *Immortality* (1991), Pt.3, 'The Brilliant Ally of His Own Gravediggers'

5 When distant and unfamiliar and complex things are communicated to great masses of people, the truth suffers a considerable and often a radical distortion. The complex is made over into the simple, the hypothetical into the dogmatic, and the relative into an absolute.

Walter Lippmann (1889–1974), U.S. journalist: *The Public Philosophy* (1955), Ch.2, Sct.3

6 And now for something completely different.

Monty Python's Flying Circus: John Cleese, as a newsreader, in *Monty Python's Flying Circus* (TV series 1969–74). The words became a catchphrase, used by various characters as a link between sketches. Monty Python episodes were written and performed by Graham Chapman (1941–1989), John Cleese (b.1939), Terry Gilliam (b.1940), Eric Idle (b.1943), Terry Jones (b.1942) and Michael Palin (b.1943)

7 Newsmen believe that news is a tacitly acknowledged fourth branch of the federal system. This is why most news about government sounds as if it were federally mandated – serious, bulky and blandly worthwhile, like a high-fiber diet set in type.

P.J. O'Rourke (b.1947), U.S. journalist: *Parliament of Whores* (1991), 'The Dictatorship of Boredom; The Winners Go to Washington D.C.'

8 The conflict between the men who make and the men who report the news is as old as time. News may be true, but it is not truth, and reporters and officials seldom see it the same way. ... In the old days, the reporters or couriers of bad news were often put to the gallows; now they are given the Pulitzer Prize, but the conflict goes on.

James Reston (b.1909), U.S. journalist: *The Artillery of the Press* (1966), 'The Tug of History'

9 I'm confused about who the news belongs to. I always have it in my head that if your name's in the news, then the news should be paying you. Because it's *your news* and they're taking it and selling it as their product. ... If people didn't give the news their news, and if everybody kept their news to themselves, the news wouldn't have any news.

Andy Warhol (c.1928–1987), U.S. Pop artist: *From A to B and Back Again* (1975), Ch.5

NEWSPAPERS

1 I read the newspapers avidly. It is my one form of continuous fiction.

Aneurin Bevan (1897–1960), British Labour politician: in *The Times* (London), 29 March 1960

2 Frankly, despite my horror of the press, I'd love to rise from the grave every ten years or so and go buy a few newspapers.

Luis Buñuel (1900–1983), Spanish film-maker: *My Last Breath* (autobiography, 1983), Ch.21

3 The *New York Times* is the best and the worst newspaper on earth, a daily monument to the sloppy and extravagant simplification of the overdone; the *Daily Mirror* is the worst and the best newspaper, a gymnastic in the dedicated technical expertise of the persuasive non-think. I have worked for them both, but I cannot yet determine which I like least.

James Cameron (1911–1985), British journalist: *Point of Departure* (1967), Ch.4

4 Their constant yelping about a free press means, with a few honorable exceptions, freedom to peddle scandal, crime, sex, sensationalism, hate, innuendo and the political and financial uses of propaganda. A newspaper is a

business out to make money through advertising revenue. That is predicated on the circulation and you know what circulation depends on.

Raymond Chandler (1880–1959), U.S. author: Harlan Potter, in *The Long Goodbye* (1954), Ch.32

5 What appears in newspapers is often new but seldom true.

Patrick Kavanagh (1905–1967), Irish poet and author: *Collected Pruse* (1967), 'Signposts'

6 A good newspaper is never nearly good enough but a lousy newspaper is a joy forever.

Garrison Keillor (b.1942), U.S. author: 'That Old "Picayune-Moon"', publ. in *Harper's Magazine* (New York), Sept. 1990

7 A good newspaper, I suppose, is a nation talking to itself.

Arthur Miller (b.1915), U.S. playwright: quoted in *The Observer* (London), 26 Nov. 1961

8 To read a newspaper for the first time is like coming into a film that has been on for an hour. Newspapers are like serials. To understand them you have to take knowledge to them; the knowledge that serves best is the knowledge provided by the newspaper itself.

V.S. Naipaul (b.1932), Trinidadian-born British writer: on reading the *New York Times* for the first time, in *The Enigma of Arrival* (1987), 'The Journey'

9 People are always dying in the *The Times* who don't seem to die in other papers, and they die at greater length and maybe even with a little more grace.

James Reston (b.1909), U.S. journalist: in *New Leader* (New York), 7 Jan. 1963

10 When other helpers fail and comforts flee, when the senses decay and the mind moves in a narrower and narrower circle, when the grasshopper is a burden and the postman brings no letters, and even the Royal Family is no longer quite what it was, an obituary column stands fast.

Sylvia Townsend Warner (1893–1978), British author: *Autumn River* (1966), 'Their Quiet Lives'

See also EDITORS; *The Sun* on ELECTIONS; THE PRESS; PRESS BARONS

NICARAGUA

1 Violence has been Nicaragua's most important export to the world.

Ronald Reagan (b.1911), U.S. Republican politician and president: speech to Congress, 27 April 1983, publ. in *Speaking My Mind* (1989)

2 They are our brothers, these freedom fighters. … They are the moral equal of our Founding Fathers and the brave men and women of the French Resistance. We cannot turn away from them, for the struggle here is not right versus left; it is right versus wrong.

Ronald Reagan: on the Nicaraguan Contra fighters, in speech, 1 March 1985, to Conservative Political Action Conference, Washington D.C., publ. in *Speaking My Mind* (1989)

3 One's own country can be a place of exile, can be Egypt, or Babylon … in fact Somocista Nicaragua had literally *not been* these people's country … the revolution had really been an act of migration, for the locals as well as the resettled men. They were inventing their country, and, more than that, themselves.

Salman Rushdie (b.1947), Indian-born British author: on a recurrent theme expressed by the people of Nicaragua, in 'Eating the Eggs of Love', publ. in *Granta* (Cambridge), No.20, winter 1986

NIGHT

1 There is something … not quite right about night life, something shadowy in every sense. However efficiently artificial light annihilates the difference between night and day, it never wholly eliminates the primitive suspicion that night people are up to no good.

A. Alvarez (b.1929), British critic, poet and novelist: preface to *Night: An Exploration Of Night Life, Night Language, Sleep and Dreams* (1995)

2 I cannot walk through the suburbs in the solitude of the night without thinking that the night pleases us because it suppresses idle details, just as our memory does.

Jorge Luis Borges (1899–1986), Argentinian author: *Labyrinths* (1964), 'A New Refutation of Time'

3 Men use the night to erase us…. The annihilation of a woman's personality, individuality, will, character, is prerequisite to male sexuality, and so the night is the sacred time of male sexual celebration, because it is dark and in the dark it is easier not to see: not to see who she is. Male sexuality, drunk on its intrinsic contempt for all life, but especially for women's lives, can run wild, hunt down random victims, use the dark for cover, find in the dark solace, sanctuary, cover.

Andrea Dworkin (b.1946), U.S. feminist critic: *Letters from a War Zone* (1988), p.14 of Secker & Warburg edn. (1988)

4 Downtown Manhattan, clear winter noon,
    and I've been up all night, talking, talking,
    reading the Kaddish aloud, listening to
    Ray Charles blues shout blind on the
    phonograph

Allen Ginsberg (b.1926), U.S. poet: 'Kaddish', Sct.1, publ. in *Kaddish and Other Poems* (1960)

5 Beware thoughts that come in the night. They aren't turned properly; they come in askew, free of sense and restriction, deriving from the most remote of sources.
William Least Heat-Moon [William Trogdon] (b.1939), U.S. author: opening words of *Blue Highways: A Journey into America* (1983)

6 In the day we sweat it out in the streets of a
  runaway American dream
At night we ride through mansions of glory in
  suicide machines.
Bruce Springsteen (b.1949), U.S. rock musician: 'Born to Run' (song) on the album *Born to Run* (Bruce Springsteen and the E Street Band, 1975)

7 To begin at the beginning: It is spring, moonless night in the small town, starless and bible-black, the cobblestreets silent and the hunched courters'-and-rabbits' wood limping invisible down to the sloeblack, slow, black, crowblack, fishingboat-bobbing sea.
Dylan Thomas (1914–1953), Welsh poet: *Under Milk Wood* (1954)

NIHILISM

1 Nihilism is not only despair and negation, but above all the desire to despair and to negate.
Albert Camus (1913–1960), French-Algerian philosopher and author: *The Rebel* (1951; tr.1953), Pt.2, 'The Rejection of Salvation'

2 Nothing requires a greater effort of thought than arguments to justify the rule of non-thought.
Milan Kundera (b.1929), Czech-born French author and critic: the Bear, in *Immortality* (1991), Pt.3, 'The Brilliant Ally of his Own Gravediggers'

3 What every artist should try to prevent is the car, in which is our civilized life, plunging over the side of the precipice – the exhibitionist extremist promoter driving the whole bag of tricks into a nihilistic nothingness or zero.
Wyndham Lewis (1882–1957), British author and painter: *The Demon of Progress in the Arts* (1954), 'There Is a Limit, Beyond Which There Is Nothing'

4 Nihilism is best done by professionals.
Iggy Pop (b.1947), U.S. rock musician: in *The Independent* (London), 12 July 1990

5 When there's no future
How can there be sin
We're the flowers in the dustbin
We're the poison in your human machine
We're the future
Your future
God Save the Queen.
Sex Pistols (1976–1979), British punk band: 'God Save the Queen' (song) on the album *Never Mind the Bollocks* (1977)

See also Cioran on DENIAL

THE 1940s

1 It is true that the men of my generation have seen too many things to imagine that the world of today can retain the atmosphere of a children's book. They know that there are also prisons and mornings of execution. ... But this is not despair. This is lucidity.
Albert Camus (1913–1960), French-Algerian philosopher and author: written response to questions for an interview on Radio-Algérie, 1948, quoted in *Camus: A Biography* by Herbert R. Lottman (1979), Ch.33

2 England was still so completely Victorian in those years, so strangely prudish. It seems hard to understand how a whole generation of men who had been through the toughest of wars – and won – could be reduced to the level of schoolchildren, and be told what to read and what not to read by a conglomerate of spinsters and bowler-hatted policemen.
Maurice Girodias (1919–1990), French publisher: introduction to *The Olympia Reader* (ed. Maurice Girodias, 1965)

3 Quite convinced that this is a twilight phase, a period of running down, which may be protracted but cannot be altered in its essential character. ... We, now living, have rehearsed one play, and find ourselves appearing in another, quite different.
Malcolm Muggeridge (1903–1990), British journalist and broadcaster: journal entry, 31 Dec. 1949, publ. in *Like It Was* (ed. John Bright-Holmes, 1981)

4 The fashionable female torso of the forties was not flesh but metal, a *cuirass*. It was armour. The whole popular mode was armour. We used it to conceal our distress and confusion, but our distress and confusion arose from our hatred of lies so the shield, the mask, had to drop.
Jeff Nuttall (b.1933), British poet, painter and musician: *The Bomb Culture* (1968), 'Pop', Sct.3

THE 1950s

1 These are the fifties, you know. The disgusting, posturing fifties.
Hannah Arendt (1906–1975), German-born U.S. political philosopher: said to author and poet Frederic Prokosch, quoted in Prokosch's *Voices: A Memoir* (1983), 'The Monster'

2 Roll over, Beethoven,
And tell Tchaikovsky the news.
Chuck Berry (b.1926), U.S. rock musician: 'Roll Over, Beethoven' (song, 1956)

3 In 1953, excess is always a comfort, and sometimes a career.

Albert Camus (1913–1960), French-Algerian philosopher and author: *The Rebel* (1951; tr.1953), Pt.5, 'Moderation and Excess'

4 The 1950s to me is darkness, hidden history, perversion behind most doors waiting to creep out. The 1950s to most people is kitsch and Mickey Mouse watches and all this intolerable stuff...
James Ellroy (b.1948), U.S. crime author: quoted in *Into The Badlands* by John Williams (1991), Ch.4

5 The fifties – they seem to have taken place on a sunny afternoon that asked nothing of you except a drifting belief in the moment and its power to satisfy.
Elizabeth Hardwick (b.1916), U.S. critic and author: *Bartleby in Manhattan and Other Essays* (1983), 'Domestic Manners'

6 These are the tranquilized *Fifties*, and I am forty. Ought I to regret my seedtime?
Robert Lowell (1917–1977), U.S. poet: 'Memories of West Street and Lepke', publ. in *Life Studies* (1959)

7 Let us be frank about it: most of our people have never had it so good.
Harold Macmillan (1894–1986), British Conservative politician and prime minister: speech, 20 July 1957, Bedford, quoted in *The Times* (London), 22 July 1957. The slogan was already current in the United States by the end of World War II (*See: The Dictionary of Catch-Phrases*, ed. Eric Partridge, rev. Paul Beale, 1985)

8 We live in an era of revolution – the revolution of rising expectations.
Adlai Stevenson (1900–1965), U.S. Democratic politician: in *Look* (New York), 22 Sept. 1953, rep. in *The Papers of Adlai E. Stevenson*, Vol.V (1974)

9 The Fifties was the most sexually frustrated decade ever: ten years of foreplay.
Lily Tomlin (b.1939), U.S. comedienne: *Lily Tomlin on Stage* (album, 1977; material written by Lily Tomlin and Jane Wagner), 'Glenna – A Child of the Sixties'

THE 1960s

1 The defiance of established authority, religious and secular, social and political, as a world-wide phenomenon may well one day be accounted the outstanding event of the last decade.
Hannah Arendt (1906–1975), German-born U.S. political philosopher: *Crises of the Republic* (1972), 'Civil Disobedience'

2 All that Swinging Sixties nonsense, we all thought it was passé at the time.
David Bailey (b.1938), British photographer: interview in *The Face* (London), Dec. 1984

3 That's what this decade is: the Decade of the Experts and the Decade of the Assassins. and neither one of them is worth crystallized dog turds.
Charles Bukowski (1920–1994), U.S. author and poet: *Notes of a Dirty Old Man* (1969), p.46 of City Lights edn. (1973)

4 In the late 1950s, perhaps 5 per cent of the girls went to bed with men; in the late 1960s, perhaps 5 per cent didn't.
Nigel Dempster (b.1941), British journalist: interview in *Singular Encounters* by Naim Attallah (1990), 'Nigel Dempster'

5 We were that generation called 'silent,' but we were silent neither, as some thought, because we shared the period's official optimism nor, as others thought, because we feared its official repression. We were silent because the exhilaration of social action seemed to many of us just one more way of escaping the personal, of masking for a while that dread of the meaningless which was man's fate.
Joan Didion (b.1934), U.S. essayist: 'On the Morning After the Sixties' (1970), rep. in *The White Album* (1979)

6 Many people I know in Los Angeles believe that the Sixties ended abruptly on August 9, 1969, ended at the exact moment when word of the murders on Cielo Drive traveled like brushfire through the community, and in a sense this is true. The tension broke that day. The paranoia was fulfilled.
Joan Didion: of the Charles Manson murders, in 'The White Album: A Chronicle of Survival in the Sixties', publ. in *New West*, 4 June 1979

7 The order is
Rapidly fadin'.
And the first one now
Will later be last
For the times they are a-changin'.
Bob Dylan (b.1941), U.S. singer and songwriter: 'The Times They Are A-Changin'' (song) on the album *The Times They Are A-Changin'* (1964)

8 People today are still living off the table scraps of the sixties. They are still being passed around – the music and the ideas.
Bob Dylan: in *The Guardian* (London), 13 Feb. 1992

9 For me, the lame part of the Sixties was the political part, the social part. The real part was the spiritual part.
Jerry Garcia (1942–1995), U.S. rock musician: in *Rolling Stone* (New York), 30 Nov. 1989

10 Today, as those who were young then, or just becoming adults, are passing into middle age, the 60s seem the most inescapable of all those nostalgia-girt decades. Whether hymned by

ageing hippies, still wreathed in rosy fantasies, or vilified by contemporary politicians, desperately hunting an easy scapegoat for over-complex ills, the image remains: something happened.

Jonathon Green (b.1948), British anthologist: introduction to *Days in the Life* (1988)

11 What a long strange trip it's been.

Robert Hunter, U.S. rock lyricist: 'Truckin'' (song) on the album *American Beauty* (The Grateful Dead, 1971). This best known of The Grateful Dead's lyrics ('WALSTIB' to dedicated fans) has been adopted as the title of numerous books and articles evoking the 1960s

12 The Great Society is a place where every child can find knowledge to enrich his mind and to enlarge his talents. ... It is a place where the city of man serves not only the needs of the body and the demands of commerce but the desire for beauty and the hunger for community. ... It is a place where men are more concerned with the quality of their goals than the quantity of their goods.

Lyndon B. Johnson (1908–1973), U.S. Democratic politician and president: speech, 22 May 1964, Ann Arbor, Michigan, publ. in *Public Papers of the Presidents of the United States: Lyndon B. Johnson, 1963–64*. The slogan 'Great Society' had been current for several years, but became closely associated with Johnson's presidency, featuring in his acceptance speech at the Democratic Party National Convention, Aug. 1964, the inspiration of Richard N. Goodwin, secretary general of the International Peace Corps Secretariat and occasional speechwriter (*See* Hugh Sidey's *A Very Personal Presidency*, 1968)

13 We stand today on the edge of a new frontier – the frontier of the 1960s, a frontier of unknown opportunities and perils, a frontier of unfulfilled hopes and threats.

John F. Kennedy (1917–1963), U.S. Democratic politician and president: acceptance speech, 15 July 1960, at the Democratic Convention, Los Angeles. The speech was drafted by Theodore C. Sorensen, according to his biography, *Kennedy* (1965), Ch.6.

14 We were all on this ship in the sixties, our generation, a ship going to discover the New World. And the Beatles were in the crow's nest of that ship.

John Lennon (1940–1980), British rock musician: interview for French TV, March 1974, publ. in *Imagine* (ed. Andrew Solt and Sam Egan, 1988)

15 I like to think of my behavior in the sixties as a 'learning experience.' Then again, I like to think of anything stupid I've done as a 'learning experience.' It makes me feel less stupid.

P.J. O'Rourke (b.1947), U.S. journalist: 'Second Thoughts About the Sixties', speech, Oct. 1987, Second Thoughts Conference, Washington D.C., rep. in *Give War A Chance* (1992)

16 My generation of the Sixties, with all our great ideals, destroyed liberalism, because of our excesses.

Camille Paglia (b.1947), U.S. author and critic: 'The MIT Lecture: Crisis in the American Universities', 19 Sept. 1991, publ. in *Sex, Art, and American Culture* (1992)

17 The Sixties, of course, was the worst time in the world to try and bring up a child. They were exposed to all these crazy things going on.

Nancy Reagan (b.1923), wife of President Ronald Reagan: quoted in *Parade* (New York), 8 Nov. 1981

18 I knew the youthfulness of the sixties: Talitha and Paul Getty lying on a starlit terrace in Marrakesh, beautiful and damned, and a whole generation assembled as if for eternity where the curtain of the past seemed to lift before an extraordinary future.

Yves Saint Laurent (b.1936), French fashion designer: interview in *Ritz* (London), No.85, 1984

19 History is hard to know, because of all the hired bullshit, but even without being sure of 'history' it seems entirely reasonable to think that every now and then the energy of a whole generation comes to a head in a long fine flash, for reasons that nobody really understands at the time – and which never explain, in retrospect, what actually happened.

Hunter S. Thompson (b.1939), U.S. journalist: *Fear and Loathing in Las Vegas* (1971), Ch.8

20 The Sixties was like coitus interruptus. The only thing we didn't pull out of was Vietnam.

Lily Tomlin (b.1939), U.S. comedienne: *Lily Tomlin on Stage* (album, 1977; material written by Lily Tomlin and Jane Wagner), 'Glenna – A Child of the Sixties'

21 Never before has a civilization reached such a degree of a contempt for life; never before has a generation, drowned in mortification, felt such a rage to live.

Raoul Vaneigem (b.1934), Belgian Situationist philosopher: *The Revolution of Everyday Life* (1967; tr.1983), Ch.5

22 The sixties have a name now, all the contradictory tensions neatly resolved in a few Golden Age images.

Peter York (b.1950), British journalist: 'Recycling the Sixties', first publ. in *Harpers & Queen* (London), Jan. 1978, rep. in *Style Wars* (1980)

23 The sad thing about the Sixties was the weak-mindedness of the so-called radicals and the way that they managed to get co-opted. I think one of the things that helped that happen was LSD. It's the only chemical known to mankind that will convert a hippy to a yuppie.

Frank Zappa (1940–1993), U.S. rock musician: quoted in the *Independent on Sunday* (London), 26 Jan. 1992

See also Dylan on THE GENERATION GAP

THE 1970s

1   The victim style of the 1970s has a behavioural style to match. They never smile, these infants of the recession: they sneer. Defiant untouchables, tattooed at the extremities and accessoried with offensive weapons, lips and fingernails stained black and blue and the skin round their eyes painted up like rococo window-frames.
    Angela Carter (1940–1992), British author: 'Ups and Downs for the Babes in Bondage', first publ. in *New Society* (London), 22 Dec. 1977, rep. in *The Faber Book of Pop* (ed. Hanif Kureishi and Jon Savage, 1995), Pt.7

2   For me, the attraction of the Seventies is that it was a bit off, a bit eccentric, a bit wrong. Music and fashion and culture became stupidly exaggerated and then eventually imploded.
    Jarvis Cocker (b.1963), British rock musician: interview in *Select Magazine* (London), quoted in *Pulp: The Tomorrow People* by Susan Wilson (1996), Ch.1. Elsewhere in the interview, Cocker remarked, 'The seventies was the last future-looking decade'

3   Sure I remember the Seventies. There were a lot of drawn blinds and dark rooms.
    Dennis Hopper (b.1935), U.S. actor and filmmaker: interview in *The Face* (London), May 1993

4   If anything characterizes the cultural life of the seventies in America, it is an insistence on preventing failures of communication.
    Richard Dean Rosen (b.1949), U.S. journalist and critic: *Psychobabble: Fast Talk and Quick Cure in the Era of Feeling* (1977), 'Psychobabble'

5   For the longest time everyone kept saying the seventies hadn't started yet. There was no distinctive style for the decade, no flair, no slogans. The mistake we made was that we were all looking for something as startling as the Beatles, acid, Pop Art, hippies and radical politics. What actually set in was a painful and unexpected working out of the terms the sixties had so blithely tossed off.
    Edmund White (b.1940), U.S. author: 'Fantasia on the Seventies' (1977), rep. in *The Burning Library* (1994)

6   We are now in the Me Decade – seeing the upward roll of ... the third great religious wave in American history.
    Tom Wolfe (b.1931), U.S. author and journalist: *Mauve Gloves and Madmen, Clutter and Vine* (1976), 'The Me Decade and the Third Great Awakening'

7   In the Golden Age, that is the 1970's, the Phoney Wars were ... style wars.... Style became a weapon to forge your own legend.
    Peter York (b.1950), British journalist: *Style Wars* (1980), 'Style Wars'

THE 1980s

1   Maybe in the '90s or possibly in the next century people will look upon the '80s as the age of masturbation, when it was taken to the limit; that might be all that's going on right now in a big way.
    Bob Dylan (b.1941), U.S. singer and songwriter: interview, 1985, for *Biograph* box set (1985), notes to 'Every Grain of Sand'

2   In economics, we borrowed from the Bourbons; in foreign policy, we drew on themes fashioned by the nomad warriors of the Eurasian steppes. In spiritual matters, we emulated the braying intolerance of our archenemies, the Shi'ite fundamentalists.
    Barbara Ehrenreich (b.1941), U.S. author and columnist: of the 'traditional values' adopted by Americans in the 1980s, in *The Worst Years of Our Lives* (1991), 'Family Values'. These values formed 'part of what may someday be known as the "Reagan renovation", that finely balanced mix of cosmetic refinement and moral coarseness which brought $200,000 china to the White House dinner table and mayhem to the beleaguered peasantry of Central America'

3   We can safely abandon the doctrine of the eighties, namely that the rich were not working because they had too little money, the poor because they had much.
    J.K. Galbraith (b.1908), U.S. economist: in *The Guardian* (London), 20 Nov. 1991

4   I wouldn't wish the eighties on anyone, it was the time when all that was rotten bubbled to the surface. If you were not at the receiving end of this mayhem you could be unaware of it. It was possible to live through the decade preoccupied by the mortgage and the pence you saved on your income tax. It was also possible for those of us who saw what was happening to turn our eyes in a different direction; but what, in another decade, had been a trip to the clap clinic was now a trip to the mortuary.
    Derek Jarman (1942–1994), British film-maker, artist and author: *At Your Own Risk: A Saint's Testament* (1992), '1980's'

5   The new puritanism. Sloth, gluttony, recreational drugs were out. Narcissism, blind ambition and greed by contrast were free of side- or after-effects, at least in this life, and who was counting on the other anymore?
    Jay McInerney (b.1955), U.S. author: *Brightness Falls* (1992), Ch.10

6   I spent most of the Eighties, most of my *life*, riding around in somebody else's car, in possession of, or ingested of, something illegal, on my way from something illegal to something illegal with many illegal things happening all around me.

Iggy Pop (b.1947), U.S. rock musician: interview in *The Guardian* (London), 17 Feb. 1996

7 I think what's happening now is people want to forget. There was Vietnam, there was Watergate, there was Iran. We were beaten, we were hustled, and then we were humiliated. And I think people got a need to feel good about the country they live in. But what's happening, I think, is that the need – which is a good thing – is gettin' manipulated and exploited. And you see the Reagan reelection ads on TV. You know: 'It's morning in America.' And you say, well, it's not morning in Pittsburgh. It's not morning above 125th Street in New York. It's midnight, and, like, there's a bad moon risin'.
Bruce Springsteen (b.1949), U.S. rock musician: interview in *Rolling Stone* (New York), Dec. 1984

8 Technology itself has changed. Not for us the giant steam snorting wonders of the past: the Hoover Dam, the Empire State Building, the nuclear power plant. Eighties tech sticks to the skin, responds to the touch: the personal computer, the Sony Walkman, the portable telephone, the soft contact lens.
Bruce Sterling (b.1954), U.S. science fiction author: preface to *Mirrorshades* (ed. Bruce Sterling, 1986). Sterling went on to write: 'The Eighties are an era of reassessment, of integration, of hybridized influences, of old notions shaken loose and reinterpreted with a new sophistication, a broader perspective'

9 The last best hope of earth, two trillion dollars in debt, is spinning out of control, and all we can do is stare at a flickering cathode-ray tube as Ollie 'answers' questions on TV while the press, resolutely irrelevant as ever, asks politicians if they have committed adultery. From V-J Day 1945 to this has been, my fellow countrymen, a perfect nightmare.
Gore Vidal (b.1925), U.S. novelist and critic: *A View from the Diner's Club* (1991), 'Ollie'

10 Pornography was the great vice of the Seventies; plutography – the graphic depiction of the acts of the rich – is the great vice of the Eighties.
Tom Wolfe (b.1931), U.S. author and journalist: interview in *The Sunday Times* (London), 10 Jan. 1988

11 The eighties are a long story about fun, greed and money. The eighties are what happened when what looked like the majority went out and took what the minority had previously thought of as its own. It was a bloodless revolution.
Peter York (b.1950), British journalist: *Peter York's The Eighties* (written with Charles Jennings, 1996), Ch.1

THE 1990s

1 The reason the press in this country are so aggressively superficial is because they are living in the nineties. It's a fuck-up decade, there's such appetite, there are so many papers, so many television programmes, and you have to know that every six months they are going to want someone else.
Damon Albarn (b.1967), British rock musician: quoted in *The Face* (London), April 1996

2 Everything's so repressive now – it's the No generation. You can't do anything, you can't eat anything, you have to abstain.
Michael Douglas (b.1944), U.S. actor: quoted in the *Independent on Sunday* (London), 5 April 1992

3 1992 is not a year I shall look back on with undiluted pleasure. In the words of one of my more sympathetic correspondents, it has turned out to be an Annus Horribilis.
Elizabeth II (b.1926), Queen of Great Britain and Northern Ireland: speech, 24 Nov. 1992, Guildhall, London, quoted in *The Times* (London), 25 Nov. 1992. The Queen's reference to John Dryden's long poem *Annus Mirabilis* (1667) was lost on much of the nation, producing headlines such as 'One's Bum Year' in *The Sun*. Dryden had described the events of 1666 as a 'year of marvels', which included the Great Fire of London; a few days before the Queen's speech, which commemorated her 40 years on the throne, a fire had gutted some of the State Apartments in Windsor Castle. Other personal disasters included the separation of the Prince and Princess of Wales, and a fierce press campaign against the royal family

4 Once we get out of the 80s, the 90s are going to make the 60s seem like the 50s.
Dennis Hopper (b.1935), U.S. actor and filmmaker: the fugitive (Hopper), in *Flashback* (film; screenplay by David Loughery, directed by Franco Amurri, 1990)

5 Thirty years ago it was 'the conservative establishment' that was at fault, a conspiracy largely composed of university professors, bureaucrats, and TV executives who couldn't play guitar and trembled at the sound of Dylan's harmonica. Now it is 'the liberal establishment' that is at fault, a conspiracy largely composed of university professors, bureaucrats, and TV executives who tremble before the wisdom of Arianna Huffington.
Lewis H. Lapham (b.1935), U.S. essayist and editor: *Harper's Magazine* (New York), March 1996

6 The 1990's, after the reign of terror of academic vandalism, will be a decade of restoration: restoration of meaning, value, beauty, pleasure, and emotion to art and restoration of art to its audience.

Camille Paglia (b.1947), U.S. author and
critic: book review in the *Washington Post Book
World*, 10 March 1991, rep. in *Sex, Art, and
American Culture* (1992), 'The Critic at Graceful
Ease'

RICHARD NIXON

1   I think that Richard Nixon will go down in
history as a true folk hero, who struck a vital
blow to the whole diseased concept of the
revered image and gave the American virtue of
irreverence and skepticism back to the people.
William Burroughs (1914–1997), U.S. author: *The
Adding Machine* (1985), 'A Word to the Wise Guy'

2   Do you realize the responsibility I carry? I'm
the only person between Nixon and the White
House.
John F. Kennedy (1917–1963), U.S. Democratic
politician and president: teasing remark to a liberal
supporter during the 1960 election campaign;
quoted in *Kennedy* by Theodore C. Sorensen (1965),
Pt.2, Ch.7. In the event, Nixon won 49.6 per cent of
the total vote, giving Kennedy the narrowest victory
in a presidential election since 1888

3   To have striven so hard, to have molded a
public personality out of so amorphous an
identity, to have sustained that superhuman
effort only to end with every weakness dis-
closed and every error compounding the
downfall – that was a fate of biblical proportions. Evidently the Deity would not tolerate
the presumption that all can be manipulated;
an object lesson of the limits of human presumption was necessary.
Henry Kissinger (b.1923), U.S. Republican
politician and secretary of state: on the downfall of
Richard Nixon, in *Years of Upheaval* (1982), Ch.25,
'The End of the Road'

4   As I leave you I want you to know – just think
how much you're going to be missing. You
won't have Nixon to kick around any more
because, gentlemen, this is my last press conference.
Richard Nixon (1913–1992), U.S. Republican
politician and president: press conference, 5 Nov.
1962, following his defeat in the California
gubernatorial election, quoted in the *New York
Times*, 8 Nov. 1962

5   Nixon is the kind of politician who would cut
down a redwood tree, then mount the stump
for a speech on conservation.
Adlai Stevenson (1900–1965), U.S. Democratic
politician: quoted in *The Fine Art of Political Wit*
by Leon Harris (1965), Ch.10

6   The trouble with Nixon is that he's a serious
politics junkie. He's totally hooked ... and like
any other junkie, he's a bummer to have
around: especially as President.

Hunter S. Thompson (b.1939), U.S. journalist: *The
Great Shark Hunt* (1979), 'Jacket Copy for Fear and
Loathing in Las Vegas'

See also Stevenson on THE UNITED STATES: THE
PRESIDENT

NOISE

1   For twenty-five centuries, Western knowledge
has tried to look upon the world. It has failed to
understand that the world is not for the
beholding. It is for hearing. It is not legible,
but audible. Our science has always desired to
monitor, measure, abstract, and castrate
meaning, forgetting that life is full of noise and
that death alone is silent: work noise, noise of
man, and noise of beast. Noise bought, sold, or
prohibited. Nothing essential happens in the
absence of noise.
Jacques Attali (b.1943), Algerian-born French
economist and writer: opening sentences of *Noise:
The Political Economy of Music* (1977), Ch.1

2   I have felt and hoped to have led other people
to feel that the sounds of their environment
constitute a music which is more interesting
than the music which they would hear if they
went into a concert hall.
John Cage (1912–1992), U.S. composer: interview
in *Soho Weekly News* (New York), 12 Sept. 1974,
rep. in *Conversing with Cage* (ed. Richard
Kostelanetz, 1988), 'His Own Music (to 1970)'

3   The world is never quiet, even its silence eternally resounds with the same notes, in vibra-
tions which escape our ears. As for those that
we perceive, they carry sounds to us, occasionally a chord, never a melody.
Albert Camus (1913–1960), French-Algerian
philosopher and author: *The Rebel* (1951; tr.1953),
'Rebellion and Art'

4   There is something terribly wrong with a
culture inebriated by noise and gregariousness.
George Steiner (b.1929), French-born U.S. critic
and novelist: in *The Daily Telegraph* (London),
23 May 1989

See also Bellow on TELEVISION

NONSENSE

1   Supercalifragilisticexpialidocious!
Even though the sound of it is something quite
    atrocious!
If you say it loud enough you'll always sound
    precocious.
Supercalifragilisticexpialidocious!
Julie Andrews (b.1934), British actress and singer:
'Supercalifragilisticexpialidocious!' (song; written
by Richard and Robert Sherman) in *Mary Poppins*
(film, 1964)

2 It is a far, far better thing to have a firm anchor in nonsense than to put out on the troubled seas of thought.
J.K. Galbraith (b.1908), U.S. economist: referring to the resistance of conventional wisdom to 'the economics of affluence', in *The Affluent Society* (1958), Ch.11, Sct.4

NONVIOLENCE

1 It is my contention that civil disobedients are nothing but the latest form of voluntary association, and that they are thus quite in tune with the oldest traditions of the country.
Hannah Arendt (1906–1975), German-born U.S. political philosopher: *Crises of the Republic* (1972), 'Civil Disobedience'

2 The point of nonviolence is to build a floor, a strong new floor, beneath which we can no longer sink. A platform which stands a few feet above napalm, torture, exploitation, poison gas, A and H bombs, the works. Give man a decent place to stand.
Joan Baez (b.1941), U.S. singer: *Daybreak* (1968), 'What Would You Do If?'

3 The people in power will not disappear voluntarily, giving flowers to the cops just isn't going to work. This thinking is fostered by the establishment; they like nothing better than love and nonviolence. The only way I like to see cops given flowers is in a flower pot from a high window.
William Burroughs (1914–1997), U.S. author: *The Job: Interviews with Daniel Odier* (1969), 'Prisoners of the Earth Come Out'

4 Only a philosophy of eternity, in the world today, could justify non-violence.
Albert Camus (1913–1960), French-Algerian philosopher and author: *The Rebel* (1951; tr.1953), Pt.5, 'Historic Murder'

5 In a nonviolent movement there must be a latent threat of eruption, a dormant possibility of sudden and violent action if concessions are to be won, respect gained, and the established order altered. That nonviolent theory is practicable in civilized lands among civilized people, the Asians and Africans, but a look at European history shows that anything of great value that ever changed hands was taken by force of arms.
George Jackson (1942–1971), U.S. black activist: letter to his mother, March 1967, from Soledad Prison, publ. in *Soledad Brother* (1970)

6 We who engage in nonviolent direct action are not the creators of tension. We merely bring to the surface the hidden tension that is already alive.
Martin Luther King Jr. (1929–1968), U.S. clergyman and civil rights leader: 'Letter from Birmingham Jail', open letter to clergymen, 16 April 1963, publ. in *Why We Can't Wait* (1963)

7 To be deeply committed to negotiations, to be opposed to a particular war or military action, is not only considered unpatriotic, it also casts serious doubt on one's manhood.
Myriam Miedzian, U.S. author: *Boys Will Be Boys* (1991), Ch.2

NORMALITY

1 The only effort of my life, the rest having been given to me, and largely (except for wealth, to which I am indifferent): to live the life of a normal man. I didn't want to be a man of the abyss. This overwhelming effort was useless. Little by little, instead of succeeding more and more in my endeavour, I see the abyss approaching.
Albert Camus (1913–1960), French-Algerian philosopher and author: journal entry, Sept.1949, quoted in *Camus: A Biography* by Herbert R. Lottman (1979), Ch.35

2 Normality highly values its normal man. It educates children to lose themselves and to become absurd, and thus to be normal. Normal men have killed perhaps 100,000,000 of their fellow normal men in the last fifty years.
R.D. Laing (1927–1989), British psychiatrist: *The Politics of Experience* (1967), Ch.1

3 There is no such thing as a normal human being. Nobody looks so eccentric as the man who is trying to look normal.
Auberon Waugh (b.1939), British journalist and novelist: 'Way of the World', column in *The Daily Telegraph* (London), 6 Nov.1995

NORTHERN IRELAND *see under* IRELAND

NOSTALGIA

1 People have this obsession. They want you to be like you were in 1969. They want you to, because otherwise their youth goes with you.... It's very selfish, but it's understandable.
Mick Jagger (b.1942), British rock musician: quoted in *The Observer* (London), 10 Jan.1993

2 Time has lost all meaning in that nightmare alley of the Western world known as the American mind. We wallow in nostalgia but manage to get it all wrong. True nostalgia is an ephemeral composition of disjointed memories ... but American-style nostalgia is about as ephemeral as copyrighted déjà vu.
Florence King (b.1936), U.S. author: *Reflections in a Jaundiced Eye* (1989), 'Déjà Views'

3 A society that has made 'nostalgia' a market-able commodity on the cultural exchange quickly repudiates the suggestion that life in the past was in any important way better than life today.
Christopher Lasch (1932–1994), U.S. historian: preface to *The Culture of Narcissism* (1979)

4 I don't like nostalgia unless it's mine.
Lou Reed (b.1944), U.S. rock musician: in the *Evening Standard* (London), 8 June 1989

5 Even while I protest the assembly-line pro-duction of our food, our songs, our language, and eventually our souls, I know that it was a rare home that baked good bread in the old days. Mother's cooking was with rare excep-tions poor, that good unpasteurized milk touched only by flies and bits of manure crawled with bacteria, the healthy old-time life was riddled with aches, sudden death from unknown causes, and that sweet local speech I mourn was the child of illiteracy and ignor-ance. It is the nature of a man as he grows older, a small bridge in time, to protest against change, particularly change for the better.
John Steinbeck (1902–1968), U.S. author: *Travels With Charley: in Search of America* (1962), Pt.2

6 For us, the best time is always yesterday.
Tatyana Tolstaya (b.1951), Russian author: of the Russians, in *The Independent* (London), 31 May 1990

See also Rich on TIME: PAST

NOVELTY

1 The new always happens against the over-whelming odds of statistical laws and their probability, which for all practical, everyday purposes amounts to certainty; the new there-fore always appears in the guise of a miracle.
Hannah Arendt (1906–1975), German-born U.S. political philosopher: *The Human Condition* (1958), Pt.5, Ch.24

2 The New is not a fashion, it is a value.
Roland Barthes (1915–1980), French semiologist: *The Pleasure of the Text* (1975), 'Modern'

3 An old thing becomes new if you detach it from what usually surrounds it.
Robert Bresson (b.1907), French film-maker: *Notes on the Cinematographer* (1975), '1950–1958: on Poverty'

THE NUCLEAR AGE

1 If you ask a member of this generation two simple questions: 'How do you want the world to be in fifty years?' and 'What do you want your life to be like five years from now?' the answers are quite often preceded by 'Provided there is still a world' and 'Provided I am still alive.' ... To the often-heard question, Who are they, this new generation? one is tempted to answer, Those who hear the ticking. And to the other question, Who are they who utterly deny them? the answer may well be, Those who do not know, or refuse to face, things as they really are.
Hannah Arendt (1906–1975), German-born U.S. political philosopher: *Crises of the Republic* (1972), 'On Violence', Sct.1

2 REST IN PEACE. THE MISTAKE SHALL NOT BE REPEATED.
Hiroshima cenotaph: inscription on the cenotaph at Hiroshima, Japan

3 No country without an atom bomb could properly consider itself independent.
Charles de Gaulle (1890–1970), French statesman and soldier: quoted in the *New York Times Magazine*, 12 May 1968

4 The unleashed power of the atom has changed everything save our modes of thinking and we thus drift toward unparalleled catastrophe.
Albert Einstein (1879–1955), German-born U.S. theoretical physicist: telegram sent to prominent Americans, 24 May 1946, publ. in the *New York Times*, 25 May 1946

5 What has kept the world safe from the bomb since 1945 has not been deterrence, in the sense of fear of specific weapons, so much as it's been memory. The memory of what happened at Hiroshima.
John Hersey (1914–1993), U.S. novelist and journalist: interview in *Writers at Work* (Eighth Series, ed. George Plimpton, 1988)

6 The base emotions Plato banned
have left a radio-active and not radiant land.
Libby Houston (b.1941), British poet: 'Judging Lear', publ. in *At the Mercy* (1981)

7 What happened at Hiroshima was not only that a scientific breakthrough ... had occurred and that a great part of the population of a city had been burned to death, but that the prob-lem of the relation of the triumphs of modern science to the human purposes of man had been explicitly defined.
Archibald MacLeish (1892–1982), U.S. poet: 'The Great American Frustration', first publ. in the *Saturday Review* (New York), 9 July 1968, rep. in *Riders on Earth* (1978) as 'Return from the Excursion'

8 The flame from the angel's sword in the garden of Eden has been catalysted into the atom bomb; God's thunderbolt became blunted, so man's dunderbolt has become the steel star of destruction.
Sean O'Casey (1884–1964), Irish playwright: *Sunset and Evening Star* (sixth volume of autobiography, 1954), 'And Evening Star'

9 J. Robert Oppenheimer, witnessing the first test of a nuclear weapon, confessed to tasting sin. But he and all his colleagues knew from the beginning what lay waiting at the end of the project. And which was the stronger flavor, the sin, or the satisfaction of having stolen fire from the gods?

Theodore Roszak (b.1933), U.S. social critic: *Where the Wasteland Ends* (1972), Ch.6. *See* Oppenheimer on PHYSICS

10 There is no evil in the atom; only in men's souls.

Adlai Stevenson (1900–1965), U.S. Democratic politician: 'The Atomic Future', speech, 18 Sept. 1952, Hartford, Connecticut, publ. in *Speeches* (1953)

11 The terror of the atom age is not the violence of the new power but the speed of man's adjustment to it – the speed of his acceptance.

E.B. White (1899–1985), U.S. author and editor: *The Second Tree From the Corner* (1954), 'Notes on Our Time'

See also Bevan on DISARMAMENT

NUCLEAR TESTING

1 What a city, what a night, what a crowd, what a bomb, what a mistake, what a wanker you have for a president.

Bono (b.1960), Irish rock musician: on French nuclear testing in the Pacific, in acceptance speech at MTV Europe Music Awards in Paris, quoted in *Mojo* (London), Jan. 1996

2 Now, standing up unsteadily from the sea, was the famous Mushroom. ... It climbed like a fungus; it looked like a towering mound of firm cream shot with veins and rivers of wandering red; it mounted tirelessly through the clouds as though it were made of denser, solider stuff, as no doubt it was. The only similes that came to mind were banal: a sundae, red ink in a pot of distemper. From behind me I heard a frenetic ticking of typewriters; very soon I found I was fumbling with my own. The reportage had begun. Many of us will never live it down.

James Cameron (1911–1985), British journalist: on the first atomic-bomb test on the Bikini atoll, summer 1946, in *Point of Departure* (1969), Ch.3

3 We test and then they test and we have to test again. And you build up until somebody uses them.

John F. Kennedy (1917–1963), U.S. Democratic politician and president: remark, 1961, quoted in *A Thousand Days* by Arthur M. Schlesinger Jr. (1965), Ch.17

NUCLEAR WAR

1 For myself and my loved ones, I want the heat, which comes at the speed of light. I don't want to have to hang about for the blast, which idles along at the speed of sound.

Martin Amis (b.1949), British author: introduction to *Einstein's Monsters* (1987)

2 It is a secret from nobody that the famous random event is most likely to arise from those parts of the world where the old adage 'There is no alternative to victory' retains a high degree of plausibility.

Hannah Arendt (1906–1975), German-born U.S. political philosopher: *Crises of the Republic* (1972), 'On Violence', Sct.1

3 It is in our ancient tradition to murder each other; but only we, in the present, should pay the price of our abominable stupidity. Nothing that concerns us, in our brief moment of history, gives us the right to stop time, to blot out the future, to end the continuing miracles and glories and tragedies and wretchedness of the human race.

Martha Gellhorn (b.1908), U.S. journalist and author: introduction (1959), to *The Face of War* (1967), appendix

4 I'm not saying we wouldn't get our hair mussed, Mister President, but I do say not more than ten to twenty million dead depending on the breaks.

Stanley Kubrick (b.1928), U.S. film-maker: General 'Buck' Turgidson (George C. Scott), in *Dr Strangelove; or, How I Learned to Stop Worrying and Love the Bomb* (film; screenplay by Stanley Kubrick, Terry Southern and Peter George, directed by Stanley Kubrick, 1963)

5 If the Third World War is fought with nuclear weapons, the fourth will be fought with bows and arrows.

Louis Mountbatten (1900–1979), British naval commander and statesman: in *Maclean's* (Toronto), 17 Nov. 1975

6 At last, after innumerable glamorous and frightful years, mankind approaches a war which is *totally predictable from beginning to end*.

Frederic Raphael (b.1931), British author and critic: in *New Society* (London), 10 May 1984

7 That even an apocalypse can be made to seem part of the ordinary horizon of expectation constitutes an unparalleled violence that is being done to our sense of reality, to our humanity.

Susan Sontag (b.1933), U.S. essayist: *AIDS and Its Metaphors* (1989), Ch.8

8   We are heading towards catastrophe. I think the world is going to pieces. I am very pessimistic. Why? Because the world hasn't been punished yet, and the only punishment that could be adequate is the nuclear destruction of the world.
Elie Wiesel (b.1928), Rumanian-born U.S. writer: interview in *Writers at Work* (Eighth Series, ed. George Plimpton, 1988)

See also Sontag on THE END

NUDITY

1   Nakedness reveals itself. Nudity is placed on display. ... The nude is condemned to never being naked. Nudity is a form of dress.
John Berger (b.1926), British author and critic: *Ways of Seeing* (1972), Ch.3

2   In the NUDE, all that is not beautiful is obscene.
Robert Bresson (b.1907), French film-maker: *Notes on the Cinematographer* (1975), 'Further Notes 1960–1974'

3   Nudity is the uniform of the other side ... nudity is a shroud.
Milan Kundera (b.1929), Czech-born French author and critic: *The Book of Laughter and Forgetting* (1978; tr.1980), Pt.7, Ch.8

4   The part never calls for it. And I've never ever used that excuse. The box office calls for it.
Helen Mirren (b.1946), British actress: quoted in *The Guardian* (London), 31 Dec.1994

5   It's not true I had nothing on. I had the radio on.
Marilyn Monroe (1926–1962), U.S. actress: in *Time* (New York), 1952

6   Basically collectors want nudes. So I have supplied for them nude cars, nude telephones, nude electric plugs, nude switches, nude fans, newd electretcetera and sew on.
Claes Oldenburg (b.1929), Swedish-born U.S. artist: quoted in Moderna Museet Gallery catalogue, Stockholm, 1966, rep. in *Icons and Images of the Sixties* by Nicholas and Elena Calas (1971), 'Pop Art: Claes Oldenburg's Contented Objects'

7   Being naked approaches being revolutionary; going barefoot is mere populism.
John Updike (b.1932), U.S. author and critic: 'Going Barefoot', first publ. in the anthology *On the Vineyard* (1980), rep. in *Hugging the Shore* (1983)

8   My advice to those who think they have to take off their clothes to be a star is, once you're boned, what's left to create the illusion? Let'em wonder. I never believed in givin' them too much of me.

Mae West (1892–1980), U.S. actress: quoted in David Ray Johnson's 'Biographical Study', appendix to *On Sex, Health and ESP* (1975)

NUMBERS

1   People have been counting, as they have been talking, in every culture. Arithmetic, like language, begins in legend.
Jacob Bronowski (1908–1974), British scientist and author: *The Ascent of Man* (1973), Ch.5

2   Seven is for something. What's seven for? One for a glorious golden grave – two for a terrible torch of tin; three for a hundred hollow horses; four for a knight with a spur of speargrass; five for a fish with fortunate fins, six – I've forgotten six, and seven – what's seven for? Eight for a frog with eyes like marbles, nine, what's nine? Nine for a – nine, nine – ten for a tower of turbulent toast – but what is seven. What is seven?
Mervyn Peake (1911–1968), British author and illustrator: spoken by Fuschia, after she has counted seven clouds through her bedroom window, in *Titus Groan* (1946), 'Prunesquallor's Knee Cap'

See also Thompson on PUBLISHING; STATISTICS

OBSCENITY

1   Would you approve of your young sons, young daughters – because girls can read as well as boys – reading this book? Is it a book that you would have lying around in your own house? Is it a book that you would even wish your wife or your servants to read?
Mervyn Griffith-Jones (1909–1979), British lawyer: opening address to jury during the prosecution of Penguin Books Ltd., 20 Oct.1961, publ. in *The Trial of Lady Chatterley* (ed. C.H. Rolph, 1961). Griffith-Jones was senior prosecuting counsel in the case brought against Penguin for publishing an unexpurgated edition of D.H. Lawrence's *Lady Chatterley's Lover*

2   Obscenity is a moral concept in the verbal arsenal of the Establishment, which abuses the term by applying it, not to expressions of its own morality but to those of another.
Herbert Marcuse (1898–1979), U.S. political philosopher: *An Essay on Liberation* (1969), Ch.1

3   Obscenity is whatever happens to shock some elderly and ignorant magistrate.
Bertrand Russell (1872–1970), British philosopher and mathematician: in *Look* (New York), 23 Feb.1954

4   Shocking writing is like murder: the questions the jury must decide are the questions of motive and intent.

E.B. White (1899–1985), U.S. author and editor: interview in *Writers at Work* (Eighth Series, ed. George Plimpton, 1988)

See also Miller on PORNOGRAPHY

OBSCURITY

1   More significant than the fact that poets write abstrusely, painters paint abstractly, and composers compose unintelligible music is that people should admire what they cannot understand; indeed, admire that which has no meaning or principle.
Eric Hoffer (1902–1983), U.S. philosopher: *Reflections on the Human Condition* (1973), Aph.104

2   Obscurantism is the academic theorist's revenge on society for having consigned him or her to relative obscurity – a way of proclaiming one's superiority in the face of one's diminished influence.
David Lehman (b.1948), U.S. poet, editor and critic: *Signs of the Times* (1991), Ch.3, 'Archie Debunking'

3   The mind's passion is all for singling out. Obscurity has another tale to tell.
Adrienne Rich (b.1929), U.S. poet: 'Focus', St.7, publ. in *Necessities of Life* (1966)

OBSESSION

1   Everyone who's any good is obsessive.
Alan Bates (b.1934), British actor: quoted in the *Independent on Sunday* (London), 9 May 1993

2   I envy people who can just look at a sunset. I wonder how you can shoot it. There is nothing more grotesque to me than a vacation.
Dustin Hoffman (b.1937), U.S. actor: in *The Observer* (London), 19 Feb. 1989

3   I have met women who loved football, and go to watch a number of games a season, but I have not yet met one who would make that Wednesday night trip to Plymouth. And I have met women who love music, and can tell their Mavis Staples from their Shirley Browns, but I have never met a woman with a huge and ever-expanding and neurotically alphabeticised record collection. They always seem to have lost their records, or to have relied on somebody else in the house – a boyfriend, a brother, a flatmate, usually a male – to have provided the physical details of their interests. Men cannot allow that to happen. ...
I am not saying that the anally retentive woman does not exist, but she is vastly outnumbered by her masculine equivalent; and while there are women with obsessions, they are usually, I think, obsessive about people, or

the focus for their obsession changes frequently.
Nick Hornby (b.1957), British author: *Fever Pitch* (1992), '1976–1986: Boys and Girls'

See also FANATICS; Bates on FANS

THE OBVIOUS

1   To spell out the obvious is often to call it in question.
Eric Hoffer (1902–1983), U.S. philosopher: *The Passionate State of Mind* (1955), Aph.220

2   In saying what is obvious, never choose cunning. Yelling works better.
Cynthia Ozick (b.1928), U.S. novelist and short-story writer: 'We are the Crazy Lady and Other Feisty Feminist Fables', publ. in *The First Ms. Reader* (ed. Francine Klagsbrun, 1972)

THE OFFICE

1   A molehill man is a pseudo-busy executive who comes to work at 9am and finds a molehill on his desk. He has until 5pm to make this molehill into a mountain. An accomplished molehill man will often have his mountain finished before lunch.
Fred Allen (1894–1957), U.S. radio comic: *Treadmill to Oblivion* (1954), Pt.2

2   He [Robert Benchley] and I had an office so tiny that an inch smaller and it would have been adultery.
Dorothy Parker (1893–1967), U.S. humorous writer: interview in *Writers at Work* (First Series, ed. Malcolm Cowley, 1958). Benchley himself probably originated this remark, ascribed to him in the *New Yorker*, 5 Jan. 1946: 'One square foot less and it would be adulterous'

3   An office party is not, as is sometimes supposed, the Managing Director's chance to kiss the tea-girl. It is the tea-girl's chance to kiss the Managing Director (however bizarre an ambition this may seem to anyone who has seen the Managing Director face on). Bringing down the mighty from their seats is an agreeable and necessary pastime, but no one supposes that the mighty, having struggled so hard to get seated, will enjoy the dethronement.
Katharine Whitehorn (b.1926), British journalist: *Roundabout* (1962), 'The Office Party'

ON THE ROAD

1   I'm out here a thousand miles from my home, Walkin' a road other men have gone down. I'm seein' your world of people and things,

Your paupers and peasants and princes and
kings.

Bob Dylan (b.1941), U.S. singer and songwriter:
'Song to Woody' (song) on the album *Bob Dylan*
(1962)

2 Do you know there's a road that goes down to
Mexico and all the way to Panama? – and
maybe all the way to the bottom of South
America where the Indians are seven feet tall
and eat cocaine on the mountainside? Yes! You
and I, Sal, we'd dig the whole world with a car
like this because, man, the road must eventually lead to the whole world. Ain't nowhere
else it can go – right?

Jack Kerouac (1922–1969), U.S. author: Dean
Moriarty, in *On the Road* (1957), Pt.3, Ch.9

3 I keep finding myself getting off the freeway at
familiar landmarks that turn out to be
unfamiliar. On the way to appointments.
Wandering down streets I thought I recognized that turn out to be replicas of streets I
remember. Streets I misremember. Streets I
can't tell if I've lived on or saw in a postcard.

Sam Shepard (b.1943), U.S. playwright and actor:
Austin, in *True West* (1980), Act 2, Sc.8

4 If you ever plan to motor west,
travel my way, take the highway that's the best
--
Get your kicks on Route 66.

Bobby Troup, U.S. songwriter: 'Route 66' (song,
1946)

OPERA

1 The opera ain't over till the fat lady sings.

Anonymous: there is no precise origin for this
modern proverb, though both *The Concise Oxford
Dictionary of Proverbs* (ed. John Simpson, 1982),
and *Bartlett's Familiar Quotations* (16th ed., 1992),
cite sports commentator Dan Cook in the
Washington Post, 13 June 1978. *Bartlett's* notes
another version in *Southern Words and Sayings* (ed.
Fabia Rue Smith and Charles Rayford Smith, 1976):
'Church ain't out till the fat lady sings'

2 If music in general is an imitation of history,
opera in particular is an imitation of human
willfulness; it is rooted in the fact that we not
only have feelings but insist upon having them
at whatever cost to ourselves. ... The quality
common to all the great operatic roles,
e.g., Don Giovanni, Norma, Lucia, Tristan,
Isolde, Brünnhilde, is that each of them is a
passionate and willful state of being. In real life
they would all be bores, even Don Giovanni.

W.H. Auden (1907–1973), Anglo-American poet:
The Dyer's Hand (1962), Pt.8, 'Notes on Music and
Opera'

3 Opera once was an important social instrument – especially in Italy. With Rossini and

Verdi people were listening to opera together
and having the same catharsis with the same
story, the same moral dilemmas. They were
holding hands in the darkness. That has gone.
Now perhaps they are holding hands watching
television.

Luciano Berio (b.1925), Italian composer:
interview in *The Observer* (London), 5 Feb. 1989

4 Opera, next to Gothic architecture, is one of
the strangest inventions of Western man. It
could not have been foreseen by any logical
process.

Kenneth Clark (1903–1983), British art historian:
Civilisation (1970), Ch.9

5 A Librettist is a mere drudge in the world of
opera.

Robertson Davies (1913–1995), Canadian novelist
and journalist: 'The Happy Intervention of
Robertson Davies', first publ. in *Opera Canada*
Spring 1982, rep. in *The Enthusiasms of Robertson
Davies* (1990)

6 If I weren't reasonably placid, I don't think I
could cope with this sort of life. To be a diva,
you've got to be absolutely like a horse.

Joan Sutherland (b.1926), Australian opera singer:
quoted in *Divas: Impressions of Six Opera
Superstars* by Winthrop Sargeant (1959), 'Joan
Sutherland'

7 I have always believed that opera is a planet
where the muses work together, join hands and
celebrate all the arts.

Franco Zeffirelli (b.1922), Italian stage and film
director: in the *International Herald Tribune* (Paris),
21 March 1990

OPINION

1 Opinions are formed in a process of open
discussion and public debate, and where no
opportunity for the forming of opinions exists,
there may be moods – moods of the masses
and moods of individuals, the latter no less
fickle and unreliable than the former – but no
opinion.

Hannah Arendt (1906–1975), German-born
U.S. political philosopher: *On Revolution* (1963),
Ch.6

2 My basic view of things is – not to have any
basic view of things.

Ingmar Bergman (b.1918), Swedish stage and film
writer-director: interview in *Bergman on Bergman*
(1970), 'Solna, 25 June 1968'

3 It rarely adds anything to say, 'In my opinion'
– not even modesty. Naturally a sentence is
only your opinion; and you are not the Pope.

Paul Goodman (1911–1972), U.S. author, poet and
critic: *Five Years* (1966), '1959', Sct.2

4 A point of view can be a dangerous luxury when substituted for insight and understanding.
Marshall McLuhan (1911–1980), Canadian communications theorist: *The Gutenberg Galaxy* (1962), 'Typographic Man Can Express but is Helpless to Read the Configuration of Print Technology'

5 It's not that I don't have opinions, rather that I'm paid not to think aloud.
Yitzhak Navon (b.1921), Israeli politician and president: quoted in *The Observer* (London), 16 Jan. 1983

6 The more opinions you have, the less you see.
Wim Wenders (b.1945), German film-maker: in the *Evening Standard* (London), 25 April 1990

See also Stevenson on FREEDOM OF EXPRESSION; Auden on FRIENDS

OPPOSITES

1 The world is not dialectical – it is sworn to extremes, not to equilibrium, sworn to radical antagonism, not to reconciliation or synthesis. This is also the principle of evil.
Jean Baudrillard (b.1929), French semiologist: *Fatal Strategies* (1983; tr.1990), 'Ecstasy and Inertia'

2 War is peace. Freedom is slavery. Ignorance is strength.
George Orwell (1903–1950), British author: 'Ingsoc' party slogan, in *Nineteen Eighty-four* (1949), Pt.1, Ch.1

3 All human beings are born either introvert or extrovert; they are either Greeks or Trojans, Apollonian or Dionysian; Classic or Romantic. This is the divide in the human spirit which produces the opposites and the tensions that provide human beings with their energies of change and renewal.
Laurens van der Post (1906–1996), South African writer and philosopher: *A Walk with a White Bushman* (1986), p.94 of Chatto & Windus edn.

OPPOSITION

1 I respect only those who resist me; but I cannot tolerate them.
Charles de Gaulle (1890–1970), French general and president: quoted in the *New York Times Magazine*, 12 May 1966

2 It is easy and dismally enervating to think of opposition as merely perverse or actually evil – far more invigorating to see it as essential for honing the mind, and as a positive good in itself. For the day that moral issues cease to be fought over is the day the word 'human' disappears from the race.
Jill Tweedie (1936–1993), British author and journalist: in *The Independent* (London), May 1989

OPPRESSION

1 You know, it's not the world that was my oppressor, because what the world does to you, if the world does it to you long enough and effectively enough, you begin to do to yourself.
James Baldwin (1924–1987), U.S. author: in conversation with Nikki Giovanni, London, 4 Nov. 1971, publ. in *A Dialogue* (1973)

2 Powerlessness breeds a race of beggars who smile at the enemy and swear at him in the sanctity of their toilets; who shout 'Baas' willingly during the day and call the White man a dog in their buses as they go home. Once again the concept of fear is at the heart of this two-faced behaviour on the part of the conquered Blacks.
Steve Biko (1946–1977), South African anti-apartheid activist: 'I Write What I Like: Fear – an Important Determinant in South African Politics' (written under the pseudonym of Frank Talk), publ. in Appendix to *Steve Biko: Black Consciousness in South Africa* (ed. Millard Arnold, 1978)

3 The will to domination is a ravenous beast. There are never enough warm bodies to satiate its monstrous hunger. Once alive, this beast grows and grows, feeding on all the life around it, scouring the earth to find new sources of nourishment. This beast lives in each man who battens on female servitude.
Andrea Dworkin (b.1946), U.S. feminist critic: 'Our Blood: The Slavery of Women in Amerika', speech, 23 Aug. 1975, to the National Organization for Women, Washington D.C., publ. in *Our Blood* (1976), Ch.8

4 The native's muscles are always tensed. You can't say that he is terrorized, or even apprehensive. He is in fact ready at a moment's notice to exchange the role of the quarry for that of the hunter. The native is an oppressed person whose permanent dream is to become the persecutor.
Frantz Fanon (1925–1961), Martiniquan psychiatrist, philosopher and political activist: *The Wretched of the Earth* (1961), Ch.1

5 True enough, the country is calm. Calm as a morgue or a grave, would you not say?
Václav Havel (b.1936), Czech playwright and president: of the situation in Czechoslovakia under the Communist régime, in *Living in Truth* (1986), Pt.1, 'Letter to Dr Gustáv Husák', 8 April 1975

6 Do not be misled by the fact that you are at liberty and relatively free; that for the moment

you are not under lock and key: you have simply been granted a reprieve.

Ryszard Kapuściński (b.1932), Polish journalist: 'A Warsaw Diary', publ. in *Granta* (Cambridge), No.15, 1985

7 Loss of freedom seldom happens overnight. Oppression doesn't stand on the doorstep with toothbrush moustache and swastika armband – it creeps up insidiously ... step by step, and all of a sudden the unfortunate citizen realises that it is gone.

Baron Lane (b.1918), British judge, Lord Chief Justice of England: referring to proposed legal reforms, quoted in *The Independent* (London), 3 Feb. 1990

8 The web of domination has become the web of Reason itself, and this society is fatally entangled in it.

Herbert Marcuse (1898–1979), U.S. political philosopher: *One-Dimensional Man* (1964), Ch.5

9 First we kill all the subversives; then, their collaborators; later, those who sympathize with them; afterward, those who remain indifferent; and finally, the undecided.

Iberico Saint Jean, Argentinian soldier and politician: quoted in *Boletin de las Madres de Plaza de Mayo*, May 1985, rep. in *The Demon Lover* by Robin Morgan (1989), Ch.4. General Iberico Saint Jean was governor of the province of Buenos Aires during the military rule in Argentina

10 Hey! Do you see it, can't you feel it
It's all in the air
I can't stand oppression much longer
Somebody say a prayer.

Alabama's got me so upset
Tennessee made me lose my rest
And everybody knows about Mississippi –
 Goddam.

Nina Simone (b.1933), U.S. singer, songwriter and pianist: 'Mississippi – Goddam' (song, 1964), publ. in *The Poetry of Soul* (ed. A.X. Nicholas, 1971)

See also Biko on BLACK CONSCIOUSNESS/BLACK POWER; King on FREEDOM; Kapuściński on SURVIVAL; Orwell on TIME: FUTURE

OPTIMISM

---

1 If you think that historical forces are sending everybody straight to hell you can either go resignedly with the procession or hold out, and hold out not from pride or other personal motives, but from admiration and love for human abilities and powers to which, without exaggeration, the words 'miracle' and 'sublimity' can be applied.

Saul Bellow (b.1915), U.S. novelist: *More Die of Heartbreak* (1987), Ch.2

2 If Christianity is pessimistic as to man, it is optimistic as to human destiny. Well, I can say that, pessimistic as to human destiny, I am optimistic as to man.

Albert Camus (1913–1960), French-Algerian philosopher and author: address to monks of Latour-Maubourg, 1948, publ. in *Resistance, Rebellion and Death* (1961), 'The Unbeliever and Christians'

3 Optimism is the opium of the people.

Milan Kundera (b.1929), Czech-born French author and critic: *The Joke* (1967; tr.1982), Pt.3, Ch.3. Written by Ludvik on a postcard, the line was used by the Party as incriminating evidence against him, though it was only meant as 'a joke'

4 The happy ending is our national belief.

Mary McCarthy (1912–1989), U.S. author and critic: 'America the Beautiful: The Humanist in the Bathtub' (Sept. 1947), rep. in *On the Contrary* (1962), Pt.1

5 Some things in life are bad
They can really make you mad
Other things just make you swear and curse
When you're chewing on life's gristle
Don't grumble, give a whistle
And this'll help turn things out for the best ...
And ... always look on the bright side of life.

Monty Python's Flying Circus: Mr Frisbee III (Eric Idle), in *Monty Python's Life of Brian* (film; written by Graham Chapman (1941–1989), John Cleese (b.1939), Terry Gilliam (b.1940), Eric Idle (b.1943), Terry Jones (b.1942) and Michael Palin (b.1943) and directed by Terry Jones, 1979)

6 Nothing bad's going to happen to us. If we get fired, it's not failure; it's a midlife vocational reassessment.

P.J. O'Rourke (b.1947), U.S. journalist: in *Rolling Stone* (New York), 30 Nov. 1989

7 In these times you have to be an optimist to open your eyes when you wake in the morning.

Carl Sandburg (1878–1967), U.S. poet: in the *New York Post*, 9 Sept. 1960

8 She would rather light a candle than curse the darkness, and her glow has warmed the world.

Adlai Stevenson (1900–1965), U.S. Democratic politician: comment on learning of Eleanor Roosevelt's death, quoted in the *New York Times*, 8 Nov. 1962. Stevenson was quoting the motto of the Christopher Society, 'It is better to light one candle than curse the darkness.' According to *Brewer's Quotations* (ed. Nigel Rees, 1994), this in turn is a Chinese proverb

9 As both capitalist and communist states – not to mention the technological world – have evolved under the illusion that men purposefully built them, ideological optimism seeps into every niche of our lives. It is made worse by mass culture which feeds our most destructive illusions, fostering the belief that if we're only justified (and who isn't?) – if we only

calculate things correctly, if we only *do the right thing* (and who doesn't?) – then the future must yield the desired results. There must always be a way. And so hubris turns to false certainties, everyone expects to be a winner, and each morning is a mind-blowing surprise.

Stephen Vizinczey (b.1933), Hungarian novelist and critic: 'One of the Very Few', an appreciation of Stendhal first publ. in *The Times* (London), 11 May 1968, rep. in *Truth and Lies in Literature* (1986)

ORDER

1 That man is a creature who needs order yet yearns for change is the creative contradiction at the heart of the laws which structure his conformity and define his deviancy.

Freda Adler (b.1934), U.S. educator and author: *Sisters in Crime* (1975), Ch.8

2 The symbols of social order – the police, the bugle-calls in the barracks, military parades and the waving flags – are at one and the same time inhibitory and stimulating: for they do not convey the message 'Don't dare to budge'; rather, they cry out 'Get ready to attack'.

Frantz Fanon (1925–1961), Martiniquan psychiatrist, philosopher and political activist: *The Wretched of the Earth* (1961), Ch.1

3 There is a quality even meaner than outright ugliness or disorder, and this meaner quality is the dishonest mask of pretended order, achieved by ignoring or suppressing the real order that is struggling to exist and to be served.

Jane Jacobs (b.1916), U.S. author: introduction to *The Death and Life of Great American Cities* (1961)

4 Despite crime's omnipresence, things *work* in society, because biology compels it. Order eventually restores itself, by psychic equilibrium.

Camille Paglia (b.1947), U.S. author and critic: *Sex, Art, and American Culture* (1992), 'Sexual Personae: The Cancelled Preface'

5 There seems to be a kind of order in the universe, in the movement of the stars and the turning of the earth and the changing of the seasons, and even in the cycle of human life. But human life itself is almost pure chaos. Everyone takes his stance, asserts his own rights and feelings, mistaking the motives of others, and his own.

Katherine Anne Porter (1890–1980), U.S. short-story writer and novelist: interview in *Writers at Work* (Second Series, ed. George Plimpton, 1963)

See also Miller on THE WORLD

ORGANIZATION

1 Any consideration of the life and larger social existence of the modern corporate man ... begins and also largely ends with the effect of one all-embracing force. That is organization – the highly structured assemblage of men, and now some women, of which he is a part. It is to this, at the expense of family, friends, sex, recreation and sometimes health and effective control of alcoholic intake, that he is expected to devote his energies.

J.K. Galbraith (b.1908), U.S. economist: 'Corporate Man'. first publ. in the *New York Times*, 22 Jan. 1984, rep. in *A View from the Stands* (1986)

2 One of the many reasons for the bewildering and tragic character of human existence is the fact that social organization is at once necessary and fatal. Men are forever creating such organizations for their own convenience and forever finding themselves the victims of their home-made monsters.

Aldous Huxley (1894–1963), British author: *Themes and Variations* (1950), 'Variations on a Philosopher', Sct.2

ORGASM

1 I finally had an orgasm and my doctor told me it was the wrong kind.

Woody Allen (b.1935), U.S. film-maker: Polly (Lisa Farrow), in *Manhattan* (film; screenplay by Woody Allen and Marshall Brickman, directed by Woody Allen, 1979)

2 I may not be a great actress but I've become the greatest at screen orgasms. Ten seconds of heavy breathing, roll your head from side to side, simulate a slight asthma attack and die a little.

Candice Bergen (b.1946), U.S. actress: in the *Daily Mirror*, 1971, quoted in *Halliwell's Filmgoer's Companion* (ed. Leslie Halliwell, 1984)

3 There is the pleasurable orgasm, like a rising sales graph, and there is the unpleasurable orgasm, slumping ominously like the Dow Jones in 1929.

William Burroughs (1914–1997), U.S. author: *The Adding Machine* (1985), 'My Experiences with Wilhelm Reich's Orgone Box'

4 I'll have what she's having.

Nora Ephron (b.1941), U.S. author and journalist: woman diner to waiter, having observed Sally Albright (Meg Ryan) acting an orgasm, in *When Harry Met Sally...* (film; screenplay by Nora Ephron, directed and co-produced by Rob Reiner, 1989)

5 Women are learning that nobody gives you an orgasm, nobody makes you sexual, except yourself.

Nancy Friday (b.1937), U.S. author: *Men in Love* (1980), Ch.1

6 Orgasmism is a Western neurosis, but I say once you've had one, you've had them all.

Germaine Greer (b.1939), Australian feminist writer: interview in *A Little Light Friction* by Val Hennessy (1989), 'Germaine Greer'

7 An enema under the influence of Ecstasy would probably feel much like this.

Germaine Greer: on D.H. Lawrence's description of the female orgasm in *Lady Chatterley's Lover*, in the *Independent on Sunday* (London), 3 June 1990

8 An orgasm joins you to the past. Its timelessness becomes the brotherhood; the brethren are lovers; they extend the 'family'. I share that sexuality. It was then, is now and will be in the future.

Derek Jarman (1942–1994), British film-maker, artist and author: *At Your Own Risk: A Saint's Testament* (1992), '1950's'

9 Oh Doris Lessing, my dear – your Anna is *wrong* about orgasms. They are no proof of love – any more than that other Anna's fall under the wheels of that Russian train was a proof of love. It's all female shenanigans, cultural *mishegoss*, conditioning, brainwashing, male mythologizing. What does a woman want? She wants what she has been told she ought to want. Anna Wulf wants orgasm, Anna Karenina, death. Orgasm is no proof of anything. Orgasm is proof of orgasm. Someday every woman will have orgasms – like every family has color TV – and we can all get on with the real business of life.

Erica Jong (b.1942), U.S. author: *How To Save Your Own Life* (1977), 'The street where I lived...'

10 The orgasm has replaced the Cross as the focus of longing and the image of fulfillment.

Malcolm Muggeridge (1903–1990), British journalist and broadcaster: *Tread Softly for You Tread on My Jokes* (1966), 'Down with Sex'

11 Women liked me because I made them laugh. And what is an orgasm, except laughter of the loins?

Mickey Rooney (b.1920), U.S. actor and entertainer: *Life is Too Short* (autobiography, 1991), Ch.32

ORIGINALITY

1 The true is inimitable, the false untransformable.

Robert Bresson (b.1907), French film-maker: *Notes on the Cinematographer* (1975), '1950–1958: The Real'

2 The first man to compare the cheeks of a young woman to a rose was obviously a poet; the first to repeat it was possibly an idiot.

Salvador Dali (1904–1989), Spanish painter: preface to *Dialogues with Marcel Duchamp* (ed. Pierre Cabanne, 1968; tr.1971)

3 A man is original when he speaks the truth that has always been known to all good men.

Patrick Kavanagh (1905–1967), Irish poet and author: *Collected Pruse* (1967), 'Signposts'

4 Original thought is like original sin: both happened before you were born to people you could not have possibly met.

Fran Lebowitz (b.1951), U.S. journalist: *Social Studies* (1981), 'People'

5 No one can be profoundly original who does not avoid eccentricity.

André Maurois (1885–1967), French author and critic: *The Art of Writing* (1960), 'Turgenev'

OTHER PEOPLE

1 I recommend limiting one's involvement in other people's lives to a pleasantly scant minimum. This may seem too stoical a position in these madly passionate times, but madly passionate people rarely make good on their madly passionate promises.

Quentin Crisp (b.1908), British author: *Manners from Heaven* (1984), Ch.8

2 The thing that's between us is fascination, and the fascination resides in our being alike. Whether you're a man or a woman, the fascination resides in finding out that we're alike.

Marguerite Duras (1914–1996), French author and film-maker: *Practicalities* (1987; tr.1990), 'Men'

3 What we know of other people
Is only our memory of the moments
During which we knew them.

T.S. Eliot (1888–1965), Anglo-American poet and critic: Unidentified Guest, later identified as Sir Henry Harcourt-Reilly, in *The Cocktail Party* (1950), Act 1, Sc.3

4 We demand that people should be true to the pictures we have of them, no matter how repulsive those pictures may be: we prefer the true portrait (as we have conceived it), in all its homogeneity, to one with a detail added which refuses to fit in.

Pamela Hansford Johnson (1912–1981), British author and critic: *Night and Silence, Who is Here? – An American Comedy* (1962), Ch.23

5 The human crowd has been the lesson of my life. I can come to it with the born timidity of the poet, with the fear of the timid, but once I am in its midst, I feel transfigured. I am part of

the essential majority, I am one more leaf on the great human tree.

Pablo Neruda (1904–1973), Chilean poet: *Memoirs* (1974), Ch.11, 'Living with the Language'

6 The odds of not meeting in this life are so great that every meeting is like a miracle. It's a wonder that we don't make love to every single person we meet.

Yoko Ono (b.1933), Japanese-born U.S. artist: sleevenotes on the album *Feeling the Space* (1973)

7 Men often treat others worse than they treat themselves, but they rarely treat anyone better. It is the height of folly to expect consideration and decency from a person who mistreats himself.

Thomas Szasz (b.1920), U.S. psychiatrist: *The Second Sin* (1973), 'Personal Conduct'

See also STRANGERS; Sartre on SUBJECTIVITY; Merton on SUCCESS

OUTCASTS

1 In an expanding universe, time is on the side of the outcast. Those who once inhabited the suburbs of human contempt find that without changing their address they eventually live in the metropolis.

Quentin Crisp (b.1908), British author: *The Naked Civil Servant* (1968), Ch.1

2 I am an invisible man. ... I am a man of substance, of flesh and bone, fiber and liquids – and I might even be said to possess a mind. I am invisible, understand, simply because people refuse to see me.

Ralph Ellison (b.1914), U.S. author: the narrator, in prologue to *The Invisible Man* (1952)

OUTLAWS

1 To live outside the law, you must be honest.

Bob Dylan (b.1941), U.S. singer and songwriter: 'Absolutely Sweet Marie' (song) on the album *Blonde on Blonde* (1968). A similar line appears in Don Siegel's 1958 film, *The Line-Up*

2 The lyricism of marginality may find inspiration in the image of the 'outlaw', the great social nomad, who prowls on the confines of a docile, frightened order.

Michel Foucault (1926–1984), French philosopher: *Discipline and Punish: The Birth of the Prison* (1975), Pt.4, Ch.3

3 An outlaw by profession, an inlaw by marriage. His tail lights were deteriorating, but his collection of porcelain remained a constant companion.

John Lennon (1940–1980), British rock musician: *Skywriting by Word of Mouth* (ed. Yoko Ono, 1986), 'Spare Me the Agony of Your Birth Control'

OXFORD UNIVERSITY

1 The greatest gift that Oxford gives her sons is, I truly believe, a genial irreverence toward learning, and from that irreverence love may spring.

Robertson Davies (1913–1995), Canadian novelist and journalist: 'Shakespeare Over the Port', first publ. in *Stratford Papers on Shakespeare* (1960), rep. in *The Enthusiasms of Robertson Davies* (1990)

2 Oxford is, and always has been, full of cliques, full of factions, and full of a particular non-social snobbiness.

Mary Warnock (b.1924), British philosopher: in *The Observer* (London), 2 Nov. 1980

PAIN

1 Imaginary pains are by far the most real we suffer, since we feel a constant need for them and invent them because there is no way of doing without them.

E.M. Cioran (1911–1995), Rumanian-born French philosopher: *The Trouble with Being Born* (1973), Ch.3

2 This horror of pain is a rather low instinct and ... if I think of human beings I've known and of my own life, such as it is, I can't recall any case of pain which didn't, on the whole, enrich life.

Malcolm Muggeridge (1903–1990), British journalist and broadcaster: *Meeting Point*, BBC1, 11 Aug. 1963, publ. in *Muggeridge Through the Microphone* (1967), 'The Problem of Pain'

3 They can rule the world while they can persuade us
our pain belongs in some order.
Is death by famine worse than death by suicide,
than a life of famine and suicide ...?

Adrienne Rich (b.1929), U.S. poet: 'Hunger', publ. in *The Dream of a Common Language* (1978)

4 Pain is real when you get other people to believe in it. If no one believes in it but you, your pain is madness or hysteria.

Naomi Wolf (b.1962), U.S. author: *The Beauty Myth* (1990), 'Violence'

PAINTING *see under* ART

PALESTINE

1 Palestine is the cement that holds the Arab world together, or it is the explosive that blows it apart.
Yasir Arafat (b.1929), Palestinian leader: in *Time* (New York), 11 Nov. 1974

2 There was no such thing as a Palestinian people ... it is not as though there was a Palestinian people and we came and threw them out and took their country away from them. They did not exist.
Golda Meir (1898–1978), Israeli politician and prime minister: in *The Sunday Times* (London), 29 June 1969

3 Should there be maniacs who raise the idea, they will encounter an iron fist which will leave no trace of such attempts.
Yitzhak Shamir (b.1915), Israeli politician and prime minister: on Palestinian self-government, quoted in *The Times* (London), 11 Aug. 1988

4 Even the pyramids might one day disappear, but not the Palestinians longing for their homeland.
Eduard Shevardnadze (b.1927), Georgian politician and diplomat: in *The Daily Telegraph* (London), 24 Feb. 1989

5 The hijacker is not a hero. If we could liberate Palestine by hijacking, then yes, let us train 300 hijackers. We would be terrorists but at least we would have a purpose. But we cannot liberate Palestine that way.
Salah Tamari, P.L.O. commander: quoted in *The Palestinians* by Jonathan Dimbleby (1979), Ch.8

6 In the past, Arafat always tried to make an ally of the strongest power in the region. That, of course, was always Arab. Now it is Israeli. And it is far too big for him. Truly, he has put himself in the belly of the whale. He is a part of the state of Israel.
Abbas Zaki, P.L.O. leader: quoted in *The Guardian* (London), 15 April 1995

PARADISE

1 It gets to seem as if way back in the Garden of Eden after the Fall, Adam and Eve had begged the Lord to forgive them and He, in his boundless exasperation, had said, 'All right, then. Stay. Stay in the Garden. Get civilized. Procreate. Muck it up.' And they did.
Diane Arbus (1923–1971), U.S. photographer: on a seedy nudist camp, from classes given in 1971, publ. in *Diane Arbus: An Aperture Monograph* (1972)

2 Santa Barbara is a paradise; Disneyland is a paradise; the U.S. is a paradise. Paradise is just paradise. Mournful, monotonous, and super-ficial though it may be, it is paradise. There is no other.
Jean Baudrillard (b.1929), French semiologist: *America* (1986; tr.1988), 'Utopia Achieved'

3 They paved paradise
And put up a parking lot
With a pink hotel,
A boutique, and a swinging hot spot.
Joni Mitchell (b.1943), Canadian-born U.S. singer and songwriter: 'Big Yellow Taxi' (song), on the album *Ladies of the Canyon* (1970)

4 It is difficult to write a paradiso when all the superficial indications are that you ought to write an apocalypse. It is obviously much easier to find inhabitants for an inferno or even a purgatorio.
Ezra Pound (1885–1972), U.S. poet and critic: interview in *Writers at Work* (Second Series, ed. George Plimpton, 1963)

PARANOIA

1 The paranoiac is the exact image of the ruler. The only difference is their position in the world.... One might even think the paranoiac the more impressive of the two because he is sufficient unto himself and cannot be shaken by failure.
Elias Canetti (1905–1994), Austrian novelist and philosopher: *Crowds And Power* (1960; tr.1962), 'The Case of Schreber: II'

2 Something is happening here
But you don't know what it is
Do you, Mister Jones?
Bob Dylan (b.1941), U.S. singer and songwriter: 'Ballad of a Thin Man' (song) on the album *Highway 61 Revisited* (1968)

3 Even a paranoid can have enemies.
Henry Kissinger (b.1923), U.S. Republican politician and secretary of state: quoted in *Time* (New York), 24 Jan. 1977

4 I envy paranoids; they actually feel people are paying attention to them.
Susan Sontag (b.1933), U.S. essayist: quoted in *Time Out* (London), 19 Aug. 1992

PARENTS

1 It's a sad moment, really, when parents first become a bit frightened of their children.
Ama Ata Aidoo (b.1942), Ghanaian scholar and poet: 'The Message', publ. in *Fragment from a Lost Diary and Other Stories* (ed. Naomi Katz and Nancy Milton, 1973)

2 It's frightening to think that you mark your children merely by being yourself.... It seems unfair. You can't assume the responsibility for everything you do – or don't do.

Simone de Beauvoir (1908–1986), French novelist and essayist: *Les Belles Images* (1966; tr.1968), Ch.3

3 Let me go to hell, that's all I ask, and go on cursing them there, and them look down and hear me, that might take some of the shine off their bliss.

Samuel Beckett (1906–1989), Irish playwright and novelist: *From an Abandoned Work* (1958)

4 Fathers and mothers have lost the idea that the highest aspiration they might have for their children is for them to be wise ... specialized competence and success are all that they can imagine.

Allan Bloom (1930–1992), U.S. educator and author: *The Closing of the American Mind* (1987), Pt.1, 'The Clean Slate'

5 There are lots of things that you can brush under the carpet about yourself until you're faced with somebody whose needs won't be put off.

Angela Carter (1940–1992), British author: on being a mother for the first time, aged 43, in interview in *Marxism Today* (London), Jan. 1985

6 No matter how calmly you try to referee, parenting will eventually produce bizarre behavior, and I'm not talking about the kids. *Their* behavior is always normal.

Bill Cosby (b.1937), U.S. comedian and actor: *Fatherhood* (1986), Ch.4

7 No matter how hard you try, you can never be more than twelve years old with your parents. Parents earnestly try not to inflame, but their comments contain no scale and a strange focus.

Douglas Coupland (b.1961), Canadian author: the narrator (Andy), in *Generation X* (1991), 'Define Normal'

8 My mother protected me from the world and my father threatened me with it.

Quentin Crisp (b.1908), British author: *The Naked Civil Servant* (1968), Ch.5

9 If you have never been hated by your child, you have never been a parent.

Bette Davis (1908–1989), U.S. actress: *The Lonely Life* (1962), Ch.19

10 There are times when parenthood seems nothing but feeding the mouth that bites you

Peter De Vries (1910–1993), U.S. author: *The Tunnel of Love* (1954), Ch.5

11 The thing that impresses me most about America is the way parents obey their children.

Edward, Duke of Windsor (1894–1972), formerly King Edward VIII of Great Britain and Northern Ireland: in *Look* (New York), 5 March 1957

12 You don't have to deserve your mother's love. You have to deserve your father's. He's more particular. ... The father is always a Repub-

lican towards his son, and his mother's always a Democrat.

Robert Frost (1874–1963), U.S. poet: interview in *Writers at Work* (Second Series, ed. George Plimpton, 1963)

13 Do they know they're old,
These two who are my father and my
   mother
Whose fire from which I came, has now grown
   cold?

Elizabeth Jennings (b.1926), British poet: 'One Flesh', publ. in *Collected Poems* (1967)

14 Selective ignorance, a cornerstone of child rearing. You don't put kids under surveillance: it might frighten you. Parents should sit tall in the saddle and look upon their troops with a noble and benevolent and extremely near-sighted gaze.

Garrison Keillor (b.1942), U.S. author: *Leaving Home* (1987), 'Easter'

15 If you bungle raising your children, I don't think whatever else you do well matters very much.

Jacqueline Kennedy (1929–1994), U.S. First Lady: quoted in *Kennedy* by Theodore C. Sorenson (1965), Pt.4, Ch.15

16 They fuck you up, your mum and dad.
   They may not mean to, but they do.
They fill you with the faults they had
   And add some extra, just for you.

Philip Larkin (1922–1986), British poet: 'This Be The Verse', St.1, publ. in *High Windows* (1974). In a letter, 6 June 1982, Larkin complained of the notoriety of this poem, which 'will clearly be my "Lake Isle of Innisfree". I fully expect to hear it recited by a thousand Girl Guides before I die' (*Selected Letters*, 1992)

17 Your responsibility as a parent is not as great as you might imagine. You need not supply the world with the next conqueror of disease or major motion-picture star. If your child simply grows up to be someone who does not use the word 'collectible' as a noun, you can consider yourself an unqualified success.

Fran Lebowitz (b.1951), U.S. journalist: *Social Studies* (1981), 'Parental Guidance'

18 The pressures of being a parent are equal to any pressure on earth. To be a conscious parent, and really look to that little being's mental and physical health, is a responsibility which most of us, including me, avoid most of the time because it's too hard.

John Lennon (1940–1980), British rock musician: interview in *Playboy* (Chicago), Sept. 1980. Lennon added, 'To put it loosely, the reason why kids are crazy is because nobody can face the responsibility of bringing them up'

19 Oh, high is the price of parenthood,
   And daughters may cost you double.

You dare not forget, as you thought you could,
That youth is a plague and a trouble.
Phyllis McGinley (1905–1978), U.S. poet and
author: 'Homework for Anabelle', publ. in *Times
Three* (1960)

20 'Father?'
'Yes, son?'
'I want to kill you.'
'Mother, I want to...'
Jim Morrison (1943–1971), U.S. rock musician:
'The End' (song, written with other members of the
Doors) on the album *The Doors* (The Doors, 1967)

21 The relationship between a son and his mother
is not a historical relationship, it is a purely
interior, private relationship which is outside
history, indeed it is meta-historical, and therefore ideologically unproductive, whereas what
produces history is the relationship of hatred
and love between father and son.
Pier Paolo Pasolini (1922–1975), Italian film-
maker and essayist: 'Perche quella di Edipo e una
storia' (introduction to the film *Oedipus Rex*, 1967),
rep. in *Pasolini Requiem* by David Barth Schwartz
(1992), Ch.20

22 Parents ... are sometimes a bit of a disappointment to their children. They don't fulfil the
promise of their early years.
Anthony Powell (b.1905), British novelist:
Stringham, in *A Buyer's Market* (1952), Ch.2

23 Man can build a magnificent reality in adulthood out of what was only an illusion in early
childhood – his loving, joyous, trusting, ingenuous, unrealistic over-idealization of his two
parents.
Benjamin Spock (b.1903), U.S. paediatrician and
author: *Baby and Child Care* (1946), 'The Parents'
Part', Sct.13

24 Perhaps the best function of parenthood is to
teach the young creature to love with *safety*, so
that it may be able to venture unafraid when
later emotion comes; the thwarting of the
instinct to love is the root of all sorrow and not
sex only but divinity itself is insulted when it is
repressed. To disapprove, to condemn – the
human soul shrivels under barren righteousness.
Freya Stark (1893–1993), British travel writer:
Traveller's Prelude (1950), Ch.10

25 The educating of the parents is really the education of the child: children tend to live what is
unlived in the parents, so it is vital that parents
should be aware of their inferior, their dark
side, and should press on getting to know
themselves.
Laurens van der Post (1906–1996), South African
writer and philosopher: *A Walk with a White
Bushman* (1986), p.49 of Chatto & Windus edn.

26 Once you bring life into the world, you must

protect it. We must protect it by changing the
world.
Elie Wiesel (b.1928), Rumanian-born U.S. writer:
interview in *Writers at Work* (Eighth Series, ed.
George Plimpton, 1988)

27 No test tube can breed love and affection. No
frozen packet of semen ever read a story to a
sleepy child.
Shirley Williams (b.1930), British Liberal-
Democrat politician: in the *Daily Mirror* (London),
2 March 1978

PARIS *see under* FRANCE

PARLIAMENT

1 This place is the longest running farce in the
West End.
Cyril Smith (b.1928), British Liberal politician:
comment, July 1973, quoted in *Big Cyril*
(autobiography, 1977), Ch.8

2 Parliament must not be told a direct untruth,
but it's quite possible to allow them to mislead
themselves.
Norman Tebbit (b.1931), British Conservative
politician: quoted in *The Observer* (London),
17 March 1991

PARLIAMENT: the House of Commons

1 Most of them are buffers, or demi-buffers, of
buffers-aspirant. They amount to nothing.
Alan Clark (b.1928), British Conservative
politician: referring to backbenchers in the House of
Commons, in journal entry, 18 Nov. 1986, publ. in
Diaries (1993)

2 The House of Commons starts its proceedings
with a prayer. The chaplain looks at the
assembled members with their varied intelligence and then prays for the country.
Lord Denning (b.1899), British judge: in *The Daily
Telegraph* (London), 12 Oct. 1989

3 Anybody who enjoys being in the House of
Commons probably needs psychiatric care.
Ken Livingstone (b.1945), British Labour
politician: in the *Evening Standard* (London),
26 Feb. 1988

PARLIAMENT: the House of Lords

1 The House of Lords is the British Outer Mongolia for retired politicians.
Tony Benn (b.1925), British Labour politician:
comment made during his campaign to disclaim his
hereditary peerage, quoted in the *New York Times*,
11 Feb. 1962

2 We are fortunate to have inherited an institu-

tion which we certainly should never have had the intelligence to create. We might have been landed with something like the American Senate.

Lord Esher (b.1913), British architect: in the *Wall Street Journal* (New York), 2 May 1963

PARODY

1 The parody is the last refuge of the frustrated writer. Parodies are what you write when you are associate editor of the Harvard *Lampoon*. The greater the work of literature, the easier the parody. The step up from writing parodies is writing on the wall above the urinal.

Ernest Hemingway (1899–1961), U.S. author: quoted in *Papa Hemingway* by A.E. Hotchner (1966 edn.), Pt.1, Ch.4

2 So much contemporary art and design is a parody, a joke, and full of allusions to the past. It's like that because it is the end of an era, like the end of the nineteenth century. Not such a comfortable period to live in. Everything must be a kind of caricature to register, everything must be larger than life.

Christian Lacroix (b.1951), French fashion designer: quoted in *The Sunday Times* (London), Oct. 1987, rep. in *Sultans of Style* by Georgina Howell (1990), 'Christian Lacroix'

See also McMurtry on AGE: AGING

PARTIES

1 Fasten your seat belts. It's going to be a bumpy night.

Bette Davis (1908–1988), U.S. actress: Margo Channing (Davis), bracing for a rocky party, in *All About Eve* (film; written and directed by Joseph L. Mankiewicz, 1950)

2 Another all night party over.
Another night of passages,
Stairs, and angelic messages.

Thom Gunn (b.1929), British poet: 'Another All Night Party', publ. in *The Passages of Joy* (1982)

3 At every party there are two kinds of people – those who want to go home and those who don't. The trouble is, they are usually married to each other.

Ann Landers (b.1918), U.S. advice columnist: in the *International Herald Tribune* (Paris), 19 June 1991

4 A party is like a marriage ... making itself up while seeming to follow precedent, running on steel rails into uncharted wilderness while the promises shiver and wobble on the armrests like crystal stemware.

Jay McInerney (b.1955), U.S. author: Corrine, in *Brightness Falls* (1992), Ch.1

5 All the people at this party, they've got a lot of style,
They've got stamps of many countries, they've got passport smiles.
Some are friendly, some are cutting, some are watchin' it from the wings,
Some are standin' in the center givin' to get something.

Joni Mitchell (b.1943), Canadian-born U.S. singer and songwriter: 'People's Parties' (song) on the album *Court and Spark* (1974)

PARTNERSHIP

1 We sit down together and discuss things carefully and in detail. Sam has his say and I have mine. And then we reach a decision and agree that I am right.

Brian Clough (b.1935), British footballer and manager: on working with Sam Longson, chairman of Derby County Football Club, in *Clough: The Autobiography* (1994), Ch.9

2 By the time a partnership dissolves, it has dissolved.

John Updike (b.1932), U.S. author and critic: *Couples* (1968), Ch.5

See also Bush on RONALD REAGAN

PASSION

1 What the public wants is the image of passion, not passion itself.

Roland Barthes (1915–1980), French semiologist: *Mythologies* (1957), 'Le monde où l'on catche'

2 What is passion? It is surely the becoming of a person. Are we not, for most of our lives, marking time? Most of our being is at rest, unlived. In passion, the body and the spirit seek expression outside of self. Passion is all that is other from self. Sex is only interesting when it releases passion. The more extreme and the more expressed that passion is, the more unbearable does life seem without it. It reminds us that if passion dies or is denied, we are partly dead and that soon, come what may, we will be wholly so.

John Boorman (b.1933), British film-maker: journal entry, 16 May 1991, publ. in *Projections* (ed. John Boorman and Walter Donohue, 1992)

3 Passion makes the world go round. Love just makes it a safer place.

Ice-T (b.1958), U.S. rapper: *The Ice Opinion* (written with Heidi Sigmund, 1994), Ch.4

4 A man who has not passed through the inferno of his passions has never overcome them.

Carl Jung (1875–1961), Swiss psychiatrist: *Memories, Dreams, Reflections* (1962), Ch.9

5 You shake my nerves and you rattle my brain.
   Too much love drives a man insane.
   You broke my will, but what a thrill.
   Goodness gracious, great balls of fire!
   Jerry Lee Lewis (b.1935), U.S. rock musician:
   'Great Balls of Fire' (song, written by Jack Hammer
   and Otis Blackwell, 1957)

PASSIVITY

1 To *make* oneself an object, to *make* oneself
   passive, is a very different thing from *being* a
   passive object.
   Simone de Beauvoir (1908–1986), French novelist
   and essayist: *The Second Sex* (1949; tr.1953), Bk.2,
   Pt.4, Ch.3

2 Silence, indifference and inaction were Hitler's principal allies.
   Lord Jakobovits (b.1921), Chief Rabbi of the
   British Commonwealth: on the prosecution of
   alleged war criminals, in *The Independent* (London),
   5 Dec. 1989

3 We will have to repent in this generation not
   merely for the hateful words and actions of the
   bad people but for the appalling silence of the
   good people.
   Martin Luther King Jr. (1929–1968), U.S.
   clergyman and civil rights leader: 'Letter from
   Birmingham Jail', open letter to clergymen, 16 April
   1963, publ. in *Why We Can't Wait* (1964)

PATRIOTISM

1 God and Country are an unbeatable team; they
   break all records for oppression and bloodshed.
   Luis Buñuel (1900–1983), Spanish film-maker: *My
   Last Breath* (autobiography, 1983), Ch.14

2 I thank God for all the freedom we have in this
   country, I cherish it – even the right to burn
   the flag. But we also have the right to bear arms
   and if you burn my flag – *I'll shoot you!*
   Johnny Cash (b.1932), U.S. country singer: quoted
   by Tony Parsons in 'Standing Up For God and
   Country', first publ. in *The Daily Telegraph*, 10
   April 1992, rep. in *Dispatches from the Front Line of
   Popular Culture* (Tony Parsons, 1994). The speech
   was a routine preamble to Cash's hymn to the Stars
   and Stripes, *Ragged Old Flag*, usually to a standing
   ovation

3 Everyone loathes his own country and countrymen if he is any sort of artist.
   Lawrence Durrell (1912–1990), British author:
   letter, March 1948, to Henry Miller, publ. in *The
   Durrell-Miller Letters 1935–80* (1988)

4 No matter that patriotism is too often the
   refuge of scoundrels. Dissent, rebellion, and
   all-around hell-raising remain the true duty of
   patriots.

Barbara Ehrenreich (b.1941), U.S. author and
columnist: *The Worst Years of Our Lives* (1991),
'Family Values'

5 Nationalism is our form of incest, is our
   idolatry, is our insanity. 'Patriotism' is its cult.
   It should hardly be necessary to say, that by
   'patriotism' I mean that attitude which puts
   the own nation above humanity, above the
   principles of truth and justice; not the loving
   interest in one's own nation, which is the
   concern with the nation's spiritual as much as
   with its material welfare – never with its power
   over other nations. Just as love for one individual which excludes the love for others is not
   love, love for one's country which is not part of
   one's love for humanity is not love, but
   idolatrous worship.
   Erich Fromm (1900–1980), U.S. psychologist: *The
   Sane Society* (1955), Ch.3, 'Rootedness –
   Brotherliness vs. Incest'

6 It seems that American patriotism measures
   itself against an outcast group. The right
   Americans are the right Americans because
   they're not like the wrong Americans, who are
   not really Americans.
   Eric Hobsbawm (b.1917), British historian: in
   Marxism Today (London), Jan. 1988

7 My fellow Americans, ask not what your country can do for you – ask what you can do for
   your country.
   John F. Kennedy (1917–1963), U.S. Democratic
   politician and president: inaugural address, 20 Jan.
   1961, Washington D.C., quoted in *Kennedy* by
   Theodore C. Sorenson (1965), Pt.3, Ch.9. Kennedy
   continued, 'My fellow citizens of the world, ask not
   what America will do for you, but what together we
   can do for the freedom of man.' He had previously
   expressed this idea in a televised campaign address,
   20 Sept. 1960. Many antecedents have been cited,
   including Oliver Wendell Holmes Sr. in his
   Memorial Day Address, 1884: 'It is now the moment
   ... to recall what our country has done for each of us,
   and to ask ourselves what we can do for our country
   in return'

8 Patriotism to me was not something static, a
   sentiment of good things to be conserved. It
   was something dynamic and creative, seeking
   to build a better and more modern nation, constantly adapted to the development of the age
   and inspiring it.
   Oswald Mosley (1896–1980), British fascist leader:
   My Life (1968), Ch.5

9 What do we mean by patriotism in the context
   of our times? I venture to suggest that what we
   mean is a sense of national responsibility ... a
   patriotism which is not short, frenzied outbursts of emotion, but the tranquil and steady
   dedication of a lifetime.
   Adlai Stevenson (1900–1965), U.S. Democratic
   politician: 'The Nature of Patriotism', speech,

27 Aug. 1952, to American Legion Convention, New York City, publ. in *Speeches* (1953)

See also Forster on CAUSES

PEACE

1 I see little hope for a peaceful world until men are excluded from the realm of foreign policy altogether and all decisions concerning international relations are reserved for women, preferably married ones.
W.H. Auden (1907–1973), Anglo-American poet: *A Certain World* (1970), 'Penis Rivalry'

2 When it's a question of peace one must talk to the Devil himself.
Édouard Herriot (1872–1957), French statesman: quoted in *The Observer* (London), 21 Sept. 1953

3 All we are saying is give peace a chance.
John Lennon (1940–1980), British rock musician: 'Give Peace a Chance' (song, 1969), on the album *Shaved Fish* (1975). The song is also credited to Paul McCartney

4 You either get tired fighting for peace, or you die.
John Lennon: press conference, June 1970, Toronto, Canada, publ. in *The Ballad of John and Yoko* (ed. Jonathan Cott and Christine Doudna, 1982), Pt.2, 'John, Yoko and Year One'

5 You can't separate peace from freedom because no one can be at peace unless he has his freedom.
Malcolm X (1925–1965), U.S. black leader: 'Prospects for Freedom in 1965', speech, 7 Jan. 1965, New York City, publ. in *Malcolm X Speaks* (1965), Ch.12

6 Peace is no more than a dream as long as we need the comfort of the clan.
Peter Nichols (b.1927), British playwright: in *The Independent* (London), 1 Sept. 1990

7 To many men ... the miasma of peace seems more suffocating than the bracing air of war.
George Steiner (b.1929), French-born U.S. critic and novelist: 'Has Truth a Future?', Bronowski Memorial Lecture, 1978

8 Since wars begin in the minds of men, it is in the minds of men that the defences of peace must be constructed.
UNESCO constitution (1945)

9 Peace is not something we are entitled to but an illusory respite we earn. On both the personal and national level, islands of truce created by balances of terror and potential violence are the best we can hope for.
John Updike (b.1932), U.S. author and critic: *Self-Consciousness* (1989), Ch.2

See also Lennon on PUBLICITY; Jackson on RIOTS

THE PEOPLE

1 What's important is promising something to the people, not actually keeping those promises.... The people have always lived on hope alone.
Hermann Broch (1886–1951), Austrian novelist: Mother Gisson, in *The Spell* (1976; tr.1987), Ch.13

2 If all power is in the people, if there is no higher law than their will, and if by counting their votes, their will may be ascertained – then the people may entrust all their power to anyone, and the power of the pretender and the usurper is then legitimate. It is not to be challenged since it came originally from the sovereign people.
Walter Lippmann (1889–1974), U.S. journalist: 'The American Idea', address at the unveiling of the statue of George Washington in Washington Cathedral, 3 Feb. 1947, later publ. in a shortened version in the *New York Herald Tribune*, 22 Feb. 1954, rep. in *The Essential Lippman* (1982), Pt.1, Sct.1

3 There used to be a thing or a commodity we put great store by. It was called the People. Find out where the People have gone. I don't mean the square-eyed toothpaste-and-hair-dye people or the new-car-or-bust people, or the success-and-coronary people. Maybe they never existed, but if there ever were the People, that's the commodity the Declaration was talking about, and Mr Lincoln.
John Steinbeck (1902–1968), U.S. author: quoting a political correspondent in conversation with Steinbeck, in *Travels With Charley: in Search of America* (1962), Pt.3

PERCEPTION

1 Nothing exists until or unless it is observed. An artist is making something exist by observing it. And his hope for other people is that they will also make it exist by observing it. I call it 'creative observation.' Creative viewing.
William Burroughs (1914–1997), U.S. author: *Painting and Guns* (1992), 'The Creative Observer'

2 No two people see the external world in exactly the same way. To every separate person a thing is what he thinks it is – in other words, not a thing, but a think.
Penelope Fitzgerald (b.1916), British author: Shippey, in *The Gate of Angels* (1990), Ch.6

3 Whether the scouring, sexless eye of the bird or beast of prey disperses and sees all or concentrates and evades all saving that for which it searches, it is certain that the less powerful eye of the human cannot grasp, even after a life of training, a scene in its entirety. No eye may see dispassionately. There is no comprehension at

a glance. Only the recognition of damsel, horse or fly and the assumption of damsel, horse or fly; and so with dreams and beyond, for what haunts the heart will, when it is found, leap foremost, blinding the eye and leaving the main of Life in darkness.

Mervyn Peake (1911–1968), British author and illustrator: *Titus Groan* (1946), 'Near and Far'

4   If only we could pull out our brain and use only our eyes.

Pablo Picasso (1881–1973), Spanish artist: in the *Saturday Review* (New York), 1 Sep 1956

See also Stevens on REALITY

PERFECTION

1   Perfection can be a fetish.

Bernard Leach (1887–1979), British potter: *The Potter's Challenge* (1976), Ch.1

2   The essence of being human is that one does not seek perfection, that one *is* sometimes willing to commit sins for the sake of loyalty, that one does not push asceticism to the point where it makes friendly intercourse impossible, and that one is prepared in the end to be defeated and broken up by life, which is the inevitable price of fastening one's love upon other human individuals.

George Orwell (1903–1950), British author: *Shooting an Elephant* (1950), 'Reflections on Gandhi'

See also Tarkovsky on ARTISTS

PERFORMANCE

1   I think it's the height of arrogance to go onstage and *not* be extraordinary and brilliant. It's the height of arrogance to make average music. You know, people are listening.

Brett Anderson (b.1967), British rock musician: in *New Musical Express* (London), 1992, quoted in *NME Book of Quotes* (1995), 'Music'

2   The ultimate sin of any performer is contempt for the audience.

Lester Bangs (1948–1982), U.S. rock journalist: in *Village Voice* (New York), 29 Aug. 1977, rep. in *Psychotic Reactions & Carburetor Dung* (1987), 'Where Were You When Elvis Died?'

3   The majority of people perform well in a crisis and when the spotlight is on them; it's on the Sunday afternoons of this life, when nobody is looking, that the spirit falters.

Alan Bennett (b.1934), British playwright: journal entry, 13 Oct. 1984, publ. in *Writing Home* (1994), 'Diaries 1980–1990'

4   The reason I'm in this business, I assume all performers are – it's 'Look at me, Ma!' It's

acceptance, you know – 'Look at me, Ma, look at me, Ma, look at me, Ma.' And if your mother watches, you'll show off till you're exhausted; but if your mother goes, *Ptshew!*

Lenny Bruce (1925–1966), U.S. satirical comedian: *The Essential Lenny Bruce* (ed. John Cohen, 1967), 'Performing and the Art of Comedy'

5   The most difficult performance in the world is acting naturally, isn't it? Everything else is artful.

Angela Carter (1940–1992), British author: *Fireworks* (1974), 'Flesh and the Mirror'

6   The thing about performance, even if it's only an illusion, is that it is a celebration of the fact that we do contain within ourselves infinite possibilities.

Daniel Day-Lewis (b.1957), British actor: interview in *Rolling Stone* (New York), 8 Feb. 1990

7   The only performance that makes it, that really makes it, is the one that ends in madness.

Mick Jagger (b.1942), British rock musician: Turner (Jagger) in *Performance* (film; screenplay by Donald Cammell, directed by Donald Cammell and Nicolas Roeg, 1971)

8   A bad performance of a work by Mozart is always the fault of the performer. But a bad performance of a piece of contemporary music is always the fault of the composer – every listener knows that!

Witold Lutoslawski (1913–1994), Polish composer: *Conversations with Witold Lutoslawski* (ed. Tadeusz Kaczyński, 1972; tr.1984), Ch.11

9   When I'm onstage, I feel this incredible, almost spiritual experience ... lost in a naturally induced high. Those great rock 'n' roll experiences are getting harder and harder to come by, because they have to transcend a lot of drug-induced stupor. But when they occur, they are sacred.

Peter Townshend (b.1945), British rock musician: interview in *Playboy* (Chicago), June 1974

THE PERMISSIVE SOCIETY

1   Sexual liberation, as a slogan, turns out to be another kind of bondage. For a woman it offers orgasm as her ultimate and major fulfillment; it's better than motherhood.

Victoria Billings (b.1945), U.S. journalist and author: *The Womansbook* (1974), 'What Is Individuality?'

2   When anything goes, it's women who lose.

Camille Paglia (b.1947), U.S. author and critic: in *The Observer* (London), 15 Dec. 1991

3   The sexual freedom of today for most people is really only a convention, an obligation, a social

duty, a social anxiety, a necessary feature of the consumer's way of life.

Pier Paolo Pasolini (1922–1975), Italian film-maker and essayist: 'Sono Contro l'Aborto', first publ. in *Il Corriere della Sera* (Milan), 19 Jan. 1975, rep. in *Scritti Corsari* (1975)

4   Permissiveness is the principle of treating children as if they were adults; and the tactic of making sure they never reach that stage.

Thomas Szasz (b.1920), U.S. psychiatrist: *The Second Sin* (1973), 'Social Relations'

5   Modern society is in certain respects extremely permissive. In matters that are irrelevant to the functioning of the system we can generally do what we please. We can believe in any religion we like (as long as it does not encourage behavior that is dangerous to the system). We can go to bed with anyone we like (as long as we practise 'safe sex'). We can do anything we like as long as it is UNIMPORTANT.

Unabomber, U.S. radical: *Industrial Society and Its Future*, 'Disruption of the Power Process in Modern Society', Sct.72, publ. in the *Washington Post*, 19 Sept. 1995

PERSONALITY

1   I am what is mine. Personality is the original personal property.

Norman O. Brown (b.1913), U.S. philosopher: *Love's Body* (1967), Ch.8

2   Man's main task in life is to give *birth* to himself, to become what he potentially is. The most important product of his effort is his own personality.

Erich Fromm (1900–1980), U.S. psychologist: *Man For Himself* (1947), Ch.4

3   Personality is the glitter that sends your little gleam across the footlights and the orchestra pit into that big black space where the audience is.

Mae West (1892–1980), U.S. actress: quoted in David Ray Johnson's 'Biographical Study', Ch.2, appendix to *On Sex, Health and ESP* (1975)

PERSUASION

1   'For your own good' is a persuasive argument that will eventually make a man agree to his own destruction.

Janet Frame (b.1924), New Zealand novelist and poet: *Faces in the Water* (1961), Ch.4

2   The real persuaders are our appetites, our fears and above all our vanity. The skillful propagandist stirs and coaches these internal persuaders.

Eric Hoffer (1902–1983), U.S. philosopher: *The Passionate State of Mind* (1955), Aph.218

3   Folks don't like to have somebody around knowin' more than they do. It aggravates 'em. You're not gonna change any of them by talkin' right, they've got to want to learn themselves, and when they don't want to learn there's nothing you can do but keep your mouth shut or talk their language.

Harper Lee (b.1926), U.S. author: Calpurnia, in *To Kill a Mockingbird* (1960), Pt.2, Ch.12

4   Neither in religious practices, nor in royal ceremonial or in politics is any lasting advantage gained by playing the monkey on the barrel-organ of transient fashion. In the end, conversion depends on ability, sympathy, example and conviction.

Oswald Mosley (1896–1980), British fascist leader: *My Life* (1968), Ch.2

5   One of the best ways to persuade others is with your ears – by listening to them.

Dean Rusk (1909–1994), U.S. Democratic politician: in *Reader's Digest* (Pleasantville, N.Y.), July 1961

PESSIMISM

1   Pessimists are the people who have no hope for themselves or for others. Pessimists are also people who think the human race is beneath their notice, that they're better than other human beings.

James Baldwin (1924–1987), U.S. author: in conversation with Nikki Giovanni, 4 Nov. 1971, London, publ. in *A Dialogue* (1973)

2   Pessimists are not boring. Pessimists are right. Pessimists are superfluous.

Elias Canetti (1905–1994), Austrian novelist and philosopher: *The Secret Heart Of The Clock: Notes, Aphorisms, Fragments 1973–1985* (1991), '1982'

3   I don't consider myself a pessimist at all. I think of a pessimist as someone who is waiting for it to rain. And I feel completely soaked to the skin.

Leonard Cohen (b.1934), Canadian singer, poet and novelist: quoted in the *Independent on Sunday* (London), 2 May 1993

4   Man, at least when educated, is a pessimist. He believes it safer not to reflect on his achievements; Jove is known to strike such people down.

J.K. Galbraith (b.1908), U.S. economist: *The Age of Uncertainty* (1977), Ch.12

5   If we see light at the end of the tunnel, It's the light of the oncoming train.

Robert Lowell (1917–1977), U.S. poet: 'Since 1939', publ. in *Day by Day* (1977)

6 One has to have the courage of one's pessimism.

Ian McEwan (b.1948), British author: in *The Guardian* (London), 26 May 1983

7 I like to burn my bridges before I come to them.

Leonard Rossiter (1926–1984), British comic actor: Reginald Perrin (Rossiter), in *The Fall and Rise of Reginald Perrin* (TV series, 1976–79, created by David Nobbs)

8 The taste for worst-case scenarios reflects the need to master fear of what is felt to be uncontrollable. It also expresses an imaginative complicity with disaster.

Susan Sontag (b.1933), U.S. essayist: *AIDS and Its Metaphors* (1989), Ch.8

PHILOSOPHERS

1 The profoundest thoughts of the philosophers have something tricklike about them. A lot disappears in order for something to suddenly appear in the palm of the hand.

Elias Canetti (1905–1994), Austrian novelist and philosopher: *The Secret Heart Of The Clock: Notes, Aphorisms, Fragments 1973–1985* (1991), '1973'

2 Philosophers have ended up worrying about the meaning of history in a way a shipping company worries about weather forecasts. Thought no longer dares take flight unless it can fly straight to the haven of victory.

Emmanuel Levinas (b.1905), French Jewish philosopher: 'The Meaning of History' (1963), rep. in *Difficult Freedom* (1990), Pt.5

3 The usual picture of Socrates is of an ugly little plebeian who inspired a handsome young nobleman to write long dialogues on large topics.

Richard Rorty (b.1931), U.S. philosopher: *Contingency, Irony, and Solidarity* (1989), Ch.6, 'From Ironist Theory to Private Allusions'

4 Reason, progress, unselfishness, a wide historical perspective, expansiveness, generosity, enlightened self-interest. I had heard it all my life, and it filled me with despair.

Katherine Tait (b.1923), daughter of Bertrand Russell: of her life with Bertrand Russell, quoted in afterword to *Bertrand Russell* by Caroline Moorehead (1992)

See also de Gaulle on DISSENT

PHILOSOPHY

1 In the information age, you don't teach philosophy as they did after feudalism. You perform it. If Aristotle were alive today he'd have a talk show.

Timothy Leary (1920–1996), U.S. psychologist: in the *Evening Standard* (London), 8 Feb. 1989

2 In philosophy if you aren't moving at a snail's pace you aren't moving at all.

Iris Murdoch (b.1919), British novelist and philosopher: Socrates, in *Acastos: Two Platonic Dialogues* (1986), 'Above the Gods: A Dialogue about Religion'

3 Jerking off the universe is perhaps what all philosophy, all abstract thought is about: an intense, and not very sociable pleasure, which has to be repeated again and again.

Susan Sontag (b.1933), U.S. essayist: *Against Interpretation* (1966), 'Sartre's *Saint Genet*'

4 Our most visible philosophies – visible in the sense of the media – are arcane juggleries. They play with words.

George Steiner (b.1929), French-born U.S. critic and novelist: 'Modernity, Mythology and Magic', lecture at the 1994 Salzburg Festival, publ. in *The Guardian* (London), 6 Aug. 1994

PHOTOGRAPHY

1 A photograph is a secret about a secret. The more it tells you the less you know.

Diane Arbus (1923–1971), U.S. photographer: quoted in preface to *Diane Arbus: A Biography* by Patricia Bosworth (1985)

2 The virtue of the camera is not the power it has to transform the photographer into an artist, but the impulse it gives him to keep on looking.

Brooks Atkinson (1894–1984), U.S. critic and essayist: *Once Around the Sun* (1951), '28 Aug.'

3 It takes a lot of imagination to be a good photographer. You need less imagination to be a painter, because you can invent things. But in photography everything is so ordinary; it takes a lot of looking before you learn to see the ordinary.

David Bailey (b.1938), British photographer: interview in *The Face* (London), Dec. 1984

4 The photographic image ... *is a message without a code.*

Roland Barthes (1915–1980), French semiologist: 'The Photographic Message', first publ. in *Communications* (Paris), No.1, 1961, rep. in *Image-Music-Text* (1977)

5 Most things in life are moments of pleasure and a lifetime of embarrassment; photography is a moment of embarrassment and a lifetime of pleasure.

Tony Benn (b.1925), British Labour politician: quoted in *The Independent* (London), 21 Oct. 1989

6 Unlike any other visual image, a photograph is not a rendering, an imitation or an interpretation of its subject, but actually a trace of it. No painting or drawing, however naturalist, *belongs* to its subject in the way that a photograph does.
John Berger (b.1926), British author and critic: *About Looking* (1980), 'Uses of Photography'

7 The camera can photograph thought. It's better than a paragraph of sweet polemic.
Dirk Bogarde (b.1921), British actor: quoted in *The Independent* (London), 28 Jan. 1990

8 The most refined skills of color printing, the intricate techniques of wide-angle photography, provide us pictures of trivia bigger and more real than life. We forget that we see trivia and notice only that the reproduction is so good. Man fulfils his dream and by photographic magic produces a precise image of the Grand Canyon. The result is not that he adores nature or beauty the more. Instead he adores his camera – and himself.
Daniel J. Boorstin (b.1914), U.S. historian: *The Image* (1961), Ch.4

9 The camera is a killing chamber, which speeds up the time it claims to be conserving. Like coffins exhumed and prised open, the photographs put on show what we were and what we will be again.
Peter Conrad (b.1948), Australian author and critic: *Down Home: Revisiting Tasmania* (1988), Pt.5, 'Seeing Tasmania'

10 You can't help but wonder at just how sweet and sad and innocent all moments of life are rendered by the tripping of a camera's shutter, for at that point the future is still unknown and has yet to hurt us, and also for that brief moment, our poses are accepted as honest.
Douglas Coupland (b.1961), Canadian author: the narrator (Andy), in *Generation X* (1991), 'I Am Not a Target Market'

11 A hundredth of a second here, a hundredth of a second there – even if you put them end to end, they still only add up to one, two, perhaps three seconds, snatched from eternity.
Robert Doisneau (1912–1994), French photographer: in *The Guardian* (London), 4 April 1992

12 The camera has an interest in turning history into spectacle, but none in reversing the process. At best, the picture leaves a vague blur in the observer's mind; strong enough to send him into battle perhaps, but not to have him understand why he is going.
Denis Donoghue (b.1928), Irish educator and author: 'Radio Talk', publ. in *The State of the Language* (ed. Christopher Ricks, 1980)

13 The magic of photography is metaphysical. What you see in the photograph isn't what you saw at the time. The real skill of photography is organised visual lying.
Terence Donovan (1936–1996), British photographer: in *The Guardian* (London), 19 Nov. 1983

14 When you photograph a face ... you photograph the soul behind it.
Jean-Luc Godard (b.1930), French film-maker and author: Bruno Forestier (Michel Subor), in *Le Petit Soldat* (film; written and directed by Jean-Luc Godard, 1960)

15 Photography is just one way, albeit the most direct, by which physical existence can modulate a two-dimensional surface.
Richard Hamilton (b.1922), British artist: 'Photography and Painting', first publ. in *Studio International*, March 1969, rep. in *Collected Words 1953–1982* (1982), 'Notes on Photographs'

16 The camera is an instrument that teaches people how to see without a camera.
Dorothea Lange (1895–1979), U.S. photographer: quoted in the *Los Angeles Times*, 13 Aug. 1978

17 Photographers never have much incentive to show the world as it is.
William Leith (b.1960), British journalist: in the *Independent on Sunday* (London), 13 Sept. 1992

18 Giving a camera to Diane Arbus is like putting a live grenade in the hands of a child.
Norman Mailer (b.1923), U.S. author: in *Newsweek* (New York), 22 Oct. 1984

19 The photographer is an armed version of the solitary walker reconnoitering, stalking, cruising the urban inferno, the voyeuristic stroller who discovers the city as a landscape of voluptuous extremes.
Susan Sontag (b.1933), U.S. essayist: *On Photography* (1977), 'Melancholy Objects'

20 The camera doesn't rape, or even possess, though it may presume, intrude, trespass, distort, exploit, and, at the farthest reach of metaphor, assassinate – all activities that, unlike the sexual push and shove, can be conducted from a distance, and with some detachment.
Susan Sontag: *On Photography* (1977), 'Plato's Cave'

21 This century has needed witnesses more than it has needed artists. The camera asserts what it has seen. The artists are just looking.
Mark Wallinger (b.1959), British artist: in *The Guardian* (London), 13 Jan. 1996

22 The camera is a weapon against the tragedy of things, against their disappearing.
Wim Wenders (b.1945), German film-maker: reply to a questionnaire, in *The Logic of Images* (1988; tr.1991), 'Why do you make films?'

23 We *regard* the photograph, the picture on our wall, as the object itself (the man, landscape, and so on) depicted there. This need not have been so. We could easily imagine people who did not have this relation to such pictures. Who, for example, would be repelled by photographs, because a face without colour and even perhaps a face in reduced proportions struck them as inhuman.
Ludwig Wittgenstein (1889–1951), Austrian-born British philosopher: *Philosophical Investigations* (1953), Pt.2, Sct.11

See also Godard on CINEMA

PHOTOGRAPHY: and Painting

1 All photographs are there to remind us of what we forget. In this – as in other ways – they are the opposite of paintings. Paintings record what the painter remembers. Because each one of us forgets different things, a photo more than a painting may change its meaning according to who is looking at it.
John Berger (b.1926), British author and critic: *Keeping a Rendezvous* (1992), 'How Fast Does It Go?'

2 Now at least we know everything that painting isn't.
Pablo Picasso (1881–1973), Spanish artist: said in Rome, 1949, in answer to whether figurative painting was still possible after the advances made by photography and cinema, reported by artist Renato Guttuso in his journals, quoted in *Scritti di Picasso* by Mario De Micheli (1964)

3 The painter constructs, the photographer discloses.
Susan Sontag (b.1933), U.S. essayist: *On Photography* (1977), 'The Heroism of Vision'

PHYSICS

1 One aim of the physical sciences has been to give an exact picture of the material world. One achievement of physics in the twentieth century has been to prove that that aim is unattainable.
Jacob Bronowski (1908–1974), British scientist and author: *The Ascent of Man* (1973), Ch.11

2 When you are courting a nice girl an hour seems like a second. When you sit on a red-hot cinder a second seems like an hour. That's relativity.
Albert Einstein (1879–1955), German-American theoretical physicist: quoted in the *News Chronicle*, 14 March 1949

3 People like us, who believe in physics, know that the distinction between past, present and future is only a stubbornly persistent illusion.
Albert Einstein: letter, March 1955, publ. in *Albert Einstein, Michele Besso: Correspondence 1903–1955* (1972), Letter 215

4 In some sort of crude sense, which no vulgarity, no humor, no overstatement can quite extinguish, the physicists have known sin; and this is a knowledge which they cannot lose.
J. Robert Oppenheimer (1904–1967), U.S. physicist: 'Physics in the Contemporary World', lecture at Massachusetts Institute of Technology, 25 Nov. 1947, first publ. in *Technology Review*, No.50, 1948, rep. in *Open Mind* (1955). Oppenheimer's remark became notorious after it was quoted in *Time* (New York), 23 Feb. 1948 and 8 Nov. 1948

5 It would be a poor thing to be an atom in a universe without physicists, and physicists are made of atoms. A physicist is an atom's way of knowing about atoms.
George Wald (1906–1997), U.S. biochemist: foreword to *The Fitness of the Environment* by L.J. Henderson (1959)

PHYSIQUE

1 Outside every fat man there was an even fatter man trying to close in.
Kingsley Amis (1922–1995), British novelist and poet: Roger Micheldene, 'a shortish fat Englishman of forty', musing over a particularly heavy lunch, in *One Fat Englishman* (1963), Ch.3. This is one of a series of variations on a theme which probably originated with George Orwell's *Coming Up For Air*, (1939), Pt.1, Ch.3: 'I'm fat, but I'm thin inside. Has it ever struck you that there's a thin man inside every fat man, just as they say there's a statue inside every block of stone?' In *The Unquiet Grave* (1944, rev.1951), Cyril Connolly wrote, 'Imprisoned in every fat man a thin one is wildly signalling to be let out'

2 Every day the fat woman dies a series of small deaths.
Shelley Bovey, U.S. author: *Being Fat Is Not a Sin* (1989), Ch.1

3 I don't mind that I'm fat. You still get the same money.
Marlon Brando (b.1924), U.S. actor: in the *International Herald Tribune* (Paris), 9 Oct. 1989

4 Exercise is the yuppie version of bulimia.
Barbara Ehrenreich (b.1941), U.S. author and columnist: 'Food Worship' (1985), rep. in *The Worst Years of Our Lives* (1991)

5 I'm perfect. The areas that I need help on are not negotiable. They have to do with gravity.
Jane Fonda (b.1937), U.S. actress: in *People* (New York), 12 Nov. 1990

6 it's a sex object if you're pretty
and no love
or love and no sex if you're fat

Nikki Giovanni (b.1943), U.S. poet: 'Woman Poem', publ. in *Black Feeling/Black Talk/Black Judgement* (1970),

7 Our growing softness, our increasing lack of physical fitness, is a menace to our security.
John F. Kennedy (1917–1963), U.S. Democratic politician and president: 'The Soft America' (1960), rep. in *Sport and Society: an Anthology* (ed. John T. Talamini and Charles H. Page, 1973)

8 Some people are born to fatness. Others have to get there.
Les Murray (b.1938), Australian poet: in the *Independent on Sunday* (London), 15 April 1990

9 Fat is a social disease, and fat is a feminist issue.
Susie Orbach (b.1946), British psychotherapist and author: introduction to *Fat is a Feminist Issue* (1978)

10 Modern bodybuilding is ritual, religion, sport, art, and science, awash in Western chemistry and mathematics. Defying nature, it surpasses it.
Camille Paglia (b.1947), U.S. author and critic: book review in the *Boston Globe*, 27 Jan. 1991, rep. in *Sex, Art, and American Culture* (1992), 'Alice in Muscle Land'

11 There is no need to worry about mere size. We do not necessarily respect a fat man more than a thin man. Sir Isaac Newton was very much smaller than a hippopotamus, but we do not on that account value him less.
Bertrand Russell (1872–1970), British philosopher and mathematician: 'The Expanding Mental Universe', publ. in the *Saturday Evening Post* (New York), 2 July 1959

12 *I going to bite them young ladies, partner,*
like a hot dog or a hamburger
and if you thin, don't be in a fright
is only fat women I going to bite.
Derek Walcott (b.1930), West Indian poet and playwright: 'The Spoiler's Return', publ. in *The Fortunate Traveller* (1981)

13 To ask women to become unnaturally thin is to ask them to relinquish their sexuality.
Naomi Wolf (b.1962), U.S. author: *The Beauty Myth* (1990), 'Hunger'

14 The phrase pops into his head at that very instant: *social X-rays*. ...They keep themselves so thin, they look like X-ray pictures.... You can see lamplight through their bones ... while they're chattering about *interiors* and *landscape gardening* ... and encasing their scrawny shanks in metallic Lycra tubular tights for their Sports Training classes.
Tom Wolfe (b.1931), U.S. author and journalist: *The Bonfire of the Vanities* (1987), Ch.1

PABLO PICASSO

1 No theoretician, no writer on art, however interesting he or she might be, could be as interesting as Picasso. A good writer on art may give you an insight to Picasso, but, after all, Picasso was there first.
David Hockney (b.1937), British artist: *Hockney on Photography* (conversations with Paul Joyce, ed. Wendy Brown, 1988), 'Mexico City: May 1984'

2 Today, as you know, I am famous and very rich. But when I am alone with myself, I haven't the courage to consider myself an artist, in the great and ancient sense of that word ... I am only a public entertainer, who understands his age.
Pablo Picasso (1881–1973), Spanish artist: *Le Spectacle du Monde* (Paris), Nov. 1962, rep. in *The Trousered Ape* by Duncan Williams (1971), Ch.2

3 A painter like Picasso, who runs through many periods and phases, ends up by saying all those things which are on the tip of the tongue of the age to say, and finally sterilizes the originality of his contemporaries and juniors.
Norbert Wiener (1894–1964), U.S. mathematician, educator and founder of cybernetics: *The Human Use of Human Beings* (1950), Ch.7

PLAGIARISM

1 Out of the closets and into the museums, libraries, architectural monuments, concert halls, bookstores, recording studios and film studios of the world. Everything belongs to the inspired and dedicated thief. ... Words, colors, light, sounds, stone, wood, bronze belong to the living artist. They belong to anyone who can use them. Loot the Louvre! *A bas l'originalité*, the sterile and assertive ego that imprisons us as it creates. *Vive le sol* – pure, shameless, total. We are not responsible. Steal anything in sight.
William Burroughs (1914–1997), U.S. author: *The Adding Machine* (1985), 'Les Voleurs'

2 Ideas improve. The meaning of words participates in the improvement. Plagiarism is necessary. Progress implies it. It embraces an author's phrase, makes use of his expressions, erases a false idea, and replaces it with the right idea.
Guy Debord (1931–1994), French Situationist philosopher: *The Society of the Spectacle* (1967; tr.1977), Ch.8, Sct.207

3 I am a thief and I glory in it. I steal from the present and from the glorious past ... so I stand accused – I am a thief – but with this reservation – I think I know the value of that I steal

and I treasure it for all time – not as a possession but as a heritage and as legacy.
Martha Graham (1894–1991), U.S. dancer and choreographer: *The Notebooks of Martha Graham* (1973), 'Center of the Hurricane'

4 We all steal, but if we're smart, we steal from great directors. Then we can call it influence.
Krzysztof Kieślowski (1941–1996), Polish film-maker: quoted in appreciation in *The Guardian* (London), 14 March 1996

5 Stealing things is a glorious occupation, particularly in the artworld.
Malcolm McLaren (b.1946), British rock impresario: 'Punk and History', transcript of discussion, 24 Sept. 1988, New York, publ. in *Discourses: Conversations in Postmodern Art and Culture* (ed. Russell Ferguson *et al.*, 1990)

6 I steal from every single movie ever made. I love it – if my work has anything it's that I'm taking this from this and that from that and mixing them together. If people don't like that, then tough titty, don't go and see it, all right? I steal from everything. Great artists steal, they don't do homages.
Quentin Tarantino (b.1958), U.S. film-maker: interview in *Empire* (London), Nov. 1994, quoted in *Quentin Tarantino: The Man and His Movies* by Jami Bernard (1995), Ch.11

7 So much of what I am I got from you. I had no idea how much of it was secondhand.
Pete Townshend (b.1945), British rock musician: addressed to the Rolling Stones at the 1989 Rock and Roll Hall of Fame induction ceremony, Jan. 1989, quoted in *Rolling Stone* (New York), 8 Feb. 1990

8 Immature artists imitate. Mature artists steal.
Lionel Trilling (1905–1975), U.S. critic: in *Esquire* (New York), Sept. 1962

See also Bastos on IMITATION

PLANNING

1 In preparing for battle I have always found that plans are useless, but planning is indispensable.
Dwight D. Eisenhower (1890–1969), U.S. general, Republican politician and president: one of Eisenhower's favourite maxims, quoted by Richard Nixon in *Six Crises* (1962), 'Khrushchev'

2 For the happiest life, days should be rigorously planned, nights left open to chance.
Mignon McLaughlin (b.1915?), U.S. author and editor: in *Atlantic Monthly* (Boston), July 1965

3 Planning ahead is a measure of class. The rich and even the middle class plan for future generations, but the poor can plan ahead only a few weeks or days.

Gloria Steinem (b.1934), U.S. feminist writer and editor: 'The Time Factor', first publ. in *Ms.* (New York), March 1980, rep. in *Outrageous Acts and Everyday Rebellions* (1983)

PLEASURE

1 Pleasure is continually disappointed, reduced, deflated, in favour of strong, noble values: Truth, Death, Progress, Struggle, Joy, etc. Its victorious rival is Desire: we are always being told about Desire, never about Pleasure.
Roland Barthes (1915–1980), French semiologist: *The Pleasure of the Text* (1975), 'Oppositions'

2 Pleasure only starts once the worm has got into the fruit, to become delightful happiness must be tainted with poison.
Georges Bataille (1897–1962), French novelist and critic: the Mother, in *My Mother* (1966; tr.1979), p.65 of Marion Boyars edn. (1989)

3 Give yourself to absolute pleasure.
Tim Curry (b.1946), British actor: Dr Frank N. Furter (Curry), in *The Rocky Horror Picture Show* (film; screenplay by Jim Sharman and Richard O'Brien, based on Richard O'Brien's stage musical, directed by Jim Sharman, 1975)

4 Pleasure that isn't paid for is as insipid as everything else that's free.
Anita Loos (1893–1981), U.S. novelist and screenwriter: *Kiss Hollywood Good-by* (1974), Ch.2

5 Pleasure is but a mirage of happiness – a false vision of shade and refreshment seen across parched sand.
Malcolm Muggeridge (1903–1990), British journalist and broadcaster: *Woman's Hour* (radio broadcast), 5 Oct. 1965, publ. in *Muggeridge Through the Microphone* (1967), 'Happiness'

6 Marred pleasure's best, shadow makes the sun strong.
Stevie Smith (1902–1971), British poet and novelist: 'The Queen and the Young Princess', publ. in *Not Waving But Drowning* (1957)

7 The eruption of lived pleasure is such that in losing myself I find myself; forgetting that I exist, I realize myself.
Raoul Vaneigem (b.1934), Belgian Situationist philosopher: *The Revolution of Everyday Life* (1967; tr.1983), Ch.20, Sct.2

8 The vocabulary of pleasure depends on the imagery of pain.
Marina Warner (b.1946), British author and critic: 'Fighting Talk', publ. in *The State of the Language* (ed. Christopher Ricks and Leonard Michaels, 1990)

See also HAPPINESS

PLURALISM

1 Our flag is red, white and blue, but our nation is a rainbow – red, yellow, brown, black and white – and we're all precious in God's sight.
Jesse Jackson (b.1941), U.S. clergyman and civil rights leader: speech, 16 July 1984, Democratic National Convention, San Francisco, quoted in *The Harper Book of American Quotations* (ed. Gorton Carruth and Eugene Ehrlich, 1988)

2 Ultimately, America's answer to the intolerant man is diversity, the very diversity which our heritage of religious freedom has inspired.
Robert Kennedy (1925–1968), U.S. Democratic politician and attorney general: *The Pursuit of Justice* (1964), Pt.3, 'Extremism, Left and Right'

3 Of course I'm a black writer. ... I'm not *just* a black writer, but categories like black writer, woman writer and Latin American writer aren't marginal anymore. We have to acknowledge that the thing we call 'literature' is more pluralistic now, just as society ought to be. The melting pot never worked. We ought to be able to accept on equal terms everybody from the Hasidim to Walter Lippmann, from the Rastafarians to Ralph Bunche.
Toni Morrison (b.1931), U.S. novelist and editor: quoted in *Newsweek* (New York), 30 March 1981

4 In our wish to make ourselves heard, we tend very often to forget that the world is a crowded place, and that if everyone were to insist on the radical purity or priority of one's voice, all we would have would be the awful din of unending strife, and a bloody political mess, the true horror of which is beginning to be perceptible here and there in the re-emergence of racist politics in Europe, the cacophony of debates over political correctness and identity politics in the United States, and ... the intolerance of religious prejudice and illusionary promises of Bismarckian despotism, *à la* Saddam Hussein and his numerous Arab epigones and counterparts.
Edward Said (b.1935), Lebanese-born U.S. social and literary critic: introduction to *Culture and Imperialism* (1993)

5 If I've got one thing to offer – because of where I come from and because I've been through the long rinse cycle – through college and Fleet Street and radio and telly and everything else and finally ending up at the BBC – my agenda is to reflect what I see as the reality, that Britain is made up of a whole mixture of people – not just white males.
Janet Street-Porter (b.1946), British broadcaster and programme-maker: interview in the *Independent on Sunday* (London), 20 Dec. 1992

See also MULTICULTURALISM

POETRY

1 There is the view that poetry should improve your life. I think people confuse it with the Salvation Army.
John Ashbery (b.1927), U.S. poet and critic: in the *International Herald Tribune* (Paris), 2 Oct. 1989

2 Rhymes, metres, stanza forms, etc., are like servants. If the master is fair enough to win their affection and firm enough to command their respect, the result is an orderly happy household. If he is too tyrannical, they give notice; if he lacks authority, they become slovenly, impertinent, drunk and dishonest.
W.H. Auden (1907–1973), Anglo-American poet: *The Dyer's Hand* (1962), Pt.1, 'Writing'

3 I cannot accept the doctrine that in poetry there is a 'suspension of belief'. A poet must never make a statement simply because it sounds poetically exciting; he must also believe it to be true.
W.H. Auden: *A Certain World* (1970), 'Writing'

4 Poetry is one of the destinies of speech. ... One would say that the poetic image, in its newness, opens a future to language.
Gaston Bachelard (1884–1962), French scientist, philosopher and literary theorist: *The Poetics of Reverie* (1960; tr.1969), 'Introduction', Sct.2

5 In the works of the better poets you get the sensation that they're not talking to people any more, or to some seraphical creature. What they're doing is simply talking back to the language itself – as beauty, sensuality, wisdom, irony – those aspects of language of which the poet is a clear mirror. Poetry is not an art or a branch of art, it's something more. If what distinguishes us from other species is speech, then poetry, which is the supreme linguistic operation, is our anthropological, indeed genetic, goal. Anyone who regards poetry as an entertainment, as a 'read', commits an anthropological crime, in the first place, against himself.
Joseph Brodsky (1940–1996), Russian-born U.S. poet and critic: interview in *Writers at Work* (Eighth Series, ed. George Plimpton, 1988)

6 I have nothing to say
    and I am saying   and that is
poetry.
John Cage (1912–1992), U.S. composer: 'Lecture on Nothing', publ. in *Silence* (1961)

7 An age which is incapable of poetry is incapable of any kind of literature except the cleverness of a decadence.
Raymond Chandler (1880–1959), U.S. author: letter, 5 Jan. 1947, to *Atlantic Monthly* editor Charles W. Morton, publ. in *Raymond Chandler*

Speaking (ed. Dorothy Gardiner and Kathrine S. Walker, 1962)

8 Poetry is indispensable – if I only knew what for.

Jean Cocteau (1889–1963), French author and film-maker: quoted in *The Necessity of Art* by Ernst Fischer (1959), Ch.1

9 The Thames runs, bones rattle, rats creep;
Tiresias fancies a peep –
A typist is laid,
A record is played –
Wei la la. After that it gets deep.

Wendy Cope (b.1945), British poet: 'Waste Land Limericks', publ. in *Making Cocoa for Kingsley Amis* (1986)

10 We read poetry because the poets, like our-selves, have been haunted by the inescapable tyranny of time and death; have suffered the pain of loss, and the more wearing, continuous pain of frustration and failure; and have had moods of unlooked-for release and peace.

Elizabeth Drew (1887–1965), Anglo-American author and critic: *Poetry: A Modern Guide to Its Understanding and Enjoyment* (1959), Pt.2, Ch.7

11 Poetry, the genre of purest beauty, was born of a truncated woman: her head severed from her body with a sword, a symbolic penis.

Andrea Dworkin (b.1946), U.S. feminist critic: *Pornography* (1981), Ch.4

12 I would define the poetic effect as the capacity that a text displays for continuing to generate different readings, without ever being com-pletely consumed.

Umberto Eco (b.1932), Italian semiologist and novelist: *Reflections on the Name of the Rose* (1983; tr.1984), 'Telling the Process'

13 The writing of a poem is like a child throwing stones into a mineshaft. You compose first, then you listen for the reverberation.

James Fenton (b.1949), British poet and critic: 'Ars Poetica', No.22, in the *Independent on Sunday* (London), 24 June 1990

14 Poetry is at least an elegance and at most a revelation.

Robert Fitzgerald (1910–1985), U.S. scholar and translator: interview in *Writers at Work* (Eighth Series, ed. George Plimpton, 1988)

15 Poetry is a way of taking life by the throat.

Robert Frost (1874–1963), U.S. poet: quoted in *Robert Frost: the Trial by Existence* by Elizabeth S. Sergeant (1960), Ch.18

16 Poetry is the language in which man explores his own amazement ... says heaven and earth in one word ... speaks of himself and his pre-dicament as though for the first time. It has the virtue of being able to say twice as much as prose in half the time, and the drawback, if you do not give it your full attention, of seeming to say half as much in twice the time.

Christopher Fry (b.1907), British playwright: in *Time* (New York), 3 April 1950

17 Just as a new scientific discovery manifests something that was already latent in the order of nature, and at the same time is logically related to the total structure of the existing science, so the new poem manifests something that was already latent in the order of words.

Northrop Frye (1912–1991), Canadian literary critic: *Anatomy of Criticism* (1957), 'Mythical Phase: Symbol as Archetype'

18 Poetry comes out of the barrel of a gun.

Dan Georgakas (b.1938), U.S. poet: manifesto in *Black Mask* (New York), Feb./April 1967, rep. in *Black Mask* (1993)

19 I have a new method of poetry. All you got to do is look over your notebooks ... or lay down on a couch, and think of anything that comes into your head, especially the miseries.... Then arrange in lines of two, three or four words each, don't bother about sentences, in sections of two, three or four lines each.

Allen Ginsberg (b.1926), U.S. poet: letter, 1952, to Jack Kerouac and Neal Cassady, publ. in *Ginsberg: A Biography* by Barry Miles (1989), Ch.5

20 If there's no money in poetry, neither is there poetry in money.

Robert Graves (1895–1985), British poet and novelist: speech, 6 Dec. 1963, London School of Economics, publ. in *Mammon and the Black Goddess* (1965), 'Mammon'

21 Every poem is a momentary defeat of pessi-mism.

Tony Harrison (b.1953), British poet: interview in *Poetry Review* (London), Jan. 1984

22 When power leads man towards arrogance, poetry reminds him of his limitations. When power narrows the area of man's concern, poetry reminds him of the richness and diver-sity of existence. When power corrupts, poetry cleanses.

John F. Kennedy (1917–1963), U.S. Democratic politician and president: Kennedy's last major public address, at dedication of Robert Frost Library, Amherst College, 26 Oct. 1963, quoted in the *New York Times*, 27 Oct. 1963. Previously, in a speech at Harvard, 14 June 1956, Kennedy said, 'If more politicians knew poetry, and more poets knew politics, I am convinced the world would be a little better place to live'

23 I have no ideas about poetry at all. For me, a poem is the crossroads of my thoughts, my feelings, my imaginings, my wishes, and my verbal sense: normally these run parallel; often two or more cross; but only when all cross at one point do you get a poem. Yippee!

Philip Larkin (1922–1985), British poet: letter, 10 July 1951, publ. in *Selected Letters* (ed. Anthony Thwaite, 1992)

24 A poem is usually a highly professional artificial thing, a verbal device designed to reproduce a thought or emotion indefinitely.
Philip Larkin: letter, 12 March 1965, publ. in *Selected Letters* (ed. Anthony Thwaite, 1992)

25 Most people ignore most poetry
          because
most poetry ignores most people.
Adrian Mitchell (b.1932), British poet and author: epigraph to *Poems* (1964)

26 I see no reason for calling my work poetry except that there is no other category in which to put it.
Marianne Moore (1887–1972), U.S. poet: on accepting the National Book Award for poetry, quoted in the *New York Mirror*, 31 May 1959

27 And it was at that age ... Poetry arrived
in search of me. I don't know, I don't know
     where
it came from, from winter or a river.
I don't know how or when,
no, they were not voices, they were not
words, nor silence,
but from the street I was summoned,
from the branches of night,
abruptly from the others,
among violent fires
or returning alone,
there I was without a face
and it touched me.
Pablo Neruda (1904–1973), Chilean poet: 'La Poesia', publ. in *Memorial de Isla Negra* (1964),

28 Poetry is adolescence fermented, and thus preserved.
José Ortega y Gasset (1883–1955), Spanish essayist and philosopher: 'In Search of Goethe from Within', first publ. in *Partisan Review* (New Brunswick, N.J.), Dec. 1949, rep. in *The Dehumanization of Art and Other Essays* (1968)

29 It is no longer possible for lyric poetry to express the immensity of our experience. Life has grown too cumbersome, too complicated. We have acquired values which are best expressed in prose.
Boris Pasternak (1890–1960), Russian poet, novelist and translator: interview in *Writers at Work* (Second Series, ed. George Plimpton, 1963)

30 When in public poetry should take off its clothes and wave to the nearest person in sight; it should be seen in the company of thieves and lovers rather than that of journalists and publishers.
Brian Patten (b.1946), British poet: 'Prose Poem Towards a Definition of Itself', publ. in *Little Johnny's Confession* (1967)

31 To read a poem is to hear it with our eyes; to hear it is to see it with our ears.
Octavio Paz (b.1914), Mexican poet and essayist: *Alternating Current* (1967), 'Recapitulations'

32 No verse is *libre* for the man who wants to do a good job.
Ezra Pound (1885–1972), U.S. poet and critic: interview in *Writers at Work* (Second Series, ed. George Plimpton, 1963)

33 Now, again, poetry
violent, arcane, common,
hewn of the commonest living substance
into archway, portal, frame
I grasp for you, your bloodstained splinters,
     your
ancient and stubborn poise
– as the earth trembles –
burning out from the grain
Adrienne Rich (b.1929), U.S. poet: 'The Fact of a Doorframe', St.3, publ. in *The Fact of a Doorframe* (1974)

34 To a poet the mere making of a poem can seem to solve the problem of truth ... but only a problem of art is solved in poetry.
Laura Riding (1901–1991), U.S. poet: preface to *Selected Poems: In Five Sets* (1975)

35 Ordering a man to write a poem is like commanding a pregnant woman to give birth to a red-headed child.
Carl Sandburg (1878–1967), U.S. poet: quoted in *Reader's Digest* (Pleasantville, N.Y.), Feb. 1978

36 Every age has its own poetry; in every age the circumstances of history choose a nation, a race, a class to take up the torch by creating situations that can be expressed or transcended only through poetry.
Jean-Paul Sartre (1905–1980), French philosopher and author: 'Orphée Noir', preface to *Anthologie de la Nouvelle Poésie Nègre et Malgache* (1948)

37 If poetry should address itself to the same needs and aspirations, the same hopes and fears, to which the Bible addresses itself, it might rival it in distribution.
Wallace Stevens (1879–1955), U.S. poet: 'Imagination as Value', lecture, 1948, Columbia University, first publ. 1949, rep. in *The Necessary Angel* (1951)

38 Poetry, which is perfection's sweat but which must seem as fresh as the raindrops on a statue's brow, combines the natural and the marmoreal; it conjugates both tenses simultaneously: the past and the present, if the past is the sculpture and the present the beads of dew or rain on the forehead of the past.
Derek Walcott (b.1930), West Indian poet: Nobel Lecture, 1992, publ. in *The Antilles, Fragments of Epic Memory* (1993)

See also Smith on INSPIRATION

POETS

1 Poets ... are the only ones to whom love is not only a crucial, but an indispensable experience, which entitles them to mistake it for a universal one.
Hannah Arendt (1906–1975), German-born U.S. political philosopher: *The Human Condition* (1958), footnote in Ch.33

2 It is a sad fact about our culture that a poet can earn much more money writing or talking about his art than he can by practising it.
W. H. Auden (1907–1973), Anglo-American poet: opening words of Foreword to *The Dyer's Hand* (1962)

3 One of the good things about Larkin is that he still has you firmly by the hand as you cross the finishing-line, whereas reading Auden is like doing a parachute drop: for a while the view is wonderful, but then you end up on your back in the middle of a ploughed field and in the wrong country.
Alan Bennett (b.1934), British playwright: *Writing Home* (1994), 'Instead of a Present'

4 Every individual ought to know at least one poet from cover to cover: if not as a guide through the world, then as a yardstick for the language.
Joseph Brodsky (1940–1996), Russian-born U.S. poet and critic: 'To Please a Shadow', Sct.5 (1983), rep. in *Less Than One: Selected Essays* (1986). Brodsky recommended W.H. Auden as qualified on both counts

5 The earnings of a poet could be reckoned by a metaphysician rather than a bookkeeper.
Edward Dahlberg (1900–1977), U.S. author and critic: *Alms for Oblivion* (1964), 'For Sale'

6 Constantly risking absurdity
　and death
whenever he performs
　above the heads
　　of his audience
the poet like an acrobat
　climbs on rime
　　to a high wire of his own making.
Lawrence Ferlinghetti (b.1919), U.S. poet and publisher: *Coney Island of the Mind* (1958), Sct.15

7 Is encouragement what the poet needs? Open question. Maybe he needs discouragement. In fact, quite a few of them need more discouragement, the most discouragement possible.
Robert Fitzgerald (1910–1985), U.S. scholar and translator: interview in *Writers at Work* (Eighth Series, ed. George Plimpton, 1988)

8 He repeated until his dying day that there was no one with more common sense, no stone-cutter more obstinate, no manager more lucid or dangerous, than a poet.
Gabriel García Márquez (b.1928), Colombian author: of Florentino Ariza's father, in *Love in the Time of Cholera* (1985; tr.1988), p.168 of Penguin edn. (1989)

9 To be a poet is a condition rather than a profession.
Robert Graves (1895–1985), British poet and novelist: 'The Cost of Letters', reply to questionnaire in *Horizon* (London), Sept. 1946

10 Nine-tenths of English poetic literature is the result either of vulgar careerism or of a poet trying to keep his hand in. Most poets are dead by their late twenties.
Robert Graves: quoted in *The Observer* (London), 11 Nov. 1962

11 In this nadir of poetic repute, when the only verse that most people read from one year's end to the next is what appears on greetings cards, it is well for us to stop and consider our poets. ... Poets are the leaven in the lump of civilization.
Elizabeth Janeway (b.1913), U.S. author and critic: *The Writer's Book* (ed. Helen Hull, 1950), Ch.30

12 Poets ... are literal-minded men who will squeeze a word till it hurts.
Archibald MacLeish (1892–1982), U.S. poet: 'Apologia', publ. in the *Harvard Law Review* (Cambridge, Mass.), June 1972, rep. in *Riders on Earth* (1978) as 'Art and Law'

13 If, as Shelley believed, poets are the unacknowledged legislators of the world, they take a very long time getting their bills passed through the parliament of mankind.
Theodore Roszak (b.1933), U.S. social critic: preface to *Where the Wasteland Ends* (1972; rev.1989)

14 A poet's work is to name the unnameable, to point at frauds, to take sides, start arguments, shape the world, and stop it going to sleep.
Salman Rushdie (b.1947), Indian-born British author: quoted in *The Independent* (London), 18 Feb. 1989

15 The poet must be free to love or hate as the spirit moves him, free to change, free to be a chameleon, free to be an *enfant terrible*. He must above all never worry about his effect on other people. Power requires that one do just that all the time. Power requires that the inner person never be unmasked. No, we poets have to go naked. And since this is so, it is better that we stay private people; a naked public person would be rather ridiculous, what?
May Sarton (b.1912), U.S. poet and novelist: Hilary Stevens, in *Mrs Stevens Hears the Mermaids Singing* (1965), Pt.2

16 At a time when pimpery, lick-spittlery, and picking the public's pocket are the order of the

day – indeed, officially proclaimed as virtue – the poet must play the madcap to keep his balance. And ours.

Studs Terkel (b.1912), U.S. author and broadcaster: *Talking to Myself* (1977), Bk.4, Ch.4

See also Brodsky on LITERATURE: AND SOCIETY

POLAND

1 It is often said that Poland is a country where there is anti-semitism and no Jews, which is pathology in its purest state.

Bronislaw Geremek (b.1932), Polish politician and historian: in the *International Herald Tribune* (Paris), 17 Feb. 1992

2 In Poland a man must be one thing: white or black, here or there, with us or against us – clearly, openly, without hesitations. ... We lack the liberal, democratic tradition rich in all its gradations. We have instead the tradition of struggle: the extreme situation, the final gesture.

Ryszard Kapuściński (b.1932), Polish journalist: 'A Warsaw Diary', publ. in *Granta* (Cambridge), No.15, 1985

3 The Poles do not know how to hate, thank God.

Stefan Wyszynski (1901–1981), Polish ecclesiastic and archbishop: quoted in *The Observer* (London), 8 June 1986

THE POLICE

1 He may be a very nice man. But I haven't got the time to figure that out. All I know is, he's got a uniform and a gun and I have to relate to him that way. That's the only way to relate to him because one of us may have to die.

James Baldwin (1924–1987), U.S. author: of the police, in a conversation with Nikki Giovanni, 4 Nov. 1971, London, publ. in *A Dialogue* (1973)

2 A *functioning* police state needs no police.

William Burroughs (1914–1997), U.S. author: Dr Benway, in *The Naked Lunch* (1959), 'Benway'

3 However low a man sinks he never reaches the level of the police.

Quentin Crisp (b.1908), British author: *The Naked Civil Servant* (1968), Ch.12

4 Fuck tha police coming straight out the underground
A young nigger got it bad cause I'm brown
And not the other color.

Eazy-E (1963–1995), U.S. rapper: 'Fuck tha Police' (song) on the album *Straight Outta Compton* (N.W.A., 1989). The lyrics provoked a storm of controversy in the United States because of their overtly inflammatory tone

5 We now in the United States have more security guards for the rich than we have police services for the poor districts. If you're looking for personal security, far better to move to the suburbs than to pay taxes in New York.

J.K. Galbraith (b.1908), U.S. economist: in *The Guardian* (London), 23 May 1992

6 I'm not against the police; I'm just afraid of them.

Alfred Hitchcock (1899–1980), British film-maker: quoted in *New Society* (London), 10 May 1984

7 You're a real blue flame special, aren't you son? Young, dumb and full of come, I know. What I don't know is how you got assigned here. Guess we must have ourselves an asshole shortage, huh?

Pete Iliff, U.S. screenwriter: Ben Harp (John McGinley), grilling FBI agent (Keanu Reeves), newly posted to an L.A. police department, in *Point Break* (film; screenplay by Pete Iliff, directed by Kathryn Bigelow, 1991)

8 Every society gets the kind of criminal it deserves. What is equally true is that every community gets the kind of law enforcement it insists on.

Robert Kennedy (1925–1968), U.S. Democratic politician and attorney general: *The Pursuit of Justice* (1964), Pt.3, 'Eradicating Free Enterprise in Organized Crime'

9 Policemen so cherish their status as keepers of the peace and protectors of the public that they have occasionally been known to beat to death those citizens or groups who question that status.

David Mamet (b.1947), U.S. playwright: *Writing in Restaurants* (1986), 'Some Thoughts on Writing in Restaurants'

10 Evenin' all.

Jack Warner (1895–1981), British actor: George Dixon (Warner), in *Dixon of Dock Green* (TV series, created by Ted Willis, 1955–1976). Each episode of the series ended with Dixon's familiar salute and 'evenin' all'

POLICY

1 The longest suicide note in history.

Gerald Kaufman (b.1930), British Labour politician: referring to the Labour Party's manifesto for the 1983 general election, *New Hope For Britain*, quoted in *The Time of My Life* by Denis Healey (1989), Ch.23. 'The scale of our defeat was devastating,' Healey wrote of the results of the election

2 Where's the beef?

Walter Mondale (b.1928), U.S. Democratic politician and vice president: campaign slogan for 1984 Democratic presidential nomination. Originally used to advertise Wendy's Hamburgers, the line was adopted by Mondale's campaign team after a televised debate in which the candidate told rival Democratic nominee Gary Hart, 'When I hear your new ideas I'm reminded of that ad, *Where's the beef?*' (11 March 1984)

3   A public man must never forget that he loses his usefulness when he as an individual, rather than his policy, becomes the issue.
    Richard Nixon (1913–1992), U.S. Republican politician and president: in *Life* (New York), 8 June 1959. This observation appeared in a tribute to secretary of state John Foster Dulles following his death. Dulles, Nixon asserted, recognized this 'fundamental truth'

4   You do the policy, I'll do the politics.
    Dan Quayle (b.1947), U.S. Republican politician and vice president: remark to aide, quoted in the *International Herald Tribune* (Paris), 13 Jan. 1992

POLITICAL CORRECTNESS

1   It is silly to call fat people 'gravitationally challenged' – a self-righteous fetishism of language which is no more than a symptom of political frustration.
    Terry Eagleton (b.1943), British critic: in *The Guardian* (London), 27 Oct. 1992

2   During the years 1945–1965 (I am referring to Europe), there was a certain way of thinking correctly, a certain style of political discourse, a certain ethics of the intellectual. One had to be on familiar terms with Marx, not let one's dreams stray too far from Freud. ... These were the ... requirements that made the strange occupation of writing and speaking a measure of truth about oneself and one's time acceptable.
    Michel Foucault (1926–1984), French philosopher: preface to *Anti-Oedipus* by Gilles Deleuze and Félix Guattari (1972)

3   We want to create a sort of linguistic Lourdes, where evil and misfortune are dispelled by a dip in the waters of euphemism.
    Robert Hughes (b.1938), Australian author and critic: *Culture of Complaint* (1993), Ch.1

4   We have needed to define ourselves by reclaiming the words that define us. They have used language as weapons. When we open ourselves to what they say and how they say it, our narrow prejudices evaporate and we are nourished and armed.
    Selma James (b.1930), U.S. author and political activist: *The Ladies and the Mammies: Jane Austen and Jean Rhys* (1983), Ch.1

5   Political correctness is the natural continuum from the party line. What we are seeing once again is a self-appointed group of vigilantes imposing their views on others. It is a heritage of communism, but they don't seem to see this.

Doris Lessing (b.1919), British novelist: in *The Sunday Times* (London), 10 May 1992

6   It is about people trying to talk their way into heaven, cheap virtue. I could do something about racism, I could do something about the plight of the inner cities in America, I could donate time, I could donate money, but how much easier to say 'African American' instead of 'black' and feel enormously good about myself and feel I have accomplished something.
    P.J. O'Rourke (b.1947), U.S. journalist: interview in *The Guardian* (London), 25 Nov. 1995

7   Political correctness is a concept invented by hard-rightwing forces to defend their right to be racist, to treat women in a degrading way and to be truly vile about gay people. They invent this idea of people who are politically correct, with a rigid, monstrous attitude to life so they can attack them. But we have all had to learn to modify our language. That's all part of being a decent human being.
    Clare Short (b.1946), British Labour politician: interview in *The Guardian* (London), 18 Feb. 1995

8   It seems our fate to be incorrect ... and in our incorrectness stand.
    Alice Walker (b.1944), U.S. author and critic: interview first publ. in *Interviews with Black Writers* (ed. John O'Brien, 1973), rep. in *In Search of Our Mothers' Gardens* (1983), 'From an Interview'

9   The thing has been blown up out of all proportion. PC language is *not* enjoined on one and all – there are a lot more places where you can say 'spic' and 'bitch' with impunity than places where you can smoke a cigarette.
    Katharine Whitehorn (b.1926), British journalist: in *The Observer* (London), 25 Aug. 1991

See also Sontag on BOOKS: Classics; Orwell on LANGUAGE

POLITICAL PARTIES

1   Political organizations have slowly substituted themselves for the Churches as the places for believing practices. ... Politics has once again become religious.
    Michel de Certeau (1925–1986), French author and critic: *The Practice of Everyday Life* (1974), Ch.13, 'An Archeology: The Transits of Believing'

2   The two-party system has given this country the war of Lyndon Johnson, the Watergate of Nixon, and the incompetence of Carter. Saying we should keep the two-party system simply because it is working is like saying the Titanic voyage was a success because a few people survived on life-rafts.
    Eugene J. McCarthy (b.1916), U.S. Democratic senator and author: in the *Chicago Tribune*, 10 Sept. 1978

3 As usual the Liberals offer a mixture of sound and original ideas. Unfortunately none of the sound ideas is original and none of the original ideas is sound.

Harold Macmillan (1894–1986), British Conservative politician and prime minister: speech, 7 March 1961, London, quoted in *The Times* (London), 8 March 1961

4 The strangest parliamentary malady of modern times is that fundamentally the parties appear to agree about everything; when anything goes wrong they just adopt each other's policies, but abuse each other for doing it. All very practical, perhaps.

Oswald Mosley (1896–1980), British fascist leader: *My Life* (1968), Ch.5

5 The lounge of the main hotel is full of jollity, with large comfortable men sitting in braces; the bar is packed with talkative intellectuals, full of witty disloyalties. ... The next week the main hotel is suddenly full of dinner-jackets and large hats. The girls are dressed as if for a weekend in the country. ... When one of the great men of the party comes through, the crowd edges respectfully away, murmuring loyal noises.

Anthony Sampson (b.1926), British journalist and author: describing respectively the Labour and Conservative Party Conferences, in *The Anatomy of Britain Today* (1965), Ch.5

6 The Republican party makes even its young men seem old; the Democratic Party makes even its old men seem young.

Adlai Stevenson (1900–1965), U.S. Democratic politician: comparing Richard Nixon, the Republican Party nominee for vice-president, with the septuagenarian Democratic vice-president Alben Barkley, during the 1952 presidential race, quoted in *Richard Nixon: A Political and Personal Portrait* by Earl Mazo (1959), Ch.7

7 The two real political parties in America are the *Winners* and the *Losers*. The people don't acknowledge this. They claim membership in two imaginary parties, the *Republicans* and the *Democrats*, instead.

Kurt Vonnegut (b.1922), U.S. novelist: *Wampeters, Foma and Granfalloons* (1974), 'In a Manner that Must Shame God Himself'

See also THE CONSERVATIVE PARTY; THE LABOUR PARTY

POLITICIANS

1 It is no part of my business ... to discuss what gets politicians into office or debars them from it, but in the case of two noteworthy contenders of our time, J. Enoch Powell and Anthony Wedgwood Benn, the reason for their failure to reach the top is surely obvious. They both look barmy.

Kingsley Amis (1922–1995), British novelist and poet: *Memoirs* (1991), 'Enoch Powell'

2 A political leader must keep looking over his shoulder all the time to see if the boys are still there. If they aren't still there, he's no longer a political leader.

Bernard Baruch (1870–1965), U.S. financier: quoted in obituary, in the *New York Times*, 21 June 1965

3 It only takes a politician believing in what he says for the others to stop believing him.

Jean Baudrillard (b.1929), French semiologist: *Cool Memories* (1987; tr.1990), Ch.5

4 I never would have thought about doing what I'm doing: receiving heads of state, prime ministers from foreign countries, addressing Parliament. These things are contrary to my nature! So while a politician likes these things, I can't bear doing them! I suffer doing these things. Suffer physically. Suffer. Suffer.

Silvio Berlusconi (b.1936), Italian businessman and politician: interview in *Vanity Fair* (New York), Jan. 1995

5 The Prime Minister has an absolute genius for putting flamboyant labels on empty luggage.

Aneurin Bevan (1897–1960), British Labour politician: referring to Harold Macmillan, in Queen's Speech debate, House of Commons, 3 Nov. 1959, quoted in *Aneurin Bevan* by Michael Foot (1973), Vol.II, Ch.16

6 We all know the principal preoccupation of politicians is how they can do down their colleagues so that they can advance their own careers.

Alan Clark (b.1928), British Conservative politician: interview with John Humphries, in *On the Ropes*, BBC Radio 4, 16 May 1995. Clark explained that his main regret from his political career was in not destabilizing his boss at the Ministry of Defence, Tom King

7 You campaign in poetry. You govern in prose.

Mario Cuomo (b.1932), U.S. Democratic politician: in *New Republic* (Washington D.C.), 8 April 1985

8 It is our experience that political leaders do not always mean the opposite of what they say.

Abba Eban (b.1915), Israeli politician: quoted in *The Observer* (London), 5 Dec. 1971

9 It is not necessary that every time he rises he should give his famous imitation of a semi-house-trained polecat.

Michael Foot (b.1913), British Labour politician: of Norman Tebbit, in speech to House of Commons, 2 March 1978, publ. in *Hansard*, Col.668

10 It's important for people not to hold a high opinion of politicians, and one of the strengths of the British is that they don't on the whole. Even Mrs Thatcher, the most successful politician of our time, who has done more than anyone, is not liked very much in her own country, and that's a good attitude. The danger begins when people start admiring politicians.

Richard Ingrams (b.1937), British journalist and editor: interview in *Singular Encounters* by Naim Attollah (1990), 'Richard Ingrams'

11 You slam a politician, you make out he's the devil, with horns and hoofs. But his wife loves him, and so did all his mistresses.

Pamela Hansford Johnson (1912–1981), British author and critic: Dr Wohlgemutt, in *Night and Silence, Who is Here? – An American Comedy* (1962), Ch.23

12 Politicians are the same all over: they promise to build a bridge even where there is no river.

Nikita Khrushchev (1894–1971), Soviet premier: quoted in the *New York Herald Tribune*, 22 Aug. 1963. The remark had earlier been ascribed to Khrushchev at a press conference at Glen Cove, New York, Oct. 1960

13 Successful democratic politicians are insecure and intimidated men. They advance politically only as they placate, appease, bribe, seduce, bamboozle, or otherwise manage to manipulate the demanding and threatening elements in their constituencies. The decisive consideration is not whether the proposition is good but whether it is popular – not whether it will work well and prove itself but whether the active talking constituents like it immediately. Politicians rationalize this servitude by saying that in a democracy public men are the servants of the people.

Walter Lippmann (1889–1974), U.S. journalist: *The Public Philosophy* (1955), Ch.2, Sct.4

14 The American, if he has a spark of national feeling, will be humiliated by the very prospect of a foreigner's visit to Congress – these, for the most part, illiterate hacks whose fancy vests are spotted with gravy, and whose speeches, hypocritical, unctuous, and slovenly, are spotted also with the gravy of political patronage, these persons are a reflection on the democratic process rather than of it; they expose it in its underwear.

Mary McCarthy (1912–1989), U.S. author and critic: 'America the Beautiful', first publ. in *Commentary* (New York) Sept. 1947, rep. in *On the Contrary* (1961)

15 At home you always have to be a politician. When you're abroad you almost feel yourself a statesman.

Harold Macmillan (1894–1986), British Conservative politician and prime minister: speech, 17 Feb. 1958, Melbourne, Australia, during the first visit to Australia by a British prime minister, quoted in *Look* (New York), 15 April 1958

16 The politician who never made a mistake never made a decision.

John Major (b.1943), British Conservative politician and prime minister: interview on *The World This Weekend*, BBC Radio 4, 25 Nov. 1990

17 One has to be a lowbrow, a bit of a murderer, to be a politician, ready and willing to see people sacrificed, slaughtered, for the sake of an idea, whether a good one or a bad one.

Henry Miller (1891–1980), U.S. author: interview in *Writers at Work* (Second Series, ed. George Plimpton, 1963)

18 Political image is like mixing cement. When it's wet, you can move it around and shape it, but at some point it hardens and there's almost nothing you can do to reshape it.

Walter Mondale (b.1928), U.S. Democratic politician: quoted in the *Independent on Sunday* (London), 12 May 1991

19 Napoleon at Waterloo appears in modern research to have been a burnt-out old man, although he was almost exactly the same age as politicians now recommended by the parties to head government and opposition as conspicuous examples of young statesmanship.

Oswald Mosley (1896–1980), British fascist leader: *My Life* (1968), Ch.6

20 Don't fall in love with politicians, they're all a disappointment. They can't help it, they just are.

Peggy Noonan (b.1950), U.S. author and presidential speechwriter: *What I Saw at the Revolution* (1990), 'Another Epilogue'

21 We assume that politicians are without honor. We read their statements trying to crack the code. The scandals of their politics: not so much that men in high places lie, only that they do so with such indifference, so endlessly, still expecting to be believed. We are accustomed to the contempt inherent in the political lie.

Adrienne Rich (b.1929), U.S. poet: 'Women and Honor: Some Notes on Lying', paper read at Hartwick College, New York, June 1975, first publ. 1977, rep. in *On Lies, Secrets, and Silence* (1980)

22 People start parades – politicians just get out in front and act like they're leading.

Dana Gillman Rinehart (b.1946), U.S. politician and mayor of Columbus, Ohio: quoted in *The Observer* (London), 22 May 1988

23 A politician is a statesman who approaches every question with an open mouth.

Adlai Stevenson (1900–1965), U.S. Democratic politician: quoted in *The Fine Art of Political Wit* by Leon Harris (1964), Ch.10

24 A politician is a man who understands government and it takes a politician to run a government. A statesman is a politician who's been dead ten or fifteen years.
Harry S Truman (1884–1972), U.S. Democratic politician and president: speech, 11 April 1958, Reciprocity Club, Washington D.C., quoted in the *New York World-Telegram and Sun*, 12 April 1958

25 People with high ideals don't necessarily make good politicians. If clean politics is so important, we should leave the job to scientists and the clergy.
Michio Watanabe (b.1923), Japanese Liberal Democratic politician: quoted in *Newsweek* (New York), 12 June 1989

26 It is my settled opinion, after some years as a political correspondent, that no one is attracted to a political career in the first place unless he is socially or emotionally crippled.
Auberon Waugh (b.1939), British journalist and author: quoted in *A Ford, Not a Lincoln* by Richard Reeves (1975), Ch.1

27 A politician's words reveal less about what he thinks about his subject than what he thinks about his audience.
George F. Will (b.1941), U.S. political columnist: quoted in *A Ford, Not a Lincoln* by Richard Reeves (1975), Ch.1

See also Baker on INDECISION; Nixon on SPEECHES

POLITICS

1 Nothing is irreparable in politics.
(*Rien n'est irréparable en politique*.)
Jean Anouilh (1910–1987), French playwright: Warwick, in *The Lark* (1953; tr.1955), Pt.1

2 Politics is about putting yourself in a state of grace.
Paddy Ashdown (b.1941), British Liberal Democrat politician: in *The Daily Telegraph* (London), 16 Sept. 1992

3 The belief that politics can be scientific must inevitably produce tyrannies. Politics cannot be a science, because in politics theory and practice cannot be separated, and the sciences depend upon their separation. ... Empirical politics must be kept in bounds by democratic institutions, which leave it up to the subjects of the experiment to say whether it shall be tried, and to stop it if they dislike it, because, in politics, there is a distinction, unknown to science, between Truth and Justice.
W.H. Auden (1907–1973), Anglo-American poet: *A Certain World* (1970), 'Tyranny'

4 Every political system is an accumulation of habits, customs, prejudices, and principles that have survived a long process of trial and error and of ceaseless response to changing circumstances. If the system works well on the whole, it is a lucky accident – the luckiest, indeed, that can befall a society.
Edward C. Banfield (b.1916), U.S. political scientist: quoted in *Newsweek* (New York), 12 June 1989

5 The history of American politics is littered with bodies of people who took so pure a position that they had no clout at all.
Ben C. Bradlee (b.1921), U.S. editor: quoted in *Talking to Myself* by Studs Terkel (1977), Bk.1, Ch.7

6 Politics are usually the executive expression of human immaturity.
Vera Brittain (1896–1970), British author and pacifist: *The Rebel Passion* (1964), Ch.1

7 A passion for politics stems usually from an insatiable need, either for power, or for friendship and adulation, or a combination of both.
Fawn M. Brodie (1915–1981), U.S. biographer: *Thomas Jefferson* (1974), Ch.1

8 Religion is organized to satisfy and guide the soul – politics does the same thing for the body.
Joyce Cary (1888–1957), British author: interview in *Writers at Work* (First Series, ed. Malcolm Cowley, 1958)

9 I think politics is an instrument of the devil. Just that clear. I think politics is what kills; it doesn't bring anything alive. Politics is corrupt: I mean, anybody knows that.
Bob Dylan (b.1941), U.S. singer and songwriter: interview in *Rolling Stone* (New York), June 1984

10 Politics ought to be the part-time profession of every citizen who would protect the rights and privileges of free people and who would preserve what is good and fruitful in our national heritage.
Dwight D. Eisenhower (1890–1969), U.S. general, Republican politician and president: speech, broadcast 28 Jan. 1954, publ. in *Public Papers of the Presidents of the United States* (1954)

11 Some things stay there, some things go out of the other ear, and some things don't go in at all.
Elizabeth II (b.1926), Queen of Great Britain and Northern Ireland: on her weekly meetings with prime ministers, quoted in *The Guardian* (London), 20 April 1996

12 Mediocrity in politics is not to be despised. Greatness is not needed.
Hans Magnus Enzensberger (b.1929), German poet and critic: *The Late Show*, BBC2, 5 Nov. 1990

13 It may be that war as strategy is a continuation of politics. But it must not be forgotten that 'politics' has been conceived as a continuation, if not exactly and directly of war, at least of the

military model as a fundamental means of preventing civil disorder.

Michel Foucault (1926–1984), French philosopher: *Discipline and Punish: The Birth of the Prison* (1975), 'Docile Bodies'

14 Politics is not the art of the possible. It consists in choosing between the disastrous and the unpalatable.

J.K. Galbraith (b.1908), U.S. economist: letter to President Kennedy, 2 March 1962, written while serving as U.S. ambassador in India, publ. in *Ambassador's Journal* (1969), Ch.15. Galbraith was referring to Bismarck's celebrated saying, *Die Politik ist die Lehre von Möglichen* ('Politics is the art of the possible')

15 In politics, being ridiculous is more damaging than being extreme.

Roy Hattersley (b.1932), British Labour politician: in the *Evening Standard* (London), 9 May 1989

16 Politics is a choice of enemas. You're gonna get it up the ass, no matter what you do.

George V. Higgins (b.1939), U.S. novelist: Ed Cobb, in *Victories* (1991), Ch.7

17 Here we are the way politics ought to be in America. The politics of happiness, the politics of purpose and the politics of joy.

Hubert H. Humphrey (1911–1978), U.S. Democratic politician and vice president: speech, 28 April 1968, Washington D.C., quoted in the *New York Times*, 28 April 1968

18 Son, in politics you've got to learn that overnight chicken shit can turn to chicken salad.

Lyndon B. Johnson (1908–1973), U.S. Democratic politician and president: quoted in *Richard Nixon: The Shaping of his Character* by Fawn Brodie (1983), Ch.25. Johnson, who had previously referred to Nixon as 'chicken shit', was replying to a reporter who had questioned him on his embracing Richard Nixon on the latter's return from a vice presidential tour of South America in May 1958, during which he had been mobbed by an angry crowd in Caracas. Walter Lippmann called the tour 'a diplomatic Pearl Harbor' and the *Boston Globe* said it was 'one of the most ineptly handled episodes in this country's foreign relations'

19 Most of us are conditioned for many years to have a political viewpoint – Republican or Democratic, liberal, conservative, or moderate. The fact of the matter is that most of the problems ... that we now face are technical problems, are administrative problems. They are very sophisticated judgments, which do not lend themselves to the great sort of passionate movements which have stirred this country so often in the past. [They] deal with questions which are now beyond the comprehension of most men.

John F. Kennedy (1917–1963), U.S. Democratic politician and president: press conference, May 1962, quoted in 'Policy-Planning for the Establishment' by David Eakins, publ. in *A New History of Leviathan* (ed. Ronald Radosh and Murray Rothbard, 1972)

20 In politics, it seems, retreat is honorable if dictated by military considerations and shameful if even *suggested* for ethical reasons.

Mary McCarthy (1912–1989), U.S. author and critic: *Vietnam* (1967), 'Solutions'

21 Politics is the enemy of the imagination.

Ian McEwan (b.1948), British author: quoted in the *Independent on Sunday* (London), 5 July 1992

22 Politics will eventually be replaced by imagery. The politician will be only too happy to abdicate in favor of his image, because the image will be much more powerful than he could ever be.

Marshall McLuhan (1911–1980), Canadian communications theorist: quoted in *Maclean's* (Toronto), June 1971

23 The first requirement of politics is not intellect or stamina but patience. Politics is a very long run game and the tortoise will usually beat the hare.

John Major (b.1943), British Conservative politician and prime minister: in the *Daily Express* (London), 25 July 1989

24 I learnt ... to work with my hands both in farming and carpentry, and must admit that I was better at shovelling muck than in the fine work of joinery; both aptitudes have their use in political life.

Oswald Mosley (1896–1980), British fascist leader: on his childhood, in *My Life* (1968), Ch.1

25 The one thing sure about politics is that what goes up comes down and what goes down often comes up.

Richard Nixon (1913–1992), U.S. Republican politician and president: quoted in *Richard Nixon: A Political and Personal Portrait* by Earl Mazo (1959), Ch.17

26 I played by the rules of politics as I found them.

Richard Nixon: in *The Times* (London), 26 March 1990

27 Beware the politically obsessed. They are often bright and interesting, but they have something missing in their natures; there is a hole, an empty place, and they use politics to fill it up. It leaves them somehow misshapen.

Peggy Noonan (b.1950), U.S. author and presidential speechwriter: *What I Saw at the Revolution* (1990), 'Another Epilogue'

28 Politics are for foreigners with their endless wrongs and paltry rights. Politics are a lousy way to get things done. Politics are, like God's infinite mercy, a last resort.

P.J. O'Rourke (b.1947), U.S. journalist: preface to the British edition of *Parliament of Whores* (1991)

29 In our time, political speech and writing are largely the defence of the indefensible.

George Orwell (1903–1950), British author: 'Politics and the English Language' (1946), rep. in *Shooting an Elephant* (1950)

30 In politics people give you what they think you deserve and deny you what they think you want.

Cecil Parkinson (b.1932), British Conservative politician: television interview, ITV, 19 Nov. 1990

31 Politics is still crucially important. Our choices are vital, and we've got to make them, and not just say, 'Oh, they're all the same'. They *are* all the same in certain ways, alas – a political animal is such an animal. But lurking somewhere behind their rhetoric and their spittle are important choices that we should make.

Dennis Potter (1935–1994), British dramatist and screenwriter: interview with Melvyn Bragg, Channel 4, 5 April 1994

32 All political lives, unless they are cut off in mid-stream at a happy juncture, end in failure.

Enoch Powell (b.1912), British Conservative politician: in *The Sunday Times* (London), 6 Nov. 1977

33 Politics is just like show business, you have a hell of an opening, coast for a while, and then have a hell of a close.

Ronald Reagan (b.1911), U.S. Republican politician and president: said, to aide Stuart Spencer, 1966, quoted in *There He Goes Again* (ed. Mark Green and Gail MacColl, 1983)

34 All politics ... are based on the indifference of the majority.

James Reston (b.1909), U.S. journalist: in the *New York Times*, 12 June 1968

35 Politics in the United States consists of the struggle between those whose change has been arrested by success or failure, on one side, and those who are still engaged in changing themselves, on the other. Agitators of arrested metamorphosis versus agitators of continued metamorphosis. The former have the advantage of numbers (since most people accept themselves as successes or failures quite early), the latter of vitality and visibility (since self-transformation, though it begins from within, with ideology, religion, drugs, tends to express itself publicly through costume and jargon).

Harold Rosenberg (1906–1978), U.S. art critic and author: *Discovering the Present* (1973), Pt.4, Ch.24

36 To bemoan the messiness of politics is not just a folly; it betrays a dangerous impatience with basic human realities. It is like becoming disturbed that people do not fall in love sensibly – and so deciding to computerize the problem.

Theodore Roszak (b.1933), U.S. social critic: *Where the Wasteland Ends* (1972), Ch.7

37 To 'know your place' is a good idea in politics. That is not to say 'stay in your place' or 'hang on to your place', because ambition or boredom may dictate upward or downward mobility, but a sense of place – a feel for one's own position in the control room – is useful in gauging what you should try to do.

William Safire (b.1929), U.S. journalist: prologue to *Before The Fall* (1975)

38 Only very intelligent people don't wish they were in politics, and I'm dumb enough to want to be in there.

Orson Welles (1915–1985), U.S. film-maker and actor: interview in *The Americans* by David Frost (1970), 'Can a Martian Survive by Pretending to be a Leading American Actor?'

39 Politics should share one purpose with religion: the steady emancipation of the individual through the education of his passions.

George F. Will (b.1941), U.S. political columnist: *Statecraft as Soulcraft: What Government Does* (1984), Ch.2

40 A week is a long time in politics.

Harold Wilson (1916–1995), British Labour politician and prime minister: attributed. In *Sayings of the Century* by Nigel Rees (1984), 'Prime Ministers: A Word from No.10', Rees reports that in 1977, Wilson was unable to remember when or even if he had uttered this dictum always associated with him. Rees suggests the words were probably said in 1964, shortly after Wilson became prime minister, though a journalist recalled Wilson saying 'Forty-eight hours is a long time in politics' at a party conference in 1960

41 The principal purpose of politics [is] the evolution and maintenance of a securely established ruling class with a justified sense of its own honourable superiority.

Peregrine Worsthorne (b.1923), British journalist: quoted in the *New Socialist* (London), Nov. 1985, rep. in *We, the Nation* by A.J. Davies (1995), Ch.3

See also ACTIVISM & PROTEST; ART: POLITICAL ART; IDEOLOGY; POLITICAL PARTIES; POLITICIANS; WOMEN: IN POLITICS

POLLUTION

1 Raise a million filters and the rain will not be clean, until the longing for it be refined in deep confession. And still we hear, If only this nation had a soul, or, Let us change the way we trade, or, Let us be proud of our region.

Leonard Cohen (b.1934), Canadian singer, poet and novelist: *Book of Mercy* (1984), Sct.30

2 Even the most ardent environmentalist doesn't really want to stop pollution. If he thinks about it and doesn't just talk about it, he wants to have the *right amount* of pollution. We can't really *afford* to eliminate it – not without abandoning all the benefits of technology that we not only enjoy but on which we depend.

Milton Friedman (b.1912), U.S. economist: introduction to *There's No Such Thing as a Free Lunch* (1975)

3 Approximately 80% of our air pollution stems from hydrocarbons released by vegetation, so let's not go overboard in setting and enforcing tough emission standards from man-made sources.

Ronald Reagan (b.1911), U.S. Republican politician and president: *Sierra* 10 Sept. 1980, quoted in *Reagan's Reign of Error* (ed. Mark Green and Gail MacColl, 1987), 'Killer Trees'. Reagan later amended this figure to 93%

4 When industrial pollutants finally make the air unbreathable, we will be advised to cover the cities over with plastic domes and air-condition them. Technological optimism is the snake oil of urban-industrialism.

Theodore Roszak (b.1933), U.S. social critic: *Where the Wasteland Ends* (1972), Ch.2

5 The new American finds his challenge and his love in the traffic-choked streets, skies nested in smog, choking with the acids of industry, the screech of rubber and houses leashed in against one another while the townlets wither a time and die.

John Steinbeck (1902–1968), U.S. author: *Travels With Charley: in Search of America* (1961), Pt.2. Steinbeck added, 'This is not offered in criticism but only as observation. And I am sure that, as all pendulums reverse their swing, so eventually will the swollen cities rupture like dehiscent wombs and disperse their children back to the countryside'

See also THE ECOLOGY MOVEMENT; THE ENVIRONMENT

POP ART *see under* ART

POP MUSIC *see under* MUSIC

POPULAR CULTURE

1 Popular art is the dream of society; it does not examine itself.

Margaret Atwood (b.1939), Canadian novelist, poet and critic: 'A Question of Metamorphosis', interview first publ. in *Malahat Review*, No.41,

1977, rep. in *Conversations* (ed. Earl G. Ingersoll, 1990)

2 The bastard form of mass culture is humiliated repetition ... always new books, new programmes, new films, news items, but always the same meaning.

Roland Barthes (1915–1980), French semiologist: *The Pleasure of the Text* (1975), 'Modern'

3 If people must worship, let them worship Madonna rather than McCarthy; if they must be diverted, let them be diverted by MTV rather than bear-baiting.

Julie Burchill (b.1960), British journalist and author: *Damaged Gods* (1986), 'Damaged Gods'

4 Popular art is normally decried as vulgar by the cultivated people of its time; then it loses favor with its original audience as a new generation grows up; then it begins to merge into the softer lighting of 'quaint', and cultivated people become interested in it, and finally it begins to take on the archaic dignity of the primitive.

Northrop Frye (1912–1991), Canadian literary critic: *Anatomy of Criticism* (1957), 'Mythical Phase: Symbol as Archetype'

5 If the artist is not to lose much of his ancient purpose he may have to plunder the popular arts to recover the imagery which is his rightful inheritance.

Richard Hamilton (b.1922), British Pop artist: 'For the Finest Art Try – POP', first publ. in *Gazette* No.1, 1961, rep. in *Collected Words 1953–1982* (1982)

6 There is no comparing the brutality and cynicism of today's pop culture with that of forty years ago: from *High Noon* to *Robocop* is a long descent.

Charles Krauthammer (b.1950), U.S. editor and columnist: in the *International Herald Tribune* (Paris), 31 Oct. 1990

7 The mistake which most critics make is to persist in trying to evaluate pop culture as if it were something else: the equivalent of insisting on considering a bicycle as if it were a horse.

George Melly (b.1926), British jazz musician, critic and author: introduction to *Revolt into Style* (1970)

8 Popular culture is the new Babylon, into which so much art and intellect now flow. It is our imperial sex theater, supreme temple of the western eye. We live in the age of idols. The pagan past, never dead, flames again in our mystic hierarchies of stardom.

Camille Paglia (b.1947), U.S. author and critic: *Sexual Personae* (1990), Ch.4

9 The fact is popular art dates. It grows quaint. How many people feel strongly about Gilbert and Sullivan today compared to those who felt strongly in 1890?

Stephen Sondheim (b.1930), U.S. composer and lyricist: in the *International Herald Tribune* (Paris), 20 June 1989

10 The violent illiteracies of the graffiti, the clenched silence of the adolescent, the nonsense-cries from the stage-happening, are resolutely strategic. The insurgent and the freak-out have broken off discourse with a cultural system which they despise as a cruel, antiquated fraud. They will not bandy words with it. Accept, even momentarily, the conventions of literate linguistic exchange, and you are caught in the net of the old values, of the grammars that can condescend or enslave.

George Steiner (b.1929), French-born U.S. critic and novelist: *In Bluebeard's Castle* (1971), Ch.4

11 All forms of pop culture go through doldrums; they catch cold when society sneezes.

Bruce Sterling (b.1954), U.S. science fiction author: preface to *Burning Chrome* by William Gibson (1986)

12 We now have a whole culture based on the assumption that people know nothing and so anything can be said to them.

Stephen Vizinczey (b.1933), Hungarian novelist and critic: book review in *The Observer* (London), 24 June 1990

13 Nobody seriously questions the principle that it is the function of mass culture to maintain public morale, and certainly nobody in the mass audience objects to having his morale maintained.

Robert Warshow (1917–1955), U.S. author: 'The Gangster as Tragic Hero', first publ. in *Partisan Review* (New Brunswick, N.J.), 1948, rep. in *The Immediate Experience* (1970)

See also ART: POP ART; MUSIC: ROCK & POP

POPULARITY

1 Everybody hates me because I'm so universally liked.

Peter De Vries (1910–1993), U.S. author: the narrator (Joe Sandwich), in *The Vale of Laughter* (1967), Pt.1, Ch.1

2 I'd like to be a queen of people's hearts, in people's hearts, but I don't see myself being Queen of this country.

Diana, Princess of Wales (1961–1997): interview on *Panorama*, BBC1, 20 Nov. 1995, publ. in *The Times* (London), 21 Nov. 1995

3 What most people in our culture mean by being lovable is essentially a mixture between being popular and having sex appeal.

Erich Fromm (1900–1980), U.S. playwright: *The Art of Loving* (1956), Ch.1

4 He's liked, but he's not well liked.

Arthur Miller (b.1915), U.S. playwright: Biff, referring to Bernard, his schoolmate, in *Death of a Salesman* (1949), Act 1

POPULATION

1 The purpose of population is not ultimately peopling earth. It is to fill heaven.

Graham Leonard (b.1921), British churchman and bishop of London: speech to Church of England Synod, 10 Feb. 1983, quoted in *The Observer* (London), 13 Feb. 1983

2 We have been God-like in our planned breeding of our domesticated plants and animals, but we have been rabbit-like in our unplanned breeding of ourselves.

A.J. Toynbee (1889–1975), British historian: on population growth, in speech to World Food Congress, Washington D.C., quoted in the *National Observer* (Maryland), 10 June 1963

3 Think of the earth as a living organism that is being attacked by billions of bacteria whose numbers double every forty years. Either the host dies, or the virus dies, or both die.

Gore Vidal (b.1925), U.S. novelist and critic: 'Gods and Greens', first publ. in *The Observer* (London), 27 Aug. 1989, rep. in *A View from the Diner's Club* (1991)

PORNOGRAPHY

1 What I wanted to get at is the value difference between pornographic playing-cards when you're a kid, and pornographic playing-cards when you're older. It's that when you're a kid you use the cards as a substitute for a real experience, and when you're older you use real experience as a substitute for the fantasy.

Edward Albee (b.1928), U.S. playwright: Jerry, in *The Zoo Story* (1959)

2 There's only one good test of pornography. Get twelve normal men to read the book, and then ask them, 'Did you get an erection?' If the answer is 'Yes' from a majority of the twelve, then the book is pornographic.

W.H. Auden (1907–1973), Anglo-American poet: *The Table Talk of W.H. Auden* (comp. Alan Ansen, ed. Nicholas Jenkins, 1990), 'March 17, 1947'

3 A widespread taste for pornography means that nature is alerting us to some threat of extinction.

J.G. Ballard (b.1930), British author: *Myths of the Near Future* (1982), 'News from the Sun'

4 Pornography is the quadrophonics of sex. It adds a third and fourth track to the sexual act. It is the hallucination of detail that rules. Science has already habituated us to this microscopics, this excess of the real in its microscopic detail, this voyeurism of exactitude.

Jean Baudrillard (b.1929), French semiologist: *Seduction* (1979; tr.1990), Ch.1

5 Soft core porn ... is a form of eroticised sentimentality.

Angela Carter (1940–1992), British author: 'Ups and Downs for the Babes in Bondage', first publ. in *New Society* (London), 22 Dec. 1977, rep. in *The Faber Book of Pop* (ed. Hanif Kureishi and Jon Savage, 1995), Pt.7

6 Pornographers are the enemies of women only because our contemporary ideology of pornography does not encompass the possibility of change, as if we were the slaves of history and not its makers. ... Pornography is a satire on human pretensions.

Angela Carter: *The Sadeian Woman* (1979), 'Polemical Preface'

7 Pornography is rather like trying to find out about a Beethoven symphony by having somebody tell you about it and perhaps hum a few bars.

Robertson Davies (1913–1995), Canadian novelist and journalist: *The Enthusiasms of Robertson Davies* (1990), 'The Table Talk of Robertson Davies'

8 The utopian male concept which is the premise of male pornography is this – since manhood is established and confirmed over and against the brutalized bodies of women, men need not aggress against each other; in other words, women absorb male aggression so that men are safe from it.

Andrea Dworkin (b.1946), U.S. feminist critic: 'The Root Cause', speech, 26 Sept. 1975, Massachusetts Institute of Technology, publ. in *Our Blood* (1976), Ch.9

9 Women, for centuries not having access to pornography and now unable to bear looking at the muck on the supermarket shelves, are astonished. Women do not believe that men believe what pornography says about women. But they do. From the worst to the best of them, they do.

Andrea Dworkin: *Pornography* (1981), Ch.5

10 Those Romans who perpetrated the rape of the Sabines, for example, did not work themselves up for the deed by screening *Debbie Does Dallas*, and the monkish types who burned a million or so witches in the Middle Ages had

almost certainly not come across *Boobs and Buns* or related periodicals.

Barbara Ehrenreich (b.1941), U.S. author and columnist: 'Our Neighborhood Porn Committee', first publ. in *Mother Jones*, 1986, rep. in *The Worst Years of Our Lives* (1991)

11 It's red hot, mate. I hate to think of this sort of book getting in the wrong hands. As soon as I've finished this, I shall recommend they ban it.

Tony Hancock (1924–1968), British comedian: 'The Missing Page', *Hancock's Half-Hour*, BBC, 26 Feb. 1960 (series scripted by Ray Galton and Alan Simpson)

12 Much of what *Playboy* is really all about is the projection of the adolescent fantasies I have never really lost. The boy has been father to the man.

Hugh Hefner (b.1926), U.S. publisher: quoted in *Hefner* by Frank Brady (1974), Ch.11

13 Pornography is literature designed to be read with one hand.

Angela Lambert (b.1940), British journalist: in the *Independent on Sunday* (London), 18 Feb. 1990

14 The pornography of violence of course far exceeds, in volume and general acceptance, sexual pornography, in this Puritan land of ours. Exploiting the apocalypse, selling the holocaust, is a pornography. ... For the ultimate selling job on ultimate violence one must read those works of fiction issued by our government as manuals of civil defense, in which ... you learn that there's nothing to be afraid of if you've stockpiled lots of dried fruit.

Ursula K. Le Guin (b.1929), U.S. author: 'Facing It', speech, Dec. 1982, Portland Fellowship of Reconciliation, Maine, publ. in *Dancing at the Edge of the World* (1989)

15 If pornography is part of your sexuality, then you have no right to your sexuality.

Catharine A. MacKinnon (b.1946), U.S. lawyer and critic: quoted in the *San Francisco Examiner*, 29 Nov. 1992

16 There's a subterranean impetus towards pornography so powerful that half the business world is juiced by the sort of half sex that one finds in advertisements.

Norman Mailer (b.1923), U.S. author: 'Petty Notes on some Sex in America', interview first publ. in *Playboy* (Chicago), 1962–3, rep. in *Cannibals and Christians* (1966)

17 Obscenity is a cleansing process, whereas pornography only adds to the murk.

Henry Miller (1891–1980), U.S. author: interview in *Writers at Work* (Second Series, ed. George Plimpton, 1963). Miller is quoted as saying, 'I am for obscenity and against pornography'

18 Pornography is human imagination in tense

theatrical action; its violations are a protest against the violations of our freedom by nature.

Camille Paglia (b.1947), U.S. author and critic: *Sexual Personae* (1990), Ch.1

19 Any pornographic film is better than any ordinary television programme; there is much more reality in the ugliest porno film than in all the programming of a year of television.

Pier Paolo Pasolini (1922–1975), Italian film-maker and essayist: *La fiera letteraria*, 10 Nov. 1974, rep. in *Pasolini Requiem* by David Barth Schwartz (1992), Ch.22

20 What pornographic literature does is precisely to drive a wedge between one's existence as a full human being and one's existence as a sexual being – while in ordinary life a healthy person is one who prevents such a gap from opening up. Normally we don't experience, at least don't want to experience, our sexual fulfillment as distinct from or opposed to our personal fulfillment. But perhaps in part they are distinct, whether we like it or not.

Susan Sontag (b.1933), U.S. essayist: 'The Pornographic Imagination', Sct.3, first publ. in *Partisan Review* (New Brunswick, N.J.), spring 1967, rep. in *Styles of Radical Will* (1969)

21 Pornographers subvert this last, vital privacy; they do our imagining for us. They take away the words that were of the night and shout them over the roof-tops, making them hollow.

George Steiner (b.1929), French-born U.S. critic and novelist: *Language and Silence* (1967), 'Nightworks'

22 The MacDworkinite idea that pornography is violence against women insults the many women who experience actual, brutal, three-dimensional violence in their real lives. ... I certainly would like nothing better than to find a simple, fast route to equality and safety for women. But censoring sexual speech is really a detour or, worse, a dead end.

Nadine Strossen, U.S. civil rights lawyer and author: referring to the anti-pornography stance of Andrea Dworkin and Catharine MacKinnon, in *Defending Pornography* (1995), Ch.13

23 I have all the curiosity of the anthropologist and the frank hope of the voyeur. Porno-graphy's texture is shamelessness; it maps the limits of my shame. ... The message of porno-graphy, by its very existence, is that our sexual selves are real.

Sallie Tisdale (b.1957), U.S. author and feminist: in *Harper's Magazine* (New York), Feb. 1992

24 The only thing pornography has been known to cause is solitary masturbation; as for corrup-tion, the only immediate victim is English prose.

Gore Vidal (b.1925), U.S. novelist and critic: quoted in *The Observer* (London), 28 Jan. 1996

See also Steinem on EROTICISM

POSING

1 Let the world know you as you are, not as you think you should be, because sooner or later, if you are posing, you will forget the pose, and then where are you?

Fanny Brice (1891–1951), U.S. entertainer: quoted in *The Fabulous Fanny* by Norman Katkov (1952), Ch.24

2 We are more afraid of being pretentious than of being dishonest.

Stephen Fry (b.1957), British comic actor and author: quoted in *The Guardian* (London), 31 Dec. 1994

3 Our greatest pretenses are built up not to hide the evil and the ugly in us, but our emptiness. The hardest thing to hide is something that is not there.

Eric Hoffer (1902–1983), U.S. philosopher: *The Passionate State of Mind* (1955), Aph.217

4 Few persons who have ever sat for a portrait can have felt anything but inferior while the process is going on.

Anthony Powell (b.1905), British novelist: quoted in *The Observer* (London), 9 Jan. 1983

POSITIVISM

1 Positivism has not only been a philosophy or a methodology; it has been one of those *schools of suspicion* that the modern era has seen grow and prosper.

Pope John Paul II [Karol Wojtyla] (b.1920), Polish ecclesiastic: *Crossing the Threshold of Hope* (1994), '"Proof": Is It Still Valid?'

2 The positivist is really the secret blood brother of the dogmatic theologian. The one nails his literalism to creed and scripture, the other to empirical verification. The one dismisses whatever lacks doctrinal authority, the other whatever lacks empirical fact.

Theodore Roszak (b.1933), U.S. social critic: *Where the Wasteland Ends* (1972), Ch.11

POSSESSIONS

1 Americans are uneasy with their possessions, guilty about power, all of which is difficult for Europeans to perceive because they are themselves so truly materialistic, so versed in the uses of power.

Joan Didion (b.1934), U.S. essayist: '7000 Romaine, Los Angeles' (1967), rep. in *Slouching Towards Bethlehem* (1968)

2 People who get through life dependent on other people's possessions are always the first to lecture you on how little possessions count.
Ben Elton (b.1959), British author and comic: *Stark* (1989), 'Strategic Decisions'

3 Possession denies independent existence. To have is to refuse to be.
Emmanuel Levinas (b.1905), French Jewish philosopher: 'Ethics and Spirit' (1952), rep. in *Difficult Freedom* (1990), Pt.1

See also MATERIALISM

POSSIBILITY

1 Today Americans are overcome not by the sense of endless possibility but by the banality of the social order they have erected against it.
Christopher Lasch (1932–1994), U.S. historian: *The Culture of Narcissism* (1979), Ch.1, 'The Therapeutic Sensibility'

2 I am neither an optimist nor pessimist, but a possibilist.
Max Lerner (1902–1992), U.S. author and columnist: entry in *Who's Who in America* (1992)

3 The becoming of man is the history of the exhaustion of his possibilities.
Susan Sontag (b.1933), U.S. essayist: *Styles of Radical Will* (1969), '"Thinking Against Oneself": Reflections on Cioran'

See also Steiner on LANGUAGE: GRAMMAR, SPELLING & PUNCTUATION; POTENTIAL

POSTERITY

1 The flattery of posterity is not worth much more than contemporary flattery, which is worth nothing.
Jorge Luis Borges (1899–1986), Argentinian author: *Dreamtigers* (1960), 'Dead Men's Dialogue'

2 History will absolve me.
(*La historia me absolverá.*)
Fidel Castro (b.1926), Cuban revolutionary, premier: *La Historia Me Absolverá* (pamphlet, 1953). Castro spoke the words during his trial in 1953, referring to his unsuccessful assault on the Moncada barracks. Though sentenced to fifteen years' imprisonment, he was released under an amnesty within a year and returned from exile in 1958 to oust the Batista régime and assume power

3 Men of genius are not to be analyzed by commonplace rules. The rest of us who have been or are leaders, more commonplace in our quality, will do well to remember two things. One is *never to forget posterity when devising a policy*. The other is *never to think of posterity when making a speech*.
Robert Menzies (1894–1978), Australian Liberal politician and prime minister: *The Measure of the Years* (1970), Ch.1

POSTMODERNISM

1 Postmodernism is, almost by definition, a transitional cusp of social, cultural, economic and ideological history when modernism's high-minded principles and preoccupations have ceased to function, but before they have been replaced with a totally new system of values. It represents a moment of suspension before the batteries are recharged for the new millennium, an acknowledgment that preceding the future is a strange and hybrid interregnum that might be called the last gasp of the past.
Gilbert Adair, British author and critic: in *The Sunday Times* (London), 21 April 1991

2 Postmodernity is the simultaneity of the destruction of earlier values and their reconstruction. It is renovation within ruination.
Jean Baudrillard (b.1929), French semiologist: *Cool Memories* (1987; tr.1990), Ch.4

3 I think the adjective 'post-modernist' really means 'mannerist'. Books about books is fun but frivolous.
Angela Carter (1940–1992), British author: *Novelists in Interview* (ed. John Haffenden, 1985)

4 Postmodernism is among other things a sick joke at the expense of ... revolutionary avant-gardism.
Terry Eagleton (b.1943), British critic: 'Capitalism, Modernism and Postmodernism' (1985), rep. in *Against The Grain* (1986), Ch.9

5 The postmodern reply to the modern consists of recognizing that the past, since it cannot really be destroyed, because its destruction leads to silence, must be revisited: but with irony, not innocently. I think of the post-modern attitude as that of a man who loves a very cultivated woman and knows he cannot say to her, 'I love you madly', because he knows that she knows (and that she knows that he knows) that these words have already been written by Barbara Cartland. Still, there is a solution. He can say, 'As Barbara Cartland would put it, I love you madly.'
Umberto Eco (b.1932), Italian semiologist and novelist: *Reflections on the Name of the Rose* (1983; tr.1984), 'Postmodernism, Irony, the Enjoyable'

6 Post-modernism is modernism with the optimism taken out.
Robert Hewison (b.1943), British cultural historian: *The Heritage Industry* (1987), Ch.6

7 A work can become modern only if it is first postmodern. Postmodernism thus understood is not modernism at its end but in the nascent state, and this state is constant.

Jean François Lyotard (b.1924), French philosopher: 'Answering the Question: What is Postmodernism?', first publ. in *Critique* (Paris), April 1982, rep. in *The Postmodern Condition: A Report on Knowledge* (1979, rev.1986)

8 Postmodernism refuses to privilege any one perspective, and recognizes only difference, never inequality, only fragments, never conflict.

Elizabeth Wilson (b.1936), British journalist and author: *Hallucinations* (1988), Ch.23

POTENTIAL

1 Knowing what you can *not* do is more important than knowing what you can do. In fact, that's good taste.

Lucille Ball (1911–1989), U.S. actress and producer: quoted in *The Real Story of Lucille Ball* by Eleanor Harris (1954), Ch.1

2 I think that if you love passionately, you can hate passionately. I think everyone is capable of all things – we all have the potential for great evil and great good.

Nick Cave (b.1957), Australian musician and author: interview in *Dazed and Confused* (London), Feb.1996

3 And what is the potential man, after all? Is he not the sum of all that is human? *Divine*, in other words?

Henry Miller (1891–1980), U.S. author: 'A Devil in Paradise' (1956), rep. in *Big Sur and the Oranges of Hieronymus Bosch* (1957), Pt.3, as 'Paradise Lost'

4 Our being is subject to all the chances of life. There are so many things we are capable of, that we could be or do. The potentialities are so great that we never, any of us, are more than one-fourth fulfilled.

Katherine Anne Porter (1890–1980), U.S. short-story writer and novelist: interview in *Writers at Work* (Second Series, ed. George Plimpton, 1963)

See also POSSIBILITY

POVERTY

1 Poor illiterate boys from the slums and starving children from southern villages obviously know all they need to know even before they begin to speak. Those who never learn to read have a clear uncluttered mind: they do not have to forget what others have to learn. How old are the little boys in Naples who steal bags from parked cars and procure prostitutes for sailors on shore-leave? They are born decrepit.

Luigi Barzini (1908–1984), Italian author: *The Italians* (1964), Ch.10

2 The poverty of our century is unlike that of any other. It is not, as poverty was before, the result of natural scarcity, but of a set of priorities imposed upon the rest of the world by the rich. Consequently, the modern poor are not pitied ... but written off as trash. The twentieth-century consumer economy has produced the first culture for which a beggar is a reminder of nothing.

John Berger (b.1926), British author and critic: 'The Soul and the Operator', first publ. in *Expressen* (Stockholm), 19 March 1990, rep. in *Keeping a Rendezvous* (1992)

3 The poverty from which I have suffered could be diagnosed as 'Soho' poverty. It comes from having the airs and graces of a genius and no talent.

Quentin Crisp (b.1908), British author: *The Naked Civil Servant* (1968), Ch.7

4 I used to think I was poor. Then they told me I wasn't poor, I was needy. Then they told me it was self-defeating to think of myself as needy, I was deprived. Then they told me deprived was a bad image, I was underprivileged. Then they told me underprivileged was overused, I was disadvantaged. I still don't have a dime. But I sure have a great vocabulary.

Jules Feiffer (b.1929), U.S. cartoonist: cartoon caption, 1965, quoted in *Political Dictionary* by William Safire (1968; rev.1978), 'Disadvantaged'

5 That the poor are invisible is one of the most important things about them. They are not simply neglected and forgotten as in the old rhetoric of reform; what is much worse, they are not seen.

Michael Harrington (1928–1989), U.S. social scientist and author: *The Other America* (1962), Ch.1, Sct.1

6 If a free society cannot help the many who are poor, it cannot save the few who are rich.

John F. Kennedy (1917–1963), U.S. Democratic politician and president: inaugural address, 20 Jan. 1961, Washington D.C., publ. in *Public Papers of the Presidents of the United States: John F. Kennedy, 1961*

7 You don't seem to realize that a poor person who is unhappy is in a better position than a rich person who is unhappy. Because the poor person has hope. He thinks money would help.

Jean Kerr (b.1923), U.S. author and playwright: Sydney, in *Poor Richard* (1963), Act 1

8 In verity ... we are the poor. This humanity we would claim for ourselves is the legacy, not only of the Enlightenment, but of the thousands and thousands of European peasants and poor townspeople who came here bringing their humanity and their sufferings with them. It is the absence of a stable upper class that is responsible for much of the vulgarity of the American scene. Should we blush before the visitor for this deficiency?

Mary McCarthy (1912–1989), U.S. author and critic: 'America the Beautiful', first publ. in *Commentary* (New York), Sept. 1947, rep. in *On the Contrary* (1961)

9 The greatest poverty is not to live
In a physical world, to feel that one's desire
Is too difficult to tell from despair.
Wallace Stevens (1879–1955), U.S. poet: 'Esthètique du Mal', publ. in *Transport to Summer* (1947), Sct.15m

10 Our life of poverty is as necessary as the work itself. Only in heaven will we see how much we owe to the poor for helping us to love God better because of them.
Mother Teresa (1910–1997), Albanian-born Roman Catholic missionary: *A Gift for God* (1975), 'Carriers of Christ's Love'

11 Do we look at the poor with compassion? They are hungry not only for food, they are hungry to be recognised as human beings. They are hungry for dignity and to be treated as we are treated. They are hungry for our love.
Mother Teresa: *A Simple Path* (ed. Lucinda Vardey, 1995), 'The Fruit of Faith is Love'

12 As poverty has been reduced in terms of mere survival, it has become more profound in terms of our way of life.
Raoul Vaneigem (b.1934), Belgian Situationist philosopher: 'Basic Banalities I', first publ. in *Internationale Situationiste* 7, April 1962, rep. in *Situationist International Anthology* (ed. K. Knabb, 1981)

13 At present cats have more purchasing power and influence than the poor of this planet. Accidents of geography and colonial history should no longer determine who gets the fish.
Derek Wall (b.1965), British ecologist: *Getting There* (1990), Ch.1

See also Harrington on DRESS; Trilling on LIBERALS; Vaneigem on WEALTH

POWER

1 Power is not only what you have but what the enemy thinks you have.
Saul Alinsky (1909–1972), U.S. political activist: *Rules for Radicals* (1971), 'Tactics'

2 Power tires only those who do not have it.
Giulio Andreotti (b.1919), Italian Christian Democrat politician and prime minister: reply when asked how he had survived in power so long, quoted in the *Independent on Sunday* (London), 5 April 1992

3 The relationship of morality and power is a very subtle one. Because ultimately power without morality is no longer power.

James Baldwin (1924–1987), U.S. author: in conversation with Nikki Giovanni, 4 Nov. 1971, London, publ. in *A Dialogue* (1973)

4 I call the discourse of power any discourse that engenders blame, hence guilt, in its recipient.
Roland Barthes (1915–1980), French semiologist: 'Leçon', inaugural lecture at Collège de France, 7 Jan. 1977 (1978), rep. in *Barthes: Selected Writings* (1982)

5 Contact with men who wield power and authority still leaves an intangible sense of repulsion. It's very like being in close proximity to faecal matter, the faecal embodiment of something unmentionable, and you wonder what it is made of and when it acquired its historically sacred character.
Jean Baudrillard (b.1929), French semiologist: *Cool Memories* (1987; tr.1990), Ch.3

6 The purpose of getting power is to be able to give it away.
Aneurin Bevan (1897–1960), British Labour politician: quoted in *Aneurin Bevan* by Michael Foot (1962), Vol.I, Ch.1

7 From Paul to Stalin, the popes who have chosen Caesar have prepared the way for Caesars who quickly learn to despise popes.
Albert Camus (1913–1960), French-Algerian philosopher and author: *The Rebel* (1951; tr.1953), Pt.2, 'The Rejection of Salvation'

8 All personal, psychological, social, and institutionalized domination on this earth can be traced back to its source: the phallic identities of men.
Andrea Dworkin (b.1946), U.S. feminist critic: 'The Rape Atrocity and the Boy Next Door', speech, 1 March 1975, State University of New York, Stony Brook, publ. in *Our Blood* (1976), Ch.4

9 Power is not an institution, and not a structure; neither is it a certain strength we are endowed with; it is the name that one attributes to a complex strategical situation in a particular society.
Michel Foucault (1926–1984), French philosopher: *The History of Sexuality*, Vol.I (1976), Pt.4, Ch.2

10 In the United States, though power corrupts, the expectation of power paralyzes.
J.K. Galbraith (b.1908), U.S. economist: 'The United States', publ. in *New York*, 15 Nov. 1971, rep. in *A View from the Stands* (1986)

11 'Power may be at the end of a gun', but sometimes it's also at the end of the shadow or the image of a gun.
Jean Genet (1910–1986), French playwright and novelist: on the notion that armed struggle is the only way to achieve revolutionary change, in *Prisoner of Love* (1986; tr.1989), Pt.1. Mao Zedong asserted that 'political power grows out of the barrel of a gun' (1938)

12 The strongest and most effective [force] in guaranteeing the long-term maintenance of ... power is not violence in all the forms deployed by the dominant to control the dominated, but consent in all the forms in which the dominated acquiese in their own domination.
Maurice Godelier (b.1934), French anthropologist: preface to *The Mental and the Material: Thought Economy and Society* (1986)

13 The exercise of power is determined by thousands of interactions between the world of the powerful and that of the powerless, all the more so because these worlds are never divided by a sharp line: everyone has a small part of himself in both.
Václav Havel (b.1936), Czech playwright and president: *Disturbing the Peace* (1986; tr.1990), Ch.5

14 Power is the great aphrodisiac.
Henry Kissinger (b.1923), U.S. Republican politician and secretary of state: quoted in the *New York Times*, 19 Jan. 1971

15 The quality of the will to power is, precisely, growth. Achievement is its cancellation. To be, the will to power must increase with each fulfillment, making the fulfillment only a step to a further one. The vaster the power gained the vaster the appetite for more.
Ursula K. Le Guin (b.1929), U.S. author: *The Lathe of Heaven* (1971), Ch.9

16 Power? It's like a dead sea fruit. When you achieve it, there's nothing there.
Harold Macmillan (1894–1986), British Conservative politician and prime minister: quoted in Anthony Sampson's *The New Anatomy of Britain* (1971), Ch.37

17 By the power elite, we refer to those political, economic, and military circles which as an intricate set of overlapping cliques share decisions having at least national consequences. In so far as national events are decided, the power elite are those who decide them.
C. Wright Mills (1916–1962), U.S. sociologist: *The Power Elite* (1956), Ch.1, 'The Higher Circles'

18 Power is not a means, it is an end. One does not establish a dictatorship in order to safeguard a revolution; one makes the revolution in order to establish the dictatorship.
George Orwell (1903–1950), British author: O'Brien, in *Nineteen Eighty-four* (1949), Pt.3, Ch.3

19 Power-worship blurs political judgement because it leads, almost unavoidably, to the belief that present trends will continue. Whoever is winning at the moment will always seem to be invincible.
George Orwell: *Shooting an Elephant* (1950), 'Second Thoughts on James Burnham'

20 Power, after all, is not just military strength. It is the social power that comes from democracy, the cultural power that comes from freedom of expression and research, the personal power that entitles every Arab citizen to feel that he or she is in fact a citizen, and not just a sheep in some great shepherd's flock.
Edward Said (b.1935), Lebanese-born U.S. social and literary critic: on Arab 'powerlessness', in 'A Powerless People', publ. in *The Guardian* (London), 25 April 1996

21 You only have power over people so long as you don't take *everything* away from them. But when you've robbed a man of *everything* he's no longer in your power – he's free again.
Alexander Solzhenitsyn (b.1918), Russian novelist: Bobynin, in *The First Circle* (1968), Ch.17

22 Power can be taken, but not given. The process of the taking is empowerment in itself.
Gloria Steinem (b.1934), U.S. feminist writer and editor: 'Far From the Opposite Shore', first publ. in *Ms.* (New York), July 1978 and July/Aug. 1982, rep. in *Outrageous Acts and Everyday Rebellions* (1983)

23 It is difficult to find a reputable American historian who will acknowledge the crude fact that a Franklin Roosevelt, say, wanted to be President merely to wield power, to be famed and to be feared. To learn this simple fact one must wade through a sea of evasions: history as sociology, leaders as teachers, bland benevolence as a motive force, when, finally, power *is* an end to itself, and the instinctive urge to prevail the most important single human trait, the necessary force without which no city was built, no city destroyed.
Gore Vidal (b.1925), U.S. novelist and critic: *Rocking the Boat* (1963), 'Robert Graves and the Twelve Caesars'

24 Powerful men in particular suffer from the delusion that human beings have no memories. I would go so far as to say that the distinguishing trait of powerful men is the psychotic certainty that people forget acts of infamy as easily as their parents' birthdays.
Stephen Vizinczey (b.1933), Hungarian novelist and critic: 'Commentary on a Poem', publ. in *Horizon* (London), Oct. 1976, rep. in *Truth and Lies in Literature* (1986)

See also Todd on PRINCIPLES; Vaneigem on WEALTH

PRAISE

1 Praise out of season, or tactlessly bestowed, can freeze the heart as much as blame.
Pearl S. Buck (1892–1973), U.S. author: *To My Daughters, With Love* (1967), 'First Meeting'

2 One should use praise to recognize what one is not.
Elias Canetti (1905–1994), Austrian novelist and philosopher: *The Secret Heart Of The Clock: Notes, Aphorisms, Fragments 1973–1985* (1991), '1976'

3 I love eulogies. They are the most moving kind of speech because they attempt to pluck meaning from the fog, and on short order, when the emotions are still ragged and raw and susceptible to leaps.
Peggy Noonan (b.1950), U.S. author and presidential speechwriter: *What I Saw at the Revolution* (1990), Ch.13

PRAYER

1 To pray is to pay attention to something or someone other than oneself. Whenever a man so concentrates his attention – on a landscape, a poem, a geometrical problem, an idol, or the True God – that he completely forgets his own ego and desires, he is praying. ... The primary task of the schoolteacher is to teach children, in a secular context, the technique of prayer.
W.H. Auden (1907–1973), Anglo-American poet: *A Certain World* (1970), 'Prayer, Nature of'

2 A childish soul not inoculated with compulsory prayer is a soul open to any religious infection.
Alexander Cockburn (b.1941), Anglo-Irish journalist: 'Heatherdown' (1985), rep. in *Corruptions of Empire* (1988), Pt.1

3 Prayer is translation. A man translates himself into a child asking for all there is in a language he has barely mastered.
Leonard Cohen (b.1934), Canadian singer, poet and novelist: 'F.', in *Beautiful Losers* (1970), Sct.18

4 Prayer is not an old woman's idle amusement. Properly understood and applied, it is the most potent instrument of action.
Mohandas K. Gandhi (1869–1948), Indian political and spiritual leader: *Non-Violence in Peace and War* (1948), Vol.II, Ch.77

5 There is no greater distance than that between a man in prayer and God.
Ivan Illich (b.1926), Austrian-born U.S. theologian and author: *Celebration of Awareness* (1969), Ch.4

6 Our Father which art in heaven
Stay there
And we will stay on earth
Which is sometimes so pretty.
Jacques Prévert (1900–1977), French poet: opening lines of 'Pater Noster', publ. in *Paroles* (1946; rev.1949; tr. Lawrence Ferlinghetti, 1958)

7 I hate it when people pray on the screen. It's not because I hate praying, but whenever I see an actor fold his hands and look up in the spotlight, I'm lost. There's only one other thing in the movies I hate as much, and that's sex. You just can't get in bed or pray to God and convince me on the screen.
Orson Welles (1915–1985), U.S. film-maker and actor: interview in *The Americans* by David Frost (1970), 'Can a Martian Survive by Pretending to be a Leading American Actor?'

See also Szasz on GOD; Todd on PRINCIPLES

PRECEDENT

1 It is in the very nature of things human that every act that has once made its appearance and has been recorded in the history of mankind stays with mankind as a potentiality long after its actuality has become a thing of the past.
Hannah Arendt (1906–1975), German-born U.S. political philosopher: epilogue to *Eichmann in Jerusalem* (1963)

2 Judicial judgment must take deep account ... of the day before yesterday in order that yesterday may not paralyze today.
Felix Frankfurter (1882–1965), U.S. judge: quoted in the *National Observer* (Silver Spring, Md.), 1 March 1965

PREDICTION

1 No one can possibly know what is about to happen: it is happening, each time, for the first time, for the only time.
James Baldwin (1924–1987), U.S. author: 'The Devil Finds Work', Sct.1 (1976), rep. in *The Price of the Ticket* (1985)

2 Legends of prediction are common throughout the whole Household of Man. Gods speak, spirits speak, computers speak. Oracular ambiguity or statistical probability provides loopholes, and discrepancies are expunged by Faith.
Ursula K. Le Guin (b.1929), U.S. author: *The Left Hand of Darkness* (1969), Ch.4

3 The cock that perceives the dawn, that senses in the night, a few moments in advance, the approach of light: what an admirable symbol of intelligence! An intelligence that knows the meaning of History before the event, and does not simply divine it after it has happened.
Emmanuel Levinas (b.1905), French Jewish philosopher: *Difficult Freedom* (1990), Pt.2, 'Messianic Texts'

4 Don't ask what the teacups hold.
I'll tell you: you can bank
on days upon days like windfalls
and more. Don't mope in corners.

David Malouf (b.1934), Australian novelist and poet: 'Four Odes of Horace', publ. in *Bicycle and Other Poems* (1970). The poem is based on Horace's *Odes*, Bk.1, No.9

See also PROPHECY

PREGNANCY

1 Childbearing is glorified in part because women die from it.
Andrea Dworkin (b.1946), U.S. feminist critic: *Pornography* (1981), Ch.2

2 If men were equally at risk from this condition – if they knew their bellies might swell as if they were suffering from end-stage cirrhosis, that they would have to go nearly a year without a stiff drink, a cigarette, or even an aspirin, that they would be subject to fainting spells and unable to fight their way onto commuter trains – then I am sure that pregnancy would be classified as a sexually transmitted disease and abortions would be no more controversial than emergency appendectomies.
Barbara Ehrenreich (b.1941), U.S. author and columnist: *The Worst Years of Our Lives* (1991), 'Their Dilemma and Mine'

3 These wretched babies don't come until they are ready.
Queen Elizabeth II (b.1926), Queen of Great Britain and Northern Ireland: of the imminent birth of her fifth grandchild (the first child of the Duke and Duchess of York), quoted in *Today* (London), 4 Aug. 1988. A girl, Beatrice, was born five days later

4 If pregnancy were a book they would cut the last two chapters.
Nora Ephron (b.1941), U.S. author and journalist: Meryl Streep (Rachel Samstrat), in *Heartburn* (film; screenplay by Nora Ephron adapted from her own novel, directed by Mike Nichols, 1986)

5 If men could get pregnant, abortion would be a sacrament.
Florynce R. Kennedy (b.1916), U.S. lawyer and civil rights activist: quoted by Gloria Steinem in 'The Verbal Karate of Florynce R. Kennedy, Esq.', publ. in *Ms.* (New York), March 1973

6 Pregnancy demonstrates the deterministic character of woman's sexuality. Every pregnant woman has body and self taken over by a chthonian force beyond her control. In the welcome pregnancy, this is a happy sacrifice. But in the unwanted one, initiated by rape or misadventure, it is a horror. Such unfortunate women look directly into nature's heart of darkness. For a fetus is a benign tumor, a vampire who steals in order to live. The so-called miracle of birth is nature getting her own way.
Camille Paglia (b.1947), U.S. author and critic: *Sexual Personae* (1990), Ch.1

See also CHILDBIRTH

ELVIS PRESLEY

1 He moved as if he was sneering with his legs.
Anonymous critic: quoted in *The Fifties* by Peter Lewis (1978), 'Youthquake'

2 Elvis was a hero to most
But he never meant shit to me you see.
Chuck D. (b.1960), U.S. rapper: 'Fight the Power' (theme song to Spike Lee's film *Do The Right Thing*) on the album *Fear of a Black Planet* (Public Enemy, 1990)

3 When I first heard Elvis's voice I just knew that I wasn't going to work for anybody and nobody was gonna be my boss. Hearing him for the first time was like busting out of jail.
Bob Dylan (b.1941), U.S. singer and songwriter: comment on the anniversary of Presley's death, in *U.S.* (New York), Aug. 1987

4 Commercial to the core, Elvis was the kind of singer dear to the heart of the music business. For him to sing a song was to sell a song. His G clef was a dollar sign.
Albert Goldman (1927–1994), U.S. author and critic: *Elvis* (1981), Ch.14

5 Distorting hackneyed words in hackneyed songs
He turns revolt into a style, prolongs
The impulse to a habit of the time.
Thom Gunn, (b.1929), British poet: 'Elvis Presley', publ. in *The Sense of Movement* (1957). The poem gave George Melly the title for his study of the pop arts in Britain: *Revolt into Style* (1970)

6 Elvis' disappearing body is like a flashing event horizon at the edge of the black hole that is America today.
Arthur Kroker (b.1945), **David Cook** (b.1946) and **Marilouise Kroker** (dates unknown), Canadian sociologists: *Panic Encyclopedia* (1989), 'Why Panic?'

7 I'm not putting Elvis down, but he was a shitass, a yellow belly, and I hated the fucker.
Jerry Lee Lewis (b.1935), U.S. rock musician: in *New Musical Express* (London), 1988, quoted in *NME Book of Quotes* (1995), 'Rivals'

8 Elvis transcends his talent to the point of dispensing with it altogether.
Greil Marcus (b.1945), U.S. rock journalist: *Mystery Train* (1976), 'Elvis: Presliad'

9 No-one dares say so, but he was one almighty pain in the arse. He never knew when to stop. It could be 3am, and if he decided to begin a 4-hour conversation, or wanted you to ride snomobiles, or take a plane somewhere to go and buy his favourite hamburgers you just didn't dare say 'no'.

Dee Presley (b.1925), step-mother of Elvis Presley: interview in *A Little Light Friction* by Val Hennessy (1989), 'Dee Presley'

10 I wish not to be given a title or an appointed position. I can and will do more good if I were made a Federal Agent at Large, and I will help best by doing it my way through my communications with people of all ages. First and Foremost I am an entertainer but all I need is the Federal Credentials.

Elvis Presley (1935–1977), U.S. singer: letter, 19 Dec. 1970, to President Nixon, offering Presley's services as a Federal Agent to work to curb drug abuse by young people. Elvis was made an agent of the Bureau of Narcotics and Dangerous Drugs by Nixon, receiving an enamel shield which, according to biographer Albert Goldman, became one of his most treasured possessions

11 I don't aim to let this fame business get me. God gave me a voice. If I turned against God, I'd be finished.

Elvis Presley: quoted in *All You Need is Love* by Tony Palmer (1976), 'Hail! Hail! Rock 'n' Roll!'

See also Moore on MUSIC: BLUES

THE PRESS

1 We may be scum, but at least we're *la crème de la scum.*

Anonymous: Member of the 'Royal Ratpack' – journalists assigned to report on the royal family – quoted in *The Sunday Times* (London), 13 Nov. 1988

2 The press and politicians. A delicate relationship. Too close, and danger ensues. Too far apart and democracy itself cannot function without the essential exchange of information. Creative leaks, a discreet lunch, interchange in the Lobby, the art of the unattributable telephone call, late at night.

Howard Brenton (b.1942) and David Hare (b.1947), British playwrights: Quince, in *Pravda* (1985), Act 1, Sc.4

3 When the seagulls follow the trawler, it is because they think sardines will be thrown into the sea.

Eric Cantona (b.1966), French footballer: remark in May 1995, on the press coverage of his conviction for assault on a hostile fan that January, quoted in *The Guardian* (London), 30 Dec. 1995

4 When I see them around all the time, it is like being raped.

Diana, Princess of Wales (1961–1997): on press photographers, quoted in *The Guardian* (London), 30 Dec. 1995

5 I sometimes compare press officers to riflemen on the Somme – mowing down wave upon wave of distortion, taking out rank upon rank of supposition, deduction and gossip.

Bernard Ingham (b.1932), British government press officer: in *The Independent* (London), 8 Feb. 1990

6 It is impossible to read the daily press without being diverted from reality. You are full of enthusiasm for the eternal verities – life is worth living, and then out of sinful curiosity you open a newspaper. You are disillusioned and wrecked.

Patrick Kavanagh (1905–1967), Irish poet and author: *Collected Pruse* (1967), 'Signposts'

7 There is a terrific disadvantage in not having the abrasive quality of the press applied to you daily. ... Even though we never like it, and even though we wish they didn't write it, and even though we disapprove, there isn't any doubt that we could not do the job at all in a free society without a very, very active press.

John F. Kennedy (1917–1963), U.S. Democratic politician and president: of Khrushchev's control of the Soviet press, quoted in *Kennedy* by Theodore C. Sorensen (1965), Pt.3, Ch.12

8 The job of the press is to encourage debate, not to supply the public with information.

Christopher Lasch (1932–1994), U.S. historian: 'Journalism, Publicity, and the Lost Art of Political Argument', first publ. in the *Gannett Center Journal* (New York), Spring 1990, rep. as 'The Lost Art of Political Argument' in *Harper's Magazine* (New York), Sept. 1990

9 The tabloids are like animals, with their own behavioural patterns. There's no point in complaining about them, any more than complaining that lions might eat you.

David Mellor (b.1949), British Conservative politician: in *The Independent* (London), 3 Nov. 1992. Mellor was forced to resign his government position in 1992 largely as a result of pressure from the British press

10 The rising power of the United States in world affairs...requires, not a more compliant press, but a relentless barrage of facts and criticism. ... Our job in this age, as I see it, is not to serve as cheerleaders for our side in the present world struggle but to help the largest possible number of people to see the realities of the changing and convulsive world in which American policy must operate.

James Reston (b.1909), U.S. journalist: introduction to *The Artillery of the Press* (1966)

See also JOURNALISM; MAGAZINES; NEWSPAPERS

PRESS BARONS

1 In my opinion, any man who can afford to buy a newspaper should not be allowed to own one.

Roy Hattersley (b.1932), British Labour politician: quoted in *Maxwell: the Outsider* by Tom Bower (1988; rev.1991), Ch.13

2 When I fire someone it is like a thunderclap. My primary duty is to hire and fire editors. I treat them like a Field Marshal.

Robert Maxwell (1923–1991), British tycoon: in *The Independent* (London), 13 May 1990

3 He aspired to power instead of influence, and as a result forfeited both.

A.J.P. Taylor (1906–1990), British historian: referring to Lord Northcliffe, in *English History, 1914–1945* (1965), Ch.1. Northcliffe notoriously made *The Times* (London) and other newspapers mouthpieces for his political ambitions

4 [He] has made a fortune from selling excrement and, in the process, has debauched our culture and corrupted our youth, producing a generation of lager louts, sex maniacs and morons.

Francis Wheen, British journalist: referring to Rupert Murdoch, quoted by William Shawcross in the *Evening Standard* (London), 8 Sept. 1992

PRINCIPLES

1 The principles which men give to themselves end by overwhelming their noblest intentions.

Albert Camus (1913–1960), French-Algerian philosopher and author: *The Rebel* (1951; tr.1953), Pt.3, 'State Terrorism and Rational Terror'

2 The proclamation and repetition of first principles is a constant feature of life in our democracy. Active adherence to these principles, however, has always been considered un-American. We recipients of the boon of liberty have always been ready, when faced with discomfort, to discard any and all first principles of liberty, and, further, to indict those who do not freely join with us in happily arrogating those principles.

David Mamet (b.1947), U.S. playwright: *Writing in Restaurants* (1986), 'First Principles'

3 How much better it is to hold great principles without personal animosity than to have no principles and yet to feel enmity.

Oswald Mosley (1896–1980), British fascist leader: *My Life* (1968), Ch.5

4 You don't have power if you surrender all your principles – you have office.

Ron Todd (b.1927), British trade unionist: in *The Daily Telegraph* (London), 17 June 1988

5 The left takes an accepted moral principle, adopts it as its own, and then accuses mainstream society of violating that principle. Examples: racial equality, equality of the sexes, helping poor people, peace as opposed to war, nonviolence generally, freedom of expression, kindness to animals.

Unabomber, U.S. radical: *Industrial Society and Its Future*, 'Oversocialization', Sct.28, publ. in the *Washington Post*, 19 Sept. 1995

6 Americans are willing to go to enormous trouble and expense defending their principles with arms, very little trouble and expense advocating them with words. Temperamentally we are ready to die for certain principles (or, in the case of overripe adults, send youngsters to die), but we show little inclination to advertise the reasons for dying.

E.B. White (1899–1985), U.S. author and editor: 'The Thud of Ideas', first publ. in the *New Yorker*, 23 Sept. 1950, rep. in *Writings from the New Yorker 1927–1976* (ed. Rebecca M. Dale, 1991)

PRISON

1 Prison is a second-by-second assault on the soul, a day-to-day degradation of the self, an oppressive steel and brick umbrella that transforms seconds into hours and hours into days.

Mumia Abu-Jamal (b.1954), U.S. journalist and environmentalist: on being a death-row prisoner, in *Live from Death Row* (1995), Pt.1, 'Nightraiders meet rage'

2 If you want to know who your friends are, get yourself a jail sentence.

Charles Bukowski (1920–1994), U.S. author and poet: *Notes of a Dirty Old Man* (1969), p.166 of City Lights edn. (1973)

3 To assert in any case that a man must be absolutely cut off from society because he is absolutely evil amounts to saying that society is absolutely good, and no-one in his right mind will believe this today.

Albert Camus (1913–1960), French-Algerian philosopher and author: *Resistance, Rebellion and Death* (1961), 'Reflections on the Guillotine'

4 In jail a man has no personality. He is a minor disposal problem and a few entries on reports. Nobody cares who loves or hates him, what he looks like, what he did with his life. Nobody reacts to him unless he gives trouble. Nobody abuses him. All that is asked of him is that he go quietly to the right cell and remain quiet when he gets there. There is nothing to fight against, nothing to be mad at. The jailers are quiet men without animosity or sadism. All this stuff you read about men yelling and screaming, beating against the bars, running spoons along them, guards rushing in with clubs – all that is for the big house. A good jail is one of the quietest places in the world. ... Life in jail is in suspension.

Raymond Chandler (1880–1959), U.S. author: *The Long Goodbye* (1953), Ch.8

5 In prison, those things withheld from and denied to the prisoner become precisely what he wants most of all.
Eldridge Cleaver (b.1935), U.S. black leader and writer: 'On Becoming', written in Folsom Prison, 25 June 1965, publ. in *Soul on Ice* (1968)

6 I see my light come shining
From the west unto the east
Any day now, any day now,
I shall be released.
Bob Dylan (b.1941), U.S. singer and songwriter: 'I Shall Be Released' (song, recorded 1967), on the album *The Basement Tapes* (1975)

7 Attica is a machine for elimination, a form of prodigious stomach, a kidney which consumes, destroys, breaks up and then rejects, and which consumes in order to eliminate what it has already eliminated.
Michel Foucault (1926–1984), French philosopher: on Attica prison, New York, after visiting it in 1974, in interview in *Telos*, No.19, quoted in *The Lives of Michel Foucault* by David Macey (1993), Ch.11

8 We are aware of all the inconvenience of prison, and that it is dangerous when it is not useless. And yet one cannot 'see' how to replace it. It is the detestable solution, which one seems unable to do without.
Michel Foucault: *Discipline and Punish: The Birth of the Prison* (1975), 'Complete and Austere Institutions'

9 *There is a close relationship between flowers and convicts*. The fragility and delicacy of the former are of the same nature as the brutal insensitivity of the latter.
Jean Genet (1910–1986), French playwright and novelist: *The Thief's Journal* (1949; tr.1965)

10 The prisoner is not the one who has committed a crime, but the one who clings to his crime and lives it over and over.
Henry Miller (1891–1980), U.S. author: *Sexus* (1949), Ch.14

11 Prison *is* punishment, it is not *for* punishment.
David Ramsbotham (b.1934), British general and prisons inspector: opposing calls for harsher prison régimes, in interview on the *World at One*, BBC Radio 4, 14 March 1996

12 In order to understand birds
You have to be a convict.
And if you share your bread –
It means your time is done.
Irina Ratushinskaya (b.1954), Russian poet: 'The Sparrows of Butyrki', publ. in *No, I'm Not Afraid* (1986)

13 We tend to send men, under 25, who come from broken homes and did very badly at school because they didn't try very hard and played truant, what one might call yobs. ... These boys will come out bitter, not trained and not fit for work in the community we live in. And they're going to be with us for another 50 years.
Stephen Tumim (b.1930), British judge and chief inspector of prisons: on the typical prison population, interview in *The Guardian* (London), 13 April 1996

14 It isn't true that convicts live like animals: animals have more room to move around.
Mario Vargas Llosa (b.1936), Peruvian novelist: *The Real Life of Alejandro Mayta* (1984; tr.1986), Ch.10

See also Abu-Jamal on TELEVISION

PRIVACY

1 Privacy is not something that I'm merely entitled to, it's an absolute prerequisite.
Marlon Brando (b.1924), U.S. actor: quoted in *Marlon Brando* by David Shipman (1974, rev.1989), Ch.11

2 Who could deny that privacy is a jewel? It has always been the mark of privilege, the distinguishing feature of a truly urbane culture. Out of the cave, the tribal tepee, the pueblo, the community fortress, man emerged to build himself a house of his own with a shelter in it for himself and his diversions. Every age has seen it so. The poor might have to huddle together in cities for need's sake, and the frontiersman cling to his neighbors for the sake of protection. But in each civilization, as it advanced, those who could afford it chose the luxury of a withdrawing-place.
Phyllis McGinley (1905–1978), U.S. poet and author: *The Province of the Heart* (1959), 'A Lost Privilege'

3 May we agree that private life is irrelevant? Multiple, mixed, ambiguous at best – out of it we try to fashion the crystal clear, the singular, the absolute, and that is what *is* relevant; that is what matters.
May Sarton (b.1912), U.S. poet and novelist: Hilary Stevens, in *Mrs Stevens Hears the Mermaids Singing* (1965), Pt.2

PRIVILEGE

1 There are some things in which, by the decree of the Almighty, the rich are less privileged. They've no privileges in relation to fresh air; they've no privileges in relation to sea-bathing. Shortly they'll have to discover that they've no real privilege in relation to justice.

Lord Goodman (1913–1995), British lawyer and public figure: interview in *Singular Encounters* by Naim Attallah (1990), 'Lord Goodman'

2 I was born with a plastic spoon in my mouth.
Pete Townshend (b.1945), British rock musician: 'Substitute' (song) on the album *My Generation* (The Who, 1965)

3 If you don't have a policeman to stop traffic and let you walk across the street like you are somebody, how are you going to know you are somebody?
John C. White (b.1924), U.S. Democratic politician: on the perks of working in Washington D.C., in the *International Herald Tribune* (Paris), 23 March 1992

PROBLEMS

1 I have yet to see any problem, however complicated, which, when you looked at it in the right way, did not become still more complicated.
Poul Anderson (b.1926), U.S. science fiction writer: in the *New Scientist* (London), 25 Sept. 1969

2 The truth is that we live out our lives putting off all that can be put off; perhaps we all know deep down that we are immortal and that sooner or later all men will do and know all things.
Jorge Luis Borges (1899–1986), Argentinian author: *Labyrinths* (1956; tr.1962), 'Funes the Memorious'

3 I am immensely and continuously conscious of a world of nuclear bombs, of vast hunger, of curable injustice, of a meretricious press and cheapjack television, of perilous and apparently endless international division, of unreasonable cruelty and suffering for which almost nobody cares, and of my own silly efforts to make money to provide me with irrelevant comforts or necessities like drink and to ensure some measure of security for my family. And I know that it is not the answer, because there is truthfully only one answer, which is absolute pacifism and absolute communism – not in the dreary dogmatic party-political sense, but in the sense that my father would have called religious: the sense of mortal community. Not only do I know it; I knew it all along.
James Cameron (1911–1985), British journalist: *Point of Departure* (1967), Ch.4

4 I thought a lot about our nation and what I should do as president. And Sunday night before last, I made a speech about two problems of our country – energy and malaise.
Jimmy Carter (b.1924), U.S. Democratic politician and president: speech at town meeting, 31 July 1979, Bardstown, Kentucky, publ. in *Public Papers of the*

Presidents of the United States: Jimmy Carter, 1979. The speech referred to by Carter, broadcast on 15 July, from the White House, did not include the word *malaise*

5 But Jesus, when you don't have any money, the problem is food. When you have money, it's sex. When you have both, it's health, you worry about getting ruptured or something. If everything is simply jake then you're frightened of death.
J.P. Donleavy (b.1926), U.S. author: O'Keefe, in *The Ginger Man* (1955), Ch.5

6 It is characteristic of all deep human problems that they are not to be approached without some humor and some bewilderment.
Freeman Dyson (b.1923), British-born U.S. physicist and author: *Disturbing the Universe* (1979), Pt.1, Ch.1

7 Any solution to a problem changes the problem.
R.W. Johnson (b.1916), U.S. journalist and newspaper executive: in *The Washingtonian* (Washington D.C.), Nov. 1979

8 The problems of the world, AIDS, cancer, nuclear war, pollution, are, finally, no more solvable than the problem of a tree which has borne fruit: the apples are overripe and they are falling – what can be done? ... *Nothing* can be done, and nothing needs to be done. Something *is* being done – the organism is preparing to rest.
David Mamet (b.1947), U.S. playwright: *Writing in Restaurants* (1986), 'Decay: Some Thoughts for Actors'

9 The problems of this world are only truly solved in two ways: by extinction or duplication.
Susan Sontag (b.1933), U.S. essayist: *I, Etcetera* (1978), 'The Dummy'

10 Somehow we should learn to know that our problems are our most precious possessions. They are the raw materials of our salvation: no problem, no redemption.
Laurens van der Post (b.1906), South African writer and philosopher: *A Walk with a White Bushman* (1986), p.71 of Chatto & Windus edn.

PROCREATION

1 Sperm is a bandit in its pure state.
(*Le spermatozoïde est le bandit à l'état pur.*)
E.M. Cioran (1911–1995), Rumanian-born French philosopher: *Syllogismes de L'Amertune* (1952), 'Aux Sources du Vide'

2 Media mystifications should not obfuscate a simple, perceivable fact; Black teenage girls do not create poverty by having babies. Quite the contrary, they have babies at such a young age

precisely because they are poor – because they do not have the opportunity to acquire an education, because meaningful, well-paying jobs and creative forms of recreation are not accessible to them ... because safe, effective forms of contraception are not available to them.

Angela Davis (b.1944), U.S. political activist: 'Facing Our Common Foe,' speech, 15 Nov. 1987, rep. in *Women, Culture and Politics* (1989)

3 We've done our duty to civilization: We've procreated and now we can die.

Paul Mazursky (b.1930), U.S. film-maker: Nick Fifer (Woody Allen), in *Scenes from a Mall* (film; screenplay by Roger L. Simon and Paul Mazursky, directed by Paul Mazursky, 1991)

4 It is so characteristic, that just when the mechanics of reproduction are so vastly improved, there are fewer and fewer people who know how the music should be played.

Ludwig Wittgenstein (1889–1951), Austrian-born British philosopher: conversation in 1949, publ. in *Personal Recollections* (ed. Rush Rhees, 1981), Ch.6

PROFESSIONALS

1 C'mon, guys, nobody wants this. We're supposed to be fuckin' professionals.

Quentin Tarantino (b.1958), U.S. film-maker: Mr Pink (Steve Buscemi), as the gang-members point guns at each other, in *Reservoir Dogs* (film; written and directed by Quentin Tarantino, 1992)

2 My objective is to be the ultimate professional. Regardless of whatever happens, the job has to be done. That's what being a professional is.

Mike Tyson (b.1966), U.S. boxer: quoted in the *New York Times*, 28 June 1988

PROFIT

1 A corporate executive's responsibility is to make as much money for the stockholders as possible, as long as he operates within the rules of the game. When an executive decides to take action for reasons of social responsibility, he is taking money from someone else – from the stockholders, in the form of lower dividends; from the employees, in the form of lower wages; or from the consumer, in the form of higher prices.

Milton Friedman (b.1912), U.S. economist: introduction to *There's No Such Thing as a Free Lunch* (1975)

2 What is a man if he is not a thief who openly charges as much as he can for the goods he sells?

Mohandas K. Gandhi (1869–1948), Indian political and spiritual leader: *Non-Violence in Peace and War* (1949), Vol.II, Ch.124

3 There is no secret strategy other than to make money.

Robert Maxwell (1923–1991), British tycoon: comment, 1986, on his intricate financial dealings, quoted in *Maxwell: The Outsider* by Tom Bower (1988; rev.1991), Ch.14

PROGRESS

1 It's the same each time with progress. First they ignore you, then they say you're mad, then dangerous, then there's a pause and then you can't find anyone who disagrees with you.

Tony Benn (b.1925), British Labour politician: quoted in *The Observer* (London), 6 Oct. 1991

2 Nothing recedes like progress.

e e cummings (1894–1962), U.S. poet: 'Jottings', publ. in *Wake*, No.10, 1951, rep. in *A Miscellany* (ed. George J. Firmage, 1958)

3 Perhaps the best definition of progress would be the continuing efforts of men and women to narrow the gap between the convenience of the powers that be and the unwritten charter.

Nadine Gordimer (b.1923), South African author: 'Speak Out: The Necessity for Protest', lecture, 11 Aug. 1971, University of Natal, South Africa, publ. in *The Essential Gesture* (ed. Stephen Clingman, 1988). Gordimer was referring to a passage by Mohandas K. Gandhi in *Satyagraha in South Africa* (rev.1928): 'The convenience of the powers that be is the law in the final analysis'

4 Progress everywhere today does seem to come so *very* heavily disguised as Chaos.

Joyce Grenfell (1910–1979), British actress and writer: *Stately as a Galleon* (1978), 'English Lit.'

5 Enthusiastic partisans of the idea of progress are in danger of failing to recognize ... the immense riches accumulated by the human race. ... By underrating the achievements of the past, they devalue all those which still remain to be accomplished.

Claude Lévi-Strauss (b.1908), French anthropologist: *Tristes Tropiques* (1955), Ch.38

See also Camus on INJUSTICE

PROJECTS

1 All this will not be finished in the first hundred days. Nor will it be finished in the first thousand days, nor in the life of this administration, nor even perhaps in our lifetime on this planet. But let us begin.

John F. Kennedy (1917–1963), U.S. Democratic politician and president: describing his programme of reforms in inaugural address, 20 Jan. 1961, Washington D.C., publ. in prologue to *A Thousand Days* by Arthur M. Schlesinger Jr. (1965). Kennedy's administration lasted a little over 1,000 days, as described in Schlesinger's account

2 I want to see us build a country that is at ease with itself, a country that is confident, and a country that is prepared and willing to make the changes necessary to provide a better quality of life for all our citizens. I don't promise you that it will be easy, and I don't promise you that it will be quick, but I believe it is an immensely worthwhile job. Now, if you will forgive me, because it will be neither easy nor quick, I will go into Number 10 straight away and make a start right now.

John Major (b.1943), British Conservative politician and prime minister: speech, outside No.10 Downing Street, 28 Nov. 1990, after winning the election for the leadership of the Conservative Party, thus becoming Prime Minister, quoted in *John Major* by Nesta Wyn Ellis (1991), Ch.1

3 In case I conk out, this is provisionally what I have to do: I must clarify obscurities; I must make clearer definite ideas or dissociations. I must find a verbal formula to combat the rise of brutality – the principle of order versus the split atom.

Ezra Pound (1885–1972), U.S. poet and critic: interview in *Writers at Work* (Second Series, ed. George Plimpton, 1963)

4 The road to hell is paved with works-in-progress.

Philip Roth (b.1933), U.S. author: in the *New York Times Book Review*, 15 July 1979

PROMISCUITY

1 To sleep around is absolutely wrong for a woman; it's degrading and it completely ruins her personality. Sooner or later it will destroy all that is feminine and beautiful and idealistic in her.

Barbara Cartland (b.1901), British novelist: interview in *Speaking Frankly* by Wendy Leigh (1978)

2 What happens is that, as with drugs, he needs a stronger shot each time, and women are just women. The consumption of one woman is the consumption of all. You can't double the dose.

Ian Fleming (1908–1964), British author: describing a man's progress from woman to woman, in notebook entry, quoted in *The Life of Ian Fleming* by John Pearson (1966), Ch.8, Sct.1

3 Certainly my sexual partners are too numerous to count, I often can't remember whether I *did* or *didn't* when I see men grinning familiarly across rooms or at parties, but then I say to myself that if I *did* and I can't remember then it couldn't have been a very big deal, I don't hold it against them. I've *never* been totally indiscriminate, occasionally I have been known to leap out of strange beds and hop on the 49 bus in the middle of the action when things have proved insipid.

Germaine Greer (b.1939), Australian feminist writer: interview in *A Little Light Friction* by Val Hennessy (1989), 'Germaine Greer'

4 I have known a number of Don Juans who were good studs and who cavorted between the sheets without a psychiatrist to guide them. But most of the busy love-makers I knew were looking for masculinity rather than practicing it. They were fellows of dubious lust.

Ben Hecht (1893–1964), U.S. journalist, author and screenwriter: of sex in Hollywood, in *A Child of the Century* (1954), Bk.5, 'Don Juan in Hollywood'. Of Don Juan's 'conquests', Hecht noted 'a similar lack': 'Their female sexuality was nearly all in their clothes, their mannerisms and their reputations. ... The ladies hopping from lover to lover brought more ambition to bed than passion'

5 *Si non oscillas, noli tintinnare.*
(If you don't swing, don't ring.)

Hugh Hefner (b.1926), U.S. publisher: sign in the Playboy Mansion, Chicago, quoted in *Hefner* by Frank Brady (1974), Ch.1

6 You were born with your legs apart. They'll send you to the grave in a Y-shaped coffin.

Joe Orton (1933–1967), British playwright: Dr Prentice to his wife, in *What the Butler Saw* (1969), Act 1

7 When sexual indulgence has reduced a man to the shape of Lord Hailsham, sexual continence involves no more than a sense of the ridiculous.

Reginald Paget (1908–1990), British Labour politician: speech, 17 June 1963, House of Commons, during a debate on the Profumo scandal, quoted in *The Fine Art of Political Wit* by Leon Harris (1964), Ch.12

8 Promiscuity in men may cheapen love but sharpen thought. Promiscuity in women is illness, a leakage of identity. The promiscuous woman is self-contaminated and incapable of clear ideas. She has ruptured the ritual integrity of her body.

Camille Paglia (b.1947), U.S. author and critic: *Sexual Personae* (1990), Ch.1

9 If you can't be with the one you love,
Love the one you're with.

Stephen Stills (b.1945), U.S. rock musician: 'Love the One You're With' (song) on the album *Stephen Stills* (1970). The lyrics recall the 1947 song by Yip Harburg, 'When I'm Not Near the Girl I Love': 'When I'm not near the girl I love, I love the girl I'm near'

10 The right to have sex, even to look for it, has been so stringently denied to gays for so many centuries that the drive toward sexual freedom remains a bright, throbbing banner in the fierce winds whipping over the ghetto.

Edmund White (b.1940), U.S. author: 'Sexual Culture', first publ. in *Vanity Fair*, 1983, rep. in *The Burning Library* (1994)

See also Pasolini on THE PERMISSIVE SOCIETY

PROPAGANDA

1 Propaganda is a soft weapon; hold it in your hands too long, and it will move about like a snake, and strike the other way.
Jean Anouilh (1910–1987), French playwright: Warwick, in *The Lark* (1953; adapted by Lillian Hellman, 1955)

2 Propaganda has a bad name, but its root meaning is simply to disseminate through a medium, and all writing therefore is propaganda for *something*. It's a seeding of the self in the consciousness of others.
Elizabeth Drew (1887–1965), Anglo-American author and critic: *Poetry: A Modern Guide to Its Understanding and Enjoyment* (1959), Pt.2, Ch.10

3 All propaganda or popularization involves a putting of the complex into the simple, but such a move is instantly deconstructive. For if the complex *can* be put into the simple, then it cannot be as complex as it seemed in the first place; and if the simple can be an adequate medium of such complexity, then it cannot after all be as simple as all that.
Terry Eagleton (b.1943), British critic: *Against The Grain* (1986), Ch.10, 'The Critic as Clown'

4 The successor to politics will be propaganda. Propaganda, not in the sense of a message or ideology, but as the impact of the whole technology of the times.
Marshall McLuhan (1911–1980), Canadian communications theorist: quoted in *Maclean's* (Toronto), June 1971

5 In our country the lie has become not just a moral category but a pillar of the State.
Alexander Solzhenitsyn (b.1918), Russian novelist: of the U.S.S.R., quoted in *The Observer* (London), 29 Dec. 1974

6 Words that are saturated with lies or atrocity, do not easily resume life.
George Steiner (b.1929), French-born U.S. critic and novelist: 'K' (1963), rep. in *Language and Silence* (1967)

PROPHECY

1 Man has an incurable habit of not fulfilling the prophecies of his fellow men.
Alistair Cooke (b.1908), British broadcaster and journalist: *Talk About America* (1968), Ch.8

2 Prophecy today is hardly the romantic business that it used to be. The old tools of the trade, like the sword, the hair shirt, and the long fast in the wilderness, have given way to more contemporary, mundane instruments of doom – the book, the picket and the petition, the sit-in … at City Hall.
Jane Kramer (b.1938), U.S. author: *Off Washington Square* (1963), 'The Ranks and Rungs of Mrs Jacobs' Ladder'

3 Monotheism has not only a horror of idols, but a nose for false prophecy. A special patience – Judaism – is required to refuse all premature messianic claims.
Emmanuel Levinas (b.1905), French Jewish philosopher: 'Judaism and the Present' (1969), rep. in *Difficult Freedom* (1990), Pt.5

4 Since the time of the French Revolution, while the moral surface of prophetical protest has been skimmed by modern radicalism, its religious vision has been transmuted into purely secular ideologies. The thunder of Amos still reverberates in the pronouncements of Marx – but now the poetic ecstasy has been flattened into power political prose.
Theodore Roszak (b.1933), U.S. social critic: *Where the Wasteland Ends* (1972), Ch.3

PROPHETS

1 The people who were honored in the Bible were the false prophets. It was the ones we call the prophets who were jailed and driven into the desert, and so on.
Noam Chomsky (b.1928), U.S. linguist and political analyst: interview in *The Guardian* (London), 23 Nov. 1992

2 And I'll tell it and think it and speak it and
   breathe it,
And reflect it from the mountain so all souls
   can see it,
Then I'll stand on the ocean until I start
   sinkin',
But I'll know my song well before I start
   singin',
And it's a hard, it's a hard, it's a hard, it's a
   hard,
It's a hard rain's a-gonna fall.
Bob Dylan (b.1941), U.S. singer and songwriter: 'A Hard Rain's A-Gonna Fall' (song) on the album *The Freewheelin' Bob Dylan* (1963)

3 Fear prophets … and those prepared to die for the truth, for as a rule they make many others die with them, often before them, at times instead of them.
(*Temi … i profeti e coloro disposti a morire per la verità, di solito fan morire moltissimi con loro, spesso prima di loro, talvolta al posto loro.*)

Umberto Eco (b.1932), Italian semiologist and novelist: Brother William, in *The Name of the Rose* (1980; tr.1983), 'Seventh Day: Night (2)'

4 The prophet who fails to present a bearable alternative and yet preaches doom is part of the trap that he postulates. Not only does he picture us caught in a tremendous man-made or God-made trap from which there is no escape, but we must also listen to him day in, day out, describe how the trap is inexorably closing. To such prophecies the human race, as presently bred and educated and situated, is incapable of listening. So some dance and some immolate themselves as human torches; some take drugs and some artists spill their creativity in sets of randomly placed dots on a white ground.

Margaret Mead (1901–1978), U.S. anthropologist: introduction to *Culture and Commitment* (1970)

5 There is no question but that if Jesus Christ, or a great prophet from another religion, were to come back today, he would find it virtually impossible to convince anyone of his credentials ... despite the fact that the vast evangelical machine on American television is predicated on His imminent return among us sinners.

Peter Ustinov (b.1921), British actor, writer and director: in *The Independent* (London), 25 Feb. 1989

PROSTITUTION

1 The women who take husbands not out of love but out of greed, to get their bills paid, to get a fine house and clothes and jewels; the women who marry to get out of a tiresome job, or to get away from disagreeable relatives, or to avoid being called an old maid – these are whores in everything but name. The only difference between them and my girls is that my girls gave a man his money's worth.

Polly Adler (1900–1962), U.S. brothel-keeper: *A House Is Not a Home* (1953), Ch.10

2 Prostitution is the supreme triumph of capitalism. ... Worst of all, prostitution reinforces all the old dumb clichés about women's sexuality; that they are not built to enjoy sex and are little more than walking masturbation aids, things to be DONE TO, things so sensually null and void that they have to be *paid* to indulge in fornication, that women can be had, bought, as often as not sold from one man to another. When the sex war is won prostitutes should be shot as collaborators for their terrible betrayal of all women, for the moral tarring and feathering they give indigenous women who have had the bad luck to live in what they make their humping ground.

Julie Burchill (b.1960), British journalist and author: *Damaged Gods* (1986), 'Born again Cows'

3 The whore is despised by the hypocritical world because she has made a realistic assessment of her assets and does not have to rely on fraud to make a living. In an area of human relations where fraud is regular practice between the sexes, her honesty is regarded with a mocking wonder.

Angela Carter (1940–1992), British author: *The Sadeian Woman* (1979), 'Desecration of the Temple'

4 A country without bordels is like a house without bathrooms.

Marlene Dietrich (1904–1992), German-born U.S. actress: *Marlene Dietrich's ABC* (1962), 'Bordel'

5 Actually, if my business was legitimate, I would deduct a substantial percentage for depreciation of my body.

Xaviera Hollander (b.1936), U.S. prostitute: *The Happy Hooker* (written with Robin Moore and Yvonne Dunleavy, 1972), Ch.14

6 I was like a social worker for lepers. My clients had a chunk of their body they wanted to give away; for a price I was there to receive it. Crimes, sins, nightmares, hunks of hair: it was surprising how many of them had something to dispose of. The more I charged, the easier it was for them to breathe freely once more.

Tama Janowitz (b.1957), U.S. author: *Slaves of New York* (1986), 'Modern Saint 271'

7 The degradation in which the prostitute is held and holds herself, the punitive attitude society adopts toward her, are but reflections of a culture whose general attitudes toward sexuality are negative and which attaches great penalties to a promiscuity in women it does not think to punish in men.

Kate Millett (b.1934), U.S. feminist author: *Sexual Politics* (1970), Ch.3

8 The prostitute is not, as feminists claim, the victim of men but rather their conqueror, an outlaw who controls the sexual channel between nature and culture.

Camille Paglia (b.1947), U.S. author and critic: 'Elizabeth Taylor: Hollywood's Pagan Queen', first publ. in *Penthouse* (New York), March 1992, rep. in *Sex, Art, and American Culture* (1992)

9 If it weren't for us there would be more murders in America, because a stiff penis has no conscience.

Miss Prissy, U.S. prostitute: quoted in *The Independent* (London), 29 April 1990. Miss Prissy ran for the 1990 mayoral race in Washington D.C., explaining, 'I'm the greatest whore in the world, so I know I'll be the greatest mayor ... I decided to become a whore so I could learn politics'

10 He would, wouldn't he?

Mandy Rice-Davies (b.1944), British call-girl: remark in court, 29 June 1963, responding to the statement that one of her alleged clients denied having had sex with her, quoted in *The Guardian* (London), 1 July 1963. The exchange took place in the wake of the Profumo affair, in which a member of Macmillan's government was found to have compromised national security by consorting with Rice-Davies' friend, Christine Keeler

11 Punishing the prostitute promotes the rape of all women. When prostitution is a crime, the message conveyed is that women who are sexual are 'bad', and therefore legitimate victims of sexual assault. Sex becomes a weapon to be used by men.
Margo St James (b.1937), U.S. prostitute and activist: quoted in the *San Francisco Examiner*, 29 April 1979

12 There is no more defiant denial of one man's ability to possess one woman exclusively than the prostitute who refuses to redeemed.
Gail Sheehy (b.1937), U.S. author and critic: *Hustling* (1971), Ch.1

See also Duke of Edinburgh on WIVES

PROTESTANTISM

1 The White Protestant's ultimate sympathy must be with science, factology, and committee rather than with sex, birth, heat, flesh, creation, the sweet and the funky; they must vote, manipulate, control, and direct, these Protestants who are the center of power in our land, they must go for what they believe is reason when it is only the Square logic of the past.
Norman Mailer (b.1923), U.S. author: *Advertisements for Myself* (1959), Pt.5, 'Advertisement for "Games and Ends"'

2 The Protestant thrust is always toward didactic preaching, interpretation, and loquacious explaining. The pulpit crowds out the altar.
Theodore Roszak (b.1933), U.S. social critic: *Where the Wasteland Ends* (1972), Ch.4

PROVINCIALISM

1 When I was growing up I used to think that the best thing about coming from Des Moines was that it meant you didn't come from anywhere else in Iowa. By Iowa standards, Des Moines is a mecca of cosmopolitanism, a dynamic hub of wealth and education, where people wear three-piece suits and dark socks, often simultaneously.
Bill Bryson (b.1951), U.S. author and journalist: *The Lost Continent: Travels in Small Town America* (1989), Ch.1

2 Great things happen in small places. Jesus was born in Bethlehem. Jesse Jackson was born in Greenville.
Jesse Jackson (b.1941), U.S. clergyman and civil rights leader: in the *Daily Mail* (London), 9 March 1988

3 Being a Georgia author is a rather specious dignity, on the same order as, for the pig, being a Talmadge ham.
Flannery O'Connor (1925–1964), U.S. author: 'The Regional Writer', first publ. in *Esprit* (University of Scranton, Pennsylvania), winter 1963, rep. in *Mystery and Manners* (ed. Sally and Robert Fitzgerald, 1972)

4 When you're growing up in a small town
You know you'll grow down in a small town
There is only one good use for a small town
You hate it and you know you'll have to leave.
Lou Reed (b.1944), U.S. rock musician: 'Small Town' (song) on the album *Songs for Drella* (Lou Reed and John Cale, 1990)

PSYCHEDELIA

1 Acid had changed consciousness entirely. The U.S. has changed in the last few years and it's because that whole first psychedelic thing meant: here's this new consciousness, this new freedom, and it's here in yourself.
Jerry Garcia (1942–1995), U.S. rock musician: quoted in *Rock 'n' Roll Babylon* by Gary Herman (1982), Ch.3

2 Purple haze all in my brain,
Lately things don't seem the same,
Actin' funny, but I don't know why,
'Suse me while I kiss the sky.
Jimi Hendrix (1942–1970), U.S. rock musician: 'Purple Haze' (song) on the album *Are You Experienced?* (The Jimi Hendrix Experience, 1967)

3 Remember what the dormouse said:
'Feed your head.'
Grace Slick (b.1939), U.S. rock musician: 'White Rabbit' (song) on the album *Surrealistic Pillow* (Jefferson Airplane, 1967). In an interview in 1977, Slick explained: '"Feed your head" doesn't mean take every fucking drug that comes along, "Feed your head" means read ... listen and read' (quoted in *Shaman Woman, Mainline Lady*, ed. Cynthia Palmer and Michael Horowitz, 1982)

PSYCHIATRIC INSTITUTIONS

1 I myself spent nine years in an insane asylum and I never had the obsession of suicide, but I know that each conversation with a psychiatrist, every morning at the time of his visit, made me want to hang myself, realizing that I would not be able to cut his throat.
Antonin Artaud (1896–1948), French theatre producer, actor and theorist: *Van Gogh, the Man Suicided by Society* (1947), rep. in *Selected Writings* (ed. Susan Sontag, 1976), Pt.33

2 Every morning I woke in dread, waiting for the day nurse to go on her rounds and announce from the list of names in her hand whether or not I was for shock treatment, the new and fashionable means of quieting people and of making them realize that orders are to be obeyed and floors are to be polished without anyone protesting and faces are to be made to be fixed into smiles and weeping is a crime.

Janet Frame (b.1924), New Zealand novelist and poet: *Faces in the Water* (1961), Ch.1

3 Pound's crazy. All poets are.... They have to be. You don't put a poet like Pound in the loony bin. For history's sake we shouldn't keep him there.

Ernest Hemingway (1899–1961), U.S. author: of Ezra Pound's detention in St Elizabeth's Hospital in Washington D.C., quoted in the *New York Post*, 24 Jan. 1957

4 Involuntary mental hospitalization is like slavery. Refining the standards for commitment is like prettifying the slave plantations. The problem is not how to improve commitment, but how to abolish it.

Thomas Szasz (b.1920), U.S. psychiatrist: *The Second Sin* (1973), 'Mental Hospitalization'

PSYCHIATRY

1 It is almost impossible to be a doctor and an honest man, but it is obscenely impossible to be a psychiatrist without at the same time bearing the stamp of the most incontestable madness: that of being unable to resist that old atavistic reflex of the mass of humanity, which makes any man of science who is absorbed by this mass a kind of natural and inborn enemy of all genius.

Antonin Artaud (1896–1948), French theatre producer, actor and theorist: *Van Gogh, the Man Suicided by Society* (1947), rep. in *Selected Writings* (ed. Susan Sontag, 1976), Pt.33

2 If the nineteenth century was the age of the editorial chair, ours is the century of the psychiatrist's couch.

Marshall McLuhan (1911–1980), Canadian communications theorist: introduction to *Understanding Media* (1964)

3 A psychiatrist is a man who goes to the Folies-Bergère and looks at the audience.

Mervyn Stockwood (1913–1995), British churchman and author: quoted in *The Observer* (London), 15 Oct. 1961

4 The professional must learn to be moved and touched emotionally, yet at the same time stand back objectively: I've seen a lot of damage done by tea and sympathy.

Anthony Storr (b.1920), British psychiatrist: in *The Times* (London), 22 Oct. 1992

5 Institutional psychiatry is a continuation of the Inquisition. All that has really changed is the vocabulary and the social style. The vocabulary conforms to the intellectual expectations of our age: it is a pseudo-medical jargon that parodies the concepts of science. The social style conforms to the political expectations of our age: it is a pseudo-liberal social movement that parodies the ideals of freedom and rationality.

Thomas Szasz (b.1920), U.S. psychiatrist: *The Manufacture of Madness* (1971), Ch.1

PSYCHOANALYSIS

1 I was depressed ... I was suicidal; as a matter of fact, I would have killed myself but I was in analysis with a strict Freudian and if you kill yourself they make you pay for the sessions you miss.

Woody Allen (b.1935), U.S. film-maker: Alvy Singer (Allen), in *Annie Hall* (film; screenplay by Woody Allen and Marshall Brickman, directed by Woody Allen, 1977). The gag originated in a stand-up routine recorded live in San Francisco, Aug. 1968, on the album *The Nightclub Years* (1968), 'Second Marriage'

2 Freud thought he was bringing the plague to the U.S.A, but the U.S.A. has victoriously resisted the psychoanalytical frost by real deep freezing, by mental and sexual refrigeration. They have countered the black magic of the Unconscious with the white magic of 'doing your own thing', air conditioning, sterilization, mental frigidity and the cold media of information.

Jean Baudrillard (b.1929), French semiologist: *Cool Memories* (1987; tr.1990), Ch.2

3 Psycho-analysis pretends to investigate the Unconscious. The Unconscious by definition is what you are not conscious of. But the Analysts already know what's in it – they should, because they put it all in beforehand.

Saul Bellow (b.1915), U.S. novelist: Albert Corde, in *The Dean's December* (1982), Ch.18

4 Psychoanalysis can unravel some of the forms of madness; it remains a stranger to the sovereign enterprise of unreason. It can neither limit nor transcribe, nor most certainly explain, what is essential in this enterprise.

Michel Foucault (1926–1984), French essayist and philosopher: *Madness and Civilization* (1961; tr.1965), 'The Birth of the Asylum'

5 Freud is the father of psychoanalysis. It had no mother.

Germaine Greer (b.1939), Australian feminist writer: *The Female Eunuch* (1970), 'The Psychological Sell'

6　Considered in its entirety, psychoanalysis won't do. It's an end product, moreover, like a dinosaur or a zeppelin; no better theory can ever be erected on its ruins, which will remain for ever one of the saddest and strangest of all landmarks in the history of twentieth-century thought.
Peter Medawar (1915–1987), British immunologist: *The Hope of Progress* (1972), 'Further Comments on Psychoanalysis'

7　Aided and abetted by corrupt analysts, patients who have nothing better to do with their lives often use the psychoanalytic situation to transform insignificant childhood hurts into private shrines at which they worship unceasingly the enormity of the offenses committed against them. This solution is immensely flattering to the patients – as are all forms of unmerited self-aggrandizement; it is immensely profitable for the analysts – as are all forms pandering to people's vanity; and it is often immensely unpleasant for nearly everyone else in the patient's life.
Thomas Szasz (b.1920), U.S. psychiatrist: *The Second Sin* (1973), 'Psychoanalysis'

PSYCHOLOGY

1　Analytical psychology is fundamentally a natural science, but it is subject far more than any other science to the personal bias of the observer. The psychologist must depend therefore in the highest degree upon historical and literary parallels if he wishes to exclude at least the crudest errors in judgement.
Carl Jung (1875–1961), Swiss psychiatrist: *Memories, Dreams, Reflections* (1962), Ch.7

2　Psychology, we must remember, is the study of the soul, therefore the discipline closest to the religious life. An authentic psychology discards none of the insights gained from spiritual discipline.
Theodore Roszak (b.1933), U.S. social critic: *Where the Wasteland Ends* (1972), Ch.11

3　A large part of the popularity and persuasiveness of psychology comes from its being a sublimated spiritualism: a secular, ostensibly scientific way of affirming the primacy of 'spirit' over matter.
Susan Sontag (b.1933), U.S. essayist: *Illness As Metaphor* (1978), Ch.7

4　There is no psychology; there is only biography and autobiography.
Thomas Szasz (b.1920), U.S. psychiatrist: *The Second Sin* (1973), 'Psychology'

See also THE BRAIN

THE PUBLIC

1　The reading public is intellectually adolescent at best, and it is obvious that what is called 'significant literature' will only be sold to this public by exactly the same methods as are used to sell it toothpaste, cathartics and automobiles.
Raymond Chandler (1880–1959), U.S. author: letter, 29 Jan. 1946, to crime novelist Erle Stanley Gardner, publ. in *Raymond Chandler Speaking* (ed. Dorothy Gardiner and Kathrine S. Walker, 1962)

2　I don't believe that the public knows what it wants; this is the conclusion that I have drawn from my career.
Charlie Chaplin (1889–1977), British comic actor and film-maker: quoted in *Cinema: Art and Industry* (1976), Ch.10

3　The basic idea which runs right through modern history and modern liberalism is that the public has got to be marginalized. The general public are viewed as no more than ignorant and meddlesome outsiders, a bewildered herd.
Noam Chomsky (b.1928), U.S. linguist and political analyst: interview in *The Guardian* (London), 23 Nov. 1992

4　If you have got the public in the palm of your hand, you can be sure that is where they want to be.
Cliff Richard (b.1940), British singer: in *The Observer* (London), 4 Dec. 1988

See also Barthes on PASSION

PUBLIC LIFE

1　You're not an M.P., you're a gastronomic pimp.
Aneurin Bevan (1897–1960), British Labour politician: to a colleague who complained of attending too many public dinners, quoted in *Aneurin Bevan* by Michael Foot (1973), Vol.II, Ch.6

2　The measure of your quality as a public person, as a citizen, is the gap between what you do and what you say.
Ramsey Clark (b.1927), U.S. attorney general: in the *International Herald Tribune* (Paris), 18 June 1991

3　We are not here to laugh.
(*On n'est pas là pour rigoler.*)
Charles de Gaulle (1890–1970), French general and president: said on frequent occasions, quoted in *The Independent* (London), 21 April 1990 on the centenary of de Gaulle's birth.

4　Everywhere I go I smell fresh paint.

Diana, Princess of Wales (1961–1997): on her ceremonial duties, quoted in *The Daily Telegraph* (London), 28 Jan. 1988

5 I never know when I press these whether I am going to blow up Massachusetts or start the project...

John F. Kennedy (1917–1963), U.S. Democratic politician and president: speech, Sept. 1963, at Salt Lake City, Utah, where Kennedy pulled a switch to activate generators in the Colorado river basin, 150 miles distant, quoted in *The Wit of President Kennedy* (ed. Bill Adler, 1964), 'The Presidency'

6 The more you stay in this kind of job, the more you realize that a public figure, a major public figure, is a lonely man.

Richard Nixon (1913–1992), U.S. Republican politician and president: said when vice-president in an interview with Stewart Alsop, quoted in Appendix to Alsop's *Nixon and Rockefeller: A Double Portrait* (1960), 'A Talk with Nixon'

7 The General has dedicated himself so many times, he must feel like the cornerstone of a public building.

Adlai Stevenson (1900–1965), U.S. Democratic politician: of President Eisenhower, quoted in *The Fine Art of Political Wit* by Leon Harris (1964), Ch.10

PUBLIC OPINION

1 Opinion is made, even created, by the continual pressure of a wild variety of facts, or semi-facts, which vary between the banal and the cosmic, all of which bear in some way on the human situation. How this charivaria of information is transmuted into public opinion is a most mysterious thing.

James Cameron (1911–1985), British journalist: *Point of Departure* (1967), Ch.4

2 Where mass opinion dominates the government, there is a morbid derangement of the true functions of power. The derangement brings about the enfeeblement, verging on paralysis, of the capacity to govern. This breakdown in the constitutional order is the cause of the precipitate and catastrophic decline of Western society. It may, if it cannot be arrested and reversed, bring about the fall of the West.

Walter Lippmann (1889–1974), U.S. journalist: *The Public Philosophy* (1955), Ch.1, Sct.4

3 The total collapse of the public opinion polls shows that this country is in good health. A country that developed an airtight system of finding out in advance what was in people's minds would be uninhabitable.

E.B. White (1899–1985), U.S. author and editor: on Truman's surprise win in the 1948 presidential election, in 'Polling', first publ. in the *New Yorker*, 13 Nov. 1948, rep. in *Writings from the New Yorker 1927–1976* (ed. Rebecca M. Dale, 1991)

PUBLIC SCHOOLS *see under* SCHOOL

PUBLICITY

1 All publicity is good, except an obituary notice.

Brendan Behan (1923–1964), Irish playwright: quoted in the *Sunday Express* (London), 5 Jan. 1964

2 Publicity is the life of this culture – in so far as without publicity capitalism could not survive – and at the same time publicity is its dream.

John Berger (b.1926), British author and critic: *Ways of Seeing* (1972), Ch.7

3 With publicity comes humiliation.

Tama Janowitz (b.1957), U.S. author: in the *International Herald Tribune* (Paris), 8 Sept. 1992

4 Of course I'm a publicity hound. Aren't all crusaders? How can you accomplish anything unless people know what you are trying to do?

Vivien Kellems (1896–1975), U.S. industrialist and lecturer: quoted in *Reader's Digest* (Pleasantville, N.Y.), Oct. 1975

5 The Blue Meanies, or whatever they are, still preach violence all the time in every newspaper, every TV show and every magazine. The least Yoko and I can do is hog the headlines and make people laugh. We're quite willing to be the world's clowns if it will do any good. For reasons known only to themselves, people print what I say. And I say 'peace'.

John Lennon (1940–1980), British rock musician: on the peace campaign waged by John Lennon and Yoko Ono, quoted in *Shout! The True Story of the Beatles* by Philip Norman (1981), Pt.4, 'May 1969'

6 In America, the race goes to the loud, the solemn, the hustler. If you think you're a great writer, you must say that you are.

Gore Vidal (b.1925), U.S. novelist and critic: interview in *Writers at Work* (Fifth Series, ed. George Plimpton, 1981)

See also Sharpton on THE MEDIA

PUBLISHING

1 The minute you try to talk business with him he takes the attitude that he is a gentleman and a scholar, and the moment you try to approach him on the level of his moral integrity he starts to talk business.

Raymond Chandler (1880–1959), U.S. author: on publishers in general, in letter, 2 June 1947, publ. in *Raymond Chandler Speaking* (ed. Dorothy Gardiner and Kathrine S. Walker, 1962)

2 A publisher is a specialised form of bank or building society, catering for customers who cannot cope with life and are therefore forced to write about it.

Colin Haycraft (1929–1994), British publisher: letter to *The Sunday Times* (London), 11 Feb. 1990. 'Hype,' added Haycraft, 'springs eternal in every publisher's breast'

3 Having books published is very destructive to writing. It is even worse than making love too much. Because when you make love too much at least you get a damned clarte that is like no other light. A very clear and hollow light.

Ernest Hemingway (1899–1961), U.S. author: letter, 2 Oct. 1952, to poet and critic Bernard Berenson, publ. in *Selected Letters* (ed. Carlos Baker, 1981)

4 When you publish a book, it's the world's book. The world edits it.

Philip Roth (b.1933), U.S. author: in the *New York Times Book Review*, 2 Sept. 1979

5 Publishers are notoriously slothful about numbers, unless they're attached to dollar signs – unlike journalists, quarterbacks, and felony criminal defendants who tend to be keenly aware of numbers at all times.

Hunter S. Thompson (b.1939), U.S. journalist: *Songs Of The Doomed* (1991), 'A Letter to *The Champion*: a publication of the National Assoc. of Criminal Defense Lawyers' (July 1990)

See also EDITING

PUNISHMENT

1 Retaliation is related to nature and instinct, not to law. Law, by definition, cannot obey the same rules as nature.

Albert Camus (1913–1960), French-Algerian philosopher and author: *Resistance, Rebellion and Death* (1961), 'Reflections on the Guillotine'

2 In its function, the power to punish is not essentially different from that of curing or educating.

Michel Foucault (1926–1984), French philosopher: *Discipline and Punish: The Birth of the Prison* (1975), Pt.4, Ch.3

3 A great deal in life depends on who smacked your hand at breakfast when you were a child.

Krzysztof Kieślowski (1941–1996), Polish film-maker: *Kieślowski on Kieślowski* (1993), Ch.1

4 Our system is the height of absurdity, since we treat the culprit both as a child, so as to have the right to punish him, and as an adult, in order to deny him consolation.

Claude Lévi-Strauss (b.1908), French anthropologist: of the justice system, in *Tristes Tropiques* (1955), Ch.38

5 If he who breaks the law is not punished, he who obeys it is cheated. This, and this alone, is why lawbreakers ought to be punished: to authenticate as good, and to encourage as useful, law-abiding behavior. The aim of criminal law cannot be correction or deterrence; it can only be the maintenance of the legal order.

Thomas Szasz (b.1920), U.S. psychiatrist: *The Second Sin* (1973), 'Punishment'

6 I'm all for bringing back the birch, but only between consenting adults.

Gore Vidal (b.1925), U.S. novelist and critic: TV interview with David Frost, quoted in *The Sunday Times* (London), 16 Sept. 1973

PUNK

1 At its best New Wave/punk represents a fundamental and age-old Utopian dream: that if you give people the license to be as outrageous as they want in absolutely any fashion they can dream up, *they'll be creative about it*, and do something good besides.

Lester Bangs (1948–1982), U.S. rock journalist: in *New Musical Express* (London), 24 Dec. 1977, rep. in *Psychotic Reactions & Carburetor Dung* (1987), 'The Clash'

2 Punk, far from being a peasants' revolt, was just another English spectacle, like the Royal Wedding: a chance for us to congratulate ourselves on our talent for tableaux ... and to cock a snook at envious Americans.

Julie Burchill (b.1960), British journalist: in *Modern Review* (London), autumn 1991

3 The heavy irony of the punks blunts the style's offensive edge before it can even wound you. It makes you feel old, that is the cruellest thing, but it is basically a style of self-mockery. Arguing, perhaps, a low state of self-esteem in those who sport it. Warpaint was never put on to frighten the other side so much as to bolster the faint hearts of the wearers.

Angela Carter (1940–1992), British author: 'Ups and Downs for the Babes in Bondage', first publ. in *New Society* (London), 22 Dec. 1977, rep. in *The Faber Book of Pop* (ed. Hanif Kureishi and Jon Savage, 1995), Pt.7

4 Oh dead punk lady with the knack
Of looking fierce in pins and black,
The suburbs wouldn't want you back.

Thom Gunn (b.1929), British poet: 'The Victim', publ. in *The Passages of Joy* (1982)

5 Punks in their silly leather jackets are a cliché. I have never liked the term and have never discussed it. I just got on with it and got out of it when it became a competition.

John Lydon [formerly Johnny Rotten] (b.1957), British rock musician: in *The Observer* (London), 4 May 1986

6 Punk to me was a form of free speech. It was a moment when suddenly all kinds of strange voices that no reasonable person could ever have expected to hear in public were being heard all over the place.

Greil Marcus (b.1945), U.S. rock journalist: 'Punk and History', transcript of a discussion, 24 Sept. 1988, New York, publ. in *Discourses: Conversations in Postmodern Art and Culture* (ed. Russell Ferguson *et al.*, 1990)

7 Actually we're not into music. ... We're into chaos.

Sex Pistols (1976–1979), British punk band: a member of the band, quoted in *New Musical Express* (London), 25 Feb. 1976, '1976: Don't Look Over Your Shoulder, but the Sex Pistols are Coming', rep. in *The Faber Book of Pop* (ed. Hanif Kureishi and Jon Savage, 1995), Pt.7

See also Sex Pistols on REBELS

PURITY

1 No one is more dangerous than he who imagines himself pure in heart: for his purity, by definition, is unassailable.

James Baldwin (1924–1987), U.S. author: 'The Black Boy Looks at the White Boy', first publ. in *Esquire* (New York), May 1961, rep. in *Nobody Knows My Name* (1961)

2 I'm as pure as the driven slush.

Tallulah Bankhead (1903–1968), U.S. actress: quoted in the *Saturday Evening Post* (New York), 12 April 1947

3 In order for the wheel to turn, for life to be lived, impurities are needed, and the impurities of impurities in the soil, too, as is known, if it is to be fertile. Dissension, diversity, the grain of salt and mustard are needed: Fascism does not want them, forbids them, and that's why you're not a Fascist; it wants everybody to be the same, and you are not. But immaculate virtue does not exist either, or if it exists it is detestable.

Primo Levi (1919–1987), Italian chemist and author: *The Periodic Table* (1975; tr.1984), 'Zinc'

See also Burchill on HAIR

QUARRELS

1 The last sound on the worthless earth will be two human beings trying to launch a homemade spaceship and already quarreling about where they are going next.

William Faulkner (1897–1962), U.S. novelist: speech to UNESCO Commission, quoted in the *New York Times*, 3 Oct. 1959

2 Break a vase, and the love that reassembles the fragments is stronger than that love which took its symmetry for granted when it was whole.

Derek Walcott (b.1930), West Indian poet and playwright: 'Dissolving the Sigh of History', publ. in *The Guardian* (London), 16 Dec. 1992

DAN QUAYLE

1 That's the really neat thing about Dan Quayle, as you must have realized from the first moment you looked into those lovely blue eyes: *impeachment insurance.*

Barbara Ehrenreich (b.1941), U.S. author and columnist: addressing George Bush, in 'My Reply to George' (1989), rep. in *The Worst Years of Our Lives* (1991)

2 Quayle was a twink. He got all the way through the sixties without dying from an overdose, being institutionalized by his parents or getting arrested for nude violation of the Mann Act on a motorcycle. At least he was a draft-dodger – although Dan timidly joined the National Guard instead of bravely going to his physical in panty hose.

P.J. O'Rourke (b.1947), U.S. journalist: *Parliament of Whores* (1991), 'Attack of the Midget Vote Suckers'

QUESTIONS & ANSWERS

1 The real questions are the ones that obtrude upon your consciousness whether you like it or not, the ones that make your mind start vibrating like a jackhammer, the ones that you 'come to terms with' only to discover that they are still there. The real questions refuse to be placated. They barge into your life at the times when it seems most important for them to stay away. They are the questions asked most frequently and answered most inadequately, the ones that reveal their true natures slowly, reluctantly, most often against your will.

Ingrid Bengis (b.1944), U.S. author: *Combat in the Erogenous Zone* (1973), 'Man-Hating'

2 The answer my friend is blowin' in the wind, The answer is blowin' in the wind.

Bob Dylan (b.1941), U.S. singer and songwriter: 'Blowin' in the Wind' (song) on the album *The Freewheelin' Bob Dylan* (1962). On the sleeve notes to the record, Dylan wrote: 'The first way to answer the questions in the song is by asking them. But lots of people have to first find the wind'

3 What is the answer to the question? The problem. How is the problem resolved? By displacing the question. ... We must think problematically rather than question and answer dialectically.

Michel Foucault (1926–1984), French philosopher: 'Theatrum Philosophicum', publ. in *Language,*

Counter-Memory, Practice (ed. Donald Bouchard and Simon Sherry, 1977), Pt.2, 'Counter-Memory: The Philosophy of Difference'

4   Just before she died she asked, 'What *is* the answer?' No answer came. She laughed and said, 'In that case, what is the question?' Then she died.

     Gertrude Stein (1874–1946), U.S. author: quoted in *Gertrude Stein, A Biography of Her Work* by Donald Sutherland (1951), Ch.6. Sutherland concludes the biography: 'Those were her last words, but they say what she had always been saying'

QUOTATION

1   Quotes from Mao, Castro, and Che Guevara ... are as germane to our highly technological, computerized society as a stagecoach on a jet runway at Kennedy airport.

     Saul Alinsky (1909–1972), U.S. political activist: prologue to *Rules for Radicals* (1971),

2   When one begins to live by habit and by quotation, one has begun to stop living.

     James Baldwin (1924–1987), U.S. author: 'White Racism or World Community?', first publ. in the *Ecumenical Review*, Oct. 1968, rep. in *The Price of the Ticket* (1985)

3   Life itself is a quotation.

     Jorge Luis Borges (1899–1986), Argentinian author: heard by Jean Baudrillard at a lecture given in Paris, quoted in Baudrillard's *Cool Memories* (1987; tr.1990), Ch.5

4   To be apt in quotation is a splendid and dangerous gift. Splendid, because it ornaments a man's speech with other men's jewels; dangerous, for the same reason.

     Robertson Davies (1913–1995), Canadian novelist and journalist: 'Dangerous Jewels', publ. in the *Toronto Daily Star*, 1 Oct. 1960, rep. in *The Enthusiasms of Robertson Davies* (1990). 'Too much traffic with a quotation book begets a conviction of ignorance in a sensitive reader,' Davies wrote. 'Not only is there a mass of quotable stuff he never quotes, but an even vaster realm of which he has never heard'

5   Quotations are useful in periods of ignorance or obscurantist beliefs.

     Guy Debord (1931–1994), French Situationist philosopher: *Panegyric* (first volume of autobiography, 1989), Pt.1

6   We rarely quote nowadays to appeal to authority ... though we quote sometimes to display our sapience and erudition. Some authors we quote against. Some we quote not at all, offering them our scrupulous avoidance, and so make them part of our 'white mythology'. Other authors we constantly invoke, chanting their names in cerebral rituals of propitiation or ancestor worship.

     Ihab Hassan (b.1925), U.S. critic: 'The Critic as Innovator', publ. in the *Chicago Review*, winter 1977, rep. in *The Right Promethean Fire* (1980)

7   Fidelity to the subject's thought and to his characteristic way of expressing himself is the sine qua non of journalistic quotation.

     Janet Malcolm (b.1934), U.S. author: *The Journalist and the Murderer* (1990), 'Afterword'. Malcolm was at the centre of a legal dispute in which she was accused of fabricating quotations. In her book, Malcolm argued that accurate quotation is impossible: 'When we talk with somebody, we are not aware of the language we are speaking. Our ear takes it in as English, and only if we see it transcribed verbatim do we realize that it is a kind of foreign tongue'

8   Great speeches have always had great sound-bites. The problem now is that the young technicians who put together speeches are paying attention only to the soundbite, not to the text as a whole, not realizing that all great soundbites happen by accident, which is to say, all great soundbites are yielded up inevitably, as part of the natural expression of the text. They are part of the tapestry, they aren't a little flower somebody sewed on.

     Peggy Noonan (b.1950), U.S. author and presidential speechwriter: *What I Saw at the Revolution* (1990), Ch.5

9   That's the nice thing about this job. You get to quote yourself shamelessly. If you don't, Larry Speakes will.

     Ronald Reagan (b.1911), U.S. Republican politician and president: in *The Daily Telegraph* (London), 14 April 1988. Speakes was press secretary at the White House

10   The taste for quotations (and for the juxtaposition of incongruous quotations) is a Surrealist taste.

     Susan Sontag (b.1933), U.S. essayist: *On Photography* (1977), 'Melancholy Objects'

11   In the dying world I come from quotation is a national vice. It used to be the classics, now it's lyric verse.

     Evelyn Waugh (1903–1966), British novelist: Dennis Barlow, in *The Loved One* (1948), p.108 of Penguin edn. (1951)

RACE

1   It is a great shock at the age of five or six to find that in a world of Gary Coopers you are the Indian.

     James Baldwin (1924–1987), U.S. author: speech, 17 Feb. 1965, Cambridge Union, Cambridge University, quoted in the *New York Times Magazine*, 7 March 1965

2   Whites must be made to realize that they are only human, not superior. Same with blacks. They must be made to realize that they are also human, not inferior.

Steve Biko (1946–1977), South African anti-apartheid activist: quoted in the *Boston Globe*, 26 Oct. 1977

3 The new grammar of race is constructed in a way that George Orwell would have appreciated, because its rules make some ideas impossible to express – unless, of course, one wants to be called a racist.
Stephen Carter (b.1954), U.S. lawyer and author: *Reflections of an Affirmative Action Baby* (1992), Ch.8

4 There are only two races on this planet – the intelligent and the stupid.
John Fowles (b.1926), British novelist: in *The Daily Telegraph* (London), 15 Aug. 1991

5 A white face goes with a white mind. Occasionally a black face goes with a white mind. Very seldom a white face will have a black mind.
Nikki Giovanni (b.1943), U.S. poet: in conversation with James Baldwin, London, 4 Nov. 1971, publ. in *A Dialogue* (1973)

6 No one has been barred on account of his race from fighting or dying for America – there are no 'white' or 'colored' signs on the foxholes or graveyards of battle.
John F. Kennedy (1917–1963), U.S. Democratic politician and president: message to Congress, 19 June 1963, referring to the proposed civil rights bill, quoted in the *New York Times*, 20 June 1963

7 In this country American means white. Everybody else has to hyphenate.
Toni Morrison (b.1931), U.S. novelist and editor: in *The Guardian* (London), 29 Jan. 1992

8 There's no such thing as a race and barely such a thing as an ethnic group. If we were dogs, we'd be the same breed. ... Trouble doesn't come from Slopes, Kikes, Niggers, Spics or White Capitalist Pigs; it comes from the heart.
P.J. O'Rourke (b.1947), U.S. journalist: introduction to *Holidays in Hell* (1988)

9 To me, the black black woman is our essential mother – the blacker she is the more us she is – and to see the hatred that is turned on her is enough to make me despair, almost entirely, of our future as a people.
Alice Walker (b.1944), U.S. author and critic: 'If the Present Looks Like the Past, What Does the Future Look Like?' (July 1982), rep. in *In Search of our Mothers' Gardens* (1983)

See also BLACK CONSCIOUSNESS/BLACK POWER; Malcolm X on MULTICULTURALISM; WHITES

RACISM

1 At bottom, to be colored means that one has been caught in some utterly unbelievable cosmic joke, a joke so hideous and in such bad taste that it defeats all categories and definitions.
James Baldwin (1924–1987), U.S. author: 'Color', first publ. in *Esquire* (New York), Dec. 1962, rep. in *The Price of the Ticket* (1985)

2 Racism? But isn't it only a form of misanthropy?
Joseph Brodsky (1940–1996), Russian-born U.S. poet and critic: *Less Than One: Selected Essays* (1986), 'Flight from Byzantium', Sct.9

3 It is exasperating to see little brown men and little yellow men from the mysterious Orient, and the opaque black men of Africa (to say nothing of those impudent American Negroes!) who come to the U.N. and talk smart to us, who are scurrying all over *our* globe in their strange modes of dress – much as if they were new, unpleasant arrivals from another planet. Many whites believe in their ulcers that it is only a matter of time before the Marines get the signal to round up these truants and put them back securely in their cages.
Eldridge Cleaver (b.1935), U.S. black leader and writer: *Soul on Ice* (1968), 'The White Race and Its Heroes'

4 What I did not yet know so intensely was the hatred of the white American for the black, a hatred so deep that I wonder if every white man in this country, when he plants a tree, doesn't see *Negroes* hanging from its branches.
Jean Genet (1910–1986), French playwright and novelist: introduction to *Soledad Brother: The Prison Letters of George Jackson* (1970)

5 As the global expansion of Indian and Chinese restaurants suggests, xenophobia is directed against foreign people, not foreign cultural imports.
Eric Hobsbawm (b.1917), British historian: lecture to the American Anthropological Association, publ. in the *New Statesman* (London), 24 April 1992

6 Racism as a form of skin worship, and as a sickness and a pathological anxiety for America, is so great, until the poor whites – rather than fighting for jobs or education – fight to remain pink and fight to remain white. And therefore they cannot see an alliance with people that they feel to be inherently inferior.
Jesse Jackson (b.1941), U.S. clergyman and civil rights leader: interview with David Frost in Frost's *The Americans* (1970), 'When Whites Are Unemployed, It's Called a Depression'

7 I have a dream that my four little children will one day live in a nation where they will not be judged by the color of their skin but by the content of their character.
Martin Luther King Jr. (1929–1968), U.S. clergyman and civil rights leader: 'I Have a Dream',

speech, 28 Aug. 1963, at civil rights march, Washington D.C., publ. in *A Testament of Hope: Essential Writings* (ed. James Melvin Washington, 1986)

8 As you grow older, you'll see white men cheat black men every day of your life, but let me tell you something and don't you forget it – whenever a white man does that to a black man, no matter who he is, how rich he is, or how fine a family he comes from, that white man is trash.
Harper Lee (b.1926), U.S. author: Atticus Finch to his son Jem, in *To Kill a Mockingbird* (1960), Pt.2, Ch.23

9 Racism is when you have laws set up, systematically put in a way to keep people from advancing, to stop the advancement of a people. Black people have never had the power to enforce racism, and so this is something that white America is going to have to work out themselves. If they decide they want to stop it, curtail it, or to do the right thing ... then it will be done, but not until then.
Spike Lee (b.1956), U.S. film-maker: interview in *Roger Ebert's Home Movie Companion* (1990)

10 Anti-Semitism is a horrible disease from which nobody is immune, and it has a kind of evil fascination that makes an enlightened person draw near the source of infection, supposedly in a scientific spirit, but really to sniff the vapors and dally with the possibility.
Mary McCarthy (1912–1989), U.S. author and critic: 'Settling the Colonel's Hash' (1954), rep. in *On the Contrary* (1961), Pt.3

11 If you're born in America with a black skin, you're born in prison, and the masses of black people in America today are beginning to regard our plight or predicament in this society as one of a prison inmate.
Malcolm X (1925–1965), U.S. black leader: interview, June 1963, publ. in *Malcolm X: The Man and His Times* (ed. John Henrik Clarke, 1969), Pt.3, 'Malcolm X Talks with Kenneth B. Clark'

12 Until the philosophy which holds one race superior and another inferior is finally and permanently discredited and abandoned, everywhere is war ... and until there are no longer first-class and second-class citizens of any nation, until the colour of a man's skin is of no more significance than the colour of his eyes, me seh war. And until the basic human rights are equally guaranteed to all without regard to race, there is war. And until that day, the dream of lasting peace, world citizenship, rule of international morality, will remain but a fleeting illusion to be pursued, but never attained ... now everywhere is war.
Bob Marley (1945–1981), Jamaican reggae musician: 'War' (song) on the album *Rastaman Vibration* (Bob Marley and the Wailers, 1976). The words of the song are based on a speech given to the United Nations by the Ethiopian emperor Haile Selassie in 1968

13 The worst mistake I made was that stupid, suburban prejudice of anti-Semitism.
Ezra Pound (1885–1972), U.S. poet and critic: in conversation with Allen Ginsberg in June 1968, quoted in *A Serious Character* by Humphrey Carpenter (1988), Pt.5

14 I do not think white America is committed to granting equality to the American Negro ... this is a passionately racist country; it will continue to be so in the foreseeable future.
Susan Sontag (b.1933), U.S. essayist: 'What's Happening in America (1966)', first publ. in *Partisan Review* (New Brunswick, N.J.), winter 1967, rep. in *Styles of Radical Will* (1969)

15 Whatever you do, be bloody good at it, better than the white person next to you. That's the way it is.
Meera Syal (b.1963), British actress and writer: quoting her father's advice, in interview in *The Guardian* (London), 6 April 1996

16 I am fifty-two years of age. I am a bishop in the Anglican Church, and a few people might be constrained to say that I was reasonably responsible. In the land of my birth I cannot vote, whereas a young person of eighteen can vote. And why? Because he or she possesses that wonderful biological attribute – a white skin.
Desmond Tutu (b.1931), South African churchman and archbishop: quoted in *The Guardian Weekly* (London), 8 April 1984

17 Come on now! You kick out the gooks, the next thing you know, you have to kick out the chinks, the spicks, the spooks, the kikes and all that's going to be left is a couple of brain-dead rednecks.
Robin Williams (b.1952), U.S. actor and comedian: Adrian Cronauer (Williams), in *Good Morning, Vietnam* (film; screenplay by Mitch Markowitz, directed by Barry Levinson, 1987)

See also Malcolm X on BROTHERHOOD; Eazy-E on THE POLICE; Fanon on SCAPEGOATS; SEGREGATION

RADICALS

1 *Radical* simply means 'grasping things at the root'.
Angela Davis (b.1944), U.S. political activist: 'Let Us All Rise Together', speech, 25 June 1987, Spellman College, rep. in *Women, Culture and Politics* (1989)

2 People who regard themselves as radical fill the air with their desire to do their own thing, get rid of the establishment and centralized control, and so on. But when you ask them how

they are going to do it, the answer is always by giving government more power.

Milton Friedman (b.1912), U.S. economist: *There's No Such Thing as a Free Lunch* (1975), Ch.11

3 Radical Chic, after all, is only radical in Style; in its heart it is part of Society and its traditions – Politics, like Rock, Pop, and Camp, has its uses.

Tom Wolfe (b.1931), U.S. author and journalist: *Radical Chic and Mau-Mauing the Flak-Catchers* (1970, from an essay first publ. in *New York*, 8 June 1970)

See also Arendt on REVOLUTIONARIES

RADIO

1 Radio football is football reduced to its lowest common denominator. Shorn of the game's aesthetic pleasures, or the comfort of a crowd that feels the same way as you, or the sense of security that you get when you see that your defenders and goalkeeper are more or less where they should be, all that is left is naked fear.

Nick Hornby (b.1957), British author: *Fever Pitch* (1992), '1976–1986: Filling a Hole'

2 We fight our way through the massed and leveled collective safe taste of the Top 40, just looking for a little something we can call our own. But when we find it and jam the radio to hear it again it isn't just ours – it is a link to thousands of others who arc sharing it with us. As a matter of a single song this might mean very little; as culture, as a way of life, you can't beat it.

Greil Marcus (b.1945), U.S. rock journalist: *Mystery Train* (1976), 'Randy Newman'

3 TV gives everyone an image, but radio gives birth to a million images in a million brains.

Peggy Noonan (b.1950), U.S. author and presidential speechwriter: *What I Saw at the Revolution* (1990), Ch.2

See also DISC JOCKEYS; Lang on STORY-TELLING

RAIN

1 There's always a period of curious fear between the first sweet-smelling breeze and the time when the rain comes cracking down.

Don DeLillo (b.1926), U.S. author: James Axton, in *The Names* (1982), Ch.12

2 The rain in Spain stays mainly in the plain.

Alan Jay Lerner (1918–1986), U.S. songwriter: 'The Rain in Spain' (song) from *My Fair Lady* (stage show, 1956; film, 1964). The words were a phonetic exercise devised by Henry Higgins for Eliza Doolittle

3 The sound of the rain is like the voices of tens of thousands of monks reading sutras.... No-one's words can compete with this mercilessly powerful rain. The only thing that can compete with the sound of this rain, that can smash this deathlike wall of sound, is the shout of a man who refuses to stoop to this chatter, the shout of a simple spirit that knows no words.

Yukio Mishima (1925–1970), Japanese author: *Thirst for Love* (*Ai No Kawaki*, 1950; tr.1969), Ch.4

4 Rain is grace; rain is the sky condescending to the earth; without rain, there would be no life.

John Updike (b.1932), U.S. author and critic: *Self-Consciousness: Memoirs* (1989), Ch.1

See also Dylan on PROPHETS

RAP *see under* MUSIC

RAPE

1 It is little wonder that rape is one of the least-reported crimes. Perhaps it is the only crime in which the victim becomes the accused and, in reality, it is she who must prove her good reputation, her mental soundness, and her impeccable propriety.

Freda Adler (b.1934), U.S. educator and author: *Sisters in Crime* (1975), Ch.9

2 Rape is a culturally fostered means of suppressing women. Legally we say we deplore it, but mythically we romanticize and perpetuate it, and privately we excuse and overlook it.

Victoria Billings (b.1945), U.S. journalist and author: *The Womansbook* (1974), 'Sex: We Need Another Revolution'

3 Rape is no excess, no aberration, no accident, no mistake – it embodies sexuality as the culture defines it. As long as these definitions remain intact – that is, as long as men are defined as sexual aggressors and women arc defined as passive receptors lacking integrity – men who are exemplars of the norm will rape women.

Andrea Dworkin (b.1946), U.S. feminist critic: 'The Rape Atrocity and the Boy Next Door', speech, 1 March 1975, State University of New York, Stony Brook, publ. in *Our Blood* (1976), Ch.4

4 As long as there is rape ... there is not going to be any peace or justice or equality or freedom. You are not going to become what you want to become or who you want to become. You are not going to live in the world you want to live in.

Andrea Dworkin: 'Feminism: An Agenda', speech, 8 April 1983, publ. in *Letters from a War-Zone* (1987)

5 I don't want to know about the constitution of the rapist – I want to kill him! I don't care if he is white or black, if he is middle-class or poor, if his mother hung him from the clothesline by his balls: I only want to *kill* him! Any woman who has been raped will agree.
Diamanda Galás (b.1955), U.S. singer: interview in *Re/Search* (San Francisco), No.13, 1991, 'Angry Women'

6 Politically, I call it rape whenever a woman has sex and feels violated.
Catharine A. MacKinnon (b.1946), U.S. lawyer and feminist critic: *Feminism Unmodified* (1987), p.82 of Harvard University Press edn. (1987)

7 And after this quick bash in the dark
You will rise and go
Thinking of how empty you have grown
And of whether all the evening's care in front
    of mirrors
And the younger boys disowned
Led simply to this.
Brian Patten (b.1946), British poet: 'Portrait of a Young Girl Raped at a Suburban Party', publ. in *Notes to the Hurrying Man* (1969)

8 Rape is a part of war; but it may be more accurate to say that the capacity for dehumanizing another which so corrodes male sexuality is carried over from sex into war.
Adrienne Rich (b.1929), U.S. poet: 'Caryatid', first publ. in the *American Poetry Review* (Philadelphia), May/June 1973, rep. in *On Lies, Secrets, and Silence* (1980)

9 The idea that men don't know what women mean when women say no stems from something deeper and more complicated than feminist concerns with rape. The conservative thrust of the movement against date rape is that women need to be protected from men who don't share their social background.
Katie Roiphe (b.1969), U.S. feminist writer: *The Morning After* (1993), 'The Rape-Crisis, or "Is Dating Dangerous?"'

See also Pritchett on BOOKS: BESTSELLERS; Dworkin on SEDUCTION

THE RAT RACE

1 People nowadays like to be together not in the old-fashioned way of, say, mingling on the piazza of an Italian Renaissance city, but, instead, huddled together in traffic jams, bus queues, on escalators and so on. It's a new kind of togetherness which may seem totally alien, but it's the togetherness of modern technology.
J.G. Ballard (b.1930), British author: interview in *Penthouse* (London), April 1979

2 You know what? I'll tell you the problem. Agents. Time differences. New York. Paris. Barcelona. Milan. Los Angeles. They call me at seven in the morning, start giving me all the options, who wants me, where I have to go...
Naomi Campbell (b.1970), British model: quoted in *Naomi* by Lesley-Ann Jones (1993), Ch.6

3 You have to be a bastard to make it, and that's a fact. And the Beatles are the biggest bastards on earth.
John Lennon (1940–1980), British rock musician: *Lennon Remembers* (ed. Jann Wenner, 1970), p.87 of Penguin edn. (1972)

4 Until their brains snap open
I have no love for those who rush
about its mad business;
put their children on a starting line and push
into Christ knows what madness.
Brian Patten (b.1946), British poet: 'Note to the Hurrying Man', publ. in *Notes to the Hurrying Man* (1969)

5 A rat race is for rats. We're not rats. We're human beings. Reject the insidious pressures in society that would blunt your critical faculties to all that is happening around you, that would caution silence in the face of injustice lest you jeopardize your chances of promotion and self-advancement. This is how it starts and, before you know where you are, you're a fully paid-up member of the rat pack. The price is too high.
Jimmy Reid, British trade union official: rectorial address, Glasgow University, April 1972, quoted in *Writings on the Wall* (ed. Tony Benn, 1984), Pt.1

REACTIONARIES

1 He is a man walking backwards with his face to the future.
Aneurin Bevan (1897–1960), British Labour politician: of Conservative politician Sir Walter Elliot, quoted in *The Fine Art of Political Wit* by Leon Harris (1964), Ch.9

2 All the reputedly powerful reactionaries are merely paper tigers. The reason is that they are divorced from the people. Look! Was not Hitler a paper tiger? Was Hitler not overthrown? ... U.S. imperialism has not yet been overthrown and it has the atomic bomb. I believe it also will be overthrown. It, too, is a paper tiger.
Mao Zedong (1893–1976), Chinese leader: speech to International Congress of Communist and Workers' Parties, Moscow, 18 Nov. 1957, publ. in *Quotations from Chairman Mao Tse-Tung* (1967), Ch.6. Mao's first recorded reference to 'paper tigers' was in 1946, in 'Talk with the American correspondent Anne Louise Strong', Aug. 1946, publ. in *Selected Works*, Vol.IV (1961)

3 Those old faces, in Pasadena, California, and Tucson, Arizona, and Dallas, crumpling in hatred and fear at the mention of the United Nations or those liberals in government who constitute for them the fifth column of communism, yearn for an America that is as far from the society of the present as is the extended family system in village India.

Ronald Segal (b.1932), South African author: *America's Receding Future* (1968), Ch.1

READING

1 I feel about the reader the way I feel about my children. When they come to stay, I want them to have a great time. I want to give them treats, I want to buy them toys and make them laugh. I also want to stimulate their imaginations, use all their emotions and give them something exciting to be going on with; like a party bag with nuts and oranges and a balloon. Also, I want to torture them a bit.

Martin Amis (b.1949), British author: interview in *The Guardian* (London), 18 March 1995

2 To feel most beautifully alive means to be reading something beautiful, ready always to apprehend in the flow of language the sudden flash of poetry.

Gaston Bachelard (1884–1962), French scientist, philosopher and literary theorist: *Fragments of a Poetics of Fire* (1988; tr.1990), 'A Retrospective Glance at the Lifework of a Master of Books'

3 The world may be full of fourth-rate writers but it's also full of fourth-rate readers.

Stan Barstow (b.1928), British novelist and playwright: in the *Daily Mail* (London), 15 Aug. 1989

4 When we read a story, we inhabit it. The covers of the book arc like a roof and four walls. What is to happen next will take place within the four walls of the story. And this is possible because the story's voice makes everything its own.

John Berger (b.1926), British author and critic: 'Ev'ry Time We Say Goodbye', first publ. in *Expressen* (Stockholm), 3 Nov. 1990, rep. in *Keeping a Rendezvous* (1992)

5 The failure to read good books both enfeebles the vision and strengthens our most fatal tendency – the belief that the here and now is all there is.

Allan Bloom (1930–1992), U.S. educator and author: *The Closing of the American Mind* (1987), Pt.1, 'Books'

6 A conventional good read is usually a bad read, a relaxing bath in what we know already. A true good read is surely an act of innovative creation in which we, the readers, become conspirators.

Malcolm Bradbury (b.1932), British author and critic: in *The Sunday Times* (London), 29 Nov. 1987

7 Americans will listen, but they do not care to read. *War and Peace* must wait for the leisure of retirement, which never really comes: meanwhile it helps to furnish the living room. Blockbusting fiction is bought as furniture. Unread, it maintains its value. Read, it looks like money wasted. Cunningly, Americans know that books contain a person, and they want the person, not the book.

Anthony Burgess (1917–1993), British author and critic: *You've Had Your Time* (1990), Ch.2

8 Reading a book is like re-writing it for yourself.... You bring to a novel, anything you read, all your experience of the world. You bring your history and you read it in your own terms.

Angela Carter (1940–1992), British author: in *Marxism Today* (London), Jan. 1985

9 The novel can't compete with cars, the movies, television, and liquor. A guy who's had a good feed and tanked up on good wine gives his old lady a kiss after supper and his day is over. Finished.

Louis-Ferdinand Céline (1894–1961), French author: interview, 1 June 1960, publ. in *Critical Essays on Louis-Ferdinand Céline* (ed. William F. Buckley, 1989)

10 Readers are less and less seen as mere non-writers, the subhuman 'other' or flawed derivative of the author; the lack of a pen is no longer a shameful mark of secondary status but a positively enabling space, just as within every writer can be seen to lurk, as a repressed but contaminating antithesis, a reader.

Terry Eagleton (b.1943), British critic: 'The Revolt of the Reader' (1982), rep. in *Against The Grain* (1986), Ch.13

11 A reader who quarrels with postulates, who dislikes *Hamlet* because he does not believe that there are ghosts or that people speak in pentameters, clearly has no business in literature. He cannot distinguish fiction from fact, and belongs in the same category as the people who send cheques to radio stations for the relief of suffering heroines in soap operas.

Northrop Frye (1912–1991), Canadian literary critic: *Anatomy of Criticism* (1957), 'Literal and Descriptive Phases'

12 The unread story is not a story; it is little black marks on wood pulp. The reader, reading it, makes it live: a live thing, a story.

Ursula K. Le Guin (b.1929), U.S. author: *Dancing at the Edge of the World* (1989), 'Where Do You Get Your Ideas From?'

13 Until I feared I would lose it, I never loved to read. One does not love breathing.
Harper Lee (b.1926), U.S. author: Scout, in *To Kill a Mockingbird* (1960), Pt.1, Ch.2

14 With one day's reading a man may have the key in his hands.
Ezra Pound (1885–1972), U.S. poet and critic: Canto 74 in *Pisan Cantos* (1948)

15 She could give herself up to the written word as naturally as a good dancer to music or a fine swimmer to water. The only difficulty was that after finishing the last sentence she was left with a feeling at once hollow and uncomfortably full. Exactly like indigestion.
Jean Rhys (1894–1979), British author: 'The Insect World', publ. in *Sleep It Off, Lady* (1976)

16 A great book should leave you with many experiences, and slightly exhausted at the end. You live several lives while reading it.
William Styron (b.1925), U.S. novelist: interview in *Writers at Work* (First Series, ed. Malcolm Cowley, 1958)

17 I always begin at the left with the opening word of the sentence and read toward the right and I recommend this method.
James Thurber (1894–1961), U.S. humorist and illustrator: on editors' reading habits, in memo to the *New Yorker* in 1959, first publ. in the *New York Times Book Review*, 4 Dec. 1988

RONALD REAGAN

1 I'm proud to be his partner. We've had triumphs, we've made mistakes, we've had sex.
George Bush (b.1924), U.S. Republican politician and president: speech, 6 May 1988, College of Southern Idaho, quoted by Alexander Cockburn in the *New Statesman* (London), 27 May 1988, rep. in Cockburn's *Corruptions of Empire* (1988). Bush's gaffe occurred in a speech extolling the Reagan/Bush administration. He corrected himself: '... setbacks, we've had setbacks ... I feel like the javelin competitor who won the toss and elected to receive.'

2 Are you more likely to tolerate drivel than you were four years ago? I think the answer is yes. Four years of Reagan has deadened the senses against a barrage of uninterrupted nonsense.
Alexander Cockburn (b.1941), Anglo-Irish journalist: 'Balancing Acts', first publ. in *The Nation* (New York), 27 Oct. 1984, rep. in *Corruptions of Empire* (1988), Pt.2

3 Someday our grandchildren will look up at us and say, 'Where were you, Grandma, and what were you doing when you first realized that President Reagan was, er, not playing with a full deck?'

Barbara Ehrenreich (b.1941), U.S. author and columnist: 'The Unfastened Head of State' (1987), rep. in *The Worst Years of Our Lives* (1991)

4 Reagan was a flesh and blood version of any other mute national emblem, say the Statue of Liberty. Everyone knows what she represents, but no one would dream of asking her opinion.
Simon Hoggart (b.1946), British journalist: *America: A User's Guide* (1990), Ch.11

5 The battle for the mind of Ronald Reagan was like the trench warfare of World War I: Never have so many fought so hard for such barren terrain.
Peggy Noonan (b.1950), U.S. author and presidential speechwriter: *What I Saw at the Revolution* (1990), Ch.14. Noonan worked as a special assistant and speechwriter to Reagan 1984–8

6 We're an ideal political family, as accessible as Disneyland.
Maureen Reagan (b.1941), daughter of President Ronald Reagan: quoted in *The Guardian* (London), 24 Dec. 1984

7 As the age of television progresses the Reagans will be the rule, not the exception. To be perfect for television is all a President has to be these days.
Gore Vidal (b.1925), U.S. novelist and critic: quoted in *The Observer* (London), 7 Feb. 1982. In *The Observer*, 26 April 1981, Vidal was quoted as describing Reagan as 'a triumph of the embalmer's art'

See also Cher on ACTING

REALISM

1 Realism should only be the means of expression of religious genius ... or, at the other extreme, the artistic expressions of monkeys which are quite satisfied with mere imitation. In fact, art is never realistic though sometimes it is tempted to be. To be really realistic a description would have to be endless.
Albert Camus (1913–1960), French-Algerian philosopher and author: *The Rebel* (1951; tr.1953), Pt.4, 'Rebellion and Style'

2 Realism is a bad word. In a certain sense everything is realistic. I see no dividing line between imagination and reality. I see a great deal of reality in imagination. I don't feel it's my responsibility to arrange everything neatly on one universally valid level. I have an infinite capacity for amazement, and I don't see why I should set up a pseudo-rational screen to protect me from being amazed.
Federico Fellini (1920–1993), Italian film-maker: *Fellini on Fellini* (ed. Anna Keel and Christian Strich, 1974; tr.1977), 'Miscellany III', Sct.8

3 Realism, whether it be socialist or not, falls short of reality. It shrinks it, attenuates it, falsifies it; it does not take into account our basic truths and our fundamental obsessions: love, death, astonishment. It presents man in a reduced and estranged perspective. Truth is in our dreams, in the imagination.

Eugène Ionesco (1912–1994), Rumanian-born French playwright: 'Experience of the Theatre', publ. in *Nouvelle N.R.F.*(Paris), No.62, 1958, rep. in *Notes and Counter Notes* (1962)

4 I have found that anything that comes out of the South is going to be called grotesque by the Northern reader, unless it *is* grotesque, in which case it is going to be called realistic.

Flannery O'Connor (1925–1964), U.S. author: 'Some Aspects of The Grotesque in Southern Fiction', lecture, Wesleyan College for Women, Macon, Georgia, autumn 1960, first publ. in *Cluster Review* (Macon University), 1965, rep. in *Mystery and Manners* (ed. Sally and Robert Fitzgerald, 1972)

REALITY

1 Given that external reality is a fiction, the writer's role is almost superfluous. He does not need to invent the fiction because it is already there.

J.G. Ballard (b.1930), British author: interview in *Friends* (London), 30 Oct. 1970, rep. in *Re/Search* (San Francisco), No.8/9, 1984

2 The very definition of the real becomes: *that of which it is possible to give an equivalent reproduction.* ... The real is not only what can be reproduced, but *that which is always already reproduced.* The hyperreal.

Jean Baudrillard (b.1929), French semiologist: *Simulations* (1983), Pt.2, 'The Hyperrealism of Simulation'

3 One may be tired of the world – tired of the prayer-makers, the poem-makers, whose rituals are distracting and human and pleasant but worse than irritating because they have no reality – while reality itself remains very dear. One wants glimpses of the real. God is an immensity, while this disease, this death, which is in me, this small tightly defined pedestrian event, is merely and perfectly real, without miracle – or instruction.

Harold Brodkey (1930–1996), U.S. author: 'Passage into Non-Existence', publ. in the *Independent on Sunday* (London), 11 Feb. 1996. The article was Brodkey's last piece of published writing before his death from AIDS

4 In an age of synthetic images and synthetic emotions, the chances of an accidental encounter with reality are remote indeed.

Serge Daney (1944–1992), French film critic: 'Falling out of Love', publ. in *Sight and Sound* (London), July 1992

5 Reality is that which, when you stop believing in it, doesn't go away.

Philip K. Dick (1928–1982), U.S. science fiction writer: definition given in 1972, quoted by Dick in his Introduction to *I Hope I Shall Arrive Soon* (1986), 'How to Build a Universe That Doesn't Fall Apart Two Days Later'

6 Reality in our century is not something to be faced.

Graham Greene (1904–1991), British novelist: Hasselbacher, in *Our Man in Havana* (1958), Pt.1, Ch.1, Sct.1

7 Reality leaves a lot to the imagination.

John Lennon (1940–1980), British rock musician: *The Way It Is*, CBC-TV, June 1969, publ. in *Imagine* (ed. Andrew Solt and Sam Egan, 1988)

8 Reality is a question of perspective; the further you get from the past, the more concrete and plausible it seems – but as you approach the present, it inevitably seems more and more incredible.

Salman Rushdie (b.1947), Indian-born British author: *Midnight's Children* (1981), Bk.2, 'All-India Radio'

9 What our eyes behold may well be the text of life but one's meditations on the text and the disclosures of these meditations are no less a part of the structure of reality.

Wallace Stevens (1879–1955), U.S. poet: 'Three Academic Pieces', No.1 (1947), rep. in *The Necessary Angel* (1951)

10 In the American metaphysic, reality is always material reality, hard, resistant, unformed, impenetrable, and unpleasant.

Lionel Trilling (1905–1975), U.S. critic: *The Liberal Imagination* (1950), 'Reality in America'

REASON

1 Reason itself is fallible, and this fallibility must find a place in our logic.

Nicola Abbagnano (1901–1990), Italian philosopher: quoted in appreciation in *The Daily Telegraph* (London), 14 Sept. 1990

2 Reason transformed into prejudice is the worst form of prejudice, because reason is the only instrument for liberation from prejudice.

Allan Bloom (1930–1992), U.S. educator and author: *The Closing of the American Mind* (1987), Pt.3, 'From Socrates' *Apology* to Heidegger's *Rektoratsrede*'

3 In relying on his absolute rationalism, one places historical values above the values that we are accustomed by education or by prejudice to consider valid. Therefore if we rely on absolute rationalism or on one or another idea of progress, we accept the principle that the end justifies the means.

Albert Camus (1913–1960), French-Algerian philosopher and author: 'Neither Victims nor Executioners', publ. in *Combat*, Nov. 1947, rep. in *Actuelles*, 1950, quoted in *Camus: A Biography* by Herbert R. Lottman (1979), Ch.30

4 The more you reason the less you create.
Raymond Chandler (1880–1959), U.S. author: letter, 28 Oct. 1947, publ. in *Raymond Chandler Speaking* (ed. Dorothy Gardiner and Kathrine S. Walker, 1962)

5 Reason is a whore, surviving by simulation, versatility, and shamelessness.
E.M. Cioran (1911–1995), Rumanian-born French philosopher: *The Temptation to Exist* (1956), 'Rages and Resignations: Luther'

6 Just as love is an orientation which refers to all objects and is incompatible with the restriction to one object, so is reason a human faculty which must embrace the whole of the world with which man is confronted.
Erich Fromm (1900–1980), U.S. psychologist: *The Sane Society* (1955), Ch.3, 'The Need for a Frame of Orientation and Devotion – Reason vs. Irrationality'

7 Reason is a faculty far larger than mere objective force. When either the political or the scientific discourse announces itself as the voice of reason, it is playing God, and should be spanked and stood in the corner.
Ursula K. Le Guin (b.1929), U.S. author: Bryn Mawr Commencement Address (1986), publ. in *Dancing at the Edge of the World* (1989)

8 The fact that logic cannot satisfy us awakens an almost insatiable hunger for the irrational.
A.N. Wilson (b.1950), British author: book review in *The Guardian* (London), 30 Sept. 1989

See also Hawking on THE COSMOS; Fromm on INTELLIGENCE

REBELLION

1 Whoever thinks of stopping the uprising before it achieves its goals, I will give him ten bullets in the chest.
Yasir Arafat (b.1929), Palestinian leader: on the Intifada, quoted in *The Daily Telegraph* (London), 19 Jan. 1989

2 Every act of rebellion expresses a nostalgia for innocence and an appeal to the essence of being.
Albert Camus (1913–1960), French-Algerian philosopher and author: *The Rebel* (1951; tr.1953), Pt.3

3 It's not wise to violate rules until you know how to observe them.

T.S. Eliot (1888–1965), Anglo-American poet, critic: interview in *Writers at Work* (Second Series, ed. George Plimpton, 1963)

4 All men should have a drop of treason in their veins, if nations are not to go soft like so many sleepy pears.
Rebecca West (1892–1983), British author: *The Meaning of Treason* (1949), Pt.4, 'Conclusion'

REBELS

1 What've ya got?
Marlon Brando (b.1924), U.S. actor: Johnny (Brando), on being asked what he is rebelling against, in *The Wild One* (film; screenplay by John Paxton from a story by Mick Rooney, directed by Laslo Benedek, 1953)

2 The rebel can never find peace. He knows what is good and, despite himself, does evil. The value which supports him is never given to him once and for all – he must fight to uphold it, unceasingly.
Albert Camus (1913–1960), French-Algerian philosopher and author: *The Rebel* (1951; tr.1953), Pt.5, 'Nihilistic Murder'

3 No one can go on being a rebel too long without turning into an autocrat.
Lawrence Durrell (1912–1990), British author: Pursewarden writing to D.H. Lawrence, in *Balthazar* (1958), Pt.2, Ch.6

4 I wouldn't have turned out the way I was if I didn't have all those old-fashioned values to rebel against.
Madonna (b.1959), U.S. singer and actress: in *Time* (New York) 17 Dec. 1990, quoted in *Madonna: Blonde Ambition* by Mark Bego (1992), Ch.11

5 To be a rebel is not to be a revolutionary. It is more often but a way of spinning one's wheels deeper in the sand.
Kate Millett (b.1934), U.S. feminist author: *Sexual Politics* (1970), Ch.8, Sct.2

6 I'm interested in anything about revolt, disorder, chaos, especially activity that appears to have no meaning. It seems to me to be the road toward freedom.
Jim Morrison (1943–1971), U.S. rock musician: quoted in *Time* (New York), 24 Jan. 1968

7 Bad white boys, unlike their female counterparts, can draw upon a long history of benign tolerance for their rebel roles, while their male and female counterparts of color are marked as a pathological criminal class. The values of the white male outlaw are often those of the creative maverick universally prized by entrepreneurial or libertarian individualism.
Andrew Ross (b.1956), British social theorist: *Strange Weather* (1991), Ch.4

8   I am an Anti-Christ
I am an anarchist
Don't know what I want but I know where to
   get it
I wanna destroy passers-by
Because I wanna be anarchy!

Sex Pistols (1976–1979), British punk band:
'Anarchy in the U.K.' (song, 1976) on the album
Never Mind the Bollocks (1977)

9   I guess I was born, naturally born, born bad.

Quentin Tarantino (b.1958), U.S. film-maker:
sung by Mallory (Juliette Lewis) in prison, in
Natural Born Killers (film; screenplay by Quentin
Tarantino, directed by Oliver Stone, 1995). In a
dispute with Stone, Tarantino later disowned the
film

RECESSION

1   Few can believe that suffering, especially by
others, is in vain. Anything that is disagreeable
must surely have beneficial economic effects.

J.K. Galbraith (b.1908), U.S. economist: on
austerity measures proposed by politicians to ride
out a recession, in *The Age of Uncertainty* (1977),
Ch.7

2   In a society of little economic development,
universal inactivity accompanies universal
poverty. You survive not by struggling against
nature, or by increasing production, or by relentless labour; instead you survive by expending as little energy as possible, by striving
constantly to achieve a state of immobility.

Ryszard Kapuściński (b.1932), Polish journalist: 'A
Warsaw Diary', publ. in *Granta* (Cambridge),
No.15, 1985

3   So-called 'austerity', the stoic injunction, is
the path towards universal destruction. It is
the old, the fatal, competitive path. 'Pull in
your belt' is a slogan closely related to 'gird up
your loins', or the guns-butter metaphor.

Wyndham Lewis (1882–1957), British author and
painter: *America and Cosmic Man* (1948), 'The Case
Against Roots'

RECLUSIVES

1   I withdrew from the world not because I had
enemies there, but because I had friends. Not
because they did me an injustice as usually
happens, but because they believed me better
than I am. It's a lie I can't accept.

Albert Camus (1913–1960), French-Algerian
philosopher and author: journal entry, Jan. 1948,
while taking an eight-month break in Switzerland,
quoted in *Camus: A Biography* by Herbert R.
Lottman (1979), Ch.33

2   I've been up the mountain and I had a choice.
Should I come down? So I came down. God

said, 'Okay, you've been up on the mountain,
now you go down. You're on your own,
free. Check in later, but now you're on your
own.'

Bob Dylan (b.1941), US singer and songwriter: on
his decision to return to live performances in 1975,
quoted in *Dylan: Behind the Shades* by Clinton
Heylin (biography, 1991), Ch.22. Shortly after,
Dylan embarked on the 'Rolling Thunder Review'
tour of small venues in America

3   The monk in hiding himself from the world
becomes not less than himself, not less of a
person, but more of a person, more truly and
perfectly himself: for his personality and individuality are perfected in their true order, the
spiritual, interior order, of union with God,
the principle of all perfection.

Thomas Merton (1915–1968), U.S. religious writer
and poet: *The Seven Storey Mountain* (autobiography, 1948), Pt.3, Ch.2

4   In this world without quiet corners, there can
be no easy escapes from history, from hulla-
baloo, from terrible, unquiet fuss.

Salman Rushdie (b.1947), Indian-born British
author: 'Outside the Whale', essay (1984), rep. in
Imaginary Homelands (1991)

REFORM

1   You begin saving the world by saving one man
at a time; all else is grandiose romanticism or
politics.

Charles Bukowski (1920–1994), U.S. author and
poet: *Tales of Ordinary Madness* (1967), 'Too
Sensitive'

2   If there are people who feel that God wants
them to change the structures of society, that is
something between them and their God. We
must serve him in whatever way we are called.
I am called to help the individual; to love each
poor person. Not to deal with institutions. I am
in no position to judge.

Mother Teresa (1910–1997), Albanian-born
Roman Catholic missionary: *A Gift for God* (1975),
'Carriers of Christ's Love'

3   Men must be capable of imagining and executing and insisting on social change if they are to
reform or even maintain civilization, and capable too of furnishing the rebellion which is
sometimes necessary if society is not to perish
of immobility.

Rebecca West (1892–1983), British author: *The
Meaning of Treason* (1949), Pt.4, 'Conclusion'

See also PROGRESS

REGGAE *see under* MUSIC

REGRET

1 To look back is to relax one's vigil.
Bette Davis (1908–1989), U.S. actress: *The Lonely Life* (autobiography, 1962), Ch.1

2 Maybe all one can do is hope to end up with the right regrets.
Arthur Miller (b.1915), U.S. playwright: Tom, in *The Ride Down Mount Morgan* (1991), Act 1

3 *Non! Rien de rien...*
Non, je ne regrette rien!
Ni le bien qu'on m'a fait,
Ni le mal. Tout ça m'est bien égal!
(No, I regret nothing...
Neither the good nor the bad,
It's all the same for me.)
Edith Piaf (1918–1963), French singer: 'Non, Je Ne Regrette Rien' (song; written by Charles Dumont and Michael Vaucaire, 1961)

4 Hindsight is always twenty-twenty.
Billy Wilder (b.1906), U.S. film-maker: quoted in *Wit and Wisdom of the Moviemakers* (ed. John Robert Columbo, 1979), Ch.7

See also REMORSE; TIME: PAST

RELATIONSHIPS

1 Tenderness between people is nothing other than awareness of the possibility of relations without purpose.
Theodor W. Adorno (1903–1969), German philosopher, sociologist and music critic: *Minima Moralia* (1951; tr. G.F.N. Jephcott, 1978), Ch.20

2 A relationship, I think, is like a shark, you know? It has to constantly move forward or it dies. And I think what we got on our hands is a dead shark.
Woody Allen (b.1935), U.S. film-maker: Alvy Singer (Allen), reaching the end of his affair with Annie Hall (Diane Keaton), in *Annie Hall* (film; screenplay by Woody Allen and Marshall Brickman, directed by Woody Allen, 1977)

3 Now the whole dizzying and delirious range of sexual possibilities has been boiled down to that one big, boring, bulimic word. RELATIONSHIP.
Julie Burchill (b.1960), British journalist and author: 'The Dead Zone', first publ. in *Arena* (London), 1988, rep. in *Sex and Sensibility* (1992)

4 People who are having a love-sex relationship are continuously lying to each other because the very nature of the relationship demands that they do, because you have to make a love object of this person, which means that you editorialize about them. ... You cut out what you don't want to see, you add this if it isn't there. And so therefore you're building a lie.
Truman Capote (1924–1984), U.S. author: interview in *The Americans* by David Frost (1970), 'When does a Writer Become a Star?'

5 In the mythic schema of all relations between men and women, man proposes, and woman is disposed of.
Angela Carter (1940–1992), British author: *The Sadeian Woman* (1979), 'Polemical Preface'

6 In the beginning of all relationships you are out there bungee jumping every weekend but after six months you are renting videos and buying corn chips just like everyone else – and the next day you can't even remember what video you rented.
Douglas Coupland (b.1961), Canadian author: *Life After God* (1994), 'Gettysburg'

7 It is explained that all relationships require a little give and take. This is untrue. Any partnership demands that we give and give and give and at the last, as we flop into our graves exhausted, we are told that we didn't give enough.
Quentin Crisp (b.1908), British author: *How to Become a Virgin* (1981), Ch.4

8 The formula for achieving a successful relationship is simple: you should treat all disasters as if they were trivialities but never treat a triviality as if it were a disaster.
Quentin Crisp: *Manners from Heaven* (1984), Ch.7

9 Maybe the most you can expect from a relationship that goes bad is to come out of it with a few good songs.
Marianne Faithfull (b.1946), British singer: on her relationship with Mick Jagger, in *Faithfull* (1994), 'Colston Hall'

10 It is easier to live through someone else than to become complete yourself.
Betty Friedan (b.1921), U.S. feminist writer: *The Feminine Mystique* (1963), Ch.14

11 Kindness and intelligence don't always deliver us from the pitfalls and traps: there are always failures of love, of will, of imagination. There is no way to take the danger out of human relationships.
Barbara Grizzuti Harrison (b.1941), U.S. author and publicist: 'Secrets Women Tell Each Other', in *McCall's* (New York), Aug. 1975

12 We can never establish with certainty what part of our relations with others is the result of our emotions – love, antipathy, charity, or malice – and what part is predetermined by the constant power play among individuals.

Milan Kundera (b.1929), Czech-born French author and critic: *The Unbearable Lightness of Being* (1984), Pt.7, Ch.2

13 Long-term commitment to an intimate relationship with one person of whatever sex is an essential need that people have in order to breed the qualities out of which nurturant thought can rise.

Gerda Lerner (b.1920), U.S. educator and author: quoted in *Ms.* (New York), Sept. 1981

14 There is no substitute for the comfort supplied by the utterly taken-for-granted relationship.

Iris Murdoch (b.1919), British novelist and philosopher: Martin Lynch-Gibbons, in *A Severed Head* (1961), Ch.28

15 What you want
Baby, I got it.
What you need,
You know I got it.
All I'm askin' for's
A little respect, baby,
When you come home, hey, baby,
When you get home.

Otis Redding (1941–1967), U.S. soul singer: 'Respect' (song, 1965), publ. in *The Poetry of Soul* (ed. A.X. Nicholas, 1971). The song is best known in the 1967 version by Aretha Franklin

16 Nobody on this planet ever really chooses each other. I mean, it's all a question of quantum physics, molecular attraction and timing.

Ron Shelton (b.1945), U.S. film-maker: Annie Savoy (Susan Sarandon), in *Bull Durham* (film; written and directed by Ron Shelton, 1988)

17 It is only when we no longer compulsively need someone that we can have a real relationship with them.

Anthony Storr (b.1920), British psychiatrist: *The Integrity of the Personality* (1960), Ch.9

See also FRIENDSHIP; LOVE; MARRIAGE; MONOGAMY

RELIGION

1 No one is safe from religious ideas and confessional phenomena. ... We can fall victim to them when we least expect it. It's like Mao 'flu, or being struck by lightning.

Ingmar Bergman (b.1918), Swedish stage and film writer-director: interview in *Bergman on Bergman* (1970), 'Rasunda, 3 July 1968'

2 Culture's essential service to a religion is to destroy intellectual idolatry, the recurrent tendency in religion to replace the object of its worship with its present understanding and forms of approach to that object.

Northrop Frye (1912–1991), Canadian literary critic: *Anatomy of Criticism* (1957), 'Anagogic Phase: Symbol as Monad'

3 Religion is doing; a man does not merely *think* his religion or feel it, he 'lives' his religion as much as he is able, otherwise it is not religion but fantasy or philosophy.

George Gurdjieff (c.1877–1949), Greek-Armenian religious teacher and mystic: quoted in *In Search of the Miraculous* by P.D. Ouspensky (1949), Ch. 15

4 It's incongruous that the older we get, the more likely we are to turn in the direction of religion. Less vivid and intense ourselves, closer to the grave, we begin to conceive of ourselves as immortal.

Edward Hoagland (b.1932), U.S. novelist and essayist: 'The Ridge-Slope Fox and The Knife-Thrower', first publ. in *Harper's Magazine* (New York), Jan. 1977, rep. in *Heart's Desire* (1988)

5 Pure Spirit, one hundred degrees proof – that's a drink that only the most hardened contemplation-guzzlers indulge in. Bodhisattvas dilute their Nirvana with equal parts of love and work.

Aldous Huxley (1894–1963), British author: Susila, in *Island* (1962), Ch.15

6 Talk to me about the truth of religion and I'll listen gladly. Talk to me about the duty of religion and I'll listen submissively. But don't come talking to me about the consolations of religion or I shall suspect that you don't understand.

C.S. Lewis (1898–1963), British author: *A Grief Observed* (1961), Pt.2

7 I daresay anything can be made holy by being sincerely worshipped.

Iris Murdoch (b.1919), British novelist and philosopher: Maisie Tether, in *The Message to the Planet* (1989), Pt.5

8 Religion to me has always been the wound, not the bandage.

Dennis Potter (1935–1994), British dramatist and screenwriter: interview with Melvyn Bragg, Channel 4, 5 April 1994

9 Religion is probably, after sex, the second oldest resource which human beings have available to them for blowing their minds.

Susan Sontag (b.1933), U.S. essayist: 'The Pornographic Imagination', Sct.3, first publ. in *Partisan Review* (New Brunswick, N.J.), spring 1967, rep. in *Styles of Radical Will* (1969)

10 Religion is the state of being grasped by an ultimate concern, a concern which qualifies all other concerns as preliminary and which itself contains the answer to the question of a meaning of our life.

Paul Tillich (1886–1965), German-born U.S. theologian: *Christianity and the Encounter of the World Religions* (1963), Ch.1

11 Religion enables us to ignore nothingness and get on with the jobs of life.
John Updike (b.1932), U.S. author and critic: *Self-Consciousness: Memoirs* (1989), Ch.6

12 Now is a great time for new religions to pop up. There are people who get religious about jogging, they get religious about sex, and you talk to some of these people who are avowed swingers – they'll bore your head off. God, it's just painful to listen to them. Health foods have become the basis of a religion. Let's see, ESP, of course, flying saucers, anything is fertile ground now. There's a new messiah born every day.
Tom Wolfe (b.1931), U.S. author and journalist: interview in *Rolling Stone* (New York), Aug. 1980

See also BUDDHISM; CHRISTIANITY; GOD; ISLAM; JUDAISM; PRAYER; Fry on THE SUPERNATURAL

REMORSE

1 Classic remorse, as all the moralists are agreed, is a most undesirable sentiment. If you have behaved badly, repent, make what amends you can and address yourself to the task of behaving better next time. On no account brood over your wrongdoing. ROLLING IN THE MUCK IS NOT THE BEST WAY OF GETTING CLEAN.
Aldous Huxley (1894–1963), British author: introduction written in 1946, to *Brave New World* (1932)

2 Only in your imagination can you revise.
Fay Wray (b.1907), U.S. actress: in the *International Herald Tribune* (Paris), 22 Feb. 1989

See also REGRET

REPRESSION

1 If they take you in the morning, they will be coming for us that night.
James Baldwin (1924–1987), U.S. author: 'Open Letter to my Sister, Angela Davis', in the *New York Review of Books*, 7 Jan. 1971

2 The only justification for repressive institutions is material and cultural deficit. But such institutions, at certain stages of history, perpetuate and produce such a deficit, and even threaten human survival.
Noam Chomsky (b.1928), U.S. linguist and political analyst: 'Language and Freedom', lecture at Loyola University, Chicago, Jan. 1970, rep. in *For Reasons of State* (1973)

3 If repression has indeed been the fundamental link between power, knowledge, and sexuality since the classical age, it stands to reason that

we will not be able to free ourselves from it except at a considerable cost.
Michel Foucault (1926–1984), French philosopher: *The History of Sexuality* (1976; tr.1984), Vol.I, Pt.1

4 People with a culture of poverty suffer much less from repression than we of the middle class suffer and indeed, if I may make the suggestion with due qualification, they often have a hell of a lot more fun than we have.
Brian Friel (b.1929), Irish playwright and author: Dodds, in *The Freedom of the City* (1974), Act 1

5 Life cannot be destroyed for good, neither ... can history be brought entirely to a halt. A secret streamlet trickles on beneath the heavy lid of inertia and pseudo-events, slowly and inconspicuously undercutting it. It may be a long process, but one day it must happen: the lid will no longer hold and will start to crack. This is the moment when something once more begins visibly to *happen*, something truly new and unique ... something truly historical, in the sense that *history* again demands to be heard.
Václav Havel (b.1936), Czech playwright and president: *Living in Truth* (1986), Pt.1, 'Letter to Dr Gustáv Husák', 8 April 1975

6 Blow the dust off the clock. Your watches are behind the times. Throw open the heavy curtains which are so dear to you – you do not even suspect that the day has already dawned outside.
Alexander Solzhenitsyn (b.1918), Russian novelist: letter to the Secretariat of the Soviet Writer's Union, 12 Nov. 1969, publ. in *Solzhenitsyn: A Documentary Record* (ed. Leopold Labedz, 1970), 'Expulsion'

See also Crews on WILD AT HEART

REPUTATION

1 Never do anything you wouldn't want to be caught dead doing.
John Carradine (1906–1988), U.S. actor: advice to his son, David Carradine, quoted in *Brewer's Cinema* (1995)

2 My reputation is a media creation.
John Lydon [formerly Johnny Rotten] (b.1957), British rock musician: in *The Observer* (London), 4 May 1986

RESEARCH

1 Not many appreciate the ultimate power and potential usefulness of basic knowledge accumulated by obscure, unseen investigators who, in a lifetime of intensive study, may never see any practical use for their findings but who go

on seeking answers to the unknown without thought of financial or practical gain.

Eugenie Clark (b.1922), U.S. marine biologist and author: *The Lady and the Sharks* (1969), Ch.1

2 After all, the ultimate goal of all research is not objectivity, but truth.

Helene Deutsch (1884–1982), U.S. psychiatrist: preface to *The Psychology of Women* (1944–45), Vol.I

3 Data is what distinguishes the dilettante from the artist.

George V. Higgins (b.1939), U.S. novelist: in *The Guardian* (London), 17 June 1988

4 If politics is the art of the possible, research is surely the art of the soluble. Both are immensely practical-minded affairs.

Peter Medawar (1915–1987), British immunologist: 'The Act of Creation', first publ. in the *New Statesman* (London), 19 June 1964, rep. in *The Art of the Soluble* (1967)

5 Research is usually a policeman stopping a novel from progressing.

Brian Moore (b.1921), Irish novelist: in *The Sunday Times* (London), 15 April 1990

RESENTMENT

1 In ceremonies of the horsemen,
Even the pawn must hold a grudge.

Bob Dylan (b.1941), U.S. singer and songwriter: 'Love Minus Zero/No Limit' (song) on the album *Bringing it All Back Home* (1965)

2 To have a grievance is to have a purpose in life.

Eric Hoffer (1902–1983), U.S. philosopher: *The Passionate State of Mind* (1955), Aph.166. Hoffer added: 'It not infrequently happens that those who hunger for hope give their allegiance to him who offers them a grievance'

RESISTANCE

1 You may write me down in history
With your bitter, twisted lies,
You may trod me in the very dirt
But still, like dust, I'll rise.

Maya Angelou (b.1928), U.S. author: 'Still I Rise', publ. in *And Still I Rise* (1978)

2 Fight the power that be. Fight the power.

Public Enemy, U.S. rap group: 'Fight the Power' (song), written and performed by Carlton Ridenhour, Keith Shocklee (James Henry Boxley) & Eric Sadler, of Public Enemy, used as theme song in *Do the Right Thing* (film; written, directed and co-produced by Spike Lee, 1989). Lyrics are printed in *Rap: The Lyrics* ed. Lawrence A. Stranley (1992)

See also Kundera on MEMORY

RESPECTABILITY

1 Decency ... must be an even more exhausting state to maintain than its opposite. Those who succeed seem to need a stupefying amount of sleep.

Quentin Crisp (b.1908), British author: *The Naked Civil Servant* (1968), Ch.9

2 In order to acquire a growing and lasting respect in society, it is a good thing, if you possess great talent, to give, early in your youth, a very hard kick to the right shin of the society that you love. After that, be a snob.

Salvador Dali (1904–1989), Spanish painter: journal entry, 11 May 1956, in *Diary of a Genius* (1966)

3 *I'm* the bad guy? ... How did that happen? I did everything they told me to. Did you know I build missiles? I help to protect America. You should be rewarded for that.

Michael Douglas (b.1944), U.S. actor: D-Fens (Douglas), in *Falling Down* (film; screenplay by Ebbe Roe Smith, directed by Joel Schumacher, 1993)

4 We're like bad architecture or an old whore. If you stick around long enough, eventually you get respectable.

Jerry Garcia (1942–1995), U.S. rock musician: referring to the Grateful Dead rock group, quoted in *Captain Trips* by Sandy Troy (1994), Ch.9

5 Prestige is the shadow of money and power. Where these are, there it is. Like the national market for soap or automobiles and the enlarged arena of federal power, the national cash-in area for prestige has grown, slowly being consolidated into a truly national system.

C. Wright Mills (1916–1962), U.S. sociologist: *The Power Elite* (1956), Ch.4

6 My life has been one long descent into respectability.

Mandy Rice-Davies (b.1944), British call-girl: quoted by journalist Lynn Barber in the *Independent on Sunday* (London), 31 March 1991, in connection with reports that Rice-Davies was on social terms with Sir Denis Thatcher, husband of ex-prime minister Margaret Thatcher

RESPONSIBILITY

1 What does it mean to say that government might have a responsibility? Government can't have a responsibility any more than the business can. The only entities which can have responsibilities are people.

Milton Friedman (b.1912), U.S. economist: *There's No Such Thing as a Free Lunch* (1975), Ch.11

2   Responsibility is what awaits outside the Eden of Creativity.
    Nadine Gordimer (b.1923), South African author: 'The Essential Gesture', lecture, 12 Oct. 1984, University of Michigan, first publ. in *The Tanner Lectures on Human Values* (ed. Sterling M. McMurrin, 1985), rep. in *The Essential Gesture* (ed. Stephen Clingman, 1988)

3   Man is free and therefore *responsible*. His is a personal and social responsibility, a responsibility before God, a responsibility which is his greatness.
    Pope John Paul II [Karol Wojtyla] (b.1920), Polish ecclesiastic: *Crossing the Threshold of Hope* (1994), 'Does "Eternal Life" Exist?'

4   We are responsible for actions performed in response to circumstances for which we are not responsible.
    Allan Massie (b.1938), British author: Etienne, in *A Question of Loyalties* (1989), Pt.3, Ch.22

5   The most dangerous aspect of present-day life is the dissolution of the feeling of individual responsibility. Mass solitude has done away with any difference between the internal and the external, between the intellectual and the physical.
    Eugenio Montale (1896–1981), Italian poet: *Poet In Our Time* (1972), p.16 of Marion Boyars edn. (1976)

6   Mum, you've absolved yourself of responsibility. You live from self-induced-crisis to self-induced-crisis. Someone chooses what you wear. Someone does your brain. Someone tells you what to eat, and, three times a week, someone sticks a hose up your bum and flushes it all out for you.
    Jennifer Saunders (b.1957), British comedian: Saffron (Julia Sawalha), in *Absolutely Fabulous*, 'Fashion' (TV series written by Jennifer Saunders, first series, broadcast 1993). Edina replies, 'It's called colonic irrigation, darling, and it's not to be sniffed at'

7   The buck stops here.
    Harry S Truman (1884–1972), U.S. Democratic politician and president: motto on Truman's desk at the White House, quoted in *The Man from Missouri* by Alfred Steinberg (1962)

See also Smith on JESUS CHRIST

RESTAURANTS

1   In the United States all business not transacted over the telephone is accomplished in conjunction with alcohol or food, often under conditions of advanced intoxication. This is a fact of the utmost importance for the visitor of limited funds ... for it means that the most expensive restaurants are, with rare exceptions, the worst.
    J.K. Galbraith (b.1908), U.S. economist: 'The United States', publ. in *New York*, 15 Nov. 1971, rep. in *A View from the Stands* (1986)

2   My little breasts, my face, my hips,
    My legs they study while they feed
    Are not found on the list they read.
    Thom Gunn (b.1929), British poet: 'Waitress', publ. in *The Passages of Joy* (1982)

3   You can get anything you want at Alice's Restaurant.
    Arlo Guthrie (b.1947), U.S. singer and songwriter: 'Alice's Restaurant Massacree' (song) on the album *Alice's Restaurant* (1967)

4   A restaurant is a fantasy – a kind of living fantasy in which diners are the most important members of the cast.
    Warner LeRoy, founder of Maxwell's Plum restaurant, New York City: in the *New York Times*, 9 July 1976

5   In a restaurant one is both observed and unobserved. Joy and sorrow can be displayed and observed 'unwittingly', the writer scowling naively and the diners wondering, What the *hell* is he doing?
    David Mamet (b.1947), U.S. playwright: *Writing in Restaurants* (1986), 'Some Thoughts on Writing in Restaurants'

6   I don't tip because society says I gotta. I tip when somebody deserves a tip. When somebody really puts forth an effort, they deserve a little extra something. But this tipping automatically, that's shit for the birds. ... It would appear that waitresses are one of the groups in society the government fucks in the ass on a regular basis. That's fucked up.
    Quentin Tarantino (b.1958), U.S. film-maker: Mr Pink (Steve Buscemi), in *Reservoir Dogs* (film; written and directed by Quentin Tarantino, 1992)

See also MCDONALD'S

RESTRAINT

1   People don't deserve the restraint we show by not going into delirium in front of them. To hell with *them!*
    Louis-Ferdinand Céline (1894–1961), French author: letter, 30 June 1947, publ. in *Critical Essays on Louis-Ferdinand Céline* (ed. William K. Buckley, 1989)

2   Moderation is a virtue only in those who are thought to have an alternative.
    Henry Kissinger (b.1923), U.S. Republican politician and secretary of state: quoted in *The Observer* (London), 24 Jan. 1982

RETIREMENT

1   Men and women approaching retirement age should be recycled for public service work, and their companies should foot the bill. We can no longer afford to scrap-pile people.
Maggie Kuhn (1905–1995), U.S. civil rights activist and author: 'Gray Panthers Versus Ageism', publ. in *Ms*. (New York), July 1973

2   Retire, retire into a fungus basement
Where nothing moves except the draught
And the light and dark grey figures
Doubling their money on the screen;
Where the cabbages taste like the mummy's hand
And the meat tastes of feet;
Where there is nothing to say except:
'Remember?' or 'Your turn to dust the cat.'
Adrian Mitchell (b.1932), British poet and author: 'Old Age Report', publ. in *Ride the Nightmare* (1971)

3   I am a free man. I feel as light as a feather.
Javier Perez de Cuéllar (b.1920), Peruvian diplomat: on stepping down as secretary-general of the U.N., quoted in *The Times* (London), 2 Jan. 1992

4   Eating's going to be a whole new ball game. I may even have to buy a new pair of trousers.
Lester Piggott (b.1935), British champion jockey: on his retirement, quoted in *The Sunday Times* (London), 29 Dec. 1985. Piggott later came out of retirement

REVENGE

1   Revenge today pursues not merely individuals but whole peoples, and the flames of animosity are stoked continuously with a propaganda hitherto confined to time of war.
Oswald Mosley (1896–1980), British fascist leader: *My Life* (1968), Ch.5

2   God shrive my soul, for it'll need it! ... God shrive it when I find the evil thing! For absolution, or no absolution – there'll be *satisfaction* found. ... Let them touch him. For every hair that's hurt I'll stop a heart. If grace I have when turbulence is over – so be it; and if not – what then?
Mervyn Peake (1911–1968), British author and illustrator: Gertrude, Countess of Groan, swears vengeance on the revolutionary, Steerpike, in *Titus Groan* (1946), 'Countess Gertrude'

3   No one can kill Americans and brag about it. No one.
Ronald Reagan (b.1911), U.S. Republican politician and president: following the U.S. attack on Libya, 15 April 1986, quoted in *The Observer* (London), 27 April 1986. The attack followed the bombing of a discotheque in West Berlin, at which

two American servicemen were killed and 200 injured. The attack on Libya killed about a hundred civilians

4   Somebody's stickin' a red hot poker up our asses and we gotta find out whose name is on the handle.
Quentin Tarantino (b.1958), U.S. film-maker: Mr Pink (Steve Buscemi), in *Reservoir Dogs* (film; written and directed by Quentin Tarantino, 1992)

REVOLUTION

1   The idea that a revolution in the West could be based on a small minority, however active and militant, is totally absurd. It is a view of revolution advanced only by those who fear the masses. Or by those products of 1968 who, despairing of the mass parties and their domination of working-class politics, have abandoned politics and picked up sub machine-guns and bombs.
Tariq Ali (b.1943), Pakistani-born British activist and author: *1968 and After: Inside the Revolution* (1978), Ch.7

2   Revolutions are celebrated when they are no longer dangerous.
Pierre Boulez (b.1925), French composer and conductor: on the bicentenary celebrations of the French Revolution, in *The Guardian* (London), 13 Jan. 1989

3   Revolution sounds very romantic, you know. but it ain't. it's blood and guts and madness; it's little kids who don't understand what the fuck is going on. it's your whore, your wife ripped in the belly with a bayonet and then raped in the ass while you watch. it's men torturing men who used to laugh at Mickey Mouse cartoons.
Charles Bukowski (1920–1994), U.S. author and poet: *Notes of a Dirty Old Man* (1969), p.64 of City Lights edn. (1973)

4   I had such a wonderful feeling last night, walking beneath the dark sky while cannon boomed on my right and guns on my left ... the feeling that I could change the world only by being there.
Viorica Butnariu, student at Bucharest University, Rumania: on the Rumanian revolution, in letter to American friend, 23 Dec. 1989, publ. in *The Observer* (London), 31 Dec. 1989

5   More and more, revolution has found itself delivered into the hands of its bureaucrats and doctrinaires on the one hand, and to enfeebled and bewildered masses on the other.
Albert Camus (1913–1960), French-Algerian philosopher and author: *The Rebel* (1951; tr.1953), Pt.3, 'State Terrorism and Rational Terror'

6   I began revolution with 82 men. If I had [to] do it again, I do it with 10 or 15 and absolute faith.

It does not matter how small you are if you have faith and plan of action.

Fidel Castro (b.1926), Cuban revolutionary and premier: in the *New York Times*, 22 April 1959

7 All revolutions go down in history, but history does not fill up; the rivers of revolution return from whence they came, only to flow again.

Guy Debord (1931–1994), French Situationist philosopher: *Panegyric* (autobiography, 1989), Pt..2

8 All successful revolutions are the kicking in of a rotten door. The violence of revolutions is the violence of men who charge into a vacuum.

J.K. Galbraith (b.1908), U.S. economist: *The Age of Uncertainty* (1977), Ch.3

9 The main object of a revolution is the liberation of man ... not the interpretation and application of some transcendental ideology.

Jean Genet (1910–1986), French playwright and novelist: *Prisoner of Love* (1986; tr.1989), Pt.1

10 The surest guide to the correctness of the path that women take is *joy in the struggle*. Revolution is the festival of the oppressed.

Germaine Greer (b.1939), Australian feminist writer: *The Female Eunuch* (1970), 'Revolution'

11 The revolution is made by man, but man must forge his revolutionary spirit from day to day.

Ernesto 'Che' Guevara (1928–1967), Argentinian revolutionary leader: 'Socialism and Man in Cuba', open letter to the editor of a Uruguayan newspaper *La Marcha*, 1967, rep. in *Che Guevara on Revolution* (ed. Jay Mallin, 1969)

12 Revolutions are notorious for allowing even non-participants – even women! – new scope for telling the truth since they are themselves such massive moments of truth, moments of such massive participation.

Selma James (b.1930), U.S. author and political activist: *The Ladies and the Mammies: Jane Austen and Jean Rhys* (1983), Ch.1

13 Although a system may cease to exist in the legal sense or as a structure of power, its values (or anti-values), its philosophy, its teachings remain in us. They rule our thinking, our conduct, our attitude to others. The situation is a demonic paradox: we have toppled the system but we still carry its genes.

Ryszard Kapuściński (b.1932), Polish journalist: in the *Independent on Sunday* (London), 1 Sept. 1991

14 Those who make peaceful revolution impossible will make violent revolution inevitable.

John F. Kennedy (1917–1963), U.S. Democratic politician and president: speech, 13 March 1962, the White House, addressing the diplomatic corps of the Latin American republics, publ. in *Public Papers of the Presidents of the United States: John F. Kennedy, 1962*

15 If we were to promise people nothing better than only revolution, they would scratch their heads and say: 'Is it not better to have good goulash?'

Nikita Khrushchev (1894–1971), Soviet premier: quoted in *The Observer* (London), 12 Sept. 1971

16 The children of the revolution are always ungrateful, and the revolution must be grateful that it is so.

Ursula K. Le Guin (b.1929), U.S. author: 'Reciprocity of Prose and Poetry', address, 1983, in Poetry Series, Folger Shakespeare Library, Washington D.C., publ. in *Dancing at the Edge of the World* (1989)

17 It is easier to run a revolution than a government.

Ferdinand E. Marcos (1917–1981), Filipino politician and president: in *Time* (New York), 6 June 1977

18 The word 'revolution' itself has become not only a dead relic of Leftism, but a key to the deadendedness of male politics: the 'revolution' of a wheel which returns in the end to the same place; the 'revolving door' of a politics which has 'liberated' women only to use them, and only within the limits of male tolerance.

Adrienne Rich (b.1929), U.S. poet: 'Power and Danger: Works of a Common Woman', Introduction to *The Work of a Common Woman: The Collected Poetry of Judy Grahn, 1964–1977* (1977), rep. in *On Lies, Secrets, and Silence* (1980)

19 The differences between revolution in art and revolution in politics are enormous. ... Revolution in art lies not in the will to destroy but in the revelation of what has already been destroyed. Art kills only the dead.

Harold Rosenberg (1906–1978), U.S. art critic and author: *The Tradition of the New* (1960), Ch.6

20 Life in this society being, at best, an utter bore and no aspect of society being at all relevant to women, there remains to civic-minded, responsible, thrill-seeking females only to overthrow the government, eliminate the money system, institute complete automation and destroy the male sex.

Valerie Solanas (1936–1988), U.S. actress and writer: 'The SCUM Manifesto' (1968), rep. in *Sisterhood is Powerful* (ed. Robin Morgan, 1970). The acronym *SCUM* stood for Society for Cutting Up Men

21 You better stop, hey,
What's that sound?
Everybody look what's goin' down.

Stephen Stills (b.1945), U.S. singer and songwriter: 'For What it's Worth' (song) on the album *Buffalo Springfield Again* (The Buffalo Springfield, 1967). The song, written after the LA riots in 1967, became a protest anthem about police brutality

22 I'll tip my hat to the new constitution
Take a vow for the new revolution;

Smiling free at the change all around me;
Pick up my guitar and play;
Just like yesterday.
Then I'll get on my knees and pray
We don't get fooled again.

Pete Townshend (b.1945), British rock musician:
'Won't Get Fooled Again' (song) on the album
Who's Next (The Who, 1971)

23 Two tasks confront those who hate the
servitude to which the industrial system is
reducing the human race. First, we must work
to heighten the social stresses within the
system so as to increase the likelihood that it
will break down or be weakened sufficiently so
that a revolution against it becomes possible.
Second, it is necessary to develop and propa-
gate an ideology that opposes technology and
industrial society if and when the system
becomes sufficiently weakened. And such an
ideology will help to assure that, if and when
industrial society breaks down, its remnants
will be smashed beyond repair, so that system
cannot be reconstituted. The factories should
be destroyed, technical books burned, etc.

Unabomber, U.S. radical: *Industrial Society and
Its Future*, 'Human Race at a Crossroads', Sct.165,
publ. in the *Washington Post*, 19 Sept. 1995

24 People who talk about revolution and class
struggle without referring explicitly to everyday life, without understanding what is subversive about love and what is positive in the
refusal of constraints, such people have a
corpse in their mouth.

Raoul Vaneigem (b.1934), Belgian Situationist
philosopher: *The Revolution of Everyday Life* (1967;
tr.1983), Ch.1, Sct.4. The last words were graffitied
onto walls in Paris during the 1968 revolt

See also Dylan on THE 1960S

REVOLUTIONARIES

1 Naturally revolutionaries cannot be certain
what will be the outcome of a particular
struggle or battle. We are not soothsayers who
promise success. What we do insist on is that
our methods are more educative so that even in
cases of defeats the masses, in reality, assimi-
late the causes of the setback and are better
prepared for the next encounter.

Tariq Ali (b.1943), Pakistani-born British activist
and author: *1968 and After: Inside the Revolution*
(1978), Ch.4

2 It is well known that the most radical revolutionary will become a conservative the day
after the revolution.

Hannah Arendt (1906–1975), German-born U.S.
political philosopher: in the *New Yorker*, 12 Sept.
1970

3 Every revolutionary ends by becoming either
an oppressor or a heretic.

Albert Camus (1913–1960), French-Algerian
philosopher and author: *The Rebel* (1951; tr.1953),
Ch.3, 'Rebellion and Revolution'

4 I feel my belief in sacrifice and struggle getting
stronger. I despise the kind of existence that
clings to the miserly trifles of comfort and self-
interest. I think that a man should not live
beyond the age when he begins to deteriorate,
when the flame that lighted the brightest
moment of his life has weakened.

Fidel Castro (b.1926), Cuban revolutionary and
president: letter, 19 Dec. 1953, publ. in Carlos
Franqui's *Diary of the Cuban Revolution* (1980),
p.67

5 Normal life cannot sustain revolutionary
attitudes for long.

Milovan Djilas (1911–1995), Yugoslav political
leader and writer: in *The Guardian* (London),
9 April 1990

6 The peasants alone are revolutionary, for they
have nothing to lose and everything to gain.
The starving peasant, outside the class system,
is the first among the exploited to discover that
only violence pays. For him there is no compromise, no possible coming to terms.

Frantz Fanon (1925–1961), Martiniquan
psychiatrist, philosopher and political activist: *The
Wretched of the Earth* (1961), Ch.1

7 Let me say, with the risk of appearing ridiculous, that the true revolutionary is guided by
strong feelings of love. It is impossible to think
of an authentic revolutionary without this
quality.

Ernesto 'Che' Guevara (1928–1967), Argentinian
revolutionary leader: 'Socialism and Man in Cuba',
open letter to the editor of a Uruguayan newspaper
La Marcha, 1967, publ. in *Che Guevara on
Revolution* (ed. Jay Mallin, 1969)

8 True revolutionaries are like God – they create
the world in their own image. Our awesome
responsibility to ourselves, to our children,
and to the future is to create ourselves in the
image of goodness, because the future depends
on the nobility of our imaginings.

Barbara Grizzuti Harrison (1941), U.S. author
and publicist: *Unlearning the Lie: Sexism in School*
(1973), Ch.9

9 The first duty of a revolutionary is to get away
with it.

Abbie Hoffman (1935–1989), U.S. political activist:
attributed, in *The Heretic's Handbook of Quotations*
(ed. Charles Bufe, 1988; rev.1991)

10 Revolutions are brought about by men, by
men who think as men of action and act as men
of thought.

Kwame Nkrumah (1900–1972), Ghanaian
president: *Consciencism* (1964), Ch.2

11 If not us, who? If not now, when?

Slogan by Czech university students in Prague, November 1989, quoted in *The Observer* (London), 26 November 1989

12 Revolutionaries should have as many children as they can. There is strong scientific evidence that social attitudes are to a significant extent inherited.

Unabomber, U.S. radical: *Industrial Society and Its Future*, 'Strategy', Sct.204, publ. in the *Washington Post*, 19 Sept. 1995

13 You said 'They're harmless dreamers and they're loved by the people.' – 'What,' I asked you, 'is harmless about a dreamer, and what,' I asked you, 'is harmless about the love of the people? – Revolution only needs good dreamers who remember their dreams.'

Tennessee Williams (1911–1983), U.S. playwright: Gutman, speaking to the Generalissimo, in *Camino Real* (1953), Block 2

THE RICH

1 And being rich is about acting too, isn't it? A style, a pose, an interpretation that you force upon the world? Whether or not you've made the stuff yourself, you have to set about pretending that you merit it, that money chose right in choosing you, and that you'll do right by money in your turn. Moneymad or just moneysmug, you have to pretend it's the natural thing.

Martin Amis (b.1949), British author: *Money* (1984), p.333 of Penguin edn. (1985)

2 Every man thinks God is on his side. The rich and powerful know he is.

Jean Anouilh (1910–1987), French playwright: Charles, in *The Lark* (1953; adapted by Lillian Hellman, 1955)

3 The rich are different – they have scandal.

Julie Burchill (b.1960), British journalist and author: *Girls on Film* (1986), Ch.3

4 The saddest thing I can imagine is to get used to luxury.

Charlie Chaplin (1889–1977), British comic actor and film-maker: *My Autobiography* (1960), Ch.22

5 There is a gigantic difference between earning a great deal of money and being rich.

Marlene Dietrich (1904–1992), German-born U.S. actress: *Marlene Dietrich's ABC* (1962), 'Earning'

6 Of all classes the rich are the most noticed and the least studied.

J.K. Galbraith (b.1908), U.S. economist: *The Age of Uncertainty* (1977), Ch.2

7 No, not rich. I am a poor man with money, which is not the same thing.

Gabriel García Márquez (b.1928), Colombian author: Uncle Leo XII, in *Love in the Time of Cholera* (1985; tr.1988), p.167 of Penguin edn. (1989)

8 A certain kind of rich man afflicted with the symptoms of moral dandyism sooner or later comes to the conclusion that it isn't enough merely to make money. He feels obliged to hold views, to espouse causes and elect Presidents, to explain to a trembling world how and why the world went wrong. The spectacle is nearly always comic.

Lewis H. Lapham (b.1935), U.S. essayist and editor: *Money and Class in America* (1988), Ch.7

9 I don't care how rich he is – as long as he has a yacht, his own private railroad car, and his own toothpaste.

Marilyn Monroe (1926–1962), U.S. actress: Sugar Kane (Monroe), in *Some Like It Hot* (film; screenplay by Billy Wilder and I.A.L. Diamond, produced and directed by Billy Wilder, 1959)

10 I have no idea what a poor Rothschild would look like. I suppose he would vanish in anonymity.

Guy de Rothschild (b.1909), French banker: *The Whims of Fortune* (1985), Ch.1

11 The trouble is that rich people, well-to-do people, very often don't really know who the poor are; and that is why we can forgive them, for knowledge can only lead to love, and love to service. And so, if they are not touched by them, it's because they do not know them.

Mother Teresa (1910–1997), Albanian-born Roman Catholic missionary: *A Gift for God* (1975), 'Riches'

12 To be rich nowadays merely means to possess a large number of poor objects.

Raoul Vaneigem (b.1934), Belgian Situationist philosopher: *The Revolution of Everyday Life* (1967; tr.1983), Ch.7, Sct.2

See also Goodman on PRIVILEGE; TYCOONS; WEALTH

RIOTS

1 Burn, baby, burn!

Black extremist slogan, following the August 1965 race riots in Watts, Los Angeles, quoted in *I Hear America Talking* by Stuart Berg Flexner (1976), 'The Blacks'

2 Perhaps having built a barricade when you're sixteen provides you with a sort of safety rail. If you've once taken part in building one, even inadvertently, doesn't its usually latent image reappear like a warning signal whenever you're tempted to join the police, or support any manifestation of Law and Order?

Jean Genet (1910–1986), French playwright and novelist: *Prisoner of Love* (1986; tr.1989), Pt.1

3 The absence of noise is not the presence of peace.

Jesse Jackson (b.1941), U.S. politician: speech, 17 April 1994, referring to the 1992 LA riots in the wake of the acquittal of the LAPD officers in the Rodney King case, quoted in *The Ice Opinion* by Ice-T and Heidi Sigmund (1994), Ch.5

4 White riot! I wanna riot!
White riot! a riot of my own.

Joe Strummer (b.1952) and **Mick Jones** (b.1956), British rock musicians: 'White Riot' (song) on the album *The Clash* (The Clash, 1977)

RITUAL

1 Only in rites
can we renounce our oddities
and be truly entired.

W.H. Auden (1907–1973), Anglo-American poet: 'Archaeology', publ. in *Thank You, Fog* (1974)

2 Any serious attempt to try to do something worthwhile is ritualistic.

Derek Walcott (b.1930), West Indian poet and playwright: interview in *Writers at Work* (Eighth Series, ed. George Plimpton, 1988)

RIVERS

1 If I had wings and I could fly,
I know where I would go.
But right now I'll just sit here so contentedly
And watch the river flow.

Bob Dylan (b.1941), U.S. singer and songwriter: 'Watching the River Flow' (song, 1971) on the album *Greatest Hits Vol.II* (1971)

2 A river seems a magic thing. A magic, moving, living part of the very earth itself – for it is from the soil, both from its depth and from its surface, that a river has its beginning.

Laura Gilpin (1891–1979), U.S. photographer: introduction to *The Rio Grande* (1949)

3 I may be smelly, and I may be old,
Rough in my pebbles, reedy in my pools,
But where my fish float by I bless their
    swimming
And I like people to bathe in me, especially
women.

Stevie Smith (1902–1971), British poet and novelist: 'The River God', publ. in *Harold's Leap* (1950)

ROADS

1 The 20th century reaches just about its highest expression on the highway. Everything is there, the speed and violence of our age, its love of stylization, fashion, the organized side of things – what I call the elaborately signalled landscape.

J.G. Ballard (b.1930), British author: interview in *Penthouse* (London), Sept. 1970

2 A route differs from a road not only because it is solely intended for vehicles, but also because it is merely a line that connects one point with another. A route has no meaning in itself; its meaning derives entirely from the two points that it connects. A road is a tribute to space. Every stretch of road has meaning in itself and invites us to stop. A route is the triumphant devaluation of space, which thanks to it has been reduced to a mere obstacle to human movement and a waste of time.

Milan Kundera (b.1929), Czech-born French author and critic: *Immortality* (1991), Pt.5, Ch.3

See also Sam on ACTIVISM & PROTEST; Didion on THE UNITED STATES: LOS ANGELES

ROCK & POP *see under* MUSIC

ROLE-PLAYING

1 The main interest in life is to become someone else that you were not at the beginning. ... The game is worthwhile insofar as we don't know what will be the end.

Michel Foucault (1926–1984), French philosopher: *Technologies of the Self* (ed. Luther Martin, Huck Gutman and Patrick Hutton, 1988), 'Truth, Power, Self: An Interview with Michel Foucault'

2 Nothing is ever simple. What do you do when you discover you *like* parts of the role you're trying to escape?

Marilyn French (b.1929), U.S. author and critic: Mira, in *The Women's Room* (1977), Ch.5, Sct.6

3 There comes a point in many people's lives when they can no longer play the role they have chosen for themselves. When that happens, we are like actors finding that someone has changed the play.

Brian Moore (b.1921), Irish novelist: in *The Sunday Times* (London), 15 April 1990. 'What I write about,' Moore added, 'is the mess that follows'

ROMANCE

1 The essence of romantic love is that wonderful beginning, after which sadness and impossibility may become the rule.

Anita Brookner (b.1938), British novelist and art historian: Rachel, referring to Michael Sandberg, in *A Friend From England* (1987), Ch.10

2 Romance, like the rabbit at the dog track, is the elusive, fake, and never attained reward which,

for the benefit and amusement of our masters, keeps us running and thinking in safe circles.
Beverly Jones (b.1927), U.S. feminist writer: *The Florida Paper on Women's Liberation* (1970), 'The Dynamics of Marriage and Motherhood'

3 The concept of romantic love affords a means of emotional manipulation which the male is free to exploit, since love is the only circumstance in which the female is (ideologically) pardoned for sexual activity.
Kate Millett (b.1934), U.S. feminist author: *Sexual Politics* (1970), Ch.2, Sct.4

ROMANTICISM

1 Romanticism is not just a mode; it literally eats into every life. Women will never get rid of just waiting for the right man.
Anita Brookner (b.1938), British novelist and art historian: interview in *Women Writers Talk* (ed. Olga Kenyon, 1989)

2 Romanticism is the struggle to save the reality of experience from evaporating into theoretical abstraction or disintegrating into the chaos of bare, empirical fact. It is a critical counterpart of the imperial advance of science.
Theodore Roszak (b.1933), U.S. social critic: *Where the Wasteland Ends* (1972), Ch.8. Of the term 'Romanticist', Roszak also wrote: 'The adjective, well exercised in abusive criticism, drips contempt or condescension: a diagnosis of emotional indigestion. Moonstruck lovers and Byronic seizures, great cloudy symbols and Faustian ardour no longer appeal to more sophisticated tastes' (Ch.7)

ROME *see under* ITALY

ROOTS

1 For Africa to me ... is more than a glamorous fact. It is a historical truth. No man can know where he is going unless he knows exactly where he has been and exactly how he arrived at his present place.
Maya Angelou (b.1928), U.S. author: quoted in the *New York Times*, 16 April 1972

2 It is rightly said that when a griot dies, it is as if a library has burned to the ground. The griots symbolize how all human ancestry goes back to some place, and some time, where there was no writing. Then, the memories and the mouths of ancient elders was the only way that early histories of mankind got passed along ... for all of us today to know who we are.
Alex Haley (1921–1992), U.S. author: of the transmitters of oral history in west African villages, in *Roots* (1976), 'Acknowledgements'

3 No American worth his salt should go around looking for a root. I advance this in all modesty, as a not unreasonable opinion.
Wyndham Lewis (1882–1957), British author and painter: *America and Cosmic Man* (1948), 'The Case Against Roots'

4 To explain why we become attached to our birthplaces we pretend that we are trees and speak of roots. Look under your feet. You will not find gnarled growths sprouting through the soles. Roots, I sometimes think, are a conservative myth, designed to keep us in our places.
Salman Rushdie (b.1947), Indian-born British author: *Shame* (1983), Ch.5

THE ROYAL FAMILY

1 At first we thought it was Radio 2 married to Radio 4, but now it's more like Radio 1 married to Radio 3.
Anonymous member of the 'Royal Ratpack' – journalists assigned to report on the royal family – of Diana and Charles, quoted in *The Sunday Times* (London), 13 Nov. 1988

2 All the time I feel I must justify my existence.
Charles, Prince of Wales (b.1948): quoted in *The Observer* (London), 2 Jan. 1983

3 I have nothing against the Queen of England. Even in my heart I never resented her for not being Jackie Kennedy. She is, to my mind, a very gallant lady, victimized by whoever it is who designs the tops of her uniforms.
Leonard Cohen (b.1934), Canadian singer, poet and novelist: *Beautiful Losers* (1970), Bk.2, 'A Long Letter from F'

4 The lager louts of today are the parents of tomorrow, and I do not believe that their children will feel any empathy towards the royal family or think that Prince Charles is a good egg. The people who think Prince Charles a good egg are those around at the moment, and the only reason why the royal family is in favour is because Princess Diana is a pin-up, a jolly good pin-up too. In twenty-five years' time this country will have grown out of the idea of kings or queens, and when Charles ascends the throne ... I think the gig is up.
Nigel Dempster (1941), British journalist: interview in *Singular Encounters* by Naim Attallah (1990), 'Nigel Dempster'

5 Everyone said I was the Marilyn Monroe of the 1980s and I was adoring every minute of it. Actually I've never sat down and said: 'Hooray how wonderful.' Never. The day I do we're in trouble.

Diana, Princess of Wales (1961–1997): quoted in *Diana: Her True Story* by Andrew Morton (1992), Ch.9

6 I declare before you all that my whole life, whether it be long or short, shall be devoted to your service and the service of our great Imperial family to which we all belong.

Elizabeth II (b.1926), Queen of Great Britain and Northern Ireland: speech to the Commonwealth, 21 April 1947, Cape Town, quoted in *The Times* (London), 22 April 1947

7 Like all the best families, we have our share of eccentricities, of impetuous and wayward youngsters and of family disagreements.

Elizabeth II: quoted in the *Daily Mail* (London), 19 Oct. 1989

8 In a few years there will be only five kings in the world – the King of England and the four kings in a pack of cards.

Farouk I (1920–1965), King of Egypt (1936–1952): remark to Lord Boyd-Orr, quoted in *Life* (New York), 10 April 1950

9 The metaphor of the king as the shepherd of his people goes back to ancient Egypt. Perhaps the use of this particular convention is due to the fact that, being stupid, affectionate, gregarious, and easily stampeded, the societies formed by sheep are most like human ones.

Northrop Frye (1912–1991), Canadian literary critic: *Anatomy of Criticism* (1957), 'Theory of Archetypal Meaning'

10 We live in what virtually amounts to a museum – which does not happen to a lot of people.

Philip, Duke of Edinburgh (b.1921): remark, 25 Feb. 1964, quoted in *Anatomy of Britain Today* by Anthony Sampson (1965), Pt.1, Ch.2

11 Once you touch the trappings of monarchy, like opening an Egyptian tomb, the inside is liable to crumble.

Anthony Sampson (b.1926), British journalist and author: *Anatomy of Britain Today* (1965), Pt.1, Ch.2

12 She deserves better than to be perpetuated as an old-age pensioner about to lose her bungalow.

Brian Sewell, British art critic: on the portrait by Anthony Williams to mark the Queen's 70th birthday, quoted in the *Independent on Sunday* (London), 12 May 1996

13 If your job is to leaven ordinary lives with elevating spectacle, be elevating or be gone.

George F. Will (b.1941), U.S. political columnist: of the British royal family, in the *International Herald Tribune* (Paris), 25 June 1992

See also Anonymous on THE PRESS

THE RUSHDIE AFFAIR

1 When you write, when you try to instruct and entertain, you want the world to sit up and take notice. But not literally. And here on the evening news are the pulsing flashpoints on the colour-coded worldmap, Bombay, Los Angeles, Brussels, riot, fire and murder. What's the story? You are the story; your book is the story. And now another chapter of crossed lines, ungot ironies, atrocious misunderstandings.

Martin Amis (b.1949), British author: in *Vanity Fair* (New York), 1990, rep. in *Visiting Mrs Nabokov* (1993), 'Salman Rushdie'

2 Its blasphemy enabled man
to break free from the Bible and Koran
with their life-denying fundamentalists
and hell fire such fanatics love to fan.

Tony Harrison (b.1953), British poet: referring to *The Satanic Verses*, in *The Blasphemers' Banquet*, BBC1, 31 July 1989, televised poem in defence of Salman Rushdie, first publ. in *Tony Harrison: Bloodaxe Critical Anthologies 1* (ed. Neil Astley, 1991)

3 I would like to inform all the intrepid Muslims in the world that the author of the book entitled *The Satanic Verses*, which has been compiled, printed and published in opposition to Islam, the prophet and the Qur'an, as well as those publishers who were aware of its contents, have been declared *madhur el dam* ['those whose blood must be shed']. I call on all zealous Muslims to execute them quickly, wherever they find them, so that no one will dare to insult Islam again. Whoever is killed in this path will be regarded as a martyr.

Ruhollah Khomeini (1900–1989), Iranian religious and political leader: Fatwa, or legal ruling, issued 14 Feb. 1989, quoted in *A Satanic Affair* by Malise Ruthven (1990), Ch.5

4 I don't think it is given to any of us to be impertinent to great religions with impunity.

John Le Carré (b.1931), British author: referring to *The Satanic Verses*, in the *International Herald Tribune* (Paris), 23 May 1989

5 Your blasphemy, Salman, can't be forgiven. ...
To set your words against the Words of God.

Salman Rushdie (b.1947), Indian-born British author: Mahound, speaking to Salman the Persian, in *The Satanic Verses* (1988), 'Return to Jahilia'. Despite his crime – of pitting 'his Word against mine' – Salman the Persian is spared the death-sentence

6 As author of *The Satanic Verses* I recognise that Moslems in many parts of the world are genuinely distressd by the publication of my novel. I profoundly regret the distress that publication has occasioned to sincere followers

of Islam. Living as we do in a world of many faiths this experience has served to remind us that we must all be conscious of the sensibilities of others.

Salman Rushdie: statement following Khomeini's fatwa, publ. in *The Observer* (London), 19 Feb. 1989. A statement issued by the Ayatollah's office the following day declared: 'Even if Salman Rushdie repents and becomes the most pious person of this age, it is still the duty of all Muslims to use all their efforts, wealth and lives to send him to hell'

See also Rushdie on ISLAM

RUSSIA

1 Moscow, breathing fire like a human volcano with its smouldering lava of passion, ambition and politics, its hurly-burly of meetings and entertainment. ... Moscow seethes and bubbles and gasps for air. It's always thirsting for something new, the newest events, the latest sensation. Everyone wants to be the first to know. It's the rhythm of life today.

Svetlana Alliluevya (b.1925), Russian writer and daughter of Josef Stalin: 'Introduction' (1963) to *Twenty Letters to a Friend* (1967)

2 The so-called new Russian man is characterized mainly by his complete exhaustion. You may find yourself wondering if he has the strength to enjoy his new-found freedom. He is like a long-distance runner who, on reaching the finishing line, is incapable even of raising his hands in a gesture of victory.

Ryszard Kapuściński (b.1932), Polish journalist: in the *Independent on Sunday* (London), 27 Oct. 1991

3 One question that people always ask at home is never asked here: 'What happened to Communism in Russia?' Everybody yawns when a visitor brings it up, because the answer is so obvious to every Russian. The answer is that there never was Communism in Russia; there were only communists.

Arthur Koestler (1905–1983), Hungarian-born British novelist and essayist: 'The Shadow of a Tree' (1953), rep. in *The Trail of the Dinosaur* (1955), Pt.2

4 You ask can we ever trust the Bear? ... I will give you several answers at once. The first is no, we can never trust the Bear. For one reason, the Bear doesn't trust himself. The Bear is threatened and the Bear is frightened and the Bear is falling apart. The Bear is disgusted with his past, sick of his present and scared stiff of his future. He often was. The Bear is broke, lazy, volatile, incompetent, slippery, dangerously proud, dangerously armed, sometimes brilliant, often ignorant. Without his claws, he'd be just another chaotic member of the Third World. ... The second answer is yes, we can trust the Bear completely. The Bear has never been so trustworthy. The Bear is begging to be part of us, to submerge his problems in us, to have his own bank account with us, to shop in our High Street and be accepted as a dignified member of our forest as well as his.... The Bear needs us so desperately that we may safely trust him to need us.

John Le Carré (b.1931), British author: Smiley, in *The Secret Pilgrim* (1990), Ch.12

5 Everything established, settled, everything to do with home and order and the common round, has crumbled into dust and been swept away in the general upheaval and reorganization of the whole of society. The whole human way of life has been destroyed and ruined. All that's left is the bare, shivering human soul, stripped to the last shred, the naked force of the human psyche for which nothing has changed because it was always cold and shivering and reaching out to its nearest neighbour, as cold and lonely as itself.

Boris Pasternak (1890–1960), Russian poet, novelist and translator: Lara, speaking of life in communist Russia, in *Doctor Zhivago* (1957; tr. 1958), Ch.13, Sct.13

6 My fellow Americans, I am pleased to tell you today that I've signed legislation which outlaws Russia forever. The bombing begins in five minutes.

Ronald Reagan (b.1911), U.S. Republican politician and president: radio test broadcast, 11 Aug. 1984, quoted in *Reagan's Reign of Error* (ed. Mark Green and Gail MacColl, 1987), 'Defense and Russia'

7 For us in Russia, communism is a dead dog, while, for many people in the West, it is still a living lion.

Alexander Solzhenitsyn (b.1918), Russian novelist: radio broadcast on BBC Russian service, publ. in *The Listener* (London), 15 Feb. 1979

8 In Russia, people suffer from the stillness of time.

Tatyana Tolstaya (b.1951), Russian author: in *The Independent* (London), 31 May 1990

9 Oh, where is the poet or bard who will compose an ode to Russian rumours? Thanks to the chronic shortage of truthful (or even false) information, our people live on rumours.

Boris Yeltsin (b.1931), Russian politician and president: *Against the Grain* (1990), Ch.9

See also Tolstaya on NOSTALGIA; THE U.S.S.R.

THE SACRED & PROFANE

1 Sacred cows make the best hamburgers.

Abbie Hoffman (1935–1989), U.S. political activist: attributed, quoted in *The Heretic's Handbook of Quotations* (ed. Charles Bufe, 1988; rev.1991)

2   The idea of the sacred is quite simply one of the most conservative notions in any culture, because it seeks to turn other ideas – uncertainty, progress, change – into crimes.

Salman Rushdie (b.1947), Indian-born British author: 'Is Nothing Sacred?', Herbert Read Memorial Lecture, ICA, London, 6 Feb. 1990, publ. in *The Guardian* (London), 7 Feb. 1990.

3   I've always believed there was no such thing as the sacred without the profane – and in some cases it's hard to tell the difference.

Andres Serrano (b.1950), U.S. photographer: quoted in *Contemporary Photographers* (3rd edn., ed. Martin Marix Evans, 1995). Serrano achieved notoriety with his 1987 work *Piss Christ*

4   I've never liked you. You wanna know why? You don't curse. I don't trust the man who doesn't curse. Not a fuck or a shit in all these years. Real men curse, Prendergast.

Ebbe Roe Smith, U.S. screenwriter: Capt. Yardley (Raymond J. Barry) bidding farewell to Prendergast (Robert Duvall) on his last day on the force, in *Falling Down* (film; screenplay by Ebbe Roe Smith, directed by Joel Schumacher, 1993)

SACRIFICE

1   There is no moral authority like that of sacrifice.

Nadine Gordimer (b.1923), South African author: 'The Essential Gesture', lecture, 12 Oct. 1984, University of Michigan, first publ. in *The Tanner Lectures on Human Values* (ed. Sterling M. McMurrin, 1985), rep. in *The Essential Gesture* (ed. Stephen Clingman, 1988)

2   The whole point of a sacrifice is that you give up something you never really wanted in the first place. ... People are doing it around you all the time. They give up their careers, say – or their beliefs – or sex.

John Osborne (1929–1994), British playwright: Jimmy Porter, in *Look Back in Anger* (1956), Act 3, Sc.1

3   Greater love hath no man than this, that he lay down his friends for his life.

Jeremy Thorpe (b.1929), British Liberal politician: remark, 1962, following a Cabinet 'reorganization' – in which many members of the Cabinet were sacked – by Prime Minister Harold Macmillan, quoted in *The General Election of 1964* by D.E. Butler and Anthony King (1965), Ch.1. The remark echoes the words of Jesus in *Mark* 15:13, 'Greater love hath no man than this, that a man lay down his life for his friends'

4   As for the negative consequences of eliminating industrial society – well, you, can't eat your

cake and have it too. To gain one thing you have to sacrifice another.

Unabomber, U.S. radical: *Industrial Society and Its Future*, 'Strategy', Sct.185, publ. in the *Washington Post*, 19 Sept. 1995

SADISM

1   Sade has a curious ability to render every aspect of sexuality suspect, so that we see how the chaste kiss of the sentimental lover differs only in degree from the vampirish love-bite that draws blood, we understand that a disinterested caress is only quantitatively different from a disinterested flogging.

Angela Carter (1940–1992), British author: *The Sadeian Woman* (1979), 'Polemical Preface'

2   Sexual sadism actualizes male identity. Women are tortured, whipped, and chained; women are bound and gagged, branded and burned, cut with knives and wires; women are pissed on and shit on; red-hot needles are driven into breasts, bones are broken, rectums are torn, mouths are ravaged, cunts are savagely bludgeoned by penis after penis, dildo after dildo – and all of this to establish in the male a viable sense of his own worth.

Andrea Dworkin (b.1946), U.S. feminist critic: 'The Root Cause', speech, 26 Sept. 1975, Massachusetts Institute of Technology, publ. in *Our Blood* (1976), Ch.9

3   'Must we burn Sade?' asks Mme de Beauvoir. Now that you mention it, why not? The world is littered with literature. And Sade teaches us little about human nature which we couldn't gather from a few minutes of honest introspection.

D.J. Enright (b.1920), British poet and critic: 'The Marquis and the Madame' (1953), rep. in *Conspirators and Poets* (1966)

4   One can say that S and M is the eroticisation of power, the eroticisation of strategic relations.... Of course there are roles, but everyone knows very well that those roles can be reversed. Sometimes the scene begins with the master and slave, and at the end the slave has become the master.

Michel Foucault (1926–1984), French philosopher: 'An Interview: Sex, Power and the Politics of Identity', in *Advocate* Aug. 1984, quoted in *The Lives of Michel Foucault* by David Macey (1993), Ch.14

5   Sadism is the necessary outcome of the belief that one sex is passive and suffers sex at the hands of another. If we are to escape any of the hideous effects of this mythology, effects which include war and capital punishment, we must regain the power of the cunt.

Germaine Greer (b.1939), Australian feminist writer: 'Lady Love Your Cunt', first publ. in *Suck*

(London) 1971, rep. in *The Madwoman's Underclothes* (1986)

6 Shiny, shiny, shiny boots of leather
Whiplash girlchild in the dark
Comes in bells your servant, don't forsake him
Strike dear mistress and cure his heart.
Lou Reed (b.1944), U.S. rock musician: 'Venus in Furs' (song) on the album *The Velvet Underground and Nico* (The Velvet Underground, 1967)

7 Sadomasochism has always been the furthest reach of the sexual experience: when sex becomes most purely sexual, that is, severed from personhood, from relationships, from love. It should not be surprising that it has become attached to Nazi symbolism in recent years. Never before was the relation of masters and slaves so consciously aestheticized. Sade had to make up his theater of punishment and delight from scratch, improvising the decor and costumes and blasphemous rites. Now there is a master scenario available to everyone. The color is black, the material is leather, the seduction is beauty, the justification is honesty, the aim is ecstasy, the fantasy is death.
Susan Sontag (b.1933), U.S. essayist: 'Fascinating Fascism' (1974), *Under the Sign of Saturn* (1980)

8 Sado-masochism is a futile effort to reduce ubiquitous cruelty to the comprehensible scope of sex.
Edmund White (b.1940), U.S. author: 'Sado Machismo', first publ. in *New Times* (New York), 8 Jan. 1979, rep. in *The Burning Library* (1994)

SAINTS

1 Saintliness is also a temptation.
(*La sainteté aussi est une tentation.*)
Jean Anouilh (1910–1987), French playwright: Thomas à Becket, in *Becket* (1959; tr.1961), Act 3

2 It's impossible to represent a saint [in Art]. It becomes boring. Perhaps because he is, like the *Saturday Evening Post* people, in the position of having almost infinitely free will.
W.H. Auden (1907–1973), Anglo-American poet: *The Table Talk of W.H. Auden* (comp. Alan Ansen, ed. Nicholas Jenkins, 1990), 'November 16, 1946'

3 What after all
Is a halo? It's only one more thing to keep clean.
Christopher Fry (b.1907), British playwright: Thomas, in *The Lady's Not for Burning* (1949), Act 1

4 People who are born even-tempered, placid and untroubled – secure from violent passions or temptations to evil – those who have never needed to struggle all night with the Angel to emerge lame but victorious at dawn, never become great saints.

Eva Le Gallienne (1899–1991), U.S. actress and producer: *The Mystic in the Theatre: Eleanora Duse* (1965), Ch.1

5 Saints should always be judged guilty until they are proved innocent.
George Orwell (1903–1950), British author: *Shooting an Elephant* (1950), 'Reflections on Gandhi'. Orwell was deeply sceptical of the desire for sainthood: 'It is probable,' he wrote, 'that some who achieve or aspire to sainthood have never felt much temptation to be human beings'

6 We must have a real living determination to reach holiness. 'I will be a saint' means I will despoil myself of all that is not God; I will strip my heart of all created things; I will live in poverty and detachment; I will renounce my will, my inclinations, my whims and fancies, and make myself a willing slave to the will of God.
Mother Teresa (1910–1997), Albanian-born Roman Catholic missionary: *A Gift for God* (1975), 'Willing Slaves to the Will of God'

7 Saints are simply men & women who have fulfilled their natural obligation which is to approach God.
Evelyn Waugh (1903–1966), British novelist: letter, 26 Aug. 1946, to Nancy Mitford, publ. in *The Letters of Evelyn Waugh* (ed. M. Amory, 1980)

SALES & MARKETING

1 In fast-moving, progress-conscious America, the consumer expects to be dizzied by progress. If he could completely understand advertising jargon he would be badly disappointed. The half-intelligibility which we expect, or even hope, to find in the latest product language personally reassures each of us that progress *is* being made: that the pace exceeds our ability to follow.
Daniel J. Boorstin (b.1914), U.S. historian: *The Image* (1961), Ch.5

2 When producers want to know what the public wants, they graph it as curves. When they want to tell the public what to get, they say it in curves.
Marshall McLuhan (1911–1980), Canadian communications theorist: *The Mechanical Bride* (1951), 'Eye Appeal'

3 For a salesman, there is no rock bottom to the life. He don't put a bolt to a nut, he don't tell you the law or give you medicine. He's a man way out there in the blue, riding on a smile and a shoeshine. And when they start not smiling back – that's an earthquake. And then you get yourself a couple of spots on your hat, and you're finished. Nobody dast blame this man.

A salesman is got to dream, boy. It comes with the territory.

Arthur Miller (b.1915), U.S. playwright: Charley, in *Death of a Salesman* (1949), 'Requiem'

SALVATION

1 When you have understood that nothing *is*, that things do not even deserve the status of appearances, you no longer need to be saved, you are saved, and miserable forever.
(*Quand on a compris que rien n'est, que les choses ne méritent même pas le statut d'apparences, on n'a plus besoin d'être sauvé, on est sauvé, et malheureux à jamais.*)

E.M. Cioran (1911–1995), Rumanian-born French philosopher: *The New Gods* (*Le Mauvais Démiurge*, 1969; tr. 1974), 'Encounters with Suicide'

2 It is the final proof of God's omnipotence that he need not exist in order to save us.

Peter De Vries (1910–1993), U.S. author: the Reverend Andrew Mackerel, in *The Mackerel Plaza* (1958), Ch.1. 'This aphorism,' wrote De Vries, 'seemed to his hearers so much better than anything Voltaire had said on the subject that he was given an immediate hike in pay and invited out to more dinners than he could possibly eat'

3 Don't matter how much money you got, there's only two kinds of people: there's saved people and there's lost people.

Bob Dylan (b.1941), U.S. singer and songwriter: on stage at Tempe, Arizona, 26 Nov. 1979, quoted in *Wanted Man* (ed. John Bauldie, 1990), 'Saved: Bob Dylan's Conversion to Christianity'

4 The salvation of this human world lies nowhere else than in the human heart, in the human power to reflect, in human meekness and human responsibility.

Václav Havel (b.1936), Czech playwright and president: in the *International Herald Tribune* (Paris), 21 Feb. 1990

5 People get ready
There's a train a-coming
You don't need no baggage
You just get on board
All you need is faith to hear the diesels humming
Don't need no ticket you just thank the Lord.

Curtis Mayfield (b.1942), U.S. singer: 'People Get Ready' (song, 1964), publ. in *The Poetry of Soul* (ed. A.X. Nicholas, 1971)

See also Montessori on CHILDREN

SAN FRANCISCO *see under* THE UNITED STATES

SATIRE

1 The writer has a grudge against society, which he documents with accounts of unsatisfying sex, unrealized ambition, unmitigated loneliness, and a sense of local and global distress. The square, overpopulation, the bourgeois, the bomb and the cocktail party are variously identified as sources of the grudge. There follows a little obscenity here, a dash of philosophy there, considerable whining overall, and a modern satirical novel is born.

Renata Adler (b.1938), U.S. author and film critic: 'Salt into Old Scars' (1963), rep. in *Toward a Radical Middle* (1971)

2 Satire is tragedy plus time. You give it enough time, the public, the reviewers will allow you to satirize it. Which is rather ridiculous, when you think about it.

Lenny Bruce (1925–1966), U.S. satirical comedian: *The Essential Lenny Bruce* (ed. John Cohen, 1967), 'Performing and the Art of Comedy'

3 The satirist is prevented by repulsion from gaining a better knowledge of the world he is attracted to, yet he is forced by attraction to concern himself with the world that repels him.

Italo Calvino (1923–1985), Italian author and critic: 'Definitions of Territories: Comedy', first publ. in *Il Caffé* (Rome), Feb. 1967, rep. in *The Literature Machine* (1987)

4 What arouses the indignation of the honest satirist is not, unless the man is a prig, the fact that people in positions of power or influence behave idiotically, or even that they behave wickedly. It is that they conspire successfully to impose upon the public a picture of themselves as so very sagacious, honest and well-intentioned.

Claud Cockburn (1904–1981), British author and journalist: *I, Claud* (1967), 'The Worst Possible Taste'

5 It's the gap between how they *think* they are coming over and how they *actually* come over. In their case, it's the *gulf* between their self-perception and the reality. The job of a satirist is to point it out.

Ian Hislop (b.1960), British journalist: on what makes Princess Diana, James Goldsmith and Jeffrey Archer natural subjects for satire, in interview in *The Guardian* (London), 27 April 1996

6 Does it really make a valuable contribution to our society to destroy both in our eyes and in those of the world at large our major national asset of incorruptibility in public life – to replace it with a belief that the instincts of the piggery motivate our public servants and successful entrepreneurs?

Robert Maxwell (1923–1991), British tycoon: reviewing a history of the satirical magazine *Private Eye*, Nov. 1982, quoted in *Maxwell: The Outsider* by Tom Bower (1988, rev.1991), Ch.14. Maxwell had long been the subject of facetious comment in *Private Eye*, in which he was also the model for a strip cartoon. His irritation culminated in a successful libel suit taken against the magazine in 1985 (*see* Ingrams on LITIGATION), and a call for it to be closed down

See also Vidal on MOCKERY

SCANDAL

1 Mistakes, scandals, and failures no longer signal catastrophe. The crucial thing is that they be made credible, and that the public be made aware of the efforts being expended in that direction. The 'marketing' immunity of governments is similar to that of the major brands of washing powder.
Jean Baudrillard (b.1929), French semiologist: *America* (1986; tr.1988), 'The End of U.S. Power?'

2 I have a Dalinian thought: the one thing the world will never have enough of is the outrageous.
Salvador Dali (1904–1989), Spanish painter: journal entry, 30 Aug. 1953, in *Diary of a Genius* (1966)

3 History is made in the class struggle and not in bed.
Alex Mitchell, British left-wing journalist: remark following deposition of Gerry Healey, leader of the Workers' Revolutionary Party, in the wake of a sex scandal, quoted in *The Sunday Times* (London), 29 Dec. 1985

SCAPEGOATS

1 Collective guilt is borne by what is conventionally called the scapegoat. Now the scapegoat for white society – which is based on myths of progress, civilization, liberalism, education, enlightenment, refinement – will be precisely the force that opposes the expansion and the triumph of these myths. This brutal opposing force is supplied by the Negro.
Frantz Fanon (1925–1961), Martiniquan psychiatrist, philosopher and political activist: *Black Skins, White Masks* (1952; tr.1967), Ch.6

2 Anything remotely resembling a student can, in time of crisis, be gunned down, gassed, and bayoneted by the authorities with impunity, indeed, with the applause of millions of voters. Black Panthers and hippies have become for cynical opportunists like Governor Reagan the scapegoat equivalent of Hitler's Jews.
Theodore Roszak (b.1933), U.S. social critic: *Where the Wasteland Ends* (1972), Ch.2

3 Authoritarian political ideologies have a vested interest in promoting fear, a sense of the imminence of takeover by aliens – and real diseases are useful material.
Susan Sontag (b.1933), U.S. essayist: *AIDS and Its Metaphors* (1989), Ch.6

See also White on CROSS-DRESSING

SCHOLARSHIP

1 The ceaseless, senseless demand for original scholarship in a number of fields, where only erudition is now possible, has led either to sheer irrelevancy, the famous knowing of more and more about less and less, or to the development of a pseudo-scholarship which actually destroys its object.
Hannah Arendt (1906–1975), German-born U.S. political philosopher: *Crises of the Republic* (1972), 'On Violence'

2 In the same way that we need statesmen to spare us the abjection of exercising power, we need scholars to spare us the abjection of learning.
Jean Baudrillard (b.1929), French semiologist: *Cool Memories* (1987; tr.1990), Ch.5

3 The professors laugh at themselves, they laugh at life; they long ago abjured the bitch-goddess Success, and the best of them will fight for his scholastic ideals with a courage and persistence that would shame a soldier. The professor is not afraid of words like *truth*; in fact he is not afraid of words at all.
Catherine Drinker Bowen (1897–1973), U.S. author: *Adventures of a Biographer* (1946), Ch.5

4 By the worldly standards of public life, all scholars in their work are of course oddly virtuous. They do not make wild claims, they do not cheat, they do not try to persuade at any cost, they appeal neither to prejudice nor to authority, they are often frank about their ignorance, their disputes are fairly decorous, they do not confuse what is being argued with race, politics, sex or age, they listen patiently to the young and to the old who both know everything. These are the general virtues of scholarship, and they are peculiarly the virtues of science.
Jacob Bronowski (1908–1974), British scientist and author: 'The Sense of Human Dignity', lecture, 19 March 1953, Massachusetts Institute of Technology, publ. in *Science and Human Values* (1961), Pt.3, Sct.4

5 I am an old scholar, better-looking now than when I was young. That's what sitting on your ass does to your face.
Leonard Cohen (b.1934), Canadian singer, poet and novelist: *Beautiful Losers* (1970), Bk.1, 'The History of Them All'

6 Art and religion first; then philosophy; lastly science. That is the order of the great subjects of life, that's their order of importance.

Muriel Spark (b.1918), British novelist: Miss Brodie, in *The Prime of Miss Jean Brodie* (1961), Ch.2

See also ACADEMIA

SCHOOL

1 I was allowed to ring the bell for five minutes until everyone was in assembly. It was the beginning of power.

Jeffrey Archer (b.1940), British Conservative politician and novelist: on his schooldays, in *The Daily Telegraph* (London), 16 March 1988

2 A school is not a factory. Its raison d'être is to provide opportunity for experience.

J.L. Carr (1912–1994), British novelist: *The Harpole Report* (1972), Ch.6

3 School divides life into two segments, which are increasingly of comparable length. As much as anything else, schooling implies custodial care for persons who are declared undesirable elsewhere by the simple fact that a school has been built to serve them.

Ivan Illich (b.1926), Austrian-born U.S. theologian and author: *Celebration of Awareness* (1969), Ch.8

4 No one can look back on his schooldays and say with truth that they were altogether unhappy.

George Orwell (1903–1950), British author: 'Such, Such Were the Joys' (1947), rep. in *The Collected Essays, Journalism and Letters of George Orwell* (ed. Sonia Orwell and Ian Angus, 1968), Vol.IV

5 I am putting old heads on your young shoulders; all my pupils are the crème de la crème.

Muriel Spark (b.1918), British novelist: Miss Brodie, in *The Prime of Miss Jean Brodie* (1961), Ch.1

6 I owe everything to a system that made me learn by heart till I wept. As a result I have thousands of lines of poetry by heart. I owe everything to this.

George Steiner (b.1929), French-born U.S. critic and novelist: in *The Guardian* (London), 26 March 1992

7 The Founding Fathers in their wisdom decided that children were an unnatural strain on parents. So they provided jails called schools, equipped with tortures called an education. School is where you go between when your parents can't take you and industry can't take you.

John Updike (b.1932), U.S. author and critic: George Caldwell, in *The Centaur* (1963), Ch.4

SCHOOL: Public Schools

1 Three years of remorseless nastiness at Eton squeezed every last trace of confidence from me.

Ranulph Fiennes (b.1945), British explorer: quoted in *The Independent* (London), 30 March 1996

2 They'd rather gie a merchant school old boy with severe brain damage a job in nuclear engineering than gie a schemie wi a Ph.D. a post as a cleaner in an abattoir.

Irvine Welsh (b.1958), Scottish author: Renton, in *Trainspotting* (1994), 'Kicking'

SCIENCE

1 Science has nothing to be ashamed of even in the ruins of Nagasaki. The shame is theirs who appeal to other values than the human imaginative values which science has evolved.

Jacob Bronowski (1908–1974), British scientist and author: 'The Sense of Human Dignity', lecture, 19 March 1953, Massachusetts Institute of Technology, publ. in *Science and Human Values* (1961), Pt.3, Sct.11

2 Science has a simple faith, which transcends utility. Nearly all men of science, all men of learning for that matter, and men of simple ways too, have it in some form and in some degree. It is the faith that it is the privilege of man to learn to understand, and that this is his mission.

   If we abandon that mission under stress we shall abandon it forever, for stress will not cease. Knowledge for the sake of understanding, not merely to prevail, that is the essence of our being. None can define its limits, or set its ultimate boundaries.

Vannevar Bush (1890–1974), U.S. electrical engineer and physicist: *Science Is Not Enough* (1967), 'The Search for Understanding'. During World War II Bush, a champion of the 'missionary' function of science, led the U.S. Office of Scientific Research and Development, directing such programmes as the development of the first atomic bomb

3 Thus will the fondest dream of Phallic science be realized: a pristine new planet populated entirely by little boy clones of great scientific entrepreneurs ... free to smash atoms, accelerate particles, or, if they are so moved, build pyramids – without any social relevance or human responsibility at all.

Barbara Ehrenreich (b.1941), U.S. author and columnist: 'Phallic Science' (1988), rep. in *The Worst Years of Our Lives* (1991)

4 The whole of science is nothing more than a refinement of everyday thinking.
Albert Einstein (1879–1955), German-born U.S. theoretical physicist: *Out of My Later Years* (1950), Ch.12

5 The pace of science forces the pace of technique. Theoretical physics forces atomic energy on us; the successful production of the fission bomb forces upon us the manufacture of the hydrogen bomb. *We* do not choose our problems, we do not choose our products; we are pushed, we are forced – by what? By a system which has no purpose and goal transcending it, and which makes man its appendix.
Erich Fromm (1900–1980), U.S. psychologist: *The Sane Society* (1955), Ch.5, 'Nineteenth-Century Capitalism'

6 The real accomplishment of modern science and technology consists in taking ordinary men, informing them narrowly and deeply and then, through appropriate organization, arranging to have their knowledge combined with that of other specialized but equally ordinary men. This dispenses with the need for genius. The resulting performance, though less inspiring, is far more predictable.
J.K. Galbraith (b.1908), U.S. economist: *The New Industrial State* (1967), Ch.6

7 To overturn orthodoxy is no easier in science than in philosophy, religion, economics, or any of the other disciplines through which we try to comprehend the world and the society in which we live.
Ruth Hubbard (b.1924), U.S. biologist: 'Have Only Men Evolved?', publ. in *Women Look at Biology Looking At Women* (ed. Ruth Hubbard, Mary Sue Henifin and Barbara Fried, 1979)

8 In order to imbue civilization with sound principles and enliven it with the spirit of the gospel, it is not enough to be illuminated with the gift of faith and enkindled with the desire of forwarding a good cause. For this end it is necessary to take an active part in the various organizations and influence them from within. And since our present age is one of outstanding scientific and technical progress and excellence, one will not be able to enter these organizations and work effectively from within unless he is scientifically competent, technically capable and skilled in the practice of his own profession.
Pope John XXIII (1881–1963): encyclical, 10 April 1963: *Pacem in Terris*, Pt.5

9 It seems I am of a literary rather than a scientific turn. An example is the fact that I can't write numbers properly. They end up looking like the decorative ancient cursive syllabary. Learning to drive a car is out of the question; I am incapable of operating an ordinary still camera or even putting fluid in a cigarette lighter. My son tells me that when I use the telephone it's as if a chimpanzee were trying to place a call.
Akira Kurosawa (b.1910), Japanese film-maker: *Something Like an Autobiography* (1982), 'The Goblin's Nose'

10 Science is all metaphor.
Timothy Leary (1920–1996), U.S. psychologist: interview, 24 Sept. 1980, publ. in *Contemporary Authors* (1983), Vol.CVII

11 The scientific mind does not so much provide the right answers as ask the right questions.
Claude Lévi-Strauss (b.1908), French anthropologist: *The Raw and the Cooked* (1964), 'Overture', Sct.1

12 Pure science in modern times offers the decisive choice of the ages, utter destruction or unlimited progress, the abyss or the heights. All politics are in this, and all the future. The problem of war and peace became one with the arrival of science ... the question of life or death.
Oswald Mosley (1896–1980), British fascist leader: *My Life* (1968), Ch.3

13 Traditional scientific method has always been at the very *best*, 20–20 hindsight. It's good for seeing where you've been. It's good for testing the truth of what you think you know, but it can't tell you where you *ought* to go.
Robert M. Pirsig (b.1928), U.S. author: *Zen and the Art of Motorcycle Maintenance* (1974), Pt.3, Ch.24

14 Science may be described as the art of systematic over-simplification.
Karl Popper (1902–1994), Anglo-Austrian philosopher: quoted in *The Observer* (London), 1 Aug. 1982

15 What science can measure is only a portion of what man can know. Our knowing reaches out to embrace the sacred; what bars its way, though it promises us dominion, condemns us to be prisoners of the empirical lie.
Theodore Roszak (b.1933), U.S. social critic: *Where the Wasteland Ends* (1972), Ch.2

16 The effort to understand the universe is one of the very few things that lifts human life a little above the level of farce, and gives it some of the grace of tragedy.
Steven Weinberg (b.1933), U.S. theoretical physicist: closing sentence of *The First Three Minutes* (1977), Ch.8

See also ASTRONOMY; CHEMISTRY; ENGINEERING; MATHEMATICS; PHYSICS; TECHNOLOGY

SCIENCE: and Society

1 No science is immune to the infection of politics and the corruption of power.
Jacob Bronowski (1908–1974), British scientist and author: in *Encounter* (London), July 1971

2 I hate Science. It denies a man's responsibility for his own deeds, abolishes the brotherhood that springs from God's fatherhood. It is a hectoring, dictating expertise, which makes the least lovable of the Church Fathers seem liberal by contrast. It is far easier for a Hitler or a Stalin to find a mock-scientific excuse for persecution than it was for Dominic to find a mock-Christian one.
Basil Bunting (1900–1985), British poet: letter to the poet Louis Zukofsky, 1 Jan. 1947, quoted in *The Poetry of Basil Bunting* by Victoria Forde (1991), Ch.6

3 Science is an integral part of culture. It's not this foreign thing, done by an arcane priesthood. It's one of the glories of the human intellectual tradition.
Stephen Jay Gould (b.1941), U.S. scientist: in *The Independent* (London), 24 Jan. 1990

4 There is not much that even the most socially responsible scientists can do as individuals, or even as a group, about the social consequences of their activities.
Eric Hobsbawm (b.1917), British historian: in the *New York Review of Books*, 19 Nov. 1970

5 We have genuflected before the god of science only to find that it has given us the atomic bomb, producing fears and anxieties that science can never mitigate.
Martin Luther King Jr. (1929–1968), U.S. clergyman and civil rights leader: *Strength Through Love* (1963), Ch.13

6 The future of humanity is uncertain, even in the most prosperous countries, and the quality of life deteriorates; and yet I believe that what is being discovered about the infinitely large and infinitely small is sufficient to absolve this end of the century and millennium. What a very few are acquiring in knowledge of the physical world will perhaps cause this period not to be judged as a pure return of barbarism.
Primo Levi (1919–1987), Italian chemist and author: *Other People's Trades* (1985; tr.1989), 'News from the Sky'

7 Science is intimately integrated with the whole social structure and cultural tradition. They mutually support one other – only in certain types of society can science flourish, and conversely without a continuous and healthy development and application of science such a society cannot function properly.
Talcott Parsons (1902–1979), U.S. sociologist: *The Social System* (1951), Ch.8

8 Objective knowing is alienated knowing; and alienated knowing is, sooner or later, ecologically disastrous knowing. Before the earth could become an industrial garbage can it had first to become a research laboratory.
Theodore Roszak (b.1933), U.S. social critic: *Where the Wasteland Ends* (1972), Ch.7

9 Can a society in which thought and technique are scientific persist for a long period, as, for example, ancient Egypt persisted, or does it necessarily contain within itself forces which must bring either decay or explosion...?
Bertrand Russell (1872–1970), British philosopher and mathematician: 'Can a Scientific Community be Stable?', Lloyd Roberts Lecture to the Royal Society of Medicine, London, 29 Nov. 1949

SCIENCE FICTION *see under* FICTION

SCIENTISTS

1 But how is one to make a scientist understand that there is something unalterably deranged about differential calculus, quantum theory, or the obscene and so inanely liturgical ordeals of the precession of the equinoxes?
Antonin Artaud (1896–1948), French theatre producer, actor and theorist: *Van Gogh, the Man Suicided by Society* (1947), rep. in *Selected Writings* (ed. Susan Sontag, 1976), Pt.33

2 When I find myself in the company of scientists, I feel like a shabby curate who has strayed by mistake into a drawing room full of dukes.
W.H. Auden (1907–1973), Anglo-American poet: *The Dyer's Hand* (1962), Pt.2, 'The Poet and the City'

3 Dissent is the native activity of the scientist, and it has got him into a good deal of trouble in the last years. But if that is cut off, what is left will not be a scientist. And I doubt whether it will be a man.
Jacob Bronowski (1908–1974), British scientist and author: 'The Sense of Human Dignity', lecture, 19 March 1953, Massachusetts Institute of Technology, publ. in *Science and Human Values* (1961), Pt.3, Sct.5

4 They tend to be suspicious, bristly, paranoid-type people with huge egos they push around like some elephantiasis victim with his distended testicles in a wheelbarrow terrified no doubt that some skulking ingrate of a clone student will sneak into his very brain and steal his genius work.
William Burroughs (1914–1997), U.S. author: *The Adding Machine* (1985), 'Immortality'

5 Everybody's a mad scientist, and life is their lab. We're all trying to experiment to find a way to live, to solve problems, to fend off madness and chaos.

David Cronenberg (b.1943), Canadian film-maker: *Cronenberg on Cronenberg* (ed. Chris Rodley, 1992), Ch.1

6 The man of science is a poor philosopher.

Albert Einstein (1879–1955), German-born U.S. theoretical physicist: *Out of My Later Years* (1950), Ch.12

7 If they don't depend on true evidence, scientists are no better than gossips.

Penelope Fitzgerald (b.1916), British author: Herbert Flowerdew, in *The Gate of Angels* (1990), Ch.3

8 The mythology of science asserts that with many different scientists all asking their own questions and evaluating the answers independently, whatever personal bias creeps into their individual answers is cancelled out when the large picture is put together. This might conceivably be so if scientists were women and men from all sorts of different cultural and social backgrounds who came to science with very different ideologies and interests. But since, in fact, they have been predominantly university-trained white males from privileged social backgrounds, the bias has been narrow and the product often reveals more about the investigator than about the subject being researched.

Ruth Hubbard (b.1924), U.S. biologist: 'Have Only Men Evolved?', publ. in *Women Look at Biology Looking At Women* (ed. Ruth Hubbard, Mary Sue Henifin and Barbara Fried, 1979)

9 There comes a time when every scientist, even God, has to write off an experiment.

P.D. James (b.1920), British author: Jonah the tramp, in *Devices and Desires* (1989), Ch.40

10 It is a good morning exercise for a research scientist to discard a pet hypothesis every day before breakfast. It keeps him young.

Konrad Lorenz (1903–1989), Austrian ethologist: *On Aggression* (1963; tr.1966), Ch.2

11 People may still nostalgically honor prescientific faiths, but no one – no priest or prophet – any longer speaks with authority to us about the nature of things except the scientists.

Theodore Roszak (b.1933), U.S. social critic: *Where the Wasteland Ends* (1972), Ch.2

12 Aristotle could have avoided the mistake of thinking that women have fewer teeth than men, by the simple device of asking Mrs Aristotle to keep her mouth open while he counted.

Bertrand Russell (1872–1970), British philosopher and mathematician: *Unpopular Essays* (1950), 'An Outline of Intellectual Rubbish'

13 If we ask, are they more ethical, more socially aware, more disciplined, more relevant to the happiness of the whole, then our scientists have failed the age they claim to have created. The masses are fobbed off with gadgets, while the real science takes place behind closed doors, the preserve of the pharmaceuticals and the military. Genetic control will be the weapon of the future. Doctors will fill the ranks of the New Model Army. And of course you will trust me won't you, when I tell you that with my help, your unborn child will be better off? The white coat will replace the khaki fatigues as the gun gives way to the syringe.

Jeanette Winterson (b.1959), British author: *Art and Lies* (1994), 'Handel', p.107 of Jonathan Cape edn.

See also ALBERT EINSTEIN; ENGINEERING

SCOTLAND *see under* BRITAIN

SCULPTURE *see under* ART

THE SEA

1 There is something about going to sea. A little bit of discipline, self-discipline and humility are required.

Prince Andrew (b.1960), Duke of York: in *The Daily Telegraph* (London), 7 Oct. 1988

2 Those who live by the sea can hardly form a single thought of which the sea would not be part.

Hermann Broch (1886–1951), Austrian novelist: foreword to *The Spell* (1976; tr.1987)

3 As usual I finish the day before the sea, sumptuous this evening beneath the moon, which writes Arab symbols with phosphorescent streaks on the slow swells. There is no end to the sky and the waters. How well they accompany sadness!

Albert Camus (1913–1960), French-Algerian philosopher and author: journal entry, 3 July 1949, written while crossing the Atlantic *en route* to South America, publ. in *American Journals* (1978; tr.1988)

4 for whatever we lose (like a you or a me) it's always ourselves we find in the sea

e e cummings (1894–1962), U.S. poet: 'maggie and milly and molly and may', publ. in *95 Poems* (1958)

5 The ocean, whose tides respond, like women's menses, to the pull of the moon, the ocean which corresponds to the amniotic fluid in

which human life begins, the ocean on whose surface vessels (personified as female) can ride but in whose depth sailors meet their death and monsters conceal themselves ... it is unstable and threatening as the earth is not; it spawns new life daily, yet swallows up lives; it is changeable like the moon, unregulated, yet indestructible and eternal.

Adrienne Rich (b.1929), U.S. poet: *Of Woman Born* (1976), Ch.4

6   The sea is mother-death and she is a mighty female, the one who wins, the one who sucks us all up.

Anne Sexton (1928–1974), U.S. poet: journal entry, 19 Nov. 1971, in 'A Small Journal', publ. in *The Poet's Story* (ed. Howard Moss, 1974)

7   The peace of white horses
The pastures of ports
The litany of islands
The rosary of archipelagoes

Derek Walcott (b.1930), West Indian poet and playwright: 'A Sea-Chantey', publ. in *In a Green Night* (1962)

SEASONS

1   Ah, summer, what power you have to make us suffer and like it.

Russell Baker (b.1925), U.S. journalist: in the *New York Times*, 27 June 1965

2   Often in winter the end of the day is like the final metaphor in a poem celebrating death: there is no way out.

Agustin Gomez-Arcos (b.1939), Spanish author: *A Bird Burned Alive* (1988), Ch.1

3   One of the joys our technological civilisation has lost is the excitement with which seasonal flowers and fruits were welcomed; the first daffodil, strawberry or cherry are now things of the past, along with their precious moment of arrival. Even the tangerine – now a satsuma or clementine – appears de-pipped months before Christmas.

Derek Jarman (1942–1994), British film-maker, artist and author: journal entry, 7 Feb. 1989, in *Modern Nature: The Journals of Derek Jarman* (1991)

4   Too often summer days appear
Emblems of perfect happiness
I can't confront: I must await
A time less bold, less rich, less clear:
An autumn more appropriate.

Philip Larkin (1922–1985), British poet: 'Mother, Summer, I', written 1953, publ. in *Collected Poems* (1988)

5   Indoors or out, no one relaxes
In March, that month of wind and taxes,
The wind will presently disappear,

The taxes last us all the year.

Ogden Nash (1902–1971), U.S. poet: 'Thar She Blows', publ. in *Versus* (1949)

6   Snow, snow over the whole land
across all boundaries.
The candle burned on the table,
the candle burned.

Boris Pasternak (1890–1960), Russian poet, novelist and translator: 'Winter Night', St.1, publ. in *Doctor Zhivago: the Poems* (1958; tr.1985)

See also Nordern on SPORT: CRICKET

SECRETS

1   You know there are no secrets in America. It's quite different in England, where people think of a secret as a shared relation between two people.

W.H. Auden (1907–1973), Anglo-American poet: *The Table Talk of W.H. Auden* (comp. Alan Ansen, ed. Nicholas Jenkins, 1990), '16 March, 1948'

2   Secrecy is the badge of fraud.

John Chadwick (b.1941), British judge: in *The Independent* (London), 26 July 1990

3   Men with secrets tend to be drawn to each other, not because they want to share what they know but because they need the company of the like-minded, the fellow afflicted.

Don DeLillo (b.1926), U.S. author: Walter Everett Jr., in *Libra* (1988), Pt.1, '17 April'

4   There is no better means of intensifying the treasured feeling of individuality than the possession of a secret which the individual is pledged to guard. The very beginnings of societal structures reveal the craving for secret organisations. When no valid secrets really exist, mysteries are invented or contrived to which privileged initiates are admitted.

Carl Jung (1875–1961), Swiss psychiatrist: *Memories, Dreams, Reflections* (1962), Ch.12, Sct.2

SEDUCTION

1   A gentleman doesn't pounce ... he glides.

Quentin Crisp (b.1908), British author: *Manners from Heaven* (1984), Ch.6

2   Seduction is often difficult to distinguish from rape. In seduction, the rapist often bothers to buy a bottle of wine.

Andrea Dworkin (b.1946), U.S. feminist critic: 'Sexual Economics: the Terrible Truth', speech, 1976, publ. in *Letters from a War-Zone* (1987)

3 You have to penetrate a woman's defenses. Getting into her head is a prerequisite to getting into her body.

Bob Guccione (b.1930), U.S. publisher: interview in *Speaking Frankly* by Wendy Leigh (1978)

4 Mrs Robinson, you're trying to seduce me. Aren't you?

Dustin Hoffman (b.1937), U.S. actor: Ben Braddock (Hoffman), in *The Graduate* (film; screenplay by Calder Willingham and Buck Henry, based on the novel by Charles Webb, directed by Mike Nichols, 1967)

5 You rip! Boom! Boom! Boom! Let's get together.

Tommy Lee (b.1962), U.S. rock musician: chat-up line to *Bay Watch* star Pamela Anderson, whom he married five days later, quoted in *FHM* (London), March 1996

6 The trouble with Ian is that he gets off with women because he can't get on with them.

Rosamond Lehmann (1903–1990), British author: of novelist Ian Fleming, quoted in *The Life of Ian Fleming* by John Pearson (1966), Ch.8, Sct.1. Fleming is portrayed as having a voracious – and cynical – sexual appetite: *see* Fleming on PROMISCUITY and SEX

7 Pursuit and seduction are the essence of sexuality. It's part of the sizzle.

Camille Paglia (b.1947), U.S. author and critic: interview in *Playboy* (Chicago), Oct. 1991, rep. in *Sex, Art, and American Culture* (1992), 'The Rape Debate'

SEGREGATION

1 The difference between *de jure* and *de facto* segregation is the difference between open, forthright bigotry and the shamefaced kind that works through unwritten agreements between real estate dealers, school officials, and local politicians.

Shirley Chisholm (b.1924), U.S. congresswoman: *Unbought and Unbossed* (1970), Pt.4, Ch.14

2 In America, you can segregate the people, but the problems will travel. From slavery to equal rights, from state suppression of dissent to crime, drugs and unemployment, I can't think of a supposedly Black issue that hasn't wasted the original Black target group and then spread like measles to outlying white experience.

June Jordan (b.1936), U.S. poet and civil rights activist: 'Problems of Language in a Democratic State' (1982), rep. in *Moving Towards Home: Political Essays* (1989)

3 Segregation now, segregation tomorrow and segregation forever!

George Wallace (b.1919), U.S. Democratic politician: inaugural address as Governor of Alabama, Jan. 1963, publ. in *Birmingham World*, 19 Jan. 1963. Wallace persisted in refusing to implement President Kennedy's desegregation laws. His speechwriter, Asa Carter (1926–1979), was a Ku Klux Klansman who went on to have literary success under the name of Forrest Carter, with two books: one, *Gone to Texas*, was made into a film by Clint Eastwood, *The Outlaw Josey Wales* (1976); the other, *The Education of Little Tree* (1976), purported to be Carter's memoir describing his upbringing by Cherokee grandparents and became a bestseller

SELF

1 The boundary line between self and external world bears no relation to reality; the distinction between ego and world is made by spitting out part of the inside, and swallowing in part of the outside.

Norman O. Brown (b.1913), U.S. philosopher: *Love's Body* (1967), Ch.8

2 It is ironic that the one thing that all religions recognize as separating us from our creator – our very self-consciousness – is also the one thing that divides us from our fellow creatures. It was a bitter birthday present from evolution.

Annie Dillard (b.1945), U.S. author and poet: *Pilgrim at Tinker Creek* (1974), Ch.6

3 Me, what's that after all? An arbitrary limitation of being bounded by the people before and after and on either side. Where they leave off, I begin, and vice versa.

Russell Hoban (b.1932), U.S. author: William G, in *Turtle Diary* (1975), Ch.11

4 The self is now the sacred cow of American culture, self-esteem is sacrosanct.

Robert Hughes (b.1938), Australian author and critic: *Culture of Complaint* (1993), Ch.1

5 I suppose everyone continues to be interested in the quest for the self, but what you feel when you're older, I think, is that ... you really must *make* the self. It is absolutely useless to look for it, you won't find it, but it's possible in some sense to make it. I don't mean in the sense of making a mask, a Yeatsian mask. But you finally begin in some sense to make and choose the self you want.

Mary McCarthy (1912–1989), U.S. author and critic: interview in *Writers at Work* (Second Series, ed. George Plimpton, 1963)

6 You have for company the best companion you will ever have – the modest, defeated, plodding workaday self which has a name and can be identified in public registers in case of accident or death. But the real self, the one who has taken over the reins, is almost a stranger. He is the one who is filled with ideas; he is the one who is writing in the air; he is the one who, if

you become too fascinated with his exploits, will finally expropriate the old, worn-out self, taking over your name, your address, your wife, your past, your future.

Henry Miller (1891–1980), U.S. author: *Sexus* (1949), Ch.2

7   Man is not merely the sum of his masks. Behind the shifting face of personality is a hard nugget of self, a genetic gift. ... The self is malleable but elastic, snapping back to its original shape like a rubber band. Mental illness is no myth, as some have claimed. It is a disturbance in our sense of possession of a stable inner self that survives its personae.

Camille Paglia (b.1947), U.S. author and critic: *Sex, Art, and American Culture* (1992), 'Sexual Personae: the Cancelled Preface'

8   The more the development of late capitalism renders obsolete or at least suspect the real possibilities of self, self-fulfillment and actualization, the more they are emphasized as if they could spring to life through an act of will alone.

Richard Dean Rosen (b.1949), U.S. journalist and critic: *Psychobabble: Fast Talk and Quick Cure in the Era of Feeling* (1977), 'Psychobabble'

9   All I can tell you with certainty is that I, for one, have no self, and that I am unwilling or unable to perpetrate upon myself the joke of a self. ... What I have instead is a variety of impersonations I can do, and not only of myself – a troupe of players that I have internalised, a permanent company of actors that I can call upon when a self is required. ... I am a theater and nothing more than a theater.

Philip Roth (b.1933), U.S. novelist: Nathan Zuckerman, writing to Maria, in *The Counterlife* (1986), Ch.5

10   The world is made for people who aren't cursed with self-awareness.

Susan Sarandon (b.1946), U.S. actress: Annie Savoy (Sarandon), in *Bull Durham* (film; written and directed by Ron Shelton, 1988)

11   There is no me. I do not exist. There used to be a me but I had it surgically removed,

Peter Sellers (1925–1980), British comic: in *Time* (New York), 3 March 1980

12   It's awkward, in a society where the cult of the individual has never been preached with greater force, and where many of our collective ills are a result of that force, to say that it is to the Self to which one must attend. But the Self is not a random collection of stray desires striving to be satisfied, nor is it only by suppressing such desires, as women are encouraged to do, that any social cohesion is possible. Our broken society is not born out of the triumph of the individual, but out of his effacement.

Jeanette Winterson (b.1959), British author: *Art and Lies* (1994), 'Handel', p.24 of Jonathan Cape edn.

13   *To become oneself, with all one's strength.* Difficult. A bomb, a speech, a rifle shot – and the world can look a different place. And then where is this 'self'?

Christa Wolf (b.1929), German novelist: *The Quest for Christa T* (1968; tr.1982), Ch.17

See also EGOTISM

SELF-ABSORPTION

1   For an introvert his environment is himself and can never be subject to startling or unforeseen change.

Quentin Crisp (b.1908), British author: *The Naked Civil Servant* (1968), Ch.24

2   I have often wished I had time to cultivate modesty. ... But I am too busy thinking about myself.

Edith Sitwell (1887–1964), British poet: quoted in *The Observer* (London), 30 April 1950

3   Happiness lies outside yourself, is achieved through interacting with others. Self-forgetfulness should be one's goal, not self-absorption. The male, capable of only the latter, makes a virtue of an irremediable fault and sets up self-absorption, not only as a good but as a Philosophical Good.

Valerie Solanas (1936–1988), U.S. actress and writer: *The SCUM Manifesto* (1968)

See also INTROSPECTION

SELF-ASSERTION

1   A successful social technique consists perhaps in finding unobjectionable means for individual self-assertion.

Eric Hoffer (1902–1983), U.S. philosopher: *The Passionate State of Mind* (1955), Aph.26

2   If we are to be men again we must stop working for nothing, competing against each other for the little they allow us to possess, stop selling our women or allowing them to be used and handled against their will, stop letting our children be educated by the barbarian, using their language, dress, and customs, and most assuredly stop turning our cheeks.

George Jackson (1942–1971), U.S. black activist: letter to his father, 30 March 1965, from Soledad Prison, publ. in *Soledad Brother* (1970)

3   Back in the days when men were hunters and chestbeaters and women spent their whole lives worrying about pregnancy or dying in childbirth, they often had to be taken against their will. Men complained that women were

cold, unresponsive, frigid. ... They wanted their women wanton. They wanted their women wild. Now women were finally learning to be wanton and wild – and what happened? The men wilted.

Erica Jong (b.1942), U.S. author: the narrator (Isadora Wing), in *Fear of Flying* (1973), Ch.16

4　To me, the whole process of being a brushstroke in someone else's painting is a little difficult.

Madonna (b.1959), U.S. singer and actress: in *Vanity Fair* (New York), April 1991

SELF-CONFIDENCE

1　The people I respect most behave as if they were immortal and as if society was eternal.

E.M. Forster (1879–1970), British novelist and essayist: *Two Cheers for Democracy* (1951), 'What I Believe'

2　I probably have been made to look a fool but I'm not a man with phobias and complexes. I'm not a man who needs sleeping pills. I don't care what you think about me. ... I'm not ashamed of anything I've done.

Robert Maxwell (1923–1991), British tycoon: interview with Lynda Lee-Potter in the *Daily Mail* (London), 15 June 1973, quoted in *Maxwell* by Joe Haines (1988), Ch.1

3　The greatest violence is when you attack somebody with the notion that they're hopeless; that they can't change. That is violence.

Sean Penn (b.1960), U.S. actor: quoted in *The Guardian* (London), 23 March 1996

SELF-CRITICISM

1　You see it's awfully hard to talk or write about your own stuff because if it is any good you yourself know about how good it is – but if you say so yourself you feel like a shit.

Ernest Hemingway (1899–1961), U.S. author: letter to poet and critic Malcolm Cowley, 17 Oct. 1945, publ. in *Selected Letters* (ed. Carlos Baker, 1981)

SELF-DECEPTION

1　Most of our platitudes notwithstanding, self-deception remains the most difficult deception. The tricks that work on others count for nothing in that very well-lit back alley where one keeps assignations with oneself: no winning smiles will do here, no prettily drawn lists of good intentions.

Joan Didion (b.1934), U.S. essayist: *Slouching Towards Bethlehem* (1968), 'On Self-Respect'

2　We lie loudest when we lie to ourselves.

Eric Hoffer (1902–1983), U.S. philosopher: *The Passionate State of Mind* (1955), Aph. 70

SELF-DESTRUCTIVENESS

1　It's all false pressure; you put the heat on yourself, you get it from the networks and record companies and movie studios, and then you put more pressure on yourself to make everything that much harder because work is no longer challenging. You say, 'Well, I'll get all screwed up and then it'll be a real challenge again'. So stupid – I've often wondered why people do these things. You're so much happier if you don't, but I guess happiness is not a state you want to be in all the time.

John Belushi (1949–1982), U.S. comedian, singer and actor: interview in *Cosmopolitan* (New York) Dec. 1981, quoted in *Wired: The Short Life and Fast Times of John Belushi* by Bob Woodward (1984), Pt.2, Ch.14

2　When the beginnings of self-destruction enter the heart it seems no bigger than a grain of sand.

John Cheever (1912–1982), U.S. author: journal entry, 1952, in *John Cheever: The Journals* (ed. Robert Gottlieb, 1991), 'The Late Forties and the Fifties'

3　When man meets an obstacle he can't destroy, he destroys himself.

Ryszard Kapuściński (b.1932), Polish journalist: 'A Warsaw Diary', publ. in *Granta* (Cambridge), No.15, 1985

SELF-EXPRESSION

1　I am into my own expression; expression of what goes through my head or expression of whatever inspires me to be a creative person in the first place. It just so happens that I was brought up on a diet of rock 'n' roll, and at the time, it seemed to be my canvas. It really is as basic as that, it's just an artist's materials.

David Bowie (b.1947), British rock musician: interview, June 1973, rep. in *Bowie in His Own Words* (ed. Miles, 1980), 'Rock'n'Roll'

2　One can create a masterpiece by using any means of expression, no matter how absurd, just as one can make a beautiful gesture lying at the edge, or even the bottom, of a precipice.

Witold Lutoslawski (1913–1994), Polish composer: *Conversations with Witold Lutoslawski* (ed. Tadeusz Kaczyński, 1972; tr.1984), Ch.9

3　A gesture cannot be regarded as the expression of an individual, as his creation (because no individual is capable of creating a fully original gesture, belonging to nobody else), nor can it even be regarded as that person's instrument; on the contrary, it is gestures that use us as their instruments, as their bearers and incarnations.

Milan Kundera (b.1929), Czech-born French author and critic: *Immortality* (1991), Pt.1, Ch.2

4 One's prime is elusive. You little girls, when you grow up, must be on the alert to recognize your prime at whatever time of your life it may occur. You must then live it to the full.

Muriel Spark (b.1918), British novelist: Miss Brodie, in *The Prime of Miss Jean Brodie* (1961), Ch.1

SELF-IMAGE

1 I think it's one of the scars in our culture that we have too high an opinion of ourselves. We align ourselves with the angels instead of the higher primates.

Angela Carter (1940–1992), British author: in *Marxism Today* (London), Jan. 1985

2 If we could see ourselves as others see us, we would vanish on the spot.

E.M. Cioran (1911–1995), Rumanian-born French philosopher: *The Trouble with Being Born* (1973), Ch.3

3 Every morning I walk to the toilet, look in the mirror and tell myself I'm the baddest muthafucker alive. But I always flush before I leave, so I can't be that bad.

George Clinton (b.1940), U.S. funk and rap musician: in *New Musical Express* (London), 1985, quoted in *NME Book of Quotes* (1995), 'Ego'

4 The very purpose of existence is to reconcile the glowing opinion we have of ourselves with the appalling things that other people think about us.

Quentin Crisp (b.1908), British author: *How to Become a Virgin* (1981), Ch.2

5 To see ourselves as others see us can be eye-opening. To see others as sharing a nature with ourselves is the merest decency. But it is from the far more difficult achievement of seeing ourselves amongst others, as a local example of the forms human life has locally taken, a case among cases, a world among worlds, that the largeness of mind, without which objectivity is self-congratulation and tolerance a sham, comes.

Clifford Geertz (b.1926), U.S. anthropologist: introduction to *Local Knowledge* (1983)

6 Women are reputed never to be disgusted. The sad fact is that they often are, but not with men; following the lead of men, they are most often disgusted with themselves.

Germaine Greer (b.1939), Australian feminist writer: *The Female Eunuch* (1970), 'Loathing and Disgust'

7 Anyone who takes himself too seriously always runs the risk of looking ridiculous; anyone who can consistently laugh at himself does not.

Václav Havel (b.1936), Czech playwright and president: *Disturbing the Peace* (1986; tr.1990), Ch.2

8 No matter what our achievements might be, we think well of ourselves only in rare moments. We need people to bear witness against our inner judge, who keeps book on our shortcomings and transgressions. We need people to convince us that we are not as bad as we think we are.

Eric Hoffer (1902–1983), U.S. philosopher: *Reflections on the Human Condition* (1973), Aph. 144

9 It is terrible to destroy a person's picture of himself in the interests of truth or some other abstraction.

Doris Lessing (b.1919), British novelist: *The Grass is Singing* (1950), Ch.2

10 I always felt I was a nobody, and the only way for me to be somebody was to be – well, somebody else. Which is probably why I wanted to act.

Marilyn Monroe (1926–1962), U.S. actress: quoted in *Marilyn Monroe: the Biography* by Donald Spoto (1993), Ch.15

See also MacLiammóir on COMPLACENCY

SELF-IMPROVEMENT

1 Let's not forget James Brown picked cotton. James Brown shined shoes. And yet James Brown is still active. Because James Brown worked all the way to the top. ... I first started out tryin' to get a decent meal, a decent pair of shoes, so when I got to where I could do that, I thought I was on the top anyway.

James Brown (b.1928), U.S. soul singer: in the *Los Angeles Weekly*, 18 April 1984

2 I used to live in a sewer. Now I live in a swamp. I've come up in the world.

Linda Darnell (1921–1965), U.S. actress: Edie Johnson (Darnell), in *No Way Out* (film; screenplay by Lesser Samuels and Joseph L. Mankiewicz, directed by Joseph L. Mankiewicz, 1950)

SELF-INTEREST

1 Some people's self-interest is to save the world. Some people's self-interest is to do good for others. Florence Nightingale pursued her own self-interest through charitable activities. Rockefeller pursued his self-interest in setting up the Rockefeller foundation. But for

most people, most of the time, self-interest is greed.

Milton Friedman (b.1912), U.S. economist: introduction to *There's No Such Thing as a Free Lunch* (1975)

2 The punters know that the horse named Morality rarely gets past the post, whereas the nag named Self-Interest always runs a good race.

Gough Whitlam (b.1916), Australian Labor politician and prime minister: in *The Daily Telegraph* (London), 19 Oct. 1989

3 Long before Einstein told us that matter is energy, Machiavelli and Hobbes and other modern political philosophers defined man as a lump of matter whose most politically relevant attribute is a form of energy called 'self-interestedness'. This was not a portrait of man 'warts and all'. It was all wart.

George F. Will (b.1941), U.S. political columnist: *Statecraft as Soulcraft: What Government Does* (1984), Ch.2

SELF-KNOWLEDGE

1 The self-explorer, whether he wants to or not, becomes the explorer of everything else. He learns to see himself, but suddenly, provided he was honest, all the rest appears, and it is as rich as he was, and, as a final crowning, richer.

Elias Canetti (1905–1994), Austrian novelist and philosopher: *The Secret Heart Of The Clock: Notes, Aphorisms, Fragments 1973–1985* (1991), '1975'

2 If you don't understand yourself you don't understand anybody else.

Nikki Giovanni (b.1943), U.S. poet: in conversation with James Baldwin, 4 Nov. 1971, London, publ. in *A Dialogue* (1973)

3 Our lives teach us who we are.

Salman Rushdie (b.1947), Indian-born British author: in the *Independent on Sunday* (London), 4 Feb. 1990

4 I feel there are territories within us that are totally unknown. Huge, mysterious, and dangerous territories. We think we know ourselves, when we really know only this little bitty part. We have this social person that we present to each other. We have all these galaxies inside of us. And if we don't enter those in art of one kind or another, whether it's playwriting, or painting, or music, or whatever, then I don't understand the point of doing anything. It's the reason I write. I try to go into parts of myself that are unknown.

Sam Shepard (b.1943), U.S. playwright and actor: quoted in *The Other American Drama* by Marc Robinson (1994), Ch.3

5 In the lifelong romance each man has with himself, he should know which vows he's sworn.

Edmund White (b.1940), U.S. author: 'The Gay Philosopher', written 1969, publ. in *The Burning Library* (1994)

SELF-LOVE

1 Self-love depressed becomes self-loathing.

Sally Kempton (b.1943), U.S. author: 'Cutting Loose', publ. in *Esquire* (New York), July 1970

2 Self-love seems so often unrequited.

Anthony Powell (b.1905), British novelist: the narrator (Nicholas Jenkins), in *The Acceptance World* (1955), Ch.1

3 Narcissist: psychoanalytic term for the person who loves himself more than his analyst; considered to be the manifestation of a dire mental disease whose successful treatment depends on the patient learning to love the analyst more and himself less.

Thomas Szasz (b.1920), U.S. psychiatrist: *The Second Sin* (1973), 'Psychoanalysis'

4 A narcissist is someone better looking than you are.

Gore Vidal (b.1925), U.S. novelist and critic: quoted in the *San Francisco Chronicle*, 12 April 1981

SELF-PORTRAITS

1 I'm not as normal as I appear.

Woody Allen (b.1935), U.S. film-maker: in *Time* (New York), 14 April 1976

2 I'm not worldly, a bit of a savage really. I love the trees, the isolation, the soul. I've a mystic temperament, an independence that prevents me from constantly looking into myself. I'm not suicidal but alive, excessive, bloody-minded, above all a traveller without need for medicaments to assist my journey.

Gérard Depardieu (b.1948), French actor: in *The Observer* (London), 3 April 1985

3 I have invented myself entirely: a childhood, a personality, longings, dreams and memories, all in order to enable me to tell them.

Federico Fellini (1920–1993), Italian film-maker: *Fellini on Fellini* (ed. Anna Keel and Christian Strich, 1974; tr.1977), 'Miscellany I', Sct.10

4 I am astonished, disappointed, pleased with myself. I am distressed, depressed, rapturous. I am all these things at once, and cannot add up the sum. I am incapable of determining ultimate worth or worthlessness; I have no judgement about myself and my life. There is

nothing I am quite sure about. I have no definite convictions – not about anything really. I only know that I was born and exist, and it seems to me that I have been carried along.

Carl Jung (1875–1961), Swiss psychiatrist: *Memories, Dreams, Reflections* (1962), 'Retrospect'

5 I'm roughly six foot one. I've got blue eyes. I've got a gap in the front of my teeth. I've got ears that stick out. I don't shave everyday. My favourite colour is black. My favourite places are Tipperary, New York, Thailand and London. I like the Dubliners, Bo Diddley, Nick Cave, John Turturro and Clint Eastwood. I find journalists annoying. I don't like being depressed. And I don't like being poor.

Shane MacGowan (b.1957), Anglo-Irish rock musician: interview in *The Face* (London), Nov. 1994

6 As for me, I am – or think I am – hard-nosed, small-eyed, sparse of hair, swollen in the abdomen, long-legged, broad-footed, yellow-complexioned, generous in love, impossible at figures, confused by words, tender-handed, slow-walking, pure-hearted, fond of stars and tides and swells, an admirer of beetles, a walker of sands, institutionally dull, perpetually Chilean, friend to my friends, silent to my enemies, meddlesome among birds, bad-mannered at home, timid in gatherings, daring in solitude, repentant without reason ... persistently in disorder, brave out of necessity, a coward without guilt, lazy by vocation, lovable to women, congenitally active, a poet by curse, and a first-rate fool.

Pablo Neruda (1904–1973), Chilean poet: 'Panorama', in *Defectos escogidos* (1973), quoted in *Neruda: An Intimate Biography* (1985; tr.1992), Pt.8, Sct.182

7 Trying to define yourself is like trying to bite your own teeth.

Alan Watts (1915–1973), British-born U.S. philosopher and author: in *Life* (New York), 21 April 1961

SELF-PROMOTION

1 I am the greatest.

Muhammad Ali (b.1942), U.S. boxer: slogan, used from c.1962, quoted in *The Dictionary of Catchphrases* (ed. Paul Beale, 1986)

2 Movie stars are created by other people – they're a product. I created myself – I invented myself. I not only invented myself, I re-invented myself.

Hugh Hefner (b.1926), U.S. publisher: interview in the *Independent on Sunday* (London), 1 May 1994

3 The final key to the way I promote is bravado. I play to people's fantasies. People may not always think big themselves, but they can still get very excited by those who do. That's why a little hyperbole never hurts.

Donald Trump (b.1946), U.S. businessman: *Trump: The Art of the Deal* (written with Tony Schwartz, 1987), Ch.2

SELF-RESPECT

1 To have that sense of one's intrinsic worth which constitutes self-respect is potentially to have everything: the ability to discriminate, to love and to remain indifferent. To lack it is to be locked within oneself, paradoxically incapable of either love or indifference.

Joan Didion (b.1934), U.S. essayist: *Slouching Towards Bethlehem* (1968), 'On Self-Respect'

2 Self-respect is nothing to hide behind. When you need it most it isn't there.

May Sarton (b.1912), U.S. poet and novelist: Hilary Stevens, in *Mrs Stevens Hears the Mermaids Singing* (1965), 'Epilogue: Mar'

SELF-SUFFICIENCY

1 The history of this country was made largely by people who wanted to be left alone. Those who could not thrive when left to themselves never felt at ease in America.

Eric Hoffer (1902–1983), U.S. philosopher: *Reflections on the Human Condition* (1973), Aph. 53

2 The proverb warns that 'You should not bite the hand that feeds you.' But maybe you should, if it prevents you from feeding yourself.

Thomas Szasz (b.1920), U.S. psychiatrist: *The Second Sin* (1973), 'Control and Self-control'

SELFISHNESS

1 You have no idea how promising the world begins to look once you have decided to have it all for yourself. And how much healthier your decisions are once they become entirely selfish.

Anita Brookner (b.1938), British novelist and art historian: Mr Neville, in *Hotel du Lac* (1984), Ch.7

2 Selfish persons are incapable of loving others, but they are not capable of loving themselves either.

Erich Fromm (1900–1980), U.S. psychologist: *Man for Himself* (1947), Ch.4

3 Selfishness is like listening to good jazz
With drinks for further orders and a huge fire.

Philip Larkin (1922–1985), British poet: 'None of the books have time', written 1960, publ. in *Collected Poems* (1988)

SENSATION

1 Reciprocity of sensation is not possible because to share is to be robbed.

Angela Carter (1940–1992), British author: *The Sadeian Woman* (1979), 'Speculative Finale'

2 A sensation must have fallen very low to deign to turn into an idea.

E.M. Cioran (1911–1995), Rumanian-born French philosopher: *Anathemas and Admirations* (1986), 'On the Verge of Existence'

SENSITIVITY

1 It is ... axiomatic that we should all think of ourselves as being more sensitive than other people because, when we are insensitive in our dealings with others, we cannot be aware of it at the time: conscious insensitivity is a self-contradiction.

W.H. Auden (1907–1973), Anglo-American poet: foreword to Dag Hammarskjöld's *Markings* (1964)

2 I am continually fascinated at the difficulty intelligent people have in distinguishing what is controversial from what is merely offensive.

Nora Ephron (b.1941), U.S. author and journalist: 'Barney Collier's Book', publ. in *Esquire* (New York), Jan. 1976

3 How frail the human heart must be – a mirrored pool of thought...

Sylvia Plath (1932–1963), U.S. poet: 'I Thought That I Could Not Be Hurt', first poem written aged 14, quoted in introduction by Aurelia Schober Plath to *Letters Home: Correspondence 1950–1963* (1975)

4 What we think of as our sensitivity is only the higher evolution of terror in a poor dumb beast. We suffer for nothing. Our own death wish is our only real tragedy.

Mario Puzo (b.1920), U.S. novelist: Merlyn, in *Fools Die* (1978), Ch.55

5 I can't stand a naked light bulb, any more than I can a rude remark or a vulgar action.

Tennessee Williams (1911–1983), U.S. playwright: Blanche DuBois, in *A Streetcar Named Desire* (1947), Sc.3

6 I allow myself to be vulnerable. It's not something I do consciously. But I am. It just happens that way. I'm vulnerable and people say, 'Poor thing. She has big hips too.'

Oprah Winfrey (b.1954), U.S. chat-show host: quoted in *Oprah!* by Robert Waldron (1987), 'A Day with Oprah'

SENTIMENTALITY

1 Sentimentality is a form of fatigue.

Leonora Carrington (b.1917), British surrealist artist and writer: the Happy Corpse, in 'The Happy Corpse Story', written 1971, first publ. in a French translation in *Le Nouveau Commerce*, Nos.30–31 (1975), rep. in *The Seventh Horse and Other Tales* (1988)

2 What's wrong with sentimental? Sentimental means you *love*, you *care*, you *like* stuff. The thing is, we're *frightened* to be sentimental.

Paul McCartney (b.1942), British rock musician: interview in *Smash Hits* (London), 24 Nov. 1983

3 Sentimentality is the emotional promiscuity of those who have no sentiment.

Norman Mailer (b.1923), U.S. author: *Cannibals and Christians* (1966), 'My Hope for America'

4 *Quand il me prend dans ses bras*
Il me parle tout bas
Je vois la vie en rose.
(When he takes me in his arms
He speaks to me in a low voice
I see *la vie en rose*.)

Edith Piaf (1918–1963), French singer: 'La Vie en Rose' (song; written by Louis Louiguy, Piaf and Mal Davis, 1946)

See also Burroughs on GRIEF

SERENITY

1 You must learn to be still in the midst of activity and to be vibrantly alive in repose.

Indira Gandhi (1917–1984), Indian politician and prime minister: quoted in *People* (New York), 30 June 1975

2 There is no such thing as inner peace. There is only nervousness or death. Any attempt to prove otherwise constitutes unacceptable behavior.

Fran Lebowitz (b.1951), U.S. journalist: *Metropolitan Life* (1978), 'Manners'

SERVANTS

1 There is something gracious and graceful about serving. ... The truth is, our history in this country has been the history of the servers.... In Africa it is a great honor to serve.

Maya Angelou (b.1928), U.S. author: 'The Black Scholar Interviews Maya Angelou', first publ. Jan./Feb. 1977, rep. in *Conversations with Maya Angelou* (ed. Jeffrey M. Elliot, 1989)

2 Me? What am I? Nothing. The legs on which dinner comes to the table, the arms by which

cocktails enter the living room, the hands that drive cars. I am the eyes that see nothing, the ears that don't hear. I'm invisible too. They look and don't see me. When they move, I have to guess their direction and get myself out of the way.

Shirley Ann Grau (b.1929), U.S. author: *The Condor Passes* (1971), 'Stanley'

SEX

1   Is sex dirty? Only if it's done right.

Woody Allen (b.1935), U.S. film-maker: 'Chapter' title, in *Everything You Always Wanted to Know About Sex (But Were Afraid to Ask)* (film; written and directed by Woody Allen, 1972)

2   That was the most fun I've ever had without laughing.

Woody Allen: Alvy Singer (Allen), in *Annie Hall* (film; screenplay by Woody Allen and Marshall Brickman, directed by Woody Allen, 1977)

3   You have to see the sex act comically, as a child.

W.H. Auden (1907–1973), Anglo-American poet: *The Table Talk of W.H. Auden* (comp. Alan Ansen, ed. Nicholas Jenkins, 1990), 'March 17, 1947'

4   Sex – the great inequality, the great miscalculator, the great Irritator.

Enid Bagnold (1889–1981), British novelist and playwright: *Autobiography* (1969), Ch.6

5   The question of sexual dominance can exist only in the nightmare of that soul which has armed itself, totally, against the possibility of the changing motion of conquest and surrender, which is love.

James Baldwin (1924–1987), U.S. author: 'The Devil Finds Work', Sct.2 (1976), rep. in *The Price Of The Ticket* (1985)

6   I've tried several varieties of sex. The conventional position makes me claustrophobic and the others give me a stiff neck or lockjaw.

Tallulah Bankhead (1903–1968), U.S. actress: quoted in *Miss Tallulah Bankhead* by Lee Israel (1972)

7   My husband complained to me, he said 'I can't remember when we last had sex', and I said, 'Well I can and that's why we ain't doing it.'

Roseanne Barr (b.1952), U.S. stand-up comedienne and actress: *Roseanne* (U.S. sitcom, from 1988), quoted in *Funny Business* by David Housham and John Frank-Keyes (1992), 'Roseanne Barr'

8   Sex pleasure in woman ... is a kind of magic spell; it demands complete abandon; if words or movements oppose the magic of caresses, the spell is broken.

Simone de Beauvoir (1908–1986), French novelist and essayist: *The Second Sex* (1949; tr.1953), Bk.2, Pt.4, Ch.3

9   Sex has never been an obsession with me. It's just like eating a bag of crisps. Quite nice, but nothing marvellous.

Boy George (b.1961), British rock singer: quoted in *The Sun* (London), 21 Oct. 1982, rep. in *The Faber Book of Pop* (ed. Hanif Kureishi and Jon Savage, 1995), Pt.8, '1982: Mister (or is it Miss) Weirdo'

10   Sexual intercourse is kicking death in the ass while singing.

Charles Bukowski (1920–1994), U.S. author and poet: *Notes of a Dirty Old Man* (1969), p.166 of City Lights edn. (1973)

11   If the devil were to offer me a resurgence of what is commonly called virility, I'd decline. 'Just keep my liver and lungs in good working order,' I'd reply, 'so I can go on drinking and smoking!'

Luis Buñuel (1900–1983), Spanish film-maker: *My Last Breath* (autobiography, 1983), Ch.6

12   Sex. Rule One: the sun will rise in the East. Rule Two: wherever there are rich men trying not to feel old there will be young girls trying not to feel poor.

Julie Burchill (b.1960), British journalist and author: *Girls on Film* (1986), Ch.3

13   In love, as in gluttony, pleasure is a matter of the utmost precision.

Italo Calvino (1923–1985), Italian author and critic: introduction to *Theory of the Four Movements* by Charles Fourier (1971), rep. in *The Literature Machine* (1987)

14   We do not go to bed in single pairs; even if we choose not to refer to them, we still drag there with us the cultural impedimenta of our social class, our parents' lives, our bank balances, our sexual and emotional expectations, our whole biographies – all the bits and pieces of our unique existences.

Angela Carter (1940–1992), British author: *The Sadeian Woman* (1979), 'Polemical Preface'

15   Every man has been brought up with the idea that decent women don't pop in and out of bed; he has always been told by his mother that 'nice girls don't'. He finds, of course, when he gets older that this may be untrue – but only in a certain section of society.

Barbara Cartland (b.1901), British novelist: interview in *Speaking Frankly* by Wendy Leigh (1978)

16   The real problem between the sexes is that for men, sex is a gender-underliner, they need it for their egos. We don't need sex to make us feel we are the person we need to be.

Carol Clewlow (b.1947), British novelist: interview in *The Observer* (London), 19 Feb. 1989

17   Sex is the last refuge of the miserable.

Quentin Crisp (b.1908), British author: *The Naked Civil Servant* (1968), Ch.8

18 Women need a reason to have sex. Men just need a place.

Billy Crystal (b.1947), U.S. actor: Mitch Robbins (Crystal), in *City Slickers* (film; screenplay by Lowell Ganz and Babaloo Mandel, directed by Ron Underwood, 1991)

19 Sex is a short cut to everything.

Anne Cumming (b.1917), British author: opening line of *The Love Quest* (autobiography, 1991), Ch.1

20 The act of sex, gratifying as it may be, is God's joke on humanity. It is man's last desperate stand at superintendency.

Bette Davis (1908–1989), U.S. actress: *The Lonely Life* (autobiography, 1962), Ch.20

21 I finally understand what all the fuss is about now. It's just like a whole other ball game.

Geena Davis (b.1957), U.S. actress: Thelma (Davis), in *Thelma and Louise* (film; screenplay by Callie Khouri, directed and co-produced by Ridley Scott, 1991)

22 Women's Liberation calls it enslavement but the real truth about the sexual revolution is that it has made of sex an almost chaotically limitless and therefore unmanageable realm in the life of women.

Midge Decter (b.1927), U.S. author, editor and social critic: *The New Chastity and Other Arguments Against Women's Liberation* (1972), Ch.2

23 Sex. In America an obsession. In other parts of the world a fact.

Marlene Dietrich (1904–1992), German-born U.S. actress: *Marlene Dietrich's ABC* (1962), 'Sex'

24 You can't remember sex. You can remember the fact of it, and recall the setting, and even the details, but the sex of the sex cannot be remembered, the substantive truth of it, it is by nature self-erasing, you can remember its anatomy and be left with a judgment as to the degree of your liking of it, but whatever it is as a splurge of being, as a loss, as a charge of the conviction of love stopping your heart like your execution, there is no memory of it in the brain, only the deduction that it happened and that time passed, leaving you with a silhouette that you want to fill in again.

E.L. Doctorow (b.1931), U.S. novelist: the narrator (Billy Bathgate), in *Billy Bathgate* (1989), Ch.16

25 No woman needs intercourse; few women escape it.

Andrea Dworkin (b.1946), U.S. feminist critic: *Right-Wing Women* (1978), Ch.3

26 What will happen to sex after liberation? Frankly, I don't know. It is a great mystery to all of us.

Nora Ephron (b.1941), U.S. author and journalist: 'Women', publ. in *Esquire* (New York), July 1972

27 We do not understand these Americans who, like adolescents, always speak of sex, and who, like adolescents, all of a sudden have discovered that sex is good not only for procreating children.

Oriana Fallaci (b.1930), Italian author: *The Egotists* (1963), 'Hugh Hefner'

28 Sex is two plus two making five, rather than four. Sex is the X ingredient that you can't define, and it's that X ingredient between two people that make both a man and a woman good in bed. It's all relative. There are no rules.

Marty Feldman (1933–1982), British comedian: interview in *Speaking Frankly* by Wendy Leigh (1978)

29 Older women are best, because they always think they may be doing it for the last time.

Ian Fleming (1908–1964), British author: notebook entry, quoted in *The Life of Ian Fleming* by John Pearson (1966), Ch.8, Sct.1

30 Instead of fulfilling the promise of infinite orgastic bliss, sex in the America of the feminine mystique is becoming a strangely joyless national compulsion, if not a contemptuous mockery.

Betty Friedan (b.1921), U.S. feminist writer: *The Feminine Mystique* (1963), Ch.11

31 If I were asked for a one line answer to the question 'What makes a woman good in bed?' I would say, 'A man who is good in bed'.

Bob Guccione (b.1930), U.S. publisher: interview in *Speaking Frankly* by Wendy Leigh (1978)

32 I prod, you react. Thus to and fro
We turn, to see ourselves perform the same
Comical acts inside the tragic game.

Thom Gunn (b.1929), British poet: 'Carnal Knowledge', publ. in *Fighting Terms* (1954)

33 Sex is everywhere, symbolized in the glamour of mass-produced luxury – the interplay of fleshy plastic and smooth, fleshier metal. This relationship of woman and appliance is a fundamental theme in our culture.

Richard Hamilton (b.1922), British Pop artist: referring to images of women in advertising in the 1950s, in 'An Exposition of $he', first publ. in *Architectural Design*, Oct. 1962, rep. in *Collected Words 1953–1982* (1982)

34 Sex can no longer be the germ, the seed of fiction. Sex is an episode, most properly conveyed in an episodic manner, quickly, often ironically. It is a bursting forth of only one of the cells in the body of the omnipotent 'I', the one who hopes by concentration of tone and voice to utter the sound of reality.

Elizabeth Hardwick (b.1916), U.S. critic and author: 'Seduction and Betrayal', address, 1972,

Vassar College, publ. in *Seduction and Betrayal: Women and Literature* (1974)

35 I find it extraordinary that a straightforward if inelegant device for ensuring the survival of the species should involve human beings in such emotional turmoil. Does sex have to be taken so seriously?

P.D. James (b.1920), British author: Alice, in *Devices and Desires* (1989), Ch.16

36 I can live without it all –
love with its blood pump,
sex with its messy hungers,
men with their peacock strutting,
their silly sexual baggage,
their wet tongues in my ear.

Erica Jong (b.1942), U.S. author: 'Becoming a Nun', publ. in *About Women* (ed. Stephen Berg and S.J. Marks, 1973)

37 The zipless fuck is absolutely pure. It is free of ulterior motives. There is no power game. The man is not 'taking' and the woman is not 'giving'. No one is attempting to cuckold a husband or humiliate a wife. No one is trying to prove anything or get anything out of anyone. The zipless fuck is the purest thing there is. And it is rarer than the unicorn. And I have never had one.

Erica Jong: *Fear of Flying* (1973), Ch.1. Jong explained, 'Zipless ... because the incident has all the swift compression of a dream and is seemingly free of all remorse and guilt'

38 Sexual intercourse began
In nineteen sixty-three
(Which was rather late for me) –
Between the end of the *Chatterley* ban
And the Beatles' first LP.

Philip Larkin (1922–1986), British poet: 'Annus Mirabilis', St.1, publ. in *High Windows* (1974)

39 That our popular art forms have become so obsessed with sex has turned the USA into a nation of hobbledehoys; as if grown people don't have more vital concerns, such as taxes, inflation, dirty politics, earning a living, getting an education, or keeping out of jail.

Anita Loos (1893–1981), U.S. novelist and screenwriter: *Kiss Hollywood Good-by* (1974), Ch.21

40 Sex is two minutes of squelching.

John Lydon [formerly Johnny Rotten] (b.1957), British rock musician: quoted by Tony Parsons in *Vox* (London), March 1994, rep. in *Dispatches from the Front Line of Popular Culture* (Tony Parsons, 1994)

41 I think men talk to women so they can sleep with them and women sleep with men so they can talk to them.

Jay McInerney (b.1955), U.S. author: Jeff, in *Brightness Falls* (1992), Ch.8

42 For those for whom the sex act has come to seem mechanical and merely the meeting and manipulation of body parts, there often remains a hunger which can be called metaphysical but which is not recognized as such, and which seeks satisfaction in physical danger, or sometimes in torture, suicide, or murder.

Marshall McLuhan (1911–1980), Canadian communications theorist: title essay of *The Mechanical Bride* (1951)

43 There is nothing safe about sex. There never will be.

Norman Mailer (b.1923), U.S. author: in the *International Herald Tribune* (Paris), 24 Jan. 1992

44 Continental people have sex lives; the English have hot-water bottles.

George Mikes (1912–1987), Hungarian-born British humorist: *How to be an Alien* (1946), Ch.1, Sct.6. Thirty years later, Mikes referred to this notorious pronouncement: 'Things *have* progressed. Not on the continent, where people still have sex lives; but they have progressed here because the English now have electric blankets. It's a pity that electricity so often fails in this country' (*How to be Decadent*, 1977)

45 Sex is one of the nine reasons for reincarnation. The other eight are unimportant.

Henry Miller (1891–1980), U.S. author: *Sexus* (1949), Ch.21

46 Coitus can scarcely be said to take place in a vacuum; although of itself it appears a biological and physical activity, it is set so deeply within the larger context of human affairs that it serves as a charged microcosm of the variety of attitudes and values to which culture subscribes. Among other things, it may serve as a model of sexual politics on an individual or personal plane.

Kate Millett (b.1934), U.S. feminist author: *Sexual Politics* (1970), Ch.2

47 Sex is the mysticism of materialism and the only possible religion in a materialistic society.

Malcolm Muggeridge (1903–1990), British journalist and broadcaster: BBC1, 21 Oct. 1965, quoted in *Muggeridge Through the Microphone* (1967), 'The American Way of Sex'

48 You have to accept the fact that part of the sizzle of sex comes from the danger of sex. You can be overpowered.

Camille Paglia (b.1947), U.S. author and critic: interview in the *San Francisco Examiner*, 7 July 1991, rep. in *Sex, Art, and American Culture* (1992), 'The Rape Debate'

49 I know it does make people happy, but to me it is just like having a cup of tea.

Cynthia Payne (b.1934), British housewife and brothel-keeper: remark, 8 Nov. 1987, after being acquitted of running a brothel in Streatham, South London, in the 'sex-for-luncheon-vouchers' case, quoted in the *Sunday Correspondent* (London), 24 Dec. 1989

50 Everything you always wanted to know about sex, but were afraid to ask.

David Reuben (b.1933), U.S. psychiatrist: *Everything You Always Wanted to Know About Sex, But Were Afraid to Ask* (book title) (1969). Reuben's manual became America's number-one nonfiction bestseller, giving the title to Woody Allen's satirical movie released in 1972

51 In this era of Just Say No and No Means No, we don't have many words for embracing experience. Now instead of liberation and libido, the emphasis is on trauma and disease. Now the idea of random encounters, of joyful, loveless sex, raises eyebrows. The possibility of adventure is clouded by the specter of illness. It's a difficult backdrop for conducting one's youth.

Katie Roiphe (b.1969), U.S. feminist writer: *The Morning After* (1993), 'The Blue-Light System'

52 Making love is like hitting a baseball. You just gotta relax and concentrate.

Susan Sarandon (b.1946), U.S. actress: Annie Savoy (Sarandon), in *Bull Durham* (film; written and directed by Ron Shelton, 1988)

53 Making love? It's a communion with a woman. The bed is the holy table. There I find passion – and purification.

Omar Sharif (b.1932), Egyptian actor: quoted in *City Limits* (London), 18 Dec. 1986

54 I believe in the theory that anyone can get laid, it's just a matter of lowering your standards enough.

Michael Stipe (b.1960), U.S. rock musician with the band REM: quoted in *The Observer* (London), 1 Jan. 1995

55 All nature's creatures join to express nature's purpose. Somewhere in their mounting and mating, rutting and butting is the very secret of nature itself.

Graham Swift (b.1949), British author: *Shuttlecock* (1981), Ch.11

56 Sex is like money; only too much is enough.

John Updike (b.1932), U.S. author and critic: Piet Hanema, in *Couples* (1968), Ch.5

57 Sex is a conversation carried out by other means. If you get on well out of bed, half the problems of bed are solved.

Peter Ustinov (b.1921), British actor, writer and director: interview in *Speaking Frankly* by Wendy Leigh (1978)

58 Sex is. There is nothing more to be done about it. Sex builds no roads, writes no novels and sex certainly gives no meaning to anything in life but itself.

Gore Vidal (b.1925), U.S. novelist and critic: 'Norman Mailer's Self-Advertisements', first publ. in *The Nation* (New York), 2 Jan. 1960, rep. in *Homage to Daniel Shays: Collected Essays 1952–1972* (1974)

59 Sex is more exciting on the screen and between the pages than between the sheets.

Andy Warhol (c.1928–1987), U.S. Pop artist: *From A to B and Back Again* (1975), Ch.3

60 Writings on sex which claim a special telephone line to the truth should be treated with a great deal of suspicion. Writing is a resource, to be played with, chewed over, debated, and above all used; but never trusted.

Jeffrey Weeks (b.1945), British sexologist: introduction to *Against Nature* (1991)

61 What is sex after all? It's self-expression.

Vivienne Westwood (b.1941), British fashion designer: quoted in *Fashion and Perversity* by Fred Vermorel (1996), Pt.1

62 Perhaps sex and sentiment *should* be separated. Isn't sex, shadowed as it always is by jealousy and ruled by caprice, a rather risky basis for a sustained, important relationship?

Edmund White (b.1940), U.S. author: 'Fantasia on the Seventies' (1977), rep. in *The Burning Library* (1994)

63 I am, I must confess, suspicious of those who denounce others for having 'too much' sex. At what point does a 'healthy' amount become 'too much'? There are, of course, those who suffer because their desire for sex has become compulsive; in their case the drive (loneliness, guilt) is at fault, not the activity as such. ... When 'morality' is discussed I invariably discover, halfway into the conversation, that what is meant are not the great ethical questions ... but the rather dreary business of sexual habit, which to my mind is an aesthetic rather than an ethical issue.

Edmund White: *States of Desire: Travels in Gay America* (1980), Ch.2

See also CELIBACY; CINEMA: SEX & VIOLENCE; Tomlin on DEATH: THE AFTERLIFE; FRIGIDITY; IMPOTENCE; LOVE: AND SEX; LUST; Allen on MASTURBATION; ORGASM; PROCREATION; PROMISCUITY; SEDUCTION

SEX SYMBOLS

1 Sex appeal is fifty percent what you've got and fifty percent what people think you've got.

Sophia Loren (b.1934), Italian actress: quoted in *Halliwell's Filmgoer's Companion* (ed. Leslie Halliwell, 1984)

2 Being a sex symbol has to do with an attitude, not looks. Most men think it's looks, most women know otherwise.
Kathleen Turner (b.1956), U.S. actress: quoted in *The Observer* (London), 27 April 1986

SEXISM

1 In the beginning, I wanted to enter what was essentially a man's field. I wanted to prove I could do it. Then I found that when I did as well as the men in the field I got more credit for my work because I am a woman, which seems unfair.
Eugenie Clark (b.1922), U.S. marine biologist and author: quoted in *Ms.* (New York), Aug. 1979

2 Sexism is the foundation on which all tyranny is built. Every social form of hierarchy and abuse is modeled on male-over-female domination.
Andrea Dworkin (b.1946), U.S. feminist critic: 'Redefining Nonviolence', speech, 5 April 1975, Boston College, publ. in *Our Blood* (1976), Ch.6

3 A woman is handicapped by her sex, and handicaps society, either by slavishly copying the pattern of man's advance in the professions, or by refusing to compete with man at all.
Betty Friedan (b.1921), U.S. feminist writer: *The Feminine Mystique* (1963), Ch.14

4 If any of us hopes to survive, s/he must meet the extremity of the American female condition with immediate and political response. The thoroughly destructive and indefensible subjugation of the majority of Americans cannot continue except at the peril of the entire body politic.
June Jordan (b.1936), U.S. poet and civil rights activist: 'The Case for the Real Majority' (1982), rep. in *Moving Towards Home: Political Essays* (1989)

5 There are very few jobs that actually require a penis or vagina. All other jobs should be open to everybody.
Florynce R. Kennedy (b.1916), U.S. lawyer and civil rights activist: quoted by John Brady in 'Freelancer with No Time to Write', publ. in *Writer's Digest* (Cincinnati), Feb. 1974

6 The misogyny that shapes every aspect of our civilization is the institutionalized form of male fear and hatred of what they have denied and therefore cannot know, cannot share: that wild country, the being of women.
Ursula K. Le Guin (b.1929), U.S. author: 'Woman/Wilderness', speech, June 1986, University of California at Davis, publ. in *Dancing at the Edge of the World* (1989)

7 Much of the ill-tempered railing against women that has characterized the popular writing of the last two years is a half-hearted attempt to find a way back to a more balanced relationship between our biological selves and the world we have built. So women are scolded both for being mothers and for not being mothers, for wanting to eat their cake and have it too, and for not wanting to eat their cake and have it too.
Margaret Mead (1901–1978), U.S. anthropologist: *Male and Female* (1949), Ch.8

8 However muted its present appearance may be, sexual dominion obtains nevertheless as perhaps the most pervasive ideology of our culture and provides its most fundamental concept of power.
Kate Millett (b.1934), U.S. feminist author: *Sexual Politics* (1970), Ch.2

9 No man can call himself liberal, or radical, or even a conservative advocate of fair play, if his work depends in any way on the unpaid or underpaid labor of women at home, or in the office.
Gloria Steinem (b.1934), U.S. feminist writer and editor: in the *New York Times*, 26 Aug. 1971

10 Any woman who chooses to behave like a full human being should be warned that the armies of the status quo will treat her as something of a dirty joke. That's their natural and first weapon. She will *need* her sisterhood.
Gloria Steinem: 'Sisterhood', first publ. in *Ms.* (New York), spring 1972, rep. in *Outrageous Acts and Everyday Rebellions* (1983)

11 Society's double behavioral standard for women and for men is, in fact, a more effective deterrent than economic discrimination because it is more insidious, less tangible. Economic disadvantages involve ascertainable amounts, but the very nature of societal value judgments makes them harder to define, their effects harder to relate.
Anne Tucker (b.1945), U.S. editor and critic: introduction to *The Woman's Eye* (1973)

See also MacKinnon on WORDS

SEXUAL DEVIATIONS

1 I believe that sex is a beautiful thing between two people. Between five, it's fantastic.
Woody Allen (b.1935), U.S. film-maker: live recording, San Francisco, Aug. 1968, on *The Third Woody Allen Album* (1968), 'Second Marriage'

2 There is no such thing as a value-free concept of deviance; to say homosexuals are deviant because they are a statistical minority is, in practice, to stigmatize them. Nuns are rarely classed as deviants for the same reason,

although if they obey their vows they clearly differ very significantly from the great majority of people.

Dennis Altman (b.1943), Australian sociologist: *The Homosexualization of America* (1982), Ch.1

3 People will begin to explore all the sidestreets of sexual experience, but they will do it intellectually.... Sex won't take place in the bed, necessarily – it'll take place in the head!

J.G. Ballard (b.1930), British author: interview in *Penthouse* (London), Sept. 1970

4 Philosophically, incest asks a fundamental question of our shifting mores: not simply what is normal and what is deviant, but whether such a thing as deviance exists at all in human relationships if they seem satisfactory to those who share them.

Elizabeth Janeway (b.1913), U.S. author and critic: 'Incest: A Rational Look at the Oldest Taboo', publ. in *Ms.* (New York), Nov. 1981

5 How many modern transsexuals are unacknowledged shamans? Perhaps it is to poets they should go for counsel, rather than surgeons.

Camille Paglia (b.1947), U.S. author and critic: *Sexual Personae* (1990), Ch.2

6 The variables are surprisingly few. ... One can whip or be whipped; one can eat excrement or quaff urine; mouth and private part can be met in this or that commerce. After which there is the grey of morning and the sour knowledge that things have remained fairly generally the same since man first met goat and woman.

George Steiner (b.1929), French-born U.S. critic and novelist: *Language and Silence* (1967), 'Nightworks'

7 I'm gonna git Medieval on your ass.

Quentin Tarantino (b.1958), U.S. film-maker: Marsellus Wallace (Ving Rhames), speaking to Zed as he prepares to sodomize him, in *Pulp Fiction* (film; written and directed by Quentin Tarantino, 1994)

See also CHILD ABUSE; CROSS-DRESSING; SADISM

SEXUAL FANTASY

1 What we're getting is a whole new order of sexual fantasies, involving a different order of experiences, like car crashes, like travelling in jet aircraft, the whole overlay of new technologies, architecture, interior design, communications, transport, merchandising. These things are beginning to reach into our lives and change the interior design of our sexual fantasies.

J.G. Ballard (b.1930), British author: interview in *Penthouse* (London), Sept. 1970

2 A partner evoked by sophisticated electric brain stimulation could be as real and much more satisfying than the boy or girl next door. ... All the stars in Hollywood living or dead are there for your pleasure. Sated with superstars, you can lay Cleopatra, Helen of Troy, Isis, Madame Pompadour, or Aphrodite. You can get fucked by Pan, Jesus Christ, Apollo or the Devil himself.

William Burroughs (1914–1997), U.S. author: *The Adding Machine* (1985), 'Civilian Defense'

3 Fantasies are the triumph of love over rage.

Nancy Friday (b.1937), U.S. author: *Men in Love* (1980), Ch.22

4 His mind dwindled on her soft posterity, her robust excess... Remembering the mornings they had spent wrapped in each other's hardware... her hair smouldering softly in his face, her buttocks almost clean... 'Take me,' she breathed. 'Take me somewhere decent.'

John Lennon (1940–1980), British rock musician: *Skywriting by Word of Mouth* (ed. Yoko Ono, 1986), 'Spare Me the Agony of Your Birth Control'

SEXUAL HARASSMENT

1 In most cases an act of unwelcome sex is no more bother than being vaccinated, so there's no point going on about it as if it were a fate worse than death. With skill and good manners you can avoid having to make the sacrifice, but should you find yourself in a compromising situation largely of your own making, you should stop defending your virtue and start worrying about your maturity. It will give you something to think about while the savage pumper bangs away.

Quentin Crisp (b.1908), British author: *Manners from Heaven* (1984), Ch.6

2 A man assumes that a woman's refusal is just part of a game. Or, at any rate, a lot of men assume that. When a man says no, it's no. When a woman says no, it's yes, or at least maybe. There is even a joke to that effect. And little by little, women begin to believe in this view of themselves,

Erica Jong (b.1942), U.S. author: the narrator (Isadora Wing), in *Fear of Flying* (1973), Ch.16

3 Profanation and violation are part of the perversity of sex, which never will conform to liberal theories of benevolence. Every model of morally or politically correct sexual behavior *will be subverted*, by nature's daemonic law.

Camille Paglia (b.1947), U.S. author and critic: *Sexual Personae* (1990), Ch.1

4 People have the right to leer at whomever they want to leer at. By offering protection to the woman against the leer, the movement against

sexual harassment is curtailing her personal power. This protection implies the need to be protected. It paints her as defenseless against even the most trivial of male attentions. This protection assumes that she never ogles, leers, or makes sexual innuendos herself.

Katie Roiphe (b.1969), U.S. feminist writer: *The Morning After* (1993), 'Reckless Eyeballing: Sexual Harassment on Campus'

SEXUALITY

1 The American *ideal* ... of sexuality appears to be rooted in the American ideal of masculinity. This idea has created cowboys and Indians, good guys and bad guys, punks and studs, tough guys and softies, butch and faggot, black and white. It is an ideal so paralytically infantile that it is virtually forbidden – as an unpatriotic act – that the American boy evolve into the complexity of manhood.

James Baldwin (1924–1987), U.S. author: 'Freaks and the American Ideal of Manhood', first publ. in *Playboy* (Chicago), Jan. 1985, rep. in *The Price of the Ticket* (1985), 'Here be Dragons'

2 Admittedly, a homosexual can be conditioned to react sexually to a woman, or to an old boot for that matter. In fact, both homo- and heterosexual experimental subjects *have* been conditioned to react sexually to an old boot, and you can save a lot of money that way.

William Burroughs (1914–1997), U.S. author: *The Adding Machine* (1985), 'Civilian Defense'

3 Much more than our other needs and endeavours, it is sexuality that puts us on an even footing with our kind: the more we practice it, the more we become like everyone else: it is in the performance of a reputedly bestial function that we prove our status as citizens: nothing is more *public* than the sexual act.

E.M. Cioran (1911–1995), Rumanian-born French philosopher: *The Temptation to Exist* (1956), 'Rages and Resignations: Gogol'

4 A woman can look both moral and exciting – if she also looks as if it was quite a struggle.

Edna Ferber (1887–1968), U.S. author: quoted in *Reader's Digest* (Pleasantville, N.Y.), Dec. 1954

5 Everyone probably thinks that I'm a raving nymphomaniac, that I have an *insatiable* sexual appetite, when the truth is I'd rather read a book.

Madonna (b.1959), U.S. singer and actress: in *Q Magazine* (London), June 1991

6 The sexual parts are not only vivid examples of the body's dominion; they are also apertures whose damp emissions and ammoniac smells testify to the mysterious putrefaction of the body.

Roger Scruton (b.1944), British philosopher and author: *Sexual Desire* (1986), Ch.6

7 Tamed as it may be, sexuality remains one of the demonic forces in human consciousness – pushing us at intervals close to taboo and dangerous desires, which range from the impulse to commit sudden arbitrary violence upon another person to the voluptuous yearning for the extinction of one's consciousness, for death itself. Even on the level of simple physical sensation and mood, making love surely resembles having an epileptic fit at least as much as, if not more than, it does eating a meal or conversing with someone.

Susan Sontag (b.1933), U.S. essayist: 'The Pornographic Imagination', Sct.3, first publ. in *Partisan Review* (New Brunswick, N.J.), spring 1967, rep. in *Styles of Radical Will* (1969)

8 Fear of sexuality is the new, disease-sponsored register of the universe of fear in which everyone now lives.

Susan Sontag: *AIDS and Its Metaphors* (1989), Ch.7

9 In asking forgiveness of women for our mythologizing of their bodies, for being *unreal* about them, we can only appeal to their own sexuality, which is different but not basically different, perhaps, from our own. For women, too, there seems to be that tangle of supplication and possessiveness, that descent toward infantile undifferentiation, that omnipotent helplessness, that merger with the cosmic mother-warmth, that flushed pulse-quickened leap into overestimation, projection, general mix-up.

John Updike (b.1932), U.S. author and critic: 'The Female Body', publ. in the *Michigan Quarterly Review* (1990), rep. in *The Best American Essays, 1991* (ed. Joyce Carol Oates, 1991)

10 We're in danger now, in the late twentieth century, of forcing everyone to become a sexual hero, a sexual superstar when there are probably a number of alternative ways of working out the basic erotic patterns of your life.

John Updike: interview in *Singular Encounters* by Naim Attallah (1990), 'John Updike'

11 There is no such thing as a homosexual or a heterosexual person. There are only homo- or heterosexual acts. Most people are a mixture of impulses if not practices.

Gore Vidal (b.1925), U.S. novelist and critic: *Armageddon? Essays 1983–1987* (1987), 'Tennessee Williams: Someone to Laugh at the Squares With', Sct.1

12 It is only possible to express the feelings of the body through the lacework of meanings that

envelop it. Sexuality is as much about language as it is about sexual organs.
Jeffrey Weeks (b.1945), British sexologist: introduction to *Against Nature* (1991)

13 Women are on the whole more sensual than sexual, men are more sexual than sensual.
Mai Zetterling (1925–1994), Swedish actress and director: in *The Times* (London), 17 May 1989

See also BISEXUALITY; Deneuve on CINEMA: SEX & VIOLENCE; HETEROSEXUALITY; HOMOSEXUALITY; LESBIANISM

WILLIAM SHAKESPEARE

1 Alive today he would undoubtedly have written and directed motion pictures, plays and God knows what. Instead of saying 'This medium is not good,' he would have used it and made it good. If some people called some of his work cheap (which some of it is), he wouldn't have cared a rap, because he would know that without some vulgarity there is no complete man.
Raymond Chandler (1880–1959), U.S. author: letter, 22 April 1949, to publisher Hamish Hamilton, publ. in *Raymond Chandler Speaking* (ed. Dorothy Gardiner and Kathrine S. Walker, 1962)

2 As a practical man, with practical human concerns, Shakespeare doesn't ask to be canonised, but to live alongside and illuminate the modern realities of human life. ... The marginalising of Shakespeare seems to be symptomatic of a general flight from our great literary heritage.
Charles, Prince of Wales (b.1948): Shakespeare Birthday Lecture, 22 April 1991, Stratford-upon-Avon, quoted in *The Prince of Wales: a Biography* by Jonathan Dimbleby (1994), Ch.23

3 The remarkable thing about Shakespeare is that he is really very good – in spite of all the people who say he is very good.
Robert Graves (1895–1985), British poet and novelist: quoted in *The Observer* (London), 6 Dec. 1964

4 Shakespeare was the great one before us. His place was between God and despair.
Eugène Ionesco (1912–1994), Rumanian-born French playwright: in the *International Herald Tribune* (Paris), 17 June 1988

5 My brain is hurting. I have just had two pages of *Macbeth* to translate into English.
Sue Townsend (b.1946), British author: Adrian Mole's journal entry for 21 Jan., in *The Secret Diary of Adrian Mole aged 13¾* (1982)

6 I think that in the end, far more than political power, ideology, political sciences and philosophies, Shakespeare and all he inspired may

save India, as he will save the English-speaking world itself.
Laurens van der Post (1906–1996), South African writer and philosopher: *A Walk with a White Bushman* (1986), p.120 of Chatto & Windus edn.

SHAME

1 The basis of shame is not some personal mistake of ours, but the ignominy, the humiliation we feel that we must be what we are without any choice in the matter, and that this humiliation is seen by everyone.
Milan Kundera (b.1929), Czech-born French author and critic: *Immortality* (1991), Pt.5, Ch.12

2 We who have grown up on a diet of honour and shame can still grasp what must seem unthinkable to peoples living in the aftermath of the death of God and of tragedy: that men will sacrifice their dearest love on the implacable altars of their pride. ... Between shame and shamelessness lies the axis upon which we turn; meteorological conditions at both these poles are of the most extreme, ferocious type. Shamelessness, shame: the roots of violence.
Salman Rushdie (b.1947), Indian-born British author: *Shame* (1983), Ch.7

SHOES

1 Shoes are the first adult machines we are given to master.
Nicholson Baker (b.1957), U.S. author: *The Mezzanine* (1988), Ch.2

2 It is the fragrant lack of practicality that makes high-heeled shoes so fascinating: in terms of static mechanics they induce a sort of insecurity which some find titillating. If a woman wears a high-heeled shoe it changes the apparent musculature of the leg so that you get an effect of twanging sinew, of tension needing to be released. Her bottom sticks out like an offering. At the same time, the lofty perch is an expression of vulnerability, she is effectively hobbled and unable to escape. There is something arousing about this declaration that she is prepared to sacrifice function for form. A glossy finish enhances the effect: there is simply no knowing what a girl who offers herself in this way wouldn't do in pursuit of superficial pleasure.
Stephen Bayley (b.1951), British design critic: *Taste* (1991), Pt.2, 'Fashion: Being and Dressing'

3 But don't you step on my Blue Suede Shoes. You can do anything but lay off my Blue Suede Shoes.
Carl Perkins (b.1932), U.S. rock musician: 'Blue Suede Shoes' (song, 1956)

SHOPPING

1 Economists are wrong: the law of diminishing marginal utility of goods states that when survival needs are satisfied, the appetite for consumption declines. It is demonstrably a false law. In an age robbed of religious symbols, going to the shops replaces going to church.

Stephen Bayley (b.1951), British design critic: *Taste* (1991), Pt.2, 'The Sport of Things'

2 Shopping is a feeling.

David Byrne (b.1952), U.S. rock musician: quoted in introduction to *Shopping in Space* by Elizabeth Young and Graham Caveney (1992)

3 We feel that we have to go out in the world and find things. When people were primitive they would hunt for things like food to eat. We don't need to do that anymore, so we hunt for other things. I hunt through Oxfam shops and jumble sales.

Jarvis Cocker (b.1963), British rock musician: interview in *i-D* (London), Dec. 1993

4 You think I'm the thief? ... You see, I'm not the thief. I'm not the one charging 85 cents for a stinking soda! You're the thief. I'm just standing up for my rights as a consumer.

Michael Douglas (b.1944), U.S. actor: D-Fens (Douglas) to a Korean grocer whose shop he has just trashed, in *Falling Down* (film; screenplay by Ebbe Roe Smith, directed by Joel Schumacher, 1993)

5 Americans are fascinated by their own love of shopping. This does not make them unique. It's just that they have more to buy than most other people on the planet. And it's also an affirmation of faith in their country, its prosperity and limitless bounty. They have shops the way that lesser countries have statues.

Simon Hoggart (b.1946), British journalist: *America: A User's Guide* (1990), Ch.6

See also SUPERMARKETS

SHOPPING MALLS

1 The new shopping malls make possible the synthesis of all consumer activities, not least of which are shopping, flirting with objects, idle wandering, and all the permutations of these.

Jean Baudrillard (b.1929), French semiologist: 'Consumer Society', publ. in *La Société de Consommation* (1970), rep. in *Selected Writings* (ed. Mark Poster, 1988)

2 Shopping malls are liquid TVs for the end of the twentieth century. A whole micro-circuitry of desire, ideology and expenditure for processed bodies drifting through the cyber-space of ultracapitalism.

Arthur Kroker (b.1945), David Cook (b.1946), and Marilouise Kroker, Canadian sociologists: *Panic Encyclopedia* (1989), 'Panic (Shopping) Malls'

SHOW BUSINESS

1 Whom God wishes to destroy, He first makes successful in show business.

Francis Ford Coppola (b.1939), U.S. film-maker: memorandum from Coppola to staff at Zoetrope studios, 1977, quoted in *Coppola* by Peter Cowie (1989), Ch.8

2 All my shows are great. Some of them are bad. But they are all great.

Lew Grade (b.1906), British film and TV entrepreneur: quoted in *The Observer* (London), 14 Sept. 1975

3 Show business offers more solid promises than Catholicism

John Guare (b.1938), U.S. playwright: in *The Independent* (London), 25 April 1992

4 That's what show business is – sincere insincerity.

Benny Hill (1925–1992), British comedian: quoted in *The Observer* (London), 12 June 1977

5 Show business is the best possible therapy for remorse.

Anita Loos (1893–1981), U.S. novelist and screenwriter: *Kiss Hollywood Good-by* (1974), Ch.13

6 Show business is really 90 per cent luck and 10 per cent being able to handle it when it gets offered to you.

Tommy Steele (b.1936), British actor and singer: in *The Listener* (London), 10 Oct. 1974

SHYNESS

1 When the excessively shy force themselves to be forward, they are frequently surprisingly unsubtle and overdirect and even rude: they have entered an extreme region beyond their normal personality, an area of social crime where gradations don't count. Unavailable to them are the instincts and taboos that booming extroverts, who know the territory of self-advancement far better, can rely on.

Nicholson Baker (b.1957), U.S. author: *U And I: A True Story* (1991), Ch.9

2 Shyness is just egotism out of its depth.

Penelope Keith (b.1939), British actress: in the *Daily Mail* (London), 27 June 1988

See also INHIBITION

SILENCE

1 There is no such thing as silence.
John Cage (1912–1992), U.S. composer:
'Everything We Do is Music', interview in the
Saturday Evening Post, 19 Oct. 1968, rep. in
Conversing with Cage (ed. Richard Kostelanetz,
1988), 'His Own Music (to 1970)'

2 Speech and silence. We feel safer with a madman who talks than with one who cannot open
his mouth.
E.M. Cioran (1911–1995), Rumanian-born French
philosopher: *The New Gods* (*Le Mauvais Démiurge*
1969; tr. 1974), 'Strangled Thoughts', Sct.3

3 It takes more time and effort and delicacy to
learn the silence of a people than to learn its
sounds. Some people have a special gift for
this. Perhaps this explains why some missionaries, notwithstanding their efforts, never
come to speak properly, to communicate
delicately through silences. Although they
'speak with the accent of natives' they remain
forever thousands of miles away. The learning
of the grammar of silence is an art much more
difficult to learn than the grammar of sounds.
Ivan Illich (b.1926), Austrian-born U.S. theologian
and author: *Celebration of Awareness* (1969), Ch.4

4 Do not the most moving moments of our lives
find us all without words?
Marcel Marceau (b.1923), French mime artist:
quoted in *Reader's Digest* (Pleasantville, N.Y.), June
1958

5 People talking without speaking,
People hearing without listening,
People writing songs that voices never share
And no one dares disturb the sound of silence.
Paul Simon (b.1941), U.S. singer and song-
writer: 'The Sound of Silence' (song, 1965) on the
album *Sounds of Silence* (Simon and Garfunkel,
1966)

6 We need to find God, and he cannot be found
in noise and restlessness. God is the friend of
silence. See how nature – trees, flowers, grass –
grows in silence; see the stars, the moon and
the sun, how they move in silence. ... We need
silence to be able to touch souls.
Mother Teresa (1910–1997), Albanian-born
Roman Catholic missionary: *A Gift for God* (1975),
'Willing Slaves to the Will of God'

See also Cage on MUSIC: COMPOSITION; Cage on
POETRY

SILLINESS

1 Ying tong iddle I po.
Spike Milligan (b.1918), British comedian and
humorous writer: Ned Seagoon (Harry Secombe), in

The Goon Show (BBC radio comedy series, 1951–60,
written by Spike Milligan), publ. in *The Goon Show
Scripts* (ed. Spike Milligan, 1972). The words were
later set to music and released as 'The Ying Tong
Song', Oct. 1956

2 Never stay up on the barren heights of clever-
ness, but come down into the green valleys of
silliness.
Ludwig Wittgenstein (1889–1951), Austrian-born
British philosopher: journal entry, 1948, publ. in
Culture and Value (ed. G.H. von Wright with Heikki
Nyman, 1980)

SIMPLICITY

1 An intellectual is a man who says a simple thing
in a difficult way; an artist is a man who says a
difficult thing in a simple way.
Charles Bukowski (1920–1994), U.S. author and
poet: *Notes of a Dirty Old Man* (1969), p.166 of City
Lights edn. (1973)

2 Successful ideas generally have the appearance
of simplicity because they seem inevitable.
Sol LeWitt (b.1928), U.S. artist: 'Paragraphs on
Conceptual Art', first publ. in *Artform*, June 1967,
rep. in *Twentieth-Century Artists on Art* (ed. Dore
Ashton, 1985)

SIN

1 Perhaps there is only one cardinal sin:
impatience. Because of impatience we were
driven out of Paradise, because of impatience
we cannot return.
W.H. Auden (1907–1973), Anglo-American poet:
The Dyer's Hand (1962), Pt.3, 'The I Without a Self'

2 A 'sin' is something which is not necessary.
George Gurdjieff (c.1877–1949), Greek-Armenian
religious teacher and mystic: quoted in *In Search
of the Miraculous* by P.D. Ouspensky (1949),
Ch.17

3 Sin has always been an ugly word, but it has
been made so in a new sense over the last half-
century. It has been made not only ugly but
passé. People are no longer sinful, they are only
immature or underprivileged or frightened or,
more particularly, sick.
Phyllis McGinley (1905–1978), U.S. poet and
author: *The Province of the Heart* (1959), 'In
Defense of Sin'

4 Sins become more subtle as you grow
older: you commit sins of despair rather than
lust.
Piers Paul Read (b.1941), British author: in *The
Daily Telegraph* (London), 3 Oct. 1990

5 You don't make up for your sins in church.
You do it on the streets. You do it at home. The
rest is bullshit and you know it.

Martin Scorsese (b.1942), U.S. film-maker: voiceover, in *Mean Streets* (film; screenplay by Martin Scorsese and Mardik Martin, directed by Martin Scorsese, 1973)

See also Auden on ADDICTION

SINCERITY

1 Sincerity: if you can fake it, you've got it made.
   Dan Schorr (b.1916), U.S. journalist and broadcaster: in the *International Herald Tribune* (Paris), 18 May 1992

2 Everyone says he's sincere, but everyone isn't sincere. If everyone was sincere who says he's sincere there wouldn't be half so many insincere ones in the world and there would be lots, lots, lots more really sincere ones!
   Tennessee Williams (1911–1983), U.S. playwright: Esmeralda, in *Camino Real* (1953), Block 12

SLACKING

1 I may live badly – but at least I don't have to work to do it.
   Richard Linklater (b.1962), U.S. film-maker: *Slacker* (film; written and directed by Richard Linklater, 1991)

2 Some people are born slack – others have slacking thrust upon them.
   Will Self (b.1961), British author: 'Slack Attack', first publ. in *The Observer* (London), 2 Jan. 1994, rep. in *Junk Mail* (1995)

SLANDER

1 I don't care what anybody says about me as long as it isn't true.
   Truman Capote (1924–1984), U.S. author: interview in *The Americans* by David Frost (1970), 'When does a Writer Become a Star?'

2 People, family and friends have been recklessly attacked for years. We have exposed once and for all that they will publish anything for profit. They do not check their sources, they do not have the guts to apologise or withdraw. They are pedlars of lies and filth.
   Robert Maxwell (1923–1991), British tycoon: statement on winning a libel action against the satirical magazine *Private Eye*, Nov. 1985, quoted in *Maxwell: The Outsider* by Tom Bower (1988; rev.1991), Ch.14. On being asked what he would do with the £50,000 damages, Maxwell answered, 'The money might go to AIDS research. After all it came from an infected organ and will go to help cure another.' *See* Maxwell on SATIRE

3 I have been thinking that I would make a proposition to my Republican friends. That if they will stop telling lies about Democrats, we will stop telling the truth about them.
   Adlai Stevenson (1900–1965), U.S. Democratic politician: campaign speech, 10 Sept. 1952, Fresno, California, quoted in *Adlai Stevenson of Illinois* by John Bartlow Martin (1976), Ch.8. The remark has been earlier attributed to Republican Chauncey Depew (senator 1899–1911) – though with the party-names reversed

4 It is harder to kill a whisper than even a shouted calumny.
   Mary Stewart (b.1916), British novelist: *The Last Enchantment* (1979), Bk.1, Ch.1

5 If you know somebody is going to be awfully annoyed by something you write, that's obviously very satisfying, and if they howl with rage or cry, that's honey.
   A.N. Wilson (b.1950), British author: quoted in the *Independent on Sunday* (London), 13 Sept. 1992

SLAVERY

1 Slavery is so intolerable a condition that the slave can hardly escape deluding himself into thinking that he is choosing to obey his master's commands when, in fact, he is obliged to. Most slaves of habit suffer from this delusion and so do some writers, enslaved by an all too 'personal' style.
   W.H. Auden (1907–1973), Anglo-American poet: *The Dyer's Hand* (1962), Pt.1, 'Writing'

2 The genius of any slave system is found in the dynamics which isolate slaves from each other, obscure the reality of a common condition, and make united rebellion against the oppressor inconceivable.
   Andrea Dworkin (b.1946), U.S. feminist critic: 'Our Blood: the Slavery of Women in Amerika', speech to the National Organization for Women, Washington D.C., 23 Aug. 1975, publ. in *Our Blood* (1976), Ch.8

3 There're two people in the world that are not likeable: a master and a slave.
   Nikki Giovanni (b.1943), U.S. poet: in conversation with James Baldwin, London, 4 Nov. 1971, publ. in *A Dialogue* (1973)

4 To relive the relationship between owner and slave we can consider how we treat our cars and dogs – a dog exercising a somewhat similar leverage on our mercies and an automobile being comparable in value to a slave in those days.
   Edward Hoagland (b.1932), U.S. novelist and essayist: 'Virginie and the Slaves', first publ. in *Travel and Leisure* (New York), Feb. 1976, rep. in *Heart's Desire* (1988)

5 You can be up to your boobies in white satin, with gardenias in your hair and no sugar cane

for miles, but you can still be working on a plantation.
Billie Holiday (1915–1959), U.S. blues singer: *Lady Sings the Blues* (written with William Dufty, 1956, rev.1975), Ch.11

SLEEP

1   A sleeping presence is always a mystery, present and absent at the same time, seemingly peaceful, yet in reality off on wild adventures in strange landscapes.
A. Alvarez (b.1929), British critic, poet and novelist: *Night* (1995), 'The Sleep Laboratory', Sct.2

2   The repose of sleep refreshes only the body. It rarely sets the soul at rest. The repose of the night does not belong to us. It is not the possession of our being. Sleep opens within us an inn for phantoms. In the morning we must sweep out the shadows.
Gaston Bachelard (1884–1962), French scientist, philosopher and literary theorist: *The Poetics of Reverie* (1960; tr.1969), Ch.2, Sct.3

3   There is between sleep and us something like a pact, a treaty with no secret clauses, and according to this convention it is agreed that, far from being a dangerous, bewitching force, sleep will become domesticated and serve as an instrument of our power to act. We surrender to sleep, but in the way that the master entrusts himself to the slave who serves him.
Maurice Blanchot (b.1907), French literary theorist and author: *The Space of Literature* (1955; tr.1982), 'Sleep, Night'

4   Sleep is when all the unsorted stuff comes flying out as from a dustbin upset in a high wind.
William Golding (1911–1993), British author: *Pincher Martin* (1956), Ch.6

SLEEP: Insomnia

1   Impossible to spend sleepless nights and accomplish anything: if, in my youth, my parents had not *financed* my insomnias, I should surely have killed myself.
E.M. Cioran (1911–1995), Rumanian-born French philosopher: *Anathemas and Admirations* (1986), 'On the Verge of Existence'

2   The last refuge of the insomniac is a sense of superiority to the sleeping world.
Leonard Cohen (b.1934), Canadian singer, poet and novelist: Lawrence Breavman, in *The Favourite Game* (1963), Bk.4, Sct.12

3   Counting the beats,
Counting the slow heart beats,

The bleeding to death of time in slow heart beats,
Wakeful they lie.
Robert Graves (1895–1985), British poet and novelist: 'Counting the Beats', publ. in *Poems and Satires* (1951)

SLOANE RANGERS

1   Sloaneness, some people would say, is a track to be liberated from.
Peter York (b.1950), British journalist: 'The Sloane Rangers', first publ. in *Harpers & Queen* (London), Oct. 1975, rep. in *Style Wars* (1980)

2   Sloane minds are undeveloped but intuitive, wild places where they go out to bag an idea or see how things are going. They do *not* like theory, unless it produces a joke.
Peter York (b.1950) and **Ann Barr**, British journalists: *The Official Sloane Ranger Handbook* (1982), 'Sloane Language'

SMILING

1   If you have only one smile in you, give it to the people you love. Don't be surly at home, then go out in the street and start grinning 'Good morning' at total strangers.
Maya Angelou (b.1928), U.S. author: quoting her mother's advice, in *Singin' and Swingin' and Gettin' Merry Like Christmas* (third volume of autobiography, 1976), Ch.5

2   Smile and others will smile back. Smile to show how transparent, how candid you are. Smile if you have nothing to say. Most of all, do not hide the fact you have nothing to say nor your total indifference to others. Let this emptiness, this profound indifference shine out spontaneously in your smile.
Jean Baudrillard (b.1929), French semiologist: *America* (1986; tr.1988), 'Astral America'

SNOBBERY

1   Snobbery? But it's only a form of despair.
Joseph Brodsky (1940–1996), Russian-born U.S. poet and critic: *Less Than One: Selected Essays* (1986), 'Flight from Byzantium', Sct.9

2   I am ... by tradition and long study a complete snob. P. Marlowe and I do not despise the upper classes because they take baths and have money; we despise them because they are phony.
Raymond Chandler (1880–1959), U.S. author: letter, 7 Jan. 1945, publ. in *Raymond Chandler Speaking* (ed. Dorothy Gardiner and Kathrine S. Walker, 1962)

3   Laughter would be bereaved if snobbery died.

Peter Ustinov (b.1921), British actor, writer and director: quoted in *The Observer* (London), 13 March 1955

SOAP OPERAS

1 In its artless cruelty, *Dallas* is superior to any 'intelligent' critique that can be made of it. That is why intellectual snobbery meets its match here.
Jean Baudrillard (b.1929), French semiologist: *Cool Memories* (1987; tr.1990), Ch.3

2 Watching the English soap operas is like viewing the tiny lives of mice in a cage. Watching the American series is like watching expensive leopards prowling round a luxurious cage. Either way it's not the jungle of life, just a zoo.
The Daily Telegraph: review of *Eastenders*, 1986, quoted in *Fields of Vision* by D.J. Enright (1988), 'Television: Mice in Cages'

3 A sceptic finds Dallas absurd. A cynic thinks the public doesn't.
Clive James (b.1939), Australian writer and critic: introduction to *Glued to the Box* (1983)

4 I've finally figured out why soap operas are, and logically should be, so popular with generations of housebound women. *They are the only place in our culture where grown-up men take seriously all the things that grown-up women have to deal with all day long.*
Gloria Steinem (b.1934), U.S. feminist writer and editor: 'Night Thoughts of a Media Watcher', first publ. in *Ms.* (New York), Nov. 1981, rep. in *Outrageous Acts and Everyday Rebellions* (1983)

THE SOCIAL SCIENCES

1 Sociology begins in the dustbin, and sociologists have always been licensed rag-and-bone men trundling their carts round the backyards of the posher academic establishments.
Alan Bennett (b.1934), British playwright: *Writing Home* (1994), 'Cold Sweat'

2 Like the Pentagon, our social science often reduces all phenomena to dollars and body counts. Sexuality, family unity, kinship, masculine solidarity, maternity, motivation, nurturing, all the rituals of personal identity and development, all the bonds of community, seem 'sexist', 'superstitious', 'mystical', 'inefficient', 'discriminatory'. And, of course, they are – and they are also indispensable to a civilized society.
George Gilder (b.1939), U.S. editor, speechwriter and author: introduction to *Sexual Suicide* (1973)

3 There are no better terms available to describe [the] difference between the approach of the natural and the social sciences than to call the former 'objective' and the latter 'subjective'. ... While for the natural scientist the contrast between objective facts and subjective opinions is a simple one, the distinction cannot as readily be applied to the object of the social sciences. The reason for this is that the object, the 'facts' of the social sciences are also opinions – not opinions of the student of the social phenomena, of course, but opinions of those whose actions produce the object of the social scientist.
Friedrich August von Hayek (1899–1992), Austrian-born British economist: *The Counter-Revolution of Science* (1952), Pt.1, Ch.3

4 He ... was a sociologist; he had got into an intellectual muddle early on in life and never managed to get out.
Iris Murdoch (b.1919), British novelist and philosopher: *The Philosopher's Pupil* (1983), 'The Events in Our Town'

SOCIALISM

1 Socialists make the mistake of confusing individual worth with success. They believe you cannot allow people to succeed in case those who fail feel worthless.
Kenneth Baker (b.1934), British Conservative politician: quoted in *The Observer* (London), 13 July 1986

2 Socialism is finished. That's why I got into Buddhism... In fact I thought that, being a little orphan of Marx, here at least was another space where I could feel comfortable.
Bernardo Bertolucci (b.1940), Italian filmmaker: referring to his film *Little Buddha*, quoted in the *Independent on Sunday* (London), 1 May 1994

3 Socialism with a human face.
Alexander Dubček (1921–1992), Czechoslovakian politician: Dubček's words, repeated in various forms on different occasions, became a slogan of the 'Prague Spring' of 1968, which led to his replacement as first secretary of the party by Gustav Husak, and the withdrawal of his party membership in 1970

4 Real socialism is inside man. It wasn't born with Marx. It was in the communes of Italy in the Middle Ages. You can't say it is finished.
Dario Fo (b.1926), Italian playwright and actor: in *The Times* (London), 6 April 1992

5 Socialisms do not need a new freedom charter or a new declaration of rights: easy, therefore useless. If they want to deserve being loved, and not to repel, if they want to be desired, they have to answer the question of power and of its exercise. They have to discover a way of

exercising power that does not instil fear. That would be something new.

Michel Foucault (1926–1984), French philosopher: 'Crimes et châtiments en URSS et ailleurs...', publ. in *Le Nouvel Observateur* (Paris), 26 Jan. 1976, quoted in *The Lives of Michel Foucault* by David Macey (1993), Ch.15

6   Socialism is not like pregnancy. We can be, as we are, a little or even more than a little socialist without going all the way. Yet it is the ideal that animates our actions. If the ideal is false, perhaps we should reconsider the steps that we have taken, or are prepared to take, in its name.

Milton Friedman (b.1912), U.S. economist: on creeping socialism in the U.S., in *There's No Such Thing as a Free Lunch* (1975), Ch.11

7   Socialism is young and makes mistakes. We revolutionaries often lack the knowledge and the intellectual audacity to face the task of the development of a new man by methods different from the conventional ones.

Ernesto 'Che' Guevara (1928–1967), Argentinian revolutionary leader: 'Socialism and Man in Cuba', open letter to the editor of a Uruguayan newspaper, *La Marcha*, 1967, publ. in *Che Guevara on Revolution* (ed. Jay Mallin, 1969)

8   By concentrating on what is good in people, by appealing to their idealism and their sense of justice, and by asking them to put their faith in the future, socialists put themselves at a severe disadvantage.

Ian McEwan (b.1948), British author: in *City Limits* (London), 27 May 1983

9   Every reasonable human being should be a moderate Socialist.

Thomas Mann (1875–1955), German author and critic: in the *New York Times*, 18 June 1950, quoted in *Thomas Mann: A Critical Study* by R.J. Hollingdale (1971), Ch.2

10   It may well be an error to use the term socialism because it is an emotive word which repulses many people, and is capable of so many different interpretations that in the end it has come to mean almost nothing except a mild shock to complacent guardians of the status quo.

Oswald Mosley (1896–1980), British fascist leader: *My Life* (1968), Ch.9

11   WOT IZZA COMIN'?
     'I'll tell you wot izza comin'
     Sochy-lism is a-comin''

Ezra Pound (1885–1972), U.S. poet and critic: canto 77 in *Pisan Cantos* (1948)

12   It is certainly safe, in view of the movement to the right of intellectuals and political thinkers, to pronounce the brain death of socialism.

Norman Tebbit (b.1931), British Conservative politician: in *The Times* (London), 26 April 1988

13   Socialism can only arrive by bicycle.
     (*El socialismo puede llegar sólo en bicicleta*.)

José Antonio Viera Gallo (b.1943), Chilean politician in Allende's government: quoted in foreword to *Energy and Equity* by Ivan Illich (1974)

14   It wasn't idealism that made me, from the beginning, want a more secure and rational society. It was an intellectual judgement, to which I still hold. When I was young its name was socialism. We can be deflected by names. But the need was absolute, and is still absolute.

Raymond Williams (1921–1988), British novelist and critic: Norman Braose, in *Loyalties* (1985), Pt.5, Ch.5

SOCIETY

1   Society is held together by our need; we bind it together with legend, myth, coercion, fearing that without it we will be hurled into that void, within which, like the earth before the Word was spoken, the foundations of society are hidden.

James Baldwin (1924–1987), U.S. author: 'Everybody's Protest Novel', first publ. in *Partisan Review* (New Brunswick, N.J.), June 1949, rep. in *Notes of a Native Son* (1955), Pt.1

2   We can imagine a society in which no one could survive as a social being because it does not correspond to biologically determined perceptions and human social needs. For historical reasons, existing societies might have such properties, leading to various forms of pathology.

Noam Chomsky (b.1928), U.S. linguist and political analyst: *Language and Responsibility* (1979), 'A Philosophy of Language'

3   No society has been able to abolish human sadness, no political system can deliver us from the pain of living, from our fear of death, our thirst for the absolute. It is the human condition that directs the social condition, not vice versa.

Eugène Ionesco (1912–1994), Rumanian-born French playwright: 'The Playwright's Role', first publ. in *The Observer* (London), 29 June 1958, rep. in *Notes and Counter-Notes* (1962), Pt.2

4   It is something other than a coexistence of a multitude of humans, or a participation in new and complex laws imposed by the masses. Society is the miracle of moving out of oneself.

Emmanuel Levinas (b.1905), French Jewish philosopher: 'Ethics and Spirit' (1952), rep. in *Difficult Freedom* (1990), Pt.1

5   The principles of the good society call for a concern with an order of being – which cannot

be proved existentially to the sense organs – where it matters supremely that the human person is inviolable, that reason shall regulate the will, that truth shall prevail over error.

Walter Lippmann (1889–1974), U.S. journalist: *The Public Philosophy* (1955), Ch.11, Sct.4

6 There can never be a perfectly good society – there can only be a decent society, and that depends on freedom and order and circumstances and an endless tinkering which can't be programmed from a distance. It's all accidental, but the values are absolute.

Iris Murdoch (b.1919), British novelist and philosopher: Gerard Hernshaw (quoting Rose Curtland), in *The Book and the Brotherhood* (1987), Pt.3, 'Spring'

7 Our society is not a community, but merely a collection of isolated family units.

Valerie Solanas (1936–1988), U.S. actress and writer: *The SCUM Manifesto* (1968)

8 One set of messages of the society we live in is: Consume. Grow. Do what you want. Amuse yourselves. The very working of this economic system, which has bestowed these unprecedented liberties, most cherished in the form of physical mobility and material prosperity, depends on encouraging people to defy limits.

Susan Sontag (b.1933), U.S. essayist: *AIDS and Its Metaphors* (1989), Ch.7

9 There is no such thing as society: there are individual men and women, and there are families.

Margaret Thatcher (b.1925), British Conservative politician and prime minister: interview in *Woman's Own* (London), 31 Oct. 1987

See also ART: AND SOCIETY; Tarkovsky on IDEAS; SCIENCE: AND SOCIETY; Major on UNDERSTANDING

SOLITUDE

1 One of the conditions of being human, and even if we're surrounded by others, we essentially live our lives alone: real life takes place inside us.

Paul Auster (b.1947), U.S. author: interview, 1989/90, publ. in *The Red Notebook* (1995), 'Interview with Larry McCaffery and Sinda Gregory'

2 Ah, *mon cher*, for anyone who is alone, without God and without a master, the weight of days is dreadful.

Albert Camus (1913–1960), French-Algerian philosopher and author: the narrator (Jean-Baptiste Clamence), in *The Fall* (1956), p.99 of Hamish Hamilton edn. (1957)

3 Alone, even doing nothing, you do not waste your time. You do, almost always, in company.

No encounter with yourself can be altogether sterile: Something necessarily emerges, even if only the hope of some day meeting yourself again.

E.M. Cioran (1911–1995), Rumanian-born French philosopher: *The New Gods* (*Le Mauvais Démiurge*, 1969; tr. 1974), 'Strangled Thoughts', Sct.2

4 We are a most solitary people, and we live, repelled by one another, in the gray, outcast cities of Cain.

Edward Dahlberg (1900–1977), U.S. author and critic: *Alms for Oblivion* (1964), 'No Love and No Thanks'

5 In the tumult of men and events, solitude was my temptation; now it is my friend. What other satisfaction can be sought once you have confronted History?

(*Dans le tumulte des hommes et des événements, la solitude était ma tentation. Maintenant, elle est mon amie. De quelle autre se contenter quand on a rencontré l'Histoire?*)

Charles de Gaulle (1890–1970), French general and president: *War Memoirs*, Vol.III (1959; tr.1960), Ch.7

6 True solitude is a din of birdsong, seething leaves, whirling colors, or a clamor of tracks in the snow.

Edward Hoagland (b.1932), U.S. novelist and essayist: in *The Guardian* (London), 20 Jan. 1990

7 With some people solitariness is an escape not from others but from themselves. For they see in the eyes of others only a reflection of themselves.

Eric Hoffer (1902–1983), U.S. philosopher: *The Passionate State of Mind* (1955), Aph.211

8 Solitude is un-American.

Erica Jong (b.1942), U.S. author: *Fear of Flying* (1973), Ch.1

9 Solitude: a sweet absence of looks.

Milan Kundera (b.1929), Czech-born French author and critic: *Immortality* (1991), Pt.1, Ch.6

10 I see life more as an affair of solitude diversified by company than an affair of company diversified by solitude.

Philip Larkin (1922–1985), British poet: interview in *The Observer* (London), 1979, rep. in *Required Writing* (1983)

11 Being human cannot be borne alone. We need other presences. We need soft night noises – a mother speaking downstairs. ... We need the little clicks and sighs of a sustaining otherness. We need the gods.

John Updike (b.1932), U.S. author and critic: *Self-Consciousness: Memoirs* (1989), Ch.6

See also RECLUSIVES

SOLUTIONS

1 It's been said that today, you're part of the solution or you're part of the problem. There is no middle ground.
   Eldridge Cleaver (b.1935), U.S. black leader and writer: 'Stanford speech', 1 Oct. 1968, San Francisco, publ. in *Eldridge Cleaver, Post Prison Writings and Speeches* (ed. R. Scheer, 1969)

2 Increasingly in recent times we have come first to identify the remedy that is most agreeable, most convenient, most in accord with major pecuniary or political interest, the one that reflects our available faculty for action; then we move from the remedy so available or desired back to a cause to which that remedy is relevant.
   J.K. Galbraith (b.1908), U.S. economist: 'The Convenient Reverse Logic of our Time', Commencement Address at the American University, 1984, rep. in *A View from the Stands* (1986)

3 In this age, which believes that there is a short cut to everything, the greatest lesson to be learned is that the most difficult way is, in the long run, the easiest.
   Henry Miller (1891–1980), U.S. author: preface to *The Books in My Life* (1951)

4 If a doctor diagnoses a tumour and prescribes an operation, it does not mean that he desires the illness of the patient, but that he tells the truth as he sees it. He is then liable to be very unpopular if all the other physicians are prescribing a slight dose of salts and a little gentle massage for a passing malaise.
   Oswald Mosley (1896–1980), British fascist leader: *My Life* (1968), Ch.15

See also Johnson on PROBLEMS

SONG

1 Precisely because we do not communicate by singing, a song can be out of place but not out of character; it is just as credible that a stupid person should sing beautifully as that a clever person should do so.
   W.H. Auden (1907–1973), Anglo-American poet: *The Dyer's Hand* (1962), Pt.8, 'Notes on Music and Opera'

2 To sing is to love and to affirm, to fly and soar, to coast into the hearts of the people who listen, to tell them that life is to live, that love is there, that nothing is a promise, but that beauty exists, and must be hunted for and found.
   Joan Baez (b.1941), U.S. singer: *Daybreak* (1968), 'Singing'

3 Hey! Mr Tambourine Man, play a song for me.
   I'm not sleepy and there is no place I'm going to.
   Hey! Mr Tambourine Man, play a song for me.
   In the jingle jangle morning I'll come following you.
   Bob Dylan (b.1941), U.S. singer and songwriter: 'Mr Tambourine Man' (song) on the album *Bringing It All Back Home* (1965)

4 A song is anything that can walk by itself.
   Bob Dylan: sleeve notes on the album *Bringing It All Back Home* (1965)

5 The lullaby is the spell whereby the mother attempts to transform herself back from an ogre to a saint.
   James Fenton (b.1949), British poet and critic: 'Ars Poetica', No.7, publ. in the *Independent on Sunday* (London), 11 March 1990

6 I can't stand to sing the same song the same way two nights in succession, let alone two years or ten years. If you can, then it ain't music, it's close-order drill or exercise or yodeling or something, not music.
   Billie Holiday (1915–1959), U.S. blues singer: *Lady Sings the Blues* (written with William Dufty, 1956; rev.1975), Ch.4

7 Cheap songs, so-called, actually do have something of the Psalms of David about them. They do say the world is other than it is. They do illuminate. This is why people say, 'Listen, they're playing our song'. It's not because that particular song actually expresses the depth of the feelings that they felt when they met each other and heard it. It is that somehow it re-evokes it, but with a different coating of irony and self-knowledge. Those feelings come bubbling back.
   Dennis Potter (1935–1994), British dramatist and screenwriter: interview with Melvyn Bragg, Channel 4, 5 April 1994

See also Dylan on MUSIC: COMPOSITION

SOPHISTICATION

1 I have always thought of sophistication as rather a feeble substitute for decadence.
   Christopher Hampton (b.1946), British playwright: Braham, in *The Philanthropist* (1970), Sc.3

2 Hip is the sophistication of the wise primitive in a giant jungle.
   Norman Mailer (b.1923), U.S. author: 'The White Negro', Sct.3, first publ. in *Dissent*, summer 1957, rep. in *Advertisements for Myself* (1959)

SORROW

1 The lives of happy people are dense with their own doings – crowded, active, thick. ... But the sorrowing are nomads, on a plain with few landmarks and no boundaries; sorrow's horizons are vague and its demands are few.
Larry McMurtry (b.1936), U.S. screenwriter, novelist and essayist: *Some Can Whistle* (1989), Pt.4, Ch.9

2 Jesus, Buddha, Mahommed, great as each may be, their highest comfort given to the sorrowful is a cordial introduction into another's woe. Sorrow's the great community in which all men born of woman are members at one time or another.
Sean O'Casey (1884–1964), Irish playwright: *Rose and Crown* (fifth volume of autobiography, 1952), 'Wild Life in New Amsterdam'

3 Pain and fear and hunger are effects of causes which can be foreseen and known: but sorrow is a debt which someone else makes for us.
Freya Stark (1893–1993), British travel writer: *Perseus in the Wind* (1948), Ch.16

See also GRIEF; UNHAPPINESS

THE SOUL

1 I rather feel that deep in the soul of mankind there is a reflection as on the surface of a mirror, of a mirror-calm lake, of the beauty and harmony of the universe. ... So much depends, I think, on how each one of us is introduced to and made aware of that reflection within us.
Charles, Prince of Wales (b.1948): speech, 4 May 1986, Prince George (British Columbia), quoted in *The Prince of Wales: a Biography* by Jonathan Dimbleby (1994), Ch.20

2 Developing the muscles of the soul demands no competitive spirit, no killer instinct, although it may erect pain barriers that the spiritual athlete must crash through.
Germaine Greer (b.1939), Australian feminist writer: *The Change: Women, Ageing and the Menopause* (1991), Ch.2

3 There is nothing deep down inside us except what we have put there ourselves.
Richard Rorty (b.1931), U.S. philosopher: *Consequences of Pragmatism* (1982), 'Pragmatism and Philosophy'. Rorty was arguing against the notion that there is some metaphysical 'truth' about human beings – i.e., an answer within us to the problems presented to us by the world

SOUTH AFRICA

1 The White strategy so far has been to systematically break down the resistance of the Blacks to the point where the latter would accept crumbs from the White table. This we have shown we reject unequivocally; and now the stage is therefore set for a very interesting turn of events.
Steve Biko (1946–1977), South African anti-apartheid activist: 'I Write What I Like: Fear – an Important Determinant in South African Politics' (written under the pseudonym of Frank Talk), publ. in appendix to *Steve Biko: Black Consciousness in South Africa* (ed. Millard Arnold, 1978)

2 Christ in this country would quite likely have been arrested under the Suppression of Communism Act.
Joost de Blank (1908–1968), South African churchman: quoted in *The Observer* (London), 27 Oct. 1963. Joost de Blank was archibishop of Cape Town 1957–63

3 There is only one element that can break the Afrikaner, and that is the Afrikaner himself. It is when the Afrikaner, like a baboon shot in the stomach, pulls out his own intestines. We must guard against that.
P.W. Botha (b.1916), South African politician and prime minister: speech, 26 April 1984, quoted in the *Independent on Sunday* (London), 15 March 1992

4 Today we have closed the book on apartheid.
F.W. de Klerk (b.1936), South African president: on the results of the referendum endorsing his proposals for constitutional and political reform, quoted in *The Independent* (London), 19 March 1992

5 South Africa used to seem so far away. Then it came home to me. It began to signify the meaning of white hatred here. That was what the sheets and the suits and the ties covered up, not very well. That was what the cowardly guys calling me names from their speeding truck wanted to happen to me, to all of me: to my people. That was what would happen to me if I walked around the corner into the wrong neighborhood. That was Birmingham. That was Brooklyn. That was Reagan. That was the end of reason. South Africa was how I came to understand that I am not against war; I am against losing the war.
June Jordan (b.1936), U.S. poet and civil rights activist: 'South Africa: Bringing It All Back Home', written 1981, first publ.1985, rep. in *Moving Towards Home: Political Essays* (1989)

6 The drama can only be brought to its climax in one of two ways – through the selective bru-

tality of terrorism or the impartial horrors of war.

Kenneth Kaunda (b.1924), Zambian politician and president: of the situation in South Africa, in *Kaunda on Violence* (1980), Pt.2

7 Together, hand in hand, with that stick of matches, with our necklace, we shall liberate this country.

Winnie Mandela (b.1934), South African politician: speech in black townships, quoted in *The Guardian* (London), 15 April 1986

8 The people who want sanctions remind me a lot of missionaries, who are anchored off an island full of prancing savages and cannibals whom they say they want to convert, but refuse to disembark and go among them, shouting instead, 'If you stop being cannibals, we will bring you the Bible!' This is metaphorically what they are trying to do with sanctions in South Africa.

Laurens van der Post (1906–1996), South African writer and philosopher: *A Walk with a White Bushman* (1986), p.279 of Chatto & Windus edn.

9 Is not our role to stand for the one thing which means our own salvation here but with which it will also be possible to save the world, and with which Europe will be able to save itself, namely the preservation of the white man and his state?

Hendrik Verwoerd (1901–1966), South African politician and prime minister: speech, 1964, quoted in *The Oxford History of South Africa* (ed. M. Wilson and L. Thompson, 1971), Vol.II, Ch.10

10 As far as criticism is concerned, we don't resent that unless it is absolutely biased, as it is in most cases.

John Vorster (1915–1983), South African politician and prime minister: quoted in *The Observer* (London), 9 Nov. 1969

See also Slovo on CAPITALISM; Tutu on RACISM

SPACE

1 Don't tell me that man doesn't belong out there. Man belongs wherever he wants to go – and he'll do plenty well when he gets there.

Wernher von Braun (1912–1977), German-born U.S. rocket engineer: in *Time* (New York), 17 Feb. 1958

2 Man is an artifact designed for space travel. He is not designed to remain in his present biologic state any more than a tadpole is designed to remain a tadpole.

William Burroughs (1914–1997), U.S. author: *The Adding Machine* (1985), 'Civilian Defense'

3 The question that will decide our destiny is not whether we shall expand into space. It is: shall we be one species or a million? A million species will not exhaust the ecological niches that are awaiting the arrival of intelligence.

Freeman Dyson (b.1923), British-born U.S. physicist and author: *Disturbing the Universe* (1979), Pt.1, Ch.21

4 Our passionate preoccupation with the sky, the stars, and a God somewhere in outer space is a homing impulse. We are drawn back to where we came from.

Eric Hoffer (1902–1983), U.S. philosopher: on the first moon-landing, in the *New York Times*, 21 July 1969

5 Space isn't remote at all. It's only an hour's drive away if your car could go straight upwards.

Fred Hoyle (b.1915), British astronomer: in *The Observer* (London), 9 Sept. 1979

6 Prometheus is reaching out for the stars with an empty grin on his face.

Arthur Koestler (1905–1983), Hungarian-born British novelist and essayist: on the first moon-landing, in the *New York Times*, 21 July 1969

7 Space is almost infinite. As a matter of fact, we think it is infinite.

Dan Quayle (b.1947), U.S. Republican politician and vice president: in *The Daily Telegraph* (London), 8 March 1989

8 Space – the final frontier. These are the voyages of the starship *Enterprise*. Its five-year mission: to explore strange new worlds, to seek out new life and new civilizations, to boldly go where no man has gone before.

Gene Roddenberry (1921–1991), U.S. TV producer and writer: voiceover in *Star Trek* (television series, 1966–69). This preamble to each episode includes what is probably the most famous split infinitive ever recorded

9 It is marvelous indeed to watch on television the rings of Saturn close; and to speculate on what we may yet find at galaxy's edge. But in the process, we have lost the human element; not to mention the high hope of those quaint days when flight would create 'one world'. Instead of one world, we have 'star wars', and a future in which dumb dented human toys will drift mindlessly about the cosmos long after our small planet's dead.

Gore Vidal (b.1925), U.S. novelist and critic: *Armageddon? Essays 1983–1987* (1987), 'On Flying', Sct.3

10 It was a thunderingly beautiful experience – voluptuous, sexual, dangerous, and expensive as hell.

Kurt Vonnegut (b.1922), U.S. novelist: on the Apollo launches, in *Wampeters, Foma and Granfallons* (1974), 'Playboy Interview, 1973'

See also Sharman on MEN & WOMEN; THE MOON

SPEECH

1 Wherever the relevance of speech is at stake, matters become political by definition, for speech is what makes man a political being.
Hannah Arendt (1906–1975), German-born U.S. political philosopher: prologue to *The Human Condition* (1958)

2 It's a damn shame we have this immediate ticking off in the mind about how people sound. On the other hand, how many people really want to be operated upon by a surgeon who talks broad cockney?
Eileen Atkins (b.1934), British actress: in *The Daily Telegraph* (London), 5 Feb. 1992

3 Language is legislation, speech is its code. We do not see the power which is in speech because we forget that all speech is a classification, and that all classifications are oppressive.
Roland Barthes (1915–1980), French semiologist: *Leçon* (1978), inaugural lecture, Collège de France, 7 Jan. 1977, rep. in *Barthes: Selected Writings* (1982)

4 The basic rule of human nature is that powerful people speak slowly and subservient people quickly – because if they don't speak fast nobody will listen to them.
Michael Caine (b.1933), British actor: in *The Times* (London), 26 Aug. 1992

5 From my earliest days I have enjoyed an attractive impediment in my speech. I have never permitted the use of the word 'stammer'. I can't say it myself.
Patrick Campbell (1913–1980), Irish humorist: *The P-P-Penguin Patrick Campbell* (1965), 'Unaccustomed As I Am'

6 For mankind, speech with a capital S is especially meaningful and committing, more than the content communicated. The outcry of the newborn and the sound of the bells are fraught with mystery more than the baby's woeful face or the venerable tower.
Paul Goodman (1911–1972), U.S. author, poet and critic: *Five Years* (1966), 'Summer 1957, in Europe', Sct.3

7 What has influenced my life more than any other single thing has been my stammer. Had I not stammered I would probably ... have gone to Cambridge as my brothers did, perhaps have become a don and every now and then published a dreary book about French literature.
W. Somerset Maugham (1874–1965), British author: in *Newsweek* (New York), 23 May 1960

8 Man does not speak because he thinks; he thinks because he speaks. Or rather, speaking is no different than thinking: to speak is to think.
Octavio Paz (b.1914), Mexican poet and essayist: *Alternating Current* (1967), 'André Breton or the Quest of the Beginning'

9 People resent articulacy, as if articulacy were a form of vice.
Frederic Raphael (b.1931), British author and critic: in *The Guardian* (London), 8 June 1989

10 The world does not speak. Only we do. The world can, once we have programmed ourselves with a language, cause us to hold beliefs. But it cannot propose a language for us to speak. Only other human beings can do that.
Richard Rorty (b.1931), U.S. philosopher: *Contingency, Irony, and Solidarity* (1989), Ch.1, 'The Contingency of Language'

11 Many great writers have been extraordinarily awkward in daily exchange, but the greatest give the impression that their style was nursed by the closest attention to colloquial speech.
Thornton Wilder (1897–1975), U.S. author: interview in *Writers at Work* (First Series, ed. Malcolm Cowley, 1958)

12 There are remarks that sow and remarks that reap.
Ludwig Wittgenstein (1889–1951), Austrian-born British philosopher: journal entry, 1948, publ. in *Culture and Value* (ed. G.H. von Wright with Heikki Nyman, 1980)

See also Cioran on SILENCE

SPEECHES

1 I do not object to people looking at their watches when I am speaking. But I strongly object when they start shaking them to make certain they are still going.
Lord Birkett (1883–1962), British lawyer and Liberal politician: quoted in *The Observer* (London), 30 Oct. 1960

2 My husband and I...
Elizabeth II (b.1926), Queen of Great Britain and Northern Ireland: Christmas message, 1953, New Zealand. These opening words became a regular feature of the Queen's speeches, though the alternative 'Prince Philip and I...' appeared in the 1960s when it was apparent that the familiar formula was becoming a joke

3 Commencement oratory ... must eschew anything that smacks of partisan politics, political preference, sex, religion or unduly firm opinion. Nonetheless, there must be a speech: speeches in our culture are the vacuum that fills a vacuum.
J.K. Galbraith (b.1908), U.S. economist: commencement address at the American University, Washington D.C., publ. in *Time* (New York), 18 June 1984

4 I feel like Zsa Zsa Gabor's fifth husband. I know what I'm supposed to do but I don't know if I can make it interesting.
Albert Gore (b.1948), U.S. Democratic politician and vice president: on being 23rd speaker at a political dinner, quoted in *Today* (London), 1 March 1989

5 His speech was rather like being savaged by a dead sheep.
Denis Healey (b.1917), British Labour politician: referring to a criticism of Healey's Budget proposals by Shadow Chancellor Geoffrey Howe, in speech to House of Commons, 14 June 1978, publ. in *Hansard* col.1027. According to Healey's memoirs, this off-the-cuff remark was inspired by Winston Churchill's comment that an attack by Labour politician Clement Attlee was 'like being savaged by a pet lamb' (*The Time of My Life*, Pt.3, Ch.21, 1989). In 1983, after being congratulated by Healey on his appointment as Foreign Secretary, Howe commented that it was 'like being nuzzled by an old ram'. Healey's rejoinder: 'It would be the end of a beautiful friendship if he accused me of necrophilia'

6 The choice is whether you start sober and end drunk, or start drunk and end sober. The former is much better, both for the health of the speaker and for the effect on the audience.
Oswald Mosley (1896–1980), British fascist leader: on public speaking, in *My Life* (1968), Ch.5

7 The mark of a true politician is that he is never at a loss for words because he is always half-expecting to be asked to make a speech.
Richard Nixon (1913–1992), U.S. Republican politician and president: *Six Crises* (1962), 'The Campaign of 1960'

8 A speech is poetry: cadence, rhythm, imagery, sweep! A speech reminds us that words, like children, have the power to make dance the dullest beanbag of a heart.
Peggy Noonan (b.1950), U.S. author and presidential speechwriter: *What I Saw at the Revolution* (1990), Ch.5

SPEED

1 Speed, it seems to me, provides the one genuinely modern pleasure.
Aldous Huxley (1894–1963), British author: *Music at Night and Other Essays* (1949), 'Wanted, a New Pleasure'

2 Beep! Beep!
Chuck Jones (b.1912), U.S. animator: the Road Runner at full sprint, in *Looney Tunes/Merrie Melodies* (Warner Brothers cartoon, from 1949). This only line of dialogue between the Road Runner and Wile E. Coyote, was voiced by Mel Blanc. The characters were created by Chuck Jones (who directed most of the episodes) and Michael Maltese, and first introduced in a Warner Brothers' *Looney Tunes* cartoon called *Fast and Furry-Ous* (1949)

3 Get on with it, keep moving, keep in, speed, the nerves, their speed, the perceptions, theirs, the acts, the split second acts, the whole business, keep it moving as fast as you can, citizen ... fast, there's the dogma.
Charles Olson (1910–1970), U.S. poet and critic: 'Projective Verse', first publ. in *Poetry New York* (1950), rep. in *The Poetics of the New American Poetry* (ed. Donald M. Allen and Warren Tallman, 1973)

4 Speed is scarcely the noblest virtue of graphic composition, but it has its curious rewards. There is a sense of getting somewhere fast, which satisfies a native American urge.
James Thurber (1894–1961), U.S. humorist and illustrator: preface to *A Thurber Garland* (1955)

SPONSORSHIP

1 I would rather have as my patron a host of anonymous citizens digging into their own pockets for the price of a book or a magazine than a small body of enlightened and responsible men administering public funds. I would rather chance my personal vision of truth striking home here and there in the chaos of publication that exists than attempt to filter it through a few sets of official, honorably public-spirited scruples.
John Updike (b.1932), U.S. author and critic: testimony given before the House of Representatives Committee on Education and Labor, 30 Jan. 1978, Boston, publ. in appendix to Updike's *Hugging the Shore* (1983)

2 The most puzzling thing about TV is the steady advance of the sponsor across the line that has always separated news from promotion, entertainment from merchandising. The advertiser has assumed the role of originator, and the performer has gradually been eased into the role of peddler.
E.B. White (1899–1985), U.S. author and editor: 'Split Personalities', publ. in the *New Yorker*, 19 Feb. 1955, rep. in *Writings from the New Yorker 1927–1976* (ed. Rebecca M. Dale, 1991)

SPORT

1 Playing snooker gives you firm hands and helps to build up character. It is the ideal recreation for dedicated nuns.
Luigi Barbarito (b.1922), Italian churchman and archbishop: in *The Daily Telegraph* (London), 15 Nov. 1989

2 There are people who think that wrestling is an ignoble sport. Wrestling is not sport, it is a spectacle, and it is no more ignoble to attend a wrestled performance of suffering than a performance of the sorrows of Arnolphe or Andromaque.

Roland Barthes (1915–1980), French semiologist: *Mythologies* (1957; tr.1972), 'The World of Wrestling'. 'What wrestling is above all meant to portray,' Barthes added, 'is a purely moral concept: that of justice. The idea of "paying" is essential to wrestling, and the crowd's "Give it to him" means above all else "Make him pay"'

3 For many sportsmen, coming face to face with irrefutable evidence of their mortality is the moment they dread above all others.
Ian Botham (b.1955), British cricketer: on sustaining injuries, in *Botham: My Autobiography* (1994), Ch.1

4 What principle governed the British sporting event? It appeared that, in exchange for a few pounds, you received one hour and forty-five minutes characterized by the worst possible weather, the greatest number of people in the smallest possible space and the greatest number of obstacles – unreliable transport, no parking, an intensely dangerous crush at the only exit, a repellent polio pond to pee into, last minute changes of the starting time – to keep you from ever attending a match again.
Bill Buford (b.1954), U.S. editor and author: *Among the Thugs* (1991), Pt.1, 'A Station Outside Cardiff'

5 Courage and grace is a formidable mixture. The only place to see it is the bullring.
Marlene Dietrich (1904–1992), German-born U.S. actress: *Marlene Dietrich's ABC* (1962), 'Matador'

6 Take a look at them. All nice guys. They'll finish last. Nice guys. Finish last.
Leo Durocher (1906–1991), U.S. baseball coach: remark, 6 July 1946, referring to the New York Giants, quoted in *Nice Guys Finish Last* by Leo Durocher (1975), Pt.1

7 I'm fanatical about sport: there seems to me something almost religious about the fact that human beings can organise play, the spirit of play.
Simon Gray (b.1936), British playwright: interview in the *Independent on Sunday* (London), 19 Feb. 1995

8 A sporting system is the by-product of society and its political system, and it is just boyhood dreaming to suppose you can ever take politics out of sport.
Peter Hain (b.1950), British political activist and Labour politician: in *The Observer* (London), 2 May 1971

9 Be tolerant of those who describe a sporting moment as their best ever. We do not lack imagination, nor have we had sad and barren lives; it is just that real life is paler, duller, and contains less potential for unexpected delirium.
Nick Hornby (b.1957), British author: *Fever Pitch* (1992), '1986–1992: the Greatest Moment Ever'

10 Unlike any other business in the United States, sports must preserve an illusion of perfect innocence. The mounting of this illusion defines the purpose and accounts for the immense wealth of American sports. It is the ceremony of innocence that the fans pay to see – not the game or the match or the bout, but the ritual portrayal of a world in which time stops and all hope remains plausible, in which everybody present can recover the blameless expectations of a child, where the forces of light always triumph over the powers of darkness.
Lewis H. Lapham (b.1935), U.S. essayist and editor: *Money and Class in America* (1988), Ch.5, Sct.2

11 We want beans, not goals.
(*Queremos frijoles, no goles.*)
Mexican steelworkers' banner at opening ceremony of World Cup games, June 1986

12 People in the States used to think that if girls were good at sports their sexuality would be affected. Being feminine meant being a cheerleader, not being an athlete. The image of women is changing now. You don't have to be pretty for people to come and see you play. At the same time, if you're a good athlete, it doesn't mean you're not a woman.
Martina Navratilova (b.1956), Czech-born U.S. tennis player: *Martina Navratilova – Being Myself* (1985), Ch.8

See also GAMES; GOLF

SPORT: Athletics

1 *Why runners make lousy communists.* In a word, *individuality*. It's the one characteristic all runners, as different as they are, seem to share. ... Stick with it. Push yourself. Keep running. And you'll never lose that wonderful sense of individuality you now enjoy. Right, comrade?
Advertisement for running shoes at the 1984 Olympic Games in Los Angeles: quoted in *The Guardian* (London), 29 Dec. 1984

2 Athletes have studied how to leap and how to survive the leap some of the time and return to the ground. They don't always do it well. But they are our philosophers of actual moments and the body and soul in them, and of our manoeuvres in our emergencies and longings.
Harold Brodkey (1930–1996), U.S. author: 'Meditations on an Athlete', publ. in *Cape* (London), July 1992

SPORT: Baseball

1 In the great department store of life, baseball is the toy department.

Anonymous, Los Angeles sportscaster: quoted in *The Independent* (London), 28 Sept. 1991

2 Whoever wants to know the heart and mind of America had better learn baseball, the rules and realities of the game.

Jacques Barzun (b.1907), U.S. scholar: quoted in *The Joy of Sports* by Michael Novak (1976), Pt.1

3 A ball player's got to be kept hungry to become a big leaguer. That's why no boy from a rich family ever made the big leagues.

Joe DiMaggio (b.1914), U.S. baseball player: in the *New York Times*, 30 April 1961

4 I believe in the Church of Baseball. I tried all the major religions and most of the minor ones. I've worshipped Buddha, Allah, Brahma, Vishnu, Siva, trees, mushrooms and Isadora Duncan. I know things. For instance: there are 108 beads in a Catholic rosary and there are 108 stitches in a baseball. When I learned that, I gave Jesus a chance.

Ron Shelton (b.1945), U.S. film-maker: opening monologue in *Bull Durham* (film; written and directed by Ron Shelton, 1988)

5 I don't think I can be expected to take seriously any game which takes less than three days to reach its conclusion.

Tom Stoppard (b.1937), British playwright and cricket enthusiast: on baseball, quoted in *The Guardian* (London), 24 Dec. 1984

6 Baseball, it is said, is only a game. True. And the Grand Canyon is only a hole in Arizona. Not all holes, or games, are created equal.

George F. Will (b.1941), U.S. political columnist: *Men at Work: The Craft of Baseball* (1990), 'Conclusion'

SPORT: Boxing

1 It's just a job. Grass grows, birds fly, waves pound the sand. I beat people up.

Muhammad Ali (b.1942), U.S. boxer: in the *New York Times*, 6 April 1977

2 Boxing is just show business with blood.

Frank Bruno (b.1961), British boxer: in *The Guardian* (London), 19 Nov. 1991

3 Probably the greatest of all arguments for banning boxing is the audience it attracts. No young people – all too busy learning a martial art or painting their toenails. Few blacks (outside the ring). No sentient girls, only middle-aged bits of fluff who look like Miss TV Times 1957. The *noise* that comes from their wretched throats indicates that, with a

boxing crowd, brain damage is also in the head of the beholder.

Julie Burchill (b.1960), British journalist and author: *Damaged Gods* (1986), 'Only a Game'

4 I want to keep fighting because it is the only thing that keeps me out of the hamburger joints. If I don't fight, I'll eat this planet.

George Foreman (b.1948), U.S. boxer: in *The Times* (London), 17 Jan. 1990

5 Sure the fight was fixed. I fixed it with a right hand.

George Foreman: quoted in *The Sunday Times* (London), 18 Dec. 1994

6 All fighters are prostitutes and all promotors are pimps.

Larry Holmes (b.1949), U.S. boxing champion: quoted in *The Guardian* (London), 24 Dec. 1984

7 He can run. But he can't hide.

Joe Louis (1914–1981), U.S. boxer: quoted in *Louis: My Life Story* (1947), p.176. The threat was addressed to Billy Conn, his opponent in a World Championship match, 19 June 1946, which Louis won

8 It's the boxers who attract the real women, after all, with their raw primeval strength, beautifully toned bodies and just a touch of vulnerability.

Eamonn McCabe (b.1948), British journalist and photographer: in *The Guardian/Elle Supplement* (London), 9 Jan. 1992

9 Boxing got me started on philosophy. You bash them, they bash you and you think, what's it all for?

Arthur Mullard (1910–1995), British comic actor and boxer: quoted in the *Independent on Sunday* (London), 17 Dec. 1995

See also MUHAMMAD ALI; Tyson on PROFESSIONALS

SPORT: Cricket

1 In cricket, as in no other game, a great master may well go back to the pavilion scoreless.... In no other game does the law of averages get to work so potently, so mysteriously.

Neville Cardus (1889–1975), British journalist and critic: *Cardus on the Ashes* (1989), '1961 Illustrious Pages of History'

2 Cricket is first and foremost a dramatic spectacle. It belongs with the theatre, ballet, opera and the dance.

C.L.R. James (1901–1989), Trinidadian political activist and cricket enthusiast: *Beyond a Boundary* (1963), Pt.6, Ch.16

3 There is no essential discrepancy between the game's time-honoured virtues and the world

we live in. It is a matter of creatively adapting the form in order to preserve the content. So far much valuable time has been wasted on quibbling over what 'isn't cricket', and not much has been devoted to what cricket should become.

Imran Khan (b.1952), Pakistani cricketer: *All Round View* (1988), Ch.13

4 It's a funny kind of month, October. For the really keen cricket fan it's when you discover that your wife left you in May.

Denis Nordern (b.1922), British humorist: in *She* (London), Oct. 1977

5 I tend to believe that cricket is the greatest thing that God ever created on earth.

Harold Pinter (b.1930), British playwright: 'Pinter on Pinter', in *The Observer* (London), 5 Oct. 1980

See also Keneally on AUSTRALIA

SPORT: Football

1 Football is a sport with a great future behind it.

Julie Burchill (b.1960), British journalist and author: *Damaged Gods* (1986), 'Only a Game'

2 People stress the violence. That's the smallest part of it. Football is brutal only from a distance. In the middle of it there's a calm, a tranquility. The players accept pain. There's a sense of order even at the end of a running play with bodies strewn everywhere. When the systems interlock, there's a satisfaction to the game that can't be duplicated. There's a harmony.

Don DeLillo (b.1926), U.S. author: Emmett Creed, describing American football, in *End Zone* (1972), Ch.28

3 I am in favour of soccer passion as I am in favour of drag racing, of competition between motorcycles on the edge of a cliff, and of wild parachute jumping, mystical mountain climbing, crossing oceans in rubber dinghies, Russian roulette, and the use of narcotics. Races improve the race, and all these games lead fortunately to the death of the best, allowing mankind to continue its existence serenely with normal protagonists, of average achievement.

Umberto Eco (b.1932), Italian semiologist and novelist: 'The World Cup and its Pomps' (1978), rep. in *Travels in Hyperreality* (1986)

4 The point about football in Britain is that it is not just a sport people take to, like cricket or tennis or running long distances. It is inherent in the people. It is built into the urban psyche, as much a common experience to our children as are uncles and school. It is not a phenomenon; it is an everyday matter. There is more eccentricity in deliberately disregarding it than

in devoting a life to it. It has more significance in the national character than theatre has.

Arthur Hopcraft (b.1932), British author: introduction to *The Football Man* (1968)

5 Even though there is no question that sex is a nicer activity than watching football (no nil-nil draws, no offside trap, no cup upsets, *and* you're warm), in the normal run of things, the feelings it engenders are simply not as intense as those brought about by a once-in-a-lifetime last-minute Championship winner.

Nick Hornby (b.1957), British author: *Fever Pitch* (1992), '1986–1992: the Greatest Moment Ever'

6 The one thing that has never changed in the history of the game is the shape of the ball.

Denis Law (b.1940), British footballer: quoted in *The Sunday Times* (London), 18 Dec. 1994

7 Conventional wisdom notwithstanding, there is no reason either in football or in poetry why the two should not meet in a man's life if he has the weight and cares about the words.

Archibald MacLeish (1892–1982), U.S. poet: *Riders on Earth* (1978), 'Moonlighting on Yale Field'

8 The goal was scored a little bit by the hand of God, a little by the head of Maradona.

Diego Maradona (b.1960), Argentinian footballer: on the fisted goal that ousted England from the World Cup finals in Mexico, quoted in *The Observer* (London), 29 June 1986

9 Football combines the two worst things about America: it is violence punctuated by committee meetings.

George F. Will (b.1941), U.S. political columnist: on American football, in the *International Herald Tribune* (Paris), 7 May 1990

See also Clough on MANAGEMENT

SPORT: Tennis

1 New Yorkers love it when you spill your guts out there. Spill your guts at Wimbledon and they make you stop and clean it up.

Jimmy Connors (b.1952), U.S. tennis player: quoted in *The Guardian* (London), 24 Dec. 1984

2 Good shot, bad luck and hell are the five basic words to be used in a game of tennis, though these, of course, can be slightly amplified.

Virginia Graham (b.1914), U.S. author and commentator: *Say Please* (1949), Ch.8

3 I'm not just involved in tennis but committed. Do you know the difference between involvement and commitment? Think of ham and eggs. The chicken is involved. The pig is committed.

Martina Navratilova (b.1956), Czech-born U.S. tennis player: quoted in the *International Herald Tribune* (Paris), 3 Sept. 1982

JOSEF STALIN

1 He is gone, but his shadow still stands over all of us. It still dictates to us and we, very often, obey.
Svetlana Alliluevya (b.1925), Russian writer and daughter of Josef Stalin: *Twenty Letters to a Friend* (1967), Ch.2

2 Everyone can err, but Stalin considered that he never erred, that he was always right. He never acknowledged to anyone that he made any mistake, large or small, despite the fact that he made not a few mistakes in the matter of theory and in his practical activity.
Nikita Khrushchev (1894–1971), Soviet premier: speech to 20th Congress of Soviet Communist Party, Feb. 1956, quoted in *Stalin* (ed. T.H. Rigby, 1966), Pt.2, Ch.6

See also Khrushchev on INDIVIDUALITY

STARDOM

1 Five minutes of stardom means another 65 years of emptiness.
Marc Almond (b.1956), British rock musician: in *New Musical Express* (London), 1983, quoted in *NME Book of Quotes* (1995), 'Fame'

2 When you're sucked through this media machine and run under the wheels of the star machine, you can go to bed with a cup of cocoa and wake up looking like Bela Lugosi in the morning.
Brett Anderson (b.1967), British rock musician: interview in *i-D* (London), Oct. 1994

3 I stopped believing in Santa Claus when I was six. Mother took me to see him in a department store and he asked for my autograph.
Shirley Temple Black (b.1928), U.S. actress: quoted in *Halliwell's Filmgoer's Companion* (ed. Leslie Halliwell, 1984)

4 You're not a star until they can spell your name in Karachi.
Humphrey Bogart (1899–1957), U.S. actor: quoted in *Star Billing* by David Brown (1985), p.5 of Weidenfeld & Nicolson edn.

5 The star is the ultimate American verification of Jean Jacques Rousseau's *Emile*. His mere existence proves the perfectibility of any man or woman. Oh wonderful pliability of human nature, in a society where anyone can become a celebrity! And where any celebrity ... may become a star!
Daniel J. Boorstin (b.1914), U.S. historian: *The Image* (1961), Ch.4

6 What makes a star a star is not that 'indefinable something extra' the low-browed girls and high-heeled boys talk about in reverent, quiet-in-the-library murmurs – what makes a star a star is that indefinable something MISSING.
Julie Burchill (b.1960), British journalist and author: *Damaged Gods* (1986), 'Damaged Gods'

7 Richard Burton is now my epitaph, my cross, my title, my image. I have achieved a kind of diabolical fame. It has nothing to do with my talents as an actor. That counts for little now. I am the diabolically famous Richard Burton.
Richard Burton (1925–1984), British actor: interview, 1963, quoted in *Elizabeth Taylor* by Ruth Waterbury (1964), Ch.21

8 Being at the centre of a film is a burden one takes on with innocence – the first time. Thereafter, you take it on with trepidation.
Daniel Day-Lewis (b.1957), British actor: interview in *City Limits* (London), 7 April 1988

9 [Being] a Hollywood star is death as far as acting is concerned. I don't want people to recognize me in the streets. I don't want to do what real stars have to do – repeat themselves in film after film, always being themselves.
Robert De Niro (b.1943), U.S. actor: interview in *Screen International* (London), May 1976

10 Better to be a king for a night than a schmuck for a lifetime.
Robert De Niro: Rupert Pupkin (De Niro), in *The King of Comedy* (film; screenplay by Paul Zimmerman, directed by Martin Scorsese, 1983)

11 As far as the filmmaking process is concerned, stars are essentially worthless – and absolutely essential.
William Goldman (b.1931), U.S. screenwriter and novelist: *Adventures in the Screen Trade* (1983), Ch.1

12 One thing about being successful is that I stopped being afraid of dying. Once you're a star you're dead already. You're embalmed.
Dustin Hoffman (b.1937), U.S. actor: quoted in *Halliwell's Filmgoer's Companion* (ed. Leslie Halliwell, 1984)

13 You have to know exactly what you want out of your career. If you want to be a star, you don't bother with other things.
Marilyn Horne (b.1934), U.S. opera singer: quoted in *Divas: Impressions of Six Opera Superstars* by Winthrop Sargeant (1959)

14 It's nice to be a part of history but people should get it right. I may not be perfect, but I'm bloody close.
John Lydon [formerly Johnny Rotten] (b.1957), British rock musician: in *The Observer* (London), 4 May 1986

15 I'm a minute commodity.
River Phoenix (1970–1993), U.S. actor: quoted in *Sight and Sound* (London), Feb. 1994

16 I'm just a normal everyday kind of goddess.

Sandie Shaw (b.1947), British singer: in *New Musical Express* (London), 1988, quoted in *NME Book of Quotes* (1995), 'Ego'

17 I could go on stage and make a pizza and they'd still come to see me.

Frank Sinatra (b.1915), U.S. singer and actor: quoted in the *Independent on Sunday* (London), 31 May 1992

18 I *am* big. It's the pictures that got small.

Gloria Swanson (1897–1983), U.S. actress: Norma Desmond (Swanson), in *Sunset Boulevard* (film; screenplay by Billy Wilder, Charles Brackett and D.M. Marsham Jr., directed by Billy Wilder, 1950). The remark is a riposte to Joe Gillis (William Holden), in one of their opening scenes together: 'You're Norma Desmond! You used to be in silent pictures. Used to be big'

19 Do we really want to know HOW Michael Jackson makes his music? NO. We want to understand why he needs the bones of the Elephant Man – and, until he tells us, it doesn't make too much difference whether or not he really is 'bad'.

Frank Zappa (1940–1993), U.S. rock musician: *The Real Frank Zappa Book* (written with Peter Occhiogrosso, 1989), Ch.11

See also Swanson on ACTORS; FAME

STARS

1 Admirer as I think I am
Of stars that do not give a damn,
I cannot, now I see them, say
I missed one terribly all day.

W.H. Auden (1907–1973), Anglo-American poet: 'The More Loving One', publ. in *Homage to Clio* (1960)

2 He said he'd take me to the stars. Spinning waltzes in those empty spaces. Nothing can be more remote than the stars, François, or colder. Not even your lying heart.

Ruth Morgan (1920–1978), U.S. novelist: Roberta, the closing words of *Jeu d'Esprit* (1968), Ch.21

THE STATE

1 In the twentieth century one of the most personal relationships to have developed is that of the person and the state. ... It's become a fact of life that governments have become very intimate with people, most always to their detriment.

E.L. Doctorow (b.1931), U.S. novelist: interview in *Writers at Work* (Eighth Series, ed. George Plimpton, 1988)

2 The State has but one face for me: that of the police. To my eyes, all of the State's ministries have this single face, and I cannot imagine the ministry of culture other than as the police of culture, with its prefect and commissioners.

Jean Dubuffet (1901–1985), French sculptor and painter: *Asphyxiating Culture* (1968), rep. in *Asphyxiating Culture and Other Writings* (1986; tr.1988)

3 The vital interests of the state, which are always about power, have nothing to do with the vital interests of the citizens, which are private and simple and are always about a better life for themselves and their children. You do not kill for such interests, you work for them.

Martha Gellhorn (b.1908), U.S. journalist and author: introduction to *The Face of War* (1959; rev.1967)

4 In a free society the state does not administer the affairs of men. It administers justice among men who conduct their own affairs.

Walter Lippmann (1889–1974), U.S. journalist: *The Good Society* (1937), Ch.12

5 BIG BROTHER IS WATCHING YOU.

George Orwell (1903–1950), British author: caption to 'Ingsoc' poster, in *Nineteen Eighty-four* (1949), Pt.1, Ch.1. The poster is described as 'one of those pictures which are so contrived that the eyes follow you about when you move'

6 My thinking tends to be libertarian. That is, I oppose intrusions of the state into the private realm – as in abortion, sodomy, prostitution, pornography, drug use, or suicide, all of which I would strongly defend as matters of free choice in a representative democracy.

Camille Paglia (b.1947), U.S. author and critic: introduction to *Sex, Art, and American Culture* (1992)

7 Statecraft is soulcraft. Just as all education is moral education because learning conditions conduct, much legislation is moral legislation because it conditions the action and the thought of the nation in broad and important spheres of life.

George F. Will (b.1941), U.S. political columnist: *Statecraft as Soulcraft: What Government Does* (1984), Ch.1

STATISTICS

1 Like dreams, statistics are a form of wish fulfilment.

Jean Baudrillard (b.1929), French semiologist: *Cool Memories* (1987; tr.1990), Ch.4

2 It was only one of those sums one is forever being quoted, like the number of cocaine addicts in the country, of the dead in the Great War, or a figure for the daily loss of brain cells.

Saul Bellow (b.1915), U.S. novelist: *More Die of Heartbreak* (1987), Ch.3

3 I will stand on, and continue to use, the figures I have used, because I believe they are correct. Now, I'm not going to deny that you don't now and then slip up on something; no one bats a thousand.

Ronald Reagan (b.1911), U.S. Republican politician and president: news conference, Philadelphia, quoted in the *Washington Post*, 20 April 1980

STEREOTYPES

1 All stereotypes turn out to be true. This is a horrifying thing about life. All those things you fought against as a youth: you begin to realize they're stereotypes because they're true.

David Cronenberg (b.1943), Canadian film-maker: *Cronenberg on Cronenberg* (ed. Chris Rodley, 1992), Ch.1

2 It is very prevalent in modern culture, the way in which things become more and more archetypal or stereotypical; even human beings become more that way, through films, so you tend to locate your friends in terms of characters in movies. It's been the case that, more and more, images take the place of reality.

Claes Oldenburg (b.1929), Swedish-born U.S. artist: quoted in *The Independent* (London), 7 Sept. 1991

3 Out with stereotypes, feminism proclaims. But stereotypes are the west's stunning sexual personae, the vehicles of art's assault against nature. The moment there is imagination, there is myth.

Camille Paglia (b.1947), U.S. author and critic: *Sexual Personae* (1990), Ch.1

4 Do you really have to be the ice queen intellectual or the slut whore? Isn't there some way to be both?

Susan Sarandon (b.1946), U.S. actress: in *The Observer* (London), 14 Sept. 1991

See also Greer on WOMEN

THE STOCK MARKET

1 The freedom to make a fortune on the Stock Exchange has been made to sound more alluring than freedom of speech.

John Mortimer (b.1923), British barrister and novelist: quoted in *The Independent* (London), 29 Oct. 1988

2 We make the rules. The news, war, peace, famine, upheaval, the price of paper clips. We pick that rabbit out of the hat while everybody stands around wondering how the hell we did it. Now, you're not naive enough to think we're living in a democracy, are you, buddy? It's a free market – are you with me?

Oliver Stone (b.1946), U.S. film-maker: Gordon Gekko (Michael Douglas), in *Wall Street* (film; screenplay by Stanley Weiser and Oliver Stone, directed by Oliver Stone, 1987)

3 The only reason to invest in the market is because you think you know something others don't.

R. Foster Winans (b.1948), U.S. journalist: in *Newsweek* (New York), 1 Dec. 1986. Winans, a *Wall Street Journal* reporter, was tried and convicted for 'insider dealing'

4 On Wall Street he and a few others – how many? – three hundred, four hundred, five hundred? – had become precisely that ... Masters of the Universe.

Tom Wolfe (b.1931), U.S. author and journalist: of bond dealer Sherman McCoy, in *The Bonfire of the Vanities* (1979), Ch.1

STORY-TELLING

1 It is not the voice that commands the story: it is the ear.

Italo Calvino (1923–1985), Italian author and critic: Marco Polo, in *Invisible Cities* (1972; tr.1974), p.135 of Secker & Warburg edn. (1974)

2 A good story cannot be devised; it has to be distilled.

Raymond Chandler (1880–1959), U.S. author: letter, 7 March 1947, publ. in *Raymond Chandler Speaking* (ed. Dorothy Gardiner and Kathrine S. Walker, 1962)

3 I'm a liar, but an honest one. People reproach me for not always telling the same story the same way. But this happens because I've invented the whole tale from the start and it seems boring to me and unkind to other people to repeat myself.

Federico Fellini (1920–1993), Italian film-maker: *Fellini on Fellini* (ed. Anna Keel and Christian Strich, 1974; tr.1977), 'Miscellany I', Sct.4

4 If a nation loses its storytellers, it loses its childhood.

Peter Handke (b.1942), Austrian author, playwright and poet: in *The Independent* (London), 9 June 1988

5 Twenty or thirty years ago, in the army, we had a lot of obscure adventures, and years later we tell them at parties, and suddenly we realize that those two very difficult years of our lives have become lumped together into a few episodes that have lodged in our memory in a standardized form, and are always told in a standardized way, in the same words. But in fact that lump of memories has nothing whatsoever to do with our experience of those

two years in the army and what it has made of us.
Václav Havel (b.1936), Czech playwright and president: *Disturbing the Peace* (1986; tr.1990), Ch.4

6 Are you sitting comfortably? Then I'll begin.
Julia Lang (b.1921), British broadcaster: introductory words to *Listen with Mother* (daily children's stories on BBC radio, 1950–82)

7 In the tale, in the telling, we are all one blood. Take the tale in your teeth, then, and bite till the blood runs, hoping it's not poison; and we will all come to the end together, and even to the beginning: living, as we do, in the middle.
Ursula K. Le Guin (b.1929), U.S. author: 'It Was a Dark and Stormy Night; Or, Why Are We Huddling About the Campfire?', speech, 1979, University of Chicago, publ. in *Dancing at the Edge of the World* (1989)

8 We are lonesome animals. We spend all our life trying to be less lonesome. One of our ancient methods is to tell a story begging the listener to say – and to feel – 'Yes, that's the way it is, or at least that's the way I feel it. You're not as alone as you thought'.
John Steinbeck (1902–1968), U.S. author: 'In Awe of Words', first publ. in 75th-anniversary edition of *The Exonian* (Exeter University), rep. in *Writers at Work* (Fourth Series, ed. George Plimpton, 1977)

9 Stories give people the feeling that there is meaning, that there is ultimately an order lurking behind the incredible confusion of appearances and phenomena that surrounds them. ... Stories are substitutes for God. Or maybe the other way round.
Wim Wenders (b.1945), German film-maker: 'Impossible Stories', talk given at a colloquium on narrative technique, 1982, publ. in *The Logic of Images* (1988; tr.1991)

STRANGERS

1 Every time a man unburdens his heart to a stranger he reaffirms the love that unites humanity.
Germaine Greer (b.1939), Australian feminist writer: *The Female Eunuch* (1970), 'The Ideal'

2 Some enchanted evening,
You may see a stranger,
You may see a stranger,
Across a crowded room.
Oscar Hammerstein II (1895–1960), U.S. songwriter: 'Some Enchanted Evening' (song) in *South Pacific* (stage musical, 1949; film, 1958)

3 I have always depended on the kindness of strangers.
Tennessee Williams (1911–1983), U.S. playwright: the final words of Blanche DuBois, in *A Streetcar Named Desire* (1947), Sc.11

STRESS

1 When you suffer an attack of nerves you're being attacked by the nervous system. What chance has a man got against a system?
Russell Hoban (b.1932), U.S. author: the bookshop owner, in *The Lion of Boaz-Jachin and Jachin-Boaz* (1973), Ch.13

2 If you can't stand the heat, get out of the kitchen.
Harry S Truman (1884–1972), U.S. Democratic politician and president: favourite saying of Truman's, previously ascribed to an adviser, quoted in *Mr Citizen* (1960), Ch.15

See also Rushdie on RECLUSIVES

STRUCTURALISM

1 Post-structuralism is among other things a kind of theoretical hangover from the failed uprising of '68 – a way of keeping the revolution warm at the level of language, blending the euphoric libertarianism of that moment with the stoical melancholia of its aftermath.
Terry Eagleton (b.1943), British critic: in *The Guardian* (London), 27 Oct. 1992

2 The (post) structuralist temper requires too great a depersonalization of the writing/speaking subject. Writing becomes plagiarism; speaking becomes quoting. Meanwhile, we do write, we do speak.
Ihab Hassan (b.1925), U.S. critic: 'The Re-Vision of Literature', publ. in *New Literary History*, autumn 1976, rep. in *The Right Promethean Fire* (1980)

3 By day, Structuralists constructed the structure of meaning and pondered the meaning of structure. By night, Deconstructivists pulled the cortical edifice down. And the next day the Structuralists started in again...
Tom Wolfe (b.1931), U.S. author and journalist: *From Bauhaus to Our House* (1981), Ch.5

STUPIDITY

1 The question now is: Can we understand our stupidity? This is a test of intellect, not of character.
John King Fairbank (1907–1991), U.S. historian and educator: quoted in *The Observer* (London), 4 May 1975

2 Stupid is as stupid does.
Tom Hanks (b.1957), U.S. actor: Forrest Gump (Hanks) quoting his mother, in *Forrest Gump* (film;

screenplay by Eric Roth based on a novel by Winston Groom, directed by Robert Zemeckis, 1994)

3 To accuse another of having weak kidneys, lungs, or heart, is not a crime; on the contrary, saying he has a weak brain is a crime. To be considered stupid and to be told so is more painful than being called gluttonous, mendacious, violent, lascivious, lazy, cowardly: every weakness, every vice, has found its defenders, its rhetoric, its ennoblement and exaltation, but stupidity hasn't.
Primo Levi (1919–1987), Italian chemist and author: *Other People's Trades* (1985; tr.1989), 'The Irritable Chess-players'

4 You're not too smart, are you? I like that in a man.
Kathleen Turner (b.1954), U.S. actress: Matty Walker (Turner), in *Body Heat* (film; written and directed by Lawrence Kasdan, 1981)

5 Strange as it may seem, no amount of learning can cure stupidity, and formal education positively fortifies it.
Stephen Vizinczey (b.1933), Hungarian novelist and critic: 'Europe's Inner Demons' (review of *An Inquiry Inspired by the Great Witch-Hunt* by Norman Cohn), in *The Sunday Telegraph* (London), 2 March 1975, rep. in *Truth and Lies in Literature* (1986)

STYLE

1 Style is not neutral; it gives moral directions.
Martin Amis (b.1949), British author: *Novelists in Interview* (ed. John Haffenden, 1985)

2 The most durable thing in writing is style, and style is the most valuable investment a writer can make with his time. It pays off slowly, your agent will sneer at it, your publisher will misunderstand it, and it will take people you have never heard of to convince them by slow degrees that the writer who puts his individual mark on the way he writes will always pay off.
Raymond Chandler (1880–1959), U.S. author: letter, 7 March 1947, publ. in *Raymond Chandler Speaking* (ed. Dorothy Gardiner and Kathrine S. Walker, 1962)

3 A style does not go out of style as long as it adapts itself to its period. When there is an incompatibility between the style and a certain state of mind, it is never the style that triumphs.
Coco Chanel (1883–1971), French *couturière*: quoted in *Coco Chanel: Her Life, Her Secrets* by Marcel Haedrich (1971), Ch.21

4 What is line? It is life. A line must live at each point along its course in such a way that the artist's presence makes itself felt above that of the model. ... With the writer, line takes

precedence over form and content. It runs through the words he assembles. It strikes a continuous note unperceived by ear or eye. It is, in a way, the soul's style, and if the line ceases to have a life of its own, if it only describes an arabesque, the soul is missing and the writing dies.
Jean Cocteau (1889–1963), French author and film-maker: *The Difficulty of Being* (1947), 'De la Ligne'

5 Style is a fraud. I always felt the Greeks were hiding behind their columns.
Willem de Kooning (1904–1997), Dutch-born U.S. artist: 'A Desperate View', talk in New York, 1949, publ. in *Collected Writings* (ed. George Scrivani, 1988)

6 To me style is just the outside of content, and content the inside of style, like the outside and the inside of the human body – both go together, they can't be separated.
Jean-Luc Godard (b.1930), French film-maker and author: quoted in introduction (1967) to *Godard* by Richard Roud (1970)

7 I might say that what amateurs call a style is usually only the unavoidable awkwardnesses in first trying to make something that has not heretofore been made.
Ernest Hemingway (1899–1961), U.S. author: interview in *Writers at Work* (Second Series, ed. George Plimpton, 1963)

8 Happy the society whose deepest divisions are ones of style.
Peter McKay (b.1940), British Conservative politician: in the *Evening Standard* (London), 31 Jan. 1990

9 Always, however brutal an age may actually have been, its style transmits its music only.
André Malraux (1901–1976), French man of letters and statesman: quoted in *The Journey* by Lillian Smith (1955), Ch.15

10 Style [is] the hallmark of a temperament stamped on the material in hand.
André Maurois (1885–1967), French author and critic: *The Art of Writing* (1960), 'The Writer's Craft', Sct.2

11 Using language like clothes or the skin on your body, with its sleeves, its patches, its transpirations, and its blood and sweat stains, that's what shows a writer's mettle. This is style.
Pablo Neruda (1904–1973), Chilean poet: *Memoirs* (1974), Ch.11, 'Living with the Language'

12 A cultivated style would be like a mask. Everybody knows it's a mask, and sooner or later you must show yourself – or at least, you show yourself as someone who could not afford to show himself, and so created something to hide behind. ... You do not create a style. You work, and develop yourself; your style is an emanation from your own being.

Katherine Anne Porter (1890–1980), U.S. short-story writer and novelist: interview in *Writers at Work* (Second Series, ed. George Plimpton, 1963)

13 Fashions fade, style is eternal.
Yves Saint Laurent (b.1936), French fashion designer: *Andy Warhol's Interview* (New York), 13 April 1975

14 In the final analysis, 'style' is art. And art is nothing more or less than various modes of stylized, dehumanized representation.
Susan Sontag (b.1933), U.S. essayist: *Against Interpretation* (1966), 'On Style'

See also Mies van der Rohe on MINIMALISM; York on THE 1970S

THE SUBCONSCIOUS

1 The subconscious is ceaselessly murmuring, and it is by listening to these murmurs that one hears the truth.
Gaston Bachelard (1884–1962), French scientist, philosopher and literary theorist: *The Poetics of Reverie* (1960; tr.1969), Ch.2, Sct.2

2 The unconscious is the ocean of the unsayable, of what has been expelled from the land of language, removed as a result of ancient prohibitions.
Italo Calvino (1923–1985), Italian author and critic: 'Cybernetics and Ghosts', lecture, Nov. 1969, Turin, publ. in *The Literature Machine* (1987)

3 The images of the unconscious place a great responsibility upon a man. Failure to understand them, or a shirking of ethical responsibility, deprives him of his wholeness and imposes a painful fragmentariness on his life.
Carl Jung (1875–1961), Swiss psychiatrist: *Memories, Dreams, Reflections* (1963), Ch.6

4 The Yanks have colonized our subconscious.
Wim Wenders (b.1945), German film-maker: Robert Lander (Hans Zischler), in *Kings of the Road* (film; written and directed by Wim Wenders, 1976)

SUBJECTIVITY

1 Bias and impartiality is in the eye of the beholder.
Lord Barnett (b.1923), British Conservative politician: in *The Independent* (London), 12 July 1990

2 When you're in the muck you can only see muck. If you somehow manage to float above it, you still see the muck but you see it from a different perspective. And you see other things too. That's the consolation of philosophy.
David Cronenberg (b.1943), Canadian film-maker: *Cronenberg on Cronenberg* (ed. Chris Rodley, 1992), Ch.3

3 Balance is the enemy of art.
Richard Eyre (b.1943), British theatre, film and TV director: in *The Independent* (London), 28 Oct. 1992

4 I shut my eyes and all the world drops dead;
I lift my eyes and all is born again.
Sylvia Plath (1932–1963), U.S. poet: 'Mad Girl's Love Song', publ. in *Mademoiselle* (New York), Aug. 1953

5 I look at the people passing by: I say, 'human beings'. All at once I am a human being. But if I have objectified my subjectivity, at the same time I have projected all my subjectivity upon them.
Jean-Paul Sartre (1905–1980), French philosopher and author: *Notebooks for an Ethics* (1983; tr.1992), Notebook 1

SUBMISSION

1 At fifteen life had taught me undeniably that surrender, in its place, was as honorable as resistance, especially if one had no choice.
Maya Angelou (b.1928), US author: *I Know Why the Caged Bird Sings* (first volume of autobiography, 1969), Ch.31

2 The sovereign being is burdened with a servitude *that crushes him*, and the condition of free men is deliberate servility.
Georges Bataille (1897–1962), French novelist and critic: *L'Abbé C* (1950), Pt.4, "The Diary of Chianine"

SUBURBS

1 Being born on the outskirts of London, being able to just peer in but not quite see what's going on, is a really tantalising thing – it makes you hungry and gives you a certain amount of ambition.
Brett Anderson (b.1967), British rock musician: interview in the *Independent on Sunday* (London), 21 March 1993

2 Everywhere – all over Africa and South America ... you see these suburbs springing up. They represent the optimum of what people want. There's a certain sort of logic leading towards these immaculate suburbs. And they're terrifying, because they are the *death of the soul*. ... *This* is the prison this planet is being turned into.
J.G. Ballard (b.1930), British author: interview, 30 Oct. 1982, in *Re/Search* (San Francisco), No.8/9, 1984

3 Let's face it, we became ingrown, clannish, and retarded. Cut off from the mainstream of humanity, we came to believe that pink is 'flesh-color', that mayonnaise is a nutrient, and that Barry Manilow is a musician.

6 Don't look forward to the day you stop suffering, because when it comes you'll *know* you're dead.
Tennessee Williams (1911–1983), U.S. playwright: quoted in *The Observer* (London), 26 Jan. 1958

See also Orwell on FUN; Allen on LOVE

SUICIDE

1 No one is promiscuous in his way of dying. A man who has decided to hang himself will never jump in front of a train.
A. Alvarez (b.1929), British critic, poet and novelist: *The Savage God* (1971), Pt.5

2 Men are never convinced of your reasons, of your sincerity, of the seriousness of your sufferings, except by your death. So long as you are alive, your case is doubtful; you have a right only to your scepticism.
Albert Camus (1913–1960), French-Algerian philosopher and author: the narrator (Jean-Baptiste Clamence), in *The Fall* (1956) p.56 of Hamish Hamilton edn. (1957)

3 It is not worth the bother of killing yourself, since you always kill yourself *too late*.
E.M. Cioran (1911–1995), Rumanian-born French philosopher: *The Trouble with Being Born* (1973), Ch.2

4 Thank you all from the pit of my burning, nauseous stomach.
Kurt Cobain (1967–1994), U.S. rock musician: suicide note, publ. in *Cobain* (ed. *Rolling Stone* magazine, 1994), p.94. Parts of Kurt Cobain's suicide note were read out by Courtney Love at a memorial ceremony in Seattle, 10 April 1994

5 Would Hamlet have felt the delicious fascination of suicide if he hadn't had an audience, and lines to speak?
Jean Genet (1910–1986), French playwright and novelist: *Prisoner of Love* (1986; tr.1989), Pt.1

6 However great a man's fear of life, suicide remains the courageous act, the clear-headed act of a mathematician. The suicide has judged by the laws of chance – so many odds against one that to live will be more miserable than to die. His sense of mathematics is greater than his sense of survival.
Graham Greene (1904–1991), British novelist: Dr Magiot, in *The Comedians* (1966), Bk.3, Pt.1, Ch.1, Sct.1

7 Fatigue dulls the pain, but awakes enticing thoughts of death. So! *that* is the way in which you are tempted to overcome your loneliness – by making the ultimate escape from life. – No! It may be that death is to be your ultimate gift to life: it must not be an act of treachery against it.
Dag Hammarskjöld (1905–1961), Swedish statesman and secretary-general of U.N.: note, written 1952, publ. in *Markings* (1963), 'Night is Drawing Nigh'

8 Sometimes I wonder if suicides aren't in fact sad guardians of the meaning of life.
Václav Havel (b.1936), Czech playwright and president: *Disturbing the Peace* (1986; tr.1990), Ch.5

9 If you are of the opinion that the contemplation of suicide is sufficient evidence of a poetic nature, do not forget that actions speak louder than words.
Fran Lebowitz (b.1951), U.S. journalist: *Metropolitan Life* (1978), 'Letters'

10 The lieutenant's eyes fixed his wife with an intense, hawk-like stare. Moving the sword around to his front, he raised himself slightly on his hips and let the upper half of his body lean over the sword point. That he was mustering his whole strength was apparent from the angry tension of the uniform at his shoulders. The lieutenant aimed to strike deep into the left of his stomach. His sharp cry pierced the silence of the room.
Yukio Mishima (1925–1970), Japanese author: 'Patriotism', publ. in *Death in Midsummer and Other Stories* (1966). Mishima himself chose to die by this traditional method of death among the Japanese warrior class – *hara-kiri* (or *seppuku*)

11 At great periods you have always felt, deep within you, the temptation to commit suicide. *You gave yourself to it*, breached your own defences. You were a child. The idea of suicide was a protest against life; by dying, you would escape this longing for death.
Cesare Pavese (1908–1950), Italian poet, novelist and translator: journal entry, 1 Jan. 1950, publ. in *This Business of Living* (1952; tr.1961). Suicide was a continuing theme in Pavese's diaries; he took his own life on 27 Aug. 1950, shortly after being awarded the Strega Prize for literature

12 The woman is perfected.
Her dead
Body wears the smile of accomplishment.
Sylvia Plath (1932–1963), U.S. poet: 'Edge', publ. in *Ariel* (1965). These are the opening lines of Sylvia Plath's last poem, written a week before her suicide

13 I have always thought the suicide shd bump off at least one swine before taking off for parts unknown.
Ezra Pound (1885–1972), U.S. poet and critic: letter, 10 Sept. 1956, to poet Archibald MacLeish, quoted in *A Serious Character* by Humphrey Carpenter (biography, 1988), Pt.5, Ch.3

14 Dear World, I am leaving you because I am bored. I am leaving you with your worries. Good luck.

George Sanders (1906–1972), British actor: suicide note left by Sanders, quoted in *Brewer's Cinema* (1995)

15 But suicides have a special language.
Like carpenters they want to know *which tools.*
They never ask *why build.*
Anne Sexton (1928–1974), U.S. poet: 'Wanting to Die', St.3, publ. in *Live or Die*, 1966). Sexton committed suicide in October 1974, after several failed attempts

16 Oh, no no no no, it was too cold always
(Still the dead one lay moaning)
I was much too far out all my life
And not waving but drowning.
Stevie Smith (1902–1971), British poet and novelist: 'Not Waving But Drowning', publ. in *Not Waving But Drowning* (1957)

17 He who does not accept and respect those who want to reject life does not truly accept and respect life itself.
Thomas Szasz (b.1920), U.S. psychiatrist: *The Second Sin* (1973), 'Suicide'

See also Berryman on THE WORLD

THE SUN

1 And before you let the sun in, mind it wipes its shoes.
Dylan Thomas (1914–1953), Welsh poet: Mrs Ogmore-Pritchard, in *Under Milk Wood* (1954)

2 The most beautiful thing under the sun is being under the sun.
Christa Wolf (b.1929), German novelist: *A Model Childhood* (1976; tr.1980), Ch.8

SUNDAYS

1 Sometimes there's nothing but Sundays for weeks on end. Why can't they move Sunday to the middle of the week so you could put it in the OUT tray on your desk?
Russell Hoban (b.1932), U.S. author: 'The tightly furled man', in *The Lion of Boaz-Jachin and Jachin-Boaz* (1973), Ch.13. 'Forgive us our Sundays,' he added, 'as we forgive those who Sunday against us'

2 Why do I do this every Sunday? Even the book reviews seem to be the same as last week's. Different books – same reviews.
John Osborne (1929–1994), British playwright: Jimmy Porter, in opening words of *Look Back in Anger* (1956), Act 1

3 Sunday – the doctor's paradise! Doctors at country clubs, doctors at the seaside, doctors with mistresses, doctors with wives, doctors in church, doctors in yachts, doctors everywhere resolutely being people, not doctors.

Sylvia Plath (1932–1963), U.S. poet: the narrator (Esther Greenwood), in *The Bell Jar* (1963), Ch.19

4 The feeling of Sunday is the same everywhere, heavy, melancholy, standing still. Like when they say, 'As it was in the beginning, is now, and ever shall be, world without end.'
Jean Rhys (1894–1979), British author: the narrator (Anna Morgan), in *Voyage in the Dark* (1934), Act 4

5 Anybody can observe the Sabbath, but making it holy surely takes the rest of the week.
Alice Walker (b.1944), U.S. author and critic: *In Search of Our Mothers' Gardens* (1983), 'To the Editors of *Ms.* Magazine'

See also WEEKENDS

SUPERMARKETS

1 In my hungry fatigue, and shopping for images, I went into the neon fruit supermarket, dreaming of your enumerations!
Allen Ginsberg (b.1926), U.S. poet: 'A Supermarket in California', publ. in *Howl and Other Poems* (1956)

2 There should be supermarkets that sell things and supermarkets that buy things back, and until that equalizes, there'll be more waste than there should be.
Andy Warhol (c.1928–1987), U.S. Pop artist: *From A to B and Back Again* (1975), Ch.10

THE SUPERNATURAL

1 The more enlightened our houses are, the more their walls ooze ghosts.
Italo Calvino (1923–1985), Italian author and critic: 'Cybernetics and Ghosts', lecture, Nov. 1969, Turin, publ. in *The Literature Machine* (1987)

2 Religion
Has made an honest woman of the supernatural,
And we won't have it kicking over the traces again.
Christopher Fry (b.1907), British playwright: Tappercoom, in *The Lady's Not for Burning* (1949), Act 2

See also MAGIC; MIRACLES

THE SUPERPOWERS

1 Greece is a sort of American vassal; the Netherlands is the country of American bases that grow like tulip bulbs; Cuba is the main sugar plantation of the American monopolies; Turkey is prepared to kow-tow before any United States pro-consul and Canada is the

boring second fiddle in the American symphony.

Andrei Andreyevich Gromyko (1909–1989), Soviet statesman and diplomat: in the *New York Herald Tribune*, 30 June 1953

2 The superpowers often behave like two heavily-armed blind men feeling their way around a room, each believing himself in mortal peril from the other, whom he assumes to have perfect vision.

Henry Kissinger (b.1923), U.S. Republican politician and secretary of state: quoted in *The Observer* (London), 30 Sept. 1979

3 There are far too many politicized people on earth today for any nation readily to accept the finality of America's historical mission to lead the world.

Edward Said (b.1935), Lebanese-born U.S. social and literary critic: *Culture and Imperialism* (1993), Ch.4, Sct.1

4 In April 1917 the illusion of isolation was destroyed, America came to the end of innocence, and of the exuberant freedom of bachelor independence. That the responsibilities of world power have not made us happier is no surprise. To help ourselves manage them, we have replaced the illusion of isolation with a new illusion of omnipotence.

Barbara Tuchman (1912–1989), U.S. historian: 'How We Entered World War I', publ. in the *New York Times Magazine*, 5 May 1967

SUPERSTITION

1 Superstitions are habits rather than beliefs.

Marlene Dietrich (1904–1992), German-born U.S. actress: *Marlene Dietrich's ABC* (1962), 'Superstition'

2 We would be a lot safer if the Government would take its money out of science and put it into astrology and the reading of palms.... Only in superstition is there hope. If you want to become a friend of civilization, then become an enemy of the truth and a fanatic for harmless balderdash.

Kurt Vonnegut (b.1922), U.S. novelist: *Wampeters, Foma and Granfallons* (1974), 'When I Was Twenty-One'

See also ASTROLOGY

SURPRISE

1 Nobody expects the Spanish Inquisition!

Monty Python's Flying Circus: Michael Palin, in *Monty Python's Flying Circus* (BBC TV comedy series, 1969–74), 2nd series, episode 2, first broadcast 22 Sept. 1970. Monty Python episodes were written and performed by Graham Chapman

(1941–1989); John Cleese (b.1939); Terry Gilliam (b.1940); Eric Idle (b.1943); Terry Jones (b.1942), and Michael Palin (b.1943)

2 Stupefaction, when it persists, becomes stupidity.

José Ortega y Gasset (1883–1955), Spanish essayist and philosopher: 'In Search of Goethe from Within', first publ. in *Partisan Review* (New Brunswick, N.J.), Dec. 1949, rep. in *The Dehumanization of Art and Other Essays* (1968)

SURREALISM

1 Surrealism ... is the forbidden flame of the proletariat embracing the insurrectional dawn – enabling us to rediscover at last the revolutionary moment: the radiance of the workers' councils as a life profoundly adored by those we love.

Arab Surrealist Movement Manifesto (1975): quoted in *What is Surrealism?* (ed. Franklin Rosemont, 1971), 'Surrealist Glossary'

2 Instead of stubbornly attempting to use surrealism for purposes of subversion, it is necessary to try to make of surrealism something as solid, complete and classic as the works of museums.

Salvador Dali (1904–1989), Spanish painter: *The Secret Life of Salvador Dali* (1948), Ch.14

3 Like all revolutions, the surrealist revolution was a reversion, a restitution, an expression of vital and indispensable spiritual needs.

Eugène Ionesco (1912–1994), Rumanian-born French playwright: 'Experience of the Theatre', first publ. in *N.R.F.* (Paris), Feb. 1958, rep. in *Notes and Counter Notes* (1962), Pt.1

4 To be a surrealist ... means barring from your mind all remembrance of what you have seen, and being always on the lookout for what has never been.

René Magritte (1898–1967), Belgian surrealist painter: in *Time* (New York), 21 April 1947, quoted in 'Sightless Vision' by Uwe M. Scheede, publ. in *Max Ernst* (ed. Werner Spies, 1991)

5 Surrealism is not a school of poetry but a movement of liberation.... A way of rediscovering the language of innocence, a renewal of the primordial pact, poetry is the basic text, the foundation of the human order. Surrealism is revolutionary because it is a return to the beginning of all beginnings.

Octavio Paz (b.1914), Mexican poet and essayist: *Alternating Current* (1967), 'André Breton or the Quest of the Beginning'

6 All of us may be surrealists in our dreams, but in our worries we are incorrigibly bourgeois.

Adam Phillips, British psychoanalyst and author: 'Worrying and its Discontents', first publ. in *Raritan*

(London), Vol.IX, No.9, 1989, rep. in *On Kissing, Tickling and Being Bored* (1993)

7 Surrealism is a bourgeois disaffection; that its militants thought it universal is only one of the signs that it is typically bourgeois.

Susan Sontag (b.1933), U.S. essayist: *On Photography* (1977), 'Melancholy Objects'. For Sontag, 'surrealism in painting amounted to little more than the contents of a meagrely stocked dream world: a few witty fantasies, mostly wet dreams and agoraphobic nightmares'

SURVIVAL

1 The values by which we are to survive are not rules for just and unjust conduct, but are those deeper illuminations in whose light justice and injustice, good and evil, means and ends are seen in fearful sharpness of outline.

Jacob Bronowski (1908–1974), British scientist and author: concluding sentence of 'The Sense of Human Dignity', lecture, 19 March 1953, Massachusetts Institute of Technology, publ. in *Science and Human Values* (1961), Pt.3, Sct.11

2 As long as I know how to love, I know I'll stay alive,
   I've got all my life to live, I've got so much love to give,
   I will survive! I will survive!

Gloria Gaynor (b.1949), U.S. soul singer: 'I Will Survive' (song; written by Dino Fekaris and Freddie Perren, 1979). Unusually for a disco song, this multi-million-seller became a feminist and gay anthem

3 Survival, with honor, that outmoded and all-important word, is as difficult as ever and as all-important to a writer. Those who do not last are always more beloved since no one has to see them in their long, dull, unrelenting, no-quarter-given-and-no-quarter-received, fights that they make to do something as they believe it should be done before they die. Those who die or quit early and easy and with every good reason are preferred because they are understandable and human. Failure and well-disguised cowardice are more human and more beloved.

Ernest Hemingway (1899–1961), U.S. author: interview in the *Paris Review* (Flushing, N.Y.), spring 1958, rep. in *Writers at Work* (Second Series, ed. George Plimpton, 1963)

4 A population weakened and exhausted by battling against so many obstacles – whose needs are never satisfied and desires never fulfilled – is vulnerable to manipulation and regimentation. The struggle for survival is, above all, an exercise that is hugely time-consuming, absorbing and debilitating. If you create these 'anti-conditions', your rule is guaranteed for a hundred years.

Ryszard Kapuściński (b.1932), Polish journalist: 'A Warsaw Diary', publ. in *Granta* (Cambridge), No.15, 1985

5 I'm one of the world's great survivors. I'll always survive because I've got the right combination of wit, grit and bullshit.

Don King (b.1931), U.S. boxing promoter: quoted in *The Sunday Times* (London), 18 Dec. 1994

6 We have survived again.

Akira Kurosawa (b.1910), Japanese film-maker: the samurai Kanbei to Shichiroji, after they have battled to save a village from a bandit attack, in *The Seven Samurai* (film; screenplay by Shinobu Hashimoto, Hideo Oguni and Akira Kurosawa, directed by Akira Kurosawa, 1954)

7 The notion that one will not survive a particular catastrophe is, in general terms, a comfort since it is equivalent to abolishing the catastrophe.

Iris Murdoch (b.1919), British novelist and philosopher: Franca Sheerwater, in *The Message to the Planet* (1989), Pt.6

8 Once one determines that he or she has a mission in life, that it's not going to be accomplished without a great deal of pain, and that the rewards in the end may not outweigh the pain – if you recognize historically that that always happens, then when it comes, you survive it.

Richard Nixon (1913–1992), U.S. Republican politician and president: remark to interviewer, Sept. 1980, quoted in *Exile: The Unquiet Oblivion of Richard M. Nixon* by Robert Sam Anson (1984), Ch.17

9 All I'm trying to do is not join my ancestral spirits just yet.

Joshua Nkomo (b.1917), Zimbabwean politician: in *The Observer* (London), 20 March 1983

10 As a lone ant from a broken ant-hill
    from the wreckage of Europe, ego scriptor.

Ezra Pound (1885–1972), U.S. poet and critic: canto 76 in *The Pisan Cantos* (1948)

11 Humans make the mistake of believing that it's their right to survive. Species die out on this planet all the time without anybody noticing. The planet will still be here, and we must lose this attitude of divine right, that something will save us, which we've developed over the centuries. The Martians aren't going to come down and save us. God isn't going to save us.

Sting (b.1951), British rock musician: interview in *Rolling Stone* (New York), Sept. 1983

12 We must lighten ourselves to survive. We must not cling. Safety lies in lessening, in becoming random and thin enough for the new to enter.

John Updike (b.1932), U.S. author and critic: on the 'natural principle of divestment', in *The Witches of Eastwick* (1984), Pt.1

13 Nobody is stonger, nobody is weaker than someone who came back. There is nothing you can do to such a person because whatever you could do is less than what has already been done to him. We have already paid the price.
Elie Wiesel (b.1928), Rumanian-born U.S. writer: interview in *Writers at Work* (Eighth Series, ed. George Plimpton, 1988)

See also Bowie on ERROR

SUSPICION

1 The suspicious mind believes more than it doubts. It believes in a formidable and ineradicable evil lurking in every person.
Eric Hoffer (1902–1983), U.S. philosopher: *The Passionate State of Mind* (1955), Aph.184

2 Suspicion ... is one of the morbid reactions by which an organism defends itself and seeks another equilibrium.
Nathalie Sarraute (b.1900), French novelist: 'The Age of Suspicion' (Feb. 1950), rep. in *The Age of Suspicion* (1956)

3 We have to distrust each other. It is our only defence against betrayal.
Tennessee Williams (1911–1983), U.S. playwright: Marguerite Gautier, in *Camino Real* (1953), Block 10

SWIMMING POOLS

1 As suburban children we floated at night in swimming pools the temperature of blood; pools the color of Earth as seen from outer space.
Douglas Coupland (b.1961), Canadian author: *Life After God* (1994), '1,000 Years (Life after God)'

2 A pool is, for many of us in the West, a symbol not of affluence but of order, of control over the uncontrollable. A pool is water, made available and useful, and is, as such, infinitely soothing to the western eye.
Joan Didion (b.1934), U.S. essayist: 'Holy Water' (1977), rep. in *The White Album* (1979)

SWITZERLAND

1 Berne... is twice the size of the cemetery in Vienna but only half as amusing.
Luciano De Crescenzo (b.1928), Italian author: the Professor, in *Thus Spake Bellavista* (1977; tr.1988), Ch.7

2 This is a strange little complacent country, in many ways a U.S.A. in miniature but of course nearer the center of disturbance!
Eleanor Roosevelt (1884–1962), U.S. columnist, lecturer and wife of F.D. Roosevelt: letter to her daughter from Geneva, 2 May 1951, publ. in *Mother and Daughter: The Letters of Eleanor and Anna Roosevelt* (1982)

3 There is a vast and vital difference between Swiss neutrality and, say, Swedish or Irish neutrality. The Swiss is a commitment, the others an evasion and, at best, a hope to keep out of trouble.
Laurens van der Post (1906–1996), South African writer and philosopher: *A Walk with a White Bushman* (1986), p.167 of Chatto & Windus edn.

4 In Italy for thirty years under the Borgias they had warfare, terror, murder, bloodshed – they produced Michelangelo, Leonardo da Vinci and the Renaissance. In Switzerland they had brotherly love, five hundred years of democracy and peace, and what did they produce? The cuckoo clock!
Orson Welles (1915–1985), U.S. film-maker and actor: Harry Lime (Welles), in *The Third Man* (film; screenplay by Graham Greene adapted from his own novella, directed by Carol Reed, 1949). Welles starred in the film, and contributed the speech to Greene's screenplay; he later claimed that the speech was based on a fragment of an old Hungarian play. Welles played the role of Cesare Borgia in the film *Prince of Foxes*, also released in 1949

SYMBOLISM

1 There is no symbolic content to my work. It is not like a chemical formula but like a chemical reaction. A good work of art, once it is offered in display and shown to other people, is a social fact.
Carl André (b.1935), U.S. artist: symposium at Wyndham College, Vermont, 30 April 1968, publ. in *Twentieth-Century Artists on Art* (ed. Dore Ashton, 1985)

2 Great symbols swallow us whole. They lead us on into themselves ... we pursue ... but we never capture their whole meaning. Not because the symbol is mindlessly obscure (though there are literary vices of this kind too) but because it is radically, authentically enigmatic.
Theodore Roszak (b.1933), U.S. social critic: *Where the Wasteland Ends* (1972), Ch.4

3 What the nuns told us in school when I was going to religious instruction was that we worship not the crucifix but Christ... We aren't supposed to worship the symbol or give it the same level of reverence that we give Christ because it's only a representation.
Andres Serrano (b.1950), U.S. photographer: on the depiction of the crucifix in his 1987 work, *Piss Christ*, in interview in the *Boston Globe*, 20 Aug. 1989, quoted in *Body and Soul* (ed. Brian Wallis, 1995), 'Andres Serrano: Invisible Power'. Serrano's

image caused enormous controversy in the United States and Britain

SYMPATHY

1 One cannot weep for the entire world, it is beyond human strength. One must choose.
(*On ne peut pas en verser sur tout le monde. C'est au-dessus des forces humaines. It faut choisir.*)
Jean Anouilh (1910–1987), French playwright: Le Chevalier, in *Cécile* (1951)

2 The force of truth that a statement imparts, then, its prominence among the hordes of recorded observations that I may optionally apply to my own life, depends, in addition to the sense that it is argumentatively defensible, on the sense that someone like me, and someone I like, whose voice is audible and who is at least notionally in the same room with me, does or can possibly hold it to be compellingly true.
Nicholson Baker (b.1957), U.S. author: *U and I: A True Story* (1991), Ch.4

3 When times get rough,
And friends just can't be found
Like a bridge over troubled water
I will lay me down.
Paul Simon (b.1949), U.S. singer and songwriter: 'Bridge Over Troubled Water' (song) on the album *Bridge Over Troubled Water* (Simon and Garfunkel, 1970)

4 I am those women. I am every one of them. And they are me. That's why we get along so well.
Oprah Winfrey (b.1954), U.S. chat-show host: quoted in *Oprah!* by Robert Waldron (1987), 'A Day with Oprah'

See also COMPASSION; Greene on MISERY; Elton on VICTIMS

TABOO

1 The type of fig leaf which each culture employs to cover its social taboos offers a twofold description of its morality. It reveals that certain unacknowledged behavior exists and it suggests the form that such behavior takes.
Freda Adler (b.1934), U.S. educator and author: *Sisters in Crime* (1975), Ch.3

2 I think the greatest taboos in America are faith and failure.
Michael Malone (b.1942), U.S. author: in *The Guardian* (London), 7 July 1989

3 Whenever a taboo is broken, something good happens, something vitalizing. ... Taboos after

all are only hangovers, the product of diseased minds, you might say, of fearsome people who hadn't the courage to live and who under the guise of morality and religion have imposed these things upon us.
Henry Miller (1891–1980), U.S. author: interview in *Writers at Work* (Second Series, ed. George Plimpton, 1963)

See also Tarantino on WORDS

TALENT

1 It takes little talent to see clearly what lies under one's nose, a good deal of it to know in which direction to point that organ.
W.H. Auden (1907–1973), Anglo-American poet: *The Dyer's Hand* (1962), Pt.1, 'Writing'

2 There are two kinds of talent, man-made talent and God-given talent. With man-made talent you have to work very hard. With God-given talent, you just touch it up once in a while.
Pearl Bailey (1918–1990), U.S. singer, writer and diplomat: in *Newsweek* (New York), 4 Dec. 1967

3 I don't believe that talented people today have less gifts than their artistic ancestors. The *times* are exhausted – stories come from the structure of ideas, ethics, beliefs, actualities of the times. Our *times* are exhausted – not our artists.
Francis Ford Coppola (b.1939), U.S. film-maker: quoted in *Coppola* by Peter Cowie (1989), Ch.8

4 Talent is an amalgam of high sensitivity; easy vulnerability; high sensory equipment (seeing, hearing, touching, smelling, tasting – *intensely*); a vivid imagination as well as a grip on reality; the desire to communicate one's own experience and sensations, to make one's self heard and seen.
Uta Hagen (b.1919), U.S. actress: *Respect for Acting* (1973), Pt.1, Ch.1

5 If you have this enormous talent, it's got you by the balls, it's a *demon*. You can't be a family man and a husband and a caring person and *be* that animal. Dickens wasn't that nice a guy.
Dustin Hoffman (b.1937), U.S. actor: in *Empire* (London), Aug. 1992

6 Everyone has talent. What is rare is the courage to follow the talent to the dark place where it leads.
Erica Jong (b.1942), U.S. author: 'The Artist as Housewife', publ. in *The First Ms. Reader* (ed. Francine Kragbrun, 1972)

7 I think this is the most extraordinary collection of talent, of human knowledge, that has ever been gathered together at the White House –

with the possible exception of when Thomas Jefferson dined alone.

John F. Kennedy (1917–1963), U.S. Democratic politician and president: remark at a dinner for Nobel prizewinners, 29 April 1962, Washington D.C., publ. in *Public Papers of the Presidents of the United States: John F. Kennedy, 1962*

8 Talent is cheaper than table salt. What separates the talented individual from the successful one is a lot of hard work.

Stephen King (b.1946), U.S. author: quoted in the *Independent on Sunday* (London), 10 March 1996

9 A man with a talent does what is expected of him, makes his way, constructs, is an engineer, a composer, a builder of bridges. It's the natural order of things that he construct objects outside himself and his family. The woman who does so is aberrant. ... We have to *expiate* for this cursed talent someone handed out to us, by mistake, in the black mystery of genetics.

May Sarton (b.1912), U.S. poet and novelist: Hilary Stevens, in *Mrs Stevens Hears the Mermaids Singing* (1965), Pt.2

10 Talent is a misfortune, for on the one hand it entitles a person to neither merit nor respect, and on the other it lays on him tremendous responsibilities; he is like the honest steward who has to protect the treasure entrusted to his keeping without ever making use of it.

Andrey Tarkovsky (1932–1986), Russian film-maker: journal entry, 14 Aug. 1971, publ. in *Time Within Time: The Diaries 1970–1986* (1989; tr.1994)

TASTE

1 Everyone has taste, yet it is more of a taboo subject than sex or money. The reason for this is simple: claims about your attitudes to or achievements in the carnal and financial arenas can be disputed only by your lover and your financial advisers, whereas by making statements about your taste you expose body and soul to terrible scrutiny. Taste is a merciless betrayer of social and cultural attitudes. Thus, while anybody will tell you as much (and perhaps more than) you want to know about their triumphs in bed and at the bank, it is taste that gets people's nerves tingling.

Stephen Bayley (b.1951), British design critic: *Taste* (1991), Pt.1, 'Taste: the Story of an Idea'

2 Common persists. It's not a distinction I'd want to be directed making but to myself I make it still. There are some lace (or more likely nylon) curtains popular nowadays that are gathered up for some reason in the middle. They look to me like a woman who's been to

the lav and got her underskirt caught up behind her.... They're common.

Alan Bennett (b.1934), British playwright: introduction to *Talking Heads* (1988)

3 Lovers of painting and lovers of music are people who openly display their preference like a delectable ailment that isolates them and makes them proud.

Maurice Blanchot (b.1907), French literary theorist and author: 'Reading', first publ. in *The Space of Literature* (1955), rep. in *The Gaze of Orpheus, & Other Literary Essays* (ed. P. Adams Sitney, 1981)

4 Bad taste is the key to the emerging seventies style, I think. In a changing world, amidst a bewildering welter of variables, at least you know where you are when you can evoke offence.

Angela Carter (1940–1992), British author: 'Ups and Downs for the Babes in Bondage', first publ. in *New Society* (London), 22 Dec. 1977, rep. in *The Faber Book of Pop* (ed. Hanif Kureishi and Jon Savage, 1995), Pt.7

5 Every orientation presupposes a disorientation.

Hans Magnus Enzensberger (b.1929), German poet and critic: 'Topological Studies in Modern Literature', publ. in *Sur* (Buenos Aires), May/June 1966

6 To achieve harmony in bad taste is the height of elegance.

Jean Genet (1910–1986), French playwright and novelist: *The Thief's Journal* (1949; tr.1965)

7 I like stuff that's cool, I don't like stuff that sucks.

Mike Judge (b.1963), U.S. musician: Butt-head, in *Beavis and Butt-head* (cartoon created and voiced by Mike Judge, written by Sam Johnson and Chris Marcil, shown on MTV from Sept. 1992)

8 Errors of taste are very often the outward sign of a deep fault of sensibility.

Jonathan Miller (b.1936), British doctor, humorist and director: in *The Guardian* (London), 21 May 1992

9 The English are the most tasteless nation on earth, which is why they set such store by it.

Joe Orton (1933–1967), British playwright: in the *Radio Times* (London), 29 Aug. 1964, quoted in *Prick Up Your Ears: the Biography of Joe Orton* by John Lahr (1978), Ch.4

10 Ah, good taste! What a dreadful thing! Taste is the enemy of creativeness.

Pablo Picasso (1881–1973), Spanish artist: quoted in *Quote* (Anderson, S.C.), 24 March 1957

11 The discovery of the good taste of bad taste can be very liberating. The man who insists on high and serious pleasures is depriving himself of pleasure; he continually restricts what he

can enjoy; in the constant exercise of his good taste he will eventually price himself out of the market, so to speak.

Susan Sontag (b.1933), U.S. essayist: 'Notes on "Camp"', Note 54 (1964), rep. in *Against Interpretation* (1966). 'Here Camp taste supervenes upon good taste as a daring and witty hedonism,' Sontag added. 'It makes the man of good taste cheerful, where before he ran the risk of being chronically frustrated. It is good for the digestion'

12 The hard truth is that what may be acceptable in elite culture may not be acceptable in mass culture, that tastes which pose only innocent ethical issues as the property of a minority become corrupting when they become more established. Taste is context, and the context has changed.

Susan Sontag: on the fashion for 'fascist art', in 'Fascinating Fascism' (1974), rep. in *Under the Sign of Saturn* (1980)

13 I think 'taste' is a social concept and not an artistic one. I'm willing to show good taste, if I can, in somebody else's living room, but our reading life is too short for a writer to be in any way polite. Since his words enter into another's brain in silence and intimacy, he should be as honest and explicit as we are with ourselves.

John Updike (b.1932), U.S. author and critic: interview in the *New York Times Book Review*, 10 April 1977, rep. in appendix to *Hugging the Shore* (1984)

See also CAMP; Auden on FRIENDS; Muggeridge on HUMOUR

TAXES

1 Read my lips: no new taxes.

George Bush (b.1924), U.S. Republican politician and president: acceptance speech, 18 Aug. 1988, New Orleans, quoted in the *New York Times*, 19 Aug. 1988. The expression, 'Read my lips', has been in general usage since at least the 1970s. Bush eventually raised taxes

2 Can't Pay? Won't Pay!
(*Non si paga, non si paga.*)

Dario Fo (b.1926), Italian dramatist: *Can't Pay? Won't Pay!* (play, 1974; tr.1978). The words were adopted as a slogan by anti-Poll-Tax protesters in Britain in the 1990s. The play's title was originally translated as *We Can't Pay? We Won't Pay!*

3 The fear of raising taxes is a matter of political error. Power has passed to the people who are conservative and comfortable and who are able to do without the public services which are so important to those in our central cities and to the poor. This is one of the great misfortunes of our time.

J.K. Galbraith (b.1908), U.S. economist: interview in *Singular Encounters* by Naim Attallah (1990), 'John Kenneth Galbraith'

4 We don't pay taxes. Only the little people pay taxes.

Leona Helmsley (b.1920), U.S. businesswoman: quoted by Helmsley's former housekeeper during her trial for tax evasion, as reported in the *New York Times*, 12 July 1989. Leona Helmsley was sentenced to four years' imprisonment in March 1992

5 Our tax law is a 1,598–page hydra-headed monster and I'm going to attack and attack and attack until I have ironed out every fault in it.

Vivien Kellems (1896–1975), U.S. industrialist and lecturer: quoted in the *Los Angeles Times*, 26 Jan. 1975

6 All money nowadays seems to be produced with a natural homing instinct for the Treasury.

Philip, Duke of Edinburgh (b.1921): quoted in *The Observer* (London), 26 May 1963

ELIZABETH TAYLOR

1 Elizabeth Taylor is pre-feminist woman. This is the source of her continuing greatness and relevance. She wields the sexual power that feminism cannot explain and has tried to destroy. Through stars like Taylor, we sense the world-disordering impact of legendary women like Delilah, Salome, and Helen of Troy.

Camille Paglia (b.1947), U.S. author and critic: 'Elizabeth Taylor: Hollywood's Pagan Queen', publ. in *Penthouse* (New York), March 1992, rep. in *Sex, Art, and American Culture* (1992). Paglia claims to have collected 599 pictures of Taylor during her teenage years

2 Liz Taylor, in being late fifty times and then early once, must be applying the same principle that I do by having my hair gray so when I do something with a normal amount of energy it seems 'young'. Liz Taylor when she's on time seems 'early'. It's like you get a new talent all of a sudden by being so bad at something for so long, and then suddenly one day being not quite so bad.

Andy Warhol (c.1928–1987), U.S. Pop artist: *From A to B and Back Again* (1975), Ch.7

TEA

1 The trouble with tea is that originally it was quite a good drink. So a group of the most eminent British scientists put their heads together, and made complicated biological experiments to find a way of spoiling it. To the

eternal glory of British science their labour bore fruit.

George Mikes (1912–1987), Hungarian-born British humorist: *How To Be an Alien* (1946), Ch.1, Sct.5

2 Our trouble is that we drink too much tea. I see in this the slow revenge of the Orient, which has diverted the Yellow River down our throats.

J.B. Priestley (1894–1984), British author: quoted in *The Observer* (London), 15 May 1949

TEACHERS

1 Teaching is not a lost art, but the regard for it is a lost tradition.

Jacques Barzun (b.1907), U.S. scholar: in *Newsweek* (New York), 5 Dec. 1955

2 Life is amazing: and the teacher had better prepare himself to be a medium for that amazement.

Edward Blishen (1920–1996), British author: *Donkey Work* (autobiography, 1983), Pt.2, Ch.5

3 There is no real teacher who in practice does not believe in the existence of the soul, or in a magic that acts on it through speech.

Allan Bloom (1930–1992), U.S. educator and author: preface to *The Closing of the American Mind* (1987)

4 Housework is a breeze. Cooking is a pleasant diversion. Putting up a retaining wall is a lark. But teaching is like climbing a mountain.

Fawn M. Brodie (1915–1981), U.S. biographer: quoted in the *Los Angeles Times Home Magazine*, 20 Feb. 1977

5 We teachers can only help the work going on, as servants wait upon a master.

Maria Montessori (1870–1952), Italian educationist: *The Absorbent Mind* (1949), Ch.1

6 Give me a girl at an impressionable age, and she is mine for life!

Muriel Spark (b.1918), British novelist: Miss Brodie, in *The Prime of Miss Jean Brodie* (1961), Ch.1

7 A teacher should have maximal authority, and minimal power.

Thomas Szasz (b.1920), U.S. psychiatrist: *The Second Sin* (1973), 'Education'

See also Gurdjieff on KNOWLEDGE

TECHNIQUE

1 Technique is communication: the two words are synonymous in conductors.

Leonard Bernstein (1918–1990), U.S. composer and conductor: in *The Times* (London), 27 June 1989

2 Do not pursue skills, technique will follow the idea. The idea will find technique, it is included in the real gift.

Bernard Leach (1887–1979), British potter: *The Potter's Challenge* (1976), Ch.1

3 Technique is the test of sincerity. If a thing isn't worth getting the technique to say, it is of inferior value.

Ezra Pound (1885–1972), U.S. poet and critic: interview in *Writers at Work* (Second Series, ed. George Plimpton, 1963)

TECHNOLOGY

1 Technology is making gestures precise and brutal, and with them men. It expels from movements all hesitation, deliberation, civility.

Theodor W. Adorno (1903–1969), German philosopher, sociologist and music critic: *Minima Moralia* (1951: tr. G.F.N. Jephcott, 1978), Ch.19

2 Science and technology multiply around us. To an increasing extent they dictate the languages in which we speak and think. Either we use those languages, or we remain mute.

J.G. Ballard (b.1930), British author: introduction (1974) to the French edition of *Crash* (1973)

3 Technology ... is one aspect of today that is truly fresh and brimming with new tunes and story turns. ... So there is and can be *content* in technology – new tunes we've never heard before because they've never been possible before.

Francis Ford Coppola (b.1939), U.S. film-maker: quoted in *Coppola* by Peter Cowie (1989), Ch.8

4 I've never met anyone who has entered the technological realm and not come out of it happier, enhanced and more fulfilled.

Douglas Coupland (b.1961), Canadian author: *Without Walls: J'Accuse – Technonerds*, Channel 4, 19 March 1996

5 If we had a reliable way to label our toys good and bad, it would be easy to regulate technology wisely. But we can rarely see far enough ahead to know which road leads to damnation. Whoever concerns himself with big technology, either to push it forward or to stop it, is gambling in human lives.

Freeman Dyson (b.1923), British-born U.S. physicist and author: *Disturbing the Universe* (1979), Pt.1, Ch.1

6 Technology ... the knack of so arranging the world that we don't have to experience it.

Max Frisch (1911–1991), Swiss author and architect: Hanna, in *Homo Faber* (1957; tr.1959), 'Second Stop'

7 If there is technological advance without social advance, there is, almost automatically, an

increase in human misery, in impoverishment.

Michael Harrington (1928–1989), U.S. social scientist and author: *The Other America* (1962), appendix, Sct.1

8 Space-ships and time machines are no escape from the human condition. Let Othello subject Desdemona to a lie-detector test; his jealousy will still blind him to the evidence. Let Oedipus triumph over gravity; he won't triumph over his fate.

Arthur Koestler (1905–1983), Hungarian-born British novelist and essayist: 'The Boredom of Fantasy' (1953), rep. in *The Trail of the Dinosaur* (1955), Pt.2

9 Persons grouped around a fire or candle for warmth or light are less able to pursue independent thoughts, or even tasks, than people supplied with electric light. In the same way, the social and educational patterns latent in automation are those of self-employment and artistic autonomy.

Marshall McLuhan (1911–1980), Canadian communications theorist: *Understanding Media* (1964), Ch.33

10 By his very success in inventing labor-saving devices, modern man has manufactured an abyss of boredom that only the privileged classes in earlier civilizations have ever fathomed.

Lewis Mumford (1895–1990), U.S. social philosopher: *The Conduct of Life* (1951), 'The Challenge of Renewal'

11 When you see something that is technically sweet, you go ahead and do it and you argue about what to do about it only after you have had your technical success. That is the way it was with the atomic bomb.

J. Robert Oppenheimer (1904–1967), U.S. physicist: said during hearings investigating allegations of past communist associations, in connection with Oppenheimer's involvement in the Los Alamos project to develop the atomic bomb, publ. in *In the Matter of J. Robert Oppenheimer, USAEC Transcript of Hearing Before Personnel Security Board* (1954), p.81

12 Technology is not an image of the world but a way of operating on reality. The nihilism of technology lies not only in the fact that it is the most perfect expression of the will to power ... but also in the fact that it lacks meaning.

Octavio Paz (b.1914), Mexican poet and essayist: *Alternating Current* (1967), 'The Channel and the Signs'

13 The Church welcomes technological progress and receives it with love, for it is an indubitable fact that technological progress comes from God and, therefore, can and must lead to Him.

Pope Pius XII [Eugenio Pacelli] (1876–1958), Italian ecclesiastic: Christmas message, 1953, publ. in *The Harvest of a Quiet Eye* (ed. Alan L. Mackay, 1977)

14 There are three roads to ruin; women, gambling and technicians. The most pleasant is with women, the quickest is with gambling, but the surest is with technicians.

Georges Pompidou (1911–1974), French politician and president: quoted in *The Sunday Telegraph* (London), 26 May 1968

15 We can no more afford to see ourselves as unavoidably victims of technological development than as happy beneficiaries of a future that has already been planned and exploited. Such an attitude does not lead to empowerment.

Andrew Ross (b.1956), British social theorist: *Strange Weather* (1991), Ch.3

16 I have no doubt that it is possible to give a new direction to technological development, a direction that shall lead it back to the real needs of man, and that also means: *to the actual size of man.* Man is small, and, therefore, small is beautiful. To go for giantism is to go for self-destruction.

E.F. Schumacher (1911–1977), German-born British economist: *Small is Beautiful* (1973), Pt.2, Ch.10

17 Imagine an alcoholic sitting with a barrel of wine in front of him. Suppose he starts saying to himself, 'Wine isn't bad for you if used in moderation. Why, they say small amounts of wine are even good for you! It won't do me any harm if I take just one little drink...' Well you know what is going to happen. Never forget that the human race with technology is just like an alcoholic with a barrel of wine.

Unabomber, U.S. radical: *Industrial Society and Its Future*, 'Strategy', Sct.203, publ. in the *Washington Post*, 19 Sept. 1995

18 The only points on which we absolutely insist are that the single overriding goal must be the elimination of modern technology, and that no other goal can be allowed to compete with this one.

Unabomber: *Industrial Society and Its Future*, 'Strategy', Sct.206, publ. in the *Washington Post*, 19 Sept. 1995

19 The white heat of the technological revolution.

Harold Wilson (1916–1995), British Labour politician and prime minister: quoted in *Sayings of the Century* by Nigel Rees (1984), 'Prime Ministers: A Word from No.10'. The actual words spoken by Wilson, in a speech to the Labour Party Conference in Scarborough, 1 Oct. 1963, were: 'We are redefining and we are restating our socialism in terms of the scientific revolution.... The Britain that is going to be forged in the white heat of this revolution will be no place for restrictive practices or for outdated methods on either side of industry.' Wilson succeeded in associating his government with technological innovation, in contrast to the perceived old-fashioned ideas in the Conservative Party.

See also COMPUTER TECHNOLOGY; Sterling on THE 1980S

TEENAGERS

1   What promises does maturity hold for a teenager: a dull job, a dull life, television, freezers, babies and baby sitters, a guaranteed annual wage, taxes, social security, hospitalization insurance, and death.

Pauline Kael (b.1919), U.S. film critic: *I Lost it at the Movies* (1965), 'The Glamour of Delinquency'

2   Remember that as a teenager you are at the last stage in your life when you will be happy to hear that the phone is for you.

Fran Lebowitz (b.1951), U.S. journalist: *Social Studies* (1981), 'Tips for Teens'

3   Having a thirteen-year-old in the family is like having a general-admission ticket to the movies, radio and TV. You get to understand that the glittering new arts of our civilization are directed to the teen-agers, and by their suffrage they stand or fall.

Max Lerner (1902–1992), U.S. author and columnist: 'Teen-ager', first publ. in the *New York Post*, 4 June 1952, rep. in *The Unfinished Country* (1959), Pt.1

4   Ahead
lay our fifteenth birthdays,
acne, deodorants, crabs, salves,
butch haircuts, draft registration,
the military and political victories
of Dwight Eisenhower, who brought us
Richard Nixon with wife and dog.
Any wonder we tried gin.

Philip Levine (b.1928), U.S. poet: 'Gin', publ. in *What Work Is* (1991)

5   No doubt about it: teenagers – in some senses, at any rate – ripen more quickly than they used to.

Colin MacInnes (1914–1976), British author: 'Pop Songs and Teenagers', publ. in *Twentieth Century* (London), Feb. 1958, rep. in *England, Half English* (1961)

6   This teenage ball had had a real splendour in the days when the kids discovered that, for the first time since centuries of kingdom-come, they'd money, which hitherto had always been denied to us at the best time in life to use it, namely, when you're young and strong, and also before the newspapers and telly got hold of this teenage fable and prostituted it as conscripts seem to do to everything they touch.

Yes, I tell you, it had a real savage splendour in the days when we found that no one couldn't sit on our faces any more because we'd loot to spend at last, and our world was to be our world, the one we wanted and not standing on the doorstep of somebody else's waiting for honey, perhaps.

Colin MacInnes: the narrator in *Absolute Beginners* (1959), 'in June'

7   Teenage boys, goaded by their surging hormones ... run in packs like the primal horde. They have only a brief season of exhilarating liberty between control by their mothers and control by their wives.

Camille Paglia (b.1947), U.S. author and critic: 'Homosexuality at the Fin de Siècle', first publ. in *Esquire* (New York), Oct. 1991, rep. in *Sex, Art, and American Culture* (1992)

8   All over the world people were in love with the life of the American teenager. It was so much freer than it was anywhere else. Anything the young wanted to do they could do in an automobile. On Saturday nights the drive-in was the automobile meeting ground where carloads of boys and girls would go to do anything from picking up each other to picking a fight.

Tom Wolfe (b.1931), U.S. author and journalist: of the U.S. in the 1950s, quoted in *The Fifties* by Peter Lewis (1978), 'Youthquake'

See also ADOLESCENCE

TEETH

1   Americans may have no identity, but they do have wonderful teeth.

Jean Baudrillard (b.1929), French semiologist: *America* (1986; tr.1988), 'Astral America'

2   I had very good dentures once. Some magnificent gold work. It's the only form of jewelry a man can wear that women fully appreciate.

Graham Greene (1904–1991), British novelist: Mr Visconti, in *Travels With My Aunt* (1969), Pt.2, Ch.7

3   Some were kicked out, most of them rotted away. I don't fancy having clean white totally regular teeth. I think they look stupid.

Shane MacGowan (b.1957), Anglo-Irish rock musician: interview in *The Face* (London), Nov. 1994

TELEVISION

1   Many inmates use TV as an umbilical cord, a psychological connection to the world they have lost. They depend on it, in the way that lonely people turn to TV for the illusion of companionship, and they dread separation

from it. For many, loss of TV is too high a price to pay for any show to resistance.

Mumia Abu-Jamal (b.1954), U.S. journalist and environmentalist: *Live from Death Row* (1995), Pt.1, 'Teetering on the brink between life and death'

2 There is nothing more mysterious than a TV set left on in an empty room. It is even stranger than a man talking to himself or a woman standing dreaming at her stove. It is as if another planet is communicating with you.

Jean Baudrillard (b.1929), French semiologist: *America* (1986; tr.1988), 'Astral America'

3 TV is the principal source of the noise peculiar to our time – an illuminated noise that claims our attention not in order to concentrate it but to disperse it. Watching the tube, we are induced to focus on nothing in particular.

Saul Bellow (b.1915), U.S. novelist: *It All Adds Up* (1994), 'The Distracted Public'

4 Sometimes, because of its immediacy, television produces a kind of electronic parable. Berlin, for instance, on the day the Wall was opened. Rostropovich was playing his cello by the Wall that no longer cast a shadow, and a million East Berliners were thronging to the West to shop with an allowance given them by West German banks! At that moment the whole world saw how materialism had lost its awesome historic power and become a shopping list.

John Berger (b.1926), British author and critic: 'The Soul and the Operator', first publ. in *Expressen* (Stockholm), 19 March 1990, rep. in *Keeping a Rendezvous* (1992)

5 It's like a kaleidoscope. No matter how many little colours you put in it, that kaleidoscope will make those colours have a pattern ... and that's what happens with TV – it doesn't matter who puts what in the TV, by the end of the year there's a whole format that the TV put together. The TV puts over its own plan.

David Bowie (b.1947), British rock musician: interview, Aug. 1975, rep. in *Bowie In His Own Words* (ed. Miles, 1980), 'Politics'

6 Television's perfect. You turn a few knobs, a few of those mechanical adjustments at which the higher apes are so proficient, and lean back and drain your mind of all thought. And there you are watching the bubbles in the primeval ooze. You don't have to concentrate. You don't have to react. You don't have to remember. You don't miss your brain because you don't need it. Your heart and liver and lungs continue to function normally. Apart from that, all is peace and quiet. You are in the man's nirvana. And if some poor nasty minded person comes along and says you look like a fly on a can of garbage, pay him no mind. He probably hasn't got the price of a television set.

Raymond Chandler (1880–1959), U.S. author: letter, 22 Nov. 1950, publ. in *Raymond Chandler Speaking* (ed. Dorothy Gardiner and Kathrine S. Walker, 1962)

7 You can always tell a detective on TV. He never takes his hat off.

Raymond Chandler: Philip Marlowe, in *Playback* (1958), Ch.14

8 What is a television apparatus to man, who has only to shut his eyes to see the most inaccessible regions of the seen and the never seen, who has only to imagine in order to pierce through walls and cause all the planetary Baghdads of his dreams to rise from the dust?

Salvador Dali (1904–1989), Spanish painter: *The Secret Life of Salvador Dali* (1948), Ch.11

9 Television thrives on unreason, and unreason thrives on television. It strikes at the emotions rather than the intellect.

Robin Day (b.1915), British broadcaster: in the *Financial Times* (London), 8 Nov. 1989

10 You have debased [my] child.... You have made him a laughing-stock of intelligence ... a stench in the nostrils of the gods of the ionosphere.

Lee De Forest (1873–1961), U.S. inventor of the audion tube: speech to National Association of Broadcasters, quoted in obituary in *Time* (New York), 7 July 1961

11 So why do people keep on watching? The answer, by now, should be perfectly obvious: we love television because television brings us a world in which television does not exist. In fact, deep in their hearts, this is what the spuds crave most: a rich, new, participatory life.

Barbara Ehrenreich (b.1941), U.S. author and columnist: of 'couch potatoes', in 'Spudding Out' (1988), rep. in *The Worst Years of Our Lives* (1991)

12 It is a medium of entertainment which permits millions of people to listen to the same joke at the same time, and yet remain lonesome.

T.S. Eliot (1888–1965), Anglo-American poet and critic: in the *New York Post*, 22 Sept. 1963

13 Let's face it, there are no plain women on television.

Anna Ford (b.1943), British radio and television journalist: quoted in *The Observer* (London), 23 Sept. 1979

14 TV is the place
Where the pursuit of happiness has become
   the pursuit of trivia
Where toothpaste and cars have become sex
   objects
Where imagination is sucked out of children
   by a cathode ray nipple.
TV is the only wet nurse that would create a
   cripple.

Television, the drug of the nation,
Breeding ignorance and feeding radiation.

Michael Franti, U.S. rapper: 'Television, The
Drug of the Nation' (song) on the album *Hypocrisy is
the Greatest Luxury* (Disposable Heroes of
Hiphoprisy, 1992)

15 Hello, good evening, and welcome.

David Frost (b.1939), British broadcaster: *The
Frost Report* (TV show, 1966–67). The words were
used to open each show as well as subsequent Frost
series

16 A three- to four- to five-hour experience with
nothingness.

Frederic Glezer (b.1937), U.S. literacy lobbyist and
librarian: on watching TV, quoted in *Newsweek*
(New York), 1 Dec. 1986

17 The BBC keeps us all honest.

Michael Grade (b.1943), British broadcasting
executive, head of Channel 4: quoted in the
Independent on Sunday (London), 19 Feb. 1995

18 The invention of television can be compared to
the introduction of indoor plumbing. Fundamentally it brought no change in the public's
habits. It simply eliminated the necessity of
leaving the house.

Alfred Hitchcock (1899–1980), British film-maker:
Screen Producers Guild dinner, 7 March 1965, publ.
in *Hitchcock on Hitchcock* (ed. Sidney Gottlieb,
1995), 'After-Dinner Speech'

19 Television has brought back murder into the
home – where it belongs.

Alfred Hitchcock: quoted in *The Observer*
(London), 19 Dec. 1965

20 Television is becoming a collage – there are so
many channels that you move through them
making a collage yourself. In that sense, everyone sees something a bit different.

David Hockney (b.1937), British artist: *Hockney On
Photography* (ed. Wendy Brown, 1988), 'New York:
November 1985'

21 The contest between education and TV –
between argument and conviction by spectacle
– has been won by television.

Robert Hughes (b.1938), Australian author and
critic: *Culture of Complaint* (1993), Ch.1

22 Most of us no longer watch television; we
graze, zapping back and forth between channels whenever our boredom threshold is
triggered. No one does any one thing at a time.
A new culture has taken shape which caters for
people with the attention span of a flea.

Michael Ignatieff (b.1947), Canadian author and
critic: *Three Minute Culture*, BBC 2, 15 Jan. 1989

23 Anyone afraid of what he thinks television does
to the world is probably just afraid of the
world.

Clive James (b.1939), Australian writer and critic:
introduction to *Glued to the Box* (1983)

24 Watching old movies is like spending an evening with those people next door. They bore us,
and we wouldn't go out of our way to see them;
we drop in on them because they're so close. If
it took some effort to see old movies, we might
try to find out which were the good ones, and if
people saw only the good ones maybe they
would still respect old movies. As it is, people
sit and watch movies that audiences walked out
on thirty years ago. Like Lot's wife, we are
tempted to take another look, attracted not by
evil but by something that seems much more
shameful – our own innocence.

Pauline Kael (b.1919), U.S. film critic: *Kiss Kiss
Bang Bang* (1968), 'Movies on Television'

25 Television, despite its enormous presence,
turns out to have added pitifully few lines to
the communal memory.

Justin Kaplan (b.1925), U.S. literary historian,
biographer and editor: on editing the new (1992)
edition of *Bartlett's Familiar Quotations*, quoted in
The Observer (London), 9 June 1991

26 There's a good deal in common between the
mind's eye and the TV screen, and though the
TV set has all too often been the boobtube, it
could be, it can be, the box of dreams.

Ursula K. Le Guin (b.1929), U.S. author: 'Working
on "The Lathe"', publ. in *Horizon* (New York),
1980, rep. in *Dancing at the Edge of the World*
(1989)

27 Do not, on a rainy day, ask your child what he
feels like doing, because I assure you that what
he feels like doing, you won't feel like watching.

Fran Lebowitz (b.1951), U.S. journalist: *Social
Studies* (1981), 'Parental Guidance'

28 The difference between writing a book and
being on television is the difference between
conceiving a child and having a baby made in a
test tube.

Norman Mailer (b.1923), U.S. author: 'The Siege
of Mailer: Hero to Historian', first publ. in *Village
Voice* (New York), 21 Jan. 1971, rep. in
Conversations with Norman Mailer (ed. J. Michael
Lennon, 1988)

29 In the theater, while you recognized that you
were looking at a house, it was a house in
quotation marks. On screen, the quotation
marks tend to be blotted out by the camera.

Arthur Miller (b.1915), U.S. playwright: on a
television production of *Death of a Salesman*, in the
New York Times, 15 Sept. 1985

30 Television was not invented to make human
beings vacuous, but is an emanation of their
vacuity.

Malcolm Muggeridge (1903–1990), British
journalist and broadcaster: *Tread Softly For You
Tread on My Jokes* (1966), 'I Like Dwight'

31 Much of what passes for quality on British television is no more than a reflection of the narrow elite which controls it and has always thought that its tastes were synonymous with quality.
Rupert Murdoch (b.1931), Australian-born U.S. media tycoon: address to the 1989 Edinburgh Television Festival, quoted in *The Guardian* (London), 1 Jan. 1990

32 Man watches his history on the screen with apathy and an occasional passing flicker of horror or indignation.
Conor Cruise O'Brien (b.1917), Irish historian, diplomat and critic: quoted in the *Irish Times* (Dublin), 16 July 1969

33 The television screen, so unlike the movie screen, sharply reduced human beings, revealed them as small, trivial, flat, in two banal dimensions, drained of color. Wasn't there something reassuring about it! – that human beings were in fact merely images of a kind registered in one another's eyes and brains, phenomena composed of microscopic flickering dots like atoms. They *were* atoms – nothing more. A quick switch of the dial and they disappeared and who could lament the loss?
Joyce Carol Oates (b.1938), U.S. author: *You Must Remember This* (1987), Pt.1, Ch.13

34 Television is actually closer to reality than anything in books. The madness of TV is the madness of human life.
Camille Paglia (b.1947), U.S. author and critic: in *Harper's Magazine* (New York), March 1991

35 Already we Viewers, when not viewing, have begun to whisper to one another that the more we elaborate our means of communication, the less we communicate.
J.B. Priestley (1894–1984), British author: *Thoughts in the Wilderness* (1957), 'Televiewing'

36 The great networks are there to prove that ideas can be canned like spaghetti. If everything ends up by tasting like everything else, is that not the evidence that it has been properly cooked?
Frederic Raphael (b.1931), British author and critic: 'The Language of Television', publ. in *The State of the Language* (ed. Christopher Ricks, 1980)

37 TV is not where truly innovative ideas end up any more. Why? Because TV isn't fun any more and fun is where ideas breed. A terminal blight has hit the TV industry nipping fun in the bud and stunting our growth. This blight is management – the dreaded Four Ms: male, middle class, middle-aged and mediocre.
Janet Street-Porter (b.1946), British broadcaster and programme-maker: MacTaggart Lecture, Edinburgh Television Festival, 25 Aug. 1995, publ. in *The Guardian* (London), 26 Aug. 1995

38 For me the British Broadcasting Corporation might have better called itself the Stateless Persons Broadcasting Corporation for it certainly did not reflect the mood of the British people who finance it.
Norman Tebbit (b.1931), British Conservative politician: on the BBC's coverage of the Falklands War, in *Upwardly Mobile* (1988), Ch.8

39 It is on – like the light. The ordinary viewer ... he, she, we, the moblike broken family, goes back and forth, like leopards in our cage, while TV is 'on', six or seven hours a day. The world works by way of TV: that is where marketing occurs; that is how politicians play at running the country; and that is where news is defined and focused. It is lamentable, if you want to take that view. Though I suspect a greater damage to our culture and our ideas came earlier, in permitting photography. That was the first great drug, and it trained us for the others.
David Thomson (b.1941), British author and film critic: *A Biographical Dictionary of Film* (1975; rev.1994), 'Dennis Potter'

40 If we had had the right technology back then, you would have seen Eva Braun on the Donahue show and Adolf Hitler on Meet the Press.
Ed Turner (b.1935), U.S. TV executive and author: quoted in *The Daily Telegraph* (London), 5 Sept. 1990

41 I hate television. I hate it as much as peanuts. But I can't stop eating peanuts.
Orson Welles (1915–1985), U.S. film-maker and actor: in the *New York Herald Tribune*, 12 Oct. 1956

42 Television hangs on the questionable theory that whatever happens anywhere should be sensed everywhere. If everyone is going to be able to see everything, in the long run all sights may lose whatever rarity value they once possessed, and it may well turn out that people, being able to see and hear practically everything, will be specially interested in almost nothing.
E.B. White (1899–1985), U.S. author and editor: 'Television', first publ. in the *New Yorker*, 4 Dec. 1948, rep. in *Writings from the New Yorker 1927–1976* (ed. Rebecca M. Dale, 1991)

43 What do a few lies on TV matter? They can be swallowed, digested and excreted, or follow people when they doze off to sink into oblivion.
Zhang Jie (b.1937), Chinese author: Teacher Li, in *As Long as Nothing Happens, Nothing Will* (1988), 'What's Wrong with Him?'

See also CHAT SHOWS; Raphael on CRITICS; Allen on LIFE; SOAP OPERAS; White on SPONSORSHIP

TENNIS *see under* SPORT

TERRORISM

1 It's not the bullet with my name on it that worries me. It's the one that says 'To whom it may concern'.
Anonymous Belfast resident: quoted in *The Guardian* (London), 16 Oct. 1991

2 I have always denounced terrorism. I must also denounce a terrorism which is exercised blindly, in the streets of Algiers for example, and which some day could strike my mother or my family. I believe in justice, but I shall defend my mother above justice.
Albert Camus (1913–1962), French-Algerian philosopher and author: debate at University of Stockholm, 1957, quoted in *Camus, A Biography* by Herbert R. Lottman (1979), Pt.5, Ch.45. Camus received much criticism for his remarks, taken as a betrayal of the struggle for Algerian independence

3 After seeing *Rambo* last night I know what to do next time this happens.
Ronald Reagan (b.1911), U.S. Republican politician and president: following the hijack of an aeroplane carrying U.S. passengers in 1985, quoted in *City Limits* (London), 16 Dec. 1987. *Rambo* star Sylvester Stallone was quoted in the *Sunday Express*, 17 July 1988, as saying, 'When President Reagan stood up and said: "Having seen *Rambo* I know what to do with Libya", it was the kiss of death. He made Rambo a Republican.' *See* Stallone on CINEMA: SEX AND VIOLENCE

4 The terrible thing about terrorism is that ultimately it destroys those who practise it. Slowly but surely, as they try to extinguish life in others, the light within them dies.
Terry Waite (b.1939), British religious adviser and hostage in Lebanon: in *The Guardian* (London), 20 Feb. 1992

5 Fighting terrorism is like being a goalkeeper. You can make a hundred brilliant saves but the only shot that people remember is the one that gets past you.
Paul Wilkinson (b.1937), British scholar and author on terrorism: in *The Daily Telegraph* (London), 1 Sept. 1992

TEXAS *see under* THE UNITED STATES

MARGARET THATCHER

1 Sexuality is ... an underrated factor in her appeal (or repellence). Envy of it among women, consciousness of its unavailability among men, retains power even when advancing age should have disposed of it. But Mrs Thatcher's enemies cannot admit it in those terms and call her cold, unsympathetic, schoolmarmish, suburban, etc.
Kingsley Amis (1922–1995), British novelist and poet: *Memoirs* (1991), 'Margaret Thatcher'

2 What Mrs Thatcher did for women was to demonstrate that if a woman had enough desire she could do what she wanted, do anything a man could do.... Mrs Thatcher did not have one traditional feminine cell in her body.
Julie Burchill (b.1960), British journalist and author: *Damaged Gods* (1986), 'Born again Cows'

3 I am not prepared to accept the economics of a housewife.
Jacques Chirac (b.1932), French politician and prime minister: of Margaret Thatcher, quoted in *The Sunday Times* (London), 27 Dec. 1987

4 She's made a new class of spiv. Now, whether the spiv would have risen without Mrs Thatcher I don't know, but she has given the green light to spivvery.
Nigel Dempster (b.1941), British journalist: interview in *Singular Encounters* by Naim Attallah (1990), 'Nigel Dempster'

5 For us she is not the iron lady. She is the kind, dear Mrs Thatcher.
Alexander Dubček (1921–1992), Czechoslovakian politician: quoted in the *Independent on Sunday* (London), 30 Dec. 1990

6 She's the best man in England.
Ronald Reagan (b.1911), U.S. Republican politician and president: said to reporters, quoted in *The Observer* (London), 16 Jan. 1983

7 She really is a woman just like my mum.
Cliff Richard (b.1940), British singer: in *The Guardian* (London), 17 Aug. 1988

8 Gradually it was becoming clear that she was a Prime Minister unlike any since Churchill. Nonetheless, the 'wets', the weaker willed, the craven-hearted and the embittered failures amongst the Conservative Party still hoped she would go away and let them go back to their old ways.
Norman Tebbit (b.1931), British Conservative politician: on Mrs Thatcher's record by the summer of 1981, in *Upwardly Mobile* (memoirs, 1988), Ch.8

9 To those waiting with bated breath for that favourite media catchphrase, the U-turn, I have only this to say. You turn, if you want; the lady's not for turning.
Margaret Thatcher (b.1925), British Conservative politician and prime minister: speech to the Conservative Party Conference, Brighton, 10 Oct. 1980, publ. in *The Times* (London), 11 Oct. 1980. The phrase is a play on the title *The Lady's not for Burning* by Christopher Fry (play, 1946)

See also Bennett on CHURCHES

THEATRE

1   The theatre
    is the state
    the place
    the point
    where we can get hold of man's anatomy and
    through it heal and dominate life.
    Antonin Artaud (1896–1948), French theatre
    producer, actor and theorist: *Aliéner l'Acteur*, 12
    May 1947, rep. in *Artaud* by Martin Esslin (1976),
    Ch.4

2   Drama is based on the Mistake. I think some-
    one is my friend when he really is my enemy,
    that I am free to marry a woman when in fact
    she is my mother, that this person is a cham-
    bermaid when it is a young nobleman in
    disguise, that this well-dressed young man is
    rich when he is really a penniless adventurer,
    or that if I do this such and such a result will
    follow when in fact it results in something very
    different. All good drama has two movements,
    first the making of the mistake, then the
    discovery that it was a mistake.
    W.H. Auden (1907–1973), Anglo-American poet:
    The Dyer's Hand (1962), Pt.8, 'Notes on Music And
    Opera'

3   The theatre is a gross art, built in sweeps and
    over-emphasis. Compromise is its second
    name.
    Enid Bagnold (1889–1981), British novelist and
    playwright: *Autobiography* (1969), Ch.3

4   It's one of the tragic ironies of the theatre that
    only one man in it can count on steady work –
    the night watchman.
    Tallulah Bankhead (1903–1968), U.S. actress:
    Tallulah (1952), Ch.1

5   I can't do the same thing every night, the same
    gestures ... it's like putting on dirty panties
    every day.
    Brigitte Bardot (b.1934), French actor: of acting in
    the theatre, quoted in *Bébé: The Films of Brigitte
    Bardot* by Tony Crawley (1975), 'The BBeginning'

6   I submit all my plays to the National Theatre
    for rejection. To assure myself I am seeing
    clearly.
    Howard Barker (b.1946), British poet and
    playwright: in *The Guardian* (London), 13 Feb.
    1992

7   We need a type of theatre which not only
    releases the feelings, insights and impulses
    possible within the particular historical field of
    human relations in which the action takes
    place, but employs and encourages those
    thoughts and feelings which help transform
    the field itself.
    Bertolt Brecht (1898–1956), German playwright
    and poet: 'A Short Organum for the Theatre',

para.35 (1949), rep. in *Brecht on Theatre* (ed. and tr.
John Willett, 1964)

8   Let's face it, sweetheart, without Jews, fags,
    and Gypsies, there is no theatre.
    Mel Brooks (b.1926), U.S. film-maker and actor:
    Frederick Bronski (Brooks), in *To Be or Not To Be*
    (film; screenplay by Thomas Meehan and Ronny
    Graham, directed by Alan Johnson, 1983; a remake
    of Ernst Lubitsch's 1942 film of the same title)

9   The primary function of a theater is not to
    please itself, or even to please its audience. It is
    to serve talent.
    Robert Brustein (b.1927), U.S. stage director,
    author and critic: *Who Needs Theatre?* (1987), Pt.3,
    'The Humanist and the Artist'

10 The stage is life, music, beautiful girls, legs,
    breasts, not talk or intellectualism or dried-up
    academics.
    Harold Clurman (1901–1980), U.S. stage director
    and critic: quoted in *Who Needs Theatre?* by Robert
    Brustein (1987), Pt.1, 'The Vitality of Harold
    Clurman'

11 Theater people are always pining and agoniz-
    ing because they're afraid that they'll be for-
    gotten. And in America they're quite right.
    They will be.
    Agnes De Mille (1908–1993), U.S. choreographer
    and dancer: quoted in *Life* (New York), 15 Nov. 1963

12 One of the complaints made by the orthodox
    supporters of the arts on the right is that right-
    wing plays are never put on. The answer is
    simple. There aren't any right-wing plays. Go
    and search for them.
    Lord Goodman (1913–1995), British lawyer and
    public figure: interview in *Singular Encounters* by
    Naim Attallah (1990), 'Lord Goodman'

13 The theatre is the best way of showing the gap
    between what is said and what is seen to be
    done, and that is why, ragged and gap-toothed
    as it is, it has still a far healthier potential than
    some poorer, abandoned arts.
    David Hare (b.1947), British playwright: 'The
    Playwright as Historian', publ. in *The Sunday Times*
    (London), 26 Nov. 1978

14 I think theatre should always be somewhat
    suspect.
    Václav Havel (b.1936), Czech playwright and
    president: *Disturbing the Peace* (1986; tr.1990), Ch.2

15 If you want to see your plays performed the
    way you wrote them, become President.
    Václav Havel: speech to Institute of Contemporary
    Arts, London, quoted in *The Independent* (London),
    24 March 1990

16 The novel is more of a whisper, whereas the
    stage is a shout.
    Robert Holman (b.1936), British playwright: in
    The Independent (London), 8 Oct. 1990

17 I write plays for people who wouldn't be seen dead in the theatre.

Barrie Keeffe (b.1945), British playwright: in the *Evening Standard* (London), 8 June 1989

18 The art of the theater is action. It is the study of commitment. The word is an act. To *say* the word in such a way as to make it heard and understood by all in the theater is a commitment – it is the highest art to see a human being out on a stage speaking to a thousand of his or her peers saying, 'These words which I am speaking are the *truth* – they are not an approximation of any kind. They are the God's truth, and I support them with my life,' which is what the actor does on stage. Without this commitment, acting becomes prostitution and writing becomes advertising.

David Mamet (b.1947), U.S. playwright: *Writing in Restaurants* (1986), 'Against Amplification'

19 By whatever means it is accomplished, the prime business of a play is to arouse the passions of its audience so that by the route of passion may be opened up new relationships between a man and men, and between men and Man. Drama is akin to the other inventions of man in that it ought to help us to know more, and not merely to spend our feelings.

Arthur Miller (b.1915), U.S. playwright: introduction, Sct.7, to *Collected Plays* (1958)

20 A playwright ... is ... the litmus paper of the arts. He's got to be, because if he isn't working on the same wave length as the audience, no one would know what in hell he was talking about. He is a kind of psychic journalist, even when he's great.

Arthur Miller: interview in the *Paris Review* (Flushing, N.Y.), summer 1966

21 The drama's altar isn't on the stage: it is candle-sticked and flowered in the box office. There is the gold, though there be no frankincense or myrrh; and the gospel for the day always The Play will Run for a Year. The Dove of Inspiration, of the desire for inspiration, has flown away from it; and on its roof, now, the commonplace crow caws candidly.

Sean O'Casey (1884–1964), Irish playwright: *Sunset and Evening Star* (sixth volume of autobiography, 1954), 'And Evening Star'

22 I always say to myself that the theatre is the Temple of Dionysus, and not Apollo. You do the Dionysus thing on your typewriter, and then you allow a little Apollo in, just a little to shape and guide it along certain lines you may want to go along. But you can't allow Apollo in completely.

Joe Orton (1933–1967), British playwright: interview on BBC Radio, 28 July 1964, quoted in *Prick Up Your Ears: the Biography of Joe Orton* by John Lahr (1978), Ch.1

23 Inside every playwright there is a Falstaff, gathering like a boil to be lanced by his liege employers – fashion and caprice.

John Osborne (1929–1994), British playwright: *Almost a Gentleman* (1991), Ch.18

24 Ideas emerge from plays, not the other way round.

Sam Shepard (b.1943), U.S. playwright and actor: 'Language, Visualization and the Inner Library', publ. in *American Dreams* (ed. Bonnie Marranca, 1981)

25 If a playwright tried to see eye to eye with everybody, he would get the worst case of strabismus since Hannibal lost an eye trying to count his nineteen elephants during a snowstorm while crossing the Alps.

James Thurber (1894–1961), U.S. humorist and illustrator: in the *New York Times*, 21 Feb. 1960

26 One of the things that I promised myself that we might see at this theatre was that drama should be re-established to the same level of eminence that it attained with the Greeks; that the theatre should be a place where great matters of public concern were presented.... In these days, when the churches are empty, there is nowhere except the theatre where such matters can be properly debated as the Greeks debated them: matters of supreme conscience, of the highest level of importance, moral concern with great events and the motives behind them. That is what theatre is for.

Kenneth Tynan (1927–1980), British critic: board meeting at the National Theatre, 24 April 1967, as remembered by Laurence Olivier in appendix to his memoirs, *Confessions of an Actor* (1982)

27 A talent for drama is not a talent for writing, but is an ability to articulate human relationships.

Gore Vidal (b.1925), U.S. novelist and critic: in the *New York Times*, 17 June 1956

28 The theater needs continual reminders that there is nothing more debasing than the work of those who do well what is not worth doing at all.

Gore Vidal: in *Newsweek* (New York), 25 March 1968

29 I want to give the audience a *hint* of a scene. No more than that. Give them too much and they won't contribute anything themselves. Give them just a suggestion and you get them working with you. That's what gives the theater meaning: when it becomes a social act.

Orson Welles (1915–1985), U.S. film-maker and actor: quoted in *Citizen Welles* by Frank Brady (1989), Ch.8

30 The theatre is supremely fitted to say: 'Behold! These things are.' Yet most dramatists employ

it to say: 'This moral truth can be learned from beholding this action.'

Thornton Wilder (1897–1975), U.S. author: interview in *Writers at Work* (First Series, ed. Malcolm Cowley, 1958)

31 Every now and then, when you're on stage, you hear the best sound a player can hear. It's a sound you can't get in movies or in television. It is the sound of a wonderful, deep silence that means you've hit them where they live.

Shelley Winters (b.1922), U.S. actress: in *Theatre Arts*, June 1956

See also Brustein on AUDIENCES; Miller on BROADWAY; Thurber on BROADWAY

THEORY

1 There never comes a point where a theory can be said to be true. The most that one can claim for any theory is that it has shared the successes of all its rivals and that it has passed at least one test which they have failed.

A.J. Ayer (1910–1989), British philosopher: *Philosophy in the Twentieth Century* (1982), Ch.4

2 To insure the adoration of a theorem for any length of time, faith is not enough, a police force is needed as well.

Albert Camus (1913–1960), French-Algerian philosopher and author: *The Rebel* (1951; tr.1953), Pt.3, 'The Regicides'

3 Every theory is a self-fulfilling prophecy that orders experience into the framework it provides.

Ruth Hubbard (b.1924), U.S. biologist: 'Have Only Men Evolved?', publ. in *Women Look at Biology Looking At Women* (ed. Ruth Hubbard, Mary Sue Henifin and Barbara Fried, 1979)

4 Everything that explains the world has in fact explained a world that does not exist, a world in which men are at the center of the human enterprise and women are at the margin 'helping' them. Such a world does not exist – never has.

Gerda Lerner (b.1920), U.S. educator and author: quoted in *Ms.* (New York), Sept. 1981

THINGS

1 Inanimate objects are classified scientifically into three major categories – those that don't work, those that break down and those that get lost.

Russell Baker (b.1925), U.S. journalist: in the *New York Times*, 18 June 1968

2 The art of losing isn't hard to master; so many things seem filled with the intent to be lost that their loss is no disaster.

Elizabeth Bishop (1911–1979), US poet: 'One Art', publ. in *Geography III* (1976)

3 We live in a world of things, and our only connection with them is that we know how to manipulate or to consume them.

Erich Fromm (1900–1980), U.S. psychologist: *The Sane Society* (1955), Ch.5

4 Objects exist, and if one pays more attention to them than to people, it is precisely because they exist more than these people. Dead objects are still alive. Living people are often already dead.

Jean-Luc Godard (b.1930), French film-maker and author: *Deux ou Trois Choses que Je Sais d'Elle* (film, 1967), quoted in *Godard* by Richard Roud (1967; rev.1968), Ch.5

THE THIRD WORLD

1 From all around the Third World,
You hear the same story;
Rulers
Asleep to all things at
All times –
Conscious only of
Riches, which they gather in a
Coma –
Intravenously

Ama Ata Aidoo (b.1942), Ghanaian scholar and poet: 'The Plum', publ. in *Wayward Girls and Wicked Women* (ed. Angela Carter, 1986)

2 The Third World is not a reality but an ideology.

Hannah Arendt (1906–1975), German-born U.S. political philosopher: *Crises of the Republic* (1972), 'On Violence', Sct.1

3 In the under-developed countries ... the leader stands for moral power, in whose shelter the thin and poverty-stricken bourgeoisie of the young nation decides to get rich.

Frantz Fanon (1925–1961), Martiniquan psychiatrist, philosopher and political activist: *The Wretched of the Earth* (1961), Ch.3

4 To the United States the Third World often takes the form of a black woman who has been made pregnant in a moment of passion and who shows up one day in the reception room on the forty-ninth floor threatening to make a scene. The lawyers pay the woman off; sometimes uniformed guards accompany her to the elevators.

Lewis H. Lapham (b.1935), U.S. essayist and editor: *Money and Class in America* (1988), Ch.5, Sct.1

5 We face neither East nor West: we face forward.

Kwame Nkrumah (1900–1972), Ghanaian president: conference speech, Accra, 7 April 1960, quoted in *Axioms of Kwame Nkrumah* (1967)

6 The greatest single contribution America could make to the development of the poor countries would be to abolish the CIA tomorrow ... and the Chase Manhattan Bank the day after.
Theodore Roszak (b.1933), U.S. social critic: *Where the Wasteland Ends* (1972), Ch.12

See also Fanon on INTELLECTUALS

THOUGHT

1 True thoughts are those alone which do not understand themselves.
Theodor W. Adorno (1903–1969), German philosopher, sociologist and music critic: *Minima Moralia* (1951: tr.1978), Pt.3, Sct.122, 'Monograms'

2 Like many rich men, he thought in anecdotes; like many simple women, she thought in terms of biography.
Anita Brookner (b.1938), British novelist and art historian: of Bertie and Blanche Vernon, in *The Misalliance* (1986), Ch.1

3 The freeing of difference requires thought without contradiction, without dialectics, without negation; thought that accepts divergence; affirmative thought whose instrument is disjunction; thought of the multiple – of the nomadic and dispersed multiplicity that is not limited or confined by the constraints of similarity.
Michel Foucault (1926–1984), French philosopher: 'Theatrum Philosophicum', publ. in *Language, Counter-Memory, Practice* (ed. Donald Bouchard and Simon Sherry, 1977), Pt.2, 'Counter-Memory: the Philosophy of Difference'

4 It is clear that all verbal structures with meaning are verbal imitations of that elusive psychological and physiological process known as thought, a process stumbling through emotional entanglements, sudden irrational convictions, involuntary gleams of insight, rationalized prejudices, and blocks of panic and inertia, finally to reach a completely incommunicable intuition.
Northrop Frye (1912–1991), Canadian literary critic: *Anatomy of Criticism* (1957), 'Formal Phase: Symbol as Image'

5 The beginning of thought is in disagreement – not only with others but also with ourselves.
Eric Hoffer (1902–1983), U.S. philosopher: *The Passionate State of Mind* (1955), Aph.266

6 Man cannot produce a single work without the assistance of the slow, assiduous, corrosive worm of thought.
Eugenio Montale (1896–1981), Italian poet: *Poet In Our Time* (1972), p.17 of Marion Boyars edn. (1976)

7 We do not live to think, but, on the contrary, we think in order that we may succeed in surviving.
José Ortega y Gasset (1883–1955), Spanish essayist and philosopher: 'In Search of Goethe from Within', first publ. in *Partisan Review* (New Brunswick, N.J.), Dec. 1949, rep. in *The Dehumanization of Art and Other Essays* (1968)

8 Modern man likes to pretend that his thinking is wide-awake. But this wide-awake thinking has led us into the mazes of a nightmare in which the torture chambers are endlessly repeated in the mirrors of reason.
Octavio Paz (b.1914), Mexican poet and essayist: *The Labyrinth of Solitude* (1950; tr.1961), Ch.9

9 Man
You beheld the saddest and dreariest of all the flowers of the earth
And as with other flowers you gave it a name
You called it Thought.
(*Homme*
Tu as regardé la plus triste la plus morne de toutes les fleurs de la terre
Et comme aux autres fleurs tu lui as donné un nom
Tu l'as appelée Pensée.)
Jacques Prévert (1900–1977), French poet: 'Flowers and Wreaths', publ. in *Paroles* (1946; tr. Lawrence Ferlinghetti, 1958)

10 The birth of thought in the depths of the spirit, the shaping and ordering of it into periods, the translation into signs, and above all the transference of it from one spirit to another, the communication that is, if only for an instant, the meeting of two beings, with the unforeseeable consequences that such a meeting always causes, is in fact a miracle; except that the moment one stops to think about it one can't even write a letter.
Salvatore Satta (1902–1975), Italian jurist and novelist: *The Day of Judgment* (1979), Ch.20

11 A man's thinking goes on within his consciousness in a seclusion in comparison with which any physical seclusion is an exhibition to public view.
Ludwig Wittgenstein (1889–1951), Austrian-born British philosopher: *Philosophical Investigations* (1953), Pt.2, Sct.2

See also CONSCIOUSNESS; Galbraith on NONSENSE; PHILOSOPHY

THRILLERS *see under* FICTION

TIME

1 Modern thought has transferred the spectral character of Death to the notion of time

itself. Time has become Death triumphant over all.

John Berger (b.1926), British author and critic: 'That Which Is Held', first publ. in *Village Voice* (New York), 13 April 1982, rep. in *Keeping a Rendezvous* (1992)

2 Time is the substance from which I am made. Time is a river which carries me along, but I am the river; it is a tiger that devours me, but I am the tiger; it is a fire that consumes me, but I am the fire.

Jorge Luis Borges (1899–1986), Argentinian author: *Labyrinths* (1964), 'A New Refutation of Time'

3 The best way to fill time is to waste it.

Marguerite Duras (1914–1996), French author and film-maker: *Practicalities* (1987; tr.1990), 'Wasting Time'

4 City people try to buy time as a rule, when they can, whereas country people are prepared to kill time, although both try to cherish in their mind's eye the notion of a better life ahead.

Edward Hoagland (b.1932), U.S. novelist and essayist: 'The Ridge-Slope Fox and The Knife-Thrower', first publ. in *Harper's Magazine* (New York), Jan. 1977, rep. in *Heart's Desire* (1988)

5 We must use time as a tool, not as a couch.

John F. Kennedy (1917–1963), U.S. Democratic politician and president: quoted in *The Observer* (London), 10 Dec. 1961

6 We all run on two clocks. One is the outside clock, which ticks away our decades and brings us ceaselessly to the dry season. The other is the inside clock, where you are your own time-keeper and determine your own chronology, your own internal weather and your own rate of living. Sometimes the inner clock runs itself out long before the outer one, and you see a dead man going through the motions of living.

Max Lerner (1902–1992), U.S. author and columnist: 'Fifty', first publ. in the *New York Post*, 18 Dec. 1952, rep. in *The Unfinished Country* (1959), Pt.1

7 For tribal man space was the uncontrollable mystery. For technological man it is time that occupies the same role.

Marshall McLuhan (1911–1980), Canadian communications theorist: *The Mechanical Bride* (1951), 'Magic that Changes Mood'

8 American time has stretched around the world. It has become the dominant tempo of modern history, especially of the history of Europe.

Harold Rosenberg (1906–1978), U.S. art critic and author: *The Tradition of the New* (1960), Ch.14

9 Time is the only critic without ambition.

John Steinbeck (1902–1968), U.S. author: *Writers at Work* (Fourth Series, ed. George Plimpton, 1977), 'On Critics'

10 Time is such a simple, almost primitive idea. It is ... just a means of communication. We are swaddled in it, cocooned, and there is nothing to stop us tearing off the wadding of centuries that envelops us so that all our awareness should be common, one, simultaneous.

Andrey Tarkovsky (1932–1986), Russian film-maker: journal entry, 12 Dec. 1979, publ. in *Time Within Time: The Diaries 1970–1986* (1989; tr.1994)

11 Our lives are dominated by symbols of our own making. Once we had invented time by differentiating one year from another, we became in thrall to the notion of the decade, the century, the millennium. Every twenty years the middle-aged celebrate the decade of their youth.

Gore Vidal (b.1925), U.S. novelist and critic: 'Gods and Greens', first publ. in *The Observer* (London), 27 Aug. 1989, rep. in *A View from the Diner's Club* (1991)

12 Punctuality is the virtue of the bored.

Evelyn Waugh (1903–1966), British novelist: journal entry, 26 March 1962, publ. in *The Diaries of Evelyn Waugh* (ed. Michael Davie, 1976)

13 Time rushes toward us with its hospital tray of infinitely varied narcotics, even while it is preparing us for its inevitably fatal operation.

Tennessee Williams (1911–1983), U.S. playwright: *The Rose Tattoo* (1951), 'The Timeless World of a Play'

14 It haunts me, the passage of time. I think time is a merciless thing. I think life is a process of burning oneself out and time is the fire that burns you. But I think the spirit of man is a good adversary.

Tennessee Williams: in the *New York Post*, 30 April 1958

15 Without music to decorate it, time is just a bunch of boring production deadlines or dates by which bills must be paid.

Frank Zappa (1940–1993), U.S. rock musician: *The Real Frank Zappa Book* (written with Peter Occhiogrosso, 1989), Ch.8

TIME: Future

1 I would sum up my fear about the future in one word: *boring*. And that's my one fear: that everything has happened; nothing exciting or new or interesting is ever going to happen again ... the future is just going to be a vast, conforming *suburb of the soul*.

J.G. Ballard (b.1930), British author: interview, 30 Oct. 1982, in *Re/Search* (San Francisco), No.8/9, 1984

2 I don't try to describe the future. I try to prevent it.

Ray Bradbury (b.1920), U.S. science fiction author: quoted by Arthur C. Clarke in *The Independent* (London), 16 July 1992

3 Real generosity towards the future lies in giving all to the present.

Albert Camus (1913–1960), French-Algerian philosopher and author: *The Rebel* (1951; tr.1953), Pt.5, 'Beyond Nihilism'

4 The future? Like unwritten books and unborn children, you don't talk about it.

Dietrich Fischer-Dieskau (b.1925), German baritone singer: in *The Daily Telegraph* (London), 14 Oct. 1988

5 The danger of the past was that men became slaves. The danger of the future is that men may become robots. True enough, robots do not rebel. But given man's nature, robots cannot live and remain sane, they become 'Golems', they will destroy their world and themselves because they cannot stand any longer the boredom of a meaningless life.

Erich Fromm (1900–1980), U.S. psychologist: *The Sane Society* (1955), Ch.9. Fromm was echoing a speech made by Adlai Stevenson at Columbia University in 1954: 'We are not in danger of becoming slaves any more, but of becoming robots'

6 Things are getting faster and faster and stranger and stranger and it's almost comforting to think that some sort of crystal moment will arrive and a new order will snap out and suddenly everything will be different.

William Gibson (b.1948), U.S. science fiction author: interview in *Rapid Eye 3* (ed. Simon Dwyer, 1995)

7 The old futures have a way of hanging around.... I think now that everyone sort of knows that the real future is going to be cluttered with all the same junk we have today, except it will be old and beat up and there will be more of it.

William Gibson: interview in *Sight and Sound* (London), July 1995

8 We already have the statistics for the future: the growth percentages of pollution, over-population, desertification. The future is already in place.

Günter Grass (b.1927), German author: interview in the *New Statesman and Society* (London), 22 June 1990

9 People are always shouting they want to create a better future. It's not true. The future is an apathetic void of no interest to anyone. The past is full of life, eager to irritate us, provoke and insult us, tempt us to destroy or repaint it. The only reason people want to be masters of the future is to change the past.

Milan Kundera (b.1929), Czech-born French author and critic: *The Book of Laughter and Forgetting* (1978; tr.1982), Pt.1, Sct.17

10 I don't 'ave a future. Nobody 'as a future. The party's over. Take a look around you, man. It's all breakin' up.

Mike Leigh (b.1943), British film-maker: Johnny (David Thewlis), in *Naked* (film; written and directed by Mike Leigh, 1993)

11 A fixed image of the future is in the worst sense ahistorical.

Juliet Mitchell (b.1940), New Zealand author: 'Women – The Longest Revolution', publ. in the *New Left Review* (London), Nov./Dec. 1966

12 It was a bright, cold day in April and the clocks were striking thirteen.

George Orwell (1903–1950), British author: opening words of *Nineteen Eighty-four* (1949)

13 If you want a vision of the future, imagine a boot stamping on a human face – forever.

George Orwell: O'Brien, in *Nineteen Eighty-four* (1949), Pt.3, Ch.3

See also Warhol on FAME; Murdoch on TIME: PRESENT

TIME: Past

1 One must always maintain one's connection to the past and yet ceaselessly pull away from it. To remain in touch with the past requires a love of memory. To remain in touch with the past requires a constant imaginative effort.

Gaston Bachelard (1884–1962), French scientist, philosopher and literary theorist: *Fragments of a Poetics of Fire* (1988; tr.1990), 'A Retrospective Glance at the Lifework of a Master of Books'

2 The past grows gradually around one, like a placenta for dying.

John Berger (b.1926), British author and critic: *And Our Faces, My Heart, Brief As Photos* (1984), Pt.2

3 We are well advised to keep on nodding terms with the people we used to be, whether we find them attractive company or not. Otherwise they turn up unannounced and surprise us, come hammering on the mind's door at 4am of a bad night and demand to know who deserted them, who betrayed them, who is going to make amends. We forget all too soon the things we thought we could never forget.

Joan Didion (b.1934), U.S. essayist: *Slouching Towards Bethlehem* (1968), 'On Keeping a Notebook'

4 It is not the literal past, the 'facts' of history, that shape us, but images of the past embodied in language.

Brian Friel (b.1929), Irish playwright and author: Hugh, in *Translations* (1981), Act 3

5 We live in a world where amnesia is the most wished-for state. When did history become a bad word?
   John Guare (b.1938), U.S. playwright: in the *International Herald Tribune* (Paris), 13 June 1990

6 The past is a foreign country; they do things differently there.
   L.P. Hartley (1895–1972), British author: opening sentence of *The Go-Between* (1953), 'Prologue'

7 If the past cannot teach the present and the father cannot teach the son, then history need not have bothered to go on, and the world has wasted a great deal of time.
   Russell Hoban (b.1932), U.S. author: Jachin-Boaz, in *The Lion of Boaz-Jachin and Jachin-Boaz* (1973), Ch.1

8 Who controls the past controls the future: who controls the present controls the past.
   George Orwell (1903–1950), British author: 'Ingsoc' party slogan, in *Nineteen Eighty-four* (1949), Pt.1, Ch.3

9 I think we should always look back on our own past with a sort of tender contempt. As long as the tenderness is there but also please let some of the contempt be there, because we know what we're like, we know how we hustle and bustle and shove and push, and you sometimes use grand words to cloak it.
   Dennis Potter (1935–1994), British dramatist and screenwriter: interview with Melvyn Bragg, Channel 4, 5 April 1994

10 Every journey into the past is complicated by delusions, false memories, false namings of real events.
   Adrienne Rich (b.1929), U.S. poet: foreword to *Of Woman Born* (1976)

11 When we think of the past we tend to assume that people were simpler in their functions, and shaped by forces that were primary and irreducible. We take for granted that our forebears were imbued with a deeper purity of purpose than we possess nowadays, and a more singular set of mind, believing, for example, that early scientists pursued their ends with unbroken 'dedication' and that artists worked in the flame of some perpetual 'inspiration'. But none of this is true. Those who went before us were every bit as wayward and unaccountable and unsteady in their longings as people are today.
   Carol Shields (b.1935), U.S.-born Canadian author: *The Stone Diaries* (1993), Ch.3

12 The past itself, as historical change continues to accelerate, has become the most surreal of subjects – making it possible ... to see a new beauty in what is vanishing.
   Susan Sontag (b.1933), U.S. essayist: *On Photography* (1977), 'Melancholy Objects'

13 It is not the literal past that rules us, save, possibly, in a biological sense. It is images of the past. ... Each new historical era mirrors itself in the picture and active mythology of its past or of a past borrowed from other cultures. It tests its sense of identity, of regress or new achievement, against that past.
   George Steiner (b.1929), French-born U.S. critic and novelist: *In Bluebeard's Castle* (1971), Ch.1

See also Hewison on HERITAGE; Sontag on MEMORY; NOSTALGIA; REGRET

TIME: Present

1 I am prisoner of a gaudy and unlivable present, where all forms of human society have reached an extreme of their cycle and there is no imagining what new forms they may assume.
   Italo Calvino (1923–1985), Italian author and critic: the Great Khan, in *Invisible Cities* (1972; tr.1974) p.135–6 of Secker & Warburg edn. (1974)

2 No one has lived in the past and no one will live in the future. The present is the form of all life, and there are no means by which this can be avoided.
   Jean-Luc Godard (b.1930), French film-maker and author: the voice of the computer, Alpha 60, in *Alphaville* (film; written and directed by Jean-Luc Godard, 1965)

3 The present reeks of mediocrity and the atom bomb.
   René Magritte (1898–1967), Belgian surrealist painter: quoted in *Magritte* by Suzi Gablik (1970), Ch.5. 'I don't want to belong to my own time, or for that matter, to any other,' Magritte added

4 We shall be better prepared for the future if we see how terrible, how *doomed* the present is.
   Iris Murdoch (b.1919), British novelist and philosopher: David Crimond, in *The Book and the Brotherhood* (1987), Pt.2, 'Midwinter'

5 We are always acting on what has just finished happening. It happened at least 1/30th of a second ago. We think we're in the present, but we aren't. The present we know is only a movie of the past.
   Tom Wolfe (b.1931), U.S. author and journalist: Ken Kesey's philosophy, as explained in *The Electric Kool-Aid Acid Test* (1968), Ch.11

6 The present is the ever moving shadow that divides yesterday from tomorrow. In that lies hope.
   Frank Lloyd Wright (1869–1959), U.S. architect: closing words of *The Living City* (1958), Pt.5, 'Night is But a Shadow Cast by the Sun'

See also Potter on DEATH: DYING

TOBACCO

1 If alcohol is queen, then tobacco is her consort. It's a fond companion for all occasions, a loyal friend through fair weather and foul. People smoke to celebrate a happy moment, or to hide a bitter regret. Whether you're alone or with friends, it's a joy for all the senses. What lovelier sight is there than that double row of white cigarettes, lined up like soldiers on parade and wrapped in silver paper? ... I love to touch the pack in my pocket, open it, savour the feel of the cigarette between my fingers, the paper on my lips, the taste of tobacco on my tongue. I love to watch the flame spurt up, love to watch it come closer and closer, filling me with its warmth.
Luis Buñuel (1900–1983), Spanish film-maker: *My Last Breath* (autobiography, 1983), Ch.6. Buñuel concluded this eulogy: 'Finally, dear readers, allow me to end these ramblings on tobacco and alcohol, delicious fathers of abiding friendships and fertile reveries, with some advice: Don't drink and don't smoke. It's bad for your health'

2 Pull out a Monte Cristo at a dinner party and the political liberal turns into the nicotine fascist.
Martyn Harris (b.1952), British journalist and author: in *The Daily Telegraph* (London), 20 Jan. 1989

3 But when I don't smoke I scarcely feel as if I'm living. I don't feel as if I'm living unless I'm killing myself.
Russell Hoban (b.1932), U.S. author: William G, in *Turtle Diary* (1975), Ch.7

4 Tobacco may kill you but it's slow and it's rather a pleasure. People smoke for their mental health don't they? It's part of their total health, I'd say.
David Hockney (b.1937), British artist: on taking up smoking after a period of abstinence, in interview in *The Guardian* (London), 25 March 1995

5 It is their uselessness that ensures the aesthetic appeal of cigarettes – the sublimely, darkly beautiful pleasure that cigarettes bring to the lives of smokers. It is a pleasure that is democratic, popular, and universal; it is a form of beauty that the world of high as well as popular culture has for more than a century recognized and explicitly celebrated, in prose and poetry, in images both still and moving.
Richard Klein, U.S. author: introduction to *Cigarettes Are Sublime* (1993)

6 I would say nicotine is the hardest thing to quit of all – it's the perfect drug, it's your best buddy. It just happens to have a coupla bad side effects.
Lou Reed (b.1943), U.S. rock musician: interview in *Mojo* (London), March 1996

7 There are some circles in America where it seems to be more socially acceptable to carry a hand-gun than a packet of cigarettes.
Katharine Whitehorn (b.1926), British journalist: in *The Observer* (London), 30 Oct. 1988

TOOLS

1 There is a great satisfaction in building good tools for other people to use.
Freeman Dyson (b.1923), British-born U.S. physicist and author: *Disturbing the Universe* (1979), Pt.1, Ch.1

2 A worker may be the hammer's master, but the hammer still prevails. A tool knows exactly how it is meant to be handled, while the user of the tool can only have an approximate idea.
Milan Kundera (b.1929), Czech-born French author and critic: *The Book of Laughter and Forgetting* (1978; tr.1980), Pt.7, Ch.8

TORTURE

1 One of the most horrible, yet most important, discoveries of our age has been that, if you really wish to destroy a person and turn him into an automaton, the surest method is not physical torture, in the strict sense, but simply to keep him awake, i.e., in an existential relation to life without intermission.
W.H. Auden (1907–1973), Anglo-American poet: *The Dyer's Hand* (1962), Pt.3, 'Hic et Ille', Sct.C

2 Torment, for some men, is a need, an appetite, and an accomplishment.
(*Le tourment chez certains est un besoin, un appétit, et un accomplissement.*)
E.M. Cioran (1911–1995), Rumanian-born French philosopher: *The New Gods* (*Le Mauvais Démiurge* 1969, tr. 1974), 'Strangled Thoughts', Sct.3

3 There is only one thing that arouses animals more than pleasure, and that is pain. Under torture you are as if under the dominion of those grasses that produce visions. Everything you have heard told, everything you have read returns to your mind, as if you were being transported, not toward heaven, but toward hell. Under torture you say not only what the inquisitor wants, but also what you imagine might please him, because a bond (this, truly, diabolical) is established between you and him.
Umberto Eco (b.1932), Italian semiologist and novelist: Brother William, in *The Name of the Rose* (1980; tr.1983), 'First Day: Sext'

4 I don't really give a fuck what you know or don't know, but I'm going to torture you anyway, regardless.
Quentin Tarantino (b.1958), U.S. film-maker: Mr Blonde (Michael Madsen), about to slice off a cop's

ear, in *Reservoir Dogs* (film; written and directed by
Quentin Tarantino, 1992)

TOTALITARIANISM

1 Totalitarianism is never content to rule by
external means, namely, through the state and
a machinery of violence; thanks to its peculiar
ideology and the role assigned to it in this
apparatus of coercion, totalitarianism has
discovered a means of dominating and ter-
rorizing human beings from within.
Hannah Arendt (1906–1975), German-born U.S.
political philosopher: *The Origins of Totalitarianism*
(1951), Ch.10, Sct.1

2 One leader, one people, signifies one master
and millions of slaves.
Albert Camus (1913–1960), French-Algerian
philosopher and author: *The Rebel* (1951; tr.1953),
Pt.3, 'State Terrorism and Irrational Terror'

3 People who live in the post-totalitarian system
know only too well that the question of
whether one or several political parties are in
power, and how these parties define and label
themselves, is of far less importance than the
question of whether or not it is possible to live
like a human being.
Václav Havel (b.1936), Czech playwright and
president: *Living in Truth* (1986), Pt.1, 'The Power
of the Powerless', Sct.11. 'Post-totalitarianism' was
the term used by Havel – writing before the
dissolution of the Iron Curtain – to describe
Czechoslovakia and other East European states:
'totalitarian in a way fundamentally different from
classical dictatorships'

4 The only successful revolution of this century
is totalitarianism.
Bernard-Henri Lévy (b.1948), French philosopher:
in *Time* (New York), 12 Sept 1977

TOURISM

1 I am leaving the town to the invaders: increasingly numerous, mediocre, dirty, badly
behaved, shameless tourists.
Brigitte Bardot (b.1933), French actress: on leaving
her home at Saint Tropez, quoted in the
International Herald Tribune (Paris), 10 Aug. 1989

2 Should we have stayed at home and thought of
here?
Where should we be today?
Is it right to be watching strangers in a play
in this strangest of theatres?
Elizabeth Bishop (1911–1979), U.S. poet:
'Questions of Travel', St.2, publ. in *Questions of
Travel* (1965). Bishop, an avid traveller, spent the
last 16 years of her life in Brazil

3 Modern tourist guides have helped raised
tourist expectations. And they have provided

the natives – from Kaiser Wilhelm down to the
villagers of Chichacestenango – with a detailed
and itemized list of what is expected of them
and when. These are the up-to-date scripts for
actors on the tourists' stage.
Daniel J. Boorstin (b.1914), U.S. historian: *The
Image* (1961), Ch.3

4 The *personal appropriation of clichés* is a
condition for the spread of cultural tourism.
Serge Daney (1944–1992), French film critic:
'Falling out of Love', publ. in *Sight and Sound*
(London), July 1992

5 Tourism, human circulation considered as
consumption ... is fundamentally nothing
more than the leisure of going to see what has
become banal.
Guy Debord (1931–1994), French Situationist
philosopher: *The Society of the Spectacle* (1967;
tr.1977), Ch.7, Sct.168

6 Tourism is the march of stupidity. You're
expected to be stupid. The entire mechanism
of the host country is geared to travelers acting
stupidly. You walk around dazed, squinting
into fold-out maps. You don't know how to
talk to people, how to get anywhere, what the
money means, what time it is, what to eat or
how to eat it. Being stupid is the pattern, the
level and the norm. You can exist on this level
for weeks and months without reprimand or
dire consequence. Together with thousands,
you are granted immunities and broad freedoms. You are an army of fools, wearing bright
polyesters, riding camels, taking pictures of
each other, haggard, dysenteric, thirsty. There
is nothing to think about but the next shapeless
event.
Don DeLillo (b.1926), U.S. author: James Axton, in
The Names (1982), Ch.3

7 Sailin' 'round the world in a dirty gondola
Oh, to be back in the land of Coca-Cola!
Bob Dylan (b.1941), U.S. singer and songwriter:
'When I Paint My Masterpiece' (song, 1971) on the
album *Greatest Hits Vol.II* (1971)

8 The country of the tourist pamphlet always is
another country, an embarrassing abstraction
of the desirable that, thank God, does not exist
on this planet, where there are always ants and
bad smells and empty Coca-Cola bottles to
keep the grubby finger-print of reality upon
the beautiful.
Nadine Gordimer (b.1923), South African author:
A World of Strangers (1958), Ch.1

9 The tourist who moves about to see and hear
and open himself to all the influences of the
places which condense centuries of human
greatness is only a man in search of excellence.
Max Lerner (1902–1992), U.S. author and
columnist: 'Lo, the Poor Sightseer', first publ. in the

New York Post, 15 Sept. 1954, rep. in *The Unfinished Country* (1959), Pt.1

10 In the middle ages people were tourists because of their religion, whereas now they are tourists because tourism is their religion.
Robert Runcie (b.1921), British ecclesiastic and archbishop of Canterbury: quoted in *The Independent* (London), 7 Dec. 1988

11 Inter-railers are the ambulatory equivalent of McDonald's, walking testimony to the erosion of French culture.
Alice Thompson (b.1963), British travel writer and journalist: 'Ticket to Ride the Rails of France', publ. in *The Times* (London), 16 July 1992

See also Allen on FRANCE: PARIS; THE UNITED STATES: AMERICANS ABROAD

TRADE UNIONS

1 The trade union movement is learning again that it needs a political party to represent working people in Parliament. Non-political trade unionism, on the American model, would fail here, as it has done there. For those without personal wealth or political authority a trade union card and a ballot paper are the only two routes to political power.
Tony Benn (b.1925), British Labour politician: *Arguments for Democracy* (1981), Ch.9

2 If you mean by capitalism the God-given right of a few big corporations to make all the decisions that will affect millions of workers and consumers and to exclude everyone else from discussing and examining those decisions, then the unions are threatening capitalism.
Max Lerner (1902–1992), U.S. author and columnist: *Actions and Passions* (1949), 'A Look at the Books and a Share of the Pie'

3 When the next Conservative government comes to power, many trade unionists will have put it there. Millions of them vote for us at every election. I want to say this to them and all our supporters in industry: go out and join in the work of your unions: go to their meetings and stay to the end, and learn the rules as well as the far left knows them. Remember that if parliamentary democracy dies, free trades unions die with it.
Margaret Thatcher (b.1925), British Conservative politician and prime minister: speech to Conservative Party Conference, Blackpool, 1975, quoted in *Tories* by Rupert Morris (1991), Ch.9

TRADITION

1 In America nothing dies easier than tradition.
Russell Baker (b.1925), U.S. journalist: in the *New York Times*, 14 May 1991

2 The assumption must be that those who can see value only in tradition, or versions of it, deny man's ability to adapt to changing circumstances.
Stephen Bayley (b.1951), British design critic: *Commerce and Culture* (1989), Ch.3

3 As soon as tradition has come to be recognized as tradition, it is dead.
Allan Bloom (1930–1992), U.S. educator and author: *The Closing of the American Mind* (1987), Pt.1, 'The Clean Slate'

4 Tradition! We scarcely know the word anymore. We are afraid to be either proud of our ancestors or ashamed of them. We scorn nobility in name and in fact. We cling to a bourgeois mediocrity which would make it appear we are all Americans, made in the image and likeness of George Washington.
Dorothy Day (1897–1980), U.S. religious leader: *The Long Loneliness* (1952), Pt.1

5 I like to keep my values scripturally straight ... I like to stay a part of that stuff that don't change.
Bob Dylan (b.1941), U.S. singer and songwriter: sleeve notes on *Biograph* box set (1985)

TRAGEDY

1 I have spent more than half a lifetime trying to express the tragic moment.
Marcel Marceau (b.1923), French mime artist: in *The Guardian* (London), 11 Aug. 1988

2 The closer a man approaches tragedy the more intense is his concentration of emotion upon the fixed point of his commitment, which is to say the closer he approaches what in life we call fanaticism.
Arthur Miller (b.1915), U.S. playwright: introduction, Sct.1, to *Collected Plays* (1958)

3 A tragic situation exists precisely when virtue does *not* triumph but when it is still felt that man is nobler than the forces which destroy him.
George Orwell (1903–1950), British author: *Shooting an Elephant* (1950), 'Lear, Tolstoy and the Fool'

4 It's not the tragedies that kill us, it's the messes.
Dorothy Parker (1893–1967), U.S. humorous writer: interview in *Writers at Work* (First Series, ed. Malcolm Cowley, 1958)

5 When you close your eyes to tragedy, you close your eyes to greatness.
Stephen Vizinczey (b.1933), Hungarian novelist and critic: 'Who Killed Kleist?' (review of *Kleist: A Biography* by Joachim Maass), publ. in *The Sunday Telegraph* (London), 5 Jan. 1984, rep. in *Truth and Lies in Literature* (1986)

TRAINING

1 Coaching is for kids. If a player can't trap a ball and pass it by the time he's in the team, he shouldn't be there in the first place. I told Roy McFarland to go and get his bloody hair cut – that's coaching at this level.

Brian Clough (b.1935), British footballer and manager: *Clough: The Autobiography* (1994), Ch.8

2 It's all to do with the training: you can do a lot if you're properly trained.

Elizabeth II (b.1926), Queen of Great Britain and Northern Ireland: television documentary, BBC1, 6 Feb. 1992

TRAMPS

1 I know you like a book, ya little tramp. You'd sell out you're own mother for a piece of fudge. ... You've got a great big dollar there where most women have a heart.

Sterling Hayden (1916–1986), U.S. actor: Johnny Clay (Hayden), in *The Killing* (film; screenplay by Stanley Kubrick and Jim Thompson, adapted from the *The Clean Break* by Lionel White, directed by Stanley Kubrick, 1956)

2 I'm a man of means by no means
King of the road.

Roger Miller (1936–1992), U.S. country singer: 'King of the Road' (song) on the album *The Return of Roger Miller* (1965)

3 You're nothing else but a wild animal, when you come down to it. You're a barbarian. And to put the old tin lid on it, you stink from arsehole to breakfast time.

Harold Pinter (b.1930), British playwright: Mick, speaking to Davies, in *The Caretaker* (1960), Act 3

See also Springsteen on WILD AT HEART

TRANSLATION

1 The test of a given phrase would be: Is it worthy to be immortal? To 'make a beeline' for something. That's worthy of being immortal and is immortal in English idiom. 'I guess I'll split' is not going to be immortal and is excludable, therefore excluded.

Robert Fitzgerald (1910–1985), U.S. scholar and translator: on his criteria for translating Homeric Greek, in *Writers at Work* (Eighth Series, ed. George Plimpton, 1988). Fitzgerald's translations of Homer's *Odyssey* and *The Iliad* appeared in 1961 and 1974

2 Poetry is what is lost in translation.

Robert Frost (1874–1963), U.S. poet: quoted in *Robert Frost: a Backward Look* by Louis Untermeyer (1964), Ch.1. Frost's formula echoes a passage from Coleridge's *Biographia Literaria* (1817), Ch.22: 'In poetry, in which every line, every phrase, may pass the ordeal of deliberation and deliberate choice, it is possible, and barely possible, to attain that *ultimatum* which I have ventured to propose as the infallible test of a blameless style; namely: its *untranslatableness* in words of the same language without injury to the meaning.'

3 To translate, one must have a style of his own, for otherwise the translation will have no rhythm or nuance, which come from the process of artistically thinking through and molding the sentences; they cannot be reconstituted by piecemeal imitation. The problem of translation is to retreat to a simpler tenor of one's own style and creatively adjust this to one's author.

Paul Goodman (1911–1972), U.S. author, poet and critic: *Five Years* (1966), 'Summer 1957, in Europe', Sct.8

4 Translation is entirely mysterious. Increasingly I have felt that the art of writing is itself translating, or more like translating than it is like anything else. What is the other text, the original? I have no answer. I suppose it is the source, the deep sea where ideas swim, and one catches them in nets of words and swings them shining into the boat ... where in this metaphor they die and get canned and eaten in sandwiches.

Ursula K. Le Guin (b.1929), U.S. author: 'Reciprocity of Prose and Poetry', speech, 1983, in Poetry Series, Folger Shakespeare Library, Washington D.C., publ. in *Dancing at the Edge of the World* (1989)

5 Translation is the paradigm, the exemplar of all writing. ... It is translation that demonstrates most vividly the yearning for transformation that underlies every act involving speech, that supremely human gift.

Harry Mathews (b.1930), U.S. novelist: *Country Cooking and Other Stories* (1980), 'The Dialect of the Tribe'

TRANSPORT

1 My experience of ships is that on them one makes an interesting discovery about the world. One finds one can do without it completely.

Malcolm Bradbury (b.1932), British author: Dr Jochum, in *Stepping Westward* (1965), Bk.1, Ch.2

2 I have done almost every human activity inside a taxi which does not require main drainage.

Alan Brien (b.1925), British novelist and humorist: in *Punch* (London), 5 July 1972

3 A solitary traveller can sleep from state to state, from day to night, from day to day, in the long womb of its controlled interior. It is the cradle

that never stops rocking after the lullaby is over. It is the biggest sleeping tablet in the world, and no one need ever swallow the pill, for it swallows them.

Lisa St Aubin de Terán (b.1953), British author: on trains in the U.S., publ. in *Off the Rails* (1989), Ch.15

4 I am struck by the way people behave on the Tube. They look at each other beadily and inquisitively, and something goes on in their thoughts which must be equivalent to the way dogs and other animals, when they meet, sniff each other's arses and nuzzle each other's fur.

Graham Swift (b.1949), British author: *Shuttlecock* (1981), Ch.3

See also AEROPLANES; BICYCLES; CARS

TRASH

1 No cash a passion for trash.

John Cooper Clarke (b.1950), British punk poet: 'Psycle Sluts: Pt.1', on the album *Poetry Olympics Live* (1982), publ. in *Ten Years in an Open Necked Shirt* (1993)

2 Almost all of us at some time settle for trash, even though we may know better.

Richard Hoggart (b.1918), British critic: in the *Independent on Sunday* (London), 19 Feb. 1995

TRAVEL

1 Of all possible subjects, travel is the most difficult for an artist, as it is the easiest for a journalist.

W.H. Auden (1907–1973), Anglo-American poet: *The Dyer's Hand* (1962), Pt.6, 'The American Scene'

2 A part, a large part, of travelling is an engagement of the ego v. the world. ... The world is hydra headed, as old as the rocks and as changing as the sea, enmeshed inextricably in its ways. The ego wants to arrive at places safely and on time.

Sybille Bedford (b.1911), British author: 'The Quality of Travel', first publ. in *Esquire* (New York), Nov. 1961, rep. in *As It Was* (1990)

3 Ours is the century of enforced travel ... of disappearances. The century of people helplessly seeing others, who were close to them, disappear over the horizon.

John Berger (b.1926), British author and critic: 'Ev'ry Time We Say Goodbye', first publ. in *Expressen* (Stockholm), 3 Nov. 1990, rep. in *Keeping a Rendezvous* (1992)

4 Travelling, you realize that differences are lost: each city takes to resembling all cities, places exchange their form, order, distances, a shapeless dust cloud invades the continents.

Italo Calvino (1923–1985), Italian author and critic: Marco Polo, in *Invisible Cities* (1972; tr.1974), p.137 of Secker & Warburg edn. (1974)

5 The travel writer seeks the world we have lost – the lost valleys of the imagination.

Alexander Cockburn (b.1941), Anglo-Irish journalist: 'Bwana Vistas', first publ. in *Harper's Magazine* (New York), Aug. 1985, rep. in *Corruptions of Empire* (1988), Pt.1

6 When one realizes that his life is worthless he either commits suicide or travels.

Edward Dahlberg (1900–1977), U.S. author and critic: *Reasons of the Heart* (1965), 'On Futility'

7 Journeys, like artists, are born and not made. A thousand differing circumstances contribute to them, few of them willed or determined by the will – whatever we may think.

Lawrence Durrell (1914–1991), British author: opening words of *Bitter Lemons* (1957), 'Towards an Eastern Landfall'

8 It would be nice to travel if you knew where you were going and where you would live at the end or do we ever know, do we ever live where we live, we're always in other places, lost, like sheep.

Janet Frame (b.1924), New Zealand novelist and poet: *You Are Now Entering the Human Heart* (1983), 'The Day of the Sheep'

9 The important thing about travel in foreign lands is that it breaks the speech habits and makes you blab less, and breaks the habitual space-feeling because of different village plans and different landscapes. It is less important that there are different mores, for you counteract these with your own reaction-formations.

Paul Goodman (1911–1972), U.S. author, poet and critic: *Five Years* (1966), 'Summer 1957, in Europe', Sct.3

10 I have no interest in sailing round the world. Not that there is any lack of requests for me to do so.

Edward Heath (b.1916), British Conservative politician and prime minister: in *The Observer* (London), 19 June 1977

11 A disruptive minority of humankind regarded journeys, even short ones, as the occasion for pleasant encounters. There were people ready to inflict intimacies on strangers. Such travellers were to be avoided if you belonged to the majority for whom a journey was the occasion for silence, reflection, daydream. The requirements were simple: an obstructed view of a changing landscape, however dull, and freedom from the breath of other passengers, their body warmth, sandwiches and limbs.

Ian McEwan (b.1948), British author: *The Child in Time* (1987), Ch.3

12 If we are always arriving and departing, it is also true that we are eternally anchored. One's destination is never a place but rather a new way of looking at things.
Henry Miller (1891–1980), U.S. author: *Big Sur and the Oranges of Hieronymous Bosch* (1957), 'The Oranges of the Millennium'

13 Life, as the most ancient of all metaphors insists, is a journey; and the travel book, in its deceptive simulation of the journey's fits and starts, rehearses life's own fragmentation. More even than the novel, it embraces the contingency of things.
Jonathan Raban (b.1942), British author and critic: *For Love and Money* (1987), Pt.5

14 Travelling is like flirting with life. It's like saying, 'I would stay and love you, but I have to go; this is my station'.
Lisa St Aubin de Terán (b.1953), British author: *Off the Rails* (1989), Ch.2

15 An involuntary return to the point of departure is, without doubt, the most disturbing of all journeys.
Iain Sinclair (b.1943), British author: *Downriver* (1991), 'Riverside Opportunities', Sct.9

16 A journey is like marriage. The certain way to be wrong is to think you control it.
John Steinbeck (1902–1968), U.S. author: *Travels With Charley: in Search of America* (1961), Pt.1

17 Extensive traveling induces a feeling of encapsulation, and travel, so broadening at first, contracts the mind.
Paul Theroux (b.1941), U.S. novelist and travel writer: *The Great Railway Bazaar* (1975), Ch.21

18 Travel is glamorous only in retrospect.
Paul Theroux: quoted in *The Observer* (London), 7 Oct. 1979

See also TOURISM; TRANSPORT

TREES

1 Tall poplars – human beings of this earth!
(*Ihr hohen Pappeln – Menschen dieser Erde!*)
Paul Celan (1920–1970), German poet and translator: 'Landscape', first publ. in *Von Schwelle zu Schwelle* (1955), rep. in *Paul Celan: Poems* (ed./tr. Michael Hamburger, 1980)

2 The trees are coming into leaf
Like something almost being said.
Philip Larkin (1922–1985), British poet: 'The Trees', publ. in *High Windows* (1974)

3 A tree's a tree. How many more do you need to look at?
Ronald Reagan (b.1911), U.S. Republican politician and president: speech, 12 Sept. 1965, quoted in *Sacramento Bee* (California), 12 March 1966. Reagan later denied having made this statement

See also Sting on THE ENVIRONMENT

TRIALS

1 I was court-martialled in my absence, and sentenced to death in my absence, so I said they could shoot me in my absence.
Brendan Behan (1923–1964), Irish playwright: Pat, on his experiences in the IRA, in *The Hostage* (1958), Act 1

2 Courts are places where the ending is written first and all that precedes is simply vaudeville.
Charles Bukowski (1920–1994), U.S. author and poet: *Notes of a Dirty Old Man* (1969), p.62 of City Lights edn. (1973)

3 When the judge calls the criminal's name out he stands up, and they are immediately linked by a strange biology that makes them both opposite and complementary. The one cannot exist without the other. Which is the sun and which is the shadow? It's well known some criminals have been great men.
Jean Genet (1910–1986), French playwright and novelist: *Prisoner Of Love* (1986; tr.1989), Pt.1.

4 A criminal trial is like a Russian novel: it starts with exasperating slowness as the characters are introduced to a jury, then there are complications in the form of minor witnesses, the protagonist finally appears and contradictions arise to produce drama, and finally as both jury and spectators grow weary and confused the pace quickens, reaching its climax in passionate final argument.
Clifford Irving (b.1930), U.S. author and hoaxer: in *The Sunday Times* (London), 14 Aug. 1988

5 I'm no idealist to believe firmly in the integrity of our courts and in the jury system – that is no ideal to me, it is a living, working reality. Gentlemen, a court is no better than each man of you sitting before me on this jury. A court is only as sound as its jury, and a jury is only as sound as the men who make it up.
Harper Lee (b.1926), U.S. author: speech to the jury by Atticus Finch, in *To Kill a Mockingbird* (1960), Pt.2, Ch.20

6 I'm trusting in the Lord and a good lawyer.
Oliver North (b.1943), U.S. marine officer: on investigations into the 'Iran-Contra' scandal, quoted in *The Observer* (London), 7 Dec. 1986

7 Ladies and gentlemen, let me tell you again what you are to presume. [The defendant] is innocent. I am the judge. I am telling you that. Presume he is innocent. When you sit there, I

want you to look and say to yourself, There sits an innocent man.

Scott Turow (b.1949), U.S. lawyer and author: Judge Larren Lyttle addressing the jury, in *Presumed Innocent* (1987), Ch.26. Judge Lyttle begins the selection of the jury by asking one member whether the defendant committed the crime, and, on receiving the answer, 'I wouldn't know, Judge,' dismissed the juror

8 He maintained that the case was lost or won by the time the final juror had been sworn in; his summation was set in his mind before the first witness was called. It was all in the orchestration, he claimed: in knowing how and where to pitch each and every particular argument; who to intimidate; who to trust, who to flatter and court; who to challenge; when to underplay and exactly when to let out all the stops.

Dorothy Uhnak (b.1933), U.S. novelist: *The Investigation* (1977), Pt.1, Ch.14

See also Thompson on LAWYERS

TRICKERY

1 I do not believe that in a great age government by small tricks will work for long, and always maintain that great things can only be done in a great way.

Oswald Mosley (1896–1980), British fascist leader: *My Life* (1968), Ch.12

2 It seems to me that there are two kinds of trickery: the 'fronts' people assume before one another's eyes, and the 'front' a writer puts on the face of reality.

Françoise Sagan (b.1935), French novelist and playwright: interview in *Writers at Work* (First Series, ed. Malcolm Cowley, 1958)

TRIVIALITY

1 Not many people know that.

Michael Caine (b.1933), British stage and actor: catch-phrase and book title (1984). Caine's catch-phrase, which found its way into his films and was made the title of a collection of trivial information compiled by him, is said to have been his comment when habitually offering information garnered from *The Guinness Book of Records*

2 I'm proud to say I've made a career out of being trivial. I think it's an art form.

Janet Street-Porter (b.1946), British broadcaster and programme-maker: on starting a new column in *The Observer* (London), 12 Nov. 1995

TROUBLE

1 Trouble and pain were what kept a man alive. Or trying to avoid trouble and pain. It was a full time job.

Charles Bukowski (1920–1994), U.S. author: the narrator (Nicky Belane), in *Pulp* (1994), Ch.26

2 Lately ... Americans have begun to understand that trouble does not start somewhere on the other side of town. It seems to originate inside the absolute middle of the homemade cherry pie. In our history, the state has failed to respond to the weak. ... You could be white, male, Presbyterian and heterosexual besides, but if you get fired or if you get sick tomorrow, you might as well be Black, for all the state will want to hear from you.

June Jordan (b.1936), U.S. poet and civil rights activist: 'Problems of Language in a Democratic State' (1982), rep. in *Moving Towards Home: Political Essays* (1989)

TRUST

1 *Trust me*, he said, *you will, won't you?* Trust him to what, she wondered. Which men could one trust? Any man carrying a musical instrument, perhaps? Any man walking along reading a book? Most doctors – with reservations about those wearing bow ties. *Trust you to what?* she asked.

Connie Bensley (b.1929), British poet: 'Politeness', publ. in *Choosing to be a Swan* (1994)

2 Everyone realizes that one can believe little of what people say about each other. But it is not so widely realized that even less can one trust what people say about themselves.

Rebecca West (1892–1983), British author: in *The Sunday Telegraph* (London), 1975, quoted as epigraph to Victoria Glendinning's biography, *Rebecca West: A Life* (1987)

TRUTH

1 No blame should attach to telling the truth. But it does, it does.

Anita Brookner (b.1938), British novelist and art historian: Rachel, in *A Friend From England* (1987), Ch.10

2 Truth is used to vitalize a statement rather than devitalize it. Truth implies more than a simple statement of fact. 'I don't have any whisky,' may be a fact but it is not a truth.

William Burroughs (1914–1997), U.S. author: *The Adding Machine* (1985), 'On Coincidence'

3 Perhaps our only sickness is to desire a truth which we cannot bear rather than to rest content with the fictions we manufacture out of each other.

Lawrence Durrell (1912–1990), British author: Justine, in *Clea* (1960), Ch.1, Sct.3

4 Perhaps the mission of those who love mankind is to make people laugh at the truth, *to make truth laugh*, because the only truth lies in learning to free ourselves from insane passion for the truth.

Umberto Eco (b.1932), Italian semiologist and novelist: Brother William, in *The Name of the Rose* (1980; tr.1983), 'Seventh Day: Night (2)'

5 The truth isn't always beauty, but the hunger for it is.

Nadine Gordimer (b.1923), South African author: 'A Bolter and the Invincible Summer', first publ. in *London Magazine*, May 1963, rep. in *The Essential Gesture* (ed. Stephen Clingman, 1988)

6 The truth has never been of any real value to any human being – it is a symbol for mathematicians and philosophers to pursue. In human relations kindness and lies are worth a thousand truths.

Graham Greene (1904–1991), British novelist: Scobie, in *The Heart of the Matter* (1948), Bk.1, Pt.1, Ch.2, Sct.4

7 The truth is not simply what you think it is; it is also the circumstances in which it is said, and to whom, why, and how it is said.

Václav Havel (b.1936), Czech playwright and president: *Disturbing the Peace* (1986; tr.1990), Ch.2

8 There are times when we must sink to the bottom of our misery to understand truth, just as we must descend to the bottom of a well to see the stars in broad daylight.

Václav Havel: *Living in Truth* (1986), Pt.1 'The Power of the Powerless', Sct.16

9 Truth-telling, I have found, is the key to responsible citizenship. The thousands of criminals I have seen in forty years of law enforcement have had one thing in common: every single one was a liar.

J. Edgar Hoover (1895–1972), U.S. director of the FBI: in *Family Weekly* (New York), 14 July 1963

10 Truth must be the foundation stone, the cement to solidify the entire social edifice.

Pope John Paul II [Karol Wojtyla] (b.1920), Polish ecclesiastic: quoted in *The Times* (London), 18 May 1988

11 In the society of men the truth resides now less in what things are than in what they are not. Our social realities are so ugly if seen in the light of exiled truth, and beauty is no longer possible if it is not a lie.

R.D. Laing (1927–1989), British psychiatrist: introduction to *The Politics of Experience* (1967)

12 There are no new truths, but only truths that have not been recognized by those who have perceived them without noticing. A truth is something that everybody can be shown to know and to have known, as people say, all along.

Mary McCarthy (1912–1989), U.S. author and critic: 'The Vita Activa', first published in the *New Yorker*, 18 Oct. 1958, rep. in *On the Contrary* (1961)

13 You cannot have both truth and what you call civilisation.

Iris Murdoch (b.1919), British novelist and philosopher: Honor Klein, in *A Severed Head* (1961), Ch.9

14 As for truth – well, it's like brown – it's not in the spectrum. ... Truth is *sui generis*.

Iris Murdoch: Rozanov, in *The Philosopher's Pupil* (1983), 'The Events in Our Town'

15 Let us begin by committing ourselves to the truth, to see it like it is and tell it like it is, to find the truth, to speak the truth and to live the truth.

Richard Nixon (1913–1992), U.S. Republican politician and president: speech accepting the Republican presidential nomination, 8 Aug. 1968, Miami, quoted in the *New York Times*, 9 Aug. 1968

16 I preach there are all kinds of truth, your truth and somebody else's. But behind all of them there is only one truth and that is that there's no truth.

Flannery O'Connor (1925–1964), U.S. author: the preacher Hazel Motes, in *Wise Blood* (1952), Ch.10

17 Truth is simply a compliment paid to sentences seen to be paying their way.

Richard Rorty (b.1931), U.S. philosopher: quoted in the *New York Times Magazine*, 12 Feb. 1990

18 It is not because the truth is too difficult to see that we make mistakes. It may even lie on the surface; but we make mistakes because the easiest and most comfortable course for us is to seek insight where it accords with our emotions – especially selfish ones.

Alexander Solzhenitsyn (b.1918), Russian novelist: 'Peace and Violence', Sct.2, first publ. in *Index* (London), No.4, 1973, rep. in *Solzhenitsyn: A Documentary Record* (ed. Leopold Labedz, 1974), 'Trials in Détente'

19 The truth is always something that is told, not something that is known. If there were no speaking or writing, there would be no truth about anything. There would only be what is.

Susan Sontag (b.1933), U.S. essayist: *The Benefactor* (1963), Ch.1

20 The truth is balance, but the opposite of truth, which is unbalance, may not be a lie.

Susan Sontag: *Against Interpretation* (1966), 'Simone Weil'

21 Truth should not be forced; it should simply manifest itself, like a woman who has in her privacy reflected and coolly decided to bestow

herself upon a certain man. She will *dawn* upon that man.

John Updike (b.1932), U.S. author and critic: *Self-Consciousness: Memoirs* (1989), Ch.6

22 The truth is really an ambition which is beyond us.

Peter Ustinov (b.1921), British actor, writer and director: in the *International Herald Tribune* (Paris), 12 March 1990

See also Ford on GOVERNMENT

THE TWENTIETH CENTURY

1 The marriage of reason and nightmare which has dominated the 20th century has given birth to an ever more ambiguous world. Across the communications landscape move the spectres of sinister technologies and the dreams that money can buy. Thermonuclear weapons systems and soft drink commercials coexist in an overlit realm ruled by advertising and pseudo-events, science and pornography. Over our lives preside the great twin leitmotifs of the 20th century – sex and paranoia.

J.G. Ballard (b.1930), British author: introduction (1974), to the French edition of *Crash* (1973)

2 At no previous period has mankind been faced by a half-century which so paradoxically united violence and progress. Its greater and lesser wars and long series of major assassinations have been strangely combined with the liberation of more societies and individuals than ever before in history, and by the transformation of millions of second-class citizens – women, workers and the members of subject races – to a stage at which first-rate achievement is no longer inhibited even if opportunities are not yet complete.

Vera Brittain (1893–1970), British author: *The Rebel Passion* (1964), Ch.12

3 The real passion of the twentieth century is servitude.

Albert Camus (1913–1960), French-Algerian philosopher and author: *The Rebel* (1951; tr.1953), Pt.3, 'State Terrorism and Rational Terror'

4 In the nineteenth century the problem was that *God is dead*; in the twentieth century the problem is that *man is dead*.

Erich Fromm (1900–1980), U.S. psychologist: *The Sane Society* (1955), Ch.9

5 The horror of the Twentieth Century was the size of each new event, and the paucity of its reverberation.

Norman Mailer (b.1923), U.S. author: *A Fire on the Moon* (1970), Pt.1, Ch.1

6 It is the mission of the twentieth century to elucidate the irrational.

Maurice Merleau-Ponty (1907–1961), French philosopher: quoted in *Witness of Decline* by Lev Braun (1974), Ch.8

7 This filthy twentieth century. I hate its guts.

A.L. Rowse (1903–1997), British historian and critic: in *Time* (New York), 13 Nov. 1978

8 Please wash your hands before leaving the 20th century.

Slogan, 1960s: quoted in *The Incomplete Works of Jamie Reid* by Jamie Reid and Jon Savage (1987), 'Death'. Reid used the words as the title for his itinerant multi-media exhibition in the 1970s

9 All in all, I would not have missed this century for the world.

Gore Vidal (b.1925), U.S. novelist and critic: in *The Observer* (London), 31 Dec. 1989

See also DeLillo on CINEMA; THE 1940S; THE 1950S; THE 1960S; THE 1970S; THE 1980S; THE 1990S; Wallinger on PHOTOGRAPHY

TYCOONS

1 It is impossible to think of Howard Hughes without seeing the apparently bottomless gulf between what we say we want and what we do want, between what we officially admire and secretly desire, between, in the largest sense, the people we marry and the people we love. In a nation which increasingly appears to prize social virtues, Howard Hughes remains not merely antisocial but grandly, brilliantly, surpassingly, asocial. He is the last private man, the dream we no longer admit.

Joan Didion (b.1934), U.S. essayist: '7000 Romaine, Los Angeles' (1967), rep. in *Slouching Towards Bethlehem* (1968)

2 There's a certain part of the contented majority who love anybody who is worth a billion dollars.

J.K. Galbraith (b.1908), U.S. economist: of millionaire presidential candidate H. Ross Perot, in *The Guardian* (London), 23 May 1992

3 I wasn't satisfied just to earn a good living. I was looking to make a statement.

Donald Trump (b.1946), U.S. businessman: *Trump: The Art of the Deal* (written with Tony Schwartz, 1987), Ch.2

See also THE RICH; WEALTH

TYRANNY

1 Under conditions of tyranny it is far easier to act than to think.

Hannah Arendt (1906–1975), German-born U.S. political philosopher: quoted in *A Certain World* by W.H. Auden (1970), 'Tyranny'

2 Tyranny destroys or strengthens the individual; freedom enervates him, until he becomes no more than a puppet. Man has more chances of saving himself by hell than by paradise.
E.M. Cioran (1911–1995), Rumanian-born French philosopher: *Anathemas and Admirations* (1986), 'On the Verge of Existence'

See also TOTALITARIANISM

UGLINESS

1 I seated ugliness on my knee, and almost immediately grew tired of it.
Salvador Dali (1904–1989), Spanish painter: journal entry, 1 Aug. 1953, in *The Diary of a Genius* (1966). Dali's words echo those of Rimbaud: 'One evening I sat Beauty on my knees – And I found her bitter – And I reviled her' (*Une Saison en Enfer*, 1874)

2 Against the beautiful and the clever and the successful, one can wage a pitiless war, but not against the unattractive: then the millstone weighs on the breast.
Graham Greene (1904–1991), British novelist: *The Heart of the Matter* (1948), Bk.1, Pt.1, Ch.2, Sct.2

UNCERTAINTY

1 The quest for certainty blocks the search for meaning. Uncertainty is the very condition to impel man to unfold his powers.
Erich Fromm (1900–1980), U.S. psychologist: *Man for Himself* (1947), Ch.3

2 Hesitation increases in relation to risk in equal proportion to age.
Ernest Hemingway (1899–1961), U.S. author: quoted in *Papa Hemingway* by A.E. Hotchner (1966 edn.), Pt.1, Ch.3

3 All my life I believed I knew something. But then one strange day came when I realized that I knew nothing, yes, I knew nothing. And so words became void of meaning... I have arrived too late at ultimate uncertainty.
Ezra Pound (1885–1972), U.S. poet and critic: in *Época* (Milan), March 1963

See also DOUBT

UNDERSTANDING

1 The way a child discovers the world constantly replicates the way science began. You start to notice what's around you, and you get very curious about how things work. How things interrelate. It's as simple as seeing a bug that

intrigues you. You want to know where it goes at night; who its friends are; what it eats.
David Cronenberg (b.1943), Canadian film-maker: *Cronenberg on Cronenberg* (ed. Chris Rodley, 1992), Ch.1

2 In the long course of history, having people who understand your thought is much greater security than another submarine.
J. William Fulbright (1905–1995), U.S. Democratic politician: of the Fulbright scholarship programme, in the *New York Times*, 26 June 1986

3 If one does not understand a person, one tends to regard him as a fool.
Carl Jung (1875–1961), Swiss psychiatrist: *Mysterium Coniunctionis* (1955–6), rep. in *Collected Works*, Vol.XIV (ed. William McGuire, 1963), para.147

4 Shallow understanding from people of good will is more frustrating than absolute misunderstanding from people of ill will.
Martin Luther King Jr. (1929–1968), U.S. clergyman and civil rights leader: 'Letter from Birmingham Jail', open letter to clergymen, 16 April 1963, publ. in *Why We Can't Wait* (1963)

5 Society needs to condemn a little more and understand a little less.
John Major (b.1943), British Conservative politician and prime minister: interview in *The Mail on Sunday* (London), 21 Feb. 1993

6 Is an intelligent human being likely to be much more than a large-scale manufacturer of misunderstanding?
Philip Roth (b.1933), U.S. novelist: Nathan Zuckerman, in *The Counterlife* (1986), Ch.5

7 Once something becomes discernible, or understandable, we no longer need to repeat it. We can destroy it.
Robert Wilson (b.1941), U.S. theatre director and designer: quoted in *The Sunday Times* (London), 17 Nov. 1991

UNEMPLOYMENT

1 Gizza job, go on, gizzit!
Alan Bleasdale (b.1946), British playwright and novelist: Yosser Hughes, in *The Boys from the Blackstuff* (TV series, 1983). The catchphrase is usually quoted, 'gissa job!'

2 I lost my job. Actually I didn't lose it; it lost me. I'm overeducated and underskilled – or maybe it's the other way around, I forget. I'm obsolete. I'm not 'economically viable'. I can't even support my own kid.
Michael Douglas (b.1944), U.S. actor: D-Fens (Douglas), in *Falling Down* (film; screenplay by Ebbe Roe Smith, directed by Joel Schumacher, 1993)

3 Being out of a job makes you passive. You spend a lot of time in bed, and you can't be angry while you're asleep.

Roddy Doyle (b.1950), Irish author: referring to Jimmy in *The Snapper*, in interview in the *Independent on Sunday* (London), 14 April 1996

4 When we're unemployed, we're called lazy; when the whites are unemployed it's called a depression.

Jesse Jackson (b.1941), U.S. clergyman and civil rights leader: interview in *The Americans* by David Frost (1970), 'When Whites Are Unemployed, It's Called a Depression'

5 Unemployment insurance is a pre-paid vacation for freeloaders.

Ronald Reagan (b.1911), U.S. Republican politician and president: *Sacramento Bee* (California), 28 April 1966. None the less, on 31 March 1982, Reagan claimed that, 'We have, in some of the hardest-hit states, extended the unemployment insurance. There's nothing that strikes to my heart more than the unemployed...' (quoted in *Reagan's Reign of Error*, ed. Mark Green and Gail MacColl, 1987, 'Want Ads')

6 The left demands full employment for all – we demand full unemployment for all. The world owes us a living!

Jerry Rubin (1938–1994), U.S. essayist and radical leader: *Do It!* (1970), 'Yippie!', Extract 13

7 Career opportunities, the ones that never knock,
Every job they offer you is to keep you out the dock.

Joe Strummer (b.1952) and **Mick Jones** (b.1956), British rock musicians: 'Career Opportunities' (song) on the album *The Clash* (The Clash, 1977)

8 He didn't riot. He got on his bike and looked for work.

Norman Tebbit (b.1931), British Conservative politician: speech to Conservative Party Conference, Blackpool, 15 Oct. 1981, quoted in *The Daily Telegraph* (London), 16 Oct. 1981. Tebbit's speech, contrasting his unemployed father's self-help approach during the Depression with the attitude of rioters in Britain the previous summer, was received with a rousing ovation at the Conservative conference, but provoked widespread controversy in the country at a time when unemployment stood at three million

9 When skilled workers are put out of a job by technical advances and have to undergo 're-training', no one asks whether it is humiliating for them to be pushed around in this way. It is simply taken for granted that everyone must bow to technical necessity.

Unabomber, U.S. radical: *Industrial Society and Its Future*, 'Restriction of Freedom is Unavoidable in Industrial Society', Sct.119, publ. in the *Washington Post*, 19 Sept. 1995

UNHAPPINESS

1 Nothing is funnier than unhappiness, I grant you that. ... Yes, yes, it's the most comical thing in the world.

Samuel Beckett (1906–1989), Irish playwright and novelist: Nell, in *Endgame* (1957; tr.1958)

2 Unhappiness is best defined as the difference between our talents and our expectations.

Edward de Bono (b.1933), British writer on thinking processes: quoted in *The Observer* (London), 12 June 1977

3 He felt the loyalty we feel to unhappiness – the sense that that is where we really belong.

Graham Greene (1904–1991), British novelist: referring to Harris, in *The Heart of the Matter* (1948), Bk.2, Pt.2, Ch.1, Sct.1

4 It's not what isn't, it's what you wish *was* that makes unhappiness. ... I think I think too much. That's why I drink.

Janis Joplin (b.1943), U.S. rock musician: quoted in *Rock 'n' Roll Babylon* by Gary Herman (1982), Ch.3

See also GRIEF; MISERY; SORROW

UNIQUENESS

1 Losing faith in your own singularity is the start of wisdom, I suppose; also the first announcement of death.

Peter Conrad (b.1948), Australian author and critic: *Down Under: Revisiting Tasmania* (1988), Pt.6, 'In the Family'

2 Today, we have something in which is a desire for individual recognition. We strive for this recognition by trying to achieve perfection, and we deceive ourselves into calling the result heaven. We want whatever we do to be unique.

Bernard Leach (1887–1979), British potter: *The Potter's Challenge* (1976), Ch.1

3 One of the supreme debts one great writer can owe another is the realization of unlikeness.

F.R. Leavis (1895–1978), British literary critic: *The Great Tradition* (1948), Ch.1

THE UNITED NATIONS

1 The U.N. is not just a product of do-gooders. It is harshly real. The day will come when men will see the U.N. and what it means clearly. Everything will be all right – you know when? When people, just people, stop thinking of the United Nations as a weird Picasso abstraction, and see it as a drawing they made themselves.

Dag Hammarskjöld (1905–1961), Swedish statesman and secretary-general of the U.N.: in *Time* (New York), 27 June 1955

2   This organization is created to prevent you from going to hell. It isn't created to take you to heaven.
    Henry Cabot Lodge Jr. (1902–1985), U.S. Republican senator and U.N. delegate: in the *New York Times*, 28 Jan. 1954

3   The United Nations cannot do anything, and never could; it is not an animate entity or agent. It is a place, a stage, a forum and a shrine ... a place to which powerful people can repair when they are fearful about the course on which their own rhetoric seems to be propelling them.
    Conor Cruise O'Brien (b.1917), Irish historian, diplomat and critic: in the *New Republic* (Washington D.C.), 4 Nov. 1985

4   I am like a doctor. I have written a prescription to help the patient. If the patient doesn't want all the pills I've recommended that's up to him. But I must warn that next time I will have to come as a surgeon with a knife.
    Javier Perez de Cuéllar (b.1920), Peruvian diplomat and secretary-general of the U.N.: on the introduction of cost-cutting measures at the U.N., quoted in *The Guardian* (London), 10 May 1986, rep. in *Lords of Poverty* by Graham Hancock (1989), Pt.3

THE UNITED STATES

1   America fears the unshaven legs, the unshaven men's cheeks, the aroma of perspiration, and the limp prick. Above all it fears the limp prick.
    Walter Abish (b.1931), Austrian-born U.S. author: *In The Future Perfect* (1975), 'In So Many Words'

2   God bless the U.S.A., so large,
    So friendly, and so rich.
    W.H. Auden (1907–1973), Anglo-American poet: 'On the Circuit', publ. in *Collected Poems* (1976)

3   What you have to do is enter the fiction of America, enter America as fiction. It is, indeed, on this fictive basis that it dominates the world.
    Jean Baudrillard (b.1929), French semiologist: *America* (1986; tr.1988), 'Astral America'

4   The spirit is at home, if not entirely satisfied, in America.
    Allan Bloom (1930–1992), U.S. educator and author: *The Closing of the American Mind* (1987), Pt.2, 'Two Revolutions and Two States of Nature'

5   The most important American addition to the World Experience was the simple surprising fact of America. We have helped prepare mankind for all its later surprises.
    Daniel J. Boorstin (b.1914), U.S. historian: Reith Lecture, Oct. 1975, publ. in *The Exploring Spirit: America and the World Experience* (1976), Lecture 6

6   In America, you can sell a record but you can't sell a look. ... They don't identify with glamour, they just identify with jeans and a leather jacket.
    Boy George (b.1961), British singer: interview in *Smash Hits* (London), 23 Dec. 1982

7   One could view America today as a sort of Good Guys' Convention that has lasted two hundred years.
    Julie Burchill (b.1960), British journalist and author: *Girls on Film* (1986), Ch.2

8   America is not so much a nightmare as a *nondream*. The American non-dream is precisely a move to wipe the dream out of existence. The dream is a spontaneous happening and therefore dangerous to a control system set up by the non-dreamers.
    William Burroughs (1914–1997), U.S. author: *The Job: Interviews with Daniel Odier* (1969), 'Prisoners of the Earth Come Out'

9   I want a kinder, gentler nation.
    George Bush (b.1924), U.S. Republican politician and president: acceptance speech, 18 Aug. 1988, Republican National Convention, New Orleans, quoted in the *New York Times*, 19 Aug. 1988. Charlie Chaplin had used a similar form of words at the end of *The Great Dictator* (1940), when he urged, 'More than cleverness, we need kindness and gentleness'

10 I have no further use for America. I wouldn't go back there if Jesus Christ was President.
    Charlie Chaplin (1889–1977), British comic actor and film-maker: quoted in *Halliwell's Filmgoer's Companion* (ed. Leslie Halliwell, 1984)

11 America is the world's living myth. There's no sense of wrong when you kill an American or blame America for some local disaster. This is our function, to be character types, to embody recurring themes that people can use to comfort themselves, justify themselves and so on. We're here to accommodate. Whatever people need, we provide. A myth is a useful thing.
    Don DeLillo (b.1926), U.S. author: James Axton, in *The Names* (1982), Ch.5

12 I like America, just as everybody else does. I love America, I gotta say that. But America will be judged.
    Bob Dylan (b.1941), U.S. singer and songwriter: on stage at Tempe, Arizona, 26 Nov. 1979, quoted in *Wanted Man* (ed. John Bauldie, 1990), 'Saved: Bob Dylan's Conversion to Christianity'

13 Two centuries ago, a former European colony decided to catch up with Europe. It succeeded so well that the United States of America became a monster, in which the taints, the

sickness and the inhumanity of Europe have grown to appalling dimensions.
Frantz Fanon (1925–1961), Martiniquan psychiatrist, philosopher and political activist: *The Wretched of the Earth* (1961), Ch.4

14 America is rather like life. You can usually find in it what you look for. ... It will probably be interesting, and it is sure to be large.
E.M. Forster (1879–1970), British novelist and essayist: 'Impressions of the United States', first publ. in *The Listener* (London), 4 Sept. 1947, rep. in *Two Cheers for Democracy* (1951) as 'The United States'

15 What the United States does best is to understand itself. What it does worst is understand others.
Carlos Fuentes (b.1928), Mexican author: in *Time* (New York), 16 Jun 1986

16 America is still mostly xenophobic and racist. That's the nature of America, I think.
Jerry Garcia (1942–1995), U.S. rock musician: interview in *Rolling Stone* (New York), 30 Nov. 1989

17 America I'm putting my queer shoulder to the wheel.
Allen Ginsberg (b.1926), U.S. poet: last line of 'America', publ. in *Howl and Other Poems* (1956)

18 Ours is the only country deliberately founded on a good idea.
John Gunther (1901–1970), U.S. journalist: foreword to *Inside U.S.A.* (1947)

19 In Washington, the first thing people tell you is what their job is. In Los Angeles you learn their star sign. In Houston you're told how rich they are. And in New York they tell you what their rent is.
Simon Hoggart (b.1946), British journalist: *America: A User's Guide* (1990), Ch.1

20 America is the number one killer of people; a superpower that the world has never seen before in its history. America made it cool to be violent.
Ice Cube (b.1969), U.S. rapper: in *New Musical Express* (London), 1994, quoted in *NME Book of Quotes* (1995), 'Travel'

21 The United States has now achieved what critics of socialism have always posited as the end result of a socialist state: a prosperous, empty, uninspiring uniformity. If we do not have exactly what Marx meant by a classless society, we do have something so close to it that the term is certainly no longer an alluring goal.
Pauline Kael (b.1919), U.S. film critic: *I Lost it at the Movies* (1965), 'The Glamour of Delinquency'

22 The United States has to move very fast to even stand still.
John F. Kennedy (1917–1963), U.S. Democratic politician and president: quoted in *The Observer* (London), 21 July 1963

23 I don't like America. It's too big. There are too many people. Everyone runs around too quickly. There's too much commotion, too much uproar. Everybody pretends too hard that they're happy there. But I don't believe in their happiness, I think they're just as unhappy as we are, except that we still talk about it sometimes but they only say that everything's fine, that it's fantastic. ... If I had to be confronted for a whole year with people saying that everything's fantastic then I simply couldn't stand it.
Krzysztof Kieślowski (1941–1996), Polish filmmaker: *Kieślowski on Kieślowski* (1993), Ch.4

24 America is not a democracy, it's an absolute monarchy ruled by King Kid. In a nation of immigrants, the child is automatically more of an American than his parents. ... Americans regard children as what Mr Hudson in 'Upstairs, Downstairs' called 'betters'. Aping their betters, American adults do their best to turn themselves into children. Puerility exercises *droit de seigneur* everywhere.
Florence King (b.1936), U.S. author: *Reflections in a Jaundiced Eye* (1989), 'Good King Herod'

25 I feel most at home in the United States, not because it is intrinsically a more interesting country, but because no one really belongs there any more than I do. We are all there together in its wholly excellent vacuum.
Wyndham Lewis (1882–1957), British author and painter: *America and Cosmic Man* (1948), 'The Case Against Roots'

26 America is like one of those old-fashioned six-cylinder truck engines that can be missing two sparkplugs and have a broken flywheel and have a crankshaft that's 5000 millimetres off fitting properly, and two bad ball-bearings, and still runs. We're in that kind of situation. We can have substantial parts of the population committing suicide, and still run and look fairly good.
Thomas McGuane (b.1939), U.S. novelist: in the *Sunday Correspondent* (London), 1 April 1990

27 There is one expanding horror in American life. It is that our long odyssey toward liberty, democracy and freedom-for-all may be achieved in such a way that utopia remains forever closed, and we live in freedom and hell, debased of style, not individual from one another, void of courage, our fear rationalized away.
Norman Mailer (b.1923), U.S. author: 'My Hope for America' (review of book by Lyndon B. Johnson), rep. in *Cannibals and Christians* (1966), Pt.1

28 I don't see America as a mainland, but as a sea, a big ocean. Sometimes a storm arises, a formidable current develops, and it seems it will engulf everything. Wait a moment, another current will appear and bring the first one to naught.
Jacques Maritain (1882–1973), French philosopher: *Reflections on America* (1948), Ch.4

29 Is America a land of God where saints abide for ever? Where golden fields spread fair and broad, where flows the crystal river? Certainly not flush with saints, and a good thing, too, for the saints sent buzzing into man's ken now are but poor-mouthed ecclesiastical film stars and cliché-shouting publicity agents.
Their little knowledge bringing them nearer to
    their ignorance,
Ignorance bringing them nearer to death,
But nearness to death no nearer to God.
Sean O'Casey (1884–1964), Irish playwright: *Rose and Crown* (fifth volume of autobiography, 1952), 'Only Five Minutes More'

30 Our democracy, our culture, our whole way of life is a spectacular triumph of the blah. ... Maybe our national mindlessness is the very thing that keeps us from turning into one of those smelly European countries full of pseudo-reds and crypto-fascists and greens who dress like forest elves.
P.J. O'Rourke (b.1947), U.S. journalist: *Parliament of Whores* (1991), 'On the Blandwagon'

31 I take SPACE to be the central fact to man born in America. ... I spell it large because it comes large here. Large and without mercy.
Charles Olson (1910–1970), U.S. poet and critic: *Call Me Ishmael* (1947), Sct.1

32 It is capitalist America that produced the modern independent woman. Never in history have women had more freedom of choice in regard to dress, behavior, career, and sexual orientation.
Camille Paglia (b.1947), U.S. author and critic: 'The Big Udder', first publ. in the *Philadelphia Enquirer*, 12 May 1991, rep. in *Sex, Art, and American Culture* (1992)

33 The North American system only wants to consider the positive aspects of reality. Men and women are subjected from childhood to an inexorable process of adaptation; certain principles, contained in brief formulas, are endlessly repeated by the Press, the radio, the churches, and the schools, and by those kindly, sinister beings, the North American mothers and wives. A person imprisoned by these schemes is like a plant in a flowerpot too small for it: he cannot grow or mature.
Octavio Paz (b.1914), Mexican poet and essayist: *The Labyrinth of Solitude* (1950; tr.1961), Ch.1

34 There's an enduring American compulsion to be on the side of the angels. Expediency alone has never been an adequate American reason for doing anything. When actions are judged, they go before the bar of God, where Mom and the Flag closely flank His presence.
Jonathan Raban (b.1942), British author and critic: *For Love and Money* (1987), Pt.2

35 Thank God we're living in a country where the sky's the limit, the stores are open late and you can shop in bed thanks to television.
Joan Rivers (b.1935), U.S. comedienne: in the *International Herald Tribune* (Paris), 31 May 1989

36 America is the civilization of people engaged in transforming themselves. In the past, the stars of the performance were the pioneer and the immigrant. Today, it is youth and the Black.
Harold Rosenberg (1906–1978), U.S. art critic and author: *Discovering the Present* (1973), Pt.4, Ch.24

37 I like to be in America!
OK by me in America!
Ev'rything free in America
For a small fee in America!
Stephen Sondheim (b.1930), U.S. songwriter: 'America' (song) in *West Side Story* (stage musical, 1957; film, 1961)

38 The quality of American life is an insult to the possibilities of human growth ... the pollution of American space, with gadgetry and cars and TV and box architecture, brutalizes the senses, making gray neurotics of most of us, and perverse spiritual athletes and strident self-transcenders of the best of us.
Susan Sontag (b.1933), U.S. essayist: 'What's Happening in America (1966)', first publ. in *Partisan Review* (New Brunswick, N.J.), winter 1967, rep. in *Styles of Radical Will* (1969)

39 This monster of a land, this mightiest of nations, this spawn of the future, turns out to be the macrocosm of microcosm me.
John Steinbeck (1902–1968), U.S. author: *Travels With Charley: in Search of America* (1962), Pt.3

40 In America, everybody is in show business, and fame is almost within everybody's grasp. All the taxi drivers are showbiz taxi drivers, and nobody isn't an actor. ... Every walk of life in America has its counterpart in television. There are situation comedies and dramas about every walk of life, and everyone has a kind of stage rhetoric that he or she uses. Everyone is aware of the camera, whether it exists or not, and it seems that everybody in this country aspires to be famous.
Sting (b.1951), British rock musician: interview in *Rolling Stone* (New York), Sept. 1983

41 The biggest difference between ancient Rome and the U.S.A. is that in Rome the common man was treated like a dog. In America he sets

the tone. This is the first country where the common man could stand erect.

I.F. Stone (1907–1989), U.S. author: remark to Clive James, quoted in his *Flying Visits* (1984), 'Postcard from Washington'

42 In a nation ruled by swine, all pigs are upward-mobile – and the rest of us are fucked until we can put our acts together: not necessarily to win, but mainly to keep from losing completely. We owe that to ourselves and our crippled self-image as something better than a nation of panicked sheep.

Hunter S. Thompson (b.1939), U.S. journalist: *The Great Shark Hunt* (1979), 'Jacket Copy for Fear and Loathing in Las Vegas'

43 America is a vast conspiracy to make you happy.

John Updike (b.1932), U.S. author and critic: *Problems* (1980), 'How to Love America and Leave it at the Same Time'

44 It's the movies that have really been running things in America ever since they were invented. They show you what to do, how to do it, when to do it, how to feel about it, and how to look how you feel about it. Everybody has their own America, and then they have the pieces of a fantasy America that they think is out there but they can't see.

Andy Warhol (c.1928–1987), U.S. Pop artist: quoted in *Warhol* by Victor Bokris (1989), 'The Education of Andy Warhol 1937–45'

45 A man is not expected to love his country, lest he make an ass of himself. Yet our country, seen through the mists of smog, is curiously lovable, in somewhat the way an individual who has got himself into an unconscionable scrape seems lovable – or at least deserving of support.

E.B. White (1899–1985), U.S. author and editor: 'A Busy Place', first publ. in the *New Yorker*, 5 July 1976, rep. in *Writings from the New Yorker 1927–1976* (ed. Rebecca M. Dale, 1991)

46 The gap between ideals and actualities, between dreams and achievements, the gap that can spur strong men to increased exertions, but can break the spirit of others – this gap is the most conspicuous, continuous landmark in American history. It is conspicuous and continuous not because Americans achieve little, but because they dream grandly. The gap is a standing reproach to Americans; but it marks them off as a special and singularly admirable community among the world's peoples.

George F. Will (b.1941), U.S. political columnist: *Statecraft as Soulcraft: What Government Does* (1984), Ch.4

See also Marcus on ADVERSITY; THE AMERICAN DREAM; Gibson on CITIES: URBAN CULTURE;

Thurber on DISSENT; EUROPE: AND AMERICA; HOLLYWOOD; Chomsky on THE MEDIA; Vidal on THE MEDIA; Noonan on MODERN LIFE; THE NEW WORLD; Vonnegut on POLITICAL PARTIES; Bradlee on POLITICS; Rosenberg on POLITICS; Vidal on PUBLICITY; Morrison on RACE; Genet on RACISM; Sontag on RACISM; Trilling on REALITY; Hughes on SELF; Jong on SOLITUDE; Barzun on SPORT: BASEBALL; Malone on TABOO; Wolfe on TEENAGERS; Brown on VIOLENCE; Scott on WAR

THE UNITED STATES: African Americans

1 The fact that the adult American Negro female emerges a formidable character is often met with amazement, distaste and even belligerence. It is seldom accepted as an inevitable outcome of the struggle won by survivors, and deserves respect if not enthusiastic acceptance.

Maya Angelou (b.1928), U.S. author: *I Know Why the Caged Bird Sings* (first volume of autobiography, 1969), Ch.34

2 When you're called a nigger you look at your father because you think your father can rule the world – every kid thinks that – and then you discover that your father cannot do anything about it. So you begin to despise your father and you realize, oh, that's what a nigger is.

James Baldwin (1924–1987), U.S. author: in conversation with Nikki Giovanni, London, 4 Nov. 1971, publ. in *A Dialogue* (1973)

3 To be black and an intellectual in America is to live in a box.... On the box is a label, not of my own choosing.

Stephen Carter (b.1954), U.S. lawyer and author: introduction to *Reflections of an Affirmative Action Baby* (1992)

4 To be a Negro is to participate in a culture of poverty and fear that goes far deeper than any law for or against discrimination. ... After the racist statutes are all struck down, after legal equality has been achieved in the schools and in the courts, there remains the profound institutionalized and abiding wrong that white America has worked on the Negro for so long.

Michael Harrington (1928–1989), U.S. social scientist and author: *The Other America* (1962), Ch.4

5 If you wake up in the morning and think you're white, you're bound to meet someone before five o'clock who will let you know you are just another nigger.

Jesse Jackson (b.1941), U.S. clergyman and civil rights leader: in *The Sun* (London), 20 Sept. 1989

6 Body and soul, Black America reveals the extreme questions of contemporary life, questions of freedom and identity: *How can I be who I am?*

June Jordan (b.1936), U.S. poet and civil rights activist: 'Black Studies: Bringing Back the Person', first publ. in the *Evergreen Review* (New York), Oct. 1969, rep. in *Moving Towards Home: Political Essays* (1989)

7 We were here before the mighty words of the Declaration of Independence were etched across the pages of history. Our forebears labored without wages. They made cotton 'king'. And yet out of a bottomless vitality, they continued to thrive and develop. If the cruelties of slavery could not stop us, the opposition we now face will surely fail.... Because the goal of America is freedom, abused and scorned tho' we may be, our destiny is tied up with America's destiny.

Martin Luther King Jr. (1929–1968), U.S. clergyman and civil rights leader: 'Letter from Birmingham Jail', open letter to clergymen, 16 April 1963, publ. in *Why We Can't Wait* (1963). The last sentence of this extract recalls a speech by abolitionist Frederick Douglass, in Boston, 12 Feb. 1862: 'The destiny of the colored American ... is the destiny of America'

8 The common goal of 22 million Afro-Americans is respect as *human beings*, the God-given right to be a *human being*. Our common goal is to obtain the *human rights* that America has been denying us. We can never get civil rights in America until our *human rights* are first restored. We will never be recognized as citizens there until we are first recognized as *humans*.

Malcolm X (1925–1965), U.S. black leader: 'Racism: the Cancer that is Destroying America', publ. in *Egyptian Gazette* (Cairo), 25 Aug. 1964. See Gregory on CIVIL RIGHTS

9 The Afro-American experience is the only real culture that America has. Basically, every American tries to walk, talk, dress and behave like African Americans.

Hugh Masakela (b.1939), South African jazz trumpeter: in the *International Herald Tribune* (Paris), 17 May 1990

10 The warped, distorted frame we have put around every Negro child from birth is around every white child also. Each is on a different side of the frame but each is pinioned there. And ... what cruelly shapes and cripples the personality of one is as cruelly shaping and crippling the personality of the other.

Lillian Smith (1897–1966), U.S. author: *Killers of the Dream* (1949; rev.1961), Pt.1, Ch.1

11 The trouble with our people is as soon as they got out of slavery they didn't want to give the white man nothing else. But the fact is, you got to give 'em something. Either your money, your land, your woman or your ass.

Alice Walker (b.1944), U.S. author and critic: Pa, in

The Color Purple (1982), p.155 of Women's Press edn. (1983)

12 People see me and they see that I am black, that's something that I celebrate. But I don't feel that it's something that I need to wave a banner about, which used to cause me all kinds of problems in college. I was not a dashiki-wearing kind of woman.

Oprah Winfrey (b.1954), U.S. chat-show host: interview on *60 Minutes* (U.S. TV show), quoted in *Oprah!* by Robert Waldron (1987), Ch.5

See also BLACK CULTURE; BLACK CONSCIOUSNESS/BLACK POWER

THE UNITED STATES: Americans

1 If a stranger taps you on the ass and says, 'How's the little lady today!' you will probably cringe. But if he's an American, he's only being friendly.

Margaret Atwood (b.1939), Canadian novelist, poet and critic: 'A Question Of Metamorphosis', interview first publ. in *Malahat Review*, No.41, 1977, rep. in *Conversations* (ed. Earl G. Ingersoll, 1990)

2 Americans, unhappily, have the most remarkable ability to alchemize all bitter truths into an innocuous but piquant confection and to transform their moral contradictions, or public discussion of such contradictions, into a proud decoration, such as are given for heroism on the battle field.

James Baldwin (1924–1987), U.S. author: 'Many Thousands Gone', first publ. in *Partisan Review* (New Brunswick, N.J.), Nov./Dec. 1951, rep. in *Notes of a Native Son* (1955), Pt.1

3 There is a constant in the average American imagination and taste, for which the past must be preserved and celebrated in full-scale authentic copy; a philosophy of immortality as duplication. It dominates the relation with the self, with the past, not infrequently with the present, always with History and, even, with the European tradition.

Umberto Eco (b.1932), Italian semiologist and novelist: *Travels in Hyperreality* (1986), 'Travels in Hyperreality: the Fortresses of Solitude'

4 To be an American (unlike being English or French or whatever) is precisely to *imagine* a destiny rather than to inherit one; since we have always been, insofar as we are Americans at all, inhabitants of myth rather than history.

Leslie Fiedler (b.1917), U.S. critic: 'Cross the Border – Close the Gap', first publ. in *Playboy* (Chicago), Dec. 1969, rep. in *Collected Essays* Vol.II (1971)

5 Americans see history as a straight line and themselves standing at the cutting edge of it as representatives for all mankind. They believe

in the future as if it were a religion; they believe that there is nothing they cannot accomplish, that solutions wait somewhere for all problems, like brides.

Frances Fitzgerald (b.1940), U.S. journalist and author: *Fire in the Lake* (1972), Pt.1, Ch.1

6 The American character looks always as if it had just had a rather bad haircut, which gives it, in our eyes at any rate, a greater humanity than the European, which even among its beggars has an all too professional air.

Mary McCarthy (1912–1989), U.S. author and critic: 'America the Beautiful', first publ. in *Commentary* (New York), Sept. 1947, rep. in *On the Contrary* (1961)

7 The American mood, perhaps even the American character, has changed. There are few manifestations any longer of the old American self-assurance which so irritated Dickens. ... Instead, there is a sense of frustration so perceptible that even our politicians ... have attempted to exploit it.

Archibald MacLeish (1892–1982), U.S. poet: 'The Great American Frustration', first publ. in the *Saturday Review* (New York), 9 July 1968, rep. in *Riders on Earth* (1978) as 'Return from the Excursion'

8 Sitting at the table doesn't make you a diner, unless you eat some of what's on that plate. Being here in America doesn't make you an American. Being born here in America doesn't make you an American.

Malcolm X (1925–1965), U.S. black leader: 'The Ballot or the Bullet', speech, 3 April 1964, Cleveland, Ohio, publ. in *Malcolm X Speaks* (1965), Ch.3

9 People in America, of course, live in all sorts of fashions, because they are foreigners, or unlucky, or depraved, or without ambition; people live like that, but *Americans* live in white detached houses with green shutters. Rigidly, blindly, the dream takes precedence.

Margaret Mead (1901–1978), U.S. anthropologist: *Male and Female* (1949), Ch.12

10 Perhaps I am still very much of an American. That is to say, naïve, optimistic, gullible. ... In the eyes of a European, what am I but an American to the core, an American who exposes his Americanism like a sore. Like it or not, I am a product of this land of plenty, a believer in superabundance, a believer in miracles.

Henry Miller (1891–1980), U.S. author: 'A Devil in Paradise' (1956), rep. as 'Paradise Lost' in *Big Sur and the Oranges of Hieronymous Bosch* (1957), Pt.3

11 Being blunt with your feelings is very American. In this big country, I can be as brash as New York, as hedonistic as Los Angeles, as sensuous as San Francisco, as brainy as Boston, as proper as Philadelphia, as brawny as Chicago, as warm as Palm Springs, as friendly as my adopted home town of Dallas, Fort Worth, and as peaceful as the inland waterway that rubs up against my former home in Virginia Beach.

Martina Navratilova (b.1956), Czech-born U.S. tennis player: *Martina Navratilova – Being Myself* (1985), Ch.1

12 A trait no other nation seems to possess in quite the same degree that we do – namely, a feeling of almost childish injury and resentment unless the world as a whole recognizes how innocent we are of anything but the most generous and harmless intentions.

Eleanor Roosevelt (1884–1962), U.S. columnist, lecturer and wife of F.D. Roosevelt: 'My Day', syndicated newspaper column, 11 Nov. 1946

13 The story of Americans is the story of arrested metamorphoses. Those who achieve success come to a halt and accept themselves as they are. Those who fail become resigned and accept themselves as they are.

Harold Rosenberg (1906–1978), U.S. art critic and author: *Discovering the Present* (1973), Pt.4, Ch.24

14 American 'energy'...is the energy of violence, of free-floating resentment and anxiety unleashed by chronic cultural dislocations which must be, for the most part, ferociously sublimated. This energy has mainly been sublimated into crude materialism and acquisitiveness. Into hectic philanthropy. Into benighted moral crusades, the most spectacular of which was Prohibition. Into an awesome talent for uglifying countryside and cities. Into the loquacity and torment of a minority of gadflies: artists, prophets, muckrakers, cranks, and nuts. And into self-punishing neuroses. But the naked violence keeps breaking through, throwing everything into question.

Susan Sontag (b.1933), U.S. essayist: 'What's Happening in America (1966)', first publ. in *Partisan Review* (New Brunswick, N.J.), winter 1967, rep. in *Styles of Radical Will* (1969)

15 Being American is to eat a lot of beef steak, and boy, we've got a lot more beef steak than any other country, and that's why you ought to be glad you're an American. And people have started looking at these big hunks of bloody meat on their plates, you know, and wondering what on earth they think they're doing.

Kurt Vonnegut (b.1922), U.S. novelist: in *City Limits* (London), 11 March 1983

16 That impersonal insensitive friendliness which takes the place of ceremony in that land of waifs and strays.

Evelyn Waugh (1903–1966), British novelist: of Aimée Thanatogenos, an American, in *The Loved One* (1948), p.71 of Penguin edn. (1951)

17 The ideal American type is perfectly expressed by the Protestant, individualist, anti-

conformist, and this is the type that is in the process of disappearing. In reality there are few left.

Orson Welles (1915–1985), U.S. film-maker and actor: interview in *Hollywood Voices* (ed. Andrews Sarris, 1971)

See also Harrington on DRESS; Hobsbawm on PATRIOTISM; Lewis on ROOTS; Baldwin on SEXUALITY; Baudrillard on TEETH; Muggeridge on YOUTH

THE UNITED STATES: Americans Abroad

1 When Americans look out on the world, they see nothing but dark and menacing strangers who appear to have no sense of rhythm at all, nor any respect or affection for white people; and white Americans really do not know what to make of all this, except to increase the defense budget.

James Baldwin (1924–1987), U.S. author: *The Price of the Ticket* (1985), 'Notes on the House of Bondage'

2 The modern American tourist now fills his experience with pseudo-events. He has come to expect both more strangeness and more familiarity than the world naturally offers. He has come to believe that he can have a lifetime of adventure in two weeks and all the thrills of risking his life without any real risk at all.

Daniel J. Boorstin (b.1914), U.S. historian: *The Image* (1961), Ch.3

3 You can always tell a Midwestern couple in Europe because they will be standing in the middle of a busy intersection looking at a wind-blown map and arguing over which way is west. European cities, with their wandering streets and undisciplined alleys, drive Mid-westerners practically insane.

Bill Bryson (b.1951), U.S. author and journalist: *The Lost Continent: Travels in Small Town America* (1989), Ch.2

4 Americans are rather like bad Bulgarian wine: they don't travel well.

Bernard Falk (1943–1990), British broadcaster and author: quoted in *The Observer* (London), 27 April 1986

5 If a foreign country doesn't look like a middle-class suburb of Dallas or Detroit, then ob-viously the natives must be dangerous as well as badly dressed.

Lewis H. Lapham (b.1935), U.S. essayist and editor: *Money and Class in America* (1988), Ch.5, Sct.1

6 Does this boat go to Europe, France?

Marilyn Monroe (1926–1962), U.S. actress: Lorelei Lee (Monroe), in *Gentlemen Prefer Blondes* (film; screenplay by Charles Lederer, based on the original novel by Anita Loos, directed by Howard Hawkes, 1953)

THE UNITED STATES: Boston

1 I have just returned from Boston, it is the only sane thing to do if you find yourself up there.

Fred Allen (1894–1957), U.S. radio comic: quoted in *The Groucho Letters* by Groucho Marx (1967), 'Touching on Television'

2 I guess God made Boston on a wet Sunday.

Raymond Chandler (1880–1959), U.S. author: letter, 21 March 1949, publ. in *The Selected Letters of Raymond Chandler* (1981)

THE UNITED STATES: Chicago

1 Chicago – is – oh well a façade of skyscrapers facing a lake, and behind the façade every type of dubiousness.

E.M. Forster (1879–1970), British novelist and essayist: letter, 5 June 1947, publ. in *Selected Letters of E.M. Forster* Vol.II (ed. Mary Lago and P.N. Furbank, 1985)

2 New York is one of the capitals of the world and Los Angeles is a constellation of plastic, San Francisco is a lady, Boston has become Urban Renewal, Philadelphia and Baltimore and Washington blink like dull diamonds in the smog of Eastern Megalopolis, and New Orleans is unremarkable past the French Quarter. Detroit is a one-trade town, Pitts-burgh has lost its golden triangle, St Louis has become the golden arch of the corporation, and nights in Kansas City close early. The oil depletion allowance makes Houston and Dallas naught but checkerboards for this sort of game. But Chicago is a great American city. Perhaps it is the last of the great American cities.

Norman Mailer (b.1923), U.S. author: *Miami and the Siege of Chicago* (1969), opening paragraph of 'The Siege of Chicago'

THE UNITED STATES: Foreign Policy

1 U.S. international and security policy ... has as its primary goal the preservation of what we might call 'the Fifth Freedom', understood crudely but with a fair degree of accuracy as the freedom to rob, to exploit and to dominate, to undertake any course of action to ensure that existing privilege is protected and advanced.

Noam Chomsky (b.1928), U.S. linguist and poli-tical analyst: preface to *The Culture of Terrorism* (1988)

2 Americans think of themselves collectively as a huge rescue squad on twenty-four-hour call to

any spot on the globe where dispute and conflict may erupt.

Eldridge Cleaver (b.1935), U.S. black leader and writer: *Soul on Ice* (1968), Pt.2, 'Rallying Round the Flag'

3 The American foreign policy trauma of the sixties and seventies was caused by applying valid principles to unsuitable conditions.

Henry Kissinger (b.1923), U.S. Republican politician and secretary of state: arguing against a role for the U.S. as world policeman, in *The Guardian* (London), 16 Dec. 1992

4 Our policy is directed not against any country or doctrine, but against hunger, poverty, desperation and chaos. Its purpose should be the revival of a working economy in the world so as to permit the emergence of political and social conditions in which free institutions can exist.

George Marshall (1880–1959), U.S. general and Democratic politician: speech, 5 June 1947, Harvard University, describing what became known as the Marshall Plan for recovery in post-war Europe, quoted in *The Harper Book of American Quotations* (ed. Gorton Carruth and Eugene Ehrlich, 1988)

5 Whatever it is that the government does, sensible Americans would prefer that the government do it to somebody else. This is the idea behind foreign policy.

P.J. O'Rourke (b.1947), U.S. journalist: *Parliament of Whores* (1991), 'Very Foreign Policy'

6 We cannot play innocents abroad in a world that is not innocent.

Ronald Reagan (b.1911), U.S. Republican politician and president: speech, 6 Feb. 1985, publ. in *Speaking My Mind* (1989), 'The Wit and Wisdom of Ronald Reagan'

7 Strangely, and despite its intercontinental range and its genuinely various elements, American domination is insular. The foreign-policy elite has no long standing tradition of direct rule overseas, as was the case with the British or the French, so American attention works in spurts; great masses of rhetoric and huge resources are lavished somewhere (Vietnam, Libya, Iraq, Panama), followed by virtual silence.

Edward Said (b.1935), Lebanese-born U.S. social and literary critic: *Culture and Imperialism* (1993), Ch.4, Sct.1

See also Lippmann on ALLIANCES; Gromyko on THE SUPERPOWERS; Said on THE SUPERPOWERS; Lapham on THE THIRD WORLD; Roszak on THE THIRD WORLD; Ehrenreich on WAR

THE UNITED STATES: Los Angeles

1 I don't wanna live in a city where the only cultural advantage is that you can make a right turn on a red light.

Woody Allen (b.1935), U.S. film-maker: Alvy Singer (Allen), comparing Los Angeles unfavourably with Manhattan, in *Annie Hall* (film; screenplay by Woody Allen and Marshall Brickman, directed by Woody Allen, 1977)

2 It is in love with its limitless horizontality, as New York may be with its verticality.

Jean Baudrillard (b.1929), French semiologist: *America* (1986; tr.1988), 'Astral America'

3 It's like a jumble of huts in a jungle somewhere. I don't understand how you can live there. It's really, completely dead. Walk along the street, there's nothing moving. I've lived in small Spanish fishing villages which were literally sunny all day long everyday of the week, but they weren't as boring as Los Angeles.

Truman Capote (1924–1984), U.S. author: *Conversations With Truman Capote* (ed. Lawrence Grobel, 1985), Ch.7, 'Hollywood'

4 Billboards, billboards, drink this, eat that, use all manner of things, EVERYONE, the best, the cheapest, the purest and most satisfying of all their available counterparts. Red lights flicker on every horizon, airplanes beware; cars flash by, more lights. Workers repair the gas main. Signs, signs, lights, lights, streets, streets.

Neal Cassady (1926–1968), U.S. beat hero: 'Leaving LA by Train at Night, High...', publ. in *The First Third and Other Writings* (1971)

5 I used to like this town. ... Los Angeles was just a big dry sunny place with ugly homes and no style, but good-hearted and peaceful. ... Now ... we've got the big money, the sharpshooters, the percentage workers, the fast dollar boys, the hoodlums out of New York and Chicago and Detroit – and Cleveland. We've got the flash restaurants and night clubs they run, and the hotels and apartment houses they own, and the grifters and con men and female bandits that live in them. The luxury trades, the pansy decorators, the Lesbian dress designers, the riff-raff of a big hardboiled city with no more personality than a paper cup.

Raymond Chandler (1888–1959), U.S. author: Philip Marlowe, in *The Little Sister* (1949), Ch.26

6 Twenty-four hours a day somebody is running, somebody else is trying to catch him. Out there in the night of a thousand crimes people were dying, being maimed, cut by flying glass, crushed against steering wheels or under heavy car tyres. People were being beaten, robbed,

strangled, raped, and murdered. People were hungry, sick, bored, desperate with loneliness or remorse or fear, angry, cruel, feverish, shaken by sobs. A city no worse than others, a city rich and vigorous and full of pride, a city lost and beaten and full of emptiness.

Raymond Chandler: Philip Marlowe, describing Los Angeles, in *The Long Goodbye* (1953), Ch.38

7 The freeway experience ... is the only secular communion Los Angeles has. ... Actual participation requires a total surrender, a concentration so intense as to seem a kind of narcosis, a rapture-of-the-freeway. The mind goes clean. The rhythm takes over.

Joan Didion (b.1934), U.S. essayist: 'The Bureaucrats' (1976), rep. in *The White Album* (1979)

8 Everybody in Los Angeles lives miles away, not from anywhere, because there isn't actually anywhere to live away from, but from each other.

Simon Gray (b.1936), British playwright: *How's That for Telling 'Em, Fat Lady?* (1988), Ch.2

9 Prejudices are useless. Call Los Angeles any dirty name you like – Six Suburbs in Search of a City, Paradise with a Lobotomy, anything – but the fact remains that you are already living in it before you get there.

Clive James (b.1939), Australian writer and critic: 'Postcard from Los Angeles 1', first publ. in *The Observer* (London), 16 June 1979, rep. in *Flying Visits* (1984)

10 There are two modes of transport in Los Angeles: car and ambulance. Visitors who wish to remain inconspicuous are advised to choose the latter

Fran Lebowitz (b.1951), U.S. journalist: *Social Studies* (1981), 'Lesson 1'

11 Of all the world's storied thoroughfares, it must be confessed that none produces quite the effect of Hollywood Boulevard. I have been downcast in Piccadilly, chopfallen on the Champs Elysées, and *doloroso* on the Via Veneto, but the avenues themselves were blameless. Hollywood Boulevard, on the contrary, creates an instant and malign impression in the breast of the beholder. Viewed in full sunlight, its tawdriness is unspeakable; in the torrential downpour of the rainy season, as we first saw it, it inspired an anguish similar to that produced by the engravings of Piranesi.

S.J. Perelman (1904–1979), U.S. writer and humorist: *The Last Laugh* (1981), 'The Marx Brothers'

THE UNITED STATES: Native Americans

1 The Indians knew that life was equated with the earth and its resources, that America was a paradise, and they could not comprehend why the intruders from the East were determined to destroy all that was Indian as well as America itself.

Dee Brown (b.1908), U.S. author: introduction to *Bury My Heart at Wounded Knee* (1970)

2 Land of opportunity, land for the huddled masses – where would the opportunity have been without the genocide of those Old Guard, bristling Indian tribes?

Edward Hoagland (b.1932), U.S. novelist and essayist: 'Lament the Red Wolf', first publ. in *Sports Illustrated* (New York), 14 Jan. 1974, rep. in *Heart's Desire* (1988)

3 Whoever the last true cowboy in America turns out to be, he's likely to be an Indian.

William Least Heat-Moon [William Trogdon] (b.1939), U.S. author: *Blue Highways: A Journey into America* (1983), Pt.5, Ch.2

THE UNITED STATES: New England

1 The New England conscience ... does not stop you from doing what you shouldn't – it just stops you from enjoying it.

Cleveland Amory (b.1917), U.S. author: in *New York*, 5 May 1980

2 The most serious charge which can be brought against New England is not Puritanism but February.

Joseph Wood Krutch (1893–1970), U.S. author and editor: *Twelve Seasons* (1949), 'February'

3 There is no pleasing New Englanders, my dear, their soil is all rocks and their hearts are bloodless absolutes.

John Updike (b.1932), U.S. author and critic: Buchanan, in *Buchanan Dying* (1974), Act 2

THE UNITED STATES: New York

1 New York ... is a city of geometric heights, a petrified desert of grids and lattices, an inferno of greenish abstraction under a flat sky, a real Metropolis from which man is absent by his very accumulation.

Roland Barthes (1915–1980), French semiologist: 'Buffet Finishes off New York', first publ. in *Arts* (Paris), 1959, rep. in *The Eiffel Tower and Other Mythologies* (1979)

2 It is a world completely rotten with wealth, power, senility, indifference, puritanism and mental hygiene, poverty and waste, technological futility and aimless violence, and yet I cannot help but feel it has about it something of the dawning of the universe.

Jean Baudrillard (b.1929), French semiologist: *America* (1986; tr.1988), 'New York'

3 I think that New York is not the cultural center of America, but the business and administrative center of American culture.

Saul Bellow (b.1915), U.S. novelist: BBC radio interview, publ. in *The Listener* (London), 22 May 1969

4 Everybody ought to have a lower East Side in their life.

Irving Berlin (1888–1989), U.S. songwriter: in *Vogue* (New York), 1 Nov. 1962

5 I like it here in New York. I like the idea of having to keep eyes in the back of your head all the time.

John Cale (b.1940), British rock musician: in *The Times* (London), 27 Sept. 1989

6 I loved New York, with that powerful love that at times leaves you full of uncertainty and abhorrence: there are times when one needs an exile.

Albert Camus (1913–1960), French-Algerian philosopher and author: 'Pluies de New York' (1946), quoted in *Camus: A Biography* by Herbert R. Lottman (1979), Ch.29

7 New York has never learnt the art of growing old by playing on all its pasts. Its present invents itself, from hour to hour, in the act of throwing away its previous accomplishments and challenging the future. A city composed of paroxysmal places in monumental reliefs.

Michel de Certeau (1925–1986), French author and critic: *The Practice of Everyday Life* (1974), Ch.7

8 New York is more now than the sum of its people and buildings. It makes sense only as a mechanical intelligence, a transporter system for the daily absorbing and nightly redeploying of the human multitudes whose services it requires.

Peter Conrad (b.1948), Australian author and critic: *The Art of the City* (1984), Ch.13

9 In Manhattan, every flat surface is a potential stage and every inattentive waiter an unemployed, possibly unemployable, actor.

Quentin Crisp (b.1908), British author: 'Love Lies Bleeding', Channel 4, 6 Aug. 1991, publ. in the *New Statesman and Society* (London), 9 Aug. 1991

10 New York, you are an Egypt! But an Egypt turned inside out. For she erected pyramids of slavery to death, and you erect pyramids of democracy with the vertical organ-pipes of your skyscrapers all meeting at the point of infinity of liberty!

Salvador Dali (1904–1989), Spanish painter: *The Secret Life of Salvador Dali* (1948), Ch.11

11 New York is full of people ... with a feeling for the tangential adventure, the risky adventure, the interlude that's not likely to end in any double-ring ceremony.

Joan Didion (b.1934), U.S. essayist: in *Mademoiselle* (New York), Feb. 1961

12 Living in New York is like being at some terrible late-night party. You're tired, you've had a headache since you arrived, but you can't leave because then you'd miss the party.

Simon Hoggart (b.1946), British journalist: *America: A User's Guide* (1990), Ch.1

13 New York is what Paris was in the twenties ... the centre of the art world. And we want to be in the centre. It's the greatest place on earth ... I've got a lot of friends here and I even brought my own cash.

John Lennon (1940–1980), British rock musician: *The Tomorrow Show*, NBC-TV, April 1975, publ. in *Imagine* (ed. Andrew Solt and Sam Egan, 1988). Lennon was given his long-awaited residency status in the U.S. the following year

14 After nearly collapsing in bankruptcy during the seventies, their adoptive city had experienced a gold rush of sorts; prospecting with computers and telephones, financial miners had discovered fat veins of money coursing beneath the cliffs and canyons of the southern tip of Manhattan. ... The electronic buzz of fast money hummed beneath the wired streets.

Jay McInerney (b.1955), U.S. author: *Brightness Falls* (1992), Ch.1

15 This city is neither a jungle nor the moon.... In long shot: a cosmic smudge, a conglomerate of bleeding energies. Close up, it is a fairly legible printed circuit, a transistorized labyrinth of beastly tracks, a data bank for asthmatic voice-prints.

Susan Sontag (b.1933), U.S. essayist: 'Debriefing', first publ. in the *American Review* (New York), Sept. 1973, rep. in *I, Etcetera* (1978)

16 New York, home of the vivisectors of the mind, and of the mentally vivisected still to be reassembled, of those who live intact, habitually wondering about their states of sanity, and home of those whose minds have been dead, bearing the scars of resurrection.

Muriel Spark (b.1918), British novelist: *The Hothouse by the East River* (1973), Ch.1

17 The only difference between the pyramids and the Empire State Building is that the Egyptians didn't have unions.

Oliver Stone (b.1946), U.S. film-maker: Carl Fox (Martin Sheen), in *Wall Street* (film; screenplay by Stanley Weiser and Oliver Stone, directed by Oliver Stone, 1987)

18 The characteristic face in New York these days is seasoned, wry, weathered by drama and farce. ... Suddenly it's OK to be thirty, forty, even fifty, to have a streak of white crazing your beard, to have a deviated septum or eyes set too close together.

Edmund White (b.1940), U.S. author: 'Fantasia on the Seventies' (1977), rep. in *The Burning Library* (1994)

19 New York is the biggest mouth in the world. It appears to be prime example of the herd instinct, leading the universal urban conspiracy to beguile man from his birthright (the good ground), to hang him by his eyebrows from skyhooks above hard pavement, to crucify him, sell him, or be sold by him.

Frank Lloyd Wright (1869–1959), U.S. architect: *The Living City* (1958), Pt.1, 'The-Shadow-of-the-Wall – Primitive Instincts Still Alive'

See also BROADWAY; Hoagland on CITIES: URBAN CULTURE

THE UNITED STATES: the President

1 You don't need to know who's playing on the White House tennis court to be a good president. A president has many roles.

James Baker (b.1930), U.S. Republican politician and secretary of state: on the president's overall knowledge and accountability, quoted in *Miami* by Joan Didion (1987), Ch.15. Baker was White House Chief of Staff at the time

2 All Presidents start out to run a crusade but after a couple of years they find they are running something less heroic and much more intractable: namely the presidency. The people are well cured by then of election fever, during which they think they are choosing Moses. In the third year, they look on the man as a sinner and a bumbler and begin to poke around for rumours of another Messiah.

Alistair Cooke (b.1908), British broadcaster and journalist: *Talk About America* (1968), Ch.31

3 But even the President of the United States Sometimes must have To stand naked.

Bob Dylan (b.1941), U.S. singer and songwriter: 'It's Alright Ma (I'm Only Bleeding)' (song) on the album *Bringing it All Back Home* (1965)

4 I don't have any problem with a reporter or a news person who says the President is uninformed on this issue or that issue. I don't think any of us would challenge that. I do have a problem with the singular focus on this, as if that's the only standard by which we ought to judge a president. What we learned in the last administration was how little having an encyclopedic grasp of all the facts has to do with governing.

David R. Gergen (b.1942), U.S. editor and former White House communications director: in the *New York Times*, 10 Jan. 1984

5 We want a president who is as much like an American tourist as possible. Someone with the same goofy grin, the same innocent intentions, the same naive trust; a president with no conception of foreign policy and no discernible connection to the U.S. government, whose Nice Guyism will narrow the gap between the U.S. and us until nobody can tell the difference.

Florence King (b.1936), U.S. author: *Reflections in a Jaundiced Eye* (1989), 'Nice Guyism'

6 A President is best judged by the enemies he makes when he has really hit his stride.

Max Lerner (1902–1992), U.S. author and columnist: 'The Education of Harry Truman', first publ. in the *New York Star*, 9 Jan. 1949, rep. in *The Unfinished Country* (1959), Pt.4

7 When the President does it, that means that it is not illegal.

Richard Nixon (1913–1992), U.S. Republican politician and president: TV interview with David Frost, 20 May 1977, quoted in *I Gave Them a Sword* by David Frost (1978), Ch.8

8 In our brief national history we have shot four of our presidents, worried five of them to death, impeached one and hounded another out of office. And when all else fails, we hold an election and assassinate their character.

P.J. O'Rourke (b.1947), U.S. journalist: *Parliament of Whores* (1991), 'The President'

9 A president, however, must stand somewhat apart, as all great presidents have known instinctively. Then the language which has the power to survive its own utterance is the most likely to move those to whom it is immediately spoken.

J.R. Pole (b.1922), British historian: 'The Language of American Presidents', publ. in *The State of the Language* (ed. Christopher Ricks, 1980)

10 In America any boy may become President, and I suppose it's just one of the risks he takes!

Adlai Stevenson (1900–1965), U.S. Democratic politician: speech, 26 Sept. 1952, Indianapolis, publ. in *Major Campaign Speeches of Adlai E. Stevenson: 1952* (1953)

11 The Republican Vice Presidential Candidate ... asks you to place him a heartbeat from the Presidency.

Adlai Stevenson: referring to Richard Nixon, in 'The Hiss Case', speech, 23 Oct. 1952, Cleveland, Ohio, publ. in *Speeches* (1953). Nixon became vice president in 1952 (re-elected 1956)

12 From now on, I think it is safe to predict, neither the Democratic nor the Republican Party will ever nominate for President a candidate without good looks, stage presence, theatrical delivery, and a sense of timing.

James Thurber (1894–1961), U.S. humorist and illustrator: of the Kennedy–Nixon TV debates, from an unpublished manuscript, dated 20 March 1961, later publ. in *James Thurber Collecting Himself* (1989)

13 When you get to be President, there are all those things, the honors, the twenty-one gun salutes, all those things. You have to remember it isn't for you. It's for the Presidency.
Harry S Truman (1884–1972), U.S. Democratic politician and president: *Plain Speaking: Conversations with Harry S Truman* by Merle Miller (1973), Ch.15

14 To be President of the United States, sir, is to act as advocate for a blind, venomous, and ungrateful client; still, one must make the best of the case, for the purposes of Providence.
John Updike (b.1932), U.S. author and critic: President James Polk, in *Buchanan Dying* (1974), Act 2

See also Nixon on CORRUPTION; GERALD FORD; THE KENNEDYS; Kissinger on LOYALTY; RICHARD NIXON; RONALD REAGAN; Truman on RESPONSIBILITY

THE UNITED STATES: San Francisco

1 We wandered around, carrying our bundles of rags in the narrow romantic streets. Everybody looked like a broken-down movie extra, a withered starlet; disenchanted stunt-men, midget auto-racers, poignant California characters with their end-of-the-continent sadness, handsome, decadent, Casanova-ish men, puffy-eyed motel blondes, hustlers, pimps, whores, masseurs, bellhops – a lemon lot, and how's a man going to make a living with a gang like that?
Jack Kerouac (1922–1969), U.S. author: on arriving in San Francisco, in *On the Road* (1957), Pt.2, Ch.9

2 San Francisco is where gay fantasies come true, and the problem the city presents is whether, after all, we wanted these particular dreams to be fulfilled – or would we have preferred others? Did we know what price these dreams would exact? Did we anticipate the ways in which, vivid and continuous, they would unsuit us for the business of daily life? Or should our notion of daily life itself be transformed?
Edmund White (b.1940), U.S. author: *States of Desire: Travels in Gay America* (1980), Ch.2

THE UNITED STATES: the South

1 The South *is* very beautiful but its beauty makes one sad because the lives that people live here, and have lived here, are so ugly.
James Baldwin (1924–1987), U.S. author: 'They Can't Turn Back', first publ. in *Mademoiselle* (New York), Aug. 1960, rep. in *The Price of the Ticket* (1985)

2 The average Southerner has the speech patterns of someone slipping in and out of consciousness. I can change my shoes and socks faster than most people in Mississippi can speak a sentence.
Bill Bryson (b.1951), U.S. author and journalist: *The Lost Continent: Travels in Small Town America* (1989), Ch.7

3 While the South is hardly Christ-centered, it is most certainly Christ-haunted.
Flannery O'Connor (1925–1964), U.S. author: 'Some Aspects of the Grotesque in Southern Fiction', lecture at Wesleyan College for Women, Macon, Georgia, autumn 1960, first publ. in *Cluster Review* (Macon University, 1965), rep. in *Mystery and Manners* (ed. Sally and Robert Fitzgerald, 1972)

4 Storytelling and copulation are the two chief forms of amusement in the South. They're inexpensive and easy to procure.
Robert Penn Warren (b.1905), U.S. poet and novelist: in *Newsweek* (New York), 25 Aug. 1980

See also O'Connor on PROVINCIALISM; O'Connor on REALISM

THE UNITED STATES: Texas

1 It is very considerably smaller than Australia and British Somaliland put together. As things stand at present there is nothing much the Texans can do about this, and ... they are inclined to shy away from the subject in ordinary conversation, muttering defensively about the size of oranges.
Alex Atkinson, British humorous writer: 'The Eyes of Texas Are Upon You', first publ. in *Punch* (London), 1959, rep. in *Present Laughter* (ed. Alan Coren, 1982)

2 It was part of the Texas ritual. We're rich as son-of-a-bitch stew but look how homely we are, just as plain-folksy as Grandpappy back in 1836. We know about champagne and caviar but we talk hog and hominy.
Edna Ferber (1887–1968), U.S. author: *Giant* (1952), Ch.2

3 If a man's from Texas, he'll tell you. If he's not, why embarrass him by asking?
John Gunther (1901–1970), U.S. journalist: joke quoted in *Inside U.S.A.* (1947), Ch.47, 'Some Texas Jokes'

4 Many people have believed that they were Chosen, but none more baldly than the Texans.
Edward Hoagland (b.1932), U.S. novelist and essayist: 'Lament the Red Wolf', first publ. in *Sports Illustrated* (New York), 14 Jan. 1974, rep. in *Heart's Desire* (1988)

5 Fish have water, the bushmen of the Kalahari have sand, and Houstonians have interior décor.

Simon Hoggart (b.1946), British journalist: *America: A User's Guide* (1990), Ch.1

6 Texas is a state of mind. Texas is an obsession. Above all, Texas is a nation in every sense of the word. ... A Texan outside of Texas is a foreigner.

John Steinbeck (1902–1968), U.S. author: *Travels With Charley: in Search of America* (1962), Pt.4

7 Maybe we're kind of old-fashioned, but our standards of conduct aren't the same, say, as they are in the east or middle-west. Out here you say yes ma'am and no ma'am to anything with skirts on; anything white, that is. Out here, if you catch a man with his pants down, you apologize ... even if you have to arrest him afterwards. Out here you're a man, a man and a gentleman, or you aren't anything. And God help you if you're not.

Jim Thompson (1906–1977), U.S. author: the narrator (Lou Ford), in *The Killer Inside Me* (1952), Ch.2

8 For most Northerners, Texas is the home of real men. The cowboys, the rednecks, the outspoken self-made right-wing millionaires strike us as either the best or worst examples of American manliness. ... The ideal is not an illusion nor is it contemptible, no matter what damage it may have done. Many people who scorn it in conversation want to submit to it in bed. Those who believe machismo reeks of violence alone choose to forget it once stood for honor as well.

Edmund White (b.1940), U.S. author: *States of Desire: Travels in Gay America* (1980), Ch.5

THE UNITED STATES: Washington D.C.

1 In Washington, success is just a training course for failure.

Simon Hoggart (b.1946), British journalist: *America: A User's Guide* (1990), Ch.1

2 Washington is a city of southern efficiency and northern charm.

John F. Kennedy (1917–1963), U.S. Democratic politician and president: remark, Nov. 1961, quoted in *A Thousand Days* by Arthur M. Schlesinger Jr. (1965), Ch.25

3 Washington is a very easy city for you to forget where you came from and why you got there in the first place.

Harry S Truman (1884–1972), U.S. Democratic politician and president: *Plain Speaking: Conversations with Harry S Truman* by Merle Miller (1973), Ch.11

THE UNITED STATES: the West

1 It used to be said that you had to know what was happening in America because it gave us a glimpse of our future. Today, the rest of America, and after that Europe, had better heed what happens in California, for it already reveals the type of civilisation that is in store for all of us.

Alistair Cooke (b.1908), British broadcaster and journalist: *Talk About America* (1968), Ch.38

2 There is no weather in Palm Springs – just like TV. There is also no middle class, and in that sense the place is medieval.

Douglas Coupland (b.1961), Canadian author: the narrator (Andy), in *Generation X* (1991), 'Our Parents Had More'

3 It's no surprise that user-friendliness is a concept developed on the West Coast. The guy who invented the Smiley face is running for mayor of Seattle – for real.

Douglas Coupland: *Microserfs* (1995), 'Microserfs; Thursday'

4 California is a place in which a boom mentality and a sense of Chekhovian loss meet in uneasy suspension; in which the mind is troubled by some buried but ineradicable suspicion that things had better work here, because here, beneath that immense bleached sky, is where we run out of continent.

Joan Didion (b.1934), U.S. essayist: 'Notes From a Native Daughter', essay (1965), rep. in *Slouching Towards Bethlehem* (1968)

5 California is a tragic country – like Palestine, like every Promised Land.

Christopher Isherwood (1904–1986), British author: 'Los Angeles', first publ. in *Horizon* (London), 1947, rep. in *Exhumations* (1966)

6 Wherever I looked, there was nothing to see but more long streets and thousands of cars going along them, and dried-up country on each side of the streets. It was like the Sahara, only dirty.

Mohammed Mrabet (b.1940), Moroccan author: of California, in *Look and Move On* (tr. Paul Bowles, 1976), Ch.11. 'Like the Sahara Only Dirty' was the title of this chapter in Mrabet's novelistic autobiography

7 They are a very decent generous lot of people out here and *they don't expect you to listen.* ... It's the secret of social ease in this country. They talk entirely for their own pleasure. Nothing they say is designed to be heard.

Evelyn Waugh (1903–1966), British novelist: Sir Francis Hinsley, a British expatriate in California, in *The Loved One* (1948), p.8 of Penguin edn. (1951)

8 The almost Oriental politeness of the West Coast is one of its distinctive regional features, in marked contrast to the contentiousness of the East Coast. ... So few human contacts in Los Angeles go unmediated by glass (either a TV screen or an automobile windshield), that the direct confrontation renders the participants docile, stunned, sweet.
   Edmund White (b.1940), U.S. author: *States of Desire: Travels in Gay America* (1980), Ch.1

See also THE UNITED STATES: LOS ANGELES; THE UNITED STATES: SAN FRANCISCO

THE UNIVERSE

1 This is a war universe. War all the time. That is its nature. There may be other universes based on all sorts of other principles, but ours seems to be based on war and games.
   William Burroughs (1914–1997), U.S. author: 'The War Universe', taped conversation first publ. in *Grand Street* (New York), No.37, rep. in *Painting and Guns* (1992) in a slightly different form

2 Anyone informed that the universe is expanding and contracting in pulsations of eighty billion years has a right to ask, 'What's in it for me?'
   Peter De Vries (1910–1993), U.S. author: the narrator (Jim Tickler), in *The Glory of the Hummingbird* (1974), Ch.1

3 If that's how it all started, then we might as well face the fact that what's left out there is a great deal of shrapnel and a whole bunch of cinders (one of which is, fortunately, still hot enough and close enough to be good for tanning).
   Barbara Ehrenreich (b.1941), U.S. author and columnist: of the Big Bang, in 'Blocking the Gates to Heaven' (1986), rep. in *The Worst Years of Our Lives* (1991)

4 The universe seems to me infinitely strange and foreign. At such a moment I gaze upon it with a mixture of anguish and euphoria; separate from the universe, as though placed at a certain distance outside it; I look and I see pictures, creatures that move in a kind of timeless time and spaceless space, emitting sounds that are a kind of language I no longer understand or ever register.
   Eugène Ionesco (1912–1994), Rumanian-born French playwright: *Notes and Counter-Notes* (1962), Pt.2, 'Interviews: Brief Notes for Radio'

5 Just as the individual is not alone in the group, nor any one in society alone among the others, so man is not alone in the universe
   Claude Lévi-Strauss (b.1908), French anthropologist: *Tristes Tropiques* (1955), Ch.40

6 The more the universe seems comprehensible, the more it also seems pointless.
   Steven Weinberg (b.1933), U.S. theoretical physicist: *The First Three Minutes* (1977), Ch.8

UNIVERSITY

1 The most important function of the university in an age of reason is to protect reason from itself.
   Allan Bloom (1930–1992), U.S. educator and author: *The Closing of the American Mind* (1987), Pt.3, 'From Socrates' *Apology* to Heidegger's *Rektoratsrede*'

2 The University is a Mecca to which students come with something less than perfect faith. It is important that students bring a certain ragamuffin, barefoot irreverence to their studies; they are not here to worship what is known, but to question it.
   Jacob Bronowski (1908–1974), British scientist and author: *The Ascent of Man* (1973), Ch.11

3 Within the university ... you can study without waiting for any efficient or immediate result. You may search, just for the sake of searching, and try for the sake of trying. So there is a possibility of what I would call playing. It's perhaps the only place within society where play is possible to such an extent.
   Jacques Derrida (b.1930), Algerian-born French literary theorist: interview, 1985, publ. in *Criticism in Society* (ed. Imre Salusinski, 1987)

4 I think that universities, where leisure and academic freedom are considered to be interchangeable, are a model for economic life in general. ... Maybe we should have more opportunity for paid vacations, and paid sabbatical leave for people who have to do heavy manual labour. We consider both of those very desirable things for college professors.
   J.K. Galbraith (b.1908), U.S. economist: interview in *Singular Encounters* by Naim Attallah (1990), 'John Kenneth Galbraith'

5 My own experience is that a certain kind of genius among students is best brought out in bed.
   Allen Ginsberg (b.1926), U.S. poet: interview, Feb. 1981, Michigan State University, publ. in the *Washington Post*, 29 July 1984

6 University degrees are a bit like adultery: you may not want to get involved with that sort of thing, but you don't want to be thought incapable.
   Peter Imbert (b.1933), British police commissioner: in *The Times* (London), 11 Oct. 1992

7 As to our universities, I've come to the conclusion that they are élitist where they should be egalitarian and egalitarian where they should be élitist.

David Lodge (b.1935), British novelist and critic:
Charles, in *Nice Work* (1988), Pt.5, Ch.4

8　I am told that today rather more than 60 per
cent of the men who go to university go on a
Government grant. This is a new class that has
entered upon the scene. It is the white-collar
proletariat. ... They do not go to university to
acquire culture but to get a job, and when they
have got one, scamp it. They have no manners
and are woefully unable to deal with any social
predicament. Their idea of a celebration is to
go to a public house and drink six beers. They
are mean, malicious and envious. ... They are
scum.

W. Somerset Maugham (1874–1966), British
author: referring to the generation of 'Angry Young
Men' as portrayed in Kingsley Amis's 1954 novel
Lucky Jim, in *The Sunday Times* (London), 25 Dec.
1955. These people, Maugham continued, 'will in
due course leave the university. Some will doubtless
sink back, perhaps with relief, into the modest social
class from which they emerged; some will take to
drink, some to crime and go to prison. ... A few will
go into Parliament, become Cabinet Ministers and
rule the country. I look upon myself as fortunate that
I shall not live to see it'

9　I don't think one 'comes down' from Jimmy's
university. According to him, it's not even red
brick, but white tile.

John Osborne (1929–1994), British playwright:
Alison, in *Look Back in Anger* (1956), Act 2, Sc.1

10　Our major universities are now stuck with an
army of pedestrian, toadying careerists, Fifties
types who wave around Sixties banners to
conceal their record of ruthless, beaverlike
tunneling to the top.

Camille Paglia (b.1947), U.S. author and critic:
introduction to *Sex, Art, and American Culture*
(1992)

See also ACADEMIA; CAMBRIDGE UNIVERSITY;
OXFORD UNIVERSITY

THE UNKNOWN

1　There is nothing that man fears more than the
touch of the unknown. He wants to *see* what
is reaching towards him, and to be able to
recognize or at least classify it. Man always
tends to avoid physical contact with anything
strange.

Elias Canetti (1905–1994), Austrian novelist and
philosopher: opening lines of *Crowds and Power*
(1960; tr.1962), 'The Fear of Being Touched'

2　The mind loves the unknown. It loves images
whose meaning is unknown, since the meaning
of the mind itself is unknown.

René Magritte (1898–1967), Belgian surrealist
painter: quoted in *Magritte* by Suzi Gablik (1970),
Ch.1

THE U.S.S.R.

1　As a result of half a century of Soviet rule
people have been weaned from a belief in
human kindness.

Svetlana Alliluevya (b.1925), Russian writer and
daughter of Josef Stalin: *Only One Year* (1969),
'The Journey's End'

2　I believe, as Lenin said, that this revolutionary
chaos may yet crystallize into new forms of life.

Mikhail Gorbachev (b.1931), Russian political
leader: to journalists, of the secession of the Baltic
republics and other regional disputes, quoted in *The
Times* (London), 18 May 1990

3　Nothing an interested foreigner may have to
say about the Soviet Union today can compare
with the scorn and fury of those who inhabit
the ruin of a dream.

Christopher Hope (b.1944), South African author:
in *The Sunday Times* (London), 15 April 1990

4　Visitors who come from the Soviet Union and
tell you how marvellous it is to be able to look at
public buildings without advertisements stuck
all over them are just telling you that they can't
decipher the cyrillic alphabet.

Clive James (b.1939), Australian writer and critic:
introduction to *Glued to the Box* (1983)

5　When your house is on fire, you can't be
bothered with the neighbours. Or, as we say in
chess, if your king is under attack you don't
worry about losing a pawn on the queen's side.

Gary Kasparov (b.1963), Russian chess player: of
Mikhail Gorbachev's attitude to changes in Eastern
Europe, in interview in *The Observer* (London),
3 Dec. 1989

6　Those who wait for that must wait until a
shrimp learns to whistle.

Nikita Khrushchev (1894–1971), Soviet premier:
on the possibility of the Soviet Union rejecting
communism, in speech, 17 Sept. 1955, Moscow,
quoted in the *New York Times*, 18 Sept. 1955

7　The Régime did not want Communists; it
wanted robots. It will take at least a generation
to change them back into humans again.

Arthur Koestler (1905–1983), Hungarian-born
British novelist and essayist: *The Trail of the
Dinosaur* (1955), Pt.2, 'The Shadow of a Tree'

8　Let us be aware that while they preach the
supremacy of the state, declare its omnipotence over individual man, and predict its
eventual domination of all peoples of the earth
– they are the focus of evil in the modern world.

Ronald Reagan (b.1911), U.S. Republican
politician and president: statement, 8 March 1983,
quoted in *Reagan's Reign of Error* (ed. Mark Green
and Gail MacColl, 1987), 'Focus of Evil'

9 If the Soviet Union let another political party come into existence, they would still be a one-party state, because everybody would join the other party.
Ronald Reagan: said to Polish Americans in Chicago, 23 June 1983, publ. in *Speaking My Mind* (1989), 'The Wit and Wisdom of Ronald Reagan'

10 Under Russian influence, they inherit a weakness for the secret police methods of the Holy Alliance and have been weighed down by dimwitted, often vicious party hacks whose tastes are a musty legacy from the court of the Czars.
Theodore Roszak (b.1933), U.S. social critic: of the governments of the Soviet bloc, in *Where the Wasteland Ends* (1972), Ch.2

11 In the Soviet Union everything happens slowly. Always remember that.
A.N. Shevchenko (b.1930), defecting Soviet diplomat: quoted in *The Observer* (London), 2 Jan. 1983

12 I have not had major experience of talking with people once pronounced brain-dead, but I think we could be safe in saying he did not have great zip.
Howard Smith (b.1919), ex-British ambassador to Moscow: of Soviet premier Leonid Brezhnev, in *The Times* (London), 8 Sept. 1988

13 They were right. The Soviet régime is not the embodiment of evil as you think in the West. They have laws and I broke them. I hate tea and they love tea. Who is wrong?
Alexander Zinoviev (b.1922), Soviet philosopher: on his forced exile from the Soviet Union, in *The Sunday Times* (London), 3 May 1981

See also Khrushchev on THE COLD WAR; Ford on EUROPE: EASTERN EUROPE; Solzhenitsyn on REPRESSION; Khrushchev on REVOLUTION; RUSSIA

THE U.S.S.R.: Glasnost & Perestroika

1 *Perestroika* basically is creating material incentives for the individual. Some of the comrades deny that, but I can't see it any other way. In that sense human nature kinda goes backwards. It's a step backwards. You have to realize the people weren't quite ready for a socialist production system.
Gus Hall (b.1910), general secretary of the Communist Party of the U.S.A.: interview in *The Independent* (London), 19 May 1990

2 Democratization is not democracy; it is a slogan for the temporary liberalization handed down from an autocrat. Glasnost is not free speech; only free speech, constitutionally guaranteed, is free speech.
Gail Sheehy (b.1937), U.S. journalist and author: *Gorbachev* (1991), 'Looking for Mikhail Gorbachev'

3 The clock of communism has stopped striking. But its concrete building has not yet come crashing down. For that reason, instead of freeing ourselves, we must try to save ourselves from being crushed by its rubble.
Alexander Solzhenitsyn (b.1918), Russian novelist: opening sentence of essay, 'How We Must Rebuild Russia', publ. in *Komosomolskaya Pravda* (Moscow), 18 Sept. 1990

UTOPIA

1 In our wildest aberrations we dream of an equilibrium we have left behind and which we naively expect to find at the end of our errors. Childish presumption which justifies the fact that child-nations, inheriting our follies, are now directing our history.
Albert Camus (1913–1960), French-Algerian philosopher and author: 'Helen's Exile' (1948), rep. in *The Myth of Sisyphus and Other Essays* (1955)

2 Utopias are presented for our inspection as a critique of the human state. If they are to be treated as anything but trivial exercises of the imagination, I suggest there is a simple test we can apply. ... We must forget the whole paraphernalia of social description, demonstration, expostulation, approbation, condemnation. We have to say to ourselves, 'How would I myself live in this proposed society? How long would it be before I went stark staring mad?'
William Golding (1911–1993), British author: 'Utopias and Antiutopias', speech to Les Anglicistes, Lille, France, 13 Feb. 1977, rep. in *A Moving Target* (1982)

3 If people would forget about utopia! When rationalism destroyed heaven and decided to set it up here on earth, that most terrible of all goals entered human ambition. It was clear there'd be no end to what people would be made to suffer for it.
Nadine Gordimer (b.1923), South African author: Bernard, in *Burger's Daughter* (1979), Pt.2

4 I shall speak of ... how melancholy and utopia preclude one another. How they fertilize one another. ... Of the revulsion that follows one insight and precedes the next. ... Of superabundance and surfeit. Of stasis in progress. And of myself, for whom melancholy and utopia are heads and tails of the same coin.
Günter Grass (b.1927), German author: *From the Diary of a Snail* (1972), 'On Stasis in Progress'

5 The trouble with kingdoms of heaven on earth is that they're liable to come to pass, and then their fraudulence is apparent for all to see. We

need a kingdom of heaven in Heaven, if only because it can't be realised.

Malcolm Muggeridge (1903–1990), British journalist and broadcaster: *Jesus Rediscovered* (1979), 'Me and Myself'

6   We are at heart so profoundly anarchistic that the only form of state we can imagine living in is Utopian; and so cynical that the only Utopia we can believe in is authoritarian.

Lionel Trilling (1905–1975), U.S. critic: notebook entry, 1948, publ. in *Partisan Review 50th Anniversary Edition* (ed. William Philips, 1985)

See also Vonnegut on COMMUNITIES

VALUES

1   First you destroy those who create values. Then you destroy those who know what the values are, and who also know that those destroyed before were in fact the creators of values. But real barbarism begins when no one can any longer judge or know that what he does is barbaric.

Ryszard Kapuściński (b.1932), Polish journalist: 'A Warsaw Diary', publ. in *Granta* (Cambridge), No.15, 1985

2   Values are tapes we play on the Walkman of the mind: any tune we choose so long as it does not disturb others.

Jonathan Sacks (b.1948), British Chief Rabbi: 'The Persistence of Faith', 1990 Reith Lecture

VANITY

1   Looking at yourself in a mirror isn't exactly a study of life.

Lauren Bacall (b.1924), U.S. actress: in the *Daily Mail* (London), 1 Nov. 1990

2   If there is a single quality that is shared by all great men, it is vanity. But I mean by 'vanity' only that they appreciate their own worth. Without this kind of vanity they would not be great. And with vanity alone, of course, a man is nothing.

Yousef Karsh (b.1908), Turkish-born Canadian photographer: in *Cosmopolitan* (New York), Dec. 1955

3   Possibly, more people kill themselves and others out of hurt vanity than out of envy, jealousy, malice or desire for revenge.

Iris Murdoch (b.1919), British novelist and philosopher: *The Philosopher's Pupil* (1983), 'The Events in Our Town'

4   The vanity of men, a constant insult to women, is also the ground for the implicit feminine claim of superior sensitivity and morality.

Patricia Meyer Spacks (b.1929), U.S. literary critic: *The Female Imagination* (1975), Ch.1

VENICE *see under* ITALY

VICE

1   So much of our lives is given over to the consideration of our imperfections that there is no time to improve our imaginary virtues. The truth is we only perfect our vices, and man is a worse creature when he dies than he was when he was born.

Edward Dahlberg (1900–1977), U.S. author and critic: *Alms for Oblivion* (1964), 'Moby-Dick: A Hamitic Dream'

2   Never support two weaknesses at the same time. It's your combination sinners – your lecherous liars and your miserly drunkards – who dishonor the vices and bring them into bad repute.

Thornton Wilder (1897–1975), U.S. novelist and playwright: Malachi, in *The Matchmaker* (1954), Act 3

VICTIMS

1   Oh, the holiness of always being the injured party. The historically oppressed can find not only sanctity but safety in the state of victimization. When access to a better life has been denied often enough, and successfully enough, one can use the rejection as an excuse to cease all efforts. After all, one reckons, 'they' don't want me, 'they' accept their own mediocrity and refuse my best, 'they' don't deserve me.

Maya Angelou (b.1928), U.S. author: *Singin' and Swingin' and Gettin' Merry Like Christmas* (third volume of autobiography, 1976), Ch.9

2   It is a very rare man who does not victimize the helpless.

James Baldwin (1924–1987), U.S. author: 'No Name in the Street' (1972), rep. in *The Price Of The Ticket* (1985)

3   Sympathy for victims is always counterbalanced by an equal and opposite feeling of resentment towards them.

Ben Elton (b.1959), British author and comic: *Stark* (1989), 'On the Business of Stark'

4   The range of victims available ten years ago – blacks, chicanos, Indians, women, homosexuals – has now expanded to include every permutation of the halt, the blind, the lame and the short, or, to put it correctly, the differently abled, the other-visioned and the vertically challenged. Never before in human history were so many acronyms pursuing identity. It's as though all human encounter were one big

sore spot, inflamed with opportunities to unwittingly give, and truculenty receive, offence.

Robert Hughes (b.1938), Australian author and critic: *Culture of Complaint* (1993), Ch.1

5 Don't agonize. Organize.

Florynce R. Kennedy (b.1916), U.S. lawyer and civil rights activist: quoted by Gloria Steinem, in *Ms.* (New York), March 1973, 'The Verbal Karate of Florynce R. Kennedy, Esq'

6 I hate victims who respect their executioners.

Jean-Paul Sartre (1905–1980), French philosopher and author: Leni, in *The Condemned of Altona* (1959; tr.1961), Act 1, Sc.1

7 Victims suggest innocence. And innocence, by the inexorable logic that governs all relational terms, suggests guilt.

Susan Sontag (b.1933), U.S. essayist: *AIDS and Its Metaphors* (1989), Ch.1

8 I understand that there are a lot of sick people in the world. I understand that many people are victimized, and some people certainly more horribly than I have been. But you have to be responsible for claiming your own victories, you really do. If you live in the past and allow the past to define who you are then you never grow.

Oprah Winfrey (b.1954), U.S. chat-show host: quoted in *Oprah!* by Robert Waldron (1987), Ch.2

VICTORY

1 Victory is gay only back home. Up front it is joyless.

Marlene Dietrich (1904–1992), German-born U.S. actress: *Marlene Dietrich's ABC* (1962), 'Victory'

2 Democracies are notorious for a tendency to obey the feelings rather than the mind; thus the nature of democracies often makes it difficult to conclude a peace after a hard-won war. Generous victors are rare.

Amos Elon (b.1926), Israeli author and journalist: in the *New Yorker*, 23 April 1990

3 The moment of victory is much too short to live for that and nothing else.

Martina Navratilova (b.1956), Czech-born U.S. tennis player: in *The Guardian* (London), 21 June 1989

4 Rejoice, rejoice...

Margaret Thatcher (b.1925), British Conservative politician and prime minister: on the recapture of South Georgia during the Falklands conflict, 25 April 1982, quoted in *The Daily Telegraph* (London), 26 April 1982

See also WINNING

VIDEO CULTURE

1 I recently learned something quite interesting about video games. Many young people have developed incredible hand, eye, and brain coordination in playing these games. The air force believes these kids will be our outstanding pilots should they fly our jets.

Ronald Reagan (b.1911), U.S. Republican politician and president: statement, 8 August 1983, quoted in *Reagan's Reign of Error* (ed. Mark Green and Gail MacColl, 1987), 'Temptation of Pride'

2 The currents rage deep inside us
This is the age of video violence.

Lou Reed (b.1944), U.S. rock musician: 'Video Violence' (song) on the album *Mistrial* (1986)

VIETNAM

1 The logic of war dictated that the Americans *should* win, but this logic had been superseded by one superior and infinitely more powerful: the logic of revolution. It remains a logic which can never be properly understood: its richness and diversity always excludes the minds of its opponents.

Tariq Ali (b.1943), Pakistani-born British activist and author: *1968 and After: Inside the Revolution* (1978), Ch.1

2 The war was won on both sides: by the Vietnamese on the ground, by the Americans in the electronic mental space. And if the one side won an ideological and political victory, the other made *Apocalypse Now* and that has gone right around the world.

Jean Baudrillard (b.1929), French semiologist: *America* (1986; tr.1988), 'Astral America'

3 Vietnam was *not* a war, it was one long atrocity – I realize that our American friends, living in a country built on genocide, may not appreciate the difference, so I will makes allowances for them – and the miracle of Vietnam is that the massacred won the war.

Julie Burchill (b.1960), British journalist and author: *Girls on Film* (1986), Ch.14

4 Our mission was not to win terrain, or seize positions, but simply to kill: to kill Communists and to kill as many of them as possible. Stack 'em like cordwood. Victory was a high body-count, defeat a low-kill ratio, war a matter of arithmetic.

Philip Caputo (b.1941), U.S. author, journalist and Vietnam veteran: prologue to *A Rumor of War* (1977)

5 Nothing else in the world smells like that... I love the smell of napalm in the morning... It smells like victory.

Francis Ford Coppola (b.1939), U.S. film-maker: Colonel Kilgore (Robert Duvall), in *Apocalypse Now* (film; screenplay by Michael Herr, John Milius and Francis Ford Coppola, produced and directed by Francis Ford Coppola, 1979)

6 You have a row of dominoes set up; you knock over the first one, and what will happen to the last one is that it will go over very quickly.

Dwight D. Eisenhower (1890–1969), U.S. general, Republican politician and president: referring to the situation in Southeast Asia after the defeat of the French by the Viet-Minh, in press conference, 7 April 1954, publ. in *Public Papers of the Presidents of the United States: Dwight D. Eisenhower, 1954*

7 Saigon was an addicted city, and we were the drug: the corruption of children, the mutilation of young men, the prostitution of women, the humiliation of the old, the division of the family, the division of the country – it had all been done in our name. ... The French city ... had represented the opium stage of the addiction. With the Americans had begun the heroin phase.

James Fenton (b.1949), British poet and critic: 'The Fall of Saigon', first publ. in *Granta* (Cambridge), No.15, 1985, rep. in *All the Wrong Places* (1988)

8 By intervening in the Vietnamese struggle the United States was attempting to fit its global strategies into a world of hillocks and hamlets, to reduce its majestic concerns for the containment of communism and the security of the Free World to a dimension where governments rose and fell as a result of arguments between two colonels' wives.

Frances Fitzgerald (b.1940), U.S. journalist and author: *Fire in the Lake* (1972), Pt.1, Ch.1

9 America has made no reparation to the Vietnamese, nothing. We are the richest people in the world and they are among the poorest. We savaged them, though they had never hurt us, and we cannot find it in our hearts, our honor, to give them help – because the government of Vietnam is Communist. And perhaps because they won.

Martha Gellhorn (b.1908), U.S. journalist and author: *The Face of War* (1959; rev.1986), 'The War in Vietnam – Vietnam Again, 1986'. Gellhorn went on to say: 'After all this time I still cannot think calmly about that war. It was the only war I reported on the wrong side'

10 Vietnam was what we had instead of happy childhoods.

Michael Herr (b.1940), U.S. journalist: *Dispatches* (1977), 'Colleagues', Sct.3

11 All the wrong people remember Vietnam. I think all the people who remember it should forget it, and all the people who forgot it should remember it.

Michael Herr: in *The Observer* (London), 15 Jan. 1989

12 We are not about to send American boys 9 or 10,000 miles away from home to do what Asian boys ought to be doing for themselves.

Lyndon B. Johnson (1908–1973), U.S. Democratic politician and president: speech, 21 Oct. 1964, Akron University, Ohio, publ. in *Public Papers of the Presidents of the United States, Lyndon B. Johnson: 1963–64*

13 Vietnam presumably taught us that the United States could not serve as the world's policeman; it should also have taught us the dangers of trying to be the world's midwife to democracy when the birth is scheduled to take place under conditions of guerrilla war.

Jeane Kirkpatrick (b.1926), U.S. public official and diplomat: 'Dictatorship and Double Standards', publ. in *Commentary* (New York), Nov. 1979

14 Some of the critics viewed Vietnam as a morality play in which the wicked must be punished before the final curtain and where any attempt to salvage self-respect from the outcome compounded the wrong. I viewed it as a genuine tragedy. No one had a monopoly on anguish.

Henry Kissinger (b.1923), U.S. Republican politician and secretary of state: *The White House Years* (1979), Ch.8

15 And it's one, two, three what are we fightin' for?
Don't ask me I don't give a damn, next stop is Vietnam!
And it's five, six, seven, open up the pearly gates,
There ain't no time to wonder why,
Whoopee! – we're all going to die.

Country Joe McDonald (b.1942), U.S. singer and songwriter: 'I-Feel-Like-I'm-Fixin'-to-Die-Rag' (song, 1965) on the album *I-Feel-Like-I'm-Fixin'-to-Die-Rag* (Country Joe and the Fish, 1968). The song became a feature of the anti-war rallies and festivals at which Country Joe appeared

16 Television brought the brutality of war into the comfort of the living room. Vietnam was lost in the living rooms of America – not on the battlefields of Vietnam.

Marshall McLuhan (1911–1980), Canadian communications theorist: quoted in the *Montreal Gazette*, 16 May 1975

17 Above all, Vietnam was a war that asked everything of a few and nothing of most in America.

Myra MacPherson, U.S. author: epilogue to *Long Time Passing: Vietnam and the Haunted Generation* (1984)

18 Let us understand: North Vietnam cannot defeat or humiliate the United States. Only Americans can do that.

Richard Nixon (1913–1992), U.S. Republican politician and president: television broadcast, 3 Nov. 1969, quoted in *Nixon: The Triumph of a Politician* by Stephen Ambrose (1989), Ch.14. In his *Memoirs*, Nixon commented: 'Very few speeches actually influence the course of history. The November 3 speech was one of them'

19 No event in American history is more misunderstood than the Vietnam War. It was misreported then, and it is misremembered now.

Richard Nixon: 'No More Vietnams', publ. in the *New York Times*, 28 March 1985

20 We are at war with the most dangerous enemy that has ever faced mankind in his long climb from the swamp to the stars, and it has been said if we lose that war, and in so doing lose this way of freedom of ours, history will record with the greatest astonishment that those who had the most to lose did the least to prevent its happening.

Ronald Reagan (b.1911), U.S. Republican politician and president: 'A Time for Choosing', television address, 27 Oct. 1964, publ. in *Speaking My Mind* (1989)

21 We should declare war on North Vietnam. ... We could pave the whole country and put parking strips on it, and still be home by Christmas.

Ronald Reagan: *Fresno Bee* (California), 10 Oct. 1965, quoted in *Reagan's Reign of Error* (ed. Mark Green and Gail MacColl, 1987), 'Vietnam, a Noble Cause'

22 I was proud of the youths who opposed the war in Vietnam because they were my babies.

Benjamin Spock (b.1903), U.S. paediatrician and author: in *The Times* (London), 2 May 1988

23 The war against Vietnam is only the ghastliest manifestation of what I'd call imperial provincialism, which afflicts America's whole culture – aware only of its own history, insensible to everything which isn't part of the local atmosphere.

Stephen Vizinczey (b.1933), Hungarian novelist and critic: 'Condemned World, Literary Kingdom' (review of Norman Mailer's *Armies of the Night*), publ. in *The Times Saturday Review* (London), 21 Sept. 1968, rep. in *Truth and Lies in Literature* (1986)

24 Out here, due process is a bullet.

John Wayne (1907–1979), U.S. actor: Col. Mike Kirby (Wayne), in *The Green Berets* (film; screenplay by James Lee Barrett, directed by John Wayne and Ray Kellogg, 1968)

VIOLENCE

1 The old guard may grumble and occasionally sue, but in a society where *Portnoy's Complaint* is a record-breaking best-seller sexual permissiveness is no longer an issue. The real resistance now is to an art which forces its audience to recognize and accept imaginatively, in their nerve-ends, not the facts of life but the facts of death and violence: absurd, random, gratuitous, unjustified, and inescapably part of the society we have created.

A. Alvarez (b.1929), British critic, poet and novelist: *The Savage God* (1971), Pt.4, 'The Savage God'

2 Power and violence are opposites; where the one rules absolutely, the other is absent. Violence appears where power is in jeopardy, but left to its own course it ends in power's disappearance.

Hannah Arendt (1906–1975), German-born U.S. political philosopher: *Crises of the Republic* (1972), 'On Violence'

3 The only thing that's been a worse flop than the organization of nonviolence has been the organization of violence.

Joan Baez (b.1941), U.S. singer: *Daybreak* (1968), 'What Would You Do If?'

4 Perhaps violence, like pornography, is some kind of an evolutionary standby system, a last-resort device for throwing a wild joker into the game?

J.G. Ballard (b.1930), British author: *Myths of the Near Future* (1982), 'News from the Sun'

5 I write about violence as naturally as Jane Austen wrote about manners. Violence shapes and obsesses our society, and if we do not stop being violent we have no future.

Edward Bond (b.1934), British playwright: preface to *Lear* (1972). Two of Bond's plays were banned in the 1960s for their violent content, provoking a furore which contributed to ending censorship on the stage in Britain

6 Violence is as American as cherry pie.

H. Rap Brown (b.1943), U.S. radical and author: press conference, July 1967, quoted in the *Evening Star* (Washington D.C.), 27 July 1967

7 Violence is one of the most intensely lived experiences and, for those capable of giving themselves over to it, is one of the most intense pleasures.

Bill Buford (b.1954), U.S. editor and author: *Among the Thugs* (1991), Pt.2, 'Dawes Road, Fulham'

8 We are supposed to be the children of Seth; but Seth is too much of an effete nonentity to deserve ancestral regard. No, we are the sons of

Cain, and with violence can be associated the attacks on sound, stone, wood and metal that produced civilisation.

Anthony Burgess (1917–1993), British author and critic: book review in *The Observer* (London), 26 Nov. 1989

9 Men are rewarded for learning the practice of violence in virtually any sphere of activity by money, admiration, recognition, respect, and the genuflection of others honoring their sacred and proven masculinity. In male culture, police are heroic and so are outlaws; males who enforce standards are heroic and so are those who violate them.

Andrea Dworkin (b.1946), U.S. feminist critic: *Pornography* (1981), Ch.2

10 There are situations in life to which the only satisfactory response is a physically violent one. If you don't make that response, you continually relive the unresolved situation over and over in your life.

Russell Hoban (b.1932), U.S. author: *Novelists in Interview* (ed. John Haffenden, 1985)

11 Some people draw a comforting distinction between 'force' and 'violence'.... I refuse to cloud the issue by such word-play.... The power which establishes a state is violence; the power which maintains it is violence; the power which eventually overthrows it is violence.... Call an elephant a rabbit only if it gives you comfort to feel that you are about to be trampled to death by a rabbit.

Kenneth Kaunda (b.1924), Zambian president: quoted in *Kaunda on Violence* (1980), Pt.1

12 A society that presumes a norm of violence and celebrates aggression, whether in the subway, on the football field, or in the conduct of its business, cannot help making celebrities of the people who would destroy it.

Lewis H. Lapham (b.1935), U.S. essayist and editor: 'Citizen Goetz', publ. in *Harper's Magazine* (New York), March 1985

13 Violence is not to be found only in the collision of one billiard ball with another, or the storm that destroys a harvest, or the master who mistreats his slave, or a totalitarian State that vilifies its citizens, or the conquest and subjection of men in war. Violence is to be found in any action in which one acts as if one were alone to act: as if the rest of the universe were there only to *receive* the action.

Emmanuel Levinas (b.1905), French Jewish philosopher: 'Ethics and Spirit' (1952), rep. in *Difficult Freedom* (1990), Pt.1

14 In violence we forget who we are.

Mary McCarthy (1912–1989), U.S. author and critic: *On the Contrary* (1961), Pt.3, 'Characters in Fiction'

15 In America all too few blows are struck into flesh. We kill the spirit here, we are experts at that. We use psychic bullets and kill each other cell by cell.

Norman Mailer (b.1923), U.S. author: contrasting the U.S. with Cuba, where 'hatred runs over into the love of blood', in *The Presidential Papers* (1963), 'The Fourth Presidential Paper – Foreign Affairs: letter to Castro'

16 If human beings are to survive in a nuclear age, committing acts of violence may eventually have to become as embarrassing as urinating or defecating in public are today.

Myriam Miedzian, U.S. author: *Boys Will Be Boys* (1991), Ch.3

17 I had a repugnance for violence, and in particular for its brutal and unnecessary use. Later in politics I had to prove my capacity and determination to meet violence with force and by leadership and organisation to overcome it. The sad fact is that in human affairs this is sometimes necessary.

Oswald Mosley (1896–1980), British fascist leader: *My Life* (1968), Ch.2

18 Violence, like Achilles' lance, can heal the wounds that it has inflicted.

Jean-Paul Sartre (1905–1980), French philosopher and author: on revolutionary struggle, in preface to *The Wretched of the Earth* by Frantz Fanon (1961)

19 Violence can only be concealed by a lie, and the lie can only be maintained by violence. Any man who has once proclaimed violence as his method is inevitably forced to take the lie as his principle.

Alexander Solzhenitsyn (b.1918), Russian novelist: Nobel Prize lecture, 1973, publ. in *Solzhenitsyn: A Documentary Record* (ed. Leopold Labedz, 1974)

20 Violence is one of the most fun things to watch.

Quentin Tarantino (b.1958), U.S. film-maker: said at the screening of his movie *Pulp Fiction* in Cannes, March 1994, quoted in *Quentin Tarantino: The Man and His Movies* by Jami Bernard (1995), Ch.11

See also CINEMA: SEX & VIOLENCE; Penn on SELF-CONFIDENCE

VIRGINITY

1 An isolated outbreak of virginity ... is a rash on the face of society. It arouses only pity from the married, and embarrassment from the single.

Charlotte Bingham (b.1942), British author: *Lucinda* (1966), Ch.1

2 The great majority of people in England and America are modest, decent and pure-minded

and the amount of virgins in the world today is stupendous.

Barbara Cartland (b.1901), British novelist: interview in *Speaking Frankly* by Wendy Leigh (1978). But on another occasion, Cartland was reported as saying: 'Only the English and the Americans are improper. East of Suez everyone wants a virgin'

3   Men are afraid of virgins, but they have a cure for their own fear and the virgin's virginity: fucking.

Ursula K. Le Guin (b.1929), U.S. author: 'The Space Crone', first publ. in *The Co-Evolution Quarterly*, summer 1976, rep. in *Dancing at the Edge of the World* (1989)

4   I always thought of losing my virginity as a career move.

Madonna (b.1959), U.S. singer and actress: quoted in epilogue to *Madonna Unauthorized* by Christopher Andersen (1991)

See also CELIBACY

VIRTUE

1   Virtue cannot separate itself from reality without becoming a principle of evil.

Albert Camus (1913–1960), French-Algerian philosopher and author: *The Rebel* (1951; tr.1953), Pt.5, 'Moderation and Excess'

2   Vice is its own reward. It is virtue which, if it is to be marketed with consumer appeal, must carry Green Shield stamps.

Quentin Crisp (b.1908), British author: *The Naked Civil Servant* (1968), Ch.2

3   Nothing in our times has become so unattractive as virtue.

Edward Dahlberg (1900–1977), U.S. author and critic: *Alms for Oblivion* (1964), 'The Expatriates: A Memoir'

4   People who are in a fortunate position always attribute virtue to what makes them so happy.

J.K. Galbraith (b.1908), U.S. economist: in *The Guardian* (London), 23 May 1992

5   All art is a struggle to be, in a particular sort of way, virtuous.

Iris Murdoch (b.1919), British novelist and philosopher: quoted in *Novelists in Interview* (ed. John Haffenden, 1985)

6   I don't like people who have never fallen or stumbled. Their virtue is lifeless and it isn't of much value. Life hasn't revealed its beauty to them.

Boris Pasternak (1890–1960), Russian poet, novelist and translator: Zhivago, in *Doctor Zhivago* (1957; tr.1958), Ch.13, Sct.12

7   A man oughta do what he thinks is right.

John Wayne (1907–1979), U.S. actor: Hondo Lane (Wayne), in *Hondo* (film; screenplay by James Edward Grant, directed by John Farrow, 1953)

See also Burroughs on FUNCTION; Cleaver on GOD; Fry on SAINTS

VISIONARIES

1   Nothing is so easy to fake as the inner vision.

Robertson Davies (1913–1995), Canadian novelist and journalist: Saraceni, in *What's Bred in the Bone* (1985), Pt.4, 'What Would Not Out of the Flesh?'

2   It doesn't matter with me now. Because I've been to the mountaintop. And I don't mind. Like anybody, I would like to live a long life. Longevity has its place. But I'm not concerned about that now. I just want to do God's will. And He's allowed me to go up to the mountain. And I've looked over, and I've seen the promised land. ... Mine eyes have seen the glory of the coming of the Lord.

Martin Luther King Jr. (1929–1968), U.S. clergyman and civil rights leader: 'I See the Promised Land', speech, 3 April 1968, Memphis, publ. in *A Testament of Hope: Essential Writings* (ed. James Melvin Washington, 1986). The speech was made the day before Martin Luther King's assassination

3   St Teresa of Avila described our life in this world as like a night at a second-class hotel.

Malcolm Muggeridge (1903–1990), British journalist and broadcaster: quoted in *The Observer* (London), 20 March 1983

4   Each day I live in a glass room
Unless I break it with the thrusting
Of my senses and pass through
The splintered walls to the great landscape.

Mervyn Peake (1911–1968), British author and illustrator: 'Each Day I Live in a Glass Room', publ. in *A Reverie of Bone* (1967)

VITALITY

1   We derive our vitality from our store of madness.

E.M. Cioran (1911–1995), Rumanian-born French philosopher: title essay of *The Temptation to Exist* (1956)

2   I suppose if you had to choose just one quality to have that would be it: vitality.

John F. Kennedy (1917–1963), U.S. Democratic politician and president: quoted in *A Thousand Days* by Arthur M. Schlesinger Jr. (1965), Ch.25

3   Oh heavens, how I long for a little ordinary human enthusiasm. Just enthusiasm – that's all. I want to hear a warm, thrilling voice cry out Hallelujah! Hallelujah! I'm alive!

John Osborne (1929–1994), British playwright: Jimmy Porter, in *Look Back in Anger* (1956), Act 1

4 Although none of the rules for becoming more alive is valid, it is healthy to keep on formulating them.
Susan Sontag (b.1933), U.S. essayist: 'Debriefing', first publ. in the *American Review* (New York), Sept. 1973, rep. in *I, Etcetera* (1978)

VOCATION

1 Once you get into this great stream of history you can't get out. You can drown. Or you can be pulled ashore by the tide. But it is awfully hard to get out when you are in the middle of the stream – if it is intended that you stay there.
Richard Nixon (1913–1992), U.S. Republican politician and president: on revoking his decision to retire in 1954, quoted in *Richard Nixon: A Political and Personal Portrait* by Earl Mazo (1959), Ch.10

2 I want to preserve the level of quality. Like Atlas holding the earth on his shoulders. He could, after all, have thrown it off when he got tired. But he didn't; for some reason he went on holding it up.
Andrey Tarkovsky (1932–1986), Russian film-maker: journal entry, 2 June 1979, publ. in *Time Within Time: The Diaries 1970–1986* (1989; tr.1994). 'That, incidentally, is the most remarkable point of the legend,' Tarkovsky noted: 'not the fact that he held it up for so long, but the fact that he did not become disillusioned and throw it down'

3 Many people mistake our work for our vocation. Our vocation is the love of Jesus.
Mother Teresa (1910–1997), Albanian-born Roman Catholic missionary: from *Mother Teresa* (documentary film), quoted in the *New York Times*, 28 Nov. 1986

VOTING

1 Constantly choosing the lesser of two evils is still choosing evil.
Jerry Garcia (1942–1995), U.S. rock musician: in *Rolling Stone* (New York), 30 Nov. 1989

2 It's not the voting that's democracy, it's the counting.
Tom Stoppard (b.1937), British playwright: Dotty, in *Jumpers* (1972), Act 1

3 Voters don't decide issues, they decide *who* will decide issues.
George F. Will (b.1941), U.S. political columnist: in *Newsweek* (New York), 8 March 1976

See also ELECTIONS

VULGARITY

1 It's only with great vulgarity that you can achieve real refinement, only out of bawdry that you can get tenderness.
Lawrence Durrell (1912–1990), British author: interview in *Writers at Work* (Second Series, ed. George Plimpton, 1963)

2 Vulgarity is, in reality, nothing but a modern, chic, pert descendant of the goddess Dullness.
Edith Sitwell (1887–1964), British poet and critic: *Taken Care Of* (1965), Ch.19

WALES *see under* BRITAIN

WAR

1 The chief reason warfare is still with us is neither a secret death-wish of the human species, nor an irrepressible instinct of aggression, nor, finally and more plausibly, the serious economic and social dangers inherent in disarmament, but the simple fact that no substitute for this final arbiter in international affairs has yet appeared on the political scene.
Hannah Arendt (1906–1975), German-born U.S. political philosopher: *Crises of the Republic* (1972), 'On Violence, Sct.1

2 There is the guilt all soldiers feel for having broken the taboo against killing, a guilt as old as war itself. Add to this the soldier's sense of shame for having fought in actions that resulted, indirectly or directly, in the deaths of civilians. Then pile on top of that an attitude of social opprobrium, an attitude that made the fighting man feel personally morally responsible for the war, and you get your proverbial walking time bomb.
Philip Caputo (b.1941), U.S. author, journalist and Vietnam veteran: referring to Vietnam veterans, in *Playboy* (Chicago), Jan.1982

3 A 'just war' is hospitable to every self-deception on the part of those waging it, none more than the certainty of virtue, under whose shelter every abomination can be committed with a clear conscience.
Alexander Cockburn (b.1941), Anglo-Irish journalist: in the *New Statesman & Society* (London), 8 Feb. 1991

4 America is addicted to wars of distraction.
Barbara Ehrenreich (b.1941), U.S. author and columnist: in *The Times* (London), 22 April 1991

5 Those who actually set out to see the fall of a city ... or those who choose to go to a front line, are obviously asking themselves to what extent they are cowards. But the tests they set themselves – there is a dead body, can you bear

to look at it? – are nothing in comparison with the tests that are sprung on them. It is not the obvious tests that matter (do you go to pieces in a mortar attack?) but the unexpected ones (here is a man on the run, seeking your help – can you face him honestly?).

James Fenton (b.1949), British poet and critic: 'The Fall of Saigon', first publ. in *Granta* (Cambridge), No.15, 1985, rep. in *All the Wrong Places* (1988)

6 Either war is obsolete or men are.

R. Buckminster Fuller (1895–1983), U.S. architect and engineer: in the *New Yorker*, 8 Jan. 1966

7 After a lifetime of war-watching, I see war as an endemic human disease, and governments the carriers.

Martha Gellhorn (b.1908), U.S. journalist and author: introduction to *The Face of War* (1959; rev.1967)

8 What if someone gave a war and Nobody came?
Life would ring the bells of Ecstasy and
Forever be Itself again.

Allen Ginsberg (b.1926), U.S. poet: 'Graffiti 12th Cubicle Men's Room Syracuse Airport', publ. in *The Fall of America* (1972). The words were current during the anti-war protests of the 1960s, and were adopted as the title of a 1970 film, *Suppose They Gave a War and Nobody Came?*, starring Brian Keith and Tony Curtis. The originator was probably a line from another poem, 'The People, Yes' by Carl Sandburg (1936)

9 The war was a mirror; it reflected man's every virtue and every vice, and if you looked closely, like an artist at his drawings, it showed up both with unusual clarity.

George Grosz (1893–1959), German artist: referring to World War I, in *A Small Yes and a Big No* (1955; tr.1982), Ch.7

10 There's a rule saying I have to ground anyone who's crazy ... there's a catch. Catch-22. Anyone who wants to get out of combat duty isn't really crazy.

Joseph Heller (b.1923), U.S. author: Doc Daneeka, in *Catch-22* (1955), Ch.5. The narrator explains: 'Orr would be crazy to fly more missions and sane if he didn't, but if he was sane he had to fly them. If he flew them he was crazy and didn't have to; but if he didn't want to he was sane and had to'

11 Frankly, I'd like to see the government get out of war altogether and leave the whole field to private industry.

Joseph Heller: Milo Minderbinder, in *Catch-22* (1955), Ch.24

12 War has been the most convenient pseudo-solution for the problems of twentieth-century capitalism. It provides the incentives to modernisation and technological revolution which the market and the pursuit of profit do only fitfully and by accident, it makes the

unthinkable (such as votes for women and the abolition of unemployment) not merely thinkable but practicable.... What is equally important, it can re-create communities of men and give a temporary sense to their lives by uniting them against foreigners and outsiders. This is an achievement beyond the power of the private enterprise economy ... when left to itself.

Eric Hobsbawm (b.1917), British historian: in *The Observer* (London), 26 May 1968

13 What we believe is more important than our material existence, therefore warfare is a legitimate extension of values.

Edward Johnson (b.1915), U.S. author and educator: in *The Independent* (London), 26 April 1988

14 The most persistent sound which reverberates through man's history is the beating of war drums.

Arthur Koestler (1905–1983), Hungarian-born British novelist and essayist: *Janus: A Summing Up* (1978), 'Prologue: the New Calendar', Sct.1

15 Those who have been immersed in the tragedy of massive death during wartime, and who have faced it squarely, never allowing their senses and feelings to become numbed and indifferent, have emerged from their experiences with growth and humanness greater than that achieved through almost any other means.

Elisabeth Kübler-Ross (b.1926), Swiss-born U.S. psychiatrist: *Death: The Final Stage of Growth* (1975), Ch.5

16 The more prosperous and settled a nation, the more readily it tends to think of war as a regrettable accident; to nations less fortunate the chance of war presents itself as a possible bountiful friend.

Lewis H. Lapham (b.1935), U.S. essayist and editor: 'Notebook: Brave New World', publ. in *Harper's Magazine* (New York), March 1991

17 Oh what a lovely war!

Joan Littlewood (b.1914), British stage director: song and title of stage musical (1963) and film (1969), written with Charles Chilton (b.1914) and Gerry Raffles (1924–1975)

18 Blunders are an inescapable feature of war, because choice in military affairs lies generally between the bad and the worse.

Allan Massie (b.1938), British author: Marshal Pétain, in *A Question of Loyalties* (1989), Pt.3, Ch.11

19 The quickest way of ending a war is to lose it.

George Orwell (1903–1950), British author: 'Second Thoughts on James Burnham', first publ. in *Polemic* (London), May 1946, rep. in *Shooting an Elephant* (1950)

20 Wars are made to make debt.

Ezra Pound (1885–1972), U.S. poet and critic: interview in *Writers at Work* (Second Series, ed. George Plimpton, 1963)

21 Of the four wars in my lifetime, none came about because the U.S. was too strong.
Ronald Reagan (b.1911), U.S. Republican politician and president: quoted in *The Observer* (London), 29 June 1980

22 I had supposed until that time that it was quite common for parents to love their children, but the war persuaded me that it is a rare exception. I had supposed that most people liked money better than almost anything else, but I discovered that they liked destruction even better. I had supposed that intellectuals frequently loved truth, but I found here again that not ten per cent of them prefer truth to popularity.
Bertrand Russell (1872–1970), British philosopher and mathematician: referring to World War I, in *The Autobiography of Bertrand Russell*, Vol.II (1968), Ch.1

23 All this stuff you heard about America not wanting to fight, wanting to stay out of the war, is a lot of horse dung. Americans, traditionally, love to fight. All real Americans love the sting of battle. ... Americans play to win all the time. I wouldn't give a hoot in hell for a man who lost and laughed. That's why Americans have never lost – and will never lose – a war, because the very thought of losing is hateful to Americans.
George C. Scott (b.1926), U.S. actor: General George S. Patton Jr. (Scott), in *Patton* (film; screenplay by Francis Ford Coppola and Edmund H. North, directed by Franklin J. Schaffner, 1970). In this opening speech, Patton addresses the audience as though they were his troops. The screenplay was based on Ladislas Farago's *Patton: Ordeal and Triumph* (1966) and General Omar Brady's *A Soldier's Story* (1951)

24 Funny thing – in the war you do a lot of chopping and you get a medal for it. You come back and do the same thing and they fry you for it.
Frank Sinatra (b.1915), U.S. singer and actor: Johnny Baron (Sinatra), in *Suddenly* (film; screenplay by Richard Sale, directed by Lewis Allen, 1954)

25 War...
What is it good for?
Absolutely nothing.
Edwin Starr (b.1942), U.S. soul singer: 'War' (song; written by Norman Whitfield and Barrett Strong, 1970)

26 To say that war is madness is like saying that sex is madness: true enough, from the standpoint of a stateless eunuch, but merely a provocative epigram for those who must make their arrangements in the world as given.

John Updike (b.1932), U.S. author and critic: *Self-Consciousness: Memoirs* (1989), Ch.4

27 What war has always been is a puberty ceremony. It's a very rough one, but you went away a boy and came back a man, maybe with an eye missing or whatever but godammit you were a man and people had to call you a man thereafter.
Kurt Vonnegut (b.1922), U.S. novelist: interview in *City Limits* (London), 11 March 1983

See also Vonnegut on APPEASEMENT; BOSNIA; THE COLD WAR; GUERRILLA WARFARE; Scott on HEROES; IRAQ & THE SECOND GULF WAR; Foucault on POLITICS; VIETNAM; WORLD WAR II

WAR CORRESPONDENTS

1 Who could not be moved by the sight of that poor, demoralized rabble, outwitted, outflanked, outmanoeuvered by the U.S. military? Yet, given time, I think the press will bounce back.
James Baker (b.1930), U.S. Republican politician and secretary of state: of the Second Gulf War, quoted in *The Guardian* (London), 26 March 1991

2 I plied my trade as a war-correspondent in the uniform of a fighting force, and while I did not bear arms I was part of a community that did, and while I killed no one – nor could for that matter have defended myself against anyone who proposed to kill me – I was part of a machine whose only purpose was that of killing people, in circumstances of considerable wretchedness. I do not yet know whether I was wrong or right about that. In both cases, had I not done so I would have been unable to protest with experience and conviction at what I had seen, but I am far from persuaded that these horrible and dangerous times were not for me the easy way out.
James Cameron (1911–1985), British journalist: of his experiences in Korea and Indo-China, in *Point of Departure* (1967), Ch.4

3 It took nine years, and a great depression, and two wars ending in defeat, and one surrender without war, to break my faith in the benign power of the press. Gradually I came to realize that people will more readily swallow lies than truth, as if the taste of lies was homey, appetizing: a habit.
Martha Gellhorn (b.1908), U.S. journalist and author: introduction to *The Face of War* (1959)

4 We came to fear something more complicated than death, an annihilation less final but more complete, and we got out. Because ... we all knew that if you stayed too long you became

one of those poor bastards who had to have a war on all the time, and where was that?

Michael Herr (b.1940), U.S. journalist: *Dispatches* (1977), 'Colleagues', Sct.3

WAR CRIMES

1 A trial cannot be conducted by announcing the general culpability of a civilization. Only the actual deeds which, at least, stank in the nostrils of the entire world were brought to judgement.

Albert Camus (1913–1960), French-Algerian philosopher and author: *The Rebel* (1951; tr.1953), Pt.3, 'State Terrorism and Irrational Terror'

2 You cannot do justice to the dead. When we talk about doing justice to the dead we are talking about retribution for the harm done to them. But retribution and justice are two different things.

William Shawcross (b.1902), British lawyer: discussing the War Crimes Bill, which proposed to prosecute ex-Nazis living in Britain, in *The Daily Telegraph* (London), 1 May 1991. Lord Shawcross was chief British prosecutor at the Nuremberg War Trials

3 There is no such thing as collective guilt.

Kurt Waldheim (b.1918), Austrian diplomat and president: on charges levelled against him of collaboration with the Nazi regime in Austria, in the *International Herald Tribune* (Paris), 11 March 1988

ANDY WARHOL

1 Ultimately Warhol's private moral reference was to the supreme kitsch of the Catholic church.

Allen Ginsberg (b.1926), U.S. poet: *Andy Warhol: A Retrospective* (1986), 'A Collective Portrait of Andy Warhol'

2 Andy passes through things, but so do we. He sat down and had a talk with me. 'You gotta decide what you want to do. Do you want to keep just playing museums from now on and the art festivals? Or do you want to start moving into other areas? Lou, don't you think you should think about it?' So I thought about it, and I fired him.

Lou Reed (b.1944), U.S. rock musician: interview in *Rolling Stone* (New York), 4 May 1989

3 My image is a statement of the symbols of the harsh, impersonal products and brash materialistic objects on which America is built today. It is a projection of everything that can be bought and sold, the practical but impermanent symbols that sustain us.

Andy Warhol (c.1928–1987), U.S. Pop artist: 'New Talent U.S.A.', publ. in *Art in America* (New York), Vol.L, No.1, 1962

4 If you want to know all about Andy Warhol, just look at the surface: of my paintings and films and me, and there I am. There's nothing behind it.

Andy Warhol: 'Warhol in his Own Words', first publ. in the *Los Angeles Free Press*, 17 March 1967, rep. in *Andy Warhol: A Retrospective* (1986)

5 The man whose heart is as warm as a hanky soaked in ethyl chloride.

Edmund White (b.1940), U.S. author: *States of Desire: Travels in Gay America* (1980), Ch.1

6 He was the person who created Attitude. Before Warhol, in artistic circles, there was Ideology – you took a stance against the crassness of American life. Andy Warhol turned that on its head, and created an attitude. And that attitude was 'It's so awful, it's wonderful. It's so tacky, let's wallow in it.'

Tom Wolfe (b.1931), U.S. author and journalist: comment made a few days after Warhol's death, 22 Feb. 1987, quoted in *Rolling Stone* (New York), 9 April 1987

WASHINGTON D.C. *see under* THE UNITED STATES

WATERGATE

1 If the national security is involved, *anything goes*. There are no rules. There are people so lacking in roots about what is proper and what is improper that they don't know there's anything wrong in breaking into the headquarters of the opposition party.

Helen Gahagan Douglas (1900–1980), U.S. author, actress and congresswoman: quoted in *Ms.* (New York), Oct. 1973

2 Our long national nightmare is over. Our Constitution works; our great Republic is a government of laws and not of men. Here the people rule.

Gerald Ford (b.1913), U.S. Republican politician and president: speech on succeeding Richard Nixon as president, 9 Aug. 1974, publ. in *Public Papers of the Presidents, 1974*

3 There can be no whitewash at the White House.

Richard Nixon (1913–1992), U.S. Republican politician and president: television address on Watergate, 30 April 1973, quoted in the *New York Times*, 1 May 1973. In July 1972, agents of Nixon's re-election committee were arrested in the Democratic Party headquarters after an attempt to tap telephones there, of which Nixon denied all knowledge

4 There had been no thievery or venality. We had all simply wandered into a situation unthinkingly, trying to protect ourselves from

what we saw as a political problem. Now, suddenly, it was like a Rorschach ink blot: others, looking at our actions, pointed out a pattern that we ourselves had not seen.

Richard Nixon: *The Memoirs of Richard Nixon* (1978), 'The Presidency 1973'

5 Maybe this is like the Old Testament. It was visited upon us and maybe we're going to benefit from it.

Nelson A. Rockefeller (1908–1979), U.S. Republican politician and vice president: speech, 17 July 1973, New York, quoted in the *New York Times*, 18 July 1973

WEAKNESS

1 The weak are the most treacherous of us all. They come to the strong and drain them. They are bottomless. They are insatiable. They are always parched and always bitter. They are everyone's concern and like vampires they suck our life's blood.

Bette Davis (1908–1989), U.S. actress: *The Lonely Life* (autobiography, 1962), Ch.20

2 The weak are more likely to make the strong weak than the strong are likely to make the weak strong.

Marlene Dietrich (1904–1992), German-born U.S. actress: *Marlene Dietrich's ABC* (1962), 'Weakness'

3 It is a talent of the weak to persuade themselves that they suffer for something when they suffer from something; that they are showing the way when they are running away; that they see the light when they feel the heat; that they are chosen when they are shunned.

Eric Hoffer (1902–1983), U.S. philosopher: *The Passionate State of Mind* (1955), Aph.49

WEALTH

1 The secret point of money and power in America is neither the things that money can buy nor power for power's sake ... but absolute personal freedom, mobility, privacy. It is the instinct which drove America to the Pacific, all through the nineteenth century, the desire to be able to find a restaurant open in case you want a sandwich, to be a free agent, live by one's own rules.

Joan Didion (b.1934), U.S. essayist: '7000 Romaine, Los Angeles' (1967), rep. in *Slouching Towards Bethlehem* (1968)

2 Wealth is not without its advantages and the case to the contrary, although it has often been made, has never proved widely persuasive.

J.K. Galbraith (b.1908), U.S. economist: opening words of *The Affluent Society* (1958), Ch.1, Sct.1

3 Wealth, in even the most improbable cases, manages to convey the aspect of intelligence.

J.K. Galbraith: in the *Sydney Morning Herald*, 22 May 1982

4 If you can actually count your money, then you are not really a rich man.

J. Paul Getty (1892–1976), U.S. oil millionaire and arts patron: quoted in *The Observer* (London), 3 Nov. 1957

5 I've been rich and I've been poor. Believe me, rich is better.

Gloria Grahame (1924–1981), U.S. actress: Debby Marsh (Grahame), in *The Big Heat* (film; screenplay by Sidney Boehm, adapted from William P. McGivern's novel, directed by Fritz Lang, 1953). The words may have been borrowed from U.S. singer Sophie Tucker's book, *Some of These Days* (1945)

6 Wealth often takes away chances from men as well as poverty. There is none to tell the rich to go on striving, for a rich man makes the law that hallows and hollows his own life.

Sean O'Casey (1884–1964), Irish playwright: *Rose and Crown* (fifth volume of autobiography, 1952), 'Pennsylvanian Visit'

7 Money doesn't make you happy. I now have $50 million but I was just as happy when I had $48 million.

Arnold Schwarzenegger (b.1947), U.S. actor: quoted in *Brewer's Cinema* (1995)

8 There must be a reason why some people can afford to live well. They must have worked for it. I only feel angry when I see waste. When I see people throwing away things that we could use.

Mother Teresa (1910–1997), Albanian-born Roman Catholic missionary: *A Gift for God* (1975), 'Riches'

9 Purchasing power is a licence to purchase power.

Raoul Vaneigem (b.1934), Belgian Situationist philosopher: *The Revolution of Everyday Life* (1967; tr.1983), Ch.7, Sct.3

See also THE RICH

WEATHER

1 All we need is a meteorologist who has once been soaked to the skin without ill effect. No one can write knowingly of the weather who walks bent over on wet days.

E.B. White (1899–1985), U.S. author and editor: 'Dismal?', first publ. in the *New Yorker*, 25 Feb. 1950, rep. in *Writings from the New Yorker 1927–1976* (ed. Rebecca M. Dale, 1991)

2 People get a bad impression of it by continually trying to treat it as if it was a bank clerk, who ought to be on time on Tuesday next, instead

of philosophically seeing it as a painter, who may do anything so long as you don't try to predict what.

Katharine Whitehorn (b.1926), British journalist: of the English climate, in *The Observer* (London), 7 Aug. 1966

3 It was so cold I almost got married.

Shelley Winters (b.1922), U.S. actress: quoted in the *New York Times*, 29 April 1956

See also RAIN

WEDDINGS

1 Wedding invitations now are apt to bring to mind divorce statistics, sexual instability, reflections on the sexual revolution and on venereal disease, on the effects of herpes and AIDS on marital infidelity. ... Your contemporary wedding guest has been transported by modern forces of malign magic into a sphere of distraction where instead of hearing village musicians he is blasted by a great noise – the modern noise.

Saul Bellow (b.1915), U.S. novelist: *It All Adds Up* (1994), 'The Distracted Public'

2 It's pretty easy. Just say 'I do' whenever anyone asks you a question.

Richard Curtis (b.1956), British screenwriter: Carrie (Andie MacDowell), in *Four Weddings and a Funeral* (film; screenplay by Richard Curtis, directed by Mike Newell, 1994)

3 I'm getting married in the morning,
Ding! dong! the bells are gonna chime.
Pull out the stopper;
Let's have a whopper;
But get me to the church on time!

Alan Jay Lerner (1918–1986), U.S. songwriter: 'Get Me to the Church on Time' (song), in *My Fair Lady* (stage show, 1956; film, 1964)

See also MARRIAGE

WEEKENDS

1 One non-revolutionary weekend is infinitely more bloody than a month of permanent revolution.

Graffiti, School of Oriental Languages, London, 1968: quoted in *Leaving the 20th Century: The Incomplete Work of the Situationist International* (ed./tr. Christopher Gray, 1974)

2 Your hair may be brushed, but your mind's untidy,
You've had about seven hours' sleep since Friday,
No wonder you feel that lost sensation;
You're sunk from a riot of relaxation.

Ogden Nash (1902–1971), U.S. poet: 'We'll All Feel Better By Wednesday', publ. in *Versus* (1949)

See also SUNDAYS

WELFARE

1 Mothers born on relief have their babies on relief. Nothingness, truly, seems to be the condition of these New York people. ... They are nomads going from one rooming house to another, looking for a toilet that functions.

Elizabeth Hardwick (b.1916), U.S. author and critic: 'The Insulted and Injured: Books About Poverty' (1961), rep. in *A View of My Own* (1962)

2 Social Security is a government program with a constituency made up of the old, the near old and those who hope or fear to grow old. After 215 years of trying, we have finally discovered a special interest that includes 100 percent of the population. Now we can vote ourselves rich.

P.J. O'Rourke (b.1947), U.S. journalist: *Parliament of Whores* (1991), 'Graft for the Millions: Social Security'

See also Reagan on UNEMPLOYMENT

THE WEST

1 So-called Western Civilization, as practised in half of Europe, some of Asia and a few parts of North America, is better than anything else available. Western civilization not only provides a bit of life, a pinch of liberty and the occasional pursuance of happiness, it's also the only thing that's ever tried to. Our civilization is the first in history to show even the slightest concern for average, undistinguished, none-too-commendable people like us.

P.J. O'Rourke (b.1947), U.S. journalist: introduction to *Holidays in Hell* (1988)

2 Western man represents himself, on the political or psychological stage, in a spectacular world-theater. Our personality is innately cinematic, light-charged projections flickering on the screen of Western consciousness.

Camille Paglia (b.1947), U.S. author and critic: *Sex, Art, and American Culture* (1992), 'Sexual Personae: the Cancelled Preface'

3 In dealing with dissent, its strength lies in having learned to substitute the absorbency of the sponge for the brute force of the truncheon.

Theodore Roszak (b.1933), U.S. social critic: on Western democracy, in *Where the Wasteland Ends* (1972), Ch.2

4　The greatest disease in the West today is not TB or leprosy, it is being unwanted, unloved and uncared for.

Mother Teresa (1910–1997), Albanian-born Roman Catholic missionary: *A Simple Path* (ed. Lucinda Vardey, 1995), 'Love'

5　You in the West have a problem. You are unsure when you are being lied to, when you are being tricked. We do not suffer from this; and unlike you, we have acquired the skill of reading between the lines.

Zdeněk Urbánek (b.1917), Czech translator and essayist: interview with John Pilger, Aug. 1977, quoted in *The Guardian* (London), 12 Feb. 1990

6　Who wants a world in which the guarantee that we shall not die of starvation entails the risk of dying of boredom?

Raoul Vaneigem (b.1934), Belgian Situationist philosopher: introduction to *The Revolution of Everyday Life* (1967; tr.1983)

7　You have riches and freedom here but I feel no sense of faith or direction. You have so many computers, why don't you use them in the search for love?

Lech Walesa (b.1943), Polish trade union leader and president: said in Paris on his first visit out of the Soviet Bloc, quoted in *The Daily Telegraph* (London), 14 Dec. 1988

See also Greer on CHILDREN; Ross on HOLISM; Appelfeld on LITERATURE: AND SOCIETY

WESTERNS

1　In Westerns you were permitted to kiss your horse but never your girl.

Gary Cooper (1901–1961), U.S. actor: 'Well, It Was This Way', publ. in the *Saturday Evening Post* (New York), 17 March 1958

2　Everybody knows nobody ever stood in the street and let the heavy draw first. That's where I disagree with the [John] Wayne concept. I do all the stuff Wayne would never do. I play bigger-than-life characters but I'll shoot a guy in the back. I go by the expediency of the moment.

Clint Eastwood (b.1930), U.S. actor and film-maker: in *Variety* (New York), 14 Sept. 1976

3　Head 'em up, move 'em out, rope 'em in, head 'em off, pull 'em down, move 'em on.

Charles Marquis Warren (1917–1990), U.S. writer, director and producer: preamble to *Rawhide* (TV series, created by Charles Marquis Warren, 1959–66). The series, which ran for 217 episodes and included Clint Eastwood among its stars, was based on the 1866 diary of drover and pioneer cowboy George Duffield

4　I wouldn't say when you've seen one Western you've seen the lot; but when you've seen the lot you get the feeling you've seen one.

Katharine Whitehorn (b.1926), British journalist: *Sunday Best* (1976), 'Decoding the West'

WHITES

1　As far as I knew white women were never lonely, except in books. White men adored them, Black men desired them and Black women worked for them.

Maya Angelou (b.1928), U.S. author: *Singin' and Swingin' and Gettin' Merry Like Christmas* (third volume of autobiography, 1976), Ch.1

2　The reason people think it's important to be white is that they think it's important not to be black.

James Baldwin (1924–1987), U.S. author: in conversation with Nikki Giovanni, 4 Nov. 1971, London, publ. in *A Dialogue* (1973)

3　You can't steal nothing from a white man, he's
　　already stole it he owes
you anything you want, even his life. All the
　　stores will open if you
will say the magic words. The magic words are:
　　Up against the wall mother
fucker this is a stick-up!

Amiri Baraka [formerly Leroi Jones] (b.1934), U.S. poet and playwright: 'Black People!', publ. in the *Evergreen Review* (New York), summer 1967, rep. in *Black Magic* (1969). The poem/manifesto was read out by the judge at Baraka's trial for illegal arms possesion, in Newark, July 1967, with the obscenities omitted. Baraka was involved with the anarchist group Up Against the Wall Motherfucker

4　At best ... Blacks see whiteness as a concept that warrants being despised, hated, destroyed and replaced by an aspiration with more human content in it. At worst Blacks envy White society for the comfort it has usurped and at the centre of this envy is the wish – nay, the secret determination – in the innermost minds of most Blacks who think like this, to kick Whites off those comfortable garden chairs that one sees as he rides in a bus, out of town, and to claim them for themselves.

Steve Biko (1946–1977), South African anti-apartheid activist: 'I Write What I Like: Fear – an Important Determinant in South African Politics' (written under the pseudonym of Frank Talk), publ. in appendix to *Steve Biko: Black Consciousness in South Africa* (ed. Millard Arnold, 1978)

5　Every time I embrace a black woman I'm embracing slavery, and when I put my arms around a white woman, well, I'm hugging freedom. The white man forbade me to have the white woman on pain of death. ... I will not be free until the day I can have a white woman in my bed.

Eldridge Cleaver (b.1935), U.S. black leader and writer: Lazarus, in *Soul on Ice* (1968), 'Allegory of the Black Eunuchs'

6 We do not deride the fears of prospering white America. A nation of violence and private property has every reason to dread the violated and the deprived.

June Jordan (b.1936), U.S. poet and civil rights activist: 'Black Studies: Bringing Back the Person', first publ. in the *Evergreen Review* (New York), Oct. 1969, rep. in *Moving Towards Home: Political Essays* (1989)

7 In the tropics the white feels weakened, or downright weak, whence comes the heightened tendency to outbursts of aggression. People who are polite, modest or even humble in Europe fall easily into a rage here, get into fights, destroy other people, start feuds, fall prey to megalomania, grow touchy about their prestige and significance and go around completely devoid of self-criticism, bragging about the position and the influence they have at home.

Ryszard Kapuściński (b.1932), Polish journalist: *The Soccer War* (1990), 'The Plan of the Never-Written Book', Sct.32

8 The fact that white people readily and proudly call themselves 'white', glorify all that is white, and whitewash all that is glorified, becomes unnatural and bigoted in its intent only when these same whites deny persons of African heritage who are Black the natural and inalienable right to readily − proudly − call themselves 'black', glorify all that is black, and blackwash all that is glorified.

Abbey Lincoln (b.1930), U.S. singer: 'Who Will Revere the Black Woman?', publ. in the *Negro Digest*, Sept. 1966

9 The truth is that Mozart, Pascal, Boolean algebra, Shakespeare, parliamentary government, baroque churches, Newton, the emancipation of women, Kant, Marx, and Balanchine ballets don't redeem what this particular civilization has wrought upon the world. The white race *is* the cancer of human history.

Susan Sontag (b.1933), U.S. essayist: 'What's Happening in America (1966)', first publ. in *Partisan Review* (New Brunswick, N.J.), spring 1967, rep. in *Styles of Radical Will* (1969)

10 Be nice to the whites, they need you to rediscover their humanity.

Desmond Tutu (b.1931), South African churchman and archbishop: quoted in the *New York Times*, 19 Oct. 1984

11 The good news may be that Nature is phasing out the white man, but the bad news is that's who She thinks we all are.

Alice Walker (b.1944), U.S. author and critic: 'Nuclear Madness: What You Can Do', first publ. in *Black Scholar* (New York), spring 1982, rep. in *In Search of our Mothers' Gardens* (1983)

See also Fanon on SCAPEGOATS

WILD AT HEART

1 I think all of us have a very thin veneer of civilization painting over what underneath is a savage and marauding beast.

Harry Crews (b.1935), U.S. author: interview in *Dazed and Confused* (London), April 1995

2 This whole world is wild at heart and weird on top.

David Lynch (b.1947), U.S. film-maker: Lula (Laura Dern), in *Wild at Heart* (film; written by David Lynch, adapted from Barry Gifford's novel, directed by David Lynch, 1990)

3 Take a walk on the wild side.

Lou Reed (b.1943), U.S. rock musician: 'Walk on the Wild Side' (song) on the album *Transformer* (1972). *A Walk on the Wild Side* was the title of a novel by Nelson Algren (1956)

4 Life is too small a container for certain individuals.

Tom Robbins (b.1936), U.S. author: *Jitterbug Perfume* (1984), Pt.3

5 Baby this town rips the bones from your back,
It's a death trap, it's a suicide rap,
We gotta get out while we're young
'Cause tramps like us baby we were born to run.

Bruce Springsteen (b.1949), U.S. rock musician: 'Born to Run' (song) on the album *Born to Run* (Bruce Springsteen and the E Street Band, 1975)

THE WILDERNESS

1 Wildness and silence disappeared from the countryside, sweetness fell from the air, not because anyone wished them to vanish or fall but because throughways had to floor the meadows with cement to carry the automobiles which advancing technology produced. ... Tropical beaches turned into high-priced slums where thousand-room hotels elbowed each other for glimpses of once-famous surf not because those who loved the beaches wanted them there but because enormous jets could bring a million tourists every year − and therefore did.

Archibald MacLeish (1892–1982), U.S. poet: on the advance of technology in the U.S., in 'The Great American Frustration', first publ. in the *Saturday Review* (New York), 9 July 1968, rep. in *Riders on Earth* (1978) as 'Return from the Excursion'

2 Once, perhaps, the God-intoxicated few could abscond to the wild frontiers, the forests, the desert places to keep alive the perennial wisdom that they harbored. But no longer. They must now become a political force or their tradition perishes. Soon enough, there will be no solitude left for the saints to roam but its air will shudder with a noise of great engines that drowns out all prayers.

Theodore Roszak (b.1933), U.S. social critic: *Where the Wasteland Ends* (1972), Ch.3

See also THE DESERT

WIMPS

1 I'm not the heroic type. I was beaten up by Quakers.

Woody Allen (b.1935), U.S. film-maker: Victor Shakapopolis (Allen), in *Sleeper* (film; screenplay by Woody Allen and Marshall Brickman, directed by Woody Allen, 1973)

2 Someone has to stand up for wimps.

Barbara Ehrenreich (b.1941), U.S. author and columnist: 'Wimps', first publ. in the *New York Times*, 1985, rep. in *The Worst Years of Our Lives* (1991)

WINE

1 Wine is a part of society because it provides a basis not only for a morality but also for an environment; it is an ornament in the slightest ceremonials of French daily life, from the snack ... to the feast, from the conversation at the local café to the speech at a formal dinner.

Roland Barthes (1915–1980), French semiologist: *Mythologies* (1957; tr.1972), 'Wine and Milk'

2 Elderberry? It is shires dreaming wine.

Seamus Heaney (b.1939), Irish poet: 'Glanmore Sonnets', publ. in *Field Work* (1979)

3 We want the finest wines available to humanity. And we want them *here*, and we want them *now*.

Bruce Robinson (b.1946), British film-maker: Withnail (Richard E. Grant), in *Withnail and I* (film; written and directed by Bruce Robinson, 1987)

See also COCKTAILS; DRINK

WINNING

1 Winning is everything. The only ones who remember when you come second are your wife and your dog.

Damon Hill (b.1960), British racing driver: quoted in *The Sunday Times* (London), 18 Dec. 1994

2 Would you go out there and win one for the Gipper?

Ronald Reagan (b.1911), U.S. Republican politician and president: speech, 7 Nov. 1988, San Diego, publ. in *Speaking My Mind* (1989). One of Reagan's favourite sayings, this is associated with the football star George Gipp (1895–1931), whom he played in the film *Knute Rockne – All-American* (1940)

See also VICTORY

WISDOM

1 Wisdom we know is the knowledge of good and evil – not the strength to choose between the two.

John Cheever (1912–1982), U.S. author: journal entry, 1956, in *John Cheever: The Journals* (ed. Robert Gottlieb, 1991), 'The Late Forties and the Fifties'

2 History teaches us that men and nations behave wisely once they have exhausted all other alternatives.

Abba Eban (b.1915), Israeli politician: speech, 16 Dec. 1970, London, quoted in *The Times* (London), 17 Dec. 1970

3 There often seems to be a playfulness to wise people, as if either their equanimity has as its source this playfulness or the playfulness flows from the equanimity; and they can persuade other people who are in a state of agitation to calm down and manage a smile.

Edward Hoagland (b.1932), U.S. novelist and essayist: 'Other Lives', first publ. in *Harper's Magazine* (New York), July 1973, rep. in *Heart's Desire* (1988)

WISHING

1 Wouldn't it be loverly...

Alan Jay Lerner (1918–1986), U.S. songwriter: 'Wouldn't it be Loverly' (song) sung by Eliza Doolittle, in *My Fair Lady* (stage show, 1956; film, 1964)

2 O to be a dragon
a symbol of the power of Heaven – of silkworm size or immense; at times invisible.
Felicitous phenomenon!

Marianne Moore (1887–1972), U.S. poet: 'O To Be a Dragon', publ. in *O To Be a Dragon* (1959)

WIT

1 You can make a sordid thing sound like a brilliant drawing-room comedy. Probably a fear we have of facing up to the real issues. Could you say we were guilty of Noel Cowardice?

Peter De Vries (1910–1993), U.S. author: *Comfort Me With Apples* (1956), Ch.15

2 The witty woman is a tragic figure in American life. Wit destroys eroticism and eroticism destroys wit, so women must choose between taking lovers and taking no prisoners.

Florence King (b.1936), U.S. author: *Reflections in a Jaundiced Eye* (1989), 'The State of the Funny Bone'

3 There's a helluva distance between wisecracking and wit. Wit has truth in it; wisecracking is simply calisthenics with words.

Dorothy Parker (1893–1967), U.S. humorous writer: interview in *Writers at Work* (First Series, ed. Malcolm Cowley, 1958)

4 Humor does not include sarcasm, invalid irony, sardonicism, innuendo, or any other form of cruelty. When these things are raised to a high point they can become wit, but unlike the French and the English, we have not been much good at wit since the days of Benjamin Franklin.

James Thurber (1894–1961), U.S. humorist and illustrator: letter, 25 June 1954, publ. in *Horn Book Magazine*, April 1962

WIVES

1 A woman asking 'Am *I* good? Am I satisfied?' is extremely selfish. The less women fuss about themselves, the less they talk to other women, the more they try to please their husbands, the happier the marriage is going to be.

Barbara Cartland (b.1901), British novelist: interview in *Speaking Frankly* by Wendy Leigh (1978)

2 The majority of persons choose their wives with as little prudence as they eat. They see a trull with nothing else to recommend her but a pair of thighs and choice hunkers, and so smart to void their seed that they marry her at once. They imagine they can live in marvelous contentment with handsome feet and ambrosial buttocks. Most men are accredited fools shortly after they leave the womb.

Edward Dahlberg (1900–1977), U.S. author and critic: *The Carnal Myth* (1968), Ch.1

3 Many a promising career has been wrecked by marrying the wrong sort of woman. The right sort of woman can distinguish between Creative Lassitude and plain shiftlessness.

Robertson Davies (1913–1995), Canadian novelist and journalist: 'The Writer's Week', first publ. in the *Toronto Daily Star*, 28 March 1959, rep. in *The Enthusiasms of Robertson Davies* (1990)

4 A man would prefer to come home to an unmade bed and a happy woman than to a neatly made bed and an angry woman.

Marlene Dietrich (1904–1992), German-born U.S. actress: *Marlene Dietrich's ABC* (1962), 'Unmade Bed'

5 If you want to know about a man you can find out an awful lot by looking at who he married.

Kirk Douglas (b.1916), U.S. actor: in the *Daily Mail* (London), 9 Sept. 1988

6 The argument between wives and whores is an old one; each one thinking that whatever she is, at least she is not the other.

Andrea Dworkin (b.1946), U.S. feminist critic: *Right-Wing Women* (1978), Ch.2

7 I have only one regret remaining now in this matter of Adolf. It is simply that I was unable to look down upon her open coffin and, like that bird in the Book of Tobit, drop a good, large mess in her eye.

John Osborne (1929–1994), British playwright: *Almost a Gentleman* (1991), Ch.28. 'Adolf' was Osborne's name for his wife, Jill Bennett. Tobit, a pious Jew in the Apocrypha's Book of Tobit, was blinded by sparrows' droppings

8 I don't think a prostitute is more moral than a wife, but they are doing the same thing.

Philip, Duke of Edinburgh (b.1921): speech, 6 Dec. 1988, quoted in the *Daily Mail* (London), 7 Dec. 1988. Prince Philip was discussing the morality of blood-sports

WOMEN

1 Men themselves have wondered
What they see in me.
They try so much
But they can't touch
My inner mystery.
When I try to show them,
They say they still can't see.
I say,
It's in the arch of my back,
The sun of my smile,
The ride of my breasts,
The grace of my style.
I'm a woman
Phenomenally.
Phenomenal woman,
That's me.

Maya Angelou (b.1928), U.S. author: 'Phenomenal Woman', publ. in *And Still I Rise* (1978)

2 One is not born, but rather becomes, a woman.

Simone de Beauvoir (1908–1986), French novelist and essayist: *The Second Sex* (1949; tr.1953), Bk.2, Pt.4, Ch.1

3 It will be a pity if women in the more conventional mould are to be phased out, for there will never be anyone to go home to.

Anita Brookner (b.1938), British novelist and art historian: Rachel, in *A Friend from England* (1987), Ch.10

4 A complete woman is probably not a very admirable creature. She is manipulative, uses

other people to get her own way, and works within whatever system she is in.

Anita Brookner: interview in *Writers at Work* (Eighth Series, ed. George Plimpton, 1988)

5   A woman who looks like a girl and thinks like a man is the best sort, the most enjoyable to be and the most pleasurable to have and to hold.

Julie Burchill (b.1960), British journalist and author: *Damaged Gods* (1986), 'Born again Cows'

6   If *Miss* means respectably unmarried, and *Mrs.* respectably married, then *Ms.* means nudge, nudge, wink, wink.

Angela Carter (1940–1992), British author: 'The Language of Sisterhood', publ. in *The State of the Language* (ed. Christopher Ricks, 1980)

7   Don't you realize that as long as you have to sit down to pee, you'll never be a dominant force in the world? You'll never be a convincing technocrat or middle manager. Because people will know. She's in there *sitting down*.

Don DeLillo (b.1926), U.S. author: James Axton to his wife Kathryn, in *The Names* (1982), Ch.5

8   It's only women who are not really quite women at all, frivolous women who have no idea, who neglect repairs.

Marguerite Duras (1914–1996), French author and film-maker: *Practicalities* (1987; tr.1990), 'House and Home'

9   There are only three things to be done with a woman. You can love her, suffer for her, or turn her into literature.

Lawrence Durrell (1912–1990), British author: Clea, in *Justine* (1957), Pt.1

10   Woman is not born: she is made. In the making, her humanity is destroyed. She becomes symbol of this, symbol of that: mother of the earth, slut of the universe; but she never becomes herself because it is forbidden for her to do so.

Andrea Dworkin (b.1946), U.S. feminist critic: *Pornography* (1981), Ch.4

11   She takes just like a woman, yes she does
She makes love just like a woman, yes she does
And she aches just like a woman
But she breaks just like a little girl.

Bob Dylan (b.1941), U.S. singer and songwriter: 'Just Like a Woman' (song) on the album *Blonde on Blonde* (1968)

12   We're all sisters under the mink.

Gloria Grahame (1924–1981), U.S. actress: Debby Marsh (Grahame), in *The Big Heat* (film; screenplay by Sidney Boehm, adapted from William P. McGivern's novel, directed by Fritz Lang, 1953)

13   Maybe I couldn't make it. Maybe I don't have a pretty smile, good teeth, nice tits, long legs, a cheeky arse, a sexy voice. Maybe I don't know how to handle men and increase my market value, so that the rewards due to the feminine will accrue to me. Then again, maybe I'm sick of the masquerade. I'm sick of pretending eternal youth. I'm sick of belying my own intelligence, my own will, my own sex. I'm sick of peering at the world through false eyelashes, so everything I see is mixed with a shadow of bought hairs; I'm sick of weighting my head with a dead mane, unable to move my neck freely, terrified of rain, of wind, of dancing too vigorously in case I sweat into my lacquered curls. I'm sick of the Powder Room. I'm sick of pretending that some fatuous male's self-important pronouncements are the objects of my undivided attention, I'm sick of going to films and plays when someone else wants to, and sick of having no opinions of my own about either. I'm sick of being a transvestite. I refuse to be a female impersonator. I am a woman, not a castrate.

Germaine Greer (b.1939), Australian feminist writer: *The Female Eunuch* (1970), 'Soul: the Stereotype'

14   A woman might claim to retain some of the child's faculties, although very limited and defused, simply because she has not been encouraged to learn methods of thought and develop a disciplined mind. As long as education remains largely induction ignorance will retain these advantages over learning and it is time that women impudently put them to work.

Germaine Greer: *The Female Eunuch* (1970), 'Womanpower'

15   It is not women's fault if we are so tender. It is in the nature of the lives *we* live. And further, it would be a terrible catastrophe if men had to live men's lives and women's also. Which is precisely what has happened today – to women.

Selma James (b.1930), U.S. author and political activist: *The Ladies and the Mammies: Jane Austen and Jean Rhys* (1983), Ch.1

16   Like their personal lives, women's history is fragmented, interrupted; a shadow history of human beings whose existence has been shaped by the efforts and the demands of others.

Elizabeth Janeway (b.1913), U.S. author and critic: *Women: Their Changing Roles* (1973), 'Reflections on the History of Women'

17   Growing up female in America. What a liability! You grew up with your ears full of cosmetic ads, love songs, advice columns, whoreoscopes, Hollywood gossip, and moral dilemmas on the level of TV soap operas. What

litanies the advertisers of the good life chanted at you! What curious catechisms!

Erica Jong (b.1942), U.S. author: the narrator (Isadora Wing), in *Fear of Flying* (1973), Ch.1

18 Women are natural guerrillas. Scheming, we nestle into the enemy's bed, avoiding open warfare, watching the options, playing the odds.

Sally Kempton (b.1943), U.S. author: 'Cutting Loose', publ. in *Esquire* (New York), July 1970

19 Woman is the future of man. That means that the world which was once formed in man's image will now be transformed to the image of woman. The more technical and mechanical, cold and metallic it becomes, the more it will need the kind of warmth that only the woman can give it. If we want to save the world, we must adapt to the woman, let ourselves be led by the woman, let ourselves be penetrated by the *Ewigweibliche*, the eternally feminine!

Milan Kundera (b.1929), Czech-born French author and critic: Paul, in *Immortality* (1991), Pt.7, Ch.3

20 To me the 'female principle' is, or at least historically has been, basically anarchic. It values order without constraint, rule by custom not by force. It has been the male who enforces order, who constructs power structures, who makes, enforces, and breaks laws.

Ursula K. Le Guin (b.1929), U.S. author: 'Is Gender Necessary?', first publ. in *Aurora* (ed. Susan Anderson and Vonda McIntyre, 1976), rep. in *Dancing at the Edge of the World* (1989)

21 We are volcanoes. When we women offer our experience as our truth, as human truth, all the maps change. There are new mountains.

Ursula K. Le Guin: Bryn Mawr Commencement Address, 1986, publ. in *Dancing at the Edge of the World* (1989)

22 Being a woman is of special interest only to aspiring male transsexuals. To actual women it is merely a good excuse not to play football.

Fran Lebowitz (b.1951), U.S. journalist: *Metropolitan Life* (1978), 'Letters'

23 If woman is inconstant,
good, I am faithful to
ebb and flow, I fall
in season and now
is a time of ripening.

Denise Levertov (b.1923), U.S. poet: 'Stepping Westward', publ. in *The Sorrow Dance* (1967)

24 But if God had wanted us to think just with our wombs, why did He give us a brain?

Clare Boothe Luce (1903–1987), U.S. diplomat and writer: Nora, in *Slam the Door Softly* (1970)

25 Women are the fulfilled sex. Through our children we are able to produce our own immortality, so we lack that divine restlessness which sends men charging off in pursuit of fortune or fame or an imagined Utopia. That is why we number so few geniuses among us. The wholesome oyster wears no pearl, the healthy whale no ambergris, and as long as we can keep on adding to the race, we harbor a sort of health within ourselves.

Phyllis McGinley (1905–1978), U.S. poet and author: *The Province of the Heart* (1959), 'Some of My Best Friends...'

26 Coming to terms with the rhythms of women's lives means coming to terms with life itself, accepting the imperatives of the body rather than the imperatives of an artificial, man-made, perhaps transcendentally beautiful civilization. Emphasis on the male work-rhythm is an emphasis on infinite possibilities; emphasis on the female rhythms is an emphasis on a defined pattern, on limitation.

Margaret Mead (1901–1978), U.S. anthropologist: *Male and Female* (1949), Ch.8

27 Aren't women prudes if they don't and prostitutes if they do?

Kate Millett (b.1934), U.S. feminist author: speech, 22 March 1975, Women's Writer's Conference, Los Angeles, quoted in *The Quotable Woman* (ed. Elaine Partnow, 1982)

28 Women reminded him of lilies and roses.
Me they remind rather of blood and soap,
Armed with a warm rag, assaulting noses
Ears, neck, mouth and all the secret places.

Elena Mitchell (b.1919), British poet: 'Thoughts after Ruskin', publ. in *The Poor Man in the Flesh* (1976)

29 I think being a woman is like being Irish. ... Everyone says you're important and nice, but you take second place all the same.

Iris Murdoch (b.1919), British novelist and philosopher: Frances Bellman, in *The Red and the Green* (1965), Ch.2. Iris Murdoch was born in Dublin

30 Woman is the nigger of the world.

Yoko Ono (b.1933), Japanese-born U.S. artist: interview in *Nova* (London), 1968, quoted in *The Lennon Tapes* (1981). The words – used by John Lennon as a song title on the album *Some Time in New York City* (1972) – recall those of Zora Neale Hurston: 'De nigger woman is de mule uh de world so fur as Ah can see.' (*Their Eyes Were Watching God* (1937), Ch.2)

31 If civilization had been left in female hands we would still be living in grass huts.

Camille Paglia (b.1947), U.S. author and critic: quoted in introduction to *Sex, Art, and American Culture* (1992)

32 Every woman adores a Fascist,
The boot in the face, the brute
Brute heart of a brute like you.

Sylvia Plath (1932–1963), U.S. poet: 'Daddy', St.10, first publ. in *Encounter* (London), Oct. 1963, rep. in *Ariel* (1965)

33 If women got a slap round the face more often, they'd be a bit more reasonable.
Charlotte Rampling (b.1945), British actress: quoted in *The Observer* (London), 6 March 1983

34 A woman is like a teabag – only in hot water do you realize how strong she is.
Nancy Reagan (b.1923), wife of President Ronald Reagan: quoted in *The Observer* (London), 29 March 1981. The quote has also been ascribed to Eleanor Roosevelt, as quoted by Hillary Clinton

35 Yes, I am wise, but it's wisdom born of pain
Yes, I've paid the price, but look how much
　　I've gained
If I have to, I can do anything
I am strong, I am invincible, I am woman.
Helen Reddy (b.1942), Australian singer and songwriter: 'I am Woman' (song) on the album *I Am Woman* (Helen Reddy, 1972). The song, which reached No.1 in the U.S., became an anthem for the Women's Movement in the 1970s

36 The connections between and among women are the most feared, the most problematic, and the most potentially transforming force on the planet.
Adrienne Rich (b.1929), U.S. poet: 'Disloyal to Civilization: Feminism, Racism, Gynophobia', first publ. in *Chrysalis*, No.7 (1979), rep. in *On Lies, Secrets, and Silence* (1980)

37 For my part I distrust *all* generalizations about women, favourable and unfavourable, masculine and feminine, ancient and modern; all alike, I should say, result from paucity of experience.
Bertrand Russell (1872–1970), British philosopher and mathematician: *Unpopular Essays* (1950), 'An Outline of Intellectual Rubbish'

38 The cliché that women, more consistently than men, turn inward for sustenance seems to mean, in practice, that women have richly defined the ways in which imagination creates possibility; possibility that society denies.
Patricia Meyer Spacks (b.1929), U.S. literary critic: *The Female Imagination* (1975), 'Afterword'

39 Some of us are becoming the men we wanted to marry.
Gloria Steinem (b.1934), U.S. feminist writer and editor: speech, Sept. 1981, Yale University, New Haven, Connecticut, quoted in *The Quotable Woman* (ed. Elaine Partnow, 1982). Steinem's words reappeared in an article in *Ms.* (New York), July/Aug. 1982

40 Women are not little children. Women are not weak, not victims. Pleasure and danger go together, of course they do. We want the pleasure, and we can cope with danger.

Nadine Strossen, U.S. civil rights lawyer and author: on calls to censor negative images of women, in interview in *The Observer* (London), 28 Jan. 1996

41 From birth to 18 a girl needs good parents. From 18 to 35, she needs good looks. From 35 to 55, good personality. From 55 on, she needs good cash. I'm saving my money.
Sophie Tucker (1884–1966), Russian-born U.S. singer: remark from 1953, quoted in *Sophie* by Michael Freedland (1978), 'When They Get Too Wild for Everyone Else'

42 A typical minority group stereotype – woman as nigger – if she knows her place (home), she is really a quite lovable, loving creature, happy and childlike.
Naomi Weisstein (b.1939), U.S. psychologist and author: 'Woman as Nigger', publ. in *Psychology Today* (New York), Oct. 1969

43 The New Women! I could barely recognise them as being of the same sex as myself, their buttocks arrogant in tight jeans, openly inviting, breasts falling free and shameless and feeling no apparent obligation to smile, look pleasant or keep their voices low. And how they live! Just look at them to know how! If a man doesn't bring them to orgasm, they look for another who does. If by mistake they fall pregnant, they abort by vacuum aspiration. If they don't like the food, they push the plate away. If the job doesn't suit them, they hand in their notice. They are satiated by everything, hungry for nothing. They are what I wanted to be; they are what I worked for them to be: and now I see them, I hate them.
Fay Weldon (b.1933), British novelist: the narrator (Praxis Duveen), in *Praxis* (1978), Ch.2

See also THE CHURCH: AND WOMEN; Parsons on DRINK: DRUNKS; FEMININITY; FEMINISM; GIRLS; Harrison on INTIMACY; Nasreen on ISLAM; MEN & WOMEN; THE MENOPAUSE; MENSTRUATION; MOTHERS; PREGNANCY; Hornby on OBSESSION; RAPE; Fleming on SEX; Greer on SELF-IMAGE; Sarton on TALENT

WOMEN: and the Arts

1 I think it's a question which particularly arises over women writers: whether it's better to have a happy life or a good supply of tragic plots.
Wendy Cope (b.1945), British poet: in *The Independent* (London), 9 March 1992

2 Men like women who write. Even though they don't say so. A writer is a foreign country.
Marguerite Duras (1914–1996), French author and film-maker: *Practicalities* (1987; tr.1990), 'The M.D. Uniform'

3 If you want your writing to be taken seriously, don't marry and have kids, and above all, don't

die. But if you have to die, commit suicide. They approve of that.

Ursula K. Le Guin (b.1929), U.S. author: 'Prospects for Women in Writing', speech, Sept. 1986, Conference on Women in the Year 2000, Portland, Maine, publ. in *Dancing at the Edge of the World* (1989)

4 Literature takes shape and life in the body, in the wombs of the mother tongue: always: and the Fathers of Culture get anxious about paternity. They start talking about legitimacy. They steal the baby. They ensure by every means that the artist, the writer, is male. This involves intellectual abortion by centuries of women artists, infanticide of works by women writers, and a whole medical corps of sterilizing critics working to purify the Canon, to reduce the subject matter and style of literature to something Ernest Hemingway could have understood.

Ursula K. Le Guin: Bryn Mawr Commencement Address, 1986, publ. in *Dancing at the Edge of the World* (1989)

5 There is no female Mozart because there is no female Jack the Ripper.

Camille Paglia (b.1947), U.S. author and critic: in the *International Herald Tribune* (Paris), 26 April 1991

6 As artists they're rot, but as providers they're oil wells; they gush. Norris said she never wrote a story unless it was fun to do. I understand Ferber whistles at her typewriter. And there was that poor sucker Flaubert rolling around on his floor for three days looking for the right word.

Dorothy Parker (1893–1967), U.S. humorous writer: interview in *Writers at Work* (First Series, ed. Malcolm Cowley, 1958)

7 The woman who needs to create works of art is born with a kind of psychic tension in her which drives her unmercifully to find a way to balance, to make herself whole. Every human being has this need: in the artist it is mandatory. Unable to fulfill it, he goes mad. But when the artist is a woman she fulfills it at the *expense* of herself as a woman.

May Sarton (b.1912), U.S. poet and novelist: Hilary Stevens, in *Mrs Stevens Hears the Mermaids Singing* (1965), Pt.2

8 Paradoxically, the most constructive thing women can do ... is to write, for in the *act* of writing we deny our mutedness and begin to eliminate some of the difficulties that have been put upon us.

Dale Spender (b.1943), Australian feminist author: *Man Made Language* (1980), Ch.7

WOMEN: in Business

1 It's so much easier for men. They don't have to paint their nails for a meeting.

Eve Pollard (b.1945), British journalist and editor: remark in June 1995, quoted in *The Guardian* (London), 30 Dec. 1995

2 I think that business practices would improve immeasurably if they were guided by 'feminine' principles – qualities like love and care and intuition.

Anita Roddick (b.1943), British businesswoman and founder of the Body Shop: *Body and Soul* (1991), Ch.1

WOMEN: the Male View

1 Tall, gelid, aloof Teutonic-Prussian girls. I adore villagey-looking blondes. I like a girl who's arrogant, spoiled and dirty, but brilliant and beautiful.

Woody Allen (b.1935), U.S. film-maker: in reply to the question, 'What kind of girls turn you on?' in interview in *Playboy* (Chicago), May 1967, quoted in *The Woody Allen Companion* by Stephen J. Spignesi (1993), Ch.4

2 The white American man makes the white American woman maybe not superfluous but just a little kind of decoration. Not really important to the turning around of the wheels of state. Well the black American woman has never been able to feel that way. No black American man at any time in our history in the United States has been able to feel that he didn't need that black woman right against him, shoulder to shoulder – in that cotton field, on the auction block, in the ghetto, wherever.

Maya Angelou (b.1928), U.S. author: 'A Conversation with Maya Angelou', interview, broadcast 21 Nov. 1973, publ. in *Conversations with Maya Angelou* (ed. Jeffrey M. Elliot, 1989)

3 She even had a kind of special position among men: she was an exception, she fitted none of the categories they commonly used when talking about girls; she wasn't a cock-teaser, a cold fish, an easy lay or a snarky bitch; she was an honorary person. She had grown to share their contempt for most women.

Margaret Atwood (b.1939), Canadian novelist, poet and critic: 'The Man From Mars', first publ. in the *Ontario Review* 1977, rep. in *Dancing Girls* (1984)

4 Every woman is like a timezone. She is a nocturnal fragment of your journey. She brings you unflaggingly closer to the next night.

Jean Baudrillard (b.1929), French semiologist: *Cool Memories* (1987; tr.1990), Ch.5

5 Women are most fascinating between the ages of thirty-five and forty, after they have won a few races and know how to pace themselves. Since few women ever pass forty, maximum fascination can continue indefinitely.
Christian Dior (1905–1957), French couturier: in *Collier's Magazine*, 10 June 1955

6 Upscale young men seem to go for the kind of woman who plays with a full deck of credit cards, who won't cry when she's knocked to the ground while trying to board the six o'clock Eastern shuttle, and whose schedule doesn't allow for a sexual encounter lasting more than twelve minutes.
Barbara Ehrenreich (b.1941), U.S. author and columnist: 'The Cult of Busyness', first publ. in the *New York Times*, 1985, rep. in *The Worst Years of Our Lives* (1991)

7 Women have very little idea of how much men hate them.
Germaine Greer (b.1939), Australian feminist writer: *The Female Eunuch* (1970), 'Loathing and Disgust'

8 From the viewpoint of many men, there are two stages in a woman's life: prey and invisible. After a certain age, when they don't want to fuck you anymore, they don't see you at all.
Cynthia Heimel, U.S. columnist: 'Why I Hate Marilyn', first publ. in *Playboy* (Chicago), 1987, rep. in *If You Can't Live Without Me, Why Aren't You Dead Yet?* (1991), 'Women'

9 If the Lord made anything better than a woman, he kept it for himself.
Jerry Lee Lewis (b.1935), U.S. rock musician: quoted in *Early Rockers* by Howard Elson (1982), Ch.9

10 All dames are alike. They reach down your throat so they can grab your heart, they pull it out, they throw it on the floor and they step on it with their high heels. They spit on it. They shove it in the oven and they cook the shit out of it. Then they slice it into little pieces, slam it on a hunk of toast and serve it to you. And they expect you to say: thanks honey, it's delicious!
Steve Martin (b.1945), U.S. comedian and screenwriter: Rigby Reardon (Martin), in *Dead Men Don't Wear Plaid* (film; screenplay by George Gipe, Carl Reiner and Steve Martin, directed by Carl Reiner, 1982)

11 It is not her body that he wants but it is only through her body that he can take possession of another human being, so he must labor upon her body, he must enter her body, to make his claim.
Joyce Carol Oates (b.1938), U.S. author: *Unholy Loves* (1979), 'In the Founders' Room'

12 There's no way that you, nor any other man, could ever understand what it is that you men make us women think of our bodies.

Dennis Potter (1935–1994), British dramatist and screenwriter: Jessica, in *Blackeyes* (television series, BBC, 1989)

13 Listen to the woman very carefully. Women know shit. I mean, even if you don't get the words, even if you don't know what the hell she's talking about, just listen.
Ron Shelton (b.1945), U.S. film-maker: Sidney Deane (Wesley Snipes), in *White Men Can't Jump* (film; written and directed by Ron Shelton, 1992)

14 Man, born of woman, has found it a hard thing to forgive her for giving him birth. The patriarchal protest against the ancient matriarch has borne strange fruit through the years.
Lillian Smith (1897–1966), U.S. author: *Killers of the Dream* (1949; rev.1961), Pt.2, Ch.4

15 If there hadn't been women we'd still be squatting in a cave eating raw meat, because we made civilization in order to impress our girl friends. And they tolerated it and let us go ahead and play with our toys.
Orson Welles (1915–1985), U.S. film-maker and actor: interview in *The Americans* by David Frost (1970), 'Can a Martian Survive by Pretending to be a Leading American Actor?'

See also Savile on BEAUTY

WOMEN: and Men

1 I've always had this penchant for what I call kamikaze women. I call them kamikaze because they crash their plane. They're self-destructive – but they crash it into you, taking you with them.
Woody Allen (b.1935), U.S. film-maker: Gabe Roth (Allen), in *Husbands and Wives* (film; written and directed by Woody Allen, 1992)

2 It seems as though women keep growing. Eventually they can have little or nothing in common with the men they chose long ago.
Eugenie Clark (b.1922), U.S. marine biologist and author: quoted in *Ms.* (New York), Aug. 1979

3 To be completely woman you need a master, and in him a compass for your life. You need a man you can look up to and respect. If you dethrone him it's no wonder that you are discontented, and discontented women are not loved for long.
Marlene Dietrich (1904–1992), German-born U.S. actress: *Marlene Dietrich's ABC* (1962), 'Married Love'

4 Once a man is on hand, a woman tends to stop believing in her own beliefs.
Colette Dowling (b.1939), U.S. author: *The Cinderella Complex* (1981), Ch.6

5 Women are an enslaved population – the crop we harvest is children, the fields we work are houses. Women are forced into committing sexual acts with men that violate integrity because the universal religion – contempt for women – has as its first commandment that women exist purely as sexual fodder for men.
Andrea Dworkin (b.1946), U.S. feminist critic: 'Pornography: the New Terrorism', speech, 1977, University of Massachusetts, publ. in *Letters From A War-Zone* (1988)

6 I think women rule the world, and that no man has ever done anything that a woman hasn't allowed him to do or encouraged him to do.
Bob Dylan (b.1941), U.S. singer and songwriter: interview in *Rolling Stone* (New York), June 1984

7 When a woman behaves like a man why doesn't she behave like a nice man?
Edith Evans (1888–1976), British actress: quoted in *The Observer* (London), 30 Sept. 1956

8 Perhaps ... women have always been in closer contact with reality than men: it would seem to be the just recompense for being deprived of idealism.
Germaine Greer (b.1939), Australian feminist writer: *The Female Eunuch* (1970), 'Womanpower'

9 Women receive
the insults of men
with tolerance,
having been bitten
in the nipple
by their toothless gums.
Dilys Laing (1906–1960), Canadian poet and editor: 'Veterans', publ. in *Collected Poems* (1967)

10 Once women begin to question the inevitability of their subordination and to reject the conventions formerly associated with it, they can no longer retreat to the safety of those conventions. The woman who rejects the stereotype of feminine weakness and dependence can no longer find much comfort in the cliché that all men are beasts. She has no choice except to believe, on the contrary, that men are human beings, and she finds it hard to forgive them when they act like animals.
Christopher Lasch (1932–1994), U.S. historian: *The Culture of Narcissism* (1979), Ch.8, 'Feminism and the Intensification of Sexual Warfare'

11 There are always women who will take men on their own terms. If I were a man I wouldn't bother to change while there are women like that around.
Ann Oakley (b.1944), British sociologist and author: quoted in *The Observer* (London), 27 Oct. 1991

12 A woman without a man is like a fish without a bicycle.
Gloria Steinem (b.1934), U.S. feminist writer and editor: attributed. Although the quote is generally ascribed to Steinem, the words were current as graffiti in the 1970s, in the form, 'A woman needs a man like a fish needs a bicycle'

WOMEN: in Politics

1 Life here is hellish for a woman in politics unless she is elderly and ugly.
Edith Cresson (b.1934), French politician and prime minister: on becoming France's first woman prime minister, quoted in *The Guardian* (London), 16 May 1991

2 Like all successful politicians I married above myself.
Dwight D. Eisenhower (1890–1969), U.S. general, Republican politician and president: quoted by Richard Nixon in *Six Crises* (1962), 'The Campaign of 1960'

3 My father was a statesman, I'm a political woman. My father was a saint. I'm not.
Indira Gandhi (1917–1984), Indian politician and prime minister: of her father Pandit Jawaharlal Nehru, quoted in 'Indira's Coup' by Oriana Fallaci, in the *New York Review of Books*, 18 Sept. 1975

4 Man made one grave mistake: in answer to vaguely reformist and humanitarian agitation he admitted women to politics and the professions. The conservatives who saw this as the undermining of our civilization and the end of the state and marriage were right after all; it is time for the demolition to begin.
Germaine Greer (b.1939), Australian feminist writer: *The Female Eunuch* (1970), 'Revolution'

5 To put a woman on the ticket would challenge the loyalty of women everywhere to their sex, because it would be made to seem that the defeat of the ticket meant the defeat for a hundred years of women's chance to be truly equal with men in politics.
Clare Boothe Luce (1903–1987), U.S. diplomat and writer: quoted in the *New York World-Telegram*, 28 June 1948

6 It certainly must have been a relief for the women of the country to realize that one could be a woman and a lady and yet be thoroughly political.
Agnes Meyer (1887–1970), U.S. author and journalist: letter to Eleanor Roosevelt, 25 July 1952, quoted in *Eleanor: The Years Alone* by Joseph P. Lash (1972), Ch.10

7 No woman in my time will be Prime Minister or Chancellor or Foreign Secretary – not the top jobs. Anyway I wouldn't want to be Prime Minister. You have to give yourself 100%.
Margaret Thatcher (b.1925), British Conservative politician and prime minister: interview in *The Sunday Telegraph* (London), 26 Oct. 1969. Mrs Thatcher was then shadow education spokesperson

8 In politics if you want anything said, ask a man. If you want anything done, ask a woman.
Margaret Thatcher: in *People* (New York), 15 Sept. 1975

See also Auden on PEACE

WOMEN: Single Women

1 There is simply no dignified way for a woman to live alone. Oh, she can get along financially perhaps (though not nearly as well as a man), but emotionally she is never left in peace. Her friends, her family, her fellow workers never let her forget that her husbandlessness, her childlessness – her *selfishness*, in short – is a reproach to the American way of life.
Erica Jong (b.1942), U.S. author: the narrator (Isadora Wing), in *Fear of Flying* (1973), Ch.1

2 He travels fastest who travels alone, and that goes double for she. Real feminism is spinsterhood.
Florence King (b.1936), U.S. author: *Reflections in a Jaundiced Eye* (1989), 'Spinsterhood is Powerful'

3 I'm anal retentive. I'm a workaholic. I have insomnia. And I'm a control freak. That's why I'm not married. Who could stand me?
Madonna (b.1959), U.S. singer and actress: quoted in *Madonna Unauthorized* by Christopher Andersen (1991), Ch.22

4 A woman without a man is like a trailer without a car; it ain't going nowhere.
Billy Wilder (b.1906), U.S. film-maker: Polly the Pistol (Kim Novak), in *Kiss me, Stupid* (film; written and directed by Billy Wilder, 1964)

WONDER

1 Sometimes I think the people to feel the saddest for are people who once knew what profoundness was, but who lost or became numb to the sensation of wonder – people who closed the door that leads us into the secret world – or who had the doors closed for them by time and neglect and decisions made in time of weakness.
Douglas Coupland (b.1961), Canadian author: *Life After God* (1994), 'My Hotel Year'

2 Our brains are no longer conditioned for reverence and awe. We cannot imagine a Second Coming that would not be cut down to size by the televised evening news, or a Last Judgment not subject to pages of holier-than-Thou second-guessing in the *New York Review of Books*.
John Updike (b.1932), U.S. author and critic: *Self-Consciousness: Memoirs* (1989), Ch.6

WORDS

1 I am a dreamer of words, of written words. I think I am reading; a word stops me. I leave the page. The syllables of the word begin to move around. Stressed accents begin to invert. The word abandons its meaning like an overload which is too heavy and prevents dreaming. Then words take on other meanings as if they had the right to be young. And the words wander away, looking in the nooks and crannies of vocabulary for new company, bad company.
Gaston Bachelard (1884–1962), French scientist, philosopher and literary theorist: *The Poetics of Reverie* (1960; tr.1969), 'Introduction', Sct.6

2 Today the discredit of words is very great. Most of the time the media transmit lies. In the face of an intolerable world, words appear to change very little. State power has become congenitally deaf, which is why – but the editorialists forget it – terrorists are reduced to bombs and hijacking.
John Berger (b.1926), British author and critic: 'Lost Off Cape Wrath', first publ. in the *Threepenny Review*, winter 1988, rep. in *Keeping a Rendezvous* (1992)

3 My general theory since 1971 has been that the word is literally a virus, and that it has not been recognised as such because it has achieved a state of relatively stable symbiosis with its human host; that is to say, the word virus (the Other Half) has established itself so firmly as an accepted part of the human organism that it can now sneer at gangster viruses like smallpox and turn them in to the Pasteur Institute.
William Burroughs (1914–1997), U.S. author: *The Adding Machine* (1985), 'Ten Years and a Billion Dollars'

4 Euphemisms are not, as many young people think, useless verbiage for that which can and should be said bluntly; they are like secret agents on a delicate mission, they must airily pass by a stinking mess with barely so much as a nod of the head, make their point of constructive criticism and continue on in calm forbearance. Euphemisms are unpleasant truths wearing diplomatic cologne.
Quentin Crisp (b.1908), British author: *Manners from Heaven* (1984), Ch.5

5 The basic tool for the manipulation of reality is the manipulation of words. If you can control the meaning of words, you can control the people who must use the words.
Philip K. Dick (1928–1982), U.S. science fiction writer: introduction to *I Hope I Shall Arrive Soon* (1986), 'How to Build a Universe That Doesn't Fall Apart Two Days Later'

6 There can be no doubt that distrust of words is less harmful than unwarranted trust in them. Besides, to distrust words, and indict them for the horrors that might slumber unobtrusively within them – isn't this, after all, the true vocation of the intellectual?

Václav Havel (b.1936), Czech playwright and president: speech accepting a peace prize, Oct. 1989, Germany, quoted in *The Independent* (London), 9 Dec. 1989

7 Actually if a writer needs a dictionary he should not write. He should have read the dictionary at least three times from beginning to end and then have loaned it to someone who needs it. There are only certain words which are valid and similies (bring me my dictionary) are like defective ammunition (the lowest thing I can think of at this time).

Ernest Hemingway (1899–1961), U.S. author: letter to the critic Bernard Berenson, 20 March 1953, publ. in *Selected Letters* (ed. Carlos Baker, 1981)

8 Poor Faulkner. Does he really think big emotions come from big words? He thinks I don't know the ten-dollar words. I know them all right. But there are older and simpler and better words, and those are the ones I use.

Ernest Hemingway: quoted in *Papa Hemingway* by A.E. Hotchner (1966), Pt.1, Ch.4. Hemingway's rebuke was made after being informed (by Hotchner) that William Faulkner considered Hemingway 'had no courage' and 'had never been known to use a word that might send the reader to the dictionary'. Hemingway referred to Faulkner as 'Old Corndrinking Mellifluous' (quoted in Carlos Baker, *Ernest Hemingway, A Life Story*, 1969; rev.1973)

9 The word is the first small step
to freedom
from oneself.

Miroslav Holub (b.1923), Czech biologist and poet: 'Brief Reflection on the Word Pain', publ. in *On the Contrary and Other Poems* (1984)

10 Without words to objectify and categorize our sensations and place them in relation to one another, we cannot evolve a tradition of what is real in the world.

Ruth Hubbard (b.1924), U.S. biologist: 'Have Only Men Evolved?', publ. in *Women Look at Biology Looking at Women* (ed. Ruth Hubbard, Mary Sue Henifin and Barbara Fried, 1979)

11 As a poet and writer, I deeply love and I deeply hate words. I love the infinite evidence and change and requirements and possibilities of language; every human use of words that is joyful, or honest or new, because experience is new. ... But as a Black poet and writer, I hate words that cancel my name and my history and the freedom of my future: I hate the words that condemn and refuse the language of my people in America.

June Jordan (b.1936), U.S. poet and civil rights activist: 'White English/Black English: the Politics of Translation' (1972), rep. in *Moving Towards Home: Political Essays* (1989)

12 Words can have no single fixed meaning. Like wayward electrons, they can spin away from their initial orbit and enter a wider magnetic field. No one owns them or has a proprietary right to dictate how they will be used.

David Lehman (b.1948), U.S. poet, editor and critic: *Signs of the Times* (1991), Ch.1, 'The End of the Word'

13 Sometimes I think words are like girlfriends – can't find a good one to save your life when you're actually looking, but when you don't need any they're falling out of the goddamned trees!

Jay McInerney (b.1955), U.S. author: Jeff, in *Brightness Falls* (1992), Ch.47

14 In a society in which equality is a fact, not merely a word, words of racial or sexual assault and humiliation will be nonsense syllables.

Catharine A. MacKinnon (b.1946), U.S. lawyer and feminist critic: *Only Words* (1993), Ch.3

15 The word
was born in the blood,
grew in the dark body, beating,
And flew through the lips and the mouth.

Pablo Neruda (1904–1973), Chilean poet: opening lines of 'La Palabra', publ. in *Plenos Poderes* (1962)

16 The minute any word has that much power, everyone on the planet should scream it.

Quentin Tarantino (b.1958), U.S. film-maker: on the frequent use of the word 'nigger' in the script of *Pulp Fiction* (film, 1994), quoted in *Quentin Tarantino: The Man and His Movies* by Jami Bernard (1995), Ch.11

17 The supply of words in the world market is plentiful but the demand is falling. Let deeds follow words now.

Lech Walesa (b.1943), Polish trade union leader and president: in *Newsweek* (New York), 27 Nov. 1989

18 One forgets words as one forgets names. One's vocabulary needs constant fertilizing or it will die.

Evelyn Waugh (1903–1966), British novelist: journal entry, 25 Dec. 1962, publ. in *The Diaries of Evelyn Waugh* (ed. Michael Davie, 1976)

19 What are words worth?
Words in papers
Words in books
Words on TV
Words are crooks
Words of comfort
Words of peace
Words to make the fighting cease
Words to tell you what to do
Words are working hard for you.

Tina Weymouth (b.1950) and **Chris Frantz** (b.1951), U.S. rock musicians: 'Wordy Rappinghood' (song) on the album *Genius of Love* (Tom Tom Club, 1981)

See also Steiner on PROPAGANDA

WORK

1 Something made greater by ourselves and in turn that makes us greater.
Maya Angelou (b.1928), U.S. author: definition of work, in 'The Black Scholar Interviews Maya Angelou' (Jan./Feb. 1977), rep. in *Conversations with Maya Angelou* (ed. Jeffrey M. Elliot, 1989). 'I do believe that a person, a human being without his or her work is like a peapod where the peas have shrivelled before they have come to full growth,' Angelou declared

2 In order that people may be happy in their work, these three things are needed: They must be fit for it: they must not do too much of it: and they must have a sense of success in it – not a doubtful sense, such as needs some testimony of others for its confirmation, but a sure sense, or rather knowledge, that so much work has been done well, and fruitfully done, whatever the world may say or think about it.
W.H. Auden (1907–1973), Anglo-American poet: *A Certain World* (1970), 'Work, Labour, and Play'

3 After all, it is hard to master both life and work equally well. So if you are bound to fake one of them, it had better be life.
Joseph Brodsky (1940–1996), Russian-born U.S. poet and critic: interview in *Writers at Work* (Eighth Series, ed. George Plimpton, 1988)

4 Work's a curse, Saturno. I say to hell with the work you have to do to earn a living! That kind of work does us no honour; all it does is fill up the bellies of the pigs who exploit us. But the work you do because you like to do it, because you've heard the call, you've got a vocation – that's ennobling! We should all be able to work like that. Look at me, Saturno – I don't work. And I don't care if they hang me, I *won't* work! Yet I'm alive! I may live badly, but at least I don't have to work to do it!
Luis Buñuel (1900–1983), Spanish film-maker: Don Lope (Fernando Rey), in *Tristana* (film; written and directed by Luis Buñuel, 1970). Buñuel's screenplay is largely derived from the novel of the same name by the Spanish novelist and dramatist Benito Pérez Galdós, but where Galdós criticized his character for laziness, Buñuel praises him

5 I never forget that work is a curse – which is why I've never made a habit of it.
Blaise Cendrars (1887–1961), Swiss-born novelist and poet: interview in *Writers at Work* (Third Series, ed. George Plimpton, 1967)

6 McJob: A low-pay, low-prestige, low-dignity, low-benefit, no-future job in the service sector.
Douglas Coupland (b.1961), Canadian author: note in *Generation X* (1991), 'The Sun is Your Enemy'

7 Let us reject tedious work. It goes against human nature, against the cosmic rhythms, it goes against man himself, to take the trouble where none is needed. ... Tedious work is inhuman and repugnant, every work which shows signs of it is ugly. It is pleasure and ease, without harshness and constraint, which create grace in every human gesture.
Jean Dubuffet (1901–1985), French sculptor and painter: 'Notes for the Well-Lettered', first publ. in *Prospectus* (1946), rep. in *Art in Theory* (ed. Charles Harrison and Paul Wood, 1992), Pt.5B

8 Personally, I have nothing against work, particularly when performed, quietly and unobtrusively, by someone else. I just don't happen to think it's an appropriate subject for an 'ethic'.
Barbara Ehrenreich (b.1941), U.S. author and columnist: 'Goodbye to the Work Ethic' (1988), rep. in *The Worst Years of Our Lives* (1991)

9 One of the saddest things is that the only thing that a man can do for eight hours a day, day after day, is work. You can't eat eight hours a day nor drink for eight hours a day nor make love for eight hours – all you can do for eight hours is work. Which is the reason why man makes himself and everybody else so miserable and unhappy.
William Faulkner (1897–1962), U.S. novelist: interview in *Writers at Work* (First Series, ed. Malcolm Cowley, 1958). 'The best job that was ever offered to me was to become a landlord in a brothel,' Faulkner remarked. 'In my opinion it's the perfect milieu for an artist to work in'

10 Clearly the most unfortunate people are those who must do the same thing over and over again, every minute, or perhaps twenty to the minute. They deserve the shortest hours and the highest pay.
J.K. Galbraith (b.1908), U.S. economist: *Made to Last* (1964), Ch.4

11 Melancholy has ceased to be an individual phenomenon, an exception. It has become the class privilege of the wage earner, a mass state of mind that finds its cause wherever life is governed by production quotas.
Günter Grass (b.1927), German author: *From the Diary of a Snail* (1972), 'On Stasis in Progress'

12 I have long been of the opinion that if work were such a splendid thing the rich would have kept more of it for themselves.
Bruce Grocott (b.1940), British Labour politician: quoted in *The Observer* (London), 22 May 1988

13 Why should I let the toad *work*
Squat on my life?
Can't I use my wit as a pitchfork
And drive the brute off?

Philip Larkin (1922–1986), British poet: 'Toads',
St.1, publ. in *The Less Deceived* (1955)

14 Work is life, you know, and without it, there's
nothing but fear and insecurity.

John Lennon (1940–1980), British rock musician:
Twenty-Four Hours, BBC, 15 Dec. 1969, publ. in
Imagine (ed. Andrew Solt and Sam Egan, 1988)

15 The bond between a man and his profession is
similar to that which ties him to his country; it
is just as complex, often ambivalent, and in
general it is understood completely only when
it is broken: by exile or emigration in the case
of one's country, by retirement in the case of a
trade or profession.

Primo Levi (1919–1987), Italian chemist and
author: *Other People's Trades* (1985; tr.1989), 'Ex-
Chemist'

16 Labor is work that leaves no trace behind it
when it is finished, or if it does, as in the case of
the tilled field, this product of human activity
requires still more labor, incessant, tireless
labor, to maintain its identity as a 'work' of
man.

Mary McCarthy (1912–1989), U.S. author and
critic: 'The Vita Activa', first publ. in the *New
Yorker*, 18 Oct. 1958, rep. in *On the Contrary*
(1961)

17 Where the whole man is involved there is no
work. Work begins with the division of labor.

Marshall McLuhan (1911–1980), Canadian
communications theorist: *Understanding Media*
(1964), Ch.14

18 I suspect that American workers have come to
lack a work ethic. They do not live by the sweat
of their brow.

Kiichi Miyazawa (b.1919), Japanese politician and
prime minister: in *The Daily Telegraph* (London),
5 Feb. 1992

19 All work and no play makes Jack a dull boy.

Jack Nicholson (b.1937), U.S. actor: Jack Torrance
(Nicholson), in *The Shining* (film; screenplay by
Stanley Kubrick and Diane Johnson, produced and
directed by Stanley Kubrick, 1980). The words
typed by Nicholson cover the pages of the
manuscript he is supposed to be working on

20 Work! Labour the *aspergas me* of life; the one
great sacrament of humanity from which all
other things flow – security, leisure, joy, art,
literature, even divinity itself.

Sean O'Casey (1884–1964), Irish playwright: *Rose
and Crown* (fifth volume of autobiography, 1952),
'In New York Now'

21 Work expands so as to fill the time available for
its completion. General recognition of this fact

is shown in the proverbial phrase 'It is the
busiest man who has time to spare'.

C. Northcote Parkinson (1909–1993), British
historian and political scientist: opening words of
Parkinson's Law, or The Pursuit of Progress (1958)

22 The greatest analgesic, soporific, stimulant,
tranquilizer, narcotic, and to some extent even
antibiotic – in short, the closest thing to a
genuine panacea – known to medical science is
work.

Thomas Szasz (b.1920), U.S. psychiatrist: *The
Second Sin* (1973), 'Medicine'

23 There is always the danger that we may just do
the work for the sake of the work. This is where
the respect and the love and the devotion come
in – that we do it to God, to Christ, and that's
why we try to do it as beautifully as possible.

Mother Teresa (1910–1997), Albanian-born
Roman Catholic missionary: *A Gift for God* (1975),
'Imitation of Christ'

24 Work to survive, survive by consuming, survive to consume: the hellish cycle is complete.

Raoul Vaneigem (b.1934), Belgian Situationist
philosopher: *The Revolution of Everyday Life* (1967;
tr.1983), Ch.7, Sct.2

25 I suppose I have a really loose interpretation of
'work', because I think that just being alive is
so much work at something you don't always
want to do. ... The machinery is always going.
Even when you sleep.

Andy Warhol (c.1928–1987), U.S. Pop artist: *From
A to B and Back Again* (1975), Ch.6

26 'What do you do?' is the party line, where
doing is a substitute for being, and where the
shame of not doing wipes away the thin chalk
outline that sketches Husband Wife Banker
Actor even Thief.

Jeanette Winterson (b.1959), British author: *Art
and Lies* (1994), 'Handel', p.24 of Jonathan Cape
edn.

See also CAREERS; THE OFFICE; TRADE UNIONS;
UNEMPLOYMENT

THE WORKING CLASS

1 The working class – a piece of language that
serves to reinforce certain social customs and a
way of talking and that obscures the fact that
the only thing hiding behind it is a highly
mannered suburban society stripped of culture
and sophistication and living only for its
affectations: a bloated code of maleness, an
exaggerated embarrassing patriotism, a violent
nationalism, an array of bankrupt antisocial
habits. This bored, empty, decadent generation consists of nothing more than what it
appears to be. It is a lad culture without
mystery, so deadened that it uses violence to

wake itself up. It pricks itself so that it has feeling, burns its flesh so that it has smell.

Bill Buford (b.1954), U.S. editor and author: *Among the Thugs* (1991), Pt.3, 'Düsseldorf'

2 The worst fault of the working classes is telling their children they're not going to succeed, saying: 'There is life, but it's not for you'.

John Mortimer (b.1923), British barrister and novelist: in the *Daily Mail* (London), 31 May 1988

3 The trouble with the working class today is that they are such peasants. Something has died in them – a sense of grace, all feelings of community, their intelligence, decency and wit. Socialism is finished here because it is no longer possible to feel sentimental about the workers. They love their country – eat shit, you Argie sheep-shaggers – but they don't care enough about the street they live on to bother binning their rubbish.

Tony Parsons (b.1955), British journalist: 'The Tattooed Jungle', publ. in *Arena* (London), Sept./Oct. 1989, rep. in *Dispatches from the Front Line of Popular Culture* (1994)

4 Admiration of the proletariat, like that of dams, power stations, and aeroplanes, is part of the ideology of the machine age.

Bertrand Russell (1872–1970), British philosopher and mathematician: *Unpopular Essays* (1950), 'The Superior Virtue of the Oppressed'

5 The same people who are murdered slowly in the mechanized slaughterhouses of work are also arguing, singing, drinking, dancing, making love, holding the streets, picking up weapons and inventing a new poetry.

Raoul Vaneigem (b.1934), Belgian Situationist philosopher: *The Revolution of Everyday Life* (1967; tr.1983), Ch.5

6 That's what being in the working class is all about – how to get out of it.

Neville Kenneth Wran (b.1926), Australian barrister and politician: in the *Sydney Morning Herald*, 19 June 1982

THE WORLD

1 Our lives don't really belong to us, you see – they belong to the world, and in spite of our efforts to make sense of it, the world is a place beyond our understanding.

Paul Auster (b.1947), U.S. author: interview, 1989/90, publ. in *The Red Notebook* (1995), 'Interview with Larry McCaffery and Sinda Gregory'

2 The world is gradually becoming a place Where I do not care to be any more.

John Berryman (1914–1972), U.S. poet: *His Toy, His Dream, His Rest*, No.149 (1968). Berryman

ended his life by jumping off a bridge over the Mississippi river

3 We could say, then, that man is an instrument the world employs to renew its own image constantly.

Italo Calvino (1923–1985), Italian author and critic: introduction to Saul Steinberg's *Still Life and Architecture* (1982), rep. in *The Literature Machine* (1987)

4 The Sage of Toronto ... spent several decades marvelling at the numerous freedoms created by a 'global village' instantly and effortlessly accessible to all. Villages, unlike towns, have always been ruled by conformism, isolation, petty surveillance, boredom and repetitive malicious gossip about the same families. Which is a precise enough description of the global spectacle's present vulgarity.

Guy Debord (1931–1994), French Situationist philosopher: of Marshall McLuhan's notion of the 'global village', in *Comments on the Society of the Spectacle* (1988; tr.1990), Ch.12

5 Despite everybody who has been born and has died, the world has just gone on. I mean, look at Napoleon – but we went right on. Look at Harpo Marx – the world went around, it didn't stop for a second. It's sad but true. John Kennedy, right?

Bob Dylan (b.1941), U.S. singer and songwriter: interview with Robert Shelton, 1966, publ. in *No Direction Home* by Robert Shelton (biography, 1986), Ch.10

6 A lot of people experience the world with the same incredulity as when a magician pulls a rabbit out of a hat. ... We know that the world is not all sleight of hand and deception because we are in it, we are part of it. Actually we *are* the white rabbit being pulled out of the hat. The only difference beween us and the white rabbit is that the rabbit does not realize it is taking part in a magic trick.

Jostein Gaarder (b.1952), Norwegian philosopher: *Sophie's World* (1991), 'The Top Hat'

7 The world is not black and white. More like black and grey.

Graham Greene (1904–1991), British novelist: quoted in *The Observer* (London), 2 Jan. 1983

8 I have no other pictures of the world apart from those which express evanescence, and callousness, vanity and anger, emptiness, or hideous useless hate. Everything has merely confirmed what I had seen and understood in my childhood: futile and sordid fits of rage, cries suddenly blanketed by the silence, shadows swallowed up for ever by the night.

Eugène Ionesco (1912–1994), Rumanian-born French playwright: 'Testimony: When I Write' (April 1958), rep. in *Notes and Counter-Notes* (1962), Pt.2

9 If we cannot accept the importance of the world, which considers itself important, if in the midst of that world our laughter finds no echo, we have but one choice: to take the world as a whole and make it the object of our game; to turn it into a toy.
Milan Kundera (b.1929), Czech-born French author and critic: *Immortality* (1991), Pt.7, Ch.5

10 The world has *not* to be put in order: the world *is* order incarnate. It is for us to put ourselves in unison with this order.
Henry Miller (1891–1980), U.S. author: *Sexus* (1949), Ch.9

11 Perhaps when distant people on other planets pick up some wave-length of ours all they hear is a continuous scream.
Iris Murdoch (b.1919), British novelist and philosopher: Alfred Ludens, in *The Message to the Planet* (1989), Pt.6

12 The world is a funny paper read backwards. And that way it isn't so funny.
Tennessee Williams (1911–1983), U.S. playwright: self-interview, in *The Observer* (London), 7 April 1957

See also Lévi-Strauss on THE END; Baldwin on OPPRESSION

WORLD WAR II

1 Yalta in a number of ways was the modern equivalent of Vienna. Those who signed their initials on a scrap of paper or embedded their seals on the parchment before them were not to know that the masses had and still have an awkward way of making themselves heard above the roars of the loudest cannon or gunfire and at a time when it is least expected of them.
Tariq Ali (b.1943), Pakistani-born British activist and author: comparing the 1945 Yalta agreement with the Peace of Vienna in 1815, in prologue to *1968 and After: Inside the Revolution* (1978)

2 We had won. Pimps got out of their polished cars and walked the streets of San Francisco only a little uneasy at the unusual exercise. Gamblers, ignoring their sensitive fingers, shook hands with shoeshine boys. ... Beauticians spoke to the shipyard workers, who in turn spoke to the easy ladies. ... I thought if war did not include killing, I'd like to see one every year. Something like a festival.
Maya Angelou (b.1928), U.S. author: prologue to *Gather Together in My Name* (second volume of autobiography, 1974)

3 Springtime for Hitler and Germany, Winter for France and Poland.

Mel Brooks (b.1926), U.S. film-maker and actor: Max Bialystok (Zero Mostel), in *The Producers* (film; written and directed by Mel Brooks, 1968)

4 If the 1945 victory demonstrates that in history, vice is ultimately punished and virtue recognized, we do not wish once more to bear the brunt of this demonstration.
Emmanuel Levinas (b.1905), French Jewish philosopher: 'The Diary of Leon Brunschvicg' (1949), rep. in *Difficult Freedom* (1990), Pt.1

See also Cleese on GERMANY

WRITERS

1 Writers must fortify themselves with pride and egotism as best they can. The process is analogous to using sandbags and loose timbers to protect a house against flood. Writers are vulnerable creatures like anyone else. For what do they have in reality? Not sandbags, not timbers. Just a flimsy reputation and a name...
Brian Aldiss (b.1925), British science fiction writer: *Bury My Heart at W.H. Smith's* (1990), 'Apéritif'

2 The hard necessity of bringing the judge on the bench down into the dock has been the peculiar responsibility of the writer in all ages of man.
Nelson Algren (1909–1981), U.S. author: preface added to his prose-poem *Chicago: City on the Make* (1961; original work publ.1951)

3 Every writer hopes or boldly assumes that his life is in some sense exemplary, that the particular will turn out to be universal.
Martin Amis (b.1949), British author: in *The Observer* (London), 30 Aug. 1987

4 You can't be consumed by another person if you're a writer because your relationship is basically with yourself. You're being intimate with your abilities, with your talent. This means in some very viable sense that for a lot of the time you're just having a wank.
Martin Amis: interview in *The Guardian* (London), 18 March 1995

5 Everyone thinks writers must know more about the inside of the human head, but that is wrong. They know less, that's why they write. Trying to find out what everyone else takes for granted.
Margaret Atwood (b.1939), Canadian novelist, poet and critic: *Dancing Girls* (1977), 'Lives of the Poets'

6 No poet or novelist wishes he were the only one who ever lived, but most of them wish they were the only one alive, and quite a number fondly believe their wish has been granted.
W.H. Auden (1907–1973), Anglo-American poet: *The Dyer's Hand* (1962), Pt.1, 'Writing'

7 Who wants to become a writer? And why? Because it's the answer to everything. To 'Why am I here?' To uselessness. It's the streaming reason for living. To note, to pin down, to build up, to create, to be astonished at nothing, to cherish the oddities, to let nothing go down the drain, to make something, to make a great flower out of life, even if it's a cactus.

Enid Bagnold (1889–1981), British novelist and playwright: *Autobiography* (1969), Ch.3

8 The responsibility of a writer is to excavate the experience of the people who produced him.

James Baldwin (1924–1987), U.S. author: in conversation with Nikki Giovanni, 4 Nov. 1971, London, publ. in *A Dialogue* (1973)

9 I was an only child. I lost both my parents. By the time I was twenty I was bald. I'm homosexual. In the way of circumstances and background to transcend I had everything an artist could possibly want. It was practically a blueprint. I was programmed to be a novelist or a playwright.

Alan Bennett (b.1934), British playwright: Halliwell, in *Prick up Your Ears: The Screenplay* (1987), p.70 of Faber & Faber edn.

10 A writer never reads his work. For him, it is the unreadable, a secret, and he cannot remain face to face with it. A secret, because he is separated from it.

Maurice Blanchot (b.1907), French literary theorist and author: *The Space of Literature* (1955), 'The Essential Solitude'

11 Every writer 'creates' his own precursors. His work modifies our conception of the past, as it will modify the future.

Jorge Luis Borges (1899–1986), Argentinian author: 'Kafka and his Precursors' (1951), rep. in *Other Inquisitions* (1960; tr.1964)

12 For your born writer, nothing is so healing as the realization that he has come upon the right word.

Catherine Drinker Bowen (1897–1973), U.S. author: *Adventures of a Biographer* (1946), Ch.11

13 Every writing career starts as a personal quest for sainthood, for self-betterment. Sooner or later, and as a rule quite soon, a man discovers that his pen accomplishes a lot more than his soul.

Joseph Brodsky (1940–1996), Russian-born U.S. poet and critic: 'The Power of the Elements' (1980), rep. in *Less Than One: Selected Essays* (1986)

14 Great writers are the saints for the godless.

Anita Brookner (b.1938), British novelist and art historian: *Novelists in Interview* (ed. John Haffenden, 1985)

15 If I die, I hope to go with my head on that typewriter. It's my battlefield.

Charles Bukowski (1920–1994), U.S. author and poet: interview in the *Los Angeles Times*, 1987, quoted in obituary in the *Los Angeles Times*, 10 March 1994

16 Novelists are perhaps the last people in the world to be entrusted with opinions. The nature of a novel is that it has no opinions, only the dialectic of contrary views, some of which, all of which, may be untenable and even silly. A novelist should not be too intelligent either, although ... he may be permitted to be an intellectual.

Anthony Burgess (1917–1993), British author and critic: *You've Had Your Time* (1990), Ch.2

17 The task of an American writer is not to describe the misgivings of a woman taken in adultery as she looks out of a window at the rain but to describe four hundred people under the lights reaching for a foul ball. This is ceremony.

John Cheever (1912–1982), U.S. author: journal entry, 1963, in *John Cheever: The Journals* (ed. Robert Gottlieb, 1991), 'The Sixties'

18 What has a writer to be bombastic about? Whatever good a man may write is the consequence of accident, luck, or surprise, and nobody is more surprised than an honest writer when he makes a good phrase or says something truthful.

Edward Dahlberg (1900–1977), U.S. author and critic: *Alms for Oblivion* (1964), 'No Love and No Thanks'

19 I think of an author as somebody who goes into the marketplace and puts down his rug and says, 'I will tell you a story,' and then he passes the hat.

Robertson Davies (1913–1995), Canadian novelist and journalist: *The Enthusiasms of Robertson Davies* (1990), 'The Table Talk of Robertson Davies'

20 The writer's language is to some degree the product of his own action; he is both the historian and the agent of his own language.

Paul de Man (1919–1983), Belgian-born U.S. literary critic: *Blindness and Insight* (1971), Ch.8

21 Writers are always selling somebody out.

Joan Didion (b.1934), U.S. essayist: preface to *Slouching Towards Bethlehem* (1968)

22 If a writer has to rob his mother, he will not hesitate; the 'Ode on a Grecian Urn' is worth any number of old ladies.

William Faulkner (1897–1962), U.S. novelist: interview in *Writers at Work* (First Series, ed. Malcolm Cowley, 1958)

23 The writer probably knows what he meant when he wrote a book, but he should imme-

diately forget what he meant when he's written it.

William Golding (1911–1993), British author: *Novelists in Interview* (ed. John Haffenden, 1985)

24 They're fancy talkers about themselves, writers. If I had to give young writers advice, I would say don't listen to writers talking about writing or themselves.

Lillian Hellman (1905–1984), U.S. playwright: in the *New York Times*, 21 Feb. 1960

25 The most essential gift for a good writer is a built-in, shock-proof, shit detector. This is the writer's radar and all great writers have had it.

Ernest Hemingway (1899–1961), U.S. author: interview first publ. in the *Paris Review* (Flushing, N.Y.), spring 1958, rep. in *Writers at Work* (Second Series, ed. George Plimpton, 1963)

26 We are all apprentices in a craft where no one ever becomes a master.

Ernest Hemingway: in the *New York Journal-American*, 11 July 1961

27 I'd rather be a lightning rod than a seismograph.

Ken Kesey (b.1935), U.S. author: quoted in *The Electric Kool-Aid Acid Test* by Tom Wolfe (1968), Ch.1

28 I believe that it is my job not only to write books but to have them published. A book is like a child. You have to defend the life of a child.

George Konrád (b.1933), Hungarian writer and politician: in *The Sunday Correspondent* (London), 15 April 1990

29 Don't ask a writer what he's working on. It's like asking someone with cancer about the progress of his disease.

Jay McInerney (b.1955), U.S. author: Jeff, in *Brightness Falls* (1992), Ch. 1

30 I was brought up in the great tradition of the late nineteenth century: that a writer never complains, never explains and never disdains.

James A. Michener (1907–1997), U.S. novelist: quoted in *The Observer* (London), 26 Nov. 1989

31 A man writes to throw off the poison which he has accumulated because of his false way of life. He is trying to recapture his innocence, yet all he succeeds in doing (by writing) is to inoculate the world with a virus of his disillusionment. No man would set a word down on paper if he had the courage to live out what he believed in.

Henry Miller (1891–1980), U.S. author: *Sexus* (1949), Ch.1

32 A writer is unfair to himself when he is unable to be hard on himself.

Marianne Moore (1887–1972), U.S. poet: interview in *Writers at Work* (Second Series, ed. George Plimpton, 1963)

33 The shelf life of the modern hardback writer is somewhere between the milk and the yoghurt.

John Mortimer (b.1923), British barrister and novelist: quoted in *The Sunday Times* (London), 27 Dec. 1987

34 I'm the kind of writer that people think other people are reading.

V.S. Naipaul (b.1932), Trinidadian-born British writer: in the *Radio Times* (London), 24 March 1979

35 He is a man of thirty-five, but looks fifty. He is bald, has varicose veins and wears spectacles, or would wear them if his only pair were not chronically lost. If things are normal with him, he will be suffering from malnutrition, but if he has recently had a lucky streak, he will be suffering from a hangover. At present it is half past eleven in the morning, and according to his schedule he should have started work two hours ago; but even if he had made any serious effort to start he would have been frustrated by the almost continuous ringing of the telephone bell, the yells of the baby, the rattle of an electric drill out in the street, and the heavy boots of his creditors clumping up the stairs. The most recent interruption was the arrival of the second post, which brought him two circulars and an income-tax demand printed in red. Needless to say this person is a writer.

George Orwell (1903–1950), British author: 'Confessions of a Book Reviewer' (1946), rep. in *The Collected Essays, Journalism and Letters of George Orwell* (ed. Sonia Orwell and Ian Angus, 1968), Vol.IV

36 All writers are vain, selfish and lazy, and at the very bottom of their motives lies a mystery. Writing a book is a long, exhausting struggle, like a long bout of some painful illness. One would never undertake such a thing if one were not driven by some demon whom one can neither resist nor understand.

George Orwell: 'Why I Write' (1947), rep. in *Collected Essays* (1961)

37 One reason writers write is out of revenge. Life hurts; certain ideas and experiences hurt; one wants to clarify, to set out illuminations, to replay the old bad scenes and get the *Treppenworte* said – the words one didn't have the strength or ripeness to say when those words were necessary for one's dignity or survival.

Cynthia Ozick (b.1928), U.S. novelist and short-story writer: *Writers at Work* (Eighth Series, ed. George Plimpton, 1988). Later in the interview Ozick compared the writer to 'a beast howling inside a coal-furnace, heaping the coals on itself to increase the fire'

38 Writers, you know, are the beggars of Western society.

Octavio Paz (b.1914), Mexican poet and essayist: quoted in the *Independent on Sunday* (London), 30 Dec. 1990

39 Great writers arrive among us like new diseases – threatening, powerful, impatient for patients to pick up their virus, irresistible.

Craig Raine (b.1944), British poet and critic: in the *Independent on Sunday* (London), 18 Nov. 1990

40 I cannot and do not live in the world of discretion, not as a writer, anyway. I would prefer to, I assure you – it would make life easier. But discretion is, unfortunately, not for novelists.

Philip Roth (b.1933), U.S. novelist: 'Philip', to his wife, in *Deception* (1990), p.190 of Jonathan Cape edn.

41 Whores and writers, Mahound. We are the people you can't forgive.

Salman Rushdie (b.1947), Indian-born British author: the 'famous satirist' Baal, in *The Satanic Verses* (1988), 'Return to Jahilia'. Mahound, Prophet of Jahilia, replies, 'Writers and whores. I see no difference...'

42 I make no complaint. I am a writer. I do not accept my condition; I will strive to change it; but I inhabit it, I am trying to learn from it.

Salman Rushdie: in the *Independent on Sunday* (London), 4 Feb. 1990

43 After Proust, there are certain things that simply cannot be done again. He marks off for you the boundaries of your talent.

Françoise Sagan (b.1935), French novelist and playwright: interview in *Writers at Work* (First Series, ed. Malcolm Cowley, 1958)

44 I cringe when critics say I'm a master of the popular novel. What's an unpopular novel?

Irwin Shaw (b.1913), U.S. author: in *The Observer* (London), 6 March 1983

45 The writer is either a practising recluse or a delinquent, guilt-ridden one; or both. Usually both.

Susan Sontag (b.1933), U.S. essayist: 'When Writers Talk among Themselves', in the *New York Times*, 5 Jan. 1986

46 People do not become writers out of healthy literary impulse, but out of a deep loneliness, a deficiency, a kind of dysfunction ... and on the positive side, they turn to books for solace. It's all sorts of things. It's conceit. It's signalling for attention. People who are normal don't become writers.

Paul Theroux (b.1941), U.S. novelist and travel writer: interview in *The Guardian* (London), 11 Nov. 1995

47 He uses those short, sharp words just like hooks and upper cuts. You always know what he's saying 'cause he says it very clearly.

Mike Tyson (b.1966), U.S. boxer: on discovering a liking for the works of Ernest Hemingway while in his prison cell, quoted in the *Independent on Sunday* (London), 13 Feb. 1994

48 Many writers who choose to be active in the world lose not virtue but time, and that stillness without which literature cannot be made.

Gore Vidal (b.1925), U.S. novelist and critic: in *Réalités*, Aug. 1966. 'That is sad,' Vidal added, 'until one recalls how many bad books the world may yet be spared because of the busyness of writers'

49 Each writer is born with a repertory company in his head. Shakespeare has perhaps 20 players, and Tennessee Williams has about 5, and Samuel Beckett one – and maybe a clone of that one. I have 10 or so, and that's a lot. As you get older, you become more skillful at casting them.

Gore Vidal: in the *Times Herald* (Dallas), 18 June 1978

50 In a sense the world dies every time a writer dies, because, if he is any good, he has been a wet nurse to humanity during his entire existence and has held earth close around him, like the little obstetrical toad that goes about with a cluster of eggs attached to his legs.

E.B. White (1899–1985), U.S. author and editor: 'Doomsday', first publ. in the *New Yorker*, 17 Nov. 1945, rep. in *Writings from the New Yorker 1927–1976* (ed. Rebecca M. Dale, 1991)

See also THE ANGRY YOUNG MEN; Crews on ARTISTS; Appelfeld on LITERATURE: AND SOCIETY; Forster on LITERATURE: AND SOCIETY; DeLillo on MADNESS; O'Connor on MANNERS; Adler on SATIRE; Wilder on SPEECH; Handke on STORY-TELLING; Leavis on UNIQUENESS

WRITING

1 Writing is no longer an act of free will for me, it's a matter of survival. An image surges up inside me, and after a time I begin to feel cornered by it, to feel that I have no choice but to embrace it. A book starts to take shape after a series of such encounters.

Paul Auster (b.1947), U.S. author: interview, 1989/90, publ. in *The Red Notebook* (1995), 'Interview with Larry McCaffery and Sinda Gregory'

2 A word is a bud attempting to become a twig. How can one not dream while writing? It is the pen which dreams. The blank page gives the right to dream.

Gaston Bachelard (1884–1962), French scientist, philosopher and literary theorist: *The Poetics of Reverie* (1960; tr.1969), 'Introduction', Sct.6

3 To write is to make oneself the echo of what cannot cease speaking – and since it cannot, in

order to become its echo I have, in a way, to silence it. I bring to this incessant speech the decisiveness, the authority of my own silence.
Maurice Blanchot (b.1907), French literary theorist and author: *The Space of Literature* (1955; tr.1982), Ch.1, 'The Essential Solitude'

4 Writing is more than anything a compulsion, like some people wash their hands thirty times a day for fear of awful consequences if they do not. It pays a whole lot better than this type of compulsion, but it is no more heroic.
Julie Burchill (b.1960), British journalist and author: introduction to *Sex and Sensibility* (1992)

5 The trouble began with Forster. After him it was considered ungentlemanly to write more than five or six novels.
Anthony Burgess (1917–1993), British author and critic: in *The Guardian* (London), 24 Feb. 1989. Burgess himself wrote more than twenty novels

6 The process of writing has something infinite about it. Even though it is interrupted each night, it is one single notation.
Elias Canetti (1905–1994), Austrian novelist and philosopher: *The Secret Heart Of The Clock: Notes, Aphorisms, Fragments 1973–1985* (1991), '1973'

7 Writing is to descend like a miner to the depths of the mine with a lamp on your forehead, a light whose dubious brightness falsifies everything, whose wick is in permanent danger of explosion, whose blinking illumination in the coal dust exhausts and corrodes your eyes.
Blaise Cendrars (1887–1961), Swiss-born novelist and poet: *Le Lotissement du Ciel* (1949), quoted in Mary Anne Caws's introduction to *Selected Poems: Blaise Cendrars* (1979)

8 There is something about the literary life that repels me, all this desperate building of castles on cobwebs, the long-drawn acrimonious struggle to make something important which we all know will be gone forever in a few years, the miasma of failure which is to me almost as offensive as the cheap gaudiness of popular success.
Raymond Chandler (1880–1959), U.S. author: letter to publisher Hamish Hamilton, 22 April 1949, publ. in *Raymond Chandler Speaking* (ed. Dorothy Gardiner and Kathrine S. Walker, 1962)

9 If you describe things as better than they are, you are considered to be a romantic; if you describe things as worse than they are, you will be called a realist; and if you describe things exactly as they are, you will be thought of as a satirist.
Quentin Crisp (b.1908), British author: *The Naked Civil Servant* (1968), Ch.24

10 To write is a humiliation.
Edward Dahlberg (1900–1977), U.S. author and critic: introduction to *The Carnal Myth* (1968)

11 The ambivalence of writing is such that it can be considered both an act and an interpretive process that follows after an act with which it cannot coincide. As such, it both affirms and denies its own nature.
Paul de Man (1919–1983), Belgian-born U.S. literary critic: 'Literary History and Literary Modernity', lecture, Sept. 1969, publ. in *Blindness and Insight* (1971; rev.1983)

12 Writing is a socially acceptable form of schizophrenia.
E.L. Doctorow (b.1931), U.S. novelist: interview in *Writers at Work* (Eighth Series, ed. George Plimpton, 1988)

13 Writing is turning one's worst moments into money.
J.P. Donleavy (b.1926), Irish-American novelist: in *Playboy* (Chicago), May 1979

14 Writing a novel without being asked seems a bit like having a baby when you have nowhere to live.
Lucy Ellman (b.1956), U.S. novelist: in *The Guardian* (London), 16 Jan. 1992

15 A pathological business, writing, don't you think? Just look what a writer actually does: all that unnatural tense squatting and hunching, all those rituals: pathological!
Hans Magnus Enzensberger (b.1929), German poet and critic: quoted in *The Guardian* (London), 30 Aug. 1990

16 My own experience has been that the tools I need for my trade are paper, tobacco, food, and a little whisky.
William Faulkner (1897–1962), U.S. novelist: interview in *Writers at Work* (First Series, ed. Malcolm Cowley, 1958)

17 Ultimately, literature is nothing but carpentry. With both you are working with reality, a material just as hard as wood.
Gabriel García Márquez (b.1928), Colombian author: interview in *Writers at Work* (Sixth Series, ed. George Plimpton, 1985)

18 Do you remember how old Ford was always writing how Conrad suffered so when he wrote? How it was un metier de chien etc. Do you suffer when you write? I don't at all. Suffer like a bastard when don't write, or just before, and feel empty and fucked out afterwards. But never feel as good as while writing.
Ernest Hemingway (1899–1961), U.S. author: of the writers Ford Madox Ford and Joseph Conrad, in letter to poet and critic Malcolm Cowley, 14 Nov. 1945, publ. in *Selected Letters* (ed. Carlos Baker, 1981)

19 Writing and travel broaden your ass if not your mind and I like to write standing up.
Ernest Hemingway: letter, 9 July 1950, publ. in *Selected Letters* (ed. Carlos Baker, 1981)

20 Writing, at its best, is a lonely life. Organizations for writers palliate the writer's loneliness, but I doubt if they improve his writing. He grows in public stature as he sheds his loneliness and often his work deteriorates. For he does his work alone and if he is a good enough writer he must face eternity, or the lack of it, each day.
Ernest Hemingway: address recorded for the Nobel Prize Committee, accepting the Nobel Prize for literature, 10 Dec. 1954, publ. in *Hemingway: the Writer as Artist* by Carlos Baker (3rd edn., 1963), Ch.13

21 The requirements for prose and verse are the same, i.e. *blow* – What a man most wishes to hide, revise, and unsay, is precisely what Literature is waiting and bleeding for. Every doctor knows, every Prophet knows the convulsion of truth.
Jack Kerouac (1922–1969), U.S. author: letter to Malcolm Cowley, 11 Sept. 1955, publ. in *Selected Letters 1940–1956* (ed. Ann Charters, 1995). Malcolm Cowley was then an editor at Viking Press

22 The reason we write books is that our kids don't give a damn. We turn to an anonymous world because our wife stops up her ears when we talk to her.
Milan Kundera (b.1929), Czech-born French author and critic: *The Book of Laughter and Forgetting* (1978; tr.1982), Pt.4, Sct.9

23 It's hard enough to write a good drama, it's much harder to write a good comedy, and it's hardest of all to write a drama with comedy. Which is what life is.
Jack Lemmon (b.1925), U.S. actor: in *The Independent* (London), 21 Feb. 1990

24 The only phenomenon with which writing has always been concomitant is the creation of cities and empires, that is the integration of large numbers of individuals into a political system, and their grading into castes or classes. ... It seems to have favoured the exploitation of human beings rather than their enlightenment.
Claude Lévi-Strauss (b.1908), French anthropologist: *Tristes Tropiques* (1955), Ch.28

25 You enter a state of controlled passivity, you relax your grip and accept that even if your declared intention is to justify the ways of God to man, you might end up interesting your readers rather more in Satan.
Ian McEwan (b.1948), British author: on novel-writing, in preface to *A Move Abroad* (1989)

26 I think writing does come out of a deep well of loneliness and a desire to fill some kind of gap. No one in his right mind would sit down to write a book if he were a well-adjusted, happy man.

Jay McInerney (b.1955), U.S. author: interview in the *Independent on Sunday* (London), 19 April 1992

27 You expect far too much of a first sentence. Think of it as analogous to a good country breakfast: what we want is something simple, but nourishing to the imagination. Hold the philosophy, hold the adjectives, just give us a plain subject and verb and perhaps a wholesome, nonfattening adverb or two.
Larry McMurtry (b.1936), U.S. screenwriter, novelist and essayist: Godwin, in *Some Can Whistle* (1989), Pt.1, Ch.3

28 Writing books is the closest men ever come to childbearing.
Norman Mailer (b.1923), U.S. author: 'Mr Mailer Interviews Himself', first publ. in the *New York Times Book Review*, 17 Sept. 1965, rep. in *Conversations with Norman Mailer* (ed. J. Michael Lennon, 1988)

29 The need to express oneself in writing springs from a maladjustment to life, or from an inner conflict which the adolescent (or the grown man) cannot resolve in action. Those to whom action comes as easily as breathing rarely feel the need to break loose from the real, to rise above, and describe it. ... I do not mean that it is enough to be maladjusted to become a great writer, but writing is, for some, a method of resolving a conflict, provided they have the necessary talent.
André Maurois (1885–1967), French author and critic: *The Art of Writing* (1960), 'The Writer's Craft', Sct.1

30 Writing is like getting married. One should never commit oneself until one is amazed at one's luck.
Iris Murdoch (b.1919), British novelist and philosopher: *The Black Prince* (1973), 'Bradley Pearson's Foreword'. The narrator is here discussing his own literary output: three short books in 40 years

31 Style and Structure are the essence of a book; great ideas are hogwash.
Vladimir Nabokov (1899–1977), Russian-born U.S. novelist and poet: interview in *Writers at Work* (Fourth Series, ed. George Plimpton, 1976)

32 The only way out is the way through, just as you cannot escape from death except by dying. Being unable to write, you must examine in writing this being unable, which becomes for the present – henceforth? – the subject to which you are condemned.
Howard Nemerov (1920–1991), U.S. poet, novelist and critic: *Journal of the Fictive Life* (1965), 'Reflexions of the Novelist Felix Ledger', Sct.B

33 If you're going to write, don't pretend to write down. It's going to be the best you can do, and

it's the fact that it's the best you can do that kills you.

Dorothy Parker (1893–1967), U.S. humorous writer: interview in *Writers at Work* (First Series, ed. Malcolm Cowley, 1958)

34 You sit in front of the typewriter and the first thing you have to deal with is the government of the mind, the super-ego, sitting up there on top of your head.

Bruce Robinson (b.1946), British film-maker: interview in *The Idler* (London), Nov./Dec. 1995

35 Books choose their authors; the act of creation is not entirely a rational and conscious one.

Salman Rushdie (b.1947), Indian-born British author: in the *Independent on Sunday* (London), 4 Feb. 1990

36 Writing is a question of finding a certain rhythm. I compare it to the rhythms of jazz. Much of the time life is a sort of rhythmic progression of three characters. If one tells oneself that life is like that, one feels it less arbitrary.

Françoise Sagan (b.1935), French novelist and playwright: interview in *Writers at Work* (First Series, ed. Malcolm Cowley, 1958)

37 Writing is not a profession, but a vocation of unhappiness.

Georges Simenon (1903–1985), French mystery writer: interview in *Writers at Work* (First Series, ed. Malcolm Cowley, 1958)

38 The best emotions to write out of are anger and fear or dread. ... The least energizing emotion to write out of is admiration. It is very difficult to write out of because the basic feeling that goes with admiration is a passive contemplative mood.

Susan Sontag (b.1933), U.S. essayist: taped conversation, 1980, in *With William Burroughs: A Report from the Bunker* by Victor Bockris (1981), 'On Writing'

39 The discipline of the written word punishes both stupidity and dishonesty.

John Steinbeck (1902–1968), U.S. author: 'In Awe of Words', first publ. in 75th anniversary edition of *The Exonian* (Exeter University), rep. in *Writers at Work* (Fourth Series, ed. George Plimpton, 1977)

40 What you're trying to do when you write is to crowd the reader out of his own space and occupy it with yours, in a good cause. You're trying to take over his sensibility and deliver an experience that moves from mere information.

Robert Stone (b.1937), U.S. novelist: interview in *Writers at Work* (Eighth Series, ed. George Plimpton, 1988)

41 Let's face it, writing is hell.

William Styron (b.1925), U.S. novelist: interview in *Writers at Work* (First Series, ed. Malcolm Cowley, 1958). Writing, Styron said in the same

interview, is a 'fine therapy for people who are perpetually scared of nameless threats ... for jittery people'

42 When all things are equal, translucence in writing is more effective than transparency, just as glow is more revealing than glare.

James Thurber (1894–1961), U.S. humorist and illustrator: memo to the *New Yorker* in 1959, first publ. in the *New York Times Book Review*, 4 Dec. 1988

43 No doubt I shall go on writing, stumbling across tundras of unmeaning, planting words like bloody flags in my wake. Loose ends, things unrelated, shifts, nightmare journeys, cities arrived at and left, meetings, desertions, betrayals, all manner of unions, adulteries, triumphs, defeats ... these are the facts.

Alexander Trocchi (1925–1983), Scottish novelist, poet and translator: *Cain's Book* (1960), p.3 of Quarto edn. (1973)

44 Writing saved me from the sin and inconvenience of violence.

Alice Walker (b.1944), U.S. author and critic: '*One Child of One's Own*', publ. in *Ms*. (New York), Aug. 1979

45 I am often mad, but I would hate to be nothing but mad: and I think I would lose what little value I may have as a writer if I were to refuse, as a matter of principle, to accept the warming rays of the sun, and to report them, whenever, and if ever, they happen to strike me.

E.B. White (1899–1985), U.S. author and editor: interview in *Writers at Work* (Eighth Series, ed. George Plimpton, 1988)

46 Writing is not like painting where you add. It is not what you put on the canvas that the reader sees. Writing is more like a sculpture where you remove, you eliminate in order to make the work visible. Even those pages you remove somehow remain.

Elie Wiesel (b.1928), Rumanian-born U.S. writer: interview in *Writers at Work* (Eighth Series, ed. George Plimpton, 1988)

47 It is dangerous to leave written that which is badly written. A chance word, upon paper, may destroy the world. Watch carefully and erase, while the power is still yours, I say to myself, for all that is put down, once it escapes, may rot its way into a thousand minds, the corn become a black smut, and all libraries, of necessity, be burned to the ground as a consequence.

Only one answer: write carelessly so that nothing that is not green will survive.

William Carlos Williams (1883–1963), U.S. poet: *Paterson* (1949, rev.1963), Bk.3, 'The Library,' Sct.3

See also AUTOBIOGRAPHY; BIOGRAPHY; FICTION; Miller on INSPIRATION; Smith on INSPIRATION;

LITERATURE; Chandler on STYLE; Neruda on STYLE; Spender on WOMEN: AND THE ARTS

WRITING: Scripts & Screenplays

1 The most ordinary word, when put into place, suddenly acquires brilliance. That is the brilliance with which your images must shine.
Robert Bresson (b.1907), French film-maker: *Notes on the Cinematographer* (1975), '1950–1958: Exercises'

2 You sell a screenplay like you sell a car. If someone drives it off a cliff, that's it.
Rita Mae Brown (b.1944), U.S. feminist writer: in *Newsweek* (New York), 19 Aug. 1985

3 Out of the thousand writers huffing and puffing through movieland there are scarcely fifty men and women of wit or talent. The rest of the fraternity is deadwood. Yet, in a curious way, there is not much difference between the product of a good writer and a bad one. They both have to toe the same mark.
Ben Hecht (1893–1964), U.S. journalist, author and screenwriter: *A Child of the Century* (1954), Bk.5, 'Money is the Root'

4 A good film script should be able to do completely without dialogue.
David Mamet (b.1947), U.S. playwright: in *The Independent* (London), 11 Nov. 1988

5 I could be just a writer very easily. I am not a writer. I am a *screen*writer, which is half a film-maker. ... But it is *not* an art form, because screenplays are not works of art. They are invitations to others to collaborate on a work of art.
Paul Schrader (b.1946), U.S. director and screenwriter: quoted in preface to *Writers in Hollywood 1915–1951* by Ian Hamilton (1990)

YOUTH

1 I've never understood why people consider youth a time of freedom and joy. It's probably because they have forgotten their own.
Margaret Atwood (b.1939), Canadian novelist, poet and critic: the narrator, in 'Hair Jewelry', first publ. in *Ms.* (New York), 1976, rep. in *Dancing Girls* (1977)

2 Time misspent in youth is sometimes all the freedom one ever has.
Anita Brookner (b.1938), British novelist and art historian: Blanche Vernon, in *The Misalliance* (1986), Ch.10

3 The young always have the same problem – how to rebel and conform at the same time. They have now solved this by defying their parents and copying one another.
Quentin Crisp (b.1908), British author: *The Naked Civil Servant* (1968), Ch.19

4 The hatred of the youth culture for adult society is not a disinterested judgment but a terror-ridden refusal to be hooked into the, if you will, ecological chain of breathing, growing, and dying. It is the demand, in other words, to remain children.
Midge Decter (b.1927), U.S. author, editor and social critic: *The New Chastity and Other Arguments Against Women's Liberation* (1972), Ch.1

5 Youth itself is a talent – a perishable talent.
Eric Hoffer (1902–1983), U.S. philosopher: *The Passionate State of Mind* (1955), Aph.32

6 *We need the enthusiasm of the young.* We need their *joie de vivre*. In it is reflected something of the original joy God had in creating man. The young experience this same joy within themselves. This joy is the same everywhere, but it is also ever new and original. The young know how to express this joy in their own special way.
Pope John Paul II [Karol Wojtyla] (b.1920), Polish ecclesiastic: *Crossing the Threshold of Hope* (1994), 'Is There Really Hope in the Young?'

7 As for the boys and girls, the dear young absolute beginners, I sometimes feel that if they only *knew* this fact, this very simple fact, namely how powerful they really are, then they could rise up overnight and enslave the old taxpayers, the whole damn lot of them – toupets and falsies and rejuvenators and all – even though they number millions and sit in the seats of strength.
Colin MacInnes (1914–1976), British author: the narrator in *Absolute Beginners* (1959), 'in June'. The narrator added: 'Youth has power, a kind of divine power straight from mother nature'

8 Youth possesses the impulse to resist and the impulse to surrender, in equal measure. One might re-define these as the impulse to be free and the impulse to die. The manifestation of these impulses, no matter how political the form it assumes, is like an electric current that results from a difference in electrical charge – in other words, from the fundamental contradictions of human existence.
Yukio Mishima (1925–1970), Japanese author: *Mishima on Hagakure* (1977), '*Hagakure* is Alive Today'

9 The pursuit of happiness, which American citizens are obliged to undertake, tends to involve them in trying to perpetuate the moods, tastes and aptitudes of youth.
Malcolm Muggeridge (1903–1990), British journalist and broadcaster: *The Most of Malcolm Muggeridge* (1966), 'Women of America'

10 Youth has no age.

Pablo Picasso (1881–1973), Spanish artist: *Arts de France* (Paris), No.6, 1946, rep. in *Picasso on Art* by Dore Ashton (1972)

11 Well, youth is the period of assumed personalities and disguises. It is the time of the sincerely insincere.

V.S. Pritchett (1900–1997), British author and critic: *Midnight Oil* (second volume of memoirs, 1971), Ch.8

12 When the newspapers have got nothing else to talk about, they cut loose on the young. The young are always news. If they are up to something, that's news. If they aren't, that's news too.

Kenneth Rexroth (1905–1982), U.S. poet, critic and translator: *Assays* (1961), 'The Students Take Over'

13 There is a period near the beginning of every man's life when he has little to cling to except his unmanageable dream, little to support him except good health, and nowhere to go but all over the place.

E.B. White (1899–1985), U.S. author and editor: 'The Years of Wonder' (1961), rep. in *Essays of E.B. White* (1977)

See also Townshend on THE GENERATION GAP; Rubin on GROWING UP

YUPPIES

1 The Yuppies are not defectors from revolt, they are a new race, assured, amnestied, exculpated, moving with ease in the world of performance, mentally indifferent to any objective other than that of change and advertising.

Jean Baudrillard (b.1929), French semiologist: *America* (1986; tr.1988), 'The End of U.S. Power?'

2 Yuppies never gamble, they calculate. They have no aura: ever been to a yuppie party? It's like being in an empty room: empty hologram people walking around peeking at themselves in mirrors and surreptitiously misting their tonsils with Bianca spray, just in case they have to kiss another ghost like themselves. There's just nothing *there*.

Douglas Coupland (b.1961), Canadian author: Dag, in *Generation X* (1991), 'I Am Not a Target Market'

3 The media have just buried the last yuppie, a pathetic creature who had not heard the news that the great pendulum of public conciousness has just swung from Greed to Compassion and from Tex-Mex to meatballs.

Barbara Ehrenreich (b.1941), U.S. author and columnist: 'Goodbye To The Work Ethic' (1988), rep. in *The Worst Years of Our Lives* (1991)

4 You will belong to that minority which, according to current Washington doctrine, must be protected in its affluence lest its energy and initiative be impaired. Your position will be in contrast to that of the poor, to whom money, especially if it is from public sources, is held to be deeply damaging.

J.K. Galbraith (b.1908), U.S. economist: in *The Guardian* (London), 28 July 1989

5 The yuppie idea of a future ain't my idea of a future. Your safe car, and home, and job, and all the time rushing between the three – let's make people feel they can grow up and have some education, some interest in life! That's what counts!

Joe Strummer (b.1952), British rock musician: interview in *Melody Maker* (London), 23 July 1988

INDEX OF AUTHORS

DEATH: DYING; FAME; HERITAGE; HOMOSEXUALITY; HOTELS; LIBRARIES; PERFORMANCE; POETS; THE SOCIAL SCIENCES; TASTE; WRITERS
Bensley, Connie: MEDICINE; TRUST
Berdyaev, Nicolai A: ATHEISM
Bergen, Candice: ORGASM
Berger, John: ACTORS; ANIMALS; ART: AND SOCIETY; AUTOBIOGRAPHY; THE BODY: BODILY FUNCTIONS; BOREDOM; CHILDHOOD; CITIES; COMMON SENSE; COMPASSION; COUNTRY LIFE; THE DEAD; DOCTORS; EMIGRATION & EXILE; ENVY; EVIL; FRANCE: PARIS; GLAMOUR; IMAGINATION; LANGUAGE; THE MEDIA; MEN & WOMEN; NATIONALISM; NUDITY; PHOTOGRAPHY; PHOTOGRAPHY: AND PAINTING; POVERTY; PUBLICITY; READING; TELEVISION; TIME; TIME: PAST; TRAVEL; WORDS
Bergman, Ingmar: AGE: OLD AGE; CINEMA; CINEMA: THE MOVIE-MAKERS; THE END; INDIVIDUALITY; MORALITY; OPINION; RELIGION
Berio, Luciano: OPERA
Berlin, Irving: SUCCESS; THE UNITED STATES: NEW YORK
Berlusconi, Silvio: ITALY; POLITICIANS
Bernikow, Louise: MEN
Bernstein, Carl: CHAT SHOWS; CULTURE; JOURNALISM; NEWS
Bernstein, Leonard: TECHNIQUE
Berry, Chuck: THE 1950S
Berryman, John: ANIMALS; ARTISTS; BOREDOM; THE WORLD
Bertolucci, Bernardo: HOLLYWOOD; SOCIALISM
Betjeman, John: CHRISTMAS; HOUSE & HOME
Bevan, Aneurin: CLEMENT ATTLEE; BUREAUCRACY; WINSTON CHURCHILL; THE CONSERVATIVE PARTY; DISARMAMENT; FASCISM; FREEDOM; INDECISION; INDUSTRY; THE LABOUR PARTY; NEWSPAPERS; POLITICIANS; POWER; PUBLIC LIFE; REACTIONARIES; SUEZ
Bigelow, Kathryn: BIKERS; CINEMA: SEX & VIOLENCE; see also Cameron on THE END
Biko, Steve: ADVERSITY; BLACK CONSCIOUSNESS/BLACK POWER; CAUSES; DEFIANCE; DRESS; MARTYRDOM; OPPRESSION; RACE; SOUTH AFRICA; WHITES
Billings, Victoria: COUPLES; MONEY; MOTHERS; THE PERMISSIVE SOCIETY; RAPE
Bingham, Charlotte: VIRGINITY
Bird, Caroline: FEMININITY
Birkett, Lord: SPEECHES
Birtwistle, Harrison: MUSIC
Bishop, Elizabeth: DREAMING; THINGS; TOURISM
Bisset, Jacqueline: CHARACTER
Bjork: MASTURBATION
Black, Conrad: JOURNALISM
Black, Shirley Temple: STARDOM
Blair, Tony: EDUCATION; LEADERS
Blanchot, Maurice: DIARIES; GERMANY: BERLIN; SLEEP; TASTE; WRITERS; WRITING

Blank, Joost De: SOUTH AFRICA
Bleasdale, Alan: AGE: THE 50S; UNEMPLOYMENT
Blishen, Edward: EDITING; EDUCATION; TEACHERS
Bloom, Allan: CULTURE; EDUCATION; IGNORANCE; KNOWLEDGE; PARENTS; READING; REASON; TEACHERS; TRADITION; THE UNITED STATES; UNIVERSITY
Bloom, Harold: ACADEMIA
Bly, Robert: MASCULINITY
Blythe, Ronald: AGE: OLD AGE
Boesky, Ivan F.: GREED
Bogarde, Dirk: PHOTOGRAPHY
Bogart, Humphrey: GUNS; STARDOM
Bolt, Robert: MORALITY
Bombeck, Erma: FAMILIES; HUMOUR
Bond, Edward: VIOLENCE
Bono: IRELAND; NUCLEAR TESTING
Bookchin, Murray: HOLISM
Boorman, John: PASSION
Boorstin, Daniel J.: ADVERTISING; THE AMERICAN DREAM; CRIME; EVENTS; FAME; HEROES; JOURNALISM; PHOTOGRAPHY; SALES & MARKETING; STARDOM; TOURISM; THE UNITED STATES; THE UNITED STATES: AMERICANS ABROAD
Borges, Jorge Luis: THE FALKLANDS CONFLICT; LITERATURE; NIGHT; POSTERITY; PROBLEMS; QUOTATION; TIME; WRITERS
Botha, P.W.: SOUTH AFRICA
Botham, Ian: FAME: UPS & DOWNS; FUND-RAISING; SPORT
Bottome, Phyllis: EDUCATION
Boulez, Pierre: REVOLUTION
Bovey, Shelley: PHYSIQUE
Bowen, Catherine Drinker: BIOGRAPHY; BRITAIN; SCHOLARSHIP; WRITERS
Bowen, Elizabeth: MEMORY
Bowie, David: AIDS; ART; ARTISTS; BISEXUALITY; ERROR; EXTREMISM; FASCISM; FASHION; THE GENERATION GAP; HEROES; HIPPIES; ADOLF HITLER; LIBERALS; THE MEDIA; MUSIC: COMPOSITION; MUSIC: ROCK & POP; SELF-EXPRESSION; TELEVISION
Boy George: GLAMOUR; HOMOSEXUALITY; MOTTOS & MAXIMS; SEX; THE UNITED STATES
Boyd, William: HUMAN NATURE
Bradbury, Malcolm: HISTORY; INNOCENCE; MANNERS; READING; TRANSPORT
Bradbury, Ray: TIME: FUTURE
Bradlee, Ben C.: POLITICS
Bradley, Omar Nelson: GENERALS
Bragg, Melvyn: BRITAIN
Branagh, Kenneth: ADULTHOOD; FRIENDSHIP
Brando, Marlon: ACTING; ACTORS; BIKERS; JAMES DEAN; FACES; FAILURE; PHYSIQUE; PRIVACY; REBELS
Braun, Wernher von: SPACE
Brautigan, Richard: NEUROSIS
Breathed, Berke: CARTOONS
Brecht, Bertolt: GERMANY: BERLIN; THE MEDIA; THEATRE
Brenton, Howard, and David Hare: THE PRESS

Breslin, Jimmy: JOURNALISM
Bresson, Robert: CINEMA: THE MOVIE-MAKERS; INSPIRATION; THE MEDIA; MODELS; NOVELTY; NUDITY; ORIGINALITY; WRITING: SCRIPTS & SCREENPLAYS
Brice, Fanny: AUDIENCES; CLOWNS; FRIGIDITY; POSING
Brien, Alan: COUNTRY LIFE; TRANSPORT
Brittain, Vera: DIVORCE; POLITICS; THE TWENTIETH CENTURY
Broch, Hermann: DEATH; HATE; MADNESS; THE PEOPLE; THE SEA
Brodie, Fawn M: AUTOBIOGRAPHY; BIOGRAPHY; FARMING; POLITICS; TEACHERS
Brodkey, Harold: REALITY; SPORT: ATHLETICS
Brodsky, Joseph: AESTHETICS; ASIA; BOOKS; CONSCIOUSNESS; EMIGRATION & EXILE; EVIL; LITERATURE: AND SOCIETY; POETRY; POETS; RACISM; SNOBBERY; WORK; WRITERS
Brolly, Francie: IRELAND: NORTHERN IRELAND
Bron, Eleanor: FAULTS
Bronowski, Jacob: ASTRONOMY; DISSENT; NUMBERS; PHYSICS; SCHOLARSHIP; SCIENCE; SCIENCE: AND SOCIETY; SCIENTISTS; SURVIVAL; UNIVERSITY
Brookner, Anita: BOOKS; CHARM; EXISTENTIALISM; FICTION; FRIENDSHIP; INTROSPECTION; JUDAISM; LOVE; LOVERS; LUCK; MIDDLE AGE; ROMANCE; ROMANTICISM; SELFISHNESS; THOUGHT; TRUTH; WOMEN; WRITERS; YOUTH
Brooks, Gwendolyn: ABORTION
Brooks, James L.: INSECURITY
Brooks, Mel: THEATRE; WORLD WAR II
Brower, John: JOHN LENNON
Brown, Craig: JOURNALISM
Brown, Dee: THE UNITED STATES: NATIVE AMERICANS
Brown, H. Rap: VIOLENCE
Brown, Hux: MUSIC: REGGAE
Brown, James: BLACK CULTURE; SELF-IMPROVEMENT
Brown, Norman O.: THE BODY; FREEDOM; MONEY; PERSONALITY; SELF
Brown, Rita Mae: WRITING: SCRIPTS & SCREENPLAYS
Bruce, Lenny: CATHOLICISM; COMEDIANS; COMEDY; DRUGS: ADDICTIONS; HUMOUR; JESUS CHRIST; JUDAISM; LIBERALS; PERFORMANCE; SATIRE
Bruno, Frank: SPORT: BOXING
Brustein, Robert: AUDIENCES; THEATRE
Bryson, Bill: FARMING; FOOD; MOTTOS & MAXIMS; PROVINCIALISM; THE UNITED STATES: AMERICANS ABROAD; THE UNITED STATES: THE SOUTH
Buchanan, Patrick: CATHOLICISM; ISRAEL
Buchman, Frank: GREED
Buchwald, Art: THE ESTABLISHMENT; FRANCE

TIME; THE UNITED STATES: NATIVE
AMERICANS; THE UNITED STATES:
TEXAS; WISDOM
Hoban, Russell: ANIMALS;
LANGUAGE; MEN & WOMEN; SELF;
STRESS; SUNDAYS; TIME: PAST;
TOBACCO; VIOLENCE
Hobsbawm, Eric: FOREIGNERS;
NATIONALISM; PATRIOTISM;
RACISM; SCIENCE: AND SOCIETY;
WAR
Hockney, David: ART: AND SOCIETY;
ARTISTS; DESIGN; PABLO PICASSO;
TELEVISION; TOBACCO
Hoffer, Eric: ACTION; ADOLESCENCE;
AMBITION; ANIMALS; BIGOTRY;
CAPITALISM; COWARDICE;
CREDULITY; DEPRESSION;
DISAPPOINTMENT; DISSENT;
DISSIPATION; ENDS & MEANS;
ESCAPISM; FAITH; FAVOURS;
GENERALIZATIONS; GIVING;
GREATNESS; IMITATION;
LOQUACITY; MALICE; THE MASSES;
MEDIOCRITY; MISANTHROPY;
NECESSITY; OBSCURITY; THE
OBVIOUS; PERSUASION; POSING;
RESENTMENT; SELF-ASSERTION;
SELF-DECEPTION; SELF-IMAGE;
SELF-SUFFICIENCY; SOLITUDE;
SPACE; SUSPICION; THOUGHT;
WEAKNESS; YOUTH
Hoffman, Abbie: REVOLUTIONARIES;
THE SACRED & PROFANE
Hoffman, Dustin: THE BEATLES;
OBSESSION; SEDUCTION; STARDOM;
TALENT
Hoggart, Richard: TRASH
Hoggart, Simon: WALT DISNEY;
RONALD REAGAN; SHOPPING;
THE UNITED STATES; THE
UNITED STATES: NEW YORK; THE
UNITED STATES: TEXAS;
THE UNITED STATES: WASHINGTON
D.C.
Holiday, Billie: DRUGS; DRUGS:
ADDICTIONS; SLAVERY; SONG
Holland, Jack: iRELAND: NORTHERN
IRELAND
Holland, Jools: NAGGING
Hollander, Xaviera: PROSTITUTION
Holleran, Andrew: DANCE
Hollingdale, R.J.: GOD
Holm, Ian: ALIENS
Holman, Robert: THEATRE
Holmes, Larry: SPORT: BOXING
Holmes, Richard: BIOGRAPHY
Holub, Miroslav: HUMANITY;
LAUGHTER; THE WORLD
Hooker, John Lee: MUSIC: BLUES
Hoover, J. Edgar: TRUTH
Hopcraft, Arthur: SPORT: FOOTBALL
Hope, Bob: AGE: OLD AGE; DRESS;
GOLF
Hope, Christopher: THE U.S.S.R.
Hopper, Dennis: ARTISTS; THE
GENERATION GAP; THE 1970S
Hornby, Nick: DEATH; FANS;
FATHERS; GROWING UP; OBSESSION;
RADIO; SPORT; SPORT: FOOTBALL
Horne, Marilyn: STARDOM
Hospital, Janette Turner: NARRATIVE
Houston, Libby: IDEALISM; THE
NUCLEAR AGE
Howe, Louise Kapp: FAMILIES
Hoyle, Fred: SPACE

Hubbard, Ruth: SCIENCE;
SCIENTISTS; THEORY; WORDS
Hudson, Rock: INTERVIEWS
Huffington, Arianna: CREATIVITY;
FEMINISM; GENDER; MEN
Hughes, Robert: EXTREMISM;
POLITICAL CORRECTNESS; SELF;
TELEVISION; VICTIMS
Hughes, Ronnie: MEN: THE NEW MAN
Hull, Richard: THE ARMY
Hume, Basil: MORALITY
Humphrey, Hubert H.: CIVIL RIGHTS;
POLITICS
Hunter, Robert: THE 1960S
Hurd, Douglas: AID
Hussein, Saddam: IRAQ & THE SECOND
GULF WAR
Huston, John: ACTORS; CRIME;
HOLLYWOOD
Hutton, Lauren: MODELS
Huxley, Aldous: THE CHURCH; DEATH;
DRUGS; FICTION; INTELLIGENCE;
ORGANIZATION; RELIGION;
REMORSE; SPEED
Huxley, Elspeth: CHANGE
Hynde, Chrissie: MEAT
Ice Cube: THE UNITED STATES
Ice-T: CRIME; MUSIC: RAP;
PASSION
Ignatieff, Michael: TELEVISION
Iliff, Pete: THE POLICE
Illich, Ivan: ALTRUISM; DEATH: THE
AFTERLIFE; LATIN AMERICA;
MISSIONARIES; PRAYER; SCHOOL;
SILENCE
Imbert, Peter: UNIVERSITY
Indiana, Gary: AFFECTION; AIDS
Ingham, Bernard: THE PRESS
Inglis, Brian: DRUGS
Ingrams, Richard: LITIGATION;
POLITICIANS
Ionesco, Eugène: ALIENATION; ART;
THE AVANT-GARDE; BANALITY;
BEAUTY; CRISES; DEATH; MEMORY;
MYTH; REALISM; WILLIAM
SHAKESPEARE; SOCIETY;
SURREALISM; THE UNIVERSE; THE
WORLD
Irving, Clifford: TRIALS
Isherwood, Christopher: THE UNITED
STATES: THE WEST
Jackson, George: MARTIN LUTHER
KING; LAW; MOTHERS;
NONVIOLENCE; SELF-ASSERTION
Jackson, Glenda: ACTING
Jackson, Jesse: BLACK CULTURE;
DREAMING; FUND-RAISING;
MULTICULTURALISM; PLURALISM;
PROVINCIALISM; RACISM; RIOTS;
UNEMPLOYMENT; THE UNITED
STATES: AFRICAN AMERICANS
Jackson, Mahalia: INDEPENDENCE;
MUSIC: BLUES
Jackson, Michael: FICTION: SCIENCE
FICTION
Jacobs, Jane: CITIES: URBAN
CULTURE; ORDER
Jagger, Mick: NOSTALGIA;
PERFORMANCE; see also Jagger, Mick
and Keith Richards
Jagger, Mick, and Keith Richards:
DESIRE; THE KENNEDYS; MUSIC:
ROCK & POP
Jaine, Tom: COOKERY
Jakobovits, Lord: PASSIVITY
James, C.L.R.: SPORT: CRICKET

James, Clive: CINEMA; GERMANY;
IMPOTENCE; LITERARY CRITICISM;
SOAP OPERAS; TELEVISION; THE
UNITED STATES: LOS ANGELES; THE
U.S.S.R.
James, P.D.: EFFORT; FICTION:
THRILLERS; KINDNESS;
LITERATURE; NATURE; SCIENTISTS;
SEX
James, Selma: POLITICAL
CORRECTNESS; REVOLUTION;
WOMEN
Janeway, Elizabeth: ANIMALS; CHILD
ABUSE; CONTEMPLATION; POETS;
SEXUAL DEVIATIONS; WOMEN
Janowitz, Tama: INSECTS;
PROSTITUTION; PUBLICITY
Jarman, Derek: AIDS; CINEMA; DEATH:
DYING; DEPARTURES; GARDENS;
HOMOSEXUALITY; LABELS; MEN;
THE 1980S; ORGASM; SEASONS
Jastrzębska, Maria: LESBIANISM
Jay, Anthony: FRANCE
Jellicoe, Geoffrey: ARCHITECTURE
Jencks, Charles: CAMP
Jenkins, David: BELIEF; GOD; JESUS
CHRIST
Jennings, Elizabeth: MIDDLE AGE;
PARENTS
Jiang Qing: INTERNATIONAL
RELATIONS
John, Elton: MARILYN MONROE
John XXIII, Pope: SCIENCE
John Paul II, Pope: ABORTION; THE
CHURCH: AND SOCIETY;
CIVILIZATION; COMMUNISM;
FAMILIES; FEAR; FEMINISM; HUMAN
RIGHTS; LEBANON; LOVE;
MARRIAGE; POSITIVISM;
RESPONSIBILITY; TRUTH; YOUTH
Johnson, Edward: WAR
Johnson, Lady Bird: THE KENNEDYS
Johnson, Linton Kwesi: MUSIC:
REGGAE
Johnson, Lyndon B.: BROTHERHOOD;
GERALD FORD; THE 1960S; POLITICS;
VIETNAM
Johnson, Pamela Hansford:
MORALITY; OTHER PEOPLE;
POLITICIANS
Johnson, Paul: THE BEATLES;
FAMILIES
Johnson, Philip: ARCHITECTS;
ARCHITECTURE
Johnson, R.W.: PROBLEMS
Jones, Beverly: HOUSEWIVES;
ROMANCE
Jones, Chuck: SPEED
Jones, Leroi: see Baraka, Amiri
Jones, Mick: see Strummer, Joe, and
Mick Jones
Jones, Quincy: MUSIC: BLUES
Jong, Erica: ADVICE; ARTISTS; BLAME;
THE CIRCUS; FRIENDS; GOSSIP;
HOLLYWOOD; HOUSEWIVES;
JEALOUSY; LOVE; MAKE-UP;
MARRIAGE: FAILED; MEN & WOMEN;
MENSTRUATION; MISERY; NAMES;
ORGASM; SELF-ASSERTION; SEX;
SEXUAL HARASSMENT; SOLITUDE;
TALENT; WOMEN; WOMEN: SINGLE
WOMEN
Joplin, Janis: UNHAPPINESS
Jordan, June: BLACK CULTURE;
CHILDREN; FEMINISM; HIPPIES;
INTERVENTION; MARTIN LUTHER

INDEX OF KEY WORDS

Orthodox modern a. is progressive:
ARCHITECTURE: MODERN
ARCHITECTURE: 25:4

argue: When you a. with your inferiors:
ARGUMENT: 25:1

aristocracy: thing that shows there is no
a.: GUNS: 190:4

Aristotle: A. could have avoided the
mistake: SCIENTISTS: 412:12

arithmetic: A. ... begins in legend:
NUMBERS: 326:1

armament: mental magic to modern a.:
THE ARMS INDUSTRY: 25:3

arms: a. race a giant misunderstanding:
THE ARMS RACE: 26:6

world in a. is not spending money:
THE ARMS RACE: 25:3

army: one nice thing about the A.: THE
ARMY: 26:2

arriving: If we are always a. and
departing: TRAVEL: 479:12

arrogance: turn and trick to British a.:
BRITAIN: 57:2

arse: almighty pain in the a.: ELVIS
PRESLEY: 367:9

art: a. ... an adventure of the mind: ART:
27:18

a. appears, life disappears: ART: 28:25

A. attracts us only: ART: 27:16

a. can teach us to reproduce: ART: 27:6

A. ... cannot avoid cheating truth:
ART: 28:27

a. changes morals: ART: MODERN
ART: 29:11

a. exists under the shadow of the
historian: ART: 28:28

A. for art's sake: ART: 27:7

a. has judged the judges: ART: AND
SOCIETY: 31:4

a. is a community effort: ART:
27:15

a. is a flock of sheep: ART: 27:9

A. is a fruit: ART: 26:2

a. is a means of expurgation: ART:
27:21

a. is a revolt against man's fate: ART:
27:22

a. is a strictly ... individual function:
ART: AND SOCIETY: 31:5

a. is a struggle to be ... virtuous:
VIRTUE: 506:5

A. is an experience ... of a problem:
ART: 26:1

A. is aristocratic: ART: 27:10

A. is dangerous: ART: 26:5

A. is good when it springs from
necessity: ART: 27:8

A. is on the side of the oppressed: ART:
AND SOCIETY: 31:8

A. is parasitic on life: ART: 28:32

a. is seduction: ART: 28:30

A. is so wonderfully irrational: ART:
27:17

A. is the final cunning: ART: 28:23

a. is the laboratory for making new
men: ARTISTS: 34:31

A. ... is the lighthouse: ART: 27:13

A. is the most passionate orgy: ART:
27:12

A. is the objectification of feeling:
ART: 27:20

A. is too serious: ART: 28:26

A. kills only the dead: REVOLUTION:
398:19

a. must show the world as changeable:
ART: AND SOCIETY: 31:6

a. of the last thirty-five years: ART:
MODERN ART: 29:5

a. ... replacement for ... the love of god:
ART: 28:29

A. should be Divine Inspiration: ART:
28:31

A. should be usable: ART: 26:4

a. that is political-erotical-mystical:
ART: 28:24

A. ... the bafflement of the public:
ART: MODERN ART: 29:4

Advanced a. today is no longer a cause:
ART: POLITICAL ART: 30:5

All works of a. are commissioned:
CREATIVITY: 104:2

denounce any work of a.: ART:
POLITICAL ART: 30:4

falsely mystical view of a.: ART: AND
SOCIETY: 32:14

Feminist a. is not some tiny creek:
ART: POLITICAL ART: 30:2

first mistake of A.: ART: 26:3

great a. ... must appear extreme: ART:
AND SOCIETY: 32:17

great work of a. has two faces: ART:
AND SOCIETY: 31:2

history of experimental a.: ART:
MODERN ART: 29:10

How easily a. and nature overlap:
ITALY: 230:3

I never thought a. could change things:
ART: AND SOCIETY: 31:1

In a., one idea is as good as another:
ART: 27:11

in a. things have a shape: ART: 27:14

Modern a. has been ... explosions:
ART: MODERN ART: 29:9

no a. remains shocking: ART: AND
SOCIETY: 31:7

primary function of a. and thought:
ART: AND SOCIETY: 32:16

Progressive a. can assist: ART:
POLITICAL ART: 30:1

public accepts ... anything in Modern
A.: ART: MODERN ART: 29:12

public history of modern a.: ART:
MODERN ART: 29:7

purpose of a. is to intensify: ART: AND
SOCIETY: 32:12

tragedy that we call modern a.: ART:
MODERN ART: 29:3

Twentieth-century a. may start
with nothing: ART: MODERN ART:
29:1

understand a great work of a.: ART:
28:34

What distinguishes modern a.: ART:
MODERN ART: 29:8

work of a. must start an argument:
ART: 28:33

arteriosclerosis: Civilization is the a. of
culture: CIVILIZATION: 87:5

articulacy: People resent a.: SPEECH:
439:9

artist: a. ... finally he dies blind:
ARTISTS: 32:5

a. is a being who strives: ARTISTS:
34:32

a. is a creature driven by demons:
ARTISTS: 33:11

a. ... is a researcher: ARTISTS: 33:18

a. is extremely lucky: ARTISTS: 32:3

a. is forced by others to paint:
ARTISTS: 33:9

a. ... is really needed: ART: AND
SOCIETY: 31:9

a. is touched by some social condition:
ART: AND SOCIETY: 32:11

a. must always have one skin too few:
ARTISTS: 33:14

a. must be a reactionary: ART: AND
SOCIETY: 32:18

a. needs both knowledge:
ABSTINENCE: 1:2

a. should be grateful for a naïve grace:
ARTISTS: 32:2

a. was that privileged being: ARTISTS:
34:30

a.'s originality is balanced: ARTISTS:
33:15

aim of an a. is just to investigate:
ARTISTS: 32:4

contemporary a. has a responsibility:
ARTISTS: 33:16

distinguishes an a. from a performer:
MUSIC: JAZZ: 304:11

enemy of America is the a.: ART: AND
SOCIETY: 32:13

Everybody's an a.: ARTISTS: 34:26

for the a. to have a world: ART: AND
SOCIETY: 31:3

good a. should be isolated: ARTISTS:
34:33

No a. is ahead of his time: ARTISTS:
33:13

nothing fiercer than a failed a.:
ARTISTS: 33:20

One of the dangers of the American a.:
ARTISTS: 34:34

only meet him as an a.: ARTISTS: 32:6

prerogative of an a. ... is to make a fool:
ARTISTS: 33:21

primary distinction of the a.: ARTISTS:
32:1

product of the a. has become less
important: ARTISTS: 33:23

task of the a. ... to discover: ARTISTS:
34:29

work of the a.: ARTISTS: 34:28

artistic: 'Oh what an a. animal is our
little Man': ILLUSION: 213:4

artists: a. are indestructible: ARTISTS:
34:27

A. are never allowed to let things alone:
ARTISTS: 32:7

A. are not engineers of the soul: ART:
AND SOCIETY: 31:10

a. are the first men: ARTISTS: 34:25

a. don't have the patience to make art:
ARTISTS: 33:22

a., ... independent *craftsmen*:
ARTISTS: 34:35

a. must disorientate their minds:
ARTISTS: 33:19

all a. were ... housewives:
HOUSEWIVES: 204:4

for us a. there waits the joyous
compromise: ARTISTS: 33:10

Immature a. imitate: PLAGIARISM:
346:8

There are only a.: ARTISTS: 33:12

times are exhausted – not our a.:
TALENT: 457:3

two kinds of a. left: MUSIC: ROCK &
POP: 306:14

arts: a. ... a consolation for loneliness:
THE ARTS: 35:3

a. are not just instantaneous pleasure:
THE ARTS: 35:2

techniques of the a.: THE ARTS: 35:5

Asiatic: long-feared A. colossus: ASIA:
35:5

brains: B. evolved after bowels: FOOD: 170:1
Until their b. snap open: THE RAT RACE: 386:4
With my b. and your looks: COUPLES: 104:3
brainwashing: b. and propaganda blitzes: ELECTIONS: 140:9
Brando: Mr B. is the man for the job: MARLON BRANDO: 57:1
brands: great b. are far more than labels: CONSUMERISM: 100:11
Brazilian: B. without land or money: THE ENVIRONMENT: 145:7
bread: b. they have cast on the waters: ABUSE: 2:2
breadwinner: 'b. ethic': MEN: 282:11
breasts: My little b., my face, my hips: RESTAURANTS: 396:2
protruding b. were pressed flat: BREASTS: 57:3
breathing: One does not love b.: READING: 388:13
breeding: unplanned b. of ourselves: POPULATION: 359:2
breeze: first sweet-smelling b.: RAIN: 385:1
Brian: It's an ordinary day for B.: DRUGS: 134:31
bribe: b. ... changes a relation: CORRUPTION: 102:3
bridge: Like a b. over troubled water: SYMPATHY: 457:3
bridges: I like to burn my b.: PESSIMISM: 342:7
Never burn b.: CAREERS: 65:5
bright: look on the b. side of life: OPTIMISM: 330:5
they're not that b.: FANS: 160:3
brinkmanship: boasting of his b.: THE COLD WAR: 89:9
Britain: B. is made up of a whole mixture: PLURALISM: 347:5
B. will play a vital part within Europe: EUROPE: 148:6
B. will still be the country: BRITAIN: ENGLAND: 58:9
Great B. has lost an Empire: BRITAIN: 57:1
British: B. do not expect happiness: BRITAIN: 57:4
nothing the B. like better: BRITAIN: 57:3
word 'B.' harder ... to use: BRITAIN: 57:6
broadcasting: all day b. on the radio and TV: IRAQ & THE SECOND GULF WAR: 227:6
Broadway: every play that comes to B.: BROADWAY: 59:3
wide wonder of B.: BROADWAY: 59:2
brother: BIG B. IS WATCHING YOU: THE STATE: 445:5
most dangerous word ... is the word for b.: BROTHERHOOD: 60:9
brotherhood: b. of man is evoked: BROTHERHOOD: 60:7
I believe in the b. of man: BROTHERHOOD: 60:8
ideal of b. of man: BROTHERHOOD: 59:1
together at the table of b.: BROTHERHOOD: 60:5
brotherly: b. feelings grounded in ... common baseness: BROTHERHOOD: 60:6

brothers: recognition of all men as our b.: BROTHERHOOD: 60:2
Brown: James B. and Frank Sinatra: MUSIC: ROCK & POP: 306:4
Let's not forget James B. picked cotton: SELF-IMPROVEMENT: 417:1
brushstroke: b. in someone else's painting: SELF-ASSERTION: 416:4
brutal: small minority ... who like being b.: EVIL: 151:12
buck: b. stops here: RESPONSIBILITY: 396:7
Buddha: B. the Godhead, resides: BUDDHISM: 60:1
Buddhism: B. has offered a rhetoric of dissent: BUDDHISM: 60:2
Budget: closer to balancing the B.: THE ECONOMY: 137:3
buffers: Most of them are b.: PARLIAMENT: THE HOUSE OF COMMONS: 336:1
building: b. becomes a theatrical demonstration: ARCHITECTURE: MODERN ARCHITECTURE: 25:3
buildings: job of b. is to improve: ARCHITECTURE: 24:3
We shape our b.: ARCHITECTURE: 24:2
built: It is not what they b.: CITIES: 84:6
bullet: b. with my name on: TERRORISM: 466:1
due process is a b.: VIETNAM: 504:24
bullets: B. cannot be recalled: DISARMAMENT: 124:1
bum: Instead of a b., which is what I am: FAILURE: 155:3
bumpy: It's going to be a b. night: PARTIES: 337:1
burden: b. of being black: BLACK CULTURE: 50:6
bureaucracy: b. disposes: BUREAUCRACY: 61:5
B., ... the modern form of despotism: BUREAUCRACY: 61:4
efficient b. is the greatest threat: BUREAUCRACY: 61:3
bureaucrat: b. that does not like a poem: BUREAUCRACY: 61:11
bureaucrats: envied are like b.: ENVY: 145:1
buried: never bear to be b. with people: BURIAL: 61:2
Burma: Be careful about B.: ASIA: 35:2
burn: B., baby, burn: RIOTS: 400:1
those who b. themselves alive: ACTIVISM & PROTEST: 5:9
Burton: diabolically famous Richard B.: STARDOM: 444:7
bury: We will b. you: THE COLD WAR: 89:5
Bush: Consider the vice president, George B.: GEORGE BUSH: 61:2
business: b. practices would improve: WOMEN: IN BUSINESS: 520:2
good b. is the best art: BUSINESS: 62:12
try to talk b.: PUBLISHING: 379:1
busy: how *not* to be b.: EFFORT: 139:2
busyness: utopian principle – absolute b.: MODERN LIFE: 291:5
butterfly: Float like a b.: MUHAMMAD ALI: 18:1
buzzard: I'd want to come back a b.: DEATH: THE AFTERLIFE: 115:3

cabaret: Im C.! Au Cabaret: ENTERTAINMENT: 144:1
cabbage: like a human c.: FUND-RAISING: 178:1
caffeine: C. has been the chemical adjunct: COFFEE: 88:3
Cain: we are the sons of C.: VIOLENCE: 504:8
California: better heed what happens in C.: THE UNITED STATES: THE WEST: 497:1
C. ... in which a boom mentality: THE UNITED STATES: THE WEST: 497:4
C. is a tragic country: THE UNITED STATES: THE WEST: 497:5
calm: C. as a morgue or a grave: OPPRESSION: 329:5
Cambridge: most difficult feat for a C. male: CAMBRIDGE UNIVERSITY: 62:2
Camelot: one brief shining moment ... known/As C.: THE KENNEDYS: 237:6
camels: C. are snobbish: ANIMALS: 21:7
camera: c. asserts what it has seen: PHOTOGRAPHY: 343:21
c. can photograph thought: PHOTOGRAPHY: 343:7
c. doesn't rape: PHOTOGRAPHY: 343:20
c. has an interest in turning history: PHOTOGRAPHY: 343:12
c. is a killing chamber: PHOTOGRAPHY: 343:9
c. is a weapon: PHOTOGRAPHY: 343:22
c. is an instrument that teaches: PHOTOGRAPHY: 343:16
Giving a c. to Diane Arbus: PHOTOGRAPHY: 343:8
man ... adores his c. – and himself: PHOTOGRAPHY: 343:8
tripping of a c.'s shutter: PHOTOGRAPHY: 343:10
virtue of the c.: PHOTOGRAPHY: 342:2
caméra-stylo: age of *c*.: CINEMA: THE NEW WAVE: 82:1
camp: C. is the modern dandyism: CAMP: 63:2
campaign: You c. in poetry: POLITICIANS: 353:7
camps: c. pose the supreme riddle: CONCENTRATION CAMPS: 96:3
police terror and the concentration c.: CONCENTRATION CAMPS: 96:1
can't: things you just c. do in life: MOTTOS & MAXIMS: 299:5
Canada: C. is a country where nothing: CANADA: 63:7
C. is not really a place where: CANADA: 63:3
Canadian: beginning of C. cultural nationalism: CANADA: 63:1
Canadians: C. look down on the United States: CANADA: 63:5
cancer: C. patients are lied to: CANCER: 63:4
We 'need' c.: CANCER: 63:1
candidates: Which one of the three c.: ELECTIONS: 140:7
candle: Like a c. in the wind: MARILYN MONROE: 295:4
capital: c. punishment has another power: CAPITAL PUNISHMENT: 64:2
capitalism: c. ... condition for political freedom: CAPITALISM: 64:3

C. ... in a noncapitalist environment: CAPITALISM: 64:6
C. is an art form: CAPITALISM: 64:7
ideology of c. makes us all: CAPITALISM: 65:9
In culture, c. has given all: CAPITALISM: 63:4
most eloquent eulogy of c.: CAPITALISM: 64:1
Predatory c. created a complex: CAPITALISM: 64:2
predict the collapse of c.: FIN DE SIÈCLE: 169:2
unacceptable face of c.: CAPITALISM: 64:5
What breaks c. ... is capitalists: CAPITALISM: 65:11
capitalist: c. roots of the racial miseries: CAPITALISM: 64:8
captains: C. go down with their ships: BUSINESS: 62:6
car: c. has become the carapace: CARS: 66:7
c. ... is on the way out: CARS: 65:2
carbuncle: monstrous c. on the face of a ... friend: MUSEUMS & GALLERIES: 301:1
carcinoma: To sing of rectal c.: CANCER: 63:3
cards: Never play c. with a man called Doc: MOTTOS & MAXIMS: 299:1
care: don't c. what anybody says: SLANDER: 431:1
take better c. of myself: LIVE FAST, DIE YOUNG: 259:1
career: C. opportunities ... that never knock: UNEMPLOYMENT: 484:7
whole c. playing myself: ACTING: 4:17
careers: People don't choose their c.: CAREERS: 65:1
carpet: brush under the c.: PARENTS: 335:5
cars: c. ... the great Gothic cathedrals: CARS: 65:3
giant finned c. nose forward: CARS: 65:6
reason American c. don't sell: CARS: 65:5
cartooning: relationship between c. and people: CARTOONS: 66:2
case: c. was lost or won: TRIALS: 480:8
cash: c. register mind: MONEY: 294:19
Castro: C. couldn't even go to the bathroom: CUBA: 110:4
Everything was blamed on C.: CUBA: 110:5
'I like Fidel C. and his beard': CUBA: 109:1
cat: c. is a diagram and pattern: CATS: 67:5
c. transformed into a woman: BRIGITTE BARDOT: 42:1
One c. in a house: CATS: 67:2
catastrophe: abolishing the c.: SURVIVAL: 455:7
c. is the natural human environment: DISASTERS: 125:3
Catch-22: there's a catch. C.: WAR: 508:10
catcher: c. in the rye: CHILDREN: 75:19
catechism: struggles with the Catholic c.: CATHOLICISM: 67:9
cathedral: c. is a decorated shed: CHURCHES: 77:3
Catholic: C. Church has never ... come to terms: CATHOLICISM: 67:12

One cannot ... be a C. and grown up: CATHOLICISM: 67:8
Today's C. church: CATHOLICISM: 66:4
you may as well be a C.: CATHOLICISM: 67:10
Catholicism: C. is not a soothing religion: CATHOLICISM: 66:6
cats: Authors like c.: CATS: 67:3
C. are autocrats of naked self-interest: CATS: 67:6
c. have more purchasing power: POVERTY: 364:12
C. seem to go on the principle: CATS: 67:4
catwalk: c. is theatre: MODELS: 291:9
caught: be c. dead doing: REPUTATION: 394:1
cause: c. bigger than himself: CAUSES: 68:10
c. of freedom versus tyranny: CAUSES: 67:1
fight in your own c.: CAUSES: 68:8
good c. can become bad: CAUSES: 67:3
Truth never damages a c.: CAUSES: 68:5
causes: aren't any good, brave c. left: CAUSES: 68:11
I hate the idea of c.: CAUSES: 68:4
people who believe in c.: CAUSES: 68:7
cave: Own Your Own C.: HOUSE & HOME: 204:8
ceiling: One Man's C.: COMMUNITIES: 94:5
celebrity: C. is a mask that eats: FAME: 157:11
c. is a person who is known: FAME: 157:2
C. is good for kick-starting ideas: FAME: 157:10
In the world of the c.: FAME: 157:6
To become a c. is to become a brand name: FAME: 157:9
where any c. ... may become a star: STARDOM: 444:5
celibacy: C. is not just ... not having sex: CELIBACY: 68:3
celibates: c. are no more deranged: CELIBACY: 68:2
Some perks belong/ ... to all unwilling c.: CELIBACY: 68:1
celluloid: most expensive habit in the world is c.: CINEMA: THE MOVIE-MAKERS: 81:14
cemetery: c. of the victims of human cruelty: ABORTION: 1:4
censor: To c. is to destroy: CENSORSHIP: 68:3
censors: C. ... confuse reality with illusion: CENSORSHIP: 68:2
censorship: C. is a political issue: CENSORSHIP: 69:7
c. is necessary: CENSORSHIP: 69:10
C. is never over: CENSORSHIP: 68:4
centipede: 'And here is my good big c.!': INSECTS: 221:1
century: As the end of the c. approaches: FIN DE SIÈCLE: 169:1
lesson of the c.: NATIONS: 311:3
missed for the world: THE TWENTIETH CENTURY: 482:9
ceremonies: learn which c. may be breached: CEREMONY: 69:3
ceremony: c. is a book: CEREMONY: 69:2

certain: we are never c.: CERTAINTY: 69:1
certainty: quest for c. blocks the search: UNCERTAINTY: 483:1
cesspit: human c. of their own making: AIDS: 16:2
chance: C. is a part of reality: LUCK: 265:1
C. is the one thing you can't buy: LUCK: 265:4
chancre: dignity of a hard c.: EVIL: 151:8
change: c., continuing change: CHANGE: 70:3
c. is gonna come: CHANGE: 70:6
C. means movement: CHANGE: 70:1
c. the structures of society: REFORM: 391:2
c. the world only by being there: REVOLUTION: 397:4
If a man like Malcolm X could c.: CHANGE: 70:5
in constant state of c.: CHANGE: 70:2
insisting on social c.: REFORM: 391:3
nature of a man ... to protest against c.: NOSTALGIA: 324:5
wind of c. is blowing: DECOLONIZATION: 117:2
word c., so dear to our Europe: CHANGE: 70:9
changed: as eager to be c.: CHANGE: 70:4
not have c. a single item: COMPLACENCY: 95:2
changes: Today the world c. so quickly: CHANGE: 70:11
changing: things ... must always be c.: CHANGE: 70:8
chaos: C. is a name for any order: CHAOS: 71:2
revolutionary c. may yet crystallize: THE U.S.S.R.: 499:2
We're into c.: PUNK: 381:7
Chaplin: Charlie C.'s genius: COMEDIANS: 90:4
character: All that endures is c.: CHARACTER: 71:8
C. contributes to beauty: CHARACTER: 71:1
pipe down about 'c. issues': ELECTIONS: 140:5
tell a lot about a fellow's c.: CHARACTER: 71:7
To keep your c. intact: CHARACTER: 71:5
charivaria: c. of information: PUBLIC OPINION: 379:1
Charles: Prince C. is a good egg: THE ROYAL FAMILY: 402:4
charm: forced to rely upon physical c.: CHARM: 71:4
man of such obvious and exemplary c.: CHARM: 71:1
What is c. then: CHARM: 71:3
You know what c. is: CHARM: 71:2
Chaucer: C. was a class traitor: LITERATURE: AND SOCIETY: 257:8
cheeks: compare the c. of a young woman: ORIGINALITY: 332:2
stop turning our c.: SELF-ASSERTION: 415:2
cheese: c. may disappoint: FOOD: 170:8
246 different kinds of c.: FRANCE: 173:8
chemistry: c. represented an indefinite cloud: CHEMISTRY: 72:1
nothing colder than c.: CHEMISTRY: 72:2

Without a c., I am not a man: NATIONS: 311:2

You can't be a Real C. unless: NATIONS: 311:4

couple: human c. is the metaphor par excellence: COUPLES: 104:5

courage: C. and grace is a formidable mixture: SPORT: 441:5

c. is only an accumulation of small steps: COURAGE: 104:3

C. is when you have choices: HOSTAGES: 203:1

c. of the woman who gives birth: CHILDBIRTH: 73:1

no man can be sure of his c.: COURAGE: 104:1

court: c. is only as sound as its jury: TRIALS: 479:5

courtesy: His c. was somewhat extravagant: LETTERS: 250:6

courts: C. are places where the ending is written: TRIALS: 479:2

Couture: Haute C. should be fun: HAUTE COUTURE: 192:1

cowardice: guilty of Noel C.: WIT: 515:1

When c. is made respectable: COWARDICE: 104:1

cowboy: last true c. in America: THE UNITED STATES: NATIVE AMERICANS: 493:3

cradle: c. rocks above an abyss: EXISTENCE: 152:7

crash: car c. harnesses ... eroticism: ACCIDENTS: 3:1

crazy: Pound's c. All poets are: PSYCHIATRIC INSTITUTIONS: 377:3

create: Whoever undertakes to c.: CREATIVITY: 105:11

creative: c. imagination as a fruit machine: CREATIVITY: 105:8

c. person ... has to face the fact: CREATIVITY: 105:12

c. spirits of our time: CREATIVITY: 105:9

contribution to the c. act: CREATIVITY: 105:4

creativity: Americans worship c.: CREATIVITY: 105:6

don't merely give over your c.: ACTING: 3:4

Our current obsession with c.: CREATIVITY: 105:5

True c. often starts: CREATIVITY: 105:7

credulity: Our c. is greatest: CREDULITY: 105:1

sin of c.: CREDULITY: 105:2

credulous: Man is a c. animal: CREDULITY: 105:3

creed: at the back of every c.: CREEDS: 106:1

If you have embraced a c.: CREEDS: 106:3

crème: pupils are the c. de la crème: SCHOOL: 409:5

cricket: c. is the greatest thing: SPORT: CRICKET: 443:5

C. is ... a dramatic spectacle: SPORT: CRICKET: 442:2

quibbling over what 'isn't c.': SPORT: CRICKET: 442:3

crime: c. ... a lefthanded form of human endeavor: CRIME: 106:7

C. is a fact of the human species: CRIME: 106:3

C. is an equal-opportunity employer: CRIME: 106:8

c. is anything that a group in power: CRIME: 106:1

C. seems to change character: CRIME: 106:5

original 'c.' of 'niggers': DISSENT: 127:10

world of c. ... is a last refuge: CRIME: 106:4

crimes: C. of which a people is ashamed: CRIME: 106:6

criminal: c. and the soldier: COMMITMENT: 91:3

society gets the kind of c. it deserves: THE POLICE: 351:8

criminals: c. have been great men: TRIALS: 479:3

c. ... organize a forbidden universe: CRIMINALS: 106:1

crises: history is nothing but ... 'c.': CRISES: 106:2

crisis: C. can indeed be an agony: CRISES: 107:4

can't be a c. next week: CRISES: 107:3

in a c. ... Americans see other people: CRISES: 106:1

turn political c. into armed crisis: GUERRILLA WARFARE: 189:2

critic: Any c. is entitled to wrong judgments: CRITICS: 108:4

c. is a bundle of biases: CRITICS: 108:1

Give a c. an inch: CRITICS: 108:5

good drama c. perceives: CRITICS: 108:6

literary c. ... may detach himself: LITERARY CRITICISM: 255:6

television c. ... does not labour: CRITICS: 108:3

critical: c. method which denies literary modernity: LITERARY CRITICISM: 254:2

C. remarks are only made: CRITICISM: 107:3

Good c. writing is measured: CRITICISM: PROFESSIONAL: 107:5

criticism: As far as c. is concerned: SOUTH AFRICA: 438:10

C. is a misconception: LITERARY CRITICISM: 254:1

C. is ceremonial revivification: CRITICISM: PROFESSIONAL: 108:14

C. is getting all mixed up: BIOGRAPHY: 47:4

C. should be a casual conversation: CRITICISM: PROFESSIONAL: 107:3

C. takes longer to change: CRITICISM: PROFESSIONAL: 107:2

function of c.: CRITICISM: PROFESSIONAL: 108:15

Honest c. means nothing: CRITICISM: PROFESSIONAL: 108:11

lots of c. is written by characters: LITERARY CRITICISM: 254:5

meditative background that is c.: CRITICISM: PROFESSIONAL: 107:9

Much literary c. comes from people: LITERARY CRITICISM: 254:4

people ... cower before c.: CRITICISM: 107:2

Social c. begins with grammar: MEANING: 278:5

Unless c. refuses to take itself: CRITICISM: PROFESSIONAL: 107:8

Writing c. is to writing fiction: LITERARY CRITICISM: 255:8

critics: children one's 'mature' c. often are: CRITICS: 108:7

time to listen to the c.: CRITICISM: PROFESSIONAL: 107:7

crook: if you're a c. you're ... up-there: CROOKS: 108:5

Well, I'm not a c.: CORRUPTION: 102:5

cross: hero is so dreadfully c.: THE ANGRY YOUNG MEN: 20:1

cross-section: c. of any plan of a big city: CITIES: 85:15

crowd: human c. has been the lesson of my life: OTHER PEOPLE: 332:5

crowded: forget that the world is a c. place: PLURALISM: 347:4

crucify: They're going to c. me: ADVERSITY: 8:3

cruelty: c. will not make us humane: CRUELTY: 109:1

crusade: c. against Communism: COMMUNISM: 93:16

Party is a moral c.: THE LABOUR PARTY: 241:6

Cuba: give C. a chance to breathe: CUBA: 109:2

cuckoo clock: what did they produce? The c.: SWITZERLAND: 456:4

culpability: general c. of a civilization: WAR CRIMES: 510:1

culprit: treat the c. both as a child: PUNISHMENT: 380:4

cult: c. is a religion with no political power: CULTS: 110:4

What is a c.: CULTS: 110:1

culture: all phases of c. are alive: CULTURE: 111:11

bastard form of mass c.: POPULAR CULTURE: 358:2

c. has reached a dead end: MYTH: 309:7

C. is a sort of theatre: CULTURE: 111:12

c. is what is done to us: CULTURE: 110:2

C.'s essential service to a religion: RELIGION: 393:2

creating ... the idiot c.: CULTURE: 110:5

essence of imaginative c.: CULTURE: 111:9

national c. is not a folklore: CULTURE: 111:8

This c. is authentic: CULTURE: 110:3

When I hear the word c.: CINEMA: THE MOVIE-MAKERS: 81:6

whole c. based on the assumption: POPULAR CULTURE: 359:12

cultures: All c. are involved in one another: MULTICULTURALISM: 300:6

history of other c. is non-existent: ABROAD: 1:4

cunt: regain the power of the c.: SADISM: 405:5

curiosity: that gift would be c.: CURIOSITY: 111:3

curse: You don't c.: SACRED & PROFANE, THE: 405:4

curtain: born at the rise of the c.: ACTORS: 6:9

iron c. has descended: THE COLD WAR: 89:3

cyberpunk: c. is very much a pop phenomenon: LITERATURE: MODERN LITERATURE: 256:1

cyberspace: C. is where a long distance phone call: THE INTERNET: 225:2

cycle: women ... c. every month: MENSTRUATION: 286:5

cynic: c. ... is prematurely disappointed: CYNICISM: 110:2

cynicism: C. is cheap: CYNICISM: 111:1

Czars: legacy from the court of the C.: THE U.S.S.R.: 500:10

Daily Mirror: D. is the worst and the best newspaper: NEWSPAPERS: 315:3

Dallas: *D.* is superior: SOAP OPERAS: 433:1

sceptic finds D. absurd: SOAP OPERAS: 433:3

dames: All d. are alike: WOMEN: THE MALE VIEW: 521:10

damnation: final measure of d.: GOODNESS: 186:5

dance: D. then wherever you may be: DANCE: 111:2

how many of us can d. ... the gombe sugu: DANCE: 112:6

dancing: d. in the street: DANCE: 112:7

dangerous: everything is d.: DANGER: 112:2

Danish: you're yesterday's D.: FAME: UPS & DOWNS: 158:2

darkness: d. of mere being: EXISTENCE: 152:4

Darwinian: validity of the D. theory: EVOLUTION: 152:6

data: D. is what distinguishes the dilettante: RESEARCH: 395:3

more the d. banks record: INFORMATION: 220:4

daughter: two rules for my newly born d.: GIRLS: 183:3

dawning: something of the d. of the universe: THE UNITED STATES: NEW YORK: 493:2

day: Go ahead. Make my d.: FAVOURS: 163:1

daydream: d. is a meal at which images: DAYDREAMS: 112:1

days: What are d. for: DAYS: 112:1

dead: actually *already d*.: THE DEAD: 113:3

close relations of the walking d.: LIBRARIES: 252:1

not more than ten to twenty million d.: NUCLEAR WAR: 325:4

We are close to d.: THE END: 142:7

deals: D. are my art form: BUSINESS: 62:11

Dean: dialogue of James D.'s films: JAMES DEAN: 113:3

Mr D. appears to be wearing: JAMES DEAN: 113:1

death: at ... d. I hope to be surprised: DEATH: THE AFTERLIFE: 115:4

body must become familiar with its d.: DEATH: 114:12

call of d. is a call of love: DEATH: 114:13

chief problem about d.: DEATH: THE AFTERLIFE: 115:2

composing myself to thoughts of d.: DEATH: 114:22

confrontation of d.: DANGER: 112:1

d. can itself be a politicizing thing: MARTYRDOM: 273:2

D. does determine life: LIFE: AND DEATH: 254:2

D. is a displaced name: DEATH: 113:4

D. is an endless night: DEATH: 114:23

D. is someone you see very clearly: DEATH: 114:18

D. is the last enemy: DEATH: 113:7

d. is the obscene mystery: DEATH: 114:21

d. makes everything certain: THE DEAD: 112:1

d. merely set a seal: CONCENTRATION CAMPS: 96:2

d. row inmates are not 'doing time': CAPITAL PUNISHMENT: 64:1

D. stay thy phantoms: DEATH: 113:9

d. terrifies men less: DEATH: 115:24

d. will be someone's/ Milestone: DEATH: 114:20

d. ... your ultimate gift to life: SUICIDE: 452:7

D.'s at the bottom of everything: DEATH: 113:10

facts of d. and violence: VIOLENCE: 504:1

force of a d. should be enormous: KILLING: 238:3

I'm not afraid of d.: DEATH: DYING: 116:6

Let me die a youngman's d.: LIVE FAST, DIE YOUNG: 259:4

more complicated than d.: WAR CORRESPONDENTS: 509:4

No d. may be called futile: DEATH: 114:19

No one's d. comes to pass: DEATH: 113:3

One lives one's d.: EXISTENCE: 153:8

people who say 'There is no d.': DEATH: 114:17

resigned to d.: DEATH: 114:11

sign of creeping inner d.: MISANTHROPY: 289:1

Since the d. instinct exists: DEATH: 114:16

tragedy of massive d. during wartime: WAR: 508:15

Welcome to Pennsylvania's d. row: DEATH: 113:1

debauchery: True d. is liberating: DEBAUCHERY: 116:1

decade: D. of the Experts: THE 1960S: 318:3

decadence: d. is indispensable to rebirth: DECADENCE: 117:2

d. ... ours is apathetic: DECADENCE: 117:3

decadent: d. civilization compromises: DECADENCE: 117:1

deceived: men I d. the most: BETRAYAL: 46:1

deceiving: Adults find pleasure in d. a child: CHILDREN: 74:6

decency: D. ... an even more exhausting state: RESPECTABILITY: 395:1

decent: Better d. than indecent: ATHEISM: 36:4

'Take me somewhere d.': SEXUAL FANTASY: 426:4

decision: don't take a d. until you have to: DECISIONS: 117:3

Every d. is liberating: DECISIONS: 117:1

hard, fast and specific d.: GOVERNMENT: 188:10

decisions: how much healthier your d. are: SELFISHNESS: 419:1

on the eve of great d.: CANDOUR: 64:3

deck: not playing with a full d.: RONALD REAGAN: 388:3

decolonization: D., which sets out to change: DECOLONIZATION: 117:1

deconstruction: D. ... insists not that truth is illusory: DECONSTRUCTION: 117:3

d. is affirmation: DECONSTRUCTION: 117:2

fall into the abyss of d.: DECONSTRUCTION: 117:1

deconstructive: air of last things ... about so much d.: DECONSTRUCTION: 117:4

Deconstructivists: D. pulled the cortical edifice down: STRUCTURALISM: 447:3

defeat: D. doesn't finish a man: DEFEAT: 118:3

Man is not made for d.: DEFEAT: 118:1

ordeal of recurrent d.: DEFEAT: 118:2

stumble from d. to defeat: ADVERSITY: 8:2

defences: My d. were so great: INHIBITION: 220:3

penetrate a woman's d.: SEDUCTION: 414:3

defending: military is ... incapable of d.: DEFENCE: 118:2

deference: Nothing is more immobilizing than ... d: DELINQUENTS: 119:5

defiance: d. of established authority: THE 1960S: 318:1

define: Trying to d. yourself: SELF-PORTRAITS: 419:7

degrees: University d. are a bit like adultery: UNIVERSITY: 498:6

delay: d. makes pleasure great: ANTICIPATION: 22:1

delegate: d. authority: DELEGATION: 119:2

democracy: D.! Bah: DEMOCRACY: 120:8

D. don't rule the world: DEMOCRACY: 120:5

D. is largely a sham: DEMOCRACY: 119:3

D. is supposed to give you ... choice: DEMOCRACY: 120:11

D. is the menopause of Western society: DEMOCRACY: 119:2

d. on the American continent: MULTICULTURALISM: 299:1

not the voting that's d.: VOTING: 507:2

Two cheers for D.: DEMOCRACY: 120:6

understand the meaning of d.: JUSTICE: 237:6

democratization: D. is not democracy: THE U.S.S.R.: GLASNOST & PERESTROIKA: 500:2

denies: In so far as one d. what is: DENIAL: 120:2

dentopedalogy: D. is the science of opening your mouth: FAUX-PAS: 163:2

dentures: I had very good d. once: TEETH: 462:2

departure: Now is the time of d.: DEPARTURES: 120:2

return to the point of d.: TRAVEL: 479:15

has-been: better to be a h.: FAME: UPS & DOWNS: 158:3

hasta: H. la vista, baby: FAREWELLS: 160:2

hat: h. is not for the street: HATS: 192:1
leopard-skin pill-box h.: HATS: 192:2

hate: h. layer of opinion and emotion: MCCARTHYISM: 266:2
H. traps us by binding us: HATE: 192:7
people are capable of real h.: HATE: 192:8

hated: I never h. a man enough: HATE: 192:5
To make oneself h. is more difficult: HATE: 192:9

hating: price of h. other human beings: HATE: 192:4

hatred: H. becomes a pleasure: HATE: 192:2
h. of the white American: RACISM: 383:4
h. only perceives the topmost surface: HATE: 191:1
H. preserves: HATE: 192:3
What we need is h.: HATE: 192:6

hats: H. divide generally into three classes: HATS: 192:3

having: I'll have what she's h.: ORGASM: 331:4

head: 'Feed your h.': PSYCHEDELIA: 376:3
H. 'em up: WESTERNS: 513:3
h. for business: THE BODY: 52:11
human h. is monstrous: THE MIND: 288:3

head-hunter: H. to his friends: DRUGS: THE DEALERS: 135:3

healing: 'H./ ... is not a science': HEALTH: 192:1

health: Bad h. is a sign of the moral failing: HEALTH: 192:2
concept of 'mental h.': CONFORMITY: 97:6
Health is a state of ... well-being: HEALTH: 193:4

heart: hard to get your h. and head together: HOLISM: 198:1
learn by h. till I wept: SCHOOL: 409:6

heartbeat: h. from the Presidency: THE UNITED STATES: THE PRESIDENT: 495:11

heat: h., which comes at the speed of light: NUCLEAR WAR: 325:1
If you can't stand the h.: STRESS: 447:2
white h. of the technological revolution: TECHNOLOGY: 461:19

heaven: trouble with kingdoms of h. on earth: UTOPIA: 500:5

hedgerow: more violence in an English h.: NATURE: 311:5

hell: belief in h.: DEATH: 114:15
H. is not horror: HELL: 193:4
H. is oneself,/Hell is alone: HELL: 193:2
Let me go to h.: PARENTS: 335:3
literally to get out of h.: CREATIVITY: 104:1
prevent you from going to h.: THE UNITED NATIONS: 485:2
To be in a world which is a h.: HELL: 193:3

hells: institutional h. of the present century: HELL: 193:1

help: not helpful to h. a friend: AID: 16:2
with a little h. from my friends: FRIENDS: 177:6

hen: better take a wet h.: COMPROMISE: 95:1

heresies: most interesting ideas are h.: BOOKS: CLASSICS: 55:6

heritage: fetishism of the cultural h.: FRANCE: 172:2
use of the word 'h.': HERITAGE: 193:1

hero: become a sexual h.: SEXUALITY: 427:10
h. acts: HEROES: 194:12
h. as someone who understands: HEROES: 194:6
h. is a man who would argue: HEROES: 194:11
I'm a h. wid coward's legs: COWARDICE: 104:2
'paper tiger' h.: HEROES: 194:5

heroes: fame of h. owes little: HEROES: 194:8
h. are inspiring: HEROES: 194:16
individuals who don't want to be h.: MEDIOCRITY: 279:3
They wouldn't be h.: HEROES: 193:1
true h. tend to be anonymous: HEROES: 193:3
unless he believes in h.: CINEMA: 80:31
We can be h./Just for one day: HEROES: 194:4
we do not require our h. to be subtle: HEROES: 194:7
world doesn't make any h. anymore: HEROES: 194:9

heroic: society without a h. dimension: HEROES: 193:2

heroism: All this anonymous h.: HEROES: 194:13
opportunities for h. are limited: HEROES: 194:15

herring: h. encased in a block of ice: ANTHROPOLOGY: 22:3

hesitation: H. increases in relation to risk: UNCERTAINTY: 483:2

heteros: h. make love while gays have sex: HOMOSEXUALITY: 201:5

heterosexual: In h. love there's no solution: HETEROSEXUALITY: 194:2
no sensitive h. alive: HOMOSEXUALITY: 202:20

heterosexuality: Competence in h.: HETEROSEXUALITY: 195:4
failed to convert me to h.: HETEROSEXUALITY: 195:3
I have decided to give up h.: LESBIANISM: 250:8

hide: He can run. But he can't h.: SPORT: BOXING: 442:7

hierarchy: In a h. every employee tends to rise: BUSINESS: 62:8

high: Eight miles h.: DRUGS: 133:20
H., the Middle, and the Low: CLASS: 87:7
how low you go to get h.: DRUGS: 133:18
lost in a naturally induced h.: PERFORMANCE: 340:9

high-heeled: If a woman wears a h. shoe: SHOES: 428:2

highway: highest expression on the h.: ROADS: 401:1

hijacker: h. is not a hero: PALESTINE: 334:5

hilarity: h. was like a scream from a crevasse: HUMOUR: 208:7

hillbilly: before you can sing like a h.: MUSIC: COUNTRY: 303:2

him: It is either h. or us: SUEZ: 451:3

hindsight: H. is always twenty-twenty: REGRET: 392:4

hip: H. is the sophistication: SOPHISTICATION: 436:2
hard to be h. over thirty: AGE: THE 30s: 12:1

hippie: h. is the scion of surplus value: HIPPIES: 195:5
turned in for the H. model: HIPPIES: 195:7

hippies: lazy, self-obsessed h.: HIPPIES: 195:3
Old h. don't die: HIPPIES: 195:4
when the h. came along: HIPPIES: 195:1
When we heard about the h.: HIPPIES: 195:6

Hippocrates: In the name of H.: LONGEVITY: 260:1

hippy: h. movement seemed ... a worldwide movement: HIPPIES: 195:9

Hiroshima: memory of what happened at H.: THE NUCLEAR AGE: 324:5
What happened at H.: THE NUCLEAR AGE: 324:7

historian: h.'s job is to aggrandize: HISTORIANS: 196:1
I am not a professional h.: HISTORIANS: 196:2

historians: H. are left forever chasing shadows: HISTORIANS: 196:3
H. are to nationalism: NATIONALISM: 310:4

historical: bases for h. knowledge: HISTORY: 196:6

history: all h. originates in human flesh: HISTORY: 196:8
bugle note of h.: WINSTON CHURCHILL: 78:1
country losing touch with its own h.: HISTORY: 197:17
English h. is all about men: HISTORY: 196:3
great stream of h.: VOCATION: 507:1
h. finds its revenge: HISTORY: 197:15
H. has no 'meaning': HISTORY: 196:9
h. has shape, order, and meaning: HISTORY: 197:13
H. is a relay of revolutions: HISTORY: 196:1
H. is made in the class struggle: SCANDAL: 408:3
h. is on our side: THE COLD WAR: 89:5
H. is the myth ... of man's fall: HISTORY: 196:11
H. is the present: HISTORY: 196:7
H. is ... the study of questions: HISTORY: 196:5
H. only exists ... for God: HISTORY: 196:4
H. teaches us that men: WISDOM: 515:2
H. will absolve me: POSTERITY: 362:2
h. you do not know: HISTORY: 197:16
meaning of H. before the dawn: PREDICTION: 366:3
recorded in the h. of mankind: PRECEDENT: 366:1
Western h. and our philosophy of history: HISTORY: 196:10

M.P.: not an M., you're a gastronomic pimp: PUBLIC LIFE: 378:1
Ma: I got nothing, M., to live up to.: ALIENATION: 18:2
Maastricht: M. has become an obscure mockery: THE EUROPEAN UNION: 150:4
Macbeth: two pages of *M.* to translate: WILLIAM SHAKESPEARE: 428:5
McCarthyism: M. is Americanism with its sleeves rolled: MCCARTHYISM: 266:3
McDonald's: M. is good for the world: MCDONALD'S: 266:2
M. was given licence to invade: MCDONALD'S: 266:1
most beautiful thing in Tokyo is M.: MCDONALD'S: 267:3
MacDworkinite: M. idea that pornography is violence: PORNOGRAPHY: 361:22
machine: m. has had a pernicious effect: MACHINES: 267:1
We are living in the m. age: COMEDIANS: 90:1
machismo: tragedy of m.: MASCULINITY: 275:6
mad: I am not m.: ARTISTS: 33:8
I am often m.: WRITING: 534:45
Men are m. most of their lives: MADNESS: 267:5
only people for me are the m. ones: THE BEAT GENERATION: 42:4
We all are born m.: MADNESS: 267:3
We all go a little m. sometimes: MADNESS: 268:13
madman: what is an authentic m.: MADNESS: 267:1
madmen: usefulness of m. is famous: MADNESS: 268:12
madness: M. cannot be found in a wild state: MADNESS: 267:7
m. is the only freedom: MADNESS: 267:2
M. need not be all breakdown: MADNESS: 267:9
only given a little spark of m.: MADNESS: 268:14
To a writer, m. is a final distillation: MADNESS: 267:6
world has ... gone through periods of m.: MADNESS: 267:4
Madonna: M. is the true feminist: MADONNA: 268:4
M.'s ambition is to rule the world: MADONNA: 268:2
M.'s protean quality: MADONNA: 268:1
maelstrom: fate threw me into this m.: DESTINY: 122:4
Mafia: M. kills the servants of the State: ASSASSINATION: 35:2
magazine: great danger with a m.: MAGAZINES: 268:2
Having a high-profile m.: MAGAZINES: 268:1
magic: Black m. operates most effectively: MAGIC: 269:1
kind of civic m.: MENTAL ILLNESS: 286:2
walk in the aura of m.: MAGIC: 269:2
Magnum: being this is a .44 M.: LUCK: 266:5
maidenhood: impulse to m.: FEMINISM: AND MEN: 166:1

mainstream: Cut off from the m. of humanity: SUBURBS: 449:3
Major: John M. is the Antichrist: JOHN MAJOR: 269:2
majority: doesn't abide by m. rule: THE MAJORITY: 269:2
M. rule is a precious, sacred thing: THE MAJORITY: 269:3
safer to be wrong with the m.: INSTITUTIONS: 223:1
wrong-headed m. assailed by truth: THE MAJORITY: 269:1
Malaya: Everything takes a long ... time in M.: ASIA: 35:3
Malcolm X: If we became students of M.: BLACK CULTURE: 50:9
male: I love the m. body: MEN: 282:23
m. and female are really two cultures: MEN & WOMEN: 285:10
m. behavior is taken to be the norm: MEN: 282:21
M. supremacy is fused into the language: LANGUAGE: 242:10
males: m. have got to ... justify their existence: MEN: 283:30
malice: how much a pinch of m. enhances: MALICE: 269:1
M. is only another name for mediocrity: MALICE: 269:2
malignant: trouble was not 'm.': CANCER: 63:6
malls: new shopping m. make possible: SHOPPING MALLS: 429:1
Shopping m. are liquid TVs: SHOPPING MALLS: 429:2
Mama: What is wrong with you, M.: MOTHERS: 298:7
mammaries: Thanks for the m.: BREASTS: 57:2
man: essentially a m.'s field: SEXISM: 425:1
Every m. needs two women: LOVERS: 265:2
harder to be a m.: MEN: 282:16
just call me a m.: HOMOSEXUALITY: HOMOPHOBIA: 203:2
m. falls in love through his eyes: LOVE: 264:58
m. has every season: AGE: 12:4
m. in love is incomplete: MARRIAGE: AND LOVE: 273:3
m. in love is like a clipped coupon: LOVE: 264:54
m. is an instrument the world employs: THE WORLD: 527:3
m. is the missing link: HUMANITY: 207:7
M. made one grave mistake: WOMEN: IN POLITICS: 522:4
M. ... the animal that can say 'I': IDENTITY: 211:2
m. will always be Prometheus: HUMANITY: 206:3
m. will teach his wife what is needed: MARRIAGE: 271:5
new m. is the result: MEN: THE NEW MAN: 284:1
Once a m. is on hand: WOMEN: AND MEN: 521:4
problem is that *m. is dead*: THE TWENTIETH CENTURY: 482:4
sentence will suffice for modern m.: MODERN LIFE: 291:1
She's the best m. in England: MARGARET THATCHER: 466:6

study of m. is just beginning: HUMANITY: 206:1
To be sure he's a 'M.': GENDER: 180:4
To call a m. an animal: MEN: 283:28
want to know about a m.: WIVES: 516:5
what distinguishes m. so sharply: HUMAN NATURE: 206:3
You may marry the m. of your dreams: HUSBANDS: 209:2
manager: m. may be tough and practical: MANAGEMENT: 270:5
Manhattan: Downtown M., clear winter noon: NIGHT: 316:4
In M., every flat surface: THE UNITED STATES: NEW YORK: 494:9
manhood: Only when m. is dead: MEN: 282:10
serious doubt on one's m.: NONVIOLENCE: 323:7
mankind: CAME IN PEACE FOR ALL M.: THE MOON: 296:9
no longer expect/anything from m.: MISANTHROPY: 289:2
manners: don't mind if you don't like my m.: MANNERS: 270:1
Good m. have much to do with the emotions: MANNERS: 270:6
in England people have good table m.: FOOD: 171:14
M. are especially the need of the plain: MANNERS: 270:7
M. are love in a cool climate: MANNERS: 270:3
M. are of such great consequence: MANNERS: 270:5
Maradona: by the head of M.: SPORT: FOOTBALL: 443:8
March: In M., that month of wind: SEASONS: 413:5
marijuana: I experimented with m.: DRUGS: 132:4
Is m. addictive: DRUGS: 133:22
M. is ... self-punishing: DRUGS: 133:23
One's condition on m.: DRUGS: 133:21
Marilyn: In death M. has become strangely sexless: MARILYN MONROE: 294:1
M. who was every man's love affair: MARILYN MONROE: 295:5
M., Hollywood's Joan of Arc: MARILYN MONROE: 295:9
marital: In Europe we tend to see m. love: MARRIAGE: 271:4
market: It's a free m.: THE STOCK MARKET: 446:2
m. came with the dawn of civilization: FREE ENTERPRISE: 174:3
only reason to invest in the m.: THE STOCK MARKET: 446:3
Marlon: Living with M. is like an afternoon: MARLON BRANDO: 57:2
marriage: American woman's concept of m.: MARRIAGE: 272:19
Chains do not hold a m. together: MARRIAGE: 272:31
curse which lies upon m.: MARRIAGE: 271:3
different brands of m.: MARRIAGE: 272:27
Every m. tends to consist of an aristocrat: MARRIAGE: 273:35
happy m. perhaps represents the ideal: MARRIAGE: 273:33
how to combine m. and a career: CAREERS: 65:4

In almost every m. there is a selfish: MARRIAGE: 272:29

In m. there are no manners to keep up: MARRIAGE: 271:2

institution of m. in all societies: MARRIAGE: 272:28

M. ... a marvellous thing for other people: MARRIAGE: 272:21

M. accustomed one to the good things: MARRIAGE: 271:13

M. as an institution developed from rape: MARRIAGE: 271:10

M. is an act of will: MARRIAGE: 272:17

m. is just a way of getting out: MARRIAGE: 271:8

M. is like the Middle East: MARRIAGE: 271:7

m. is ... more interesting than any romance: MARRIAGE: AND LOVE: 273:1

M. is nothing like being in prison: MARRIAGE: 273:34

m. is punishment for shoplifting: MARRIAGE: 272:30

M. is socialism among two people: MARRIAGE: 271:11

m. neutered the appeal: COUPLES: 104:4

problem with m.: MARRIAGE: 271:14

Progress of a m.: MARRIAGE: 272:22

rhythm to the ending of a m.: MARRIAGE: FAILED: 273:1

That a m. ends is less than ideal: MARRIAGE: FAILED: 273:2

There were three of us in this m.: MARRIAGE: 271:9

We treat the failure of m.: MARRIAGE: FAILED: 273:3

marriages: M. will survive despite enormous strains: MARRIAGE: 271:6

married: all proper men are m.: MARRIAGE: 273:36

getting m. in the morning: WEDDINGS: 512:3

I m. above myself: WOMEN: IN POLITICS: 522:2

m. are those who have taken the ... risk: MARRIAGE: 271:16

M. life requires shared mystery: MARRIAGE: 271:12

They're either m. or gay: MEN: THE FEMALE VIEW: 283:5

You can't stay m.: DIVORCE: 128:7

marry: Those who m. God: THE CHURCH: 77:3

When two people m.: MARRIAGE: 270:1

marrying: M. a man is like buying something: MARRIAGE: 272:18

martyrs: M. ... must choose: MARTYRDOM: 274:3

Marx: theories of Karl M.: MARXISM: 274:1

Marxism: M. exists in nineteenth-century thought: MARXISM: 274:6

M. is not scientific: MARXISM: 274:3

something about M. that brings out warts: MARXISM: 274:10

M. vision of man without God: MARXISM: 274:11

right of every M. scholar: MARXISM: 274:7

Marxist: M. analysis has got nothing to do: MARXISM: 274:2

Marxists: whether or not we are M.: MARXISM: 274:9

masculine: m. imagination has very little appreciation: MEN: 281:3

m. imagination lives in ... revolt: MASCULINITY: 275:1

values of the m. mystique: MASCULINITY: 275:8

masculinity: American ideal of m.: MASCULINITY: 275:2

M. is not something given to you: MASCULINITY: 275:7

M. is risky and elusive: MASCULINITY: 275:9

relaxed m. is at bottom empty: MASCULINITY: 275:5

tendency to destroy m. in American men: MEN: 282:20

masks: m. always in peril of smearing: FACES: 154:9

masochism: spirit of national m. prevails: INTELLECTUALS: 224:1

mass: function of m. culture: POPULAR CULTURE: 359:13

grandeur in the uniformity of the m.: THE MASSES: 276:4

once the authentic m. man takes over: THE MASSES: 275:1

Massachusetts: whether I am going to blow up M.: PUBLIC LIFE: 379:5

massacre: m. of the whole of mankind: BAN THE BOMB: 41:4

masses: anything said about the m.: THE MASSES: 276:6

dehumanized into 'the m.': THE MASSES: 276:7

only freedom ... left to the m.: THE MASSES: 275:2

tremendous energy of the m.: THE MASSES: 276:5

master: not likeable: a m. and a slave: SLAVERY: 431:1

one m. and millions of slaves: TOTALITARIANISM: 475:2

To be completely woman you need a m.: WOMEN: AND MEN: 521:3

masters: had become ... M. of the Universe: THE STOCK MARKET: 446:4

masterpiece: create a m. by using any means: SELF-EXPRESSION: 416:2

masturbate: I tell women, 'Go and m.': MASTURBATION: 276:2

masturbation: don't knock m.: MASTURBATION: 276:1

M. ... an expression of self-regard: MASTURBATION: 276:3

M.: the primary sexual activity: MASTURBATION: 276:6

m. ... void of meaning: MASTURBATION: 276:4

Women are denied m.: MASTURBATION: 276:5

mate: people should m. for life: MONOGAMY: 294:1

materialism: believe in m.: MATERIALISM: 277:4

mathematical: Only m. thought manages to free itself: MATHEMATICS: 277:5

mathematician: How happy the lot of the m.: MATHEMATICS: 277:1

mathematics: laws of m. refer to reality: MATHEMATICS: 277:2

maturity: True m. is only reached: MATURITY: 277:3

MBE: M. ... we received ours for entertaining: AWARDS: 40:3

me: I'd like to be a better m.: IDENTITY: 211:4

I'm glad I'm not m.: BOB DYLAN: 135:1

M., what's that after all: SELF: 414:3

There is no m.: SELF: 415:11

We are now in the M. Decade: THE 1970s: 320:6

meaning: Everywhere one seeks to produce m.: MEANING: 277:1

experience of an absence of m.: MEANING: 278:4

fact that life has no m.: MEANING: 278:3

Life is – or has – m.: LIFE: 253:10

means: m. by which we live: ENDS & MEANS: 143:3

Perfection of m.: ENDS & MEANS: 143:1

mechanical: Never let anything m. know: MACHINES: 267:4

sex has come to seem m.: SEX: 423:42

media: Acceptance of the mass m. entails: CULTURE: 110:1

bosses of our mass m.: DISASTERS: 125:2

futility of everything ... from the m.: THE MEDIA: 278:1

m. network has its idols: THE MEDIA: 278:2

m. no longer ask those who know: INTERVIEWS: 226:3

m. overestimates its own importance: THE MEDIA: 279:11

m. transforms the great silence: THE MEDIA: 278:6

m., even with tricks: THE MEDIA: 279:10

mass m. are nearly universal: THE MEDIA: 279:9

sucked through this m. machine: STARDOM: 444:2

medicine: I wasn't driven into m.: DOCTORS: 128:5

imposing edifice of modern m.: MEDICINE: 279:3

m. is to remain a humanitarian: MEDICINE: 279:5

Some men are born m.: MEDIOCRITY: 279:1

mediocrity: M. in politics is not to be despised: POLITICS: 355:12

water of m.: MEDIOCRITY: 279:2

medium: m. is the message: THE MEDIA: 279:8

meeting: odds of not m. in this life: OTHER PEOPLE: 333:6

meetings: giving Oscars for m.: MEETINGS: 280:2

I love m. with suits: MEETINGS: 280:3

M. are a great trap: MEETINGS: 280:1

melancholy: m. and utopia are heads and tails: UTOPIA: 500:4

M. has ceased to be ... an exception: WORK: 525:11

mellow: I don't respond well to m.: DRUGS: 132:1

melting-pot: hear that m. stuff a lot: MULTICULTURALISM: 299:4

memorial: M. services are the cocktail parties: FUNERALS: 179:2

memories: difference between false m. and true: MEMORY: 280:5

pleasure to share one's m.: MEMORY:
281:14
memory: All stimulation generates a m.:
MEMORY: 280:4
effectiveness of our m. banks:
MEMORY: 281:17
genius of m., is that it is choosy:
MEMORY: 280:1
Human m. is a marvellous ...
instrument: MEMORY: 280:9
light of m. ... is the palest: MEMORY:
280:7
m. becomes water overflowing:
MEMORY: 280:3
m. is ... a distortion of his past:
AUTOBIOGRAPHY: 39:4
M. is a parade of dead men: MEMORY:
280:11
m. is what makes our lives: MEMORY:
280:2
m. of most men is an abandoned
cemetery: MEMORY: 281:18
My m. is so very untrustworthy:
MEMORY: 280:13
my major preoccupation – m.:
MEMORY: 281:15
only our m. of the moments: OTHER
PEOPLE: 332:3
selective m. isn't selective enough:
MEMORY: 280:10
men: all m. are as strange as hell: MEN:
282:22
All real m. are gentle: MEN: 281:8
before everything else, m. are men:
MEN: 282:9
Bloody m. are like bloody buses: MEN:
281:6
breed of m. who claim to be
feminists: FEMINISM: AND MEN:
166:3
During the feminist seventies m.:
MEN: THE NEW MAN: 284:3
if more m. wanted to become women:
MEN & WOMEN: 284:4
M. act and women appear: MEN &
WOMEN: 284:1
M. and women, women and men: MEN
& WOMEN: 284:7
m. are afraid that they will not be men:
MEN & WOMEN: 285:12
M. are gentle, honest: MEN & WOMEN:
285:11
M. are not ... irreplaceable: MEN:
281:7
M. are not to be told anything ...
painful: MEN: 281:2
M. are the enemies of women: MEN:
282:24
M. have defined the parameters:
DEFINITION: 118:1
M. know they are sexual exiles: MEN:
283:25
M. like women who write: WOMEN:
AND THE ARTS: 519:2
m. make us women think: WOMEN:
THE MALE VIEW: 521:12
M., not women, are the weaker sex:
MEN: 283:26
m. ... portrayed as the bad guys: MEN &
WOMEN: 285:16
m. talk to women so they can sleep:
SEX: 423:41
m. want quick ... sexual adventure:
LUST: 266:5
m. we wanted to marry: WOMEN:
519:39

m. who are discriminated against:
FEMINISM: AND MEN: 166:4
M. who care passionately for women:
INFATUATION: 219:4
M. who want to support women:
FEMINISM: AND MEN: 166:2
Poor little m.: MEN: 281:1
possible *not* to live in the world of m.:
MEN: 281:5
so much easier for m.: WOMEN: IN
BUSINESS: 520:1
special position among m.: WOMEN:
THE MALE VIEW: 520:3
world m. inhabit ... is rather bleak:
MEN: 282:13
mendacity: M. is a system that we live
in: LIES: 252:8
menopause: m. is probably the least
glamorous topic: MENOPAUSE:
285:2
menstrual: not m. blood per se which
disturbs: MENSTRUATION:
285:3
tasting your m. blood:
MENSTRUATION: 285:1
menstruate: If men could m.:
MENSTRUATION: 286:6
mental illness: 'm.' is not the name:
MENTAL ILLNESS: 286:8
mentally: regard themselves ... as m.
unwell: MENTAL ILLNESS: 286:1
mess: drop a ... large m. in her eye:
WIVES: 516:7
We are ... in a m.: HUMANITY: 207:9
Messiah: failed to say anything about the
M.: THE MESSIAH: 286:1
new m. born every day: RELIGION:
394:12
Messianic: M. concept ... is a great
victory: THE MESSIAH: 287:2
metaphors: M. are much more
tenacious: IMAGERY: 213:3
metaphysics: cheating on my m. final:
METAPHYSICS: 287:1
m. ... forbidden me by my doctor:
METAPHYSICS: 287:3
meteorologist: All we need is a m.:
WEATHER: 511:1
meter: know how to use a parking m.:
MODERN LIFE: 291:2
meters: And watch the parkin' m.:
MOTTOS & MAXIMS: 299:7
Metro-Goldwyn-Mayer: born ... on a
M. lot: ACTORS: 6:6
metropolis: M. should have been
aborted: CITIES: 84:7
Mexico: M. is a nineteenth-century
country: LATIN AMERICA: 245:7
Mickey Mouse: I love M. more: WALT
DISNEY INC.: 126:2
middle: people who stay in the m. of the
road: INDECISION: 216:2
middle class: Being m. means: THE
MIDDLE CLASS: 288:3
ruined m. which makes revolutions:
THE MIDDLE CLASS: 287:2
What I call m. society: THE MIDDLE
CLASS: 287:1
Middle East: mad dog of the M.: THE
MIDDLE EAST: 288:4
tormenting dilemma of the M.: THE
MIDDLE EAST: 288:5
middle-aged: misery of the m. woman:
MIDDLE AGE: 287:3
mid-life: In m. the man wants to see:
MIDDLE AGE: 287:6

Midwestern: tell a M. couple in Europe:
THE UNITED STATES: AMERICANS
ABROAD: 491:3
militants: real m. are like cleaning
women: ACTIVISM & PROTEST: 5:10
militarisation: m. of city life: CITIES:
URBAN CULTURE: 85:2
military: m. mind is indeed a menace:
THE ARMY: 26:5
millennium: end of a m. promises
apocalypse: FIN DE SIÈCLE: 169:3
million: know what a m. dollars actually
is: MONEY: 293:8
one m. dollars here: MONEY: 294:16
millionaires: one of our least sedentary
m.: MICK JAGGER: 231:1
mind: Is there no way out of the m.: THE
MIND: 288:4
m. is the result of the torments: THE
MIND: 288:2
never m.: APATHY: 22:1
waking m. ... is the least serviceable:
CONSCIOUSNESS: 97:3
minds: best m. of my generation
destroyed: THE BEAT
GENERATION: 42:3
minorities: cannot discuss the state of
our m.: MINORITIES: 289:1
History is made by active ... m.:
MINORITIES: 289:6
minority: belong to that m.: YUPPIES:
536:4
characterizes a member of a m. group:
MINORITIES: 289:3
minute: I'm a m. commodity:
STARDOM: 444:15
miracle: m. entails a degree of
irrationality: MIRACLES: 289:2
mirror: Looking at yourself in a m.:
VANITY: 501:1
misery: another person's habitual m.:
MISERY: 290:1
Friends *love* m.: MISERY: 290:2
m.'s shadow or reflection: MISERY:
290:4
Man hands on m. to man: MISERY:
290:3
separated ... by the degree of their m.:
MISERY: 290:5
sink to the bottom of our m.: TRUTH:
481:8
Mis-shapes: M., mis-takes, mis-fits:
THE COUNTERCULTURE: 103:1
misogyny: m. that shapes every aspect:
SEXISM: 425:6
mission: m. in life: SURVIVAL: 455:8
on a m. from God: MISSIONARIES:
290:1
missionaries: what God and the M. of
Charity expect: MISSIONARIES:
290:4
mistake: M. SHALL NOT BE
REPEATED: THE NUCLEAR AGE:
324:2
mistakes: M. are a fact of life: ERROR:
147:4
M. are ... of a sacred nature: ERROR:
147:3
M., scandals, and failures: SCANDAL:
408:1
M. ... the foundations of truth: ERROR:
147:5
person who has made m.: ERROR:
147:6
watching people who make m.:
ERROR: 147:2

In p., those things withheld: PRISON: 370:5

P. is a second-by-second assault: PRISON: 369:1

P. *is* punishment: PRISON: 370:11

prisoner: p. is not the one who has committed: PRISON: 370:10

privacy: deny that p. is a jewel: PRIVACY: 370:2

P. is not something: PRIVACY: 370:1

private: agree that p. life is irrelevant: PRIVACY: 370:3

privileged: rich are less p.: PRIVILEGE: 370:1

problem: p. is food: PROBLEMS: 371:5

solution to a p. changes the problem: PROBLEMS: 371:7

yet to see any p.: PROBLEMS: 371:1

problems: characteristic of all deep human p.: PROBLEMS: 371:6

p. are our most precious possessions: PROBLEMS: 371:10

p. of the world: PROBLEMS: 371:8

p. of this world are ... solved: PROBLEMS: 371:9

two p. of our country: PROBLEMS: 371:4

procreated: We've p. and now we can die: PROCREATION: 372:3

producers: When p. want to know: SALES & MARKETING: 406:2

production: Its idea of 'p. value': HOLLYWOOD: 198:6

profession: bond between a man and his p.: WORK: 526:15

professional: to be the ultimate p.: PROFESSIONALS: 372:2

professionals: Leave death to the p.: DEATH: 113:10

p. ... play not just the necessary role: ACTORS: 6:2

supposed to be fuckin' p.: PROFESSIONALS: 372:1

professors: p. laugh at themselves: SCHOLARSHIP: 408:3

P. of literature: LITERATURE: 256:26

progress: best definition of p.: PROGRESS: 372:3

Nothing recedes like p.: PROGRESS: 372:2

P. everywhere today: PROGRESS: 372:4

P. is the injustice each generation commits: INJUSTICE: 220:2

partisans of the idea of p.: PROGRESS: 372:5

same each time with p.: PROGRESS: 372:1

proletariat: Admiration of the p.: THE WORKING CLASS: 527:4

white-collar p.: UNIVERSITY: 499:8

Prometheus: P. is reaching out for the stars: SPACE: 438:6

promiscuity: P. in women is illness: PROMISCUITY: 373:8

Promised Land: I've seen the p.: VISIONARIES: 506:2

promising: What's important is p. something: THE PEOPLE: 339:1

proofs: Literature is *without p.*: LITERATURE: 255:1

propaganda: All p. or popularization involves: PROPAGANDA: 374:3

P. has a bad name: PROPAGANDA: 374:2

P. is a soft weapon: PROPAGANDA: 374:1

successor to politics will be p.: PROPAGANDA: 374:5

prophecies: not fulfilling the p.: PROPHECY: 374:1

prophecy: P. today is hardly the romantic business: PROPHECY: 374:2

prophet: p. who fails to present: PROPHETS: 375:4

prophetical: p. protest has been skimmed: PROPHECY: 374:4

prophets: Fear p.: PROPHETS: 374:3

ones we call the p.: PROPHETS: 374:1

proposes: man p., and woman is disposed of: RELATIONSHIPS: 392:5

prose: requirements for p. and verse: WRITING: 533:21

values which are best expressed in p.: POETRY: 349:29

prosperity: P. or egalitarianism: EQUALITY: 146:10

prostitute: degradation in which the p. is held: PROSTITUTION: 375:7

p. is more moral than a wife: WIVES: 516:8

p. is not ... the victim of men: PROSTITUTION: 375:8

p. who refuses to be redeemed: PROSTITUTION: 376:12

Punishing the p. promotes the rape: PROSTITUTION: 376:11

prostitution: P. is the supreme triumph of capitalism: PROSTITUTION: 375:2

protection: p. of a ten-year-old girl: CHILD ABUSE: 72:5

protest: It wasn't just a p. camp: ACTIVISM & PROTEST: 5:7

Protestant: P. thrust is always toward: PROTESTANTISM: 376:2

P. with a horse: IRELAND: 228:1

White P.'s ultimate sympathy: PROTESTANTISM: 376:1

proud: I'm black and I'm p.: BLACK CULTURE: 50:3

Proust: After P., there are certain things: WRITERS: 531:43

provenance: not bothered by the p. of things: AUTHENTICITY: 38:4

proverb: apply the p. to his own life: MOTTOS & MAXIMS: 299:3

providers: as p. they're oil wells: WOMEN: AND THE ARTS: 520:6

providing: P. for one's family: MEN: 282:12

pseudo-event: p. comes about: EVENTS: 150:1

pseudosimplicities: p. of brutal directness: CANDOUR: 64:1

psychedelic: those p. experiences: DRUGS: 132:9

with the help of p. chemicals: HIPPIES: 195:10

psychiatrist: century of the p.'s couch: PSYCHIATRY: 377:2

obscenely impossible to be a p.: PSYCHIATRY: 377:1

p. ... goes to the Folies-Bergère: PSYCHIATRY: 377:3

psychiatry: Institutional p. is a continuation: PSYCHIATRY: 377:5

psychoanalysis: in its entirety, p. won't do: PSYCHOANALYSIS: 378:6

P. can unravel some of the forms: PSYCHOANALYSIS: 377:4

P. pretends to investigate: PSYCHOANALYSIS: 377:3

psychobabble: p. ... a set of repetitive verbal formalities: LANGUAGE: JARGON: 244:2

p., this spirit which now tyrannizes: LOQUACITY: 260:2

psychology: p. is ... a natural science: PSYCHOLOGY: 378:1

p. is the study of the soul: PSYCHOLOGY: 378:2

persuasiveness of p.: PSYCHOLOGY: 378:3

There is no p.: PSYCHOLOGY: 378:4

puberty: see in the agonies of p.: ADOLESCENCE: 7:2

public: p. figure ... is a lonely man: PUBLIC LIFE: 379:6

p. has got to be marginalized: THE PUBLIC: 378:3

p. in the palm of your hand: THE PUBLIC: 378:4

p. knows what it wants: THE PUBLIC: 378:2

p. man must never forget: POLICY: 352:3

quality as a p. person: PUBLIC LIFE: 378:2

reading p. is intellectually adolescent: THE PUBLIC: 378:1

publicity: All p. is good, except an obituary: PUBLICITY: 379:1

Of course I'm a p. hound: PUBLICITY: 379:4

P. is the life of this culture: PUBLICITY: 379:2

With p. comes humiliation: PUBLICITY: 379:3

publish: When you p. a book: PUBLISHING: 380:4

published: Having books p. is very destructive: PUBLISHING: 380:3

publisher: p. is a specialised form of bank: PUBLISHING: 380:2

publishers: P. are notoriously slothful: PUBLISHING: 380:5

punctuality: P. is the virtue of the bored: TIME: 471:12

punish: power to p. is not essentially different: PUNISHMENT: 380:2

punishment: No p. has ever possessed enough power: CRIME: 106:2

punk: dead p. lady with the knack: PUNK: 380:4

P. to me was a form of free speech: PUNK: 381:6

P. ... was just another English spectacle: PUNK: 380:2

punks: heavy irony of the p.: PUNK: 380:3

P. in their silly leather jackets: PUNK: 380:5

purchasing: P. power is a licence: WEALTH: 511:9

pure: p. as the driven slush: PURITY: 381:2

puritanism: new p.: THE 1980S: 320:5

purity: apostles of p.: FANATICS: 159:4

p. ... is unassailable: PURITY: 381:1

purple: P. haze all in my brain: PSYCHEDELIA: 376:2

walk by the color p.: COLOUR: 90:2

pursuit: P. and seduction are the essence: SEDUCTION: 414:7

Watteau: W. is no less an artist: ART: AND COMMERCE: 28:1

waving: not w. but drowning: SUICIDE: 453:16

wax: 'woman of w.' whom he could model: BRIGITTE BARDOT: 42:2

way: I did it my w.: AGE: OLD AGE: 15:21

weak: talent of the w. to persuade: WEAKNESS: 511:3

true that we are w. and sick: MISANTHROPY: 290:3

w. are more likely: WEAKNESS: 511:2

w. are the most treacherous: WEAKNESS: 511:1

weakness: dare not tempt them with w.: THE ARMS RACE: 26:4

weaknesses: Never support two w. at the same time: VICE: 501:2

wealth: cemetery of tax-deductible w.: MUSEUMS & GALLERIES: 301:4

W. is not without its advantages: WEALTH: 511:2

w. ... manages ... the aspect of intelligence: WEALTH: 511:3

W. often takes away chances: WEALTH: 511:6

weapons: W. are like money: THE ARMS RACE: 25:1

weather: he did not fear the w.: THE KENNEDYS: 237:10

weatherman: don't need a w.: NEWS: 315:2

wedding: contemporary w. guest: WEDDINGS: 512:1

week: greatest w. in the history of the world: THE MOON: 296:8

w. is a long time in politics: POLITICS: 357:40

weep: cannot w. for the entire world: SYMPATHY: 457:1

weeping: w. is a crime: PSYCHIATRIC INSTITUTIONS: 377:2

welcome: Hello, good evening, and w.: TELEVISION: 464:15

West: You in the W. have a problem: THE WEST: 513:5

West Bank: W. they think you mean Arkansas: ISRAEL: 230:2

West Coast: Oriental politeness of the W.: THE UNITED STATES: THE WEST: 498:8

Western: appearance of the epithet 'W.': HOLISM: 198:3

W. man represents himself: THE WEST: 512:2

when you've seen one W.: WESTERNS: 513:4

Westerns: In W. you were permitted to kiss: WESTERNS: 513:1

wets: 'w.' ... hoped she would go away: MARGARET THATCHER: 466:8

whip: One can w. or be whipped: SEXUAL DEVIATIONS: 426:6

whisper: harder to kill a w.: SLANDER: 431:4

white: be ... better than the w. person: RACISM: 384:15

crumbs from the W. table: SOUTH AFRICA: 437:1

I don't like w. people: BLACK CULTURE: 50:5

important to be w.: WHITES: 513:2

no 'w.' or 'colored' signs on the foxholes: RACE: 383:6

preservation of the w. man: SOUTH AFRICA: 438:9

proudly call themselves 'w.': WHITES: 514:8

w. face goes with a white mind: RACE: 383:5

w. man is trash: RACISM: 384:8

W. people really deal more with God: CHRISTIANITY: 76:2

w. race *is* the cancer: WHITES: 514:9

w. women were never lonely: WHITES: 513:1

White House: no whitewash at the W.: WATERGATE: 510:4

on the way to the W.: ELECTIONS: 140:11

Whitehall: W. envelops me: GOVERNMENT: 187:2

whites: Be nice to the w.: WHITES: 514:10

W. must be made to realize: RACE: 382:2

Where do w. fit in the New Africa: AFRICA: 11:4

who: If not us, w.: REVOLUTIONARIES: 400:11

whom: 'w.' is a word that was invented: LANGUAGE: GRAMMAR, SPELLING & PUNCTUATION: 244:7

You can't write 'W. the devil–': LANGUAGE: GRAMMAR, SPELLING & PUNCTUATION: 244:3

whore: w. is despised by the hypocritical: PROSTITUTION: 375:3

whorehouse: Nothing seems more like a w.: MUSEUMS & GALLERIES: 301:5

whores: government is a parliament of w.: GOVERNMENT: 187:8

W. and writers ... you can't forgive: WRITERS: 531:41

w. in everything but name: PROSTITUTION: 375:1

wicked: All things truly w.: INNOCENCE: 221:6

widow: W.. The word consumes itself: BEREAVEMENT: 46:6

wife: opens the car door for his w.: CHIVALRY: 76:1

wild: Born to be w.: BIKERS: 47:4

Making contact with this W. Man: MASCULINITY: 275:3

walk on the w. side: WILD AT HEART: 514:3

whole world is w. at heart: WILD AT HEART: 514:2

wilderness: redemption from W.: DEATH: 113:9

wildness: W. and silence disappeared: THE WILDERNESS: 514:1

will: believing in free w.: FREE WILL: 174:2

w. is never free: FREE WILL: 174:1

wilted: men w.: SELF-ASSERTION: 415:3

Wimbledon: Spill your guts at W.: SPORT: TENNIS: 443:1

wimps: Someone has to stand up for w.: WIMPS: 515:2

wind: great w. swept over the ghetto: BLACK CONSCIOUSNESS/BLACK POWER: 49:2

w. of change: DECOLONIZATION: 117:2

wine: W. is a part of society: WINE: 515:1

W., the Grape, the Visions: DRINK: ABSTINENCE: 131:2

wines: finest w. available: WINE: 515:3

wink: Nudge, nudge, w., wink: INNUENDO: 221:2

winning: W. is everything: WINNING: 515:1

winter: in w. the end of the day: SEASONS: 413:2

Winters: blitz of a boy is Timothy W.: BOYS: 56:1

wisdom: our physical body possesses a w.: THE BODY: 52:13

W. ... is the knowledge of good and evil: WISDOM: 515:1

W. lies neither in fixity nor in change: CHANGE: 70:13

wise: w. man who is not heeded: FOOLS: 171:2

wisecracking: distance between w. and wit: WIT: 516:3

wish: 'I w. I'd done that': DRINK: DRUNKS: 131:31

wit: W. destroys eroticism: WIT: 516:2

W. is a weapon: HUMOUR: 208:11

witches: In the past, men created w.: MENTAL ILLNESS: 286:7

withdrew: I w. from the world: RECLUSIVES: 391:1

without: two things in life you can do w.: IRRITANTS: 229:4

wives: argument between w. and whores: WIVES: 516:6

majority ... choose their w.: WIVES: 516:2

wolves: If you live among w.: INTERNATIONAL RELATIONS: 225:2

woman: Any w. who chooses to behave: SEXISM: 425:10

anything better than a w.: WOMEN: THE MALE VIEW: 521:9

be a w. and ... political: WOMEN: IN POLITICS: 522:6

being a w. is like being Irish: WOMEN: 518:29

Being a w. is of special interest: WOMEN: 518:22

complete w. is ... manipulative: WOMEN: 516:4

Every w. adores a Fascist: WOMEN: 518:32

Every w. is like a timezone: WOMEN: THE MALE VIEW: 520:4

hellish for a w. in politics: WOMEN: IN POLITICS: 522:1

I am invincible, I am w.: WOMEN: 519:35

if a w. never lets herself go: INHIBITION: 220:2

If w. is inconstant,/good: WOMEN: 518:23

making marriage work is a w.'s business: MARRIAGE: 272:26

marrying the wrong sort of w.: WIVES: 516:3

modern w. is the curse of the universe: FEMINISM: 166:23

No w. can call herself free: BIRTH CONTROL: 49:5

No w. needs intercourse: SEX: 422:25

not born, but rather becomes, a w.: WOMEN: 518:23

phenomenal w.: WOMEN: 516:1

seems as though w. keep growing: WOMEN: AND MEN: 521:2

She takes just like a w.: WOMEN: 517:11

Robert Andrews is a travel writer and the compiler of a
number of acclaimed dictionaries of quotations, including
the *Routledge Dictionary of Quotations*,
the *Columbia Dictionary of Quotations* and *Famous Lines*.